The SAGE Handbook of Counselling and Psychotherapy

Third Edition

Edited by Colin Feltham and Ian Horton

Los Angeles | London | New Delhi
Singapore | Washington DC

First edition published 2000. Reprinted 2002, 2003, 2004, 2005
Second edition published 2006. Reprinted 2007, 2009, 2010
This third edition published 2012

SAGE Publications Ltd
1 Oliver's Yard
55 City Road
London EC1Y 1SP

SAGE Publications Inc.
2455 Teller Road
Thousand Oaks, California 91320

SAGE Publications India Pvt Ltd
B 1/I 1 Mohan Cooperative Industrial Area
Mathura Road
New Delhi 110 044

SAGE Publications Asia-Pacific Pte Ltd
3 Church Street
#10-04 Samsung Hub
Singapore 049483

Library of Congress Control Number: 2011929353

British Library Cataloguing in Publication data

A catalogue record for this book is available from the British Library

ISBN 978-0-85702-325-4
ISBN 978-0-85702-326-1 (pbk)

Typeset by C&M Digitals (P) Ltd, India, Chennai
Printed in Great Britain by MPG Books Group, Bodmin, Cornwall
Printed on paper from sustainable resources

The Counselling

SAGE has been part of the global academic community since 1965, supporting high quality research and learning that transforms society and our understanding of individuals, groups, and cultures. SAGE is the independent, innovative, natural home for authors, editors and societies who share our commitment and passion for the social sciences.

Find out more at: **www.sagepublications.com**

In memory of Fay Fransella

Contents

List of Figures

List of Tables

About the Editors and Contributors

Colin Feltham is Emeritus Professor of Critical Counselling Studies at Sheffield Hallam University. His most recent publications are *What's Wrong With Us? The Anthropathology Thesis* (Wiley, 2007), *Critical Thinking in Counselling and Psychotherapy* (Sage, 2010) and *Failure* (Acumen, forthcoming). He is an independent writer, consultant, teacher and practitioner.

Ian Horton has retired as Principal Lecturer and Programme Director for the Postgraduate Diploma/MA Counselling and Psychotherapy at the University of East London. He is a Fellow of the BACP and was formerly a member of the BACP Professional Standards Committee, UPCA Council, Chair of the BACP Courses Accreditation Group and UKRC Executive Committee and has been a BACP Senior Registered Practitioner and UKRC Registered Independent Counsellor.

Suzanne Abraham is Associate Professor in the Department of Obstetrics and Gynaecology, and Co-Director of the Eating Disorders Unit at the Northside Clinic at the University of Sydney. She has written *Eating Disorders: The Facts*, now in its sixth edition, and continues to revise each edition of the *Llewellyn-Jones Fundamentals of Obstetrics and Gynaecology* with Jeremy Oats.

Geof Alred is a BPS Chartered Psychologist, a former counsellor trainer at Durham University, and counsellor in NHS Primary Care, and is currently in private practice. He is a Visiting Fellow, Centre for Individual and Organisational Development, Sheffield Hallam University, and Visiting Lecturer, University of Malta. He is co-editor of and contributor to *Experiences of Counsellor Training: Challenge, Surprise and Change* (Palgrave, 2004), and co-author of *The Mentoring Pocketbook* (Management Pocketbooks, 2010). His research interests include language in therapy and integrative practice.

Kate Anthony, DPsych FBACP, is a leading expert on the use of technology in therapy. Kate has trained practitioners and organizations worldwide in online therapy for over 10 years. She is co-editor and co-author of three textbooks on the subject, as well as numerous articles, chapters and journals. She is a Fellow of the British Association of Counselling and Psychotherapy and past President and Fellow of the International Society for Mental Health Online. She is Executive Specialist for Online Coaching for the BACP Coaching Division. She is Co-Founder of the Online Therapy Institute and the Online Coach Institute, and Co-Managing Editor of *TILT Magazine* (*Therapeutic Innovations in Light of Technology*).

Lionel Bailly is a psychoanalyst and a child and adolescent psychiatrist. He is Honorary Senior Lecturer at University College London Psychoanalysis Unit where he teaches in the MSc in Theoretical Psychoanalytic Studies and in the MSc in Psychodynamic Developmental Neuroscience (in collaboration with the Anna Freud Centre and Yale University School of Medicine). He is a Consultant in Child and Adolescent Psychiatry with North Essex Partnership NHS Foundation Trust. He has recently published a *Beginner's Guide to Lacan* (Oneworld, 2009) and is a member of the Association Lacanienne Internationale.

Clark Baim is a Senior Trainer in Psychodrama and the Co-Director of the Birmingham Institute for Psychodrama, Birmingham, England. Since 2000 he has also been the Co-Lead National Trainer for the Probation Service's Sexual Offending Groupwork Programmes in England and Wales. In 1987 he established and was the Founder Director of Geese Theatre UK, a company focusing on reha-bilitative work in criminal justice. In 2007 he received the David Kipper Scholar's Award from the American Society of Group Psychotherapy and Psychodrama.

Jill Balmont has worked as a Chartered Clinical Psychologist in the NHS in the East Midlands for over 25 years. She specializes in the field of HIV/AIDS and sexual health for Nottinghamshire Healthcare NHS Trust, and in psychodynamic psychotherapy for Derbyshire Healthcare NHS Foundation Trust.

Michael Barkham is Professor of Clinical Psychology and Director of the Centre for Psychological Services Research at the University of Sheffield. Previously he was Professor of Clinical and Counselling Psychology as well as Director of the Psychological Therapies Research Centre at the University of Leeds. He has pub-lished 150 peer-review articles in the areas of counselling and the psychological therapies and is committed to supporting the development of practice-based evi-dence as a complement to trials methodology. He is joint editor of the *British Journal of Clinical Psychology*, a Fellow of the British Psychological Society, and co-editor of *Developing and Delivering Practice-based Evidence: A Guide for the Psychological Therapies* (Wiley, 2010).

Rowan Bayne is emeritus professor of psychology and counselling at the University of East London where he was a core tutor on counselling and psychotherapy courses for over 30 years. His books include *How To Survive Counsellor Training: An A–Z guide* (with Gordon Jinks: Palgrave Macmillan, 2010) and *The Counsellor's Guide to Personality: Preferences, Motives and Life Stories* (Palgrave Macmillan, forthcoming).

Jenny Bimrose is a Professorial Fellow with the Institute for Employment Research at the University of Warwick. She has over 30 years' experience of teaching in higher education, management and research. Many of her research projects have focused on different aspects of gender and career counselling, both in the UK and internationally. She is a Fellow of the Institute of Career Guidance and Co-Editor of the *British Journal of Guidance and Counselling*.

Tim Bond is Professor and Head of the Graduate School of Education at the University of Bristol, where he uses counselling skills both therapeutically and to support problem-solving in currently challenging times for universities, teachers and the public sector. He researches and writes extensively on ethical and legal issues for counselling and psychotherapy, including *Standards and Ethics for Counselling in Action*, Third Edition (Sage, 2009).

John Boorman, DClinPsy, is a recently qualified HPC Chartered Clinical Psychologist from the Universities of Coventry and Warwick. He has developed a keen interest in acceptance and commitment therapy (ACT) over recent years, and has delivered training in this area and other contextual behavioural approaches across the UK.

John Bullough, PhD MBACP, is an integrative counsellor/psychotherapist, working at a doctor's surgery and in private practice. He is co-editor and contributing author of *EFT and Beyond: Cutting Edge Techniques for Personal Transformation* (Energy Publications, 2009) and has spoken at international conferences on subjects related to energy psychology. He has also been an active contributor to the development of professional standards within the Association for the Advancement of Meridian Energy Techniques (www.aamet.org).

Jo Cooper has been involved with NLP since the mid-1980s and is certified by Richard Bandler as a master trainer. She is a founding partner of Centre NLP, a training and consultancy partnership, and has a private practice specializing in performance enhancement.

Mick Cooper is a Professor of Counselling at the University of Strathclyde and a Chartered Counselling Psychologist. Mick is author and editor of a wide range of texts on person-centred, existential, and pluralistic approaches to therapy, including *The Handbook of Person-Centred Psychotherapy and Counselling* (Palgrave, 2007), *Working at Relational Depth in Counselling and Psychotherapy* (Sage, 2005, with Dave Mearns) *and Pluralistic Counselling and Psychotherapy* (Sage, 2011, with John McLeod). Mick has also written extensively on research findings and their implications for therapeutic practice: authoring *Essential Research Findings in Counselling and Psychotherapy: The Facts are Friendly* (Sage, 2008) as well as co-editing *Person-Centred and Experiential Therapies Work* (PCCS, 2010). Mick lives in Glasgow with his partner and four children.

Olivier Cormier-Otaño, MBACP (Accred.), is an integrative and relational counsellor and a psychosexual health therapist in private practice. After many years as a volunteer counsellor for various LGBT (lesbian, gay, bisexual, transgender) charities in London, he is mostly working with gender and sexual minority clients. He also specialises in counselling in French and Spanish. He is an Advanced Accredited Sexual Minority Therapist with Pink Therapy. He has been presenting his research on asexuality to conferences and universities.

Dominic Davies is a Fellow of BACP and a BACP Senior Registered Practitioner who has been working with gender and sexual minorities for 30 years. He is Director of Pink Therapy, the UK's largest private practice specializing in working with sexual minority clients (www.pinktherapy.com). He is co-editor (with Charles Neal) of the Pink Therapy trilogy of textbooks (Open University Press) and has written and taught extensively on the subject of sexual minority therapy in the UK and internationally.

Harbrinder Dhillon-Stevens has a doctorate in psychotherapy and is a BPS and HPC Registered Chartered Counselling Psychologist, UKCP Registered Integrative Psychotherapist and HPC Registered Child Art Psychotherapist. Currently she is Senior Lecturer in Counselling, Psychotherapy and Counselling Psychology at the University of Roehampton. She is also Primary Tutor at the Metanoia Institute on the Doctorate in Counselling Psychology and Psychotherapy (DCPsych). Harbrinder is Training Director for DhillonStevens Ltd, a specialist training and research company. She has a private practice and undertakes expert witness assessment and treatment, supervision and therapeutic work with children, young people, adults and families. She is interested in anti-oppressive practice in psychological therapies and has undertaken research and publication in this area.

Gill Donohoe is a BABCP Accredited Cognitive-Behavioural Psychotherapist, Trainer and Supervisor. She is currently working within the Improving Access to Psychological Therapies service in Sheffield Health and Social Care NHS Foundation Trust. She is also a tutor on the Post Graduate Diploma in High Intensity Psychological Interventions at the University of Sheffield. Her background is in mental health nursing and she has an interest in self-management and group approaches and is clinical lead for stress control psycho-educational courses in Sheffield.

Windy Dryden is Professor of Psychotherapeutic Studies, Goldsmiths, University of London. He is a Fellow of the BPS and BACP. He began his training in REBT in 1977 and became the first Briton to be accredited as a REBT therapist by the Albert Ellis Institute.

Christine Dunkley is an Advanced Practitioner in Psychological Therapy in an NHS trust in Hampshire. She qualified as a medical social worker in 1982 and is now a Senior Accredited Practitioner with the British Association for Counselling and Psychotherapy. She is a founder member of the award-winning Dialectical Behaviour Therapy team in Winchester and has been on the UK DBT training team since 2006. In partnership with Michaela Swales she has produced the DVD series Core Components of Dialectical Behaviour Therapy. She is an honorary lecturer at Bangor University and a director of the training company Grayrock.

Graham Dyson, PhD, DClinPsy, is an HPC registered clinical psychologist currently working in South Durham. He also works as a Senior Lecturer on the Doctorate in Clinical Psychology programme at Teesside University where he is responsible for recruitment and personal professional development. He worked as a clinical psychologist in the National Health Service for 6 years, primarily with adults in a low security setting, before setting up his own independent practice. He completed his interpersonal therapy training in 2005 and is engaged in teaching and supervision within the Durham and Teesside areas.

Michael Ellis, MA, is a UKCP Registered Psychotherapist. He is a Director of the Gestalt Centre London and a tutor on the MA Programme in Psychotherapy. He has a private practice working with individuals and couples, is a supervisor, and works with organizations as a trainer and organizational consultant.

Gail Evans, MSc, is currently Programme Director at an independent training institute, The Academy: S.P.A.C.E. A counsellor, psychosexual therapist, trainer and clinical supervisor for 20 years with Relate, she also educated counsellors at Sheffield Hallam University, following an earlier career in therapeutic social work. Gail has worked in private practice for the last 18 years, focusing mainly on relationship and sexual therapy and more recently trauma. Gail co-owns a counselling and therapy centre in Sheffield. Her first book, *Counselling Skills for Dummies*, appeared in 2007.

Rose Evison, CPsychol (Couns&Occ), business psychologist, has used and taught co-counselling for 35+ years, integrating its typical processes into her work as an independent practitioner helping individuals and organizations change. In particular, she incorporates emotionally expressive techniques in all aspects of her work; uses reciprocal role pairs for destressing and creative thinking; and evokes supportive working cultures for learning, decision making and strategic planning groups.

Fay Fransella was Founder and Director of the Centre for Personal Construct Psychology at the University of Hertfordshire, a Fellow of the BPS, and Visiting Professor in Personal Construct Psychology at the University of Hertfordshire. Sadly, Fay passed away in early 2011.

Kevin Friery is a BACP Senior Accredited Psychotherapist and Counsellor. He is Clinical Director at Right Corecare Ltd and is, at the time of writing, Chair of BACP Workplace. He maintains a private therapy and coaching practice, as well as responding regularly to media interest in articles around psychological wellbeing and the workplace.

David Geldard has worked for many years as a psychologist specializing in counselling children, young people and families, in mental health, community health and private practice settings. He is the co-author of a number of internationally published textbooks on counselling.

Kathryn Geldard, PhD, is currently an Adjunct Senior Lecturer in the Faculty of Arts and Social Sciences at the University of the Sunshine Coast, Australia. Previously she was Senior Lecturer in Counselling and Programme Leader of the Counselling Programmes at the University. Her research interests include adolescent peer counselling, and counsellor training and education. She is the author of a number of textbooks on counselling and has several years' experience in supervising and training counsellors.

Paul Gilbert is a Professor of Clinical Psychology at the University of Derby. He has published a number of books and over 150 academic papers in the areas of mood disorders, shame and self-criticism. He is a Fellow of BPS and a former President of BACBP. He is the Founder of the charity the Compassionate Mind Foundation (www.compassionatemind.co.uk) and is currently developing and researching the efficacy of compassion-focused therapy.

Sobhi Girgis, MBBCh MMedSci MRCPsych LLM (Mental Health Law), is a Consultant Psychiatrist with Sheffield Health and Social Care NHS Foundation Trust. He is trained in both general adult and forensic psychiatry. His responsibilities include the Forensic Services in the Trust. He is also the Clinical Lead for the Sheffield Asperger Syndrome Service, a National Tertiary Service. He is the Co-Chair of the Mental Health Act Group in the Trust and organizer of S12 (2) and Approved Clinician training courses in Sheffield.

Stephen Goss, MBBCh, is Principal Lecturer at the Metanoia Institute, Middlesex University, and an independent consultant in counselling and support service development, mental health technology, research and evaluation in the UK and worldwide, and offers counselling supervision by email and telephone. He co-edited *The Use of Technology in Mental Health* (Thomas, 2010), *Technology in Counselling and Psychotherapy: A Practitioner's Guide* (Palgrave, 2003) and *Evidence Based Counselling and Psychological Therapies: Research and Applications* (Routledge, 2000) among over 70 other items of public output. He is also Associate Editor for Research for the bimonthly journal *Therapeutic Innovations in Light of Technology* (*TILT Magazine*) and sits on the Editorial Board of the *British Journal of Guidance and Counselling*.

Andrew Guppy is Professor of Applied Psychology at the University of Bedfordshire and is a health psychologist and an occupational psychologist registered with the Health Professions Council. He has been involved in the provision and evaluation of counselling and other interventions in the stress, alcohol and drug fields for over 25 years.

Angela Harris is a Lecturer on the Counselling Psychology Doctorate Programme at Glasgow Caledonian University and is the Psychological Therapies Training Coordinator for NHS Lothian. She works clinically with older adults in the Edinburgh Psychology Service and also has a private practice. She trained as a counselling psychologist following a career in human resources with multinational organizations.

Colleen Heenan is a psychotherapist and Honorary Lecturer in Psychology at The University of Bolton. She was also a Co-Founder of the Leeds Women's Counselling and Therapy Service. Colleen is co-author (with Erica Burman et al.) of *Challenging Women: Psychology's Exclusions, Feminist Possibilities* (Open University Press, 1996) and *Psychology, Discourse, Practice: From Regulation to Resistance* (Taylor and Francis, 1996), is co-editor (with Bruna Seu) of *Feminism and Psychotherapy: Reflections on Contemporary Theories and Practices* (Sage, 1998), and has edited a number of special features in the journal *Feminism and Psychology* plus contributing to other texts and journals on these subjects.

Claudia Herbert, DClinPsy AFBPsS, is a Chartered Consultant Clinical Psychologist, a BABCP and UKCP Accredited Cognitive Behavioural Psychotherapist, an EMDR Consultant, an ISST Registered Schema Therapist and a Reconnective Healing Practitioner. She is the Managing Director of The Oxford Development Centre Ltd, an independent psychological therapy service, of which The Oxford Stress and Trauma Centre and The Centre for Trauma and Positive Growth form parts. She has worked in the field of trauma psychology since 1992, wrote the first therapeutic help booklet for survivors of trauma available in the UK, entitled *Understanding your Reactions to Trauma*, and has published regularly since. She lectures and trains therapists, runs specialist supervision groups for complex trauma, facilitates workshops worldwide, works as an organizational consultant and is frequently consulted by the media. She feels passionate about enabling survivors of trauma to transition into positive growth and self-development as part of their healing and recovery process.

Nick Hodge, EdD, is Principal Lecturer in Research Development and Lecturer in Autism in the Department of Education, Childhood and Inclusion at Sheffield Hallam University. Prior to joining the University in 1998, Nick's professional background was in supporting disabled children and their families in schools for over 15 years. His research interests focus around the issues that impact on the education, development and wellbeing of disabled people and their families. More information on Nick is available at shu.academia.edu/NickHodge/About.

Richard Horobin is Honorary Research Fellow in the School of Life Sciences, College of Medical, Veterinary and Life Sciences, at the University of Glasgow. He has used and taught co-counselling for 35+ years.

Peter Hughes is a person-centred counsellor and counselling supervisor in independent practice. Counselling since the mid-1980s, and supervising since the early 1990s, Peter is also a freelance counselling and groupwork trainer, principally in higher and further education.

Francesca Inskipp is a Fellow and Accredited Supervisor of the BACP. She works freelance as a trainer, supervisor and counsellor and is Editor of the Sage Skills in Counselling and Psychotherapy series.

Peter Jenkins is an experienced counsellor trainer, and author of several books on the law, including *Counselling, Psychotherapy and the Law* (2nd edn, Sage, 2007). He has extensive experience of running training workshops on legal aspects of therapy. He is a Senior Lecturer in Counselling at Manchester University and an honorary counsellor at Manchester University Counselling Service. Formerly a member of the BACP Professional Conduct Committee, he is currently a member of the UKCP Ethics Committee. His most recent publication is *Therapy with Children: Children's Rights, Confidentiality and the Law* (2nd edn, Sage, 2010), which was co-authored with Debbie Daniels.

Gordon Jinks is a Principal Lecturer in the School of Psychology at the University of East London, where he is Programme Leader for the MA/Postgraduate Diploma in Counselling and Psychotherapy. He is an integrative counsellor and trainer with particular interest in the client's experience of therapy.

Hazel Johns has been engaged in counselling, training and supervision for over 35 years. She designed and led the Counselling Training Programme at Bristol University, after earlier experience as a counsellor in schools, developing courses at the then North East London Polytechnic and as an HMI and LEA Adviser. She has presented and co-written *Principles of Counselling*, 16 programmes for BBC Radio (1978 and 1982); written *Personal Development in Counselling Training* (first published by Cassell in 1996, with a Second Edition published by Sage in 2012); and edited *Studies in Counselling Training* (Routledge, 1998). Since taking early retirement, she has worked independently as a counsellor and supervisor in Pembrokeshire. She is a BACP Accredited Counsellor and Fellow of BACP.

Stephen Kellett is a Consultant Chartered Clinical Psychologist with Sheffield Health and Social Care NHS Foundation Trust, an Accredited Cognitive Behavioural Psychotherapist and an Accredited Cognitive Analytic Psychotherapist, Trainer and Supervisor. He is currently the Programme Director for the University of Sheffield IAPT PG High and Low Intensity Psychological Interventions courses. His research interests include outcomes across the psychological modalities, compulsive hoarding, cyclothymia and psychotherapy attendance.

Janet Laffin is a Senior Lecturer at Sheffield Hallam University, and an active researcher based in the CMRU (Coaching and Mentoring Research Unit) of the Sheffield Business School. She has designed and implemented large-scale coaching programmes and acquired over 20 years' experience of coaching in the UK and Italy. Currently, she provides coach training to public and private sector organizations in the UK and internationally.

Ken Laidlaw, PhD, is an experienced practitioner and researcher in CBT with older people. He is a part-time Senior Lecturer at Edinburgh University where he is involved with the Clinical Psychology Training Programme. He also holds a senior appointment as Consultant Clinical Psychologist and Clinical Lead for Older Adults Clinical Psychology Services in Edinburgh with NHS Lothian. He is co-author of *CBT with Older People*, and co-editor of two other books: *Handbook of Emotional Disorders in Late Life* and *The Casebook of Clinical Geropsychology: International Perspectives on Practice*. Ken is currently a Board Member of the International Psychogeriatric Association.

Pam Maras is Professor in Social and Educational Psychology at the University of Greenwich, where she is Head of the Department of Psychology and Counselling and Director of the Research Centre for Children Schools and Families. She is a Chartered Psychologist and Fellow of the British Psychological Society and was President of the BPS in 2007–8. Pam's research interests are in the broad areas of social inclusion, antisocial behaviour (including AD/HD and other disorders) in schools and raising young people's aspirations. She has a particular interest in developmental trends and the impact of others on children's and young people's behaviour – specifically, changes in mid-adolescence which she has described as 'the year 10 effect'. Pam has held numerous external research grants and has published widely in these areas. Her research has been conducted in the Thames

Gateway, South East London and Kent as well as more widely in the UK and in Africa, mainland Europe, China, the US and Australia.

Brian Martindale is a Consultant Psychiatrist working in an Early Intervention in Psychosis service for Northumberland, Tyne and Wear NHS Foundation Trust, and a psychoanalyst. He is Chair of the International Society for the Psychological Treatments of the Schizophrenias and Other Psychoses (ISPS) and Editor of the ISPS book series. He is Honorary President of the European Federation of Psychoanalytic Psychotherapy, is on the Education Committee of the World Psychiatric Association, and in 2009 was winner of the BPC Award for Outstanding Professional Leadership.

John McLeod is Emeritus Professor of Counselling at the University of Abertay, Dundee. He is committed to promoting the relevance of research as a means of informing therapy practice and improving the quality of services that are available to clients. His enthusiastic search for finding ways to make research interesting and accessible for practitioners has resulted in a teaching award from the students at his own university and an award for exceptional contribution to research from the British Association for Counselling and Psychotherapy. His writing has influenced a generation of trainees in the field of counselling and psychotherapy, and his books are widely adopted on training programmes across the world.

John Mellor-Clark has been engaged in the evaluation of UK psychological therapies and counselling for the past 20 years. Originally trained as an organisational psychologist, John's special interest in quality assurance in healthcare has led him to regularly publish and present on a range of topics such as best practice development, service quality benchmarking and introducing practitioner performance appraisal. Through the mid 1990s John led the development of the CORE System as the first UK standardised quality evaluation system for psychological therapy. Today this system is used by over 250 services and 3,500 clinicians to help measure, monitor and manage therapy outcomes. The unique empirical yield from CORE helps create one of the single largest databases of practice-based evidence in the field.

DeeAnna Merz Nagel, LPC, DCC is a psychotherapist, consultant and international expert regarding online counselling and the impact of technology on mental health. She is co-founder of the Online Therapy Institute and Managing Co-Editor of *TILT Magazine – Therapeutic Innovations in Light of Technology*. DeeAnna's expertise extends to assisting individuals and families in understanding the impact of technology in their lives from normalizing the use of technology and social media to overcoming internet and cybersex addictions. Her presentations and publications include ethical considerations for the mental health practitioner with regard to online counselling, social networking, mixed reality and virtual world environments.

Anthea Millar is a psychotherapist, trainer and supervisor working in independent practice and with organisations in the UK and abroad. She coordinated the 4 year Adlerian counselling training in Cambridge for 26 years and is co-founder of Cambridge Supervision Training (www.cambridgesupervisiontraining.com). Anthea is on the training committee of the UK Adlerian Society and co-editor of their journal. She is also a co-chair of ICASSI, an Adlerian international summer school.

Eric Morris works as a consultant clinical psychologist for the South London and Maudsley NHS Foundation Trust, and has practised acceptance and commitment therapy (ACT) for the past 10 years, as well as providing teaching and training in ACT and other contextual behavioural therapies. He is involved in developing and researching mindfulness-based group and individual interventions for psychosis at the Institute of Psychiatry, King's College London.

Jill Mytton is a Chartered Counselling Psychologist in private practice. She is currently the Deputy Course Leader of the Doctorate in Existential Counselling Psychology and Psychotherapy at the New School of Psychotherapy and Counselling, London. Prior to this she was the Course Leader on the Counselling Psychology Doctoral Programme at London Metropolitan University. She has served on the Division of Counselling Psychology Committee as the lead for conference for several years. In addition to contributing chapters to three books, she is co-author with Windy Dryden of *Four Approaches to Counselling and Psychotherapy* (Routledge, 1999).

Bill O'Connell is currently the Director of Training with Focus on Solutions Limited, a company specializing in the delivery of training in the solution-focused approach. Until 2003 he was a Senior Lecturer at the University of Birmingham where he headed the MA in Solution Focused Therapy Programme. He is a Fellow of the BACP and an Accredited Counsellor. He has a background in social work and youth work. He is the author of *Solution Focused Therapy* (Sage, 1998) and *Solution Focused Stress Counselling* (Continuum/Sage, 2001), and is co-editor with Stephen Palmer of the *Handbook of Solution Focused Therapy* (Sage, 2003).

Joe Oliver is a Clinical Psychologist working in the South London and Maudsley NHS Foundation Trust. He works within an Early Intervention for Psychosis team in South London. He has clinical and research interests in the use of acceptance and commitment therapy in working with people with psychosis.

Stephen Palmer, PhD FBACP CPsychol, is Founder Director of the Centre for Stress Management and the Centre for Coaching. He is Managing Director of the International Academy for Professional Development Ltd. He is President of the International Society for Coaching Psychology. He is an Honorary Professor of Psychology at City University and Director of their Coaching Psychology Unit. He has received awards for his contribution to both counselling and coaching psychology.

He is an Albert Ellis Institute Certified REBT Supervisor and is UKCP Registered (CBT & REBT). He has written or edited 35 books on a range of topics, including coaching, management, stress, suicide, trauma, counselling and psychotherapy.

Simon Parritt, CPsychol AFBPsS MSc BSc(Hons) BA CPsSC, is a Chartered Psychologist and Psychosexual Therapist in independent practice specializing in psychosexual and relationship therapy, disability and chronic illness, in addition to his general work as a counselling psychologist dealing with a wide range of psychological and emotional issues. A former Director of the Association to Aid the Sexual and Personal Relationships of People with a Disability (SPOD), he has worked in acute geriatrics, primary care and the voluntary sector and has been a visiting lecturer at Oxford Medical School, Brighton University and various health and social care training courses. Currently, he is visiting lecturer at the Surrey University doctoral programme in Counselling Psychology on disability. He is also a member of the British Psychological Society and the College of Sexual and Relationship Therapists, and is a contributor to *Disability Now*. He has been a disabled person himself since the age of 5.

Stephen Paul is Director of the Centre for Psychological Therapies at Leeds Metropolitan University. He is a UKCP Registered Psychotherapist. He is co-editor of *The Therapeutic Relationship: Themes and Perspectives* (PCCS, 2008). He first started using groups therapeutically in the NHS in the 1970s. He has facilitated groups in adult and child psychiatry, in self help therapy, and in the training and continuing professional development of counsellors and psychotherapists. He was also head of a special school which he developed as a therapeutic community. Stephen has been teaching Higher Education courses in group therapy for 20 years.

Sara Perren is a psychodynamic counsellor and group psychotherapist interested in research. She worked for 10 years as a primary care counsellor in Yorkshire. Research includes co-authored papers in *Counseling and Psychotherapy Research* on the take-up of counselling appointments and the long-term effects of counselling. She is Senior Psychotherapist at The Tuke Centre, the outpatient service of the Retreat Hospital, York, and is also supervisor for the counselling arm of the University of York's Acupuncture, Counselling and Usual Care for Depression (ACUDep) randomized controlled trial.

David Pilgrim is Professor of Mental Health Policy, School of Social Work, University of Central Lancashire and Honorary Professor of Clinical Psychology, University of Liverpool. He has a background in both clinical psychology and medical sociology and has researched and written extensively on the sociology of mental health.

Andrew Reeves, PhD, is a counsellor/psychotherapist and supervisor at the University of Liverpool, and a freelance trainer. He has written extensively about suicide and self-harm, authoring *Counselling Suicidal Clients* (Sage, 2010). He additionally co-edited, with Professor Windy Dryden, *Key Issues for Counselling in Action* (2nd edn, Sage, 2008). He is Editor of *Counselling and Psychotherapy Research* journal and a regular contributor to *Therapy Today*.

Tom Ricketts, PhD, is a BABCP accredited cognitive-behavioural psychotherapist and nurse consultant working in the NHS. He has developed and taught both qualifying courses for cognitive-behavioural psychotherapists and introductory courses for non-specialists. He has a particular interest in widening access to cognitive-behavioural therapy through the use of self-management approaches and the training of health professionals.

Mark Rivett is a Visiting Lecturer at Exeter University and at the University of the West of England. He is also a Family Psychotherapist in South Wales and Bristol NHS Trusts. His clinical specialism is working with families where there are mental health problems but he has also worked extensively where abuse has occurred in families. This includes domestic violence and problem sexual behaviour. He has co-authored two books with Eddy Street, namely *Family Therapy in Focus* (Sage, 2003) and *Family Therapy: 100 Key Points and Techniques* (Routledge, 2009), as well as *Working with Men in Health and Social Care* (Sage, 2007) with Brid Featherstone and Jonathan Scourfield. He is currrent Editor of *Journal of Family Therapy*.

Elizabeth Robinson, PhD, completed her core professional training as a psychiatric nurse in 1986. She received her IPT training and supervision in 1997 from Professor John Markowitz and Kathleen Clougherty, both of whom were trained by Gerald Klerman, the originator of IPT. She was the principal IPT research therapist for two clinical studies; the second, a brain imaging study of IPT in treatment resistant depression, was for her PhD at Durham University. Elizabeth works part-time in private clinical practice and as an IPT trainer and supervisor as part of the government initiative Improving Access to Psychological Therapies.

Louise Robinson is Healthcare Development Manager for the British Association for Counselling and Psychotherapy. She co-authored *NHS Commissioning: A Toolkit for Psychological Therapy Providers* (BACP, 2009).

Maxine Rosenfield has over 20 years' experience as a counsellor, supervisor and trainer. She pioneered telephone counselling in the UK, writing *Counselling by Telephone* (Sage, 1997), and has contributed to counselling and social work texts in the UK and the USA. Now based in Sydney, Australia, she continues counselling, supervising, training and writing. Maxine has private practices in two Sydney locations and works by phone and Skype with clients and supervisees throughout Australia and internationally. Maxine is past President of the Counsellors and Psychotherapists Association of New South Wales and past President of Helplines Australia.

Diana Sanders, PhD, is a Counselling Psychologist in the Oxfordshire and Buckinghamshire Mental Healthcare NHS Trust and a BABCP Accredited Cognitive Psychotherapist. She works in psychological medicine, mainly in cardiology and palliative care. She has written extensively on cognitive approaches in counselling and applications in medicine.

Christiane Sanderson is a Lecturer in Psychology at the University of London, Birkbeck College, and visiting lecturer in the School of Human and Life Sciences, Roehampton University. With 22 years' experience of working with sexual violence, domestic abuse and interpersonal trauma, she has provided consultancy and training to parents, teachers, social workers, nurses, therapists, counsellors, the NSPCC and the Metropolitan Police Service. Christiane is a trustee of the charity One in Four and the author of *Introduction to Counselling Survivors of Interpersonal Trauma* (2010), *Counselling Survivors of Domestic Abuse* (2008), *Counselling Adult Survivors of Child Sexual Abuse* (3rd edn, 2006), and *The Seduction of Children: Empowering Parents and Teachers to Protect Children from Child Sexual Abuse* (2004), all published by Jessica Kingsley. She is also the author of *The Warrior Within: A One in Four Handbook to Aid Recovery from Childhood Sexual Abuse and Sexual Violence*.

Joseph Schwartz, PhD, is a psychoanalytic psychotherapist at the Bowlby Centre in London where he is a supervisor and training therapist. He is the author of numerous books and articles including *Cassandra's Daughter: A History of Psychoanalysis in Europe and America* (Penguin and Karnac). He was founding Editor of the journal *Attachment: New Directions on Psychotherapy and Relational Psychoanalysis*.

Michael Scott is a Chartered Counselling Psychologist, with a private practice in Liverpool. He has authored or edited six text books, including the best-selling *Counselling for Post-traumatic Stress Disorder* (3rd edn, with Stephen Stradling) (Sage, 2006). Recently he became external examiner for the MSc Cognitive and Behavioural Psychotherapies programme at University College, Chester.

Peter Seal is certified by Richard Bandler as a master trainer of NLP and is a founding partner of Centre NLP. He is the originator of a simple and effective approach to working directly with unconscious processes and author of programmes encouraging others to access that approach.

Pat Seber, MA, has 30 years' experience as a counsellor, trainer and manager in a number of clinical settings including the NHS. She is currently working as a Consultant to the British Association for Counselling and Psychotherapy on workforce issues and service development. Since the 1990s she has been interested in the employment conditions of counsellors and psychotherapists and is co-author of *Guidance for Best Practice: The Employment of Counsellors and Psychotherapists in the NHS* (BACP, 2004). She is author of 'Introduction to Counselling in Healthcare Settings' in *Counselling in Different Settings: The Reality of Practice* edited by Maggie Reid (Palgrave, 2004) and has written numerous articles in professional journals on changes within the NHS affecting practitioners.

Julia Segal is a Fellow of BACP. She trained with Relate and for the past 25 years has been counselling people with neurological conditions and members of their families, using the ideas of Melanie Klein to understand and illuminate everyday experience. She has written extensively on the effects of illness on relationships. Julia is best known for her books which include *Phantasy in Everyday Life* (Penguin, 1985; Karnac, 1995), *Melanie Klein: Key Figures in Counselling and Psychotherapy* (Sage, 1992) and *Helping Children with Ill or Disabled Parents* (Jessica Kingsley, 1996).

Helen Sieroda is an independent trainer, facilitator and consultant working with groups, organizations and individuals. She has been involved in the training and supervision of counsellors, psychotherapists and coaches in Europe for over 20 years and is co-chair of the Psychosynthesis and Education Trust. She is a UKCP Registered Psychotherapist and also holds an MSc in Responsibility in Business Practice. Helen has a long-standing interest in leadership development and in developing a psychospiritual response to questions of environmental sustainability.

Charlotte Sills is a psychotherapist and supervisor in private practice and a trainer in a variety of settings, including as senior tutor at Metanoia Institute UK and co-director of the Coaching Course at Ashridge College, UK. She is also a Visiting Professor at Middlesex University. She is the author or co-author of several books and articles in the field of counselling, therapy and coaching including, with Phil Lapworth *An Introduction to Transactional Analysis,* Second Edition (Sage, 2011), with Helena Hargaden *Transactional Analysis: A Relational Perspective* (Routledge, 2002) and with Heather Fowlie *Relational Transactional Analysis – Principles in Practice* (Karnac, 2011).

Jonathan P. Smith is a lecturer in psychology and also a psychotherapist and trainer. He works at the Faculty of Continuing Education at Birkbeck College and has also been a regular contributor to courses at the Guildhall School of Music and Drama, the Psychosynthesis and Education Trust, and the University of East London. He has a private practice offering Gestalt psychotherapy and runs workshops in Gestalt for various counselling organizations.

Kathy Stephenson, BA(Hons) MSc PGCE GQHP, is a Senior Lecturer at Sheffield Hallam University. She is the course leader of the Education, Psychology and Counselling degree course and previously ran the Certificate of Hypnotherapy course. She divides her time between lecturing and running a busy private hypnotherapy practice. She has developed a range of self-hypnosis audio CDs using a combination of hypnotherapeutic suggestion and NLP techniques. Kathy also runs self-hypnosis workshops: www.innerchange.co.uk.

William B. Stiles is Professor Emeritus of Psychology, Miami University, Oxford, Ohio, USA, where he taught for more than 30 years. He also taught at the University of North Carolina at Chapel Hill, and has held visiting positions at the Universities of Sheffield and Leeds in the United Kingdom, at Massey University in New Zealand, and at the University of Joensuu in Finland. He received his PhD from UCLA in 1972. He is President-Elect of Division 29 (Psychotherapy) of the American Psychological Association and a Past President of the Society for Psychotherapy Research. He has served as Editor of *Psychotherapy Research* and is currently Editor of *Person-Centered and Experiential Psychotherapies* and Associate Editor of *British Journal of Clinical Psychology*. He has published over 250 journal articles and book chapters, most dealing with psychotherapy theory, research and practice, verbal interaction and research methods.

Léonie Sugarman, PhD, is a BPS Chartered Psychologist and Emeritus Reader in Applied Psychology at the University of Cumbria. She is an Honorary Fellow and former Vice President of the British Association for Counselling and Psychotherapy. She is on the Editorial Board of the *British Journal of Guidance and Counselling*; author of *Life-Span Development: Frameworks, Accounts and Strategies* (Psychology Press, 2001) and *Counselling and the Life Course* (Sage, 2004); and co-author with R. Wright of *Occupational Therapy and Life Course Development* (Wiley, 2009).

Michaela Swales, PhD, is Consultant Clinical Psychologist, Betsi Cadwaladr University Health Board, and Senior Lecturer in Clinical Psychology, School of Psychology, Bangor University. She is co-author with Dr Heidi Heard of *Dialectical Behaviour Therapy* in the CBT Distinctive Features series (Routledge, 2009). In 2009 she was awarded the Cindy Sanderson Outstanding Educator Award by the International Society for the Improvement and Teaching of DBT at their conference in New York.

Gabrielle Syme works in private practice as a counsellor, supervisor and trainer. She is a Fellow of BACP and an Accredited Counsellor and Supervisor. Gabrielle is a former Chair of both the Association for University and College Counselling and the British Association for Counselling and Psychotherapy. She is author or co-author of books and articles in the field of bereavement, dual relationships, private practice and ethical issues. The books are *Gift of Tears* (2nd edn, Brunner-Routledge, 2004), *Counselling in Independent Practice* (Open University Press, 1994), *Dual Relationships in Counselling and Psychotherapy* (Sage, 2003), *Questions of Ethics in Counselling and Psychotherapy* (Open University Press, 2000) and *Objectives and Outcomes: Questioning the Practice of Therapy* (Open University Press, 2006).

Digby Tantam is Clinical Professor of Psychotherapy in the University of Sheffield, Honorary Visiting Senior Fellow at the University of Cambridge, and a Director of Septimus Ltd and of its subsidiary companies, Dilemma Consultancy, the New School of Psychotherapy and Counselling, Ask the Therapist and the Existential Academy.

Nick Totton is a therapist, supervisor and trainer based in West Yorkshire. He teaches and practises the style of work he has developed, embodied-relational therapy, and has written or edited 12 books, including *Body Psychotherapy: An Introduction*; *Psychotherapy and Politics*; and *Wild Therapy*. He lives in Calderdale with his partner and grows vegetables.

Michael Townend is a Reader in Cognitive Behavioural Psychotherapy at the University of Derby, where he programme leads a Doctorate of Health and Social Care Practice. His most recent major publication is *Cognitive Behavioural Therapy for Mental Health Problems,* Second Edition (Sage, 2010, with Alec Grant, Ronan Mulhern and Nigel Short). He is also an independent consultant, teacher and practitioner.

Keith Tudor has worked for nearly 30 years in the helping professions in a number of settings. He is a qualified and registered psychotherapist, group psychotherapist and facilitator, and has a private/independent practice in Sheffield offering therapy, supervision and consultancy, where he is a Director of Temenos and its postgraduate diploma/MSc course in Person-Centred Psychotherapy and Counselling. He is a teaching and supervising transactional analyst, and an Honorary Fellow in the School of Health, Liverpool John Moores University. He is a widely-published author in the field of psychotherapy and counselling, with over 60 papers and seven books to his name. He is on the editorial advisory board of three international journals and is the series editor of A*dvancing Theory in Therapy* (published by Routledge).

Dan Tully is a speciality doctor in psychiatry and psychotherapy (CAT). He works in a community mental health team in Sheffield and has an interest in personality disorder.

Emmy van Deurzen is an existential therapist, counselling psychologist, philosopher and author. She is Principal of the New School of Psychotherapy and Counselling in London where she runs masters and doctoral programmes jointly with Middlesex University. Emmy has published widely on existential psychotherapy and counselling, including her recent book *Psychotherapy and the Quest for Happiness* (Sage, 2009) and her textbook on existential therapy *Everyday Mysteries* (Routledge, 2010). She is the Founder of the Society for Existential Analysis. She lectures worldwide and her work has been translated into over a dozen languages.

Richard Velleman is Professor of Mental Health Research at the University of Bath, and is a Consultant Clinical Psychologist with the Avon and Wiltshire

Mental Health NHS Trust. He has always held dual posts in universities and the NHS. His research and practice have been both on substance misuse generally, and on the impact of substance misuse and mental health issues on family members, especially children. His broader research and practice interests are in counselling and in children and families. He has been awarded grants of more than £4,000,000 over his research career to date, and has published over 200 items including 13 books and many chapters and scientific journal papers. His latest books include *Counselling for Alcohol Problems*, Third Edition (Sage, 2011) and *Counselling and Helping*, Second Ediion (Wiley Blackwell/British Psychological Society, 2010, co-authored with Sarajane Aris).

Alison Waines is a BACP Senior Accredited Practitioner who has been counselling in private practice for 15 years. She is author of *The Self-Esteem Journal* (2004) and *Making Relationships Work* (2005). Also a qualified teacher, she has designed and presented courses on self-esteem and written extensively for *Slimming World* magazine. Alison has made live appearances on television and radio. She is also a novelist specializing in psychological thrillers.

Ida Waksberg is a Chartered Counselling Psychologist in the Derbyshire Mental Health Services NHS Trust. She works in the Clinical Psychology Service based at the Department of Genito-Urinary Medicine in Derby (HIV and Sexual Health Service). She also works privately in Nottingham and as a visiting therapist at the Derby Psychotherapy Unit, where she trained and qualified with an MA in Psychodynamic Psychotherapy.

Moira Walker, PhD MSc, lives and works in Dorset and is a Registered Psychotherapist and Fellow of the BACP. She has experience as a trainer, supervisor, practitioner and writer and has worked in the field of abuse for many years. She set up a registered charity, Dorset Action on Abuse, offering counselling and other services to survivors. She has worked extensively in universities and other settings. Her books include *Surviving Secrets: The Experience of Abuse for the Child*, *the Adult and the Helper* and *Abuse: Questions and Answers for Counsellors and Therapists*.

Jenny Warner was a Speech and Language Therapy Manager in the NHS and an Adlerian therapist, family counsellor, supervisor, author and international trainer. She is now retired.

William West, PhD, is currently Reader in Counselling Studies at the University of Manchester in Britain where he is Director of the Counselling Studies Programme and where he delights in supervising doctoral students. William's key areas of interest include: counselling and spirituality, culture, traditional healing, supervision and qualitative research methods. William has written: two authored books, *Psychotherapy and Spirituality* (Sage, 2000) and *Spiritual*

Issues in Therapy (Palgrave, 2004); one edited book, *Exploring Counselling Spirituality and Healing* (Palgrave, 2011); one co-edited book with Roy Moodley, *Integrating Traditional Healing Practices into Counseling and Psychotherapy* (Sage, 2005); and 27 academic papers, 15 book chapters and 29 professional journal papers. William is a keen cyclist, amateur poet and beginner piano player.

Emma Williams, BSc, MPhil, PhD, is a Consultant Clinical Psychologist with West London Mental Health NHS Trust, based at Broadmoor Hospital. She is also Consultant Clinical Psychologist with Berkshire Healthcare NHS Trust providing an in-reach service to HMP Reading. She has worked as a clinical psychologist in the National Health Service for over 15 years, primarily in medium and high-security psychiatric hospitals and community forensic services.

Ruth Williams MA (Jungian and Post-Jungian Studies) is a Jungian Analyst-Analytical Psychologist in private practice in London. She trained at the Association of Jungian Analysts. She is a member of the International Association for Analytical Psychology. She is a member of the Forum for Independent Psychotherapist, registered with the United Kingdom Council for Psychotherapy as part of the Council for Psychoanalysis and Jungian Analysis. She is also a member of The Minster Centre, registered with the United Kingdom Council for Psychotherapy as part of the Humanistic and Integrative Section. Ruth is also registered as a Supervisor with the British Association for Psychoanalytic and Psychodynamic Supervision (BAPPS) and is a training therapist and supervisor for a number of UKCP organizations. She is an Honorary Psychotherapist at the Royal London Hospital and is the Honorary Secretary of the Confederation for Analytical Psychology. See www.RuthWilliams.org.uk

David Winter is Professor of Clinical Psychology and Programme Director of the Doctorate in Clinical Psychology at the University of Hertfordshire. He has applied personal construct psychology in National Health Service settings for many years, and has published extensively in this area and on psychotherapy research. His books include *Personal Construct Psychology in Clinical Practice* (Routledge, 1992) and *Personal Construct Psychotherapy: Advances in Theory, Practice and Research* (with Linda Viney: Whurr, 2005). He is a Fellow of the British Psychological Society, and has chaired its Psychotherapy Section, as well as the Experiential Constructivist Section and Research Committee of the UK Council for Psychotherapy.

Wendy Wood is a Senior Lecturer within the Faculty of Education Health and Sciences at the University of Derby. She has been involved in counselling and psychotherapy training for 13 years and has been a therapist for over 20 years.

Sally Woods is Joint Programme Co-ordinator for the MSc Drug Use and Addiction at Liverpool John Moores University. She also lectures on the undergraduate Applied Psychology degree and is a member of BPS.

Val Wosket, PhD, is a BACP Senior Accredited Counsellor/Psychotherapist and Supervisor. Formerly Senior Lecturer in Counselling at York St John University, Val now works in private practice. She has particular interest and experience in working with complex trauma and dissociation and is a teaching faculty member of the UK Division of the European Society for Trauma and Dissociation (ESTD-UK). Her publications include *Egan's Skilled Helper Model: Developments and Applications in Counselling* (Routledge, 2006), *The Therapeutic Use of Self: Counselling Practice, Research and Supervision* (Routledge, 1999) and *Supervising the Counsellor: A Cyclical Model* (with Steve Page: Routledge, 2001).

Jessica Yakeley is a Consultant Psychiatrist in Forensic Psychotherapy at the Portman Clinic, and Director of Medical Education and Associate Medical Director of the Tavistock and Portman NHS Foundation Trust. She is also a Fellow of the British Psychoanalytical Society. She has a particular interest in the treatment of antisocial personality disorder and has recently published a book *Working with Violence: A Psychoanalytic Approach* (Palgrave Macmillan, 2010).

Daniel Zahl, BA MA DClinPsych, is a BPS Chartered Clinical Psychologist and a BABCP Accredited Cognitive Psychotherapist. He works in clinical health psychology for Oxford Radcliffe Hospitals and as a CBT supervisor in an NHS IAPT primary care service and in private practice.

Preface

COLIN FELTHAM AND IAN HORTON

We are pleased to introduce this third edition of what has proved a very popular textbook. This new edition aims once more to bring together comprehensively the fundamentals of counselling and psychotherapy for both trainees and experienced practitioners seeking expansion of their knowledge base. A small number of previous cntries have been removed and several new additions made by new authors to reflect some of the progress made over the past few years in theory, practice and professional development in the field of the psychological therapies, and everything in this edition has also been updated as necessary.

Notwithstanding a few welcome distinguished authors from the USA, Australia and New Zealand, this is a mainly British text, reflecting the experiences and needs of clients and therapists in a complex multicultural society, in the twenty-first century, represented by leading practitioners and academics who are all active in their fields. It brings together both the practical and the theoretical aspects of the psychological therapies, including information of an introductory and sometimes advanced nature. Finally, although it must be in the nature of a book of this kind to present a good deal of established, relatively uncontentious knowledge, we have encouraged a degree of critical thinking, in the hope that colleagues will join with us in taking responsibility for challenging any elements of counselling and psychotherapy calling for change. We have in mind those elements which have permeated our collective professional wisdom, which are repeated by each generation of practitioners, yet often remain without a clearly articulated rationale or evidence base.

COUNSELLING AND PSYCHOTHERAPY

In the first edition we acknowledged transparently the agonizing that went into the decision behind the title of the book. At different stages the central terms were to be 'counselling' or 'therapeutic counselling' or 'psychological therapy', or even 'integrative therapeutic counselling'. Finally we opted for 'counselling and psychotherapy' for the following reasons. Among those involved in the debate on what the real, if any, differences between counselling and psychotherapy are, we both belong to that group who believe the differences to be minimal and the commonalities to be vast; we hope that *all* 'clinicians' – counsellors, psychotherapists, counselling psychologists, clinical psychologists and others – may find this book useful. More contentiously and ambitiously, we hope that the blend of information, perspectives and challenges given here will activate in some small way the thrust not only towards theoretical collaboration in this field, but also towards, if not professional integration, then at least wider acknowledgement of and greater respect for different contributions of all colleagues in the field. This edition was prepared at a time when statutory regulation was being abandoned in favour of a new form of voluntary regulation and hopefully greater cooperation between relevant professions. Gratifyingly, we have been aware that many clinical and counselling psychologists who *did* take the statutory regulation route via the Health Professions Council also find this book professionally useful.

For the most part we have encouraged the convention of referring to the recipient of therapy as the client rather than the patient. Writers have been asked to avoid, for the most part, use of 'I' for stylistic reasons, but occasionally its use has been appropriate. References have usually been limited for space reasons but we trust that those appearing are useful.

SOCIO-CULTURAL PERSPECTIVES

When we declared that this was a mainly British text, our association was never with nationalism but with the recognition that there is a need to address 'local' experience with (as far as possible) local knowledge. In spite of Central European origins, most models or schools of counselling and psychotherapy for the last 60 or so years have been American or Americanized, and many influential texts in this field have been American. British society and its particular multicultural profile is quite distinct. Moghaddam and Studer (1997) rightly challenged the kind of psychology that has become an American export, or what they referred to as 'US-manufactured psychological knowledge', which, even in its guise of cross-cultural psychology, subtly marginalizes the different experiences, indigenous theorizing and unique problem-solving capacities of other cultures, particularly in the developing world. Watters (2010) too has been critical of his American colleagues' exporting of mental health norms. On the other hand Parker (2007) and other British authors have called for an overturning of psychology at home. Yet again, we might recognize that few UK texts can match the American focus on, for example, research into psychotherapy cost-effectiveness (Lazar, 2010).

Two of the very few truly 'home-grown' traditions in Britain are represented by the Independent Group (Fairbairn, Winnicott, Bowlby, Balint, Bollas, Khan and others), who pioneered object relations work and sought to avoid the extremes of other affiliations (Rayner, 1991); and cognitive analytic therapy, which welds object relations with personal construct, cognitive therapy and related theories into a short-term, NHS-adaptable therapy (Ryle, 1990). It may still be hoped – in spite of the slowness of its realization – that such traditions of locally created theory and practice will continue to respond to the histories, needs, strengths and changing conditions of British and other European societies with a culturally sensitive and pragmatically attuned consciousness. To some extent in recent years the creation of Improving Access to Psychological Therapies (IAPT) services, and the influence of the National Institute for Health and Clinical Excellence (NICE), have affected the reputations and fortunes of some theoretical models in the UK.

The priority given here to socio-cultural issues aims to recognize the necessity for all therapists actively to widen their theoretical base and clinical and personal awareness from a predominantly individualistic focus towards a socio-culturally informed and inclusive one. This focus embraces all those groups in society – women, alienated men, children, older people, the working class, gays, lesbians, bisexual and transgender people, disabled people, as well as ethnic and cultural minorities – that have been marginalized or silenced in various ways by traditional therapeutic discourse and practice. We are continuously aware of changing demographics in British society – towards greater longevity, for example, with its attendant problems of adjustment to longer employment, insufficient pensions and intergenerational strain, as well as the growth in single households, single-parent and step-family households, and the need for increasing immigration to address a falling birthrate and ensuing economic problems. While mindful of these trends, we nevertheless suspect that along with colleagues and other texts, we have our own unrecognized assumptions, resistances and 'blind spots' and that what is presented here is still a modest movement in the direction of greater socio-cultural awareness.

COMPREHENSIVENESS

Most of the larger handbooks of counselling, psychotherapy and counselling psychology have tended towards representing mainly clinical skills and interventions and/or particular theoretical orientations, or specific client groups, or settings. Our aim in this book has been to draw together in one text as much consensual information, practice wisdom, mainstream theory, and pertinently challenging material as possible. Our own original brief for ourselves and contributors was to address what practitioners 'need to know, do, think, feel, use, reflect upon, change and abandon to be of most use to clients', and this remains true for this edition. While in a text of this kind it is necessary to include a fair amount of traditional theory, we hope there is also due bias towards practicality and creative rethinking where possible. To some extent this brief has led us to incorporate an even greater number of clinical theories in this edition.

LIMITATIONS

Necessarily, the comprehensive intention behind this book means that some areas traditionally accorded considerable space – notably, the mainstream theoretical approaches – have quite limited extent. Where this is the case, we hope that such digests of information are useful and stimulating rather than frustrating, and that readers will follow up any suggestions for more comprehensive reading given by authors. One or two critics of the previous editions complained about thinness of material in certain chapters, but our aim has been to provide a good general text that remains manageable in size, and there is of course an ever-expanding literature base available for those seeking more detail.

No single volume can hope to be exhaustive and therefore this, like any other book, has its limitations. The very selection of theoretical approaches to be represented in Part V, for example, means that many have had to be excluded. While we have consciously attempted to include 'mainstream' approaches, not everyone will agree on our definition of mainstream. In Part VI, another necessary exercise in selection means that what we perceive as among the most commonly presented problems may well not match the daily clinical experiences and interpretations of all practitioner-readers. Where omissions are evident, we hope that these are due to conscious editorial decisions on space grounds, however difficult and sometimes arbitrary, rather than to negligent oversight. We are also aware that in a field that is shared by different clinical professions and different historical and institutional affiliations, our own positioning in a primarily *counselling* tradition may lead to some unintentional biases.

STRUCTURE

As before, Part I opens with a scene-setting, succinct introduction to counselling and psychotherapy, to definitions, historical background, professional affiliations and philosophical assumptions. The varied, and not always clear, goals of therapy are briefly examined, as are the formats or arenas of therapy, the settings in which it takes place and the employment prospects it holds out. Part II lays the foundation for a socio-culturally informed account of the client populations served by therapists. Part III outlines the most significant therapeutic skills, techniques and practice issues, including many in-session and ancillary skills, the latter often being taken for granted by many clinical texts. Part IV looks at professional issues relevant to all therapists, including professional development, supervision, ethics and law, insurance and advertising, private practice issues, research and evaluation, and it includes clients' views and other neglected areas. Due attention is given to certain research issues in this edition, this topic having continued to grow in importance during recent years. Psychotherapeutic theory is the focus of Part V, first by looking briefly at the need for and the place of theory and its different applications, and second via 27 distinctive, relatively mainstream theoretical models, approaches or schools of therapy. In Part VI the focus is on the question of what clients need from therapy: first, by examining the topic of psychopharmacology, and then different perspectives on psychopathology and problems of living; and second, by outlining 20 of the most commonly presented problem areas, plus special issues. Certain judicious changes have been made in these areas. Part VII again gathers together a number of specialisms, modalities and setting-specific practice topics, now including coaching and hypnotherapeutic skills.

The construction of this book has represented yet another huge collaborative effort. In any edited book there is some undeniable risk of discordant styles and discrepancies. We hope that these are, however, minimal and that the insights and information provided by the contributors collectively make for a rich source of contemporary practice wisdom, accurate data and critical challenge to improve our services to clients by reflecting continuously on this fascinating subject.

REFERENCES

Lazar, S.G. (ed.) (2010) *Psychotherapy Is Worth It: A Comprehensive Review of Its Cost-Effectiveness*. Washington, DC: American Psychiatric Publishing.

Moghaddam, F.M. and Studer, C. (1997) Cross-cultural psychology: the frustrated gadfly's promises, potentialities, and failures. In D. Fox and I. Prilleltensky (eds), *Critical Psychology: An Introduction*. London: Sage.

Parker, I. (2007) *Revolution in Psychology: Alienation to Emancipation*. London: Pluto.

Rayner, E. (1991) *The Independent Tradition in British Psychoanalysis*. London: Aronson.

Ryle, A. (1990) *Cognitive-Analytic Therapy: Active Participation in Change*. Chichester: Wiley.

Watters, E. (2010) *Crazy Like Us: The Globalization of the American Psyche*. New York: Free Press.

Acknowledgements

This third edition of the *Sage Handbook of Counselling and Psychotherapy* has genuinely entailed a great deal of concerted teamwork, particularly from Sage staff. Alice Oven helped greatly with important early decisions and structuring and has been a constant support throughout. Fulsome thanks are due to Susan Worsey, who proactively contributed crucial ideas, leads and practical assistance far beyond the call of duty. Kate Wharton has been immensely helpful throughout, with detailed attention, liaison, technical support, and encouragement. Rachel Burrows and associates have shown unusual understanding and professionalism in necessary last minute negotiations and corrections. This book would simply not have been possible without them. We also thank authors who have conscientiously revised their chapters and welcome those new authors who have sometimes stepped in at late notice. Self-evidently, this huge undertaking would not be possible without their professional expertise and skilled distillations of complex areas of knowledge.

PART I

COUNSELLING AND PSYCHOTHERAPY IN CONTEXT

What Are Counselling and Psychotherapy?

COLIN FELTHAM

DEFINITIONS AND AIMS

No single, consensually agreed definition of either counselling or psychotherapy exists in spite of many attempts across the decades in Britain, North America and elsewhere to arrive at one. The question of pinning down crucial distinctions arose in concrete terms in the UK in the first decade of the twenty-first century when the Health Professions Council (HPC) initiated preliminary steps towards legal protection of the titles 'counsellor' and 'psychotherapist'. Attempts to load the former with wellbeing-associated tasks and the latter with competencies in addressing more severe psychological problems soon broke down. For the purposes of this book, the following provisional working definition is offered:

> Counselling and psychotherapy are mainly, though not exclusively, listening-and-talking-based methods of addressing psychological and psychosomatic problems and change, including deep and prolonged human suffering, situational dilemmas, crises and developmental needs, and aspirations towards the realization of human potential. In contrast to biomedical approaches, the psychological therapies operate largely without medication or other physical interventions and may be concerned not only with mental health but with spiritual, philosophical, social and other aspects of living. Professional forms of counselling and psychotherapy are based on formal training which encompasses attention to pertinent theory, clinical and/or micro-skills development, the personal development/therapy of the trainee, and supervised practice.

A brief, tentative definition of this kind offers some parameters but omits mention of the many, ever-expanding, often competing, schools of therapy, and the arenas and the several professions (sometimes in conflict) in which they are practised. Discussions of all such conflicting claims can be found in Feltham (1995) and James and Palmer (1996). The contention advanced by this book's editors is that counselling and psychotherapy, in spite of partly different historical roots and affiliations, have much more in common than they have serious and demonstrable differences and that practitioners and the public stand to gain much more from the assumption of commonality than from spurious or infinitesimal distinctions. It is often acknowledged that 'British counselling' much more closely resembles psychotherapy as practised in the USA and parts of Europe than it does the various kinds of guidance and mentoring that it is often confused with. Certainly practitioners in this field work with many different types of goal and expectation, implicit and explicit, each of which may call for the use of somewhat different skills, but arguably little is to be gained practically from further controversy about professional titles and distinctions.

DEVELOPMENT OF PSYCHOTHERAPY AND COUNSELLING IN THE UK

Sigmund Freud was developing psychoanalysis – often considered the grandparent of most of the diverse schools in existence today – in Austria in the late nineteenth and early twentieth centuries. Before Freud there were certainly many kinds of psychologically oriented therapies and many had already used the concept of an unconscious. However, Freud has come to mark the historical pivot when previous centuries of religious, philosophical and pseudo-scientific theories and methods (from religious propitiation to shamanism, sleeping cures, magnetism, hypnotism, etc.) were challenged by serious aspirations to establish psychotherapy as a scientific discipline. Psychoanalysis is perched curiously between being perceived as a challenge to previous faith in reason (the Enlightenment) and as itself, the new grand narrative capable of rationally explaining all the psychological ills of humanity. Freud is often (although not by all) ranked with Darwin and Marx as one of the most significant scientific thinkers at the dawn of the twentieth century.

Psychoanalysis moved through Europe and North America in the first few decades of the twentieth century, the International Psychoanalytical Association being established in 1910 and the British Psychoanalytic Society in 1924. The British Association of Psychotherapists (originally the Association of Psychotherapists) was founded in 1951. In spite of much public and medical resistance to psychoanalysis (which was originally radically counter-cultural), interest and support grew, partly in connection with the two world wars and the search for remedies for 'shell shock' (the predecessor of post-traumatic stress disorder, PTSD) and other problems experienced by military personnel. Concern about scientology led in 1971 to the Foster Report which had implications for psychotherapy, and in 1978 to the publication of the Sieghart Report on the statutory regulation of psychotherapists. During the 1980s conferences regularly held at Rugby (organized by the British Association for Counselling (BAC) led eventually, in 1993, to the now United Kingdom Council for Psychotherapy (UKCP). The British Psychoanalytic Council (BPC), representing training institutions with a strictly psychoanalytic affiliation. The UKCP, containing member organizations from humanistic, cognitive-behavioural and other traditions, was established in 1991. In recent years it has extended its membership categories to include 'psychotherapeutic counsellor' and more flexible routes to membership.

The development of counselling is harder to trace, there being no single dominant figure like Freud, or monolithic theory like psychoanalysis. Hans Hoxter may, however, be credited as one outstanding individual for his part in creating the counselling movement, including bringing American training ideas to Britain. Further relevant historical information is available in Aldridge (2011). It is usually agreed that early American vocational guidance projects and associations (for example Frank Parsons's Vocation Bureau in Boston in 1908) laid the foundations of counselling, and guidance for the young generally was a strong element. This certainly features in the early career of Carl Rogers, who is probably the closest to being the 'founder' of (non-directive) counselling in the 1940s. Another player is perhaps Rollo May, who, influenced by Alfred Adler, wrote what many consider to be the first counselling text in the 1920s (May, 1992). In the USA counselling was also originally closely linked with personnel management and the workplace. In general it is true to say that counselling has *historical* roots in practical guidance and problem-solving issues, and was often agency based rather than associated with private practice. However, it is now mainly characterized as distinctly other than advice giving and as having a primarily facilitative function.

Seminal events in the UK included the establishment of the National Marriage Guidance Council in 1938, the importation of counselling training methods from the USA to the Universities of Reading and Keele in 1966 (to serve the pastoral needs of students), and the establishment of the Westminster Pastoral Foundation in 1969. The Standing Conference for the Advancement of Counselling in 1970 led to the formation of the British Association for Counselling in 1977, renamed the British Association for Counselling and Psychotherapy (BACP) in 2000. It should be said that a great deal of cross-fertilization between these developments and others in psychotherapy was taking place and the emergence of psychodynamic counselling, for example, demonstrates these close links.

Alongside these developments we should also note pertinent developments elsewhere. Originally the Association of Medical Officers of Asylums and Hospitals for the Insane (AMOAHI, founded 1841), the Royal College of Psychiatrists was so named in 1971. The British Psychological Society was established in 1901. Significant mutual aid and voluntary organizations such as Alcoholics Anonymous (1935), the Samaritans (1953) and Cruse (1959) should also be included in this brief portrait, as should the parallel existence of the personal social services and its casework tradition which closely mirrored developments in counselling and psychotherapy.

Theoretically, psychotherapy and counselling develop continuously, some might say all too prolifically, with significant departures from psychoanalytic theory and practice observable from its earliest days. Jung and Adler were among the earliest to break away from Freud, and similar schisms, factions and developments are in evidence throughout psychotherapeutic history. Hence resulted the growth of what is still thought to be the more than 400 schools (also known as theoretical orientations, approaches, brand names) of therapy we have today. The question of whether such proliferation is desirable and in clients' interests, or not, must be faced by thoughtful practitioners, and indeed the integrationist movement stemming from the 1980s represents shared concern for convergence (Cooper and McLeod, 2010). On the other hand, early twenty-first century tensions regarding statutory regulation sometimes appear to be pushing the psychoanalytic, humanistic and cognitive-behavioural therapy (CBT) camps further apart (see House and Loewenthal, 2008; Parker and Revelli, 2008; Weatherill, 2004). A summary of some of the key points of this necessarily succinct history of events is provided in Table 1.1.1. Readers may also like to consult Aldridge (2011), Dryden (1997), Ellenberger (1970) and Feltham (1995; 2007).

ALLIED PROFESSIONS

Most (but certainly not all) would agree that counselling and psychotherapy – in so far as they *are* professions or emerging professions – are part of the health professions. Although Freud battled to have psychoanalysis recognized as separate from medicine and Rogers similarly battled with psychiatric and psychological colleagues, the psychological therapies today concern themselves largely with mental health promotion and mental illness reduction even where these terms are not used and where additional or different aims are espoused, such as personal growth and development, psychoeducation, psychopractice, etc. (see Brown and Mowbray, 2002). Counsellors are therefore often found in health and social care settings along with psychotherapists, clinical and counselling psychologists, psychiatrists and mental health nurses. A second group of related professionals includes social workers, probation officers, welfare officers, personnel managers, career guidance workers, occupational therapists, speech and communication therapists, occupational and health psychologists, and so on. Teachers, nurses, priests and others in caring roles may have closely related functions. Members of the above groups, sometimes known as the 'core professions', have been considered good candidates for counselling and psychotherapy training, and typical intakes to courses include members of all these groups.

Each professional group has its own professional body, history, and traditions of training and supervision. Each has designated tasks that obviously differ from those of others, depending on context and client group. Counselling and psychotherapeutic skills are used to degrees in all these professions and, where individual workers possess dual or multiple qualifications (for example a social worker may be trained in family therapy), they may formally provide therapeutic services. However, BACP and other clinically oriented bodies strive to emphasize a distinction between casual, informal or untrained, and uncontracted use of *counselling skills*, and disciplined, contracted, ethically protected, formal counselling or psychotherapy. Parry (1996), too, distinguishes between:

- type A: psychological treatment as an integral component of mental health care
- type B: eclectic psychological therapy and counselling
- type C: formal psychotherapy.

The above-mentioned groups are also related to those involved in practising the so-called complementary therapies (often regarding their work as holistic or mind–body integrated), including acupuncture, homeopathy, reflexology, aromatherapy, Alexander technique, spiritual healing, osteopathy, naturopathy, Bach flower remedies, etc. Again, practitioners may sometimes have dual qualifications and practise both psychological therapy and somatic or sensual therapies alternately or simultaneously, having due regard for appropriate contracting (Sills, 2006). Debates about the rights of certain of these groups to aspire to professional status cannot be ignored, but nor can public scepticism. In relation to distinctions between the titles of those engaged in closely related therapeutic professions, and their putatively distinctive skills and effectiveness, see Cheshire and Pilgrim (2004), Gask (2004), James and Palmer (1996) and Milton et al. (2011). Offering resistance to the professionalizing trend, particularly via the HPC, which is sometimes perceived as unnecessarily bureaucratizing and distorting therapy, is the Independent Practitioners' Network (IPN) (see House, 2003; Postle, 2011) and the Alliance for Counselling and Psychotherapy (see also Parker and Revelli, 2008).

A BRIEF OVERVIEW OF THE VALUES OF COUNSELLING AND PSYCHOTHERAPY

The overarching values, and the professional ethics that stem from these, of counselling and psychotherapy were summed up in the concepts of integrity, impartiality

Table 1.1.1 *Key historical developments*

Year	Birth/growth of institutions and professional organizations	Significant events	Appearance of schools (approximate dates)
1900		Freud's *Interpretation of Dreams*	
1907	British Psychological Society		
	Vienna Psychoanalytic Society		
1908		First (careers) counselling center, Boston, USA (Frank Parsons)	
1910	International Psychoanalytical Association		
1913	National Vocational Guidance Association (USA)		Analytical psychology (Jung)
	London Psychoanalytic Society		
1919	Institute of Psycho-analysis		
1920	Tavistock Clinic		Behavioural psychology
1921			Psychodrama
1924	British Psychoanalytic Society		
1926	London Clinic of Psychoanalysis		
	Medico-Psychological Association (MPA; previously AMOAH I, originally 1841)		
1935	Alcoholics Anonymous		
1936	Society of Analytical Psychology		
1937		Death of Adler	
1938	National Marriage Guidance Council (now Relate)		
1939		Death of Freud	
1940			Client/person-centred approach
1948		British National Health Service T groups	
		First student counselling service (University College Leicester)	
1950	International Association for Vocational and Educational Guidance (IAVEG)		Gestalt therapy
1951			Rogers's client-centred therapy
1952	Group Analytical Society	*Diagnostic and Statistical Manual (DSM)* 1st edn	
	American Association for Counseling and Development (AACD)		
	American Counseling Association (ACA; originally NVCA)		
1953	Samaritans		
1955			Rational emotive behaviour therapy (originally RT then RET)
			Personal construct therapy B
1957			Transactional analysis
1958			Behaviour therapy

Table 1.1.1 (Continued)

Year	Birth/growth of institutions and professional organizations	Significant events	Appearance of schools (approximate dates)
1959	Cruse Scottish Pastoral Association		
1960		First fee-charging counsellor in private practice in UK	
1961		Death of Melanie Klein Death of Jung J.D. Frank's *Persuasion and Healing*	
1962			Cognitive therapy
1965		Halmos's *The Faith of the Counsellors*	
1966		Counselling training at Universities of Reading and Keele	
1969	Westminster Pastoral Foundation Association of Humanistic Psychology (USA 1962, UK 1969)		
1970	First Standing Conference for the Advancement of Counselling (annual) MPA becomes Royal College of Psychiatrists	Death of Perls and Berne	Primal therapy
1971		*Foster Report* on Scientology	
1975	National Association of Young People's Counselling and Advisory Services (later Youth Access)		Neuro-linguistic programming
1977	British Association for Counselling (BAC)		
1978		*Sieghart Report* on statutory regulation of psychotherapists	
1980	Association of Humanistic Psychology Practitioners (AHPP)		
1982		Smith et al. *The Benefits of Psychotherapy* Rugby Psychotherapy Conference (set up by BAC)	
1983	Society for the Exploration of Psychotherapy Integration (SEPI)	First BAC accreditation scheme	Solution-focused therapy
1987		Death of Carl Rogers	
1989	United Kingdom Standing Conference on Psychotherapy (UKSCP)		
1990		Death of Bowlby	Cognitive analytic therapy
1991	British Confederation of Psychotherapists	BPS Charter of Counselling Psychologists	
1992	European Association for Counselling	First UK Chair of Counselling (Windy Dryden)	
1993	United Kingdom Council for Psychotherapy (UKCP, originally UKSCP): advice, guidance, counselling and psychotherapy lead body		
1994	Independent Practitioners' Network UKCP Register of Psychotherapists	BPS Division of Counselling Psychology	

(Continued)

Table 1.1.1 (Continued)

Year	Birth/growth of institutions and professional organizations	Significant events	Appearance of schools (approximate dates)
1995		BCP Register	
1996	United Kingdom Register of Counsellors (UKRC) (individuals) World Council for Psychotherapy	NHS Psychotherapy Services in England Review NHS Psychotherapy Services in England, Department of Health (DoH) Strategic Policy Review	
1998	Association of Counsellors and Psychotherapists in Primary Care (CPC) UKRC (organizations)	Data Protection Act CORE introduced	
1999	National Institute for Health and Clinical Excellence (NICE)		
2000	BAC renamed British Association for Counselling and Psychotherapy (BACP) Universities Psychotherapy Association (UPA) adds 'Counselling' to its title, becoming UPCA	BACP's *Ethical Framework for Good Practice in Counselling and Psychotherapy*	
2001		Lord Alderdice's Psychotherapy Bill *Treatment Choice in Psychological Therapies and Counselling: Evidence-Based Clinical Practice Guidelines* (DoH) BACP's *Guidelines for Online Counselling and Psychotherapy*	
2002		Health Professions Council (HPC) is identified as the regulatory body for all health professions, including counselling and psychotherapy ('talking therapies')	
2003		UKCP establishes its Psychotherapeutic Counselling Section BACP Service Accreditation Scheme Telephone counselling (contractual) is accepted by BACP for accreditation hours	
2004	College of Psychoanalysts British Psychoanalytic Council	Graduate mental health workers in primary care British Confederation of Psychotherapists (BCP) renamed British Psychoanalytic Council (BPC)	
2006		Improving Access to Psychological Therapies	
2007		Death of Albert Ellis	
2008		BACP represented on HPC's Professional Liaison Group	
2009		HPC Register for Applied Psychologists opened	
2011		Statutory regulation plans abandoned	

and respect (Bond, 2010). These were developed and related by BACP (2002) to tenets of moral philosophy: fidelity (honouring the trust placed in the practitioner); autonomy (the client's right to be self-governing); beneficence (concern for the greatest good); non-maleficence (to cause least harm); justice (concern for fairness); and the practitioner's self-respect (self-knowledge and care of self). Such principles are not without problems, however, since in practice there sometimes are conflicts between, for example, the wishes of a client and possible damaging consequences. Also, it is sometimes the case that what may be professionally ethical and desirable will be challenged as socially undesirable or questionable by others. Hence, the goals of individual autonomy and self-actualization, which are held by many writers as central values in psychotherapy (e.g. Hinshelwood et al., 1998), have been criticized by some sociologists as leading to an 'autonomy obsession', an undermining of social responsibility and a cultural insensitivity. It is therefore important to bear in mind that what we often call *professional ethics* (as advocated in professional codes) are not necessarily coterminous with *social ethics*.

It follows from basic principles that counsellors and psychotherapists value non-judgementalism *vis-à-vis* clients, that they owe a duty of care to clients (while remaining necessarily detached to varying degrees), and that their aim is the ultimate good of the client balanced by respect for the client's own choices. Due to the weight placed on respect for self-determination, most therapists are opposed to people being coerced into therapy and into remaining in therapy when they wish to leave, and actively support the principle of informed consent to therapeutic procedures.

All professional bodies in this field have their own codes of ethics and practice – BACP's *Ethical Framework for Good Practice in Counselling and Psychotherapy* (2002) being a mature example – usually addressing issues of safety, contracting, competence, confidentiality, boundaries, law, advertising, complaints and so on. There are few specific prohibitions, although sexual contact with clients, exploitation of clients and breach of confidentiality are prohibitions shared by all professional bodies. Nevertheless, often genuine and valid differences in values do exist between members of different professional bodies (and networks, such as the IPN, which oppose professionalization) and different theoretical affiliations. Understanding and elaboration of the foundational philosophical assumptions of therapists are an area of theory and training that is taking a long time to mature (Bennett, 2005; Erwin, 1997; Feltham, 2010; Howard, 2000).

Types of Goal

COLIN FELTHAM

Counselling and psychotherapy in the UK have developed organically and according to path dependency principles (Aldridge, 2011). Some critics have said they have flowed almost promiscuously into many areas of our lives, so that exactly what they are *for*, what their goals are, is not always clear. It is possible to state that the overall goal of therapy is to facilitate clients' own resourcefulness, insight, problem-solving capacities, happiness and so on, but critics are entitled to question such global terms. As Sandler and Dreher (1996) convey well, it is far from clear to many psychoanalytic practitioners exactly what the legitimate scope and aims of their work are and should be. Freud himself expressed various aims for psychoanalysis at different times, such as symptom removal, making the unconscious conscious, restoring the capacity to love and work, helping clients to move from neurotic misery to ordinary unhappiness, and conducting research into the human psyche. Each of the contemporary 'schools' of therapy has its characteristic and sometimes conflicting aims – some being altogether wary of 'aim attachment' and some being explicitly goal oriented and driven to reach and demonstrate successful outcomes. Currently a broad distinction may be seen between short-term outcome-focused therapy (such as is found in Improving Access to Psychological Therapies (IAPT) programmes) and open-ended process-oriented therapy. Here we look at some of the range of actual and possible goals.

SUPPORT

The term 'supportive therapy' suggests that some clients may primarily need and benefit from a form of therapy that upholds current ego strength and/or coping skills and does not seek to challenge or uncover. Some may need long-term supportive therapy, while others require short-term support in crises. Support may be in the form of warm, non-judgemental listening and encouragement and, although most therapy does not become advocacy, on occasion supportive therapy or counselling may also lean in this direction. Such supportive work remains disciplined and professional and distinct from befriending or friendship. Its aim is to support the person through a difficult time and/or towards a position of independence or readiness for more challenging therapy.

PSYCHO-EDUCATIONAL GUIDANCE

A wide range of psychologically informed practices is to be found under this umbrella term. Appropriate information giving, administering of questionnaires, coaching, mentoring, provision of social skills, lifeskills training, assertiveness and relaxation training, marriage enrichment programmes, parent effectiveness training, relapse prevention programmes, stress inoculation training, emotional intelligence and positive psychology training, are all examples. All aim to identify improvable behaviour and to teach personal skills in various areas of life. The goal is not to uncover presumed psychopathology but to directly enhance cognitive, behavioural and interpersonal functioning, to assist clients in meeting developmental challenges and to equip them with concrete coping techniques and philosophies. Coaching in particular has grown in recent years.

ADJUSTMENT AND RESOURCE PROVISION

The idea that people may be helped simply to adjust to their circumstances has usually been severely criticized by counsellors and therapists. However, it is probably a fact in at least some counselling settings (e.g. employee assistance programmes (EAPs)) that clients seek short-term adjustment-oriented help that may include elements of supportive therapy, problem-solving skills, assertiveness training, brainstorming solutions, *plus* the provision of contextual information (e.g. how an organization works, how to complain about your boss harassing you, etc.) and other welfare-oriented information, such as that relating to welfare benefits, housing, childcare, pensions, etc. In such contexts counsellors may act *both* as non-directive facilitators *and* as providers of relevant information and in some cases as brokers between individual client and organizations.

CRISIS INTERVENTION AND MANAGEMENT

These terms are used broadly here to include the intervention and support of professionals in the aftermath of large-scale (e.g. plane crash, bombing incident), small-group (e.g. bank raid) or personal disasters (e.g. road traffic accidents). Survivors and witnesses of critical incidents or breakdowns of many kinds are often offered immediate help which includes debriefing, support, practical and active-directive help, referral to specialist resources, and gradual restoration of normal functioning. The aim is to provide sensitive, non-intrusive, psychologically strengthening help in the first instance, avoiding connotations of psychopathology. Crisis intervention is concerned primarily with restoration of the level of functioning that existed prior to the crisis.

PROBLEM SOLVING AND DECISION MAKING

For a certain proportion of clients, the purpose of entering counselling or therapy is to examine a life situation or dilemma and come to a (probably quite early) resolution or decision. How to cope with nuisance neighbours and difficult relationships, whether to have a termination of pregnancy, when to retire and whether to live in sheltered accommodation, whether or not to have optional surgery, are some examples. The aim is to facilitate exploration of issues, feelings and practicalities; addressing anxiety and loss may be part of the process. In some approaches, a philosophy and techniques of problem solving may be imparted as a proactive tool for living.

SYMPTOM AMELIORATION

A symptom is a usually distressing or troublesome change of condition which manifests in a crisis, inability to function as normal, or apparently inexplicable somatic phenomena. A majority of people who seek or are referred to counselling/therapy for the first time want their symptoms to go away; they wish to return to their normal mode of functioning and self-image. Sometimes their goals are hazy or implicit; a depressed client may, for example, obviously want to be simply less (or not) depressed. Probably one of the greatest mismatches between clients' and (many) therapists' goals is that while the former seek symptom amelioration or elimination, the latter often have more ambitious agendas based on belief in presenting problems as merely the tip of an iceberg, as 'defence mechanisms' masking underlying, unconscious conflicts. Exceptions to this tend to be cognitive-behavioural therapists whose main aim is the identification of problematic behaviour and its reduction or elimination in the most efficient time span; and practitioners who strive to respond to consumers' stated needs and stages of change (e.g. Burton, 1998; Elton Wilson, 1996).

INSIGHT AND UNDERSTANDING

Some clients, and many therapists, have as their primary goals the investigation of causes of problematic feelings, thoughts and behaviour. Both client and therapist may wish to pursue the search for historical causes and the reasons for persistently counterproductive behaviour in current life circumstances. ('Why did this happen to me? Why am I like this? *Aha! – now I see where this comes from.*') For some practitioners and clients, the goal of therapy may be the attainment of deeper and deeper insights or a state of continuous understanding of self, of how conflicts arise, of motivations, etc.

CURE

Almost all therapists and counsellors avoid use of the term 'cure' and any client expectations that therapy will result in final and dramatic removal of suffering. This may be due to (1) clinical experience, as clients are very seldom dramatically, comprehensively or resolutely cured; (2) dislike of medical connotations, by which suffering, problems in living, are not regarded as biological disturbances to be treated with medical interventions; or (3) resistance to engendering hopes of unrealistic outcomes (and perhaps the disappointment and even litigation that might accompany such expectations). However, at least one approach, primal therapy, conceptualizes human problems in unitary terms as *neurosis* (a psychobiological state) for which it possesses *the cure*. Increasingly, too, the pressure from the evidence-based practice lobby and the influence of the National Institute for Health and Clinical Excellence (NICE) lead practitioners to speak explicitly in terms of specifically outcome-focused work.

SELF-ACTUALIZATION

Under this heading may be included all aims towards becoming a better person, having greater self-awareness or self-knowledge, and attaining a state of fully functioning personhood. The range of goals subsumed here may include, for example, anything from 'I want to be more assertive/risk-taking/happy' to 'I want to try out everything life has to offer, I want to overcome all obstacles in my life and find the real me.' Concepts of individuation, maturation, finding the real self, being true to oneself and increasing self-awareness fit here. Most observers accept that the concept of an end-point – the fully functioning person – is somewhat mythical; self-actualization suggests a continuous process, a valuing of the journey more than a need to reach a goal; and some are highly critical of this aim altogether (Weatherill, 2004).

PERSONALITY CHANGE

Eschewed by the more cognitive-behavioural and short-term approaches, hints at least of the possibility of quite far-reaching personality change are either found in or projected into certain forms of therapy. At an illusory level, the rather retiring, somewhat unattractive and untalented person may fantasize that therapy will compensatorily convert him or her into everything that he or she is not. However, a number of client claims and testimonies based on dramatic disappearance of distressing symptoms or limitations ('Therapy completely changed/saved my life') have suggested major life changes as a desired outcome for some clients. Many, particularly humanistic, psychotherapists regard their work as 'life-transforming therapy'. This goal raises questions about the nature of the concept of 'personality' and what actually constitutes personality change.

DISCOVERY OF MEANING AND TRANSCENDENTAL EXPERIENCE

Particularly in the wake of the relative decline of formal religion and loss of spiritual and moral leaders and mentors, it seems that therapy has become for many an avenue for the exploration of existential, spiritual or metaphysical meaning and transcendental experience. The existential, humanistic and transpersonal approaches lend themselves most explicitly to such aspirations. This 'movement' has been gathering momentum in recent years and may well change the nature of at least some therapy practice (West, 2011).

SYSTEMIC, ORGANIZATIONAL OR SOCIAL CHANGE

In some forms of therapy, change within domestic partnerships, families, task groups and other groupings is clearly a goal. But counselling and psychotherapeutic skills as human relations skills (sometimes based on an understanding of unconscious conflicts, sometimes not) are also applied to conflict resolution within and between organizations. Experimentation with group counselling and therapy where more than a dozen or so participants are involved, and sometimes hundreds of members participate, has often had goals of conflict resolution and other aspects of social change.

Clients may change their goals over time, and the aims of therapy negotiated between therapist and client may change. It is not unusual for some clients to begin with modest goals and to find further, more ambitious or deeper aims to work on. It has been said that some therapists may be satisfied with the client *feeling better* as an aim, when a more enduring aim might be to *get better*. It has also to be remembered that the types of goal previously identified refer to avowed types of goal. We know that there are also 'shadow goals': some clients may wish to be in a 'sick role', to prove how incapable they are, to maintain a therapist's attention, etc.; some therapists may primarily wish to prove something to themselves, to hold power, to perpetuate a livelihood, to find vicarious intimacy. In spite of ethical codes or frameworks, requirements for training therapy, supervision and other safeguards, unhealthy covert goals cannot be eliminated altogether.

1.3

Arenas

COLIN FELTHAM

Arenas – also sometimes referred to as arrangements or modalities – may include the constellations of people receiving therapy (individuals, peers, couples, groups, families) and the media through which therapy is delivered (telephone or online counselling, art therapy, dance therapy, writing therapy, etc.). The former group is the one most commonly included under the rubric of arena. Strictly speaking, forms of self-help such as self-analysis, therapeutic writing and meditation might be included here. The interpersonal arenas are all, usually, face-to-face, verbally mediated therapies.

PEER COUNSELLING

This refers to any kind of counselling or therapy provided on an egalitarian basis (and therefore not usually 'professional' as such), with each party agreeing temporarily to take the role of counsellor with the other as client, and then reversing roles. It started perhaps in its most disciplined format with the Re-evaluation Co-counselling of Harvey Jackins but has been modified by other groups (see Part VII). Its benefits include mutuality, egalitarianism, economy and avoidance of professional intrusion; its potential problems include boundary issues, compromised ability to 'hold', and transferential dynamics.

INDIVIDUAL THERAPY

Overwhelmingly the most enduringly popular form of therapy, one-to-one therapy (client and therapist), may be conducted in the following ways:

- 50-minute sessions for up to five times a week for many years using a couch or chairs (psychoanalysis)
- 50- or 60-minute sessions (sometimes shorter or longer), once, twice or three times weekly for months or years (psychotherapy and counselling), face to face or otherwise
- single-session therapy, short-term or brief counselling or psychotherapy (e.g. six, 10, 20 sessions), open-ended, serial or intermittent patterns of attendance, or for example online.

Individual therapy clearly replicates the original relationship of infant and caregiver and professional relationships such as that between doctor and patient. This arena offers optimal confidentiality, privacy, attention, containment, intimacy and safety. The assumption that it is necessarily the best arena for each client should, however, be balanced by considerations which include the therapist's expertise (or lack of it) in various areas: potential for dependency, manipulation, acting-out and abuse. The usefulness of other arenas should always be considered instead of or in conjunction with individual therapy.

COUPLE COUNSELLING/THERAPY

Originating in marriage guidance and marital psychotherapy, couple work is now provided for unmarried as well as married people, for homosexual as well as heterosexual partners, and for other post-conventional and pluralistic forms of partnership. Like individual and other arenas, it is informed theoretically by different schools of thought. However, unique to couple counselling is the focus on the relationship between the partners. Conflicts over domestic arrangements, interpersonal and sexual issues, children, money, affairs, values – at conscious and unconscious levels – take many couples, together or separately, to counsellors and therapists. This work entails triangular dynamics and a need for conflict management skills that individual therapists do not necessarily possess. Individual therapists whose clients persist in discussing conflicts with their partners are well advised to consider referral to a couple counsellor. A caveat to this is when a client needs privacy for personal exploration or exceptionally confidential disclosures, or when cooperation between the partners is impossible. See further discussions in Parts VI and VII.

FAMILY THERAPY

Like couple counselling, where other parties (other members of a client's family) are clearly implicated, family therapy should be considered as an option for referral. A client's difficulties may be considered systemically when, for example, there are indications that the client is 'carrying' the family's secret sexual abuse or unexpressed grief and/or is being scapegoated by other family members. Counselling a client who has to remain in a disturbed or disturbing family may be counterproductive. Conversely, vulnerable clients may be unable or unwilling to participate in family therapy alongside those who are abusing or frightening them. This arena is the least likely to be offered in private practice, as it requires suitable accommodation, often with one-way mirror and/or video facilities, but is usually associated with social and family service units. Family therapy has a rich, diverse theoretical and clinical tradition. See Part VII for further details.

GROUP THERAPY

Again, there is a rich tradition of forms of group therapy and counselling (see Part VII). In groups, clients may discover that others experience similar problems as they do; that they are accepted by group members (which can generalize into everyday life); that they can give as well as receive help and insights; and that they can draw on others' experiences and perceptions. Peer or mutual aid groups like Alcoholics Anonymous derive much of their effectiveness from common experience and committed

support. Women may feel safer to explore certain issues in an all-women group. Groups can act as a bridge from individual therapy to everyday living; they can also act as a booster for therapeutic progress either after or simultaneously with individual work. Like couple and family therapists, group therapists require particular skills and this work is sometimes conducted with co-leaders or facilitators.

COUNSELLING/THERAPY VIA OTHER MEDIA

As we have mentioned, although face-to-face, individual therapy based on talking is the most common format, increasingly therapy is offered using alternative media and arenas. Child psychotherapy is a specialism in its own right, requiring particular training (see Part VII). Sex therapy, too, is usually regarded as a specialism, and may depart from conversation to behavioural rehearsal. Sometimes brief psychotherapy is considered a specialism or arena, for which all practitioners should also consider appropriate referral routes.

The expressive or arts therapies, which include art therapy, drama therapy, psychodrama, dance and movement therapy, therapeutic writing and use of other media (e.g. photography) are increasing in their extent, availability and professionalism. For certain groups (e.g. children, older people, those who dislike primarily intense verbal communication), one or another form of expressive therapy may be the arena or modality of choice. Body work may or may not fit here, but obviously is an alternative means of providing therapy; where there are clearly problems expressed somatically, therapeutic massage, breathing or other techniques may be considered viable alternatives.

It is a common assumption that most therapy or counselling is a face-to-face activity. However, the extent to which telephone helplines are used is often played down or regarded unfairly as an inferior form of therapeutic help. This assumption is increasingly, and we believe rightly, challenged (see Part VII). Some people *prefer* the safety or convenience of telephone (or other forms of 'distant' counselling, including online therapy and bibliotherapy, or recommended self-help books); and some have no other option, often by virtue of a disability, whether physical incapacity or agoraphobia, for example, or because of geographical remoteness. Advances in information and communication technology also increasingly challenge our acceptance of the best apparent help available.

Differences between counselling and psychotherapy and the use of counselling skills have already been discussed. Here it is important to point out that people often receive sufficient help from alternative professionals or para-professionals who may use counselling skills. Social workers, probation officers, guidance workers, welfare officers, nurses, teachers, mentors, coaches and others often become involved in a helping or therapeutic role and many have specific training in therapeutic knowledge and skill. It is quite likely that many people are helped by such professionals (either incidentally and by brief contact or by formal arrangement) who might not otherwise approach, trust or have access to helpers designated 'counsellors' or 'psychotherapists'.

Settings and Opportunities for Employment

COLIN FELTHAM

A brief look at the prospects for trainees and those developing a career is included here because the subject of employment, although of obvious interest, is rarely touched upon in textbooks. It is perhaps an open secret that in spite of the huge growth of interest in counselling and therapy and the expansion of their training markets, it remains the case that relatively few (full-time) jobs exist. It has been variously estimated that the UK counselling workforce may be up to 70,000 or even that employees using counselling skills make up about 1.7 per cent of total employment (half a million workers): see Aldridge (2011). The reasons for this uncertain picture are not easy to specify but no doubt include: (1) the fact that much counselling stems from and remains attached to the voluntary and pastoral sectors and a great deal of counselling is still provided as an unpaid service; (2) the continuing emergence of counselling and therapy as valid and evidence-based forms of professional service deserving of some but limited statutory funding; and (3) their relatively 'soft' image in competition with the work of, for example, psychiatrists (Gask, 2004) and clinical psychologists (Cheshire and Pilgrim, 2004). Although a great deal of therapeutic work is conducted in private practice, the extent of this (and its economic success for practitioners) is hard to measure. Alongside the number of relatively few full-time jobs, there are of course patterns of part-time and sessional (hourly paid) opportunities, private practice (usually part-time), counselling/therapy-related work (e.g. supervision, training/lecturing, consultancy, writing) and the use of counselling and therapeutic skills in other roles (e.g. social work, mentoring).

VOLUNTARY AGENCIES

These include those with national coverage such as Relate, Samaritans, Cruse, Victim Support, Mind, Turning Point, etc. Provision of local women's therapy centres, rape crisis centres, HIV/AIDS agencies, and family-oriented drug- and alcohol-related services is widespread. Many of these rely on a mixture of statutory funding, voluntary fundraising and donations, most concentrate on a specific client group, and some may offer paid positions. The work is not always purely or solely counselling or psychotherapy, but may include telephone helplines, befriending, advocacy, information and advice giving, awareness raising and so on.

RESIDENTIAL CARE

Residential care projects may be based within statutory or voluntary services and obviously focus on clients whose needs involve more than talking therapy. Client groups include children at risk, vulnerable young people, the homeless, and those with often multiple problems of poverty, domestic violence, alcohol and drug abuse, criminal behaviour, mental health problems, disabilities and special needs, illness and frailty. Quite typically such work involves degrees of physical care, welfare issues and liaison with multiple agencies (e.g. social, probation, medical and legal services). Clients are often helped by 'keyworkers', part of whose work may be to provide counselling or to refer elsewhere for counselling. Some kinds of intensive residential care are highly specialized, for example with victims of torture, those emerging from hostage or people with damaging cult experiences. There are many projects offering residential rehabilitation programmes following drug addiction and alcoholism, and which look for experience and/or qualifications in general and psychiatric nursing, social work, counselling and group work. Often this kind of work offers in-house training and may be regarded as a route towards further professional training.

EDUCATION

Schools, further and higher education and special educational projects are some of the longest-established settings in which forms of counselling and therapy take place. While some schools offer specific counselling services (and the need is still frequently alluded to), therapeutic work is still sometimes carried out by educational psychologists, behaviour support workers, mentors, and teachers with a pastoral brief, with referrals being made where necessary (and possible) to child psychotherapists. The Welsh Assembly recently undertook to ensure access for all school pupils to counsellors. Colleges of further and higher education and universities in the UK, although not providing uniform national therapeutic services for students, are an example of a setting in which counselling has been offered successfully for decades. In the transitional and vulnerable period between adolescence and adulthood, issues of career uncertainty, susceptibility to emotional, interpersonal and sexual problems, drugs and alcohol, homesickness, and educational and financial pressures require sensitive help. Student counsellors may have relatively high caseloads of self-referred clients presenting a wide range of personal concerns. Turnover is often high since the work is often crisis oriented and determined by the pressures of the academic calendar. Student counsellors (and those with psychotherapy training may be found as much as those from a counselling background) work in one of the few areas with a relatively good, clear structure of pay, conditions and progression prospects.

THE WORKPLACE

Increasingly this has been the site of developments in counselling and opportunities for employment.

Employee counselling, established in the USA for decades, has also grown considerably in Britain. Just as student retention is one of the motives behind provision of student counselling, so prevention of absenteeism is a motive behind employee counselling services. Employers' concerns include drug and alcohol abuse, stress at work, employee relations, management of change, redundancy, accidents in the workplace, etc. Many large companies provide their own in-house counselling and coaching provision, sometimes as part of occupational health; some refer out to individual counsellors or group practices; many contract the services of external employee assistance programme (EAP) providers.

COUNSELLING IN THE NATIONAL HEALTH SERVICE

This has been the area of greatest growth for counselling and psychotherapeutic services in recent years, especially in primary care (see Part VII). This is perhaps an area where divergence of interest between counsellors and some psychotherapists is apparent, since this work is typically short term. It has been estimated that over 50 per cent of counsellors are now employed by the NHS, although most counselling in primary care remains part time. It is within the primary care sector that many new challenges face practitioners wishing to secure employment. One area of outstanding employment growth but also controversy has been in IAPT stepped care schemes where attempts have been made to provide a seamless service using so-called low- and high-intensity workers delivering first-line telephone CBT, brief counselling and other services. Counsellors and psychotherapists are also sometimes to be found in specialized roles in hospitals (e.g. providing debriefing and counselling after road traffic accidents, counselling in obstetrics, infertility clinics, etc.) depending on local policies in NHS settings. At the time of writing, a probable major restructuring of the NHS is imminent, which may affect employment for better or for worse.

PRIVATE PRACTICE

Traditionally the location for most long-term psychotherapy, based typically in practitioners' own homes, and sometimes in purpose-rented offices and group premises, private practice is also fully discussed in Part V of this book. North American texts have been issuing warnings for some years that this is the practice sector most under threat from 'managed care' and from consumers' greater sophistication, awareness of outcome research and precarious personal finances. On the other hand, some now believe that NHS waiting lists, time-limited and often CBT-oriented treatment may encourage more people to use the services of independent practitioners. Small private practices probably compose an element of many counsellors' and psychotherapists' workloads, quite typically supplementing part-time incomes in other settings (Clark, 2002; Syme, 1994; Thistle, 1998).

In addition to the above settings, therapy may be offered in a wide variety of community services and voluntary agencies, e.g. Mind, Alcohol Concern, Victim Support, women's therapy centres, etc.; statutory services, e.g. psychology departments, social and probation services (although far less so now than in the past), police services and prisons; and religious and pastoral organizations, e.g. Jewish Care's Shalvata (Holocaust Survivors' Centre), Catholic Marriage Advisory Centres, etc.

As mentioned earlier, while relatively few full-time salaried posts exist, many of these offer reasonable pay levels. Some statutory employers pay well, and EAP providers – where they offer more than occasional sessional (hourly) work – can offer relatively high remuneration. Otherwise, pecuniary rewards run from nothing (particularly for trainees and those working as volunteers in community agencies) to modest hourly pay, to average wages for caring professionals. In private practice, some practitioners have been known to generate quite high incomes, but a trend towards a probable relative decline in clients being seen predictably from twice to five times a week (as in traditional psychoanalysis) for some years, and the growth in short-term therapies, is likely to undercut high incomes for all but a very few.

REFERENCES

Aldridge, S. (2011) *Counselling: An Insecure Profession? A Sociological and Historical Analysis*. Unpublished PhD thesis, University of Leicester.

BACP (2002) *Ethical Framework for Good Practice in Counselling and Psychotherapy*. Rugby: BACP.

Bennett, M. (2005) *The Purpose of Counselling and Psychotherapy*. Basingstoke: Palgrave.

Bond, T. (2010) *Standards and Ethics for Counselling in Action* (3rd edn). London: Sage.

Brown, J. and Mowbray, R. (2002) Visionary deep personal growth. In C. Feltham (ed.), *What's the Good of Counselling and Psychotherapy? The Benefits Explained*. London: Sage.

Burton, M.V. (1998) *Psychotherapy, Counselling and Primary Health Care: Assessment for Brief or Longer-term Treatment*. Chichester: Wiley.

Cheshire, K. and Pilgrim, D. (2004) *A Short Introduction to Clinical Psychology*. London: Sage.

Clark, J. (ed.) (2002) *Freelance Counselling and Psychotherapy*. London: Brunner-Routledge.

Cooper, M. and McLeod, J. (2010) *Pluralistic Counselling and Psychotherapy*. London: Sage.

Dryden, W. (ed.) (1997) *Developments in Psychotherapy: Historical Perspectives*. London: Sage.

Ellenberger, H.F. (1970) *The Discovery of the Unconscious*. New York: Basic.

Elton Wilson, J. (1996) *Time-Conscious Psychological Therapy*. London: Routledge.

Erwin, E. (1997) *Philosophy and Psychotherapy*. London: Sage.

Feltham, C. (1995) *What Is Counselling? The Promise and Problem of the Talking Therapies*. London: Sage.

Feltham, C. (2007) Individual therapy in context. In W. Dryden (ed.), *Dryden's Handbook of Individual Therapy* (5th edn). London: Sage.

Feltham, C. (2010) *Critical Thinking in Counselling and Psychotherapy*. London: Sage.

Gask, L. (2004) *A Short Introduction to Psychiatry*. London: Sage.

Hinshelwood, R.D., Holmes, J. and Lindley, R. (1998) *The Values of Psychotherapy* (2nd edn). London: Karnac.

House, R. (2003) *Therapy Beyond Modernity: Deconstructing and Transcending Profession-Centred Therapy*. London: Karnac.

House, R. and Loewenthal, D. (eds) (2008) *Against and For CBT: Towards a Constructive Dialogue?* Ross-on-Wye: PCCS.

Howard, A. (2000) *Philosophy for Counselling and Psychotherapy: Pythagoras to Postmodernism*. Basingstoke: Palgrave.

James, I. and Palmer, S. (eds) (1996) *Professional Therapeutic Titles: Myths and Realities*. Leicester: British Psychological Society.

May, R. (1992) *The Art of Counselling*. London: Souvenir.

Milton, J., Polmear, C. and Fabricius, J. (2011) *A Short Introduction to Psychoanalysis* (2nd edn). London: Sage.

Parker, I. and Revelli, S. (eds) (2008) *Psychoanalytic Practice and State Regulation*. London: Karnac.

Parry, G. (1996) *NHS Psychotherapy Services in England: Review and Strategic Policy*. Wetherby: Department of Health.

Postle, D. (2011) *Therapy Futures: Obstacles and Opportunities*. London: WLR/ipnosis.

Sandler, J. and Dreher, A.U. (1996) *What Do Psychoanalysts Want? The Problem of Aims in Psychoanalytic Therapy*. London: Routledge/Institute of Psycho-Analysis.

Sills, C. (ed.) (2006) *Contracts in Counselling* (2nd edn). London: Sage.

Syme, G. (1994) *Counselling in Independent Practice*. Buckingham: Open University Press.

Thistle, R. (1998) *Counselling and Psychotherapy in Private Practice*. London: Sage.

Weatherill, R. (2004) *Our Last Great Illusion: A Radical Psychoanalytic Critique of Therapy Culture*. Exeter: Academic.

West, W. (ed.) (2011) *Exploring Therapy, Spirituality and Healing*. Basingstoke: Palgrave.

PART II

SOCIO-CULTURAL PERSPECTIVES

2.1

Introduction

COLIN FELTHAM AND IAN HORTON

Although counselling and psychotherapy continue to be criticized for focusing on the psychology of the individual and on the internal life of the client while ignoring the impact of the social, economic and cultural environment in which people live, there are also some relevant positive developments. Well-established commentators such as Pilgrim (1997) and Samuels (1993) have been joined by various writers (Kauffman and New, 2004; Lago and Smith, 2010; Robb, 2007; Proctor et al., 2006; Smail, 2005) arguing for far better links to be made between individual and social foci.

This part of the book starts by presenting an analysis of various familiar theoretical perspectives on social contexts and then, in subsequent chapters, examines a range of issues including gender, race, culture, class, religion, age, sexuality and disability. Therapists will hopefully respond more effectively to the needs of their clients if they understand at least something of the socio-cultural factors that affect not only their own lives and the lives of their clients, but the wider societal context in which counselling and psychotherapy take place.

Implicit in this assumption are three levels at which socio-cultural factors may impact on therapy and which therapists may find useful to address in ways that are either consistent with or constructively challenge their theoretical orientation.

HUMAN DEVELOPMENT

Two extreme theoretical positions on human development can be posited. From one point of view, human development and the origin and perpetuation of psychological problems are seen as a function of the interaction between individuals and their environment. From this position the assessment or clinical formulation of client presenting problems, and the subsequent therapeutic planning or approach to working with the client, would need to be aware of and somehow to address the impact of socio-cultural factors, however this may be done (Smail, 1993; 2005). In a rapidly changing multicultural society it can no longer be assumed that everyone has a very similar pattern of development or identical needs. Proponents of this socio-culturally sensitive view may also argue that therapists need to acquire a specific working knowledge of those factors germane to the client group they are working with. The opposing theoretical position, still quite prevalent, is that the origin and/or resolution of psychological problems are located primarily within the individual. From this position it could be argued that socio-cultural factors are secondary or largely irrelevant to counselling and psychotherapy.

THERAPIST–CLIENT RELATIONSHIP

This level of awareness is concerned with the socio-cultural similarities and differences between therapist and client. What is important here is the impact of these factors on the development of rapport and therapeutic alliance (or misalliance) and on the ways in which the dynamics of the relationship may be used as a window on the client's presenting problems and as a mechanism of therapeutic change. Clearly there are wide differences between the broad theoretical orientations concerning the value and function of the qualities, characteristics and dynamics of the relationship between therapist and client.

Ponterotto et al. (2001) argue that essential elements of multicultural therapy competence are the therapist's awareness of his or her own cultural heritage, worldview and related values, biases and assumptions about human behaviour, and an understanding of the worldview of the culturally different client (see also Palmer, 2002).

COUNSELLING AND PSYCHOTHERAPY GENERALLY

Psychological therapies remain largely a construction of the white, Western, middle-class and majority culture. People generally have widely differing views about the value or otherwise of counselling or psychotherapy and its place in present-day society. Few therapists would argue that socio-cultural/economic factors do not impinge in some way on the work they do, although the importance they place on this issue varies enormously. Issues of power and social control seem relevant at this level as do the dynamics, constraints and demands of working in particular institutions or organizational settings, for example, primary health care and employment (see Part VII). Recently the UK has experienced efforts to place mental health enhancement closer to the forefront of politics and service provision, especially in the positive psychology and wellbeing tradition which tends to argue that cognitive-behavioural therapy (CBT) will promote fuller employment (Layard, 2005). An alternative argument, that economic inequality creates and exacerbates mental distress and only greater social and material equality is likely to reduce this, is put forward by Wilkinson and Pickett (2010). Environmental and economic matters are likely to press much more sharply on the psychotherapeutic agenda in the years to come but they have not to date had any major impact on training or practice in spite of occasional appeals to extend psychotherapeutic thinking into social institutions (Bracher, 2009) and to create a cultural psychotherapy (McIntosh, 2008).

Bimrose (1993) is critical of the fact that so little attention seems to have been given to social context or multicultural issues in relation to counselling and psychotherapy theory, training and practice. This part of the book is concerned with what Bimrose describes as the hitherto invisible issues. While gradually becoming more visible, these probably remain under-exposed.

REFERENCES

Bimrose, J. (1993) Counselling and social context. In R. Bayne and P. Nicolson (eds), *Counselling and Psychology for Health Professionals*. London: Chapman and Hall.

Bracher, M. (2009) *Social Symptoms and Identity Needs: Why We Have Failed To Solve Our Social Problems and What To Do About It*. London: Karnac.

Kauffman, K. and New, C. (2004) *Co-Counselling: The Theory and Practice of Re-Evaluation Counselling*. London: Routledge.

Lago, C. and Smith, B. (eds) (2010) *Anti-Discriminatory Practice in Counselling and Psychotherapy* (2nd edn). London: Sage.

Layard, R. (2005) *Happiness: Lessons from a New Science*. London: Allen Lane.

McIntosh, A. (2008) *Hell and High Water: Climate Change, Hope and the Human Condition*. Edinburgh: Birlinn.

Palmer, S. (ed.) (2002) *Multicultural Counselling: A Reader*. London: Sage.

Pilgrim, D. (1997) *Psychotherapy and Society*. London: Sage.

Ponterotto, J.G., Casas, J.M. and Alexander, C.M. (eds) (2001) *Handbook of Multicultural Counseling* (2nd edn rev). Thousand Oaks, CA: Sage.

Proctor, G., Cooper, M., Sanders, P. and Malcolm, B. (eds) (2006) *Politicizing the Person-Centred Approach: An Agenda for Social Change*. Ross-on-Wye: PCCS.

Robb, C. (2007) *This Changes Everything: The Relational Revolution in Psychology*. New York: Picador.

Samuels, A. (1993) *The Political Psyche*. London: Routledge.

Smail, D. (1993) *The Origins of Unhappiness: A New Understanding of Personal Distress*. London: HarperCollins.

Smail, D. (2005) *Power, Interest and Psychology: Elements of a Social Materialist Understanding of Distress*. Ross-on-Wye: PCCS.

Wilkinson, R. and Pickett, K. (2010) *The Spirit Level: Why Equality Is Better for Everyone*. London: Penguin.

Gender

JENNY BIMROSE

The gender of an individual refers to their membership of a particular social category, masculine or feminine, which aligns more or less to the two sexes. It is, however, different from sex, sexual orientation, sexual preference and from other categories or descriptions that relate to various behaviours and identities associated with the sexes. Gender is defined by reference to those attributes associated with 'being female' and 'being male'. These attributes are not, however, fixed. They differ between cultures or societies during any one period in history and change within the same culture or society over time. To illustrate this last point, it is quite easy for most people to identify ways in which some of the attributes associated with being female or being male in their own society have changed over, say, a 20-year period. Such changes are bound up with role changes. They are also linked to subtle changes in social attitudes and values. Gender, then, is constructed and defined by societies. Perhaps most importantly, it highlights the ways in which 'being male' and 'being female' are valued differently – different and not equal. This chapter will examine the nature of some of these inequalities and discuss approaches developed to help counsellors respond more effectively to gender differences in counselling and psychotherapy.

GENDER INEQUALITY

A study of gender focuses attention on the profound and persistent inequalities suffered by women and girls:

> Gender equality is not only a basic human right, but its achievement has enormous socio-economic ramifications. Empowering women fuels thriving economies, spurring productivity and growth. Yet gender inequalities remain deeply entrenched in every society. (United Nations, 2010: 1)

The majority of the world's poor are women and their lack of access to financial resources has a negative impact on their overall wellbeing. UK statistics show that women's wages are, on average, 20 per cent less than men's wages (Johnson and Kossykh, 2008) and they are more likely to have low-paid, low-status, vulnerable jobs, with limited or no social protection or basic rights (Women and Work Commission, 2006). Women continue to have disproportionate responsibility for unpaid work, such as caregiving, which limits their full participation in education, the labour market and public life, with women accounting for nearly two-thirds of the 776 million illiterate adults in the world (United Nations, 2010). Progress, however, has been made, particularly in developed countries, where significant changes to the way that women live their lives are discernible. In the UK, for example, women are having their first child later than ever before; divorces have increased sixfold; the number of first-time marriages has decreased; and young women account for more first-time mortgages than men (United Nations, 1995). These social changes indicate the increasing levels of freedom being experienced by women regarding their reproductive functions, their relationship to the marriage contract and their financial affairs. However, alongside these types of positive lifestyle changes, many examples of inequalities and injustices continue that have to be routinely confronted by women across a whole range of areas in their daily lives. Perhaps the most shocking relates to the statistics on violence. Violence against girls and women is described as a 'global pandemic', with a recent 10-country study revealing that between 15 and 71 per cent of women reported physical or sexual violence by their husband or partner. These acts of violence cause more deaths and disability than cancer, malaria, traffic accidents and war combined, and in 2006 women and girls comprised 79 per cent of victims of human trafficking (United Nations, 2010). In the UK, violence against women includes: acts of rape; domestic violence; sexual harassment; stalking; crimes in the name of honour; female genital mutilation; trafficking; and forced marriage (Sen and Kelly, 2007). It has been estimated that in one year, 12.9 million incidents of domestic violence (that constituted non-sexual threats or force) were committed against women compared with 2.5 million against men (Walby and Allen, 2004). In a '24 hour snapshot' study of domestic violence carried out amongst UK police forces and domestic violence support agencies on 28 September 2000, it was found that every minute, police receive a call to a victim of domestic violence. The same study revealed that nearly one in five counselling sessions held in English Relate Centres (over 900) on that same snapshot date, and over one in five counselling sessions held in Northern Ireland, included mention of domestic violence as an issue in the marriage (Stanko, 2000).

The educational achievement of girls and women in the UK, however, represents a real success story. Girls now outperform boys at ages 7, 11 and 14 years in the National Curriculum assessments in English, with achievements in maths and sciences broadly similar. They are also more successful than boys at every level of the General Certificate of Secondary Education (GCSE), the major public examination at ages 16 and 18 (Johnson and Kossykh, 2008; Ringrose, 2007). Girls in the UK even perform as well as boys in mathematics and science subjects (traditionally the subjects in which boys' achievement outstripped girls') at the age of 16 and now gain access to higher education in larger numbers than men. Despite the successes, gendered practices in education continue. For example, both teaching methods and the curricula continue to be plagued by gendered stereotypes, with girls and women consequently excluded and marginalized in the curriculum, content and practices of education (UNESCO, 2010; Weiner et al., 1997).

Patterns of women's employment in the UK have, however, been much slower to change. While their participation rates in the labour market are increasing, women continue to dominate in part-time work, which tends to be low paid and to have few promotional prospects and limited training opportunities. The gender pay gap is persistent and is widening (Rake, 2009). Gender segregation means women are persistently underrepresented in many occupational sectors (Women and Work Commission, 2009). Additionally, sexual harassment in the workplace is a strong and recurrent theme in women's employment, but is often regarded as not being a significant problem (Bimrose, 2004; 2008).

Many examples of gender inequality can be found in other areas, such as health care, legal rights, housing, training and welfare. An important question for counsellors and psychotherapists is: to what extent and in what ways should the extent and depth of these inequalities be taken into account in their practice?

GENDER AND COUNSELLING/ PSYCHOTHERAPY

The suggestion that gender represents a dimension in the therapeutic relationship which deserves special consideration can be contentious amongst professionals. Resistance to this suggestion can relate to many issues, for example, concern about stereotyping clients – because grouping clients within a grand category, such as gender, risks generalizations and detracts from the uniqueness of individuals. One other concern relates to any suggestion that women (and girls) are more deserving of special attention or consideration in counselling than men (and boys). Despite resistance from the field, gender is increasingly attracting the attention of researchers, writers and practitioners, who argue that counsellors and therapists need to be ready to adapt their approach when working with women, who often suffer psychological distress as victims of social injustice, including discrimination and prejudice (Fischer and Holz, 2007). It has been argued, for example, that counsellors may need to review, fundamentally, the adequacy of traditional theories of assessment and treatment that underpin their practice for work with all clients who are systematically disadvantaged, including women (Eriksen and Kress, 2008). The integration of new approaches is indicated, which takes account of context:

> it is often forgotten that the roots of women's so-called psychological problems have frequently been social and political rather than the individual and intrapsychic in origin. (2008: 152)

Examples of these types of new integrated approaches include multicultural combined with a social justice approach (Comstock et al., 2008) and multicultural with feminist and social justice approaches (Crethar et al., 2008).

A useful framework for reviewing existing contributions comes from multicultural counselling and therapy (MCT) (Bimrose, 1996). The multicultural literature has now matured and established itself within counselling psychology (Bimrose, 1998; Worthington et al., 2007). It is not, however, without critics (Worthington et al., 2007) and its introduction into professional training programmes and practice has been contentious (Comstock et al., 2008). Despite possible shortcomings, a particular strength is the way it helps clients understand how problems they are confronting may emanate from their ethnicity, gender, age, disability or socio-economic status, rather than internalizing problems as individual deficits for which they have to take responsibility (Constantine et al., 2007; Ivey et al., 1997). One other attractive feature of this approach is the explication of what multicultural skills and competencies are required for practice. Even qualified and experienced practitioners have reported feelings of inadequacy around working with clients who are different from themselves in some respect, especially regarding gender and ethnicity (Bimrose and Bayne, 1995). Thus a competency framework provides a practical means of developing expertise and confidence. The multicultural standards and competencies that define the multiculturally competent counsellor (Sue et al., 1995: 625) are presented in a three-by-three matrix. The three basic dimensions of this matrix are defined as: therapist awareness, understanding and skills. It is within these dimensions that approaches to gender in therapy will now be considered.

Gender-aware therapy (GAT) is one approach that specifically encourages therapists to explore gender-related experiences with both women and men (Good et al., 1990). If adopted, the principles of GAT would enhance all three dimensions of multicultural competence in practice. Five are identified: (1) gender issues must be integrated into counselling and therapy equally with women and men (for example, problems related to childcare are discussed with men in the same way as with women); (2) problems which arise in counselling must, where relevant, be linked clearly to their social origins (for example, stress and anxiety which are created by a lack of availability of quality childcare provision should be related to systems failure in the provision of this service); (3) collusion with gender stereotypical solutions to problems must be avoided (for example, women experiencing stress and anxiety because of a lack of quality childcare provision should *not* be encouraged to give up work or to work part-time); (4) collaborative therapeutic relationships must be developed in preference to an expert therapist role; (5) and most important, clients' freedom to choose must be respected, rather than a value position being imposed. Overall, an important goal of GAT is to help clients learn to act in new ways that will allow them to develop in a manner not constrained by stereotypical gender assumptions.

Applying Sue et al.'s (1995) multicultural competency framework, the second GAT principle implies increased knowledge and understanding about the precise nature and extent of gender inequalities within all aspects of society, together with their consequences. The third GAT principle implies the need for all therapists to increase their own self-awareness about gender issues as well as their awareness of gender stereotypes which operate generally. The first, fourth and fifth GAT principles imply particular skills and techniques which should be adopted by therapists in practice. For example, the first would require a conscious exploration of issues with men in therapy which relate to matters often associated only with women.

Feminist counselling approaches gender in a similar way to gender-aware therapy, highlighting the destructive potential of gender, since it limits role expectations and relegates half the population to second-class status. Chaplin (1999) describes feminist counselling as being a different approach that implicates attitudes, values and ways of thinking. She argues that it relates more to the development of a different 'feminine' value system through raising awareness and the rejection of the dominant male values and characteristics typical of the society in which we live. Feminist counselling is concerned with inequality generally, not just that associated with gender. It is eclectic in approach, so it can be used with any other approaches to therapy which accept that external factors contribute to the problems of clients. Ivey et al. (1997: 173) summarize the main features of feminist therapy as being: the creation of an egalitarian relationship in counselling; valuing and respecting individual difference; emphasizing the effect of external influences; assisting with support for clients beyond the individual therapy session (for example, mobilizing support groups, community services); an active and participatory approach to therapy (for example, using techniques like assertiveness training for women); a strong information-giving component in counselling sessions to ensure that clients understand the origins and nature of gender oppression and inequality; and helping the client to gain a more positive self-image and personal validation.

Applying the framework for multicultural competence to feminist counselling, the approach emphasizes increased counsellor self-awareness of gender inequality together with knowledge about, and understanding of, the dimensions of social inequality. Such knowledge would be used beyond individual counselling sessions to influence, even change, structures and systems that create and maintain gender inequalities. This resonates with the social justice and advocacy movement which is gaining ground in counselling psychology (Arrendondo et al., 2008; Lee and Rodgers, 2009; Lopez-Baez and Paylo, 2009; Roysircar, 2009; Toporek et al., 2001; 2009), where intervening on behalf of clients and/or taking a more active community role may be necessary to achieve the change that makes the difference to the life chances of women.

Gendered approaches to therapy are still being developed. They represent a serious and reflective attempt to address issues raised by gender in therapy. Ivey et al. (1997: 175) discuss how feminist therapy can be combined with multicultural counselling and therapy, highlighting the value that can be derived when therapists work beyond the level of the individual to, for example, the community. Indeed, a conscious approach to gender can be particularly valuable when working cross-culturally, where cultures and value systems define strongly marked gender roles.

CONCLUSION

Nearly four decades have passed since legislation was implemented in the UK that made discrimination on the grounds of gender illegal. Yet scratch the surface and it is easy to see the extent of the continuing gender discrimination, inequality and injustice. Often difficult to separate from other types of discrimination (such as that related to ethnicity, age, disability or social class), it can be subtle and hard to detect. Even so, it is no less destructive in its impact on the individual and society. Gender represents a challenge for counselling and psychotherapy. Should counselling support, 'heal' and assist clients to return to the systems and contexts which damaged them? Or should it seek to influence those systems and contexts, as well as reflecting upon and changing those values and practices inherently discriminatory in practice itself? Gender-aware therapy, feminist counselling, multicultural counselling and psychotherapy, combined with social justice approaches, are all attempts to address gender-related issues. They are still evolving, but represent a constructive attempt to pose legitimate questions about practice and incorporate new and different ways of responding to clients.

REFERENCES

Arrendondo, P., Tovar-Blank, Z.G. and Parham, A. (2008) Challenges and promises of becoming a culturally competent counselor in a sociopolitical era of change and empowerment. *Journal of Counseling & Development*, 86 (3): 261–8.

Bimrose, J. (1996) Multiculturalism. In R. Bayne, I. Horton and J. Bimrose (eds), *New Directions in Counselling* (pp. 237–47). London: Routledge.

Bimrose, J. (1998) Increasing multicultural competence. In R. Bayne, P. Nicolson and I. Horton (eds), *Counselling and Communication Skills for Medical and Health Practitioners* (pp. 88–102). Leicester: British Psychological Association.

Bimrose, J. (2004) Sexual harassment in the workplace: an ethical dilemma for career guidance practice? *British Journal of Guidance and Counselling*, 32 (1): 109–21.

Bimrose, J. (2008) Guidance with women. In J.A. Athanasou and R.V. Esbroeck (eds), *International Handbook of Career Guidance* (pp. 375–404). Dordrecht: Springer.

Bimrose, J. and Bayne, R. (1995) The multicultural framework in counsellor training. *British Journal of Guidance and Counselling*, 23 (2): 259–65.

Chaplin, J. (1999) *Feminist Counselling in Action* (2nd edn). London: Sage.

Comstock, D.L., Hammer, T.R. and Strentzsh, J. (2008) Relational-cultural theory: a framework for bridging relational, multicultural, and social justice competencies. *Journal of Counseling & Development*, 86 (3): 279–87.

Constantine, M.G., Hage, S.M., Kindaichie, M.M. and Bryant, R.M. (2007) Social justice and multicultural issues: implications for the practice and training of counselors and counseling psychologists. *Journal of Counseling & Development*, 85 (4): 24–9.

Crethar, H.C., Rivera, E.T. and Nash, S. (2008) In search of common threads: linking multicultural, feminist, and social justice counseling paradigms. *Journal of Counseling & Development*, 86 (3): 269–78.

Ericksen, J.A. and Kress, V.E. (2008) Gender and diagnosis: struggles and suggestions for counselors. *Journal of Counseling & Development*, 86 (2): 152–62.

Fischer, A.R. and Holz, K.B. (2007) Perceived discrimination and women's psychological distress: the roles of collective and personal self-esteem. *Journal of Counseling Psychology*, 54 (2): 154–64.

Good, G.E., Gilber, L.A. and Scher, M. (1990) Gender aware therapy: a synthesis of feminist therapy and knowledge about gender. *Journal of Counseling and Development*, 68: 376–80.

Ivey, A.E., Ivey, M.B. and Simek-Morgan, L. (1997) *Counseling and Psychotherapy: A Multicultural Perspective* (4th edn). Needham Heights, MA: Allyn and Bacon.

Johnson, P. and Kossykh, Y. (2008) *Early Years, Life Chances and Equality: A Literature Review*. Research report 7. Manchester. www.equality humanrights.com/uploaded_files/research/7_ earlyyears_lifechances.pdf.

Lee, C.C. and Rodgers, R.A. (2009) Counselor advocacy: affecting systemic change. *Journal of Counseling & Development*, 87 (3): 284–7.

Lopez-Baez, S.I. and Paylo, M.J. (2009) Social justice advocacy: community collaboration and systems advocacy. *Journal of Counseling & Development*, 87 (3): 276–83.

Rake, D. (2009) *Are Women Bearing the Burden of the Recession?* London: Fawcett Society. www. fawcettsociety.org.uk/documents/Arewomen bearingtheburdenoftherecession.pdf.

Ringrose, J. (2007) Successful girls? Complicating post-feminist, neoliberal discourses of educational achievement and gender equality. *Gender and Education*, 19 (4): 471–89.

Roysircar, G. (2009) The big picture of advocacy: counselor, heal society and thyself. *Journal of Counseling & Development*, 87 (3): 288–94.

Sen, P. and Kelly, L. (2007) *Violence Against Women in the UK*. London: Shadow Thematic Report for the Committee on the Elimination of all Forms of Discrimination against Women. www.iwraw-ap.org/resources/pdf/41_shadow_ reports/UK_SR_on_VAW.pdf.

Stanko, B. (2000) Enough is enough: snapshot – counting the cost of domestic violence. www. eurowrc.org/01.eurowrc/04.eurowrc_en/45. en_ewrc.htm.

Sue, D.W., Arrendondo, P. and McDavis, R.J. (1995) Multicultural counseling competencies and standards: a call to the profession. In J.G. Ponterotto, J.M. Casas, L.A. Suzuki and C.M. Alexander (eds), *Handbook of Multicultural Counseling*. Thousand Oaks, CA: Sage.

Toporek, R.L. and Liu, E.M. (2001) Advocacy in counseling: addressing race, class and gender oppression. In D.B. Pope-Davies and H.L.K. Coleman (eds), *The Intersection of Race, Class, and Gender in Multicultural Counseling*. Thousand Oaks, CA: Sage.

Toporek, R.L., Lewis, J.A. and Crethar, H.C. (2009) Promoting systemic change through the ACA competencies. *Journal of Counseling & Development*, 87 (3): 260–9.

UNESCO (2010) *Education for All Global Monitoring Report. Summary: Reaching the Marginalised*. unesdoc.unesco.org/images/0018/001865/ 186525E.pdf.

United Nations (1995) *Fourth World Conference on Women*. Report of the Fourth World Conference on Women, Beijing, China.

United Nations (2010) *UN Women: Facts and Figures on Women Worldwide*. www.unwomen. org/wp-content/uploads/2010/06/UNWomen_ FactsAndFiguresOnWomen_20100702.pdf.

Walby, S. and Allen, J. (2004) *Domestic Violence, Sexual Assault and Stalking: Findings from the British Crime Survey*. Home Office Research, Development and Statistical Directorate.

Weiner, G., Arnot, M. and David, M. (1997) Is the future female? Female success, male disadvantage, and changing gender patterns in education. In A.H. Halsey, H. Lauder, P. Brown and A.S. Wells (eds), *Education: Culture, Economy, and Society* (pp. 620–30). Oxford: Oxford University Press.

Women and Work Commission (2006) *Shaping a Fairer Future*. London: Women and Equality Unit. www.womenandequalityunit.gov.uk/ publications/wwc_shaping_fairer_future06. pdf.

Women and Work Commission (2009) *Shaping a Fairer Future: A Review of Recommendations of the Women and Work Commission Three Years On*. London: Government Equalities Office. www.equalities.gov.uk/pdf/297158_ WWC_Report_acc.pdf.

Worthington, R.L., Soth-McNett, A.M. and Moreno, M.V. (2007) Multicultural counseling competencies research: a 20 year content analysis. *Journal of Counseling Psychology*, 54 (4): 351–61.

Disability

SIMON PARRITT

The *World Report on Disability* (WHO and The World Bank, 2011) estimates that some one billion people in the world today experience disabilities of various types and degrees and 200 million experience considerable difficulties in functioning. Whilst around 80 per cent of the world's disabled people live in the developing world, according to the UN Development Programme (UNDP, 2007), it is estimated that there are more than 6 million disabled people in the UK alone. Moreover, disabled people are not evenly distributed across society, and those from economically deprived social and educational environments are more likely to fall within the definition of a disabled person, whatever that may be.

One of the problems that arises when looking at the prevalence of disability in any population or community is that there is an ongoing debate and some controversy over the definition of disability. In 1980 WHO defined disability as the deficits in performance of activities resulting from physical impairment, though this emphasis on 'physical impairment' is increasingly extended to include mental health and learning disability. Physical impairment is the deficit in structure or functioning of some part of the body. The continuing debate concerning the definition of disability which uses a model based upon 'able bodied assumption of disability' (Oliver, 1993: 61) gives rise to tensions between society and the position of the disabled person within society. Oliver sees this as not just a question of semantics but a challenge to researchers to find new ways of operationalizing 'the concept of disability based upon the notion that disability is a social creation' (1993: 66). For example, while a

person may have an impairment which means they use a wheelchair, the disability is the difficulty experienced in accessing buildings or services, the restrictions on personal and sexual relationships, and the attitudes of a predominantly non-disabled societal structure. Progress was made in recognizing the position of disabled people within society at an international level when the United Nations produced the Convention on the Rights of Persons with Disabilities which came into force on 3 May 2008 and is a legally binding international treaty on disability. It has 147 signatories and was ratified by the European Union on 23 December 2010 (United Nations Enable, 2010).

However disability is defined, prevalence increases with age. According to the Office for National Statistics (2011), in the UK there is a trend towards an ageing population, from 15 per cent over 65 in 1984 to a projected 23 per cent by 2034. However, the number of over 85s is even more dramatic, rising from 660,000 in 1984 to 1.4 million in 2009 and a projected 3.5 million by 2034, which represents approximately 5 per cent of the total population. It follows that the percentage of people who either define themselves, or are classified by others, as disabled will increase over the next few decades. In addition, the public policy of encouraging people to remain economically active to a greater age will impact upon those who are disabled and less able to participate in work and society. The Labour Force Survey of 1999 starkly showed that of those who came within the definition of the Disability Discrimination Act (DDA), 85 per cent between 16 and 59 were economically inactive as opposed to 54 per cent of the non-disabled group. An understanding of the issues and experiences of disabled people is therefore even more essential for counsellors, psychotherapists and counselling psychologists if they are to meet the needs of this substantial group of people and of society as a whole.

As a minority group, disabled people differ in one important aspect from most others, in that anyone can become a disabled person at any time in their life. Despite this, or perhaps because of this, there is often a tendency for therapists to collude with a process of denial or to distance themselves, seeing disability as something that happens to others. A substantial number of people, however, will experience disability in one form or another during their lifetime. One might in fact suggest that it is the exceptional person who will live his or her life without experiencing disability or being close to someone who is disabled. To see disability as 'other' and not to reflect upon one's own relationship to disability, chronic illness and impairment is a fundamentally flawed strategy for anyone, but especially for those of us who are counsellors, psychotherapists or counselling psychologists.

The rejection and stigmatizing of disability is rooted deep within most societies across the world. Within ancient, pre-industrial and modern society, disability has often been seen as punishment or possession. Demons, spirits and divine retribution have all been evoked as ways of making sense out of arbitrary and random events experienced by individuals and societies over which we have little control. This placed disability firmly within the domain of religion and therefore of faith healers, shamans and traditional healers. However, with the separation of the physical from the spiritual, illness and disability have increasingly become the domain of the physician and surgeon who have sought to 'cure', treat or prevent. The impact of this upon disabled people, while overtly helping through interventions which have cured or improved disabled people's lives, has also brought difficulties. It has placed disability itself within a conceptual framework which sees it as inherently bad or deviant, and therefore interventions are aimed at individuals to alter them physically or psychologically towards what a non-disabled world sees as the accepted norm, rather than what may be in their best interests.

Therapists can often be faced with clients who are forever seeking 'the' cure, but at what cost? If it takes many operations and almost half a lifetime to no longer be a wheelchair user, is this what the client wants the bulk of their life to be about? What has been lost in terms of living and what has been gained? Therapists will need to think deeply about these issues both from a philosophical standpoint and in respect of each client and the stage they are at in facing choices, or lack of them. There are no right answers, but the questions, options and choices should be aired and explored together.

The impact of a predominantly biomedical model on the development of services for disabled people has been to focus upon active physical treatment and to marginalize the psychological and socio-political experience of disabled people. For those whom medicine fails to cure or repair, interventions are aimed at helping them 'come to terms' with their disability and accept their new reduced role and usually reduced status in society. They are in danger of becoming the passive recipients of care and sympathy from others. It is this image of disability that charity advertising has historically played upon, portraying disabled people as either helpless, sad, brave or courageous; and whilst today charities and the media are more aware of this narrative, it still persists in many ways. Lip service may be paid to self-determination and empowerment, but the reality for most is that support for these aspirations in such areas as employment, entertainment, transport, sex and relationships focuses upon an economic model of a benefit culture which is cost driven. Rehabilitation and counselling intervention, particularly when delivered within the statutory sector, are often targeted at outcomes which focus upon reducing the costs to society in purely economic terms. Therapists can therefore be in danger of falling into this narrow 'rehabilitation' framework. There are obviously physical access issues, but even after recognizing economic and physical barriers it is also worth considering how the philosophy which underpins a counselling or psychotherapy service may compound the above view.

Leaving aside hospital-based services, which by the nature of the service are time and outcome focused, how much counselling or therapy is delivered from a social model perspective which proposes that people are disabled not so much by their impairments as by the environment? Much 'non-medical-based' counselling for disabled people, where it exists, is delivered by charities or self-help groups with an emphasis on perhaps just sharing experiences. Disability charities have often struggled with the problem of being organizations run for disabled people by the non-disabled rather than the disabled. Many large charities, established by the great and the good in a different era, often promote the medical model. While there is a genuine effort by some to change and encompass the social model, progress is slow and often superficial. Where disabled people do control and have a governing say in the organizations, the quality and professionalism of counselling must be an overriding consideration. While it may be important for counsellors to 'understand the issues', any service for disabled people should offer the same professional standards as would be expected by any other service user, disabled or not. Empathy is important, but it is surely not sufficient as the basis for a professional service. Equally important is access to high-quality training that addresses the fundamentals of disability for both disabled and non-disabled counsellors and therapists. At a time of economic constraints and funding reductions, training always seems to be an early casualty.

Counsellors and therapists should also be aware of the multiplicity of cultural value systems around disability, not just at a societal level but also at the individual and family level. There are many ethnically and culturally differing attitudes towards disability. However, while counsellors must be aware of cultural values and practices, they should also view disability from a cross-cultural perspective. For example, family members may expect to be present during sessions, or a young disabled client may be expected to remain dependent and cared for at home with the family as a duty, and not to work or have sexual relationships. While these attitudes can be rationalized within a particular cultural perspective, they are also common forms of oppression and disempowerment that pervade disabled people's lives throughout the world. Therapists must be sensitive to all aspects of a disabled client's lived experience and yet also be brave enough to help a client challenge oppressive and disablist beliefs and practices within both themselves and their community.

There are other, more subtle barriers which may explain why therapists see few disabled people. Attendance for counselling, so often seen as a therapeutic and funding issue, has to be viewed as potentially different, as clients' experience of transport and access problems or just being ill may be a real and genuine problem outside their control. The result can be that non-attendance is higher and throughput lower than with other counselling services, resulting in increased cost of a service per client. Counsellors and therapists need to be aware of these factors when compiling statistics and writing reports for the funding bodies, and to explain them within a well-argued philosophical social model context. It is also important to question whether time-limited work which restricts the therapeutic contract to six or eight or 10 sessions is the most suitable model for disabled clients, and to consider what the research and theoretical basis is for such contracts.

When a disabled client has been referred, there are practical issues that need to be addressed. But most counsellors or psychotherapists probably see very few disabled people, or clients perceived as disabled people. One counsellor, when asked how many disabled clients she had, was quite clear she had none. However, following a conversation about the subject, she realized that one of her long-term clients was in fact disabled with multiple sclerosis. Why had she not realized? Another experienced therapist felt unable to help in research because she also had 'no disabled clients'. Again, following discussion, she realized she had several clients with long-term impairments such as heart disease and rheumatoid arthritis.

The reason behind this 'denial' or 'invisibility' of disability is complex, but as therapists we need to become aware of all the issues in which clients themselves are immersed. The invisibility of many disabled people in society is itself a major source of oppression. Why do so few therapists have disabled clients? It may be that clients are reluctant to label themselves disabled, preferring to be ill. This can reflect either a reluctance to be associated with a stigmatized group, or a preference for being ill – as illness is something that doctors treat rather than defining who you are. Remember that most disabled people's experience of professionals is from a medical not a social model perspective. Cure and treatment are aspects of the medical approach with which disabled clients are familiar from day one of their diagnosis. Therapists need to be aware of where they are coming from and what their experiences of and reactions to impairment are, as well as how these influence their approach. They will also need to understand the client's belief system as well as their own in relation to disability, impairment and chronic illness and their role as the counsellor or therapist.

As stated earlier, the social model as outlined by Oliver (1993) and others proposes that disabled people are disabled by the environment, not by their impairments. This is clearly true at a sociological level, but for the individual client it only partly illuminates the experience of disability. Counsellors are looking to develop a therapeutic relationship with clients as unique individuals, but come to them with their own beliefs, experiences and models of working. Impairment may have little or nothing to do with what the client wants to address, or it may be central. However, therapists may at least initially be occupied by the impairment, especially if it is visible or declared prior to the first meeting or assessment.

Images of disabled people are often polarized between the 'dependent cripple' requiring sympathy, care and total support, and the strongly independent wheelchair user such as the Olympic athlete. The truth is rarely that clear-cut, and the majority of disabled people are not wheelchair users despite that being the accepted symbol for disability.

Disabled people have attempted to claim a cultural identity similar to that of other oppressed people. They need to own their identity and see it for what it is – a unique culture of experience. This does not mean all disabled people are the same or share the same view of disability. Counsellors and therapists, whether they themselves are disabled or not, have a duty to see the experience of disability in a cultural context just as they would if they were seeing a client from a different culture. For many clients, having an impairment and being a disabled person mean that they have experienced pain in various forms. It would be unrealistic to deny this. But how and to what degree this is the focus of therapy is both critical for the client and central to a wider political context in which therapy takes place. Being disabled is not necessarily a reason in itself for needing therapy.

Research has consistently shown that outcome depends more upon the quality of the therapeutic relationship than upon the theoretical model used by the therapist. It follows that the way therapists (be they non-disabled or disabled themselves) relate to their non-disabled or disabled clients is the critical factor. Here are just a few of the issues which might militate against the therapist making a successful therapeutic alliance with a disabled client:

- the association of tragedy with disability
- fear of contamination
- disgust at physical appearance
- helplessness
- pity
- a concentration on loss
- not accepting the reality of discrimination
- early life experiences and biases.

The writer has seen a few clients for whom becoming a disabled person was in retrospect an opportunity to start again, and such clients may embrace the social model as a core belief system. This reaction can cause tension, for the therapist may only see the 'loss' or 'tragedy' of becoming disabled. For such a therapist the source of distress and therefore the focus of counselling is the individual, not the wider social and political environment, and he or she therefore finds it almost impossible to empathize with a position which does not view disability *per se* as negative.

More common are clients who are distressed by their impairments, not just because of the disabling environment but because they are in pain of some kind. They may have less energy and experience a deep ongoing sense of loss at not being able to do things that were once available to them. To adopt a position where all this is seen as secondary to the real issue which is located outside the individual in the social environment would be, of course, as harmful as the previous example. Finding the balance between these two extremes is perhaps the hardest task as it requires the therapist to listen intently to the internal experience of the client, to the therapeutic process as it unfolds and to their own inner process. Supervision is of paramount importance here.

For all this, the therapeutic space is perhaps one of the few opportunities that disabled people have to explore all aspects of their life and relationships. The sad thing is that few do so, and fewer counsellors feel able to offer that space. Those counsellors who do offer therapy to disabled people often still come from a medical perspective and therefore can be in danger of not listening to how the client's experience of disability relates to their other life experiences and presenting problems.

REFERENCES

Office for National Statistics (2011) *Mid-Year Population Statistics*. www.statistics.gov.uk/cci/nugget.asp?id=949.

Oliver, M. (1993) Re-defining disability: a challenge to research. In J. Swain, V. Finklestein, S. French and M. Oliver (eds), *Disabling Barriers – Enabling Environments*. Milton Keynes: Open University Press/Sage.

UNDP (2007) *Fact Sheet on Persons with Disabilities*. New York: United Nations.

United Nations Enable (2010) *Convention on the Rights of Persons with Disabilities*. www.un.org/disabilities/.

WHO (1980) *International Classification of Impairments, Disabilities and Handicaps: A Manual of Classification Relating to the Consequences of Disease*. Geneva: World Health Organization.

WHO and The World Bank (2011) *World Report on Disability*. http://whqlibdoc.who.int/publications/2011/9789240685215_eng.pdf

RECOMMENDED READING

Hales, G. (ed.) (1996) *Beyond Disability: Towards an Enabling Society*. Milton Keynes: Open University Press.

Swain, J., Finklestein, V., French, S. and Oliver, M. (eds) (1993) *Disabling Barriers – Enabling Environments*. Milton Keynes: Open University Press/Sage.

Shakespeare, T., Gillespie-Sells, C. and Davies, D. (1996) *The Sexual Politics of Disability*. London: Cassell.

2.4

Age

LÉONIE SUGARMAN

The population of the UK is ageing. The proportion of the population aged 65 and over grew from 15 per cent in 1984 to 16 per cent in 2009, an increase of 1.7 million people. Over the same period, the proportion aged under 16 decreased from 21 to 19 per cent. This trend is projected to continue. By 2034, 23 per cent of the population is projected to be aged 65 and over compared to 18 per cent aged under 16.

The fastest population increase has been in the number of those aged 85 and over, the 'oldest old'. In 1984, there were around 660,000 people in the UK aged 85 and over. Since then the numbers have more than doubled, reaching 1.4 million in 2009. By 2034 the number of people aged 85 and over is projected to be 2.5 times larger than in 2009, reaching 3.5 million and accounting for 5 per cent of the total population (Office for National Statistics, 2011).

Age is an ever-present, but often unspoken, dimension of difference in therapy (Sugarman, 2004). It is an ambiguous concept that in some ways is becoming less significant (as with the phasing out of the default retirement age), but in other ways remains crucial (as in the contemporaneous increasing of the state pension age). A personal characteristic indicating time lived since birth, age is also a social marker that structures the way individuals interpret their experience, and organizes the ways in which people perceive and interact with each other (Gilleard and Higgs, 2000). By dividing the human lifespan into socially meaningful units, we translate calendar time into social time (Neugarten and Neugarten, 1996), resulting in an age-grade system in which life stages such as 'youth', 'midlife' and 'old age' imply not only chronological age but also a cluster of socially defined rights, responsibilities, obligations, developmental tasks and preoccupations that reflect cultural traditions, laws, values and beliefs concerning age-appropriate behaviour (Liefbroer and Billari, 2010).

Although aspects of a society's age-grade system may be enshrined by law and formal regulations, much of it is grounded in custom and practice. As we grow up we tend to internalize its dictates (Heckhausen, 1999), developing by the end of adolescence an often unarticulated concept of the 'normal expectable life course' (Neugarten, 1996) – an anticipation of the likely sequence and timing of the major transitions in education, work and family that will characterize our future. We utilize this internalized social clock to assess ourselves, and others, as being 'early', 'late' or 'on time' with regard to a wide range of life events and experiences. In the face of uncertainty, age norms and stereotypes can provide individuals with a subtle sense of security (Dannefer and Setterson, 2010) and a set of ready-made and compelling life goals against which to assess how well or poorly we are doing 'for our age'. At the same time, age norms and age-related goals can directly or indirectly restrict personal choice and serve as mechanisms of social control. A key role for therapists may be to help clients disentangle whether, in striving for such targets, they are 'being themselves' or merely 'acting their age'.

The challenging of age-graded assumptions and regulations both contributes to and is facilitated by the loosening of age norms and the blurring of life stages that have occurred in the UK and elsewhere during the last half century. We are now less sure than we were about where to put punctuation marks in the life course, and age has become a poor predictor of the timing of life events and of a person's work, family or health status (Achenbaum and Cole, 2007). Transitions – for example from education to employment or from employment to retirement – have become less standardized than previously with regard to both timing and nature, and adult life may not conform to the regularities that we anticipated when we were younger. Whilst this loosening of age norms is potentially liberating, it can leave people unsupported by social structures and more dependent than previously on personal resources and skills (Wrosch and Freund, 2001). The disorder, discontinuity and uncertainties of a fluid life cycle may propel clients into therapy as much as might the constraints of rigid age restrictions and expectations.

AGE AND THERAPY

Whilst universal themes such as attachment, separation, dependency, change and loss will permeate counselling and psychotherapy irrespective of the age or life stage of the client, they take on a different hue according to the psychosocial context of successive life stages (Jacobs, 2006). Pregnancy at age 15 is not the same as pregnancy at age 45, for example, nor is redundancy the same at ages 35 and 55.

Clients of different ages and life stages have different psychological, cognitive and sensory capacities. Thus, therapists working with children and young adolescents need to be sensitive to their level of verbal and cognitive development as well as their level of emotional maturity. With clients in late adulthood, decreasing sensory capacity (notably sight and hearing) may need to be taken into account along with the declining cognitive functioning that may – but does not inevitably – accompany the ageing process. Similarly, some issues will occur more frequently for clients within a particular age range. The design and structure of therapy services will often reflect this understanding of the meaning of different life stages, such that age may be used as a gateway to a wide range of therapy-related opportunities and resources. Whilst this is more expedient than individualized assessment of need, age and need are imperfectly correlated, and any presumed correspondence may be based on erroneous assumptions and outmoded patterns of social organization. As such, age- or life-stage-based

services may encourage the stereotyping of particular age groups as problematic, and inadvertently add to age separation and segregation (Bytheway, 2005). And yet, to deny differential treatment to particular groups identified primarily by age may be to ignore real differences in capacity, vulnerability and, in particular, power.

Access to therapy is influenced by money and power (Pilgrim, 1997). People in early and middle adulthood are most likely to be economically active and in positions not only to purchase their own therapy, but also to determine who else receives therapy or other mental health services, and for what problems. In this regard, children and older adults have much in common in that the economic power of the very young and the very old is frequently either minimal or negative – although even here one must be careful since the assumption that all older people are inevitably impoverished is itself an ageist myth. Nonetheless, the very young and the very old do frequently lack direct economic power and, as a result, they also lack social power – both of which may be needed to gain access to appropriate counselling and psychotherapy.

Children and older adults are less likely to self-refer than those in the more socially powerful and (potentially) more economically active stages of the life course. Therapists working with these clients are also likely to have contact with other family members who may have been responsible for raising the clients' need for therapeutic intervention. The question needs to be asked as to whether the services that are provided are in the best interest of the clients or of those who instigate the referral process – for example, parents and school teachers in the case of children, or children and health-care professionals in the case of vulnerable older clients. Whilst advocacy by others may be a legitimate response to clients' vulnerability and limited capacities, therapists need to be wary of patronizing ageism that defines reality on behalf of either the young or the old, and decides what interventions are required.

AGE AND THE THERAPEUTIC RELATIONSHIP

Clients' age will have an impact on how they perceive the therapist. Clients of a different age to the counsellor – be they significantly older or significantly younger – may believe that 'the world is different now' and that the therapist, being of a different generation, cannot possibly understand what they are experiencing. Thus, older clients may consider a much younger therapist to be inexperienced and/or presumptive in assuming they have anything to offer, with transference issues reflecting their relationship with their children or grandchildren. Children and adolescents may, by contrast, experience the therapist as an authority figure, and parental transference may be relevant, with clients re-experiencing and re-enacting with the counsellor aspects of the relationship they have or had with their parents.

Therapists, like clients, are embedded in a network of intergenerational relationships, and need, therefore, to develop awareness of their emotional reactions to clients of different ages, carefully considering their possible impact on the course of therapy. Younger clients may remind therapists of themselves at that age, or bring therapists' own children to mind, whilst older clients may remind them of their parents or grandparents (Knight, 2004). Older clients may trigger a deep-seated unease in young and middle-aged therapists, possibly distorting clinical judgement as they provide glimpses of problems and challenges that may lie ahead both for the therapists themselves and for their parents and grandparents (Semel, 2006). Dysfunctional emotional reactions include threat, disgust, fear, shame and guilt (Behuniak, 2011; Viney, 1993), whereby younger, healthy, cognitively alert therapists are threatened by the reminder that they too may be older, ill and cognitively impaired one day, and experience shame at this reaction, guilt at their own youth and health in comparison to that of their clients, and disgust at the indignities of extreme old age.

Therapists will remember something of what it was like to be a child or an adolescent, and draw on this knowledge in developing their relationships with younger clients. Such knowledge can be a resource and/or a hindrance. Not only is every individual's experience unique, but we are all not only of our place, but also of our time – with each generation or cohort being in some way unique, having grown up in a particular economic, political and social environment, and having particular shared experiences. This reduces the extent to which our own early life experiences can be used as a basis for our understanding of those in later or, indeed, earlier generations.

Therapists may identify readily with the issues faced by clients of a similar age to themselves and who present scenarios or exhibit behaviours that mirror issues they are also addressing. Whilst this can facilitate the development of an empathic relationship, therapists may also need to be wary of over-identifying with clients seen as 'similar to me' or of projecting onto clients their own interpretation of the scenario. Also, it cannot be assumed that clients see counsellors of the same age as 'like them'. Similarity of age may reinforce clients' sense of

inadequacy – 'How come he/she is coping so well, whereas I need help?' The myth of the superhuman counsellor can come into play here.

Whilst all therapists will have experienced young, and possibly middle, adulthood, few will have personal knowledge of late adulthood. This brings the advantage that clients can be faced without interference from the therapist's direct experience of this life stage, but increases the scope for therapists to be prey to unsubstantiated stereotypes and unarticulated assumptions concerning later life. With an ageing population, and the fastest-growing age group being the over-85s (Office for National Statistics, 2011), therapists will increasingly need to engage with this traditionally under-represented group of clients.

However, stereotypes of late adulthood as inevitably a period of dependency, decline and dysfunction have not gone unchallenged. They have been supplemented by a portrayal of later life as a time of opportunity, continued productivity, self-fulfilment and self-reliance (Rudman, 2006). Images of liberation and refurbishment have replaced (or at least joined) those of sickness and decline. But replacing stereotypes of decline and dysfunction with stereotypes of the active, autonomous, competent older person may deny the reality of ageing, placing older people under a moral obligation to resist or defy ageing through never-ending projects of self-reflection and improvement, self-marketing, risk management, lifestyle maximization and body optimization (Rudman, 2006). Such a discourse sustains ageism by promoting perpetual youthfulness as a goal, and draws attention away from the socially constructed nature of disadvantage in later life.

AGEISM

Ageism – stereotyping, prejudice and discrimination based on chronological age – affects all individuals from birth onwards (Bytheway, 2005). As with other forms of oppression, such as sexism and racism, it involves attributing characteristics to individuals simply by virtue of their membership of a particular group. As with other forms of oppression, it is reinforced by the structures of society, with age being used as a gatepost restricting access to services, privileges, entitlements and responsibilities. As a form of oppression it is unique, however, in that its nature and particular impact on an individual fluctuate and change across the life course. Thus, the 70-year-old deemed, solely on the basis of chronological age, to be unfit for jury service was once the child told to be 'seen and not heard' and the adolescent whose passion was dismissed as 'puppy love'.

Ageism is frequently discussed primarily in relation to the lives of older adults (for example Nelson, 2011). Whilst drawing attention to the prejudice and discrimination experienced by older people, this bias is problematic in that it can serve both to bury ageism directed at other age groups, and to blind us to ageism within ourselves. Seeing the concept of ageism as relevant only to older adults fosters a 'them and us' view of 'the elderly' as a minority group. If older people are seen as different and separate from the rest of society then this can be used to justify different and separate treatment.

THE AGEFUL SELF

The destructive potential of ageism and the dilution of meaningful life stages render appealing the idea of dispensing with age as a categorization, to be replaced by a focus on notions of an 'age-irrelevant', 'age-neutral' or 'ageless' self (Macnicol, 2008) that acknowledges the significance of preserving a sense of continuity as we move through the life course (Shmotkin and Eyal, 2003). However, agelessness leaves us prey to 'adultism' (Milner and O'Byrne, 2004), a particular form of ageism in which concepts of the healthily functioning adult are chauvinistically assumed to represent some sort of gold standard of functioning towards which childhood should be directed and from which older adults should unquestionably prevent themselves or be prevented from falling for as long as possible. Therapists may, as a consequence of their life stage, be focused on different life goals to their clients and this can interfere with their capacity to hear the stories clients tell about their own goals.

However, whilst age cannot by itself define individual lives (Rogoff, 2002), this does not mean that it is irrelevant. Thus, Andrews (2000) sees the self, not as ageless, but as ageful, and argues that, in the same way that difference is celebrated in axes such as race, gender, religion and nationality, we should not ignore the importance of age: 'years are not empty containers: important things happen in that time … They are the stuff of which people's lives are made' (Andrews, 1999: 309).

A plea to recognize the distinctiveness of different life stages also underpins concerns about the erosion of childhood (Palmer, 2006), as seen in Crompton's (1992) advocacy for 'childist' counselling – counselling that demands respect for the idea of childhood as well as for every individual child. It begins with the idea of seeing each child, of whatever age, as a complete person rather than an immature version of the adult he or she will become: 'An acorn is not an immature oak tree; an acorn is perfectly an acorn. It contains everything necessary for growth into an oak tree but neither acorn nor tree contains greater or lesser value and virtue. Each is entire unto itself, both are of use to other forms of life' (1992: 5).

When making the journey into the unknown territory of the life of significantly older or significantly younger clients, therapists need to be wary of unwarranted interference from their own life experience, their stereotypes about different life stages, and the chauvinistic prioritization of their own current life goals and values.

CONCLUSION

Despite its limitations, chronological age continues to be used as an expedient index of social age. Despite its ambiguous meaning and significance, an individual's age is salient throughout life. Our age affords us particular rights and obligations. We use it as a guide in accommodating to the behaviour of others, in forming and re-forming our self-image, in interpreting our experience and in contemplating time past and life still to come (Neugarten and Neugarten, 1996).

Therapists cannot escape age – their clients' or their own. Supervision can be crucial in providing therapists with an arena in which to explore their responses to age, and with the opportunity to tease out the boundaries between the personal and the professional. It is also, of course, essential to look beyond and see behind the mask of ageing (Featherstone and Hepworth, 1991). Age can, in sum, be both crucially important and (almost) totally irrelevant.

REFERENCES

Achenbaum, W.A. and Cole, T.R. (2007) Transforming age-based policies to meet fluid life-course needs. In E.A. Pruchno and M.A. Smyer (eds), *Challenges of an Aging Society: Ethical Dilemmas, Political Issues*. Baltimore, MD: Johns Hopkins University Press.

Andrews, M. (1999) The seductiveness of agelessness. *Aging and Society*, 19: 301–18.

Andrews, M. (2000) Ageful and proud. *Aging and Society*, 20: 791–5.

Behuniak, S.M. (2011) The living dead? The construction of people with Alzheimer's disease as zombies. *Ageing and Society*, 31: 70–92.

Bytheway, B. (2005) Ageism. In M.L. Johnson, V.L. Bengtson, P.G. Coleman and T.B.L. Kirkwood (eds), *The Cambridge Handbook of Age and Ageing*. Cambridge: Cambridge University Press.

Crompton, M. (1992) *Children and Counselling*. London: Arnold.

Dannefer, W.D. and Settersten, R.A. (2010) The study of the life course: implications for social gerontology. In W.D. Dannefer and C. Phillipson (eds), *International Handbook of Social Gerontology*. London: Sage.

Featherstone, M. and Hepworth, M. (1991) The mask of ageing and the postmodern life course. In M. Featherstone, M. Hepworth and B.S. Turner (eds), *The Body: Social Process and Cultural Theory*. London: Sage.

Gilleard, C. and Higgs, P. (2000) *Cultures of Ageing: Self, Citizen and the Body*. Harlow, Essex: Pearson Education.

Heckhausen, J. (1999) *Developmental Regulation in Adulthood: Age-Normative and Sociostructural Constraints as Adaptive Challenges*. Cambridge: Cambridge University Press.

Jacobs, M. (2006) *The Presenting Past: The Core of Psychodynamic Counselling and Therapy* (3rd edn). Buckingham: Open University Press.

Knight, B.G. (2004) *Psychotherapy with Older Adults* (3rd edn). Thousand Oaks, CA: Sage.

Liefbroer, A.C. and Billari, F.C. (2010) Bringing norms back in: a theoretical and empirical discussion of their importance for understanding demographic behaviour. *Population, Space and Place*, 16: 287–305.

Macnicol, J. (2008) Differential treatment by age: age discrimination or age affirmation? In R.B. Hudson (ed.), *Boomer Bust? Economic and Political Issues of the Graying Society*. Westport, CT: Praeger.

Milner, J. and O'Byrne, P. (2004) *Assessment in Counselling: Theory, Process and Decision-Making*. Basingstoke: Palgrave Macmillan.

Nelson, T.D. (2011) Ageism: the strange case of prejudice against the older you. In R.L. Wiener and S.L. Wilborn (eds), *Disability and Aging Discrimination: Perspectives in Law and Psychology*. New York: Springer.

Neugarten, B.L. (1996) Continuities and discontinuities of psychological issues in adult life. In D.A. Neugarten (ed.), *The Meaning of Age: Selected Papers of Bernice L. Neugarten*. Chicago: Chicago University Press.

Neugarten, B.L. and Neugarten, D.A. (1996) Age in the aging society. In D.A. Neugarten (ed.), *The Meaning of Age: Selected Papers of Bernice L. Neugarten*. Chicago: Chicago University Press.

Office for National Statistics (2011) *Mid-Year Population Statistics*. www.statistics.gov.uk/cci/nugget.asp?id=949, 5 February 2011.

Palmer, S. (2006) *Toxic Childhood: How the Modern World Is Damaging Our Children and What We Can Do About It*. London: Orion.

Pilgrim, D. (1997) *Psychotherapy and Society*. London: Sage.

Rogoff, B. (2002) How can we study cultural aspects of human development? *Human Development*, 45: 209–10.

Rudman, D.L. (2006) Shaping the active, autonomous and responsible modern retiree: an analysis of discursive technologies and their links with neo-liberal political rationality. *Ageing and Society*, 26: 181–201.

Semel, V.G. (2006) Countertransference and ageism: therapist reactions to older patients. In C.M. Brody and V.G. Semel (eds), *Strategies for Therapy with the Elderly: Living with Hope and Meaning* (2nd edn). New York: Springer.

Shmotkin, S. and Eyal, N. (2003) Psychological time in later life: implication for counseling. *Journal of Counseling and Development*, 81: 259–67.

Sugarman, L. (2004) *Counselling and the Life Course*. London: Sage.

Viney, L. (1993) *Life Stories: Personal Construct Therapy with the Elderly*. Chichester: Wiley.

Wrosch, C. and Freund, A.M. (2001) Self-regulation or normative and non-normative developmental challenges. *Human Development*, 44: 264–83.

Social Class

DAVID PILGRIM

This chapter deals with the topic of social class or 'socio-economic status'. A summary is offered of a number of aspects of interest to psychological therapists. Something is said about the history of class discrimination and therapy before the social class of therapists and their clients is considered. The matter of 'social gap' between the two groups is discussed and then the recent policy developments about increasing access to therapy are noted. Finally, a summary is provided of what we know from the sociological and epidemiological literature about social class and mental health in the light of the occupational hazard of psychological reductionism in the therapy trade.

THE HISTORICAL ROOTS OF CLASS DISCRIMINATION IN THERAPY

It has been pointed out elsewhere (Pilgrim, 1997) that a central question under this heading is not whether but why psychotherapy is elitist. All of our research on mental health service utilization demonstrates that poorer people receive more physical treatments than richer people and vice versa in relation to talking treatments. The class gradient in access to talking treatments can be accounted for by the following factors:

- A dominant model of psychotherapy is based upon the psychoanalytic tradition. The latter originated in middle-class outpatient work in which the fee not only became fetishized as an important symbol for interpretive work in therapy but was a practical necessity for the therapist to live. Freud made the point that 'we do analysis for two reasons – to understand the unconscious and to make a living'. Fee paying *ipso facto* debars poor clients from access to therapy; it is a discriminatory practice. However private practitioners rationalize their form of employment, its consequences are discriminatory.

- The origins of contemporary styles of psychotherapy can be traced to the growth of the 'psy complex' and the medical dominance in the state asylum system. In the early days of this in the mid nineteenth century, a brief tension existed between lay managers of asylums, who wished to encourage 'moral treatment' (a precursor of the therapeutic community), and medical superintendents who argued that mental abnormality was a genetically determined defect requiring physical restraint and treatment. By the end of the nineteenth century, the medical view prevailed and set the pattern for the next 100 years: inpatients were to be mainly treated by physical means. As there was (and is) a preponderance of poorer people in inpatient settings, poverty and biological treatment become inextricably linked. In Britain by the 1990s over 90 per cent of psychiatric patients had received drugs but only 60 per cent had received any form of psychological intervention, which included access to the private and voluntary sector for counselling and therapy (Rogers et al., 1993).

- Although the above picture shows a class gradient in type of service access, it is a gradient and not a dichotomy. Psychological treatments are provided within the public sector. However, within this, a further class process has operated over time. In Britain this can be traced to the First World War and the problem of 'shell-shock', which created a crisis for the biodeterminism of Victorian psychiatry. Those who were breaking down in the trenches were either working-class volunteers or officers and gentlemen; they were 'England's finest blood' (Stone, 1985). A eugenic (genetic) account of mental abnormality was logically incompatible with this picture and was tantamount to treason. As a result, the asylum doctors lost legitimacy for a while during war conditions, as did their professional rhetoric about biodeterminism. Their authority was replaced by that of the shell-shock doctors who imported a psychological (eclectic or Freudian) model into state-provided mental health work. After the First World War outpatient treatment centres were set up, thus changing the configuration of mental health work. After that point the ambit of psychiatry began to include an interest in the neuroses. Prior to the war, medical interest had only been in madness. However, the expanded interest of psychiatry still made important distinctions in practice: the soldier patient versus the civilian; the neurotic versus the psychotic; the outpatient versus the inpatient. Against the organizational backdrop we can see how poor mad patients continued to be treated in the way they always had been – via physical not psychological means.

Apart from these historically rooted organizational biases which produced institutional discrimination against poorer clients, another factor to consider is the class background of therapists. This is influential in a number of ways, to be considered next.

THE SOCIAL CLASS OF THERAPISTS AND PATIENTS

A general sociological point made by Horwitz (1983) is that the class position of mental health professionals inevitably biases the way in which they make their assessments and conduct their treatments. This is not to say that all the fine-grain assessment and treatment is class determined but it does make the point that the class relationship between patients and their therapists is important. For example, the closer that therapists and clients are in their class position, the greater the probability of mutual agreement and understanding. Questions

of empathy and intelligibility come into the frame here. Not surprisingly, the smaller the gap between therapists and clients, the greater the probability that the former will be empathic to the latter and the more they will be confident about intelligibility of presenting problems. By contrast, the poorer client will be understood less readily. This then spills over into labelling: poorer clients are more readily given more serious or stigmatizing labels than their richer equivalents. Middle-class clients more readily accrue diagnoses of neurosis, whereas working-class patients more readily accrue diagnoses of psychosis. During the nineteenth century, for example, poorer depressed patients were described as 'melancholic', whereas richer ones were described as 'mopish'.

The social gap and its consequences have been used as an explanation for why lower-class patients do less well in psychotherapy. However, what remains ambiguous is both the evidence for this specific claim and the responsibility for its rectification, when and if it is proved to be the case.

THE SOCIAL GAP AND ITS IMPLICATIONS

The whole question of social class and psychotherapy can be unpacked sequentially, starting with this selection. In his review of the topic, Bromley (1994) found that:

- The evidence on client expectations explaining referral bias was equivocal. Some studies showed that working-class clients express a need for exploratory psychotherapy. Other studies showed no class differences.
- The evidence on professional expectations was less equivocal. There is a consistent pattern in the studies of professionals in their referral and assessment decisions which shows that professionals have lower expectations of lower-class clients in terms of their general suitability to form a therapeutic alliance and in terms of client capacity to utilize talk in a consistent way in a process of change.
- The great majority of studies of selection demonstrate that the higher the social class of the patient, the greater the probability they will be assigned to talking treatments rather than being treated physically.
- The evidence about early dropout of working-class patients is equivocal. Some studies show early dropout but others show no class difference. In those which suggested a pattern of early dropout, it was not clear whether this was

a function of client expectations, professional expectations or an interaction between the two.

- This selection bias is accounted for partly by the fee (which is prohibitive for poorer patients) and partly by the biases of professional referrers and assessors.
- Most of the studies were from the USA but the fewer studies conducted in Britain and Scandinavia confirm a similar picture.

When I reflect on the above from personal experience of working for over 20 years in a variety of British mental health settings, in which I have only seen non-fee-paying clients, then a number of the findings make sense. I am aware of GP bias in the type of client they refer to the NHS (Pilgrim et al., 1997). I am also aware of the criteria which general psychiatrists working in acute mental health units operate about the suitability of patients for referral to some form of psychological treatment. Bias by diagnosis and class is evident. My own experience has also been that a problem-solving approach, rather than one which is either rigidly non-directive (attending only to the purported necessary and sufficient conditions of the central therapeutic triad) or psychodynamic (attending only to transference), engages and profits NHS clients whatever their class background, but especially those from a poor background.

THE POLICY CONTEXT OF EQUAL ACCESS

Here I want to note the importance of the policy context of therapy. For example, a market model, which predominates in the USA, ensures plurality on the supply side but limitations on the demand side. Demand is limited by the availability to pay and so the poor are excluded. Similarly in France, most of the availability of therapy is in the private sector (Champion, 2008). Publicly provided mental health services contain a little but not much access to talking treatments. By contrast in the UK and the Netherlands, public mental health systems receive greater funding for therapy (Hutschemaekers and Oosterhuis, 2004). These cross-national differences in access mean that market-dominated health-care systems tend to exclude the poor from therapy. More socialized systems increase access but, because of the inevitable budgetary limitations of state funding, plurality on the supply side then becomes restricted.

This point has become obvious in the UK recently with the emergence of the Improving Access to Psychological Therapies (IAPT) initiative. This has been driven overwhelmingly by those committed to variants of one model of therapy (CBT) which has been able to appeal to policy makers persuaded by the advantages of more public access to therapy (Pilgrim, 2009). CBT has been developed by scientific consensus in medicine and psychology. Its appeal is both fiscal and bureaucratic. It can be 'manualized' and access can be graduated (hence it is called 'stepped care'). It can be codified according to its application to diagnostic-related groups (DRGs), which is consistent with the dominant discourse and desires of health-care planners (hence CBT 'for depression'). It is evidence based and cost effective, according to the aggregate data evaluated by meta-analyses, and so offers the prospect of cost containment for service commissioners. This trade-off between access and acceptability is now central to debates about therapy in the public sphere. The IAPT initiative limits the type of available therapy but increases availability overall. A range of views is then provoked about that trade-off.

THERAPY, PSYCHOLOGICAL REDUCTIONISM AND SOCIAL FORCES

Therapists are used to dealing with misery (and sometimes madness) at the individual level and so their preferred models of understanding and causes are *ipso facto* psychological not social. They are, after all, *psychological* therapists and so their psychological reductionism and their limited competence about understanding psychological problems in a full social context are not surprising. This is a fair accusation, with one important caveat about the upside of the occupational hazard. There is an important role for psychological formulations to account for intra-group differences. That is, not all poor people (or, in relation to other social groups, women or black people) are mad or miserable, even if the poor as a social group are *disproportionately* mad and miserable. The latter is because of the particular causal impact of childhood adversity, especially forms of abuse and neglect. Consequently knowledge of personal relationships, in their particular social contexts, is a particularly important pathway of understanding about intra-social-group differences in mental health outcome, for individuals from seemingly similar material contexts (Pilgrim et al., 2009).

With this accusation of psychological reductionism and its caveat in mind, here I lay out some of the bare bones about mental health and inequality. For a fuller account with extensive referencing about this list see Rogers and Pilgrim (2003) and Fryers et al. (2001), as well as the aggregating literature about psychosocial pathways from socio-economic conditions to mental health problems (e.g. Fryer, 1995; James, 2007; Layard, 2005; Wilkinson and Pickett, 2010).

1   *Forms of oppression and disadvantage typically attending poverty enhance neither physical nor mental health.* Such forms include poor education, low pay or unemployment, poor neighbourhoods and poor living conditions. Class position predicts both morbidity in its broadest sense and longevity in its specific sense. Not only do the poor consistently die younger but this pattern of early death is amplified in poor people who also have a psychiatric diagnosis.

2   *A psychiatric diagnosis increases the probability of social exclusion.* The stigma and personal invalidation this brings are joined then by a good chance of exclusion from the labour market.

3   *Poor employment not unemployment has the largest detrimental impact on mental health.* The best mental health is found in higher wage earners with good task control and permanent contracts.

4   *Unemployment and low pay have direct and indirect effects on mental health.* Both ensure poverty, and with this come both the environmental effects discussed later in relation to neighbourhood and the psychological effects of low status. In the case of becoming unemployed, these effects can be compounded by multiple losses. Identity for many is bound up with work roles (loss of identity). Daily meanings are bound up with the routines of work for many (loss of daily structure). For some, being unemployed is a source of shame (loss of face). And for those whose income levels drop significantly there is the direct impact of the loss of money.

5   *Macro-economic effects are important.* Economic cycles create advantages and disadvantages for individuals. For example, one generation of young people might encounter a period of growth and can access the labour market readily. The next generation may be less fortunate. Those in insecure employment will be buffered from its effects during times of full employment but in more economically depressed times will be very vulnerable.

6   *Social class has inter-generational and intra-generational impacts on mental health.* These have been demonstrated in a UK setting by two major longitudinal studies: the 1958 National Child Development Study (NCDS) and the 1970 British Birth Cohort Study (BCS). The social position achieved in early adulthood is affected by both the father's class position and psychological problems in adolescence. About 50 per cent of the relationship between social class and mental health status is accounted for by these pathways from parental social class position and adolescent mental health problems by young adulthood. By the time the age of 33 is reached these two factors account for nearly 100 per cent of the relationship. Mental health problems persist more from adolescence to adulthood in males than in females. Women show more inter-generational social mobility than men but intra-generational social mobility is the same for men and women.

7   *Relative poverty and status discrepancies are important.* The greater the inequality in a particular society, the more likely that mental health problems will be manifest. Thus poverty needs to be understood as multidimensional in relation to different forms of capital. Apart from financial capital (income maintenance and savings), social capital and cultural capital are also important. Financial capital is most readily described in *structural* terms as social class, defined by a combination of earnings and type of employment. Cultural and social capital are correlated with these variables but are better described in *functional or instrumental* terms – the ways and means people operate consciously or unconsciously to maintain or improve their social position, wellbeing and quality of life. All three types of capital can impinge on mental health status and vice versa. Poverty is a causal antecedent for some mental health problems, and some mental health problems create economic disadvantage. But money is only part of the picture. With a poor family of origin (a risk factor in mental health problems) comes a sense of particular cultural space to do with locality, schooling and family expectations about social status and prospects. Personal identity and 'knowing one's place' are set early in childhood. This emphasis on developing a sense of one's place in life describes a person's 'cultural capital'. This is bound up with the later connectivity people develop with others as adults – their 'social capital'.

8   *Poor neighbourhoods produce unhappy people.* Urban life in socially disorganized neighbourhoods is particularly pathogenic. Urban life brings with it more social disorganization, environmental stressors (crime, vandalism, noise, litter and motor traffic) and concentrated areas of poverty. Health and wellbeing increase in country areas (but beware the ecological fallacy as rich and poor live close by in

rural localities). In areas of concentrated poverty which are socially disorganized, the impact at the individual level is profound and negative. Not surprisingly in these neighbourhoods there are raised levels of depression, anxiety and substance misuse. Apart from the direct exposure to the external 'ambient hazards' of stress described above, people in these local contexts are less likely to have regular supportive social networks, particularly if there is a high turnover of residence.

9 *There are specific and independent locality effects.* For example, some particular deteriorated localities contain higher rates of presentation of depressive symptomatology *in all social groups*, including those with higher rates of forms of capital. Similarly, aggregate neighbourhood income predicts levels of diagnosis of schizophrenia and substance misuse. People in poor areas defined at the individual level as being of the same socio-economic status as those in richer areas are more likely to perpetrate and be victims of crime than their equivalents in richer areas. This differential pattern about crime features is also evident when psychiatric patients with the same diagnosis are studied in rich and poor areas.

10 *Some neighbourhoods provide more 'opportunity structures' than others.* These refer to the cultural and environmental possibilities for stress-free or health giving public behaviour. For example, two neighbourhoods may be grossly equivalent in terms of income but one may have safer streets and more spacious green park areas than the other. Generally though, more affluent neighbourhoods provide more opportunity structures than poorer ones.

This conclusion to the chapter on class reminds us of the complex relationship between mental health and social adversity.

REFERENCES

Bromley, E. (1994) Social class and psychotherapy revisited. Paper presented at the Annual Conference of the British Psychological Society, Brighton.

Champion, F. (ed.) (2008) *Psychothérapie et société.* Paris: Armand Colin.

Fryer, D. (1995) Labour market disadvantage, deprivation and mental health. *The Psychologist*, 8 (6): 265–72.

Fryers, T., Melzer, D. and Jenkins, R. (2001) *Mental Health Inequalities Report 1: A Systematic Literature Review.* Cambridge University, Department of Public Health and Primary Care.

Horwitz, A. (1983) *The Social Control of Mental Illness.* New York: Academic.

Hutschemaekers, G. and Oosterhuis, H. (2004) Psychotherapy in The Netherlands after the Second World War. *Medical History*, 48: 429–48.

James, O. (2007) *Affluenza.* London: Vermilion.

Layard, R. (2005) *Happiness.* London: Penguin.

Pilgrim, D. (1997) *Psychotherapy and Society.* London: Sage.

Pilgrim, D. (2009) Rhetorical aspects of the contention about cognitive behavioural therapy. *History and Philosophy of Psychology*, 11 (2): 36–54.

Pilgrim, D., Rogers, A., Clarke, S. and Clarke, W. (1997) Entering psychological treatment: decision-making factors for GPs and service users. *Journal of Interprofessional Care*, 11 (3): 313–23.

Pilgrim, D., Rogers, A. and Bentall, R.P. (2009) The centrality of personal relationships in the creation and amelioration of mental health problems: the current interdisciplinary case. *Health*, 13: 235–54.

Rogers, A. and Pilgrim, D. (2003) *Mental Health and Inequality.* Basingstoke: Palgrave.

Rogers, A., Pilgrim, D. and Lacey, R. (1993) *Experiencing Psychiatry: Users' Views of Services.* London: Macmillan.

Stone, M. (1985) Shellshock and the psychologists. In W.F. Bynum, R. Porter and M. Shepherd (eds), *The Anatomy of Madness* (Vol. 2). London: Tavistock.

Wilkinson, R. and Pickett, K. (2010) *The Spirit Level: Why Equality Is Better for Everyone.* London: Penguin.

Sexual Orientation

DOMINIC DAVIES

Sexual orientation describes a pattern of emotional, romantic or sexual attraction to men, women, both men and women, neither gender, or another gender. More traditionally we might think of sexual orientation as being heterosexual, lesbian/gay or bisexual, but there is increasing evidence that some people are attracted to neither men nor women and would identify as asexual. Moreover, there is an emerging awareness of people who are attracted to individuals who might identify as 'third sex' (e.g. Hijras were recently legally recognized in India, Bangladesh and Pakistan); in the West this orientation may be expressed as *trans-oriented*, that is being attracted to people who are transsexual.

This chapter will mainly focus on homosexuality and bisexuality, although it is anticipated that by the next revision of this volume we will be seeing more published work on both asexuality and trans-oriented people.

HISTORY OF HOMOSEXUALITY AND BISEXUALITY

Representations of homosexuality and bisexuality have been found by anthropologists and historians around the world and from the earliest times. In some cultures homosexuality is seen as a natural and normal variation of human sexuality; in other cultures same-sex relationships are encouraged or given high status; and in some others still homosexuality is reviled and persecuted. What is clear, though, for anyone who has spent time exploring the issue, is that same-sex desire is a naturally occurring phenomenon. Some people see their homosexuality and bisexuality as an *essential* part of their nature. Such people may say, 'I was born this way.' They may be able to give examples of childhood same-sex attractions and desires to support their experience. Others may say they have chosen their sexuality or maybe even that they have tried sexual relationships with the 'opposite' sex or just one gender, and prefer for a variety of reasons to have relationships with the same sex. Generally speaking gay men tend to use essentialist ideas (that they were born gay) to explain their homosexuality, and lesbians and bisexuals may be more likely to use arguments of 'choice'.

Some people vary in their choice of sexual partners over time or in different situations; some are confused or questioning; some experiment; others have no sexual relations; and yet others experience no sexual feelings. There exists a vast array of expressions of sexual desire and behaviour as well as, increasingly, of 'sexual identity'.

Sociologically, views of homosexuality are divided into two camps. There are those who see sexual identity as a social or cultural construct particular to a place and time. In this view, homosexuality in, say, Thailand, Ancient Greece or Pakistan has little in common with the modern gay man living in London or New York. Others argue that, because there is evidence of people who have always been gay, in every culture and through time, there is something essential or natural about homosexual identity. These arguments continue and evidence accrues in support of both views. Is sexuality determined by nature (essentialism) or nurture (social constructionism)? Individuals seeking to understand *why* they are lesbian, gay or bisexual will find plenty of evidence to support theories of homosexuality and bisexuality as *essentialist* or *socially constructed*. Most lesbian, gay and bisexual people, however, have little interest in *why* they are the way they are; it is just a given.

Grahn (1990) highlights the fact that in many cultures lesbians and gay men are holding up a mirror to the way their society views sex, gender and sexuality. They are showing different ways of being a man or woman and of relating. In some societies this is supported by the culture; in others a separate subculture exists to support lesbian, gay or bisexual people.

People with minority sexual orientations have been among the European witches and their rites. Over a 400-year period, seven million witches were burned on piles of faggots (not simply bundles of wood, but human bodies; there is evidence that many of these people would have been strangled gay men) (Grahn, 1990). They have been among the shamans and medicine men and women of the Native Americans (among which many tribes, including the Sioux, Cherokee and Navajo, sanctioned same-sex love and held it in high regard). Lesbian, gay and bisexual people have been despised, tortured and murdered by, among others, the Nazis in Germany and the authorities in modern-day Iran, China and elsewhere.

Although individual LGBT men and women participate in both heterosexual and lesbian, gay and bisexual communities and cultures, there is an invisible thread linking all sexual minorities. This thread is the way lesbian, gay and bisexual people have manifested and worked within societies throughout the world to facilitate a crossover in the way the genders operate with each other. When a lesbian cuts her hair short and wears 'male' clothing she is not trying to look like a man. She is showing another way of being a woman, in which she, as a woman, defines how she looks, rather than allowing men to define how she should look. A gay man wearing a 'camp', perhaps effeminate outfit of a loose-fitting shirt in pastel shades is not trying to look like a woman but wants to show a different way to be a man. There is a strength that comes from being able to reinvent oneself, and to create different ways to be who and what one is.

It was only as recently as 1992 that the World Health Organization (WHO) removed homosexuality from their *International Classification of Diseases* (*ICD-9*). This was two decades after the American Psychiatric Association declassified homosexuality from the *Diagnostic and Statistical Manual III*. There are still a great many practitioners, particularly those working in the mental health sector, who erroneously believe that to be lesbian, gay or bisexual is an illness or a perversion (Bartlett et al., 2009). Therapists trained in gender and sexual minority issues believe that it is *homophobia* which is the cause of mental distress and difficulties (King et al., 2008). Homophobia means a fear, dread or hatred of homosexuals or homosexuality (Weinberg, 1972; see also Davies, 1996a for more on homophobia and heterosexism). 'Biphobia' describes equivalent attitudes towards bisexuality from either heterosexual or homosexual people.

For over 100 years most 'helping' professionals have seen homosexuality as an illness. Some of the worst atrocities have been committed by people supposedly dedicated to helping and supporting people, in the name of trying to cure people of this 'disease'. Lesbians and gay men have been subjected to electric shock treatment, aversion therapy and crude attempts at psychosurgery. Others were subjected to long-term, intensive psychotherapy where they wrestled with their natural desire to love someone of the same gender, and society's (and often their therapist's) view that this was sick or perverted. The declassification of homosexuality as a mental illness has helped end these particular persecutions. Of equal concern, however, is the way certain 'counselling' groups identifying as 'Christian' have sought to 'cure' lesbian, gay and bisexual people. Preying on confused and vulnerable people in this way, those who have religious or moral objections to homosexuality continue to bring the notion of 'helping others' into disrepute and cause untold damage to their 'clients'.

HOMOPHOBIA AS PATHOLOGY

The last three decades, however, have slowly seen a growth in what have come to be known as *sexuality affirmative* (or *gay affirmative*) models of therapy. This work, undertaken in the main by lesbian, gay and bisexual therapists in the USA and Europe, has sought to show non-pathological ways of viewing homosexuality and bisexuality. Maylon describes gay affirmative therapy thus:

> Gay affirmative psychotherapy is not an independent system of psychotherapy. Rather it represents a special range of psychological knowledge, which challenges the traditional view, that homosexual desire and fixed homosexual orientations are pathological. Gay affirmative therapy uses traditional psychotherapeutic methods but proceeds from a non-traditional perspective. This approach regards homophobia, as opposed to homosexuality, as a major pathological variable in the

development of certain symptomatic conditions among gay men. (1982: 69)

The concept 'gay affirmative' is not without dissenters among lesbian and gay therapists themselves. Du Plock (1997) and Ratigan (1998), among others, have rightly questioned who or what is being affirmed in gay affirmative therapy. The term can imply that the therapist is giving permission and is encouraging the client to be gay. This can make it difficult for the client to explore his or her own negative, internalized, self-oppressive structures, feeling that these won't be accepted or approved of by their gay affirming therapist. 'Gay affirmative' has been said to exclude other sexual minorities and gender-variant people. A more neutral term, growing in use, is *gender and sexual minority therapy*. The addition of 'gender' in the title reflects increasing links being made between gender identity and sexual identity and contemporary attention to different relationship models and lifestyles. (See Chapter 7.16 in this volume for more on working with gender and sexual minorities.)

Such non-pathologizing approaches are now slowly being integrated into the syllabus of European therapy training programmes. In lamentably few courses, however, are they located within the core curriculum of the training institutes. More often they are raised at the request of individual students (usually lesbians and gay men), and sometimes only addressed through self-directed study (Davies, 1996b; 2007). This marginalization of sexual minority therapy issues only serves to perpetuate and reinforce pathological models.

Cayleff (1986), in discussing the ethical issues involved in counselling the culturally different (in which she includes lesbians, gay men and bisexuals), questions how therapists graduating from training programmes that do not require courses in working with cultural minorities may ethically work with these populations. Since formal education is a socialization process that transmits the values of the dominant culture, the majority of counselling and therapy training programmes, through both coursework and practice, continue to explore individual development, sex, gender, coupling, family and relationship issues solely within a heterosexual context (Iasenza, 1989).

EFFECTS OF HOMOPHOBIA AND HETEROSEXISM ON LESBIAN, GAY AND BISEXUAL PEOPLE

The stress of living with a stigmatized identity, where one is seen as 'mad, bad and dangerous to know,' has been demonstrated to contribute to poor mental health (King et al., 2003; 2008; Rivers, 2004). Lesbian, gay and bisexual people may at some level feel shame about their sexuality, and this *internalized homophobia* can result in low self-esteem, self-medication through drug and alcohol misuse, overwork through trying to prove oneself valuable, and avoidance of drawing attention to oneself. Lesbian, gay and bisexual people are also prone to discrimination and violence. In the survey *Queer Bashing* (1996), Stonewall found that 34 per cent of gay and bisexual men and 24 per cent of women had experienced physical violence because of their sexuality. In another study, the same organization (Stonewall, 1993) found that 37 per cent of respondents experienced workplace discrimination and almost half (48 per cent) had been harassed because of their sexuality. Even though the UK now has anti-discrimination legislation protecting against workplace harassment, there is still a climate of fear for many lesbian, gay and bisexual people that it may happen, and of course one does not need to have experienced discrimination to *fear* it. This leaves almost all lesbians, gay and bisexual people vulnerable to anxiety and disorganization.

There are not only negative effects to living with a stigmatized identity. Lesbians, gay men and bisexuals who are open about, and comfortable with, their sexuality often experience a strong sense of identity as 'different but equal' to heterosexuals. These differences sometimes result in a freedom to reinvent themselves anew with values and attitudes that support their individual and collective identities. Lesbian, gay and bisexual people may, for example, have critiqued much about a heterosexual lifestyle and identity and decided this is inappropriate. Their culture, like those of other oppressed groups (Jews, African-Caribbean people, etc.), celebrates this diversity and different perspective in art, music, literature and other expressions.

SUMMARY AND KEY POINTS

Don't assume the client's sexual orientation is the cause of his or her difficulties. Lesbian, gay and bisexual people may present for counselling or therapy with a range of life issues (relationship breakdown, bereavement, anxiety, depression, work stress, etc.). Most of these bear little direct relevance to their sexuality, although they are often coloured by the experience of being from a sexual minority in an oppressive and discriminatory society.

Don't make assumptions about a person's sexuality. Many married, apparently heterosexual men have sexual relationships with members of their own sex.

Significant numbers of gay men have sex with women. The corollary is also true for women. Encourage clients to define themselves.

Don't make assumptions about the client's lifestyle. Clients may have different notions of what it means to be in a relationship ('monogamy' may not be the norm) or to be a family (many lesbian, gay and bisexual people will consider their friends as their family). Lesbian, gay and bisexual clients may want to be parents or may already be involved in childcare. They may be uncomfortable in available gay or lesbian subcultures, too.

Be aware of the client's hypervigilance and that you may be tested for signs of homophobia and heterosexism. Work with this and do all you can to learn more about lesbian, gay and bisexual cultures and lifestyles. Be honest about your experience and work to create an open and non-defensive relationship.

Reflect on your own attitudes to, and experience of, your sexuality and homosexuality in particular. To be able to work effectively with sexual minority clients you need to be comfortable with who you are as a sexual being and to have examined your beliefs, feelings and prejudices about same-sex love and attraction. Everyone has them. The therapist who says they are not prejudiced is a therapist to be avoided, as they are probably extremely low on self-awareness. Therapists might like to consider what impact on the therapeutic relationship there might be for a sexual minority client working with them, if they have not examined their attitudes before working with such clients.

WORKING TOWARDS GOOD PRACTICE

There are perhaps three main ways in which we can prepare ourselves for working with people whose sexual orientation differs from our own:

- *Training workshops*. These include didactic and exploratory presentations about gender and sexual minority psychology, including the various models of coming out (see Davies, 1996c), dealing with internalized homophobia and multiple identities, and the social and political context of living with a gender or sexual minority identity. Most important, perhaps, are experiential exercises aimed at addressing our attitudes to, experience of and knowledge of bisexuality and homosexuality, as well as increasing understanding of our own sexuality. A leading training provider in this field is Pink Therapy (www.pinktherapy.com) who regularly run workshops and courses for therapists wishing to improve their knowledge and skill in this area.

- *Personal therapy and self-awareness work*. This enables us to explore some of our sexual histories in some depth, with therapists who have themselves done the required work. This itself raises a complication: where does one find such people? Alongside this, specific supervision/consultation is advisable from therapists experienced in this field.

- *Spending time with lesbian, gay and bisexual people at work and in recreation*. Personal contacts through genuine friendships have been demonstrated to be powerful ways of changing opinions and behaviours. Become involved socially and politically with the lesbian, gay and bisexual communities. Manthei says, 'there is no short cut to being involved in and accepted by local communities so that you are known to be supportive and trustworthy' (1997: 31).

REFERENCES

Bartlett, A., Smith, G. and King, M. (2009) The response of mental health professionals to clients seeking help to change or redirect sexual orientation. *BMC Psychiatry*, 9 (11). www.biomedcentral.com/1471-244X/9/11.

Cayleff, S. (1986) Ethical issues in counselling gender, race and culturally distinct groups. *Journal of Counseling Development*, 64 (5): 345–7.

Davies, D. (1996a) Homophobia and heterosexism. In D. Davies and C. Neal (eds), *Pink Therapy: A Guide for Counsellors and Therapists Working with Lesbian, Gay and Bisexual Clients*. Buckingham: Open University Press.

Davies, D. (1996b) Towards a model of gay affirmative therapy. In D. Davies and C. Neal (eds), *Pink Therapy: A Guide for Counsellors and Therapists Working with Lesbian, Gay and Bisexual Clients*. Buckingham: Open University Press.

Davies, D. (1996c) Working with people coming out. In D. Davies and C. Neal (eds), *Pink Therapy: A Guide for Counsellors and Therapists Working with Lesbian, Gay and Bisexual Clients*. Buckingham: Open University Press.

Davies, D. (2007) Not in front of the students. *Therapy Today*, February: 18–21.

Du Plock, S. (1997) Sexual misconceptions: a critique of gay affirmative therapy and some thoughts on an existential-phenomenological theory of sexual orientation. *Journal of the Society for Existential Analysis*, 8 (2): 56–71.

Grahn, J. (1990) *Another Mother Tongue: Gay Words, Gay Worlds*. Boston, MA: Beacon.

Iasenza, S. (1989) Some challenges of integrating sexual orientations into counselor training and research. *Journal of Counseling and Development*, 68: 73–6.

King, M., McKeown, E., Warner, J., Ramsay, A., Johnson, K., Cort, C., Wright, L., Blizard, R. and Davidson, O. (2003) Mental health and quality of life of gay men and lesbians in England and Wales: a controlled, cross-sectional study. *British Journal of Psychiatry*, 183: 552–8.

King, M., Semlyen, J., See Tai, S., Killaspy, H., Osborn, D., Popelyuk, D. and Nazareth, I. (2008) A systematic review of mental disorder, suicide, and deliberate self harm in lesbian, gay and bisexual people. *BMC Psychiatry*, 8 (70). www.biomedcentral.com/1471-244X/8/70.

Manthei, R. (1997) *Counselling: The Skills of Finding Solutions to Problems*. London: Routledge.

Maylon, A. (1982) Psychotherapeutic implications of internalized homophobia in gay men. In J. Gonsiorek (ed.), *Homosexuality and Psychotherapy*. New York: Haworth.

Ratigan, B. (1998) Psychoanalysis and male homosexuality: queer bedfellows? In C. Shelley (ed.), *Contemporary Perspectives on Psychotherapy and Homosexualities*. London: Free Association.

Rivers, I. (2004) Recollections of bullying at school and their long term implications for lesbians, gay men and bisexuals. *Crisis*, 24 (5).

Stonewall (1993) *Less Equal than Others: A Survey of Lesbians and Gay Men at Work*. London: Stonewall.

Stonewall (1996) *Queer Bashing: A National Survey of Hate Crimes against Lesbians and Gay Men*. London: Stonewall.

Weinberg, G. (1972) *Society and the Healthy Homosexual*. New York: St Martin's Press.

RECOMMENDED READING

Carroll, L. (2010) *Counselling Sexual and Gender Minorities*. Columbus, OH: Merrill/Pearson.

Clarke, V., Ellis, S.J., Peel, E. and Riggs, D.W. (2010) *Lesbian, Gay, Bisexual, Trans and Queer Psychology*. Cambridge: Cambridge University Press.

Davies, D. and Neal, C. (eds) (1996) *Pink Therapy: A Guide for Counsellors and Therapists Working with Lesbian, Gay and Bisexual Clients*. Buckingham: Open University Press.

Religion and Spirituality

WILLIAM WEST

INTRODUCTION

It would be true to say that counselling and psychotherapy have an uneasy relationship with religion and spirituality and vice versa. At first glance this might seem strange since both deal with profound questions relating to the human condition, in particular human suffering: how to make sense of it, how to deal with it and above all how to avoid or at least minimise it. However, if we reflect on the idea that the origins of modern counselling and psychotherapy lie in the Victorian era (McLeod, 2009) and, as with modern medicine and psychology, early therapists sought to define their theory and practice as 'scientific'; if we then consider that to be 'scientific', indeed to be 'modern' at that time meant to be non- or in some cases anti-religious; then we see the challenges of putting religious and therapeutic systems alongside one another. Consequently, 'It would be a mistake to imagine that all clients reporting religious, spiritual or mystical beliefs or experiences would be understood or well received by their counsellors' (McLeod, 2009: 490).

The expectation of the decline in religion and spirituality as modernism triumphed in the Western world has not proved to be the case, and indeed the role especially of spirituality remains strong in what many now refer to as our postmodern world. Questions around the religious and spiritual beliefs of people in Britain are full of paradoxes and vary according to how the questions are posed. So if we look at the 2001 census figures (Crabtree, 2007) – see

Table 2.7.1 – we find that 76.8 per cent of the UK population had a religion, with Christianity being the most popular (71.6 per cent), while the British Social Attitudes Survey produced by the National Centre for Social Research in the same year reported that 58 per cent considered themselves to 'belong to' a religion.

Of course having a 'religion' does not necessarily involve attending places of worship, and the Tearfund report on churchgoing in 2007 found large numbers of people who claimed to have a personal relationship with God but had stopped attending churches. Of course it is possible to be spiritual and even religious without having a belief in God, but when you look at the figures it is clear that atheism

Table 2.7.1 *Main religious adherence, 2001 Census*

	Adherents	**% population**
Christian	42,079,000	71.6
No religion (inc. Jedis)	9,104,000	15.5
Muslim	1,546,626	2.7
Hindu	552,421	1.0
Jedi Knight*	390,000	0.7
Sikh	329,358	0.6
Jewish	259,927	0.5
Buddhist	144,453	0.3
Total religious	45,163,000	76.8
No answer	4,289,000	7.3

*The use of Jedi Knight was considered an organised joke.

Source: Crabtree (2007)

and agnosticism are still minority viewpoints within the UK.

Apart from the competing roles in relation to human suffering referred to above, there are tensions in the area of equality and human rights where counselling and psychotherapy accept the dominant cultural position of legal equality between men and women and the moves towards equal rights for gay, lesbian and transgendered people. However, this therapeutic support for equal rights does not necessarily extend to equality of educational opportunities or economic rights. In contrast religious groups are very often, in effect, homophobic and in many cases restrict the roles available to women. So for example women still cannot be bishops in the Church of England or imams in Muslim mosques. However, religious groups have traditionally, and currently, been involved in social actions on behalf of the poor and dispossessed.

DEFINITIONS

There are a number of differing definitions particularly of spirituality but also of religion. There seems to be a developing consensus, reflected in most dictionary definitions, that spirituality relates to personal beliefs and religion to the organised group of believers including places of worship, rituals and creeds. We shall use this distinction here. However, not everyone, especially not those of a religious nature, accepts these distinctions, and many people whether religious believers or not are dismissive of personal spirituality, especially if the phrase 'New Age' is added to the word 'spiritual'. From the viewpoint of the practitioner it is always best to explore what words mean for clients.

In terms of definitions that are useful for therapy, Elkins et al.'s (1988) research into what people mean by 'spirituality' seems especially useful, with its focus on experience; John Rowan's (2005) transpersonal work reminds us that spirituality can involve changes in our sense of self; and John Swinton (2001) reminds us that it is about connections inside, between people and with creation. Pulling their ideas together, along with those of my clients and colleagues, the following seem to me to be a useful composite description of some of the possible components of spirituality particularly relevant to therapy:

1   It is rooted in human experiencing rather than abstract theology, i.e. it helps to focus on spirituality as a human experience and what this means to people.

2   It is embodied, i.e. spiritual experience often actively involves us as physical beings.

3   It involves feeling strongly connected to other people and the universe at large.

4   It involves non-ordinary consciousness, i.e. in altered states of consciousness or trance states.

5   Active engagement with spirituality tends to make people more altruistic, less materialistic and more environmentally aware.

6   It deals with the meaning that people make of their lives.

7   It faces suffering, its causes and potentially its meaning to the individual.

8   It relates to god/goddesses and to divine/ultimate reality; these words are especially rich in meaning, and not always unproblematic.

9   It often uses the word 'soul' or 'higher self'; these words often have powerful associations and meanings for people.

10 Techniques such as prayer, meditation, contemplation, mindfulness, yoga and tai chi are often used as spiritual practices (further explored in West, 2004; 2010).

Many people continue to have experiences to which they put the word 'spiritual'. Other people having the same or similar experience may not use the word 'spiritual'. This use of the word 'spiritual' for a human experience – perhaps feeling at one with nature or a profound sense of togetherness with another human being – has many implications. For a start such experiences may not be welcome or altogether pleasant, and even if they are they may raise many issues. Such spiritual experiences are common among clients (Allman et al., 1992), inevitably happen to therapists, and sometimes occur within the therapy room (Rogers, 1980; Thorne, 2002).

PRACTICE ISSUES

The following are some largely fictional examples of the kind of religious and spiritual issues that can arise in counselling:

1   Angela is a young white English woman who has recently left a residential Buddhist community that apparently functioned as a religious cult (for useful information on cults see www. inform.ac). Although relieved to be no longer living in the community, Angela is unable to move on. She is struggling with her new life since she has lost contact with her pre-Buddhist friends and is feeling a real sense of loss for

both the people and the religious life of the community.

2   James, a young African-Caribbean man, was befriended by an evangelical Christian group at his local college. This group provided him with a real sense of home and helped him find his first job. Always confused about his sexuality, after a recent drunken night out that ended up in sexual encounter with another man, James was beginning to wonder if he was gay and if so what he should do. He knew that if he came out to his Christian friends they would want to 'cure' him.

3   Nasreen was a young second-generation Pakistani British Muslim woman whose parents were both liberal but also devout. They wanted her to marry a distant cousin from Pakistan whose family were very devout and who would expect her to give up her job, become a housewife and wear traditional clothes. Nasreen did not like this cousin, and certainly did not want to marry him; nor did she want to live a very devout life. However, she did not want to go against her parents' wishes and risk dishonouring them. She had attempted suicide before being referred for counselling.

It is worth reflecting on each of these three examples in turn, especially noticing any strong reactions to any part of the stories presented, as this may well alert us to how similar issues presented in the real world could impact on us.

IMPLICATIONS FOR COUNSELLING AND PSYCHOTHERAPY

Working with clients' religious and spiritual issues can raise questions in relation to the therapist's own attitude to religion and spirituality including any unresolved counter-transference issues (Lannert, 1991). The training of therapists is intended to equip them to deal effectively with almost any issues raised by their clients. Inevitably some of these client issues will raise questions relating to the therapist's own personal life and beliefs. So facing challenges arising from their clients' spiritual and religious beliefs should be par for the course. However, there is enough research around spirituality and therapy to show that a fair few therapists cannot rise to the challenges involved (Jenkins, 2010) and neither can some of their supervisors (West, 2000b).

It is important with a religious or spiritually minded client to clarify the role of spirituality and religion in their life. Just knowing that a client is Christian or Muslim or Jewish is not enough. There are liberal and traditional groupings in almost all religions. The extent to which a client is an active believer is also important background information, as are any tensions they may be aware of in relation to their religious beliefs and their lifestyle. Any form of client assessment should naturally include questions relating to their religious upbringing and what religious or spiritual practices they have in their current life (Richards and Bergin, 2005; West, 2000a). This not only gives the therapist some very useful information (even finding out how unreligious or anti-religious a client might be is itself important) but also gives the client permission to discuss such issues if they see fit. This implies that therapists need to have a good working knowledge of the main religious traditions – including their beliefs and practices – whilst at the same time being curious as to their clients' own perspective and also having an understanding of modern spirituality.

There are a number of ways of making sense of religion and spirituality within therapy. A detailed exploration of this topic is beyond the scope of this chapter. A few pointers however are in order:

1   Within the person-centred tradition the work of Brian Thorne (1998; 2002) is worthy of consideration. He talks of the 'mystical power of person-centred therapy' and refers to the person-centred therapist as a 'secular priest', and his writings illuminate the challenges of being present to clients' spirituality. Thorne's work is rather controversial within the person-centred community, and there are other voices who value the depth of working that he suggests without necessarily adopting a religious or spiritual perspective. See for example Mearns and Cooper (2005) who discuss relationship depth.

2   From a humanistic and transpersonal perspective, John Rowan (2005) has written extensively. His work enables us to think very clearly about how to situate our work with clients within therapeutic and spiritual frameworks which includes a careful exposition and development of Ken Wilber's model (see item 3 below). Rowan advocates that all therapists pursue their own spiritual path, which is an interesting challenge to consider.

3   One of the key authors from a transpersonal viewpoint is Ken Wilber (2000), who presents a model that integrates Western secular therapy with Eastern ideas of spiritual development. His model has aroused sufficient criticism and strong support to suggest that it has value, and it challenges us to think beyond 'one size fits all' for psychospiritual practice and to tailor our

therapeutic response to the perceived (spiritual) and developmental needs of the individual client.

4   Finally we need to view these questions within a cross-cultural perspective. Here the work of Roy Moodley (2006; 2007; Moodley and West, 2005) among others (Laungani, 2007; Moodley et al., 2010) invites us to enlarge our understandings of what makes people suffer and of the creative role that cultural factors take in the relief of suffering.

ETHICS

It is important to acknowledge a number of very crucial ethical issues involved when working with clients around issues to do with religion and spirituality. These include:

1   the respectful acceptance of clients' religious and spiritual beliefs and practices, however strange and unsettling they may appear to be
2   a recognition of the limits of both the therapist's competence and their willingness to work in the area of religion and spirituality, which should be seen not as a question of therapist inadequacy but rather as a clear boundary
3   how, when spirituality is experienced in the therapy room, there is sometimes a softening of boundaries between client and therapist and great care is then needed
4   that self-awareness of the therapist with regard to their spiritual and religious beliefs and their attitudes to the same is an important underpinning of best practice in this area (Wyatt, 2002)
5   that supervision of this part of therapeutic practice is especially important even though some supervisors are reluctant to supervise or welcome therapeutic work around spirituality and religion (West, 2003).

CONCLUSION

The tensions between those of a religious or spiritual faith and the dominant, arguably secular, modern culture are unlikely to ease. Indeed as counselling and psychotherapy continue their somewhat tortuous path towards professionalisation and perhaps statutory regulation, they may well embody some of these very tensions. It is unlikely that people will cease to have spiritual experiences (Hay and Hunt, 2000) or cease to struggle to find the help they might well need in making sense of

them. Counsellors and psychotherapists are now better placed than even 10 years ago to meet this client need, but improvements in training and supervision are still, in my view, necessary before clients receive the help they are due with regards to religion and spirituality.

ACKNOWLEDGEMENTS

Many people over the years have helped me make sense of this fascinating area of human life and therapeutic practice. These include: Allen Bergin, Terry Biddington, Jeni Boyd, Dee Brown, Fevronia Christodoulidi, Peter Gubi, the late Grace Jantzen, Chris Jenkins, the late Pittu Laungani, Roy Moodley, Ann Scott, Richard Summers, Brian Thorne, and Dori Yusef.

REFERENCES

Allman, L.S., De Las Rocha, O., Elkins, D.N. and Weathers, R.S. (1992) Psychotherapists' attitudes towards clients reporting mystical experiences. *Psychotherapy*, 29 (4): 654–9.

Crabtree, V. (2007) *Religion in the United Kingdom: Diversity, Trends and Decline*. www.weven.co.uk/religon.html, accessed 4 August 2010.

Elkins, D.N., Hedstorm, J.L., Hughes, L.L., Leaf, J.A. and Saunders, C. (1988) Toward a humanistic-phenomenological spirituality. *Journal of Humanistic Psychology*, 28 (4): 5–18.

Hay, D. and Hunt, K. (2000) *Understanding the Spirituality of People Who Don't Go To Church*. Centre for the Study of Human Relations, Nottingham University.

Jenkins, C. (2010) When the client's spirituality is denied in therapy. In W. West (ed.), *Exploring Therapy, Spirituality and Healing*. Basingstoke: Palgrave.

Lannert, J. (1991) Resistance and countertransference issues with spiritual and religious clients. *Journal of Humanistic Psychology*, 31 (4): 68–76.

Laungani, P. (2007) *Understanding Cross-Cultural Psychology*. London: Sage.

McLeod, J. (2009) *An Introduction to Counselling* (4th edn). Maidenhead: Open University Press.

Mearns, D. and Cooper, M. (2005) *Working at Relational Depth in Counselling and Psychotherapy*. London: Sage.

Moodley, R. (2006) Cultural representations and interpretations of 'subjective distress' in ethnic minority patients. In R. Moodley and S. Palmer (eds), *Race, Culture and Psychotherapy*. London: Routledge.

Moodley, R. (2007) (Re)placing multiculturalism in counselling and psychotherapy. *British Journal of Guidance & Counselling*, 35 (1): 1–22.

Moodley, R. and West, W. (eds) (2005) *Integrating Traditional Healing Practices into Counseling and Psychotherapy*. Thousand Oaks, CA: Sage.

Moodley, R., Aanchal, R. and Alladin, W. (2010) *Bridging East–West Psychology and Counselling: Exploring the Work of Pittu Laungani*. New Delhi: Sage.

Richards, P.S. and Bergin, A.E. (2005) *A Spiritual Strategy for Counselling and Psychotherapy* (2nd edn). Washington, DC: APA.

Rogers, C.R. (1980) *A Way of Being*. Boston, MA: Houghton Mifflin.

Rowan, J. (2005) *The Transpersonal: Spirituality in Psychotherapy and Counselling* (2nd edn). London: Routledge.

Swinton, J. (2001) *Spirituality in Mental Health Care*. London: Jessica Kingsley.

Tearfund Report (2007) *Church Going in the UK*. Summary at www.whychcurch.org.uk/trends.php, accessed 4 August 2010.

Thorne, B. (1998) *Person-Centred Counselling and Christian Spirituality: The Secular and the Holy*. London: Whurr.

Thorne, B. (2002) *The Mystical Power of Person-Centred Therapy: Hope Beyond Despair*. London: Whurr.

West, W. (2000a) *Psychotherapy and Spirituality: Crossing the Line between Therapy and Religion*. London: Sage.

West, W. (2000b) Supervision difficulties and dilemmas for counsellors and psychotherapists around healing and spirituality. In B. Lawton and C. Feltham (eds), *Taking Supervision Forwards: Dilemmas, Insights and Trends*. London: Sage.

West, W.S. (2003) The culture of psychotherapy supervision. *Counselling and Psychotherapy Research*, 3 (2): 123–7.

West, W. (2004) *Spiritual Issues in Therapy: Relating Experience to Practice*. Basingstoke: Palgrave.

West, W. (ed.) (2010) *Exploring Therapy, Spirituality and Healing*. Basingstoke: Palgrave.

Wilber, K. (2000) *Integral Psychology: Consciousness, Spirit, Psychology, Therapy*. London: Shambhala.

Wyatt, J. (2002) 'Confronting the Almighty God'? A study of how psychodynamic counsellors respond to clients' expressions of religious faith. *Counselling and Psychotherapy Research*, 2 (3): 177–84.

Race, Culture and Ethnicity

HARBRINDER DHILLON-STEVENS

In the area of diversity, difference and oppression, the concepts of race, culture and ethnicity are key. This chapter explores the differences between these concepts as well as looking at the literature and current research in this area and how psychological therapists can integrate their learning and build conceptual maps that will inform and enhance their clinical practice. I will be drawing from theory, experience and my own research (Dhillon-Stevens, 2004). This chapter is not a definitive source for these subjects, purely an attempt to offer the reader an introduction that may spark an interest and promote further theoretical, clinical and research mindedness in the vast literature in this area.

DEFINITIONS

In the British context 'race' is treated here in terms of black and white dynamics. 'Black' is a political term and encompasses people from Africa, the Caribbean and Asia, and ethnic minority groups who experience racism. The experience of racism is a visible difference that profoundly affects experiences at various levels: psychological, emotional, cultural, economic, political, historical and internalised. In this perspective white people do not experience racism. It is worth noting that some of these groups may not identify with such terms.

DIVERSITY WITHIN THE UK CONTEXT

Office for National Statistics figures show that the level of net migration into the UK rose by 36 per cent in 2010. An estimated 572,000 people entered the UK on a long-term basis in the year to June 2010 while 346,000 emigrated. Immigration has been from European Union countries, Eastern Europe, Commonwealth countries, Africa and South East Asia. People coming into the UK have included political refugees and asylum seekers. In 1991 the breakup of the government of Somalia led to 7500 applications being made; between 1992 and 1997 2500 Bosnians entered the UK as refugees following the breakup of the former Yugoslavia; and in 1999 heavy fighting in Sri Lanka led to 5130 applications for asylum being made to the UK. In addition to the newcomers Britain, as a result of its past historical associations, has been the beneficiary of several groups of Asians (from India, Pakistan, Bangladesh, Sri Lanka, East Africa, South Africa), African-Caribbeans and Africans, most of whom emigrated to Britain soon after the Second World War. We also have British-born populations, of first, second and third generations, who offer a different dynamic in terms of the discussions regarding race, culture and ethnicity. Data from the British Labour Force Survey (UKLFS) for the period 1993–2007 show that the 'UKLFS contains information on country of birth for first generation immigrants but no information on country of parental birth for the second generation. The standard practice is to use ethnicity as a measure of being a second (or subsequent) generation immigrant' (Algan et al., 2009: 12). In considering the background to the second or third generation of migrants, then, information has to be intuited from the data on ethnic minority communities. British-born descendants of ethnic minority immigrants represent an increasing share of the ethnic minority population in the UK. According to the UKLFS, in 1991 25.2 per cent of the individuals of working age who identified themselves as members of an ethnic minority group were born in the UK. This share increased in 2001 to 35 per cent and in 2009 to 36.6 per cent (Dustmann et al., 2010).

The makeup of different cultures, races and ethnicities from a psychological perspective offers very rich opportunities for learning, for integrating theory, practice and research, and for the development of psychological services. It also fundamentally engages us with critical reflexivity into our own identity, values, prejudices, bias and practice. Psychological services that fail to address the dynamics of race, culture and ethnicity and the experiences that relate to black people are inadequate and further alienate clients who enter the therapeutic space.

The Race Relations Act 1976 (together with the Race Relations (Amendment) Act 2000) makes it unlawful to discriminate on grounds of race, colour, nationality, or ethnic or national origin. The Act covers recruitment, promotion, training and service provision; deals with direct discrimination, indirect discrimination and victimisation; and now gives service providers a statutory general duty to promote race equality.

Palmer and Laungani raise several questions in terms of working with culture:

- How do people from different cultures bring up their own children?
- What constitutes child abuse in other cultures?
- What are the parameters which they consider important in the socialisation process?
- What are the attitudes and values towards women, towards the sick, the infirm and elderly?
- What rules govern their family structures and kinship patterns?
- How do they grieve and mourn?
- How do they perceive members of the host culture?
- How do they attempt to relate to one another?
- To what extent do they succeed or fail in forming meaningful relationships with members of other cultures?
- What effect do the dominant values of the host culture have on their own system of values? (1999: 2)

The authors state that 'cross cultural counselling is like venturing into uncharted psychic territories. One might find oneself moving into areas about which very little is known' (1999: 4). This is an area where practitioners feel they often need guidance and there is real fear of 'getting it wrong'. Perhaps this fear stems from the challenges of this area of work and how the personal is so bound up in the professional.

CONSTRUCTION OF HEALTH

The construction of health in different contexts needs to be clearly understood. In Eastern constructs the ability to fulfil a cultural role is paramount; there is more emphasis on being able to do this, and less on emotional/psychological wellbeing. Emotional and psychological wellbeing are often expressed through physical symptoms, e.g. 'my heart is heavy', 'I have a pain in my knee.'

In having a construction of health we need to understand how therapeutic processes occur in black and minority ethnic communities, how healing takes place, and to this end we need to work in a strengths model of black families rather than a deficit model (Ahmed, 1990). Fernando (1991) describes how psychiatry sees black people in a deficit model and how mental health models are culturally constructed and therefore culturally specific. Fernando asserts that

> 'culture' is used in psychiatry in an ethnocentric way. Consequently, non-Western cultures that are alien to psychiatry are themselves seen as pathological. In this way 'culture' becomes the 'problem' that accounts for the abnormal behaviour of the client. The perception of a minority group as 'having' a problem insidiously turns to perceiving them as being the problem. Thus their culture is good for 'them' but bad for 'us'. (quoted in Kareem and Littlewood, 1992: 12)

In examining the rates of serious illness or over-representation of black people in the mental health system, statistics taken from the Mental Health Minimum Data Set show that of 31.8 per cent of service users receiving care on inpatient units detained involuntarily, 53.8 per cent were black. The 2009 'Count Me In' census, which was published by the Care Quality Commission in 2010, found that 22 per cent of all patients were from a minority ethnic group compared with 20 per cent for the 2005 census. The rates of people from 'other black' and 'black Caribbean' groups detained under Section 37/41 of the Mental Health Act 1983 have remained higher than average for the last five years. And the rates of admission or detention have not reduced since 2005 for black and minority ethnic groups. How do we begin to address this?

Psychological therapy training needs to incorporate black strengths models into the assessment process. Black therapists need to be aware of how they are trained versus the tension of how they want to practise, what kind of therapeutic stance they want to adopt, and whether this is congruent with their values, knowledge, and skills that have not been identified in their training.

PHILOSOPHICAL POSITIONING

Just as in separating race, culture and ethnicity from disability, sexual orientation and gender, a particular philosophical discourse is in operation in the structure of these issues in this book (and elsewhere, e.g. Lago, 2011). Whilst understanding the need for this, it is important to discuss the multiple oppression model of difference (Dhillon-Stevens, 2004). This considers race, ethnicity, culture, gender, disability, sexual orientation, class, age, religion and language. In the multiple oppression model it is important to recognise the differences as well as the similarities between oppressions. For example, whilst white working-class people are disadvantaged, black working-class people face discrimination not only because of class but also because of their skin colour (race). Anti-oppressive practice (AOP) works within this model as well as acknowledging structural and contextual issues.

Engaging in political thought and an understanding of this is what challenges personal values and the values governing counselling and psychological therapies, and how these affect practice. Responses to a research questionnaire from therapists suggested that most therapists do not see a role in therapy for politics (Dhillon-Stevens, 2004) and this affects how they see their role in working with issues of difference, diversity and oppression. At the opposite polarity are therapists who position themselves as change agents, and this affects their use of self in the therapeutic space and how they work with issues of difference.

The terms 'multicultural counselling', 'intercultural therapy', 'cross-cultural therapy', 'transcultural therapy', 'working with difference', 'diversity, anti-racist and anti-discriminatory practice' and 'anti-oppressive practice' should not be used interchangeably as they often have been in this field. These terms relate to specific philosophical and political discourses at different points in history, and therapists need to engage in these to understand the different positioning of authors in the literature and critically evaluate their own position. For example, multicultural counselling and therapy denotes the importance of paying attention to many cultural reference points that impact on relationships. As Ponterotto et al. (1995) argue, essential elements of multicultural therapy competence are found in the therapist's awareness of his or her own cultural heritage, worldview and related values, biases and

assumptions about human behaviour, and an understanding of the worldview of the culturally different client. D'Ardenne and Mahtani (1989) give preference to the 'active and reciprocal' associations of transcultural counselling. Psychological therapists in this model are responsible for working across, through or beyond their cultural differences. Practitioners need to consider the advantages as well as disadvantages of such models. The limitations of both of the above approaches are the focus on culture and cultural interface between the client and the therapist.

DEFINING RACE, CULTURE AND ETHNICITY

In the psychological therapies literature we have paid more attention to culture as a dynamic in working with difference than to ethnicity or 'race'. Fernando (1991) suggests Western concepts of mental health are greatly influenced by racist ideology. What has become clear through research (Dhillon-Stevens, 2004) is that race in the British context creates different dynamics from other issues of oppression. The introduction of race is different from how other oppressions are understood and experienced by psychological therapists emotionally and psychologically. Race provides a different concoction in the dynamics (Dhillon-Stevens, 2011). Bell's (2001) notion of 'infusing "race" into the dialogue' creates a difference. As she states, 'infusing is a technique of slowly introducing a new or uncommon ingredient to a dish. Infusing causes a subtle yet distinctive change in taste and sometimes the texture of the dish, giving layers of complexity' (2001: 48).

The concept of 'race' has been discussed from many different perspectives by different generations. Originally the term 'race' denoted a classification system used to categorise groups of people from other forms of life on the basis of common descent or heredity. In this definition lay assumptions that the genetic heritage of each group was evident in physical characteristics, e.g. a group of people of common ancestry, distinguished from others by physical characteristics such as hair type, skin colour, eye shape, etc. Racial theories grew up and these drew on scientific means to support the hypothesis that racial differences had been ordained by nature, and that intellectual ability was determined by physical characteristics. Darwin's publication of *On the Origin of Species* in 1859 led to the understanding that there was no longer a rationale for dividing humankind into fixed racial types or for ascribing social inequalities to nature. The term 'race' from this perspective refers to the human race

(*Homo sapiens*) as a single species. Tuckwell invites us to look beyond visible differences and quotes Malik: 'the clue to the importance of race in western thought therefore lies not in biology but in society' and power domination (Tuckwell, 2002: 14). Tuckwell (2002) and Dalal (2002) provide an excellent overview of the theoretical ideas of major race theorists. In reviewing the historical literature on race, Dalal notes: 'Thus despite my attempt to be logical and examine the notion of race before that of racism, it appears that racism manifested itself before the invention of race' (2002: 13). The categorisation of people in biological terms constructed by white scientists aided the justification and systematic oppression of black people and created an ideology of racism. Scientific racism was powerfully displayed in Nazi Germany and the pursuit of anti-Semitism.

Thus this concept in contemporary British society is now commonly used to denote black and white populations. In the literature, black has always been defined in correlation to white. Thus 'race' is a social construction. Fernando's (1991) work in this area clearly locates race as a social reality and as constructed by individual and group behaviour. Institutionalised racism refers to attitudes and prejudices against individuals or groups that are embedded in the infrastructure of an organisation or a society. 'Sociopolitical and psychological ideas have converged over several centuries to support the notion of white superiority and black inferiority. In this way race has become a powerful signifier of historical and contemporary experience for black groups and white groups collectively' (Tuckwell, 2002: 27). Thus it is crucial to understand structural and societal experiences as well as the unique individual intrapsychic experiences of black and white populations. Unfortunately, in psychological therapies we are uncomfortable in drawing attention to this or even knowing how to competently engage in such a discussion. Black clients comment that this is the 'elephant in the room'. Black clients, in wanting it addressed, are interested in what a white therapist has to say about the difference from her perception and how that difference relates to the therapeutic space and relationship (Dhillon-Stevens, 2011). In recent years research by Tuckwell (2002) and Ryde (2009) has addressed the issues of whiteness and what this means in the debate on 'race'.

Tuckwell's *Racial Identity, White Counsellors and Therapists* (2002) explores the subject of racial identity and encourages readers to think freely about racial issues and to explore their own racial identity. With a particular focus on white identity, the book challenges white therapists to develop their understanding of a relatively unexplored field.

The author believes that self-awareness is an essential element of competency as a therapist, and she challenges all white therapists to be aware of what it means to be white, and how this influences the therapy process. Ryde's *Being White in the Helping Professions: Developing Effective Intercultural Awareness* (2009) was based upon her research and indicated that it is extremely difficult for white people to understand their position in a racial context. She comments:

> I came eventually to understand 'white' to mean the European diaspora which now dominates global culture in its economic, political, cultural and social arrangements. I also discovered that, however much we would like to deny it, we carry with us in all our interactions with those who are not white (as well as those who are) a legacy of history and this includes both slavery and colonization. In the context of our worldwide domination it is only too easy to see ourselves as just 'normal', particularly if that normality affords us an easy, privileged position in the global society. (2009: 33)

Her encouragement is to avoid prescriptive notions which advocate 'correct' ways of working in a transcultural setting and definite descriptions of different cultures. Instead she encourages self-reflection and an inquiring stance so that our own responses as well as our clients' are taken into account when we work with them.

Ethnicity has often been used to refer to black people and as a euphemism for race: it is worth remembering that white people also belong to ethnic groups. Ethnicity refers to individuals' identification with a group sharing some of the following traits: customs, lifestyles, religion, language or nationality. Culture is a sociological and anthropological concept, an identity which everyone has, based on a number of factors such as memories, ethnic identity, family attitudes to child rearing, class, money, religious or other celebrations, and the division of family roles according to gender or age. Cultures are neither superior nor inferior to each other and are fluid, as they are constantly evolving for individuals or communities. Cultural knowledge therefore is limiting in its homogeneous application to all people of that group.

WHAT IS THE RELATIONSHIP BETWEEN RACE, CULTURE AND ETHNICITY?

Dalal (2002) differentiates the three terms on the basis of three domains: how people look, how people behave, and how people think and feel. He states these three domains are mapped into ideas of race, culture and ethnicity. He further differentiates between things (which are neutral) and the 'uses' to which they are put. He states, 'the first is a fact of nature and therefore biological and the second a fact of culture and therefore sociological' (2002: 21). He offers a further stream which says that there is no such thing as race and that more meaningful descriptions of groups of people are given by the terms 'ethnicity' and 'culture':

> Thus it is common practice to put the first term of the trinity – 'race', culture and ethnicity – in quotes. The implication of this is that whilst the notion of race is problematic, the other two are less so and exist in a straightforward way. (2002: 21)

He further demonstrates that the other two are as complicated. Certainly, despite definitions, it is impossible to separate these terms and they do have points of interconnection and overlap. Another important factor to highlight, particularly in working with people from the Indian subcontinent, is the self-use of such terms. My father describes himself as a Sikh; he infuses the concepts of culture and ethnicity into his religious identity, which is the more overriding and figural concept for him. In trying to differentiate race from ethnicity from culture we perhaps get sidetracked, and the intentions behind such concepts reveal the consistent theme, which is the idea of belonging and notions of identity. The implication of this is how clients and therapists position themselves in identity formation: this might be real or imagined, it might be attributed from the inside as a felt self-definition or from the outside. How are these differences constructed and what is their significance in the therapeutic space? The importance of these concepts is more for practitioners to be aware of their own race, culture and ethnicity and how these factors influence consciously and unconsciously their values, biases and prejudices in working with clients, especially clients who are different or disadvantaged. We need to understand the importance of such terms whilst recognising the dynamics and processes that affect the way we feel, think and behave in relation to others.

In training psychological therapists and addressing the specific issues of race, culture and ethnicity, the material is often very emotional, and the theme of how to engage with anger and hurt – historical, present day and fantasised – needs to be dealt with by facilitators. The same is true of the therapeutic space in terms of client and therapist. In asking a group of white students to think about whiteness, they each reported they felt different and guilty and less of a person. One of the black students said, 'Welcome to my world.' The concepts of projection and projective identification need attention and are

extremely powerful in black/white dynamics. One white Irish client, in working with a black therapist, commented that during the session what was present for her and what she was alert to was the concept of payback, 'she's gonna get you' – the idea that black people angry about racism, colonisation and imperialism would be waiting for opportunities 'to get even' (Dhillon-Stevens, 2004). The question arose: can you really engage in authentic dialogue with someone who represents deep emotional hurt in your history? Both client and therapist need to engage in a transparent dialogue and own the reality of their experiences as well as the projective elements.

POWER

No discussion of race, culture and ethnicity is complete without acknowledgement of the concept of power. This is an essential ingredient in the discourse of difference, diversity and oppression. Little has been researched in the field of psychotherapy, apart from Proctor (2002), which explores theories of power and how they could be applied to models of therapy.

My own understanding of power comes from social work and the idea that: personal prejudice + the power to act on those prejudices = discrimination. Power can be used positively, but arguably only when one has a full appreciation of the power that is held personally in terms of role and an understanding of how power in society is structured (political, economic, social). Proctor offers historical power, and I would add from research in dialogue between client and therapist (Dhillon-Stevens, 2004) that this historical and intergenerational element and the many dimensions of who the therapist may represent for the client were very evident. In therapy we have enormous power, but how do therapists understand their power base in the therapeutic space and its use for or against the client? Constant questioning and reflecting on power bases and dynamics within the therapeutic dyad keeps us vigilant about our use and abuse of power.

Day's doctoral research entitled 'Psychotherapists' experience of power in the psychotherapy relationship' (2010) provides a rich description of how power shapes, informs and presents itself in the psychotherapy relationship. His research identified four subordinate themes from across participants' accounts. These were: the therapist's experience of both the client's and their own role power; power as a dynamic and emerging relational and social process; different forms of power dynamics in the psychotherapy relationship; and the therapist's ambivalent feelings of power. The findings highlight that power is experienced as being an inescapable phenomenon of the psychotherapy relationship – complex, constantly shifting and, at times, paradoxical. For much of the time, the power dynamic is pre-reflective and largely out of conscious awareness. Therapists experienced power to be implicit in the structure of the psychotherapy relationship and the therapeutic context. This highlights the importance of power in the practice of psychotherapy. It demonstrates the need for the therapist to tolerate the client's need to construct them as a figure of power, to be dependent upon them and to express anger, hate, rage and envy towards their power. Participants' accounts revealed that the exploration and renegotiation of the form of the power relationship between therapist and client are pivotal to the process of therapeutic change for specific clients. Therapists described how this facilitated the establishment of a collaborative relationship in which power was shared between them and clients. Therapists reported that reconfiguration of the power dynamic facilitated the client experimenting with their power in the therapeutic relationships and their relationships with others. What is evident from the findings of this study is that the phenomenon of power is central to the therapeutic relationship. It suggests that practitioners can enhance their practice by observing, exploring and negotiating the power dynamic of their relationship with their clients. Power in the therapeutic relationship therefore needs to enter the mainstream discourse and debate in the counselling, psychology and psychotherapy communities.

RECENT RESEARCH

It is worth underlining research-mindedness in this area and the notion of evidence-based practice in what can often become emotive work. Research in this area is growing, and it is of interest that the research is increasingly being undertaken by black therapists. This presents an added richness and understanding of the issues. Insider/outsider research dimensions offer richness, complexity and different positions in the debate.

We first consider 'Healing inside and outside: an examination of dialogic encounters in the area of anti-oppressive practice in counselling and psychotherapy' (Dhillon-Stevens, 2004). This doctoral research investigated issues of anti-oppressive practice (AOP) within the British counselling and psychotherapy professions. It explored how issues of AOP are defined and discussed by counsellors and psychotherapists as well as their values and attitudes towards AOP. Above all, it looked in depth at how AOP enters their work with clients. The research was conducted through the distribution of an initial exploratory questionnaire, followed by the establishment of an inquiry group that focused on various issues of AOP over eight months (one day a month). The inquiry group explored issues of AOP through role-plays between therapist and client. The role-plays were critically reflected upon by the individuals involved as well as the other inquirers. All the work of the inquiry group was recorded using video equipment. Action research was combined with cooperative inquiry to collect data and grounded theory used to articulate AOP themes and a theory of AOP. The results show therapists and counsellors need to:

- Critically examine and reflect on their personal values and the implications of these on their professional practice.
- Understand the theoretical foundations of AOP (and in relation to specific oppressions) and how this can assist them in working with clients from different oppressed groups.
- Have an acknowledgement by training organisations that the psychological impacts of AOP are different for black and white trainees. Black trainees are far more psychologically challenged in terms of their sense of self and require different supervision and training to address these issues than is currently provided.
- Examine AOP in training and realise that this can be very distressing and can cause an 'internalised sense of rupture'. For white trainees, examining what it means to be white and how to engage in dialogue with clients regarding their whiteness is vital. The inability to examine these issues (or have the practice skills) has the potential to impact on the therapeutic space, causing white therapists to lose grasp of the therapeutic process and their sense of self and professional role.
- Be aware that clients who are from oppressed groups feel a need to protect unaware therapists from their difference, thus causing further internalisation of their oppression in the therapeutic space and fragmentation of their sense of self. This highlights the need for therapists to understand and find a way to communicate this lack of awareness and reduce the potential for damage to clients.
- Challenge the professions of counselling and psychotherapy to be more proactive in considering the competence of all therapists in working with AOP issues, and to consider a framework that would actively focus and enhance AOP in curriculum, assessment and teaching outcomes. A key element of this area is rigorous and structured reflection methods to enhance critical self-reflection.

Emerging from this research were a number of products: DVD (prototype), presentations and publications for the profession of psychological therapists. The results of this project offered a challenge to the professions of counselling and psychotherapy to reconsider how ethical practice in relation to issues of AOP is considered in the training of therapists and the monitoring of counsellors', therapists' and supervisors' work, as well as the implications for researchers conducting research into this complex and challenging area.

Isha Mckenzie-Magava's (2010) research questioned how trainee counsellors in Britain understand concerns about black issues raised by themselves during their training or about clients during the therapeutic process. Her book *Black Issues in the Therapeutic Process* specifically focuses on elements of therapeutic work which address the needs and concerns of practitioners working with issues related to people of African-Caribbean heritage. The book assists readers in understanding how to work with the hurt of racism and the inherited effects of slavery and colonialism. It offers supportive techniques to assist therapeutic work with these issues, explores questions that have been asked by practising and trainee therapists, and encourages practitioners to broaden their experience of working with black issues, placing them in a global historical context. Findings demonstrated that themes such as fear and safety were features of a trainee's process of exploring and understanding black issues. Three main concepts evolved: 'shared concerns', 'finding a voice' and 'recognition trauma'.

Alleyne's (2004) research was primarily aimed at counselling and psychotherapy practitioners who meet issues of workplace conflict in their practice, and the resulting stress and trauma faced by their clients. She defines workplace conflict as complex and enduring situations arising from diverse forms of harassment. These include bullying, scapegoating and other discriminatory and oppressive practices that affect health, esteem and work performance. This doctoral research sought to understand the specific experience and nature of workplace conflict for black workers in three institutional settings: the National Health Service (NHS), the education service and the social services. The inspiration for this research came from psychotherapy practice, where it was repeatedly observed that black workers appeared to be suffering significantly more negative and damaging effects of workplace stress and trauma than white workers. She describes these experiences as workplace oppression and differentiates them from other workplace conflicts.

Bains's research titled 'An autoethnographic exploration into transforming the wounds of racism:

implications for psychotherapy' (2007) is a reflexive autoethnographic approach integrated with psychotherapy that critically uses an evocative personal narrative approach to describe, interpret, reconstruct and transform the traumatic effects of colour racism on the self. The research produced intersubjective meaning and learning within a psychological, socio-political and historical context by attempting to focus on embodied awareness and possible new ways of thinking about the familiar. The research was a collaborative activity that interwove strands of her own story and the narratives of the family group and the professional group to produce a multi-voiced narrative of racist trauma.

CONCLUSION

My intention in this chapter has been to provide a theoretical and research-based overview of the subject. In engaging in competent ethical practice in this area we need to pay close attention to our own personal and professional development and ensure we keep this area alive and renew our knowledge base and skills. In paying attention to our own process and keeping an inquiring, critically reflexive stance we will be offering our clients a relational experience where they feel therapists can hold all aspects of the self and an exchange where therapists have taken the responsibility to address these issues and not rely on clients to inform us.

REFERENCES

Ahmed, B. (1990) *Black Perspectives in Social Work*. London: Ventura.

Algan, Y., Dustmann, C., Glitz, A. and Manning, A. (2009) *The Economic Situation of First- and Second-Generation Immigrants in France, Germany, and the UK*. Centre for Research and Analysis of Migration. CReAM discussion paper series CDP no. 22/09.

Alleyne, A. (2004) The internal oppressor and black identity wounding. *Counselling and Psychotherapy Journal*, 15 (10): 48–50.

Bains, S. (2007) *An Autoethnographic Exploration into Transforming the Wounds of Racism: Implications for Psychotherapy*. Doctorate in Psychotherapy by Professional Studies, Metanoia Institute/Middlesex University.

Bell, E.F. (2001) Infusing race into the US discourse on action research. In P. Reason and

H. Bradbury (eds), *Handbook of Action Research*. London: Sage.

Dalal, F. (2002) *Race, Colour and the Process of Racialization*. Hove: Brunner-Routledge.

D'Ardenne, P. and Mahtani, A. (1989) *Transcultural Counselling in Action*. London: Sage.

Day, A. (2010) *Psychotherapists' Experience of Power in the Psychotherapy Relationship*. Doctorate in Counselling Psychology and Psychotherapy by Professional Studies, Metanoia Institute/Middlesex University.

Dhillon-Stevens, H. (2004) *Healing Inside and Outside: An Examination of Dialogic Encounters in the Area of Anti-Oppressive Practice in Counselling and Psychotherapy*. Doctorate in Psychotherapy by Professional Studies, Metanoia Institute/Middlesex University.

Dhillon-Stevens, H. (2011) Issues for psychological therapists from black and minority ethnic groups. In C. Lago (ed.), *Transcultural Counselling and Psychotherapy: Bridging the Divide*. Maidenhead: Open University.

Dustmann, C., Frattini, T. and Theodoropoulos, N. (2010) *Ethnicity and Second Generation Immigrants in Britain*. Centre for Research and Analysis of Migration. CReAM discussion paper series CDP no. 04/10.

Fernando, S. (1991) *Mental Health, Race and Culture*. London: Macmillan.

Kareem, J. and Littlewood, R. (1992) *Inter-Cultural Therapy*. Oxford: Blackwell.

Lago, C. (ed.) (2011) *The Handbook of Transcultural Counselling and Psychotherapy*. London: Open University Press.

Mckenzie-Magava, I. (2010) *Black Issues in the Therapeutic Process*. Basingstoke: Palgrave Macmillan.

Office for National Statistics (2010) *Migration Statistics Quarterly Report*. No. 6, 26 August 2010.

Palmer, S. and Laungani, P. (1999) *Counselling in a Multicultural Society*. London: Sage.

Ponterotto, J., Casas, J.M., Suzuki, L.A. and Alexander, C.M. (1995) *Handbook of Multicultural Counseling*. Thousand Oaks, CA: Sage.

Proctor, G. (2002) *The Dynamics of Power in Counselling and Psychotherapy*. Ross-on-Wye: PCCS.

Reason, P. and Bradbury, H. (2001) *Handbook of Action Research*. London: Sage.

Ryde, J. (2009) *Being White in the Helping Professions: Developing Effective Intercultural Awareness*. London: Jessica Kingsley.

Tuckwell, G. (2002) *Racial Identity, White Counsellors and Therapists*. Buckingham: Open University Press.

PART III

THERAPEUTIC SKILLS AND CLINICAL PRACTICE

Introduction

COLIN FELTHAM AND IAN HORTON

One way of looking at the many theoretical models, training issues, contexts and so on, in and against which therapy takes place, is to focus on what therapists actually *do* in sessions (Hill, 1989) and what can be consciously analysed and improved (McLeod, 2007). We acknowledge that this may not satisfy those for whom relationship and irreducible process are the key elements. In this part of the book the concentration is on what therapists actually do when they are with clients and what they do in relation to clients. We refer to this area as clinical practice to distinguish it from other necessary but often indirect professional and theoretical issues, and we are mindful that certain practitioners dislike the epithet 'clinical' and its medical associations.

Various terms are used in this context: attitudes, skills, techniques, interventions, strategies and so on. Here we make some attempt to clarify usage. *Skills* may be found at the most atomistic levels of practice, for example the micro-skills of responding to clients' utterances with apparently simple but carefully chosen supportive or reflective statements (or, as appropriate, judicious silences). A range of generic skills serves to aid the conversational flow and therapeutic communication between therapists and clients. As well as the micro-skills necessary for these therapeutically goal-directed interactions, there are the specific skills of assessment – calling for a certain cognitive acuity – and those of structuring the therapeutic process. Implied in all these skills, however intuitive they may sometimes appear to be, is an element of putting theory into practice. This, together with the exercise of putting experience and training into practice, is mediated by therapist

decision making operating rapidly at different levels of consciousness (Dryden, 1991: 100–10).

Considerable debate continues as to whether practitioners are most effectively 'produced' by training which explicitly inculcates and reinforces all such skills, or by eliciting appropriate innate or pre-existing skills. Theorists and practitioners aligned with social learning and cognitive-behavioural traditions (e.g. Neenan and Dryden, 2004), particularly those promoting manualized therapeutic procedures, belong to the first group, while many psychoanalytic and humanistic therapists, including Lomas (1993), belong to the second. 'Use of the self' is a key concept here, with psychoanalytic and humanistic practitioners drawing heavily on the idea of *therapist attitudes* and *therapist self-awareness* as cultivated by personal (training) therapy and other forms of personal development work. The use of self is closely associated with therapeutic relationship issues, such as provision of a therapeutic climate. All the above groups agree, however, that counselling and psychotherapy are in fact skilled activities. In the 2000s much work has been done attempting to map all such skills against CBT, psychodynamic, family and systemic, and humanistic therapy traditions for the UK Department of Health's Skills for Health programme (www.skillsforhealth.org.uk).

Dryden (1991: 103) has argued that *clinical strategies* lie between theory and technique, an example being the decision as to whether to provide a corrective emotional experience, which then leads on to technical implementation. The term *interventions* tends to be used differentially to refer to anything the therapist says or does or to conscious technical choices or directions, this last understanding being characterized for example by Heron (2001).

Techniques may be characterized as deliberately (strategically) employed, purposeful actions which are associated both theoretically and clinically with the therapeutic enterprise generally (e.g. empathy) and often with particular theoretical orientations (e.g. empty chair work). While some traditions rely on a relatively small number of techniques (e.g. psychoanalysis) or may eschew the concept of techniques altogether or partially (Tolan, 2003), others spawn a large number (e.g. neuro-linguistic programming) and within eclectic practice is found an openness to the deployment of techniques from various sources (Lazarus, 1981; Thompson, 1996). Again, considerable debate exists as to the wisdom of techniques being anchored in their theoretical bases, versus techniques being freely applied, almost regardless of theory, to different clients with different needs. In addition, the contentious concepts of *treatment of choice* and *technique of choice* suggest that therapists need to think strategically both within a tradition (e.g. Barber and Crits-Christoph, 1995) and across traditions (Dryden and Reeves, 2008; Karasu and Bellak, 1980; Meier and Boivin, 2011; Roth et al., 2005; Timulak, 2011).

In this part of the book are included certain clinical practice issues and ancillary skills which are also usually necessary and widely used. Obviously each therapeutic tradition emphasizes the importance of certain skills, techniques and therapeutic protocols above others. We hope that readers interested in comparative therapeutic skills and potential *rapprochement* will cross-refer as desirable to other salient parts of the book, including the skills and strategies chapters in Part V.

REFERENCES

Barber, J.P. and Crits-Christoph, P. (eds) (1995) *Dynamic Therapies for Psychiatric Disorders (Axis I).* New York: Basic.

Dryden, W. (1991) *Dryden on Counselling.* Vol. 1: *Seminal Papers.* London: Whurr.

Dryden, W. and Reeves, A. (eds) (2008) *Key Issues for Counselling in Action* (2nd edn). London: Sage.

Heron, J. (2001) *Helping the Client* (5th edn). London: Sage.

Hill, C.E. (1989) *Therapist Techniques and Client Outcomes: Eight Cases of Brief Psychotherapy.* Newbury Park, CA: Sage.

Karasu, T.B. and Bellak, L. (eds) (1980) *Specialized Techniques for Specific Clinical Problems in Psychotherapy.* Northvale, NJ: Aronson.

Lazarus, A.A. (1981) *The Practice of Multimodal Therapy: Systematic, Comprehensive, and Effective Psychotherapy.* Baltimore, MA: Johns Hopkins University Press.

Lomas, P. (1993) *Cultivating Intuition: An Introduction to Psychotherapy.* Northvale, NJ: Aronson.

McLeod, J. (2007) *Counselling Skill.* Maidenhead: Open University Press.

Meier, A. and Boivin, M. (2011) *Counselling and Therapy Techniques: Theory and Practice.* London: Sage.

Neenan, M. and Dryden, W. (2004) *Cognitive Therapy: 100 Key Points and Techniques.* London: Brunner-Routledge.

Roth, A., Fonagy, P., Parry, G. and Target, M. (2005) *What Works for Whom? A Critical Review of Psychotherapy Research* (2nd edn). New York: Guilford.

Thompson, R.A. (1996) *Counseling Techniques.* Washington, DC: Accelerated Learning.

Timulak, L. (2011) *Developing Your Counselling and Psychotherapy Skills and Practice.* London: Sage.

Tolan, J. (2003) *Skills in Person-Centred Counselling and Psychotherapy.* London: Sage.

The Client–Therapist Relationship

WILLIAM B. STILES

The sprawling literature on the client–therapist relationship, often styled as the alliance, continues to expand (e.g. Gilbert and Leahy, 2007; Muran and Barber, 2010; Norcross, 2011). What follows is a personal selection and understanding. I have practised, supervised and researched psychotherapy for some years (e.g. Stiles, 1999). My practice orientation is strongly person centred, but my understanding of the research is that widely varying theoretical approaches are similarly effective (Lambert and Ogles, 2004). Debate about this equivalence paradox – equivalent outcomes of diverse treatments despite manifestly non-equivalent intervention techniques, or 'Everybody has won and all must have prizes' (The Dodo, in Carroll, 1865/1946) – has driven psychotherapy research for generations (e.g. Beutler, 1991; Chambless, 2002; Luborsky et al., 1975; Rosenzweig, 1936; Stiles et al., 1986; Wampold, 2001).

The concept of the therapist–client relationship offers to resolve the equivalence paradox. All therapy can be said to involve a significant relationship, though the concept has to be stretched a little to encompass internet therapy and bibliotherapy. Across very diverse treatments, including cognitive and psychopharmacological treatments and treatment of couples and families, the strength of the relationship has consistently been the strongest and most consistent process correlate of treatment outcome (Castonguay et al., 2010; Escudero et al., 2010; Friedlander et al., 2011; Horvath and Bedi, 2002; Horvath et al., 2010; 2011; Krupnick et al., 1996; Leahy, 2008; Orlinsky et al., 2004; Waddington, 2002). If the relationship is therapy's main active ingredient, as some suggest, then it is understandable that any treatment approach can be effective.

But what is the client–therapist relationship? What do authors mean when they speak of the relationship, the alliance (helping alliance, working alliance, therapeutic alliance), or the therapeutic climate? This chapter considers three illustrative conceptual approaches: psychodynamic, person centred and psychometric. It concludes with some comments about research on the relationship.

PSYCHODYNAMIC CONCEPTS OF THE RELATIONSHIP

Psychoanalytic and other psychodynamic theorists have focused on a distinction between the real relationship and the transference (Freud, 1958; Horvath and Luborsky, 1993; Zetzel, 1956). Some have further distinguished the working alliance (Gelso and Carter, 1985; 1994; Greenson, 1965). Theorists have made these distinctions in various ways. Gelso and Carter (1985; 1994) offered the following relatively succinct version:

> The real relationship is seen as having two defining features: genuineness and realistic perceptions. Genuineness is defined as the ability and willingness to be what one truly is in the relationship – to be authentic, open, and honest. Realistic perceptions refer to those perceptions that are uncontaminated by transference distortions and other defences. In other words, the therapy participants see each other in an accurate, realistic way. (1994: 297)

The transference configuration   consists of both client transference and therapist counter-transference ... Transference is the repetition of past conflicts with significant others, such that feelings, attitudes, and behaviors belonging rightfully in those earlier relationships are displaced onto the therapist; and counter-transference is the therapist's transference to the client's material, both to the transference and the nontransference communications presented by the client. (1994: 297)

[The working] alliance may be seen as the alignment or joining of the reasonable self or ego of the client and the therapist's analyzing or 'therapizing' self or ego for the purpose of the work. (1994: 297)

The working alliance that exists between client and therapist both influences and is influenced by each of the other two components – the transference configuration and the real relationship. (1994: 298)

Thus, in Gelso and Carter's conception, the working alliance is only partially reality based, and may additionally incorporate positive transferential elements, such as idealizing expectations about the therapist's ability to help.

Among these aspects, psychodynamic interest has focused on the transference. The transference concept is a way of understanding how past hurts, including early environments that interfered with or failed to support healthy development, can be manifested as problems in the present. Theoretically, the problematic (and non-problematic) relational patterns that brought the client into treatment tend to be re-experienced and acted out within the therapeutic relationship. The relationship with the therapist offers an experientially immediate opportunity for problematic patterns to be acknowledged, interpreted, understood and changed. By understanding and correcting distortions that arise in his or her feelings about the therapist, the client can resolve conflicts that have been interfering with daily life outside therapy. Positive feelings for the therapist may also represent transference, and some psychoanalytic theorists (e.g. Brenner, 1979) have argued that distinguishing the transference from the alliance or the real relationship can distract attention from the importance of analysing positive transference (see review by Messer and Wolitsky, 2010).

There are, of course, alternatives to insight and analysis of the transference to understand how the therapist–client relationship might be curative (see discussion by Hatcher, 2010), even within a broadly psychodynamic framework (Messer and Wolitsky, 2010). For example, from an object relations perspective, the therapist might serve as good object; taking in the therapist in this way might be transformative in ways that do not require insight (Geller and Farber, 1993; Orlinsky et al., 1993; Zuroff and Blatt, 2006).

Psychoanalytic theorists have elaborated the concept of transference in many ways. For example, Kohut (1971; 1977) distinguished between mirroring transferences, in which the therapist is experienced as an extension of the self, as a twin, or as an appendage whose function is mainly to support the client's (unrealistically) grandiose views of the self, and idealizing transferences, in which the client draws strength or reassurance from being associated with an idealized therapist's exaggerated virtues. In this view, progress may come when the therapist fails to fulfil these unrealistic expectations. The client's resulting frustration brings the expectations into awareness, making it possible to examine and change them within the treatment.

Manifestations of the transference in treatment can be dramatic, and observations of transference phenomena have figured centrally in the psychoanalytic literature since Freud's case studies of Anna O. and Dora (Breuer and Freud, 1957; Freud, 1953). Reliable measurement has proved more difficult, however. Probably the most sustained and best-known effort has been the work on the core conflictual relationship theme (CCRT) (Luborsky, 1977; Luborsky and Crits-Christoph, 1998; Luborsky et al., 2004). Theoretically, core conflicts are likely to appear repeatedly in many significant relationships, as well as in the therapeutic relationship. Consequently, then, a client's stories about relationships in or out of therapy are likely to manifest repeated patterns or themes that reveal the core conflicts. To assess them, accounts of relationships, called relationship episodes, are excerpted from the dialogue of therapy or of interviews with clients. Each episode is then analytically dissected into three components: (1) the wish (or needs or intention) expressed by the client; (2) the response from others, actual or expected; and (3) the response of self, that is, the client's own thoughts, feelings and actions in the situation. A theme – a CCRT – is distinguished by a repetition of these components (i.e. similar wishes, responses of others and responses of self) across multiple episodes. The availability of reliable measurement of the CCRT has led to a productive line of research on psychodynamic concepts of the relationship (e.g. see reviews by Crits-Christoph, 1998; Luborsky and Crits-Christoph, 1998).

PERSON-CENTRED CONCEPTS OF THE RELATIONSHIP

Whereas psychodynamic theorists may view the transference as a distorted fragment impinging on a distinct real relationship, person-centred theorists have tended to take a holistic, here-and-now perspective (Rogers, 1957; 1980). Yes, people may transfer attitudes from past relationships to present ones, but to consider these as unreal is to deny or derogate the immediacy of the client's actual experience. Even if a client is acting on feelings derived from problematic primary relationships, those feelings are real in the present. Rather than seeking to judge and interpret client experiences, the therapist's job is to understand and accept them. Fully experiencing, acknowledging and stating ('symbolizing') experiences enables them to be considered and revalued in light of current reality (see Greenberg's 1994 commentary on Gelso and Carter, 1994). The value placed on any particular experience is up to the client, not the therapist or the theory. This conceptualization directs attention not to the historical development of the client's problems but instead to the climate or conditions that the therapist provides within the therapy.

Rogers's (1957: 95) six therapist-provided 'necessary and sufficient conditions of therapeutic personality change' have been popularly reduced to three, which may be stated succinctly (my gloss, not Rogers's) as: (1) be yourself; (2) trust the client; and (3) listen. Collectively, they prescribe a quality of openness to experience – the therapist's own experience and the client's. They demand at least tentative trust that the experience will not be overwhelmingly painful, and they underline the importance of creating a trustworthy environment. (The remaining three conditions were that client and therapist be in psychological contact; that the client is in 'a state of incongruence', and hence potentially motivated for therapy; and that the client perceives, to some degree, the presence of the other conditions: Rogers, 1957.) Although the facilitative conditions, or attitudes, can be stated simply, they can be endlessly unpacked. Rogers did it this way:

> The first element [be yourself] could be called genuineness, realness, or congruence. The more the therapist is himself or herself in the relationship, putting up no professional front or personal façade, the greater is the likelihood that the client will change and grow in a constructive manner. This means that the therapist is openly being the feelings and attitudes that are flowing within at the moment. The term 'transparent' catches the flavor of this condition: the therapist makes himself or herself transparent to the client; the client can see right through what the therapist is in the relationship; the client experiences no holding back on the part of the therapist. As for the therapist, what he or she is experiencing is available to awareness, can be lived in the relationship, and can be communicated, if appropriate. Thus, there is a close matching, or congruence, between what is being experienced at the gut level, what is present in awareness, and what is expressed to the client.

> The second attitude of importance in creating a climate for change [trust the client] is acceptance, or caring, or prizing – what I have called 'unconditional positive regard'. When the therapist is experiencing a positive, acceptant attitude toward whatever the client is at that moment, therapeutic movement or change is more likely to occur. The therapist is willing for the client to be whatever immediate feeling is going on – confusion, resentment, fear, anger, courage, love, or pride. Such caring on the part of the therapist is nonpossessive. The therapist prizes the client in a total rather than a conditional way.

> The third facilitative aspect of the relationship [listen] is empathic understanding. This means that the therapist senses accurately the feelings and personal meanings that the client is experiencing and communicates this understanding to the client. When functioning best, the therapist is so much inside the private world of the other that he or she can clarify not only the meanings of which the client is aware but even those just below the level of awareness. This kind of sensitive, active listening is exceedingly rare in our lives. We think we listen, but very rarely do we listen with real understanding, true empathy. Yet listening, of this very special kind, is one of the most potent forces for change that I know. (1980: 115–16)

Easy to say, hard to do. From a practitioner's perspective, being genuine (and distinguishing this from self-serving disclosure), accepting the client (who may hold beliefs or engage in practices contrary to your personal principles), and understanding empathically (when the client tells endless bland stories) can be difficult and taxing. Furthermore, under some circumstances, the conditions can be contradictory. If I disapprove (suicide, child molesters, etc.), do I disclose it? If I'm absorbed by my own problems, how do I empathize? Fortunately, the theory suggests that perfect adherence is not required. Approximations can be helpful, and beneficial effects can be expected to the degree that the conditions are fulfilled.

From the perspective of a therapist or a supervisor, the three conditions may seem distinct and even contradictory, but from the perspective of an observer, they can tend to merge. Although early attempts to measure therapist congruence, unconditional positive regard, and accurate empathy seemed promising, reviewers of the research found fault (Lambert et al., 1978; Mitchell et al., 1977). In my reading, central difficulties lay in distinguishing the three conditions from each other and distinguishing any of them from global positive evaluation (e.g. Rappaport and Chinsky, 1972). Nevertheless, research on these three core conditions has continued to accumulate. In volumes reporting the work of a task force of the Psychotherapy Division of the American Psychological Association on the psychotherapy relationship (an explicitly integrative, empirically based effort: Norcross, 2002; 2011), the 'effective elements of the therapy relationship' have included empathy (Elliott et al., 2011), positive regard and affirmation (Farber and Doolin, 2011) and congruence/genuineness (Kolden et al., 2011).

Some person-centred authors have suggested that fully encountering the client as a person can move the relationship beyond the alliance to permit work at *relational depth* (Mearns and Cooper, 2005; Mearns and Schmid, 2006; Schmid and Mearns, 2006). Work on relational depth suggests that therapy's power to transform proceeds from the therapist's ability 'to engage the client at a more fundamental, existential level,' so that clients 'feel met at the deepest levels at which they experience themselves' (Schmid and Mearns, 2006: 178). Relational depth can develop very quickly; former clients who had had particularly facilitative episodes of therapy said they experienced a powerful sense of connection with their therapists from the first session (McMillan and McLeod, 2006).

PSYCHOMETRIC CONCEPTS OF THE ALLIANCE

In a conceptualization that has proved seminal for psychotherapy process research, Bordin (1979; 1994) characterized the alliance as encompassing (1) the affective bond between client and therapist, (2) agreement on the goals of treatment, and (3) agreement on treatment tasks, or means of achieving those goals. Many subsequent alliance researchers have understood the alliance as multidimensional and have attempted to construct scales to assess the dimensions, for example, using ratings on items like 'I feel friendly towards my therapist' to measure bond or 'I am clear as to what my therapist wants me to do in these sessions' to measure agreement on tasks. Typically, investigators have administered a pool of such items to respondents – clients, therapists or external raters who have observed sessions or listened to recordings – and have then grouped the items into scales using factor analysis or related statistical techniques. The result is typically to confirm that items with similar meaning tend to be rated similarly (so that ratings are intercorrelated) and hence to load on the same factor. Results have offered some support for the multidimensional accounts (i.e. the factors often appear to correspond to conceptual dimensions). The factors tend to be substantially intercorrelated, however (for an example of such a factor analytic study see Agnew-Davies et al., 1998).

Although researchers have concurred in conceiving the alliance as multidimensional, they have not concurred on the boundaries of the alliance construct or on the number or names of the dimensions. Some have used Bordin's (1979; 1994) concepts of bond, agreement on tasks, and agreement on goals (notably Horvath, 1994; Horvath and Greenberg, 1986; 1989). Some have combined or relabelled Bordin's dimensions, for example, combining agreement on tasks and agreement on goals as working strategy consensus (Gaston, 1991) or partnership (Agnew-Davies et al., 1998). And others have added dimensions, such as patient working capacity and therapist understanding and involvement (Gaston, 1991; Marmar et al., 1989); patient resistance (hostile, defensive), patient motivation (acknowledged problems, wanted to overcome them) and therapist intrusiveness (fostered dependency, imposed own values) (Hartley and Strupp, 1983); confident collaboration (Hatcher and Barends, 1996); or openness and client initiative (Agnew-Davies et al., 1998). Each such additional dimension has been defined and measured by a set of self-report items.

The alliance has sustained intense interest from researchers because of its replicated positive correlations with measures of psychotherapy outcome. The finding that clients who have strong alliances with their therapists tend to have better outcomes has been the strongest and most consistent finding in the psychotherapy process–outcome literature (Horvath and Bedi, 2002; Horvath and Luborsky, 1993; Horvath et al., 2011; Leahy, 2008; Martin et al., 2000; Orlinsky et al., 2004). Moreover, there is growing evidence that the often-observed differences in the effectiveness of different therapists may be attributable to their differing ability to form strong alliances (Baldwin et al., 2007; Crits-Christoph et al., 2009; Holmqvist, 2010). The research has not consistently supported the differentiation of the varied dimensions, however, and many researchers have ignored the dimensional scores, using total or aggregate scores meant to assess the overall strength of the alliance.

Thus, there is a disjunction between the multidimensional conceptual structure of the alliance instruments and the global implementation of the measures. That is, the clients and therapists who rate the alliance seem to respond more globally than was envisioned by the measures' creators. And investigators tend to interpret their finding in terms of global alliance.

EVALUATIONS AND ENACTMENTS

The lack of differentiation in applying the alliance dimensions points to a more general problem. Researchers had difficulty distinguishing any of the subtle concepts that theorists have developed to understand the client–therapist relationship. The weak empirical differentiation of Bordin's dimensions or of Rogers's facilitative conditions is the tip of an iceberg. Theorists and clinicians use a far more differentiated repertoire of concepts than researchers measure.

A distinction between evaluation and enactment of the therapeutic relationship (Stiles and Agnew-Davies, 1999) can aid understanding of this research–practice gap. Whereas researchers tend to use terms such as 'alliance' and 'relationship' to refer to evaluations, clinicians consider the client's (changing) feelings towards the therapist as interwoven with a variety of interpersonal activities, and they use 'alliance' and 'relationship' as umbrella terms.

Evaluation involves the private experience of the participants – what they think and feel about each other, about the relationship, and about the process in which they are engaged. Thus, it is ironic that alliance evaluation has proved far more accessible empirically than has alliance enactment.

Enactments of problems and solutions within the therapeutic relationship are far more complex than can be represented adequately on a small number of evaluative (positive–negative) scales. Each alliance involves specific content, specific behaviours, specific people and specific events, and understanding of the particularities requires longitudinal observation. For example, distinguishing between a mirroring transference and an idealizing transference is crucial for self-psychologists, following Kohut (1971; 1977), but doing this requires contextual knowledge of the case. The distinction is unlikely to be captured with the standardized items of alliance inventories.

It is always mathematically possible, of course, to project a multifaceted relationship on to a one-dimensional evaluative scale. That is, participants can always be said to have some degree of positive or negative feeling as part of the real relationship, the transference, the working alliance, or the degree of empathy, congruence, or trust. Moreover, the evaluation is highly salient to participants, researchers and research consumers; the first thing people notice or want to know about a relationship (or anything else) is how good it was. But evaluations alone gloss over what makes relationships interesting and difficult (Wallerstein, 2003). Differentiated

clinical concepts like mirror transference are not so easily scaled. Studying relationships in their contextual complexity might be better investigated in theoretically guided case studies, in which the distinctions made by clinical theories can be compared with observations in individual cases (Stiles, 2003).

Worryingly, many of the relationship components considered as effective by researchers (because they correlate positively with outcomes) have the ring of evaluative rather than descriptive qualities. Thus, they were *achievements* rather than specifiable behaviours. As an illustration, in the Norcross (2002; 2011) volume on the psychotherapy relationship, most of the 'effective elements' (alliance, group cohesion, empathy, goal consensus and collaboration, positive regard, congruence/genuineness, repair of ruptures, management of countertransference, quality of relational interpretations, etc.) were clearly desired results rather than volitional actions (Stiles and Wolfe, 2006). Therapists work to achieve strong alliances, cohesive groups, empathic exchanges, high-quality interpretations and so forth; they do not just decide that they will do these things. The behaviours that contribute to a strong alliance, accurate empathy, high-quality interventions and so forth, differ across cases in response to the circumstances of each case. It is plausible that such achievements predict outcome, but it would be more informative to learn which actual activities predict outcome.

The dominance of one-dimensional evaluative scales may reflect asking people (clients particularly) to tell us things they do not know. It is too easy to assume that because people can report some things that are private and unavailable to others, they can report the thing we want to know, which is also private. They may not know whether they are having a mirroring transference, and they may not distinguish their therapist's genuineness from his or her positive regard. Consequently, they respond on rating scales in terms of something they do know, which is their global evaluation of the relationship.

Obtaining differentiated measurements of the alliance may require observational rather than self-report approaches. In this connection, Luborsky's (1976) early and widely cited *counting signs* method of assessing alliance is of more than historical interest. More recently, Ribeiro et al. (submitted) have developed an observational measure of the relationship based on the degree to which therapists work within (or outside) the client's therapeutic *zone of proximal development*, defined as the space between the client's current therapeutic developmental level and their potential therapeutic developmental level that can be reached in collaboration with the therapist. Observational coding systems have also been developed to provide more differentiated assessments of the alliance in family therapy (Escudero et al., 2010) and child therapy (McLeod and Weisz, 2005).

Of course training therapists to improve relationships also forces therapists (and trainers) to confront and enact the complexities. Strupp and Binder (1984) designed a training programme aimed at addressing negative effects of even mildly antagonistic therapist–client relationships. The subsequent application of this programme was not very successful (Bein et al., 2000). However, Crits-Christoph et al. (2006) have shown that therapists can be trained to improve alliances, with likely positive influences on outcomes (see also Summers and Barber, 2003). Indeed, Safran and Muran (2000; Muran et al., 2010) have designed a successful treatment around improving relationships.

DEVELOPMENTAL CONCEPTS AND THE RUPTURE–REPAIR HYPOTHESIS

Authors from a variety of theoretical approaches have observed that therapeutic relationships fluctuate and change over time (see review by Stiles and Goldsmith, 2010) and have offered developmental views to address some of the potential oversimplifications of static conceptions of the relationship (Horvath, 2003; Horvath et al., 2011). As one example, Gelso and Carter suggested that 'although the alliance is initially in the forefront of the relationship, it subsequently fades into the background, returning to the foreground only when needed' (1994: 301). For example, the alliance may fluctuate in connection with crises in therapy work, such as the therapist's failures to understand or the client's emerging resistances to understanding. The initially strong alliance may weaken towards the middle of therapy and rise again in a more realistic reaction to the therapist towards the ends of treatment. Some years ago, I proposed that therapeutic relationships develop in a pattern related to Erikson's (1963) 'epigenetic' (i.e. systematically emerging) sequence of stages of the life cycle. Psychotherapeutic relationships progress through issues of trust versus mistrust, autonomy versus shame and doubt, initiative versus guilt, industry versus inferiority, identity versus role confusion, intimacy versus isolation, generativity versus stagnation, and integrity versus despair, with each resolution containing the seeds of the next conflict (Stiles, 1979).

Some significant short-term fluctuations in the relationship have been described as *rupture–repair sequences* (Eubanks-Carter et al., 2010; Harper, 1994; Safran and Muran, 1996; 2000; Samstag et al., 2004). Ruptures in the therapeutic alliance may occur when previously hidden negative feelings emerge or when the therapist makes a mistake or fails to act as the client expects or wishes. Clients may then challenge the relationship by confronting the therapist or by withdrawing (Harper, 1994). If the therapist recognizes the challenge, it may prove to be an important opportunity for therapeutic interpersonal learning. Ruptures in the client's relationship with the therapist (one could say, in the transference) may recapitulate the client's relationship difficulties outside therapy. More generally, recognizing, acknowledging and overcoming relational difficulties can provide valuable experiential learning in the here-and-now of the session. Researchers are developing methods for identifying and isolating significant incidents using post-therapy interviews (Fitzpatrick and Chamodraka, 2007), detecting rupture–repair sequences in alliance ratings (Stiles et al., 2004) and in session tapes (Samstag et al., 2000), and describing steps in the task of repairing various types of rupture (Bennett et al., 2006; Harper, 1994; Safran and Muran, 2000). By bringing research attention to processes occurring moment by moment within sessions, this work may succeed in building a bridge across the research–practice gap.

CONCLUSION

Clinical concepts of the relationship are complex, subtle and central to therapeutic practice. Depending on their theoretical orientation, therapists make extensive use of such concepts as the transference and the core facilitative conditions. Researchers using questionnaire and rating-scale methods have had difficulties coming to grips with the subtleties; measures of the relationship or the alliance tend to yield global evaluations rather than differentiated descriptions. There has been a great deal of research on the relationship in psychotherapy, but much of it repeats the broad finding that evaluations of the relationship predict evaluations of treatment outcome. This well-replicated result justifies the widespread conviction that the client–therapist relationship is central to the practice of counselling and psychotherapy but falls short of confirming or elaborating the clinical theories. Work on the development of the relationship, particularly rupture–repair sequences, holds promise of more differentiated and subtle scientific underpinnings.

REFERENCES

Agnew-Davies, R., Stiles, W.B., Hardy, G.E., Barkham, M. and Shapiro, D.A. (1998) Alliance structure assessed by the Agnew Relationship Measure (ARM). *British Journal of Clinical Psychology*, 37: 155–72.

Baldwin, S.A., Wampold, B.E. and Imel, Z.E. (2007) Untangling the alliance–outcome correlation: exploring the relative importance of therapist and patient variability in the alliance. *Journal of Consulting and Clinical Psychology*, 75: 842–52.

Bein, E., Anderson, T., Strupp, H.H., Henry, W.P., Schacht, T.E., Binder, J.L. and Butler, S.F. (2000) The effects of training in time-limited dynamic psychotherapy: changes in therapeutic outcome. *Psychotherapy Research*, 10: 119–31.

Bennett, D., Parry, G. and Ryle, A. (2006) Resolving threats to the therapeutic alliance in cognitive analytic therapy of borderline personality disorder: a task analysis. *Psychology and Psychotherapy: Theory, Research, and Practice*, 79: 395–418.

Beutler, L.E. (1991) Have all won and must all have prizes? Revisiting Luborsky et al.'s verdict. *Journal of Consulting and Clinical Psychology*, 59: 226–32.

Bordin, E.S. (1979) The generalizability of the psychoanalytic concept of working alliance. *Psychotherapy: Theory, Research, and Practice*, 16: 252–60.

Bordin, E.S. (1994) Theory and research on the therapeutic working alliance: new directions. In A.O. Horvath and L.S. Greenberg (eds), *The Working Alliance: Theory, Research and Practice* (pp. 13–37). New York: Wiley.

Brenner, C. (1979) Working alliance, therapeutic alliance, and transference. *Journal of the American Psychoanalytic Association*, 27 (supplement): 137–57.

Breuer, J. and Freud, S. (1957) *Studies on Hysteria*. New York: Basic.

Carroll, L. (1865/1946) *Alice's Adventures in Wonderland*. New York: Random House.

Castonguay, L.G., Constantino, M.J., McAleavey, A.A. and Goldfried, M.R. (2010) The therapeutic alliance in cognitive-behavioral therapy. In J.C. Muran and J.P. Barber (eds), *The Therapeutic Alliance: An Evidence-Based Approach to Practice and Training* (pp. 150–71). New York: Guilford.

Chambless, D.L. (2002) Beware the dodo bird: the dangers of overgeneralization. *Clinical Psychology: Science and Practice*, 9: 13–16.

Crits-Christoph, P. (1998) The psychological interior of psychotherapy. *Psychotherapy Research*, 8: 1–16.

Crits-Christoph, P., Gibbons, M.B.C., Crits-Christoph, K., Narducci, J., Schamberger, M. and Gallop, R. (2006) Can therapists be trained to improve their alliances? A preliminary study of alliance-fostering psychotherapy. *Psychotherapy Research*, 16: 268–81.

Crits-Christoph, P., Gallop, R., Temes, C.M., Woody, G., Ball, S.A., Martino, S. and Carroll, K.M. (2009) The alliance in motivational enhancement therapy and counseling as usual for substance use problems. *Journal of Consulting and Clinical Psychology*, 77: 1125–35.

Elliott, R., Bohart, A.C., Watson, J.C. and Greenberg, L.S. (2011) Empathy. *Psychotherapy*, 48: 43–9.

Erikson, E.H. (1963) *Childhood and Society* (2nd edn). New York: Norton.

Escudero, V., Heatherington, L. and Friedlander, M.L. (2010) Therapeutic alliances and alliance building in family therapy. In J.C. Muran and J.P. Barber (eds), *The Therapeutic Alliance: An Evidence-Based Approach to Practice and Training* (pp. 240–62). New York: Guilford.

Eubanks-Carter, C., Muran, J.C. and Safran, J.D. (2010) Alliance ruptures and resolution. In J.C. Muran and J.P. Barber (eds), *The Therapeutic Alliance: An Evidence-Based Approach to Practice and Training* (pp. 74–94). New York: Guilford.

Farber, B.A. and Doolin, E.M. (2011) Positive regard and affirmation. *Psychotherapy*, 48: 58–64.

Fitzpatrick, M. and Chamodraka, M. (2007) Participant critical events: a multi-perspective method for identifying and isolating significant therapeutic incidents. *Psychotherapy Research*, 17: 622–7.

Freud, S. (1953) Fragments of an analysis of a case of hysteria. In J. Strachey (ed. and trans.), *The Standard Edition of the Complete Psychological Works of Sigmund Freud* (Vol. 7, pp. 3–122) (original work published 1905). London: Hogarth.

Freud, S. (1958) The dynamics of transference. In J. Strachey (ed. and trans.), *The Standard Edition of the Complete Psychological Works of Sigmund Freud* (Vol. 12, pp. 99–108) (original work published 1912). London: Hogarth.

Friedlander, M.L., Escudero, V., Heatherington, L. and Diamond, G.M. (2011) Alliance in couple and family therapy. *Psychotherapy*, 48: 25–33.

Gaston, L. (1991) Reliability and criterion-related validity of the California Psychotherapy Alliance Scales–Patient Version. *Psychological Assessment*, 3: 68–74.

Geller, J.D. and Farber, B.A. (1993) Factors influencing the process of internalization in psychotherapy. *Psychotherapy Research*, 3: 166–80.

Gelso, C.J. and Carter, J.A. (1985) The relationship in counseling and psychotherapy: components, consequences, and theoretical antecedents. *The Counseling Psychologist*, 2: 155–243.

Gelso, C.J. and Carter, J.A. (1994) Components of the psychotherapy relationship: their interaction and unfolding during treatment. *Journal of Counseling Psychology*, 41: 296–306.

Gilbert, P. and Leahy, R.L. (eds) (2007) *The Therapeutic Relationship in the Cognitive Behavioural Psychotherapies*. Hove: Routledge.

Greenberg, L.S. (1994) What is 'real' in the relationship? Comment on Gelso and Carter (1994). *Journal of Counseling Psychology*, 41: 307–9.

Greenson, R.R. (1965) The working alliance and the transference neuroses. *Psychoanalysis Quarterly*, 34: 155–81.

Harper, H. (1994) *Developing the New Paradigm in Psychotherapy Research: Client Confrontation Challenges to the Therapeutic Relationship in a Psychodynamic-Interpersonal Therapy*. Unpublished PhD thesis, University of Sheffield.

Hartley, D.E. and Strupp, H.H. (1983) The therapeutic alliance: its relationship to outcome in brief psychotherapy. In J. Masling (ed.), *Empirical Studies of Psychoanalytic Theories* (Vol. 1, pp. 1–37). Hillsdale, NJ: Erlbaum.

Hatcher, R.L. (2010) Alliance theory and measurement. In J.C. Muran and J.P. Barber (eds), *The Therapeutic Alliance: An Evidence-Based Approach to Practice and Training* (pp. 7–28). New York: Guilford.

Hatcher, R.L. and Barends, A.W. (1996) Patients' view of the alliance in psychotherapy: exploratory factor analysis of three alliance measures. *Journal of Consulting and Clinical Psychology*, 64: 1326–36.

Holmqvist, R. (2010) The therapist's (not the patient's) contribution to the alliance predicts outcome. Paper presented at the Society for Psychotherapy Research Meeting, Asilomar, California, June.

Horvath, A.O. (1994) Empirical validation of Bordin's pantheoretical model of the alliance: the Working Alliance Inventory perspective. In A.O. Horvath and L.S. Greenberg (eds), *The Working Alliance: Theory, Research and Practice* (pp. 109–28). New York: Wiley.

Horvath, A.O. (2003) Alliance at the crossroad: an assessment of what has been achieved and the significant challenges that lie ahead. In T. Anderson (Chair), Advances in Measuring the Therapeutic Alliance. Panel presented at the North American Society for Psychotherapy Research Meeting, Newport, Rhode Island, November.

Horvath, A.O. and Bedi, R.P. (2002) The alliance. In J.C. Norcross (ed.), *Psychotherapy Relationships that Work: Therapist Contributions and Responsiveness to Patient Needs* (pp. 37–69). New York: Oxford University Press.

Horvath, A.O. and Greenberg, L.S. (1986) The development of the Working Alliance Inventory. In L.S. Greenberg and W.M. Pinsof (eds), *The Psychotherapeutic Process: A Research Handbook* (pp. 529–56). New York: Guilford.

Horvath, A.O. and Greenberg, L.S. (1989) Development and validation of the Working Alliance Inventory. *Journal of Counseling Psychology*, 36: 223–33.

Horvath, A.O. and Luborsky, L. (1993) The role of the therapeutic alliance in psychotherapy. *Journal of Consulting and Clinical Psychology*, 61: 561–73.

Horvath, A.O., Symonds, D. and Tapia, L. (2010) Therapeutic alliances in couple psychotherapy. In J.C. Muran and J.P. Barber (eds), *The Therapeutic Alliance: An Evidence-Based Approach to Practice and Training* (pp. 210–39). New York: Guilford.

Horvath, A.O., Del Re, A.C., Flückiger, C. and Symonds, D. (2011) Alliance in individual psychotherapy. *Psychotherapy*, 48: 9–16.

Kohut, M. (1971) *The Analysis of the Self*. New York: International Universities Press.

Kohut, M. (1977) *The Restoration of the Self*. New York: International Universities Press.

Kolden, G.G., Klein, M.H., Wang, C.-C. and Austin, S.B. (2011) Congruence/genuineness. *Psychotherapy*, 48: 65–71.

Krupnick, J.L., Sotsky, S.M., Simmens, S., Moyer, J., Elkin, I., Watkins, J. and Pilkonis, P.A. (1996) The role of the therapeutic alliance in psychotherapy and pharmacotherapy outcome: findings in the National Institute of Mental Health Treatment of Depression Collaborative Research Program. *Journal of Consulting and Clinical Psychology*, 64: 532–9.

Lambert, M.J. and Ogles, B.M. (2004) The efficacy and effectiveness of psychotherapy. In M.J. Lambert (ed.), *Bergin and Garfield's Handbook of Psychotherapy and Behavior Change* (5th edn). New York: Wiley.

Lambert, M.J., DeJulio, S.S. and Stein, D.M. (1978) Therapist interpersonal skills: process, outcome, methodological considerations, and recommendations for future research. *Psychological Bulletin*, 85: 467–89.

Leahy, R.L. (2008) The therapeutic relationship in cognitive behavioural therapy. *Behavioural and Cognitive Psychotherapy*, 36: 769–77.

Luborsky, L. (1976) Helping alliances in psychotherapy: the groundwork for a study of their relationship to its outcome. In J.L. Claghorn (ed.), *Successful Psychotherapy* (pp. 92–116). New York: Brunner/Mazel.

Luborsky, L. (1977) Measuring a pervasive psychic structure in psychotherapy: the core conflictual relationship theme. In N. Freedman and S. Grand (eds), *Communicative Structures and Psychic Structures* (pp. 367–95). New York: Plenum.

Luborsky, L. and Crits-Christoph, P. (1998) *Understanding Transference: The Core-Conflictual Relationship Theme Method* (2nd edn). Washington, DC: APA Books.

Luborsky, L., Singer, B. and Luborsky, E. (1975) Comparative studies of psychotherapies: is it true that 'everybody has won and all must have prizes'? *Archives of General Psychiatry*, 32: 995–1008.

Luborsky, L., Diguer, L., Andrusyna, T., Friedman, S., Tarca, C., Popp, C.A., Ermold, J. and Silberschatz, G. (2004) A method of choosing CCRT scores. *Psychotherapy Research*, 14: 127–34.

Marmar, C.R., Weiss, D.S. and Gaston, L. (1989) Towards the validation of the California Therapeutic Alliance Rating System. *Psychological Assessment*, 1: 46–52.

Martin, D.J., Garske, J.P. and Davis, K.M. (2000) Relation of the therapeutic alliance with outcome and other variables: a meta-analytic review. *Journal of Clinical and Consulting Psychology*, 68: 438–50.

McLeod, B.D. and Weisz, J.R. (2005) The therapy process observational coding system-alliance scale: measure characteristics and prediction of outcome in usual clinical practice. *Journal of Consulting and Clinical Psychology*, 73: 323–33.

McMillan, M. and McLeod, J. (2006) Letting go: the client's experience of relational depth. *Person-Centered and Experiential Psychotherapies*, 5: 278–93.

Mearns, D. and Cooper, M. (2005) *Working at Relational Depth in Counselling and Psychotherapy*. London: Sage.

Mearns, D. and Schmid, P.F. (2006) Being-with and being-counter. Relational depth: the challenge of fully meeting the client. *Person-Centered and Experiential Psychotherapies*, 5: 255–65.

Messer, S.B. and Wolitsky, D.L. (2010) A psychodynamic perspective on the therapeutic alliance. In J.C. Muran and J.P. Barber (eds), *The Therapeutic Alliance: An Evidence-Based Approach to Practice and Training* (pp. 97–122). New York: Guilford.

Mitchell, K.M., Bozarth, J.D. and Krauft, C.C. (1977) A reappraisal of the therapeutic effectiveness of accurate empathy, non-possessive warmth and genuineness. In A.S. Gurman and A.M. Razin (eds), *Effective Psychotherapy: A Handbook of Research* (pp. 482–502). New York: Pergamon.

Muran, J.C. and Barber, J.P. (eds) (2010) *The Therapeutic Alliance: An Evidence-Based Approach to Practice and Training*. New York: Guilford.

Muran, J.C., Safran, J.D. and Eubanks-Carter, C. (2010) Developing therapist abilities to negotiate alliance ruptures. In J.C. Muran and J.P. Barber (eds), *The Therapeutic Alliance: An Evidence-Based Approach to Practice and Training* (pp. 320–40). New York: Guilford.

Norcross, J.C. (ed.) (2002) *Psychotherapy Relationships that Work: Therapist Contributions and Responsiveness to Patient Need*. New York: Oxford University Press.

Norcross, J.C. (ed.) (2011) *Psychotherapy Relationships that Work: Evidence-Based Responsiveness* (2nd edn). New York: Oxford University Press.

Orlinsky, D.E., Geller, J.D., Tarragona, M. and Farber, B.A. (1993) Patients' representations of psychotherapy: a new focus for psychodynamic research. *Journal of Consulting and Clinical Psychology*, 61: 596–610.

Orlinsky, D.E., Rønnestad, M.H. and Willutzki, U. (2004) Fifty years of process–outcome research: continuity and change. In M.J. Lambert (ed.), *Bergin and Garfield's Handbook of Psychotherapy and Behavior Change* (5th edn, pp. 307–90). New York: Wiley.

Rappaport, J. and Chinsky, J. (1972) Accurate empathy: confusion of a construct. *Psychological Bulletin*, 77: 400–4.

Ribeiro, E., Ribeiro, A.P., Gonçalves, M.M., Horvath, A.O. and Stiles, W.B. (submitted). How collaboration in therapy becomes therapeutic: the Therapeutic Collaboration Coding System. Manuscript submitted for publication.

Rogers, C.R. (1957) The necessary and sufficient conditions of therapeutic personality change. *Journal of Consulting Psychology*, 21: 95–103.

Rogers, C.R. (1980) *A Way of Being*. Boston: Houghton Mifflin.

Rosenzweig, S. (1936) Some implicit common factors in diverse methods of psychotherapy. *American Journal of Orthopsychiatry*, 6: 412–15.

Safran, J.D. and Muran, J.C. (1996) The resolution of ruptures in the therapeutic alliance. *Journal of Consulting and Clinical Psychology*, 64: 447–58.

Safran, J.D. and Muran, J.C. (2000) *Negotiating the Therapeutic Alliance: A Relational Treatment Guide*. New York: Guilford.

Samstag, L.W., Safran, J.D. and Muran, J.C. (2000) The Rupture Resolution Scale and coding manual. Unpublished manuscript, Beth Israel Medical Center, New York.

Samstag, L.W., Muran, J.C. and Safran, J.D. (2004) Defining and identifying alliance ruptures. In D.P. Charman (ed.), *Core Processes in Brief Psychodynamic Psychotherapy: Advancing Effective Practice* (pp. 187–214). Hillsdale, NJ: Erlbaum.

Schmid, P.F. and Mearns, D. (2006) Being-with and being-counter: person-centered therapy as an in-depth co-creative process of personalization. *Person-Centered and Experiential Psychotherapies*, 5: 174–90.

Stiles, W.B. (1979) Psychotherapy recapitulates ontogeny: the epigenesis of intensive interpersonal relationships. *Psychotherapy: Theory, Research, and Practice*, 16: 391–404.

Stiles, W.B. (1999) Signs and voices in psychotherapy. *Psychotherapy Research*, 9: 1–21.

Stiles, W.B. (2003) Qualitative research: evaluating the process and the product. In S.P. Llewelyn and P. Kennedy (eds), *Handbook of Clinical Health Psychology* (pp. 477–99). London: Wiley.

Stiles, W.B. and Agnew-Davies, R. (1999) Brief alliances [review of *The Therapeutic Alliance in Brief Psychotherapy* by J.D. Safran and J.C. Muran (eds)]. *Contemporary Psychology: APA Review of Books*, 44: 392–4.

Stiles, W.B. and Goldsmith, J.Z. (2010) The alliance over time. In J.C. Muran and J.P. Barber (eds), *The Therapeutic Alliance: An Evidence-Based Approach to Practice and Training* (pp. 44–62). New York: Guilford.

Stiles, W.B. and Wolfe, B.E. (2006) Relationship factors in treating anxiety disorders. In L.G. Castonguay and L.E. Beutler (eds), *Principles of Therapeutic Change that Work* (pp. 155–65). New York: Oxford University Press.

Stiles, W.B., Shapiro, D.A. and Elliott, R. (1986) Are all psychotherapies equivalent? *American Psychologist*, 41: 165–80.

Stiles, W.B., Glick, M.J., Osatuke, K., Hardy, G.E., Shapiro, D.A., Agnew-Davies, R., Rees, A. and Barkham, M. (2004) Patterns of alliance development and the rupture–repair hypothesis: are productive relationships U-shaped or V-shaped? *Journal of Counseling Psychology*, 51: 81–92.

Strupp, H.H. and Binder, J.L. (1984) *Psychotherapy in a New Key: A Guide to Time-Limited Dynamic Psychotherapy*. New York: Basic.

Summers, R.F. and Barber, J.P. (2003) Therapeutic alliance as a measurable psychotherapy skill. *Academic Psychiatry*, 27: 160–5.

Waddington, L. (2002) The therapy relationship in cognitive therapy: a review. *Behavioural and Cognitive Psychotherapy*, 30: 179–91.

Wallerstein, R.S. (2003) Psychoanalytic therapy research: its coming of age. *Psychoanalytic Inquiry*, 23: 375–404.

Wampold, B.E. (2001) *The Great Psychotherapy Debate: Models, Methods, and Findings*. Mahwah, NJ: Erlbaum.

Zetzel, E.R. (1956) Current concepts of transference. *International Journal of Psychoanalysis*, 37: 369–76.

Zuroff, D.C. and Blatt, S.J. (2006) The therapeutic relationship in brief treatment of depression: contributions to clinical improvement and enhanced adaptive capacities. *Journal of Consulting and Clinical Psychology*, 74: 130–40.

WEBSITES

Society for the Exploration of Psychotherapy Integration: sepiweb.org/

Society for Psychotherapy Research: psychotherapyresearch.org

Generic Skills

FRANCESCA INSKIPP

This chapter assumes that it is possible to identify a set of skills which are generally applicable to counselling and psychotherapy, irrespective of theoretical orientation. However, this is not a consensually agreed or proven assumption. Some of the skills, such as therapist self-disclosure, may be regarded as inconsistent with, for example, psychodynamic practice. In addition, micro-skills tend to be assumed to be present in psychotherapy training or to be imbied in training therapy or analysis, but are not necessarily taught explicitly. Nevertheless, the assumption here is that although the concept of generic skills is contested at least by some therapists, it is just as relevant and useful for all to consider what remains a very influential area of training and practice.

Therapeutic skills imply a craft, but debate continues as to whether therapy is an art or a craft. At its best it is an art created by a unique individual in helping other unique individuals. However, a competent therapist needs to be skilled, especially in interpersonal communication, in building relationships and in self-awareness and self-management.

Counselling skills, like much of counselling theory, were an import from the USA, and initially met with considerable resistance; they were first taught on counsellor courses around 1970, and now are considered an essential part of counsellor education (BACP, 2002). Carl Rogers was the first person to move the training of counsellors and therapists from the realm of the mysterious into the realm of the observable and trainable by making audiotape recordings of sessions. He says in *A Way of Being*:

Then came my transition to a full-time position at Ohio State University, where, with the help of students, I was at last able to scrounge equipment for recording my and my students' interviews. I cannot exaggerate the excitement of our learnings as we clustered about the machine that enabled us to listen to ourselves, playing over and over some puzzling point at which the interview clearly went wrong, or those moments in which the client moved significantly forward. (1980: 138)

Research by Truax and Carkhuff (1967) confirmed the three core qualities previously identified by Rogers (1957) – empathic understanding, unconditional positive regard and congruence – and their accurate communication as essential elements manifested by counsellors who helped their clients change, whatever their theoretical base; this began the development of basic counselling skills to communicate these qualities. Carkhuff (1969) later added four other essential skills: concreteness, self-disclosure, confrontation and immediacy. Ivey (1971) developed the idea of micro-skills, identifying clearly delineated discrete behaviours such as attending, paraphrasing, reflection of feeling and summarizing, teaching them systematically and then integrating them in therapy practice.

Kagan (1975) is the third influence with his interpersonal process recall (IPR) system of training. This is not focused on teaching specific communication skills but helps in the development and monitoring of the skills of internal awareness; the core of IPR is a unique recall process in which an 'inquirer' guides trainees as they review their video- or audio-recorded

Table 3.3.1 *Some typical inquirer leads*

As you recall specific interactions or situations:

What thoughts were going on in your mind?
What emotions were going on for you – any others below the surface?
What did you sense in your body? Where specifically?
How were you breathing?
What did you imagine the client was thinking/feeling about you?
What did you want the client to think/feel about you?
Does the client remind you of anyone?
Did you have any images passing through your mind?
Did you have any fantasies about the outcomes? Or about the client?

sessions with clients. The overall purpose is to encourage practitioners to become more aware of the interaction process, to study aspects of their own interpersonal behaviour and to become more attuned to their own sensations and thoughts in a safe recall situation. In developing this awareness by recall outside the session, they become more aware in the actual session, and can learn to communicate this awareness to develop the therapeutic relationship. It is based on the theory that even beginning practitioners perceive and intuitively understand much more of their communication with the client than might be expected, but often have no way of using this information. See Table 3.3.1.

IPR has not had such an impact on training in Britain, partly because it is time consuming and not easy to incorporate into basic skills courses. However, it has great potential for developing the skills which depend on internal and interpersonal awareness, for example self-disclosure and immediacy. IPR can usefully be incorporated into supervision. Further details of this training are found in Inskipp (1996).

Connor (1994) gives detailed references to the main research on skills training in both the UK and the USA. Most of the work and research on counselling and therapy skills has been with a white middle-class population, and has been undertaken by men; there is some work being done on how this relates to other cultures and, following research on brain differences in the sexes, how women may learn in different ways from men.

The competencies originally developed by the National Council for Vocational Qualifications in Advice, Guidance, Counselling and Psychotherapy (now abandoned) are used as a structure for generic skills in this chapter. Readers may also wish to refer to the Skills for Health approach to skill identification (www.skillsforhealth.org.uk).

KEY GENERIC SKILLS

The key generic skills are:

- Establish contact with clients.
- Ensure a structured therapeutic setting.
- Develop the therapeutic relationship.
- Develop and maintain interaction with clients.
- Evaluate and develop work on self.
- Monitor self within the therapeutic process.

Generic skills include basic communication skills, but also more the complex skills which a therapist needs. Skills can be learnt and practised and used as 'techniques', but the therapeutic use of them with the client depends not only on the communication skill but on the attitude and intention of the therapist – the inside 'energy' which comes from a commitment to understanding the person from his or her frame of reference.

Competent therapy depends not only on the skills therapists use to communicate with their clients, but on how well they are able to be aware of and reflect upon what is going on inside themselves and between themselves and their clients – and what they imagine is going on inside their clients. This in turn depends on awareness of the therapist's own attitudes, beliefs, values, intentions and knowledge. Casement describes this internal supervision as 'a process of self-review in the session' (1985: i). These skills of inside awareness are referred to here as 'inside', 'inner' or 'process' skills and those skills which can be seen and evaluated by an observer are referred to as 'outside' or 'outer' skills.

The 'inside skills' have not normally been taught as skills, but therapists in training have used personal development groups, experiential exercises and individual therapy to develop awareness of themselves and of themselves in interaction. Arguably counsellors and psychotherapists gain from making awareness of inner processes more specific and from finding ways to learn and practise these skills; IPR is especially useful for this.

Macro-skills and Micro-skills

To learn and practise skills it is important to be able to break down a competency such as 'contracting' into smaller units, e.g. negotiating, and further into micro-skills such as listening, paraphrasing, reflecting feelings, etc. It is these specific micro-skills that can be identified, practised, internalized and developed into the practitioner's way of working; therapy is an art but it needs a good craft background for development into a creative artist.

Table 3.3.2   *Inner and outer skills*

Inner	Outer
Observing	Attending
Listening	Greeting
Body scanning for:	Active listening
awareness of body sensations	paraphrasing
emotions	reflecting feelings
thoughts	summarizing
images	Asking questions
Impartial witnessing	Contracting
Discriminating	purpose stating
Reflecting	preference stating
	Clarifying counselling/psychotherapy and therapeutic role
	Technical skills of audio recording and introducing this to clients

Quite crucially, Rogers warns against the mechanical 'reflection of the client's feelings', a caricature of 'false empathy'. By learning and practising micro-skills, therapists can become good at 'portraying' empathy and congruence without necessarily developing the inner understanding and acceptance of the client. In a similar way therapists may become facile in analysing and give ill-judged interpretations. This emphasizes the importance of inner work running alongside outer practice.

ESTABLISH CONTACT WITH CLIENTS, AND ENSURE A STRUCTURED THERAPEUTIC SITUATION

The stages in these processes are:

- making psychological contact
- effecting intake and assessment
- introducing tape recording
- contracting and clarifying therapy
- beginning to build a relationship.

The first meeting with a client requires a wide range of skills, both inner and outer, to accomplish the tasks and monitor the process. Table 3.3.2 lists the necessary skills.

Making Psychological Contact

Rogers's conditions for constructive personality change to occur, have been immensely important in the development of counselling and therapy. However, one of the conditions, that 'two persons are in psychological contact', has often been neglected,

though it has been revived in relation to work on 'pre-therapy' (Mearns, 1994; Prouty et al., 2002). Psychological contact is hard to define; it is different from rapport, being in a relationship, or being empathic, but precedes and underlies them all. It may be seen as the intangible interpersonal process which changes from moment to moment – the 'dance' and exchange of energy between human beings.

Psychological contact between therapist and client depends on the skills, experience, attitudes and emotions that each brings to the situation. Clients present on a continuum from those who appear to make no contact to those who may seem overwhelming, invading the therapist's space. Therapists also vary in their ability to make contact, especially with a new person or possibly with clients who are different from themselves in culture, class, race, gender, age or sexual orientation.

The following skills are relevant to making psychological contact.

Inner skills

Awareness of your experience of initial interpersonal contact   This can be developed by self-reflection:

- What feelings, thoughts and bodily sensations are engendered at first interaction?
- How do these vary when meeting with different individuals?
- Have I any particular 'allergies' to people?
- How different am I in the role of therapist from my everyday self?

Impartial witnessing   This is concerned with the ability to observe inner processes without judging; to be an interested and curious observer of inner self is one of the greatest skills that can be developed. It can enable practitioners to use their thoughts, sensations, images and emotions both to build the therapeutic relationship and to promote purposeful interaction with the client.

Awareness of how others experience you in initial psychological contact

This can be developed by asking colleagues in training or supervision whether they experience you as, for example:

- warm or cool
- immediate or slow in contact
- anxious or relaxed
- engaged or distant
- congruent or incongruent
- strong or vulnerable
- fearful or open
- intrusive or distant.

They can also be asked to describe your interpersonal style and whether they see you differently in the role of therapist.

Very useful skills for exploring psychological contact, especially emotional and subtle contact, are given in Tolan (2003). Major theory and practice are discussed in Wyatt and Sanders (2002). Other examples of exploring 'inside processes', both in dyads and in groups, are given in Crouch (1997). IPR can be used to increase self-awareness of the range and level of feelings experienced in initial contacts with clients.

Outer skills

Skills of greeting appropriately and starting the interaction

These are concerned with the following kinds of issues:

- How do I encourage psychological contact?
- Does the therapist have any physical contact, e.g. shake hands?
- Does the therapist put the client 'at ease'? If so, how?
- What impression, if any, does the therapist want the client to have about him or her?
- How is the scene set which is not a social visit but is sufficiently welcoming?

How are adjustments made to a different culture or age? Some older people prefer to be addressed by their title of 'Mr' or 'Mrs' and dislike calling therapists by their first name. People from some cultures always shake hands at every meeting; some do not touch, or do not touch the opposite gender.

What does the therapist do if clients arrive early on their first visit? How should therapists indicate time is important without diminishing the welcome? How do therapists decide whether to see clients early if they are free and then later discuss punctual starting, or whether to ask them to wait outside until the time of the appointment?

These nuances of first contact are opportunities for skill development. Therapists need to be aware of their own thoughts, emotions and physical reactions. These are the skills of self-management and they enable therapists to make choices in handling beginnings – clearly mediated by the therapist's theoretical orientation.

Where a client's ability to make psychological contact seems impaired, pre-therapy is well suited as a source of inspiration and a departure point for highly concrete client–therapist interaction. The method is basically a way of making contact with the client by reflecting back concrete client behaviour and/or relevant elements from the surrounding reality, for example, 'You've come into my room and you're wondering which chair to sit in.' Although based on working with disturbed clients, these ideas can be adapted to work with clients who seem to make little or no psychological contact.

EXAMPLE

Client: [*comes in, sits down, looks out of the window and says in a very quiet voice*] Dr Evans sent me. [*therapist feels cut off, not seen*]

Therapist: You've come to see me for counselling … You're not sure what to say … I notice you're looking out of the window and I wonder what you are seeing.

Responses like this can help clients be in touch with where they are, psychologically and literally, and can help to draw them into contact. Exploring the skills for making psychological contact is a fruitful field for further work. The concept can be particularly useful in supervision to help the therapist focus on the interaction.

Effecting Intake and Assessment

In an intake interview or a formal assessment, specific skills are needed.

Asking for information

Assessment sessions may involve asking set questions and it is important for the client to know the purpose of these ques tions. If the answers are written down it is necessary to explain what will happen to the records. However, many therapists never make any form of written record *during* a session.

EXAMPLES

Therapist: I'll need to ask you some personal questions to find out if my approach would be helpful and how we might work together – is this OK?

Therapist: I will be writing down your answers on a form. This will have a coded number, not your name, and will be kept in a confidential file.

Purpose stating: what the therapist wants to happen and what must happen
This is an important skill in setting a scene of openness to clients so that they know the therapist's intentions or the purpose in asking questions. It helps the client to experience the therapist as congruent.

EXAMPLES

Therapist: Dr James suggested you came to see me, and it would be useful to spend time now talking, to decide whether therapy would be useful for you.

Therapist: You know I am a student on a counselling course, and after this session I need to check with my tutor whether I will be the most suitable counsellor for you. Have you any questions about that?

Preference stating: what the therapist would like to happen
Here the therapist says what needs to happen but is giving the client some choice.

EXAMPLE

Therapist: I would like to start by you telling me what brings you here today, but you might like to ask some questions first about psychotherapy or about me.

Saying 'no' to a client
There may be clients for whom the therapist, or the therapist's supervisor, decides they cannot offer therapy. These clients may, or may not, need to be referred to somebody

else. The issue here is how to communicate this and at the same time remain empathic, respectful and congruent.

EXAMPLES

Therapist: When we talked last week I said I would have to consult with my supervisor before setting up counselling with you. I'm sorry but it seems that I may not have the relevant experience to be able to offer you the service you need, and I would like to refer you to a more experienced therapist if you are willing.

Client: That makes me feel my problems are too difficult and I'm hopeless.

Therapist: You're feeling worse because I'm suggesting you could be helped better by a more experienced counsellor?

Client: Well you seemed a very understanding person last week when I told you all my troubles, and now I feel you're shutting me out.

The therapist gives the client time to explore feelings using paraphrasing, reflection of feelings, summarizing and restating that the referral is about his or her own inexperience.

Introducing Tape Recording

Many counsellors and psychotherapists find tape recording very hard to do but it is now often a requirement for trainees, and many experienced therapists find it a great asset in developing their work and using recordings in supervision.

Technical skills are needed to set up equipment in order to obtain a good recording. Gaining the client's consent needs practice and confidence and an inner conviction that it is acceptable and useful for the therapist and the client. It needs to be part of the initial contract.

Contracting and clarifying therapy

Contracting is dealt with in more detail elsewhere in this part of the book, so the related skills will only be listed. Negotiating a contract with a client requires particularly the multiple skills of 'active listening' – paraphrasing, reflecting feelings, summarizing – and also 'asking questions', purpose and preference stating, and the ability to be assertive enough and flexible enough. It is an ethical requirement of BACP, for example, that clients understand what they are committing themselves to, that expectations and intentions are clarified. Complaints by clients to BACP are often the result of poorly contracted arrangements.

If therapists are working in an agency or organization they also need these skills to clarify their work contract with the agency. They need skills to be able to communicate effectively with people who refer clients or manage their work, and sometimes skills to educate the agency about counselling or psychotherapy, and about what constitute suitable referrals.

Further useful skills for intake interviews, assessment and diagnosis are given in Joyce and Sills (2001).

Beginning to Build a Relationship

The ability to communicate empathic understanding of the client, to show unconditional respect, and to be perceived as congruent, requires both inner and outer, receptive and responding skills. The client needs to hear that the therapist understands him from his point of view, accepting and not judging him, and is openly present for him and genuine in the role. The 'openness' conveyed by the therapist may vary with the orientation: for example, a psychodynamic role may require more reticence.

The skills which communicate this are as follows.

Inner and outer skills

Attention giving   This is shown non-verbally by alert and relaxed posture, body lean, eye contact and gaze (not staring), facial expressions and head movements.

Accessibility is expressed by being open to being influenced and affected by the client. This is an inner attitude, dependent upon the therapist's degree of awareness of sensitivity and vulnerability. There is a degree of anxiety and threat in all interpersonal relating. Therapists tend (as human beings) to like approval and fear rejection and this can interfere with their non-verbal messages of receptiveness to the client if they are not aware of, or have not worked on, their interpersonal anxieties.

Being completely present for the client is sometimes called 'presence' and signifies that all the effort is at that moment focused on being with the client. It takes considerable energy. Some barriers which deplete that energy are:

- tiredness or being in poor physical condition
- anxieties about self, performance, role or present life
- overlap of the therapist's issues with the client's
- not liking the client; unconditional positive regard does not necessarily mean liking him, but having respect and acceptance for him as a human being as he is at this moment.

Both verbal and non-verbal behaviour can indicate an open willingness to work with the client, a commitment to helping him.

Rogers suggests:

> To be with another in this way means that for the time being, you lay aside your own views and values in order to enter another's world without prejudice. In some sense it means that you lay aside yourself; this can only be done by persons who are secure enough in themselves that they know they will not get lost in what may turn out to be the strange and bizarre world of the other, and that they can comfortably return to their own world when they wish. (1980: 143)

Some therapists find that relaxation or meditation before a session helps them to gather energy and stack their own issues on one side to be with the client. Ethically, therapists need to know when their energy is so depleted that they cannot give this attention, and refrain from therapy until they are re-energized or emotionally reasonably stable.

Feedback from others can help develop skills of good attention giving, and opportunities to view the self on video can enable therapists to check how skilled they are, or what might be improved.

Observing: what do you look for, and why are you looking?   What do you look for?

- physical appearance, posture, facial expressions, dress, grooming, tension, fidgeting, perspiration, blushing, breathing, smell
- tone and volume of voice, pace, expressiveness, speech difficulties, articulation
- awareness of and responsiveness to emotions
- thinking: slow, fast, disjointed, rational
- congruence between words and body language.

And why are you looking? You seek to pick up clues to begin to understand the client from his internal reference point – his view of himself. Looking, listening and resonating give the clues to developing empathy.

'Scanning' your own body during observation can provide clues. People are much more sensitive than they think; they know they may pick up yawning from others, but they also pick up tummy rumbling, emotions and sometimes bodily pains, so by tuning into our own body we can begin to tune in to others. Mostly we need to protect ourselves from too much contact in a crowded world; however, we need to learn to shed this protection when necessary as counsellors or therapists.

Listening and Hearing   Hearing is picking up the sounds; listening is an inner activity which is aligned with attention giving. Listening to *how* the words are said – the tone, intensity, emotional inflexion, pace and volume – and taking all this in, helps the therapist to catch the precise meaning of the speaker, and what this says about him as a person.

The barriers to good listening are the same as for attention giving. Listening takes a lot of energy. As therapists listen they are remembering, choosing and discriminating what to respond to, monitoring their own thoughts, feelings, images and bodily sensations – listening with their bodies as well as their ears.

Other barriers include the ability to block out, neutralize or dampen down painful messages or other emotions such as anger, hurt and even joy or elation. Human beings survive in a crowded, often painful world by filtering what is allowed in, not hearing the starving or the abused because of the helpless feelings they engender. Therapists need to be aware of their defences, their vulnerability to being hurt and sad, or their tendency to dampen down joy or excitement, and stay with what the client may bring, hearing his pain or joy, feeling it but not confusing it with their own.

When clients feel really listened to they are encouraged to talk and reveal themselves. Therapists will often get a lot of information in a first session without asking specific questions, allowing clients to tell their story in their own way rather than through a formal assessment. On the other hand in brief counselling or therapy, it may be important to get relevant information quickly, in which case focused questions may be the most practical way.

Accurate listening can help clients to become more aware of their 'inner flow of experiencing'. Some clients may need to be encouraged to acknowledge, experience and express their thoughts and feelings. Good listening may reduce defensiveness and this may enable clients to focus on their own behaviour rather than on what others do to them. Good listening provides psychological space and support for clients' self-exploration.

Responding or Facilitating Skills   On the whole the skills discussed above are receptive ones, communicated through body language. Therapists also need good responding or facilitating skills, sometimes called the 'active listening skills'. These demonstrate and communicate empathy and acceptance and facilitate exploration.

These skills are sometimes named 'first-level empathy' to distinguish them from 'deeper empathy'. The latter is generally used later in the relationship when the therapist has a deeper understanding of the client's inner world and can sense 'the music behind his words' or what he is not quite expressing, or perhaps emotions or thoughts with which he is not quite in touch. To use advanced empathy at an early stage is risking being inaccurate and may be too challenging for the client.

So, first-level empathy is communicating to the client how he is perceived at this moment. It needs to be as accurate as possible, without adding or subtracting, and also to identify the *level* of feeling being expressed. This is sometimes called 'the interchangeable response', meaning it mirrors exactly what the client is expressing. It can be looked at as two skills: 'paraphrasing' or picking up the meaning, and 'reflecting feelings'. This combined response is a checking, tentative one and needs to be in the form of a question – with an inflection at the end – not a definitive statement:

- *Paraphrasing*: picking up the meaning of the client's words and putting it back to him accurately, using your own words and/or his, in a tentative, almost questioning tone, checking you are understanding what he is conveying.
- *Reflecting feelings*: identifying what the client is feeling, often mainly from the non-verbals – tone of voice, bodily expression, your own bodily resonance.

EXAMPLES

Client:	My manager suggested I came to see you but I'm not sure you can help me, I don't think anybody can.
Therapist:	You're not sure about being here, whether it's possible I or anybody can help you?

Done well, this enables clients to really hear and understand themselves afresh. There is a saying, 'I don't know what I mean until I hear what I say.' Often, hearing themselves will enable clients to explore further and clarify deeper meaning for themselves.

EXAMPLES

Client: I feel upset when I hear you say that, I desperately want help, but I am in such a mess I don't know what anybody could do and I think talking about it might make it worse.

Therapist: You sound as if you really want to get some help, but you're afraid that perhaps talking to me might make you feel worse?

Paraphrasing is not parroting; it means having an extensive vocabulary to reflect accurately the feeling and the meaning, and being able to use words that match the client's vocabulary, not using jargon. Notice how the therapist starts the response with 'you' and a 'feeling' followed by a 'thought'. This focuses on the client and his feelings and thoughts – his internal frame. If the counsellor had replied, 'People are often afraid talking will make things worse', that is an outside frame and does not encourage the client to be in touch with himself.

The level of feeling is important. In our culture we often decrease the level, especially of negative feelings, saying perhaps, 'You are annoyed' when the client is angry. Therapists need to develop an emotional thesaurus of 'feeling' words, especially being able to distinguish levels. For example: raging, furious, angry, irritable, annoyed, fed up.

One student kept a notebook always with her and wrote down any feeling word she came across, so developing a very good range and an ability to reflect accurately. Sometimes getting a reflection wrong enables the client to correct, showing he can express his experience accurately – what Gendlin (1981) calls a 'felt sense'.

Inaccurate reflections can also result from the use of generalized words such as: worried, concerned, upset. These are safe in early stages of interaction but may neutralize the intensity of the feelings, avoiding painful feelings and keeping things safe, when it could be useful for the client to risk connecting with stronger feelings, deepening the process of therapy. However, therapists obviously need to be sensitive to different (e.g. class and cultural) subtleties in vocabulary (Kearney, 1996).

EXAMPLES

Client: I can't go back to school, I might break down in front of the class.

[*not*] *Therapist*: You're too upset to go back to school?

[*but*] *Therapist*: Breaking down in front of the class would be very frightening?

Some feeling words are about the situation rather than the client's feelings. For example, to respond 'You feel rejected' describes the situation or something being done to the client; the actual feeling may be sad, angry, frightened, in which case a more accurate response would be 'You feel hurt when you are rejected.' Again this depends on the therapist being able to discriminate, or help the client discriminate, the finer feelings. This is often done by noticing the non-verbal communication from the client.

Sometimes, if the therapist does not express the feelings as exactly as the client experiences them, the client is able to restate them and both can then get an enhanced understanding. However, if the therapist is inaccurate too frequently, the client can begin to feel misunderstood and lose trust in the therapist.

There are further useful exercises in developing the capacity for empathic attunement in Lister-Ford (2002).

Summarizing This is the use of a combination of the above skills to focus the therapist and client at appropriate points in the interaction. Summarizing can be used:

- as a check that you are together in your understanding
- to pull out the main thoughts and feelings if a client has talked for several minutes or longer
- as a bridge for the client to move on
- to return to something significant
- to structure the interaction if the therapist or the client is getting lost.

Asking questions Asking questions – and the kinds of question asked – depend on intentions. A danger about asking questions is that it may move clients inappropriately from their internal framework to that of the therapist. Questions which stay in the 'active listening role' are listed here with examples, followed by further suggestions for effective questioning.

- *Open questions*. These encourage the client to expand and say more on the subject:
  - I'm not sure I quite understand you – could you say a bit more about your feelings about your brother? (open and checking)
  - Would you like to say how you think therapy could help you? (open)

- *Closed questions.* In these the answer is 'yes' or 'no'. They do not encourage the client to go on talking but may be the best way of collecting facts:

  - Is this your first experience of therapy? (closed)
  - Was your last therapy useful? (closed, as opposed to the following)
  - In what way was your last therapy useful or not helpful? (open)

- *Paraphrase.* It is often helpful to follow a question with a paraphrase or reflection. This helps the client to expand further and does not set the interaction into a question/answer form which may condition the client to wait for the therapist to ask questions.

- *Non-threatening questions.* Some questions are experienced as threatening by clients because they do not know the therapist's purpose, e.g. 'What is your relationship with your father?' The therapist here is using an insight or a theory without taking the client with them in their thinking. To encourage the client to work cooperatively it is ideal to state the clear purpose of questions so that he knows where the questions are coming from – so that the therapist's agenda is explicit to him. To do this therapists need to be clear of their intentions. 'You're saying you have difficulty with male managers and men in authority and I'm wondering what your relationship was like with your father.' In this example the therapist has turned the question into a statement. Making statements instead of asking questions can be a very useful way to remove the possible threat from a question and to encourage trust in a client.

- *'Why' questions.* Questions beginning with 'Why?' are seldom useful and are sometimes threatening or confusing for the client. Questions using 'in what way', 'what' or 'how' are more encouraging for the client to explore himself: for example, *not* 'Why do you think you are depressed?' *but* 'Can you describe the sort of things that seem to bring on your depression?'

All these skills are the beginning blocks for building a relationship and for helping clients start to explore what they want from the therapist and therapy. In the main they are 'supportive' skills. Skills which continue to build the relationship and develop the interaction will be considered next. These skills are challenging, both for the client and the therapist.

DEVELOP AND MAINTAIN INTERACTION WITH CLIENTS, AND DEVELOP THE THERAPEUTIC RELATIONSHIP: MOVING THE CLIENT FORWARD

The skilful weaving together of these two areas provides the ongoing work with the client. The *inner skills* needed for developing both the relationship and the interaction include all the previous skills plus:

- self-awareness of attitudes to challenge
- scanning inner maps or theories
- reflecting and recording.

The *outer skills* needed include all the previous skills plus:

- focusing
- summarizing.

Further areas of development in *moving forward* include:

- concrete examples
- deeper empathy
- challenging
- appropriate self-disclosure
- immediacy.

As mentioned above, the skills discussed so far can be considered as *supportive* – helping clients feel safe enough to begin to explore themselves and their situation. To move on in the relationship and the interaction requires skills which will *challenge* the client to explore further – to gain new perspectives and new frameworks and see the world in a different way. How the client will receive the challenge will depend on the relationship which has been built and how it is maintained and developed; all the supportive skills will still be needed, appropriately interspersed with the challenging ones.

Inner skills

To challenge well requires inner skills of examining your own feelings about challenge. Do you dislike challenging others, are you afraid of getting angry and letting out negative feelings? Or afraid the client might get angry, leave or shut down? You may be afraid to go deeper with the client in case you get out of your depth. Alternatively you may enjoy challenge and not be sensitive enough to a client who fears challenge. Timing and tentative challenge are important. It is probably better on the whole to be somewhat reluctant to challenge rather than to be too eager.

Most of these skills require good inner awareness of the therapist's 'process' and this needs practice and attention to personal development. Clarity is needed on what theories of counselling are being used to develop the interaction. What implicit or explicit theories are guiding the chosen responses? Replaying audiotapes and reflecting on the sessions, especially in supervision, can help identify what values, beliefs, thoughts, feelings, sensations and images are guiding the choices.

Outer skills

Responsible challenging needs well-practised communication skills.

Focusing   If clients are to move forward the therapist may need to help them focus.

Summarizing   As already mentioned, summarizing provides bridges, drawing themes together and keeping track. It can be used in three specific ways:

1   Summarize and ask the client to make a *choice*.
2   Summarize and ask the client for a *contrast*.
3   Summarize and bring out the *main focus* as you see it.

EXAMPLE: CHOICE

Therapist: You're not sure Robert – you're saying your girlfriend is pregnant and is thinking about an abortion which you feel is wrong – whether you should influence her as you don't really want a permanent relationship with her. It seems as if you're confused about what you want to do, what you ought to do and what others expect of you. You'll perhaps need to explore all those, but which of those might it be useful to start with?

EXAMPLE: CONTRAST

Therapist: Robert, you're worried about Gill deciding on an abortion for your child and that, although you're in love with her, you don't think you want a permanent relationship with her. Would it be useful to look at how you would feel if she left you now and disappeared out of your life?

EXAMPLE: MAIN FOCUS

Therapist: Robert, you say Gill is considering an abortion. You feel strongly against it but are not sure how much you should influence her when you don't really want to make a commitment to her. You're also aware of your parents' feelings, but it seems as if your main confusion is about how responsible you feel for Gill, for the baby and for yourself. Would it be useful to talk a bit more about that?

Summarizing is a useful skill, requiring: (1) accurate listening; (2) the ability to sort out relevant thoughts and feelings; and (3) the ability to communicate them clearly. It is also useful at times to ask the client to summarize, perhaps at the beginning or ending of a session, or before a review of the work together. Both summarizing and focusing provide challenge to clients, as they ask them to look more closely at themselves or at what is happening.

Moving forward

Concrete examples   Sometimes it can be useful to ask clients to be more specific about their experiences or their thoughts or feelings.

EXAMPLES

Therapist: You say you feel really angry because you're always being drawn into rows with your mother. Perhaps it would help us both to see how this happens if you could describe in detail the last time this occurred for you.
Therapist: You say you are very frightened of this teacher. Perhaps it would help us both if you could tell me what it is your teacher says to you that frightens you so much.

Communicating deeper empathy   This skill is to pick up 'the music behind the words', thoughts and feelings of the client which are perhaps buried, out of reach or implied and which may come to the therapist as an intuition or a hunch. The skill is to put it into appropriate words when the timing is right.

EXAMPLE: IDENTIFYING A PATTERN OF BEHAVIOUR AND EMOTION

Therapist: It seems Jo, from several things you have said, that you don't like to look ahead and plan; you'd rather let things happen. It's almost as if you want surprises and feel life would be dull if you knew what was coming? Perhaps like wanting a surprise birthday present, even if it's not what you really want. Does that make sense to you?

Client: Yeh, I suppose that's true. I've never thought about it that way, and I suppose I often don't get what I really want because I don't want to think ahead. Surprises can be horrid sometimes.

EXAMPLE: EXPRESSING WHAT IS ONLY IMPLIED

Client: I could wait to hear from her, but I suppose there's nothing wrong in phoning her to see how she's getting on.

Therapist: You seem to be talking about getting in touch with her, but somehow I feel there doesn't seem to be much enthusiasm in your voice.

Client: You're right, I really don't want to see her – I feel so guilty – and if I get in touch with her, I'll be dragged in again.

The response moves the client on to expressing his real feelings.

Challenging
Challenging entails gently confronting clients to change their perspective, see a bigger picture, recognize strengths they are not using, note discrepancies between verbal and non-verbal behaviour, or identify behaviour which is destructive to them or others. Challenging is *an invitation to see things differently*.

EXAMPLES

Therapist: Sue, what I'm hearing from you is that at work you are a very good organizer, you consult and delegate with staff, but you don't seem to use those skills to run the home, and I'm wondering if it could be useful for you to look at that? What do you think?

Therapist: You're saying, Robert, that you can't choose which of these women you want to live with. Could you change this to 'won't choose' and see how that feels?

Therapist: You're telling me how frightened you are of your father, but you're smiling as you say it, and I'm wondering what's going on in your mind, what you're feeling inside?

Therapist: You say you want to explore your difficult relationship with your mother, but I notice you move off on to other members of the family. I imagine it's painful for you, and I wonder what would help us to stay with you and your mother?

In summary, these skills require risking moving in closer to clients, being sensitive to intentions and to timing, and being able to choose appropriate words and tone of voice. If clients get defensive, be flexible. Supportive skills can be used to explore hurt or anger; to encourage self-challenge; to earn the right to challenge by being open to challenge; to be tentative and to build on successes; to be specific; to challenge strengths rather than weaknesses; and to respect the client's values.

Self-disclosure
In some sense therapists cannot help but disclose themselves by all the ways they respond to the client, or even by not responding. By verbal and non-verbal clues the client is construing the meanings, the personality of the therapist, evaluating who and what they are. There are two sorts of therapist self-disclosure: disclosing some experience from the therapist's own life, and disclosing some thoughts or feelings the therapist has about the client or his or her experiences.

The first form of self-disclosure concerns *the therapist's own experience*. When is it helpful, purposefully, to disclose some of your experience? It is usually not helpful in the beginning stages when you are concentrating on staying with the client's experience, and it needs discrimination as to what to disclose and when. The *advantages* of therapist disclosure include:

- It can act as a model for the client to talk more openly about himself or herself.
- It can build the relationship.
- It can shorten the psychological distance between the client and counsellor, produce more intimacy, more trust.

- If the therapist discloses difficulties he or she has overcome – e.g. bereavement, addiction – it can encourage and challenge the client; many self-help groups work on this principle.

The *disadvantages* of therapist disclosure include:

- The client may feel unsafe to see the therapist as less well adjusted.
- It can be too challenging, and the increased intimacy may threaten the client.
- Clients may see themselves or their difficulties as very different from their therapist and therefore are not encouraged to help themselves.
- Self-help groups may work because they provide a 'peer' experience, but the therapist is not a peer.
- Intentional self-disclosure is considered by some therapists to be always poor practice.

As with all challenge, disclosure needs a sufficiently secure relationship. It needs to be used selectively and focused flexibly; it is an art, not a science.

EXAMPLES

Client:	Since my partner died I can't face the day, there doesn't seem any point to anything. I just feel lost all the time and my daughter worries I'm not looking after myself.
Appropriate response:	You sound as if it's hard for you to get through the day. I remember when my partner died I felt as if all the structure to my life had disappeared and it was very hard to make myself do anything.
Inappropriate response:	I know how you feel; when my partner died I was like that, but I got over it and recovery happened in time.

EXAMPLES

Client:	I don't know what it is really. I just feel very low and know I could do better but I can't make the effort. I worked hard at school to get here and I've wanted to be a lawyer for as long as I can remember, and now I'm here I should be feeling happy, but I just feel fed up and depressed.

Appropriate response:	I think when I was at university I was often critical and bored but I think I knew it was what I wanted. It seems, perhaps, it is different for you. Although you say you always wanted to be a lawyer, perhaps now you know more about it you're not sure it's what you want to do?
Inappropriate response:	I can remember my second year and I felt just like that, so I know how badly you must feel. But I managed to stick at it and get my degree and that's got me where I wanted to be.

Inappropriate responses are often just relating the therapist's experience and sometimes sounding rather smug. However similar the situation, each individual will experience it differently and may not want to be classified as similar to you, especially if they perceive you as very different in class, race, age, etc.

The second form of self-disclosure entails *the therapist sharing their own thoughts or feelings* about the client's experience. This can be useful in sharing some transferential patterns or personal thoughts.

EXAMPLES

Therapist:	I noticed I was feeling very sad when you talked about your mother and your easy relationship with her. I wondered, is there, perhaps, some sadness there for you?
Therapist:	As I think about your life, both at home and at work, I'm wondering, perhaps trying to do two full-time jobs would make *me* want to give up one of them.
Therapist:	Nasreen, I'm finding it quite hard to imagine not sharing such an important decision with your husband.

Responses such as these can be a challenge to the client, maybe to enable them to see alternative frames of reference.

Things to remember about self-disclosure are as follows:

- Don't use it too soon in a session.
- Keep the focus on the client.
- Be brief.
- Don't overburden the client with your concerns, and be flexible.

- 'If I were you' usually means 'if you were me'.
- Use only if it is for the good of the client, not for your need to share.
- Recognize your power to influence the client.

Immediacy   Immediacy is one of the most useful skills of counselling and psychotherapy, and probably the most difficult to do well. It is sometimes called 'you–me talk' or 'I messages'. It is about discussing directly and openly with the client what is happening between the therapist and the client, at the moment, or about something that has happened in the recent past. It involves awareness of what is going on inside the therapist and imagining or guessing what is happening in the client and between the therapist and the client.

EXAMPLE

Therapist: Jim, when you said you were afraid to tell me because I would disapprove of you, I admit I felt hurt that you couldn't share it with me. Would it be useful to explore how far you feel you can trust me?

It is quite a difficult thing to say, but it does help clients open up what may be a difficult area for them. It also provides a model of speaking about thoughts and feelings not usually expressed.

Immediacy can also help clients understand how their behaviour may be affecting other people.

EXAMPLE

Therapist: When you say 'that's not the way it ought to be', I feel a bit battered by you, as if you're forcing me to see your point of view, and I wonder if that's how your wife feels, and if that makes it difficult for her to discuss things with you. Do you think that might be so?

Immediacy can sometimes help when the therapeutic relationship seems otherwise to be foundering.

EXAMPLE

Therapist: I felt last week that you went home angry with me, but you didn't express it, and I wondered if I had upset you. Would it be useful to talk about it?

Immediacy is a complex skill involving competence in attending, listening, empathy, self-disclosure and making self-involving statements. It requires the therapist to be assertive, to have the courage to take risks and also, most importantly, to have an awareness of 'process', or of what is happening from moment to moment internally, inside the client and in the 'dance' between therapist and client. Using IPR can be very helpful in developing this skill. Using audio or video recall to explore these processes, and to put into words what *might* have been said, enables the therapist to become more aware and to become competent at using the skill. It is important to develop an 'impartial witness' of feelings and thoughts, not to judge but to acknowledge them and to be able to use them in the way the therapist works with the client. Practice with IPR also helps in identifying transference and counter-transference.

Part of the skill of immediacy is knowing when to use it. It can be useful when:

- A session seems bogged down.
- There is tension in the relationship.
- Trust is an issue.
- There are differences in class, race, sexuality, etc., which need to be explored.
- Dependency or attraction seems to be blocking.
- The therapist is confused by the client.

Used well, immediacy can build or repair a therapeutic relationship, promote a shared working situation, develop congruence, and deepen the interaction. It is also a very useful skill in all human relationships.

All the skills in this chapter require a lot of practice with feedback, for developing both the inner and the outer skills. This leads on to the final section.

MONITOR SELF WITHIN THE THERAPEUTIC PROCESS, AND EVALUATE AND DEVELOP OWN WORK

These competencies need all the previous skills plus the additional *self-management skills* listed here:

- developing a caring acceptance of yourself and an impartial witness of your internal processes
- identifying and using resources to meet learning, emotional, physical and spiritual needs
- ongoing identification and checking of values, beliefs and theories
- planning ongoing training and personal development
- reflecting, recording, presenting and using supervision

- reviewing with clients
- asking for feedback from clients.

The above skills are necessary to develop as a foundation for the supporting and challenging skills. It is the learning and practising of these skills that enables the therapist to translate theory into competent practice with clients. Skills do not make a counsellor or psychotherapist, but an unskilled therapist may harm rather than help clients. A useful summary of the concept of counselling skills as embedded within the work of allied professionals can be found in McLeod (2007).

REFERENCES

BACP (2002) *Accreditation of Training Courses* (4th edn). Rugby: BACP.

Carkhuff, R.R. (1969) *Helping and Human Relations I: Selection and Training*. New York: Holt, Rinehart and Winston.

Casement, P. (1985) *On Learning from the Patient*. London: Routledge.

Connor, M. (1994) *Training the Counsellor: An Integrative Model*. London and New York: Routledge.

Crouch, A. (1997) *Inside Counselling*. London: Sage.

Gendlin, E. (1981) *Focusing*. New York: Bantam.

Inskipp, F. (1996) *Skills Training for Counselling*. London: Cassell.

Ivey, A.E. (1971) *Microcounseling: Innovations in Interviewing Training*. Springfield: Thomas.

Joyce, P. and Sills, C. (2001) *Skills in Gestalt Counselling and Psychotherapy*. London: Sage.

Kagan, N. (1975) *Influencing Human Interaction*. Washington, DC: American Personnel and Guidance Association.

Kearney, A. (1996) *Counselling, Class and Politics: Undeclared Influences in Therapy*. Manchester: PCCS.

Lister-Ford, C. (2002) *Skills in Transactional Analysis Counselling and Psychotherapy*. London: Sage.

McLeod, J. (2007) *Counselling Skill*. Maidenhead: Open University Press.

Mearns, D. (1994) *Developing Person-Centred Counselling*. London: Sage.

Prouty, G., Van Werde, D. and Portner, M. (2002) *Pre-Therapy: Reaching Contact-Impaired Clients*. Ross-on-Wye: PCCS.

Rogers, C.R. (1957) The necessary and sufficient conditions of therapeutic personality change. *Journal of Consulting Psychology*, 21: 95–103.

Rogers, C.R. (1980) *A Way of Being*. Boston: Houghton Mifflin.

Tolan, J. (2003) *Skills in Person-Centred Counselling and Psychotherapy*. London: Sage.

Truax, C.B. and Carkhuff, R.R. (1967) *Toward Effective Counseling and Psychotherapy: Training and Practice*. Chicago: Aldine.

Wyatt, G. and Sanders, P. (eds) (2002) *Rogers' Therapeutic Conditions: Evolution, Theory and Practice*. Ross-on-Wye: PCCS.

Specific Strategies and Techniques

GORDON JINKS

This chapter is intended to give the reader an awareness of the range of intervention strategies available to a counsellor or therapist operating in an integrative or eclectic way. The relative merits of this as against operating from a single theoretical framework will not be discussed here except to make the pragmatic point that the use of a range of techniques from different theoretical traditions appears from the research to be very common. This is not intended to be a comprehensive manual for the use of the strategies outlined, and therapists must ensure that they have the necessary underpinning to use whatever techniques they employ and work safely with material that might be raised for the client. Counselling and therapy are contracted activities which involve a working alliance between therapist and client. The values underpinning the alliance – described as client empowerment, respect and genuineness by Egan (2009) – imply that the client has a right to take part in decisions about how they are to be helped: to set their own goals, to understand the techniques which might be used to help them, and to exercise choice about what techniques are used. There is growing evidence that techniques and approaches that make sense to clients in terms of how they understand themselves, their issues and the process of change are more likely to lead to successful outcomes (Duncan et al., 2009). It is therefore important that therapists develop the practice of listening carefully to clients' existing conceptual frameworks and become skilled at discussing possible helping strategies with clients, empowering them to take an active part in therapeutic planning. We must also be aware of the

need to use techniques genuinely at the service of the client, not in order to be seen to be doing something as a substitute for the hard work of sustained listening and empathy, or because we have preference for a particular technique. The chapter is sub-divided to cover techniques which primarily address behaviours, affects or feelings, imagery, cognitions, and interpersonal factors.

BEHAVIOURS

A wide range of techniques have been developed in behaviour therapy (see for example Wolpe, 1990), which can be adapted for eclectic or integrative therapy.

Modelling, Rehearsal, Reinforcement

The sequence of modelling, rehearsal and reinforcement is a powerful one for helping clients to develop desired new behaviours, and is frequently used in developing assertiveness or social skills, or in confronting feared situations. Modelling is based on the principles of social learning theory (Bandura, 1977): that much learning is derived from observing role models; that individuals tend to select models whom they respect, trust and perceive as competent; and that the most useful models are those whose level of performance is seen as achievable and not so skilled as to seem out of reach. Rehearsal and reinforcement are based on operant conditioning: that behaviour is most likely to be repeated if it is positively reinforced.

The process begins by the client and therapist discussing the behaviour the client would like to achieve, and trying to develop a clear picture of what it might look like. Examples of behaviours which could be addressed in this way are dealing more assertively with colleagues at work, sharing feelings more openly, public speaking, and managing conflict or aggression. The more specific the client can be about what they want to be able to do, and to what standard, the better. (An important check here is to explore any possible negative consequences of a change that the client is considering, and this may need to be returned to when the client is ready to begin putting changes into practice.) The client then observes a model of the desired behaviour. They may have identified an external role model, who behaves as they would like to in a given situation, and can be observed. Alternatively, the modelling may fall to the therapist, who can role-play a situation demonstrating the behaviour the client wishes to be able to achieve. The client should be asked to give feedback on the extent to which the therapist's performance reflects what they see as desirable and achievable, and the role-play modified until the client is satisfied with what they are seeing. The client may also develop some useful insight during this process by taking the other role in the role-play.

The client then rehearses in role-play with the therapist (or some other situation if appropriate), until they are able to achieve a performance that they are happy with and feel they can reproduce in the real situation. After each rehearsal the client should be encouraged to recognize what they were happy with about their performance, rather than focusing on shortcomings, and receive congruent praise from the therapist. In the next rehearsal the client will try to repeat what has gone well, but also develop the behaviour in other aspects – a technique known as *shaping* in the terminology of behaviour therapy. For example, in rehearsing assertive behaviour the client may be able to act assertively up to a certain point, at which something said by the other causes them to 'crumple'. It will be most useful if the client can see this as a success *up to* that point, rather than a failure *at* that point. They can subsequently try to repeat the success, but add something new to deal with the response that caused the crumple. The success of this process is influenced by the atmosphere in which it is undertaken, so the therapist's sensitivity to the needs and responses of individual clients is likely to be crucial. While it can be presented as a series of steps in a technical manner, the therapeutic benefit will be greater if the client is really engaged in the process,

and maybe even has a bit of fun, but also sees it as sufficiently realistic to be a meaningful rehearsal for the real situation. This requires the therapist to continue to relate to the client with empathy during the process, rather than adopting a detached didactic position. As ever, achieving a balance between supporting the client and challenging them to stretch themselves is an important part of what the therapist should be aiming for.

Helping the client to implement the new behaviour in the real situation benefits from careful planning. Important considerations will be the sequencing of where and when this is to be attempted, how it can be positively reinforced, and contingency planning for what might go wrong. Some will benefit from fairly elaborate timetables with target dates and reward schemes, while others may prefer a looser, more evolutionary approach, with a mechanism for monitoring of progress. The therapist will often be a useful part of the monitoring process, particularly in the early stages, but it is important that the client develops self-monitoring strategies, perhaps involving significant others, if changes are to be sustained. Ongoing reinforcement for the new behaviour can be explored with the client, and *social reinforcers* identified – ways in which the new behaviour will be rewarded by the client's social circumstances and environment. If the client is more consciously able to recognize the benefits of the changes they are making, the new behaviours are more likely to be sustained.

Desensitization

Desensitization is a structured technique designed to help individuals come to terms with anxiety-provoking stimuli in a gradual and stepwise way, using relaxation techniques as a counter-measure against the anxiety. The client must first become practised in a relaxation technique that is effective for them (see later in this chapter); they then use this prior to exposure to their feared stimulus, initially in a very mild form, then gradually increasing in strength as they become desensitized to its effect. The client can determine a suitable pace for himself or herself and advance in steps of a manageable size. The intention is that at each step of the process the strength of the anxiety-provoking stimulus will be sufficient to generate a noticeable anxious response, but not sufficient to disrupt the relaxation previously induced. The client can then experience feeling the anxiety, but being able to control it, and feeling it subside with time. The therapist's role is to explain the technique, structure the process, provide support and encouragement during sessions, and help to monitor and evaluate progress. Pacing of this process is important: the client needs to see each step as manageable and experience success, but each step also needs to be challenging enough so that meaningful progress is seen to be made. Ongoing evaluation may lead to some steps being condensed together, or other steps being inserted as a programme unfolds. If a given step does turn out to be too much, a return to the previous level and the insertion of one or two intermediate steps is called for. The client usually benefits from feeling actively involved in designing and maintaining the programme. So, for example, a client with a powerful anxiety reaction to rats was helped to draw up a programme of increasingly powerful stimuli, beginning with simple line drawings and progressing to black-and-white pictures, colour pictures, and then video. The client took control of the process, uncovering pictures when she felt ready, and using a remote control with video images. Each step was repeated by the client between sessions to reinforce success. The sessions culminated with some visits to come into contact with and handle live rats, and the client was very surprised with what she was ultimately able to achieve by taking gradual steps. A useful principle in desensitization programmes is to try to help clients reach a level which is a little beyond what they will normally have to cope with to allow room for some 'slippage' after the programme is finished. The process of dealing with difficulties in a stepwise fashion underlies a number of the techniques which follow.

Exposure

Exposure techniques rely on the fact that if one is exposed to a feared stimulus, and is able to stay with it rather than retreat, then in time the level of anxiety will inevitably decline. On a physical level this occurs because the body will not sustain the same level of stimulation in the face of an ongoing threat as is generated when the threat first appears; while on a psychological level, time spent in the presence of a feared stimulus which does not result in harm leads the individual to reassess the threat posed by the stimulus. The reduction in anxiety serves as a positive reinforcement for facing the fear. A rather extreme way of using these in-built processes is known as *flooding* and involves immersing oneself in the worst feared situation until the anxiety declines to a manageable level. While this has considerable risks as a therapeutic procedure, some clients have been known to apply this technique to themselves: 'I'm just going to get in there and face it, and if it doesn't kill me then I'll have beaten it.' However a more cautious approach or *graded exposure* is usually preferable. The client can be asked

to list feared or difficult situations, covering a range from the relatively mild to the most severe. These would be rated for difficulty, and ordered with the least difficult first. The client would be helped to develop strategies for confronting and coping with each situation in turn, including ways of managing negative emotions, such as relaxation or scripted messages to repeat to themselves. The technique of stepwise exposure to difficult situations can be applied to the level of exposure as well as to the difficulty level of the situation. Thus a given situation can be confronted in fantasy (the client imagines themselves in the situation, perhaps as an observer first, then a participant); in rehearsal or role-play; and then *in vivo* (real life). This might be used, for example, with a client who has to attend a difficult meeting or interview.

Exposure *in vivo* is often a crucial step in any programme of assisting a client to change their behaviour, as it represents the move from talking about or imagining change to actually doing it. A programme of exposure *in vivo* may be developed as homework for a client, but it is also worth considering 'therapist-assisted exposure' – being present with the client while they confront a situation – where this is practical within the established contract/boundaries. The counsellor/therapist's skills are useful in supporting and challenging the client while they take a step forward; they can assist the client in monitoring anxiety (perhaps using rating scales) and can prompt the client to employ prepared coping mechanisms. Understanding of the client is likely to be deepened and the working alliance strengthened by such activity.

Response Prevention

Response prevention is a technique which has been developed primarily for use with sufferers from obsessive compulsive states and is used in combination with various types of exposure. The technique relates to the situation where an individual feels compelled to act in a certain way in response to a given stimulus; a typical example might be someone who feels compelled to wash their hands after touching a door handle. Response prevention involves delaying that response for increasing periods to help the client gain control of the behaviour. So initially the client might wait for a minute before going to wash their hands, then two minutes, then five minutes, 10 and so on – using relaxation techniques to learn to control the anxiety in the intervening period of time. The key here is that the client is not initially denying themselves the compulsive response, but is learning to control it rather than be controlled by it. At some point it becomes unnecessary to carry out the compulsive behaviour at all. Some clients are able to adapt this technique for use with a variety of apparently compulsive behaviours such as smoking, spending, eating, self-harm, seeking reassurance or making self-deprecating remarks. Many clients also report that the period of delay tends to lessen the severity of the compulsive behaviour when it is carried out.

Homework

Various ways in which homework can be incorporated into the therapeutic process have been alluded to above. The norm for counselling and psychotherapy in the UK in many contexts seems to be moving in the direction of a relatively small number of sessions at weekly intervals, and if real change is to be achieved and sustained under such a contract it seems sensible to think carefully about the part that homework might play. At the most open-ended this might involve asking the client, 'What could you be doing between now and the next time we meet which would consolidate or develop what we've been doing today?' Many approaches would allow or even encourage the therapist to be more directive in the setting of homework tasks, but developing homework tasks in collaboration with the client will give them more ownership of the process and is desirable. Homework can have a number of different aims. Often it will be about facing a difficult situation, trying a new behaviour, or putting into practice something which has been rehearsed or prepared in a session – in a sense tasks which are part of the outcome of the therapeutic journey. However, homework might also be part of the process, and could involve reflecting on a particular aspect of one's situation, continuing to work on a list of ideas or the detail of a plan, getting feedback from others, or gathering resources. It also provides the opportunity for significant others in the client's life to be involved in the helping process by being engaged for support, reinforcement or feedback.

The therapist needs to be sensitive to the client's motivation. If a client seems reluctant to undertake a particular activity it may be useful to revisit the goal for that activity. If the client feels that this goal is worth achieving then other ways can be examined for achieving it, and hopefully a different homework activity agreed on. For example, a client was working on dissatisfaction with her social life, and had become aware of how she tended to discourage new people she met in social situations, closing down opportunities to get involved in conversation. Discussing homework, she somewhat reluctantly said that she thought she was 'going to

Table 3.4.1 *Examples of homework*

Making or expanding lists: for example, anxiety-provoking situations, desired achievements, strategies
Practising steps of desensitization or graded exposure programmes
Relaxation techniques
Diary keeping
Bibliotherapy
Classes – for example, assertiveness
Dream recall – maintaining a dream diary
Practising specific behaviours in specific situations
Writing – creative or autobiographical

have to try' to have a conversation with someone new in the next week. Previous experience of this client suggested a tendency to set herself up for failure, so it seemed appropriate to reflect on the reluctance before asking what having this conversation would achieve. It became clear that the client wanted to take the risk of being rejected, and stay with it, so other ways of achieving this which she might be more willing to try, and more likely to succeed with, were explored. The homework task settled on was visiting an acquaintance unexpectedly, and a successful conversation with someone new happened a few weeks later without formal planning. See Table 3.4.1 for a summary of examples of homework tasks.

Diary Keeping

From a behavioural standpoint, keeping a diary can be useful in exploring relationships between stimuli, behaviours and reinforcement. Sometimes patterns become apparent which might not otherwise have been so clear: for example, periods of drinking tend to follow disagreements at work, or angry outbursts are being reinforced by the allowances made by others afterwards. If a particular behaviour is to be focused on, an a–b–c (antecedent–behaviour–consequence) format can be used in the diary, whereby each incidence of the behaviour is recorded in the form of a description of what happened before it occurred, the details of the behaviour itself, and the events that followed. The client and therapist can then discuss this record and perhaps clarify patterns. Links between behaviour and other aspects of experience such as thoughts, feelings and perceptions may also become clearer as a result of diary keeping. Table 3.4.2 shows an example of a structured format for diary keeping which can be varied to suit the individual needs of the client. Once the client is engaged on a change programme, a diary can be a useful tool for monitoring progress,

Table 3.4.2   *Example of a diary format*

Day/date	Time	Significant event (*What happened?*)	Antecedents (*What had been happening before?*)	Thoughts (*What were you aware of thinking?*)	Consequences (*including feelings and behaviour*)

and can serve as both stimulus and reinforcement in itself by highlighting target dates, and being a place where success is recorded. Some clients find it useful to develop ground rules about how they will use the diary, perhaps to ensure that it does not solely become a place for complaining about others or criticizing oneself.

A diary can also be valuable as a tool for reflection, and clients may wish to do this in a structured way. A simple structure for reflecting on key events is: *what?* (description and exploration of the event); *so what?* (implications, new understanding: what have I learnt?); *now what?* (goals and actions: what am I going to do as a result?). Clients may also be able to recognize and own their feelings more effectively when they have the activity of writing about them to focus on, and those who have difficulty expressing their feelings in conversation may be able to do so on paper. Some may also enjoy using diaries not just for writing, but to include drawings, pictures, cuttings and poetry, if given permission to do so. The currently expanding field of 'therapeutic writing' (see for example Bolton et al., 2004) is worth exploring for the benefits it can offer clients.

Relaxation

There is now a wide range of resources available to help an individual learn the skills of relaxation, including self-help books, tapes, videos, alternative therapies and classes, so regular relaxation may not be the most cost-effective way a therapist and client can use their valuable time together. The therapist's role may rather be to help clients clarify their needs, and choose from the available resources. However, a counsellor or psychotherapist may still need a repertoire of relaxation techniques to deal with anxiety 'on the spot' if it becomes acute within a session, or to teach clients to use for themselves. A repertoire of techniques is important because clients vary greatly in their responses to the techniques available, and each individual may need to try several before finding one which suits them. Relaxation techniques are most useful when developed as a habit carried out every day. The habit tends to

diminish one's general level of stress or anxiety, and one also becomes skilled at inducing relaxation, which can then be done in time of need.

Relaxation involves the interplay of physical and psychological factors and the feedback loops which exist between the human body and psyche. It is difficult for the mind to remain tense when the body is relaxed, and vice versa, so relaxation techniques can focus on either physical or psychological relaxation. Physical techniques most commonly employ muscle or breathing control. The tensing and relaxing of various muscle groups in turn, working through the whole body, or just face and neck, helps the client to bring into clear awareness the differences in sensation between muscle tension and relaxation, and learn to control this for themselves. The control of breathing makes use of the powerful links that exist between breathing and state of arousal. A state of relaxation is related to a slower and deeper pattern of breathing and to the use of the abdominal and diaphragm muscles to draw in breath, rather than the chest muscles. If one can learn to adopt such a breathing pattern by conscious control it becomes very difficult to sustain a state of psychological tension.

Psychological techniques usually involve giving the mind a task to perform which is absorbing yet relaxing. Guided imagery is a common example: the client is asked to adopt a relaxed posture and close their eyes if it is comfortable to do so, before being guided in imagining a relaxing scenario or series of experiences. Care needs to be taken in constructing these experiences, first to avoid any imagery which might be distressing to a particular individual, but also in the use of language and what is specified as against what is left to the client's imagination. A general principle is to avoid specifying anything which will jar with what the client has already imagined for themselves, and to use different channels of experience as a means of elaborating an experience rather than specific detail. So, for example, if a client is instructed, 'Imagine yourself lying on a warm sandy beach', a fairly detailed image is likely to occur quite quickly for most clients. If the person guiding the relaxation then starts to specify details such as the texture of the sand, the colour of the sky, or how crowded the beach is, which are not what the client had imagined, this is unlikely to be experienced as relaxing. More useful would be instructions such as 'Notice the texture of the sand … and the colour of the sky … Focus on the sounds you can hear.' Some clients like to have tapes of guided imagery in a voice they are familiar with to assist them in practising at home.

Other psychological relaxation techniques which can be suggested to clients include immersing themselves in favourite pieces of music, and the technique of 'noticing'. Here, one focuses one's attention on a specific object, and spends a period of time attending to the object in great detail, trying to take in as much as possible about its shape, colour, texture and detail. It can be a pleasant surprise how much there is to be seen even in apparently simple objects. This technique can also be practised on a walk, where trying to notice as much detail as possible about one's environment is often experienced, paradoxically, as relaxing.

Once an individual client has learned to achieve a state of relaxation, classical conditioning can be used to help them to access that state in times of stress, by establishing a link with a key word, image or physical sensation they can bring about unobtrusively. The key word, image or sensation might be part of the relaxation technique which the client finds effective, or can be introduced into it when the client has become practised. So, for example, the word 'warm' repeated inwardly, an image of a soft blanket, or gentle pressure on the back of one's hand might be used to help a client trigger relaxation more quickly than by going through the full process they have learned.

AFFECTS OR FEELINGS

Levels of Empathy

In terms of the activity required of the therapist, empathy can be described as having four dimensions: *perception* (what the therapist hears or sees from the client), *affect* (what the therapist feels when listening to the client), *cognition* (what the therapist understands and imagines about the client's experience) and *communication*. The therapist communicates empathy both verbally and non-verbally, and this communication can selectively include each of the other three dimensions – feeding back what the therapist has heard or seen, checking the validity of understanding or imagining, and sharing the therapist's emotional response.

Levels of empathy can be defined in terms of the depth of understanding achieved and communicated

(Carkhuff, 1969; Egan, 2009). Basic or primary empathy involves understanding and communicating what has been expressed by the client directly, and is generally communicated by relatively simple empathic responses such as paraphrasing, summarizing, and reflecting feeling. Advanced empathy involves awareness of the client at a deeper level – that which has only partly been expressed or alluded to. This involves a much closer attention not just to what is said, but to how it is said, and to the therapist's own affective responses. There is more scope for inaccuracy here: the therapist may have a hunch about what is going on for the client, but should also have some awareness of the origins of the hunch, and should share it with the client only when basic empathy has been established. Advanced empathy may be expressed by interventions such as: 'I notice some tension in your face when you say … and I wonder if that might mean …', or: 'As I was listening to you I noticed that I began to feel … and I was wondering if any of that was around for you.' Some practitioners focus particularly on the client's idiosyncratic metaphors and imagery, trying to develop understanding of the complexity that is conveyed, while others (e.g. Mahrer, 1996) attempt to work wholly within the client's affective experience by closing their eyes and speaking 'with' the client: 'I'm feeling heavy, sad … .' Advanced empathy may communicate understanding of aspects of the client's experience that the client was not fully aware of, and so should be used tentatively and be seen as opening up an area for exploration if the client wishes.

The consideration of a level of empathy relating to cultural understanding seems a useful addition to the concept. Cultural empathy is about striving for understanding of the interactions between the client, the client's culture (including experiences, values and beliefs), the therapist and the therapist's culture, and recognizing that communication between therapist and client can be influenced by any of these factors. Expressing and checking one's understanding of these interactions, and inviting the client to do the same, will be useful interventions in building a strong empathic bond.

Cathartic Work

Cathartic work can be very challenging for the therapist, because it involves the client making contact with and expressing their feelings, often feelings which are painful to face or difficult to contain. All of us at times will experience reluctance towards opening the 'can of worms' which we fear we may struggle to deal with. It is equally possible, having got over this reluctance, to fall into a way of thinking that sees counselling and psychotherapy as being all about catharsis, and develop the habit of making cathartic interventions when this is not what the client has come for or wants, but rather what the therapist feels they need. Therapists need to walk a fine line here: neither discouraging clients from making contact with difficult feelings (possibly colluding in efforts to deny them), nor pulling down clients' carefully constructed defences without their permission. Clients tend to know when they are ready and able to get in touch with deeper emotions, and signal this to the therapist in some way (sometimes non-verbally, perhaps through moist eyes or clenched fists). There needs to be agreement to undertake cathartic work and clients should have a clear idea of what they are hoping to achieve. However, release of powerful emotion can occur unexpectedly, and it may sometimes be appropriate to check quickly whether the client wishes to go on, rather than to lose the moment through contracting and goal-setting procedures.

In the least structured way of approaching cathartic work, the therapist concentrates carefully on accurate empathic responses, both basic and advanced, and this will almost inevitably lead a willing client into a deeper contact with their emotions. Empathic responses in cathartic work are most effective when the work is done in the present tense and the focus is on what the client is experiencing in the here-and-now (e.g. 'You are looking very sad as you talk about your brother'). Although this may involve reliving or re-experiencing past traumas or painful memories, the therapist will communicate empathy more effectively by responding to what the client is feeling as they re-experience, rather than focusing on what they were feeling in the past. Careful pacing, appropriate use of silence, and attention to non-verbal communication will help the client to actually feel and experience, rather than talk *about* their feelings. The therapist should not be afraid of silence while the client cries or experiences their anger. Staying in touch with the client's and one's own responses, being open about sharing these, and providing a safe holding environment where the client can feel able to discharge emotion, are the essential skills in managing this process, rather than needing to be completely in control of the course of the session. Some thought needs to be given to how the boundaries of the therapeutic hour will be managed in relation to cathartic work, and whether any flexibility is to be allowed. In planned cathartic work it may be advisable to allow for a specific session to be longer (e.g. 90 minutes). Near the end of a cathartic session it is useful to ask the client what they would like to do in order to prepare themselves to leave. It will often be helpful to shift into a more cognitive processing

of what has happened, asking the client what they have discovered or learned during the session. Some clients also find brief visualization exercises helpful, for example visualizing themselves closing a book and putting it away, or symbolically packing up the contents of the session into a suitable container until they decide to look at them again.

More structured approaches to cathartic work (for example Heron, 1990; Mahrer, 1996) tend to be tailored to the type of material being worked with. Single traumatic events can be approached by retelling at different levels. The client begins with a literal description of the event, so that both parties can be clear about what happened. This is followed by a first-person present-tense account – as though it were happening now, with greater attention to the emotional content, in particular the feelings which arise for the client during the retelling. The therapist should attend carefully to the client's non-verbal communication, and listen for slips of the tongue, brief asides and throwaway comments, blocks and pauses, and elements which the client appears to skate over. Sharing what has been noticed with the client and inviting them to respond will often lead to a deeper examination of a more difficult aspect of the client's feelings.

If an event cannot be clearly recalled, the client can be invited to describe what they imagine might have happened, and work with this in a similar way. A number of cautions are important here. The client is being helped to process their present feelings about what might have happened in the past, not to uncover what actually did happen. If the client's goal is to determine what actually did happen, then asking them to imagine what might have happened is probably inappropriate, and certainly unreliable. Such cathartic work on past events will at times lead to the recovery of memory, sometimes in the form of dramatic and sudden flashbacks which can be very distressing for clients. Clients should enter this sort of work from a position of informed consent, aware of the possible consequences, and it is important to consider strategies for dealing with flashback experiences if they occur – in particular being clear about who the client can turn to for support between sessions. Clients and therapists need to be aware that the validity of such recovered memories is a matter of dispute within the legal system, but the prime concern of the therapist remains the welfare of the client. This may necessitate processing such recovered memories, whether or not they can be considered legally valid, though clearly there is a need to be very cautious in avoiding implanting suggestions.

In working with sequences of events, or recurring patterns in the client's life, catharsis can be facilitated by encouraging the client to move from generalizations towards specific and detailed descriptions of examples. They can be asked to pick an event that seems particularly significant, a typical example, perhaps the oldest, most recent, or first example that comes to mind, and explore it in more depth as described above. On the other hand, some clients find themselves getting lost in the detail of specific events, and catharsis may only occur when the therapist helps them to become aware of themes and recurring patterns. When issues of loss are involved, objects or photographs which help the client to connect with the loss can be a useful focus for cathartic work. Physical acting out of difficult emotions may also help clients who have problems experiencing them fully, for example using cushions as a focus for anger, or to hold on to. Clients can also be invited to repeat emotive phrases, address an absent person directly as 'you', use the therapist as a 'stand-in', or complete emotive sentences.

Empty Chair Work

Empty chair work (Houston, 1990; Zinker, 1977) can be very helpful for raising awareness in clients and bringing feelings, relationships or conflicts to life in the therapy room, rather than being a subject for speculation or discussion. Used judiciously, it can benefit clients who struggle to express difficult emotions such as grief or anger. The client is encouraged to act out both sides of a dialogue, perhaps between themselves and some significant other person, between different parts of themselves (for example 'confident me' and 'insecure me'), between their present self and some past or future self, or between themselves and some more abstract entity (such as the organization they work for or the place they live). The client should change position when adopting different roles, so two (or more) chairs will be used. This is a potentially powerful technique, and is probably best presented to a client as an experiment they might like to try, with no preset outcome. The therapist should suggest that clients take their time and try to feel free to go with whatever occurs to them during the exercise. Clients should be given permission to stop the process at any point if they wish to, and any resistance or reluctance should be responded to empathically and explored. As is often the case, there may be more therapeutic benefit in exploring the resistance than in forging ahead with whatever is being resisted.

The dialogue is best conducted in the first-person present tense from each position to make it more present and real. Some clients will find this a bit awkward at first and may begin with statements like, 'Well, I would say that he shouldn't be so critical of me', while looking at the therapist. A gentle suggestion to 'Say it to him', while indicating the empty chair, will often get the dialogue going. When the client seems to have expressed what they want to from one position they can be encouraged to try out the other chair and respond to what has been said, and move backwards and forwards as much as they wish, to play out the dialogue. At times the therapist may wish to share an observation or ask a question of one of the roles, but should be careful not to interrupt the flow of the dialogue too much for the client, as spontaneity will often lead to useful insights. A so-called 'top dog, underdog' dialogue may emerge, where one party appears to be in a position of power over the other or be communicating from a 'critical parent' position. The therapist can then support the underdog in expressing its point of view, and dealing assertively with the top dog. When the client has taken the dialogue as far as they wish, they can be invited to reflect on what has happened, and what seemed significant. Useful feedback to the client during this process will generally be observations, rather than interpretations. Discussion may suggest some further dialogue work, or lead into an evaluation of what has been learned or is different as a result. Clients report a variety of benefits from such work, including new insights into their feelings and conflicts, or what might be going on for others; new ideas about how to move forward or resolve conflicts; a sense of satisfaction at having got something off their chest, even if only to an empty chair; decisions made; or a raised awareness of deeper feelings. They are often surprised about how much such an exercise seems to have changed their perspective, and may need time to talk this over to make sense of it.

IMAGERY

Use of Metaphors

Metaphors can be useful either when therapists respond to the metaphorical communication of clients, encouraging them to elaborate and explore their imagery; or when therapists use metaphorical communication themselves to communicate their understanding, share a new perspective, or convey a message to clients. In either case metaphors offer an opportunity for communication that is less concrete and more creative and flexible, and can sometimes bypass normal inhibitions or limitations (see for example Riikonen and Smith, 1997).

Metaphorical communication is often ignored. When a client talks about experiencing a knot in their stomach, it would be quite normal for the therapist to assume a shared understanding of what that feels like, and proceed as though the client had described tightness or tension. The metaphor of the knot is an opportunity to work in a different way to transform the experience. The client can be asked to describe the knot in more detail as a metaphor, exploring its texture, shape and colour to engage more fully in the experience it represents, and may even wish to draw it. The client can then visualize its disentangling. In learning to take control of the image they may be able to take control of the reality, using the image of the knot being disentangled as an aid to relaxation. So in listening to clients a therapist should try to notice the images and metaphors which clients use to express themselves. The bridges, crossroads, gulfs, mountains, lights, tunnels, fogs and swamps which clients mention can all be picked up, elaborated, and used to deepen empathic understanding, and possibly to transform meaning and experience – either through visualizing changes, or through linking back to objective description by exploring what would be involved in clearing a path through the swamp, or how the bridge could be made more secure. Metaphorical communication can help clients to conceptualize their difficulties more clearly or differently, and to look for solutions from a new perspective.

Emotive Imagery

Emotive imagery techniques involve working with images or imagined scenarios to help clients change or control their emotional responses to particular stimuli. Clients will usually be encouraged to relax, using whatever means they are familiar with, before immersing themselves in a particular image, designed to provoke a predetermined emotional response. This image may have been discussed beforehand, may be described by the therapist, or may be developed by dialogue with the client (for example, 'Imagine yourself in a place where you would feel very peaceful; describe it to me as the image becomes clear'). A stimulus, which would normally generate a different emotional response, is then introduced, but at a level which will not totally disrupt the response to the initial image. In this way the emotional response induced by the initial image can be used as a means of controlling (though not replacing) the response to the introduced stimulus. For example, if a particular individual generates a very angry response in a client, which the client would like to learn to control, they may first imagine themselves relaxing in a warm, comfortable room, listening to some favourite music. When they are suitably comfortable in that image, they can introduce a small black-and-white photograph of the problem individual into the room,

and take as long as they need to become comfortable and relaxed with that. This process can be repeated with increasingly powerful stimuli being introduced (larger pictures, colour, and ultimately perhaps the person themselves, silent, then talking) until the client has learned to control their angry response to the individual.

Conversely, clients can imagine themselves in a situation where they normally have an undesired emotional response, and introduce suitable stimuli to modify that response. The technique has been adapted for use in rational emotive behaviour therapy (REBT: Ellis and Dryden, 1987), where the modifying stimuli would be the therapist or client disputing the irrational beliefs which lead to the undesired response. As with all imagery techniques it is important that clients are given permission to take control if they need to and change the image for themselves or stop the activity. Positive double binds such as 'Take as long as you need to relax' and 'Do whatever you need to do in order to feel safe' can be useful in helping clients to control imagery for themselves and feel empowered in using such techniques.

Lazarus (1989) suggests using visualization techniques to help clients not only in dealing with their presenting or immediate issues, but also as 'anti-future shock imagery', preparing themselves for changes which they are likely to have to deal with in the future. Clients are asked to identify life events (e.g. children leaving home, retirement) which are likely to lie ahead for them, and visualize themselves coping effectively with the changes. As well as preparing for potentially difficult events, such visualizations of coping positively in the future may also help clients to get in touch with what they really want from life, and identify developmental goals.

Some clients may prefer to work with imagery in a more externalized way than has been described so far, and might benefit from using objects to represent significant people, feelings or experiences. A variety of objects can be put together in a *sculpt*, where their arrangement and proximity say something about the interrelationships of the factors they represent. Clients can be invited to represent and explore the current situation in this way, and then move the objects into a more desirable arrangement, often with surprisingly powerful results. Such sculpts can be undertaken with any objects that are to hand (coins, contents of pockets, handbags), but many therapists choose to keep a box of varied stones, buttons and so on available for this purpose.

Dream Work

Clients often wish to share their dreams in therapy because they seem significant, or are a source of concern. Dreams can be seen as a means of accessing unconscious material such as repressed wishes, fears or memories, and their content seems frequently to be symbolic or metaphorical. Dreams can also be seen as a normal creative expression, part of the psyche's mechanism for maintaining healthy equilibrium, and include symbolic projections of current concerns and rehearsals for events anticipated in waking life.

Work with dreams can follow a number of different approaches (see for example Cushway and Sewell, 1992), and three techniques are outlined below. It is good practice to enable the client to work with their dreams in a way that makes sense to them, so some discussion of what the client hopes to gain from dream work and the opportunity to choose from a range of approaches are indicated. Dream work techniques can bring clients into contact with material which was previously out of their awareness, so they should enter into any work knowing this, and be able to stop or withdraw if they choose. It is often helpful to examine relationships between the themes and symbols in dreams and the client's waking life, and explore what messages or learning might be drawn from these.

Clients who wish to recall their dreams but have difficulty doing so might be encouraged to keep a dream diary. This is kept by the bed, and the client should be told to expect to wake briefly during the night to write some notes. They should make these notes immediately on waking as recall tends to fade quickly. The notes need only be reminders but in enough detail to stimulate memory later. Many find it helpful to give each dream a name that has some significance.

Dreams can be worked with in a cognitive way, discussing and trying to understand what the dream might mean and how it relates to other aspects of the client's experience. To do this, the client is first asked to recount the dream in the first-person present tense as a way of getting into contact with it again. They can then describe their *actions* during the dream in the third person as a way of adopting a more objective perspective. After this, the therapist helps the client to reflect and explore: they may ask what the client sees as central in the dream; what contrasts or similarities they perceive between characters, events or feelings; what may be symbolic; what is resolved, what is not (and how it might be); what relationships might exist between anything in this dream and other dreams or waking life. The therapist should always be clear that the dream belongs to the client, and focus on facilitating the client in making sense of the dream for themselves, not interpreting it for them. After exploring the dream content in this way it is helpful to ask the client to summarize how they see the dream now, what they have learned from it so far, and any action

they may wish to consider as a result. If working with nightmares or recurring dreams, it can help to repeat this process a number of times so that the client becomes used to confronting the dream content, and thus being less afraid of it. Where disturbing events take place in dreams with characters known in waking life, it is useful to share with the client the idea that all characters in dreams can be thought of as representations of aspects of the self. For example, this enabled a client who had dreamed of killing a close family member to examine what aspect of herself that person might represent, and thus make sense of the dream.

A more active technique for working with dreams is used by gestalt therapists to explore the richness of a dream and integrate its elements into the client's awareness. Once again the client begins by recounting the dream in the first-person present tense. The client then identifies the main elements (characters or objects) in the dream, and picks out those which generate curiosity, uncertainty or powerful feelings. (This technique also assumes that the elements in the dream represent aspects of the dreamer, and this is useful in diminishing the fear associated with some nightmare figures.) The client is invited to take on the role of some of these elements in turn, beginning with 'I am ...', and either tell the story of the dream from that perspective, or explore their feelings towards other characters or objects. The type of empty chair dialogue described earlier can be developed between key dream elements where it seems there are potential conflicts or blockages. After the client has explored whatever dialogues seem appropriate they might be asked to reflect on what messages this dream may have about how they are living their life, but the purpose of the technique is less to explain or interpret the dream than to raise the client's awareness of its elements and how they relate to each other.

A third approach to dream work involves using imagery to help the client re-enter their dream world, and take control of the dream. A number of techniques exist for doing this, and the approach outlined here has been described as an adaptation of the cultural practice of the Senoi tribe in Malaysia (Johnston, 1975). The client is encouraged to settle comfortably, relax in any way that works for them, and begin talking about an aspect of the dream which seems like a 'way in' or *key*. This might be the start, a snippet that is recalled clearly, or a particularly strong image or feeling. The client is then helped to go through a period of *embellishment* by continuing to explore the world of the dream and describing the experience in the first-person present tense. This may result in retelling the dream as it first happened, but the therapist should encourage the client to follow whatever images come to mind, rather than trying to stay close to the original dream. Often a *main figure* (most significant character or object) will become apparent as the embellishment develops, and if it does not the client can be asked to identify what seems to be the most important element in the dream and imagine engaging it in dialogue. It is useful to discuss this process with clients in advance so that they can anticipate what will be asked of them, and feel empowered to take control of their imagery. It is also helpful to agree suitable language for engaging in dialogue with inanimate objects or abstract entities. (For example, can we refer to the 'spirit' or 'essence' of an object such as a tree and communicate with it?) The client might begin dialogue with the main figure by asking, 'How can I help you?', and wait for their imagination to provide a response. The objective is to make an ally of the main figure even if it is initially hostile, and positive double binds such as 'Summon whatever help you need ...' or 'Do whatever you need to do to make things safe for yourself ...' can help the client to create a situation where they can safely communicate with the main figure. For example, a client who had recurring nightmares about swarms of insects found she was able to imagine a swarm of wasps contained in a large plastic bubble, and then allow one of the wasps to come outside to engage in dialogue. Following the dialogue, the client is encouraged to ask the main figure for a *gift* to symbolize their new alliance. If something abstract such as 'peace' is offered, it seems to be useful to suggest the client ask for a more concrete gift (to symbolize the peace). At this point the client can say goodbye to the main figure and the dream world, and return their full awareness to the present when ready to do so. After processing the experience, many clients find it helpful to represent the gift for themselves, perhaps by drawing, or finding an object which resembles what they imagined. This technique seems to be particularly useful for exploring confusing dreams, or for working with nightmares and recurring dreams. Clients can be encouraged to visualize ways to safely subdue threatening figures, which can sometimes be used if they have further nightmares, though they rarely continue to be terrorized in their dreams by a main figure after confronting it in this way.

COGNITIONS

Cognitive Restructuring

The techniques of cognitive restructuring are designed to help clients take control of what they think and

believe in certain situations and, by doing so, to enable them to change their emotional or behavioural responses. Cognitive restructuring interventions rely on clients being able to report and examine their cognitive processes, learn how these are connected to other aspects of their experience, and be amenable to challenging and changing these cognitive processes.

At the most informal level, any counsellor or psychotherapist can listen for things the client might say which indicate a tendency towards self-defeating beliefs or cognitive responses. These can be evident in a tendency to over-generalize ('Nothing I do ever works out'), to use 'musts' ('I must be more confident'), or to catastrophize ('This is terrible, I can't cope'). The therapist can challenge and begin to change such patterns of expression and thought by gently inviting the client to try expressing what they have said in a more realistic form and reflect on how it feels (in relation to the above examples, 'Try saying "A lot of things I do aren't wholly successful/I'd like to be more confident/This is hard, and it will be difficult to cope" and tell me how that feels').

Rational emotive behaviour therapy (see Part V of this book) makes the assumption that events in themselves do not necessarily lead to negative emotional consequences; rather, negative emotions are the result of what one believes about an event. If a more 'rational' belief can be substituted, then the individual will be better able to respond to events. The intervention sequence for doing this begins by helping the client to learn the A–B–C Model of REBT, where A represents an activating event; B the belief one holds about oneself, other people or the world, which is called into play by the event; and C the emotional and behavioural consequences of that belief. For example, if a client fails at a job interview (A), and believes that this is another example of *always* getting knocked back when it really matters (B), then they may be unlikely to apply for any further posts (C). If that belief can be changed to something more pragmatic, practical and reality based, such as 'although there was a candidate judged to be better on this occasion, that need not always be the case', then the outcome is likely to be different. Specific target beliefs are identified with the client, goals for change are negotiated, and then the therapist engages with the client in disputing their irrational beliefs, and helping them to learn to do this for themselves. Techniques for disputing include challenging the logic of the belief; challenging the evidence for the belief and finding exceptions; drawing attention to the ultimate consequences of holding such a belief; using humour or exaggeration; using self-disclosure; or adopting a didactic style to explain why the belief is irrational. Generally speaking, asking questions which encourage the

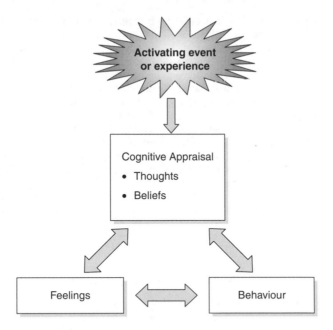

Figure 3.4.1   *Template for CBT interventions*

client to challenge their own beliefs will be preferable to therapist self-disclosure and the didactic style, as they encourage the client to focus on their own experience and see the flaws in their interpretations for themselves. Having done this, the client can be encouraged to state specifically a more rational belief, explore the effects of this and the new feeling generated, and develop a programme to practise disputing the old belief, reinforce the new belief, and put the resultant changes into operation.

Other approaches to cognitive restructuring (Beck, 1989; Meichenbaum, 1977) focus more on automatic thoughts and 'self-talk'. These can be tackled in a similar fashion, asking clients to identify problematic events and talk about the thoughts that they engender or the things they might say to themselves in such situations, and the way these are linked to their emotional and behavioural responses. It can be useful to encourage clients to explore these connections on paper, setting out events and the cognitive, emotional and behavioural responses in the form of a chart. They can rate the strength of automatic thoughts and emotions as an aid to prioritizing. The therapist then helps the client to develop a more 'adaptive' healthy response which they would like to substitute, i.e. a new thought and its emotional and behavioural consequences. The therapist can help the client to practise substituting the adaptive response by rehearsal in fantasy. The client imagines and describes the situation in order to

generate the automatic thought. When this has happened the therapist says 'Stop', or uses some other stimulus to interrupt the automatic thought pattern, and asks the client to repeat the adaptive cognitive response or positive self-talk to themselves before imagining the new desired behavioural response. This process is repeated until the client is able to stop the automatic response for themselves and substitute the adaptive response, before undertaking an action plan designed to practise and reinforce this process in real life. It is important to note that cognitive restructuring is not merely 'positive thinking', but is more personalized and subtle, and can be used as the basis for extensive personal development, not just for superficial situational help.

In recent years there has been a surge in the development of new techniques and approaches broadly under the heading of cognitive-behavioural therapy (see for example O'Donahue and Fisher, 2009). It is beyond the scope of this chapter to cover all of these in detail, and indeed it is probably beyond the scope of most integrative therapists to become conversant with every available CBT technique. However, most of these techniques can be understood from the perspective of an overarching template for CBT interventions (Figure 3.4.1) which can enable therapists to develop specific interventions in collaboration with their clients – an approach which is consistent with Beck's description of cognitive therapy as 'collaborative empiricism'.

The therapist can explore with the client their experience and responses to a particular event or experience using this diagram as a starting point or map. It is often useful to encourage the client to choose a specific example of how an issue they want to address manifests itself and examine that in some detail. The client is encouraged to consider how their cognitive appraisal of the experience or situation in question is composed of thoughts and beliefs and how these arise in response to the situation. The impact of the cognitive appraisal on the client's emotional response and the impact of the feelings thus identified, together with the cognitive appraisal, on their behaviour, can then be considered. Finally, the way that behaviour in turn affects feelings, cognition, and the course of the event or experience being considered completes the 'loop' of the cognitive-behavioural analysis. The client and therapist have then developed a sequence of causal connections between experience, thoughts, feelings, behaviour and consequences, and these connections can be examined to identify where changes might be made.

For example, the cognitive appraisal of a situation might be the initial target, and the client may be encouraged to challenge the beliefs underlying it (as in the REBT example above) or to interrupt the 'automatic thoughts' and 'self-talk' that are generated and practise substituting less self-defeating alternatives. On the other hand some clients are able to identify that there is a point of *selection* which arises in appraising an event and are able to raise their awareness of the moment of choice and exercise control at that moment. An example here might be in working with anger, when a client becomes aware that at a certain point they have a choice to interpret something someone has said as a criticism or to consider other interpretations. Once that choice has been made it might be difficult to change course because of a very quick chain of responses along the lines of perceived criticism → anger → hostile response → escalation of situation, etc. On the other hand if the initial selection of cognitive appraisal can be changed to something like 'this person is expressing dissatisfaction, but not necessarily at me', then a different set of thoughts and beliefs can come into play, resulting in a different sequence of feelings and behaviour. The key then would be for the client and therapist to develop ways to practise taking control of the selection of cognitive appraisal, perhaps by fantasy exercises or role-play.

This same example can also illustrate how a different 'causal link' in the cognitive-behavioural cycle can be targeted. If the client is struggling to have much impact on their initial appraisal of an experience, it may be that they can practise responding to perceived criticism differently, 'as if' they were taking a different view of the experience. As a result the event may unfold differently, with the client's more accepting response leading the other person involved to give a fuller explanation of their dissatisfaction, which would make it clear to the client that they were not the target (or not the only target) for criticism, thus causing them to reappraise the situation, hopefully leading to different feelings, etc. A different outcome will positively reinforce the change in behaviour and make a different appraisal more likely when similar situations occur in future. Again, specific interventions can then be developed to practise targeting this part of the cycle, perhaps through discussion, in fantasy exercises, in role-play, and through homework, diary keeping, etc.

Developing New Perspectives

New perspectives might be available to the client around ownership of problems. If they have always conceptualized themselves as being powerless in a given situation (e.g. 'My boss makes unreasonable demands of me', 'He makes me feel …') it may be very useful to encourage them to look at the situation in terms of what is within their control (e.g. 'How do you respond to these unreasonable requests?', 'What does he do, and how does that lead to your emotional response?'). Positive challenging involves helping clients to experiment with viewing things differently – problem situations as opportunities for change, difficulties as challenges, mistakes as learning opportunities – and to become more aware of the strengths and resources they are able to employ rather than focusing on weaknesses and shortcomings. Russell and Dexter (2008) provide a useful exploration of this area. The point is not that the client will feel better if only they can change their perspective on a situation, but that by experimenting they may find a perspective which gives them more autonomy. They may see a chance to act differently. This is an example of the technique of *reframing* – helping the client to find a new way of viewing the problem in which they are able to see choices, opportunities or possibilities for solution where previously they did not.

The concept of the 'empathy sandwich' for challenging interventions is useful. The intervention is preceded by an empathic response to check that the therapist has understood the client's current perspective (first layer of sandwich). The intervention to facilitate a new perspective is then offered (filling), and the therapist attends carefully to the client's reaction, which is responded to with empathy (second layer of sandwich). Hence:

Therapist: So the current situation is very difficult and you're feeling a lot of pressure, but I get the sense that you're also feeling more aware of the need to change things.

Client: [*thoughtfully*] Actually that's true, and I probably could have gone on being dissatisfied for years if things hadn't got this bad.

Therapist: So it sounds like you're thinking that this crisis might not be all bad.

The empathy sandwich can help to reinforce the new perspective if successful, but can also be a means of re-establishing an empathic relationship if the client responds with irritation or defensiveness. In this case the second layer of the sandwich may be more like, 'You seem a bit unhappy with what I've just said, maybe because it seems I don't appreciate how bad it really feels at the moment. Have I got that right?'

Making Connections, Past and Present

A useful technique for uncovering connections begins by identifying common patterns of feeling and belief. The client talks about their present situation, and the therapist listens carefully to the feelings expressed, reflects these back to ensure they are properly understood, and tries to help the client be aware of the subtleties of their emotional experience. It may seem that the client's emotional responses are not entirely explicable in terms of their current situation, so the therapist can ask the client if these feelings are familiar to them from previous experiences. If so, they can be asked to talk about these if they are prepared to. The relevance of these past situations will often be illuminated by helping the client to look at them from two different perspectives. First, the client explores how they made sense of the experience and coped with it at the developmental stage when it occurred; second, they consider what insights are possible from their current developmental stage that were not possible when the past experiences took place. Having explored past situations in this way, the client can be encouraged to look again at their present experience, and consider what new insights are available. They will often be able to understand present feelings, behaviours, irrational beliefs or automatic thoughts in terms of learning from past events, ways of coping at an earlier stage of development which are no longer appropriate, or responses which were developed in specific circumstances which have been generalized beyond their useful limits. For example, while it may be a valuable survival strategy for a child to be submissive in the face of a bullying teacher, it will be useful to have a range of ways of responding to bullying in adult life rather than be limited by the emotional response which is triggered due to connections with the past experience. If the client discovers these connections, they begin to be empowered to change their responses.

The process of connecting past and present might at times be deepened: either by developing an empty chair dialogue between the past and present selves to help one share some insight with the other, or to highlight differences in ways of understanding and coping with situations; or by encouraging the client to compose letters in which past and present selves exchange messages. If one of these selves is the individual in childhood, it may help the client to access that part of themselves by writing with their non-dominant hand. It should be noted that such techniques can bring about powerful cathartic experiences for clients, helping them access deep feelings associated with past events, or feelings of loss associated with different developmental stages, and thus need to be engaged in with caution. The client needs to be clear about what is being done, what they are hoping to achieve, and what the possible consequences are, and must give their informed consent.

If clients seem to value talking about their past and do not explicitly make connections with the present, it is likely to be useful for the therapist to invite them to do so. This can be achieved by asking the client if the feelings they have been describing in relation to past events are familiar to them in any aspects of their present, or simply if they can identify any parallels with their present experience, or interactions with others. Perhaps more obliquely, it can also be useful for the therapist to help the client become aware of the similarities and differences which are apparent between the emotions they are describing in relation to past events, and the emotions that they seem to be experiencing as they describe them. These similarities and differences can then be used as a means of bringing the client into the present and exploring the relevance of past material.

Malan's (1979) 'triangle of insight', which has the *past* ('back then'), the *present* ('out there') and the *therapy relationship* ('in here') at its corners, offers a guide to the ways that connections and parallels may be identified and worked with in therapy between any two or all three of these sets of experience. It is likely that patterns learned by the client in the past and played out in the present will also be played out in the therapy relationship. The relationship will thus provide opportunities for learning, and for experimentation with new patterns, which the client can then take 'out there'.

Identifying Personal Beliefs and Ways of Construing

The A–B–C technique from REBT outlined earlier is one way of helping clients to get in touch with their beliefs initially in relation to specific events and situations. It will often be the case that after looking at a number of situations some core beliefs about self, others and the world in general emerge. Different formulations of REBT list different sets of common irrational beliefs about how things must be in order for self, others or life in general to be acceptable – such as 'I must always succeed', 'Others must always treat me reasonably', 'The world must always be just and fair.' Encouraging the client to test their own beliefs against these can be challenging, and can help to develop a more pragmatic and reality-based outlook.

Personal construct theory (Kelly, 1991) offers some useful techniques for helping clients to be more specific about how they view themselves and others and what they believe, although the approach itself would describe this as understanding how clients construe, rather than what they believe. A 'self-characterization sketch' is a short written piece by a client describing what they see as their own most important features. The client is asked to write about themselves from the point of view of someone who knows them well and looks upon them favourably. They are asked to write about themselves fairly briefly, but in enough detail to help an actor who was preparing to take their role in a film to prepare for the part. What the client has chosen to include or leave out, and how easy it was to write from the perspective asked, can then be useful topics for further exploration.

The examination of 'bipolar constructs' can also be illuminating in helping the therapist to understand the client's worldview. Bipolar constructs are not exactly opposites in the linguistic sense, but represent concepts which an individual sees as being mutually opposed. The individual nature of such constructs is important, so that for example where one person may have the opposite pole of 'tidy' as 'messy', another may have it as 'relaxed', and these clearly represent quite different ways of looking at things. An interesting technique for eliciting such constructs from an individual is to ask them to consider three people whom they know fairly well, and develop a list of ways in which any two of them are the same as each other and different from the third, giving a name to what the two have in common and the way the third is different. (As an example, 'A and B are open while C is careful', 'B and C are optimistic while A is realistic' are statements which begin to give some insight into the construing of the individual and open up interesting avenues for discussion.) It may then be appropriate to explore how rigid or flexible the individual's constructs are and to work on new perspectives by exploring the pros and cons of opposite poles (e.g. 'What might be good/bad about being optimistic/realistic?').

The *scripts* of transactional analysis and the *schemas* of cognitive therapy represent protracted, sometimes lifelong, patterns of personal belief, which can be dysfunctional. These are analysed over a period of time in therapy, often by a process of induction from exploration of critical incidents. Client and therapist attempt to uncover patterns in relating, thinking and feeling, and the beliefs and predictions about self, others and the world, which underlie them.

Positive Asset Search

The positive asset search helps the client to re-evaluate their experience in order to find new meaning in something previously seen as negative, or new resources in themselves (Ivey et al., 1987). The technique involves the use of listening skills and selective attention to positive assets; it is not about the denial of negative aspects of a situation, but rather about the drawing of the client's attention towards positive perspectives previously overlooked. The therapist listens carefully to the client as they describe a situation or experience, paraphrasing and reflecting the feelings in what they hear in order to develop a clear empathic understanding of how the client sees the situation, but in particular drawing the client's attention to things they have said which include a neglected positive element. So, for example, when a client is describing a stressful situation in the past, the therapist should not ignore what the client is saying about how difficult they found it, but should also be listening for what is said about how they survived the situation – what internal and external resources they were able to draw on, who helped them get through, and what they learned from the situation. Achieving an appropriate balance is crucial here: clients are likely to become frustrated if the therapist seems to be ignoring their pain in order to search for positives, but the therapist can demonstrate genuine empathic understanding of a client's difficulties while at the same time helping them to find new meanings and resources in their lives.

Goal Setting

Goals can be set with the client in relation both to the therapy itself and to achievements outside the therapeutic situation. Clients will often have goals for both of these areas at some level of awareness, but may have difficulty in expressing them clearly, or in thinking explicitly in terms of wants and outcomes as opposed to problems and difficulties. Clear goals encourage a sense of self-determination and empowerment; provide a focus for activity both during and between sessions; give a sense of hope for a better future; and are something to keep in view even if specific strategies do not prove successful (Egan, 2009). Keeping goals in focus does not necessarily mean that the client will not have the opportunity to explore negative feelings or traumatic experiences, but means that they will be clear about what they are hoping to achieve in doing so, and will be 'signed up' to that as a desirable goal. This is not to deny the possibility of unintended or surprise outcomes, or to enable practitioners to tie down every aspect of the therapeutic encounter in a dry and logical process, but is to encourage both therapist and client to keep an eye on the agenda.

Clients might initially be encouraged to talk about their aims or wants in a fairly general way by asking, 'How would you like things to be?' The therapist might also try offering the client the imaginary chance to use a magic wand or to ask a 'miracle question' (De Shazer, 1985) – 'If you woke up tomorrow and a miracle had happened giving you what you want, how would you become aware that it had happened?' – as ways of helping clients free their imagination when thinking about goals. The use of other media such as drawing and sculpting can also be considered as a way of engaging the imagination. Clients can be asked to create an image to represent themselves at some point in an imagined future, when things are going well. They could also be asked to sculpt their present situation using suitable buttons, stones or other objects to represent themselves, significant others and their interrelationships; and then to move the objects to represent a more desirable configuration and talk about the changes they have made. Even if clients' initial responses to some of these interventions are not achievable, useful material can be gleaned by exploring what the client would like to be feeling, and incorporating this into a realistic goal. If clients are beginning to be able to express a rather vague goal (e.g. 'a better relationship with X'), then asking them how they will know when they have achieved that goal might well help them to state it in more measurable terms ('We'd only fall out once a week instead of every day'). The acronym SMART is often used as a guide to help clients shape up a goal from an initial statement of intent. Therapists can ask questions or prompt clients to consider how the goal can be stated specifically (S) and in a measurable form (M), to consider its appropriateness (A) and realism (R) in relation to their individual situation, and to give some thought to the time (T) by which they would like to achieve it.

It can be useful to encourage the client to look at what they want to achieve in terms of short-, medium-, and long-term goals, or perhaps to break down a major project into a series of goal steps. The technique of *scaling* (De Shazer, 1985) might be incorporated here. The client is asked to rate where they currently are on a scale for which 0 represents the worst that things could be, and 10 represents the achievement of their long-term goal, or the best that things could be. They can then be asked to specify what would be involved in moving up by one scale point, two points and so on. Once again clients are likely to benefit from recording some of this on paper as a way of productively fixing ideas, and holding on to specifics. Some clients (and indeed therapists) will find it difficult to talk about goals without quickly moving into thinking about strategies for achieving those goals, and may find the two becoming blurred: for example, is discussing one's feelings with a partner a goal or a strategy? If this seems to be occurring, the therapist might usefully try an intervention such as, 'That sounds like something that you might do, but perhaps it would be useful first to try to be clear about what you would be hoping to achieve by doing it.'

Force Field Analysis

Force field analysis (Lewin, 1969) is a technique which can be used to help clients explore the ways various factors in their situation might be operating to help or hinder them in achieving their goals or putting action plans into practice. This is a process which involves a number of steps, and it is often advisable to record the process on paper. The therapist begins by asking the client to list all the factors they can think of which might help or hinder them in achieving their goal or implementing an action plan. This can be further structured by inviting the client to consider factors about themselves, significant others, and the broader environment if appropriate. If there are a lot of factors identified, it may then be useful to ask the client to rate each on a scale from 1 to 10 in terms of its power to influence their success or otherwise, as an aid to prioritizing. The client should then be able to visualize their goal or action plan located within a 'force field' of helping and hindering factors pulling them towards success or failure, and this can be useful in assessing the realism of a given goal or plan. If the force field analogy does not appeal or make sense, clients can instead visualize a tug-of-war, with the helping and hindering factors pulling against each other.

Table 3.4.3   *Example of force field analysis*

Facilitating forces	Strength (out of 10)	Restraining forces	Strength (out of 10)
Motivation to improve the relationship	8	Guilt about not being with the children	6
Shared interests	5	Difficulty finding babysitters	3
Enjoyment we know we can have together	7	Tendency to let other priorities dominate (particularly work)	6
Chance of breaks from domestic routine	3	Inertia	4
Chance to revisit some old haunts	4	Feeling tired or stressed after work	8
Encouragement from two particular friends	6	Problems sustaining the strategy as the novelty wears off	4
		A lot of things we'd like to do cost money	5

Strategies for strengthening facilitating forces	Strategies for weakening restraining forces
List benefits of improved relationship	Plan 'quality time' around predictable work stresses
Remember current dissatisfaction	Plan 'quality time' well in advance
Careful planning and selection of things to do together that we'll both enjoy	Be more assertive at work about leaving on time
	Do things together as a family at weekends
Share feedback on 'quality time' spent together	Don't automatically take responsibility when a crisis
Spend time individually with the two friends, etc.	occurs at work, etc.

The therapist then encourages the client to examine the most powerful factors on each side and think about ways of strengthening the effects of the helping factors, and weakening the effects of the hindering factors. Specific strategies for doing this can be developed and built into the client's action plans. Table 3.4.3 shows an example of the use of this technique.

Decision Making

Strategies for helping clients with decision making can be used when a choice has to be made between competing goals, or between mutually exclusive strategies for achieving goals (e.g. career choice, college course, relationships, divorce, early retirement). Encouraging clients to adopt some form of balance-sheet method (Egan, 2009), and put their ideas down on paper, can often move them forward or get them unstuck. A balance sheet can be as simple as a list of pros and cons for each of the competing choices, but it is also possible to structure the technique to tailor it more effectively to individual needs. So, for example, a balance sheet may be composed which has two columns for each choice in which to list advantages and disadvantages, but under a series of subheadings to suit the individual, for example career, social life, home life, significant others, organization, environment and so on. The client can be asked to rate each factor listed for importance. It may also be helpful to ask clients to specify and list what is appealing to them about particular choices and what is not.

Interestingly, not all clients act on the basis of the numerical result or apparent balance of such exercises; some decide that they want to follow a particular course in spite of what the balance sheet shows them, but if they take enough time over the process, most report being clearer about what they really want as a result.

A simple but often effective technique in decision making can be used in response to the client asking the therapist what they would do. If the client is asked what response they would like or are hoping for from the therapist, the processes underlying the client's inability to make or resistance to making the decision for themselves can be explored.

Mindfulness

Evidence for the effectiveness of interventions based on the concept of mindfulness (drawn initially from Buddhist practices) has been accumulating in recent years, and has been incorporated into the development of mindfulness-based cognitive therapy (see for example Herbert and Forman, 2010). Mindfulness is based on the idea of encouraging an individual to become more consciously aware of thoughts, feelings and actions, *non-judgementally* and *in the present moment*. As such it has connections with techniques that have been practised as part of experiential and gestalt therapies, but it can also be usefully incorporated into cognitive-behavioural and integrative work. At an initial level, mindfulness can be practised by attempting to connect fully with an experience in the present. For example, when eating, focus on all of your thoughts and sensations around the experience and try to be fully in contact with them; or when observing say an object of beauty, try to *notice* as much detail as you can and be fully aware of your responses as you do so. Mindfulness meditation enables such attention to one's thoughts, feelings and experience of one's body and its responses to be practised more intentionally and regularly.

A principle of mindfulness is to recognize that the mind is continually generating a 'commentary' on experience as it unfolds, but that it is possible to raise awareness of that commentary and accept it without always being bound to act in particular ways as a result. The idea is that 'thoughts are just thoughts' and, if one is mindful of them, one can make choices about what value particular thoughts have. This principle extends also to bodily responses. One can develop heightened awareness of the responses occurring in one's body, perhaps related to anxiety, but by responding to them with acceptance in the present moment, one need not be driven by them to behave in particular ways. The view one might take would then be something like, 'I notice that I am feeling my heart beating faster and butterflies in my stomach, but that is OK, and an acceptable response to what is happening', as opposed to, 'I'm feeling really scared and that's not OK and something has to change quickly.' As a result of mindful acceptance, it is likely that feelings will change and different choices will be available in responding to a situation (sometimes including not doing anything).

INTERPERSONAL FACTORS

Interpreting Transferential Patterns

If a known client's way of being seems surprising in a particular session, perhaps charged with emotions which seem out of context, or if they seem to want the therapist to adopt a particular role with them, then it may be worth exploring the possibility of transference as an explanation. Knowledge of the client may already suggest how earlier relationships might be influencing the therapist–client interaction, but often it will not. Interpretation should not take the form of an explicit statement telling the client about the transference they are supposedly experiencing, but should be tentative and offered to the client as an area for exploration; interpreting transference can be seen as a joint activity. An initial intervention may draw attention to a behaviour or emotion that the therapist has become aware of, for example, 'I notice you've seemed quite angry

with me today'; or a sense of what the client wants, such as, 'It feels as though you'd like me to sort this out for you.' The client can then respond with their perspective on the situation, and the origins of the feelings may begin to become apparent. If this does not happen, the client can be asked if the feelings they are experiencing are familiar to them, and encouraged to talk about other instances, which will often clarify the transference. One of the relatively unusual aspects of the therapist–client relationship is that it can be discussed and examined between the parties in a way that would be difficult in many other relationships. Exploring and interpreting transference in the relationship may allow the client to understand themselves better in other relationships. It can enable them to work through issues in the relationship with the therapist which resolve past negative experiences and help them to behave differently in other present relationships. For example, if the client is able to become aware of their fear of rejection, explore its origins in past experiences, and learn to manage that fear appropriately in the relationship with their therapist, then hopefully they can also learn to manage it more effectively in other significant relationships. On the other hand, opening up exploration of transference may bring therapist–client relationship issues to the fore inappropriately, and impede the client's ability to focus on their real goals. (See Kahn, 1997 for a useful discussion.)

Clearly, a therapist needs to be aware of their own patterns of relating and responses to clients if they are to respond appropriately. If they are not, the danger exists of being flattered inappropriately by the client's positive transference, feeling inadequate in response to negative transference, or being drawn into an inappropriate co-dependent relationship. The therapist's counter-transference will often be material for supervision or personal therapy, and consideration needs to be given to the extent to which it is shared with the client. There will be times when the therapist owning their own feelings towards the client will be helpful in enabling the client to see the therapist as genuine, modelling openness in the relationship, giving feedback on how they are being received, and developing insight into the dynamics of the relationship; and other times when it would be experienced as distracting or indulgent. Once again, it is useful to be guided by the client's goals, and the extent to which these will be furthered by working with the transference relationship, and it may be helpful to involve the client in such decisions. Increasingly, forms of transference interpretation are used in even ostensibly non-psychodynamic approaches such as cognitive therapy, in order to work on cognitive distortions within the 'laboratory' of the therapeutic relationship.

Here-and-now Awareness

Therapists need to develop the habit of continually monitoring their own awareness, and learning to share this appropriately with the client. This involves attending to one's own feelings during the encounter, and processing these. The therapist can consider: how their feelings relate to the developing relationship with the client; the nature and quality of the work currently being done; and any resistance in themselves or perceived in the client. They can evaluate any hunches or intuitions they may experience in the light of what they are seeing, hearing and feeling. The therapist can choose to disclose something of their own awareness, and invite the client to reflect and share their own perspective. The skill of immediacy is used in this context. So, for example, the therapist might say, 'I'm feeling a bit confused by what you've just said, but I normally feel we understand each other quite well. How does it seem to you at the moment?'; or, 'I notice I'm feeling quite enthusiastic about the work we've done today. How is it for you?'; or, 'I'm aware that I'm feeling some anger towards X and I'm wondering what feelings are around for you.' These kinds of intervention, used intentionally and appropriately, have the potential to encourage the client to stop and think about what is happening, experience the therapist as congruent, take permission to share their own feelings or perceptions openly, and be involved in monitoring and shaping the helping process for themselves. The therapist's awareness is used as a stimulus for a joint exploration, and becomes a model for developing the client's own awareness.

If used inappropriately or excessively, such interventions also have the potential to leave the client feeling confused as to their purpose, and lacking confidence in the therapist. The therapist is again required to exercise judgement, and to have a clear intention for what might be achieved by sharing their awareness, or sufficient experience to trust their sensitivity to the situation and know when immediacy is likely to be beneficial. A thoughtful pause is often useful to check in with oneself before using such an intervention.

Corrective Emotional Experience

An example of how the therapist–client relationship can be used as a medium for correcting previous experience is given above when considering use of the transference relationship. Using the relationship intentionally to correct the client's previous learning is often a feature of work with a client who has been subject to some form of abuse in an earlier phase of their life. If, for example, the client has been the victim of a relationship where their dependence or trust has been exploited, they may have developed a range of difficulties around trust, guilt, self-esteem and responsibility, which now cause them problems in engaging in trusting relationships or a vulnerability to exploitative relationships. The counselling or psychotherapy relationship offers the opportunity to experience something different, and can be used as a model of a healthy relationship, to enable the client to have a positive experience of trust, intimacy, non-exploitative cooperation, and the maintenance of appropriate boundaries. The client can experience sharing their emotions, and understanding from another, without having their vulnerability exploited or needing to defend themselves, and they can experience being valued and trusted rather than being discounted. If this is to be effective, it requires some care from the therapist, who will ideally model congruence, acceptance, and both clarity and flexibility about boundaries. Therapists who are too rigid in their application of boundaries, for example refusing to engage in conversation with clients outside session times, can be experienced as not genuinely caring. Those who are too lax and allow the boundaries between the therapeutic relationship and friendship to become blurred can be experienced as exploitative or vulnerable to exploitation. The therapist needs to monitor the developing relationship carefully and keep in touch with their own responses, as well as learning about the client's previous experience, exploring the deficits in terms of learning about relationships, and considering how the therapeutic relationship might be used to correct these deficits. At times this might involve modelling appropriate parental behaviour: nurturing, setting limits within the relationship, or responding non-defensively but assertively to challenges and threats. Modelling such as this can enable the client to develop a more adaptive 'internal parent' and enable them to be more nurturing towards themselves, or to maintain more appropriate boundaries and limits. At other times the therapist might be involved in modelling a trusting and cooperative adult relationship, wherein both parties can share their feelings openly, accept and understand each other, and respect each other's limitations. These processes are unlikely to proceed smoothly, as clients who have been involved in exploitative relationships may well have evolved coping strategies which are experienced as hostile and rejecting, and they will probably need to test this new relationship before they are able to accept it as safe. This may involve giving the therapist the opportunity or even encouragement to exploit their position, or to reject the client, and can leave the therapist feeling angry, exposed or threatened. The therapist's ability to stay in touch with their own responses and share these with the client while maintaining the core conditions of congruence, acceptance and empathy will be vital in helping the client to gain insight into the evolving relationship, genuinely experience it as different, and learn from it.

What has been presented here is an outline of a range of techniques and strategies drawn from a wide spectrum of counselling and psychotherapeutic approaches, which individual therapists may find they can use or adapt to their own style or context. It is likely that many therapists will at least occasionally work in an eclectic fashion, even if they are unable to go along with Lazarus's (1989) assertion that it is techniques, not theories, which help clients. It seems certain at this stage in the development of knowledge about therapy that no one approach has a monopoly on the truth, and many of the techniques described above seem to have a utility which can be separated out from their theoretical rationale. The way a given technique works can be explained from a number of perspectives, so the possibilities for integration are many. Such use of techniques needs to be thoughtful, be sensitive to the client's needs, and pay due regard to contra-indications, and should give the client a voice in the way they are helped. Many therapists will feel the need for additional specialized training in relation to some of the techniques they would like to adopt, if their previous training has not provided them with an adequate framework for their use, and the skills to use them safely and deal with the possible consequences.

REFERENCES

Bandura, A. (1977) *Social Learning Theory*. Englewood Cliffs, NJ: Prentice-Hall.

Beck, A.T. (1989) *Cognitive Therapy and the Emotional Disorders*. Harmondsworth: Penguin.

Bolton, G., Howlet, S., Lago, C. and Wright, J. (eds) (2004) *Writing Cures: An Introductory Handbook of Writing in Counselling and Psychotherapy*. Hove: Brunner-Routledge.

Carkhuff, R. (1969) *Helping and Human Relations* (Vols I and II). New York: Holt, Rinehart and Winston.

Cushway, D. and Sewell, R. (1992) *Counselling with Dreams and Nightmares*. London: Sage.

De Shazer, S. (1985) *Keys to Solution in Brief Therapy*. New York: Norton.

Duncan, B., Miller, S., Wampold, B. and Hubble, M. (2009) *The Heart and Soul of Change: Delivering What Works in Therapy*. Washington: APA.

Egan, G. (2009) *The Skilled Helper* (9th edn). London: Wadsworth.

Ellis, A. and Dryden, W. (1987) *The Practice of Rational Emotive Therapy*. New York: Springer.

Herbert, J. and Forman, E. (2010) *Acceptance and Mindfulness in Cognitive Behavior Therapy: Understanding and Applying the New Therapies*. London: Wiley.

Heron, J. (1990) *Helping the Client: A Creative Practical Guide*. London: Sage.

Houston, G. (1990) *The Red Book of Gestalt* (5th edn). London: Rochester Foundation.

Ivey, A.E., Ivey, M.B. and Simek-Downing, L. (1987) *Counseling and Psychotherapy: Integrating Skills, Theory, and Practice*. Boston: Allyn and Bacon.

Johnston, J. (1975) *Elements of Senoi Dreamwork Applied to Western Culture*. San Francisco: California School for Professional Psychology.

Kahn, M. (1997) *Between Therapist and Client: The New Relationship* (2nd edn). London: St Martin's Press.

Kelly, G.A. (1991) *The Psychology of Personal Constructs*. London: Routledge.

Lazarus, A.A. (1989) *The Practice of Multimodal Therapy*. Baltimore: Johns Hopkins University Press.

Lewin, K. (1969) Quasi-stationary social equilibria and the problem of permanent change. In W.G. Bennis, K.D. Benne and R. Chinn (eds), *The Planning of Change*. New York: Holt, Rinehart and Winston.

Mahrer, A.R. (1996) *The Complete Guide to Experiential Therapy*. New York: Wiley.

Malan, D.H. (1979) *Individual Psychotherapy and the Science of Psychodynamics*. New York: Butterworth.

Meichenbaum, D. (1977) *Cognitive Behavior Modification: An Integrative Approach*. New York: Plenum.

O'Donahue, W. and Fisher, J. (2009) *Cognitive Behavior Therapy: Applying Empirically Supported Techniques in Your Practice* (2nd edn). London: Wiley.

Riikonen, E. and Smith, G.M. (1997) *Re-imagining Therapy*. London: Sage.

Russell, J. and Dexter, G. (2008) *Blank Minds and Sticky Moments in Counselling*. London: Sage.

Wolpe, J. (1990) *The Practice of Behavior Therapy* (4th edn). New York: Pergamon.

Zinker, J. (1977) *Creative in Gestalt Therapy*. New York: Vintage.

Assessment and Case Formulation

WENDY WOOD AND MICHAEL TOWNEND

INTRODUCTION

Assessment and formulation will necessarily be guided by the therapeutic modality employed. 'Thus, a psychodynamic, humanistic, existential or CBT therapist will construct and navigate through these processes in rather different ways' (Gilbert, 2008: viii). This chapter aims to examine some of the methods and tools that may be useful in assessment and formulation with any therapeutic modality.

WHEN DOES THE ASSESSMENT BEGIN?

McMahon makes some important points in regard to when assessment begins:

> Assessment starts with the receipt of any information concerning the client, be this through self-referral, referral letters, case records or an initial telephone contact, but develops more completely and perhaps more reliably, with the first therapy session. It is hard to overestimate the importance of this first session and the mutual impressions gained by the therapist and client. Mistrust and suspicion can jeopardize any future relationship … assessment can be a two-way process and not just something a counsellor or psychotherapist 'does' to a client. Whether we like it or not, clients will assess the quality of the therapeutic relationship and the effectiveness of any therapeutic plans, though some may be more able and objective than others in doing this. (2006: 110)

Taking the notion of collaboration into account, it is useful where possible to provide information for clients before the initial assessment in a brief information pack. This may help clients prepare for the session by giving them time to think through their decision making processes and formulate questions. Information provided to clients before the first session may include:

- What is counselling and psychotherapy?
- What level of experience do the counsellors and psychotherapists have?
- How long would I need to attend?
- How often would I need to attend?
- Who goes for counselling and psychotherapy?
- What kind of problems can this agency help with?
- How do I get to see a counsellor or psychotherapist?
- What happens after I have referred myself (or been referred) for counselling or psychotherapy?
- Can I choose whether I see a man or a woman?
- What happens if I need to cancel?
- What happens if I am unhappy with the service?
- How much does it cost?
- Is there a fee for cancellation of a session?
- How is confidentiality managed?
- Is the service available for all ages?
- Is the service available for people whose first language is not English?
- What hours does the service operate?
- Is there anyone to speak to between sessions?
- Are clients involved in research and service development?

WHAT IS THE PURPOSE OF THE ASSESSMENT?

The purpose of assessment is to obtain a clear and accurate understanding of a variety of factors that will assist the therapist in developing a formulation and an initial plan of potential ways of working with the client. It is important to note that the assessment and formulation are always developing. The developing nature of assessment and formulation is often the result of issues such as the development of the therapeutic relationship which may lead to increased trust and thus increased disclosure by the client. Also, as the client begins to develop greater insight and learning about their problems, the focus of work may need to be adapted to match these changes. The main areas of assessment are concerned with:

- an accurate and detailed account of the client's problems
- an understanding of the client's goals
- an understanding of how the client's past history may have influenced the development and maintenance of their problems
- past experiences of therapeutic intervention
- an understanding of why the client is coming for therapy now
- an understanding of issues that may block therapeutic change
- an understanding of how the therapeutic relationship may develop
- an understanding of the client's expectations, hopes and fears
- an understanding of practical issues that may affect therapy, such as transport, language, financial, legal, time
- an understanding of risk factors that may be evident
- an understanding of what measures may prove to be of value.

HOW IS AN ASSESSMENT CONDUCTED?

In order to make sense of the complexities of the above, many therapists use formal form-based techniques which can assist in the initial goal setting as well as a tool for evaluation as therapy progresses. The advantage of using form-based techniques is that they can assist the client and the therapist in navigating through the complexity of issues to define achievable goals. The disadvantage can be that therapists may find it difficult to balance using forms and maintaining the interpersonal skills of active listening and genuine curiosity which are important in the development of the therapeutic relationship. It is also important to note that not all clients will respond well to the use of forms and not all clients find it easy to articulate their goals. Thus, assessment is a subtle blend of art and science. Whether the intention is to use measures and other form-based techniques or not may become clearer by initially making some exploratory

enquiries. Some suggestions are as follows, in no particular order of importance:

- How would you know when things have improved for you? What would you be doing, thinking, feeling and seeing?
- What expectations do you have about how we will work together?
- Is there anything that you don't do or avoid doing to make the problem better?
- What are the things you used to do, but don't do any more because of the problem?
- What would you like to do, but don't do because of the problem?
- When does the problem not feel as bad?
- Is there anything you can think of that is really important for me to understand that will help you to get the best out of the work we do together?
- Is there anything you can think of that may hinder your progress?
- Is there anything you can think of that may help your progress?

There are many measures available. Some measures are nomothetic in nature, i.e. developed by exploring general traits observable in a general population; and some are idiosyncratic, i.e. specific to the individual. The measures listed below represent a small sample. It is certainly worth researching measures to investigate how useful they may be to the therapist's practice and to the client's understanding of their problems as well as the process of therapy. Some of the issues to take into account when deciding on measures include:

- Timing and relevance: it is important to make sure clients are not overwhelmed with measures.
- It is important to consider the cultural sensitivity of measures.
- Copyright: some measures are freely available, whilst others have to be paid for.
- Training: some measures can be used without formal specific training, whilst others are licensed to trained individuals only.
- The reliability and validity of the measures are important.
- Measures need to be used and interpreted as they were intended; understanding when and how to use them is important.

Below is a list of examples of measures that are currently freely available. Although some of the resources listed below have a research focus, the tools are as valuable for everyday practice. As discussed above, it is important to ensure that copyright conditions are followed.

- Simplified Personal Questionnaire (PQ), experiential-researchers.org/

- Goal Form, www.pluralistictherapy.com
- Clinical Outcomes in Routine Evaluation Outcome Measure (CORE-OM), www.coreims.co.uk
- Outcome Rating Scale (ORS), www.scottdmiller.com
- Patient Health Questionnaire (PHQ-9), www.pfizer.com/home/
- General Anxiety Disorder Assessment (GAD-7), www.pfizer.com/home/
- Strengths and Difficulties Questionnaire (for children and young people), www.sdqinfo.org
- Recovery Star, www.mhpf.org.uk/recoveryStar.asp

Assessing Family History

Understanding the family context of the client can be useful and in some cases very important to the client's story. Grant and Townend (2010: 40) offer the following prompts:

- Parents: relationship, changes, work.
- Siblings: relationship, changes, work.
- Is there a family psychiatric history?
- Are there any inherited disorders in the family?
- Genograms can be helpful here.

Medical History

This would include any physical or psychological problems both past and present, including any medication prescribed or none prescribed, that may have an impact on the current situation. This is worth considering as clients do not always make a connection between a medical problem and their current psychological health.

Current Health

Assessment of current health should consider the state of and any changes to the following:

- appetite
- sleep

- concentration
- energy level
- mood
- medication – prescribed or non-prescribed
- alcohol use.

Personal History

For assessing personal history Grant and Townend (2010: 40) offer the following prompts:

- What type of accommodation does the client have?
- Is there uncertainty about the accommodation?
- Who does the client live with?
- Are there any problems at home?
- Does the client work, not work, go to school, college or university?
- What does the client do with their leisure time?
- How does the client describe their personality?
- Has there been any change in personality?
- Are there any relationship or sexual problems?
- How does the client describe their relationships?
- Do they have any children? What are their ages? Any problems?

Assessing Developmental History

Using a timeline to map significant events, both positive and negative, can be very useful. An example is shown in Figure 3.5.1.

WHAT IS A FORMULATION AND HOW IS IT USED?

The use of the term 'formulation' tends to be associated with CBT. For example, Grant and Townend define case formulation as 'an individualised theory about a client's problems, based on a more general cognitive-behavioural theory' (2010: 21). Grant and Townend describe the main elements of a case formulation:

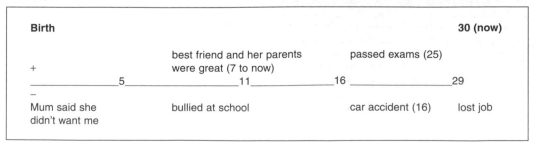

Figure 3.5.1   *Developmental history timeline*

Note: A mental state assessment may also be required (see Chapter 3.6)

Case formulation schemes usually have the following core elements: a description of presenting issues or problem list, and predisposing factors, including recent or *proximal* factors and factors more distant in time, termed *distal* factors. Case formulation schemes also describe perpetuating factors which serve to maintain the presenting problems, protective factors which function as personal and social resources and explicit guides for intervention. (2008: 54)

By drawing together the knowledge gained through the assessment and the knowledge from research, it is possible in collaboration with the client to develop an understanding of the client's problems and how they may be resolved.

Whether therapists adopt a structured approach to formulation or a more narrative approach, formulation is an explicit and an implicit process. The difficulty faced by the therapist here is how to use theories and knowledge whilst still being able to hear the client: that is, with regard to ethics, acting with respect for client autonomy and maintaining the principle of beneficence. This involves the therapist developing the skills of a reflective practitioner and asking themselves to what extent their formulation is influenced by:

- their own biases, values, attitudes, prejudices or beliefs
- their own professional and personal needs
- their theoretical orientation
- organizational issues.

Formulation also involves the skill of making sense of the various aspects of the assessment process in order to share and develop the formulation with the client in a way that makes sense to them. There are various ways to achieve this including a narrative approach, i.e. verbally exploring the formulation. There is also the opportunity to draw the formulation using shapes, symbols and/or words. Often diagrams are employed to map out the formulation. Or indeed a combination of methods may be used. Figure 3.5.2 shows a simple illustration of a continuous cycle, which assists the process of developing the formulation further at the client's pace.

SUMMARY

There is an increasingly large and rich amount of resources and ideas in regard to assessment and

Figure 3.5.2   *Example of a cycle of behaviour, thoughts and feelings*

case formulation. This chapter has attempted to provide a platform of ideas, resources and examples of techniques and tools that may assist therapists to plan assessment strategies and case formulations that can be developed, implemented and evaluated in a way that meets the needs of clients, the context in which the service is set, and the therapist's modality and choice.

REFERENCES

Gilbert, P. (2008) Foreword. In A. Grant, M. Townend, J. Mills and A. Cockx (eds), *Assessment and Case Formulation in Cognitive Behavioural Therapy.* London: Sage.

Grant, A. and Townend, M. (2008) The fundamentals of case formulation. In A. Grant, M. Townend, J. Mills and A. Cockx (eds), *Assessment and Case Formulation in Cognitive Behavioural Therapy.* London: Sage.

Grant, A. and Townend, M. (2010) Case formulation. In A. Grant, M. Townend, R. Mulhern and N. Short (eds), *Cognitive Behavioural Therapy in Mental Health Care.* London: Sage.

McMahon, G. (2006) *The SAGE Handbook of Counselling and Psychotherapy* (2nd edn). London: Sage.

Assessing Severe Mental Health Problems

DAN TULLY

INTRODUCTION

Recognising, and subsequently managing, severe mental health problems are key requirements of working with people in the therapeutic context. In keeping with other aspects of clinical practice, this chapter will focus on practical tools and frameworks to guide the individual practitioner in their day-to-day practice.

Some practitioners may not favour a diagnostic or psychiatric approach to understanding mental health problems. As with any attempt to understand or categorise the complexity of human experience and distress, it will fall short of its aim. However, the medical or psychiatric model of mental health problems is widely used, particularly within the National Health Service, and for this reason it is helpful to be familiar with that model. This chapter will therefore offer some ideas and strategies to encourage smooth transition, for the client, between individual practitioners and teams and the wealth of different approaches that exist.

Holding a clear sense of structure and understanding the value of particular aspects of a client's history can be invaluable in encouraging informed choices and a collaborative approach to clients in severe distress. In itself the process of assessment, and gathering of information, can have value in containing the sometimes highly emotive situations a professional can be faced with. It can also guide us through the balancing act that exists between the risk that the client may represent to themselves or others, confidentiality, the quality of the therapeutic relationship, and our duty of care. A thorough and pertinent assessment is also central to communication with our partners in primary care or secondary mental health teams. It can encourage a dialogic and collaborative approach to decision making, keeping the client at the heart of our work and easing the client's journey between different professionals and teams.

WHAT ARE SEVERE MENTAL HEALTH PROBLEMS?

For the purposes of this chapter and its focus on the practical aspects of recognising and managing severe mental health problems, we will consider them to be a constellation of signs, symptoms and risk that needs further or more immediate assessment and intervention. Conditions can be both acute and chronic, with a change in circumstances or risk factors pushing a client towards crisis point. A good indicator of need for intervention is social and occupational dysfunction, alongside a thorough risk assessment. Assessment of the client's ability to manage the tasks of everyday living and their physical needs, and any corresponding neglect of the self, is a strong factor in guiding us in our decision making.

We will consider below key aspects of client history and assessment and how they might relate to severity of the illness and risk. The diagnoses considered are depression, anxiety, psychotic illness, bipolar affective disorder, obsessive compulsive disorder and eating disorder. Personality disorder is not considered here but is detailed in Chapter 6.15 in this volume.

HOW TO IDENTIFY SEVERE MENTAL ILLNESS

The Assessment

The mental state examination (MSE) is a useful tool for ensuring a holistic approach to assessing the severity of a client's illness. For a more in depth account, see Sadock and Sadock (2008).

It is important to recognise that the MSE is in some ways a snapshot for the client and must be supported by a background history of the problem and a coherent sense of the client's journey through life. This framework can be used as a way of building on 'active listening' whilst conducting an assessment. Table 3.6.1 is by no means complete but is a way of capturing as much information as possible about the client's current mental state. The table contains clinical examples of signs, or symptoms, noted through an assessment and gives a suggestion of a possible diagnosis.

Background History

A wide variety of influences and circumstances create psychological distress and mental ill health. Biological, psychological and social factors each play their part in the development and perpetuation of mental health problems. Debate is ongoing as to the impact of genetic predisposition versus life experience and the impact of poverty, neglect and abuse. Building up a picture of all the factors that might predispose someone to mental illness, particularly those that we can attenuate, can guide decision making, both in the acute phase of a severe mental illness and the long-term treatment plan. Assessment should include family history of mental health problems, early life, and coping styles or personal resources to deal with stress. Loss, bereavement or significant life events, the presence of chronic pain or illness and the natural history of the presenting problem will add valuable information and avenues to treatment.

Risk Assessment

Information and risk

Assessing severe mental illness is the amalgamation of several different aspects of a client's needs, current presentation (mental state examination) and history. Alongside the face-to-face assessment and information gathered at interview, with the client's consent, it is important to access all further possible sources of information available to you. This may be primary care records, letters, occupational health reports, and where possible corroboration from carers, family and friends. In some situations these sources may be limited by confidentiality.

The therapeutic space and its inherent confidentiality are essential components of an alliance with your client. A discussion about access to other sources, although sometimes challenging, can strengthen the alliance; this is part of working together to find the best outcome.

Identifying risk

There are some situations where our duty of care, or legal obligations, outweigh the need for confidentiality. This is the area of risk. Risk can be split into four main areas as follows. Mental ill health can impact on these four domains in several ways, as in the examples given.

1 *Risk to self and suicide.* The presence of depression, and the emergence of a strong sense of hopelessness and thoughts of suicide, are strong factors in the risk of completed suicide.
2 *Risk of harm to others.* Paranoia, common in psychotic illness, can manifest in the client's perceived need for protection, sometimes leading to the use of weapons.
3 *Vulnerability to sexual or financial exploitation.* Mania or hypomania in bipolar affective disorder can lead to sexual disinhibition and a reduced ability to make sound judgements around financial (and other) decisions.
4 *Risk to physical health, i.e. dehydration or worsening of chronic illness such as diabetes.* Depression and the negative symptoms of schizophrenia can lead to marked difficulties in self-care, changes in appetite and a reduction in the motivation to manage comorbid physical problems.

Your approach will depend on your context, and different organisations work with risk in different ways. Approaching the organisation or your manager and asking for protocols or procedures, especially around managing risk, can be very helpful before facing the dilemmas detailed above. If you are a sole practitioner then contacting your professional body can be a good source of guidance. For the purposes of this section I will concentrate on risk to self and suicide.

Table 3.6.1 *Mental state assessment*

Observation	Clinical examples	Suggestive of ...
Appearance and behaviour		
General demeanour and self-care	Poorly kempt, body odour, underweight	Depression, negative symptoms of schizophrenia, eating disorder
Eye contact	Poor eye contact	Depression
Clothing	Inappropriate for the time of year	Mania or hypomania
	Exceptionally colourful	
	Hat pulled down over ears	Experiencing auditory hallucinations
Tremor	Fine or coarse tremor	Anxiety disorder, side effect of medications
How are they sitting?	On the edge of the chair	Anxiety disorder
	Restless	
Interaction	Avoiding shaking hands or touching door handle	Obsessive compulsive disorder, fear of contamination
Speech		
Rate, rhythm, tone and volume	Loud rapid and uninterruptable	Mania or hypomania
	Quiet, monosyllabic	Depression
Content of speech	Loosening of association between sentences	Thought disorder, an aspect of psychosis
Can you follow the train of thought?	Jumping from one subject to another unrelated subject or 'flight of ideas'	Mania or hypomania
	Punning	
Affect		
Predominant mood during assessment	High, overfamiliar, euphoric	Mania or hypomania
	Low, sad, hopeless, suicidal	Depression
	Restricted range of mood or emotion 'flat'	Schizophrenia
	Changeable through assessment, 'labile' or incongruent	Mania or hypomania
Mood		
Predominant mood over last few weeks	Low, tearful, hopeless, guilty	Depression
	Disturbed sleep, early morning waking, reduced appetite, lethargy	Depression and anxiety disorder

Table 3.6.1 *(Continued)*

Observation	Clinical examples	Suggestive of ...
Thought and perception		
Predominant thought processes	High, euphoric, disinhibited, overfriendly	Mania or hypomania
	Irritable, little or no sleep	
	Anxious, restless, shaky, distressed	Anxiety disorder
	Guilty, hopeless, self critical	Depression
	Difficulty making decisions, health anxieties, catastrophising	Anxiety disorder
	Preoccupation with weight (despite normal or low body mass index) and distorted body image	Eating disorder
Delusions	A fixed, false belief contrary to social background, religious beliefs and evidence	Psychosis
	Grandiose beliefs, belief in a special talent or skill, e.g. communicating directly with Jesus	Mania or hypomania
	A belief in having terminal cancer despite multiple investigations proving negative	Psychotic depression
Hallucinations	Paranoid beliefs, e.g. MI5 are watching me on covert cameras in my house	Schizophrenia, depression
	Seeing or hearing things that others do not perceive (applies to all the senses)	Schizophrenia, depression, mania
Cognition		
Understanding of time of day and day of week	Disorientation in time, place and person	'Pseudodementia' in depression
Knowing where they are and who they are speaking to		Dementia
		Intoxication
Insight		
A client's view of their own difficulties	Unaware of the possibility of mental illness	Insight can be limited in any mental illness. This has implications for management and treatment options
Their motivation to seek help and ability to engage and consent	Reluctant to engage with services	

Risk factors for suicide

During the process of assessing someone with high levels of distress or perceived risk, eliciting known risk factors is helpful in separating oneself from the powerful emotions that can be present in the room. In some senses this may represent a departure from your normal method of working depending on your background, the ethos of the organisation you work for, and the model or psychological framework within which you work. Bearing this in mind, and balancing it with the need to adhere to the model within which you work, there are relatively well-understood risk factors that can help to predict the possibility of further self-harm and completed suicide. Sometimes use of risk scales or tools can be of value, e.g. the Beck Suicide Inventory (Beck et al., 1991), although the evidence is not clear of their impact on suicide rates (Mann et al., 2005). See also Chapter 6.22 in this volume.

The following are key risk factors that may indicate a more immediate or high risk of self-harm or suicide (adapted from Cheng et al., 2000):

1   family history of suicide
2   family history of child maltreatment or neglect
3   previous suicide attempt(s)
4   history of mental disorders, particularly clinical depression
5   history of alcohol and substance misuse
6   feelings of hopelessness
7   impulsive or aggressive tendencies
8   isolation, a feeling of being cut off from other people
9   barriers to accessing mental health treatment (stigma)
10 loss (relational, social, work, or financial)
11 bereavement
12 physical illness
13 easy access to lethal methods.

Management

Following an assessment of the need for further referral on to other services, organising and communicating key information are a priority in the client's journey. Communicating to partner services can be containing for client and carers and ensure a smooth transition into another team. Barriers to communication can be wide and varied, including different outlooks on mental illness, i.e. secondary mental health services mainly adhering to the medical or psychiatric model, accident and emergency units often focusing on immediate need, and specialist teams whose remit is a particular problem or diagnosis, e.g. eating disorders. It can be useful for you as a sole practitioner or as an organisation to encourage links with local services, ask for referral criteria and familiarise yourself with local care pathways for people with severe mental illness.

Organising The Information From Your Assessment

Once agreement has been reached between you and your client of the need for referral to secondary mental health services or crisis response teams, the next stage is to draw the information together in order to communicate essential aspects of the history, formulation and current problems to an appropriate team. This can be a difficult point for clients and the professionals involved. Different perspectives on mental health problems in different settings, organisations or services can mean that language, approach and priorities can be quite disparate. For instance crisis and home treatment teams aimed at managing severe mental illness in the acute phase, alongside high levels of risk, may have an alternative view of the immediacy of your client's difficulties.

Organising information can help to mediate the boundary between services. The following is a suggested format:

1   *Background history*

   - family history of mental health problems
   - history of childhood emotional, physical or sexual abuse and neglect
   - physical illness
   - medication (current and past)
   - previous history of mental health problems
   - natural history of current episode
   - recent bereavement or loss
   - social and family support

2   *Current mental state*

   - salient positive features (symptoms and signs) of MSE
   - insight, motivation and capacity to consent to referral or treatment

3   *Risk assessment*

   - summary of risk information
   - formal risk assessment or tool

4   *Personal information*

   - full name and date of birth
   - name, address and telephone number of general practitioner
   - usual address and where they are staying now
   - home and mobile telephone number of client and carers or friends.

Clients Identified as High Risk

On completion of the assessment and recognition of a severe mental illness, and/or if associated high risk is identified in any or all of the risk domains detailed above, referral must be considered. At this point if high levels of risk have been identified, the sharing of that risk is an important part of professional duty of care. Discussion with colleagues, supervisors, managers, general practitioners and your local crisis and home treatment team or community mental health team (CMHT) can facilitate a response appropriate to your client's current presentation. This is also a way of checking out your assessment of need and risk. Working with our clients in the psychotherapeutic context means that we can be finely attuned to their thoughts, feelings and needs. The depth of our involvement, the nature of our work, the understanding of our client, and the complex dynamics involved in a therapeutic relationship can sometimes skew our assessment of risk and need. Sharing the risk with another professional or team can help contain some of our anxieties and ensure an appropriate response to the current crisis.

If a client who has been assessed as high risk does not consent to referral or sharing of information, a judgement needs to be made about the immediacy of the risk and whether the risk of significant harm outweighs the client's right to confidentiality. Sometimes severe mental illness can impact directly on a client's capacity to consent to treatment. In this situation, around a particular decision, we are able to act in the best interests of the client. With the introduction of the Mental Capacity Act 2005 we are all entitled to make 'unwise decisions' when we are able to understand the risks and consequences of our actions or choices. In some mental illness our capacity to make *specific* decisions may be reduced. For instance, some people with severe depression may present with reduced cognitive abilities or 'pseudo-dementia'. This compromises the ability to think clearly and weigh up complex problems or treatment choices.

Capacity needs to be assessed for *each* decision that may have a significant impact for our client. Capacity is not global. It is to be assessed in relation to a particular question or decision. An assessment of how much a mental illness or disorder is interrupting capacity can be completed by anyone involved in someone's care; however, if it is particularly complex, it can be requested from the general practitioner or local CMHT. It is essential that a clear record of the decision making process is kept; for further guidance see the Mental Capacity Act Code of Practice (Department for Constitutional Affairs, 2007).

REFERENCES

Beck, A.T. and Steer, R.A. (1991) *Manual for Beck Scale for Suicide Ideation*. San Antonio, TX: Psychological Corporation.

Cheng, A.T.A., Chen, T.H.H., Chen, C. and Jenkins, R. (2000) Psychosocial and psychiatric risk factors for suicide. *British Journal of Psychiatry*, 177: 360–5.

Department for Constitutional Affairs (2007) *Mental Capacity Act 2005 Code of Practice*. London: Stationery Office.

Mann, J.M.D. (2005) Suicide prevention strategies: a systematic review. *Journal of the American Medical Association*, 294: 2064–74.

Sadock, B.J. and Sadock, A.V. (2008) *Kaplan and Sadock's Concise Textbook of Psychiatry*. Philadelphia: Lippincott, Williams and Wilkins.

Structuring Work with Clients

IAN HORTON

This chapter examines the structure and process of counselling and psychotherapy. In places it overlaps with topics in the following chapters, but the emphasis here is on therapeutic phases. The assumption is made that, irrespective of theoretical orientation, it is possible to conceptualize the therapeutic process in terms of a framework of broadly defined phases or stages. Each phase is characterized by particular process goals or tasks that need to be achieved as a prerequisite of moving forward to the next phase (Beitman, 1990; Egan, 2010; McLeod, 2003). As a structural overview of the developmental process, the framework provides therapists with a sense of grounding and direction. But it is only a cognitive map and as such cannot reflect the actual experience or dynamics of a process that seldom, if ever, follows a straightforward linear progression through discrete and clearly defined phases. As the relationship between therapist and client develops, new issues may emerge, goals are evaluated and often redefined, and earlier phase-related tasks may be revisited and worked on more deeply. It is a fluid, multidimensional and complex process.

A simple generic model of the four phases of therapy – preparatory, beginning, middle and ending – is used here as a heuristic framework for examining the typical structure, process and procedures of counselling and psychotherapy. The therapist's own theoretical orientation will largely determine the relative emphasis and importance placed on the various aspects of the four-phase model. Some psychotherapists regard initial and ongoing frame management as the main, if not the

only, kind of legitimate structuring (e.g. Smith, 1991) and many psychoanalytic therapists are unconcerned with temporal and outcome issues. On the other hand, some forms of brief therapy are highly structured in terms of temporal phases.

PREPARATORY PHASE

Many practitioners believe that the therapeutic relationship actually begins before any face-to-face contact with clients. Several factors may influence both the client's and the therapist's expectations of each other and therefore the beginning of their relationship and the subsequent development of the therapeutic process. For some counsellors or psychotherapists, the normal procedure may be for a senior therapist to conduct an intake assessment, followed by allocation to a suitable therapist – a process which in itself may structure expectations and norms.

Prior Knowledge

The therapist may have a referral letter or report containing detailed information about the client and her or his presenting problem and history. Casual comments made by the receptionist or other people working in the agency or service setting may unwittingly influence the therapist's expectations of the client.

Clients themselves will often come to therapy with preconceptions about counselling or psychotherapy and project them on to the particular therapist. Previous experience of some form of psychological or psychiatric help (a phenomenon that is increasing), or accounts of the experiences of others, may similarly influence the client's expectations. The client may have heard something about the reputation of the particular therapist or agency.

Introductory Leaflet

Many agencies or therapists produce information leaflets to give to potential clients. The purpose is to inform the client about the conditions and procedures to follow and what to expect when coming for counselling or psychotherapy. The leaflet, read carefully by some potential clients and probably ignored by others, is nevertheless an opportunity to help establish positive and accurate expectations of what therapy is about. An information leaflet for clients will normally contain the following information:

- some explanation of what counselling and/or psychotherapy is about
- examples of the kinds of problems people might come with and how therapy can help
- background information about the particular agency or service offered
- qualifications, experience and professional affiliation of the therapists providing the service
- how to make an appointment
- fees and how these are paid
- cancellation procedures, fee implications and period of notice required
- typical duration and frequency of sessions and length of contract
- theoretical orientation and approach to counselling or psychotherapy
- where the counselling or therapy will take place, postal address, name and telephone number of therapist or contact person.

First Telephone Call

Often the first direct contact between client and therapist is through a telephone call. Many people do not find it easy to be a client and have to admit to others (and to themselves) that they have problems they cannot cope with. Some people agonize for some time before plucking up enough courage to make the initial telephone call. The client may be upset, diffident about making the call or sceptical about counselling or psychotherapy. The reception he or she receives, what the therapist says and how it is said, may influence the caller's feelings and attitudes. The therapist may be very busy or tired,

but if he or she is able to offer a place for an initial appointment, this is the first opportunity to start building rapport by communicating some degree of warmth and concern and perhaps by responding to callers by mirroring the way they speak. In one sense the therapeutic relationship starts at this point. The client needs to feel accepted, welcomed and understood. What happens next and what is being offered need to be explained simply and clearly.

Letter of Appointment

In some situations the letter offering a first appointment may be the first contact with the client, who, even from this limited source of information, may begin to develop some impression of the therapist and the service offered. Therapists may want to convey a balance of warmth and professional formality in what and how they write to clients. Letters, usually typed or neatly handwritten on headed A4 notepaper, would normally include information about the location, date, time and duration of the first session, as well as the contact telephone number and, if appropriate, how and by when the client should confirm acceptance of the appointment. Some examples of letters to clients can be found in Chapter 3.8 on ancillary skills in this volume.

Preparation Before the Client Arrives

Few if any therapists would disagree that it is absolutely essential to arrive on time and before the client arrives. Beginning practitioners often like to arrive early to check the room (see Chapter 3.8), read through the referral report or their case notes, and maximize their level of 'free attention'.

Practitioners vary in their attitude towards referrers' reports. Some like to study the reports carefully, noting issues to explore with the client or at least to hold as 'silent hypotheses'. Some agencies adopt a policy of asking clients to complete a pre-interview questionnaire on background history and personal details. Other practitioners want to meet the client without being influenced by the apparent facts and opinions provided by the referrer. They deliberately do not read the referral letter until after their first meeting with the client. The risk with this procedure is that the referrer might mention some critical issue which the therapist really does need to be aware of *before* meeting the client – for example, a record of frequent violent or aggressive behaviour or recent suicide attempts. The key issue is for the therapist to be aware of her or his assumptions or inferences drawn from what can sometimes be highly subjective and often dated information about the client.

Immediately prior to the expected arrival of the client, some therapists follow deliberate procedures to enable them to relax and focus attention on what they are about to do. Simple physical relaxation or breathing exercises or just sitting in silence for a few minutes can help the therapist to prepare mentally.

BEGINNING PHASE

The first face-to-face meeting with the client sows the seeds of attraction, uncertainty or dislike and the beginning of the therapist's assessment of the client. People are often unaware of the source of their feelings or immediate reactions to others, although counsellors and therapists are trained to be aware of the way in which they may prematurely interpret what they notice about the dress and demeanour of others, or may project feelings or attitudes derived from previous relationships or situations on to their clients. But of course this is a two-way process: clients will have feelings too and will make assumptions about the therapist on their first meeting. Both parties will be tentatively sizing the other up.

Initial Greeting and Seating

Practitioners vary in the degree of formality with which they greet their clients. Many do so warmly, but wait for the client to indicate tentatively whether they expect to shake hands. It is important to get the client's name correct and it is useful to become familiar with the naming conventions of different cultures. If in doubt, it is an idea to ask clients how they wish to be addressed or at least initially to adopt a more formal manner of address, leaving until later the choice to become more familiar. Some culturally different names may be difficult for therapists to pronounce. Again it would be appropriate for the therapist to ask the client how to pronounce her or his name. This at least communicates that it matters to the therapist to get the client's name right. Especially in some cultures, counsellors and psychotherapists are seen as powerful people, and clients initially feeling overwhelmed are unlikely to correct the therapist's pronunciation of their name or the mode of address and may feel put down or feel that the therapist does not really care about them as individuals.

Another concern for some therapists is whether to leave it to clients to decide where to sit or, more conventionally, whether to indicate where the client should sit. To leave it to the client may, albeit in a small way, help the client to feel more equal in an inevitably unequal relationship, but it can mean that the client has yet another unfamiliar decision to make at a time when they are already feeling anxious about what is going to happen.

Introduction

'How can I help you?', 'What brings you here?', 'We have 50 minutes together; how would you like to use the time?' are some of the ways in which therapists encourage the client to start talking as soon as possible. Some psychoanalytic therapists think it important to say *nothing* from the outset. However, other practitioners prefer to start by setting the scene, being aware that once some clients launch into telling their story it is hard to stop them, while other more reticent clients appreciate some time to relax into their new surroundings with a stranger and have little or no idea how the therapist might be able to help them or how to use the time. There is some 'collective wisdom', if not clear research evidence, that indicates a strong correlation or association between successful outcome and a shared understanding between therapist and client of the purpose of what they are doing together and how they are going to try to achieve it. This shared understanding is the basis of an effective working or therapeutic alliance. So some therapists prefer to start by saying something like: 'The purpose of our first meeting today is for us to get to know each other and for me to begin to understand something of the problems or issues that bring you here. At the end of the hour we may be in a position to decide whether we want to continue to work together and we will discuss the necessary arrangements.' Some clients may have been sent by their GP or persuaded by a friend to come and may be sceptical about the value of counselling or psychotherapy. In this situation the task is to try to establish whether or not there is a basis for working together and the therapist may suggest to the client that they leave it to a subsequent session before formally contracting to work with the client. This would give the therapist an opportunity to consult her or his clinical supervisor before seeing the client again.

Therapist's Agenda

Theoretical orientation, personal preference and style, and agency setting and organizational constraints or procedures are some of the factors that may determine the way in which the first session is structured and managed. While most therapists tend to adopt a similar way of working with all their clients, some vary what they do according to perceived client needs and expectations. The style and approach differ enormously between therapists – even those of the same orientation – and vary along a continuum from formal and highly structured to open, flexible and very much client led.

Nevertheless, whether it is explicit or not, most practitioners will have a similar agenda for the first few sessions or for the beginning phase of their work with clients. This agenda may typically include the following process goals or tasks, irrespective of whether they are achieved through listening to the client's story, intervening as appropriate as the story gradually unfolds, or asking questions in a more structured interview.

Some therapists listen for or deliberately ask about the client's expectations and previous experiences of counselling or psychotherapy. This information will help the therapist to assess the client's needs and level of readiness and to know how best to begin to facilitate a strong therapeutic alliance.

For clients for whom counselling or psychotherapy is a truly new and unfamiliar experience, the therapist may need to explain what therapy is about, the roles of therapist and client, and what is going to happen. Beginning therapists may find it a very useful exercise to prepare and rehearse the actual words they might use to define or explain counselling or psychotherapy to clients.

The whole idea of therapy as an approach to problem solving or self-development is culture bound. Seeking help with psychological problems from someone outside the family is alien to some cultures, and clients may need time to discuss and assimilate the implications and consequences of doing so. Similarly, counselling and psychotherapy goals are culture bound. For example, such concepts as self-awareness or self-actualization and the emphasis on individualism may be inappropriate as explicitly stated goals when working with some clients in cross-cultural settings.

At some point in the first (few) session(s) it is usually helpful for the therapist to say something about the ground rules or boundaries of counselling or psychotherapy. Issues about privacy, confidentiality and its limits, the length of sessions and time boundaries may need to be explained and discussed. If the therapist is culturally close to the client, some clients may feel an instant rapport and trust, but others may fear a loss of confidentiality and feel as if they risk what they say being known by everyone in their cultural community. The therapist may need to reassure the client that he or she respects confidence and that therapy is in no way compatible with socializing. Some clients may disclose something critical near the end of the session, in what feels like the safety of the session ending; other clients may

be unfamiliar with the strict timekeeping of middle-class Western practice and be left feeling resentful when invited by the therapist to raise the issue again in their next session.

Facilitating client self-disclosure is the primary task of the beginning phase of therapy. Talking about themselves and their problem is after all exactly what the client has come for. The therapist will listen to the client's story and explore the client's social and cultural background, history and experiences, the onset of the problem, current stresses and issues, coping behaviours and motivations. This will enable both the therapist and the client to begin building a picture of the problem and to consider if and how therapy might help. Some therapists start to develop a formal assessment or clinical formulation of the client's presenting problem and, from this, an initial therapeutic plan or possible therapeutic goals and approach to working with the particular client.

At this point, usually at the end of the first session, therapists need to make a decision. Basically there are four options:

- to offer counselling or psychotherapy
- to offer to refer the client to another therapist or agency
- not to offer counselling or psychotherapy if the therapist thinks it would be inappropriate or not useful to the particular client at this time
- to defer the decision to contract until a later session.

Therapists approach contracting with clients with varying degrees of formality, clarity and explicitness (Sills, 2006). It is possible to identify two types of contracting: therapeutic and business contracts. The first is concerned with negotiating and identifying with the client the sort of desired outcomes the therapy might achieve, and the initial focus or aspect of the problem that the therapist and client intend to work on together and how they might approach this. The nature of the therapeutic contract and whether it is stated explicitly and even written down will depend very much on the therapist's theoretical orientation and personal preference. Some therapists assume that the therapeutic contract is part of the client's induction into therapy and a largely unspoken yet integral part of the gradually evolving therapeutic process.

The business contract is important and few therapists disagree that it needs to be concrete and explicit. The business contract concerns such things as the duration, frequency, number, day and starting time of sessions, fees and how they are to be paid, procedures for the cancellation of sessions, and fees for missed sessions. Some therapists like to give this information in written form and include the date and time of the next appointment.

Comprehensive details of contracting from the perspectives of different theoretical orientations are given in Sills (2006).

Ending the first session is an opportunity to clarify administrative details and handle any questions the client may still have about the therapy, before confirming the next appointment and parting.

Summary: Beginning Phase
Process Goals

The beginning phase may last for one, 20 or more sessions depending on the nature of the contract, the theoretical orientation and the progress made. The process goals or tasks that need to be accomplished are summarized here:

- Build the relationship, establish rapport and an effective working alliance, clarify boundaries, conditions and the client's role, and work towards developing mutual aims about the work of therapy.
- Facilitate client self-disclosure; identify the client's presenting problem through understanding the client's worldview and experiences, exploring antecedents, precipitating events, social/cultural context and assessment of client strengths and resources. The therapist may begin to develop a tentative assessment of the nature, origins and ramifications of the client's problem(s) in a way that suggests a possible target for change. In some psychodynamic work the early fostering of a positive transference might be a key task.
- Negotiate therapeutic and business contracts, and monitor and review progress.

MIDDLE PHASE

This is typically the longest phase in counselling or psychotherapy. It is the work phase in which conflicts and problems are more clearly defined and worked through. It is within this phase that the biggest variation in practice exists. What therapists are trying to achieve and how they approach the work are largely determined by their theoretical orientation and how they explain the origin and maintenance of psychological problems and the principles and process of change. Nevertheless, at least in broad terms, it is possible to identify the kinds of process goals or tasks generally associated with this phase.

Summary: Middle Phase
Process Goals

The aspect of the counselling or psychotherapy process most strongly associated with successful outcome is the quality of the therapeutic relationship and the strength of the working alliance. In the middle phase work continues to maintain and develop further the relationship between therapist and client. Where appropriate and consistent with the therapist's theoretical orientation, the dynamics of the relationship, or what is going on within both therapist and client and between them, may be used as a basis for learning and motivation. The dynamics of the relationship between therapist and client can often provide a 'window' on the client's presenting problem and any hidden conflicts or issues.

In the middle phase the therapist is concerned with facilitating learning and change, congruent with the identified therapeutic goals and theoretical assumptions about change. It is also the phase in which sometimes unexpected memories, discoveries, obstacles, crises and ambivalence or defences may arise. The process goals of this phase may involve searching for patterns and key themes in the client's experiences and behaviours, affirming and, where possible and appropriate, using the client's strengths and ways of coping, working towards new perspectives, deeper self-awareness or understanding, and learning different ways of thinking, feeling and/or behaving.

Therapists vary in how and whether they explicitly monitor progress. Some formally contract to hold regular review sessions with their clients; others rely solely on clinical supervision, personal reflection and writing case notes to review progress; while some believe in suspending the notion of anxiety about progress altogether.

Reviewing

Some practitioners strongly advocate the need to include regular review sessions in their contract with clients, so that every five weeks or so the client will know that at least part of the session will be spent reviewing progress. Other therapists will review only informally, whenever it seems appropriate or when something comes up, or alternatively only when the work has reached an impasse, when things feel stuck and little, if any, progress is being made. However, clients are entitled to a competently delivered service that is periodically reviewed (BACP, 2002).

The arguments for explicitly monitoring progress with the client include:

- to check out the therapist's assumption about how things are going and if necessary use the opportunity to make changes or improve ways of working

- to reinforce learning and change or the conditions for change
- to share power with the client by involving the client in evaluating progress and to help re-establish that the therapist is working *with* the client rather than for, or doing something to, the client.

Arguments against any formal review sessions might be that they interrupt the whole therapeutic process and that any impasse, stuckness or resistance is better worked through as a natural part of the therapy. Review sessions could be seen as a way of avoiding or even perpetuating resistance to change and potentially damaging the transference relationship and may be misinterpreted by some clients as a review of *them*.

Review Session Structure

Review sessions will be conducted with varying degrees of structure and formality. In standard long-term psychoanalytic psychotherapy, any form of review may be discouraged, while some therapists adopt the practice of asking at *each* session 'what the client wants', 'how it went', etc. However, a full review agenda would usually involve discussing the following aspects:

- Client and therapist expectations and understanding of what it is they are trying to achieve together.
- Therapeutic goals: what has been achieved? What changes have occurred? What evidence is there of any change?
- Client's experience of the therapeutic process and relationship: what has the client found helpful, unhelpful or difficult? What problems, if any, do the therapist and client have in working together?
- Negotiate ways forward. Review and confirm, or, if necessary, revise the therapeutic goals or focus of the work, and discuss possible alternative ways of working.
- Review the business contract, and recontract for a further period before the next review session.

ENDING PHASE

The ending phase of therapy may represent a real or symbolic loss for many clients. It can provide a potent force in changing a client's frame of mind. In thinking about how best to orchestrate endings or the termination of counselling or psychotherapy, therapists will need to have views, although not necessarily clearly articulated views, on several issues (Davis, 2008; Leigh, 1998):

- How explicit is the issue of ending therapy with clients? How important is it to prepare for the ending? Some therapists discuss the ending at the beginning of their work with clients; others use a 'countdown' system to remind clients about how many sessions they have had and how many remain. Who decides when therapy should end? Is it decided by the client, by the therapist or by mutual agreement?
- How rigid is the decision about ending? Will the therapist adhere strictly to the agreed ending date? This decision is usually linked to the nature of the therapeutic goals, type of contract and sometimes negotiated or otherwise implicit completion criteria. Clearly, therapists need to be aware of what, if any, are the circumstances that justify an extension and how flexible they can be and what the ramifications are.
- What may be the special existential or development needs of the particular client around loss and ending?

For some clients, separation and loss may have been a key theme or conflict in their work with the therapist. Ending therapy may mean a reworking of earlier loss or a celebration of a new beginning. Ending may be more critical in some types of time-limited contracts and therapists need to pay attention to managing effectively client resources and deficits.

Summary: Ending Phase Process Goals

Most therapists will pay attention to some or all of the following tasks in working towards a satisfactory ending with their clients:

- seeking resolution of the client's issues around ending
- exploring ways of consolidating learning and change through helping clients to apply and assimilate change into new ways of being or living and through identifying obstacles and ways of sustaining and expanding change
- evaluating the outcomes of therapy and the effectiveness (or otherwise) of the therapeutic process and relationship.

A high percentage of counselling and psychotherapy contracts end by default rather than by design. That is, clients may just stop coming for therapy, sometimes not even letting the therapist know and not replying to the therapist's letter. Incomplete ending by default can haunt therapists for some time. It is all too easy to slip into imagining all sorts of circumstances or reasons, including the therapist's own mistakes or incompetence, for clients failing to attend to the end of a negotiated contract or agreed period of therapy. These things are best worked through in clinical supervision. However, most therapists will have the opportunity to formally complete their ending work with a client.

Ending Session Structure

Ending can be viewed as a process in itself. The aim is to help clients integrate their views of what has happened and reinforce the positive aspects of the experience. The intention is to enable clients to sustain any change.

There are five areas that can be usefully explored with clients at the end of counselling or psychotherapy:

- *What has been achieved?* What changes have occurred or are anticipated by both client and therapist? Were the goals met?
- *What still needs to be achieved?* Is it possible to anticipate any return of symptoms in particular circumstances? Will the client be able to cope with old problems using the new 'solutions' or ways of coping learned in therapy?
- *Why has change happened?* How does the client attribute cause or responsibility for change? The client's story about therapy is the best predictor of whether useful changes will last. Clients need to know the ways that they contributed to or are responsible for any change, attempts to change and the quality of the relationship.
- *What may happen in the future?* Is it possible to anticipate any stresses or 'rough spots'? What resources are available for support? Sometimes it is helpful to try to identify signs or indicators of the need to start therapy again. Will the therapist offer a one-off follow-up in say six to eight weeks, or invite the client to make contact again if necessary? What possible messages might that give to the client? What seems important is that a 'good ending' will help to ensure that clients will have positive feelings about the prospect of returning to therapy – and see it not as a failure, but as a normal occurrence in developmental change.

- *What has been the nature of the therapy relationship?* This can be threatening to the therapist, and some see it as irrelevant to identifying what qualities were helpful and/or difficult in the relationship. The client may be encouraged to identify what has been learned from the therapy relationship that may help the client in other relationships.

Many of the skills and procedures mentioned in this chapter are developed in the next chapter, on ancillary skills. Further clarification can also be found in Dryden and Reeves (2008) and Timulak (2011).

REFERENCES

BACP (2002) *Ethical Framework for Good Practice in Counselling and Psychotherapy.* Rugby: British Association for Counselling and Psychotherapy.

Beitman, B.D. (1990) Why I am an integrationist (not an eclectic). In W. Dryden and J.C. Norcross (eds), *Eclecticism and Integration in Counselling and Psychotherapy.* Loughton: Gale Centre.

Davis, D.D. (2008) *Terminating Therapy: A Professional Guide to Ending on a Positive Note.* New York: Wiley.

Dryden, W. and Reeves, A. (eds) (2008) *Key Issues for Counselling in Action* (2nd edn). London: Sage.

Egan, G. (2010) *The Skilled Helper* (9th edn). Pacific Grove, CA: Brooks/Cole.

Leigh, A. (1998) *Referral and Termination Issues for Counsellors.* London: Sage.

McLeod, J. (2003) *An Introduction to Counselling* (3rd edn). Buckingham: Open University Press.

Sills, C. (ed.) (2006) *Contracts in Counselling and Psychotherapy* (2nd edn). London: Sage.

Smith, D.L. (1991) *Hidden Conversations: An Introduction to Communicative Psychoanalysis.* London: Routledge.

Timulak, L. (2011) *Developing Your Counselling and Psychotherapy Skills and Practice.* London: Sage.

Ancillary Skills

COLIN FELTHAM

In addition to the many overt, in-session, interpersonal, therapeutic or clinical skills, there are many ancillary skills necessary for good practice. These are largely 'before and after' skills, and relate to mediated communication with clients, the setting for therapy, safety, recording and reflecting on practice; they comprise a set of skills falling somewhere between clinical and professional/business skills. While 'ancillary' may not be the best word for those internal skills of reflecting on the moment-to-moment encounter with clients, reference to these as a form of self-monitoring is nevertheless included here. To some extent how extra-therapeutic communications are managed depends on ordinary social skills, yet there are often subtle psychological and ethical considerations involved which render them quite complex. Practitioners need to find an appropriate balance between the routine and the practical, and ethically challenging issues can arise at any time (BACP, 2002).

RECEIVING REFERRALS

The manner in which clients make contact with therapists – directly or via intermediaries or certain media (letter, telephone, etc.) – depends a great deal on the nature of the practice setting. Inward referral issues are discussed here. The word 'clients' is used throughout, even though some contacts will be inquirers only.

Contact Variations

- 'Cold' contact via telephone, where the client's call is the first communication about them. This is common in private practice.
- Expected telephone contact, where an intermediary has already alerted both parties to the possibility of a referral.
- Message taken or appointment made by a receptionist, colleague or senior.
- A (usually senior) colleague allocates the client to a particular therapist following assessment.
- The client attends a 'drop-in' service and, depending on availability, may be seen almost immediately.
- Some clients initiate contact by written correspondence if they are wary, are tentative or have mobility problems.
- Formal written referral and (psychiatric, mental state, history) report from GP or psychiatrist.
- Referral via GP through Improving Access to Psychological Therapies (IAPT) services to an appropriate first professional.
- Increasingly, contacts are made via email following consultation of websites.

Two quite different scenarios are involved in all this. First, in single-handed private practice, initial contacts are typically by telephone, and frequently the caller will be completely unknown; this is especially likely when therapists advertise. This scenario immediately raises considerations of *preparation* (a practice diary, a rehearsed or spontaneous response to requests for counselling or therapy, etc.) and of *safety* (protection of client and practitioner safety). Preparation and safety issues are discussed later in this chapter.

Second, in counselling or psychotherapy agencies or private practice collectives, it is quite typical for new clients to pass through a process entailing elements of telephone inquiry, waiting lists, assessment, allocation and first appointment. Many agency-oriented issues are dealt with in Lago and Kitchin (1998) and the focus here is mainly on private practice and/or lone practitioner issues (Clark, 2002).

Telephone issues

Certain telephone skills are discussed in Part VII of this book. Clearly, it is necessary to consider who will answer the telephone (particularly in a multi-occupancy house or busy office) and what unintended first impressions clients may formulate. Background noises of children, music, television, office staff laughing, etc. are likely to detract from a professional image and could inadvertently convey the impression that the therapist or agency is too busy with other matters to give full attention to the client.

A separate practice line most usefully deals with some of the potential problems since an answerphone message can be tailored to meet the calls of clients telephoning when no one is available to answer in person. ('This is the counselling/psychotherapy practice of Paulette Jones. I'm sorry I'm unavailable at the moment. Please leave your telephone number and I will call back as soon as possible, or try calling again between 10 a.m. and 1 p.m. on Wednesdays and Fridays.') Different practitioners may disagree on the levels of warmth and informality, as opposed to neutrality and professionalism, they wish to convey by tone of voice and selection of phrases. However, therapeutic relationships begin both consciously and unconsciously at these earliest stages, and even a slightly unfriendly tone of voice or hint of impatience or incompetence may take on personalized negative proportions in some clients' minds. It is important to remember too that many people dislike telephone answering machines and there is some risk of frustrating callers and losing business or take-up of the service when no personal response is available. As in all extra-sessional (outside the session) communication with clients, sensitivity and alertness have to be exercised at all times with regard to the possibility of third parties (on your own or the clients' side) compromising confidentiality.

'I wonder if you can help me. I've been given your name by X organization. I've had a lot of problems and I've been signed off sick with stress.' This is a not unusual opening, although inquiries may of course be anywhere on a range from brief, curt and anxious to lengthy, complex and demanding. Sometimes potential clients may wish to 'interview' the therapist on the telephone, or ask for immediate opinions on their condition, or for recommendations of other therapists. Some will want to know full details of fees, available times and so on, while others may be too embarrassed or distressed to go into such details. In some instances the client's friend, partner or parent will telephone on their behalf, and the therapist needs to anticipate appropriate responses (i.e. to accept or not to accept anything other than a self-referral).

Probably only experience can teach each practitioner what suits her or his situational needs and preferences, but everyone will need to prepare to discuss early on their availability, the range of presenting concerns they feel competent to take on, and preferred referral and assessment procedures. In determining availability, therapists should allocate themselves very specific hours if possible, and anticipate all breaks, holidays and possible clashes of commitments as far in advance as they can. Some prefer to keep telephone contact minimal, for example by offering to meet at no cost for an initial assessment or 'exploratory meeting'. Others, however, offer a specific, sometimes longer initial session for which payment is due. Some have printed leaflets containing details of services, fees, availability and location, which may be sent out prior to a first meeting. Additional considerations need to be thought through in advance for any texting between client and counsellor/therapist. For comparable issues relating to online counselling, see Chapter 7.9 in this volume.

SAFETY

For ethical, legal and obvious personal reasons, all practitioners must anticipate certain issues concerning their clients' and their own physical safety and security.

Attending to client safety

Clients' physical safety may be inadvertently compromised by any of the following:

- the potentially hazardous nature of the neighbourhood in which the therapist lives or works; street lighting; transport; parking; anonymity; privacy; etc.

- hazardous features in access to residence, office and room, including slippery pathways; loose roofing slates/tiles; steep steps; loose carpets; problematic stairways; faulty wiring; fire hazards; etc.
- potential health emergencies, such as asthma attack; fainting; epilepsy; cardiac arrest; psychotic episode; etc.
- possible intrusion and assault by third parties, for example in busy agencies with a mixed clientele.

In most cases the remedy is obvious – property maintenance, adequate insurance, training in first aid, etc. – but it is recommended that self-initiated systematic surveys of potential hazards are carried out and remedies considered. Attention to outward aspects of safety is also, in an important sense, an integral reflection of the provision of psychological containment for and protection of the client. Given the increase in shared practices, it is essential that lines of responsibility and accountability are made explicit.

Practitioner Safety

Therapists owe it to themselves, and to any colleagues or family members who may be affected, to consider necessary self-protection and security measures. Again, thinking over issues of particular relevance to private practitioners (but also to others), these items are significant:

- Working alone: if possible this should be avoided, simply by having other people present in other parts of the house or building, especially if the client is a different sex from the therapist.
- In case of risk of being physically attacked, steps should be taken to install alarm buttons or other means of summoning help. Where possible, *downstairs* rooms near to exits should be used as consulting rooms.
- Careful consideration should be given to what could ensue from accepting referrals involving clients with histories of significant crime, addiction and related activities. Easily removed valuables and potentially dangerous objects should certainly be removed before seeing clients.
- Unwanted intrusions by 'out of hours' telephone calls, unexpected visits, etc. should be addressed as far as possible by clear contracting at the outset.
- While many practitioners and some clients object to tape recording of sessions, this is one way of faithfully recording what happens in sessions in case of unjustified accusations of malpractice.
- Since some therapists have unfortunately been harassed or stalked by clients or ex-clients,

thought should probably be given to prevention (e.g. rigorous assessment), and to how such eventualities will be dealt with should they occur.

- Possible aggression from clients or third parties (e.g. angry partners) should be anticipated, and appropriate methods of defusion employed when necessary. Practitioners, especially those working regularly in or with the criminal justice system, also need to consider and use supervision to reflect on issues pertaining to 'difficult clients' (Norton and McGauley, 1998) and aggressive behaviour (Sills, 2007).

A list of this kind may appear overly and unattractively defensive at first sight and some practitioners will prefer a route of optimal trust. However, the North American experience of litigation has alerted UK practitioners to these areas of concern. Professional indemnity insurance protects practitioners from unnecessary and distracting worry, thus leaving them more able to be fully present for their clients. Another valid objection to such issues is that there may simply be no way of anticipating the many anomalous challenges posed by clients. Perhaps the most that can be suggested is that careful thought be given to preparation, assessment, contracting, alertness to real threat, and robust and sensitive interpersonal skills for managing unexpected challenges.

General Risk Assessment

It could be argued that a therapist has an ethical and professional responsibility to take all reasonable steps to ensure not only their own safety but also that of their clients and, as a possible result of their client's behaviour, that of others. If called to account, therapists should be able to demonstrate that they have taken 'all reasonable steps'. This might include evidence of having conducted a general assessment of risk, either before the therapy starts, as a result of what is already known about the client or situation, or subsequently, as a result of emerging indicators of a potential risk. Evidence of the nature and severity of the hazard or risk should be identified and the likelihood that it will actually happen should be assessed.

A simple model for general risk assessment has three elements and can be applied to potential risks to self, client and/or others:

1 *Hazard severity*

- low (slight or very minor and easily managed)
- medium (potentially serious)
- high (major risk with possible risk of injury or to life)

2 *Likelihood*

- low (seldom present)
- medium (frequently present)
- high (certain or near certain that it could happen at any time)

3 *Overall risk rating*

- low (no action or low priority)
- medium
- high (urgent action and high priority).

Clearly, a written record should be kept of the evidence for each decision and the therapist would be advised to discuss the overall rating with her or his clinical supervisor and, if necessary and appropriate, with the agency manager.

PREPARING THE PHYSICAL ENVIRONMENT

Therapy has been referred to by some as a labour-intensive cottage industry requiring no equipment or props besides a room and two chairs. This is not quite true, however. Jung used the Greek term *temenos* (referring to a sacred precinct, as in 'temple') for the 'out of the ordinary' atmosphere of therapy, and some therapists have extended this metaphor to refer to the psychological significance of the physical environment of the consulting room. Considerable thought and expenditure can go into preparation of the room including, in some cases, structural alterations to buildings – creating a separate, private entrance and/or waiting area, installing soundproofing, etc. Practicalities and limited finances may often govern such matters but privacy, safety and adequate comfort must be provided, and sometimes this may necessitate specific building, conversion and decorating work.

It is important to consider what ambience will be conducive to privacy, psychological safety and reflection; and (often a neglected area) what emotional impact thoughtful aesthetics may have on clients. Those working within the humanistic tradition may wish to incorporate evocative imagery into their décor, as well as using floor cushions or other therapeutic aids. Many therapists weigh up the advantages and disadvantages of using a couch instead of a chair, and in some cases may offer the client a choice. Preferably lighting should be adjustable. It has been suggested that warm and dimly lit interiors encourage (possibly long-term) introspection, while well-lit, businesslike interiors may be suited to the outward-looking briskness of shorter-term therapy (Molnos, 1995). Heating too must be efficient and adjustable enough to provide comfort

without inducing drowsiness. Décor will obviously reflect the occupant's taste, but thought should be given to creating optimal conditions by perhaps *not* keeping personal possessions in the consulting room. A balance may be struck between sparseness (obliging the client to look inward) and usefully evocative features (pictures, artefacts, plants, etc.) which can often become therapeutically useful metaphors.

Some writers go as far as arguing that the therapeutic environment should be both minimalist and constant. In other words, furniture and other items should be no more than necessary: two chairs of the same height and style, perhaps a couch, a small table on which to place a diary, invoice, tissues, but very little else. There should be no telephone, no filing cabinet, computer or other office equipment. In no circumstances should any windows be overlooked or walls be thin enough to hear through. All such precautions provide psychological safety. Other writers and practitioners are more pragmatic, perhaps believing that clients learn as much (or more) from the normal challenges of compromised environments as from special, arguably infantilizing conditions. In many cases therapists have little choice but to practise in far from ideal agency settings. However, anticipation, thoughtfulness and planning in relation to the setting are all significant skills that can add to or detract from the therapeutic experience the client has. Guidance on many of these issues is given in Hemmings and Field (2007), Lago and Kitchin (1998) and Thistle (1998). Rowan (1988) also points out that the therapy environment can unwittingly transmit important political messages to clients.

RECORD KEEPING

Attention should be paid to all records involving clients. These often commence with a note of the first appointment in a diary. A completely separate practice diary ensures that your personal diary does not accidentally reveal details of clients' names and telephone numbers. Increasingly, therapists in institutional settings may have to keep computerized records, and in this case should consult and observe up-to-date data protection legislation. Earlier in this part of the book, suggestions are made as to useful written intake formats. It isn't always obvious that sufficient time has to be allocated within anyone's practice for administrative matters, and in some services a ratio of about 2:1 is used as an indication of practice to administration hours needed (that is, 24 one-hour practice sessions + 1 hour supervision + 12.5 hours administration (including meetings) = a

37.5 hour week). Record keeping includes appointments, case notes, financial records, reports, copies of correspondence, etc.

CASE NOTES

It is good practice to keep regular case notes, although it is not, as is sometimes claimed, necessarily unethical *not* to keep detailed notes (see Chapter 4.5 in this volume). Case notes may also help to demonstrate evidence of professional and ethical responsibility in cases of threatened or potential litigation. However, some means of monitoring one's competency and progress is always essential. The precise character of case notes will be determined by individual style, theoretical orientation and other considerations. Some therapists use pro formas, including headings such as referral source, pre-interview data, first impressions, content/process of sessions, therapeutic plan, supervision issues, etc. Others prefer a 'free writing' format – sometimes referred to as personal case notes to distinguish them from purely factual client data. These may be records of the following:

- The therapist's first impressions, observations, inferences, associations. This may be a mixture of facts, feelings and guesses – e.g. *The client is a tall, elegant man who seemed to bow as he entered the room. His very first words were 'This is cosy', and I was unsure whether this was meaningless small-talk, part of his charm, or a subtle form of defensive sarcasm.* In this example, simple visual observation and a record of actual words spoken are mixed with the therapist's speculations, possibly including implicit elements of counter-transference. Such notes do not claim to be objective and do not aim to be judgemental or diagnostic. Their purpose is (1) immediate reflection and speculation (when made very soon after a session); (2) as an *aide-mémoire*; and (3) as part of an ongoing record of progress to be reviewed from time to time.
- Significant and outstanding phrases, images, dreams, new material (e.g. first disclosure of feelings about father), declared aims, hopes, fears. Often, in a busy practice, very brief notes made immediately or soon after a session are all the therapist may have time for. *Said she'd felt better after last week's session. It had helped to get it all out in the open. She felt ready to look in more depth at the effect of her mother's death when she was 10. Mentioned her two brothers, how they seemed to protect her. She looked directly and appealingly at me several times.*

- The therapist's intentions, ongoing notes on strategies, their usefulness or otherwise, etc. *I had asked her to bring any dreams/try keeping a diary/consider using the relaxation exercise we discussed, etc. ... Today's session seemed to become stuck, arid; next time perhaps I need to challenge, to disclose how that made me feel and prompt the client to express how she feels about it ... We looked at the extent to which the client has been able to tolerate being in the supermarket; there was marked progress – 20 minutes – and it may be time to increase frequency.* It may be apparent that records of this kind are *personal* (i.e. for the therapist's use) and are *notes* (they do not have to be written in polished English, and do not have to make sense to others (unless an agency specifies this). Training in certain approaches (e.g. cognitive-behavioural therapy) may require a detailed record of the implementation of interventions and their impact. In the case of manualized therapies in particular, pro forma checklists of staged interventions may be part of regular record-keeping procedures.
- Reflections on counter-transferential patterns, congruence or transpersonal material. *Felt peculiarly drowsy today when seeing X, which seems odd, since he was talking about being beaten up ... I realize that although my grandfather used to terrify me by the look he gave me, this client really has a similar look; there is perhaps something in him that wants to terrify others ... Don't know why, but I had recurring images of a calm lake when Paul was talking today, and as if we were both floating on it.* Notes of this kind may not even make immediate sense to the writer, but can be returned to and/or taken to supervision later. Increasingly, therapists may be wary about the status of such notes.
- Matters relevant to supervision. Notes may be especially useful for marking queries, doubts, concerns, counter-transferential material and ethical matters to be brought up in supervision. Indeed it is customary in some supervision traditions for the therapist to refer directly to their notes. Additionally, therapeutic intentions arising from supervision sessions may be included in the notes, and the impact of supervision-inspired interventions can be further noted. *It had never occurred to me that I might be trying too hard to help this client ... In the next session, I consciously relaxed, allowed the silences to develop, and X suddenly burst into tears ... My supervisor suggested that I seem cynical and resistant to everything she says when I discuss Angela, and wondered whether this was the effect Angela has on me; she does!*

Case notes should be kept in a secure place, separate from any identifying details of the client concerned, and should not themselves identify clients. Coding systems and pseudonyms should be used. Notes should not be trivializing of or demeaning towards clients. Clients should be informed that records are kept and secured, and that you have plans for their safe disposal. Notes should be dated, with some indication of their 'shelf life' and who may have access to them. It is not normal practice to routinely show clients the notes made about them, but they have the right to see them. Advance thought should be given to the eventuality of the police requesting to see case notes, or of notes becoming the subject of a subpoena in court cases. Personal case notes (even when these are kept separately from 'official' notes) are not necessarily regarded as private under the law.

Counsellors and psychotherapists need to review all their record-keeping and data-processing practices to ensure compliance with the most recent Data Protection Act requirements. The Data Protection Act 1998 gives clients an increasing right to know what is recorded and written about them. It gives clients the right of access to all computerized data processing. However, 'manual' or handwritten records which are kept in some form of structured system like a card index file are also covered by the Act. Some of the key principles of the Act governing client record systems include the following:

- Data must be kept only for specific purposes.
- Data must be relevant, accurate and up-to-date.
- Data must be kept no longer than is necessary for the purpose.
- Data must be protected against misuse.
- Data must respect the client's rights, especially 'sensitive personal data' such as the client's race, religious beliefs, union membership, mental and physical health and sexual history. A counsellor's or psychotherapist's records are now classed as 'sensitive personal data'.

Ongoing Cases Summary

It may be a requirement in training situations, in certain agencies or for accreditation purposes to keep a running record of clients seen, with brief details. A simple format is given in Table 3.8.1. Obviously this can be modified as necessary. Some therapists prefer to keep a *separate* sheet for each client. A benefit to therapists themselves is that this offers an 'at-a-glance' picture of caseload, workload, length of cases, typical issues, etc. This is a quite separate exercise from data gathering which specifies items such as gender, age, ethnic identity, etc., used mainly by agencies.

CASE STUDY

A case study is a relatively formal exercise used for training, accreditation, research or publication purposes. One of its main advantages is that it

Table 3.8.1 *Record of clients seen: week beginning 14 February 2004*

Date	Client code	Session number	Presenting/major issue/outcome	Comments
14/2/09	BX5	3	Continuing conflict with partner: anger. Client needs to talk at length	
14/2/09	BX2	16	Bereavement. Reasonable progress in making new sociable contacts	Review session due in two weeks
14/2/09	CA01	1	G appears severely depressed; agreed to contact GP	GP agrees to make contact. Raised in supervision
15/2/09	BX4	6	Stress at work. Client reports feeling much better	Client wishes to end at agreed session
15/2/09	CY3	5	DNA	Wrote to extend invitation to make another appointment
15/2/09	AX9	37	Ongoing working through sexual abuse memories	
15/2/09	BY5	1	Disfigurement	Check any support groups available
16/2/09	BY4	9	DNA	Client phoned in ill
16/2/09	CY5	5	Low self-esteem. Social skills problems	Assertiveness programme well under way
16/2/09	AY3	24	Renewed motivation to overcome anxiety	Client returned after two-month interval
16/2/09	BY7	2	Complex problems of debt, loneliness, shyness, bereavement	Need for focus and prioritization
16/2/09	BX1	11	Anxiety, remorse *re* rejection by ex-partner	Counter-transference issues

obliges the therapist to think analytically, in depth, and in a detailed manner about a particular client, applying and reflecting on theory, and making links with in-session and across-session phenomena, assessment and case conceptualization skills, use of self, supervision, outcomes, and so on. Case studies in this field have been used for many decades. Freud himself was perhaps one of the most gifted writers in this genre; he certainly wrestled with the difficulties of accurate recall, but stressed the significance of detail for understanding the deeper meaning of his patients' own lapses in memory (Freud, 1977 [1925]). A case study may be written as a well-crafted narrative, but the aim is not usually to produce polished literature but to stimulate and demonstrate therapeutically significant learning.

Below are common useful ingredients of a case study. In this instance the case is retrospective, but case studies may also relate to ongoing work.

Elements of a Case Study

Depending on the specific purpose of the case study, it may include all or some of the following elements.

Initial information

- Description of the client in terms of age, appearance, demeanour, etc.
- Outline of the referral/intake process, other parties involved, etc.
- Setting in which therapy took place, including any conditions or constraints.
- First or early impressions of the client, including the therapist's own feelings, tentative hypotheses, etc.
- Initial assessment, including the client's reported problems, goals, etc.
- Contract/agreement on times, fees, etc., plus initial shared goals.
- Further personal history and relevant background material.

Assessment or clinical formulation

- Identification of patterns revealed in the client's story.
- Any classical diagnostic 'hooks' provided (whether or not these are worked with).
- Emerging themes accounting for the nature of the client's difficulties and for indications of a possible therapeutic plan.
- Observations on defence mechanisms, games, obstacles, or threats to the therapeutic alliance.

- Any subtle or tangential factors that may have some bearing on the outcome.

Therapeutic process

- A record of interventions deployed, with some indication of degree of success.
- Theoretical reflections, i.e. reference to one's training orientation and/or main theoretical allegiance and its ability to explain and predict in this case.
- Key issues and themes, as well as critical moments or turning points in the therapy.
- Specific use of supervision and a note of the usefulness of supervisory inputs.
- Reference to research evidence consulted to clarify or support the work with this client (e.g. consulting literature on outcomes in therapy with eating distress).
- An indication of the structure of sessions and pattern of change (or otherwise) across time (e.g. beginning, middle and ending phase characteristics), linked with client material and therapist interventions.
- Reflections on use of (therapist's) self, countertransference, congruence, significant components of the therapeutic relationship.

Evaluation

- Indications of success, goal attainment or client satisfaction, including any formal or informal evaluation mechanisms used.
- A statement of what the therapist has learned from this case for their own future development, including identification of any training needs, and any impact the case may have on the therapist's emerging 'personal philosophy' of therapy.

Some psychotherapy training demands extensive case study, fully documented with detailed references to clinical literature. It is quite typical for trainees in counselling to be required to write succinct case studies of anything from 1000 words upwards. A key feature is often to demonstrate coherence between theory and practice. Case studies are valuable vehicles for learning but care has to be taken that they do not become empty exercises in simply fitting the client to the theory. See McLeod (2010) for guidance on case study as research.

Protection of the client's confidentiality by (where appropriate) seeking explicit permission from them, and attending to anonymity, disguising identifying details, physically securing the written article, and limiting the readership, are essential (especially if the case study is to be published).

WRITTEN AND OTHER COMMUNICATION WITH OR FOR CLIENTS

Apart from initial telephone contact and ongoing face-to-face contact with clients (except where telephone counselling/therapy *is* the medium of therapy), the other main forms of communication are probably periodic telephone, text, online and written correspondence. The need for such communication usually arises from cancelled or missed sessions, but it can also include agreed tasks such as the goodbye letters characteristic of cognitive analytic therapy, letters of support or reports required by solicitors, notification of progress with a waiting list, and occasional correspondence of a social support or therapeutic nature.

Communication Relating to Missed Appointments

Consternation at unexpectedly missed appointments (DNAs – 'did not arrive/attend') is often expressed by trainees in supervision. What is the most appropriate way of discovering why a client did not turn up, reassuring them that they may return, and knowing where you stand with them? Such eventualities may be anticipated by comprehensive verbal contracting: for example, 'If you do not arrive for your next session, I will assume you will be here the following week at the same time, and you have agreed to pay for all missed sessions'; or, 'If you do not give at least 24 hours notice of cancellation, I will make contact with you by phone or letter.' Where leaflets are used, they may spell out exactly what happens following a non-arrival. There are numerous possible permutations here, and differing preferences and traditions. Quite typically, therapists may assume that unexpected telephone contacts may be unwelcome, and that therefore letters may be preferable. Below are two examples:

Dear Nasreen

I'm aware that you were unable to attend your last appointment with me at 3 p.m. on Tuesday 22 September. As agreed, I intend to keep the same time (3 p.m.) available for you next week on Tuesday 29 September, unless I hear from you by telephone or letter to the contrary.

I look forward to seeing you.

Yours sincerely
Margaret Smith
Practice counsellor

Dear Anthony

I'm sorry you could not attend yesterday's appointment with me. In the light of recent events in your life and your own expressed uncertainty about therapy, I assume that you don't want to continue. However, I would like you to know that you are very welcome to get in touch again at any time, either to make another appointment or simply to let me know how you're getting on.

All best wishes
Yours sincerely
Ved Patel

The first example is businesslike and reiterates a previously agreed contract. The second, written to a client after some months of therapy, is more personal, warm and tailored. There is no one correct form of correspondence in these circumstances. In spite of the norms inculcated by different training traditions, it is advisable to adapt appropriately to the unique set of demands constituted by knowledge of the client, the client's circumstances, organization or agency procedures/requirements, and ethical, professional and business considerations, as well as preconceived theoretical traditions about breaks and endings.

Other kinds of correspondence may be appropriate at times. For example, 'Here is the address of the occupational psychologist I mentioned to you'; or, 'I am writing to say that my hospital treatment is now completed and I would welcome the opportunity to resume therapy with you, if you would like to get in touch'; or, 'Thank you very much for your letter telling me why you have decided not to continue with therapy', etc. Otherwise, unsolicited communication is not advised, unless it serves specific and justifiable purposes, for example a greetings card for a special occasion. Of course, in some traditions, almost all such exceptions (including the giving or receiving of gifts) may be regarded as compromising the therapeutic frame, but in others flexible, responsible, ordinary human responses may be regarded as helpful and as particularly important with clients from some minority cultures (Ridley, 1995).

Report Writing

Counsellors and psychotherapists would not normally be required to write official reports on or for their clients unless employed by an agency with a specific brief to do so. For example, those involved in adoption counselling, or forensic psychotherapy, may have certain statutory responsibilities. Psychiatrists and clinical psychologists are the professionals more likely to be called upon for reports on clients' mental state, assessments and professional opinions. Sometimes counsellors and psychotherapists may be approached by solicitors, clients' advocates or clients themselves with requests for written reports in connection with stress at work, post-traumatic stress or marital disputes. The motivation for such requests may be straightforward but there are potential dangers: the therapist may not be a suitable 'expert', may become involved in complex disputes, and could be called to support any written statement in court. Before agreeing to any such request, a supervisor should be consulted and possible legal ramifications explored. However, an example is given below of a possible brief report.

Director of Human Resources
Zephyr-Kopf Laboratories plc
Dear Sir/Madam
re Mrs Anita Clarke (d.o.b. 13.4.58)

I write at the request of Mrs Clarke, who I have been seeing for counselling since December last year. Mrs Clarke initiated contact following a distressing incident at her workplace last November. As I believe you know, she witnessed a near fatal accident in the laboratory where she works. She tells me that since that time she has been unable to sleep normally, and has had to take several weeks off from work, and her GP has prescribed medication. I understand that she has tried returning to work but still feels too shaky to resume her full duties.

Mrs Clarke appears to have become somewhat more relaxed than when she first saw me. However, since she is still very troubled by sleeping difficulties and occasional nightmares, which in turn seem to affect her ability to concentrate at work, my recommendation is that she sees a clinical psychologist, Dr R. Brown, specializing in treating her symptoms. With her agreement I am very willing to pass contact details on to you, and I understand that you may be willing to meet any costs she may incur if seen by this psychologist.

It is my view that Mrs Clarke is suffering from a degree of post-traumatic stress but I do not claim to possess specialist assessment qualifications, and I recommend that she and you communicate with Dr Brown on this matter.

Yours sincerely
Moira McDonald, MA, DipCouns
Counsellor in Private Practice

It is important in all such communications that therapists do not claim to know more than they really do, do not make unjustified categorical statements, and use appropriately simple and tentative phrases. Obviously the client's permission is needed, and the therapist should be convinced that there is a strong case for their written intervention (for example, the client has no other professional advocate). All practitioners should be warned that even ostensibly innocent, compellingly humanitarian responses of this kind *can* backfire, and should be undertaken only with extreme care. Always consider how many parties are involved, what their respective interests are, what ulterior motives *may* be at work, and what potential minefields lie hidden beneath simple requests. Always secure the client's full permission and collaboration, perhaps by asking the client to sign a copy of the letter, and keep copies of all correspondence. Having said this, there may well be occasional requests for reports that are completely justified and appropriate. A rule of thumb is to write as factually as possible (avoiding unwarranted speculations), and concisely, although sometimes lengthier reports are necessary. Questions of related fees and any other implications should be discussed with supervisors, colleagues or employers as appropriate.

REFLECTING ON AND MONITORING ONE'S WORK

This section examines briefly the issues involved in continuing professional self-monitoring. The relevant activities include in-session self-reflection, reviewing, using supervision, and deploying suitable means of evaluating the limits of one's skills and effectiveness.

Self-reflection in The Session

Beginning therapists sometimes become caught in self-conscious 'spectatoring' as they try mentally to juggle what the client is expressing, what their trainers and supervisors have said, what they have read, and their own aspirations and self-doubts. In time this tends to be converted into a skilled form of self-observation, whereby the therapeutic process can be appropriately, undistractedly scanned and evaluated from time to time within each session. Highly experienced or gifted therapists may be able to cultivate an exquisite sensitivity to the ever-shifting nuances of their clients' moods and disclosures, while almost simultaneously tracking and testing out their own internal responses. This is what Casement (1985) has referred to as 'internal supervision'. The therapist integrates in his moment-to-moment practice a disciplined, reflexive alertness to the interaction between his statements and the client's unconsciously coded communications. This kind of awareness and *in vivo* self-supervision is increasingly incorporated into non-psychodynamic therapies, even into cognitive therapy. See Bager-Charleson (2010) and Stedmon and Dallos (2009).

Reviewing

Reviewing refers to consciously planned sessions or parts of sessions in which therapist and client agree to review their work together in terms of progress, satisfaction, problems, the relationship itself, and any new material or goals. Broadly speaking, there are probably two ends of a spectrum of opinion about reviewing. It can be argued that reviewing is a constant, vital, implicit part of the therapeutic process and needs no additional formal structure. Others, however, suggest that it is good practice to hold mini-reviews at the end of each session (quite common in cognitive therapy), reviews every four or six sessions, or, in longer-term therapy, three-monthly or six-monthly reviews.

For a review to be meaningful and not merely a compliant ritual, it may be helpful to adhere to a checklist of relevant items. For example:

- general impressions of both client and therapist
- the client's view of progress in relation to explicit goals as agreed at assessment or first meeting, including their sense of how well time has been used
- the therapist's view of progress
- the client's reservations about any aspect of therapy, disappointments, misunderstandings, need for clarification, etc.
- any impasses that are evident and how they might be addressed (Leiper and Kent, 2001)
- both parties' views on the relationship between them, its therapeutic value, any obstacles evident
- the therapist's hypotheses about obstacles, defences, gaps in the client's story
- possible alternatives to current therapy (e.g. referral elsewhere)
- any newly emerging issues or goals
- anything relating to structure, arrangements, fees, possible termination.

The nature and precise choice of the items discussed must relate to the client's needs, and to the therapist's theoretical orientation, level of competency, and ethical and professional considerations. It can be useful to give clients a checklist of this kind to think over before the agreed review session. In some therapies regular reviews are integral to the therapeutic process, rather than an optional add-on, and in some cases written records are made of them, with duplicate copies for the client. In IAPT services in particular, structured evaluation and review may be a constant process. It is *always* crucial to introduce and explain the meaning and purpose of reviews clearly and sensitively, and not to use them mechanically or in an ill-timed manner. It is also realistic to expect at least some degree of consciously or unconsciously withheld feelings and views.

Using Supervision

Counselling and psychotherapy traditions differ in regard to clinical supervision. Accredited BACP members *must* receive regular supervision (a minimum of 1.5 hours monthly) throughout their career, however experienced they are. In some professions and countries regular supervision is primarily associated mainly or exclusively with training. In certain clinical professions or specialisms 'high-dose' supervision is either recommended or mandated. Without entering into these debates (see Chapter 4.3 on clinical supervision in this volume), the focus here is on a summary of preparation for and optimal use of supervision.

Preparation

Presentation of clinical issues in supervision is touched on elsewhere. Here, a brief outline is given of the kinds of areas typically focused upon in supervision, which often require a certain amount of forethought (adapted from Horton, 1993):

- *Identification.* How will the client be 'named' or disguised? How will you describe them to the supervisor?
- *Antecedents.* How the client came to see you; the context of counselling; pre-counselling knowledge of the client; any previous contacts.
- *Presenting concerns and contract.* Summary of the main concern or concerns and their duration; precipitating factors; initial assessment; current conflicts or issues.
- *Questions for supervision.* What, exactly, do you wish to address in supervision (given that time in supervision may need to be used very efficiently)?
- *Ethical and professional issues.* It is always important to consider whether there are any

significant ethical or legal issues to be aired (BACP, 2002). More generally, therapists may wish to reflect on any continuing professional development needs that are thrown up for them by clients. 'What does the research have to say about this particular presenting problem?' is a highly relevant question here.

- *Focus on content.* How does the client see their situation? What are pertinent work and relationship factors? How does the client see himself or herself (i.e. identity)? What other elements are pertinent (e.g. early history, strengths and resources, beliefs and values, fears and fantasies, socio-cultural factors)? Part of the content focus is also (1) problem definition (how the client construes current and desired scenarios); (2) assessment and refor-mulation (how the therapist understands the presenting concern, related patterns, themes for exploration, useful theoretical constructs, helpful hunches, etc.); (3) unmentioned material, silent hypotheses, blind spots and underlying contributory factors. A therapeutic plan may or may not feature (depending on theoretical orientation). What might be the direction of future work? What goals are emerging? What criteria for change and its measurement exist? Reviewing progress and new possibilities also comes in here.
- *Focus on process.* What strategies and inter-ventions have been used? Consider therapeutic intentions, the impact of interventions and pos-sible alternative interventions. A large part of the process is of course about the relationship. What happened between you and the client? What transferential or other interpersonal pat-terns are you aware of? What variety of rela-tional factors may be at work (Feltham, 1999)? In what ways are such issues played out in the parallel process between therapist and supervi-sor? Finally, how is the process being evalu-ated? What alternatives exist?
- *Critical incident analysis.* Supervision is extremely useful for disclosing and analys-ing key moments in the therapeutic process. What did the client say or do? How did you respond (and feel internally)? What might this signify and what clues could it yield to further work?
- *Covert communication.* Supervision also offers space for considering what might be happening between therapist and client that is unspoken, subtle, taboo and so on. Supervisees can bene-ficially ask themselves how the client 'makes them feel' – what subtle sensations, images and thoughts are associated with particular clients, aside from the overt content of sessions. Recalled changes in voice quality, idiosyncratic choices of words or phrases, encoded statements – any of these may yield significant insights into non-verbal and para-verbal communication and its meaning for therapy.

Self-monitoring

It may be helpful to think of self-monitoring in the following ways:

- moment-to-moment awareness of all that may transpire consciously and unconsciously within the session
- insights, hunches; anomalous, intermittent or persistent internal (counter-transferential) reac-tions; hypotheses and conjectures, voiced to the client or otherwise
- consciously withheld thoughts, feelings, responses (relating to the client), to be noted, further developed, and/or taken to supervision
- observations about one's own occasional lapses, errors, skill deficits, or recurrent 'own material' to be taken to supervision or own (occasional, intermittent or ongoing) therapy
- awareness of times when fatigue, illness, emo-tional difficulties, etc. may amount to an impair-ment affecting competency to practise and the need to make contingency plans and take appro-priate action
- tape recordings or written notes to be studied, analysed and learned from. This is a potentially large subject in its own right and many of the practical and ethical issues involved are dis-cussed in Bor and Watts (1999)
- alternative, formal means of self-evaluation, such as a personal audit of skills, knowledge, issues of congruence or counter-transference, etc.

CONCLUSION

Reference may be made to those parts of this book addressing the wide range of generic micro-skills, clinical practice skills, strategies and techniques, professional issues and common presenting prob-lems. By checking one's therapeutic practice chal-lenges – that is, the ways in which diverse clients present with widely different issues at different levels of difficulty – against the potential range of skills and interventions, one may measure and monitor one's development in competency terms.

REFERENCES

BACP (2002) *Ethical Framework for Good Practice in Counselling and Psychotherapy*. Rugby: British Association for Counselling and Psychotherapy.

Bager-Charleson, S. (2010) *Reflective Practice in Counselling and Psychotherapy*. Poole: Learning Matters.

Bor, R. and Watts, M. (eds) (1999) *The Trainee Handbook: A Guide for Counselling and Psychotherapy Trainees*. London: Sage.

Casement, P. (1985) *On Learning from the Patient*. London: Tavistock.

Clark, J. (ed.) (2002) *Freelance Counselling and Psychotherapy: Competition and Collaboration*. London: Brunner-Routledge.

Feltham, C. (ed.) (1999) *Understanding the Counselling Relationship*. London: Sage.

Freud, S. (1977 [1925]) *Case Histories I: 'Dora' and 'Little Hans'*. Harmondsworth: Pelican.

Hemmings, A. and Field, P. (eds) (2007) *Counselling and Psychotherapy in Contemporary Private Practice*. London: Routledge.

Horton, I. (1993) Supervision. In R. Bayne and P. Nicolson (eds), *Counselling and Psychology for Health Professionals*. London: Chapman and Hall.

Lago, C. and Kitchin, D. (1998) *The Management of Counselling and Psychotherapy Agencies*. London: Sage.

Leiper, R. and Kent, R. (2001) *Working through Setbacks in Psychotherapy: Crisis, Impasse and Relapse*. London: Sage.

McLeod, J. (2010) *Case Study Research in Counselling and Psychotherapy*. London: Sage.

Molnos, A. (1995) *A Question of Time: Essentials of Brief Dynamic Psychotherapy*. London: Karnac.

Norton, K. and McGauley, G. (1998) *Counselling Difficult Clients*. London: Sage.

Ridley, C.R. (1995) *Overcoming Unintentional Racism in Counseling and Therapy*. Thousand Oaks, CA: Sage.

Rowan, J. (1988) Counselling and the psychology of furniture. *Counselling*, 64: 21–4.

Sills, C. (ed.) (2007) *Contracts in Counselling* (2nd edn). London: Sage.

Stedmon, J. and Dallos, R. (eds) (2009) *Reflective Practice in Psychotherapy and Counselling*. Maidenhead: McGraw-Hill.

Thistle, R. (1998) *Counselling and Psychotherapy in Private Practice*. London: Sage.

Clinical Practice Issues

TIM BOND, GEOF ALRED AND PETER HUGHES

LENGTH, FREQUENCY AND DURATION OF SESSIONS

In referring to length and duration of counselling and psychotherapy, there is an ambiguity about whether it is one session being discussed or a sequence of sessions. In what follows, we have referred to length of a session and duration of a sequence.

The 'therapeutic hour' is a term synonymous with 'the 50-minute hour'. Drawn from psychoanalytic psychotherapy, the 50-minute hour 'has been adopted by many psychodynamic counsellors' (Jacobs, 1999: 65), and many others, as 'long enough to get depth in interviewing but not long enough to get too tired!' (Trower et al., 1988: 37). On the other hand, person-centred therapists may be more relaxed about the length of a session, in which 'clients have wanted and benefited from sessions lasting two or three hours or even longer' (Mearns and Thorne, 1999: 123). McLeod (2003: 436) reports on research undertaken by Turner et al. (1996) in which a student counselling service 'reduced the length of each session to thirty minutes. They found that clients seemed to gain as much from these shorter sessions.' In this case, the number of sessions was retained. McLeod (2003: 436) also reports on work by Rosenbaum (1994), in which the focus was on limiting the number of sessions, preferably to one, and the length of the session 'was allowed to extend to 90–120 minutes'. A distinction between the different approaches is the extent to which significance is given to boundaries: 'Acknowledgement of the boundaries between people, demonstrated in the counselling itself, is important in the making of [more reliable interdependent]

relationships' (Jacobs, 1999: 83). Egan (2001: 36), on the other hand, with his action-oriented approach, is much more concerned with efficient use of time: 'helping can be lean and mean and still be fully human' with sessions lasting as little as five minutes.

The literature is less varied about frequency of sessions, typically opting for 'once a week, or more frequently in the case of crises' (Trower et al., 1988: 37). A person-centred approach tends to be keen to find out what the client wants, recognizing that there are people 'who may welcome a longer period between sessions' (Mearns and Thorne, 1999: 123). Perhaps it is because the lives of many people are chunked into week-long units that 'less frequent contact strains continuity and decreases the likelihood of keeping the client to the "contract"' (Trower et al., 1988: 37). However, Nelson-Jones suggests that a possible way of drawing a counselling relationship towards a conclusion 'is to *fade* the relationship by seeing the client less frequently' (1982: 295). Psychodynamic therapists, on the other hand, are likely to make use of the impact on the client of impending separation as important material.

A variety of factors impinges on the duration of a therapy sequence. Some therapy relationships are open-ended, whereas others are limited to a specified maximum. The psychoanalytic tradition pulls the psychodynamic therapy process towards several years of work. Jacobs writes of 12 weeks seeming a 'fairly short period' (1999: 84). Emmy van Deurzen-Smith (1996: 182), writing about existential therapy, considers that 'therapy ends … probably within a span of three months to a year'. Person-centred therapy is concerned to put the client in charge of the duration of the therapy, and for this reason 'person-centred therapists will find it difficult to work in agencies where policy dictates that clients can have a certain number of sessions and no more' (Mearns and Thorne, 1999: 123). However, their approximate expectation is for 'a few weeks, a month or two, or, where the difficulties seem particularly severe, a few months perhaps' (1999: 123). Whitmore (2000: 69), writing about psychosynthesis therapy, thinks 'it is advisable to set boundaries rather than leave it open-ended. Often a psychosynthesis therapist will propose an initial contract of six sessions, to be reviewed and assessed before continuing.' From a cognitive-behavioural perspective, the number of sessions suggested is 'six to ten initially, with a review at the end of the period' (Trower et al., 1988: 36).

Most counselling and psychotherapy approaches have addressed the issue of brief therapy, although what is understood by the term varies enormously: 'Malan (1976) … argues that one of the key factors in the efficacy of brief therapy (of about 30 [weekly] sessions) is the ability of the therapist to interpret the significance to the patient of the ending. Time-limited work makes a virtue out of necessity' (Jacobs, 1999: 156–7). The person-centred approach simultaneously recognizes that good work can be done even in one session alone, but that therapist or agency determination of the number of sessions is an obstacle to effective therapy (Mearns and Thorne, 1999: 124). McLeod (2003: 436) has considered research which demonstrates that a significant proportion of clients can achieve long-term improvement in their problems as a result of one (extended) therapy session. See also Chapter 7.2 in this volume.

TIME MANAGEMENT

At its simplest, the management of time in therapy concerns the start and end times of sessions. Should these times repeatedly differ from shared expectations, most therapy approaches would view such divergence as significant in terms of resistance, reluctance or stuckness. Each approach would then address the issue in its own way. Arguably, the person-centred therapist is faced with the greatest difficulty: the therapeutic imperative to enter the client's frame of reference challenges the importance of issues such as punctuality.

At a deeper level, however, time management also involves holding the therapeutic process within a session, and over a period of sessions. A significant issue is the extent to which the therapist takes responsibility for the process and its pacing, as

distinct from sharing these with the client. Egan (2001) expresses a bias towards action, and the terminology of his helping skills model points towards a process in almost perpetual forward motion, the therapist probing, challenging and looking for points of leverage. Person-centred therapists, however, are considered less effective when imposing their own values on the process (see the case study example given by Mearns and Thorne, 1999: 133–43).

CONTRACTING

Clear contracting in advance of counselling and psychotherapy is generally considered to demonstrate respect for client autonomy. Conversely, retrospective attempts to impose conditions and terms are frequently considered unethical and are unenforceable legally. Although these views are generally supported, they can be problematic to implement. In the experience of many therapists, clients may be least interested in contractual terms at the outset of therapy. Many are so concerned to unload the emotional distress or the urgency of their situation that it may be some sessions later that they are willing to consider contractual issues. One widely used way of resolving this dilemma is to provide the basic contractual terms and conditions with a pre-therapy information sheet and to review the client's understanding of these and their appropriateness. For some clients, the review will take place at the beginning of the first session. For others, the first session will involve little more than agreeing to work according to the terms of the information sheet, with more detailed discussion deferred until later.

Counselling and psychotherapy contracts tend to be complex and involve several different aspects. The first aspect concerns *administrative* matters. These include details of any fees to be charged, method(s) of payment, notice required for cancellations by clients, therapist holidays, cancellations by therapist due to illness, unavoidable delay, bad weather, etc. Level of confidentiality and limitations are also important administrative matters. In English law, limitations of confidentiality in order to protect adult clients from suicide or self-harm are legally unenforceable and would not protect a therapist from possible legal claims for breach of confidence. The law prioritizes the adult client's right to informed consent including the right to refuse life-saving treatment (*St George's Trust* v. *S.* [1998] 3 All ER at 692). In the absence of a legal requirement to disclose, therapists have professional discretion over whether to disclose to protect people other than the client from harm or to assist in the prevention and detection of child abuse. This contrasts with jurisdictions elsewhere in Europe and in the US, where there may be legal obligation to restrict confidentiality or to disclose in order to prevent suicide, harm to others and child abuse (Bond, 2009; Corey et al., 2002).

The *professional* aspects of the contract concern the nature, aims and valid considerations of therapy. Legally and ethically, it is considered unwise to promise positive outcomes, but it is appropriate to indicate methods of working and the possible benefits of therapy based on the therapist's experience or research. Some of these might be included within pre-therapy information.

The *psychological* aspects of the contract are more difficult to capture in advance as they concern the focus of the therapist's struggle. They will often involve the clarification of boundaries of responsibility and undertaking to work in specific ways by client, or therapist, or both.

Therapists vary considerably in their approach to contracts (Sills, 2007). Some treat them as rules that are unilaterally created by the therapist and non-negotiable. Others view them as bilaterally negotiable between therapist and client (Tudor, 1998). Another way of classifying contracts would be to distinguish between non-negotiable rules or negotiable terms: open-ended or fixed-term (usually short) contracts; and those that exclude or include periodic review. As with different approaches to fees, the challenge is finding the appropriate form of contract rather than assuming one type of contract is universally superior to all other types of contract.

Oral contracts are as ethically and legally binding as written contracts. However, the lack of evidence and potential for misunderstanding are considerable. Therefore it is considered best practice to record important contractual terms in writing. The methods for doing so can be quite varied. Written pre-therapy information, letters sent to clients confirming the contractual agreement, signed and dated agreements, and contemporaneous notes of agreements in the therapy records are valid forms of evidence. Perhaps the most important reason for carefully considering the contractual basis of therapy is the sense of security and clarity that a well-drawn contract can give both therapist and client.

NEGOTIATING FEES

Attitudes to charging fees vary considerably between therapists. Some attach little significance to fees, and take the view that it is simply a pragmatic transaction. For others, the exchange of services for money is full of symbolic meaning and the way the client responds may be therapeutically informative. In one of the most informative articles on the issue of fees, Tudor (1998) reflects on the significance of various omissions and errors made by clients when paying by cheque. He speculates that missing out the therapist's name may be a way of discounting the therapist; not dating the cheque may indicate withdrawal from the immediate present; leaving out the amount may indicate resentment about the amount charged; and not signing the cheque may indicate a passive-aggressive response to the therapist. Interpretations of this kind are made from the therapist's perspective. Just as therapists vary in their views about the significance of money, clients are similarly varied in their opinions. In these circumstances, it is therapeutically desirable to be systematic and clear about issues concerning fees so that areas of difficulty are minimized and their significance can be discerned as they occur.

Ethics and law reinforce the therapeutic desirability of clarity about fees. Ethical requirements from BACP state that, 'Good practice involves clarifying and agreeing the rights and the responsibilities of both the practitioner and the client at appropriate points in their working relationship' (2002: section 3) and 'Clients should be adequately informed about the nature of services being offered. Practitioners should obtain adequately informed consent from their clients and respect a client's right to choose whether to continue or withdraw' (2002: section 12). These requirements are both ethical and legal. No legal obligation to pay can be incurred without having agreed the terms of payment in advance.

In combination, therapeutic, ethical and legal considerations all reinforce the importance of the therapist having decided on a policy over fees prior to offering therapy. There are several options including setting a fixed fee, setting a variable fee usually related to the client's financial circumstances, waiving a fee by providing free therapy, bartering, and accepting fees from sources other than the client, often referred to as third-party payment. The main advantages and disadvantages of each are considered below.

Fixed fees have the advantage of being the easiest to calculate (i.e. overheads plus payment for the length of the session) and create a high degree of certainty about income and cost to therapist and client respectively. However, fixed fees may exclude people from receiving therapy who have limited income or a high number of dependants relative to their income. Many practitioners do vary their fees according to their clients' capacity to pay, or offer some of their clients reduced fees. This approach extends the availability of therapy but can sometimes create unhealthy dynamics within the therapeutic relationship, if the client feels second class or the therapist resents the reduced fee. Free therapy is one way of significantly widening the accessibility of therapy to everyone. The desirability of free therapy may be counterbalanced by the potential for the therapeutic relationship to be inhibited by the client's gratitude or the potential for widening the power imbalance between helper and helped by the dependence of the client on the therapist's charity! The bartering of therapy for goods or other services provides an alternative way of making therapy more accessible, but raises potential areas of difficulty over determining the value of what is being bartered. Establishing the value may require the involvement of someone outside the therapeutic relationship. Another complication is the potential disruption of the therapeutic relationship if the goods or services turn out to be deficient. Third-party payments, usually by an employer or a relative, may make possible the provision of adequately resourced therapy, but have the potential disadvantages of introducing additional people into the therapeutic relationship who may be more favourably motivated towards therapy than the client – for example a parent paying for a teenager. This very condensed survey of the different approaches to fees demonstrates that each has advantages and disadvantages, and the challenge is maximizing the former while minimizing the latter.

Another factor to be considered in advance is whether to require a single method of payment – for example cash, cheque or standing order – or whether the method of payment is negotiable. It is generally considered sound advice to avoid the accumulation of large sums of money owed to the therapist, both because of the way this can influence the therapist–client relationship and because of the increased risk of not being paid. Equally, any payment in advance should, in our view, be exceptional and limited to a few sessions. The usual practice is payment 'as you go' supported by clear agreements about other administrative aspects of therapy.

EVALUATION OF PROCESS AND OUTCOMES

Evaluation of process and outcomes is an integral part of therapy. It builds the initial contract (Bordin, 1994), makes significant contributions to client progress (Wills, 1997) and enhances the quality of the therapeutic alliance (Egan, 2001). Different approaches to evaluation emphasize and focus upon different dimensions of the alliance, namely the working relationship between client and therapist;

mutually agreed goals; and therapeutic tasks carried out to achieve the goals (Bordin, 1979).

In cognitive-behavioural and problem-oriented approaches, progress is evaluated primarily in terms of goals. These are set in the initial phase of therapy, and also as the therapy proceeds, and include the overall goals of the therapy, an agenda of therapeutic tasks, and homework. A straightforward example of this kind of evaluation is the goal-attainment model (Sutton, 1989) in which clients rate progress towards individual goals on a numerical scale. In cognitive analytic therapy (CAT: Ryle, 1990; Ryle and Kerr, 2002), rating scales are also used for evaluation of progress; and in the spirit of using written as well as spoken communications in CAT (Ryle, 2004), therapist and client exchange goodbye letters, making explicit outcomes and prospects for progress continuing once therapy is over. There is also evaluation of the client's progress in performing therapeutic tasks, such as disputing irrational beliefs in rational emotive behaviour therapy (REBT). Towards the end of therapy, evaluation covers learning from the therapy and how this can be sustained and built upon (Wills, 1997). Evaluation of process focuses on tasks and the working relationship as, for instance, in Egan's (2001: 38) challenge for helpers to ask in what way a technique or method contributes to the 'bottom line', that is, to outcomes that serve clients. Evaluation is an important and ongoing aspect of collaboration between client and therapist, and it also takes place formally in review sessions at regular negotiated intervals.

Sutton (1989) maintains that the goal-attainment model can be applied to any approach. This view is unlikely to be accepted by humanistic counsellors, who recognize that the achievements by the client in therapy cannot always be clearly specified, and do not always need to be. Saying specifically what has changed does not add anything to the client's conviction that she has changed, in that, for instance, she feels less anxious, or more resolved, or more in touch with people who matter to her. What helps is to appreciate the process by which change has occurred and to reflect on this, as a way to chart progress and link what goes on in therapy to what brought this client to therapy and to changes she wants to make in her life in general. Hence, evaluation takes place within the general flow of the therapeutic process and relationship, as well as in formal review sessions. Evaluation may draw upon the practitioner's own experience of the therapy process. For example, if the practitioner considers that the process is stuck, she may share this with the client and check how the client is perceiving the process at this time. Or, if the practitioner believes that the client is becoming more self-accepting, she may reflect this back to enable the client to evaluate herself. The timing of reviews is important, and there needs to be flexibility in any arrangements to review. There are times when the client is vulnerable and needy and a review would be counterproductive.

In psychodynamic therapy, as with person-centred therapy, evaluation is interwoven into the therapeutic process and relationship, and takes place at specific times. The central aim of finding meaning through interpretation and the triangle of insight provides for the client the basis for assessing progress and change. Evaluation may draw on non-specific aspects, such as the emotional atmosphere in the therapy room, as well as specific changes the client notices. A particular area of attention in psychodynamic therapy is the ending of the therapeutic relationship. This is often planned and may extend over a period of several sessions. Reviewing the therapy as a whole is part of breaking the relationship and enabling the client to experience the loss as fully and constructively as possible. See also Chapter 4.11 in this volume.

PURPOSE, SELECTION AND DEFINITION OF OUTCOME GOALS

Clients come to therapy with an intention to change their lives for the better, and to live in a more satisfactory and resourceful way. The intention may not be clearly known or articulated. The therapist responds by helping the client to establish aims in relation to areas of a client's life he or she wishes to change, and may help the client set goals, which translate aims into statements of specific desired changes. A major source of difference among counselling and psychotherapy approaches concerns those which advocate 'goal-directedness' (e.g. Dryden and Feltham, 1994; Egan, 2001) and those which pursue intentions and aims without specific goals (e.g. Jacobs, 1999; Mearns and Thorne, 1999; Worrall, 1997).

In person-centred therapy, the underlying aim is 'freeing the natural healing process in the client' (Mearns and Thorne, 1999: 146). This is not necessarily achieved by identifying specific outcomes. In relation to contracting in person-centred therapy, Worrall states that, 'Not only does such a contract not need to deal with outcomes, it is philosophically and therapeutically essential that it be independent of outcomes' (1997: 66), arguing that client distress often stems from 'contractual living' in which the individual, through seeking the approval of others, loses autonomy, sense of purpose and effectiveness.

In contrast, many practitioners employ goals to build with their clients a shared sense of therapeutic purpose. When clients are confused or distressed, they may not know what goals they have; they may feel directionless, lost or stuck. Setting goals helps to give the client a sense of direction, and a basis for charting progress and clarifying further work to be done. As the client begins to focus on what he or she wants to change, and as issues are explored, goals that are implicit in what brought the client to therapy begin to emerge. These will include goals associated with the presenting issue, of which the client has some awareness at the outset of therapy, and may also include new kinds of goals discovered in therapy. For example, through addressing a particular source of stress, a client may come to realize the value of looking at his reaction to stress in general.

There are general guidelines for goal setting, such as making them specific and achievable, which provide a useful rule of thumb, and which are given prominence in some approaches (e.g. Egan, 2001; Sutton, 1989). A more fundamental concern is ensuring that goals are negotiated and truly reflect the client's needs and desires, as 'ethically it is the client's right to determine the goals and the limits of his or her interest in counselling' (Dryden and Feltham, 1994: 31). There needs to be openness about the therapist's goals as well as those of the client, to avoid the therapist having a different, possibly more ambitious, therapeutic agenda than the client.

For therapists using an integrative or eclectic approach, a central issue is to avoid an unhelpful polarization between outcome goals and relationship, and to balance working towards specific outcome goals with attending to the relationship and its therapeutic potential. For example, Ryle states that the central task at the outset of therapy is 'to establish a working relationship, to maximize the powerful and non-specific effects of therapy on morale and to convert passive suffering to active engagement in problem-solving' (1990: 11). Attending to this balance is particularly important in brief and time-limited therapy (Bor et al., 2004; Houston, 2003; Hudson-Allez, 1997), which is essentially outcome oriented.

CONCEPTUALIZATION OF CLIENT PROBLEMS: LEVELS OF PROBLEM

This section complements material in Chapter 6.3 in this volume. A potential client may or may not have a clear idea of *what* is 'out of joint', or of what is required to *put right* what is out of joint, but is more than likely to feel, think or believe that something *is* out of joint. The person will probably present for therapy because they seek remedy for their uncertainty, unease or distress. The orientation of the therapist will not, in the first instance, restrict the therapist's awareness of the client's agenda about, say, coping with the death of a parent; or a desire to unlock the shackles of past abuse; or a yearning to leave a current partner. Remaining more central to the client's overt frame of reference is made all the easier when the client chooses a therapist who prefers to work with particular issues (e.g. bereavement) and not others (e.g. sexual abuse).

Different therapy models, however, hold divergent views about what therapy is intended to achieve (outcome), and how best to achieve it (process). Each approach conceptualizes a client's problems differently, and demands that the client accepts, or at least suspends disbelief about, some theoretical tenets central to that approach. In making this demand, the model not only attempts to conceptualize about the client, her problematic situation, and an appropriate therapeutic course of action, but also assumes that the client becomes willing to view matters in the same way.

Therefore, whose conceptualization of a client's problems prevails? This apparent polarization partly involves the extent to which the therapy addresses the client's issues from the client's phenomenological point of view, and how she talks to herself about her situation, as distinct from a more theory-laden point of view (e.g. projection and transference, stages of grieving and tasks of mourning, self-concept and organismic self).

For instance, person-centred therapy is concerned with personal growth mediated through a therapeutic relationship. The person-centred practitioner respects insight (deeper and fuller understanding) and, through the medium of the therapeutic relationship, encourages the client to value insight. The client's agenda is completely respected, and yet the process of person-centred therapy in effect transforms the client's material into footsteps towards greater self-knowledge. 'The therapist will ... focus not on problems and solutions but on communion' (Thorne, 1996: 129). Rogers (1951) describes many indicators of therapeutic movement: 'They tend to move away from façades ... from oughts ... from meeting the expectation of others.' He describes seven stages of psychological development, which for most people will be quite independent of any therapeutic endeavour, but for a client may be enhanced through the therapeutic process. A client in the earliest stages is unlikely to present for therapy, whereas a client in the latest stages is likely to be able to draw on a wide range of resources, of which therapy will be only one. A client in the middle stages of development, however, is likely to be able to make best use of person-centred therapy. For the person-centred practitioner, therefore, the client's issues are not significantly conceptualized as problems, but are seen as opportunities for the client to get to know, understand and accept herself more fully. There is little sense of level of problem, more a recognition that some clients require or desire the help – short term or long term – of a therapist in order to take them further along their journey.

Cognitive-behavioural therapy promotes the view that the client learns to think and act in different, more effective, ways. The therapist challenges what is dysfunctional and directs towards greater functionality. While a client might express the view that her shyness is problematic to her because she would like to meet new people, the therapist will consider the client's shyness to result from faulty beliefs or faulty thinking: 'emotional distress and problematic behaviour, C, are the consequences not of the events themselves, A, but of negative inferences and evaluations of these events, B' (Trower et al., 1988: 21). From the therapist's point of view, therefore, the 'problem' is how the client thinks about herself and the world she inhabits. From this perspective, the therapist's focus is not on the inconvenience or intractableness of the presenting problem, but on the range and persistence of faulty beliefs and thoughts. A client who clings tightly to a wide range of faulty thoughts and beliefs may well require longer therapy than a client who is eager to learn to challenge her own dysfunctionality.

Of all counselling models, a problem-management model, such as the skilled helper model of Egan (2001), places presenting, and subsequently revealed, problems at centre stage. 'Many clients become clients because, either in their own eyes or in the eyes of others, they are involved in problem situations they are not handling well' (2001: 4). These clients need ways of dealing with, solving or transcending their problem situations. By focusing on a clear articulation of a specific problem, and on step-by-step approaches to its solution, the problem-management model gives paramount importance to the client's stated problems and their solution. The counsellor is unlikely to restate the problem in different theoretical terms, but is likely to challenge the client to view the problem from some other perspectives to discover where leverage and opportunity exist, and to let go of inadequate solutions. It is unlikely that a problem cannot be articulated. However, a problem may be intricately entwined with other problems, in which case it is the counsellor's role to help the client tease out the different strands. A client with many intertwined problems may require more counselling than a client with only one. A client familiar with, and fluent at, personal reflection and self-challenge may require only a few sessions.

In their own unique ways, then, different counselling and psychotherapy approaches conceptualize the person of the client and her problems, the purpose of therapy and its methods, in radically different ways. Necessarily their perspectives are tied to the theoretical and philosophical foundations on which they are based.

APPROACHES TO DIAGNOSIS

Diagnosis is controversial in counselling and psychotherapy. Some practitioners are highly critical of the possibility of therapist-determined diagnosis. Practitioners working in person-centred and many other humanistic traditions are most likely to take this view. Their approach emphasizes the client's ability for self-diagnosis and capacity for self-healing, sometimes referred to as the 'wisdom of the client'. The therapist's role is to provide the conditions, particularly the quality of relationship, in which the client's wisdom can flourish. These approaches are frequently founded on a critique of the medicalization of human relationships, and a concern to avoid replicating the inherent power imbalance between patient and medical practitioner.

An alternative way of resolving some of the disempowering aspects of diagnosis is to teach clients to diagnose for themselves. Transactional analysis operates primarily in this way by teaching accessible models of the way people view themselves and interact with others and by encouraging the client to develop new insights and self-assessment (Midgley, 1998). Another very popular approach has been developed out of the Jungian psychoanalytic tradition that helps people to distinguish different personality types and understand where they stand in the Myers–Briggs classification (Bayne, 1993).

Problem management, as advocated by Egan (2001) and others, provides a variation on 'insight' models of diagnosis by combining humanistic insights into the counselling relationship with a more active counsellor facilitation of the client's problem. For example, the process of engaging the client in focusing on one of several potential issues to be considered in counselling distinguishes between different kinds of problem, e.g. contained and urgent or chronic and pervasive, and a joint counsellor–client evaluation of which should be the subject of counselling.

Some approaches to counselling and psychotherapy are much more accepting of the desirability of diagnosis. For example, family therapists are concerned to distinguish functional and dysfunctional interactions within families based on their impact on the family, which is understood as a closed or semi-closed system of relationships. The process of diagnosis and therapy is taken so seriously that it

is classically undertaken by at least two therapists working together (Waldron-Skinner and Watson, 1987). Similarly, the interventions in REBT developed by Albert Ellis (Ellis and Dryden, 1998) also depend on diagnosing dysfunctional patterns in order to challenge these and substitute ways which are considered more functional.

Psychodynamic therapists have generally been stereotyped as being most accepting of diagnostic techniques within their therapeutic approaches. In reality some are extremely reluctant to move swiftly to diagnosis. Nonetheless the notion of 'unconscious' implies something that is invisible to the client and may be visible to the therapist. In this context, diagnoses of 'resistance', 'transference' and 'defence mechanisms' as ways of understanding the therapeutic relationship may be meaningful to the therapist and eventually to the client. Some diagnoses may be problematic because they encode evaluations about suitability for therapy or imply a pessimistic prognosis, for example 'borderline' or 'sociopathic'. Some therapeutic approaches resist the implied moral judgements and the immutability of these kinds of diagnoses, and question their place in therapy.

Generally, diagnostic systems are more widely accepted in psychiatric services and clinical psychology and form an important part of the therapist's regime. The best known of the diagnostic systems has been developed by the American Psychiatric Association (2000), which is widely used as an international classification. In some countries psychologists, counsellors and psychotherapists are expected to know this system, although that is not a general expectation in Britain. However, therapists working closely in association with psychiatric and drug rehabilitation services may find it helpful to familiarize themselves with this system in order to enhance communication between services, whether or not such diagnoses are incorporated within therapy.

RELUCTANCE, RESISTANCE AND STUCKNESS

Counselling and psychotherapy approaches diverge widely, and may be distinguished from each other by their conceptualizations of the terms 'reluctance', 'resistance' and 'stuckness'. Different writers consider quite differently the sources of these features, perceive quite differently their manifestations within the therapeutic relationship, and hold quite different views about the ways in which they can most appropriately be addressed. For instance, to a person-centred practitioner, the term 'resistance' has judgemental and unempathic connotations, and is unlikely to be used, whereas a client who shows 'reluctance' is dubious or suspicious of the therapist or of therapy as a form of help for themselves, presenting the therapist with an opportunity to build trust and rapport. The term 'stuckness', in terms of lack of movement in the therapeutic process, points to the opportunity for the client to assimilate and integrate fresh insights into their frame of reference, and for the therapist to stay with and track that process (Mearns and Thorne, 1999).

In contrast, for an integrative/eclectic 'skilled helper', reluctance and resistance are similar, although recognition of the fine distinction between them may be crucial. 'Reluctance … refers to the ambiguity clients feel when they know that managing their lives better is going to exact a price. Clients are not sure that they want to pay that price. The incentives for not changing drive out the incentives for changing'. On the other hand, 'Resistance refers to the reaction of clients who in some way feel coerced. It is their way of fighting back' (Egan, 2001: 163). While Egan concedes that some resistance may be normative, he sees reluctance and resistance as features to be overcome. 'Stuckness' arises out of a failure of some part of the therapeutic process, and probably demands that the therapist takes responsibility for backtracking to the stage which was left incomplete. For Dexter and Russell (1997: 11–22), a client's resistance to the counselling process is a response to what a counsellor is doing, or not doing, and therefore the counsellor should do something differently.

'Analysis of resistance is a major part of the psychodynamic technique, freeing the client … to understand more of himself, and releasing him to make the changes which he wishes' (Jacobs, 1999: 98). Psychodynamic therapy considers that clients' failure to function fully is due to the defences they use to avoid acknowledging something:

> Resistances are the expression (or tactics) of the defences, particularly as employed in the therapeutic relationship. Both defences and resistances serve a definite … purpose, defending people either against feelings which are too strong and threaten to overwhelm them or others, or against the self-criticism of a punitive and persecutory super-ego (or conscience). (1999: 98)

In consequence, the psychodynamic therapist may go in search of resistance as a major part of the therapeutic process.

Cognitive, gestalt, psychosynthesis therapists and so on each conceptualize these terms as differently as the approaches addressed above, arising out of how each views the path and purpose of the therapy process.

CLINICAL ISSUES: TAPE RECORDING

Some (few) clients desire their therapy sessions to be recorded. They may bring a cassette tape with them to the therapy room. It would be unusual for a client to bring audio recording equipment. The recording quality of pocket-portable equipment, such as dictaphones and personal stereos, tends to be unsuitable for conversations between two or more people. An ordinary tape recorder and a multidirectional microphone are sufficient, and can be part of therapy room equipment. In this case, operation of the equipment may well fall on the therapist.

In the initial contracting process, a therapist may be able to offer the client use of audio recording facilities. This demonstrates not only a transparency about the therapy process, but also a desire for the client to listen to the content, pattern and movement in their disclosures, and to reflect on the insights, challenges and modelling of the therapist. There may be occasions when the content or manner of disclosure is traumatic in some way. Tape recordings of such material can valuably form the basis of further therapy. Parkinson (1995: 168) gives a fine example of a couple who listen in detail to each other for the first time, and gain valuable insight into their manner of communication, as a result of an audiotape recording.

Some therapists feel uncomfortable about the tape recording of sessions, and in certain psychoanalytic approaches, recording is viewed as abusive. It is seen as an unwarranted inhibition of the client's opportunity to explore sensitive and/or unconscious material. Some therapists, regardless of therapeutic orientation, are wary about requests from clients to record their sessions. They might sense that the client's request has a potentially malicious or defensive ulterior motive. Alternatively, a therapist might fear exposure of their own perceived incompetence. It is worth exploring any request by a client to audio record the session, and what value the taping of sessions has for the client. Equally, the therapist's own internal and articulated responses may hold valuable learning to be explored in counselling or psychotherapy supervision.

When it is the therapist who wishes to audio record the session, the situation is different. Parkinson (1995) is sceptical about the value to the client of a therapist analysing what a client talks about. In so far as therapy is about developing a relationship, not curing a patient's illness, his point is valid. However, the situation is different when the focus of the recording is to analyse the therapist's role in the relationship. A therapist in training may ask a client for permission to record some specific piece(s) of work. It is not unusual for therapists on training courses to be asked to analyse and present some recorded work with a client. The client may have little notion about how the therapist will subsequently listen to the disclosed material, and even if it is contractually agreed that the tape will subsequently be wiped, there is a risk that the client may feel exploited regardless of any assurances and safeguards. In an early paper, Rogers (1942) considered training/supervision to be 'probably the most significant use of [audio] recordings'. He reported that, by means of careful analysis and discussion, supported by full transcripts, trainees were able to critique their own practice in detail:

> The recorded interviews show … clearly those techniques which lead towards insight and reorientation … Such close analysis of these interviews gives to the inexperienced and experienced counselor alike a new understanding of the therapeutic process. This new understanding vitalizes and improves their treatment interviewing.

A more recent example of this kind of use of interview recording is interpersonal process recall (IPR), formulated in the early 1960s by Norman Kagan. It is appropriate for a therapist to request permission to audio record for the purposes of therapy supervision or training and to ensure both that any consent is informed about the use of the tape and that the consent is freely given. As a significant purpose of supervision and training is to enhance the quality of therapy for clients, it is likely that the costs of intrusion will be considered to be worth the benefits.

A final circumstance in which audiotaping may be used concerns research into counselling and psychotherapy. While some clients may feel uneasy about having their sessions recorded for research and refuse consent, others are willing participants. Therapists are similarly divided in their views about the validity of requesting permission to record sessions for research. Traditionally, psychodynamic therapists have the strongest reservations in contrast to others. Rogers (1942) was enthusiastic for 'electronic recording' to aid counselling research.

TESTING, PSYCHOMETRIC AND OTHER QUESTIONNAIRES

For many therapists, the idea of 'testing a client' runs counter to their core values and beliefs about what makes their work therapeutic. There are fears of labelling, dehumanizing and pathologizing people who come for therapy. However, the use of tests is common and is an integral part of the history of counselling and psychotherapy, especially in the US, both in research (e.g. Rogers and Dymond, 1954) and in practice (Watkins and Campbell, 1990). Dryden and Feltham (1994) have argued that when used flexibly and pragmatically, tests of various sorts can be of value to all practitioners. The main purposes for using questionnaires, inventories and other exercises are assessment and clarification of the client's needs; making catalytic interventions as part of the therapy process; and evaluating client progress and the effectiveness of therapy.

A wide spectrum of tests is available, ranging from standardized psychometric tests to informal information-gathering exercises. Standardized tests can be used to assess such psychological variables as anxiety, depression, social support and interpersonal functioning (Anastasi, 1992). There are inventories associated with particular therapies, such as the Beck Depression Inventory (Beck, 1978) and cognitive therapy, and Lazarus's (1981) Multimodal Life History Questionnaire and multimodal therapy. There are also questionnaires designed to gather information about specific issues, such as post-traumatic stress disorder (Scott and Stradling, 2000) and risk of suicide (Curwen, 1997).

A variety of exercises and questionnaires can be used catalytically, to initiate dialogue or to help a client get unstuck. These are not formal tests, but exercises that give sufficient structure and stimulus to reveal useful information. An example is completing sentence stems such as, 'I get sad when … .' Another, from transactional analysis, uses written or diagrammatic descriptions of key aspects of a client's situation. In reality therapy, Glasser (1989) challenges clients with questionnaires that expose problematic attitudes and behaviour.

Some tests help in deciding what therapeutic approach is most suitable for a client. This helps the therapist to adapt his approach or to consider referral. An example is the Opinions About Psychological Problems Questionnaires (Barker et al., 1983, reproduced in Dryden and Feltham, 1992) which reveal what theoretical orientation may best help a client. A more general test, the Myers–Briggs Type Indicator, assesses preferred ways in which people relate to the world and others, using Jungian concepts of psychological type. This can also be used to provide useful insights about how best to intervene with a client (Bayne, 1993).

Questionnaires can be used to assess client change and to gauge progress. This is particularly helpful with depressed or sceptical clients, who can gain concrete feedback of changes they have made. This is a feature of reality therapy and cognitive analytic therapy, and of cognitive-behavioural therapies in general. Questionnaires can also be used to evaluate a therapy service. An example is given in Carroll (1996: 222–4). See also Chapter 3.5 in this volume.

The decision to use tests, of whatever kind, depends upon a number of factors, such as the therapy setting, the therapist's theoretical orientation, and referral procedures where these are involved. The guiding principle is that the quality of the therapy is enhanced for the individual client, and over time for the therapist and the therapeutic service. This is most likely to be achieved when the rationale of a test is clearly understood and its use is closely linked to other aspects of working with the client within the therapeutic alliance.

CRISIS MANAGEMENT

Managing crises is an inevitable part of counselling and psychotherapy. Clients may seek therapy because they are already in crisis or anticipating crisis. Often, the circumstances that have created the crisis originate outside the therapy from some other aspects of the client's life, for example the ending of a close relationship or difficulties at work. Where the source of crisis is external to therapy, one of the functions of therapy is to act as a refuge, a place of relative calm and safety for the client. For the therapist this means creating an appropriately peaceful physical environment, free of interruptions, and being in a state of personal calm and order. Predictability, routine and a sense of the therapist's calm will usually be beneficial to the client.

However, the boundary between an externally generated crisis and the therapy is seldom so clearly delineated. External crises can contribute to crises within the therapeutic relationship that may be imported by the client, the therapist or someone else. Some examples of each are shown in Table 3.9.1; these may help to establish a range of circumstances in which crisis management is required.

The major challenge in managing any crisis is avoiding the sense of crisis taking over. This requires a combination of the therapist's personal/professional resourcefulness, attitude and technique. Useful techniques that have been tried and tested in practice include:

- mentally counting to 10 to allow space for initial reflection and reduce the sense of overwhelming urgency
- controlling own breathing, by breathing deeply and slowly and concentrating on exhaling

Table 3.9.1   *Sources of crisis in therapy*

Source	Example
Client	Extreme distress due to trauma, difficulties in relationship, physical or mental illness of sufficient severity to raise doubts about client's capacity to cope at end of session
Counsellor	Personal difficulties due to illness, unforeseen disruptions, own emotional issues. Practical disruptions like loss of therapy room due to fire, flood or burglary
Other	Unexpected events like client's angry partner bursting in and threatening therapist/client

- focusing personal and professional resources on managing the crisis
- breaking the source of the crisis into its component parts or more manageable 'chunks'
- maintaining a sense of hope, purpose and knowledge that the person most affected by the crisis is not alone in experiencing this kind of crisis.

The therapist's capacity to manage any crisis is considerably enhanced by preparation for such eventualities. Clinical supervision provides an excellent opportunity to review periodically the management of past crises and to anticipate other reasonably foreseeable ones. Discussion with experienced colleagues may also provide important insights.

Many therapists work alone with their clients. This is often unavoidable, especially in independent practice. However, this aspect of the work makes crisis management particularly demanding. Although therapy tends to be a professionally solitary activity, it need not be isolated. Therapists can learn from the way emergency services, such as the ambulance and fire services, manage the recurrent crises that characterize their work. Belonging to a network of therapists working in similar circumstances provides an opportunity to replicate the opportunities for informal debriefing and joint problem solving. Issues of confidentiality may prevent disclosure of the personal identity of clients, but nonetheless many of the ways of providing positive support used in emergency teams can be adopted. As in their case, formal debriefing may be required if managing the crisis has proved to be personally traumatic. The knowledge that adequate personal and professional support is available enhances the therapist's confidence to concentrate on managing the crisis without becoming unduly distracted by the personal consequences of exposure to crisis. A well-managed crisis can often prove to be both a critical and a beneficial turning point in the therapeutic process (Roberts, 2000).

ONWARD REFERRAL

There are many reasons why therapists consider making referrals to other services. Sometimes it is at the client's request. A client who is emotionally depressed by financial worries may want specialized financial advice in addition to therapy about depression. There are times when a client presents problems of such severity that they are inappropriate for therapy or may be beyond the competence of a specific therapist. For example, a client might benefit from being prescribed antidepressants by a doctor (Thistle, 1998). Ethical boundaries may also indicate the desirability of referral, for example to avoid therapy with friends and colleagues.

Most practitioners find responding to requests for referral made by clients more straightforward than raising the possibility of referral in response to their own assessment. There is the possibility of a client feeling personally rejected, or receiving implicit negative messages, when the therapist raises the possibility of referral. That is, someone who is being referred because of the therapist's concerns about their own competence may misinterpret the process as a comment on the severity of the client's problems rather than the limitations of the therapist. Considerable tact, transparency and reinforcement of key statements may be required to ensure that both therapist and client are communicating their feelings and intentions accurately.

Making a referral is likely to be an infrequent procedure in most counselling and psychotherapy services. This means that there are usually no fixed procedures and no prior expectations of the potential agency to whom the client is being referred. This can complicate any exploration of the desirability of referral and the client's active involvement in the process. It is increasingly common practice for the therapist to have discussions with the potential provider of new services about:

- the eligibility of the client to receive the service
- service availability, e.g. waiting lists
- type of service(s) available
- any requirements of the client
- confidentiality
- referral arrangements.

These discussions will usually take place with the client's consent but may also be made in ways which protect the client's identity, for example anonymously. The purpose of these discussions is to gain information, which enhances the quality of the decision to make a referral.

It is most consistent with the ethical basis of therapy to work in ways that enable clients to refer themselves to further services, especially where they are open to self-referral. However, there may be times when the client is too troubled to make a self-referral, or explicitly requests the assistance of the therapist. Some agencies will accept only professional referrals. In these circumstances, best practice is to negotiate the basis of referral with the client so that the client is clear about what is being communicated or withheld. Anecdotal evidence suggests that there is considerable variation in the amount of information passed to the receiving service. In terms of efficiency and respect for client privacy, it is usually best to restrict information to that which is relevant to the delivery of the service and which has been explicitly agreed with the client. Most receiving services would expect to be informed if the person being referred poses a threat to other service recipients or staff.

It is common practice to make referrals in writing, usually by letter or brief report. This has the potential advantage of the therapist being able to discuss the contents with a client prior to sending if it is considered personally sensitive, or of sending a copy to the client so that the process is transparent. This maximizes the client's participation. Practice varies in whether the person making the referral expects a brief report of the outcome. It is therefore best to request a report if this is considered desirable.

The major challenge in making referrals is to make them in ways consistent both with the quality of relationship and with the ways of working required for therapy (Leigh, 1998).

REFERENCES

American Psychiatric Association (2000) *Diagnostic and Statistical Manual of Mental Disorders, DSM-IV-TR* (4th edn). Washington, DC: APA.

Anastasi, A. (1992) What counselors should know about the use and interpretation of psychological tests. *Journal of Counseling and Development*, 70: 610–15.

BACP (2002) Guidance on good practice in counselling and psychotherapy. In BACP, *Ethical Framework for Good Practice in Counselling and Psychotherapy* (pp. 5–10).

Rugby: British Association for Counselling and Psychotherapy.

Barker, C., Pistrang, N. and Shapiro, D.A. (1983) Opinions about psychological problems. Unpublished manuscript. Subdepartment of Clinical Psychology, University College London.

Bayne, R. (1993) Psychological type, conversations and counselling. In R. Bayne and P. Nicholson (eds), *Counselling and Psychology for Health Professionals*. London: Chapman and Hall.

Beck, A.T. (1978) *Depression Inventory*. Philadelphia: Center for Cognitive Therapy.

Bond, T. (2009) *Standards and Ethics for Counselling in Action* (3rd edn). London: Sage.

Bor, R., Gill, S., Miller, R. and Parrot, C. (2004) *Doing Therapy Briefly*. Basingstoke: Palgrave Macmillan.

Bordin, E.S. (1979) The generalizability of the psychoanalytic concept of the working alliance. *Psychotherapy: Theory, Research and Practice*, 16: 252–60.

Bordin, E.S. (1994) Theory and research on the therapeutic working alliance. In O. Horvath and S. Greenberg (eds), *The Working Alliance: Theory, Research and Practice*. New York: Wiley.

Carroll, M. (1996) *Workplace Counselling: A Systematic Approach to Employee Care*. London: Sage.

Corey, G., Corey, M.S. and Callanan, P. (2002) *Issues and Ethics in the Caring Professions*. Pacific Grove, CA: Brooks/Cole.

Curwen, B. (1997) Medical and psychiatric assessment. In S. Palmer and G. McMahon (eds), *Client Assessment*. London: Sage.

Dexter, G. and Russell, J. (1997) *Challenging Blank Minds and Sticky Moments in Counselling*. Preston: Winckley.

Dryden, W. and Feltham, C. (1992) *Brief Counselling: A Practical Guide for Beginning Practitioners*. Buckingham: Open University Press.

Dryden, W. and Feltham, C. (1994) *Developing the Practice of Counselling*. London: Sage.

Egan, G. (2001) *The Skilled Helper: A Problem-Management and Opportunity-Development Approach to Helping* (7th edn). New York: Brooks/Cole.

Ellis, A. and Dryden, W. (1998) *The Practice of Rational Emotive Behaviour Therapy*. London: Free Association.

Glasser, N. (ed.) (1989) *Control Theory in the Practice of Reality Therapy*. London: Harper and Row.

Houston, G. (2003) *Brief Gestalt Therapy*. London: Sage.

Hudson-Allez, G. (1997) *Time-Limited Therapy in a General Practice Setting*. London: Sage.

Jacobs, M. (1999) *Psychodynamic Counselling in Action*. London: Sage.

Lazarus, A.A. (1981) *The Practice of Multimodal Therapy*. New York: McGraw-Hill.

Leigh, A. (1998) *Referral and Termination Issues for Counsellors*. London: Sage.

McLeod, J. (2003) *An Introduction to Counselling* (2nd edn). Buckingham: Open University Press.

Malan, D.H. (1976) *The Frontiers of Brief Psychotherapy*. New York: Plenum.

Mearns, D. and Thorne, B. (1999) *Person-Centred Counselling in Action* (2nd edn). London: Sage.

Midgley, D. (1998) *New Directions in Transactional Analysis Counselling: An Explorer's Handbook*. London: Free Association.

Nelson-Jones, R. (1982) *The Theory and Practice of Counselling Psychology*. London: Holt, Rinehart and Winston.

Parkinson, F. (1995) *Listening and Helping in the Workplace: A Guide for Managers, Supervisors and Colleagues Who Need to Use Counselling Skills*. London: Souvenir.

Roberts, A.R. (ed.) (2000) *Crisis Intervention Handbook: Assessment, Treatment and Research*. New York: Oxford University Press.

Rogers, C.R. (1942) The use of electronically recorded interviews in improving psychotherapeutic techniques. In H. Kirschenbaum and V.L. Hendersson (eds) (1990), *The Carl Rogers Reader* (pp. 211–19). London: Constable.

Rogers, C.R. (1951) *Client-Centered Therapy: Its Current Practice, Implications and Theory*. Boston: Houghton Mifflin.

Rogers, C.R. and Dymond, R. (eds) (1954) *Psychotherapy and Personality Change*. Chicago: Chicago University Press.

Rosenbaum, R. (1994) Single-session therapies: intrinsic integration. *Journal of Psychotherapy Integration*, 4: 229–52.

Ryle, A. (1990) *Cognitive-Analytic Therapy. Active Participation in Change: A New Integration in Brief Psychotherapy*. Chichester: Wiley.

Ryle, A. (2004) Writing by patients and therapists in cognitive analytic therapy. In G. Bolton,

S. Howlett, C. Lago and J.K. Wright (eds), *Writing Cures: An Introductory Handbook of Writing in Counselling and Therapy*. Hove: Brunner-Routledge.

Ryle, A. and Kerr, I.B. (2002) *Introducing Cognitive Analytic Therapy: Principles and Practice*. Chichester: Wiley.

Scott, M.J. and Stradling, S.G. (2000) *Counselling for Post-Traumatic Stress Disorder*. London: Sage.

Sills, C. (ed.) (2007) *Contracts in Counselling* (2nd edn). London: Sage.

Sutton, C. (1989) 'The evaluation of counselling: a goal-attainment approach. In W. Dryden (ed.), *Key Issues for Counselling in Action*. London: Sage.

Thistle, R. (1998) *Counselling and Psychotherapy in Private Practice*. London: Sage.

Thorne, B. (1996) Person-centred therapy. In W. Dryden (ed.), *Handbook of Individual Therapy* (pp. 121–46). London: Sage.

Trower, P., Casey, A. and Dryden, W. (1988) *Cognitive Behavioural Counselling in Action*. London: Sage.

Tudor, K. (1998) Value for money? Issues of fees in counselling and psychotherapy. *British Journal of Guidance and Counselling*, 26 (4): 477–93.

Turner, P.R., Valtierra, M., Talken, T.R., Miller, V.I. and DeAnda, J.R. (1996) Effect of session length on treatment outcome for college students in brief therapy. *Journal of Counseling Psychology*, 43: 228–32.

Van Deurzen-Smith, E. (1996) Existential therapy. In Windy Dryden (ed.), *Handbook of Individual Therapy in Britain* (3rd edn, pp. 166–93). London: Sage.

Waldron-Skinner, S. and Watson, D. (1987) *Ethical Issues in Family Therapy*. London: Routledge and Kegan Paul.

Watkins, C. and Campbell, V. (eds) (1990) *Testing in Counseling Practice*. Mahwah, NJ: Erlbaum.

Whitmore, D. (2000) *Psychosynthesis Counselling in Action* (2nd edn). London: Sage.

Wills, F. (1997) Cognitive counselling: a down-to-earth and accessible therapy. In C. Sills (ed.), *Contracts in Counselling*. London: Sage.

Worrall, M. (1997) Contracting within the person-centred approach. In C. Sills (ed.), *Contracts in Counselling*. London: Sage.

PART IV

PROFESSIONAL ISSUES

Introduction

COLIN FELTHAM AND IAN HORTON

Apart from what therapy attempts to do, in what settings – and its clinical or therapeutic ingredients, and the wider social context in which it takes place – there is a set of issues perhaps best described as *professional* issues. While use of this term may be usefully read against critiques of the *professionalizing* trend in therapy (see House, 2003), we believe that all practitioners, from whatever tradition, are obliged to at least consider their own version of the issues presented in this part of the book.

First, there is a cluster of matters – professional and personal development, supervision, ethical and legal considerations – that all must address in one way or another. Training institutions and professional bodies differ in their requirements for professional and personal development, but all expect that counsellors and therapists will take initial and further training seriously, and all have their own perspectives on and requirements for clinical supervision. Since the therapist's *use of self* is such a central part of the work, and it sometimes entails difficult judgements as to boundaries between subjectivity and professionalism, it behoves all therapists to weigh up carefully such issues. Equally, all must address the questions posed by ethical frameworks and the kinds of dilemma that can arise in the ethical and legal domain.

Most, if not all, practitioners will at some time need to consider the question of insurance. However, not everyone has to examine issues arising from private practice settings, including the matter of advertising; nevertheless, this is a very large area of provision and is necessarily included here. Similarly, not everyone has to consider the relevance of research, but all practitioners must weigh up their own position and the advantages that research has to offer. Quality assurance is something that many practitioners may not need urgently to confront, but increasingly many must do so and all are advised to anticipate the likelihood of future demands from employers and others for evidence-based practice informed by research and regular and systematic monitoring of clinical effectiveness. The profile of evidence-based practice continues to increase with each edition of this book.

We have also included in this part of the book a brief chapter on clients' experiences of the therapeutic enterprise, since clients both deserve and are gradually and rightfully getting a larger voice in the development and monitoring of therapy.

REFERENCE

House, R. (2003) *Therapy Beyond Modernity: Deconstructing and Transcending Profession-Centred Therapy*. London: Karnac.

Professional and Personal Development

HAZEL JOHNS

Many studies have demonstrated that in all theoretical orientations the most significant factor in terms of client outcomes is the relationship, the working alliance, between client and practitioner (McLeod, 1998; Wampold, 2001; Horvath and Bedi, 2002). That relationship is directly affected by a therapist's ability to be fully present as herself. In order to fulfil the demanding intra- and interpersonal challenge of enabling growth in others, practitioners must engage in personal and professional development, working towards self-knowledge, self-awareness, awareness of and openness to others, capacity for reflection, openness to personal growth, and self-acceptance. In a challenge to the novelist Joseph Conrad's view that 'No man ever understands quite his own artful dodges to escape from the grim shadow of self-knowledge', this chapter will argue for the primacy of personal and professional development in the training and career-long maturing of counsellors and psychotherapists.

PURPOSE AND NEEDS

The active search for self-knowledge through professional and personal development is embedded in the training and accreditation criteria of organizations in the 'psychological therapies' and related fields (for example BACP, 2009; 2010; BPS, 2005; UKCP, 1998; NHS, 2004). These two aspects of development create the essential membrane through which all other learning – theories, skills, legalities, ethics and relationships – must filter. The symbiosis of the two offers the potential to nurture in practitioners the strength and stability to question creatively self, others and systems. This should challenge arrogance, ignorance or stasis – all enemies to the helping professions. Yet, the demand for continual personal and professional development encapsulates the core tension between the imperative to work towards Egan's (1986) 'ideal helper' and the necessary acknowledgement that, being human and in order to stay sane, it is only reasonable to attempt to be good enough. In order to be effective, at whatever stage of their career, therapists are expected to aim for a professional and personal version of Socrates's 'life well lived': with forethought, self-knowledge, principle, goals and integrity, 'chosen and directed by the one who lives it, to the fullest extent possible to a human agent caught in the web of society and history', not 'a stranger mapless in a foreign land' (Grayling, 2002). Since they are human, practitioners inevitably mirror the lives and struggles of their clients, yet need also to model positive ways of grappling with 'the continual wrenching of experience', as stressed in Adams's (1995) the *Hitchhiker's Guide to the Galaxy*.

Imagine for a moment counsellors and psychotherapists in a myriad counselling rooms across the country, in colleges, GP surgeries, drop-in centres, rooms in houses and gardens, or in training establishments. What do they have in common? How are they different? Many factors are embedded in the array of individual profiles: age or life stage, physical setting, work context, nature and needs of client groups, crisis events in own and others' lives, personal fitness both physical and emotional, career ambitions, health of systems/organizations, demands and developments of professional bodies, and changes in society. Any or all of those factors will affect the precise nature of individual needs for personal and professional development, whether in initial training or as part of lifelong support for and challenge to practitioners' competence.

PROFESSIONAL DEVELOPMENT

What then does *professional* mean in therapeutic helping, especially in an activity with roots in volunteering, medical, social and vocational care for others, in neighbourliness, and in the 'barefoot counselling' movement of the 1960s? Now many practitioners hold paid posts in the public, private or voluntary sectors, shored up or trammelled (depending on the view held of the movement towards professionalism) by training, accreditation, codes and frameworks of practice. Their training should have equipped them with knowledge of the ethics and practice of therapeutic helping, theory and skills, the needs of different client groups and an ability to use supervision. Distinct from psychoanalytic approaches, which have a longer European history, many models of counselling and psychotherapy have grown in Britain in the last 50 years from infant beginnings into strapping adults. To promote and support this growth, membership and accrediting organizations have evolved, such as BACP with a current (2010) individual membership of over 33,000, BPS with its Counselling Psychology Division and UKCP with around 80 accrediting organizations. They foster those elements said to be characteristic of 'a profession' (Horton, 1997): clear standards of conduct by which the public are protected, through ethical codes of practice, complaints procedures, the monitoring of qualifications and competencies, training, accreditation and registration, accountability and evaluation through monitoring, research and evidence-based practice. All these organizations have made continuous professional development a mandatory part of registration and ongoing accreditation, enshrining in lifelong practice the concept forged in training of the 'reflective practitioner', whether alone, in supervision or with colleagues and peers.

PERSONAL DEVELOPMENT

However, none of that focus on being 'professional' is sufficient without equal or greater attention being paid to the *personal* development of counsellors and psychotherapists, since it is the self of the practitioner that has most influence on the quality and effectiveness of the therapeutic relationship. In training, and throughout working life, opportunities must be created and chosen to explore purposefully each individual's balance of strengths and limitations and the interplay between personal and professional selves. There will need to be a focus on unique patterns of values, attitudes and constructs; the elements in personal history which help or hinder the ability to feel, perceive, relate or protect/assert the self; capacities for intimacy, appropriate separation from others and emotional stability; a deeper knowledge of individual needs, fears, intolerances and blind spots; an assessment of tendencies to invade or deprive others, to use power appropriately or not; and an awareness and understanding of the self in relation to community and society, both as a person and as a therapist. The resulting self-awareness and self-knowledge should promote purposeful personal growth and further the ability to work ethically and with integrity as a counsellor or psychotherapist.

PRE-TRAINING: PREPARATION AND POTENTIAL

The person who arrives at a counselling or psychotherapy course for the selection process will, of course, have already been shaped by life experiences, by her capacity to reflect on and learn from them, by early encounters with affection and rejection, by life chances and choices concerning education, work and relationships, and by the ensuing systems of values, beliefs, and cognitive and emotional intelligences. It is the task and responsibility of training courses to select individuals who demonstrate the ability to reflect on and the strength to develop the facets of themselves necessary for creating and sustaining therapeutic relationships. This is a demanding process involving risk and courage: it should responsibly be accompanied by a 'health warning' that considerable disturbance and confusion might ensue. It must be undertaken in the interests of clients while sustaining and refining the practitioner's own emotional health. Training must, then, provide opportunities for trainees to grow in awareness of self and others, emotional stability, understanding of culture and society, flexibility of thought and attitude, knowledge and skills, in order to work ethically and purposefully with others.

TRAINING: PROFESSIONAL DEVELOPMENT

Training for counselling and psychotherapy has evolved and deepened over the last half-century; more recently, it has been formalized by the professional bodies into substantial core curricula (for example BACP, 2009). In all courses, *professional* studies include knowledge of theories and models of counselling and psychotherapy, skills and practice in one or more key theoretical orientations, ethical codes and frameworks, supervised placements, the needs of clients and client groups, input on systems/organizations, supervision, skills of evaluation and research, and all the 'how-to', 'why' and 'what-if' issues arising from the process of translating a hypothetical model of therapeutic helping into lived practical experience (Wilkins, 1997). Particular modalities will place more or less emphasis on contexts, political and cultural issues, but all must now pay attention to issues of equality, diversity, oppression and legal rights. The aim is to produce knowledgeable, skilled, competent and effective practitioners able to evaluate their work and operate in an accountable and responsible manner. After training and appropriate experience, they will be able to work within an ethical framework of practice and will be eligible for accreditation, registration or chartering.

TRAINING: PERSONAL DEVELOPMENT

There has always been considerable agreement on the substance of professional development in training, but much more debate about the mechanisms and processes through which personal development can be fostered. A number of writers have explored these concepts (Cross and Papadopoulos, 2001; Hughes and Youngson, 2009; Johns, 2012). Some have also expressed poignantly the reciprocal impact of therapeutic work on the self of the worker in the helping professions (Scaife and Walshe, 2001; Norcross, 2002) and the crucial contribution of personal development to the survival, potential and emotional stability of the counsellor, not least in modelling good practice for clients. As Rogers expressed it: 'The degree to which I can create relationships which facilitate the growth of others as separate persons is a measure of the growth I have achieved in myself' (1961: 56).

There will be a necessary focus on the individual constructs and values outlined earlier, on life stage and life space, and on patterns of coping with change or crisis. Different theoretical orientations will also add particular focus on enhanced capacities for cognitive understanding, for emotional literacy, for working with transference or with spiritual dimensions of being. Several writers have written extensively (Hughes and Youngson, 2009; Johns, 2012) about how this work may be undertaken: through individual

exploration, in journals, reflection in writing and on reading, tutorials, supervision and of course counselling/therapy; in structured activities and interactive work; and through groups of many kinds, some influenced by the theoretical model of a course and some aimed at providing trainees with a range of group experiences, combined with the potential for reflective learning and processing of experience. The place and purpose of personal counselling and therapy in training and beyond has particular resonance and has been much debated, depending in particular on the values of different theoretical models. It is, however, hard to be convinced of the integrity of any approach which could not see the importance of therapists in training experiencing what it is to be a client. However divergent opinions may be on this and any other means of personal growth, there is no disagreement that psychotherapists and counsellors operate in roles and contexts permeated by ambiguities and pressures. Personal development has, of necessity, a twofold aim: to promote personal awareness and emotional strength and to underpin optimum professional development in the best interests of clients.

POST-QUALIFICATION DEVELOPMENT

The case for career-long continuing personal and professional development is self-evident. The imperatives come from many directions: from training courses' criteria for selection; from professional organizations in their criteria for post-training accreditation, registration and chartered status; and from the determined, even strident, governmental demands for statutory regulation. Demands arise too from the bewildering pace and power of change, legally, socially, politically, since the transition to the twenty-first century: from gender politics, diversity issues, changes in employment patterns, economic refugees and asylum seekers, international terrorism, ecological fears, rampant consumerism, the cult of celebrity and, perhaps most pervasively, the identity and relationship issues arising from the internet and all forms of virtual communication. All of this affects therapists and their clients in countless unexpected, confusing and potentially conflicting ways.

RESOURCES FOR PERSONAL AND PROFESSIONAL DEVELOPMENT

What then are the means through which these demands might be met? Depending on stage of professional life, theoretical orientation, context of work, nature of client groups and personal state, practitioners will need throughout their careers to undertake some or all of the following: further training; commitment to the process of accreditation, registration or chartering after acquiring sufficient experience; engagement in career-long supervision; continuation of personal counselling/therapy; putting energy into networking with colleagues and peer support; participation in some relationship and commitment to professional organizations; recognizing and maximizing personal learning of all kinds, both planned and incidental, developmental and crisis; ensuring some balance of work, family and self-needs; and, crucially, managing self-care, emotional stability and integrity. There is also an increasing demand for and valuing of research and evaluation of practice; for writing for employment and funding purposes or for publication; for engagement with political and cultural contexts; and for the skills of the 'reflective practitioner' to be honed and applied in organizations – not least, in the struggle to survive and thrive in often destructive systems.

Further Training

The stimuli for post-qualification training can be many and varied: updating and filling gaps; desire for more depth in a core model or to acquire theoretical or practical knowledge of other approaches; needs of particular client groups; demands of employing organizations or systems; legal, social or political changes in society and the consequent need to explore any resulting ethical challenges; and experiences or crises in an individual's life which produce a need for new or deeper knowledge and understanding. Degrees, higher degrees, conferences, workshops, training days and short courses are all opportunities to extend learning in active exchange with colleagues, while purposeful reading of up-to-date books and journals can help identify trends, awareness of limitations and potential new areas for growth.

Accreditation, Registration and Chartered Status

The growth of membership organizations described earlier has been a consequence of the movement in the last 40 years towards professionalization of the 'talking therapies'. A second and demanding development has been the not-without-challenge move towards accountability through the formal processes of accreditation (BACP), registration (UKCP) and chartering (counselling division of BPS). These schemes provide standards for practitioners to work towards, recognition of their professional status and

a guarantee to clients that practitioners are trained to at least a minimum standard. The criteria include being members in good standing, not subject to complaints procedures, appropriately qualified, with sufficient experience and insurance, in regular supervision, and committed to career-long continuing professional development. A third and significant step is currently in preparation and debate: that of state regulation of the 'talking therapies', which will safeguard (for its proponents) or constrain further (for opponents) practitioners and clients. Whatever the conflicting values expressed over the rightness or disadvantages of accreditation and regulation, engagement in the written and experiential activities needed to provide evidence for approved status can be a powerful mechanism for continuing professional learning.

Supervision

Although requirements differ for ongoing supervision throughout a practitioner's career (for BACP accredited members it is mandatory, for members of other bodies it is optional after training), that working alliance is one of the most fruitful arenas for personal and professional development. The formative, normative and restorative functions of supervision, whether individually or in groups (Proctor, 2008), offer opportunities for creative support and challenge, at every stage of experience, enhancing the development of practitioners while protecting ethically the safety and welfare of clients. Effective consultant supervision, a clearly contracted collaborative relationship, can offer excellent modelling of respect, acceptance and supportive challenge and a trellis through and around which the tendrils of personal and professional growth can flourish. Therapists have a professional responsibility to conduct a continuous systematic audit of their strengths, limitations and capacity for change. Supervision at its best is the safe yet challenging place where practitioners might face their fallibility, their needs around power, belonging, shame and blame – and their triumphs, joys and laughter.

Personal Therapy and Counselling

Just as debate has raged in training courses about the place of therapy for trainees, so the jury is out on its place in the career-long personal and professional development of counsellors and psychotherapists. Some theoretical orientations insist on it, others consider it irrelevant. What may matter most is an awareness of need, often through exploration in supervision; a readiness to find the time, money and strength to undertake a period of counselling; and an understanding of how and why the process might facilitate or interfere with the practitioner's competence. The emotional and cognitive dissonances of being in the client role are powerful reminders of what being a client entails. It is also likely that life events, whether existential and age related, or crises such as bereavement or relationship break-up, will at times knock mature adult therapists off course and necessitate therapeutic support with consequent personal and professional learning. As in training, decisions have to be made about the theoretical orientation, gender, ethnicity and age of a therapist, whether through individual or group work, the safety of context, boundaries (not always simple in, for example, rural areas) and, ultimately, whether the practitioner is still 'fit for practice'

Other Sources and Resources

The many other activities that experienced counsellors and psychotherapists might engage in may depend on the stage of career, interests, ambitions, setting, personal situation or needs. Ongoing personal and professional development must meet both defensive and creative needs (Johns, 1997): defensive, to protect practitioners and clients from illegalities, unethical behaviours, incompetence, vulnerability or attacks on accountability; and creative or proactive, to increase knowledge and understanding, emotional and artistic intelligence, awareness of cultural, political and existential complexities, constantly working for clarity in values and integrity of motivation and behaviour. Writing for publication in journals or making bids for funding, undertaking small-scale personal research (McLeod, 2003), participating in a professional organization's committees and working parties, networking with colleagues in the same or related fields, applying appropriately reflective and interpersonal skills in organizations, charities or local politics: all may help to extend or refine personal and professional growth of all kinds. The parallel demands for self-care and work/life balance may also be met by introspective activities such as meditation and mindfulness practices, reflective writing (Bolton, 2010), purposeful or playful reading (Cox and Theilgaard, 1994; Knights, 1995), physical exercise and creative engagement with art, drama, music, friends and family.

CHALLENGES TO PERSONAL AND PROFESSIONAL DEVELOPMENT

Although personal and professional development is accepted as central throughout the working life of counsellors and psychotherapists, the process is not without difficulties. Development implies change and change can trigger anxiety, doubt, a sense of loss or anger at the destabilizing of self, self-image and/or relationships. There may also be very tangible obstacles – internally in terms of skills, temperament and fears, or externally in family, community or ethnic attitudes and values – which may impede or derail any growth. There are also issues of time, money and life demands, especially for counsellors juggling with careers or joblessness, children, ageing parents, health issues and the unavoidable existential challenges of being human.

In addition, there are two new challenges with implications for personal and professional development. First, research into genetics and the psychobiology of the mind is leading to as yet unknown frontiers in understandings of 'self'. Second, the growth of methods of 'virtual' communication, the plethora of internet and mobile platforms that foster and mask multiple identities, seems of major significance. They blur the essential distinction between private and public selves and militate against genuine, ethical, emotionally robust relationships. Many clients coming for therapy and many entrants to counselling and psychotherapy training will have grown up knowing only this fascinating yet fragmenting world. People are in constant communication, emailing, texting, talking, tweeting, blogging, video-phoning, yet with potentially a minimally secure sense of self or of others. Personal and professional development will have to meet those challenges and find ways of harnessing such powerful forces in the interests of ethical practice and sound, well-integrated practitioners.

REFERENCES

Adams, D. (1995) *The Hitchhiker's Guide to the Galaxy*. London: Pan.

BACP (2009) *Accreditation of Training Courses* (5th edn). Rugby: British Association for Counselling and Psychotherapy.

BACP (2010) *Ethical Framework for Good Practice in Counselling and Psychotherapy*. Rugby: British Association for Counselling and Psychotherapy.

Bolton, G. (2010) *Reflective Practice: Writing and Professional Development*. London: Sage.

BPS (2005) *Professional Practice Guidelines, Division of Counselling Psychology, Supplement to Code of Conduct, Ethical Principles and Guidelines*. Leicester: British Psychological Society.

Cox, M. and Theilgaard, A. (1994) *Shakespeare as Prompter*. London: Jessica Kingsley.

Cross, M. and Papadopoulos, L. (2001) *Becoming a Therapist: A Manual for Personal and Professional Development*. Hove: Routledge.

Egan, G. (1986) *The Skilled Helper* (3rd edn). Monterey: Brooks/Cole.

Grayling, A.C. (2002) *The Meaning of Things*. London: Phoenix.

Horton, I. (1997) *The Needs of Counsellors and Psychotherapists*. London: Sage.

Horvath, A.O. and Bedi, R.P. (2002) The alliance. In J.C. Norcross (ed.), *Psychotherapy Relationships that Work*. New York: Oxford University Press.

Hughes, J. and Youngson, S. (2009) *Personal Development and Clinical Psychology*. Chichester: BPS Blackwell.

Johns, H. (1997) Self-development: lifelong learning? In I. Horton and V. Varma (eds), *The Needs of Counsellors and Psychotherapists*. London: Sage.

Johns, H. (2012) *Personal Development in Counsellor Training* (2nd edn). London: Sage.

Knights, B. (1995) *The Listening Reader*. London: Jessica Kingsley.

McLeod, J. (1998) *An Introduction to Counselling* (2nd edn). Milton Keynes: Open University Press.

McLeod, J. (2003) *Doing Counselling Research* (2nd edn). London: Sage.

NHS (2004) *The NHS Knowledge and Skills Framework and the Development Review Process*. London: Department of Health.

Norcross, J.N. (ed.) (2002) *Psychotherapy Relationships that Work*. New York: Oxford University Press.

Proctor, B. (2008) *Group Supervision: A Guide to Creative Practice* (2nd edn). London: Sage.

Rogers, C.R. (1961) *On Becoming a Person*. London: Constable.

Scaiffe, J. and Walsh, S. (2001) The emotional climate of work and the development of self. In J. Scaife (ed.), *Supervision in the Mental Health Professions*. London: Brunner-Routledge.

UKCP (1998) *Ethical Requirements for Member Organisations*. London: United Kingdom Council for Psychotherapy.

Wampold, B.E. (2001) *The Great Psychotherapy Debate: Models, Methods, and Findings*. Mahwah, NJ: Erlbaum.

Wilkins, P. (1997) *Personal and Professional Development for Counsellors*. London: Sage.

Clinical Supervision

VAL WOSKET

WHAT IS SUPERVISION?

Supervision is a structured and formal collaborative arrangement whereby a counsellor or psychotherapist reflects regularly on their clinical work with someone who is an experienced therapist and supervisor. The aim of supervision is to promote the efficacy of the therapist–client relationship and the therapeutic work. Supervision includes a monitoring function which is intended to ensure that counsellors are working safely and ethically. Clinical supervision is *not* training, personal therapy or line management, although it may contain elements of these. BACP describes supervision as 'a process to maintain adequate standards of counselling and a method of consultancy to widen the horizons of an experienced practitioner' (2008a: 1).

Supervision at its best is a restorative process that nourishes the supervisee and helps to replenish emotional energy. As such it is a supportive process that has a preventive mental health function and can help to counteract the effects of stress. Clinical supervision does not have a disciplinary function, and within supervision the therapist should feel free to discuss their difficulties in working with clients without fear of disapproval or judgement. Supervision is different from line management in that the focus of the work is the interaction between the practitioner and the client, rather than the management of casework. Ideally practitioners are not supervised by their line managers. Where this occurs by necessity, it is important that the therapist also has access to external, objective consultative support to complement their line management supervision. In essence, then, effective supervision:

- promotes therapeutic competence, knowledge and skills development
- enhances the quality of the therapeutic work
- safeguards the welfare of clients by monitoring ethical, professional and anti-discriminatory practice
- encourages the growth of insight and self-awareness through reflective practice
- provides the therapist with a protective mechanism against stress and burnout.

Clinical supervision has three key functions, which are to support, develop and monitor the supervisee and the work that she or he is undertaking with clients. The supervisor's role is to encourage the autonomy of the practitioner within safe boundaries and limits and to provide a relationship and process that will enable the practitioner to develop their own way of working effectively with clients.

The ultimate success of supervision depends to a large extent upon the quality of the relationship between the supervisor and the therapist (Wosket, 2009). While the relationship is not an end in itself, it importantly expedites the task and process in effective supervision. An increasing number of research studies indicate that the relationship in supervision is a key determinant of its effectiveness (Gray et al., 2001; Ladany et al., 2001; Mehr et al., 2010; Nelson and Friedlander, 2001; Nelson et al., 2008; Weaks, 2002). Participants in Weaks's qualitative study which looked at what comprises 'good supervision' highlighted the quality of the supervisory relationship as of 'paramount importance' (2002: 36). Her research identified the three 'core conditions' of a good supervisory relationship as *safety*, *equality* and *challenge*. Some further key findings from research into the supervisory relationship indicate that:

- Supervisees rate the quality of the supervisory relationship as the most pivotal and crucial component of good supervision. Positive relationships with their supervisors contribute significantly to supervisees' overall satisfaction with the supervision they receive. Conversely, where supervision relationships are deemed unsatisfactory by supervisees they tend to rate these as the most significant aspect of negative supervision. In particular, inflexibility on the part of the supervisor seems to seriously inhibit supervisees' productive exploration and can lead to irreconcilable impasses.
- Supervisees who experience relationship difficulties with their supervisors learn to protect vulnerable aspects of the self by hiding certain problems and conflicts in their work from fear of an unsympathetic reaction if they reveal them to their supervisor. This experience can then be paralleled in supervisees' client work as they learn to use avoidance tactics when dealing with difficult interpersonal relationships with clients.
- There is a positive correlation between supervisees' perceived levels of rapport with their supervisors and their ability to disclose difficult and sensitive issues in supervision. Therefore the quality assurance function of supervision may be importantly mediated by the quality of the supervisory relationship.
- Supervisees value the use of self-disclosure by their supervisors where it is used judiciously to:
  - build and enhance the supervisory relationship
  - repair ruptures in the relationship when they occur
  - provide modelling about how to address conflicts and tensions in their own relationships with clients.

The willingness of a supervisor to share their vulnerability through disclosing their own struggles with therapeutic dilemmas is particularly appreciated by supervisees and helps to correct the power imbalance in the relationship. Conversely, excessive or inappropriate self-disclosure by the supervisor tends to significantly undermine the supervisory process and relationship.

REQUIREMENTS FOR SUPERVISION

Clinical supervision is stipulated in BACP's *Ethical Framework for Good Practice in Counselling and Psychotherapy* (2010) as a formal, ongoing requirement for all counsellors. Current recommendations made by BACP (2008b) advise that counsellors (including those in training) should receive a *minimum* of one and a half hours of supervision per month, irrespective of size of caseload, in order to be eligible for individual counsellor accreditation. This is considered to be an absolute minimum and BACP recommends that careful assessments based on variables such as caseloads, complexity of client issues, work setting, and experience of the counsellor are made to determine how much supervision individual practitioners need to ensure ethical and safe practice. Where supervision is undertaken in a group, counsellors may count a proportion of presentation time (rather than the total time that the group meets) towards their supervision hours. Proportions are based on the size of the group and BACP can advise on current ratios.

Other professional bodies associated with psychotherapists, psychoanalysts, clinical psychologists and counselling psychologists expect clinical practitioners to be engaged in ongoing personal and professional development including supervision, but stop short of stipulating mandatory specified amounts of career-long supervision. Increasingly, ongoing supervision for trainees and qualified practitioners is becoming embedded in the broader spectrum of mental health professions (Scaife, 2008).

TYPES OF SUPERVISION

Supervision can be undertaken in a one-to-one relationship with an individual supervisor, within a group, or between two therapists as co-supervision. Normally in individual supervision the supervisor will be a more experienced practitioner than the supervisee. Group supervision can either be peer facilitated or have a leader. Where it is led by a supervisor, group members may be supervised in turn by the leader or they may engage in peer supervision that is structured and facilitated by the leader. The latter model allows for greater use to be made of the resources and responses of all members of the group in the process of understanding and exploring the client work presented.

Peer group supervision is not recommended as the only, or main, form of supervision for trainee counsellors, who are considered to require the discipline and individual attention provided by regular one-to-one supervision with an experienced supervisor. Co-supervision occurs where two counsellors take turns in supervising one another. This form of supervision is only suitable for very experienced therapists and may not be appropriate for all practitioners.

FINDING A SUITABLE SUPERVISOR

Counsellors and psychotherapists in training will often have their supervisor appointed or recommended by their tutor from an approved register of supervisors maintained by their training institution. Where trainees are required to make their own supervision arrangements it is important that they check out the suitability of their potential supervisor to meet the requirements for the type and standard of supervision laid down by the training course. A trainee therapist should have a supervisor who is trained or well versed in (and supportive of) the core theory or model of counselling/psychotherapy that the supervisee is learning on their course. Continuity is also important for trainees. Once settled with a supervisor who suits them, it is helpful for the student to stay with the same supervisor throughout their training. The supervisor can then provide the feedback and encouragement that arise from in-depth knowledge of the student's work as it develops over time and with a variety of clients.

Qualified practitioners may benefit from supervision provided by someone who can offer a range of perspectives that extend beyond their own original training model. Therapists who work in organizations do well to choose supervisors who are willing and able to work with organizational issues and dynamics as well as interpersonal ones. Those who work in primary health care and other specialized settings, or who offer time-limited contracts or work with specific client populations, are similarly advised to seek out a supervisor who is familiar with and able to take account of the context-specific nature of their work. Therapists need to feel both supported and stretched in their learning and development. Supervision that is experienced merely as a cosy exchange of interesting observations is likely to diminish a therapist's work with clients rather than enhance it. Vigorous and active challenge, coupled with support and encouragement, are the important components of a healthy and creative supervision relationship, and without an optimum balance of these elements the supervisees and their clients are unlikely to thrive.

It is important for therapists to choose supervisors who are experienced clinical practitioners,

have sound supervisory knowledge and experience, and can offer the kind of relationship in which the supervisee feels able to reveal their concerns and dilemmas freely and honestly. BACP maintains a *Counselling and Psychotherapy Resources Directory* (available online at www.bacp.co.uk) that provides details of supervisors under geographical listings and indicates those who are accredited. Prospective supervisees should not fight shy of asking for detailed information about a supervisor's background, training, experience, style of supervision and own supervision arrangements before deciding whether to work with that person. They should expect that time will be given in an initial meeting to contracting, which includes looking at the supervisee's needs and preferences as well as what the supervisor has to offer. Supervisees can expect to have regular reviews in which mutual feedback is given and received on the supervision task, process and relationship and should ask for these if they are not offered.

NEGOTIATING A SUPERVISION CONTRACT

Once supervisor and supervisee have agreed on the possibility of working together they need to form a contract to establish ground rules for the process and relationship that are designed to ensure that the work is safely structured and proceeds in a constructive manner. Contracts can be written or verbal and should be regarded as consisting of a process as well as having content, in that they can be added to and renegotiated as the supervision work develops. Examples of supervision contracts are provided by Page and Wosket (2001) and Scaife (2008). The supervision contract will encompass a range of factors dependent on the nature and context of the supervision and whether it is with a trainee or an experienced therapist. Common to all supervision contracts are likely to be discussion and agreement on the following elements:

- *Time place, duration and frequency* of supervision meetings and arrangements for between-session contact, emergency supervision and cancellations.
- *Fees*: amount, when and how fees are to be paid and whether payment is required for sessions that are cancelled.
- *Boundaries*: in which the differences and similarities between supervision, training, therapy and line management are explored and clarified and boundaries between any (potential or

existing) overlapping roles and relationships are established.

- *Confidentiality*: where common understanding and agreement about the parameters of confidentiality governing the supervision relationship are agreed.
- *Codes of ethics and practice*: agreement on which professional codes of practice will govern the supervision and counselling work. If supervisor and supervisee adhere to different ethical frameworks they will need to familiarize themselves with one another's. Negotiation should take place on how ethical concerns will be managed if they arise.
- *Accountability and responsibility*: lines of accountability and who holds clinical responsibility for the client work need to be made explicit (BACP, 2010). In particular the supervisor should be clear with the supervisee about any responsibility they have to report back to an organization, training institution or line manager and how this will be done. It is good practice for the supervisee to have some input into any evaluation of their work through, for example, the compilation of a joint learning statement or report that includes sections written by both supervisor and supervisee.
- *Expectations and preferences* of both the supervisor and the supervisee need to be discussed. Clarification of responsibilities towards one another and the supervisee's clients should cover considerations of anti-discriminatory practice, for instance through displaying sensitivity to issues of race, disability and sexual orientation as they may arise in relation to clients and supervisees.

USING SUPERVISION EFFECTIVELY

It is important for supervisees to prepare well in order to make good and economical use of the creative learning space that supervision affords. Supervision that is largely taken up with recounting background details and blow-by-blow accounts of therapy sessions can leave little room for immediate and constructive exploration of the supervisee's issues in a way that will enhance the therapeutic work. It can be useful for the supervisee to attempt a focused presentation of their issue, for instance by being clear about what they would like help with, or by starting with a phrase such as: 'My dilemma with my client is … .' (Note that this is different from saying: 'The problem with my client is …', which may only serve to objectify the client and take the focus of thesupervision away from the interaction between client and therapist.)

PRESENTING ISSUES FOR SUPERVISION

The issues that supervisees bring to supervision can be wide ranging and extend well beyond an exploration of the content and process of counselling sessions. However, it is important that issues raised are in some way related to the client work to preserve the integrity of the supervision task and process and prevent it lapsing into something else, such as teaching or counselling. Some examples of issues which supervisees might present for supervision are: a boundary problem; a difficulty with a beginning or an ending; a sense of stuckness; a power issue; strong feelings, for instance of frustration, dread, shame, hostility or sexual attraction towards clients; a concern about working in a culturally sensitive manner; an organizational issue; feelings of stress or anxiety; a loss of motivation or commitment; a personal issue, such as pregnancy, illness or a bereavement that is impacting on the work with clients; a concern about client dependency; or, indeed, a sense of achievement or success.

Supervision issues can be presented in a number of ways, including the bringing of audio or video tapes or DVDs, case notes or transcripts of sessions. The bringing of recorded material from client sessions to supervision is especially useful in the supervision of trainees as this provides immediate and concrete examples of work that is actually taking place with clients and can enable the supervisor to give specific feedback based on behavioural observations. It is, of course, crucial that recordings of client work are presented only with the informed consent of clients. Gaining written consent is best practice (a sample consent form can be found in Page and Wosket, 2001). Where recordings are used it is important for the supervisee to select a significant portion of a session to present to their supervisor, for example where they feel they made an excellent or a very poor intervention; where the session stalled or became confusing; or where there seemed to be a sudden unexplained surge or drop in energy. Supervisor and supervisee can then explore what might have been occurring within the counselling process and relationship and consider together possible alternative interventions or responses to the client.

Creative and intuitive approaches to the presentation of client work can also be introduced, such as the use of imagery and metaphor; creative drawing; or sculpting with coins, stones or shells. Within group supervision, dramatic and active forms of supervision, such as inviting group members to represent and speak as people or parts of the client's world, can be utilized in order to make use of the dynamics of the group to throw light on the relationship between therapist and client.

WORKING WITHIN THE SUPERVISION SPACE

Whatever methods of presentation are employed, their purpose is to lead the supervisor and supervisee into a collaborative exploration of issues within the supervision space. Within this space, supervisor and therapist work together to explore possibilities, issues and dilemmas arising from the supervisee's work with clients. The focus of the work will shift according to which aspects of the supervisee's issue are most pressing. Where the focus is squarely on a particular therapy session it can be helpful for supervisor and supervisee to differentiate between:

- *Focus on the content of the session.* How is the client seeing their problem; how does the counsellor see it; are their views similar or different? What patterns and themes are emerging and what are the underlying issues, if any? What else might usefully be explored?
- *Focus on the process.* What therapeutic strategies are being used and why? How is the client responding? Would it be helpful to consider other perspectives and ways of working? How is the overall process of the work being managed and paced? Are any adjustments needed?
- *Focus on the relationship.* What is the relationship like between client and therapist? How sound is the working alliance? What impact is the therapist having on the client and the client on the therapist? What needs attention in the relationship? What might be going on in the relationship that isn't being talked about? Is anything happening in the supervisory relationship that may parallel or reveal something that is happening in the therapist–client relationship? Can any of this be named and discussed with the client?

Within the supervision space the supervisee is enabled to find their own best way of working with clients with the support and guidance of the supervisor. If effective work is taking place the therapist will feel both challenged and affirmed by the supervisor as they are helped to reflect on their work in ways that lead to the development of fresh insight and awareness. Information and suggestions about how to work more effectively with clients may be given by the supervisor if they would be welcomed by the supervisee. Trainee and novice therapists are likely to seek more guidance and advice from their supervisors than are experienced practitioners. The supervisor's role is to provide sufficient guidance for the therapist to feel securely 'held' and increasingly competent in their work,

but without disenfranchising the supervisee by taking over and standing in as a surrogate counsellor of his or her clients.

CULTURALLY SENSITIVE SUPERVISION

Responding to the many aspects of difference and diversity that arise in supervision requires a readiness on the part of the supervisor and supervisee to acquire a broad range of culture-specific knowledge, competence and sensitivity (Chang and Flowers, 2010; Lago and Smith, 2010). Ancis and Ladany (2010) have usefully identified five domains of competency within multicultural supervision that supervisors and supervisees might use to identify their strengths and areas for development as they work towards more culturally sensitive practice. Briefly, these domains include the following competencies:

1 *Personal development* (for both supervisor and supervisee). This would include exploring and challenging attitudes and biases and increasing knowledge of diverse populations and alternative approaches to helping other than those based in North American and Northern European contexts.
2 *Conceptualization.* This includes supervisors enabling their supervisees to understand the impact of racism, oppression and discrimination on clients' lives and their presenting issues and helping them to avoid pathologizing clients on the basis of cultural differences.
3 *Skills/interventions.* This involves supervisors encouraging supervisees to offer flexible interventions that do not rely solely on strategies that take the pursuit and accomplishment of individual goals as the norm and, in so doing, take proper account of group and community action and responsibility.
4 *Process.* Attending to process involves addressing power dynamics within supervision and therapy relationships. Supervisor modelling here should show the willingness to adopt a collaborative way of working with supervisees to establish jointly agreed goals, ways of working and feedback mechanisms. Supervisees are then encouraged, through such modelling, to offer respect for diversity and equality in working with their clients.
5 *Outcome/evaluation.* This involves supervisors taking responsibility for engaging in ongoing collaborative evaluation of their own and their supervisees' strengths and weaknesses in transcultural practice. Supervisors who are competent in this area recognize their duty as

gatekeepers to the professions of counselling and psychotherapy and are willing to act to ensure that their supervisees are working in culturally accountable ways and to take steps to address evident deficiencies in transcultural competency when these are apparent in their supervisees (or in themselves).

In assisting themselves and their supervisees to develop as culturally sensitive practitioners it has been suggested (Campbell, 2000) that the supervisor should attend to two crucial questions. The first of these is to ask how transcultural differences might be affecting the supervisory relationship and how the supervisor should respond to these differences. The second is to ask how transcultural issues may be affecting the client work and what response may be needed here.

In relation to the first question, supervisors have a responsibility to understand how the supervisory relationship will be mediated by cultural differences. This becomes particularly important where the supervisor has a role in evaluating the supervisee's competence. As Campbell observes, 'variables such as assertiveness, expression of feelings, sense of time, respect, and ability to function independently all have a cultural component' (2000: 175). Awareness of cultural norms should closely inform the supervisor's understanding of their supervisee and he or she should be especially careful about fixing supervisees with labels such as resistant, dependent, lacking in confidence, or reluctant to work with feelings, when these may be more indicative of cultural differences between the supervisory couple than incompetency by the supervisee.

In relation to the second question, supervisors have a duty to challenge, through supportive exploration and confrontation, supervisees' (and indeed their own) unexamined attitudes and beliefs towards clients who do not share their own cultural identifications and life experience. They need to be constantly alert to inviting supervisees to consider the impact that their own cultural identifications have on their understanding of clients' problems and the therapeutic strategies they choose to employ.

ETHICAL ISSUES IN SUPERVISION

It is good practice for supervisors to allow their supervisees to determine what they wish to explore in supervision. Counsellors should be encouraged to bring their flaws, errors, omissions and misjudgements to supervision safe in the knowledge that their vulnerability and fallibility will be accepted

and respected (Wosket, 2009). Yet at the same time the role of supervisor brings with it certain ethical responsibilities involved in monitoring the work of supervisees to ensure that the welfare of clients is safeguarded. On occasion the supervisor may have to step in and clearly indicate to the counsellor that an ethical issue needs attention. The task for both supervisor and supervisee will be more easily accomplished here if the ground has been prepared in advance, preferably at the contracting stage.

A useful question for the supervisor to ask when contracting with a supervisee is: 'If I have concerns about your practice with clients, how would you like me to address these with you?' An open invitation such as this clearly lets the supervisee know that their supervisor is comfortable with the quality assurance aspects of supervision and also allows them to have some say in how their work will be monitored. As part of the discussion the supervisor should at some point clearly declare what action they may take in the event that the counsellor appears to be engaged in practice that constitutes a breach of ethics and may lead to clients being harmed.

Where the supervisor has ethical or professional concerns about a therapist's practice this should first be raised with the supervisee, preferably invoking relevant ethical frameworks and principles so that the supervisee is clear about the rationale for the supervisor's concerns and interventions. In the unlikely event that discussion fails to resolve the issue, possible courses of action open to the supervisor are: to inform the organization and/or training institution to which the supervisee is accountable; to invoke the complaints procedure of the supervisee's professional association; and to refuse to continue to supervise the therapist. Unilateral courses of action should normally only be taken after the supervisor has consulted with their own supervisor or consultant and with the supervisee's knowledge. In all cases the clear mandate that the supervisor holds to ensure that clients are not harmed needs to be balanced against the supervisee's right to work as an autonomous practitioner.

RECENT DEVELOPMENTS AND PERSPECTIVES

Whilst the importance of supervision for therapists in training remains largely undisputed, debates about the desirability and necessity of mandatory, career-long supervision for qualified practitioners continue to be aired in the professional literature (Bond, 2010; Feltham, 1999; Lawton and Feltham, 2000). Some of the arguments voiced against career-long supervision include:

- There is a perceived lack of research evidence to show that supervision makes therapists more effective in their work with clients.
- To other professions, the requirement for obligatory, career-long supervision arguably gives out the message that counselling is a profession that needs constant surveillance and that therapists cannot be trusted to work independently.
- The requirement for mandatory supervision infantilizes the more senior and experienced members of the counselling profession.
- Practitioners may find supervision more effective if they seek it voluntarily and only when they feel the need, rather than being obliged to have a set amount at regular intervals, where the danger then exists that the activity will degenerate into empty ritual.
- Supervision is supposed to safeguard the welfare of clients, yet it relies largely on second-hand reporting of issues by counsellors. It is therefore possible that unscrupulous and unethical practitioners may simply censor what they bring to supervision and use supervision as a smokescreen to cover up bad practice.

The credibility of supervisors and the professional bodies to whom they are accountable rests, to a large degree, on their openness to critical inquiry by those within and outside their ranks. The criticisms raised here are not to be dismissed lightly and are ones which the professions of counselling, psychotherapy and supervision must continue to engage with through ongoing debate and research. One forum in which such issues have been and continue to be vigorously debated is the annual conference of the British Association for Supervision Practice and Research (BASPR). For more than a decade the annual BASPR conferences have provided a stimulating mix of keynote addresses and interactive workshops on a variety of key aspects of supervision theory and practice, including: power, authority, competence and accountability in supervision; women, femininity, intimacy and supervision; men, masculinity and supervision; and ethics and the law.

A notable contribution to the professional literature that has attempted to address concerns regarding the perceived lack of supervision research in the British context is Wheeler's systematic scoping search entitled *Research on Supervision of Counsellors and Psychotherapists* (2003). This search revealed that while most of the published research in this area at that time stemmed from America, significant studies were beginning to emerge from the United Kingdom. More recently Wheeler and Richards (2007) have conducted a systematic review of research studies which have considered what impact clinical supervision has on

counsellors/therapists, their clients and their practice. This review found some evidence that supervision impacted positively on supervisees in the following areas: self-awareness, skill development, beliefs about self-efficacy, changes and development in theoretical orientation, and their experience of support. They concluded that supervision therefore has an indirect impact on client outcomes.

A current major initiative in the field of supervision in the UK has seen the development of a comprehensive competence framework for the supervision of psychological therapies. The framework has been developed by the CORE unit in the Clinical Psychology Department of University College London (Roth and Pilling, 2010). Together with covering a wide range of generic supervision competencies, the framework initially identified the specific competences needed to supervise staff delivering high- and low-intensity CBT interventions as part of the Improving Access to Psychological Therapies (IAPT) programmes. As work on the framework has developed, further approach-specific competencies have been added for the psychoanalytical and psychodynamic, the humanistic, person-centred and experiential, and the systemic domains of supervision.

Other recent developments within the supervision field have seen creative and innovative approaches gaining greater currency. This is reflected in the literature, where topics such as the use of expressive arts, innovative technology, religion and spirituality, mindfulness, decentring (i.e. understanding multiple perspectives) and developing emotional intelligence in supervision are covered in recent publications (Culbreth and Brown, 2010; Scaife, 2010; Shohet, 2008).

It may be that a number of the questions and criticisms of supervision noted above have more to say about incompetent and ineffective supervisors than about deficiencies in the practice and function of supervision *per se*. The more supervisors take measures to effectively enhance relationships with their supervisees, and the more they attend to aspects of difference and diversity in their work and adopt flexible approaches that take account of their supervisees' differing needs and expectations as they gain experience, the more likely it is that supervision will act as a creative catalyst for supervisees' learning and development (Ladany et al., 2006). Herein, perhaps, lies the best hope that supervision has of occupying a continuing and valid place in the ongoing development of counsellors and psychotherapists as they are engaged in moving towards greater personal and professional authenticity as resourceful, culturally accountable, autonomous practitioners.

REFERENCES

Ancis, J.R. and Ladany, N. (2010) A multicultural framework for counselor supervision. In N. Ladany and L. Bradley (eds), *Counselor Supervision* (4th edn). New York: Routledge.

BACP (2008a) *What Is Supervision?* Information sheet S2. Lutterworth: British Association for Counselling and Psychotherapy.

BACP (2008b) *How Much Supervision Should You Have?* Information sheet S1. Lutterworth: British Association for Counselling and Psychotherapy.

BACP (2010) *Ethical Framework for Good Practice in Counselling and Psychotherapy*. Lutterworth: British Association for Counselling and Psychotherapy.

Bond, T. (2010) *Standards and Ethics for Counselling in Action* (3rd edn). London: Sage.

Campbell, J.M. (2000) *Becoming an Effective Supervisor: A Workbook for Counselors and Psychotherapists*. Philadelphia: Accelerated Development.

Chang, C.Y. and Flowers, L.R. (2010) Multicultural supervision competence. In J. Culbreath and L. Brown (eds), *State of the Art in Clinical Supervision*. New York: Routledge.

Culbreth, J.R. and Brown, L.L. (eds) (2010) *State of the Art in Clinical Supervision*. New York: Routledge.

Feltham, C. (ed.) (1999) *Controversies in Psychotherapy and Counselling*. London: Sage.

Gray, L.A., Ladany, N., Walker, J.A. and Ancis, J.R. (2001) Psychotherapy trainees' experience of counterproductive events in supervision. *Journal of Counseling Psychology*, 48 (4): 371–83.

Ladany, N., Walker, J.A. and Melincoff, D.S. (2001) Supervisory style: its relation to the supervisory working alliance and supervisor self-disclosure. *Counselor Education and Supervision*, 40: 263–75.

Ladany, N., Friedlander, M.L. and Nelson, M.L. (2006) *Critical Events in Psychotherapy Supervision: An Interpersonal Approach*. Washington, DC: APA.

Lago, C. and Smith, B. (eds) (2010) *Anti-Discriminatory Practice in Counselling and Psychotherapy* (2nd edn). London: Sage.

Lawton, B. and Feltham, C. (eds) (2000) *Taking Supervision Forward: Enquiries and Trends in Counselling and Psychotherapy*. London: Sage.

Mehr, K.E., Ladany, N. and Caskie, G.I. (2010) Trainee nondisclosure in supervision: what are they not telling you? *Counselling and Psychotherapy Research*, 10 (2): 103–13.

Nelson, M.L. and Friedlander, M.L. (2001) A close look at conflictual supervisory relationships: the trainee's perspective. *Journal of Counseling Psychology*, 48 (4): 384–95.

Nelson, M.L., Barnes, K.L., Evans, A.L. and Triggiano, P.J. (2008) Working with conflict in clinical supervision: wise supervisors' perspectives. *Journal of Counseling Psychology*, 55 (2): 172–84.

Page, S. and Wosket, V. (2001) *Supervising the Counsellor* (2nd edn). London: Brunner-Routledge.

Roth, A.D. and Pilling, S. (2010) *A Competence Framework for the Supervision of Psychological Therapies*. www.ucl.ac.uk/clinical-psychology/CORE/supervision_framework.htm, accessed 16 February 2011.

Scaife, J. (2008) *Supervision in Clinical Practice: A Practitioner's Guide*. London: Routledge.

Scaife, J. (2010) *Supervising the Reflective Practitioner: An Essential Guide to Theory and Practice*. London: Routledge.

Shohet, R. (ed.) (2008) *Passionate Supervision*. London: Jessica Kingsley.

Weaks, D. (2002) Unlocking the secrets of 'good supervision': a phenomenological exploration of experienced counsellors' perceptions of good supervision. *Counselling and Psychotherapy Research*, 2 (1): 33–9.

Wheeler, S. (2003) *Research on Supervision of Counsellors and Psychotherapists: A Systematic Scoping Search*. Rugby: British Association for Counselling and Psychotherapy.

Wheeler, S. and Richards, K. (2007) The impact of clinical supervision on counsellors and therapists, their practice and their clients: a systematic review of the literature. *Counselling and Psychotherapy Research*, 7 (1): 54–65.

Wosket, V. (2009) Relational ethics in supervision. In L. Gabriel and R. Casemore (eds), *Relational Ethics in Practice: Narratives from Counselling and Psychotherapy*. London: Brunner-Routledge.

Private Practice, Insurance and Advertising

GABRIELLE SYME

Psychoanalysis and psychotherapy are considerably older professions than counselling. Freud first used the word 'psychoanalysis' to describe his way of working in 1896. From the very beginning he and his successors worked only in private practice. Many people hoped that the advent of the NHS in Britain in 1948 would make both psychoanalysis and psychotherapy readily available to the general public but for a number of reasons this did not occur. Even now the provision of psychoanalysis and psychotherapy within the NHS is minimal compared with clinical psychology.

In contrast to psychoanalysis and psychotherapy, counselling started in the voluntary sector and was therefore free at the point of delivery. The first counselling was offered by volunteer lay counsellors with the National Marriage Guidance Council in the late 1940s. Shortly afterwards the first courses in counselling were set up in universities to offer teachers in-service training in counselling. Again counselling was to be offered free. In my private enquiries I found a counsellor who set up in private practice in 1960; possibly he was the first person to do so in the UK. From then on there was a slow but steady growth in private practitioners, with 127 entries in BAC's first referral directory published in 1979. From 1987 onwards there has been an accelerated growth in private practitioners. A survey by BACP in 2001 suggests that 67 per cent of its members (about 14,600 people) do some paid private practice (BACP, 2002). However, currently (2010) the number of members of BACP stating that they are in private practice when they complete the annual renewal of membership is only

2893. I am surprised that there is such discrepancy between these two figures. At least one explanation for this is that not everyone completes this section of the renewal form. In addition, some people may only state they are in private practice if this is a full-time occupation. The reduced number might also reflect the current economic situation and the retirement of some of the older members of BACP. Obviously the discrepancy between these two figures probably makes neither reliable, though I think the 2001 figure may better reflect the true situation. In both cases the actual number will be considerably larger since many private practitioners will not be members of BACP.

In many respects private practice is more difficult than working in a voluntary agency or for an organization such as a school or university. The main reason for this is the lack of both institutional and peer support. Therapists in private practice have to organize their own support and supervision, manage their own caseloads, organize their own timetables, collect their own fees and pay their bills, keep accounts, and so on. Similarly, if they are ill they have to ring their clients to cancel appointments. All these difficulties have led the UK Register of Counsellors/Psychotherapists (UKRCP) to demand higher qualifications and more experience of people registered as independent practitioners. Unfortunately not everyone working in private practice recognizes the need for this rigour.

Research is another way of checking that one's practice is up to standard in terms of quality, effectiveness and efficacy. Therapists are being encouraged, whatever their area of practice, to undertake research. At a minimal level it is important to know whether clients were satisfied with the service given to them. CORE (Clinical Outcomes in Routine Evaluation) offers the free download of a number of different tools which enable therapists to monitor their work. They can then submit their data for further analysis and comparison. These data have also enabled CORE to produce standardized data for comparisons to be made. There are also a number of online systems available to help develop a survey. One example is Survey Monkey. Apart from monitoring one's work it is easy to undertake small pieces of research, John McLeod has produced a number of excellent books to support counselling research (see Chapter 4.10 in this volume). Some issues that follow, such as insurance and advertising, are common to all counselling and psychotherapy regardless of context, but with specific detail for the private practitioner, whereas book-keeping, accounts and invoicing are more commonly issues solely for the private practitioner. Evidence of the importance of insurance cover and accurate advertising for all therapists can be seen from their mention in the *Ethical Framework for Good Practice in Counselling and Psychotherapy* published by BACP (2009), in the *Code of Ethics and Conduct* published by BPS (2009), in *Ethical Principles and Code of Professional Conduct* published by UKCP (2009) and in the *Code of Ethics* published by the BPC (2011). In addition, evidence of insurance cover is one of the essential requirements demanded by UKRCP of anyone registering or reregistering as an independent counsellor.

INSURANCE

Insurance is addressed in BACP's *Ethical Framework*. Under a heading of 'If things go wrong with own clients', the advice is as follows: 'Practitioners are strongly encouraged to ensure that their work is adequately covered by insurance for professional indemnity and liability' (2009: clause 36). Registration with UKRCP is dependent on accreditation with one of four associations – BACP, Counselling and Psychotherapy in Scotland (COSCA), Federation of Drug and Alcohol Professionals (FDAP) or UK Association for Humanistic Psychology Practitioners (UKAHPP) – all of which insist on insurance cover. BPS also requires its members to have professional indemnity insurance and publishes a leaflet to assist its members entitled 'Professional Liability Insurance' (2009). UKCP and the British Psychoanalytic Council (BPC) insist that their members are 'adequately covered by appropriate indemnity insurance' (UKCP, 2009: 12). This cover is necessary for the safety and protection of both the client and the counsellor.

Even when all reasonable steps are taken to prevent physical injury by either removing obvious sources of danger, such as wobbly chairs or sharp edges, or drawing attention to hazards such as uneven steps, accidents can still happen. Should an accident happen, the client has the right to seek compensation and to receive adequate payment for any injury. Indeed Bond states that 'there is a strong ethical case for ensuring that the client can be as adequately compensated as possible' (2009: 78). It is therefore prudent to have adequate insurance cover at a sufficient level to cover the worst possible accident with the highest likely level of damages. In fact the accidents that would happen in a therapist's premises are unlikely to draw huge compensation claims and so the premiums are relatively low.

If a therapist works from home, the ordinary household insurance will not cover injury while the counsellor is using their home for business unless this has been specifically disclosed and covered. Failure to disclose the business use may invalidate the whole policy. It is essential that this is checked out with a competent insurance broker, who will also recommend the necessary level of public liability cover. Therapists renting rooms should check with the lessors whether they hold public liability insurance. If not, the therapist is responsible for arranging this cover.

Ensuring that a client does not suffer psychological harm is considerably more burdensome than preventing physical harm. If it is proven that one has caused psychological harm through error, malpractice or omission, then the claims are frequently substantial, as are the legal costs. In addition, records show that false charges have been made by malicious clients and simply defending oneself can cost a considerable amount in legal fees. It is therefore essential to have professional indemnity insurance. However, it is important that practitioners decide for themselves, on the basis of evidence, the likely risk of being sued and therefore the appropriate cover. It should be remembered that insurance companies make money from insurance cover. The Psychologists Protection Society (PPS, 2009) gives some advice on how to assess the risk of being sued and therefore the relevant level of indemnity. The actuarial evidence is that the risk of being sued is small and therefore PPS's economy scheme (Standard Bronze Membership), which is a mutual scheme, offers £100,000 indemnity and £5 million public liability cover. This is probably adequate at the present time (2010) for a careful practitioner who minimizes the risks of being sued by following good standards of practice. However, if a higher level of insurance would reduce worry or one's employer insists on it, then £1 million cover is probably adequate. If the work is in an area of higher risk, such as reporting to courts, providing sexual or marital therapy or reporting on individuals to companies, then at least £2.5 million or even more cover may be necessary. A number of employee assistance programmes insist on £1 million. Some of these providers may be influenced by the UK having become a considerably more litigious country in recent years and by their parent company being in the USA. Another trend in the UK is that more practitioners are being investigated and disciplined by their professional associations. This can cost a considerable amount in legal expenses and therefore additional legal expenses cover for such an eventuality is also available from some insurers.

It is common for policies to include libel and slander and product insurance, though the interpretation of this, as far as counselling is concerned, is currently unclear.

A private practitioner has to consider loss of income owing to sickness or even inability to earn because of total and permanent disability following a serious illness or injury. Insurance is available to cover such eventualities but the premiums are vastly more if cover for sudden illness is wanted than if the cover is only to commence after three or even six months of illness. Cover for permanent illness or chronic disability which prevents any earnings is less expensive than insurance against sudden illness. As with all insurance issues it is essential to consult with an insurance broker, who will possibly need to have specific experience of this market.

ADVERTISING

It is always difficult, particularly when starting out in private practice, to know whether to advertise and if so where and how. In addition, the profession has regulations to prevent the public being misled. The BACP's *Ethical Framework* states, first, that 'all information about services should be honest, accurate, avoid unjustifiable claims, and be consistent with maintaining the good standing of the profession', and, second, that 'particular care should be taken over the integrity of presenting qualifications, accreditation and professional standing' (2009: clauses 52, 53). In the case of BPS, their response to the frequent requests for guidance on advertising from members and complaints from the general public was the publication of *Independent Practice*

as a Psychologist by the Professional Affairs Board (BPS, 2010). These directives are very similar to those of BACP and of UKCP, but there is considerably more detail.

Advertising can be very important when first starting out. Once one is established, most referrals come by word of mouth from satisfied clients and their networks of friends and from colleagues. Some people find it useful to place an entry in the *Yellow Pages*, although others have not found this so because few people coming by that route kept their initial appointment. Obviously advertisements can be placed in local newspapers and on notice boards in doctors' surgeries, post offices and shops. Perhaps the most effective place is an entry in a popular directory. In some cities directories of alternative therapists are published. These lists will include the names of practitioners offering a wide range of therapies, such as acupuncturists, reflexologists and aromatherapists, and including counselling and psychotherapy. In most of these directories there are no standards to be met, simply payment of a registration fee. A directory which does set standards for entry and is an effective source of referrals is the *Counselling and Psychotherapy Resources Directory*, published annually by BACP. To have one's name included, an applicant must be one or more of the following:

1. a BACP accredited counsellor/psychotherapist
2. a UKCP registered independent counsellor or psychotherapist
3. an individual member of BACP who has completed their core training as a counsellor
4. a member of the UKCP National Register of Psychotherapists
5. a member of the BPC
6. a chartered counselling psychologist or chartered psychologist with counselling training
7. a COSCA accredited counsellor
8. an Irish Association for Counselling and Psychotherapy (IACP) accredited counsellor
9. a UKAHPP accredited counsellor
10. an FDAP accredited counsellor.

The applicant's status with the relevant organization(s) is checked. This procedure offers some safety to clients in that all entrants belong to associations with codes of ethics and complaints procedures, and for the counsellor some security in being on a list with others, all of whom have been vetted and reached an agreed standard. There is an additional safeguard for clients if the counsellor is from category 3, because these people have to confirm that their work is supervised, which is a form of quality assurance. Therapists in all the other categories have to be supervised as a prerequisite of accreditation. Similar directories or registers are published by UKCP, BPS and BPC and can be found on their respective websites.

In some areas it is becoming much harder to set up in private practice. This may be because in recent years there has been a huge output of trained therapists, though the standard of courses available is very variable. Some clinical supervisors will pass a supervisee's name on to people seeking therapy if they themselves have no vacancies, but it should not be presumed that this will be the case. It is becoming more common for new counsellors and psychotherapists to inform colleagues in their locality that they have just started working and have vacancies. Many therapists are reluctant to recommend someone or even mention their name when the person and their work are unknown to them. It may be preferable to mention that there are directories to which they can refer rather than name a stranger, albeit one who is qualified as a counsellor or psychotherapist. It is clear, then, that the therapist has no responsibility for the recommendation, particularly if the recommended practitioner's work is subsequently found to be incompetent or unethical. It also has to be recognized that therapists in the private sector are in competition with each other, which can lead to rivalry. It would be naïve to think otherwise.

BOOK-KEEPING, ACCOUNTS, INVOICING

It is a legal requirement of all UK residents to pay tax on their earnings above a set threshold, and therefore an important part of professional accountability and credibility is to keep financial records so that the tax can be assessed. Laws change from time to time so it is essential to obtain or view on the website the most up-to-date versions of leaflets produced by the Inland Revenue. The current ones are 'Thinking of Working for Yourself?' and 'Working for Yourself – The Guide'. The Inland Revenue also produces free of charge to anyone starting up in business a comprehensive guide called 'Giving Your Business the Best Start with Tax'.

The self-employed are responsible for paying their own tax and, even if an accountant is employed, they remain responsible for the accuracy of the accounts. To be able to guarantee accuracy it is essential that all business transactions are separated from personal finances and are recorded, backed up by evidence of payment by clients (see later), invoices and receipts, bank statements and cheque stubs. In addition, it is important to note down immediately all postage and telephone costs and the mileage of all journeys associated with the business (the mileage driven to and from supervision is a legitimate charge). It is important to be very disciplined about this as the Inland Revenue will only allow for a small number of unsubstantiated items. Should there be no receipt for small items of cash expenditure – and this should be the exception – then make a note of what this was for, the date and the amount spent as soon as possible. I would recommend buying an account book or a computer accounts package from a commercial supplier for the book-keeping so that business income and expenses are recorded clearly and effectively. From this either you or an accountant can derive the necessary information for the annual return to the Inland Revenue. The amount of detail needed depends on the business turnover before expenses. Currently (2010), if your turnover is below £68,000 you can complete the section of the 'Full Return' (SA100) titled 'Self-employment (Short)'. With a turnover above this figure the 'Self-employment (Full)' has to be completed. There is a 'Short Return' (SA200) for those self-employed with a turnover of less than £68,000 but you cannot self-select to do this, nor is it available online, nor can it be ordered online. HMRC will send it to you based on information from the previous year's return.

The Inland Revenue do not insist that clients are given invoices, although some clients like to receive them. Nonetheless it is essential to keep a record of exactly what a client has paid. In doing so, it is important to have a system so that the client's anonymity is maintained. One way of doing this is to assign each client a unique code number, which is always stored separately from their name and address. This code number is all that is seen in the records.

The self-employed are also responsible for paying their own National Insurance contributions. Information on this can be found in 'Thinking of Working for Yourself?' and 'Giving Your Business the Best Start with Tax' (mentioned earlier) and in 'Self-employed Tax and National Insurance', all published by the Inland Revenue and on their website.

There are a very small number of self-employed therapists with sales above £70,000. They have to register for VAT.

When one is winding up a practice, the local tax office must be informed of the date on which business will cease or has ended and whether the termination is due to cessation of work or changed employment. As soon after the ending as possible, accounts must be submitted for the period of work from the last date on which prepared accounts were submitted to the Inland Revenue.

More details on all aspects of insurance, advertising, accounting and tax issues can be found in books by Syme (1994), McMahon et al. (2005), Thistle (1998) and Hemmings and Field (2007).

REFERENCES

BACP (2002) Membership survey. Released as insert in *Counselling and Psychotherapy Journal*, 14.

BACP (2009) *Ethical Framework for Good Practice in Counselling and Psychotherapy*. Rugby: British Association for Counselling and Psychotherapy.

Bond, T. (2009) *Standards and Ethics for Counselling in Action* (3rd edn). London: Sage.

BPC (2011) *Code of Ethics*. London: The British Psychoanalytic Council.

BPS (2009) *Code of Ethics and Conduct*. Leicester: The British Psychological Society.

BPS (2010) *Independent Practice as a Psychologist*. Leicester: British Psychological Society.

Hemmings, A. and Field, R. (eds) (2007) *Counselling and Psychotherapy in Contemporary Private Practice*. London: Routledge.

McMahon, G., Palmer, S. and Wilding, C. (2005) *The Essential Skills for Setting Up a Counselling and Psychotherapy Practice*. London: Routledge.

PPS (2009) *Levels of Indemnity: Guide to Thought*. Alloa: Psychologists Protection Society.

Syme, G. (1994) *Counselling in Independent Practice*. Buckingham: Open University Press.

Thistle, R. (1998) *Counselling and Psychotherapy in Private Practice*. London: Sage.

UKCP (2009) *Ethical Principles and Code of Professional Conduct*. London: United Kingdom Council for Psychotherapy.

Ethical Codes and Guidance

TIM BOND

No one reads codes of ethics for their entertainment value or their aesthetic qualities. Codes and guidelines about professional ethics are functional documents designed to fulfil many purposes. First and foremost they are written to offer guidance about the parameters of ethical behaviours that are considered acceptable conduct by the membership of a specific professional body. As someone who has been involved in the production of codes for counsellors and who has taken a wider interest in the codes of the caring professions, I have been frequently consulted about how to resolve ethical challenges within the terms of specific codes or to interpret the potential meanings of a specific ethical statement. This chapter builds on this experience by setting out a series of observations about how to get the best out of codes and guidelines by using them to inform your own capacity for ethical analysis and personal judgement. I have deliberately phrased the preceding sentence to emphasize the primacy of your ownership and control of the ethical decision making. I am also writing in the first and second person to reinforce this point.

The personal responsibility for making professional decisions is frequently understated because of the way codes are written; in particular, their 'voice' tends to be one which seems to encourage compliance rather than the exercise of personal judgement. As an individual person reading a code it is easy to be intimidated by the sense that the code states the collective voice of your professional organization. The language is often explicitly or implicitly laden with 'shoulds' or 'oughts'. Failure to observe these injunctions carries the potential for

being caught up in a professional complaints or disciplinary procedure which adds to the potentially intimidatory effect. As if to reinforce the authoritative tone, codes are usually written as though there is only one view of ethical issues, that is, the view taken by that code. Faced with the semblance of such monolithic authority, it is tempting to say, 'I submit. Just tell me what to do.'

Other factors may compound this sense of dependency on the code. In the midst of an urgent ethical crisis or dilemma, most of us do not feel at our most rational or personally robust. A pressing crisis with a client, conflict with an agency, or an impending court case can make the possibility of an authoritative answer seem very attractive. In any of these circumstances, many counsellors turn to their code as a lifeline to rescue them from the turbulent waters that sometimes surround our work. This is an understandable response. However, these are not the circumstances in which to be considering a code for the first time. The sense of personal crisis not only enhances the potential dependency but may also undermine a capacity for understanding what are in reality quite complex documents. It is said that drowning people will clutch at straws. In my experience, counsellors in acute ethical difficulty will clutch at clauses that seem to offer a degree of protection. These clauses are often taken out of context. It is a strategy that is seldom successful, because codes need to be read as a whole document. Taken out of context, an individual clause can be deceptive and the interpretation favoured by the counsellor or psychotherapist is unlikely to stand up to close scrutiny. If you find yourself clutching at clauses, it is better to recognize this as a sign of personal pressure and to seek supportive facilitation in considering the ethical issue that confronts you. However, it is much better to reduce the risk of finding yourself consulting a code for the first time in a crisis by reviewing the relevant ethical guidelines in advance of any crisis and periodically revisiting them to assess how they relate to your practice. In this way, you will acquire a sense of the totality of the contents and how different provisions are interrelated, as well as some of the strengths and weaknesses of a code for your particular area of work. This considered approach to codes will put you in the best possible position to use them constructively as a support to your practice. You will also be better placed to see through some of the authoritarian tendencies of some codes.

In the next section I will examine the authoritative voice of codes and suggest that understanding the context within which codes are produced makes them less intimidating and maximizes their capacity to be informative. This is followed by a comparison between the codes produced by three major national professional organizations for counsellors and therapists and the regulator of therapeutic psychologists. I will conclude with suggestions for ethical problem solving.

DECODING THE ETHICAL INSTRUCTION

Codes and guidelines should be taken seriously. They usually represent an important version of the collective experience of the organization that produced them. They will also have been subject to scrutiny and debate before gaining the support of a majority at an adoption meeting, usually an annual general meeting. However, they are not definitive statements. All organizations find it necessary to publish supplementary guidance and periodically to revise their codes. Some of these changes are due to changes within the profession and are in response to the challenges of new areas of work.

Other changes are determined by broader trends within society. As a result, codes and guidelines are never comprehensive. The codes currently available from the major national professional organizations all tend to share the same omissions. Ethical issues concerning counsellors or psychotherapists working with young people, within multidisciplinary teams like primary health care, and within organizational settings such as places of education and employee assistance programmes, receive relatively scant attention in comparison to the therapist

working independently with an adult client. These are issues that will doubtless receive fuller attention in the future as experience accumulates. The omission or partial treatment of a particular issue may simply indicate that practice is still evolving and no consensus has emerged about a particular issue.

There have been occasions when the publication of a code has provoked controversy about some of its provisions. Some insight into how codes are constructed will explain how these controversies emerge. The creation of codes is always a combination of ethical analysis and political process working towards creating a statement that will at least achieve majority support at its formal adoption. Within BACP and many other professional organizations, the development of a code is usually informed by a consultative process. This process will inevitably evoke a wide range of views on any issue. Those writing the code have to exercise judgement about any minority views that are incompatible with the majority view. The outcome of that judgement is likely to be that a minority view will be:

- ignored with/without debate and due consideration
- rejected with clearly articulated reasons to elicit further discussion or to encourage negotiation within the consultative process
- accommodated by 'finessing', that is artfully accommodating the minority view by creating a more inclusive and consequently more ambiguous and generalized phraseology
- treated as an exception for which special provision is made
- validated as being of sufficient importance to justify reconsidering the majority position and possibly initiating an educational programme.

As codes are designed to cover people working in a wide range of therapeutic orientations with their respective values, ethos and ethical predispositions and in a wide variety of settings with a variety of established practices and practical constraints, there are always minority issues to be taken into consideration. Depending on their composition, committees may move between actively supporting the ascendancy of a particular section of membership or taking a wider view of being as inclusive as possible of the full range of ethical practice. These are difficult judgements and like all human endeavours are fallible. It is always possible that a specific provision is unduly restrictive and may as a consequence not only be oppressive to an individual or group of counsellors or psychotherapists, but also constrain the future development of psychological therapies. On the other hand, a provision might be over-cautious in seeking to prevent unethical behaviour.

VARIATIONS BETWEEN ETHICAL GUIDELINES

Historically, there have been significant variations between professional bodies representing counsellors, psychotherapists and counselling psychologists. These differences have almost disappeared. There is general consensus around many of the essential behaviours required to be an ethical therapist. The key requirements are:

- having respect for the client, including an emphasis on enhancing the client's self-determination or autonomy and working with client consent
- protecting the client's confidences
- ensuring clarity about contracting and straightforwardness in dealings with clients
- being competent and working within the limits of competence
- being conscientious in the management of dual relationships and avoiding relationships which can damage clients or undermine the therapeutic relationship
- emphasizing the value of research and that it should be undertaken with integrity
- taking responsibility to keep oneself informed about any law applicable to one's work.

However, there are still a few areas of difference between professional bodies. The two most significant divergences concern record-keeping and supervision. I will consider each of these in turn, and in doing so will also attempt to highlight the significance of seemingly quite small variations in words.

For therapists regulated by the Health Professions Council, there is no choice about whether or not to keep records. The *Standards of Conduct, Performance and Ethics* simply states, 'You must keep records' (HPC, 2008: s. 10). Such an uncompromising requirement could be problematic. If clients refuse to have any records kept, will this mean that no therapist registered with the HPC can work with them? The *Code of Ethics and Conduct* for the British Psychological Society is more circumspect by requiring a member to 'Keep appropriate records' (BPS, 2009: s. 1.2.i). 'Appropriate' is capable of covering a wide range of practice shaped around the needs of the client and the professional, but could it include keeping no record at all if that was justified by careful consideration of the circumstances? Probably not, as there is still a positive duty to keep records, however minimally. Members of the United Kingdom Council for Psychotherapy are provided with more room for professional judgement. Their *Ethical Principles and Code of Professional Conduct* requires the psychotherapist to 'keep such records as are necessary to carry out the type of psychotherapy offered' (UKCP, 2009: s. 8.1). Presumably if records are not necessary then there is no obligation to keep them. The *Ethical Framework* of the British Association for Counselling and Psychotherapy provides the therapist with greatest discretion: 'Practitioners are advised to keep appropriate records of their work with clients unless there are good reasons for not doing so' (BACP, 2010: s. 5). A client's refusal to give consent to records being kept would be both an ethical and a legal justification for not doing so. Some counsellors working with clients who live on the fringes of the law (such as sex workers) or who feel vulnerable to persecution (such as refugees from countries in a state of civil war) may be deterred from receiving counselling by the existence of records. Practitioners working with clients who will be deterred from seeking therapy by the keeping of records could justify not doing so. These examples show how subtle changes of words may cover a range of obligations from mandatory to merely advisory.

The requirements concerning supervision are even more varied. The Health Professions Council is solely concerned with the practitioner's accountability for work undertaken on their behalf. They require that, 'You must effectively supervise tasks that you have asked other people to carry out' (HPC, 2008: s. 8). The Division of Counselling Psychology in BPS views supervision very differently. It is not a method of accountability but one of enhancing the quality of therapy being provided. Supervision support is defined as 'a contractually negotiated relationship between practitioners for the purpose of supporting, evaluating and developing professional practice. There is an ethical requirement for every practitioner to have regular supervision support' (BPS, 2005: s. 2.1). The United Kingdom Council for Psychotherapy is silent on the subject because practice over supervision is variable between different sections of its membership. Members of the British Association for Counselling and Psychotherapy are 'required to have regular and on-going formal supervision/ consultative support' (BACP, 2010: s. 7).

When these variations in ethical requirements and guidance are taken into account alongside the earlier discussion about how codes are produced, it becomes possible to identify a number of basic tips on how to consult codes and guidelines from professional organizations (see below). Following these tips should enable you to identify any requirements of your professional organization(s) for your specific therapy context. These requirements form an important component in ethical problem solving but are only part of the picture, albeit an important one.

Tips on Consulting Codes and Guidelines

- Use the most recent version. Out-of-date versions may be seriously misleading.
- Avoid taking sections out of context, by considering the document as a whole.
- Distinguish between statements on obligatory practice and those on recommended practice.
- Interpret supplementary guidance and recommendations by reference to core codes and guidelines.
- Consider the implications for your specific therapy context.

ETHICAL PROBLEM SOLVING

A useful strategy for problem management is breaking the problem down into its component parts. This helps a problem which is already overwhelming, or has that potential, to become more manageable. Effective ethical problem solving follows this approach. A six-step approach is recommended, which I know has proved to be extremely helpful to many practitioners (Bond, 2010: 227–38). Each of the steps builds progressively on the previous step(s) but does not exclude the possibility of creating new insights which might involve some reworking of an earlier step and proceeding again from that point. The steps are as follows.

Step 1: Produce a Brief Description of the Problem or Dilemma

The aim is to produce a clearer statement of the main elements in the problem. It is very difficult to make progress until the problem can be expressed clearly.

Step 2: Consider who Holds Responsibility for Resolving the Problem

Another way of approaching this step is to ask, 'Whose problem is it anyway?' This is particularly significant in therapy where a great deal of responsibility for the outcome of the therapy rests with the client, e.g. whether to confront someone, etc. There are occasions when the responsibility rests with the therapist, for example a client has started talking about someone who is already known to you in another context. Sometimes the problem is a shared responsibility and can only be resolved by discussion between therapist and client: for example, the client has selected you as therapist because of her sense of you as a person from knowing you in another context. The therapeutic orientation might determine whether the responsibility would rest with the therapist (more likely in a psychodynamic orientation) or could be resolved by joint exploration of the implications (more likely in humanistic and cognitive-behavioural approaches).

Step 3: Consider all the Relevant Ethical and Legal Guidance

It is unusual if a significant problem is resolved at this step. For all the reasons given earlier in this chapter, it is probably better to view professional guidance as establishing accepted parameters within which to exercise your ethical judgement. Sometimes you may consider that the specific circumstances of your problem challenge these parameters and that you may have to consider how to proceed against the usual guidance. This would be a major step and should be taken with professional and legal advice. Nonetheless the aim of this step is not to be prescriptive but to inform the ethical and legal decision making. At the end of this step, it ought to be possible to identify an ethical goal.

Step 4: Identify all Possible Courses of Action

It is unusual to find that there is only one possible course of action. Often there is a choice between doing nothing or doing something, which may include saying different things to your client or to someone else, or challenging accepted practice within the profession. Listing all possible courses of action avoids the frequent misconception that because one approach appears to be right, there are no other solutions. Many solutions may be possible from which a selection can be made.

Step 5: Select the Best Course of Action

A good test of your level of conviction that you have found an appropriate solution is to test it against three standards first proposed by Holly A. Stadler, a former chairperson of the American Association for Counseling and Development (now ACA):

- *Universality*

  - Could my chosen course of action be recommended to others?
  - Would I condone my proposed course of action if it was done by someone else?

- *Publicity*

  - Could I explain my chosen course of actions to other counsellors?
  - Would I be willing to have my actions and rationale exposed to scrutiny in a public forum, e.g. at a workshop, in a professional journal, in a newspaper or on radio/TV?

- *Justice*

  - Would I do the same for other clients in a similar situation?
  - Would I do the same if the client was well known or influential?

If you find yourself answering 'no' to any of these questions, you may need to reconsider your chosen outcome. A final step in identifying the best course of action may be checking whether the resources are available to implement what is proposed.

Step 6: Evaluate the Outcome

After you have implemented your course of action, it is useful to evaluate it in order to learn from the experience and to prepare yourself for any similar situations in the future:

- Was the outcome as you hoped?
- Had you considered all relevant factors, with the result that no new factors emerged after you implemented your chosen course of action?
- Would you do the same again in similar circumstances?

CONCLUSION

My aim in writing this chapter is to challenge any expectation that codes of ethics and guidance should be regarded as authoritative commandments to be followed in blind obedience. One of my colleagues on the committee responsible for professional ethics and conduct in BACP adopted a short saying to inform her work: 'Rules are for the obedience of fools and for the guidance of the wise.' This saying is a reminder that any code is a social construction and, as such, has value as a pooling of shared experience and reflection. However, no code can be universal or infallible and therefore any code must be applied with discernment. Surrendering one's personal and professional responsibility to any external authority would have the paradoxical effect of undermining the ethical basis of even the most appropriate action. Sometimes it may be ethically appropriate to inform your professional organization about a limitation or weakness in current guidance, particularly if you find it ethically desirable to override an explicit requirement. The nature of counselling or psychotherapy is such that the ethical integrity of the practitioner is paramount. All the codes of ethics and practice for therapy that are known to me share a common aim in seeking to support the development of ethical awareness and practice. Being ethical is a continual challenge.

REFERENCES

BACP (2010) *Ethical Framework for Good Practice in Counselling and Psychotherapy*. Rugby: British Association for Counselling and Psychotherapy.

Bond, T. (2010) *Standards and Ethics for Counselling in Action* (3rd edn). London: Sage.

BPS (2005) *Professional Practice Guidelines: Division of Counselling Psychology*. Leicester: British Psychological Society.

BPS (2009) *Code of Ethics and Conduct*. Leicester: British Psychological Society.

HPC (2008) *Standards of Conduct, Performance and Ethics*. London: Health Professions Council.

UKCP (2009) *Ethical Principles and Code of Professional Conduct*. London: United Kingdom Council for Psychotherapy.

Responding to Complaints

TIM BOND

Developing satisfactory ways of responding to complaints has been considered fundamental to good practice for several reasons. Pragmatically, there is only one thing more damaging to the reputation of a service than being a cause for complaint. This is allowing a complaint to go unexamined and ignored, as this compounds the sense of grievance and may eventually poison the reputation of the service. Responding to complaints is a clear indication that the service takes its responsibilities seriously. Ethically, responding to complaints is a major way of addressing possible inequalities of power between therapist and client. In some cases, the complaints procedure may be the client's only way of redressing serious abuses of power. However, complaints procedures should not be thought of solely in terms of benefiting the aggrieved client. They have often been presented as an important source of learning for the profession or organization. A good complaints procedure may be viewed as an important aspect of enhancing the quality of the entire service by drawing attention to areas of difficulty.

TYPES OF COMPLAINT

The subject matter of complaints varies in its origins and in its seriousness. Based on her experience of several years of coordinating complaints heard by the BACP and the UKCP, Palmer Barnes (1998) suggests that the causes of justifiable complaint fall into four categories. Illustrative examples from my experience as the Chair of the BACP Professional Conduct Committee have been added:

- *Error or mistake* that is the result of a slip in good practice. This might include missing an appointment due to making an entry on the wrong page of a diary, confusing the identity of two people without serious consequences, or forgetting the details of less significant parts of an oral agreement reached with the client.
- *Poor practice* is a failure to deliver good practice, whether intentional or not. Examples include a therapist working inconsistently within the therapeutic model that he has described to a client as his way of working; a therapist missing the significance of something communicated by the client relating to a therapeutically important issue; or a therapist giving out-of-date information. Poor practice and negligence are frequently indistinguishable.
- *Negligence* arises from lack of proper care or attention in circumstances where someone owes a duty of care, like a therapist to a client or a supervisor to a supervisee. An example would be a therapist, in giving a client homework between sessions, setting behavioural tasks which expose the client to serious harm or prosecution, and where the harm or illegality ought to have been known by the therapist.
- *Malpractice* is intentional misconduct. All malpractice associated with counselling and psychotherapy is serious because it undermines the trust that is so essential. However, contrary to some views, it is arguable that the level of seriousness

varies. Less serious forms of misconduct might include inappropriately blurring boundaries with clients between therapy and social contacts without significant harm to clients, or failing to honour significant but not critically important terms of an agreement made with clients. Gross misconduct includes serious exploitation of clients for the therapist's sexual, financial or other benefits; or serious misrepresentation of experience or qualifications in order to obtain clients or employment as a therapist.

Awareness of the different categories of conduct that might lead to a justifiable complaint is important because they imply different levels of culpability and seriousness, which arguably should be reflected in the kind of response that the complaint evokes. A relatively trivial mistake would not justify a full investigation by an independent investigator and an extensive adjudication leading to serious sanctions. Similarly, consideration of the seriousness of any misconduct might lead to different kinds of outcome, with the less serious first-time acts of misconduct justifying greater leniency than gross misconduct, especially if the gross misconduct has been repeated several times. Sometimes the gravity of the alleged source of grievance is not readily apparent at the outset of any procedure. However, there are times when the seriousness is readily apparent and this could inform decisions by the complainant, the complained against, and the managers of the complaints process.

INITIATING A COMPLAINTS PROCEDURE

There are two main initiators of complaints. Most complaints tend to be started by someone who is feeling aggrieved about the conduct of their service provider. A more recent and growing source of new complaints are members of the same profession who are concerned to protect the standards and conduct of their profession. The increasing emphasis on promoting client safety and wellbeing means that most professional bodies have moved from merely encouraging members of a profession to report serious concerns about the conduct of others in the same profession to making this an explicit ethical requirement. All the major professional organizations in counselling and psychotherapy include this requirement.

Whether or not the complaint is initiated by a client or another professional, it is usual practice to insist that there is an attempt to resolve the complaint informally where this would be appropriate. These informal attempts at resolving complaints are largely invisible to the profession, especially if they are successful. As a consequence, it is impossible to be confident about the level of matters that were of sufficient seriousness that someone considered making a complaint. Known levels of grievance concern those complaints that could not be resolved informally or were considered to be of sufficient seriousness to make informal resolution inappropriate. Other reasons will be considered later in this chapter for suspecting that the numbers of complaints that enter any kind of formal procedure are only a fraction of potentially valid complaints. However, if the complainant decides to initiate a complaint, she will usually have two ways of proceeding.

The main choice will usually be between seeking a remedy from the courts or using some form of professional complaints procedure. Using the county court, especially the small claims court, is an option that deserves serious consideration by fee-paying clients, especially if the grievance concerns breach of a contractual term. The procedures are user-friendly and the legal costs are relatively small with little risk of unforeseen costs. Most other types of claim are likely to fall outside the courts because of the difficulty in bringing claims for negligence against counsellors or the high cost of taking cases to more senior courts (Bond, 2010). In these circumstances, the only realistic alternative is to use a complaints procedure run by the agency providing the counselling or an appropriate professional organization. This will be the organization(s) to which the therapist belongs, as these organizations will only hear complaints against their own members.

Most agencies and organizations will only hear complaints that are made in writing against a named person who is a member of their organization and that specify the nature of the complaint. The British Psychological Society provides examples of potential complaints. These include acting beyond one's competence, breach of confidentiality, exploiting a client's trust, damaging the interests of clients or failing to obtain adequate consent (BPS, 2001). BACP (2010) currently requires that the complaint be presented as a succinct statement of the concern and the events giving rise to this concern.

THE COMPLAINTS PROCEDURE

Most organizations that hear complaints have found that, with experience, they have wanted to refine their procedures. Professional conduct hearings can be a complex and demanding process to manage, and are further complicated by the inevitable stress that is experienced by most of the people involved, but especially the complainant and the complained against. It is possible to discern a common pattern emerging in the most recently revised procedures within the talking therapies. Typically the stages include:

- An initial screening of the complaint, which must have been submitted in writing, in order to ensure that there are sufficient grounds for proceeding. Obviously ill-founded and vexatious complaints may be stopped at this or the next stage.
- An investigatory process in which usually two or more people are given the task of gathering pertinent information and recommending whether the process should move to a formal hearing for adjudication. In some procedures the investigators also have the possibility of facilitating conciliation between the complainant and the person complained against when this is appropriate. Generally conciliation is considered more appropriate to resolving issues that have arisen by error and is inappropriate to malpractice.
- The adjudication process involves hearing both sides of the complaint and usually a panel of adjudicators deciding whether or not to uphold the complaint. The way that this process is conducted varies between organizations. Some adjudication procedures may parallel the criminal law in which both parties have relatively unlimited time in which to present their case and may be legally represented. This is the process adopted by the Health Professions Council and the General Medical Council. Typically the case for upholding the complaint is taken over and presented by the professional body rather than the complainant. An alternative model is to give both the complainant and complained against equal time to present the main elements of their case, which will have already been submitted more fully in writing prior to the hearing. This creates an opportunity for both parties to question each other and for the adjudicators to ask questions. In this system legal representation may not be permitted and the power to call witnesses is restricted to the panel. This procedure is generally less costly in time and money for the people directly involved and therefore may be more accessible to a greater number of complainants. There is the possibility of the professional body taking over a complaint after a complaint has been withdrawn by the complainant, if the matter is considered sufficiently serious. However, the complainant retains the possibility of remaining more actively involved

in the complaints process, if that is desired. In many ways this process parallels the more accessible forms of civil hearings.

- The announcement of a decision and any sanctions that have been imposed typically takes place a few days after the adjudication and is given in writing.
- There is usually a set period within which any appeal against the adjudication must be lodged. Any appeal process must be completed before the next stage.
- Publication of the results of any complaint that has been upheld usually includes the name of the person concerned, the nature of the complaint or malpractice, and the sanctions that have been imposed. The complainant's name is not usually disclosed. Hearings by the Health Professions Council are fully reported on their website whereas other bodies tend to publish summaries of the key features of a case decided against a professional.

Perhaps one of the more disturbing but frequently reported findings of those most directly involved in hearing complaints against therapists is that a significant number could have been resolved at a very early stage. It is a frequent observation that the official complaints procedures would be unnecessary if the counsellor or therapist had simply apologized. This is particularly appropriate when the cause of complaint was due to error rather than malpractice. One of the motivations of complainants in pursuing a complaint is to have their sense of loss or hurt acknowledged when they believe that this is justifiable. Withholding an appropriate apology is probably not only anti-therapeutic, because it invalidates the client's personal experience, but also inflammatory.

BASIC PRINCIPLES OF HEARING COMPLAINTS

Once a complaints procedure is under way there is an ethical and often a legal obligation to ensure a fair investigation and hearing within the rules of natural justice. These consist of (1) the right to a fair hearing and (2) the rule against bias.

The exact implications of these rules are frequently considered in the courts. In general terms, the *right to a fair hearing* requires prior notice, an opportunity to be heard, a fairly conducted hearing, and a decision made supported by the reasons for it. The *rule against bias* has two main elements. The adjudicator undertaking these tasks should be independent and without any direct personal interests in the outcome. Any potential conflicts of interest that might prejudice or merely seem to prejudice the procedure ought to be declared and probably that person should withdraw. Another element requires that someone should not be judged by his accuser. Similarly it would be inappropriate for someone who has been involved in investigating a case to act as adjudicator.

Unless these rules are observed, any decision will lose moral authority. Some hearings may also be subject to judicial review, which means that the courts may overturn them. Hearings by national professional bodies in counselling and psychotherapy are subject to judicial review in the High Court.

TENSIONS BETWEEN ADJUDICATION AND THERAPY

It is not unusual to find that counsellors and psychotherapists are often uneasy about taking on a role that involves judging the behaviour of other therapists. The personal qualities and values that motivate most therapists are usually closely related to a commitment to trying to understand someone's experience, as perceived by that person. This usually involves suspending any attempt at moralizing. Some therapeutic approaches require more of the practitioner than mere abstinence from moralizing. For example, the person-centred counsellor regards non-judgemental positive regard as an essential core condition of the therapeutic relationship. In other words, the client's subjective experience is positively valued independently of any moral considerations. Almost all approaches to therapy require that understanding the client's subjective experience takes priority over making an objective assessment of behaviour against what is considered to be competent or moral.

This means that the ethos and ethic that pertain to being an effective therapist are usually very different from those which pertain to being an effective adjudicator. The role of adjudicator is much less concerned with subjective experience than with determining by objective observation and rational deduction what has occurred and then considering whether the person complained against is culpable. The adjudicator is concerned to match the imposition of any sanctions with the gravity of any malpractice. In effect the adjudicator's role could not be much further removed from that of the therapist, as each requires constructing a relationship which is almost the antithesis of the other. This may lead to therapists who take on the role of adjudicator being either too punitive or too lenient as they step outside their usual way of working. This is one of the reasons why it is highly desirable to include non-therapists in the adjudication panel. There are other reasons why this is desirable, which are considered later.

The case that brought therapeutic and psychological complaints procedures into national controversy concerned the sanctions imposed on a senior member of BPS (Lunt, 1999). Despite being found responsible for repeated inappropriate sexual relationships with clients after having been previously disciplined for similar misconduct, he neither lost his fellowship nor was expelled from membership of the Society. Instead the disciplinary board chose to accept an undertaking that he would stop seeing clients. This case has evoked an intense debate about when it is appropriate to take a constructive and formative view about helping someone back into practice, and when it is more appropriate to view a professional's behaviour as culpable and therefore subject to sanctions including expulsion. It is possible that concerns over this case prompted the professional regulation of psychological services to the public by the Health Professions Council.

I will confine my next observations to general principles rather than any specific case. The difference in attitude to wrongdoing between the courts and professional bodies over sexually inappropriate behaviour could not be more marked. When people are convicted of paedophilia, the latest practice is not simply to punish them by incarceration but also to offer treatment. On discharge they are usually dissuaded or prohibited from resuming unsupervised contact with children in order to maximize the safety of potential victims. When a professional body decides to accept an undertaking that the abusing therapist will seek treatment or will temporarily cease seeing clients until 'cured', that professional body is prioritizing the welfare of its member over the protection of the public by working towards the very situation where temptation is greatest. This may be a plausible response for a first example of malpractice where no significant harm has been caused, but it seems both implausible and irresponsible where there is sound evidence of serial abuse and a formative approach has already been tried and failed. Such responses seem to discredit the claim that the primary function of the way that a profession regulates itself is to protect the public.

There is need of a major study to discover whether professional bodies tend towards leniency in matters of serious malpractice or whether it is exceptional. In either case it would be informative to know the basis for decisions to impose sanctions and, perhaps more importantly, why they are not imposed. There may be many motivations. Seniority and prominence in the field may create an understandable reluctance to discredit a key member because to do so could seem like discrediting the entire profession. Offending therapists often offer explanations about having an alcohol problem and acting under the influence, or being untypically disinhibited by treatment for depression, or having some other reason which suggests diminished responsibility which would respond to treatment. However, some of the characteristics of sexual offenders include plausibility, which deceives others, combined with effective rationalizing, which distances them from the pain that they are causing their victims and increases self-deception. It may be that a combination of some or all these factors in a profession that values empathy creates an irresistible tendency towards mitigation. Anyone who has been involved in any of these cases knows that they are extremely hard to adjudicate. Nonetheless, it is important to the credibility of any profession's claim to be able to regulate itself that it strikes an appropriate balance between protecting the public and the welfare of an individual member. A failure to appreciate the difference between the values and expertise required for adjudication and providing therapy increases the risk that inappropriate decisions will be made by adjudicators of misconduct by therapists.

SANCTIONS

Many adjudications appear to be fairly uncontroversial and to be accepted by the professional members and others as a fair outcome. Many of the less serious examples of malpractice can be appropriately dealt with by an admonition, or a requirement for some retraining or for a period of additional supervision of practice. Temporary suspension from practice or membership can also be used in many professional hearings to mark the seriousness of what has occurred and to provide some limited protection of the public. Expulsion from membership carries different consequences according to whether the procedure forms part of a voluntary or statutory system of professional regulation. In a voluntary system such as that operated by BACP there is no way of stopping someone from continuing to practise as a counsellor after being expelled from membership. For as long as counselling and therapy are unregulated, anyone may set up as a counsellor even if they have just been discharged from prison for serious fraud or assault. Statutory regulation provides some protection by restricting the people who can make use of a particular professional title, but it is important not to exaggerate the level of protection that is offered. Even after expulsion it is possible to continue to practise in closely related roles or in organizations that are unconcerned about conforming to a system of regulation. This means that in sectors like therapy and counselling where many people are self-employed, statutory regulation will have only limited impact.

People who have had complaints upheld against them often say that their concern about the sanction that had been imposed was eclipsed by their feelings when the outcome of the hearing was published in the appropriate professional journal. The primary justification for publishing the results of adjudications is educative, in order to alert the profession to potential malpractice, as well as to identify the individual concerned. The person concerned frequently experiences a sense of loss of face and shame that is sometimes considerably greater than the seriousness of the malpractice or error appears to justify. It is one of the paradoxes of professional complaints procedures that the dissemination of the finding against someone, which is not usually viewed as a sanction, is the outcome that is most dreaded by the person concerned.

CHALLENGES TO THE IMPORTANCE OF COMPLAINTS PROCEDURES

The view that having an effective complaints procedure is an indication of a commitment to quality is widespread within the world of therapy and beyond. However, this widely accepted opinion can be challenged from a number of points of view.

Most complaints procedures managed within agencies and professional organizations are vulnerable to the suspicion that they may be no more than a mechanism for a professional group protecting its own. It is important that strategies are sought to minimize this suspicion because of the deterrent effect on well-founded complaints being presented for consideration. To be credible, a complaints procedure must involve people from outside the field of activity under consideration. A complaints procedure is only as good as its protection of its own integrity. The mere perception that a complaints procedure lacks integrity has consequences that extend beyond this area of work to damaging the reputation for integrity of the profession as a whole.

Complaints procedures are expensive to run in terms of time and resources. They are extremely difficult to run effectively within small organizations. They require a critical size in membership in order to ensure that the people representing the profession in the procedure are truly independent. They require sufficient financial resources in order to obtain adequate legal advice that can be expensive. Small organizations can overcome some of these difficulties by collaborating in the development of joint schemes. However, adequacy of resources in terms of time and funds is an important factor in being able to conduct an effective procedure.

Complaints procedures are still seen as an important method of redress for people who have well-founded grievances. However, the standing of complaints procedures as a mechanism for quality control has diminished relative to other strategies. A well-managed complaints procedure can only address those instances where there is the possibility that the quality of service has fallen below acceptable standards. Usually this will only concern a minority of the cases seen by therapists. The challenge of quality management is to enhance the standards of service of all the therapy that is provided. In particular, quality management aims to ensure that therapy which is 'rattling along the bottom but just above unacceptable standards' becomes 'good enough'. Complaints procedures make limited contributions to addressing concerns about the adequacy of quality and its consistency which are better addressed by strategies that cover the full range of service provision. It may be that the involvement of professional bodies in the development of better quality control mechanisms for use by their membership will do more to enhance the standing of the profession than has been achieved so far by the use of complaints procedures. Complaints procedures are important, especially for those who are directly involved in them, but it is equally important to be realistic about what they can achieve.

Few therapists seek to be the subject of a formal complaint or disciplinary process. Most find the process scary and confusing. Many feel that they are survivors of intense personal and professional scrutiny of something that is neither typical nor a fair representation of their work. The process of preparing a defence, presenting it at a hearing and being cross-examined and hearing the judgement is usually very stressful. The initial response to the experience is not usually positive. However, I have met people who have undoubtedly followed a journey of surviving the process and ultimately learning from it, or in Casemore's (2001) words, finding 'understanding and healing'.

REFERENCES

BACP (2010) *Ethical Framework for Good Practice in Counselling and Psychotherapy.* Rugby: British Association for Counselling and Psychotherapy.

Bond, T. (2010) *Standards and Ethics for Counselling in Action* (3rd edn). London: Sage.

BPS (2001) *Complaints about Psychologists.* Leicester: British Psychological Society.

Casemore, R. (2001) *Surviving Complaints against Therapists: Towards Understanding and Healing.* Manchester: PCCS.

Lunt, I. (1999) Disciplining psychologists. *Psychologist*, 12 (2): 59.

Palmer Barnes, F. (1998) *Complaints and Grievances in Psychotherapy: A Handbook of Ethical Practice.* London: Routledge.

Client Experiences

COLIN FELTHAM

Trainers and therapists themselves are mindful to put each unique client first, to enter the client's inner world, to learn from clients, and to respect the self-determination of the client. But therapy is now a highly organized enterprise. When therapists meet their clients they are 'armed' with experience, training, theories and a professional infrastructure. The client, however, is more often than not someone in some degree of distress who knows little if anything of the theory of therapy (although this may be changing somewhat), and their agenda may be quite different from the therapist's. In spite of requirements for therapists to have their own therapy, it is quite likely that such experiences only partially resemble those of distressed clients. For all these reasons – plus an increasing emphasis on accountability generally – this chapter looks at the client's perspective and commends an attitude of raised awareness among therapists about implications for their own practices.

WHAT CLIENTS HAVE SAID ABOUT THEIR EXPERIENCES OF THERAPY

Presented here is a collated summary of views published unprompted by consumers, formally researched, or gleaned from clinical experience.

Help-seeking Patterns

It is important to put in perspective the fact that the vast majority of people with problems resolve them themselves or with peer support, and that although up to about 20–25 per cent of the population at any one time may suffer from a diagnosable psychological problem, probably only about 5 per cent receive formal help. A slightly disproportionate number of clients are women, it being speculated that men are less ready to acknowledge personal problems, although this is probably changing too. Many people will have tried other things before turning to professionals almost as a last resort, often waiting months or years before seeking therapy. Of course many, even after presenting, may wait longer than they would like for a first appointment, and while waiting, up to about 14 per cent resolve their problems to their own satisfaction. Recent IAPT initiatives have sought to reduce waiting times. Typically, many seek word-of-mouth recommendations to private practitioners, while those eligible for services free at the point of delivery may have quite different experiences of lack of choice, waiting lists, etc. Leong et al. (1995) summarize these and many additional obstacles to effective help for ethnic minority groups. Although clients are sometimes advised to 'shop around' for a service or practitioner with whom they feel comfortable or in whom they have confidence, obviously many feel too distressed to endure such an exercise or are not sufficiently assertive to do so.

Service Anxiety and Client Fears

On top of the 'problem anxiety' that brings clients to therapists, it is common and understandable for them to feel anxious and uncertain about telephoning for an appointment, attending first appointments, knowing what to say and how to behave, and deciding whether what they are receiving is indeed helpful for them. They may have only a hazy notion of whether or not counselling can be helpful to them. In addition, it is quite typical for a power imbalance to exist, especially in counselling or psychotherapy agencies, with the therapist being styled and naturally perceived as the one who is qualified, who knows, who embodies super-sanity, whose powers may apparently border on telepathy, and who may hold the key to an exit from misery. Where discrepancies exist between the status, age, class, race, gender and sexual orientation of therapist and client, an imbalance of power may become all the more problematic and anxiety engendering. Usually the client must visit the therapist's premises (which could be experienced as frighteningly clinical, for example) and agree to the therapist's conditions, rules and ethos of therapy. Counselling and psychotherapy – we can easily forget – are for many people very strange, counter-cultural experiences: sitting sometimes silently in a room with a stranger, being (or feeling) stared at, and expected to make intimate disclosures. According to some psychoanalytic thinkers, clients are acutely aware of the necessity of consistent physical and business arrangements and will communicate unconsciously to therapists their anxieties about any inconsistencies and subtle abuses.

Service anxiety is discussed by Howe (1989). Additionally, Pipes et al. (1985) detailed some common *client fears*, which are summarized as follows:

- Is therapy what I need?
- Will I

  - be treated as a case?
  - be taken seriously?
  - be made to do things I do not want to do?
  - find out things I don't want to?
  - lose control of myself?
  - be thought of by my friends as crazy?

- Will the therapist

  - share my values?
  - think I'm a bad person?
  - think I'm more disturbed than I am?
  - discover things I don't want him or her to discover?
  - be competent?

Some research (e.g. Le Surf and Lynch, 1999; Setiawan, 2004) shows that although clients know they need help, they do not know enough or are not given enough opportunity to know about what happens in counselling. Additionally, there may be ambivalence about wanting advice and yet not wanting to be controlled.

Common Factors

Initially surprising to many in the field, but now accepted as highly significant, a majority of clients have expressed the view (or it has been inferred from their accounts) that attention from a socially sanctioned healer in a sanctioned setting plays a large part in setting positive expectations. People are often reassured by appropriate settings, a professional manner, qualifications, and an explicit rationale for therapy. For some, simply being told or reassured by a mental health professional that they are not mad is in itself 'therapeutic', and for some it is all that is required. A large proportion of clients report the importance of being taken seriously; being listened to respectfully and non-judgementally; being understood; experiencing warmth and genuine concern; feeling contained; being helped to make sense of their otherwise ostensibly chaotic life stories (Howe, 1993). Finding a therapist with whom one can make an optimally therapeutic match is increasingly regarded as significant: this *may* include theoretical orientation but is more likely to involve perceptions of warmth, attractiveness, expertness, personality and so on (Feltham, 1999). Most clients appear uninterested in clinical theories or the nomenclature attaching to them, except where this is a vital part of the ongoing therapy (as, for example, in transactional analysis or cognitive therapy). Indeed, many clients report that counsellors' and psychotherapists' publicity material is sometimes too jargon oriented and is not sympathetic to the client's perspective. If this is surprising to readers, it may be because many of us are surrounded by colleagues and friends who are therapeutically involved, whereas a statistical majority of clients, especially first-time clients, seek solutions to distress or confusion, and are very rarely fascinated by or steeped in therapeutic theory.

Scope, Depth and Length of Therapy

It has been a sobering realization for many therapists that clients not only seek crisis resolution and symptom amelioration or removal, but are often satisfied to terminate therapy when these goals have been reached. A discrepancy between the pragmatic, short-term goals of many consumers and the often more ideologically driven goals of in-depth, long-term, psychic exploration and personality overhaul of therapists is something that has to be reckoned with (Strong, 2009). Also, while many clients have appreciated the space for reflection and empathic understanding offered by therapists, they have sometimes been mystified by long unexplained silences and lack of normal social conversation, for which therapists themselves have rationales (e.g. non-directiveness and therapeutic neutrality). Rather, for some clients, a naturalistic style of therapy is preferred which may include more self-disclosure and simple practical advice than practitioners are willing to give. Related to this is the finding that many clients expect their counselling or therapy to be relatively short term (one estimate has it that therapists typically think therapy will take at least three times longer than clients think it will take) and many clients may prefer an intermittent pattern of attendance as indicated by felt need, rather than a 'once and for all time' model of therapy.

Therapist Abuse, Exploitation and Ineffectiveness

Unfortunately, for a significant number of clients, therapy has turned out to be – in spite of therapists' duty of care – a negative and damaging experience (Sands, 2000). Even allowing for media exaggeration, client bias and resistance, and a small proportion of unjustifiably litigation-oriented clients, it is clear that abuse (sexual, emotional, physical) occurs, along with other forms of exploitation and ineffectiveness of therapy. Sex between clients and therapists is perhaps the most publicized. While it is easy to *understand* how the intimacy of one-to-one therapy can slip into inappropriate sexual contact, accounts of how damaging it usually is for clients has led to its prohibition by all professional bodies. Formalized complaints procedures now offer those wronged the opportunity to seek redress, even though this may be rather too late. Emotional abuse (for example, using demeaning language, inappropriate confrontation, engaging in reciprocal emotional entanglements, 'dropping' clients who are regarded as difficult) is reported by some clients. Examples of clients being (or feeling) financially exploited are not so well publicized, but no doubt exist. The question of whether most clients prefer to pay something for their therapy, and are likely to show more commitment when paying than if they do not, has not been resolved, although increasing clinical experience might suggest that direct payment is not the critical variable in commitment and motivation that it was once assumed to be. The ineffectiveness of some counsellors, psychotherapists and their services gives cause for concern; some clients have reported spending a great deal of time and money in therapy with no discernible results

and sometimes experiencing deterioration (Striano, 1988). The extent of this is contradicted by Seligman (1995), but its sting has helped to lead to concern for evidence-based practice (Roth and Fonagy, 2006; Rowland and Goss, 2002).

Client–therapist Differences

Although no accurate figures are available, a majority of counsellors and psychotherapists in Britain are white, middle-class liberals. Therapeutic theory reflects this bias as well as certain assumptions of secular individualism and, as is pointed out elsewhere in this book, (psychology-saturated) training often marginalizes or neglects the experiences of non-dominant social groups (Palmer, 2002; Shoaib and Peel, 2003). Hence, historically, gay clients have often been assumed to need treatment to reverse their homosexuality (this is no longer permissible); the needs of clients with disabilities have been played down or ignored; women have been assumed to be 'hysterical' (and more recently all to want a career outside the home); older people have been considered too old to benefit from therapy; and different cultural norms pertaining to expressiveness, dress, religion, etc. have been either misinterpreted or ignored. There is now enough evidence from clients' reports to know that therapists can be ignorant, patronizing, and in some cases dangerous in relation to these factors. The question of *client–therapist matching* is not clear, there being mixed views on whether black people, for example, generally prefer to be seen by black therapists or not. There is concern about low awareness of counselling in Asian communities, and more information is needed about the existence and nature of counselling services (Netto et al., 2001; Setiawan, 2004). Client–therapist age difference is a similarly uncharted or disputed area. Where some trend exists, it is that many women prefer to see a woman therapist when they have a choice, and when they sense that their concerns might be better understood and more sensitively handled by another woman. Similar preferences have been shown to exist among gay and lesbian clients (Liddle, 1996). Often, clients do not want to have to explain matters of daily oppression that are obvious to them. The converse of this picture is that in some cultures it may be the norm to expect mental health professionals to be authorities to be looked up to, and who will duly dispense expert advice. All such cultural differences are mediated by *individual* differences between the parties, adding another layer of complexity. Additionally, factors of emotional distress, transference and counter-transference mean that therapists must be aware of complex interrelationships involving socio-cultural factors (including peer, family and media influences) and individual psychology.

Appreciation

The above views need to be balanced by a reminder that many consumers have expressed great satisfaction with their therapy. Client reports and formal research both affirm the overall effectiveness and/or satisfaction levels achieved by therapists (Seligman, 1995). Clients have often said that therapy 'changed my life' or that 'I couldn't have got by without counselling.' Surveys of users of mental health services have confirmed that they overwhelmingly value the talking therapies in preference to medication. Appreciating the common factors mentioned above, clients are often surprisingly unconcerned or forgiving about therapists' occasional mistakes (e.g. clumsy interpretations, forgetting factual details, etc.). Modest changes are often appreciated by clients when therapists are hoping for more radical or dramatic changes. Clients have sometimes reported having 'internalized' the therapist, that is, having a helpful inner (imaginary) dialogue with them between sessions and after therapy has ended. As might be expected, to some extent client evaluations will always represent *some* mixture of the appreciative and the negative (Bates, 2006; Dinnage, 1989; Feltham, 2002).

CONCLUSIONS

It is noteworthy that (1) discrepancies may well exist between the views and goals of therapists and clients; (2) the inherent imbalance of power in the therapeutic relationship can easily lead to forms of abuse, infantilization or insensitive treatment, and their concealment; (3) training analysis or personal therapy/counselling for the trainee is not sufficiently similar to the experience of clients to address the need for understanding; and (4) the complexity and privacy of therapeutic relationships means that clients' views have implications not only for initial training, but for ongoing development, in-session awareness and reflection, and accountability and evaluation. The objection of some therapists that an overly consumerist view of the therapeutic process is unwise must certainly also be factored into our consideration: clients do not *always* know what is best for them, and may *sometimes* unconsciously introduce confusion and revenge seeking into the enterprise (Sutherland, 1987). Nonetheless there is ongoing interest in the UK in the involvement of consumers in the audit

and evaluation of mental health services (Foster, 2007). Procedures for, and satisfactory outcomes of, monitoring and assuring quality are (increasingly) linked to continued funding.

Taking consumers' views seriously has already led to increased concern for *informed consent* (verbal and written explanations and contracts) which extends to publications advising consumers (e.g. Dryden and Feltham, 1995) and better publicized complaints procedures. Mental health agencies such as MIND have long championed users' rights to be heard, for example by taking part in management committees. New evaluation procedures seek consumers' views in order to improve services. Knowledge about the differential effectiveness of therapies in relation to different client issues, now promoted vigorously by NICE, calls for greater awareness of referral issues. Clearly, the overall trend is necessarily towards greater transparency, knowledge sharing, fairness, and constant updating of therapists' knowledge in view of clinical research results and the changing nature of society.

REFERENCES

Bates, Y. (ed.) (2006) *Shouldn't I Be Feeling Better by Now? Client Views of Therapy.* Basingstoke: Palgrave.

Dinnage, R. (1989) *One to One: Experiences of Psychotherapy.* London: Penguin.

Dryden, W. and Feltham, C. (1995) *Counselling and Psychotherapy: A Consumers' Guide.* London: Sheldon.

Feltham, C. (ed.) (1999) *Understanding the Counselling Relationship.* London: Sage.

Feltham, C. (2002) Consumers' views of the benefits of counselling and psychotherapy. In C. Feltham (ed.), *What's the Good of Counselling and Psychotherapy? The Benefits Explained.* London: Sage.

Foster, J.L.H. (2007) *Journeys through Mental Illness: Clients' Experiences and Understandings of Mental Distress.* Basingstoke: Palgrave.

Howe, D. (1989) *The Consumer's View of Family Therapy.* Aldershot: Gower.

Howe, D. (1993) *On Being a Client: Understanding the Process of Counselling and Psychotherapy.* London: Sage.

Leong, F.T.L., Wagner, N. and Tata, S.P. (1995) Racial and ethnic variations in help-seeking attitudes. In J.G. Ponterotto, J.M. Casas, L.A. Suzuki and C.M. Alexander (eds),

Handbook of Multicultural Counseling. Thousand Oaks, CA: Sage.

Le Surf, A. and Lynch, G. (1999) Exploring young people's perceptions relevant to counselling: a qualitative study. *British Journal of Guidance & Counselling*, 27 (2): 231–43.

Liddle, B. (1996) Therapist sexual orientation, gender, and counseling practices as they relate to ratings of helpfulness by gay and lesbian clients. *Journal of Counseling Psychology*, 43: 394–401.

Netto, G.S., Thanki, M., Bondi, E. and Munro, M. (2001) Perceptions and experiences of counselling services among Asian people. In G.S. Netto et al., *A Suitable Space: Improving Counselling Services for Asian People*. Bristol: Policy Press and Joseph Rowntree Foundation.

Palmer, S. (ed.) (2002) *Multicultural Counselling: A Reader*. London: Sage.

Pipes, R.B., Schartz, R. and Crouch, P. (1985) Measuring client fears. *Journal of Consulting and Clinical Psychology*, 53 (6): 933–4.

Roth, A. and Fonagy, P. (2006) *What Works for Whom? A Critical Review of Psychotherapy Research* (2nd edn). New York: Guilford.

Rowland, N. and Goss, S. (eds) (2002) *Evidence-Based Counselling and Psychological Therapies: Research and Applications*. London: Routledge.

Sands, A. (2000) *Falling for Therapy: Psychotherapy from a Client's Point of View*. Basingstoke: Palgrave Macmillan.

Seligman, M. (1995) The effectiveness of psychotherapy: the Consumer Reports Study. *American Psychologist*, 50: 96–104.

Setiawan, J.L. (2004) *Indonesian Undergraduates' Attitudes to Counselling: A Study of Areas of Concern, Perceptions Relevant to Counselling, Willingness to Seek Help and Sources of Help*. PhD thesis, University of Nottingham.

Shoaib, K. and Peel, J. (2003) Kashmiri women's perceptions of their emotional and psychological needs, and access to counselling. *Counselling and Psychotherapy Research*, 3 (2): 87–94.

Striano, J. (1988) *Can Psychotherapists Harm You?* Santa Barbara, CA: Professional.

Strong, T. (2009) Collaborative goal-setting: counsellors and clients negotiating a focus. *Counselling Psychology Review*, 24 (3 & 4): 24–37.

Sutherland, G. (1987) *Breakdown: A Personal Crisis and a Medical Dilemma* (rev. edn). London: Weidenfeld and Nicolson.

4.8

Therapy and the Law

PETER JENKINS

Therapists are discovering that they increasingly need to have at least a basic working knowledge of the law, whatever their reservations about the legal system or the law itself. Whether in terms of keeping client records, responding to requests for information by external agents such as the courts, or deciding whether to break confidentiality in order to protect a child or client at risk, therapists are finding that from time to time they urgently need access to well-informed legal advice. All too often, their basic understanding of how the law impacts on psychotherapeutic practice has been left relatively untouched by their professional training, or subjected to conflicting and sometimes even inaccurate messages about their duties and options under the law.

This chapter sets out some of the main parameters of the interface of counselling and psychotherapy and the law in the UK. The main points of reference relate to the civil law in England and Wales, with the law in Scotland and Northern Ireland operating in distinct but still broadly parallel ways. The emphasis will be on describing the key trends and professional issues to be considered by practitioners, rather than setting out the precise detail, which can be followed up in the references and resources supplied. The chapter briefly sets out:

- how legal principles applying to counselling and psychotherapy are mediated by the practitioner's context for practice, employment status and client group
- legal aspects of managing professional relationships with clients
- legal obligations and options in handling risk

- legal principles applying to the management of sensitive information
- progress towards achieving statutory regulation of therapists.

MAKING LINKS BETWEEN PSYCHOTHERAPEUTIC PRACTICE AND THE LAW

Therapists often look for general principles, and even for absolute certainty, when encountering the law. While, as practitioners, we try to encourage our clients and colleagues to contain, stay with and *work through* ambiguity and uncertainty, our own strong preference is very often to have clear and very definite answers to the professional dilemmas which we face. The following example might illustrate this process at work.

> Paul did some unpaid weekly counselling sessions for a small voluntary agency. He became concerned about his client, Sarah, who seemed to be increasingly depressed and self-absorbed, to the extent that her pre-teenage sons, who were involved in illicit drugs and joy-riding, seemed to her to be 'running wild' and almost beyond her control as a single parent. The senior counsellor at the agency was unable to
>
> *(Continued)*

(Continued)

provide any clear guidance on how he should respond to the risks he perceived for the sons, given that there was no specific evidence of child abuse. Any attempt to explore her problematic relationship with her sons, or to express his own anxiety about this situation as a counsellor, seemed to produce little response from her, possibly due to her somewhat depressed emotional state. However, Paul's supervisor was increasingly concerned about the client and the risk to the sons' welfare. His supervisor felt strongly that Paul should make contact with social services, given the apparent reluctance or inability of the client to take any action herself.

From a professional and ethical point of view, a therapist's first point of reference should be with regard to their code of ethics, such as the BACP's *Ethical Framework for Good Practice in Counselling and Psychotherapy* (2010). This case contains a classic dilemma, namely of promoting client autonomy versus protecting the welfare of the client and also of third parties. From a legal point of view the practitioner's responses will be framed by a number of key factors, which are highly specific and will vary according to:

- the *context* in which the therapist practises
- the therapist's *employment* status
- the nature of the *client group*.

The interaction of these key factors provides a clue to the complexity of the law as it relates to counselling and psychotherapy. Exploring the possible options and responses to particular legal dilemmas is often highly specific, as general principles have to be applied carefully to this particular counsellor, working in this setting, on this employment basis, with the client group. Thus, there may well be significant differences between the child protection reporting requirements faced by therapists working in a statutory setting and those for a counsellor, such as Paul, who is counselling in a voluntary agency. Alternatively, a counsellor such as Paul, who is either directly employed or who is seen by the law to approximate to 'employed' status, may have little real discretion in deciding how to respond to issues of client or third-party risk, due to agency policy. A therapist in private practice, on the other hand, generally has substantially greater freedom of action in deciding how best to work with these issues. Therapists working with children, or

with adults experiencing mental health problems, may similarly face certain pressures to act which are *not* obligatory when working with other client groups, who are deemed to be less vulnerable.

The resulting combination of legal pressures means that therapists often encounter a wider and more varied range of legal issues than do other comparable professionals, such as social workers or psychiatric nurses. Therapists need, therefore, to consider carefully how well they are prepared for recognizing and responding to such professional dilemmas, which necessarily carry a *legal* element as well as an ethical or a professional set of choices (Bond, 2009).

LEGAL ASPECTS OF MANAGING PROFESSIONAL RELATIONSHIPS WITH CLIENTS

The discussion above has emphasized the *variability* of the law as applied to different psychotherapeutic situations. The following sections now provide a brief outline of more general legal principles, which will need to be adapted to a range of specific situations. The core of counselling and psychotherapy work consists of the therapeutic relationship and its essential boundaries. These mark it as being distinct from other professional stances, such as teaching or social work, or other helping relationships, such as friendship or mentoring. From a legal perspective, the key factors relating to the therapist's therapeutic relationship with clients are framed by the concepts of:

- contract
- duty of care
- liability.

Defining a Contract

Counsellors and therapists often use the term 'contract' in a rather loose way, referring to a set of arrangements guiding contact with the client, the purpose of the counselling and psychotherapy, and arrangements for supervision and recording. While the use of formal written agreements with clients may be considered a hallmark of good practice, these documents may not be considered to constitute a contract in a proper legal sense. A legal contract requires the fulfilment of a precise set of conditions (Jenkins, 2007: 27):

- *capacity* for the parties involved, i.e. not mentally disordered or under 18 years of age
- a firm *offer* and unequivocal *acceptance*

- a clear *intention* of both parties to create a legally binding agreement
- a contract that is supported by *consideration*, i.e. an exchange of goods or services for payment.

Many therapeutic contracts would *not* meet all these conditions, particularly regarding payment, as much counselling or therapy is provided *without* charge to the client, for example in schools, in the NHS, or by voluntary agencies. In private therapy or supervision practice, however, the agreement would, in all likelihood, constitute a legal contract. As a result, a therapist, supervisor, supervisee or client could take legal action for breach of a contract in the small claims section of the county court, should there be an alleged breach of the contract (Jenkins, 2002).

Rather than applying a legal contract as such, therapists may be using a document which is actually better termed a consent form or a working agreement. This can be useful and necessary for setting out the limits to confidentiality, for example. In this way, a client may give their advance consent to their general practitioner being contacted if they become suicidal. The counsellor then has substantial protection in law against any later charge of breach of confidence from an aggrieved client. Consent forms, or working agreements, are also important in documenting the client's *informed consent* to therapy. While this is still a developing area of law, it is emerging as a significant shift within the NHS, where obtaining the patient's full, informed and *continuing* consent to physiological and psychological treatments has become part of a major policy drive on this issue.

Duty of Care

Not all counsellors or psychotherapists will be covered by the law of contract. However, therapists will be subject to a duty of care towards their client, and supervisors will be similarly bound to their supervisees. The following vignette illustrates some features of this crucial part of the law relating to psychotherapeutic practice.

Niki was a newly qualified psychotherapist, working in the NHS with clients who had been subjected to extensive domestic violence, and who often had previous histories of experiencing serious childhood sexual abuse. Interested in trauma work, Niki began experimenting by using some radical hypnotic techniques with a client, after attending a week-long workshop in the USA. Unfortunately, the client's mental condition began to deteriorate rapidly soon afterwards, and she was admitted for psychiatric treatment. Following this, she then brought a civil case against Niki as her former psychotherapist for breach of duty of care, alleging that the psychotherapeutic techniques had caused her lasting psychological damage and resultant substantial loss of earnings.

Action of this kind is brought under tort law, for the infliction of non-intentional harm, and requires the fulfilment of the following conditions:

- the existence of a duty of care between practitioner and client
- breach of that duty
- resultant foreseeable harm to the client as a direct result of the breach.

For counselling and psychotherapy clients, the alleged harm will normally be *psychological* rather than physical in nature. However, the law sets a very high threshold for such damage. It requires that the alleged harm meets the diagnostic criteria for a psychiatric illness, such as clinical depression, generalized anxiety disorder or post-traumatic stress disorder, rather than simply taking the form of the more everyday human emotions of anger, distress or disappointment.

Case Law Concerning Therapists

Many therapists are somewhat apprehensive of being sued by their clients, particularly when the latter are very aggrieved about some aspect of the therapy provided. However, the relative lack of reported cases in the UK suggests that the law actually presents very formidable barriers to clients successfully winning this type of case. Derived from medical case law, therapists subject to this type of action will be judged according to the *Bolam test*, namely whether their actions were consistent with the 'practice of competent respected professional option'. Relying on the evidence of expert witnesses, the judge needs to decide whether the therapist was working *within* the parameters of their chosen approach, such as psychodynamic, person-centred or other method. In practice, it is very difficult for clients to prove that the therapist's actions directly *caused* their psychological damage. In the case of Niki above, the client's *prior* history of abuse and possible evidence of psychiatric treatment *in the past* may well be used in court to invalidate her claim or, at the very least, reduce any damages eventually awarded to her.

Liability

Therapists are often keen to assume a professional duty of care towards their clients, as this is consistent with their overall professional stance and their obligations under a code of ethics. From a legal point of view, liability is defined in rather narrower terms and takes specific forms, which are determined by the therapist's *employment* status rather than simply by the existence of a therapeutic relationship with the client. Liability can take the form of:

- *personal* liability, where a therapist doing paid private work holds *direct* responsibility for any non-intentional harm caused to the client
- *vicarious* liability, where an *employer* holds liability for the work of employees and volunteers.

Returning to the points made earlier, Niki's liability would be primarily determined by her status as an employee of the NHS trust. The client would need to sue her *and* the NHS trust together. To that extent, a psychotherapist in Niki's position would be 'protected' by their employer, which may have its own legal department and extensive experience in responding to claims and litigation. There remains a strong case, nevertheless, for therapists to keep their own professional indemnity insurance, rather than rely totally on the goodwill of their employer. Holding such insurance gives the therapist access to independent legal advice and, if necessary, separate legal representation in court, should this be necessary (Jenkins et al., 2004).

The barriers against clients succeeding in this case remain substantial. It needs to be remembered that clients also have access to a non-legal route of redress, namely by bringing a *complaint* against the therapist, either to the therapist's employer or to their professional association. Given the shift towards establishing accessible and user-friendly complaints procedures by both sets of organizations, it is probably much more likely that counsellors and psychotherapists will face at least one serious professional or organizational complaint during their working career, rather than undergo actual litigation in court.

LEGAL OBLIGATIONS IN HANDLING RISK

Therapists often express real concern about the ethical tension and conflict existing between their obligations towards the client and those towards other members of society, who may be put at risk by the client's actions. In fact, the concept of risk can take a number of forms:

- risk to *client*, via deliberate self-harm, actual or attempted suicide
- risk to a *third party*, such as child abuse, domestic violence, serious crime or terrorism
- risk to *therapist*, via assault or stalking.

Therapists subscribe to an ethical commitment to promote the client's autonomy and to protect their wellbeing. This may come into conflict with real or imagined *legal* obligations, particularly when counterbalanced against an expectation that therapists should avoid harm to the client or others, by breaking client confidentiality if necessary. This might be in order to take preventive action by alerting the authorities concerned, for example, in the case of suspected child abuse.

As discussed below, therapists have a duty of trust and confidence towards clients. There are few overriding, absolute legal requirements to break confidentiality, and these concern instances of terrorism and drug money laundering. Therapists may be required by their contract of employment or agency policy to report suspected child abuse or threatened client self-harm or suicide when working for statutory agencies such as health, education and social services. However, even these requirements need to be balanced against the therapist's fiduciary duty of trust and confidentiality towards the client. This broad fiduciary duty to clients has been recognized by independent legal opinion, despite it conflicting on occasion with forceful employer demands for blanket policies on the reporting of risk.

In fact, in situations involving non-terrorist crime, therapists (outside Northern Ireland) have the *right*, but not necessarily a *duty*, to break confidentiality in the wider public interest. A therapist *could*, therefore, contact the police to report criminal activity by a client, such as an undetected murder, or a credible threat of revenge towards a former partner, or to report a client who was stalking the therapist herself. From an ethical, professional and therapeutic point of view, any such decision to report clearly needs to be prefaced wherever possible by discussion with the client, and consultation with a supervisor and experienced colleagues. However, the law will generally support such action if taken in a measured, responsible and accountable manner, as evidenced by the introduction of statutory provision for 'whistleblowing' facilities into the workplace.

LEGAL PRINCIPLES APPLYING TO THE MANAGEMENT OF SENSITIVE INFORMATION

Therapists learn a great deal of highly sensitive information about clients during the course of their work. In terms of the law, therapists owe a duty of confidence to clients where this would be a reasonable expectation and by virtue of the nature of the special, indeed *trusting*, relationship which underpins therapeutic work. This duty can also be assumed to apply in the case of a contract for the psychotherapeutic work (see earlier). The legal protection for client confidentiality has been further strengthened by recent statutes, such as the client's right to *respect* for privacy under human rights legislation, and, more emphatically, by the provisions of data protection law. This requires therapists to adopt transparent forms of record keeping which are consistent with the fundamental rights of citizens to know and, wherever appropriate, to have substantial access to such records. In contrast with past legislation, current data protection law covers manual records kept in systematic form, as well as computerized records, together with audio- and videotapes. The continuing impact of data protection law has spelled the end of the former practice by many therapists of keeping 'private' sets of notes on an open-ended basis for untold purposes, which were unknown to the client or agency concerned.

ACCESS BY THIRD PARTIES TO CLIENT RECORDS

Part of the therapist's role in managing sensitive client data has been to limit unauthorized access by other interested parties, such as the partner of a client undergoing therapy. What now appears to be developing is a rising interest by external agencies in requiring access to client records for use in legal proceedings. These agencies include:

- *solicitors* representing clients in legal proceedings, such as litigation for workplace stress
- *police officers* seeking evidence for a prosecution in the case of alleged child abuse
- *courts* requiring the surrender of counselling and psychotherapy records, including personal and supervision notes, to assist the court in its deliberations.

Counsellors and psychotherapists do not possess legal privilege, unlike solicitors, and cannot simply refuse to comply with court-ordered demands for notes, except at the risk of being held in contempt of court. Practitioners faced with court-authorized demands for release of client records need to take legal advice, but are faced with the reality that client confidentiality is outweighed by the wider public interest. Therapists, trainers and professional associations need to take fuller account of this issue, where client and therapist confidentiality is ultimately provided with limited protection by the law, that is when the law itself declares an interest in accessing client secrets confided within the therapy session.

STATUTORY REGULATION OF THERAPISTS

Therapists have been subject to a second wave of preparation for statutory regulation, following the unsuccessful steps taken in the late 1970s (Jenkins, 2007). This would have afforded full legal protection for the titles of 'counsellor' and 'psychotherapist', via registration of suitably qualified applicants with the Health Professions Council (HPC). While the moves towards statutory regulation were actively supported by the relevant professional associations, they were also strenuously opposed by a significant minority of therapists, including recourse to legal measures, such as judicial review. (Regulation of psychologists by the HPC has already been enacted.) The government has clearly signalled that statutory regulation will not now be enacted for counsellors and psychotherapists (Department of Health, 2011). Professional standards will be managed by voluntary registers and via professional self-regulation. This will be overseen by the Commission for Healthcare Regulatory Excellence, renamed as the Professional Standards Authority for Health and Social Care. This decision effectively closes the door to future statutory regulation of therapists and ends a period of concerted effort to achieve legal recognition for counsellors and psychotherapists, which has lasted several decades.

SUMMARY

Therapists need to be familiar with the broad outline of the civil law and the specific ways in which it impacts on their practice. In reality, the relationship of the law to counselling and psychotherapy is mediated by a number of factors, such as the therapist's context for practice, employment status and client group. In terms of managing professional relationships with clients, therapists need to be aware of the principles underlying contracts, if in private practice, and to work within the parameters of accepted professional norms in discharging their duty of care to clients. The process of managing risk presents a number of challenges to therapists, where there are relatively few absolute requirements to break client confidentiality. Data protection law has eroded previous therapist latitude regarding record keeping, and subjected it to wider principles of public transparency, access and accountability. While the law is generally supportive of client confidentiality, therapists do not possess the legal protection of privilege, and must normally comply with court-authorized demands for access to client records in the public interest. A second wave of progress towards the goal of achieving statutory regulation of counsellors and psychotherapists has been halted by a change of government policy, which favours reliance on voluntary registers and professional self-regulation.

REFERENCES

BACP (2010) *Ethical Framework for Good Practice in Counselling and Psychotherapy.* Lutterworth: British Association for Counselling and Psychotherapy.

Bond, T. (2009) *Standards and Ethics for Counselling in Action* (3rd edn). London: Sage.

Department of Health (2011) *Enabling Excellence: Autonomy and Accountability for Healthcare Workers, Social Workers and Social Care Workers.* Cm 8008. London: Stationery Office.

Jenkins, P. (ed.) (2002) *Legal Issues in Counselling and Psychotherapy.* London: Sage.

Jenkins, P. (2007) *Counselling, Psychotherapy and the Law* (2nd edn). London: Sage.

Jenkins, P., Keter, V. and Stone, J. (2004) *Psychotherapy and the Law: Questions and Answers for Counsellors and Therapists.* London: Whurr.

4.9

Mental Health Law

SOBHI GIRGIS

The care of people with mental disorder is regulated by a host of legal provisions arising from, among other sources, Acts of Parliament, secondary legislation, case law, the European Convention on Human Rights, the Human Rights Act 1998, and judgements made by the European Court of Human Rights. Detention in hospital is a significant encroachment on personal liberty. Most countries have a specific mental health law to ensure the proper use of such powers and stipulate sufficient safeguards against their misuse. Even within the UK, devolved administrations have enacted slightly different mental health laws. In England and Wales, the Mental Health Act 1983 (hereafter the MHA 1983) was recently amended by the MHA 2007 which introduced a number of significant changes, including compulsory powers in the community. Provisions for detention in hospital for treatment of mental disorder are also available through other legislation, e.g. the Children's Act 1989, the Criminal Procedure (Insanity) Act 1964 as amended by the Criminal Procedure (Insanity and Unfitness to Plead) Act 1991, and the Homicide Act 1957. The Criminal Justice Act 2003 enabled the courts to add treatment requirements when considering a community sentence if the offender agrees to comply with such requirements, e.g. mental health treatment requirement, drug treatment requirement and alcohol treatment requirement.

Legislation governing community care is a hotchpotch of conflicting statutes which have been enacted over the last 60 years or so. The National Assistance Act 1948 and the NHS and Community Care Act 1990 remain the most significant pieces of legislation in this area.

Legal provisions dealing with issues of capacity have developed over the years through common law. These were eventually codified by the Mental Capacity Act 2005 (the MCA 2005). The latter has been amended to include clear procedures and safeguards which professionals should follow when deprivation of liberty is necessary.

MHA 1983 (AS AMENDED BY MHA 2007)

The Act deals with care and treatment of people with mental disorder mainly in hospital. From 3 November 2008, clinicians have been given new powers allowing them to impose certain conditions on patients on their release from detention and enabling them to recall patients back to hospital if their mental health deteriorates or if they do not comply with the agreed conditions. Patients can be detained in hospital under 'civil' sections (Part II of the Act) or 'criminal sections' (Part III of the Act) which are issued by a court or Ministry of Justice. Part IV regulates consent to treatment. Part V deals with appealing against detention.

Mental disorder is defined for the purposes of the Act as 'any disorder or disability of the mind'. The 2007 amendment widened the definition of mental disorder and abolished the four categories included in the MHA 1983 (mental illness, mental impairment, severe mental impairment and psychopathic disorder). Learning disability is only considered to be a mental disorder for the purpose of the Act if it is associated with abnormally aggressive or seriously irresponsible behaviour. Dependence on alcohol or drugs *per se* is not considered a mental disorder and patients cannot be detained solely because of their dependence. However, psychiatric disorders arising from alcohol or drug misuse can be considered as mental disorders, e.g. intoxication, withdrawal, alcoholic psychotic disorder, etc. The 2007 amendment abolished the 'treatability' criteria for detaining patients categorised as suffering from severe mental impairment or psychopathic disorder. Instead, the Act created an appropriate medical treatment test which applies to all mental disorders. No longer can electro-convulsive therapy (ECT) be given to an adult who has capacity to consent without his/her consent unless it was a life saving treatment. The Act opened the door for professionals other than doctors, including psychologists, to become 'approved clinicians'. This allows them to act as the 'responsible clinicians' who take overall responsibility for managing patients coming under compulsion. They are also able to train to become 'approved mental health professionals' (AMHPs) and carry out the functions that used to be carried out by the 'approved social worker' before the 2007 amendment.

Medical Treatment Under the MHA 1983

The definition of medical treatment under the MHA has been widened to explicitly include psychological intervention. Medical treatment also includes nursing, psychological intervention, and specialist mental health habilitation, rehabilitation and care. The Act defines medical treatment for mental disorder as medical treatment which is for the purpose of alleviating or preventing a worsening of a mental disorder or one or more of its symptoms or manifestations. This can include treatment of physical health problems only if such treatment is part of, or ancillary to, treatment for mental disorder (e.g. treating wounds self-inflicted as a result of mental disorder). Sections 57, 58 and 58A of the Act set out types of medical treatment for mental disorder to which special rules and procedures apply, including, in many cases, the need for a certificate from a 'second opinion appointed doctor' (SOAD) approving the treatment. Unless sections 57, 58 or 58A apply, section 63 of the Act means that detained patients may be given medical treatment for any kind for mental disorder, if they consent to it; or if they have not consented to it, but the treatment is given by or under the direction of the approved clinician in charge of the treatment in question. Psychological therapies and other forms of medical treatments which, to be effective, require the patient's cooperation are not automatically

inappropriate simply because a patient does not currently wish to engage with them. Such treatments can potentially remain appropriate and available as long as it continues to be clinically suitable to offer them and they would be provided if the patient agreed to engage.

Part II of the MHA 1983

This deals with compulsory admission to hospital for assessment or treatment of mental disorder. Admission under section 2 requires two medical recommendations and an application by an approved mental health professional. It lasts for up to 28 days and cannot be renewed. Admission under section 3 is for treatment and lasts for up to six months. It can be renewed at regular intervals, initially for six months, then for another six months, then annually. Admission under section 4 is urgent detention for up to 72 hours. Section 5 deals with application for a 'holding' power order that allows a nurse for up to six hours (s. 5(4)) or a doctor for up to 72 hours (s. 5(2)) to keep a patient already in hospital to facilitate a Mental Health Act assessment. Section 7 concerns application for a guardianship order. Section 17 regulates granting leaves of absence; section 20 regulates renewal of detention; and section 23 regulates discharge.

Part III of the MHA 1983

This provides a similar framework for detention. These are orders made by the court in relation to offenders coming before them or the Ministry of Justice in relation to prisoners in need of treatment in psychiatric hospitals. Section 37 relates to a hospital order imposed by the magistrates or crown court instead of a prison sentence, if the offender is sufficiently mentally unwell at the time of sentencing to require hospitalisation. It operates in the same way as its civil counterpart under s. 3. A restriction order under s. 41 (without a limit of time) can be attached to s. 37 only by the Crown Court. The restriction order is imposed to protect the public from serious harm. The restrictions affect leave of absence, transfer between hospitals, and discharge, all of which require Ministry of Justice permission. Discharge can only be ordered by a Mental Health Tribunal or the Ministry of Justice. Section 38 provides for an interim hospital order which allows the court to remand offenders to hospital for a trial of treatment before deciding to dispose the case by way of a hospital order (s. 36). The courts also have other powers to remand offenders to hospital for assessment (s. 35) or treatment

(s. 36). Section 47 is used by the Ministry of Justice to transfer a serving prisoner to hospital. A restriction order under s. 49 (similar to s. 41) is usually attached to s. 47. Remanded prisoners can be transferred to hospital under ss. 48/49.

Part IV of the MHA 1983

This regulates medical treatment of mental disorder and issues of consent. Treatment with medication, after the first three months of its first administration, requires the patient's consent *or* the agreement of a second opinion appointed doctor (s. 58). In certain urgent cases, the responsible clinician can authorise treatment pending compliance with certification by an SOAD (s. 62). Extra safeguards have been introduced to regulate the administration of ECT (s. 58A). Treatment which could cause irreversible effects requires consent *and* the agreement of an SOAD. Only two types of treatment come under this provision: neurosurgical operation to treat mental disorder, and surgical implantation of male sex hormones to reduce sexual arousal (s. 57).

Safeguards for Patients under Compulsory Powers

The MHA gives significant powers to the nearest relative (NR). NR can object to detention in hospital for treatment (under s. 3), can order discharge of the patient, and can apply for a tribunal. Patients can apply for discharge through tribunals or hospital managers. Patients have statutory rights to be given information on their detention and any safeguards. The 2007 amendments to the MHA 1983 introduced a new right to all patients under compulsion of access to an independent mental health advocate (IMHA).

Supervised Community Treatment

The 2007 amendment introduced a new regime to apply compulsory powers in the community. New powers were given to clinicians to impose certain conditions on patients on their release from detention and enable them to recall patients back to hospital if their mental health deteriorates or if they do not comply with the agreed conditions. The aim was to stop the cycle of 'revolving door patients'. Patients who are detained in hospital for treatment (primarily s. 3 or s. 37) can be discharged but remain liable to recall if they become unwell or break the stipulated conditions attached to their community treatment order (CTO). Treatment cannot be enforced in the community, but the responsible clinician can recall the patient to hospital for up to 72 hours, where treatment

can be given. If a longer period of care is needed, the CTO can be revoked and the patient can start a new period of detention in hospital under the same section s/he was under before discharge.

Guardianship Orders

If there are concerns about the welfare of people with mental disorder, they can be placed under guardianship in the community, if deemed appropriate, rather than detained in hospital. This will require recommendations from two doctors and application by an approved mental health professional. The local authority most often takes the role of the guardian.

Powers of Entry and Police Powers (s. 135 and s. 136)

Section 135 allows an AMHP to apply to a magistrate for a warrant authorising a police officer (or other constable) to enter specific premises, by force if necessary, if there is reasonable cause to suspect that someone believed to be suffering from mental disorder

- has been or is being ill-treated, neglected or 'kept otherwise than under proper control' on the premises; or
- is living there alone and unable to care for themselves.

The police also have a special power under s. 136 in relation to people they find in a public place who appear to be suffering from mental disorder and to be in immediate need of care or control. People will then be taken to a 'place of safety' where their mental health is assessed.

Aftercare (s. 117)

All patients subject to the longer treatment sections (ss. 3, 37, 37/41, 45A, 47, 47/49) are entitled to appropriate services, according to their needs, when they leave hospital. Section 117 places obligation on primary care trusts and local authorities to provide those services free of charge.

CRIMINAL PROCEDURE (INSANITY) ACT 1964

People whom a jury accept to be legally insane are given the special verdict of 'not guilty by reason of insanity'. They can be admitted to hospital for treatment in a similar way to a s. 37 hospital order. The Act was amended in 1991 to stipulate legal provision for people who are 'unfit to plead'. People who are deemed unfit to plead cannot be tried. The jury decide whether the person has committed the act or omission. The person can be admitted to hospital for treatment.

POLICE AND CRIMINAL EVIDENCE ACT (PACE) 1984

This Act recognises the vulnerability of people with mental disorder when they come in contact with the police. The definition of 'mental disorder' in this Act is the same as in the MHA 1983. If a police constable thinks or is told in good faith that a detained person is mentally disordered, an interview cannot be conducted in the absence of an 'appropriate adult'.

HOMICIDE ACT 1957

This Act introduced the partial defence of 'diminished responsibility' to a charge of murder. This defence is available to people suffering from a mental disorder which substantially impairs their mental responsibility for the killing. They receive a conviction of manslaughter rather than murder and are invariably sentenced to a hospital order with restriction.

COMMUNITY CARE LAW

Following the establishment of the NHS in 1948 through the NHS Act 1946, a key piece of legislation was the National Assistance Act 1948. The latter abolished the workhouses, kick-started the modern system of social benefits and ended incarceration as a policy response to poverty. Other legislation followed including the Health Services and Public Health Act 1968, Chronically Sick and Disabled Persons Act 1970, National Health Service Act 1977 and Disabled Persons (Services, Consultation and Representation) Act 1986. In the 1980s there was a shift of care from psychiatric institutions to the community, with the closure of most of the long-stay asylums. Hospitals were discharging patients to nursing homes. The NHS and Community Care Act 1990 aimed at defining the relationship between health and local authorities in the provision of community

care services. This Act removed from the NHS the primary responsibility for the provision of non-hospital services for those requiring long-term care. It requires the local social services departments to assess the care needs of people whom they are either obliged or empowered to assist.

MCA 2005

This is a 'codifying' Act, as it did not create new legal principles but enshrined in statute current best practice and common law principles concerning people who lack mental capacity and those who take decisions on their behalf. It replaced existing statutory schemes for enduring powers of attorney and court of protection receivers with reformed and updated provisions. The Act is underpinned by five key principles, set out in s. 1:

1   *A presumption of capacity.* Every adult has the right to make his or her own decisions and must be assumed to have the capacity to do so unless it is proved otherwise.
2   *Individuals being supported to make their own decisions.* A person must be given all practicable help before anyone treats them as not being able to make their own decisions.
3   *Unwise decisions.* Just because an individual makes what might be seen as an unwise decision, they should not be treated as lacking capacity to make that decision.
4   *Best interests.* An act done or decision made under the Act for or on behalf of a person who lacks capacity must be done in their best interests.
5   *Least restrictive option.* Anything done for or on behalf of a person who lacks capacity should be the least restrictive of their basic rights and freedoms.

The MHA 2007 amended the MCA 2005 to introduce the deprivation of liberty safeguards (DoLs) to provide a legal framework in relation to depriving people who lack capacity of their liberty if that was deemed in their best interest. Specifically, they were introduced to prevent breaches of the European Convention on Human Rights (ECHR) such as that identified by the judgement of the European Court of Human Rights (ECtHR) in the case of *HL* v. *the United Kingdom* (application no. 45508/99, commonly referred to as the 'Bournewood' judgement). The safeguards apply to people who are either in a hospital or in registered care. DoLS contain detailed requirements about when and how deprivation of liberty may be authorised. The legislation also provides detailed arrangements for renewing and challenging the authorisation of deprivation of liberty.

HUMAN RIGHTS ACT (HRA) 1998

The UK was co-signatory of the ECHR at its inception in 1950. The Human Rights Act 1998 came into force on 2 October 2000. Its aim is to 'give further effect' in UK law to the rights contained in the ECHR. The Act makes available in UK courts a remedy for breach of a Convention right, without the need to go to the ECtHR. The HRA has sections but the ECHR has articles, given in Schedule 1 of the HRA. Some of the articles are absolute, some are qualified (by the needs of the society), and some are limited (by other legislation). The relevant ECHR articles are listed in Table 4.9.1.

Table 4.9.1 *ECHR articles*

Article 2	Right to life (absolute)
Article 3	Prohibition of torture (absolute)
Article 4	Prohibition of slavery and forced labour (absolute)
Article 5	Right to liberty and security (limited)
Article 6	Right to a fair trial (limited)
Article 7	No punishment without law (absolute)
Article 8	Right to respect for private and family life (qualified)
Article 9	Freedom of thought, conscience and religion (qualified)
Article 10	Freedom of expression (qualified)
Article 11	Freedom of assembly and association (qualified)
Article 12	Right to marry (limited)

Examples of relevance of the HRA 1998 to mental health law

Article 5 allows the detention of people with 'unsound mind' on the basis of objective medical evidence. This principle underpins the process of detaining people with mental disorder under the MHA. Medical assessment and medical recommendations provide the necessary 'objective medical evidence'. Article 5 also requires speedy review by a 'court' when people with unsound mind are detained. The mental health tribunals were given the power to discharge patients to ensure compliance with article 5. Article 6 underpins the proceedings of the tribunals and the entitlement of detained patients to free legal representation in exercising their right to a review of their detention by a tribunal.

SOME LEGAL ISSUES RELEVANT TO COUNSELLORS AND PSYCHOTHERAPISTS

The 2007 amendment of the MHA made it possible for psychologists to assume the new professional roles of approved clinician and approved mental health professional. Psychological treatment has been explicitly included in the definition of 'medical treatment'. As such, appropriate medical treatment can theoretically be limited to psychological treatment, e.g. in a personality disorders unit. As psychological treatment cannot be forced, it is provided under the authority of the responsible clinician. It is interesting that treatment is considered as 'available' even if a detained patient refuses to engage. This poses an ethical dilemma for the therapist. If psychological treatment is the main form of treatment for a detained patient, admission to a particular unit is only possible if such intervention is available in that unit.

Under s. 6 of the HRA 1998, the definition of public authority 'includes any person certain of whose functions are functions of a public nature'. Individual therapists can fall under the definition of public authority if they are working for an organisation which is a public authority itself, e.g. an NHS hospital. It is unlawful for a public authority to act in a way which is incompatible with a Convention right, e.g. the right to respect for private and family life.

RECOMMENDED READING

Mental Health Act 1983 *Code of Practice.* London: Stationery Office, 2008.

Mental Capacity Act 2005 *Code of Practice.* London: Stationery Office, 2007.

Mental Capacity Act 2005 *Deprivation of Liberty Safeguards Code of Practice.* London: Stationery Office, 2008.

Human Rights Act (HRA) 1998.

Michael Mandelstam (2008) *Community Care Practice and the Law.* London: Jessica Kingsley.

Fundamentals of Research

JOHN MCLEOD

BACKGROUND

Skills and awareness in research have become increasingly important for counsellors and psychotherapists in recent years. The professionalization of counselling and psychotherapy, and the emphasis placed within health care on evidence-based practice, has contributed to an expectation that therapists will be informed about research findings relevant to their work. There is a growing trend for institutions and agencies which fund therapy services, and also for consumer groups, to demand research evidence about effectiveness. The development of new therapy settings, client groups and interventions has also required research support.

It is widely acknowledged that there exists a 'gap' between research and practice in the field of counselling and psychotherapy. Few therapists read research articles or regard them as being useful sources of information in relation to practice. Practitioners complain that research depends too much on statistical generalizations and does not ask the appropriate questions.

At the present time there exist opposing pressures around research in therapy. On the one hand, there are demands that therapists become more tuned in to research. On the other hand, many therapists are resistant to becoming more involved in an activity that does not appear to produce advantages in respect of work with clients. The aim of this chapter is to explore some of the key issues and developments in relation to research in counselling and psychotherapy, and to demonstrate the potential value of research as a means of enhancing the quality of therapy services that are available to clients.

USING THE RESEARCH LITERATURE

The research literature represents an immense resource for therapists. It includes articles on many different kinds of therapy applied to the problems of a diversity of client groups. In the past this information was only available in university libraries. It is now possible to scan or review much of this literature using personal computer access to the internet or to online databases such as PsycLIT. Information and instruction in how to use these resources are available at most local libraries. *Bergin and Garfield's Handbook of Psychotherapy and Behavior Change*, edited by Lambert (2004) and now in its fifth edition, is an authoritative review of contemporary research and a good place to start when looking for research studies. Therapy research articles are published in a wide range of places, and among the most important journals are: *Counselling and Psychotherapy Research*; *Psychology and Psychotherapy*; *Journal of Consulting and Clinical Psychology*; *Journal of Counseling Psychology*; and *Psychotherapy Research*.

All research papers begin with an abstract which summarizes the main features and conclusions of the study. Readers can use the abstract to decide whether or not to look at the article in more detail. Although an increasing number of research studies employ qualitative methods, it is still the case that the majority rely on statistical forms of data analysis. To make sense of these papers, it is therefore necessary to have some familiarity with statistical concepts (see Barker et al., 2002; McLeod, 2011a). When reading research papers it is important to adopt a critical, questioning perspective, particularly in relation to the implications of the study for practice. In research studies, the definition and measurement of key variables, the selection of participants, or the therapeutic interventions that are used may not mirror what happens in everyday therapeutic practice.

THE THERAPIST AS RESEARCHER

There are several reasons why the participation of therapists in research is essential. If therapists do not actually engage in research, then the research base of the profession will continue to be dominated by the interests of government departments or academic psychologists and psychiatrists. However, it can also be argued that doing research can make a contribution to therapist personal and professional development (McLeod, 1997). Research is a way of reflecting on practice and on assumptions about the therapeutic process. Doing research forces therapists to think clearly, conceptualize and find ways of communicating personal experience to others. Reading the research literature exposes therapists to alternative ideas about therapy.

Therapists who appreciate the potential relevance of research are often deterred by the compromises they assume they need to make in order to collect data. For example, practitioners may be worried about compromising the confidentiality of client material, about using standardized questionnaires that do not match the client's experience, or by a perceived requirement to collect data on large numbers of cases. It is crucial in practitioner research that ethical considerations and the wellbeing of the client should take first priority. Nevertheless, there are many ways in which practitioners can engage in meaningful research, for example through systematic case study methods, qualitative analysis of therapy transcripts, or participation in practitioner inquiry groups. Various approaches to practitioner research are introduced in McLeod (2011a).

OUTCOME RESEARCH AND EVIDENCE-BASED PRACTICE

Outcome research (also described as 'efficacy', 'effectiveness' or 'evaluation' research) has the primary aim of finding out how much a particular counselling or therapy intervention has helped or benefited the client. The earliest systematic research

into counselling and therapy concentrated entirely on this issue. In the 1930s and 1940s, several studies were carried out into the effects of psychoanalysis. The results of these investigations suggested that, overall, around two-thirds of the psychoanalytic patients followed up improved, with one-third remaining the same or deteriorating after treatment. These early studies consisted of follow-up interviews with clients. The limitations of this kind of research design are readily apparent: it is possible that all, or some, of the clients who improved might have done so even if they had not received therapy. In response to this methodological critique, a later generation of outcome research employed the strategy of the randomized controlled trial (RCT), in which clients are assessed prior to receiving therapy and are randomly allocated to different treatment conditions. Within the design, any differences in outcome between the treatment groups at the end of therapy can be attributed to the effects of therapy, because all other factors have been held constant. From the 1970s, many hundreds of RCTs have been carried out into the impact of different therapy approaches on different client populations. Once a number of RCTs have been conducted, it is possible to look at whether a consistent pattern emerges regarding the relative effectiveness of competing therapy models with particular client groups. This procedure involves the use of a technique for systematic review of outcome literature, known as meta-analysis. Meta-analysis involves calculating the average amount of client change reported for each approach in each separate study, then combining these change scores to give an overall estimate of how much benefit a particular approach (such as psychoanalysis, client-centred therapy or behaviour therapy) yields over a set of studies comprising a large number of clients. The first comprehensive and systematic meta-analysis of therapy outcome was published by Smith et al. (1980), and since that time many further meta-analyses have been conducted (see Lambert, 2004 for examples). Taken as a whole, these meta-analyses suggest that counselling and psychotherapy in general are highly effective, with clients who have received treatment reporting much more benefit than those in waiting list or other control conditions. The pattern of outcome in relation to specific disorders or problem areas is more mixed. There is strong evidence for the efficacy of cognitive-behavioural therapy (CBT) for most psychological problems, but this finding may reflect the fact that more outcome studies have been carried out on CBT interventions than on other approaches. Where relevant outcome studies have been conducted, there also tends to be good evidence for the efficacy of psychodynamic, person-centred/experiential and other approaches to therapy. An accessible summary of the findings of outcome research and meta-analyses can be found in Cooper (2008).

Although there is no doubt that RCTs represent a powerful tool for examining the effectiveness of counselling and psychotherapy, it is also clear that there are many challenging methodological issues associated with the use of this methodological approach within the domain of research in counselling and psychotherapy. These issues are discussed in detail in Elliott (1998), Rowland and Goss (2000) and Westen et al. (2004). In essence, the critical factor is that the technical requirements of a good randomized trial mean that the clients who are recruited to the study, and the therapy that is provided for them, may be quite different from anything that is seen in everyday practice. As a result, the relevance of RCT findings for everyday practice can be called into question. Practice-based or naturalistic outcome studies represent a means of collecting information on the outcomes of therapy that is more faithful to the conditions of everyday therapy. In practice-based research, all clients receiving therapy from an agency or a clinic are invited to complete questionnaires at the start and end of their therapy. In the UK, the development of the CORE outcome monitoring system (Chapter 4.11 in this volume) has made it possible for many practitioners and therapy service providers to engage in practice-based audit and research. Further information on a range of research strategies that are used in practice-based outcome evaluation, including case studies and qualitative studies, can be found in Barkham et al. (2010).

Within the last decade, the findings and methods of counselling and psychotherapy have had an increasingly direct impact on therapy practice, in two areas. The accumulation of evidence about the effectiveness of different forms of therapy for different disorders has come to the attention of health services and governments committed to the development of policies of evidence-based practice. In addition, many therapy practitioners are realizing that they can use real-time feedback from outcome scales to inform their practice with clients.

The concept of evidence-based practice represents an inevitable and rational response of governments and other health-care providers to the intersection of increasing costs of health services and increasing demand from patients for new and expensive treatments. Evidence-based practice consists of a broad strategy of prioritizing those treatments for which reliable evidence of efficacy is available. It is important to recognize that the founders of evidence-based practice approaches in medicine did not intend that all treatment would be strictly determined by rigid protocols. They were always clear that evidence-based practice allowed for clinical judgement and incorporation of patient preferences, but in a context where these choices were informed by research findings. Within most of the UK, recommendations around evidence-based practice in health care are made by the National Institute for Health and Clinical Excellence (NICE); Scotland is covered by a parallel body, the Scottish Intercollegiate Guidelines Network (SIGN). These organizations are independent of but funded by government, and have the task of reviewing research into the efficacy of interventions for specific disorders, and publishing recommendations in the form of clinical guidelines which determine the types of treatment that are offered within the NHS. Guidelines emerge from a lengthy consultation process which involves all possible stakeholders including patient groups and individuals. The full version of the NICE guidelines on the treatment of depression amounts to 700 pages, with brief versions available for health professionals and patients. Current versions of all NICE guidelines are available for download at www.nice.org.uk.

There are a number of ways in which evidence-based practice policies, and the specific approach taken by NICE, can be regarded as controversial. Any form of rigorous implementation of evidence-based practice requires that counsellors and psychotherapists should assess and diagnose their clients, and only use interventions that have been supported in research studies as being efficacious for that disorder. This framework conflicts with much of current therapy practice, at least in the UK. There are many therapists who do not work in health contexts, and who do not use an illness or medical model. Even among those who are sympathetic to a diagnosis-driven approach, there is a concern that in practice very few clients fit neatly into one diagnostic category; probably the majority of people who seek help from counsellors and psychotherapists have multiple problems ('comorbidity'). Furthermore, even if a therapist is trained in one empirically validated approach to therapy, there is a tendency for practitioners to operate from a more integrative or eclectic base as they gain more experience and assimilate additional ideas and methods into their clinical repertoire. Finally, there exist many prima-facie valid approaches to therapy that have not yet been the subject of controlled outcome research, and which therefore risk being eliminated from the range of resources that are offered to clients. These are all factors that make it hard to implement strict evidence-based practice policies in the field of counselling and psychotherapy. On the other hand, the fundamental premise of the evidence-based practice movement remains sound, and there is no doubt that in recent years the counselling and psychotherapy profession has come to accept the value, in principle, of using research to inform practice. The argument centres around the detailed application of this stance. In this context, the NICE guidelines working groups have been criticized for adopting a review strategy that is too heavily dominated by RCT evidence, and which does not give sufficient weight to the contribution of other types of research (Barkham et al., 2010).

Beyond the emergence of evidence-based practice policies, the other main consequence of the proliferation of therapy outcome research has been the increasing use by practitioners of therapy outcome measures to provide real-time feedback on client progress. The leading figures in this area of development have been Lambert (2007) and Miller et al. (2005). Essentially, these initiatives involve inviting the client to complete a brief outcome measure before each session. The therapist then works out the client's score, and plots it on a graph. The pattern of improvement or deterioration that is then visible can be used by the therapist, or collaboratively by therapist and client together, as data that inform the work they are doing. This kind of information has proved to be particularly valuable in relation to managing 'off-track' clients who are getting worse, and decisions around when to end therapy. The primary reason for the value of these sources of information is that studies have shown that therapists are not good at knowing when their clients are getting worse, or when they are well enough to terminate (Lambert, 2007). Some of the projects that have been conducted involve the use of complex algorithms that predict the expected rate of improvement for a client with a particular level of problem severity at intake (Lambert, 2007). Other projects have been based on simpler graphing procedures (Miller et al., 2005). Some recent studies have examined the impact of providing therapists with checklists of potential strategies for dealing with clients who are displaying negative outcomes. Other studies have looked at the impact of feedback on the quality of the client–therapist relationship, or the client's preferences around therapy style.

The field of counselling and psychotherapy outcome research is dominated by studies that assess outcome in terms of changes in client scores on self-report measures of symptoms of anxiety, depression and other types of distress. Some researchers have sought to broaden the range of outcome research by carrying out studies that have collected data on the economic costs and benefits of therapy (Miller and Magruder, 1999) and on the way that clients and service users define and make sense of outcome in terms of their own criteria (McLeod, 2011b).

RESEARCH INTO THE PROCESS OF THERAPY

Beginning with the pioneering research programme of Carl Rogers in the 1940s, into the 'necessary and sufficient conditions' for therapeutic change, one of the key areas of research in counselling and psychotherapy has been the study of the *process* of therapy – the factors that contribute to outcome. Some of this research has used quantitative methods, such as questionnaires or rating scales completed by clients and therapists at the end of therapy sessions, or coding systems applied by independent raters to analyse processes that can be observed in video recordings of sessions. Other research has made use of qualitative methods, such as interviews with clients and therapists, and analysis of patterns of narrative and discourse in transcripts of therapy sessions (McLeod, 2011b).

The largest single body of research into the process of therapy has centred on the question of the characteristics of facilitative client–therapist relationships, for example using the Working Alliance Inventory to invite clients and therapists to record their perceptions of the strength of *bond*, *task* and *goal* dimensions of the relationship. This research has produced convincing evidence that the strength of the working alliance early in therapy, and successful resolution of ruptures in the alliance, are significant predictors of eventual good outcome in therapy (Cooper, 2008). Other research has used qualitative methods to examine the client's experience of the therapy process, and the ways that therapists use language to maintain control of therapy interactions. There is also extensive research into the nature of psychoanalytic processes in therapy, such as the role of transference and the impact in interpretations. Further information on the methods and findings of process research in therapy can be found in Cooper (2008) and Timulak (2008).

SYSTEMATIC CASE STUDY RESEARCH

The original founding figures of psychotherapy, such as Sigmund Freud and Joseph Wolpe, used case studies of their clinical practice to document and disseminate their new approaches and to explore the processes that seemed to be contributing to therapeutic change. Clinical case studies have continued to be used as a means of communicating new ideas about practice within the professional community. However, there has been a substantial amount of scepticism about the status of clinical case studies as a source of research evidence, on account of the methodological weaknesses associated with this mode of inquiry. Clinical case reports that are based solely on post-session notes made by the therapist in the case, which are then analysed and written up by that therapist, lack the kind of transparency and external scrutiny and verification that have come to be taken for granted in other spheres of counselling and psychotherapy research. As a result, there has been a decline in the number of case studies that have been published. This is regrettable, because in principle, case studies provide a unique perspective on what happens in therapy. Compared to other types of research, case studies are better able to reflect the complexity of therapy process and outcome, and to track the ways in which key change processes unfold over time. Case studies are also particularly effective at exploring the ways in which contextual factors influence the therapy process. In recent years there has been a resurgence of case study research, based on the adoption of a set of principles for systematic case inquiry (McLeod, 2010). These principles reflect two key methodological strategies: (1) the construction of a rich dataset on the case, drawn from a range of different sources of information; and (2) the analysis of case data by a group or team of researchers (usually including the therapist, and sometimes also including the client). The implementation of these principles, and the establishment of case study journals such as *Clinical Case Studies* and *Pragmatic Case Studies in Psychotherapy*, alongside the increasing willingness of other journals to publish systematic case studies, have meant that the case study method is now beginning to make a meaningful contribution to the evidence base for counselling and psychotherapy. This development is particularly welcome because it carries with it the potential to bridge the research–practice 'gap': practitioners are in a good position to collect and write up case study data, and practitioners enjoy reading case studies.

CONCLUSION

It is easy to see that, at the moment, therapy research does not always effectively relate to practice. However, it is no easy matter to remedy this situation. Therapy research at present is dominated by psychological assumptions and methods. Although there is an increasing acceptance of the idea of *methodological pluralism* (the use of many different research methods), it will only be when research techniques and ideas from fields such as sociology, anthropology and philosophy begin to make an impact on therapy research that an appreciable difference will be felt. Other critical issues

relate to the use of theory in therapy research. The emergence of eclectic and integrative approaches has been accompanied by a turning away from formal theories of the type espoused by Freud, Jung, Rogers, Kelly and other founding figures. The absence of theoretical awareness acts as a limiting factor in research because it has the result that research is restricted to recording and observing, rather than the testing of interesting and provocative hypotheses. A final issue arises in relation to the nature of the knowledge base of therapy. While disciplines like medicine, nursing and even social work are able to make use of well-defined clinical rules or procedures, therapy depends much more on the quality of the relationship between therapist and client, and the capacity of the therapist to improvise interventions rather than follow guidelines that are specified in advance. (Some branches of CBT may differ from the psychodynamic and humanistic therapies in this respect.) It is therefore difficult for therapy research to generate new clinical rules or interventions that can be 'slotted into' practice. It is important that both researchers and practitioners strive to find ways of making research more relevant for practice. It is also important to recognize that the complexity and ethical sensitivity of therapy research presents distinctive problems.

The growing emphasis that is placed on research in counselling and psychotherapy, and the multiple possible ways in which research can inform practice, have meant that it has become increasingly important for research training to be incorporated into counsellor and psychotherapist training programmes, and for research updating to be made available through continuing professional development networks. The central or core research competency that needs to be acquired during basic training is the ability to read and critically appraise the contribution that research articles and reviews can make to practice. Beyond this, trainees need to know about the strengths and weaknesses of different methods for evaluating therapy outcomes, and to be helped to develop their own position in relation to ongoing debates around the nature of evidence-based practice and the relative effectiveness of different therapy interventions for particular disorders. Finally, it is not possible to appreciate the research process without experiencing it first-hand and actually *doing* a research study of some kind. If counselling and psychotherapy are to gain and maintain credibility in a cultural environment in which the public holds expectations that professions are accountable and can produce evidence for the effectiveness of their activities, it is necessary for counsellors and psychotherapists from all sectors of the profession to come to terms with the role and meaning of research. There has been a tendency on the part of some therapists to assume that doing research and building a research base is something that CBT therapists do, and that other approaches to therapy, such as psychodynamic, transpersonal and narrative therapies, are working with processes that are not amenable to rigorous inquiry. This is a false assumption. Although there is no doubt that there is currently more evidence available around the processes and outcomes of CBT than there is for other approaches, there does exist a substantial research literature on humanistic/experiential and psychodynamic therapies, and smaller but nonetheless valuable sets of studies on most of the widely practised approaches (Cooper, 2008; Lambert, 2004; McLeod, 2011a).

REFERENCES

Barker, C., Pistrang, N. and Elliott, R. (2002) *Research Methods in Clinical Psychology: An Introduction for Students and Practitioners*. Chichester: Wiley.

Barkham, M., Hardy, G.E. and Mellor-Clark, J. (eds) (2010) *Developing and Delivering Practice-Based Evidence: A Guide for the Psychological Therapies*. Chichester: Wiley-Blackwell.

Cooper, M. (2008) *Essential Research Findings in Counselling and Psychotherapy: The Facts are Friendly*. London: Sage.

Elliott, R. (1998) A guide to the empirically supported treatments controversy. *Psychotherapy Research*, 8: 115–25.

Lambert, M. (ed.) (2004) *Bergin and Garfield's Handbook of Psychotherapy and Behavior Change* (5th edn). Chichester: Wiley.

Lambert, M.J. (2007) What we have learned from a decade of research aimed at improving psychotherapy outcome in routine care. *Psychotherapy Research*, 17 (1): 1–14.

McLeod, J. (1997) Reading, writing and research. In I. Horton and V. Varma (eds), *The Needs of Counsellors and Psychotherapists*. London: Sage.

McLeod, J. (2010) *Case Study Research in Counselling and Psychotherapy*. London: Sage.

McLeod, J. (2011a) *Doing Counselling Research* (3rd edn). London: Sage.

McLeod, J. (2011b) *Qualitative Research in Counselling and Psychotherapy* (2nd edn). London: Sage.

Miller, N.E. and Magruder, K.M. (eds) (1999) *Cost-Effectiveness of Psychotherapy: A Guide for Practitioners, Researchers and Policymakers*. New York: Oxford University Press.

Miller, S.D., Duncan, B.L. and Hubble, M.A. (2005) Outcome-informed clinical work. In J.C. Norcross and M.R. Goldfried (eds), *Handbook of Psychotherapy Integration*. New York: Oxford University Press.

Rowland, N. and Goss, S. (eds) (2000) *Evidence-Based Counselling and Psychological Therapies: Research and Applications*. London: Routledge.

Smith, M., Glass, G. and Miller, T. (1980) *The Benefits of Psychotherapy*. Baltimore: Johns Hopkins University Press.

Timulak, L. (2008) *Research in Counselling and Psychotherapy*. London: Sage.

Westen, D., Novotny, C.M. and Thompson-Brenner, H. (2004) The empirical status of empirically-supported psychotherapies: assumptions, findings, and reporting in controlled clinical trials. *Psychological Bulletin*, 130: 631–63.

Using the CORE System to Support Service Quality Development

JOHN MELLOR-CLARK AND MICHAEL BARKHAM

In the first edition of this handbook we introduced the CORE system as a quality evaluation system designed to offer a cost-free, practical and theoretical enhancement to the limitations of traditional approaches to service evaluation (Mellor-Clark and Barkham, 2000). In the second edition (Mellor-Clark and Barkham, 2006), we proposed quality evaluation as a key component to support the paradigm of practice-based evidence and profiled the CORE system as a resource for services wishing to assess and manage the relative quality of their local service delivery. In this third edition of the handbook, we update the profile of CORE's contribution to service quality development with a focus on the practical uses of the methodology for helping improve clinical effectiveness and counselling and psychotherapy service quality.

THE AIMS OF EVALUATION

In our earlier contributions, we maintained that the *raison d'être* of evaluation should be to enhance the quality of service provision and hence client care. Moreover, we emphasized that the activity of evaluation carried out by practitioners in routine settings is the means by which we can build an evidence base for counselling and psychotherapy that is grounded in practice and owned by practitioners. We referred to this as *practice-based evidence* (see Barkham et al., 2010a; 2010c) to complement the research-driven paradigm of *evidence-based practice* (see Bower and Gilbody, 2010). Practice-based evidence provides the foundations for generating questions that are grounded in the practice context and, for this reason, are seen to be relevant to practitioners and the delivery of routine services. Such questions may be pragmatic or theory driven, but they have in common a fundamental relevance to practice and provide evaluation activity that can operate at local, national or international levels via the development of practice research networks (e.g. see Andrews et al., 2011; Parry et al., 2010).

However, unfortunately all too often we observe counselling and psychological therapy services undertaking evaluation for evaluation's sake, typically relying on clients to provide most if not all information, and choosing measures on the basis of their accessibility or simplicity rather than their clinical and management utility. In short, we've asserted that it's all too common for evaluation to be about being seen to be doing the 'right' thing. To counteract this, we suggest that irrespective of whether practitioners believe that evaluation *is* the right thing, it is critical to do it for the *right reason*. This should be the primary aim of evaluation: to employ appropriate methods and measures capable of informing the quality of service provision, identify inadequacies, and thereby give information that assists in the development of service delivery. We term this activity *quality evaluation* and suggest that it should be the cornerstone of accountable service delivery and continuing professional development.

Indeed, in the previous editions of this chapter and in subsequent publications (e.g. Evans et al., 2006; Mellor-Clark et al., 2006b) we've proposed that the pragmatic aims of quality evaluation should be to measure and benchmark service quality in the following performance domains:

- develop the *appropriateness* of overall service structures by benchmarking assessment outcomes (see Cahill et al., 2006)
- enhance the *accessibility* of service provision by benchmarking and minimizing waiting time (see Trusler et al., 2006)
- improve the *acceptability* of service procedures by benchmarking and reducing unplanned endings (see Connell et al., 2006)
- increase the *effectiveness* of service practices by benchmarking and managing improvement and recovery rates (see Mullin et al., 2006)
- ensure client *safety* by benchmarking and managing clients' risk to self and others (see Bewick et al., 2006a)
- grow the *efficiency* of service delivery by benchmarking and managing the quality of outcomes data (see Bewick et al., 2006b)
- progress case mix *equity* in relation to local demographics (e.g. local age, ethnicity, employment, referral sources, etc.).

We have suggested that if evaluation methods contribute to the management and development of such performance domains, this would be a vast improvement on simply letting the need to evaluate predominate as the reason for involvement. It is in this context that we introduce the CORE system as a methodology designed for quality evaluation that we reprofile and update herein.

CORE METHODS AND SYSTEM TOOLS

The CORE system was developed by a multidisciplinary group of practitioners and researchers having a common interest in producing appropriate methods and tools to realize the benefits of quality evaluation (for full developmental accounts see Barkham et al., 2006; 2010b; Evans et al., 2002; Gray and Mellor-Clark, 2007; Mellor-Clark et al., 2006b). The content of the system was informed by extensive collaboration with practitioners, managers and service commissioners (Mellor-Clark et al., 1999).

Currently, we promote 'best practice' with the system as comprising a four-stage process involving up to six CORE measurement tools that we describe in turn hereafter.

1 At the first contact session clients should be invited to complete a *CORE Outcome Measure* (CORE-OM) to help profile their general psychological wellbeing over the last week.
2 Following this initial contact session, practitioners complete a *CORE Therapy Assessment Form* to profile the client across a standard set of case mix descriptors (e.g. demographics, social support, presenting concerns, etc.) that complement and contextualize the CORE outcome data.
3 Thereafter, on commencing therapy, clients are encouraged to complete pragmatically short subset measures (i.e. *CORE SF-A* and *SF-B*, *CORE-10* or *CORE-5*) at each ongoing therapy session, facilitating joint reflection on empirical changes using a *CORE Progress Tracking Chart*.
4 Finally, where clients attend a final discharge session they should be invited to complete a second CORE Outcome Measure whilst the practitioner completes a *CORE End of Therapy Form* to provide context on the therapy process and record practitioner-rated outcomes. Where clients initiate their own termination to therapy, practitioners should still complete an End of Therapy Form but utilize the last short measure as CORE outcome data for reflecting on empirical change.

This multidimensional data-collection strategy facilitates the collection of a comprehensive set of process and outcome data informed and evolved by the relative strengths of research, evaluation and audit. In addition, it is also informed by contemporary feedback methods and technologies (e.g. Duncan, 2010; Lambert, 2010). Descriptions of each of the tools follow.

CORE Outcome Measure

The CORE-OM (see Figure 4.11.1) is a double-sided, 34-item, client-completed questionnaire that addresses the clinical domains of *subjective wellbeing* (four items), *symptoms* (12 items which include anxiety, depression, trauma and physical symptoms) and *functioning* (12 items which include close relations, social relations and life functioning). In addition, the measure contains six items that address components of *risk or harm* that can be used as indicators of clients being at risk to themselves or to others. Each domain comprises both high- and low-intensity items to maximize sensitivity for problem severity. The measure has been found to function similarly to the PHQ-9, a measure of depression used by UK services within the Improving Access to Psychological Therapies programme (Gilbody et al., 2007).

CLINICAL

OUTCOMES in

ROUTINE

EVALUATION

OUTCOME MEASURE

Site ID — letters only / numbers only

Client ID

Therapist ID — numbers only (1) / numbers only (2)

Sub codes

Date form given — D D / M M / Y Y Y Y

Age — Male / Female

Stage Completed

S Screening
R Referral
A Assessment
F First Therapy Session
P Pre-therapy (unspecified)
D During Therapy
L Last Therapy Session
X Follow up 1
Y Follow up 2

Stage

Episode

IMPORTANT - PLEASE READ THIS FIRST

This form has 34 statements about how you have been OVER THE LAST WEEK.
Please read each statement and think how often you felt that way last week.
Then tick the box which is closest to this.
Please use a dark pen (not pencil) and tick clearly within the boxes.

Over the last week

		Not at all	Only Occasionally	Sometimes	Often	Most or all the time	OFFICE USE ONLY
1	I have felt terribly alone and isolated	0	1	2	3	4	F
2	I have felt tense, anxious or nervous	0	1	2	3	4	P
3	I have felt I have someone to turn to for support when needed	4	3	2	1	0	F
4	I have felt O.K. about myself	4	3	2	1	0	W
5	I have felt totally lacking in energy and enthusiasm	0	1	2	3	4	P
6	I have been physically violent to others	0	1	2	3	4	R
7	I have felt able to cope when things go wrong	4	3	2	1	0	F
8	I have been troubled by aches, pains or other physical problems	0	1	2	3	4	P
9	I have thought of hurting myself	0	1	2	3	4	R
10	Talking to people has felt too much for me	0	1	2	3	4	F
11	Tension and anxiety have prevented me doing important things	0	1	2	3	4	P
12	I have been happy with the things I have done	4	3	2	1	0	F
13	I have been disturbed by unwanted thoughts and feelings	0	1	2	3	4	P
14	I have felt like crying	0	1	2	3	4	W

Please turn over

(Continued)

Over the last week

		Not at all	Only Occasionally	Sometimes	Often	Most or all the time	OFFICE USE ONLY
15	I have felt panic or terror	0	1	2	3	4	P
16	I made plans to end my life	0	1	2	3	4	R
17	I have felt overwhelmed by my problems	0	1	2	3	4	W
18	I have had difficulty getting to sleep or staying asleep	0	1	2	3	4	P
19	I have felt warmth or affection for someone	4	3	2	1	0	F
20	My problems have been impossible to put to one side	0	1	2	3	4	P
21	I have been able to do most things I needed to	4	3	2	1	0	F
22	I have threatened or intimidated another person	0	1	2	3	4	R
23	I have felt despairing or hopeless	0	1	2	3	4	P
24	I have thought it would be better if I were dead	0	1	2	3	4	R
25	I have felt criticised by other people	0	1	2	3	4	F
26	I have thought I have no friends	0	1	2	3	4	F
27	I have felt unhappy	0	1	2	3	4	P
28	Unwanted images or memories have been distressing me	0	1	2	3	4	P
29	I have been irritable when with other people	0	1	2	3	4	F
30	I have thought I am to blame for my problems and difficulties	0	1	2	3	4	P
31	I have felt optimistic about my future	4	3	2	1	0	W
32	I have achieved the things I wanted to	4	3	2	1	0	F
33	I have felt humiliated or shamed by other people	0	1	2	3	4	F
34	I have hurt myself physically or taken dangerous risks with my health	0	1	2	3	4	R

THANK YOU FOR YOUR TIME IN COMPLETING THIS QUESTIONNAIRE

	(W)	(P)	(F)	(R)	All items	All minus R
Total Scores						
Mean Scores (Total score for each dimension divided by number of items completed in that dimension)						

Survey : 151 Copyright MHF and CORE System Group. Page : 2

Figure 4.11.1 *CORE Outcome Measure*

Source: CORE System Group. The CORE Outcome Measure © MHF & CORE System Group

The measure has been extensively validated (see Barkham et al., 2010b; Evans et al., 2002) and a series of publications help profile demonstrable utility for clinical assessment and service evaluation across NHS primary care services (e.g. Armstrong, 2010; Gibbard and Hanley, 2008), NHS secondary care services (e.g. Lucock et al., 2003), NHS specialist psychotherapy services (e.g. Chiesa et al., 2009), as well as higher education counselling services (e.g. Connell et al., 2008). Additionally, a wide range of unpublished local reports demonstrate equitable practical utility across a wide range of service sectors that include third-sector services; employee assistance and/or staff support; family/relationship/marital and/or sex therapy, gay and lesbian services, HIV support, and palliative care, to name but a few.

In designing, deploying and supporting the CORE-OM, there has been an emphasis on developing a user-friendly, pragmatic measure having a high level of utility for use in routine practice through simple support tools for scoring. Initially, the CORE System Group collected clinical data from a variety of service settings and client groups, including 'clients' and 'non-clients' from the general population (Evans et al., 2002). In short, the publicly available aggregated data from these two participant groups allow the practitioner to calculate easily the proportion of their caseload who scored within a client group at intake, and the proportion who moved to a 'non-client' or 'general population' group at discharge. The original process by which this is done requires the simple calculation of the mean CORE-OM score for each individual client, a comparison with the 'cut-off' scores, and a final determination as to the population the client score now most closely matches. Subsequently, the philosophy of quality evaluation places an emphasis on reviewing those cases where there was no identified change, or where there was deterioration. *The CORE System User Manual* (CORE System Group, 1998) gives more detail on these methods and can be downloaded from the CORE Support website along with copies of all CORE tools (see end of chapter).

Developments with CORE scoring have taken account of feedback from practitioners who identified the 0–4 mean score range as difficult because of the use of fractions (e.g. 1.76) and reported that it was easier to assign meaning to whole numbers rather than fractions of numbers. Consequently, the revised CORE-OM scoring method adopted a procedure of multiplying the mean score by 10 and calling this a clinical score (see Leach et al., 2006). Procedures for scoring the CORE-OM are set out in Table 4.11.1 and a look-up table of total scores and equivalent clinical scores are presented in Table 4.11.2.

Table 4.11.1   *Methods for scoring the CORE-OM*

To obtain the mean item score

Stage 1: add the total score
Stage 2: divide by the number of client completed items (i.e. 34 if none are missing)
Stage 3: result is a mean item score ranging from 0 to 4
Example: total score of 58 divided by 34; mean item score = 1.71

To obtain the clinical score

Method A: using the mean score
Stage 1: calculate the mean score (as above)
Stage 2: multiply the mean score by 10
Stage 3: result is a clinical score ranging from 0 to 40
Example: total score of 58 divided by 34, mean item score = 1.71; multiply by 10, clinical score = 17.1

Method B: using the look-up tables
Stage 1: add the total score
Stage 2: refer to look-up table (Table 4.11.2) to convert to clinical score
Example: total score of 58; look up, clinical score = 17.1

Method C: easy estimate method
Stage 1: add the total score
Stage 2: divide the total score by 10
Stage 3: multiply this score by 3
Example: total score of 58 divided by 10 gives 5.8; multiply by 3 gives 17.4. The look-up table (Table 4.11.2) shows that the actual clinical score is 17.1. Hence the estimate of 17.4 is fairly close to the true score when working at a practical level and wanting to have an immediate sense of the score

Practitioners should note that the look-up table only works correctly where clients answer all 34 questions on CORE-OM. Where clients do not respond to specific questions, the total score needs to be divided by the number of questions answered to get the mean score, and then the mean should be multiplied by 10 to produce the clinical score.

CORE-OM Subset Measures

In an attempt to improve the clinical and therapeutic utility of CORE outcome measurement, we have complemented the CORE-OM with a series of directly derived measures comprising subsets of questions from the CORE-OM. The aim has been to support 'outcomes management' (Okiishi et al., 2003) and the production of 'report cards' (Dickey, 1996) or progress charts (Duncan, 2010; Lambert, 2010) to review and, where necessary, revise or

Table 4.11.2   *Look-up table of CORE-OM scores and severity levels*

Non-clinical range

Total score	Clinical score	Simple score	Severity level
1	0.3		
2	0.6	0	
3	0.9		
4	1.2		
5	1.5	1	
6	1.8		
7	2.1		
8	2.4	2	
9	2.6		
10	2.9		Healthy
11	3.2		
12	3.5	3	
13	3.8		
14	4.1		
15	4.4	4	
16	4.7		
17	5.0		
18	5.3	5	
19	5.6		
20	5.9		
21	6.2		
22	6.5	6	
23	6.8		
24	7.1		
25	7.4	7	
26	7.6		
27	7.9		Low level
28	8.2		
29	8.5	8	
30	8.8		
31	9.1		
32	9.4	9	
33	9.7		

Clinical range — Mild, moderate, moderate to severe

Total score	Clinical score	Simple score	Severity level
Clinical cut-off level			
34	10.0		
35	10.3	10	
36	10.6		
37	10.9		
38	11.2		
39	11.5	11	
40	11.8		
41	12.1		
42	12.4		Mild level
43	12.6	12	
44	12.9		
45	13.2		
46	13.5	13	
47	13.8		
48	14.1		
49	14.4	14	
50	14.7		
51	15.0		
52	15.3	15	
53	15.6		
54	15.9		
55	16.2		
56	16.5	16	
57	16.8		
58	17.1		Moderate level
59	17.4	17	
60	17.6		
61	17.9		
62	18.2		
63	18.5	18	
64	18.8		
65	19.1		
66	19.4	19	
67	19.7		
68	20.0		
69	20.3	20	
70	20.6		
71	20.9		
72	21.2		
73	21.5	21	
74	21.8		
75	22.1		Moderate to severe level
76	22.4	22	
77	22.6		
78	22.9		
79	23.2		
80	23.5	23	
81	23.8		
82	24.1		
83	24.4	24	
84	24.7		

Clinical range — Severe

Total score	Clinical score	Simple score	Severity level
85	25.0		
86	25.3	25	
87	25.6		
88	25.9		
89	26.2		
90	26.5	26	
91	26.8		
92	27.1		
93	27.4	27	
94	27.6		
95	27.9		
96	28.2		
97	28.5	28	
98	28.8		
99	29.1		
100	29.4	29	
101	29.7		
102	30.0		
103	30.3	30	
104	30.6		
105	30.9		
106	31.2		
107	31.5	31	
108	31.8		
109	32.1		
110	32.4	32	Severe level
111	32.6		
112	32.9		
113	33.2		
114	33.5	33	
115	33.8		
116	34.1		
117	34.4	34	
118	34.7		
119	35.0		
120	35.3	35	
121	35.6		
122	35.9		
123	36.2		
124	36.5	36	
125	36.8		
126	37.1		
127	37.4	37	
128	37.6		
129	37.9		
130	38.2		
131	38.5	38	
132	38.8		
133	39.1		
134	39.4	39	
135	39.7		
136	40.0	40	

Guidance notes

The original mean item score can be readily calculated by dividing the clinical score by 10.

The 'simple' score uses the first integer only of the clinical score as a rough guide.

The reliable change index is 5 points and the cut-off level is a clinical score of 10 (or 0.5 and 1 respectively if using the traditional scoring method).

enhance therapeutic interventions. Thumbnail summaries of the derived measures follow.

CORE SF-A and CORE SF B (Cahill et al., 2006) are 18-item questionnaires that comprise differing subsets of CORE-OM questions that cover all four domains as follows: subjective wellbeing, four items (the same items in SF-A and SF-B); problems, six items; functioning, six items; and risk, two items. The primary purpose of these forms is to use alternate forms on a session-by-session basis, thereby reducing memory effects.

CORE-10 (see Figure 4.11.2) was initially designed as a screening measure to complement CORE-OM by providing a short and easy-to-score measure that is used to review progress for case management (Barkham et al., 2010b), inform supervision (Unsworth et al., 2011), and inform the calculation of pre- to post-therapy change where clients have initiated their own termination to therapy (Andrews et al., 2011).

CORE-5 was devised as an ultra-brief session-by-session monitoring tool – a thermometer (Barkham et al., 2010b) and an aid for signalling client progress. Its use differs from CORE-OM, CORE SF-A and SF-B and CORE-10 in that it is not a pre-post change measure, but a signalling measure to help flag any necessity for action where scores (for example) become static for a number of sessions.

CORE Progress Tracking Chart

To provide practical support for the scoring of session-by-session measurement, a CORE Progress Tracking Chart was developed to help inform and enhance client feedback (see Figure 4.11.3). In the illustration, the shaded bands provide a quick picture of the severity of the client's distress, as a reflection of NICE guidance steps. A score above the 'clinical cut-off' of 10 profiles the client to belong to a clinical population. Subsequent 'improvement' (statistically a five-point score change – or the movement from one severity band to another) and 'recovery' (movement below clinical cutoff) are easily recordable and visible on the chart as and when they occur. Utilizing the CORE Progress Tracking Chart at each session helps record a trajectory of progress for practitioners and clients to reflect upon. Additionally, in Figure 4.11.3 a lower dashed line marked 'Risk cut-off' shows the risk score to help record if the client is clinically at risk; if the client is at significant risk, then fuller risk assessment becomes the first priority (using CORE-OM). The cells at the bottom of the chart show the date of each consultation, the practitioner or clinician, which length measure was completed, and the treatment for each session.

CORE Therapy Assessment Form

To complement the client self-report tools (i.e. CORE-OM, CORE SF-A and SF-B, CORE-10 and CORE-5), the double-sided CORE Therapy Assessment Form (see Figure 4.11.4) helps record a 'core' set of contextual information that aids the quality of both client/patient assessment and overall service development (Mellor-Clark et al., 1999). To enhance patient assessment, the form collects important contextual information including: patient/client support; previous/concurrent attendance for psychological therapy; medication; and a categorization system to record presenting difficulties, their impact on day-to-day functioning and any associated risk. To enhance the development of service quality, the form collects data on critical assessment audit items that profile the accessibility and appropriateness of service provision. These include patient/client demographics, waiting times, and the suitability of referral.

CORE End of Therapy Form

To support client discharge, the CORE End of Therapy Form (see Figure 4.11.5) complements the other components and captures a 'core' set of treatment descriptors that aid the interpretation of CORE-OM scores to (again) help contextualize therapy outcomes and inform service development. To contextualize the outcomes of therapy, the form collects profile information that includes therapy length, type of intervention, modality and frequency. To enhance the development of service quality, the form collects data on critical discharge audit items that profile the effectiveness and efficiency of service provision. These include problem and risk review, therapy benefits, session attendance rates, and therapy ending (i.e. planned or unplanned). Ways in which users of the CORE system data are supported to help maximize the data yield for service management and development are the focus of the final part of this chapter.

CORE Population Specific Tools

Finally, to complete the full portfolio of CORE tools developed to support quality evaluation, there are derived measures for specific populations identified by the addition of a population-specific prefix/suffix. These adaptations include GP-CORE for use with *general population* samples that are not specifically clinical, such as new students enrolling for university education (see Sinclair et al., 2005). And for use with *young persons* is the YP-CORE

CLINICAL
OUTCOMES in
ROUTINE
EVALUATION

CORE-10
Screening
Measure

Site ID ☐☐☐☐☐

Client ID

☐☐ / ☐☐☐☐☐☐☐
letters only   numbers only

Sub codes

☐☐☐☐ / ☐☐☐ / ☐☐☐
Therapist ID   numbers only (1)   numbers only (2)

Date form given
D D   M M   Y Y Y Y
☐☐ / ☐☐ / ☐☐☐☐

Stage Completed
S Screening
R Referral
A Assessment
F First Therapy Session
P Pre-therapy (unspecified)
D During Therapy
L Last therapy session
X Follow up 1
Y Follow up 2

Episode ☐   Stage ☐

Gender
☐ Male   Age ☐☐
☐ Female

IMPORTANT - PLEASE READ THIS FIRST
This form has 10 statements about how you have been OVER THE LAST WEEK.
Please read each statement and think how often you felt that way last week.
Then tick the box which is closest to this.
Please use a dark pen (not pencil) and tick clearly within the boxes.

Over the last week...

	Not at all	Only occasionally	Sometimes	Often	Most or all of the time
1 I have felt tense, anxious or nervous	☐ 0	☐ 1	☐ 2	☐ 3	☐ 4
2 I have felt I have someone to turn to for support when needed	☐ 4	☐ 3	☐ 2	☐ 1	☐ 0
3 I have felt able to cope when things go wrong	☐ 4	☐ 3	☐ 2	☐ 1	☐ 0
4 Talking to people has felt too much for me	☐ 0	☐ 1	☐ 2	☐ 3	☐ 4
5 I have felt panic or terror	☐ 0	☐ 1	☐ 2	☐ 3	☐ 4
6 I have made plans to end my life	☐ 0	☐ 1	☐ 2	☐ 3	☐ 4
7 I have had difficulty getting to sleep or staying asleep	☐ 0	☐ 1	☐ 2	☐ 3	☐ 4
8 I have felt despairing or hopeless	☐ 0	☐ 1	☐ 2	☐ 3	☐ 4
9 I have felt unhappy	☐ 0	☐ 1	☐ 2	☐ 3	☐ 4
10 Unwanted images or memories have been distressing me	☐ 0	☐ 1	☐ 2	☐ 3	☐ 4

Total (Clinical Score*) ☐

---

* Procedure: Add together the item scores, then divide by the number of questions completed to get the mean score, then multiply by 10 to get the Clinical Score.
Quick method for the CORE-10 (if all items completed): Add together the item scores to get the Clinical Score.

Thank you for your time in completing this questionnaire

Figure 4.11.2   *CORE-10 Outcome Measure*

Source: CORE System Trust

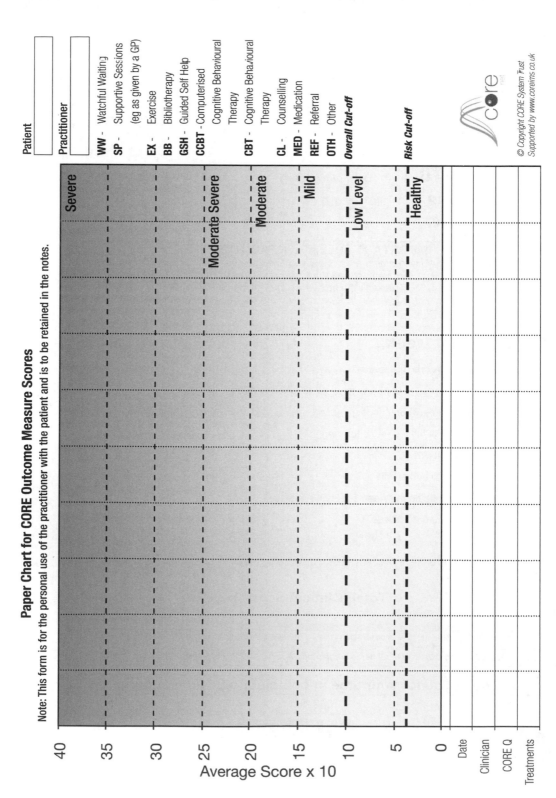

Figure 4.11.3   *CORE Progress Tracking Chart*

Source: CORE System Trust

CLINICAL
OUTCOMES in
ROUTINE
EVALUATION

**THERAPY
ASSESSMENT
FORM** v.2

Site ID	_ _ _ (letters) _ _ _ (numbers)
Client ID	_ _ _ _ _ _ _ _
Sub Codes	TH ID number _ _ _ _ SC2 numbers _ _ _ _ SC3 numbers _ _ _
Referrer(s)	_ _ _ _

Age _ _

Male ☐   Female ☐

Employment ☐   ☐

Ethnic Origin ☐   ☐

Referral date   D D / M M / Y Y Y Y

First assessment date attended   D D / M M / Y Y Y Y

Last assessment date   D D / M M / Y Y Y Y

Total number of assessments ☐

Previously seen for therapy in this service?   Yes ☐   No ☐   Episode ☐

Months since last episode _ _ _

Is this a follow-up/review appointment?   Yes ☐   No ☐

Relationships/support   *Please tick as many boxes as appropriate*

Living alone (not including dependents) ☐
Living with partner ☐
Caring for children under 5 years ☐
Caring for children over 5 years ☐
Living with parents/guardian ☐
Living with other relatives/friends ☐

Full time carer (of disabled/elderly etc) ☐
Living in shared accommodation (eg lodgings) ☐
Living in temporary accommodation (eg hostel) ☐
Living in institution/hospital ☐
Other ☐   _____

Current/previous use of services for psychological problems?
Please tick as many boxes as appropriate

		Concurrent	<12 mths	>12 mths
Primary	GP or other member of primary care team (eg practice nurse, counsellor)............	☐	☐	☐
Secondary	In primary care setting	☐	☐	☐
	In community setting	☐	☐	☐
	In hospital setting on sessional basis	☐	☐	☐
	Day care services (eg day hospital)	☐	☐	☐
	Hospital admission < =10 days	☐	☐	☐
	Hospital admission > =11 days	☐	☐	☐
Specialist	Psychotherapy/psychological treatments from specialist team (sessional)	☐	☐	☐
	Attendance at day therapeutic programme	☐	☐	☐
	Inpatient treatment	☐	☐	☐
Other	Counsellor in eg voluntary, religious, work, educational setting	☐	☐	☐

Is the client currently prescribed medication to help with their psychological problem(s)?   Yes ☐   No ☐

If yes, please indicate type of medication:

Anti-psychotics ☐ (neuroleptics/major tranquillizers)   Anti-depressants ☐   Anxiolytics/Hypnotics ☐ (minor tranquillizers)   Other ☐

(Continued)

(Continued)

Brief description of reason for referral

Identified Problems/Concerns

Severity | < 6 months | 6-12 months | > 12 months | Recurring/continuous

Depression

Anxiety/Stress

Psychosis

Personality Problems

Cognitive/Learning

Eating Disorder

Physical Problems

Addictions

Severity | < 6 months | 6-12 months | > 12 months | Recurring contin.

Trauma/abuse

Bereavement/loss

Self esteem

Interpersonal/relationship

Living/Welfare

Work/Academic

Other *(specify below)*

Risk | None | Mild | Mod | Sev

Suicide

Self Harm

Harm to others

Legal/Forensic

ICD-10 CODES

F/Z Main code Sub-code   F/Z Main Code Sub-code

1   3

F/Z Main Code Sub-code   F/Z Main Code Sub-code

2   4

What has the client done to cope with/avoid their problems? *Please tick, and then specify actions*

Positive actions   Negative actions

Assessment outcome *(tick one box only)*

Assessment/one session only

Accepted for therapy

Accepted for trial period of therapy

Long consultation

* Referred to other service

* Unsuitable for therapy at this time

*If the client is not entering therapy give brief reason

Figure 4.11.4   *CORE Therapy Assessment Form*

Source: CORE System Group. CORE Therapy Assessment Form © The CORE System Group

CLINICAL
OUTCOMES in
ROUTINE
EVALUATION

**END OF
THERAPY
FORM** V.2

Site ID — letters — numbers

Client ID

Sub Codes — Therapist ID — SC4 numbers — SC5 numbers

Date therapy commenced — D D / M M / Y Y Y Y

Date therapy completed — D D / M M / Y Y Y Y

Number of sessions planned

Number of sessions attended

Number of sessions unattended

What type of therapy was undertaken with the client? *Please tick as many boxes as appropriate*

Psychodynamic ☐	Person-centred ☐
Psychoanalytic ☐	Integrative ☐
Cognitive ☐	Systemic ☐
Behavioural ☐	Supportive ☐
Cognitive/Behavioural ☐	Art ☐
Structured/Brief ☐	Other *(specify below)* ☐

What modality of therapy was undertaken with the client? *Please tick as many boxes as appropriate*

Individual ☐	Family ☐
Group ☐	Marital/Couple ☐

What was the frequency of therapy with the client?

More than once weekly ☐	Less than once weekly ☐
Weekly ☐	Not at a fixed frequency ☐

Which of the following best describes the ending of therapy?

Unplanned ☐	**Planned** ☐
Due to crisis ☐	Planned from outset ☐
Due to loss of contact ☐	Agreed during therapy ☐
Client did not wish to continue ☐	Agreed at end of therapy ☐
Other unplanned ending *(specify below)* ☐	Other planned ending *(specify below)* ☐

(Continued)

(Continued)

Review of Identified Problems/Concerns

Severity / Therapy Issue

Depression

Anxiety/Stress

Psychosis

Personality Problems

Cognitive/Learning

Physical Problems

Eating Disorder

Addictions

Severity / Therapy Issue

Trauma/Abuse

Bereavement/Loss

Self esteem

Interpersonal/relationship

Living/Welfare

Work/Academic

Other *(specify below)*

Risk

	None	Mild	Mod	Sev
Suicide	☐	☐	☐	☐
Self Harm	☐	☐	☐	☐
Harm to others	☐	☐	☐	☐
Legal/Forensic	☐	☐	☐	☐

Contextual Factors

	Poor	Moderate	Good
Motivation	☐	☐	☐
Working Alliance	☐	☐	☐
Psychological Mindedness	☐	☐	☐

Benefits of Therapy

Improved (Yes / No) / Not addressed

Personal insight/understanding

Expression of feelings/problems

Exploration of feelings/problems

Coping strategies/techniques

Access to practical help

Other benefits
Tick box and then specify below

Improved (Yes / No) / Not addressed

Control/planning/decision making

Subjective well-being

Symptoms

Day to day functioning

Personal relationships

Has contact with this service resulted in a change of medication?   Yes ☐   No ☐   Not applicable ☐

If yes, is this change likely to be of benefit to the client?   Yes ☐   No ☐

Details of change: Started ☐   Discontinued ☐   Increased ☐   Decreased ☐   Modified ☐

Has the client been given a follow-up appointment?   **Number of months until appointment**

Yes ☐   No ☐

Survey : 78   Copyright CORE System Group   Page : 2

Figure 4.11.5   *CORE End of Therapy Form*

Source: CORE System Group. CORE End of Therapy Form © The CORE System Group

(Twigg et al., 2009), designed for people in their adolescent years (age range 11–16) and comprising four problem and four functioning items together with single items to tap risk and wellbeing. For *learning disabilities*, CORE-LD has been adapted by service users with learning difficulties (see Brooks and Davies, 2007; Marshall and Willoughby-Booth, 2007) and contains both simplified CORE-OM items and new items designed to cover the major issues faced by people with LD. To aid the ease of use of the measure, CORE-LD has a shorter Likert scale comprising a three-point rather than five-point scale, and also has graphical illustrations presented parallel to each of the 14 questions to aid comprehension. Finally, a comprehensive programme of translations is ongoing with CORE-OM (see Gray and Mellor-Clark, 2007) yielding psychometric validation papers (e.g. Palmieri et al., 2009).

UTILIZING CORE SYSTEM DATA FOR SERVICE DEVELOPMENT

When the CORE system was launched in 1998, initial support from the CORE System Group entailed data entry, data analysis, and standardized reports on batches of data sent annually to the research team. Despite initial attractive advantages, a number of limitations were quickly apparent that included: (1) lack of engagement with the aggregated results (which may be up to 12 months old); (2) critical data quality problems only being recognized retrospectively; (3) the extent of the resources required to provide the individual practitioner with personal empirical feedback; and (4) an inability for services to interact with their data by exploring clients in specific data categories. Examples of this latter limitation included a desire to explore filtered data for those clients showing deterioration, those having excessive waiting times, and those terminating therapy suddenly through a loss of contact with the service.

For these and other reasons, and in consultation with system users, the CORE system has evolved through two generations of software systems to offer cost-efficient in-house analysis and reporting provided either by a standalone personal computer (CORE-PC) format or via online internet access (CORE Net). We briefly review the relative contributions of each of these systems in turn.

CORE-PC was launched in 2001 to promote *quality evaluation* and provide services with a support resource to take control of their own evaluation on an ongoing basis to promote a 'research-practitioner' model, rather than export data to external expertise.

Over the last 10 years of deploying, refining and supporting such a relatively low-cost resource, the four key strengths have been reported to include: (1) the ability to provide information to service stakeholders as and when it was requested; (2) the ability for service practitioners to analyse their own data for personal feedback (which generated a sense of shared ownership); (3) the ability to be able to categorize easily client outcomes according to whether their CORE outcome profile categorized them as 'improved', 'deteriorated' or 'the same'; and (4) the ability to explore meaningful subsets of clients for insight into potential problems with service organization and delivery (Mellor-Clark et al., 2006a).

Between 2001 and 2010 we gathered feedback on CORE-PC from several hundred services and progressively improved the structure and utility of reporting to enhance the use of the system for service management and development. Iteratively, we promoted our philosophy of *quality evaluation* and refined it through an analytic model that pragmatically focused on tracking clients through a set of discrete stages in their journey into and through services. These stages comprised: (1) case mix equity; (2) the quality of access measured via referral to first contact waiting time; (3) the assessment outcome; (4) the engagement of the client in their therapy experience; and (5) the final measurement of clinical and/or reliable change at treatment termination. Building such a stagewise approach to data analysis encouraged services to consider the progressive attrition of their clients over the 'journey' and helped them focus on specific aspects of their CORE data that could help them understand and ultimately reduce attrition.

To help services understand the relative quality of their service provision on indicators linked to specific stages in the client's journey, we developed a set of performance indicators and service descriptors that were refined for publication in a special edition of *Counselling and Psychotherapy* (issue 1, 2006) to act as benchmarks that could be used by services for appraisal and performance management. We also compiled a series of articles on the application of the CORE system in a special issue of the *European Journal of Psychotherapy and Health* (issue 2, 2006).

In developing CORE performance indicators we wanted to help services understand the relativity of their own service profiles, while respecting and protecting the traditional culture of anonymity and confidentiality central to counselling and psychological therapy philosophy and activity. Consequently, we developed a graphical indicator that took the form of a 'thermometer' as illustrated in Figure 4.11.6. The thermometer format summarizes the range of percentages for a specific indicator (from 60 to 89 per cent in this example). In its usual coloured representation the band at the top of the thermometer is green and shows the range of percentages profiled for the top 25 per cent (i.e. quartile) of services; the second quartile band (in yellow) and the third band (in amber) show the midquartile ranges; and the lower band (in red) shows the range of percentages for the lowest quarter of all services (in this case 60–68 per cent). A percentile to the right of the thermometer is usually displayed to indicate the national average profile (in this case 75 per cent). In use, a service compares their own service profile on a specific indicator to those of the performance thermometer to get an indication of their relative performance. As stated, roughly speaking, if a service's profile is in the green, it is assumed to be high or desirable, while red equates to low or not so desirable. Where the indicator functions such that a low rate is the desired outcome, then the ordering of colours is reversed such that 'green' appears at the bottom to help illustrate that low figures are good (as in waiting times of percentage of unattended appointments).

The measures and monitoring tools described above represent work concerned with the reflective monitoring and management of service quality. Over recent years, outcome measurement systems in the UK and beyond have needed to evolve to be responsive to the developing requirements for increased transparency and accountability (see Barkham et al., 2010c). Accordingly, we have used the lessons learned from the initial decade of work to enhance the quality of the measurement system and move into a second generation of quality evaluation through our CORE Net software (Andrews et al., 2011; Gray and Mellor-Clark, 2007; Unsworth et al., 2011). This web-based technology contrasts with CORE-PC's focus on retrospective methods to promote a dynamic data capture method focused on real-time data capture, analysis and reporting whilst the client remains present. This method brings together the aforementioned CORE-10 and CORE-5 tools to be used session by session in order to generate immediate clinical feedback and flag (alert) reports that help the busy practitioner focus on matters that need attention. Thus client improvement and recovery are potentially improved in real time by practitioners' (and potentially supervisors') attention being drawn to warning flags that indicate which clients necessitate careful review. Drawing on the seminal work by Mike Lambert (2010) and Barry Duncan (2010), CORE Net also includes clinical support tools such as ARM-5 (Cahill et al., submitted) which is a five-item measure designed to help detect problems in the therapeutic alliance between client and practitioner (for a practical description of use in routine clinical practice, see

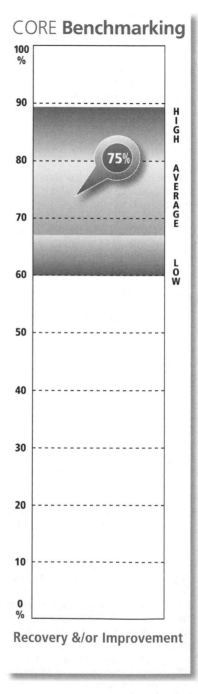

Figure 4.11.6   *Example of a CORE system performance indicator: clients meeting criteria for recovery and/or improvement*

Source: Benchmarks for Higher Education Counselling Services (CORE IMS, July 2010)

Unsworth et al., 2011). Functional profiles of CORE Net are available online at www.coreims.co.uk.

In conclusion, the CORE system methodology places considerable value on client-completed measures and has developed a wide range of self-report tools derived from the original CORE-OM, complemented by context-setting tools completed by practitioners at assessment and discharge. The tools are designed to be used either in simple ways by hand scoring and tracking, or with greater sophistication with the aid of computer software. CORE-PC offers excellent tools for retrospective data collection and reflective analysis comparative to a growing portfolio of published benchmarks. CORE Net adds more extensive tools for tracking and managing individual client progress and has been adopted widely not just for use with CORE measurement tools, but also with other tools that meet local or national measurement needs or requirements. These include support for the minimum dataset of the Improving Access to Psychological Therapies programme, along with specialist tools for eating disorder services, psychosexual therapy services, family therapy, employee assistance programmes, and higher education staff and student support services, to name but a few. Underpinning all such developments is our central philosophy that the approach of engaging and sustaining the use of such systems needs to be bottom-up. Using data routinely to improve practice needs to be rooted in daily practice so that it can then filter upwards to contribute not only to improving practice but also to enhancing the scientific evidence for the effectiveness of the psychological therapies.

RECOMMENDED READING

For a comprehensive overview of therapy research findings and their implications for clinical practice, *Essential Research Findings in Counselling and Psychotherapy* by Mick Cooper (2008) brings together a vast amount of material in a relevant and interesting way. Our own edited book, entitled *Developing and Delivering Practice-Based Evidence: A Guide for the Psychological Therapies* (2010) offers a comprehensive breadth of contributions from pioneers in the field that profile measurement methods, measurement systems, approaches to data, and improvement management practices. For those interested in the use of measurement, monitoring and feedback in clinical practice, Mike Lambert's *Prevention of Treatment Failure* (2010) provides a seminal empirical case to

promote the regular use of brief assessments to identify client progress, or lack of it, and guide change in therapy in pursuit of enhanced client outcomes. A natural complement to the Lambert text is Barry Duncan's book *On Becoming a Better Therapist* (2010), which shows how gathering feedback from clients at every session helps therapists identify and focus on the key issues, quantify when things are not going well, and make changes to improve client outcomes. The difference between Lambert's text and Duncan's is that whilst the former focuses on formal empirical investigation, the latter makes highly effective use of anecdote, offering practical guidance on how to engage clients and their resources in their own improvement. Finally, for more information on the CORE system visit www.coreims.co.uk; to access copies of our measures visit www.coreims.co.uk/forms_mailer.php; and download our portfolio publication *CORE: A Decade of Development* from www.coreims.co.uk/CORE-A-Decade-of-Development.pdf to understand how the system is used in everyday clinical practice.

REFERENCES

Andrews, W., Twigg, E., Minami, T. and Johnson, G. (2011) Piloting a practice research network: a 12-month evaluation of the human givens approach in primary care at a general medical practice. *Psychology and Psychotherapy: Theory, Research and Practice*, advance online publication. DOI 10.1111/j.2044-8341.2010.02004.x.

Armstrong, J. (2010) How effective are minimally trained/experienced volunteer mental health counsellors? Evaluation of CORE outcome data. *Counselling and Psychotherapy Research*, 10: 22–31.

Barkham, M., Mellor-Clark. J., Connell, J. and Cahill, J. (2006) A CORE approach to practice-based evidence: a brief history of the origins and applications of the CORE-OM and CORE system. *Counselling & Psychotherapy Research*, 6: 3–15.

Barkham, M., Hardy, G. and Mellor-Clark, J. (2010a) *Developing and Delivering Practice-Based Evidence: A Guide for the Psychological Therapies*. Chichester: Wiley.

Barkham, M., Mellor-Clark, J., Connell, J., Evans, C., Evans, R. and Margison, F. (2010b) Clinical Outcomes in Routine Evaluation (CORE). The CORE measures and system: measuring, monitoring and managing quality evaluation in the psychological therapies. In M. Barkham, G.E. Hardy and J. Mellor-Clark (eds), *Developing and Delivering Practice-Based Evidence: A Guide for the Psychological Therapies* (pp. 311–25). Chichester: Wiley.

Barkham, M., Stiles, W.B., Lambert, M.J. and Mellor-Clark, J. (2010c) Building a rigorous and relevant knowledge base for the psychological therapies. In M. Barkham, G.E. Hardy and J. Mellor-Clark (eds), *Developing and Delivering Practice-Based Evidence: A Guide for the Psychological Therapies* (pp. 21–61). Chichester: Wiley.

Bewick, B.M., McBride, J. and Barkham, M. (2006a) When clients and practitioners have differing views of risk: benchmarks for improving assessment and practice. *Counselling & Psychotherapy Research*, 6: 50–9.

Bewick, B.M., Trusler, K., Mullin, T., Grant, S. and Mothersole, G. (2006b) Routine outcome measurement completion rates of the CORE-OM in primary care psychological therapies and counselling. *Counselling & Psychotherapy Research*, 6: 33–40.

Bower, P. and Gilbody, S. (2010) The current view of evidence and evidence based practice. In M. Barkham, G.E. Hardy and J. Mellor-Clark (eds), *Developing and Delivering Practice-Based Evidence: A Guide for the Psychological Therapies* (pp. 3–20). Chichester: Wiley.

Brooks, M. and Davies, S. (2007) Pathways to participatory research in developing a tool to measure feelings. *British Journal of Learning Disabilities*, 36: 128–33.

Cahill, J., Barkham, M., Stiles, W.B., Twigg, E., Rees, A., Hardy, G.E. and Evans, C. (2006) Convergent validity of the CORE measures with measures of depression for clients in brief cognitive therapy for depression. *Journal of Counseling Psychology*, 53: 253–9.

Cahill, J., Stiles, W.B., Barkham, M., Hardy, G.E., Stone, G., Agnew-Davis, R. and Unsworth, G. (submitted). Two short forms of the Agnew Relationship Measure: the ARM-5 and ARM-12.

Chiesa, M., Fonagy, P., Bateman, A.W. and Mace, C. (2009) Psychiatric morbidity and treatment pathway outcomes of patients presenting to specialist NHS psychodynamic psychotherapy services: results from a multi-centre study. *Psychology and Psychotherapy: Theory, Research and Practice*, 82: 83–98.

Connell, J., Grant, S. and Mullin, T. (2006) Client initiated termination of therapy at NHS primary care counselling services. *Counselling & Psychotherapy Research*, 6: 60–7.

Connell, J., Barkham, M. and Mellor-Clark, J. (2008) The effectiveness of UK student counselling services: an analysis using the CORE system. *British Journal of Guidance and Counselling*, 36: 1–18.

Cooper, M. (2008) *Essential Research Findings in Counselling and Psychotherapy*. London: Sage.

CORE System Group (1998) *The CORE System User Manual*. Leeds: Psychological Therapies Research Centre.

Dickey, B. (1996) The development of report cards for mental health care. In L.I. Sederer and B. Dickey (eds), *Outcomes Assessment in Clinical Practice* (pp. 156–60). Baltimore: Williams & Wilkins.

Duncan, B.L. (2010) *On Becoming a Better Therapist*. Washington, DC: APA.

Evans, C., Connell, J., Barkham, M., Margison, F., Mellor-Clark, J., McGrath, G. and Audin, K. (2002) Towards a standardised brief outcome measure: psychometric properties and utility of the CORE-OM. *British Journal of Psychiatry*, 180: 51–60.

Evans, R., Mellor-Clark, J., Barkham, M. and Mothersole, G. (2006) Routine outcome measurement and service quality management in NHS primary care psychological therapy services. *European Journal of Psychotherapy and Counselling*, 8: 141–61.

Gibbard, I. and Hanley, T. (2008) A five-year evaluation of the effectiveness of person-centred counselling in routine clinical practice in primary care. *Counselling and Psychotherapy Research*, 8: 215–22.

Gilbody, S., Richards, D. and Barkham, M. (2007) Diagnosing depression in primary care using self-completed instruments: UK validation of PHQ-9 and CORE-OM. *British Journal of General Practice*, 57: 650–2.

Gray, P. and Mellor-Clark, J. (2007) *CORE: A Decade of Development*. www.coreims.co.uk/CORE-A-Decade-of-Development.pdf.

Lambert, M.J. (2010) *Prevention of Treatment Failure: The Use of Measuring, Monitoring, and Feedback in Clinical Practice*. Washington, DC: APA.

Leach, C., Lucock, M., Barkham, M., Stiles, W.B., Noble, R. and Iveson, S. (2006) Transforming between Beck Depression Inventory and CORE-OM scores in routine clinical practice. *British Journal of Clinical Psychology*, 45: 153–66.

Lucock, M., Leach, C., Iveson, S., Lynch, K., Horsefield, C. and Hall, P. (2003) A systematic approach to practice-based evidence in a psychological therapy service. *Clinical Psychology & Psychotherapy*, 10: 389–99.

Marshall, K. and Willoughby-Booth, S. (2007) Modifying the Clinical Outcomes in Routine Evaluation measure for use with people who have a learning disability. *British Journal of Learning Disabilities*, 35: 107–12.

Mellor-Clark, J. and Barkham, M. (2000) Quality evaluation: methods, measures and meaning. In C. Feltham and I. Horton (eds), *The Handbook of Counselling and Psychotherapy*. London: Sage.

Mellor-Clark, J. and Barkham, M. (2006) The CORE system: developing and delivering practice-based evidence through quality evaluation. In C. Feltham and I. Horton (eds), *The Handbook of Counselling and Psychotherapy* (2nd edn). London: Sage.

Mellor-Clark, J., Barkham, M., Connell, J. and Evans, C. (1999) Practice-based evidence and need for a standardised evaluation system: informing the design of the CORE system. *European Journal of Psychotherapy, Counselling and Health*, 2: 357–74.

Mellor-Clark, J., Barkham, M., Mothersole, G., McInnes, B. and Evans, R. (2006a) Reflections on benchmarking NHS primary care psychological therapies and counselling. *Counselling & Psychotherapy Research*, 6: 81–7.

Mellor-Clark, J., Curtis Jenkins, A., Evans, R., Mothersole, G. and McInnes, B. (2006b) Resourcing a CORE network to develop a national research database to help enhance psychological therapies and counselling service provision. *Counselling & Psychotherapy Research*, 6: 16–22.

Mullin, T., Barkham, M., Mothersole, G., Bewick, B.M. and Kinder, A. (2006) Recovery and improvement benchmarks in routine primary care mental health settings. *Counselling & Psychotherapy Research*, 6: 68–80.

Okiishi, J., Lambert, M.J., Nielsen, S.L. and Ogles, B.M. (2003) Waiting for supershrink: an empirical analysis of therapist effects. *Clinical Psychology & Psychotherapy*, 10: 361–73.

Palmieri, G., Evans, C., Hansen, V., Brancaleoni, G., Ferrari, S., Porcelli, P., Reitano, F. and Rigatelli, M. (2009) Validation of the Italian version of the Clinical Outcomes in Routine Evaluation Outcome Measure (CORE-OM). *Clinical Psychology and Psychotherapy*, 16: 444–9.

Parry, G., Castonguay, L.G., Borkovecc, T.D. and Wolf, A.W. (2010) Practice research networks and psychological services research in the UK and USA. In M. Barkham, G.E. Hardy and J. Mellor-Clark (eds), *Developing and Delivering Practice-Based Evidence: A Guide for the Psychological Therapies* (pp. 311–25). Chichester: Wiley.

Sinclair, A., Barkham, M., Evans, C., Connell, J. and Audin, K. (2005) Rationale and development of a general population well-being measure: psychometric status of the GP-CORE in a student sample. *British Journal of Guidance & Counselling*, 33: 153–74.

Trusler, K., Doherty, C., Mullin, T., Grant, S. and McBride, J. (2006) Waiting times for primary care psychological therapy and counselling services. *Counselling & Psychotherapy Research*, 6: 23–32.

Twigg, E., Barkham, M., Bewick, B.M., Mulhern, B. and Cooper, M. (2009) The YP-CORE: development and validation of a young person's version of the CORE-OM. *Counselling and Psychotherapy Research*, 9: 160–8.

Unsworth, G., Cowie, H. and Grenn, A. (2011) Therapists' and clients' perceptions of routine outcome measurement in the NHS: a qualitative study. *Counselling and Psychotherapy Research*, first published on 1 April 2011 (iFirst).

PART V

THEORY AND APPROACHES

Introduction

COLIN FELTHAM AND IAN HORTON

Counselling and psychotherapy are activities shaped, supported and guided by theory. In other words, an undeniable characteristic of the therapeutic enterprise is its theoretical underpinning. This is not to say that theory is without problems – critics have long attacked the theoretical rationale of psychoanalysis, for example, and some commentators argue that as therapists we need to be clearer about the exact place that any theory has in relation to clinical practice (Feltham, 1999; Heaton, 2010; Horton, 1996) – but it is to assert that therapy in its current form seems inseparable from various theories. Therapy or healing may well occur without or apart from theoretical preparation or influence, but is commonly driven or justified by theory.

This part of the book addresses some of the theoretical ground of therapy. First, we look at some aspects of contextual psychology, specifically developmental, social, evolutionary and positive psychology, and their relevance for practice. Psychological type theory, deriving ultimately from Jung, is examined as a valuable trans-theoretical tool. Possible reasons for, and the structures of, the myriad models of therapy and attempts at their theoretical integration are then outlined. The largest component is then given over to a selection of distinct approaches to therapy (or core theoretical models, or approach-specific theories) as described below. Hopefully the space and positioning accorded to such theories here reflect their historical importance and continuing influence, but we acknowledge our own contention that theories are not perhaps quite the crowning feature of therapy or accurate explanations of therapeutic change that they have often been considered. Readers may of course discern implicit theoretical assumptions in most other parts of the book.

REFERENCES

Feltham, C. (ed.) (1999) *Controversies in Psychotherapy and Counselling*. London: Sage.

Heaton, J. (2010) *The Talking Cure: Wittgenstein's Therapeutic Method for Psychotherapy*. London: Palgrave.

Horton, I. (1996) Towards the construction of a model: some issues. In R. Bayne, I. Horton and J. Bimrose (eds), *New Directions in Counselling*. London: Routledge.

Contextual Psychology

COLIN FELTHAM

Counselling and psychotherapy constitute a field of knowledge and practice in their own right. Although psychoanalysis was associated with nineteenth-century neuropsychiatry and speculative psychology, it evolved similarly to theology, almost as a subject *sui generis*, and also in some cases in opposition to prevailing psychologies. Counsellors and psychotherapists draw upon their own emerging tradition of knowledge which includes but is not always reliant upon psychology (Thorne and Dryden, 1993). Counselling and clinical psychologists are, of course, exceptions to this rule.

There are, however, some areas of psychology of real significance in the training of therapists: developmental and lifespan psychology, social psychology, evolutionary psychology and critical psychology. Wilkinson and Campbell (1997) include the first two of these topics in their consideration of personality, emotion, memory, thinking, states of consciousness, stress, coping, health and illness, and psychological disorders. We focus briefly here on some aspects of these as well as on the fertile fields of evolutionary psychology and psychotherapy, and positive psychology.

DEVELOPMENTAL AND LIFESPAN PSYCHOLOGY

An understanding of how human beings typically develop or grow is considered essential by some practitioners (e.g. the psychodynamic) but of far less relevance by others (e.g. those practising REBT).

Psychodynamic practitioners have their own developmental theories (e.g. Freudian, Kleinian, Eriksonian, Bowlby inspired, etc.) which are often not shared – indeed may be disputed – by classical (academic) psychologists. The concepts of early childhood memory, repression and maternal deprivation form the basis of three such disputes, for example. Nevertheless, there are certain good reasons for all therapists to familiarize themselves with the fundamentals of human development:

- Clients may present from a wide age range, from childhood to old age, and a knowledge of common age-specific characteristics can assist in assessment and therapeutic planning and referral.
- Therapists themselves will usually have analysed and grappled with their own significant developmental issues – past, present and future – and may benefit in terms of self-understanding from consulting relevant texts (Sugarman, 2004).
- All therapeutic schools inherit and generate implicit or explicit developmental theories, which are associated with different theories and practices of assessment, intervention and prognosis.
- Many therapeutic traditions rest on notions of a 'presenting past', in other words the belief that all present crises and problems in some sense represent or repeat earlier developmental stages and unresolved traumas.

Developmental psychology has traditionally focused on the years from infancy to adolescence, and perhaps to early adulthood. In some cases early life is considered, on the basis of both traditional empirical research and infant observation, somewhat deterministically (e.g. Kagan and Snidman, 2004). It is now quite usual to think in lifespan terms from birth to death. Humanistic psychology has forced on to the agenda the significance, for example, of birth (e.g. birth trauma) or even earlier formative events; and transpersonal psychology commends consideration of 'past lives', near-death and 'posthumous' experiences, as well as challenging the traditional, pessimistic assumptions of old age as decline. Increasing longevity too takes psychology into advances in psycho-gerontology, the study of old age, and many more positive accounts of older age now appear, including the growth of wisdom and spirituality (Young-Eisendrath and Miller, 2000). The emergence of evolutionary psychology commends the usefulness of examining ways in which humans as evolved beings carry forward certain archetypal behaviours, both healthy and unhealthy; and advances in transgenerational psychotherapy (Schutzenberger, 1998) also widen the potential for expansion in our understanding of human development.

In addition to simple *chronology*, lifespan psychology embraces different frameworks for understanding development, including the metaphors of journey and narrative, transitions and life events, models of the life course, and developmental tasks (Thornton, 2008). Typically, texts focus on early developmental milestones (especially cognitive achievements, following Piaget's work), attachment, moral development, family influences, etc., and thereafter on themes of physical and sexual development, identity, career seeking, forming partnerships, establishing families, and so on, into the crises, transitions and losses of midlife, retirement and old age.

Feminist and social theorists have criticized typical white, Western, individual-centred, linear models of human development propagated by psychology, particularly those focusing uncritically on the central role of the mother, and those implying direct links between statistically 'normal' development and psychological health (Burman, 1993). D'Augelli and Patterson (1995) argue for specific recognition of lesbian, gay and bisexual lifespan issues. Existential and phenomenological therapists too question orthodox deterministic models. Some Jungians interpret the life course less as a constant recovery from past hurts and general recapitulation of the past, and more in teleological terms as a forward movement to fulfil purpose and destiny.

SOCIAL PSYCHOLOGY

Traditionally social psychology has been concerned with the topics of intimate, group and wider social relationships, focusing on interpersonal perceptions, attributions, attraction, aggression, influence, power, roles and social skills. More recently, attention has been given to aspects of the self, including self-concept, schemas, subpersonalities and the body, and also to bisexual, lesbian, gay, ethnic/cultural and other psychologies of difference.

In relation to therapy, one of the most significant social psychological contributions has been that of social influence. While many therapists have concentrated on the nuances of unconscious communication in therapy, more obvious issues of power, influence, coercion, authority and attractiveness in the therapeutic context have often been neglected. Social learning theory suggests that much dysfunctional behaviour is learned in childhood by imitation, conditioning, avoidance, punishment, habit and so on. Many psychologists in the 1960s and 1970s (e.g. Claiborn, Dorn, Strong) exploited these insights via empirical work which led to the conclusion that therapists' *trustworthiness*, *attractiveness* and *expertness* were key indicators of successful therapy. In other words, clients' *perceptions* of their therapists' ability to help them were highly significant.

These developments, mirrored in the work of Carkhuff, Cormier, Egan, Ivey, Nelson-Jones, Truax and others, suggested that improvement by concerted practice of skills associated with certain therapist in-session behaviours would enhance working alliances and hence outcomes. Important work has been carried out too on the effects of judicious therapist self-disclosure, on client reactance or preference for certain relational styles, and on relevant non-verbal behaviours. Social psychological theories of close relationship development (i.e. friendships, romantic bonds, partnerships), studies of compliance with therapy, different communication styles according to gender, and psychological type have informed some therapeutic practice developments. It is now widely accepted that early consolidation of the therapeutic alliance, consciously forged by therapists, is a key to successful outcomes. Such findings have now influenced cognitive-behavioural therapists, for example, towards paying greater conscious attention to *specifically relational factors in therapy*.

These developments appear to endorse Jerome Frank's durable observations and suggestions about persuasion effected by social psychological factors in therapy, now much discussed as common factors in therapy (Feltham, 1999).

In the light of increasing disasters associated with extreme weather events or natural disasters, Cherry (2009) and others have begun to explore the impact these have on the most vulnerable members of society – usually children, families and older adults – and to look for best responses to these events.

EVOLUTIONARY PSYCHOLOGY AND PSYCHOTHERAPY

Arguably one of the missing (or inadequately developed) pieces of the counselling and psychotherapy jigsaw is a compelling account of the origins of human behaviour patterns and why they are so often entrenched, that is, why psychological dysfunctions can remain so difficult to change and what may be done to change them. While much psychoanalytic theory has focused on the deep-seated nature of psychopathology and defence mechanisms, humanistic and cognitive-behavioural approaches have shown far greater interest in understanding and implementing change processes; broadly, in understanding the nature of present behaviour and how it can be improved. Evolutionary psychology (Barrett et al., 2002), and in its clinically applied form of evolutionary psychotherapy (EP), offer explanations, for example, for proclivities towards and common experiences of depression, anxiety, obsessions, eating disorders, schizoid behaviour, schizophrenia and homosexuality, among others (Buss, 2005; Keedwell, 2009; Stevens and Price, 2000).

Where genetic explanations for behaviour start and end at the genetic level of the neurologically hard-wired, evolutionary accounts seek to speculate about the prevalence and obduracy of certain contemporary behaviours and their beginnings in the conditions in which early human beings lived. Not everyone can be a leader, and subservience has a necessary function. But too much subservience can lead to chronic low ranking and low self-esteem. On the other hand, ancient communities of humans needed their inspired, visionary and aggressive leaders. But too much of such behaviour can lead to distorted perceptions (e.g. some aspects of schizophrenia) and in-group violence (as in domestic violence, psychopathy and murder). Horrobin (2001) has suggested that schizophrenia may have roots in the distant past, being linked with changes in diet towards fatty acids, increasing brain size and a need for gifted visionary members of the group. But what was once necessary in certain circumstances backfired later in others.

It is of course unsurprising that many therapists remain either indifferent or opposed to the tenets of evolutionary psychology. Evolutionary psychotherapy may not seek to suggest that behaviour is wholly determined but, along with sociobiological accounts, does lean in this direction. If you can establish good reasons why some human beings had to act extravigilantly for long evolutionary periods, for example, you undermine to some extent the arguments that heightened anxiety is learned in our early years from parents or that it follows personal traumatic experiences. Notions of individual self-determination are undermined.

Evolutionary accounts do not in themselves suggest particular, if any, therapeutic remedies. However, in a manner typical of this field, an array of authors from Jungian, psychoanalytic, primal, cognitive-behavioural and psychopharmacological therapies have drawn selectively on evolutionary explanations for behaviour to underpin their rationales for diagnosis and treatment. Evolutionary psychology and psychotherapy offer promises for an integrative aetiology of psychological disturbances: we act in these dysfunctional ways because we have inherited certain behaviours that were once – and probably for a very long time – necessary but no longer are. Most therapists agree that *awareness* of such behavioural roots in ourselves should help us to understand how and why they function, and that they are anachronistic. But EP in itself is largely agnostic about how we can, or whether we can, reliably change such behaviour.

POSITIVE PSYCHOLOGY

Positive psychology, pioneered by Seligman (2002), Carr (2004) and others, is a relative newcomer to the discipline of psychology. Unlike the tendency of clinical and abnormal psychology to look for deficits, positive psychology looks for the causes, perpetuating factors and learned ingredients of human psychological strengths. Instead of learned helplessness, learned optimism is its focus. Although not the diametrical opposite of evolutionary psychology, positive psychology has an emphasis on functional not dysfunctional behaviours, on the study of happiness not misery, on learnable not inherited behaviours. It is unashamedly about strengths, hope, emotional intelligence, the values of relational attachment, giftedness, creativity, gratitude, forgiveness, self-esteem and even 'positive illusions'. Denial and repression, for example, are valued as sometimes necessary and helpful defence mechanisms. Optimism in the face of objective adversity is promoted.

Clearly positive psychology, which its proponents regard as not identical with positive thinking since it has a fairly sophisticated research base in academic psychology, resonates well with many aspects of humanistic psychology and psychotherapy but also with cognitive-behaviour therapy and solution-focused therapy. It is forward looking, reinforcing the significance of learning coping skills and preventing future problems. Carr (2004) advocates deep relationships, absorbing work or activity, and an optimistic outlook, all held in balance with each other, as crucial to good mental health.

Critics of positive psychology suggest that it is *not* so far from positive thinking and Pollyannaish behaviour, that it ignores the social distribution of psychological dysfunction and its myriad social causes, and that its over-reliance on positive illusions or benign self-deception is highly questionable (Ehrenreich, 2009). Carr's recipe – 'to value the future more than the present' (2004: 348) – is also open to serious criticism. Nevertheless, it chimes well with government policies for wellbeing and mental health enhancement and with an educational rather than psychopathological orientation. It represents a challenge to those therapies dwelling on uncovering past hurts.

CRITICAL PSYCHOLOGY

There are broadly two understandings of critical psychology and what we can call critique-focused psychology and critical counselling studies. The first has a history of critique within the discipline of psychology itself, particularly from radical psychologists who hope to contextualize and overhaul psychology in terms of radical politics (Parker, 2007). The second comprises those psychologists who use the tools of empirical research to mount attacks on what they regard as poorly conceived and unsupported clinical and theoretical claims (e.g. Lilienfeld et al., 2003; 2010). More broadly, texts are appearing that call for greater application of critical thinking generally to this field (Feltham, 2010).

Psychologists have been in the forefront of developing new models of mindfulness-informed therapies, and interestingly Gilbert (2010) has championed greater awareness of compassion and its constituent elements in training and practice. Given the growth of counselling psychology (Orlans and Van Scoyoc, 2009), and the positioning of clinical and counselling psychology within the Health Professions Council, it remains to be seen in what ways the more non-psychology-driven practices of counselling and psychotherapy develop.

REFERENCES

Barrett, L., Dunbar, R. and Lycett, J. (2002) *Human Evolutionary Psychology.* Basingstoke: Palgrave.

Burman, E. (1993) *Deconstructing Developmental Psychology.* London: Routledge.

Buss, D. (ed.) (2005) *The Handbook of Evolutionary Psychology.* New York: Wiley.

Carr, A. (2004) *Positive Psychology: The Science of Happiness and Human Strengths.* London: Brunner-Routledge.

Cherry, K.E. (ed.) (2009) *Lifespan Perspectives on Natural Disasters: Coping with Katrina, Rita, and Other Storms.* New York: Springer.

D'Augelli, A.R. and Patterson, C.J. (eds) (1995) *Lesbian, Gay and Bisexual Identities over the Lifespan: Psychological Perspectives.* New York: Oxford University Press.

Ehrenreich, B. (2009) *Smile or Die: How Positive Thinking Fooled America and the World.* London: Granta.

Feltham, C. (ed.) (1999) *Understanding the Counselling Relationship.* London: Sage.

Feltham, C. (2010) *Critical Thinking in Counselling and Psychotherapy.* London: Sage.

Gilbert, P. (2010) *Compassion-Focussed Therapy: Distinctive Features.* London: Routledge.

Horrobin, D. (2001) *The Madness of Adam and Eve: How Schizophrenia Shaped Humanity.* London: Corgi.

Kagan, J. and Snidman, N. (2004) *The Long Shadow of Temperament.* Cambridge, MA: Belknap.

Keedwell, P. (2009) *How Sadness Survived: The Evolutionary Basis of Depression.* Oxford: Radcliffe.

Lilienfeld, S.O., Lynn, S.J. and Lohr, J.M. (eds) (2003) *Science and Pseudoscience in Clinical Psychology.* New York: Guilford.

Lilienfeld, S.O., Lynn, S.J., Ruscio, J. and Beyerstein, B.L. (2010) *50 Great Myths of Popular Psychology.* New York: Wiley-Blackwell.

Orlans, V. and Van Scoyoc, S. (2009) *A Short Introduction to Counselling Psychology.* London: Sage.

Parker, I. (2007) *Revolution in Psychology: Alienation to Emancipation.* London: Pluto.

Schutzenberger, A.A. (1998) *The Ancestor Syndrome: Transgenerational Psychotherapy and the Hidden Links in the Family Tree.* London: Routledge.

Seligman, M. (2002) *Authentic Happiness: Using the New Positive Psychology to Realize Your Potential for Lasting Fulfilment.* New York: Free.

Stevens, A. and Price, J. (2000) *Evolutionary Psychiatry: A New Beginning* (2nd edn). London: Routledge.

Sugarman, L. (2004) *Counselling and the Lifecourse*. London: Sage.

Thorne, B. and Dryden, W. (eds) (1993) *Counselling: Interdisciplinary Perspectives*. Buckingham: Open University Press.

Thornton, S. (2008) *Understanding Human Development*. Basingstoke: Palgrave.

Wilkinson, J.D. and Campbell, E.A. (1997) *Psychology in Counselling and Therapeutic Practice*. Chichester: Wiley.

Young-Eisendrath, P. and Miller, M.E. (eds) (2000) *The Psychology of Mature Spirituality*. London: Routledge.

Psychological Type Theory

ROWAN BAYNE

Psychological type theory is Isabel Myers's clarification and development of some of Jung's ideas about personality. It has two distinctive features and several applications to counselling and psychotherapy. The distinctive features are that it takes the individuality of therapists and clients unusually seriously and its positive and constructive tone. In particular, it is intended to be a step towards understanding and valuing each person's individuality, rather than a set of restrictive and stultifying 'boxes'.

The applications that follow from these features include:

- an increased chance of quicker and deeper empathy and acceptance
- ideas about matching clients and practitioners in style and expectations of therapy
- ideas about matching clients and techniques (and perhaps especially how therapists present techniques)
- a perspective on how much clients can change.

Each of these applications is discussed briefly in this chapter. Some other applications of psychological type theory – to making decisions, choosing a counselling orientation, motives for becoming a counsellor, the idea of a 'good counsellor', time 'management' and coping with stress – are discussed in Bayne and Jinks (2010).

Myers's theory (e.g. Myers with Myers, 1980) is widely applied in organizations and with individuals. More than 2 million copies of the associated questionnaire, the Myers–Briggs Type Indicator (MBTI), are completed each year and there is a substantial research base, though much stronger for the basic level of the theory – the four preferences – than for type dynamics and type development (Bayne, forthcoming).

The key concepts are 'preference' and 'psychological type'. Tables 5.3.1 and 5.3.2 summarize the preferences, and Table 5.3.3 expands a little on their meaning in relation to aspects of 'learning style'. Preference can be defined as 'feeling most energized by and natural and comfortable with'. For example, the theory assumes that everyone behaves in both extraverted and introverted ways but that we each prefer one of them, and therefore tend to behave in that way more often and with less or no sense of effort. Each psychological type includes one from each of the four preferences, e.g. ENTP or ESTJ, and there are 16 possible combinations and therefore 16 types.

A few therapists will only work with clients who have completed the MBTI questionnaire, discussed their results, and made a provisional decision about which psychological type they are. However, most therapists who use the approach have it in the background like any other framework or concept (e.g. loss or assertiveness) to consider applying when relevant. Sometimes the application will, if the therapist has passed the appropriate training, include the MBTI questionnaire.

More often, the theory is used informally, to say for example, 'Some people like and *need* to plan ahead more than others, and that seems to be true of you', or 'You seem most comfortable making decisions through analysing the arguments for and

Table 5.3.1   *The four pairs of preferences in psychological type theory*

Extraversion (E) or Introversion (I)
Sensing (S) or Intuition (N)
Thinking (T) or Feeling (F)
Judging (J) or Perceiving (P)

against, and this usually works well for you. *This decision, though, is different and you're stuck and baffled. Would you like to try adding another element to your analysis: how right or not each possibility feels?*' In the spirit of type theory, both examples could equally well have been phrased in terms of the opposite preferences – 'perceiving' in the first example, and 'feeling' in the second.

EMPATHY AND ACCEPTANCE

Type theory illustrates in a very concrete way how difficult empathy can be. According to the theory it is impossible to *really* understand what it is like to have the opposite preference(s) to your own, even though each of us uses all of them. But at the same time, knowing this limitation and knowing how profoundly people differ may make genuine empathy more likely. It may – probably should – mean that empathy, or sufficient empathy, occurs more quickly too. The widespread assumption that 'people are like me' is less of an obstacle, more consciously (and concretely) present and therefore more readily countered.

Similarly, a knowledge of type theory should encourage quicker and deeper acceptance. It assumes that when people behave differently from ourselves it is usually because they are different and equally valid 'types', *not* because they are being awkward, weird or incompetent. Moreover, these different ways of being can be equally effective. For example, someone with a preference for perceiving (which is developed sufficiently) will tend to produce their best work at the last minute, energized by the deadline which someone with a preference for judging has probably tried to avoid by starting early, and both Js and Ps can produce excellent work.

Type theory offers a refreshing perspective on problems between people of all combinations of preferences, including those between people of the same type. Moreover, similarity is not seen as ideal. On the contrary, any combination can work well but the best work is most likely to result from partnership between people of different types who value each other's (complementary) strengths.

MATCHING

Matching clients and counsellors on type is similarly subtle, and not just or even primarily a question of INTPs being the best counsellors for other INTPs, etc. (Bayne, forthcoming; Provost, 1993). Indeed, type development is probably the most important factor: how versatile therapists can comfortably and authentically be in their use of their preferences and their non-preferences when appropriate. This is not to say that all therapists

Table 5.3.2   *Some general characteristics associated with each preference*

E	More outgoing and active	↔	More reflective and reserved	I
S	More practical and interested in facts and details	↔	More interested in possibilities and overviews	N
T	More logical and reasoned	↔	More agreeable and appreciative	F
J	More planning and coming to conclusions	↔	More easygoing and flexible	P

Table 5.3.3   *The preferences and aspects of learning style*

E	Action. Talk. Trial and error
I	Reflection. Work privately
S	Close observation of what actually happens. Start with the concrete and specific, consider ideas and theory later
N	Theory first. Links and possibilities. Surges of interest
T	Analysis and logic. Critiques. Debate
F	Harmonious atmosphere. Care about the topic
J	More formal. Organized. Clear expectations and criteria
P	Flexible. Not routine. Bursts of energy. Work as play

should aim to be so versatile. Rather, people of some psychological types (in theory, ENTP and ENFP) are more naturally versatile, and versatility for everyone tends to develop with practice (and therefore age).

According to type theory, people of the different psychological types tend to have different expectations of counselling and therapy. For example, as Table 5.3.3 implies, clients who prefer extraversion will usually want a more active approach. Similarly, some techniques will be more agreeable – though not necessarily more effective – for clients of some types, for example guided fantasy with clients who prefer intuition. Techniques can be presented playfully (in tune with SP preferences), seriously and with specificity and structure (SJ), seriously and emphasizing rationale and evidence (NT), and with lots of scope for individuality (NF).

The principle here is not a rigid, mechanistic one. Rather, it is to use the theory as a guide to being sensitive about how, when and whether to suggest a particular technique, to reviewing the outcome, and to deciding whether to continue with it or not (Provost, 1993; Bayne, forthcoming). Type theory can also make referral more acceptable to counsellors and clients.

A PERSPECTIVE ON CHANGE

We know that some behaviour can generally change quite easily – for example panic attacks, problems with being assertive, sexual problems. Type theory suggests that in normal development people develop all their preferences and, to a lesser extent, their non-preferences, but that their true preferences do not change. A 'laid-back' person

(clue for a genuine preference for perceiving) does not – at least, not without a considerable effort which continues to be a strain – change into a highly organized person. They *can*, though, develop their non-preference for J to a useful extent and without undue strain. Indeed, generally this will happen as part of life. The same applies to Js: they can benefit from developing their P qualities without losing the strengths of their true preference. This stability of type may be regarded as positive: it is part of having a sense of identity and it can lead to realistic expectations of the limits of change through counselling and psychotherapy of some (core) aspects of personality.

However, there is a special case. When someone has lived as a psychological type other than their own (usually because of an extreme upbringing), they tend not to feel 'right' and can sometimes change their typical behaviour rapidly and dramatically by expressing their true preferences.

REFERENCES

Bayne, R. (forthcoming) *The Counsellor's Guide to Personality: Preferences, Motives and Life Stories*. Basingstoke: Palgrave Macmillan.

Bayne, R. and Jinks, G. (2010) *How to Survive Counsellor Training: An A–Z Guide*. Basingstoke: Palgrave Macmillan.

Myers, I.B. with Myers, P.B. (1980) *Gifts Differing*. Palo Alto, CA: CPP.

Provost, J.A. (1993) *Applications of the Myers–Briggs Type Indicator in Counseling: A Casebook* (2nd edn). Gainesville, FL: Center for Applications of Psychological Type.

Models of Counselling and Psychotherapy

IAN HORTON

Norcross and Grencavage (1990) reviewed various surveys which indicated that between 1959 and 1986 the number of arguably different or distinct models or approaches to counselling and psychotherapy rose from 36 to over 400. The proliferation of new approaches or attempts to combine elements or aspects of existing approaches in reconstituted or integrated models seems to have continued unabated to the present day. The figure of 'over 400' has common currency but no one quite knows how many named approaches remain in use. Theoretical and clinical innovation remains something of an enduring preoccupation that exercises the imagination and creativity of some practitioners and researchers.

Historically, models or approaches to counselling and psychotherapy have tended to be seen as synonymous with psychological theories of personality with only tenuously related indicators of methods of treatment or change. However, a shift has occurred towards the view that models or approaches to counselling and psychotherapy may, but will not necessarily, subsume aspects of personality theories, and are quite distinct from them in the emphasis they place on 'therapeutic operations' (Orlinsky et al., 1994) and change processes.

The concept of model or theoretical orientation is complex. It is hard to measure. Poznanski and McLennon (1997) report that few of the multi-item self-report instruments designed to measure theoretical orientation show evidence of reliability, and even fewer of validity. They suggest that this may be explained by the evidence indicating theories or models of counselling and psychotherapy as multiple concepts made up of four positions:

1 personal therapeutic belief systems which are not always clearly articulated or accessible
2 theoretical school affiliation or the practitioner's self-reported adherence to one (or more) theoretical schools
3 espoused theory or the theoretical concepts and techniques that practitioners say they use
4 theory-in-action or what observers believe the practitioner is actually doing.

There seems to be a relatively strong link between theoretical school affiliation and espoused theory, but often a contradictory or at least a much weaker association between espoused theory and theory-in-action. Practitioners do not always seem to be doing what they say or think they do. This compounds the problems and issues faced by researchers trying to evaluate and compare the outcomes of different approaches and may be taken as evidence to support Clarkson's (1995) doubts about the usefulness of theory and Feltham's (1997) doubts about the emphasis professional bodies place on the need for a coherent core theoretical model.

What is a model or theory of counselling and psychotherapy? Relatively little has been written on this subject and there is no consensus on what actually constitutes the parts or elements of a comprehensive model or theory. However, four common elements are either explicit in the literature or can be inferred from most descriptions of particular models of counselling and psychotherapy (Horton, 2000): (1) basic assumptions or philosophy; (2) formal theory of human personality and development; (3) clinical theory which defines the goals, principles and processes of change and provides a cognitive map which gives a sense of direction and purpose; and (4) the related therapeutic operations, or skills and techniques. The basic assumptions or philosophical elements of a model or approach will typically be concerned with two aspects. The first is worldview, or how people construct reality and attribute meaning to their life experiences. In some models or approaches this may include reference to socio-cultural factors as well as psychological influences and personal values and beliefs. The second aspect is the therapeutic process and basic assumptions about the characteristics of the therapeutic relationship and the values, purpose and goals of therapy. While the basic assumptions or philosophy might be seen as setting the stage for the selection and adoption of the formal and clinical theory elements, they are not always clearly articulated or understood.

The formal theory element is concerned with human development and may contain explanations of those characteristics of a person that account for consistent patterns of behaviour and of functional or healthy development, as well as of the origin or aetiology of psychological problems and how they are perpetuated or maintained. The importance or otherwise of these aspects of theory may be explicit in the formal theory description or be inferred from how it is described. Not all models or approaches emphasize the importance of the genesis of psychological problems; some are more concerned with how problems can be modified or changed.

In a clearly articulated and internally consistent model or approach, the clinical theory element will interpret the largely abstract concepts contained in the formal theory in ways which are amenable to the delivery of therapeutic services.

Clinical theory may imply or make explicit general principles of change and account for the psychological processes which enable change to take place. Different models or approaches seem to be based on different assumptions about the mechanisms or process of change and may not necessarily be made explicit in the theory of the model. The common mechanisms or processes of change include such variables as the quality of the relationship between therapist and client; the expression of emotions or catharsis; the provision of new perspectives through some explanation or interpretation of the problem and/or of the interaction between therapist and client; reinforcement of client strengths and resources; increasing levels of 'exposure' to the problem, thus enabling clients to face and confront what was previously being avoided; and a working towards deeper understanding or awareness of unconscious processes. Some models or approaches involve psycho-educational

interventions – skills training and information giving – as an integral part of the change process. Much research still needs to be done to establish exactly what therapists do that actually contributes to helping clients change.

The most concrete and visible element of a model or approach is the therapeutic operations or the skills and strategies a therapist uses to implement the clinical theory.

This analysis of the elements of a model or approach to counselling or psychotherapy assumes a coherent and internally consistent relationship between them, with each element developing from the previous one. However, other than in very broad terms the actual relationship between the elements and how each informs the other is not always explicit. It is not always apparent how what a therapist does actually interprets his or her philosophy or theory of human development in a consistent and coherent way. More experienced therapists seem to make decreasing use of abstract concepts (Skovholt and Ronnestad, 1995), placing greater emphasis on what is referred to here as clinical theory. Bond's (2000: 319) pictorial metaphor of a 'pond' illustrates the relationship between the four elements. He describes the basic assumptions or philosophy as the 'dark, murky and stagnant water at the bottom of the pond, containing rich and fertile soil, living creatures, flora and fauna and the unregenerate sludge and detritus of our own culture'. Above that in the still relatively dark and murky water is the level of formal theory. The translucent level just below the surface represents the clinical theory, with the clearly visible water on the surface of the pond representing the therapeutic operations and what the therapist can actually be observed doing.

These four elements of a model or theory of counselling and psychotherapy are used as the basic structure for the description of the different models included later in this part of the book.

REFERENCES

Bond, T. (2000) Bond's pond. In S. Palmer and R. Woolfe (eds), *Integrative and Eclectic Counselling and Psychotherapy*. London: Sage.

Clarkson, P. (1995) *After Schoolism*. London: PHYSIS.

Feltham, C. (1997) Challenging the core theoretical model. *Counselling*, 8 (2): 121–5.

Horton, I. (2000) Principles and practice of a personal integration. In S. Palmer and R. Woolfe (eds), *Integrative and Eclectic Counselling and Psychotherapy*. London: Sage.

Norcross, J.C. and Grencavage, L.M. (1990) Eclecticism and integration in counselling and psychotherapy: major themes and obstacles. In W. Dryden and J.C. Norcross (eds), *Eclecticism and Integration in Counselling and Psychotherapy*. Loughton: Gale Centre.

Orlinsky, D.E., Grawe, K. and Parks, B.K. (1994) Process and outcome in psychotherapy – *noch einmal*. In A.E. Bergin and S.L. Garfield (eds), *Handbook of Psychotherapy and Behavior Change* (4th edn). New York: Wiley.

Poznanski, J.J. and McLennon, J. (1997) Theoretical orientation of Australian counselling psychologists. Unpublished paper. School of Social and Behavioural Sciences, Swinburne University of Technology, Victoria, Australia.

Skovholt, T.M. and Ronnestad, M.H. (1995) *The Evolving Professional Self*. Chichester: Wiley.

5.5

Integration

IAN HORTON

Most counsellors and psychotherapists, including those who espouse pure form models, tend gradually to develop their own personalized conceptual systems and individual styles of working (Skovholt and Ronnestad, 1995). Although they may not necessarily describe themselves as integrative, many practitioners appear to assimilate explanatory concepts and techniques that can be attributed to more than one theoretical perspective (Poznanski and McLennon, 1997). Skovholt and Ronnestad's (1995) model of the evolving professional self demonstrates the widespread and often significant changes in beliefs about psychological change and the ingredients of optimal therapeutic practice that occur as practitioners develop through the 'exploration', 'integration', 'individuation' and 'integrity' post-training stages of their professional development and practice. In this sense it could be argued that integration is a personal process undertaken or instinctively evolved by individual therapists and that all therapists become, to some degree, integrative practitioners. It is the view of some academics and researchers that 'pure form' approaches to practice exist only as a myth – a view that may be hotly contested by others.

In this chapter the term 'integrative' is taken to subsume ideas of technical and systematic eclecticism. Any haphazard and arbitrary pick-and-mix approach to counselling and psychotherapy ideas and methods is not considered here. For a useful discussion of the different traditions within psychotherapy integration, see Feixas and Botella (2004). They distinguish among pragmatic, theoretically guided and systematically technical eclecticisms, differentiate between hybrid and extended models

of theoretical integration, and discuss the common factors perspective.

What is clear is that there is no one approach to integrative counselling or psychotherapy. Broadly speaking it is possible to identify two types of integrative system – fixed (or relatively stable) and open – which seek to combine aspects developed originally within separate schools and approaches. For example, cognitive analytic therapy (CAT) could be described as a fixed system in that it combines identifiable and specific aspects of cognitive and analytic models in a predetermined and explicit way. Relatively fixed systems such as CAT are perhaps destined to become the single or pure form approaches of tomorrow. Arguably models or approaches such as gestalt therapy and psychosynthesis could be described as fully integrative hybrids of ideas and techniques which were previously developed or at least partially existed elsewhere, yet which have been combined and subsequently developed in such a way that in the resulting synthesis the components or influences have virtually lost their original identity and a new and distinct model of counselling or psychotherapy has emerged.

The other type of integration is within a relatively open system, utilizing some kind of overarching framework or higher-order or trans-theoretical concept that provides internal consistency while at the same time allowing for the assimilation of explanatory concepts and/or methods from other schools or approaches. The core integrative framework or concept is fixed but allows the individual practitioner to develop gradually his or her own synthesis of ideas and practice. Examples of such open system approaches might include Egan's 'skilled helper' model and other generic skills models, Andrews's 'self-confirmation' model and Garfield's 'eclectic-integrative' approach.

Integration can occur at different levels, with varying degrees of overlap between and within the different elements of a model in what can be broadly categorized as theoretical and technical integration. Theoretical integration takes place between the more abstract levels of formal theory and basic or meta-theoretical assumptions, whereas technical integration takes place primarily at the surface and more concrete levels of clinical theory and therapeutic operations. Arguably, high-level synthesis of any two or more models or part models of counselling or psychotherapy is only feasible to the extent that they share theoretical and meta-theoretical or basic assumptions. High-level integration can only take place between epistemologically compatible systems. However, the term 'high level' refers to the extent of structural integration possible between the deeper and more abstract elements of a model, rather than to the more limited degree of integration at a clinical procedural level. It should be clear that there is no evidence that high-level integration correlates with or can even be associated with the efficacy of clinical practice.

While there are some research findings supporting the effectiveness of some fixed integrative models, such as CAT, there is little if any objective and empirical research to support the effectiveness of more open integrative systems. This is largely because of the methodological problems of measuring personal and individualized combinations of ideas and methods and the existence of factors that may account for psychological change and which are common to all or most approaches.

A comprehensive account of the historical development of counselling and psychotherapy integration (Hollanders, 2000), a detailed description of some current and diverse paradigms and a useful discussion of issues and debates can be found in Palmer and Woolfe (2000).

REFERENCES

Feixas, G. and Botella, L. (2004) Psychotherapy integration: reflections and contributions from a constructivist epistemology. *Journal of Psychotherapy Integration*, 14 (2): 192–221.

Hollanders, H. (2000) Eclecticism/integrative historical developments. In S. Palmer and R. Woolfe (eds), *Integrative and Eclectic Counselling and Psychotherapy*. London: Sage.

Palmer, S. and Woolfe, R. (eds) (2000) *Integrative and Eclectic Counselling and Psychotherapy*. London: Sage.

Poznanski, J.J. and McLennon, J. (1997) Theoretical orientation of Australian counselling psychologists. Unpublished paper. School of Social and Behavioural Sciences, Swinburne University of Technology, Victoria, Australia.

Skovholt, T.M. and Ronnestad, M.H. (1995) *The Evolving Professional Self*. Chichester: Wiley.

Approaches to Counselling and Psychotherapy: Introduction

COLIN FELTHAM AND IAN HORTON

Not only are there disagreements about the exact number of therapeutic approaches in existence, but also there are disputes about how these are best grouped. In this part of the book, 27 different schools of therapy are presented in summary form. The intention has been to include a representative selection of the currently more mainstream or influential approaches. Obviously the allegedly 400 and more approaches in existence today cannot all be included. However, it has been customary to organize approaches (also often known as theoretical orientations, models, schools or brand names) according to their affiliation with the three main traditions of psychodynamic, humanistic-existential and cognitive-behavioural therapy. This convention has been utilized and extended here by adding integrative and constructivist headings, honouring the recency and trans-theoretical identity of certain approaches. Under each approach heading, alphabetical rather than chronological order has been adopted.

Even so, we are aware that some adherents may dispute the location of their approach in the present schema and, in addition, some may feel strongly about the absence of what has sometimes been called the 'fourth force', namely multicultural counselling and therapy (MCT). This is understood here not as a separate or distinct category or group, but as a theme that should permeate and enrich the psychodynamic, cognitive-behavioural, humanistic-existential and integrative approaches by focusing on issues of culture, ethnicity/race, gender, sexuality, disability, class and other factors.

Writers for each approach have been asked to give a brief history, followed by a succinct account of the basic assumptions, explanation of origins and maintenance of problems, (mechanisms of) change, skills and strategies, and any research indications, pertinent to the approach. While even this schema, with these headings, is not found completely conducive by all, we hope it will be useful in organizing and condensing a considerable amount of material in a way that facilitates comparison.

It may be useful to have a sense of the historical context of each school of therapy in order to weigh up the influences upon it and perhaps to understand how well it has endured and in what socio-cultural milieu it best operates. Every approach has some, often implicit, basic assumptions which should be understood. Possibly of more theoretical interest to many therapists is how exponents of an approach explain causes or origins of individual humans' psychological problems in living, and how these problems (or concerns, issues or disorders) persist in time. Of most clinical interest are explanations about personal change and how therapists' approach-specific skills and strategies help to effect desired changes in clients' lives. Here it should be noted that these very brief introductions to each approach are just that: there is no claim or pretence that these provide therapeutic instructions or clinical skills in a nutshell, and recommended texts should be studied by any reader wishing to gain further in-depth knowledge. Finally, any specific research relating to each approach has been highlighted, although again there are obviously major differences between approaches about valid research methodologies.

The brevity of these descriptions is acknowledged. This is very much an overview intended to demonstrate the distinctiveness of different approaches, to outline their key characteristics, and to show collectively the diversity of the field. Counselling and psychotherapy literature found elsewhere already abundantly represents the different schools of therapy. Obviously readers may adopt a 'magpie' strategy of surveying the particular attractions of these approaches. Alternatively, we might commend a reasonably systematic reading of follow-up texts towards becoming an informed student of comparative counselling and psychotherapy. To this end, the following kinds of questions may usefully be asked of these approaches, probably in conjunction with further detailed readings:

- Exactly how was each one discovered and/or constructed?
- On what kinds of knowledge, experience and methodology does it draw?
- Why do creators, developers and affiliates of therapeutic traditions have different assumptions and interpretations of distress, change and effectiveness?
- In what ways can these approaches be judged as significantly similar to or different from each other?
- What indications are there that they are philosophically defensible, empirically testable, and effective for clients in general and/or for specific kinds of presenting problems or goals?
- To what extent is this theoretical and institutional diversity helpful or unhelpful, and will such differences persist or reduce as therapies become more integrated?

THEORY AND APPROACHES

PSYCHODYNAMIC APPROACHES

Adlerian Therapy

(Alfred Adler, 1870–1937)

ANTHEA MILLAR AND JENNY WARNER

BRIEF HISTORY

Adlerian therapy has developed from the ideas and practice of Alfred Adler, a Viennese psychiatrist and contemporary of Freud and Jung. He was one of the co-founders of the Viennese Psychoanalytical Society, which he left in 1911 after a disagreement with Freud. He most particularly challenged the view of the sexual instinct as omnipotent, emphasising instead the importance of social interdependence in relationships. In 1912 Adler formed his School of Individual Psychology (expressing the indivisible nature of the human being) and continued to develop his approach, also influenced by concepts of holism and evolution. His experiences as a physician in the First World War gave further impetus to his development of the concept of community feeling and the importance of social equality, regardless of gender, culture or race. After the war, Adler returned to Vienna and focused his attention on preventive approaches and psycho-education, setting up child guidance centres, working with teachers and pupils in open sessions. He also gave lectures at the People's Institute, believing strongly that laypeople could make use of psychological insights. Adler was Jewish and, following the closure of his centres by the Nazis, he was forced to leave Vienna, emigrating to New York in 1934. Adler's ideas influenced key figures such as Viktor Frankl, Rollo May, Abraham Maslow, Albert Ellis and Carl Rogers, and also pre-empted later neo-Freudian developments, as well as cognitive constructivist approaches. After his death, a younger Viennese psychiatrist, Rudolf Dreikurs, who had also moved to the United States, further developed Adlerian therapy training and teacher and parent education. There are presently Adlerian institutes throughout the world, with the Adlerian approach of establishing democratic relationships being used in all forms of counselling and psychotherapy and in management training as well as teacher and parent education.

BASIC ASSUMPTIONS

- *Holistic*. Adler proposed a holistic view of the personality. The *individual* of 'individual psychology' is a poor translation and actually means 'indivisible'. The client's consistent overriding pattern of behaviour, goals, thoughts and emotions must be viewed as a whole. Adlerians refer to this unity of the person as the lifestyle.
- *Socially oriented*. People develop and live in a social context, and need to find a place in the group; without this the human race cannot survive. Adler considered that everyone is born with the potential to belong and contribute as a social equal. Most of us, however, also hold some feelings of inferiority, and will strive to

overcome these through feelings of superiority. *Gemeinschaftsgefühl*, commonly translated as 'social interest' or 'community feeling', describes an Adlerian concept central to mental wellbeing. Therapy aims to understand the nature of each person's way of belonging, and to identify both clients' strengths and their discouraging beliefs that block them from realising their full potential as equal human beings.

- *Goal directed*. All behaviour has a purpose and a fictional goal, mostly related to finding a way to belong. Clients' goals are identified and the purposes of their behaviour revealed. Prior to therapy clients are not usually aware of their goals, or the ideas and beliefs that underpin their movement through life.
- *Creative and responsible*. We create our own personalities or lifestyles extremely early in life, very much influenced by the interactions with our siblings and family. Our behaviour is the result of our own subjective perceptions; what we have inherited or experienced is less important than what we do with it (Adler, 1929). Our beliefs, which underpin our unconscious goals, are called our private logic; the ideas make sense to us but are not necessarily common sense. We are responsible for our goals, behaviour, beliefs and feelings and therefore it is in our power to change if we should wish to do so.
- *Unique*. Adler was a subjective psychologist, not interested in the facts *per se*, but in each person's unique perception of the facts. In order to understand people we must look at their unique subjective view of themselves, other people, the world and the decisions they have made about their movement through life.

ORIGIN AND MAINTENANCE OF PROBLEMS

Adler believed people are born with the potential to feel they belong as equal human beings, though frequently this potential is not nurtured by their early experiences. We live in a mistake-centred society where mistakes are commented upon, disruptive behaviour is responded to, competition is encouraged, and personal self-esteem is considered more important than contribution to the task in hand. When a child does not feel equal, he or she will experience inferiority feelings, or more problematically will develop an inferiority complex, which invites a compensatory superiority complex, deeply impacting on self-esteem and general health. Adler challenged the practice of corporal punishment, and stressed the importance of love and encouragement

in early childhood, decrying neglect and abuse. He also identified the danger of both pampering, which can result in a child feeling incapable and fearful about making decisions, and spoiling, when the child develops the mistaken view that they must always have what they want. If spoiling continues over the years, parents may either give in to the demands so the child gains power over them, or may punish the child. Punished children are likely to feel hurt and seek revenge. In order to hurt their parents they may also hurt themselves, for example through such revenge-seeking behaviours as failure at school, antisocial or criminal behaviour, and substance abuse.

In addition to the relationship with parents, Adler emphasised the importance of sibling influence on personality development. Each child will observe their other siblings acutely, or in the case of only children, their peers as well as significant adults. Then, as a means of ensuring some form of significance, the child will construct a unique position within the family system, even if it means behaving destructively. These role choices in the family are likely to be played out in adult life.

As inferiority feelings are so uncomfortable, people compensate for these feelings by striving for superiority; their goals involve elevated self-esteem and feeling better than others, often involving putting others down. This attitude towards others creates social and relationship problems, with engagement in power plays and competition, and concern with personal status in the group rather than cooperating and contributing to it. This leads to distancing from other people and/or a lack of intimacy and spontaneity. Goals of superiority are often unattainable, and that causes discomfort, so the person safeguards their self-esteem by developing alibis to justify why the goal is not achieved. Adler recognised neurotic behaviour in people, such as developing illnesses or disabilities or making excuses for not achieving their over-ambitious goals.

CHANGE

Where possible, Adlerian practitioners work on *prevention* of future difficulties through family and community education. Therapy, however, remains an important and hopeful process for facilitating change. The initial phase of therapy involves establishing a meaningful therapeutic relationship, based on equality and aligned goals. The therapist will first work to identify the client's strengths as a resource for future change, and then support the client in uncovering the hidden purpose of symptoms and mistaken ideas (private logic) using the therapeutic functions of insight and meaning. Clients are helped to understand that they are responsible for their own behaviour and for their decisions to change or not to change. The therapist offers both support and challenge, inviting the client to risk new attitudes and behaviours and greater flexibility in ways of being in the world.

Some clients may express a 'yes … but' attitude to change and it is up to the therapist to help them understand that they are trusted with their own destiny. This democratic cooperative relationship may be the first such experience for some clients in which they are afforded equal rights, equal respect and equal responsibility.

Clients gain insight and become aware of their beliefs and ideas and the goals (or purpose) of their behaviour, and they develop understanding of how their presenting problems have occurred due to their view of life and habitual pattern of responding. Once the goals are revealed, clients can no longer pursue them with such energy.

For reorientation, the therapist must ensure that clients want to change their personal goals and ideas and, if they do, to what extent. It takes time for the client consciously to own ideas, beliefs and goals that have been below consciousness for many years. Insight will occur first after the behaviour has taken place, then during the behaviour, and lastly before the behaviour. Carefully negotiated assignments may be set which challenge the old private logic, clients agreeing to do something they do not usually do or have never done. The therapist will now be looking towards the life tasks and the client's presenting problems. Full participation as an equal member of the community, with an ability to contribute and cooperate usefully in the three life tasks of occupation, social life and intimate relationships, was considered by Adler to be the measure of a mentally healthy person. Nowadays Adlerians take a flexible attitude towards the life tasks of occupation and intimacy: it is not possible or necessary for everyone to have paid employment, and there is appreciation that healthy emotional and sexual intimacy may be expressed in many forms.

Throughout therapy the client is taught the art of encouragement. Most people are discouraged to some extent, feeling bad about mistakes and dwelling on their failings. Many people also have unrealistic goals which are a constant source of discouragement because they are never attained. Clients are taught to focus on strengths and regard mistakes as an essential opportunity for learning, rather than evidence of failure. Once clients become more encouraged they are able to encourage others, thus creating a more optimistic yet realistic environment, which will further enhance the encouragement process. This can be especially powerful in group sessions. Realistic, attainable goals and a more flexible attitude towards life will enable clients to feel good about their achievements and worth. As their feelings of inferiority diminish and their social interest develops, they are likely to feel equal to their fellows, wishing to cooperate and make their contribution, in turn increasing a sense of mental wellbeing.

SKILLS AND STRATEGIES

- *Establishing a democratic relationship based on equality*. Adler was one of the first in therapy to use two facing chairs rather than an analytic couch. A good client–therapist relationship is based on cooperation, mutual trust and alignment of goals. This develops through the therapist's own self-awareness and authenticity as an ordinary human being. Therapists participate actively, demonstrating warmth and genuine interest, listening empathically to the client in order to understand his or her point of view. As the goal in therapy is to encourage the development of social interest, the therapist needs to model this social interest himself or herself. Whilst the therapist is free to express feelings and opinions, it is crucial to maintain a respectful, non-power-based relationship, where clients are trusted to make their own decisions.

- *Encouragement*. The encouragement process is fundamental to every stage of therapy. It is seen as the antidote to the basic problem of inferiority feelings and the resulting discouragement. Encouragement takes many forms, and involves both identifying the strengths of the client and trusting them to face challenge and gain a sense of achievement in the face of what previously felt too risky.

- *Lifestyle assessment*. In order to understand the client, a lifestyle assessment can be carried out. Information is gathered about the client and his or her presenting concerns and how the client is participating in the three life tasks. Then the therapist will elicit the client's subjective perception of their situation as a child. This involves gaining family constellation data and establishing how clients interpret their childhood position, paying special attention to birth order and sibling relationships, and the creative choices clients made to become the sort of people they are. Interpretations of the client's early memories are then explored with the client, and consistent patterns or themes identified.

- *Analysing and transforming early memories and dreams*. Early memories and dreams provide projective data for understanding a person's life-style, identifying the client's image of self, of life, of others, of the 'self-ideal' or goal, and the key strategies used to move in the direction of the self-ideal. Adler's focus on selective memory that functions in association with a person's lifestyle puts the emphasis on what is *remembered* rather than what is forgotten. Therapists need to put their own interpretations and attitudes on hold so that they can truly empathise with clients and see the world through their eyes. Each hypothesised guess will have to be checked out with the client, and the therapist needs to be sensitive to the client's reactions to their guesses. Early recollections can function as metaphors for a life situation or present-day problem, and creative work on transforming the early memory can enable new perspectives on a here-and-now situation.

- *Mutually agreed assignments*. Tasks are set that challenge the client's private logic and support new constructive behaviours.

A wide range of processes and techniques that support the above processes may be implemented; some are also used by therapists from other orientations. Some examples include psychodrama, art, music and play therapy, behavioural assignments, Socratic questioning, paradoxical intention and body work. Therapy is applied in many contexts including child guidance centres, schools, the workplace, prisons, hospitals and other institutions, and with individuals, couples, families and groups, the latter a natural fit in relation to the socially oriented view (Sonstegard and Bitter, 2004). Therapy may be short, mid or long term, all aiming to provide a positive psycho-educational and future-oriented approach, underpinned by an enabling client–therapist relationship.

RESEARCH EVIDENCE

Assessing the efficacy of the broad focus of Adlerian therapy through a medical model view of therapy raises many problems when attempting to measure such complex intra-psychic issues as the therapeutic relationship, the change in clients' subjective private logic and the development of social interest (Neukrug, 2011). Similarly, Shelley discusses the challenges of both quantitative and qualitative research methodologies when attempting 'to capture the depth and paradoxes that a depth psychology such as Individual Psychology proposes' (2008: 420). However, a good number of research studies have identified the importance of

developing a positive relationship with the client (Carlson et al., 2006) which is a critical aspect of Adlerian therapy. Other studies have confirmed the effects of birth order (Watkins, 2008), the value of analysing early memories as a projective technique (Carlson et al., 2006), and the central importance of social belongingness in a person's feeling of well-being (Curlette and Kern, 2010). More recent neuroscience research revealing the essential social embeddedness of the human being underlines this key point (Gallese et al., 2002). Also numerous studies have been conducted on the effectiveness of encouragement by teachers and parents and the positive effects of cooperation in the classroom and the benefits of education for democratic parenting (Burnett, 1988; Carns and Carns, 2008).

REFERENCES

Adler, A. (1929) *The Science of Living*. New York: Greenberg.

Burnett, P.C. (1988) Evaluation of Adlerian parenting programs. *Individual Psychology*, 44 (1): 63–76.

Carlson, J., Watts, R.E. and Maniacci, M. (2006) *Adlerian Therapy: Theory and Practice*. Washington, DC: APA.

Carns, M.R. and Carns, A.W. (2008) A review of the professional literature concerning the consistency of the definition and application of Adlerian encouragement. In J. Carlson and S. Slavik (eds), *Readings in the Theory of Individual Psychology*. New York: Routledge.

Curlette, W.L. and Kern, R.M. (2010) The importance of meeting the need to belong in lifestyle. *Journal of Individual Psychology*, 66 (1).

Gallese, V., Ferrari, P.F. and Umilta, M.A. (2002) The mirror matching system: a shared manifold for intersubjectivity. *Behavioural and Brain Sciences*, 25 (1): 35–6.

Neukrug, E.S. (2011) *Counseling Theory and Practice*. Belmont, CA: Brooks/Cole and Cengage Learning.

Shelley, C. (2008) Phenomenology and the qualitative in individual psychology. In J. Carlson and S. Slavik (eds), *Readings in the Theory of Individual Psychology*. New York: Routledge.

Sonstegard, M.A. and Bitter, J.R. (2004) *Adlerian Group Counseling and Therapy*. New York: Brunner/Routledge.

Watkins, C.E. Jr (2008) Birth order research and Adler's theory. In J. Carlson and S. Slavik (eds), *Readings in the Theory of Individual Psychology*. New York: Routledge.

RECOMMENDED READING

Adler, A. (1927) *Understanding Human Nature*. Trans. Colin Brett, Oxford: Oneworld, 1992.

Adler, A. (1931) *What Life Could Mean to You*. Trans. Colin Brett, Oxford: Oneworld, 1992.

Dreikurs, R. and Soltz, V. (1964) *Children: The Challenge*. New York: Plume, 1991.

Mosak, H.H. and Maniacci, M.P. (1999) *A Primer of Adlerian Psychology*. Philadelphia: Brunner/Mazel.

Oberst, U.E. and Stewart, A.E. (2003) *Adlerian Psychotherapy: An Advanced Approach to Individual Psychology*. Hove: Brunner-Routledge.

Analytical Psychology

(Carl Gustav Jung, 1875–1961)

RUTH WILLIAMS

BRIEF HISTORY

Analytical psychology is the term Jung coined to distinguish his form of depth psychology from Freud's psychoanalysis. It is also referred to as Jungian analysis or psychotherapy, or sometimes Jungian psychoanalysis.

Jung was born on 26 July 1875, the son of a Swiss pastor. His disappointment in his father, whose faith he saw as rooted in dogma rather than personal experience, was critical in forming Jung's view of what we might now think of as the need for personal authenticity. His mother came from one of the oldest patrician families in Basel, and he went on to marry wealthy heiress Emma Rauschenbach on Valentine's Day in 1903.

Jung worked as a psychiatrist at the Burgholzli clinic in Zurich (1900–9) under the well-known psychiatrist Eugene Blueler (who invented the term schizophrenia, hitherto known as 'dementia praecox'). During this period Jung developed the word association test, which involved a list of 100 words being given to a subject to elicit a spontaneous association to each word. Meaning was ascribed to the association itself as well as to the response time to the so-called stimulus words. Clusters of similar responses led Jung to formulate his theory of complexes. The word association test is not used in contemporary practice.

On its publication in 1900, Jung read Freud's *Interpretation of Dreams* which he recognised as having been produced by a kindred spirit. When Jung met Freud in 1906, a deep affinity was established between the two men. Freud saw Jung as his natural heir, and in Freud Jung saw a paternal figure. The relationship broke down on Jung's publication of his *Psychology of the Unconscious* (1916) when it became clear that Jung's ideas had significantly diverged from those of his mentor. The irreconcilable differences concerned whether there could be libido that was not exclusively sexual. Jung saw libido as being more broadly defined, a notion that sometimes erroneously gives rise to the idea that Jungian analysis is not concerned with sex. The trauma of this rift with Freud presaged a period of crisis for Jung during which he developed many of his most original and creative ideas using nature, creative media and dreams to explore his psyche. These explorations are now available following the long-awaited publication of *The Red Book* (2009) which gives an intimate insight into Jung's personal development in both written and artistic form. *The Red Book* presents Jung's own 'active imagination' (see definition below) giving direct access to the innermost workings of his mind in the most experimental form. Of this period Jung ([1963]1995) states:

> The years when I was pursuing my inner images were the most important of my life – in them everything essential was decided. It all began then; the later details are only supplements and clarifications of the

material that burst forth from the unconscious, and at first swamped me. It was the *prima materia* for a lifetime's work.

Some of these events are covered in abridged form in *Memories, Dreams, Reflections* ([1963] 1995, written by Jung in collaboration with Aniela Jaffé).

Jung's erudition expanded the field of his psychology to include religion (Eastern and Western) and the ancient art of alchemy, which he used as a metaphorical device to illustrate his ideas. His interest in the esoteric has attracted a wide gamut of seekers and has been incorporated into New Age thinking (see Tacey, 2001). Jung's ideas have been widely applied in cultural studies, in the arts and popular culture, perhaps especially in film.

The International Association for Analytical Psychology, with member organisations throughout the world, regulates the training and professional aspects of Jungian analysis. In Britain there are four affiliated societies with distinct features, ranging from the developmental (Society of Analytical Psychology and British Association of Psychotherapists, Jungian Section), which incorporates Kleinian ideas in regard to early human development; to the classical (Independent Group of Analytical Psychologists), which pays particular heed to myth and fairytale and thus tends to look at the personal through the lens of the collective unconscious; and to the Association of Jungian Analysts, which occupies a middle position between these approaches, holding respect for both ends of the spectrum. The history of the divisions between these societies and an in-depth account of the differences may be found in Kirsch (2000). See Samuels (1985: Chapter 1) for an account of the schools of analytical psychology; Samuels systematically delineates the features of each school which, in part, includes consideration of frequency of sessions.

There is a third strand called 'archetypal psychology', which is an important offshoot developed by James Hillman (1978) but which has not taken root as a clinical discipline.

BASIC ASSUMPTIONS

Individuation is the term used to describe the process of becoming oneself, which is the goal of analysis. It is quite distinct from individualism which is about being overly self-reliant or self-centred in a somewhat narrow way; rather, individuation implies a striving towards greater wholeness.

Jung's schema consists of a *personal unconscious* and a *collective unconscious*. The former is made up of the personal complexes, the latter of

archetypes. Archetypes may be seen as potentials. They are often referred to in the form of characters (such as Trickster, Hero, Mother, Father, Puer or Puella (eternal child), and Witch). These are all facets of personality to which we each have access and which vary in accordance with individual and cultural context. Archetypes are seen as deriving from radically differing origins by Jungian writers, ranging from the biological/evolutionary (Stevens, 1982; 2003) to the poetic (Hillman, 1983; 1994) and the developmental/neuroscientific (Knox, 2001; 2003), to name but a few.

Psychological types are central. The terms *introvert* and *extrovert* both originated with Jung and are now in common usage to describe people whose principal mode of being tends to be more internally or externally focused. Jung formulated a system whereby he then saw people as falling predominantly into one of four types: feeling, thinking, intuiting, sensation. Although this may sound restrictive and over-determined, in fact it can be used in quite a subtle fashion and enhance understanding. A person may need to give precedence to another facet of their personality to compensate (a Jungian term) for one-sidedness, and this model might help gain insight into where a person needs to develop. It is also helpful in understanding interpersonal conflicts and where people clash along the axis of different psychological type. This system gave rise to personality tests still now used in commercial settings and more rarely in a clinical context.

Jung saw life as a 'continual balancing of *opposites*' (1949: para. 1417, italics added). If a person is too 'nice', it is probable something less nice is being held at bay and needs to be balanced out in order for that person to become more rounded or authentic. The *shadow* is often referred to in this context in that it contains all the elements one does not wish to identify with or admit as part of oneself. This usually means those qualities or thoughts will burst through, like the return of the repressed.

Anima (meaning soul) and *animus* (the feminine form) are the Latin names Jung used to describe the part of ourselves which represents the internalised aspects of the gender opposite to that of the individual (see below regarding gender). These images are sometimes seen or imagined as idealised images of the beloved or desired object in dream or waking life and can be experienced as the external person being one's 'soul mate'.

Persona is sometimes seen as a mask. It is the face one presents to the world and is not necessarily 'false'.

Self is sometimes spelt with a capital 'S' in Jung to emphasise a distinction from the ordinary usage of the word 'self'. It is seen as the centre of being, sometimes with spiritual connotations. Coming more into the 'Self' is seen as an achievement in terms of *individuation*, Self being seen as the sum of all the parts.

ORIGIN AND MAINTENANCE OF PROBLEMS

One factor which might account for analytical psychology being sometimes seen as less mainstream than psychoanalysis is that Jung has been accused of being anti-Semitic. It is true that he wrote some things (regarding race, for instance) which were unwise and ill-considered, especially in the context of his time. These matters have been taken seriously by post-Jungians who have re-evaluated Jung's work from this perspective, both as historical corrective and as necessary reparation (see Samuels, 1993: 287–316).

There have likewise had to be revisions to Jung's writing in regard to gender. Jung's wife Emma (who was also a practising analyst) wrote *Animus and Anima: Two Essays* (1931), which show a more nuanced perspective than Jung's own writing in this area. See also Wehr (1987), Samuels (1989: Chapter 6) and Young-Eisendrath (2004), for instance.

There are also two new areas of study which have arisen in recent years and have contributed enormously to the field of analytical psychology. One is emergence theory, and the other is the cultural complex.

The cultural complex has been developed (by Singer and Kimbles) as an idea only since 2000. They are building on Jung's own theory of complexes (which relates to the personal level) and extrapolating those ideas on to the individual, the societal and the archetypal realm. They identify cultural complexes to be at the heart of conflicts between many groups in terms of politics, economics, sociology, etc. (Singer, 2004: 20) as well as deeply embedded in 'tribal memories, patterned behaviours in the form of rituals and strong beliefs' (Singer, 2010: 234).

Emergence theory is based on the idea that phenomena can arise without any precursor. As such it is at the cutting edge of attempts to explore the origin of archetypes (Hogenson, 2004).

CHANGE

The process of change and transformation in any psychotherapy is usually a slow one. Grappling with entrenched psychological trauma or patterns of being requires investment of time (and money if undertaken privately with an analyst or therapist) as well as deep personal application. Some see the process of *individuation* as a working through of karmic tasks. The psyche (defined in Jungian terms as encompassing the whole person) may transform through dreams or by using creative media such as art, sand tray, dance or body work, etc. (see Schaverien, 1991; 1995). Talking is usually the main means of creating a connection with the therapist/analyst in a relationship which forms the vessel in which the issues become apparent. It was in this context that Jung used the alchemical metaphor mentioned above to elucidate the process of analysis. The alchemists were striving to turn one substance into another which entailed various stages of transformation. This can be seen to mirror the psychic stages of transformation undergone during the course of an analysis or a psychotherapeutic journey. In psychoanalytic terms this refers to the transference which is the framework within which matters arise and provides the arena for working through and thus change. This is an arduous process in which one is gripped by 'real' feelings, being in a 'real' relationship. It involves coping with the vicissitudes of need and dependency. By 'working through' is meant coping with the emergence of unconscious material with a view to integrating it and gaining ways of going forward, incorporating hitherto unwanted parts of oneself. This expansion is usually felt as an enhancement of the personality and the ability to cope with and enjoy life.

SKILLS AND STRATEGIES

Dreams are central to Jungian analysis and psychotherapy. Their symbolic contents often encapsulate a situation in a way words alone cannot.

The *numinous* is a concept unique to Jungian analysis. It refers to the mysterious elements we all touch on in life at times and which may be encountered in dreams and synchronicities, for instance. Jung (1945) wrote: 'The approach to the numinous is the real therapy and inasmuch as you attain to the numinous experiences you are released from the curse of pathology.'

Active imagination was a method Jung developed during his personal crisis in which he used creativity to identify and work problems through. This is sometimes used in contemporary practice where an open mind can facilitate exploration.

Synchronicity is the term Jung introduced to describe the coincidence of two events which he saw as having an acausal link. In other words, it is not just coincidence that something happens; rather, something else happens which connects the two in an inexplicable but meaningful way. The term has of course entered common parlance. Genuine synchronicities – somewhat rare as they are – can contribute to our understanding in a clinical setting as well as outside. A dramatic example taken from Main is as follows:

> An analyst on vacation suddenly had a strong visual impression of one of her patients she knew to be suicidal. Unable to account for the impression as having arisen by any normal chain of mental associations, she immediately sent a telegram telling the patient not to do anything foolish. Two days later she learned that, just before the telegram arrived, the patient had gone into the kitchen and turned on the gas valve with the intention of killing herself. Startled by the postman ringing the doorbell, she turned the valve off; and even more struck by the content of the telegram he delivered, she did not resume her attempt. (2007: 1–2)

RESEARCH EVIDENCE

The very issue of providing research in the field of psychotherapy is somewhat contentious in as much as the work is not easily quantifiable. It is a highly subjective experience. Under pressure to conform to standards set by executive bodies, researchers put much effort into finding ways of conducting research that do justice to the work. This has become increasingly important at a time when there has been governmental pressure to statutorily regulate the profession, and in a climate where economics has been the guiding principle in the Improving Access to Psychological Therapies (IAPT) initiative. With the IAPT programme there has been a risk of losing the essential meaning of 'therapy', shifting the focus from the 'care of souls' to a manualised practice which can be evaluated in numerical form.

Jung himself regarded his life's work to be indivisible from his life and research (Stevens, 1990).

The first chair in analytical psychology was endowed at the Texas A&M University in Dallas in 1985. In Britain the first chair in analytical psychology was created in 1995 at the University of Essex. Essex has a thriving department with pioneering research programmes in analytical psychology at masters and doctoral level attracting students from around the world.

REFERENCES

Freud, S. (1900) The interpretation of dreams. In *The Standard Edition of the Complete Psychological Works of Sigmund Freud.* London: Hogarth, 1953.

Hillman, J. (1978) *The Myth of Analysis: Three Essays in Archetypal Psychology.* New York: Harper Torch.

Hillman, J. (1983) *Archetypal Psychology: A Brief Account.* Woodstock, CT: Spring.

Hillman, J. (1994) *Healing Fictions.* Woodstock, CT: Spring.

Hogenson, G.B. (2004) Archetypes: emergence and the psyche's deep structure. In J. Cambray and L. Carter (eds), *Analytical Psychology: Contemporary Perspectives in Jungian Analysis.* Hove: Brunner-Routledge.

Jung, C.G. (1916) *Psychology of the Unconscious.* London: Kegan Paul, Trench, Trubner, 1933.

Jung, C.G. (1945) Letter to P.W. Martin dated 20th August 1945. In *C.G. Jung Letters* (Vol. 1). London: Routledge and Kegan Paul, 1973.

Jung, C.G. (1949) Foreword to Neumann, *Depth Psychology and a New Ethic.* In *The Symbolic Life (Collected Works* Vol. 18). London: Routledge, 1993.

Jung, C.G. ([1963] 1995) *Memories, Dreams, Reflections.* London: Fontana, 1995.

Jung, C.G. (2009) *The Red Book.* London: Norton.

Jung, E. (1931) *Animus and Anima: Two Essays.* Woodstock, CT: Spring, 1957.

Kirsch, T. (2000) *The Jungians: A Comparative and Historical Perspective.* London: Routledge, 2000.

Knox, J. (2001) Memories, fantasies, archetypes: an exploration of some connections between cognitive science and analytical psychology. *Journal of Analytical Psychology,* 46 (4): 613–35.

Knox, J. (2003) *Archetype, Attachment, Analysis: Jungian Psychology and the Emergent Mind.* Hove: Brunner-Routledge.

Main, R. (2007) *Revelations of Chance: Synchronicity as Spiritual Experience.* New York: SUNY Press.

Samuels, A. (1985) *Jung and the Post-Jungians.* London: Routledge.

Samuels, A. (1989) *The Plural Psyche: Personality, Morality and the Father.* London: Tavistock/Routledge.

Samuels, A. (1993) *The Political Psyche.* London: Routledge.

Schaverien, J. (1991) *The Revealing Image: Analytical Art Psychotherapy in Theory and Practice*. London: Tavistock/Routledge.

Schaverien, J. (1995) *Desire and the Female Therapist: Engendered Gaze in Psychotherapy and Art Therapy*. London: Routledge.

Singer, T. (2004) Archetypal defences of the group spirit. In T. Singer and S.L. Kimbles (eds), *The Cultural Complex: Contemporary Jungian Perspectives on Psyche and Society*. Hove: Routledge.

Singer, T. (2010) The transcendent function and cultural complexes: a working hypothesis. *Journal of Analytical Psychology*, 55 (2).

Stevens, A. (1982) *Archetypes: A Natural History of the Self*. New York: Morrow.

Stevens, A. (1990) *On Jung*. London: Routledge.

Stevens, A. (2003) *Archetype Revisited: An Updated Natural History of the Self*. Toronto: Inner City.

Tacey, D. (2001) *Jung and the New Age*. Hove: Brunner-Routledge.

Wehr, D. (1987) *Jung and Feminism: Liberating Archetypes*. Boston: Beacon.

Young-Eisendrath, P. (2004) *Subject to Change: Jung, Gender and Subjectivity in Psychoanalysis*. Hove: Routledge.

RECOMMENDED READING

Bair, D. (2003) *Jung: A Biography*. London: Little Brown.

Attachment-Based Psychoanalytic Psychotherapy

JOSEPH SCHWARTZ

BRIEF HISTORY

Attachment-based psychoanalytic psychotherapy is based on the psychoanalytic tradition founded by William Alanson White (1925) and Harry Stack Sullivan (1924) in the United States in the 1920s. Known as the Interpersonal School or Washington School of Psychiatry, it had antecedents, primarily in the early work of Eugen Bleuler (1911) in Switzerland. White said: 'We must understand what the patient is trying to do' (Sullivan, 1924: 78).

After the splits of the 1940s in New York between drive theorists and relational theorists, the William Alanson White Institute in New York became the centre for training and research in a psychoanalysis based on relational conflict rather than instinctual conflict (Schwartz, 1999). What is now known as the relational turn or relational psychoanalysis (Greenberg and Mitchell, 1983; Mitchell, 1988) developed from the interpersonal psychoanalysis of White and Sullivan to include a more thorough exploration of the human inner world as pioneered by Freud. The Interpersonal School located human mental pain in the failure of relationships and felt that the Freudian use of interpretation was distancing and counterproductive clinically.

The relational school used transference and counter-transference re-enactments in the consulting room to explore how painful experience got represented in the patient's inner world. At the same time, where Freud's concept of the human being was the human being as pleasure seeking, the relational school, following the Scottish analyst Ronald Fairbairn (1946), saw the human being as fundamentally relationship seeking. The work of White and Sullivan crossed the Atlantic to Britain in the work of Ian Suttie (1935), Donald Winnicott (1965), Ronald Fairbairn (1946) and John Bowlby (1969; 1973; 1980). Based on the inadequacies of his experience of supervision with Melanie Klein and his analysis with the Kleinian analyst Joan Riviere in the 1930s, Bowlby set out to explore the effects of separation and loss on childhood emotional development. In his famous *Attachment and Loss* trilogy, Bowlby presented his attachment theory of human psychological development.

Attachment theory is now developed experimentally in the journal *Attachment and Human Development* (Routledge) and clinically in the journal *Attachment: New Directions in Psychotherapy and Relational Psychoanalysis* (Karnac). A compendium of research developments is summarized in *Handbook of Attachment: Theory, Research and Clinical Applications*, second edition (Cassidy and Shaver, 2008). Clinical work is summarized in Schwartz and Pollard (2004) and Slade (2008). Attachment-based psychoanalytic psychotherapy is not to be confused with attachment therapy which does not have psychoanalytic roots.

BASIC ASSUMPTIONS

The basic premise of attachment-based/relational work is that the human being is fundamentally relationship seeking. In the psychoanalytic context of the times, Bowlby formulated attachment theory as a drive theory, speaking loosely of attachment needs as an instinctual human drive for relationship. Bowlby's development of attachment theory can be seen as an elaboration of Fairbairn's theoretical stance as summarized late in his career (Fairbairn, 1958):

1   An ego is present from birth.
2   Libido is a function of the ego.
3   There is no death instinct; and aggression is a reaction to frustration or deprivation.
4   Since libido is a function of the ego, and aggression is a reaction to frustration or deprivation, there is no such thing as an id.
5   The ego, and therefore libido, is fundamentally object seeking.
6   The earliest and original form of anxiety, as experienced by the child, is separation anxiety.
7   Internalization of the object is a defensive measure originally adopted by the child to deal with his original object (the mother and her breast) in so far as it is unsatisfying.
8   Internalization of the object is not just a product of a phantasy of incorporating the object orally, but is a distinct psychological process.

ORIGIN AND MAINTENANCE OF PROBLEMS

Fairbairn (1958) is substantially arguing with Melanie Klein. It is the last great public dispute between relational and instinctual points of view. Klein can be credited with bringing the child's experience relevant to psychoanalysis right back to birth instead of the more classical view of psychodynamic realities starting with the Oedipus complex around age four. Latin American analysts have been particularly appreciative of Klein for bringing the role of motherhood and early childhood into psychoanalytic theory (Langer, 1989). But the theoretical resources of the 1920s were not great enough for Klein to locate the distress she observed in very young children as stemming from anxiety. Instead she took Freud's highly contested concept of the death instinct (Freud, 1920) as the foundation of her theory of childhood anger and anxiety. The breast, as in the Kleinian good breast and bad breast, became a thing instead of a channel for relationship. As Klein expressed it: 'In the earliest reality of the child it is

no exaggeration to say that the world is a breast and a belly which is filled with dangerous objects, dangerous because of the child's own impulse to attack them' (1930: 251). It took the work of Winnicott, Fairbairn and Bowlby, along with contributions from William Alanson White and Harry Stack Sullivan in the United States, to locate the distress Klein reported in young children as separation and/or abandonment anxiety. As White observed:

> When for any reason this feeling of belonging is interfered with or destroyed, when the individual is separated from as it were those whom he loves or upon whom he is dependent or to whom he looks for guidance, then there develops the separation anxiety which is at the bottom of neuroses and psychoses. (1937: 459)

And as Fairbairn summarized his views above:

> There is no death instinct; and aggression is a reaction to frustration or deprivation.

> The earliest and original form of anxiety, as experienced by the child, is separation anxiety.

Fairbairn is perhaps unusual among the early psychoanalytic theorists in stating his views clearly in opposition to other theories. But he also made attempts to understand previous formulations in light of his way of understanding the human inner world. Klein's use of the death instinct to understand childhood anxiety is relocated to be an expression of separation anxiety. Freud's premise that the human being is pleasure seeking is relocated to the human being as relationship seeking. But, perhaps uniquely in psychoanalytic theorizing, Fairbairn (1946) tried to understand how Freud could have formulated his theory of pleasure seeking. Fairbairn argued, against Freud, that pleasure seeking was a deterioration of object seeking, i.e. relationship seeking. Clinically, Fairbairn's way of understanding pleasure seeking as a deterioration of relationships is most obvious when treating womanizing men, where the sexuality involved may be pleasurable but is a sexuality of despair, a giving up of the possibility of relationship (Laschinger et al., 2004).

At present, the tensions between Kleinian and relational/attachment points of view remain strong in both the UK and the US. As the Kleinian analyst James Grotstein (2000) has vehemently argued: 'Kleinians go down deeper and come up dirtier.' At its crudest, Kleinians accuse attachment-based clinicians of being afraid of hate, while attachment-based/relational clinicians accuse the Kleinians of being afraid of love.

To this writer the evidence is clear and convincing: human beings are fundamentally relationship seeking; the earliest, most destructive form of anxiety is separation anxiety (abandonment). There is no death instinct (Schwartz, 2001). Separation anxiety is the origin and maintenance of most mental pain and problems.

CHANGE

The basic premise is that human mental pain or distress is to be located in the failure of past relationships. There is no room for genetic or instinctual hypotheses. Change happens when the pain of the failure of past relationships can be acknowledged and felt and the very real loss of what one didn't have can be mourned.

SKILLS AND STRATEGIES

As opposed to interpretation, attachment-based clinicians rely far more on counter-transference, the understanding of the full range of the therapist's feelings in the consulting room. Arguably, the therapist's feelings are the only thing that can actually be known with any degree of certainty in the consulting room. The use of the counter-transference is now routine in many schools of psychoanalytic psychotherapy. Racker (1968), for example, distinguishes between concordant counter-transference – the feelings that the therapist has that the client also has – and complementary counter-transference – the feelings that the therapist has that significant others in the client's past had in relating to the client.

Attachment-based work tends to be inclusive as opposed to the exclusivity of Freud's psychoanalysis. As Freud wrote: 'since [psychoanalysis] necessitates the devotion of long and intense attention to the individual patient, it would be uneconomical to squander such expenditure upon completely worthless persons who happen to be neurotic' (1923: 250).

Freud specifically excluded schizophrenia from psychoanalytic treatment: '[Schizophrenic patients] display two fundamental characteristics, megalomania and diversion of interest from the external world – from people and things. In consequence of the latter change, they become inaccessible to the influence of psychoanalysis and cannot be cured by our efforts' (1914: 66). Freud's view of the untreatability of psychosis was opposed in the US by the Washington School of Psychiatry who, following Bleuler's example in Switzerland, found ways to establish relationships with these severely traumatized patients: 'The incomprehensible is to be regarded as fragments of intent which has come to light after the patient has ceased his efforts at and abandoned his hopes of communicating with the

environment' (Sullivan, 1925: 72). Treatment of trauma and psychosis is a marker of the practice of attachment-based clinicians (Benemer, 2010; Badouk Epstein et al., 2011).

The clinical work in attachment-based psychoanalytic psychotherapy can be characterized by the following elements: emphasis on what Batement and Fonagy (2006) call mentalization; a recognition that transference/counter-transference entanglements are inevitable and are there to be worked through, not avoided; and an understanding that the therapist is more an experienced guide on a highly individual journey, rather than a knowing expert. Affect regulation, attunement and the processes of rupture and repair are seen to be essential to the ongoing process of co-creating what can be called a secure-enough base. The secure-enough base is then the platform from which the therapist can bear witness to childhood trauma and from which a narrative of a traumatized past can be created (Bowlby, 1979: 145–6).

The attachment strategies – secure, ambivalent, anxious, avoidant – can be useful ways to characterize the outcomes of early childhood experience. In particular, disorganized attachment, where the needed attachment figure is also a threat, can be a helpful framework for beginning work with adult survivors of physical, sexual and/or the organized abuse of paedophile rings and ritual abuse networks.

RESEARCH EVIDENCE

There has been increasing interest in the new neurobiology of human emotions in clinical work (Schore, 1994; Damasio, 2010). Schore locates counter-transference, the staple of attachment-based clinical work, as non-verbal communication from right brain to right brain. Antonio Damasio locates the human capacity to speak about feelings in the human pre-frontal cortex. As a leading neurobiologist of human emotion, Damasio argues that human beings possess what he calls secondary consciousness, that is the involvement of the pre-frontal cortex in the human capacity to be conscious of feelings, as opposed to the antelope who is afraid when chased by a lion but doesn't know it, so to speak. Many clinicians feel that the demonstration of a neurological substrate to psychoanalytic concepts is an important step towards the scientific legitimation of psychoanalytic psychotherapy.

More relevant to clinical work are the extensive research studies in exploring the attachment paradigm reported in the literature, particularly in the previously mentioned journal *Attachment and Human Development*. Issue 4, Volume 12, July 2010 is a special issue on an attachment perspective on incarcerated parents and their children. The

Handbook of Attachment, second edition (Cassidy and Shaver, 2008) contains extensive review articles on current research work.

REFERENCES

Badouk Epstein, O., Schwartz, J. and Wingfield, R. (eds) (2011) *Ritual Abuse and Mind Control: The Manipulation of Attachment Needs.* London: Karnac.

Bateman, Antony and Fonagy, Peter (2006) *Mentalization-Based Treatment for Borderline Personality Disorder: A Practical Guide.* Oxford: Oxford University Press.

Benemer, Sarah (ed.) (2010) *Telling Stories? Attachment-Based Approaches to the Treatment of Psychosis.* London: Karnac.

Bleuler, Eugen (1911) *Dementia Praecox of the Group of Schizophrenias.* Translated by J. Zinkin. New York: International Universities Press.

Bowlby, John (1969) *Attachment and Loss.* Vol. 1: *Attachment.* Harmondsworth: Penguin.

Bowlby, John (1973) *Attachment and Loss.* Vol. 2: *Separation: Anxiety and Anger.* Harmondsworth: Penguin.

Bowlby, John (1979) *The Making and Breaking of Affectional Bonds.* London: Routledge.

Bowlby, John (1980) *Attachment and Loss.* Vol. 3: *Loss: Sadness and Depression.* Harmondsworth: Penguin.

Cassidy, Jude and Shaver, Phillip R. (eds) (2008) *Handbook of Attachment: Theory, Research and Clinical Applications* (2nd edn). London: Guilford.

Damasio, Antonio R. (2010) *Self Comes to Mind. Constructing the Conscious Brain: The Evolution of Consciousness.* London: Heinemann.

Fairbairn, W.R.D. (1946) Object-relationships and dynamic structure. In W.R.D. Fairbairn, *Psychoanalytic Studies of the Personality* (pp. 137–51). London: Routledge and Kegan Paul, 1952.

Fairbairn, W.R.D. (1958) On the nature and aims of psychoanalytic treatment. *International Journal of Psychoanalysis*, 39: 374–85.

Freud, Sigmund (1914) *On the History of the Psychoanalytic Movement.* Pelican Freud Library (vol. 15, pp. 63–128). Harmondsworth: Penguin.

Freud, Sigmund (1920) *Beyond the Pleasure Principle.* New York: Norton, 1961.

Freud, Sigmund (1923) Psycho-analysis. *Standard Edition of the Complete Psychological Works of Sigmund Freud* (vol. 18, pp. 235–54).

Greenberg, J.R. and Mitchell, S.A. (1983) *Object Relations and Psychoanalytic Theory.* Cambridge, MA: Harvard University Press.

Grotstein, James S. (2000) *Who is the Dreamer Who Dreams the Dream.* Hillsdale, NJ: The Analytic Press.

Klein, Melanie (1930) The psychotherapy of the psychoses. In Melanie Klein, *Contributions to Psycho-Analysis 1921–1945* (introduction Ernest Jones) (pp. 251–3). London: Hogarth, 1948.

Langer, M. (1989) *From Vienna to Managua: Journey of a Psychoanalyst.* London: Free Association.

Laschinger, Bernice, Purnell, Chris, Schwartz, Joseph, White, Kate and Wingfield, Rachel (2004) Sexuality and attachment from a clinical point of view. *Attachment and Human Development*, 6: 151–64.

Mitchell, S.A. (1988) *Relational Concepts in Psychoanalysis: An Integration.* Cambridge, MA: Harvard University Press.

Racker, Heinrich (1968) *Transference and Countertransference.* Madison, CT: International Universities Press.

Schore, Allan N. (1994) *Affect Regulation and the Origin of the Self: The Neurobiology of Emotional Development.* Hillsdale, NJ: Erlbaum.

Schwartz, J. (1999) *Cassandra's Daughter: A History of Psychoanalysis in Europe and America.* London: Karnac.

Schwartz, Joseph (2001) Commentary on David Black: beyond the death drive detour – how can we deepen our understanding of cruelty, malice, hatred, envy and violence? *British Journal of Psychotherapy*, 18: 199–204.

Schwartz, Joseph and Pollard, James (eds) (2004) Special issue: attachment-based psychoanalytic psychotherapy. *Attachment and Human Development*, 6 (June).

Slade, Arietta (2008) Attachment theory and research: implications for the theory and practice of individual psychotherapy with adults. In Jude Cassidy and Phillip R. Shaver (eds), *Handbook of Attachment: Theory, Research and Clinical Applications* (pp. 575–94). London: Guilford.

Sullivan, Harry Stack (1924) Schizophrenia: its conservative and malignant features. *American Journal of Psychiatry*, 5 (old series v. 81): 77–91.

Sullivan, Harry Stack (1925) Peculiarity of thought processes in schizophrenia. *American Journal of Psychiatry*, 5 (old series v. 82): 21–86.

Suttie, Ian D. (1935) The taboo on tenderness. In *The Origins of Love and Hate* (Chapter 6). Republished with foreword John Bowlby, introduction Dorothy Heard, London: Free Association, 1988.

White, William Alanson (1925) Presidential address. *American Journal of Psychiatry*, 5 (old series v. 82): 1–8.

White, W.A. (1937) Review of *The Origins of Love and Hate*. *Psychoanalytic Review*, 24: 458–60.

Winnicott, D.W. (1965) *The Maturational Process and the Facilitating Environment*. New York: International Universities Press.

RECOMMENDED READING

Brisch, Karl Heinz (2002) *Treating Attachment Disorders: From Theory to Therapy*. London: Guilford.

Cortina, Mauricio and Marrone, Mario (eds) (2003) *Attachment Theory and the Psychoanalytic Process*. London: Whurr.

Diamond, Nicola and Marrone, Mario (2003) *Attachment and Intersubjectivity*. London: Whurr.

Fonagy, Peter (2001) *Attachment Theory and Psychoanalysis*. New York: Other.

Goodman, Geoff (2002) *The Internal World and Attachment*. Mahwah, NJ: Analytic.

Lacanian Therapy

(Jacques Lacan, 1901–1981)

LIONEL BAILLY

BRIEF HISTORY

In the middle decades of the twentieth century, Jacques Lacan created a model of psychoanalysis by revisiting the works of Freud in the light of developments in fields of study such as linguistics, philosophy, anthropology and mathematics.

Jacques Lacan was born in Paris on 13 April 1901. He studied medicine and psychiatry and was trained in psychiatric asylums where he acquired a wide clinical experience, including of severe psychosis. After having worked with some of the most brilliant proponents of organic psychiatry, he found in psychoanalysis the most helpful theoretical model for understanding and treating the complex patients he was dealing with. In 1938, he became a psychoanalyst of the Société Psychanalytique de Paris. Lacan believed that Freudian theory was not a perfect edifice but a work in progress, and wanted to contribute toward what he saw as a developing model. His attitude towards the development of theory was modern in that he was willing to examine any body of science that could clarify or shed new light on the phenomena he was trying to explain, and consequently he drew inspiration from biological psychiatry, genetic psychology, philosophy, structural linguistics, anthropology and even mathematics. The richness of the result has attracted students in fields far from psychoanalysis or psychiatry; but his views were

sufficiently controversial for Lacan to be banned from the International Psychoanalytic Association in 1962. In 1963, he created his own school of psychoanalysis. The new organisation proved a success, and the influence and membership of Lacanian analytic institutions has continued to grow to the present day. Jacques Lacan died in Paris on 9 September 1981.

BASIC ASSUMPTIONS

Lacan's view is that the characteristic that sets human beings apart from other animals is language: we are speaking beings. If speech is what makes us human, then the fundamentals of the human psyche should be found in the particularities and structure of spoken language. Lacan made the hypothesis of a structural mirroring between what we say, the way we think and what we are – and this also applies to the unconscious, which is structured like a language. Slips of the tongue, bungled actions and also symptoms encountered in psychopathology follow this linguistic structure and can be seen as having a metaphoric value.

The ego is a fiction, 'an imaginary narrative' that the infant starts to construct as soon as he/she is able to recognise itself in the mirror, and the building blocks of the edifice are signifiers (the spoken word). The ego is not based on a perception–consciousness system or organised by the reality principle, but exists instead by dint of *méconnaissance* (obliviousness) – the obliviousness or blindness of the subject to itself.

Drawing upon Freud's idea that thought and meaning are coded in ideational representatives, Lacan pinpointed these by means of Saussurian linguistics as being *signifiers* – the spoken part of words. Lacan emphasised the detachable quality of signifiers from what they signify, and that it is the signifier attached to an anxiogenic thought that becomes repressed into the unconscious, so that the anxious affect becomes displaced onto other, less terrifying signifiers (which might thereby acquire an irrationally worrying nature). The unconscious for Lacan is therefore a world of lost signifiers, and the task of analysis is to retrieve these and restore them to consciousness in the authentic signifying chain. The patient is the only person in possession of the unconscious knowledge, and it is by paying careful attention to the patient's discourse – especially to slips of the tongue, dreams, repetitive speech, irrational narrative or neurotic preoccupations – that the analyst is able to hear the manifestations of the unconscious. The patient has no feeling of responsibility for these manifestations, which seem to him to come from somewhere else, which Lacan calls the Other (*le grand autre*). The place occupied by this Other is that from which language and laws derive.

The unconscious discourse of the patient is directed by 'master signifiers' – the foundation stones of the individual's psychological structure. These signifiers 'orient' or give direction to the patient's preoccupations and unconscious narratives. One of the main tasks of analysis is to bring into consciousness these master signifiers, so that the patient becomes aware of how they influence his/her emotions and thoughts.

Lacan builds upon Freud's Oedipus complex to arrive at the subtler formulation known as the *paternal metaphor* to explain how a child separates psychically from its mother and accepts its status as a less-than-perfect being. In order to explain its mother's absences and preoccupations, the child must postulate an object she desires more than him/herself. This imaginary object is called the *phallus*. Lacan's view of castration is not a real physical threat, but the child's reluctant acceptance that s/he does not have what it takes to keep mother's perfect attention, and the consequent hypothesis that this most desirable object must exist 'somewhere out there' in the real world. The name-of-the-father is the first signifier that the child can accept as a representative of what mother finds more interesting than him/herself; it is a *metaphor* and the child's acceptance of it involves an important intellectual act. For Lacan, the child's submission to this formulation initiates him/her into the ability to

think metaphorically, with the flexibility of signifier substitutions that this allows, and is a keystone in the construction of the psyche.

Lacan saw desire as a condition that plays a structuring role in the subject. Desire results from the impossibility that a subject can properly articulate what it needs – the 'gap between demand and need'. The articulation of need must pass through the gates of language, and what cannot squeeze through and is left behind constitutes desire. The objects around which desire is organised are imaginary objects called 'the object cause of desire', and this has a genetic link with the original imagined perfect object, the phallus. The object cause of desire, or *object a*, is closely linked with anxiety, in that it appears in the place of a primordial experience of loss.

For Lacan, it is not the biological reality of sex that determines our gender identity; he saw gender as the result of a process of identification, and of a process he calls 'sexuation'. This has to do with how a subject situates itself in relation to the phallus and symbolic castration, and also to his/her identification with the mother.

ORIGINS AND MAINTENANCE OF PROBLEMS

Like Sigmund and Anna Freud, Lacanians think that 'human behaviour and its aberrations [are] being determined not by overt factors but by the pressure of instinctual forces emanating from the unconscious mind' (A. Freud). Besides the classical analytical views on the origin of psychopathology, the Lacanian model suggests some specific types of difficulties.

The mirror stage represents a moment at which the baby perceives itself as a unit, and also the first time the child thinks of itself as 'I' in relation to an image that he understands as representing himself. The failure to perceive oneself in this way is seen in autistic pathologies in children. In addition, the intellectual perception of oneself is an alienating experience as the image is never as perfect as the imagined self, and splits the psyche into the part that identifies with the image and the part that becomes the active agent in building a narrative about the imaginary (from image) self. The discourse that is built upon the image is the ego, which Lacan sees as a fiction maintained and nurtured throughout one's life with the help of denegation and obliviousness (*méconnaissance*). This fictional ego can be the source of the patient's discontent and request for therapeutic help.

The ego and the subject both develop in the discourse of the Other – a way of saying that the discourse, attitudes and beliefs of the main figures in a child's development have a profound structuring effect upon the subject. The individual's master signifiers, which also derive from the Other, have a crucial role in the construction of the psychological structure of an individual and can be at the root of a subject's failure and sufferings.

The submission to the paternal metaphor allows the child to situate itself within the law, to move away from an enmeshed relationship with his/her mother and to drop his/her infantile omnipotence. For Lacan the foreclosure of the paternal metaphor leads to the development of a psychotic structure, while other pathological modalities of dealing with it can lead to neurosis or perversion.

The subject's relationship with his object cause of desire defines the individual's unique way in which he/she seeks enjoyment, and both the nature of these objects and the specificity of the relationship can be the source of psychopathology.

CHANGE

Lacan was preoccupied with what exactly 'curing' means. Is it simply the disappearance of a symptom, or does one aim to change the underlying personality structure that produced it and in which it is inscribed? Is this at all achievable, and if it is, is it desirable? If it is neither achievable nor desirable, then where should curing stop – at what boundary line? Lacan clarified his position about patients and symptoms by saying that while it is reasonable that individuals expect their symptoms to disappear following an analytical treatment, the symptom has a defensive quality and it might not always be prudent to try to suppress the use of certain aspects of it. In this way, enjoyment and desire remain possible for the subject.

The Lacanian analyst knows that at some point during the course of the treatment, the patient will be faced with the decision to be cured of his/her symptom or not to be. This decision, if the treatment has been successful, could be an enlightened choice, made in the light of self-knowledge.

A patient looking to boost his/her self-esteem, or to be reassured that they are really all right and just need to rethink some of their 'coping strategies', should not go to a Lacanian analyst. Lacanians do not 'strengthen' or 'support' the ego but will try to help the patient dismantle it in order to come face to face with his/her own subject, to recognise the truth of his/her desire and the modalities of his/her enjoyment, and to emerge from treatment with an altered ego that is closer to the fullness of the subject.

SKILLS AND STRATEGIES

As in most other forms of psychotherapy, free association is the first rule. The patient is asked to say anything that comes to mind, even if it appears superficial or unrelated to what has been discussed, and is encouraged to remember and talk about their dreams. The therapist pays particular attention to the discourse of the patient, the words used, the structure of the sentences, any unusual use of a word, patterns and repetitions, etc.

The place of counter-transference in Lacanian analysis is different from that in most other schools. Lacan recognised that the therapist experiences feelings towards his patient, but suggested that he must know not only not to give into them but also how to make adequate use of them in his technique. If the analyst does not act on the basis of these feelings, it is not because his training analysis has drained away his passions, but because it has given him a desire which is even stronger than those passions: the desire to remain focused upon the treatment of the patient.

Lacanians use sessions of variable duration including short sessions. The ending of the session is a meaningful act, too important to leave to mere form. One should not end a session just because the allotted time is up, especially if the analysand is in the middle of some interesting discourse. Conversely, it may be useful to be able to end the session just at the point that the analysand says something important – so that it can 'hang in the air' for further reflection until the next time; more words will often obfuscate the realisation that was emerging. In many ways, the end of the session emphasises some particularly important aspect and works almost as an interpretation.

RESEARCH EVIDENCE

There has been no quantitative research on the outcome of psychotherapy in a Lacanian theoretical framework. In addition, a Lacanian approach would lead to questioning the ability of quantitative research to assess and measure the 'improvement' of a patient, as this can't be equated with a mere reduction in symptomatology. It is not that research is impossible but that the impact of therapy on the individual's psyche is of a complexity far beyond the reach of symptom rating scales.

REFERENCE

Freud, A. www.freud.org.uk/education/topic/40053/annafreud

RECOMMENDED READING

Bailly, L. (2009) *Lacan: A Beginner's Guide*. Oxford: One World.

Lacan, J. (1979) The neurotic's individual myth (trans. Martha Noel Evans). *Psychoanalytic Quarterly*, 48 (3): 386–425.

Lacan, J. (1982) Guiding remarks for a congress on feminine sexuality. From *Écrits* (trans. J. Rose). In J. Mitchell and J. Rose (eds), *Feminine Sexuality*. New York: Norton.

Lacan, J. (2006) *Écrits* (trans. Bruce Fink). New York: Norton.

Psychoanalytic Therapy

(Sigmund Freud, 1856–1939)

JESSICA YAKELEY

BRIEF HISTORY

Sigmund Freud is one of a handful of remarkable thinkers whose ideas helped shape the twentieth century and which continue to be influential today. Originally a neurologist in Vienna working with patients suffering from hysteria, Freud experimented with hypnosis, abreaction and catharsis before discovering the 'talking cure'. Freud initially believed that neurotic symptoms were the result of the 'damming up' of affect resulting from painful childhood experiences, and if patients could be encouraged to talk about them, they would be cured. Freud particularly focused on his patients' dreams, proposing that the dream represented an attempt by the dreamer to fulfil a wish, which was usually an erotic wish. Like dreams, Freud saw neurotic symptoms as meaningful, representing compromise formations between repressed sexual impulses and the censoring agents of the mind. As he developed his thinking further, he began to see neurosis not just as the result of real trauma or childhood seduction, but as due to conflict over unconscious fantasies of infantile sexual gratification stemming from early childhood.

Freud's ideas were ahead of his time, and his theory of infantile sexuality shocked his colleagues and the wider society of early twentieth-century Europe in which he lived. However, through extensive treatment of patients, as well as his own self-analysis, he continued to develop a methodology of treatment in which to test his theories of the mind, attracting a growing body of followers. Freud was also a prolific writer, recording the results of his research in over 20 volumes of writing (translated as the Standard Edition), which have been important in the dissemination of his ideas. Despite influential critics and controversies, Freud's ideas have endured for over a century, permeating diverse fields of thought including education, the social sciences, literary theory, philosophy and the media. Psychoanalysis, as invented by Freud, continues today as a therapeutic treatment, a body of theoretical knowledge, and a method of investigation of the human mind.

BASIC ASSUMPTIONS

Although psychoanalysis has evolved considerably since Freud, many of his basic tenets remain central to contemporary theory and practice. Key notions include unconscious mental activity, psychic determination, and the idea that childhood experiences are critical in shaping the adult personality.

The Unconscious and Models of the Mind

Part of our mind is unconscious and can never be fully known to us, but is revealed through the analysis of dreams, slips of the tongue (which Freud called *parapraxes*) and patterns of speech, which provide a window into the underlying unconscious feelings, fantasies and desires that influence our conscious thoughts and manifest behaviour. In Freud's first *topographical model*, the mind was divided into three systems: the conscious, the preconscious and the unconscious. In the *preconscious*, mental contents can easily be brought to conscious awareness by shifting awareness, whereas the mental contents of the *unconscious* are unacceptable to the conscious mind and are therefore kept from conscious awareness by the forces of *repression* but emerge in the guise of symptoms.

In Freud's second model of the mind, the *structural model*, the psychical apparatus is divided into three parts: id, ego and superego. The *id* is a reservoir of unconscious unorganized instinctual sexual and aggressive drives, which are unacceptable to the social, moral and ethical values of conscious civilized thought and must therefore be kept at bay. The id is governed by primary process thinking under the domination of the pleasure principle – the inborn tendency of the organism to avoid pain and seek pleasure via the release of tension. In the lawless world of the id, opposites coexist, wishes are fulfilled, negatives do not exist, and there is no concept of time. The *ego* mediates between the conflicting demands of id, superego and reality. It is the executive organ of the psyche, controlling motility, perception, and contact with reality; and via the defence mechanisms, which are located in the unconscious part, the ego modulates the drives coming from the id. The *superego* evolves from part of the ego as the heir to the Oedipus complex, with the internalization by the child of parental standards and goals to establish the individual's moral conscience.

Psychic Determinism

Freud believed that although we may think we have control over our lives and operate through free choice, our conscious thoughts and actions are actually shaped and controlled by unconscious forces. For example, our chosen vocation, choice of partner, or even hobbies are not randomly selected, but are unconsciously determined by our childhood experiences. Moreover, Freud proposed that a single symptom or behaviour was multi-determined, in that it could contain multiple complex meanings and serve several functions in responding to the demands of both reality and the unconscious needs of the internal world.

Drive Theory and Libido

An instinct is a hereditary pattern of behaviour, specific to a species, that unfolds in a predetermined fashion during development and is resistant to change.

Freud took this biological concept to embed his psychological theory of the mind in biology with his theory of the drives. For Freud, all instincts had a *source* in a part of the body or bodily stimulus; an *aim*, to eliminate the state of tension deriving from the source; and an *object* (often another person) which was the target of the aim. Freud described libido as 'the force by which the sexual instinct is represented in the mind'. The association with sexuality is misleading, as Freud considered libido to include the notion of pleasure as a whole. In Freud's final theory of the instincts he proposed two opposing instincts – the life instinct (Eros) and the death instinct (Thanatos). Initially aimed at self-destruction, the death instinct is later turned against the outside world and underlies aggression.

Developmental Stages

Freud believed that children were influenced by sexual drives and proposed a developmental trajectory in which the early manifestations of infantile sexuality were associated with bodily functions such as feeding and bowel control. Psychosexual development consists of libidinal energy shifting from oral to anal to phallic to genital erotogenic zones respectively, where each corresponding stage of development is characterized by particular functions and objectives, but builds upon and subsumes the accomplishments of the preceding stage. Failure to negotiate the emotional demands of each stage is linked to complex character traits in adult life. For example, excessive oral gratifications or deprivations can result in pathological narcissism and dependence on others, whereas developmental arrest at the anal stage can lead to miserliness or sadism.

The Oedipus Complex

Freud named the Oedipus complex after the Greek tragedy in which Oedipus unknowingly killed his father and married his mother. Freud proposed that the Oedipus complex was a normal stage of development occurring between the ages of three to five years, where the boy is attracted to his mother and develops feelings of rivalry and jealousy for his father. The equivalent constellation in the little girl is called the *Electra complex*. Castration anxiety refers to the boy's fear that his father will castrate him for his desire for the mother. Resolution of the Oedipus complex results in the formation of the superego. Failure to negotiate the Oedipus complex lies at the heart of neurotic illness and results in deficits in the capacity to enjoy healthy loving and sexual relations.

ORIGINS AND MAINTENANCE OF PROBLEMS

Conflict

Freud believed that neurotic illness was the result of *conflict* between the instinctual drives and the external world, or between different parts of the mind. This conflict between the ego and the id can result in neurotic symptoms, as unacceptable sexual and aggressive thoughts and feelings break through the ego's censorship barrier and are converted into substitute compromise formations to prevent them from fully entering consciousness. Conflict between the ego and the superego can give rise to feelings of low self-esteem, shame and guilt due to the ego's failure to live up to the high moral standards imposed by the superego.

Anxiety and Defence Mechanisms

The notion of anxiety is also central to Freud's formulations regarding the origin of neurosis. In Freud's earlier model, anxiety is a direct expression of undischarged sexual energy or libido. This led Freud to the concept of defence mechanisms, manoevres of the ego that protect it from both internal and external sources of danger, anxiety and unpleasure. He later revised his theory of anxiety to see anxiety as the response of the ego to the danger of internal sexual and aggressive drives.

Freud proposed that different mental states result from different constellations of anxiety and defence mechanisms. In *neurosis*, the primary defence mechanism is repression, the pushing out of consciousness of thoughts and wishes that do not fit in with one's view of one's self. In *perversion*, the ego is split via the defence mechanism of disavowal; this allows contradictory beliefs to be held simultaneously, so that the perverse person may hold a circumscribed delusional belief (such as the paedophile who believes children enjoy sexual intercourse) but the rest of the personality appears intact and functioning normally. In *psychosis*, repression fails completely; the person is overwhelmed by unconscious or id contents, and creates a delusional world via primitive defence mechanisms such as projection and omnipotence to make sense of such chaos.

Trauma

Massive trauma can also overwhelm the ego, breaking through its defences and rendering it helpless and unable to function. Freud coined the term *repetition compulsion* to describe a person's unconscious tendency in adult life to repeat past traumatic behaviour, in an attempt to resolve feelings of helplessness and conflict. Freud later explained this as a manifestation of the death instinct.

Resistance

Despite the considerable distress and disability suffered by patients who seek psychotherapeutic help for their difficulties, the patient is unconsciously opposed to changing the landscape of his internal world. Freud described such antagonism of the patient to the therapist's attempt to achieve insight and change as *resistance*, which represented a compromise between the forces that were striving towards recovery and the opposing ones. Resistances to treatment can take overt and covert forms, such as missing appointments, being late to sessions, being silent, or not hearing interpretations. Resistance can be seen as a defence mechanism that arises during treatment to avoid experiencing the psychic pain associated with previously repressed unpleasant impulses and affects that the therapy is attempting to uncover and explore.

CHANGE

Consciousness

Freud's changing views of therapeutic action reflected his evolving conceptualization of his models of the mind. His initial simple model of catharsis, in which therapy worked by releasing dammed-up affects, reflected a model of the mind in which traumas had aroused unacceptable feelings and thoughts that had to be pushed from consciousness to maintain psychic stability. Freud's mechanism of change at this time was to 'transform what is unconscious into what is conscious'.

Strengthening of the Ego

Freud's development of his topographical model of the mind led to his emphasis on the interpretation of defence and resistance as techniques to allow the unconscious mental contents into consciousness. When his structural model took priority over the topographical, his positioning of the Oedipal complex as the developmental crisis at the centre of all neurosis, and the increasing attention to ego defences, meant that the therapeutic effect now depended on alteration and redistribution of energy between the three mental agencies of ego, id and superego, and in particular the strengthening of the ego.

Transference

Freud himself recognized the central role of the transference in effecting therapeutic change, in providing a window into the patient's unconscious fantasy life. Transference is the displacement by the patient of early wishes and feelings towards people from the past, particularly the patient's parents, onto the figure of the therapist. The safety of the analytic situation allows the patient to experience those unconscious wishes and fears as they arise in relation to the analyst, to appreciate their irrationality and origins from the past, and to provide the opportunity of working through. Since Freud, increasing emphasis has been placed on the role of the transference and its interpretation in effecting therapeutic change, which includes superego modification with the introduction of a more benign superego.

Relational Experience

Whilst verbal interpretations of the meaning of the transferential experience are important, there is also a shift to believing that the relational affective experience in itself is the mutative factor. This involves the internalization of a new relationship with the therapist, who is reliable and not retaliatory, which may be very different from the relationships the patient has previously experienced.

SKILLS AND STRATEGIES

The Analytic Setting

In psychoanalytic treatment patients are encouraged to lie on the couch, with the analyst sitting behind them. The relative sensory deprivation and inability to see the analyst's facial expressions facilitates the patient in being able to focus on his inner thoughts and feelings which he is encouraged to express in free association. The reclining position is also helpful in inducing a certain degree of regression and dependency that is necessary in order to establish and work through the patient's neurotic difficulties. The boundaries of the setting or parameters of treatment are important in creating a safe environment in which therapy can occur. These boundaries include the consistency of the physical environment in which the therapy takes place, the reliability of regular

50-minute sessions that begin and end on time, and clearly defined interpersonal boundaries between patient and therapist, in which the therapist minimizes self-disclosure and maintains confidentiality.

Free Association

Free association is the cornerstone of classical Freudian psychoanalytic technique. The patient is encouraged to say whatever is in his mind, without censoring his thoughts, however embarrassing, disturbing or seemingly trivial these may be. The psychoanalyst's task, through a corresponding type of evenly suspended listening that Freud called *free-floating attention*, is to discover the unconscious themes that underlie the patient's discourse via the patient's slips of the tongue, associative links and resistances to speaking about certain topics that the patient himself is unaware of.

Spectrum of Interventions

The analyst intervenes in the form of verbal communications, which can be categorized along a spectrum that moves from the supportive to the interpretive as the therapy progresses. Thus the analyst may initially make *empathic comments*; moving to *clarifications*, using questioning or rephrasing to elucidate what the patient means; via *confrontations*, where the analyst will point out inconsistencies in the patient's account or draw his attention to subjects he may be avoiding; to *interpretations*. A classical Freudian psychoanalyst will be careful to work from surface to depth, analysing the patient's resistances and defences before interpreting the content of underlying unconscious fantasies.

Interpretations

An interpretation offers a new formulation of unconscious meaning and motivation for the patient. Many contemporary psychoanalysts view transference interpretations in the 'here-and-now' or affective interchange of the analytic session as the most mutative intervention. However, more classical Freudian analysts may wait longer before interpreting the transference, holding back until the patient himself is aware of the feelings he has towards the analyst. The Freudian analyst also focuses attentively on details of the patient's past life to make reconstructive interpretations that can help the patient understand how his current difficulties have been influenced by his history. Exploration and interpretation about the patient's current external life (extra-transference interpretations) may also be helpful, without minimizing the importance of his internal world and unconscious fantasies.

Counter-transference

Counter-transference describes the unconscious emotional reactions that the therapist has towards the patient, and is a result of both unresolved conflicts in the therapist and contributions or projections from the patient. Freud originally saw counter-transference as a resistance to treatment, but contemporary analysts see it as a source of useful information about the patient and his internal object relations, which determine the patient's pattern of relating to others.

Intensity and Duration of Treatment

Psychoanalytic therapy aims to effect long-lasting characterological change, not just alleviation of the patient's symptoms, and therefore tends to be long term, lasting years rather than months. This allows sufficient time for the *working through* of difficulties – the integration of cognitive and affective understanding and the consolidation of new ways of functioning and relating to others. Psychoanalysis is also an intensive treatment, with the patient being seen four to five times per week, whereas in psychoanalytic psychotherapy the patient is seen once to three times a week.

RESEARCH EVIDENCE

Although it is difficult to conduct outcome research on intensive psychoanalytic treatments, there is an accumulating body of empirical evidence supporting the efficacy of psychoanalytic psychotherapy. Recent meta-analyses, which pool the results of many different independent studies, including randomized controlled trials of long-term psychoanalytic psychotherapy (Leichsenring and Rabung, 2008), show that the effect sizes for psychoanalytic therapy are as large as those reported for other evidence-based therapies, such as cognitive-behavioural therapy. Moreover, patients who receive psychoanalytic therapy maintain therapeutic gains and continue to improve after cessation of treatment. The widespread scepticism regarding the scientific nature of psychoanalytic therapy is therefore not justified, and may reflect biases in the dissemination of research findings (Shedler, 2010).

REFERENCES

Leichsenring, F. and Rabung, S. (2008) Effectiveness of long-term psychodynamic psychotherapy. *Journal of the American Medical Association*, 300: 1551–65.

Shedler, J. (2010) The efficacy of psychodynamic psychotherapy. *American Psychologist*, 65: 98–109.

RECOMMENDED READING

Bateman, A. and Holmes, J. (1995) *Introduction to Psychoanalysis*. London: Routledge.

Gay, P. (1988) *Freud: A Life for Our Time*. London: Dent.

Greenson, R. (1967) *The Technique and Practice of Psychoanalysis*. New York: International Universities Press.

5.12

Psychodynamic Therapy

(Melanie Klein, 1882–1960)

JULIA SEGAL

BRIEF HISTORY

Psychoanalysis provides the basic understanding underlying insight-based counselling and psychotherapy. Melanie Klein was a psychoanalyst who came to England in 1926 from Vienna via Berlin. Her insights were deeply controversial at first but have gradually become more accepted, with Kleinian analysts receiving world recognition. Segal (1992) describes this in more detail.

Kleinian psychodynamic therapists and counsellors recognize and use the insights of Kleinian analysts while modifying their techniques to fit the different requirements of their particular settings.

Klein developed a new language with which to talk about ways we think, feel and behave; and about ideas, assumptions and beliefs people hold about themselves and others. Her discovery that babies and infants are active participants in relationships with their mothers and others around them, having both feelings and awareness, was contrary to opinion of the time. Kleinian ideas can seem strange to begin with, but bring new possibilities for understanding and new relief from anxieties.

BASIC ASSUMPTIONS

Emotional understanding is a powerful tool. An understanding relationship can allow an individual to develop their capacities to feel, to think, to understand themselves and others better.

Facing feared reality, working through the associated feelings and fantasies, and grieving for real losses brings long-term reduction in anxiety. Any kind of illusion or defence is maintained by and maintains anxiety.

People often hide their own emotions from themselves; for example, someone may light up a cigarette to prevent themselves feeling angry. Exploring emotions which are kept out of conscious awareness brings new understanding of the self in relation to others.

Difficulties in relationships with caregivers (involving accepting food and other necessities, taking in and learning, for example) underlie many problems both in the past and in the present. They manifest themselves not only in relationship difficulties but also in disturbances in the individual's relationship with themselves. (The emphasis on relations with others makes Kleinian theory an object relations theory.)

The understanding of the counsellor or therapist includes the capacity to face unpleasant, destructive, shameful feelings as well as deeply loving ones, in themselves as well as in the client. Their training should ensure that they have experienced the pains as well as the pleasures of a relationship with a therapist and that they have no sense of superiority towards their clients.

However, no relationship with a therapist or counsellor is truly one of equals. The therapist offers something which the client supposedly wants. This relationship therefore has the potential to arouse emotions such as hope, longing, desire, rivalry, envy, fear of loss, anger and aggressiveness; in therapy some of these can be understood and the associated behaviour, fears, attitudes and beliefs explored. The client's relationship with the therapist provides an opportunity to reassess the client's feelings and behaviour in connection with being cared for in the past. This can improve relations with others and with the self in the present.

The therapist's help in thinking directly about relationships with others and the self may also bring considerable relief.

The idea that we can envy and even hate those who give us what we want is particularly controversial, and distinguishes Kleinian theory from some others. These feelings manifest themselves in various forms of attack on those we love or need. We may denigrate them; or idealize them to make them useless to us; or dismiss what they say or offer, for example. Kleinian therapy involves paying close attention to such attacks by the client on the joint work of the client and therapist.

Kleinians also believe that we very much want to 'make reparation' – to repair damage which we feel we have caused by such attacks.

ORIGIN AND MAINTENANCE OF PROBLEMS

Our understanding of the world around us, and of ourselves in relation to it, grows with us. What Klein called 'phantasies' (Segal, 1981; 1985) are formed. To understand this concept, think of the way babies gradually begin to recognize people. Some kind of picture or model or 'phantasy' is formed. These phantasies are dynamic; they change and develop as the people around come and go and interact with each other. When the baby is happy, their phantasies of their world, including the people in it, are happy, loving ones; when the baby is feeling bad in some way, the phantasies may be frightening, disturbing ones.

Phantasies are unconscious constructions. We are not aware of our own contribution to our perceptions; we just see things that way. As a small child we may just *know* our father can do everything; as a teenager we may simply see him as the greatest fool in the world. One adult just knows the world is a friendly place; another lives in constant fear of attack.

As we grow up we generally begin to see those around us more realistically. Phantasies we have of other people include characteristics derived from our knowledge and experience of ourselves. So a child who is missing a parent may believe that the absent parent is sad, for example; if the child is angry with the parent for being away, they may believe the parent is angry with them. A teenager afraid of embarrassing themselves may see a parent as embarrassing.

Problems can arise if very infantile phantasies do not get modified through play and through age-appropriate relationships with real people. Problems with our parents affect our phantasies about the world. We have phantasy relationships with our parents even when they are not there; so someone whose father disappeared when they were two may expect all men to disappear from their lives after about two years, and may behave in such a way as to make it happen. Their phantasies about sexual partners and fathers may remain on a level more appropriate to the knowledge and beliefs of a two-year-old. Later experiences may lead to modifications to such beliefs, but phantasies created very early on under painful conditions (such as loss) are hard to change since recurrence of the pain is feared.

Problems arise too because of the ways we manipulate phantasies and emotions in response to conflicts. For example, bad feelings can seem so frightening that they have to be separated from good ones. In order not to feel jealous, envious, angry and left out, for example, we may see ourselves as having and being everything desirable and our mothers as poor, weak, foolish creatures with no understanding. Unfortunately such phantasies may leave us not only vulnerable to collapse when we discover we do not live up to our own expectations, but also unable then to turn to our mother for comfort.

Reality often brings emotional pain; 'splitting' is used to attempt to avoid such pain. However, the splitting itself is not only insecure but also deeply damaging. Denial, idealization and denigration (forms of splitting used in the madonna and whore images, for example) may temporarily get rid of the jealous envy attached to knowing that women in general, and our mothers in particular, can have sex as well as have children; but reliance on such splitting would prevent us from combining the two.

Phantasies that we can get rid of unbearable, uncontainable feelings into other people are common. Kleinians call this *projective identification*. This may be involved, for example, when a father of a small child finds a new lover. Instead of feeling left out of the relationship between his wife and the child, he feels that *they* are left out of his exciting new relationship. He may be trying to get rid of feelings of being cruelly left out when he was a child. He does not think to himself, 'I will leave my child, then he or she will feel the pain instead of me'; he simply feels an overwhelming urge to be cared for and loved exclusively, and the excitement helps him to split off awareness of his own cruelty. The hope must be to find a new, better solution this time; the risk is that the 'solution' will be equally or more damaging – to the father himself as well as to his family.

Both external and internal conditions can cause problems in development. A baby or child subjected to ill-treatment may respond in many ways which distort his or her long-term development. However, some babies and children seem to respond badly even to normal good and loving care, and, contrari-wise, some can make use of even the smallest opportunity for love in an otherwise problematic environment. Klein thought people had different capacities to use the good they were offered. Some babies seem to enjoy life more from the beginning; others to find it difficult and unpleasant, or even unbearable. Mothers who have to cope with diffi-cult babies often blame themselves; people with a Kleinian orientation are more likely to sympathize than to blame.

CHANGE

Change depends on modifying the underlying phan-tasies we have about the world and which we use to orient ourselves. There is increasing evidence from neuroscience (as well as from clinicians) that expe-rience, including the experience of emotion, is central to change. We can be changed by any new learning which involves an emotional element: relationships, giving birth, work and any form of creativity. All of these have the power to evoke emotions while challenging our beliefs, assump-tions and awareness of ourselves and others. However, emotions can be painful and change can be feared and avoided.

Kleinian psychodynamic practitioners have always placed emphasis on the importance of bring-ing to consciousness significant aspects of the rela-tionship with the therapist, in the room, particularly those associated with painful emotions. 'Transference interpretations', in which this rela-tionship becomes the focus of work, enable a client to become aware of their experience of the relation-ship, while being accompanied and supported by the therapist. Kleinians are always aware, for example, that endings, lateness or missed sessions all have meaning to the client which may need to be exam-ined, uncovered and addressed, even when the client does not see (at first) that they pose any problem.

In psychodynamic therapy or counselling the client has the opportunity to experience a relation-ship in which her or his emotional states can be felt, understood, tolerated and recognized in a new way.

The aim of psychodynamic counselling is to increase the client's capacity to use and accept more aspects of themselves; to free their processes of thought and feeling and to remove damaging restric-tions on them. New, better possibilities for dealing with internal and external conflicts remain after coun-selling ends. There is evidence now that improve-ments achieved during psychodynamic therapies tend to continue after the end of therapy (see below).

The significance of the relationship affects the amount of change which can be brought about. In psychoanalysis five times a week an analyst may be almost constantly 'there' in the patient's mind, and in reality reliably there and closely in touch with the client's emotional state on an almost daily basis. This relationship can contain and modify very deep anxieties. Psychodynamic psychotherapy two or three times a week can also have far-reaching effects for many clients. Counselling or therapy once a week or less, over a shorter period of time, while bringing significant relief, might not be expected to modify the deepest anxieties or change whole personality structures; however, Wallerstein (1989), in his 40-year study of outcomes of psy-choanalysis and psychodynamic psychotherapy, found that 'psychotherapies often achieved more than predicted'. (He also found that supportive interventions were more important than expected.)

Grieving can initiate powerful processes of change. Grief handled alone sometimes results in attempts to get rid of the pain by cutting off parts of the self, such as the ability to think or to feel or to see in certain areas. It can also result in attempts to get rid of unbearable pain into someone else, mak-ing them feel the pain 'instead', perhaps by hitting out at them verbally, or in some more subtle way evoking a version of the same pain in them (projec-tive identification). Grief worked through with someone (such as a psychodynamic therapist) who can help a client to tolerate painful, often humiliat-ing, thoughts and feelings may gradually bring new awareness and new strengths. The therapist them-selves must have discovered what it is like to expe-rience unexpected, painful emotions in the presence of their own therapist, and have learnt to tolerate their own (and others') failure to live up to their own previous standards.

SKILLS AND STRATEGIES

A Kleinian practitioner is expected to have an abil-ity to recognize and tolerate their own true state of mind in the presence of a client.

Since offering anything to a client has important implications for the relationship, skill is involved in knowing when and how to share an idea or to suggest a thought for the client to consider, and in picking up the consequences.

Skill is involved in deciding when to discuss an issue raised by the client in terms of the overt meaning, and when to pick up a more covert meaning. For example, a client complaining about their sister may need help in thinking about her – but they may also need help in thinking about ways in which the sister at this moment is being used to talk about some aspect of themselves or the counsellor. Negative feelings towards the therapist or therapy are often raised in such ways, providing an opportunity to draw attention to, discuss and modify processes of splitting.

Skill is also needed to interpret what clients bring to the counsellor, both verbally and non-verbally. Since feelings, both negative and positive, can often be hidden by the client from their own awareness, the therapist has to be aware of signals conveying them. As they were hidden in the first place for very powerful reasons, bringing them to the attention of the client raises many issues about the relationship with the counsellor as well as about the client's state of mind and, when it is done, has to be done skilfully.

RESEARCH EVIDENCE

Kleinian analysts and psychotherapists have been amongst the most reluctant to involve themselves in any form of quantitative measurement of their work. Rachel Blass, a Kleinian analyst, has argued that

> when psychoanalysis is regarded (as it is in Kleinian psychoanalysis) as an approach that is concerned with intra-psychic truth as it unfolds and is integrated in the long-term analysis of individuals, then the form of research that is most relevant to it continues to be the detailed description and discussion of case studies. These studies have not only demonstrated the value of this form of treatment, but also expanded understanding of intrapsychic processes and led to technical innovations. (personal communication)

Kleinian case studies (e.g. Rosenfeld, 1987; Segal, 1981; Waddell, 1998, amongst many; see the Melanie Klein Trust website www.melanie-klein-trust.org.uk) demonstrate methods of working alongside observations and deductions. At their best, these are stimulating, inspiring and practical in day-to-day work with clients. A case study is most useful for those who have the capacity to use others' insights to enhance their own. Not a book of rules, it requires a therapist to use sensitivity, thought and care when applying observations from one situation to another.

In spite of opposition, there has been some outcome research on psychodynamic psychotherapy, including both randomized controlled trials and efficacy studies, in various parts of the world. In the UK, Malan (1975) gave support to certain ideas central to the Kleinian approach. In a group of patients selected for brief insight therapy offered by a team of psychoanalytically trained analysts and psychotherapists, Malan found that effective outcomes of therapy correlated with transference interpretations. He concluded that prognosis was best when enthusiasm for treatment in both patient and therapist is high; when transference arises early and becomes a major feature of therapy; and when grief and anger at termination are important issues (1975: 274).

Attempts to measure both the outcomes and the aims of psychoanalytically inclined therapists are ongoing. Trowell et al.'s outcome study (2007) examining the role of psychotherapy for childhood depression and Jonathan Smith's (2010) meta-analysis of studies on panic disorder and generalized anxiety both provide supportive research evidence. Richardson et al. (2004) gathered an interesting collection of papers addressing the difficult technical and theoretical difficulties involved. It has been possible to demonstrate that psychodynamic therapy does produce both symptom change and personality change for a significant proportion of clients. Improvement can be shown to continue after the end of therapy, with long-term results which are better than comparison groups such as 'treatment as usual' (e.g. Leichsenring, 2005, who also found that psychoanalysis is more effective than shorter forms of psychodynamic therapy). Many of these studies have still to report and others to be confirmed. For now we can only say that more evidence is being gathered, and it is on the whole supportive for those whose own experience or understanding points in the direction of Kleinian ideas. Perhaps of note, however, is that one (so far unconfirmed) research project from Stockholm reported in Richardson et al. found that strict psychoanalytical beliefs of therapists, while predicting effectiveness in analysis five times a week, seemed less effective than a more relaxed attitude on the part of the therapist within psychodynamic psychotherapy once a week.

Neuroscience has been another source of research evidence which supports many Kleinian ideas, including the ideas that emotions are important in change; that attachment to caregivers and early relationships are highly significant for later life; and that babies actively relate to their environment and are aware of and care about the people around them. Kleinian ideas about unconscious phantasy fit well with neuroscientists' discoveries (Gerhardt, 2004;

Ledoux, 1998) about the ways we learn and experience the world.

In a lighter vein, an insurance broker examined legal actions initiated by clients against their counsellors and therapists. A list of behaviours which put therapists at risk confirmed Kleinian awareness of threats to the professional setting. Not only any form of touch other than a formal handshake, but also personal pictures or any mention of personal matters, holidays or family; any change in or carelessness about the therapist's clothing or appearance, or the arrangement of the room; any statement or behaviour which could be classed as outside the professional frame; and even changes of time or place; can all be read by certain clients as provocative invitations to a personal, often sexual, relationship, with potentially litigious consequences.

At the time of going to press, Jonathon Shedler's (2010) paper is one of the most recent and encouraging (as well as readable) pieces of research for psychodynamic therapists in general. Looking at a large number of metastudies, he concluded that:

> Empirical evidence supports the efficacy of psychodynamic therapy. Effect sizes for psychodynamic therapy are as large as those reported for other therapies that have been actively promoted as 'empirically supported' and 'evidence based'. In addition, patients who receive psychodynamic therapy maintain therapeutic gains and appear to continue to improve after treatment ends. Finally, nonpsychodynamic therapies may be effective in part because the more skilled practitioners utilize techniques that have long been central to psychodynamic theory and practice. The perception that psychodynamic approaches lack empirical support does not accord with available scientific evidence and may reflect selective dissemination of research.

We await the outcomes of future research with interest.

REFERENCES

Gerhardt, Sue (2004) *Why Love Matters: How Affection Shapes a Baby's Brain*. London: Routledge.

Ledoux, Joseph (1998) *The Emotional Brain: The Mysterious Underpinnings of Emotional Life*. London: Orion.

Leichsenring, F. (2005) Are psychodynamic and psychoanalytic therapies effective? A review of empirical data. *International Journal of Psychoanalysis*, 86 (3): 841–68.

Malan, D.H. (1975) *A Study of Brief Psychotherapy*. London: Plenum.

Richardson, P., Renlund, C. and Kachele, H. (2004) *Research on Psychoanalytic Psychotherapy with Adults*. London: Karnac.

Rosenfeld, H.A. (1987) *Impasse and Interpretation: Therapeutic and Anti-Therapeutic Factors in the Psychoanalytic Treatment of Psychotic, Borderline, and Neurotic Patients*. London: Routledge.

Segal, H. (1981) *The Work of Hanna Segal: A Kleinian Approach to Clinical Practice*. Northvale, NJ: Aronson. London: Free Association, 1986.

Segal, J.C. (1985) *Phantasy in Everyday Life*. London: Pelican. London: Karnac, 1995.

Segal, Julia (1992) *Melanie Klein*. London: Sage.

Shedler, Jonathan (2010) The efficacy of psychodynamic psychotherapy. *American Psychologist*, February–March.

Smith, Jonathan D. (2010) Panic stations: brief dynamic therapy for panic disorder and generalised anxiety. *Psychodynamic Practice*, 16 (1): 25–44.

Trowell, J., Joffe, I., Campbell, J., Clemente, C., Almqvist, F., Soininen, M., Koskenranta-Aalto, U., Weintraub, S., Kolaitis, G., Tomaras, V., Anastasopoulos, D., Grayson, K., Barnes, J. and Tsiantis, J. (2007) Childhood depression: a place for psychotherapy. An outcome study comparing individual psychodynamic psychotherapy and family therapy. *European Child & Adolescent Psychiatry*, 16 (3): 157–67.

Waddell, M. (1998) *Inside Lives: Psychoanalysis and the Growth of Personality*. London: Duckworth.

Wallerstein, Robert S. (1989) *42 Lives in Treatment: A Study of Psychoanalysis and Psychotherapy*. Report of the Psychotherapy Research Project of the Menninger Foundation, 1954–1982. New York: Guilford. Other, 2000.

PART V

THEORY AND APPROACHES

COGNITIVE-BEHAVIOURAL APPROACHES

Acceptance and Commitment Therapy

(Steven Hayes, 1948–)

JOHN BOORMAN, ERIC MORRIS AND JOE OLIVER

BRIEF HISTORY

Acceptance and commitment therapy (ACT, pronounced as a single word 'act') is part of a new 'third wave' of behavioural and cognitive psychotherapies that includes, amongst others, dialectical behaviour therapy (DBT: Linehan, 1993) and mindfulness-based cognitive therapy (Segal et al., 2002).

ACT is based upon the scientific philosophy of functional contextualism. Functional contextualism defines the goal of science to be the successful prediction and influence of an individual's behaviour, by using empirically based concepts and rules. The focus is on considering a person's actions *in the context in which they occur* (historical, situational), so that the interest is in the purpose of behaviour rather than its form. What is considered 'true' in this pragmatic philosophy are theories or rules that allow for 'successful working'. Concepts or rules that do not point to what to *do* (as a therapist or scientist) are discarded. ACT incorporates elements of both the first (behaviour therapy) and second (cognitive therapy) 'waves', whilst introducing new elements such as mindfulness, acceptance, and defusion from thoughts.

ACT was originally developed by the American psychologist Steven Hayes who, along with other colleagues, looked to expand upon the behaviour analytic principles first put forward by B.F. Skinner regarding verbal behaviour. At its inception in the late 1970s and early 1980s, ACT was originally called 'comprehensive distancing', a concept first suggested by Beck, where the therapy goal was to assist clients to develop healthy distancing from problematic thoughts and mental processes. Then followed a period spanning over 15 years when attention was centred upon development of a therapeutic model. Central to the model was the concurrent development of a behavioural account of human language and cognition, known as relational frame theory (RFT: Hayes et al., 2001). Finally, the therapy model and procedures were comprehensively explicated in the first ACT manual in 1999 (Hayes et al., 1999).

BASIC ASSUMPTIONS

ACT takes the view that psychological pain is both universal and normal and therefore is part of what makes us human. ACT therefore challenges the assumption put forward in many mainstream models of psychopathology, and perhaps by society in general, that psychological health is equated with the absence of pain, or conversely that the presence of pain is indicative of faulty or abnormal processes (biological or psychological).

Drawing upon literature into thought/emotion suppression and how humans cope with pain, ACT argues that attempts to control, avoid and/or escape from distressing thoughts and feelings can lead to an increase in distress. A core assumption of ACT is that psychological problems are maintained by excessive avoidance of painful experiences (thoughts, feelings, memories, etc.).

Based upon the research into RFT, ACT demonstrates how everyday language processes have the ability to amplify normal psychological pain. The ACT model of psychopathology assumes that psychological suffering can occur when clients believe that their private experiences (for example thoughts or memories) are accurate and literal descriptions of reality. According to the model, clients become 'fused' or entangled with the content of their minds, and literally consider that their thoughts and feelings *are what they say they are*. One of the central aims of ACT is therefore not to alter the frequency or form of distressing internal experiences, but rather to change the relationship (function) the client has with these experiences, sometimes referred to a second-order change. This is perhaps where ACT differs most from other behavioural and cognitive approaches, which primarily look to change the form or frequency of thoughts and feelings, also known as first-order change.

The emphasis on changing the function of thought (rather than frequency or form) is always in the service of assisting clients to take actions consistent with valued life directions. Values differ from goals, which are concrete and time limited, in that they are seen as life directions which don't have an end point. Examples of valued areas that clients might find important could include relationships, family, work/education, spirituality, and health. A basic assumption in ACT is to take a pragmatic view to clients solving their problems, focusing on what works to assist clients to move towards their values, as opposed to what is right or true. This stance, also known as the *pragmatic truth criterion*, is taken from the philosophy of functional contextualism.

ORIGINS AND MAINTENANCE OF PROBLEMS

Relational frame theory (RFT) offers an explanation as to how psychological distress is maintained through normal language processes, so that potentially any internal or environment stimulus (e.g. sights, sounds, smells, memories) has the capacity to induce painful thoughts and emotions. RFT views the core of human language and cognition as the learned ability to relate anything to anything (or arbitrarily), mutually and in combination. Research into RFT has shown that relational responding is a basic and learned aspect of language that serves important functions in the outside world, but can cause distress when this method of learning is applied to private experiences (Hayes et al., 2001). Importantly, relational responding (a response made to a relation) transforms the functions of any property (physical or mental) and modifies other behavioural processes such as classical and operant conditioning. Smoking may be taken as an example to explain this process. If a smoker is asked to imagine a cigarette, they may note its formal physical properties such as its colour (e.g. white), its shape (e.g. cylinder) and its contents (e.g. contains tobacco). In addition to the physical properties, however, a cigarette can also acquire informal or arbitrary properties through humans' ability to relate anything to anything (relational responding). For example, a cigarette can also be viewed as something which is 'dependable', or like a 'good friend' who is always there in times of crisis. From an RFT perspective, through the arbitrary relation of a cigarette to one's best friend, some of the functions of the cigarette are transformed and share the functions noted in a best friend.

Based upon the theory of RFT, ACT essentially sees human psychological problems in terms of a lack of psychological flexibility, which is fostered by two core processes, termed cognitive fusion and experiential avoidance.

Experiential avoidance occurs when an individual is unwilling to stay in contact with certain negative thoughts, feelings and physical sensations, and also tries to alter the content of these internal experiences even when this causes harm. Whilst engaging in such acts of avoidance can often serve to ameliorate problems in the short term, it has the potential to lead to long-term suffering. ACT views experiential avoidance as a central process in the origins and maintenance of psychological problems, the use of which is supported by folk psychology and mainstream culture (e.g. advice to 'just get over it', 'move on', etc.). ACT views psychological acceptance as the healthy and adaptive alternative to avoidance, and attempts to highlight how humans can expend lots of energy trying to escape, avoid or otherwise control these events.

Cognitive fusion occurs when individuals fail to notice a distinction between the contents of their thoughts and themselves as the *thinker*, and become *fused* with their thoughts. According to RFT, cognitive fusion becomes a source and maintenance process of psychological distress when people are unhelpfully guided more by the literal content of their thoughts than by what they directly experience in their environment. Clients are often asked to notice and observe the ebb and flow of their private experiences, in an attempt to create a helpful distance and space from their minds (*defusion*). ACT also focuses on helping clients to be in more direct contact with their actual experiences, rather than with what their thoughts are telling them is happening.

Hayes's (1989) research on verbal behaviour suggests that inflexible or unhelpful actions are frequently maintained by rigid verbal rules or beliefs, such as attempts to seek social recognition (e.g. reassurance seeking), and/or inaccurate descriptions of how thoughts and feelings work (e.g. beliefs about thought suppression, 'just get over it', etc.). Furthermore, the presence of these verbal rules can dominate such that people do not learn from their experience, especially if it does not fit with their own verbal rules. This research suggested that therapists may be more effective adopting an experiential learning approach, using metaphors and exercises that help the client to notice their own experience, rather than providing more or different verbal rules that could carry the risk of maintaining inflexibility.

Whilst ACT does not ignore or neglect biological and social factors that can cause, influence and maintain psychological distress, it places greater emphasis on the person and how they interact with their physical and internal environments (or contexts). The ACT therapist is part of the context of the client and vice versa; the focus for the ACT therapist is on creating a therapeutic context that helps the client pragmatically change their behaviour, in the service of their chosen values.

CHANGE

The main therapeutic goal of ACT is to increase an individual's psychological flexibility. ACT attempts to increase a person's psychological flexibility by:

- using acceptance and mindfulness processes
- focusing on direct behaviour change
- helping the client to be in contact with their own (actual) experiences
- focusing on increasing commitment to engaging in valued actions.

ACT endeavours to increase clients' commitment by helping them clarify what areas are important or of value in their life (e.g. family, relationships, work/education, etc.) and to notice what barriers (e.g. negative thoughts, avoidance patterns) seem to be in the way of living consistently with these values. The focus therefore is not on controlling or reducing painful thoughts or feelings, but rather on directing behaviour change according to what is important to the individual.

ACT encourages individuals to learn through their own experience that approaching life by heading in a direction that is consistent with their values often

may mean encountering and willingly accepting painful thoughts, feelings and memories. Through acceptance and mindfulness techniques, clients are taught to become more aware and notice their internal mental, physical and emotional processes. This is in the service of allowing clients the opportunity to directly observe such processes without attempting to judge, analyse or change them. Once clients become more aware of their own private experiences, they then have the opportunity to make more informed choices on whether to be guided by such thoughts or feelings. Through developing the skills of acceptance, mindfulness and a transcendent sense of self, an alternative choice is available: to be able to engage in behaviours that are consistent with their deepest values, while 'making room for' experiences.

SKILLS AND STRATEGIES

ACT therapists often adopt an experiential approach to therapeutic change through the use of metaphors and exercises carried out in the session. The aim is to help clients come into direct contact with their learning histories, as opposed to the verbal descriptions of these experiences. By noticing how their minds work and exploring the results of sensible but unworkable strategies, clients are encouraged to consider whether an alternative stance of being more in the present, while holding thoughts and feelings lightly and being in touch with personal values, may produce greater life vitality. The ACT therapist does not try to convince the client of this; the arbiter is the client's own lived experience of the workability of such an approach.

Within ACT there are six core processes; these are viewed as positive psychological skills as opposed to techniques or methods for avoiding and controlling psychological pain (see Figure 5.13.1). None of these six processes are ends in themselves; rather, ACT views them as methods and strategies for increasing psychological flexibility and allowing values-based actions. The six core therapeutic processes of ACT are:

- *Acceptance*. The aim is to actively accept what is there, without defence or judgement. The focus is on approaching whatever painful thought or feeling shows up as opposed to avoiding, distracting or controlling these. Experiential acceptance can be thought of as an alternative to experiential avoidance.
- *Defusion*. Linked to RFT's concept of literality, where humans learn to believe (literally) that the content of our minds is true. Here the aim is to notice

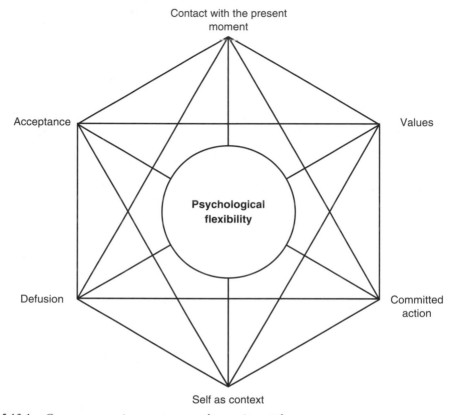

Figure 5.13.1   *Core processes in acceptance and commitment therapy*

that this process is occurring and distance oneself from unhelpful thoughts. This is achieved through a variety of ways such as getting the client to repeat a painful word or phrase over and over until it becomes what it is, a series of sounds, as opposed to the memory or event it is associated with.

- *Contacting the present moment*. This is primarily achieved through the use of a variety of mindfulness techniques whereby the therapist helps the client make contact with the here-and-now. Fundamentally the aim is to assist the client to notice their internal private content (thoughts, feelings, bodily sensations) without judging, evaluating or critiquing them.
- *Self as context*. Helping the client to become aware that they have a place or self with which they can observe difficult thoughts and feelings, without being caught up with them. Clients learn for themselves how this sense of their self remains constant, and has been with them throughout all of their life experiences.

The final two core ACT processes are known as the approach or activation strategies:

- *Values*. Clarifying with the client what areas are really important in their life. Once the client has identified particular values as important, the ACT practitioner asks the client to evaluate whether their behaviour is in accordance with these.
- *Committed action*. Clients are asked whether they are committed to develop patterns of behaviour linked to their values.

ACT also draws upon traditional behaviour analytic techniques such as functional analysis and therapeutic techniques derived from learning theory. ACT is not delivered in a prescribed or manualised way; rather, practitioners use the model to flexibly introduce strategies to the areas/domains most in need of attention.

RESEARCH EVIDENCE

The research evidence into ACT has pursued a somewhat different path to some other behavioural and cognitive psychotherapy research. Initially a significant amount of time was spent gaining empirical support for the basic theory behind ACT (RFT), before the focus shifted onto conducting outcome research on the therapeutic model. Research into RFT has yielded over 70 studies over a 15-year period. In addition to both the basic (RFT) and outcome (evaluating the effectiveness of ACT) research, a great deal of attention has also focused on examining the specific ACT process (e.g. experiential avoidance, cognitive defusion).

Whilst the outcome research into the efficacy of ACT as an intervention is undoubtedly still within the preliminary stages, there does appear to be promising evidence that ACT is useful for a variety of clinical and non-clinical problems. To date, a number of randomised controlled trials (50 in total) have been conducted with a diverse range of conditions including psychosis, anxiety, depression, substance misuse, smoking cessation, borderline personality disorder, epilepsy and weight loss. Several meta-analyses have been conducted, providing good evidence that ACT is significantly better than waiting list controls or treatment as usual (Hayes et al., 2006; Öst, 2008; Powers et al., 2009).

ACT has also been extensively examined as a treatment of chronic pain, and recently has been accepted by the American Psychological Association as an evidenced-based treatment for this condition.

Encouragingly, there continues to be a great deal of interest in further examining all avenues of research into ACT (basic, process and outcome).

REFERENCES

Hayes, S.C. (ed.) (1989) *Rule-Governed Behavior: Cognition, Contingencies, and Instructional Control*. New York: Plenum.

Hayes, S.C., Strosahl, K. and Wilson, K.G. (1999) *Acceptance and Commitment Therapy: An Experiential Approach to Behaviour Change*. New York: Guilford.

Hayes, S.C., Barnes-Holmes, D. and Roche, B. (2001) *Relational Frame Theory: A Post-Skinnerian Account of Human Language and Cognition*. New York: Kluwer.

Hayes, S.C., Luoma, J., Bond, F., Masuda, A. and Lillis, J. (2006) Acceptance and commitment therapy: model, processes, and outcomes. *Behaviour Research and Therapy*, 44 (1): 1–25.

Linehan, M.M. (1993) *Cognitive-Behavioral Treatment of Borderline Personality Disorder*. New York: Guilford.

Öst, L. (2008) Efficacy of the third wave of behavioral therapies: a systematic review and meta-analysis. *Behaviour Research and Therapy*, 46 (3): 296–321.

Powers, M.B., Vörding, M. and Emmelkamp, P.M.G. (2009) Acceptance and commitment therapy: a meta-analytic review. *Psychotherapy and Psychosomatics*, 8: 73–80.

Segal, S.V., Williams, M.G. and Teasdale, J.D. (2002) *Mindfulness-Based Cognitive Therapy for Depression*. New York: Guilford.

RECOMMENDED READING

Harris, R. (2009) *ACT Made Simple: An Easy-to-Read Primer on Acceptance and Commitment Therapy*. Oakland, CA: New Harbinger.

Luoma, J.B., Hayes., S.C. and Walser, R.D. (2007) *Learning ACT: An Acceptance and Commitment Therapy Skills-Training Manual for Therapists*. Oakland, CA: New Harbinger.

Association for Contextual Science: www.contextualpsychology.org.

Cognitive Therapy

(Aaron Beck, 1921–)

JILL MYTTON

Around the middle of the last century, two eminent American clinical psychologists, Albert Ellis and Aaron Beck, became separately dissatisfied with the psychoanalytic approach in which they were trained. Ellis went on to develop rational emotive behaviour therapy (see Chapter 5.16 in this volume) and Beck to develop what has become the most used cognitive approach to therapy today. Both these therapeutic approaches echo the ideas of the Greek, Roman and Eastern philosophers who argued that the way we think about our world and ourselves plays an important role in our emotions and behaviours. Gautama Buddha once observed, 'We are what we think. All that we are arises with our thoughts, with our thoughts we make the world.'

Aaron Beck had noticed that the dreams and thoughts of his depressed clients were focused on unrealistic negative ideas and that these thoughts seemed to precede negative emotional reactions. He noted that they seemed to be holding an internal dialogue, as if they were talking to themselves. There were three dominant schools at the time which shared 'one basic assumption: The emotionally disturbed person is victimized by concealed forces over which he has no control' (Beck, 1976: 2). At that time neuropsychiatrists believed in and sought biological causes and thus biological or physical treatments; psychoanalysis hypothesized that emotional disorders were due to unconscious psychological factors that could only be understood through psychoanalytic interpretation;

and behaviour therapy used learning theory and conditioned reflexes to explain emotional disturbance and believed that these simply needed modifying. Beck stated that these three approaches were ignoring the obvious by disregarding the person's own thoughts and reports and were in effect rendering individuals helpless to help themselves.

Beck realized that the link between thoughts and feelings was very important and that 'Man has the key to understanding and solving his psychological disturbance within the scope of his awareness' (1976: 3). In 1963 and 1964 he published two seminal papers on the relationship between thinking and depression. He analysed the dreams and psychotherapeutic sessions with 50 of his patients and found evidence of negative bias in their thinking. He later called this bias the negative cognitive triad; depressed people typically have a negative view of themselves, the world and the future. Beck hypothesized that depression was a form of 'thought disorder' and concluded that psychoanalytic theory was inadequate to account for his findings.

Over the next decade, Beck extended his ideas to other psychological disorders, in particular to anxiety. In 1976 he published *Cognitive Therapy and the Emotional Disorders* in which he described his model of cognitive processing and therapy that focused on teaching his clients to identify and change their thought patterns. Since then Beck's original model has been extended and adapted to the treatment of all forms of psychological problems including, in addition to depression and anxiety, anorexia, phobias, schizophrenia, post-traumatic stress disorder (PTSD), obsessive compulsive disorder, chronic fatigue syndrome and tinnitus. It has also been adapted for deaf clients and for hearing people with language and learning challenges (see Glickman, 2009). Cognitive therapy is used with individual clients, with families and with children. In recent times there has been increasing emphasis on adapting Western-based therapeutic approaches, taking cultural diversity into account (Hays and Iwamasa, 2006).

Beck has continued to develop cognitive therapy along with his daughter Judith (Beck, 1995), and in Britain a number of researchers such as Blackburn, Teasdale, Clarke and Salkovskis have developed and evaluated Beck's cognitive therapy. Beck's cognitive therapy is the most evidence based, influential and popular of cognitive approaches in use today. These days the term 'cognitive therapy' is often used interchangeably with the term 'cognitive-behaviour therapy' (CBT). Both the Beck Institute of Cognitive Therapy and Research and the Oxford Cognitive Therapy Centre use the term 'cognitive therapy' in the title of their organization, yet on their pages they refer frequently to cognitive-behaviour therapy. This can be confusing to people who are not aware of the historical processes leading to this situation. Since cognitive therapy has from the start used behavioural techniques, the use of the additional adjective can be said to simply reflect that fact.

Therapeutic approaches constantly evolve. Over the last decade there have been a number of developments in cognitive-behaviour therapy, including cognitive analytic therapy (Ryle, 1989), dialectical behaviour therapy (Linehan, 1993) (see Chapter 5.15 in this volume), acceptance and commitment therapy (see Chapter 5.13 in this volume) and more recently mindfulness-based cognitive therapy (MBCT) (Segal et al., 2002). MBCT brings together Eastern meditative practices with CBT perspectives. Developed mainly to prevent relapse in depression, MBCT teaches individuals to become more aware of their thoughts and see them not as facts or aspects of the self but as 'mental events'. Kabat-Zinn describes this process as 'the simple act of recognizing that your thoughts *as thoughts* can free you from the distorted reality they often create and allow for more clear-sightedness and a greater sense of manageability in your life' (1990: 70). In the last decade computerized cognitive-behaviour therapy (CCBT) has been developed; here clients interact with a computer program rather than face to face with a therapist.

BASIC ASSUMPTIONS

Human beings have cognitions. We can think, we process information coming in through our five senses, and we make interpretations, inferences and evaluations about that information. In this way we interact with our environment.

These cognitions are believed to be linked to feelings, behaviour and physiology. Thus if a situation is perceived (cognition) as a threat by someone, adrenalin will be released into the body, increasing the heart and breathing rates (physiology), the person will feel fear (affect or emotion) and will react ('flight or fight' behaviour).

Cognitions are available to our conscious minds; we can think about our thoughts and therefore we can change them. Beck described three types of cognition which strongly influence an individual's feelings and behaviour:

- *Information processing*. Individuals are constantly receiving information from the internal (for example, their own bodily reactions) and external environments which their brains process and make sense of.
- *Automatic thoughts*. Many of an individual's thoughts occur as if 'out of the blue'. Beck called these spontaneous cognitions 'automatic thoughts'. They are part of the person's internal dialogue, described as unplanned moment-to-moment thoughts that flow through our minds. Often on the edge of awareness, they can be difficult to recognize.
- *Schema*. This is a term given to hypothetical cognitive structures which act as templates to filter incoming information. They are the unspoken rules or underlying core beliefs learned through early experiences, which every individual holds about self, others and the world. When an event occurs, schemas filter out unwanted information, enabling the person to attend to that which is considered important. In some areas we have well-developed schemas. For example, when driving a car it is important for the driver to be able to filter out unimportant information to prevent overload. In new situations the schemas are less well developed and it is harder to filter out this unimportant information. Thus, people learning to drive can become confused by the variety of overwhelming information in their environment.

ORIGIN AND MAINTENANCE OF PROBLEMS

Beck's cognitive model proposes that distorted or dysfunctional thinking underlies all psychological disturbance. It is not people's experiences or situations that make them angry, depressed or anxious but the way they process the information and think about those experiences.

Schemas can be adaptive and healthy or maladaptive and unhealthy. Healthy schemas tend to be flexible and functional whereas maladaptive schemas tend to be negative, rigid and absolute. When unhealthy schemas are activated they affect all the stages of information processing. Thus a person with the maladaptive schema 'I am worthless' will tend to distort incoming information to match this belief. Positive information that would discount this belief may be ignored or distorted: 'The teacher only gave me a good mark because she wants something from me.'

When people become disturbed they tend to make errors in their information processing. Beck has identified a number of these 'logical errors', including:

- *Arbitrary inference*. People sometimes draw conclusions about events without any supporting evidence. For example, John might make the inference that when his friend Mary stares intently out of the window when he is talking to her, Mary does not like him, whereas the reality may be that Mary is watching her children at play.
- *Dichotomous thinking*. Thinking in extreme terms, for example, using the words 'never' and 'always' rather than 'sometimes', or placing experiences in one of two opposite categories such as beautiful and ugly.
- *Maximization and minimization*. Events are evaluated as much more or much less important than they really are. A normally calm mother losing her temper for the first time one day with her child may exaggerate the event and conclude that she is always a very bad mother.
- *Catastrophizing (also called fortune telling)*. Predicting the future negatively without considering more likely outcomes. For example, a student might believe that they will be too anxious in an examination and thus won't be able to function at all.
- *Mental filter (also called selective abstraction)*. Paying undue attention to one or two negative details instead of seeing the whole picture. For example, an employee getting one or two low ratings amongst many high ones will focus on the negative ones only and assume they are doing a lousy job.
- *Overgeneralization*. Making sweeping negative conclusions that go beyond the situation. For example, a partygoer might have felt uncomfortable and out of place, and from this one

experience might conclude that they are not social animals and do not have the social skills needed to make friends.
- *Personalization*. Believing that others are behaving negatively in a situation because of something you have done or said, without considering other plausible explanations for their behaviour. For example, Jane might assume the boy in her class is ignoring her and being grumpy because he does not like her, whereas he might be behaving this way because of a row he had with his parents that morning and therefore his apparent ignoring of her has nothing to do with her at all.

For more examples see Beck (1995: 119).

When unhealthy schemas are activated the individual tends to be prone to negative automatic thoughts. For example, when faced with a difficult situation, an anxious person will automatically and repeatedly think 'I can't cope with this', and a depressed person may think 'I'm useless, I'll never be able to do this, I give up.' Although healthy people can also experience such negative automatic thoughts, they are more frequent and disruptive in people with emotional problems.

Beck proposes a multi-factorial theory to explain how these maladaptive cognitive schemas, automatic thoughts and cognitive distortions leading to emotional disturbance are acquired. His model suggests that people become vulnerable to psychological problems as a result of the following interacting factors:

- *Genetic predisposition*. Individuals differ genetically in their vulnerability to different kinds of distress. For example, it has been shown that some forms of depression tend to run in families.
- *Childhood experiences*. Specific traumas and negative treatment in childhood are thought to contribute to a vulnerability to psychological problems throughout life. Underlying dysfunctional schemas are developed which can later be activated. In addition, the child-rearing practices of the parents may not have provided the child with the experiences needed to learn coping skills.
- *Social learning*. Children learn through observation of significant people in their lives. For example, they learn through imitating their parents' behaviour, and through rewards for behaviour. The child tends to learn, from its parents and other significant people, both helpful and unhelpful cognitive patterns and underlying assumptions.

Precipitating factors such as physical disease, severe and sudden external stress, and chronic external stress are thought to be responsible for activating the unhealthy cognitive processes.

Problems are thought to be maintained by the cognitive distortions. Once the unhealthy schemas are activated the individual tends to continue to think and behave in ways that maintain this activation. Any information received is filtered through the person's schema to render it consistent with their belief systems. For example, a depressed person will minimize or negate achievements and positive experiences and will maximize failures and negative experiences. This biased information processing also affects the automatic thoughts. The result is a reinforcement of the unhealthy cognitions leading to a continuation of the emotional difficulties.

- *Current thinking patterns*. Assessment is made of the client's information processing, automatic thoughts and schema.
- *Precipitating factors*. A consideration of current stressors will help the understanding of what has precipitated the present difficulties. These might be related to home, work, family or friends, and examples would include loss, illness, traumatic events or life changes.
- *Predisposing factors*. These can include past traumatic events, childhood experiences, genetic vulnerability and personality factors.

As therapy progresses, the therapeutic team of counsellor or psychotherapist and client refine the initial formulation as more information from the client is acquired.

CHANGE

Change in cognitive therapy usually means an alleviation of the emotional problems and a change in behaviour. Cognitive therapy is a goal-oriented, problem-solving and structured approach. Cognitions are the primary target for change in therapy. Cognitive therapy requires a sound therapeutic alliance and in recent years there has been an increased focus on how to use the relationship as an active ingredient in therapy. The role of collaboration between the client and the therapist and the active participation by the client in bringing about change are emphasized.

The process of change begins with the cognitive therapist educating the client about the cognitive model and the role of thoughts in emotions and behaviour. The emphasis is on conceptualizing the client's problems, teaching the cognitive model and providing some early symptom relief. The process continues with the therapist helping the client to set goals, identify and challenge cognitive errors, automatic thoughts and schemas, and plan behavioural change. Ultimately the client is helped to become their own therapist and relapse prevention is emphasized. Long-lasting change results from the modification of the person's underlying distorted and dysfunctional beliefs or schemas.

Cognitive therapy is based on the cognitive model which we have seen relates the way we think to our emotions and behaviours. This model is used to conceptualize the client's problems. Cognitive therapists believe that the clearer this formulation is, the easier it becomes to find methods to solve these problems. A formulation is a tentative hypothesis about the origins and maintenance of the client's difficulties and is conceptualized in terms of:

SKILLS AND STRATEGIES

Cognitive therapists employ an active-directive counselling style. An important skill is the ability to develop a good therapeutic relationship. Beck maintained from the early days of the development of cognitive-behaviour therapy that the context of a sound therapeutic relationship was very necessary although not sufficient to bring about change (see Beck et al., 1979). Today there is increasing recognition in the light of research that the quality of this relationship is central (Sanders and Wills, 2005). The core conditions described by Rogers (1957) of empathy, unconditional positive regard and congruence have to be in place to facilitate the effective use of cognitive and behavioural techniques.

Cognitive therapists need to be committed to the cognitive model and fully understand the rationale for this approach to therapy. The skill of being a good educator is essential to help clients understand the relationships between cognitions, emotions, physiology and behaviour. The ability to teach clients to monitor, reality test and modify their dysfunctional and distorted beliefs is crucial.

Therapists need to be able to work in a collaborative way with their clients, teaching clients to become their own therapists. Collaboration empowers clients by giving them a say in their own therapeutic process and it fosters self-efficacy.

Cognitive counselling or psychotherapy uses a variety of skills and strategies to bring about change. Techniques are chosen on the basis of the case formulation and in collaboration with the client.

Cognitive strategies are central to this approach and are used to help the client identify, examine, reality test and modify automatic thoughts, errors in information processing and schema. They include:

- *Socratic questioning.* Disciplined questioning used to explore the implications of the client's position, to stimulate rational thinking and to illuminate ideas. The therapist raises questions about the client's thoughts, feelings and actions to help the client discover things for themselves. Examples of the kind of questions used include, 'What is it about the situation that provokes these feelings of guilt?', 'What is the worst thing that could happen if it is true?', 'Is there an alternative explanation?'
- *Cost–benefit analysis.* Looking at the advantages and disadvantages of holding a particular belief.
- *Alternative perspectives.* For example, viewing their problem from the perspective of a close relative.
- *Use of automatic thought forms.* These can help clients identify their automatic thoughts and understand how they influence their emotions and behaviour. Using these forms the client might focus on a particular incident they found anxiety provoking, write down a description of the event, how they felt at the time, the thoughts they had and how strongly they believed those thoughts.
- *Reality testing.* Looking at evidence 'for' and 'against' the dysfunctional and distorted thoughts.
- *Cognitive rehearsal.* Practising coping with difficult situations either in role-play with the therapist, in imagination, or in real life.

Behavioural strategies are used to reality test clients' dysfunctional thoughts, and more specifically to reduce the physiological components of anxiety and increase the activity in people who are depressed. They include:

- *Graded exposure.* Getting clients to face step by step their fears and anxieties either in imagination or *in vivo.* For example, a woman who has had a road traffic accident may have developed a fear of driving her car again. In the early stages she will be encouraged to simply sit in the car until her anxiety levels have dropped right down. Then she can step up to the next stage which might be turning the ignition on. The stepping up continues until she is able to drive again as before.
- *Monitoring activities.* Keeping a record of daily activities and rating them on a 10-point scale for mastery and pleasure.
- *Scheduling activities.* To increase a client's activity levels, the client and counsellor schedule a number of activities into the day.
- *Behavioural experiments.* These enable the client to test out their fears. For example, a man

who has lift phobia and does not believe he can stand in a stationary lift for even five seconds can be asked to carry out this experiment and discover that, although he is uncomfortable in the lift, he can tolerate it.
- *Relaxation techniques.* These can be used to provide a coping strategy for reducing anxiety and to facilitate carrying out behavioural experiments.

Cognitive therapy advocates homework assignments to encourage clients to practise their newly learned skills and thus to enhance the therapeutic process.

RESEARCH EVIDENCE

Beck's cognitive therapy is one of the best researched approaches. Many well-controlled studies on the effectiveness of cognitive therapy have been conducted on a wide range of client problems. The general consensus is that this approach is effective in resolving problems.

The first important study was carried out by Beck and his associates (Rush et al., 1977) and demonstrated that cognitive therapy was more effective at reducing symptoms of depression than an antidepressant. As a result of this seminal study, cognitive therapy achieved academic recognition and became popular in the USA and in Europe. Roth and Fonagy (1996), in their systematic review of a large number of studies, concluded that there was good evidence of the effectiveness of CBT for a range of psychological problems. Since then a number of studies have demonstrated the efficacy of CBT for treating, for example, depression (Hollon et al., 2002; Teasdale et al., 2000), anxiety (Olatunji et al., 2010), PTSD (Blanchard et al., 2003) and panic disorder (Marchand et al., 2009). Research has recently been testing the effectiveness of emerging computerized programmes such as Blues Begone (Purves et al., 2009), and an interesting study shows that using an internet-based CBT intervention called Panic Online was comparable to face-to-face CBT (Kiropoulos et al., 2008).

CRITICISMS AND CONTROVERSIES

In the last decade in particular, cognitive therapy has received much media attention, largely due to the current discourse around wellbeing and 'happiness' (Layard, 2003). A number of controversies have developed as a result of the criticisms both of CBT and of the development of Improving Access to Psychological Therapies (IAPT: see Chapter 7.17 in this volume) which is currently having the effect of promoting CBT above all other approaches. There has been little in the way of systematic exploration of these criticisms and controversies, though the book edited by House and Loewenthal, *Against and For CBT: Toward a Constructive Dialogue* (2008), has gone some way to address this. There is only space here to mention the main criticism made, namely that the promotion of CBT is not supported by research evidence since CBT has not been shown to be more effective than any other approach. It is said by some that its elevation and endorsement by the government and the NHS are undeserved. Cognitive therapy is one approach among many and others may be more effective with particular people, with particular problems, in particular contexts. Many therapists of other persuasions believe that clients should be given a choice.

REFERENCES

Beck, A.T. (1963) Thinking and depression. I: Idiosyncratic content and cognitive distortions. *Archives of General Psychiatry*, 9: 324–33.

Beck, A.T. (1964) Thinking and depression. II: Theory and therapy. *Archives of General Psychiatry*, 10: 56–71.

Beck, A.T. (1976) *Cognitive Therapy and the Emotional Disorders*. New York: International Universities Press.

Beck, A.T., Rush, A.J., Shaw, B.F. and Emery, G. (1979) *Cognitive Therapy of Depression*. New York: Guilford.

Beck, J.S. (1995) *Cognitive Therapy: Basics and Beyond*. New York: Guilford.

Blanchard, E.B., Hickling, E.J., Devineni, T., Veazey, C.H., Galovski, T.E., Mundy, E., Malta, L.S. and Buckley, T.C. (2003) A controlled evaluation of cognitive behavioural therapy for posttraumatic stress in motor vehicle accident survivors. *Behaviour Research and Therapy*, 41 (1): 79.

Glickman, N.S. (2009) Adapting best practice in CBT for deaf and hearing persons with language and learning challenges. *Journal of Psychotherapy Integration*, 19 (4): 354–84.

Hays, P.A. and Iwamasa, G.Y. (2006) *Culturally Responsive Cognitive-Behavioral Therapy: Assessment, Practice and Supervision*. Washington, DC: APA.

Hollon, S.D., Thase, M.E. and Markowitz, J.C. (2002) Treatment and prevention of depression. *Psychological Science*, 3 (supp. 2): 39–77.

House, R. and Loewenthal, D. (eds) (2008) *Against and For CBT: Toward a Constructive Dialogue*. Ross-on-Wye: PCCS.

Kabat-Zinn, J. (1990) *Full Catastrophe Living: Using the Wisdom of Your Body and Mind to Face Stress, Pain and Illness*. New York: Dell.

Kiropoulos, L.A., Klein, B., Austin, D.W., Gilson, K., Pier, C., Mitchell, J. and Ciechomski, L. (2008) Is internet-based CBT for panic disorder and agoraphobia as effective as face-to-face CBT? *Journal of Anxiety Disorders*, 22 (8): 1273–84.

Layard, R. (2003) *Happiness: Has Social Science a Clue?* Lionel Robbins Memorial Lectures 2002/3.

Linehan, M.M. (1993) *Cognitive Behavior Therapy of Borderline Personality Disorder*. New York: Guilford.

Marchand, A., Roberge, P. and Primiano, S. (2009) A randomized, controlled trial of standard, group and brief cognitive-behavioural therapy for panic disorder with agoraphobia: a two-year follow-up. *Journal of Anxiety Disorders*, 23 (8): 1139–47.

Olatunji, B.O., Cisler, J.M. and Deacon, B.J. (2010) Efficacy of cognitive behavioral therapy for anxiety disorders: a review of meta-analytic findings. *Psychiatric Clinics of North America*, 33 (3): 557–77.

Purves, D.G., Bennett, M. and Wellman, N. (2009) An open trial in the NHS of Blues Begone: a new home based computerized CBT programme. *Behavioural and Cognitive Psychotherapy*, 37 (5): 541–51.

Rogers, C.R. (1957) The necessary and sufficient conditions of therapeutic personality change. *Journal of Consulting and Clinical Psychology*, 21: 95–103.

Roth, A. and Fonagy, P. (1996) *What Works for Whom? A Critical Review of Psychotherapy Research*. London: Guilford.

Rush, A.J., Beck, A.T., Kovacs, M. and Hollon, S.D. (1977) Comparative efficacy of cognitive therapy and pharmacotherapy in the treatment of depressed outpatients. *Cognitive Therapy and Research*, 1 (1): 17–37.

Ryle, A. (1989) *Cognitive Analytic Therapy: Active Participation in Change. A New Integration in Brief Psychotherapy*. Chichester: Wiley.

Sanders, D. and Wills, F. (2005) *Cognitive Therapy: An Introduction*. London: Sage.

Segal, Z.V., Williams, J.M.G. and Teasdale, J.D. (2002) *Mindfulness-Based Cognitive Therapy for Depression*. London: Guilford.

Teasdale, J.D., Segal, Z.V., Williams, J.M.G., Ridgeway, V., Lau, M. and Soulsby, J. (2000) Reducing risk of recurrence of major depression using mindfulness-based cognitive therapy. *Journal of Consulting and Clinical Psychology*, 68: 615.

RECOMMENDED READING

Burns, D.D. (1990) *The Feeling Good Handbook*. London: Penguin.

Padesky, C.A. and Greenberger, D. (1995) *Clinician's Guide to Mind Over Mood*. London: Guilford.

Salkovskis, P.M. (ed.) (1996) *Frontiers of Cognitive Therapy*. London: Guilford.

Trower, P., Casey, A. and Dryden, W. (1998) *Cognitive-Behavioural Counselling in Action*. London: Sage.

Westbrook, D., Kennerley, H. and Kirk, J. (2007) *An Introduction to Cognitive Behaviour Therapy*. London: Sage.

RECOMMENDED WEBSITES AND VIDEOS

The Beck Institute for Cognitive Therapy: www.beckinstitute.org

The Oxford Cognitive Therapy Centre: www.octc.co.uk/

Judith Beck PhD talks about cognitive therapy: www.youtube.com/watch?v=45U1F7cDH5k&feature=related

Beck talks about his history, how he moved from psychoanalysis to CT: www.laskerfoundation.org/2006videoawards/wm_high/clinical/html/c1.htm

To hear a former client talk about how CT helped her: www.laskerfoundation.org/2006videoawards/wm_high/clinical/html/c7.htm

Dialectical Behaviour Therapy

(Marsha Linehan, 1943–)

MICHAELA SWALES AND CHRISTINE DUNKLEY

BRIEF HISTORY

Dialectical Behaviour Therapy (DBT), developed by Marsha Linehan, evolved from the application of behaviour therapy to the treatment of suicidal behaviours. Linehan began working with women with a diagnosis of borderline personality disorder (BPD) as suicidal behaviours occur frequently in this client group. DBT is a principle-driven treatment (Swales and Heard, 2009: Chapter 1) that focuses on the treatment of specific behaviours, most commonly suicidal behaviours, in the context of a specific diagnostic group. The first trial of DBT (Linehan et al., 1991) was also the first randomised controlled trial demonstrating efficacy for any treatment for clients with a BPD diagnosis. This marked the beginning of an increasing therapeutic optimism about the treatment of BPD, where previously clinicians had been hopeless about the possibility of recovery. The treatment manuals were published in 1993 (Linehan, 1993a; 1993b) and a training programme began the same year. Since then there have been an increasing number of research trials, and clinical programmes have sprung up around the world.

BASIC ASSUMPTIONS

DBT principles are derived from three core philosophical perspectives: behaviourism, Zen and dialectics.

DBT adopts a radical behaviourist stance. Thus, DBT therapists conceptualise the diagnostic criteria for BPD as a series of behaviours, both covert and overt, that can be operationalised and changed using the principles of learning theory. If clients no longer experience and report the covert behaviours of the diagnosis, e.g. sense of emptiness, or do not engage in the overt behaviours of the diagnosis, e.g. suicidal behaviours, this means that the diagnosis no longer exists. A behavioural conceptualisation of diagnosis thus provides hope that recovery from BPD is possible.

Using this behavioural approach, DBT reorganises the diagnostic criteria into five systems of dysregulation, each subsuming different diagnostic criteria:

- emotional dysregulation (affective lability and problems with anger)
- interpersonal dysregulation (chaotic relationships and fears of abandonment)
- self dysregulation (identity disturbance and sense of emptiness)
- behaviour dysregulation (suicidal and impulsive behaviours)
- cognitive dysregulation (paranoid ideation and transient dissociated states).

Conceptually, DBT emphasises the primacy of affect: that difficulties in the management and experience of affect drive disturbance in the other domains of functioning. In turn, disturbances in these domains impact on affect and on each of the other domains. In DBT, suicidal, self-harm and impulsive behaviours are conceptualised either as a natural consequence of extreme levels of dysregulation or as attempts to reregulate affect.

In her early work, Linehan encountered several problems in applying behaviour therapy to this client group: frequently, clients did not complete homework tasks or implement solutions developed in therapy; each week clients presented with different problems to solve, driving frequent changes in treatment direction; often clients failed to return to treatment at all. In resolving these problems, Linehan hypothesised that clients struggled to engage with the therapy because the relentless focus on change fundamentally invalidated clients' experience of themselves and their capabilities. When faced with multiple life problems combined with beliefs that change is impossible or undeserved, participating in a change-focused therapy presents major challenges. Tensions build between client and therapist as the therapist pushes harder for change and the client increasingly finds change intolerable. To counterbalance the change focus Linehan turned to Zen philosophy, and mindfulness in particular. Linehan drew from this tradition a focus on acceptance. This thread of acceptance weaves throughout the therapy, informing therapist attitude, the strategies of the treatment and the skills taught to clients in treatment.

To house these two contrasting approaches, change and acceptance, Linehan turned to dialectical philosophy. Dialectics emphasises the interconnectedness and wholeness of reality such that multiple perspectives on reality are not only possible but encompass truth. Using the principles of dialectics, DBT therapists work to find the value in contrasting and opposing views on problems and solutions, to find solutions that respect the wisdom in each perspective. Embracing dialectics in this way assists to defuse the tension that often develops in a therapeutic context where the client experiences intense emotional pain and change is difficult and slow.

ORIGIN AND MAINTENANCE OF PROBLEMS

Linehan's biosocial theory of the development of BPD suggests that the disorder occurs as a result of an ongoing transactional process between emotional vulnerability in the individual and an invalidating environment. Features of emotional vulnerability include a highly sensitive nervous system with low threshold for emotional reactions. Once activated by emotional stimuli, responses are fast, extreme and slow to return to a baseline position. This pervasive emotional dysregulation adversely affects interrelated systems within the individual leading to dysregulation in cognition, interpersonal responses, identity formation and behaviour. Linehan likens the effect to a burn victim, missing a layer of 'emotional skin' and feeling each interaction as painful. When this level of vulnerability occurs in an invalidating environment a chain reaction occurs, intensifying the effects on both the environment and the individual until full BPD is evident.

The 'invalidating environment' is one which negates or dismisses the individual's internal experiences and behavioural responses regardless of their actual validity. Emotions are dismissed, as in 'you shouldn't be frightened because this isn't scary'; or criticised, such as with 'you're overreacting'; or simply ignored. As a result the individual learns to ignore her own internal responses and to search the environment for cues on how to respond. For example, a child of alcoholic parents may learn that whether she gets fed or not has nothing to do with when she is hungry, but depends on when her parents are sober. She therefore ignores internal indicators of hunger but attends avidly to signals regarding her parents' alcohol intake. The individual's internal environment becomes bewildering and their responses may seem to 'come from nowhere'. The environment often struggles to provide an effective response to such vacillations in emotional displays and may inadvertently reinforce dysfunctional behaviour. For example, an individual may repeatedly say, 'I can't bear it' when a demand is made on her, and is told, 'You can do it, it's easy.' Then she self-harms and the demand is removed. Even the most caring environment may become invalidating in an attempt to suppress dysfunctional behaviour. Linehan provides a no-blame model, looking at the transactional nature of the problems rather than seeking one point of origin.

The result of this transactional process is a skills deficit within the individual: she cannot up-regulate physiological arousal when required, and when emotionally aroused cannot turn her attention away from the stimulus. Information processing is impaired and she cannot organise behaviour in the service of her short- or long-term goals. She is likely to engage in mood-driven behaviour which may be impulsive or destructive, and at times she shuts down or freezes. Self-harming or suicidal thoughts and behaviours may function to regulate affect in the short term by providing escape from the cycle or to change an emotional state. Consequences in the environment (for example caregiving or rejection by others) can act to increase

Table 5.15.1 *Five functions of dialectical behaviour therapy*

Function	Modes in standard outpatient DBT
Enhance client capabilities	Skills training group
Improve motivational factors	Individual one-to-one therapy
Assure generalisation to the natural environment	Telephone coaching
Enhance therapist capabilities	Weekly therapist consultation meeting
Structuring the environment	Case management, family/marital/community interventions

or reduce the likelihood of further repetitions of the behaviour in a constantly evolving set of actions and reactions. In summary, DBT conceptualises clients' problems as arising from both capability and motivational deficits that are addressed in the five modalities of a comprehensive DBT programme (see below).

CHANGE

DBT therapists are working towards helping their clients to achieve a 'life worth living' by reducing behaviours that interfere with the accomplishment of this goal and at the same time increasing and strengthening skills. The change process begins with the client entering a phase of pre-treatment in which goals are identified and commitment is obtained before entering the full programme. Table 5.15.1 shows the five functions of DBT and the modes through which they are delivered in a standard outpatient programme.

DBT is a team treatment where a community of therapists treats a community of clients. A client in DBT will have one primary therapist who provides their individual therapy, and will also be expected to attend a separate skills training component of the programme. The primary therapist will also provide out-of-session help to generalise skills – usually via telephone coaching. The individual therapists and skills trainers all attend a weekly therapists' consultation meeting where they get support to adhere to the principles of the treatment.

Each modality of therapy has its own target hierarchy. Within individual therapy, behaviours are addressed in the following order:

- *Life-threatening behaviour.* Including suicidal or homicidal actions, non-suicidal self-injury, and urges to harm self or others.
- *Therapy-interfering behaviour.* Including behaviours that prevent the therapist from delivering therapy or the patient from receiving it. Examples are: missing sessions, repeatedly saying 'I don't know.'

- *Quality of life interfering behaviour.* Including severe destabilising conditions, for example behaviours leading to homelessness or unemployment. Also behaviours that are part of other comorbid conditions such as major depressive disorder or bulimia nervosa.

At the start of therapy a unique 'target hierarchy' is drawn up for each client, with specific behaviours to be changed. This may be modified during the course of treatment.

SKILLS AND STRATEGIES

The primary skill of the DBT therapist is to maintain a dialectical approach, welcoming tensions that arise as an opportunity to seek out the validity in both sides of the argument, and move towards synthesis. The therapist is modelling to the client how to move away from the characteristic black-and-white thinking by looking for what is left out and finding a both/and position. Therapists validate the functional and logical components of the client's behaviour before highlighting dysfunctional aspects. For example if the client says, 'I know people are repulsed by my scarring, so I hide at home', the therapist will validate, 'It is reasonable to think that some people are repulsed by scarring, and staying home makes sense when you want to avoid meeting that response. Are there any additional ways of addressing the problem that are less isolating?' Each problem situation is viewed as a practice opportunity for new skills, and in particular those learned in the skills training sessions (see above). The therapist favours consulting with the client on how to manage problems in her environment, rather than instructing the environment on how to manage the client.

A range of dialectical strategies is used, the main one being the balance between acceptance and change. The therapist also highlights patterns of behaviour common to BPD which Linehan (1993a) referred to as secondary targets or dialectical dilemmas:

- active passivity versus apparent competence
- unrelenting crises versus inhibited grieving
- emotional vulnerability versus self-invalidation.

The therapist moves back and forth between a reciprocal style of communication and an irreverent off-beat manner, keeping an eye on the flow of the session and altering styles strategically.

In the weekly consultation meeting therapists adhere to a number of agreements – e.g. the fallibility agreement (that all therapists are fallible) and the phenomenological empathy agreement (that all behaviours are understandable in context). The meeting begins with mindfulness and then therapists help each other to apply the principles of the therapy. The emphasis is on 'therapy for the therapist' – being alert to signs of burnout, seeking out the validity in opposing opinions to ensure nothing is being missed.

Mindfulness is considered a core skill in DBT. Therapists help clients to take control of the spotlight of their mind – being able to turn attention from distressing stimuli, to identify what would be effective, and to take action when needed. Together they acknowledge that change is inevitable, and that each situation that cannot be changed must be tolerated until natural change occurs. The therapist and client are encouraged to use skilful means and evaluate the outcome without judgement, slowly shaping more effective behaviour. The client is also taught specific emotion-regulation techniques, ways to be interpersonally effective when making requests or saying no to unwanted demands, and ways to tolerate both short-term crises and long-term distress.

RESEARCH EVIDENCE

Since the first research trial in 1991, researchers have evaluated the efficacy of DBT in different settings and with different client populations, although most research has been conducted on the original client population. Five further randomised controlled trials on chronically suicidal women with a BPD diagnosis have now been published (Clarkin et al., 2007; Koons et al., 2001; Linehan et al., 2006; McMain et al., 2009; Verheul et al., 2003) since the first trial in 1991 (Linehan et al., 1991). In summary, these trials demonstrate that DBT is efficacious in reducing suicidal behaviours (including non-suicidal self-injury and suicide ideation) and their severity, decreasing hospital stays and improving treatment retention (Koons et al., 2001; Linehan et al., 1991; 2006; Verheul et al., 2003). In later trials that have compared DBT either to a very rigorous control

condition (Linehan et al., 2006; McMain et al., 2009) or to other active treatments (Clarkin et al., 2007), benefits remain but are less marked in contrast.

DBT has also been tested for efficacy with other client groups. Two trials of DBT for women with both BPD and substance dependence demonstrated benefits in decreasing substance misuse (Linehan et al., 1999; 2002). There is also an emerging evidence base for the use of DBT with adults with a diagnosis of binge-eating disorder (Telch et al., 2001) and in older adults with comorbid depression and personality disorder (Lynch et al., 2003; 2007). Studies in inpatient settings, although not randomised, have also demonstrated the usefulness of DBT in managing behavioural disturbance (Bohus et al., 2004).

REFERENCES

Bohus, M., Haaf, B., Simms, T.M.F.L., Schmahl, C., Unckel, C., Lieb, K. and Linehan, M.M. (2004) Effectiveness of inpatient dialectical behavioral therapy for borderline personality disorder: a controlled trial. *Behaviour Research and Therapy*, 42: 487–99.

Clarkin, J.F., Levy, K.N., Lenzenweger, M.F. and Kernberg, O.F. (2007) Evaluating three treatments for borderline personality disorder: a multiwave study. *American Journal of Psychiatry*, 164: 922–8.

Koons, C.R., Robins, C.J., Tweed, J.L., Lynch, T.R., Gonzalez, A.M., Morse, J.Q., Bishop, G.K., Butterfield, M. and Bastian, L.A. (2001) Efficacy of dialectical behavior therapy in women veterans with borderline personality disorder. *Behavior Therapy*, 32: 371–90.

Linehan, M.M. (1993a) *Cognitive Behavioral Treatment of Borderline Personality Disorder*. New York: Guilford.

Linehan, M.M. (1993b) *Skills Training Manual for Borderline Personality Disorder*. New York: Guilford.

Linehan, M.M., Armstrong, H.E., Suarez, A., Allman, D. and Heard, H. (1991) Cognitive behavioral treatment of chronically suicidal borderline patients. *Archives of General Psychiatry*, 48: 1060–4.

Linehan, M.M., Schmidt, H., Dimeff, L.A., Craft, J.C., Kanter, J. and Comtois, K.A. (1999) Dialectical behavior therapy for patients with borderline personality disorder and drug-dependence. *The American Journal on Addictions* 8 (4): 279–92.

Linehan, M.M., Dimeff, L.A., Rynolds, S.K., Comtois, K.A., Shaw-Welch, S., Heagerty, P. and Kivlahan, D.R. (2002) Dialectical behavior therapy versus comprehensive validation plus 12-step for the treatment of opioid dependent women meeting criteria for borderline personality disorder. *Drug and Alcohol Dependence*, 67: 13–26.

Linehan, M.M., Comtois, K.A., Murray, A.M., Brown, M.Z., Gallop, R.J., Heard, H.H., Korslund, K.E., Tutek, D.A., Rynolds, S.K. and Lindenboim, N. (2006) Two-year randomized controlled trial and follow-up of dialectical behavior therapy vs therapy by experts for suicidal behaviors and borderline personality disorder. *Archives of General Psychiatry*, 63: 757–66.

Lynch, T.R., Morse, J.O., Mendelson, T. and Robins, C.J. (2003) Dialectical behavior therapy for depressed older adults: a randomized pilot study. *American Journal of Geriatric Psychiatry*, 11 (1): 33–45.

Lynch, T.R., Cheavens, J.S., Cukrowicz, K.C., Thorp, S., Bronner, L. and Beyer, J. (2007) Treatment of older adults with co-morbid personality disorder and depression: a dialectical behavior therapy approach. *International Journal of Geriatric Psychiatry*, 22: 131–43.

McMain, S.F., Links, P.S., Gnam, W.H., Guimond, T., Cardish, R.J., Korman, L. and Steiner, D.L. (2009) A randomized trial of dialectical behavior therapy versus general psychiatric management for borderline personality disorder. *American Journal of Psychiatry*, 166 (12): 1365–74.

Swales, M. and Heard, H. (2009) *Dialectical Behaviour Therapy*. London: Routledge.

Telch, C.F., Agras, W.S. and Linehan, M.M. (2001) Dialectical behavior therapy for binge eating disorder. *Journal of Consulting and Clinical Psychology*, 69 (6): 1061–5.

Verheul, R., van den Bosch, L.M.C., Koeter, M.W.J., De Ridder, M.A.J., Stijnen, T. and van den Brink, W. (2003) Dialectical behaviour therapy for women with borderline personality disorder: 12-month, randomised clinical trial in The Netherlands. *British Journal of Psychiatry*, 182 (2): 135–40.

Rational Emotive Behaviour Therapy

(Albert Ellis, 1913–2007)

WINDY DRYDEN

BRIEF HISTORY

Rational emotive behaviour therapy (REBT) was founded in 1955 by Albert Ellis, an American clinical psychologist who had become increasingly disaffected with psychoanalysis in which he trained in the late 1940s. Originally the approach was called rational therapy (RT) because Ellis wanted to emphasize its rational and cognitive features. In doing so, Ellis demonstrated the philosophical influences (largely Stoic) on his thinking. In 1961 he changed its name to rational-emotive therapy to show critics that it did not neglect emotions, and over 30 years later (in 1993) Ellis renamed the approach yet again, calling it rational emotive behaviour therapy to show critics that it did not neglect behaviour.

In 1962 Ellis published *Reason and Emotion in Psychotherapy*, a collection largely of previously published papers or previously delivered lectures, but which became a seminal work in the history of psychotherapy. Most of REBT's major present-day features are described in this book: the pivotal role of cognition in psychological disturbance; the principle of psychological interactionism where cognition, emotion and behaviour are seen as interacting, not separate, systems; the advantages of self-acceptance over self-esteem in helping clients with their disturbed views of their selves; and the importance of an active-directive therapeutic style, to name but a few.

Albert Ellis died in 2007 after an unfortunate period during which he was in dispute on a number of issues with the institute that continues to bear his name. Despite this, the legacy that Ellis left REBT and the wider field of psychotherapy is untarnished and unquestioned.

REBT is practised all over the world and has many different therapeutic, occupational and educational applications. However, it tends to live in the shadow of Beck's cognitive therapy, an approach to cognitive-behaviour therapy which has attracted a greater number of practitioners and is more academically respectable.

BASIC ASSUMPTIONS

Rationality is a concept that is normally applied to a person's beliefs. Rational beliefs, which are deemed to be at the core of psychological health, are flexible or non-extreme, consistent with reality, logical, and both self and relationship enhancing. Irrational beliefs, which are deemed to be at the core of psychological disturbance, are rigid or extreme, inconsistent with reality, illogical, and both self and relationship defeating.

There are four types of rational belief: non-dogmatic preferences ('I want to be approved of, but I don't have to be'); non-awfulizing beliefs ('It's bad to be disapproved of, but it isn't the end of the world'); discomfort tolerance beliefs ('It is difficult to face being disapproved of, but I can tolerate it');

and acceptance beliefs (e.g. self-acceptance, 'I can accept myself if I am disapproved of'; other acceptance, 'You are not horrible if you disapprove of me'; and life acceptance, 'Even though this tragedy happened, life is not all bad and comprises good, bad and neutral events').

Similarly, there are four types of irrational belief: rigid demands ('I must be approved of'); awfulizing beliefs ('If I'm disapproved of, it's the end of the world'); discomfort intolerance beliefs ('I can't tolerate being disapproved of'); and depreciation beliefs (e.g. self-depreciation, 'I am worthless if I am disapproved of'; other depreciation, 'You are horrible if you disapprove of me'; and life depreciation, 'Life is all bad because this tragedy happened').

REBT advocates a situational 'ABC' model of psychological disturbance and health. 'A' stands for adversity, which occurs within a situation and can be actual or inferred. 'A' represents the aspect of the situation that the person focuses on and evaluates. 'B' stands for belief (rational or irrational). 'C' stands for the consequences of holding a belief about A and can be emotional, behavioural and cognitive. Thus, 'As' do not cause 'Cs' but contribute to them. 'Bs' are seen as the prime but not the only determiners of 'Cs'.

Holding a rational belief about an 'A' leads to healthy emotions, functional behaviour, and realistic and balanced subsequent thinking. Holding an irrational belief about the same 'A' leads to unhealthy emotions, dysfunctional behaviour, and unrealistic subsequent thinking that is highly skewed to the negative.

REBT's view of human nature is realistic. Humans are seen as having the potential for both rational and irrational thinking. The ease with which we transform our strong desires into rigid demands suggests that the tendency towards irrational thinking is biologically based, but can be buffered or encouraged by environmental contexts.

Clients often have the unfortunate experience of inheriting tendencies towards disturbance and being exposed to their parents' disturbed behaviour. REBT is optimistic and realistic here. It argues that if such clients work persistently and forcefully to counter their irrational beliefs and act in ways that are consistent with their rational beliefs, then they can help themselves significantly. However, REBT also acknowledges that most clients will not put in this degree of effort over a long period of time and will therefore fall far short of achieving their potential for psychological health.

ORIGIN AND MAINTENANCE OF PROBLEMS

People are disturbed not by events but by the rigid and extreme views that they take of them. This means that while negative events contribute to the development of disturbance, particularly when these events are highly aversive, disturbance occurs when people bring their tendencies to think irrationally to these events.

REBT does not have an elaborate view of the origin of disturbance. Having said this, it does acknowledge that it is very easy for humans when they are young to disturb themselves about highly aversive events. However, it argues that even under these conditions people react differently to the same event and thus we need to understand what a person brings to and takes from a negative activating event. People learn their standards and goals from their culture, but disturbance occurs when they bring their irrational beliefs to circumstances where their standards are not met and their pursuit of their goals is blocked.

REBT has a more elaborate view of how disturbance is maintained. It argues that people perpetuate their disturbance for a number of reasons including the following:

- They lack the insight that their disturbance is underpinned by their irrational beliefs and think instead that it is caused by events.
- They wrongly think that once they understand that their problems are underpinned by irrational beliefs, this understanding alone will lead to change.
- They do not work persistently to change their irrational beliefs and to integrate the rational alternatives to these beliefs into their belief system.
- They continue to act in ways that are consistent with their irrational beliefs.
- They lack or are deficient in important social skills, communication skills, problem-solving skills and other life skills.
- They think that their disturbance has payoffs that outweigh the advantages of the healthy alternatives to their disturbed feelings and/or behaviour.
- They live in environments which support the irrational beliefs that underpin their problems and they think that as this is the case they cannot do anything to help themselves.

CHANGE

REBT therapists consider that the core facilitative conditions of empathy, unconditional acceptance and genuineness are often desirable, but neither necessary nor sufficient for constructive therapeutic change. For such change to take place, REBT therapists need to help their clients to do the following:

- realize that they largely create their own psychological problems and that while situations contribute to these problems, they are in general of lesser importance in the change process
- fully recognize that they are able to address and overcome these problems
- understand that their problems stem largely from irrational beliefs
- detect their irrational beliefs and discriminate between them and their rational beliefs
- question their irrational beliefs and their rational beliefs until they see clearly that their irrational beliefs are false, illogical and unconstructive while their rational beliefs are true, sensible and constructive
- work towards the internalization of their new rational beliefs by using a variety of cognitive (including imaginal), emotive and behavioural change methods
- refrain from acting in ways that are consistent with their old irrational beliefs
- extend this process of challenging beliefs and using multimodal methods of change into other areas of their lives and to commit to doing so for as long as necessary.

All this is best done when effective REBT therapists develop, maintain and suitably end a good working alliance with clients (Dryden, 2009). This involves:

- therapists and clients having a good working bond
- therapists and clients sharing a common view of the determinants of the latter's problems and how these can best be addressed
- therapists and clients working towards agreed goals
- therapists and clients executing agreed tasks designed to facilitate goal achievement.

SKILLS AND STRATEGIES

REBT therapists see themselves as good psychological educators and therefore seek to teach their clients the ABC model of understanding and dealing with their psychological problems. They stress that there are alternative ways of addressing these problems and strive to elicit from their clients informed consent at the outset and throughout the counselling process. If they think that a client is better suited to a different approach to therapy, they do not hesitate to effect a suitable referral.

REBT therapists frequently employ an active-directive counselling style and use both Socratic and didactic teaching methods. However, they vary their style from client to client. They begin by working with specific examples of identified client problems and help their clients to set healthy goals. They employ a sequence of steps in working on these examples which involves using the situationally based ABC framework, challenging beliefs and negotiating suitable homework assignments with their clients.

Helping clients to generalize their learning from situation to situation is explicitly built into the counselling process. So too is helping clients to identify, challenge and change core irrational beliefs which are seen as accounting for disturbance across a broad range of relevant situations.

A major therapeutic strategy involves helping clients to become their own therapists. In doing this, REBT therapists teach their clients how to use a particular skill such as challenging irrational beliefs, model the use of this skill, and sometimes give the clients written instructions on how to use the skill on their own. Constructive feedback is given to encourage the refinement of the skill. As clients learn how to use the skills of REBT for themselves, their therapists adopt a less active-directive, more prompting therapeutic style in order to encourage them to take increasing responsibility for their own therapeutic change.

REBT may be seen as an example of theoretically consistent eclecticism in that its practitioners draw upon procedures that originate from other counselling approaches, but do so for purposes that are consistent with REBT theory. REBT therapists are judiciously selective in their eclecticism and avoid the use of methods that are inefficient, or mystical, or of dubious validity.

REBT therapists have their preferred therapeutic goals for their clients, namely to help them to change their core irrational beliefs and to develop and internalize a set of core rational beliefs. However, they are ready to make compromises with their clients on these objectives when it becomes clear that their clients are unable or unwilling to change their core irrational beliefs. In such cases, REBT therapists help their clients by encouraging them to change their distorted inferences, to effect behavioural changes without necessarily changing their irrational beliefs, or to remove themselves from negative activating events.

RESEARCH EVIDENCE

There is quite a lot of research indicating that psychological disturbance is correlated with irrational beliefs (see Dryden et al., 2009), but studies indicating that these beliefs are at the core of disturbance have yet to be carried out. Most scales which measure irrational and rational beliefs are deficient in one respect or another and there is a need to develop a scale with excellent psychometric properties.

Numerous studies on the effectiveness of REBT have been carried out and various meta-analyses of REBT outcome studies have been conducted which have come to different conclusions about the effectiveness of REBT. Well-controlled trials of REBT need to be done with clinical populations, employing well-trained REBT therapists who can be shown to adhere to a properly designed REBT competency scale. Such a scale has recently been published (Dryden et al., 2010).

REFERENCES

Dryden, W. (2009) *Skills in Rational Emotive Behaviour Counselling and Psychotherapy*. London: Sage.

Dryden, W., David, D. and Ellis, A. (2009) Rational emotive behavior therapy. In K.S. Dobson (ed.), *Handbook of Cognitive-Behavioral Therapies* (3rd edn, pp. 226–76). New York: Guilford.

Dryden, W., Beal, D., Jones, J. and Trower, P. (2010) The REBT competency scale for clinical and research applications. *Journal of Rational-Emotive and Cognitive-Behavior Therapy*, 28 (4), 165–216.

Ellis, A. ([1962] 1994) *Reason and Emotion in Psychotherapy* (rev. edn). New York: Birch Lane.

RECOMMENDED READING

Dryden, W. (ed.) (1995) *A Rational Emotive Behaviour Therapy Reader*. London: Sage.

Dryden, W. (2001) *Reason to Change: A Rational Emotive Behaviour Therapy (REBT) Workbook*. Hove: Brunner-Routledge.

Dryden, W., DiGiuseppe, R. and Neenan, M. (2010) *A Primer on Rational Emotive Behaviour Therapy* (3rd edn). Champaign, IL: Research Press.

Ellis, A. (2001) *Overcoming Destructive Beliefs, Feelings, and Behaviors*. Amherst, NY: Prometheus.

THEORY AND APPROACHES

HUMANISTIC-EXISTENTIAL APPROACHES

Body Psychotherapy

NICK TOTTON

BRIEF HISTORY

While several practitioners and theories can be seen as precursors, body psychotherapy itself has one clear source: the work of Wilhelm Reich (1897–1957). Reich was one of the second generation of psychoanalysts, working originally in Vienna. Two of his particular interests led him towards engagement with the body: on the one hand his belief (following Freud's earlier views) that here-and-now sexual frustration is a crucial factor in neurosis, and on the other hand his focus on character as the key to resistance, and hence on the details of *how*, rather than *what*, the client presents, including posture, expression, gesture, tone of voice, and what we might now call vitality affect (Stern, 1985: 53–60).

During the 1920s and 1930s Reich steadily developed a clinical practice centred on inviting the client to breathe, relax, and allow bodily impulses expression, whether or not they made apparent sense. This was of course combined with verbal work, focusing on the therapeutic relationship and the means the client used to fend off or distract the therapist or distance themselves from interpretations. From this beginning as a sort of bodily free association, Reichian therapy eventually became much more strongly interventionist, with the therapist using their hands to release the client's muscular blocks and free their breathing. (The two central texts are Reich, 1972/1945; 1983/1942.) In 1934 Reich was backhandedly excluded from the International Psychoanalytic Association, mainly because of his radical politics, and he moved to the USA in 1939. After his death his work powerfully influenced the 1960s growth movement, with the result that most body psychotherapy has found its home broadly within the humanistic field.

Although many schools of body psychotherapy follow or are strongly influenced by Reichian ideas (and are often described as 'neo-Reichian'), a range of body-oriented approaches has arisen independently, for example the varieties of dance/movement therapy and of voicework; primal therapies inspired by Arthur Janov; Eugene Gendlin's focusing (Gendlin, 1981); gestalt body psychotherapy, influenced by Reich – who was for a time Fritz Perls's analyst – but developing a distinct model (Kepner, 1987; Frank, 2001; 2005); and process-centred approaches like Hakomi (Kurtz, 1990) and process-oriented psychology (Mindell, 1988; Audergon, 2005).

There are several thousand body psychotherapists around the world, with three multinational membership organisations. The European Association for Body Psychotherapy has over 700 accredited members and 10 national associations, as well as many associate members. Including body-oriented psychotherapists of all kinds, the numbers are far higher.

BASIC ASSUMPTIONS

Most body psychotherapists probably share at least the following positions:

- What happens in the mind also happens in the body, and vice versa.

- Psychological issues are sometimes best approached via the body, and vice versa.
- Many people in our culture experience problems which originate in their dissociation from their bodies.
- The more embodied a person is – that is, the more deeply they accept and identify with their bodily experience – the more likely they are, other things being equal, to be contented, productive and competent, including being able to respond to difficult experiences.
- Human beings are innately positive and creative until we encounter the oppressive circumstances of society, which become inscribed in our embodiment. This process can, at least in theory, be undone.

Some of these points will be developed in the next two sections, but I will briefly unpack them here.

Though body psychotherapists may have different philosophies, they agree that the mind/body dualism pervading Western culture and formally expressed by Descartes is both false and pernicious. Some would say that mind and body are identical; others follow Reich's view of the '*functional* identity' of mind and body, so that for each psychological process there is a bodily equivalent, and vice versa; while others see 'mind' and 'body' as different facets of the same underlying phenomenon.

In any case, body psychotherapists also recognise that although body/mind dualism is in many ways illusory, it also has very powerful effects. We frequently *experience* our minds and our bodies as distinct, and indeed as conflicting with each other; our mind wants one thing and our body 'wants' something else, for example. The strong tendency of Western culture is to privilege the wishes of the mind over those of the body, and to seek ways for the mind to impose its will. Body psychotherapy believes this is a disastrous mistake – which leads into the next section.

ORIGIN AND MAINTENANCE OF PROBLEMS

For body psychotherapists, social and cultural support for the privileging of mind over a split-away body underlies many problems people bring to therapy. It allows and encourages a denigration of bodily experience and bodily desires, in particular sexuality, but also emotional and physical expression. Our nature as human animals is treated as problematic, and there is pressure to 'rise above' embodiment and live on a spiritual or intellectual plane. This is traditionally expressed in Christianity, and most recently in the idea of virtual consciousness, in which human mind states are translated into computers.

If mind and body are one, then the notion of the mind imposing its will on the body actually means the body/mind struggling against itself. And this is what body psychotherapists see happening: no longer mainly through self-flagellation, hairshirts or cold showers, but through the pitting of muscle against muscle which creates chronic physical tension, what Reich called 'muscular armouring', embodying the psychological phenomena of repression, defence and resistance (e.g. Reich, 1983/1942: 299ff). Once muscular armouring is in place, it transforms conscious control into unconscious control, which can persist indefinitely even against the individual's conscious wishes.

According to Reich, repression is mediated through control of the breath: 'Imagine that you have been frightened or you anticipate great danger. You will involuntarily suck in your breath and hold it' (1983/1942: 306). This becomes a habitual response of children to external or internal experiences which create anxiety, and is maintained by muscular tension, initially in the diaphragm and extending to all the expressive systems of the body. And of course, less breathing means less oxygen, and hence less energy for emotional expression.

Not all body psychotherapists subscribe to this Reichian model, but in one way or another they would generally agree that the mind/body split turns the body against itself in ways which restrict spontaneity, freedom and pleasure. Many modern practitioners emphasise the role of trauma in dissociating us from our bodies (Totton, 2002; Ogden et al., 2006); while Reich does not use the term much, it is entirely consistent with his theories.

CHANGE

Body psychotherapists seek to help the client open up a space for spontaneous bodily experience, in the belief that this will kick-start a process of self-healing. This is parallel in different ways to both psychodynamic and humanistic therapies. I have suggested elsewhere (Totton, 2003: 53–61) that we can identify three different styles of working to achieve this goal through body psychotherapy: the adjustment model, the discharge model, and the process model. These are sometimes relatively distinct, but despite their different logics are often blended in various ways and proportions; which model is primary varies between individual practitioners almost as much as between schools.

The *adjustment model* is perhaps the oldest. At its simplest, it believes that helping the body achieve ideal form and function is the most effective path to freedom. Clearly this view has strong links with schools of body *work* (rather than psychotherapy) like Rolfing, Alexander Technique and massage therapy. The *discharge model*, which also has a long history, emphasises instead the embodied presence of trauma, giving rise to unexpressed emotion bound within patterns of muscular tension. Again simply put, it believes that emotional discharge with full bodily involvement clears the slate, so to speak, for a satisfying and productive life. The *process model*, which is the most recent of the three, avoids prescription and concentrates on supporting whatever is already spontaneously trying to happen in the individual body/mind, trusting the system to create its own healing.

There are clear parallels between these three approaches and those of different schools of verbal psychotherapy. This is not surprising: body psychotherapists are first and foremost *psychotherapists*, with some unique skills and concerns, but operating in the same field as other psychotherapists and facing essentially the same challenges and options.

SKILLS AND STRATEGIES

The most striking and unusual skill set employed by body psychotherapists involves direct work with and through the body. This encompasses a very large range of approaches: most challenging to the standard paradigm are those involving touch, but while a number of body psychotherapists frequently touch their clients, many do so relatively rarely, and a small minority actually abstain from touch in a similar way to most verbal therapists (Rothschild, 2003). There are in any case many other ways to interact with the client's embodiment, including observation and feedback, movement work, and consulting one's own embodied experience. I will look briefly at each of these four approaches.

Touch-based Body Work

As already mentioned, the classical Reichian method is centred on breathing and muscular tension. The client is invited to lie down on their back and focus on their breath, often also to deepen their breathing; the therapist sits beside them and offers support and feedback, and also (in most versions) uses their hands to amplify muscle tension and provoke emotional discharge, encouraging use of the voice. Although there are several manuals for this work, it cannot really be effectively manualised, and needs to be learnt through personal experience as both client and practitioner over a period of years.

This classical approach is only one of several ways in which a body psychotherapist may exercise what Don Hanlon Johnson (2000) has called 'intricate tactile sensitivity' (ITS): 'using touch to pick up complex information about the immediate and long-term state of their client's embodiment; and also to influence that state in complex ways through the quality of their touch' (Totton, 2003: 78). Johnson (2000) goes into some detail about the different subforms of ITS, which are often employed intuitively by practitioners who have developed them partly through experience rather than training, and often also through training in various body practices like craniosacral therapy or Alexander Technique.

Most body psychotherapists are also very comfortable with using touch in a more 'ordinary' way to explore and develop contact with their clients. Just as a number of verbal therapists will do, they hug clients and hold their hands when emotional support is needed; more unusually, they will also explore in a physical way their clients' impulses to push the therapist away, to hit, scratch or bite them, or to hide from them. Ethical issues around touch have been extensively explored (e.g. Tune, 2005; Totton, 2006; Caldwell, 1997).

Observation and Feedback

The use of touch depends of course on the willingness of both parties; and frequently this is not where the client wants to go. In any case it is not always the most useful direction. Often the work will focus instead on the client sharing bodily sensations and impulses, and the therapist contributing observations, interpretations and suggestions. Here is a fictional illustration:

Client: When I told you that my guts clenched up.

Therapist: Sounds as though you got a shock! What's happening to them now?

Client: Still quite tight.

Therapist: Keep your attention there … Feel into your guts … What do they want to say?

Client: [*after a moment*] Help!

Therapist: Say it again?

Client: HELP!!

This is probably within the range of many practitioners who would not describe themselves as body psychotherapists. Body psychotherapists bring more specialised skills and understandings to such work, and perhaps more confidence; they may tend to stay with it longer and take it deeper.

Movement Work

Though most body psychotherapists are not movement specialists, they are generally willing and able to get up out of the chair, and encourage their clients to do the same, in a way that most verbal therapists don't. To continue the previous fictional example:

Client:	HELP!!
Therapist:	Yes – there's a lot of energy, isn't there! How about standing up and showing it with your whole body? [*therapist stands up*]
Client:	[*standing*] HELP!! HELP ME!! [*waves arms, jumps up and down*]
Therapist:	[*coming closer*] How can I help you?
Client:	I'm drowning!
Therapist:	Shall I pull you out?
Client:	No … No, I need to get myself out.
Therapist:	Ah! OK! That sounds good. Shall we sit down and talk about it?

The Therapist's Embodiment

A core skill for body psychotherapy – perhaps its necessary and sufficient condition – is that the therapist continuously tracks her own embodied experience, asking herself at every point whether and how it relates to the client's experience and to the contact between them.

> In the therapy hour I watch not only the client's energy but also my own. I observe not only the client's breathing and constrictions, but also attend to my own … I feel what sensations emerge in my own body as the client works. (Conger, 1994: 20)

Some psychodynamic therapists call this 'embodied counter-transference' (Jacobs, 1973; Samuels, 1989: 150ff). (Harris and Sinsheimer, 2008 is an excellent discussion from an analytic perspective.) So the fictional work above could have gone in a different direction:

Client:	When I told you that my guts clenched up.

Therapist:	That's interesting – I had a similar experience myself – as if someone had punched me in the belly. It made me wonder whether you felt she was attacking you when she said that?

Or even:

Client:	When I told you that my guts clenched up.
Therapist:	That's interesting – I had a slightly different experience: I felt my guts start to clench, and then I had a sense of something releasing. I wondered whether there was also some relief for you in hearing that from her?

Verbal Work

As all this should make clear, most body psychotherapists interact verbally with their clients as much as other therapists. To do otherwise would be to support the mind/body split which body psychotherapy seeks to challenge. There tends to be a rhythmic interplay in sessions between focus on embodied aspects of the client's process, and focus on its psychological aspects – a rhythm which is clearly apparent in Reich's case histories (see Totton, 1998: 107–12).

Relational Body Psychotherapy

Most recently, particularly in the UK, body psychotherapy has joined with psychotherapy as a whole in taking a 'relational turn', using the concept and experience of embodied counter-transference as the basis for a sophisticated exploration of embodied relationship (Soth, 2005; 2006; 2009; Totton, 2005; Asheri, 2009). This constitutes a decisive shift from the traditional 'one-body' approach of the older generations of body psychotherapists.

RESEARCH EVIDENCE

Body psychotherapy is comparatively under-researched in conventional terms, if randomised controlled testing – enormously expensive, and arguably inappropriate for psychotherapy – is taken as the 'gold standard'. However, it is by no means completely without an evidence base. Much of this consists of case histories; but there is also a growing body of research into effectiveness and efficacy. The rate of development can be seen by comparing May's (2005) overview with Rohricht's (2009) overview: as the latter points out, in four years 'many more studies have been identified ... and there is now a much better evidence base for the efficacy' of body-oriented psychotherapy (2009: 146).

It should be noted that Rohricht's survey (unlike May's) covers body-*oriented* psychotherapy (BOP), a considerably wider field than body psychotherapy proper; a good deal of the research he identifies relates specifically to dance movement psychotherapy. This could be considered a spur to body psychotherapists both to develop research, and to hone their skills in movement work. In any case, Rohricht's conclusion is positive and important:

> BOP seems to have generally good effects on subjectively experienced depressive and anxiety symptoms, somatisation and social insecurity. Patients undergoing BOP appear to benefit in terms of improved general well-being, reduced motor tension and enhanced activity levels. (2009: 149)

He also notes that:

> BOP appears to offer promising additional psychotherapeutic tools in areas where traditional talking psychotherapies seem to fail so far, e.g. somatoform disorders/medically unexplained syndromes, PTSD, anorexia nervosa or chronic schizophrenia. The best example ... is the recent publication of NICE guidelines for schizophrenia in the UK ... body oriented psychotherapy is now recommended amongst other non-verbal/arts therapies as treatment of choice for chronic schizophrenia patients with predominant negative symptoms. (2009: 150)

Absence of evidence is, of course, not evidence of absence; and there is every reason to expect that body psychotherapy will in time be demonstrated to have wide-ranging value as a therapy modality.

A rather different sort of research support comes from contemporary neuroscience. This has contributed to the field's recent revitalisation through its striking confirmation of many of body psychotherapy's fundamental positions, for example, the role of the autonomic nervous system; the importance of breathing; the bodily foundations of empathy; the centrality of self-regulation; the effect of trauma; and the value of embodied relationship in developing self-calming and self-regulation. (For all of this and more, see Carroll, 2005; 2006; 2009; Totton, 2003: 32–44; Bauer and Marshall, 2009; Rohricht, 2009: 144–5.) While neuroscience undoubtedly validates body psychotherapy, there is less reason to think that it will

improve the work itself, which rests firmly on clinical experience.

REFERENCES

Asheri, S. (2009) To touch or not to touch: a relational body psychotherapy perspective. In L. Hartley (ed.), *Contemporary Body Psychotherapy: The Chiron Approach* (pp. 106–20). London: Routledge.

Audergon, J.-C. (2005) The body in process work. In N. Totton (ed.), *New Dimensions in Body Psychotherapy* (pp. 153–67). Maidenhead: Open University Press.

Bauer, J. and Marshall, E. (2009) The brain transforms psychology into biology. *Body, Movement and Dance in Psychotherapy*, 4 (3): 231–8.

Caldwell, C. (1997) Ethics and techniques for touch in somatic therapy. In C. Caldwell (ed.), *Getting in Touch: The Guide to New Body-Centered Therapies* (pp. 227–38). Wheaton, IL: Quest Books.

Carroll, R. (2005) Neuroscience and the 'law of the self'. In N. Totton (ed.), *New Dimensions in Body Psychotherapy* (pp. 13–29). Maidenhead: Open University Press.

Carroll, R. (2006) A new era for psychotherapy. In J. Corrigall, H. Payne and H. Wilkinson (eds), *About a Body: Working with the Embodied Mind in Psychotherapy* (pp. 63–82). Hove: Brunner-Routledge.

Carroll, R. (2009) Self-regulation: an evolving concept at the heart of body psychotherapy. In L. Hartley (ed.), *Contemporary Body Psychotherapy: The Chiron Approach* (pp. 89–105). London: Routledge.

Conger, J.P. (1994) *The Body in Recovery: Somatic Psychotherapy and the Self*. Berkeley, CA: Frog.

Frank, R. (2001) *Body of Awareness: A Somatic and Developmental Approach to Psychotherapy*. Cambridge, MA: Gestalt/Analytic.

Frank, R. (2005) Developmental somatic psychotherapy. In N. Totton (ed.), *New Dimensions in Body Psychotherapy* (pp. 115–27). Maidenhead: Open University Press.

Gendlin, E.T. (1981) *Focusing*. New York: Bantam.

Harris, A. and Sinsheimer, K. (2008) The analyst's vulnerability: preserving and fine-tuning analytic bodies. In F.S. Anderson (ed.), *Bodies in Treatment* (pp. 255–73). New York: Analytic.

Jacobs, T.J. (1973) Posture, gesture and movement in the analyst: cues to interpretation and countertransference. *Journal of the American Psychoanalytic Association*, 21: 77–92.

Johnson, D.H. (2000) Intricate tactile sensitivity. *Progress in Brain Research*, 122: 479–90.

Kepner, J. (1987) *Body Process: A Gestalt Approach to Working with the Body in Psychotherapy*. New York: Gestalt Institute of Cleveland Press.

Kurtz, R. (1990) *Body-Centered Psychotherapy: The Hakomi Method*. Mendocino, CA: LifeRhythm.

May, J. (2005) A review of the objective literature on body psychotherapy (2nd edition). In *Conference Proceedings, 2005* (pp. 380–98), Bethesda, MD: US Association for Body Psychotherapy.

Mindell, A. (1988) *Dreambody*. London: Arkana.

Ogden, P., Minton, K. and Pain, C. (2006) *Trauma and the Body: A Sensorimotor Approach to Psychotherapy*. New York: Norton.

Reich, W. (1972/1945) *Character Analysis*. New York: Touchstone.

Reich, W. (1983/1942) *The Function of the Orgasm*. London: Souvenir.

Rohricht, F. (2009) Body oriented psychotherapy: the state of the art in empirical research and evidence-based practice. A clinical perspective. *Body, Movement and Dance in Psychotherapy*, 4 (2): 135–56.

Rothschild, B. (2003) *The Body Remembers Casebook*. New York: Norton.

Samuels, A. (1989) *The Plural Psyche: Personality, Morality and the Father*. London: Routledge.

Soth, M. (2005) Embodied countertransference. In N. Totton (ed.), *New Dimensions in Body Psychotherapy* (pp. 40–55). Maidenhead: Open University Press.

Soth, M. (2006) What therapeutic hope for a subjective mind in an objectified body? In J. Corrigall, H. Payne and H. Wilkinson, H. (eds), *About A Body* (pp. 111–31). London: Routledge.

Soth, M. (2009) From humanistic holism via the 'integrative project' towards integral-relational body psychotherapy. In L. Hartley (ed.), *Contemporary Body Psychotherapy: The Chirpon Approach* (pp. 64–88). Hove: Routledge.

Stern, D. (1985) *The Interpersonal World of the Infant*. New York: Basic.

Totton, N. (1998) *The Water in the Glass: Body and Mind in Psychoanalysis*. London: Rebus Press/Karnac.

Totton, N. (2002) Foreign bodies: recovering the history of body psychotherapy. In T. Staunton (ed.), *Body Psychotherapy* (pp. 7–26). London: Routledge.

Totton, N. (2003) *Body Psychotherapy: An Introduction*. Maidenhead: Open University Press.

Totton, N. (2005) Embodied-Relational Therapy. In N. Totton (ed.), *New Dimensions in Body Psychotherapy* (pp. 168–81). Maidenhead: Open University Press.

Totton, N. (2006) A body psychotherapist's approach to touch. In G. Galton (ed.), *Touch Papers: Dialogues on Touch in the Psychoanalytic Space* (pp. 145–61). London: Karnac.

Tune, D. (2005) Dilemmas concerning the ethical use of touch in psychotherapy. In N. Totton (ed.), *New Dimensions in Body Psychotherapy* (pp. 70–83). Maidenhead: Open University Press.

Existential Counselling and Therapy

EMMY VAN DEURZEN

BRIEF HISTORY

Existential counselling and therapy find their origin in the ancient practice of applied philosophy. The original idea of philosophy, literally the love of wisdom, was to actively search for the secret of a well-lived life. Hellenistic philosophers used the Socratic method of dialectical discussion to reveal and unravel the truth about personal and universal issues and dilemmas. This practice fell into desuetude but was revitalized at the beginning of the twentieth century when a number of psychiatrists began applying the thinking of existential philosophers such as Kierkegaard, Nietzsche and Heidegger to their clinical work (Deurzen, 2010). Karl Jaspers, Ludwig Binswanger and Medard Boss were the first to formulate some principles for existential psychotherapy (May et al., 1958). Their work, based mainly in Germany and Switzerland, was known as *Daseinsanalysis* or existential analysis.

Authors such as Paul Tillich (1952) and Rollo May (1969) then spread the approach far more widely in the United States. Their influence on the human potential movement and on humanistic psychotherapy and counselling was extensive. There are obvious existential elements in approaches such as person-centred counselling and gestalt psychotherapy, while Irvin Yalom (1980), James Bugental (1981) and Alvin Mahrer (1996) have made direct contributions to the development of existential psychotherapy in North America.

In Europe existential psychotherapy was further developed on the Continent by Victor Frankl's ([1946] 1964) logotherapy. In the UK the work of R.D. Laing (1960) was much inspired by the existentialist writing of Jean-Paul Sartre ([1943] 1956). It facilitated the flourishing of existential psychotherapy in the UK, which was firmly established from 1988 with the founding of the Society for Existential Analysis together with its journal *Existential Analysis*. A number of training courses at the Philadelphia Association, Regent's College, Surrey University and the New School of Psychotherapy and Counselling were developed. This generated significant amounts of research and a number of noteworthy publications that made the existential approach better known and more widely spread (see Cohn, 1997; Deurzen, 1988; 2002; 2010; Spinelli, 2007).

BASIC ASSUMPTIONS

Existential therapy focuses on helping people in coming to terms with their lives rather than just with their selfhood. It enables people to take on life in all its confusing complexity.

Many of the problems that clients struggle with are the natural consequence of the challenges and limitations of the human condition.

Life is tough and most people can do with a little help in learning to live. Sooner or later many of us falter in our ability to comprehend the demands made on us and we have trouble in coping with the predicaments we find ourselves in.

The objective is not to cure people of pathology, which is often an unhelpful and misleading concept, but rather to assist them in coming to terms with the contradictions, dilemmas and paradoxes of their everyday existence.

Anxiety is a valuable instrument in helping us become more aware of reality, and should not be avoided. It needs to be embraced and understood if life is to be lived to the full.

People are never in isolation. They are always in a given world, with other people, and in a situation which influences their experience. Problems need to be seen in their cultural, social and political context.

Human beings have a tendency to hide away and deceive ourselves about life and our own position in it. The capacity for understanding self and others will increase as we face truth and aim for authenticity, though we should not fool ourselves in the belief that we can ever be fully authentic.

Self is a relative concept. It is only as I act in the world that I create a sense of self. It is only when my actions and qualities of being are named and described that my identity is established. There is no such thing as a solid, immutable self. We are in constant transformation and we respond to our environment, other people and our changing circumstances by redefining ourselves.

Existential philosophy values the exploration of the unknown and the hidden, including of those things that are in people's hearts and minds without them being aware of them. But existential therapists do not accept the idea that there is an inner place we can call 'the unconscious'. Similarly there is no such thing as absolute truth, though truth is well worth exploring and pursuing. There are multiple interpretations of reality and many layered levels of understanding and consciousness. By reflection and understanding we can expand our grasp of what is, though never know it completely.

It is essential that people tune into their own yearnings and longings. In formulating new and valuable projects, life becomes more meaningful as we rediscover new purpose and live in a more engaged manner.

Vitality is based on the acceptance of both positives and negatives. There can be no life without death and no health without illness, no happiness without unhappiness (Deurzen, 2009). Learning to work with these tensions is the *sine qua non* of being real. We live in time. Living requires us to recollect ourselves from the past and be present to ourselves now in order to project ourselves anew into the future. All these dimensions of time are equally important and in constant interaction with each other.

We live our lives on a number of dimensions. First, there is the concrete physical world where we interact with material objects. Second, there is the world with other people where we interact with those around us. Third, there is a dimension of self-representation where we constitute an inner world.

Fourth, there is an abstract dimension of spirituality where we create meaning and make sense of things.

ORIGIN AND MAINTENANCE OF PROBLEMS

Life is intrinsically problematic. Every day we encounter problems of all sorts and of various levels of magnitude. We need to build confidence in our own ability to tackle and solve these problems and improve our competence in dealing with increasingly tougher situations. We can then find pleasure in the stimulation and vitality that come with such a resolute and courageous attitude to living.

As we sometimes find life rather too difficult, we have a tendency to try and make things easier for ourselves by escaping from reality and living with illusions. One of the major ways in which we deceive ourselves is by imagining that we are condemned to be and remain what we are, instead of embracing our freedom and the responsibility of making our own choices and changes in life. This bad faith leads to passivity, which perpetuates our difficulty in dealing with our problems.

Sometimes human beings feel so overwhelmed by the complexity of the problems with which they are faced that they withdraw from the world completely, in isolation or madness, losing their foothold on reality and their remaining strength and vitality in the process.

One of our constant causes for concern is the presence of others. We often tend to see our fellow human beings as potential threats and much of our experience confirms the untrustworthiness of the other. Our destructive interactions or our avoidance of interaction with others can thus become another self-fulfilling prophecy of doom.

As fragile human beings we often live with regret over what happened yesterday, in fear of what may be demanded of us tomorrow, and in guilt over what we have not yet accomplished today. We are quite capable of emotionally paralysing ourselves in this manner.

Some people find themselves in situations that significantly restrict or constrict their outlook and their freedom of action. Genetic, developmental, accidental, class, cultural or gender factors can all generate what may seem like insurmountable obstacles. Everyone's life presents a number of difficulties that we have to learn to accommodate or overcome. Some people manage to overcome substantial initial disadvantages or adversity, whereas others squander their advantage or flounder in the face of minor contretemps.

Every problem has several solutions. Our attitude and frame of mind make all the difference to our ability to tackle difficulties. There is no point in blaming oneself, others or circumstances and remaining trapped in a particular position. Facing the situation and putting it in perspective may be hard to do, but it is always possible, given some time and with some assistance.

Being ready to face our problems leads to resolute living and to a willingness to meet whatever may come with steadfastness and in a spirit of adventure.

CHANGE

Change takes place continuously and human beings have to make considerable efforts to try and keep their situation stable. In aiming for stability and safety we may find it difficult to allow life changes to happen, even when our situation is not particularly good and change might improve it. We frequently fear the inevitable process of transformation that everything in this world is subject to and fend it off.

When clients come to psychotherapy or counselling they do so because they want to find the strength and confidence to allow a change for the better to happen in their lives. They need the therapist or counsellor to believe in them and help them to be steady when confronting their fears and doubts, so they can find their way through.

The objective of existential work is to enable clients to become more open to their own experience in all its paradoxical reality. They can be helped to be more tolerant of their own anxiety and to become more understanding of it by becoming more self-reflective. An awareness of what is the case will change what is the case, and as clients tell their story and discuss it with their therapist they will gradually alter their interpretation of their story and thus of themselves.

To enable people to be aware of their strengths, talents and abilities is as important as to help them explore the darker side of their own experience, passion and yearning.

Crisis is seen as a moment of danger and opportunity when transformation happens rapidly while everything is temporarily thrown into a state of chaos. New paths can therefore be chosen and our interaction with the world can be reorganized in a new way. Counselling and therapy ensure that the crisis is a point of breakthrough rather than breakdown.

Even when the circumstances you find yourself in are dire or unfair, it is still possible to change your attitude towards them and find new ways of improving your fate.

SKILLS AND STRATEGIES

The existential approach is in principle against techniques, as these might hamper human interaction at a deep, direct and real level. Therapeutic skill is used to help clients face vital issues and the therapeutic encounter consists of a deep and authentic human exchange.

Nevertheless, a number of conversational strategies can be recognized as belonging to an existential way of working. These include the emphasis on paradox when clients are helped to recognize their conflicts and confront reality in all its contradictions and ambiguity.

An attitude of openness is encouraged and clients are not mollycoddled, though they are treated with respect, care and understanding. In this process there is a strategic emphasis on making clients aware of the strengths they are already displaying and could learn to master more effectively.

Clients are helped to make explicit their implicit assumptions, values and beliefs, until a clear worldview emerges. This may be explored for the contradictions or implications embedded in it, allowing new purpose and meaning to come into view.

The therapist keeps track of the client's state of mind. Moods and attitudes, feelings and deep emotion are followed to their source so that a deeply felt sense of what truly matters to the person emerges. The client is taught to continue doing this emotional tracking independently.

Purpose and ultimate concerns are worked with until people feel reactivated to live life to the full in an engaged and committed manner and without hiding away from difficulties and fears. In rediscovering what it is you want to live for you get a renewed taste for your own creativity and ability, finding a new authority and playfulness on the way.

The therapist allows himself or herself to identify with the client's issues in order to find a way into and through dilemmas in a personal and direct manner. At the same time distance from the client's predicament will be preserved through the philosophical attitude, which allows problems to be seen in the broader perspective of universal human struggles.

Ideological matters might be discussed and debated and political and cultural issues will be addressed. Clarifying and creating a meaningful world is one of the important objectives. By modelling a tough and caring approach to life and others, existential therapists inspire clients with a vital desire to live to the full with courage and self-determination. This resoluteness is always set against the recognition of human and personal limitations and is matched by a growing acceptance of the forces of life and death that we are all bound by.

RESEARCH EVIDENCE

There is very little direct outcome research in existential psychotherapy and counselling because of the opposition of existential therapists to the reductionist technology of research. There is a growing body of qualitative research done largely by doctoral counselling psychology students and their tutors, using phenomenological methods and investigating various human issues. There is also a lot of research that indirectly deals with existential concerns and shows these to be at the core of change in therapy and counselling.

- Yalom (1970) in his work with groups found existential factors to be much more important to client change than he had originally thought. From then on existential psychotherapy became the focus in his subsequent work.
- Much of the research on the person-centred approach is relevant to existential therapy, especially where it demonstrates the importance of genuineness or authenticity on the part of the therapist (Carkhuff and Truax, 1965).
- Bergin and Garfield (1994) recognized a number of existential factors as determining positive outcome in psychotherapy.
- Rennie's (1992) qualitative research shows the importance of a number of existential factors.
- There is much research that shows the importance of meaning creation to the successful processing of traumatic events (Clarke, 1989).
- Recent research in positive psychology demonstrates the importance of such existential factors as authenticity (Seligman, 2002) and meaning (Baumeister, 1991).
- Much of counselling psychology research is based on qualitative research methodology and increasingly on phenomenological methods of research, as these are particularly appropriate for the investigation of human issues and concerns (Deurzen-Smith, 1990; Willig, 2001; Milton, 2010).

REFERENCES

Baumeister, R.F. (1991) *Meanings of Life*. New York: Guilford.

Bergin, A. and Garfield, S. (eds) (1994) *Handbook of Psychotherapy and Behavior Change* (4th edn). New York: Wiley.

Bugental, J.F.T. (1981) *The Search for Authenticity*. New York: Irvington.

Carkhuff, R. and Truax, C. (1965) Training in counseling and therapy: an evaluation of an integrated didactic and experiential approach. *Journal of Consulting Psychology*, 29: 333–6.

Clarke, K.M. (1989) Creation of meaning: an emotional processing task in psychotherapy. *Psychotherapy*, 26: 139–48.

Cohn, H. (1997) *Existential Thought and Therapeutic Practice*. London: Sage.

Deurzen, E. van (1998) *Paradox and Passion in Psychotherapy*. Chichester: Wiley.

Deurzen, E. van (2002) *Existential Counselling and Psychotherapy in Practice* (2nd edn). London: Sage.

Deurzen, E. van (2009) *Psychotherapy and the Quest for Happiness*. London: Sage.

Deurzen, E. van (2010) *Everyday Mysteries: Handbook of Existential Psychotherapy* (2nd edn). London: Routledge.

Deurzen-Smith, E. van (1990) Philosophical underpinnings of counselling psychology. *Counselling Psychology Review*, 5: 8–12.

Frankl, V.E. ([1946] 1964) *Man's Search for Meaning*. London: Hodder and Stoughton.

Laing, R.D. (1960) *The Divided Self*. London: Tavistock.

Mahrer, A.R. (1996) *The Complete Guide to Experiential Psychotherapy*. New York: Wiley.

May, R. (1969) *Love and Will*. New York: Norton.

May, R., Angel, E. and Ellenberger, H.F. (1958) *Existence*. New York: Basic.

Milton, M. (2010) *Therapy and Beyond: Counselling Psychology Contributions to Therapeutic and Social Issues*. Chichester: Wiley-Blackwell.

Rennie, D.L. (1992) Qualitative analysis of the client's experience of psychotherapy: the unfolding of reflexivity. In S. Toukmanian and D.L. Rennie (eds), *Psychotherapy Process Research: Paradigmatic and Narrative Approaches*. Newbury Park, CA: Sage.

Sartre, J.-P. ([1943] 1956) *Being and Nothingness: An Essay on Phenomenological Ontology* (trans. H. Barnes). New York: Philosophical Library.

Seligman, M.E.P. (2002) *Authentic Happiness*. New York: Free.

Spinelli, E. (2007) *Practising Existential Psychotherapy: The Relational World*. London: Sage.

Tillich, P. (1952) *The Courage To Be*. New Haven, CT: Yale University Press.

Willig, C. (2001) *Introducing Qualitative Research in Psychology: Adventures in Theory and Method*. Buckingham: Open University Press.

Yalom, I.D. (1970) *The Theory and Practice of Group Psychotherapy*. New York: Basic.

Yalom, I.D. (1980) *Existential Psychotherapy*. New York: Basic.

Gestalt Therapy

(Frederick Perls, 1893–1970)

MICHAEL ELLIS AND JONATHAN SMITH

BRIEF HISTORY

Gestalt theory and practice were first developed by Frederick (Fritz) Perls and Laura Perls along with Paul Goodman and others in New York in the 1950s. *Gestalt Therapy: Excitement and Growth in the Human Personality* was published in 1951. This has been for many years the definitive text on gestalt theory. Prior to this, while in South Africa, Fritz Perls published *Ego, Hunger and Aggression* (1947) in which he laid the foundations for this approach to therapy.

Perls was born in Berlin and educated at the University of Freiburg and Frederick Wilhelm University in Berlin. He received his MD in 1921. Before this he had served as a Medical Officer in the German army. He then trained in psychoanalysis in Berlin, Frankfurt and Vienna. Thus Perls brought a strong foundation in psychoanalysis, particularly influenced by Wilhelm Reich and Karen Homey. Laura Perls studied gestalt psychology with Kurt Goldstein (from which the approach takes its name), worked with Paul Tillich and was greatly influenced by Martin Buber. Paul Goodman, a philosopher, libertarian and anarchist, contributed a social and political dimension to their thinking.

Gestalt Psychology

The word *Gestalt* does not have a direct translation into English; definitions include pattern, configuration, form and whole. The work of the gestalt psychologists in the early part of the twentieth century focused primarily on perception and learning. Wertheimer and Ehrenfels proposed that we perceive our environment in terms of 'wholes'. As best as we are able, we make meaning, we create a form or gestalt, from what we experience. The gestalt includes what is 'figure' for us in relation to what is in the background. Hence the importance in gestalt work of figure and ground. An additional contribution of the gestalt psychologists was the concept of 'closure'. In its original sense it refers to the tendency of the perceptual system to 'close' or round off any incomplete shape or form.

The work of the above psychologists and others, including Koffka and Köhler, was extended into the realms of personality by Kurt Goldstein and Kurt Lewin. The work of these men was key for the development of gestalt theory and practice, although Lewin's influence has only recently been acknowledged. Goldstein developed his 'organismic theory' from gestalt principles, and particularly the centrality of 'self-actualization' for the unfolding of the individual's potential. Lewin, also an associate of Wertheimer and Kohler, developed the concept of the individual as part of a dynamic field. He emphasized the importance of the person in relation to their environment and the significance of the present forces or vectors acting on the individual from the surrounding dynamic field.

Existentialism

Gestalt theory has been influenced by a number of existentialist thinkers such as Paul Tillich, Martin Buber and Jean-Paul Sartre. It is an existential phenomenological approach and explores the individual's existence as experienced by them. There is considerable emphasis on the individual being responsible for their own existence, on the importance of the here-and-now (experience in the present) and on the meeting of therapist and client in an authentic 'I–Thou' relationship.

Eastern Religion

The influence of Eastern religions, particularly Taoism and Zen (Fritz Perls spent almost a year in Japan studying Zen), are evident in the importance of awareness of the present moment as a goal and a method in gestalt work which may lead to a 'satori'-like insight, a sudden realization which results in a reconfiguration of the phenomenal field, a new gestalt, or a reorganization of the person's experience. Also significant is the focus on 'organismic functioning' rather than an over-emphasis on thinking, and on the use of paradox and the ideas and practice of non-doing, of standing out of the way and allowing things to emerge.

Drama and Movement

Fritz Perls was very interested in the nature of theatre and drama and incorporated some of Jacob Moreno's psychodrama techniques; Laura Perls also studied dance for many years. These influences have given gestalt methodology a strong expressive/creative bias.

BASIC ASSUMPTIONS

- *Holism*. That nature is a coherent whole; different elements are in relation with each other in a continually changing process. Holistically we cannot understand ourselves by analysing aspects in isolation because 'the whole is different from the sum of the parts'.
- *Field theory*. Originally formulated by Kurt Lewin, field theory maintains that the person is never separated from their environment, both their internal physical and psychological environment and their external social and cultural context. The meaning we give to any figure, or stimulus, will then be dependent on its context or field.

- *Growth*. The process of organismic self-regulation occurs through contact with our environment, of which we are a part. In health we do this by a process of forming figures against a background based on our current most important need. At a given moment a need will emerge, become 'figural', be met, and then recede into the background as another need emerges from the 'ground'. For example, I become aware of a dry mouth, decide I need a drink, take action to get a drink, and then focus on the paper I was about to read.
- *Self-actualization*. We have an innate tendency to realize our potential, to become who we can be. Perls wrote: 'Every individual, every plant, every animal has only one inborn goal – to actualize itself as it is' (1969: 31).
- *Awareness*. Increasing awareness is at the core of gestalt practice. Through the development of 'organismic' experienced awareness (rather than just intellectual awareness) we are able to be responsible and proactive and allow the healthy flow of self-regulation for the whole organism.
- *Contact and dialogue*. Contact refers to the way we meet, interact and exchange with the environment, including other people. Gestalt work always aims for lively contact which can be enhanced through the use of dialogue. Dialogue means meeting in the here-and-now and recognizing one another 'in our uniqueness, our fullness and our vulnerability' (Hycner and Jacobs, 1995: 9). Healing occurs through meeting another as a person. Each individual, acknowledged as separate, is capable of risking meeting the other in an I–Thou relationship as defined by Martin Buber. Buber described two contrasting attitudes that an individual can take towards others: the *I–It* way of relating and the *I–Thou* way of relating. Both are needed for living. The I–It attitude is more present when there is a purpose in the meeting, when one or other or both have a goal of some sort. The I–Thou attitude is one of being as present as possible with another, without consideration of any purpose or goal, and with an appreciation of the uniqueness of the other as a person.

ORIGIN AND MAINTENANCE OF PROBLEMS

A healthy person in gestalt theory allows himself or herself a fluent exchange and adjustment in relation with the environment (organismic self-regulation). This healthy process of forming figures against the background based on our needs is known as the gestalt formation and destruction cycle and is also called the contact/withdrawal cycle.

Problems are seen as disturbances of this natural healthy functioning. Significant early relationships are important in the initial disturbance of the contact/withdrawal cycle. These disturbances may develop as a creative way of surviving in the face of danger, lack of love, care and attention. However, they become embedded in the personality and in adulthood limit any further creative adjustment with the current environment, so functioning becomes rigid, habitual and over-controlled.

Perls defined four 'neurotic mechanisms' or contact boundary disturbances which can restrict and limit individuals' healthy exchange with their environment, whether physical, emotional or intellectual. All these processes have a healthy, functional aspect; it is when they are habitual and chronic that healthy functioning is limited. The mechanisms are:

- *Introjection*. In this, something is taken in whole, 'swallowed down' without assimilation or reflection. This may be an attitude, a belief, an idea or a behaviour.
- *Projection*. Here traits, attitudes, behaviours, beliefs, etc. are attributed to others or to objects in the environment.
- *Retroflection*. This involves turning energy 'back in' against oneself which in healthy functioning would be allowed to go out to contact the environment. For example, somebody who has learnt that expressing their irritation or anger is risky may come to withhold aggressive energy, possibly causing headaches, muscle tension or other physiological distress, thus turning energy against themselves.
- *Confluence*. This is a state of being in which the individual is unclear about boundaries, with others, with the environment. There is a merging of ideas, beliefs, feelings, etc. and no clear sense of separateness.

Since Perls, more recent theorists have described another 'neurotic mechanism':

- *Deflection*. Here the individual turns away from healthy contact with the environment and the contact is experienced as unclear, weak, vague (a weak gestalt). Sometimes the impulse is redirected (deflected) towards an undeserving but convenient substitute.

These are processes by which problems are maintained and result in 'unfinished business' (incomplete gestalten) which inhibits energy and healthy functioning. If extremely chronic, this can result in severe disturbance in functioning for the individual.

CHANGE

Therapeutic change occurs with the rediscovery of the gestalt process of *organismic self-regulation*. This involves close attention to how the client does what she or he does, how they function in the world and in the relationship with the therapist.

Awareness is the key in this work: to become more aware of the sorts of disturbances described in the previous section brings a recovery of contactfulness with aspects of self and others. The sort of awareness sought is not just intellectual but is holistic in that it is an experience involving intellect, emotions and physical sensations.

As part of the therapy the client works to complete 'unfinished business' through closure and resolution of issues from the past which still affect the client's current functioning.

Another aspect of change is that of exploring/experimenting with new sorts of behaviour as the energy bound up in old patterns is released. Such experimentation develops from an underlying willingness by the client to discover more of who they are.

Change in gestalt therapy comes from becoming more fully ourselves: 'Change occurs when one becomes what he is, not when he tries to become what he is not' (Beisser, 1970: 88). This can only happen through awareness, now, of what we are actually doing and how we are functioning.

Yontef (2005) emphasizes the central role of the relationship with the therapist in the work of change. The gestalt therapist works with dialogic contact to enliven and enhance awareness. Dialogic contact requires four elements: *inclusion* (a deep entering into the world of the client); *confirmation* (the full acceptance and validation of the client's existence and experience); *presence* (the therapist bringing themselves fully and authentically to the encounter); and a surrender to the *between* (trusting the outcome of the meeting will emerge unpredictably as it unfolds).

SKILLS AND STRATEGIES

The gestalt therapist's approach is phenomenological: to facilitate clients deepening their awareness of themselves and their relationship with others through attending, engaging with the clients, exploring their experience, describing what is.

The authenticity of the therapist, their genuineness, their wholeness and presence are central. The therapist engages and participates in the relationship and also observes. The therapist interacts with the client with an I–Thou attitude, a willingness to relate authentically and meet the client as a person. What sort of contact is made and how that is 'interrupted' is the focus of the work.

Therapists must therefore use their creativity, working from a clear understanding of gestalt theory: the centrality of gestalt formation and destruction, awareness of present experience and the theory of change.

Gestalt sessions can be quite active, with the therapist suggesting behavioural or experiential experiments for the client to try out, with a view to enhancing their awareness of their feelings, aspects of their relationships with others, or subliminal thoughts or assumptions they may be carrying around with them.

Examples of such experiments might be:

- focusing on body awareness, e.g. encouraging the client to become more aware of felt sensations within the body
- exaggerating movements or phrases, repeating them and allowing them to grow or lead to some deeper awareness
- attention to language, e.g. noticing how the client constructs sentences, one aspect being whether the client uses impersonal pronouns (it, they, one) to distance themselves from their experience
- psychodramatic work, e.g. 'empty chair' work in which a client explores their relationship with others, or aspects of themselves, by imagining others to be present and engaging in dialogue with them
- exploring the contact with the therapist, by for example experimenting with sitting at different distances from each other.

Joyce and Sills (2010) discuss a variety of skills and strategies which can be used in gestalt counselling settings, although it should be remembered that the use of such interventions will arise out of the ongoing dialogue and exploration between client and therapist rather than being used merely as techniques. The aim is always to enhance the awareness of clients, to facilitate their recovery of their organismic self-regulation.

In the last 10 years, an increasing range of applications of gestalt have been explored. Houston (2003) has shown how the gestalt approach can be tailored for use in short-term, brief therapy settings. Woldt and Toman (2005) have included a number of chapters in their edited book discussing gestalt applications to a range of populations and settings including children and adolescents, families and couples, groups and organizations, community mental health, substance abuse, and in education. O'Leary et al. (2003) have explored the use of gestalt group approaches in working with older adults.

RESEARCH

Until the 1980s gestalt therapy had a limited research literature. During that decade Greenberg began to publish a series of papers exploring the benefits of two-chair work. That work was summarized by Eleanor O'Leary in 1992 in her review of the research literature, and since then an increasing number of research papers have been published. In the latest edition of *Bergin and Garfield's Handbook of Psychotherapy and Behavior Change* (Lambert, 2004), gestalt therapy is identified as one of the three 'major subapproaches' to experiential/humanistic therapy, alongside person-centred and existential approaches (Elliott et al., 2004). Another large-scale review article was published in 2004 by Strumpfel which summarized 60 studies providing some good evidence for the effectiveness of gestalt methods.

Many of the studies are concerned with the effectiveness of the two-chair technique. For example, Paivio et al. (2001) found that the degree of engagement in imagined confrontations with abusive carers in empty chair work predicted resolution of child abuse issues. Johnson and Smith (1997) compared systematic desensitization and gestalt empty chair procedures with a no-therapy control group in the treatment of phobia sufferers, and found that, following treatment, both treatment groups were significantly less phobic than the no-therapy group.

More recently gestalt therapy research has benefited from the upsurge of interest in qualitative methods. Phenomenological research methods have been a recognized approach to social science methodology generally since the 1960s (Moustakas, 1994), but their affinity with gestalt theory has only recently been highlighted. Paul Barber in particular has offered a specifically gestalt account of qualitative research (Barber, 2006; Barber and Brownell, 2008; Finlay and Evans, 2009).

REFERENCES

Barber, P. (2006) *Becoming a Practitioner-Researcher: A Gestalt Approach to Holistic Enquiry*. London: Middlesex University Press.

Barber, P. and Brownell, P. (2008) Qualitative research. In P. Brownell (ed.), *Handbook for Theory, Research and Practice in Gestalt Therapy* (pp. 37–63). Newcastle: Cambridge Scholars.

Beisser, A.R. (1970) The paradoxical theory of change. In J. Fagan and I.L. Shepherd (eds), *Gestalt Therapy Now*. Harmondsworth: Penguin.

Elliot, R.L., Greenberg, L.S. and Lietaer, G. (2004) Research on experiential psychotherapies. In M.J. Lambert (ed.), *Bergin and Garfield's Handbook of Psychotherapy and Behavior Change* (5th edn). New York: Wiley.

Finlay, L. and Evans, K. (2009) *Relational-Centred Research for Psychotherapists*. Chichester: Wiley-Blackwell.

Houston, G. (2003) *Brief Gestalt Therapy*. London: Sage.

Hycner, R.A. and Jacobs, L. (1995) *The Healing Relationship in Gestalt Therapy*. Highland, NY: Gestalt Journal Press.

Johnson, W.R. and Smith, E.W.L. (1997) Gestalt empty-chair dialogue vs systematic desensitisation in the treatment of a phobia. *Gestalt Review*, 1: 150–62.

Joyce, P. and Sills, C. (2010) *Skills in Gestalt Counselling and Psychotherapy*. (2nd edn). London: Sage.

Lambert, M.J. (ed.) (2004) *Bergin and Garfield's Handbook of Psychotherapy and Behavior Change* (5th edn). New York: Wiley.

Moustakas, C. (1994) *Phenomenological Research Methods*. London: Sage.

O'Leary, E. (1992) *Gestalt Therapy: Theory, Practice and Research*. London: Chapman and Hall.

O'Leary, E., Sheedy, G., O'Sullivan, K. and Thoreson, C. (2003) Cork Older Adult Intervention Project: outcomes of a gestalt therapy group with older adults. *Counselling Psychology Quarterly*, 16 (2): 131–43.

Paivio, S.C., Hall, I.E., Holowaty, K.A.M., Jellis, J.B. and Tran, N. (2001) Imaginal confrontation for resolving child abuse issues. *Psychotherapy Research*, 11: 433–53.

Perls, F. (1947) *Ego, Hunger and Aggression: A Revision of Freud's Theory and Method*. London: Allen and Unwin.

Perls, F. (1969) *Gestalt Therapy Verbatim*. Moab, UT: Real People.

Perls, F., Hefferline, R. and Goodman, P. (1951) *Gestalt Therapy: Excitement and Growth in the Human Personality*. New York: Julian.

Strumpfel, U. (2004) Research on gestalt therapy. *International Gestalt Journal*, 12 (1): 9–24.

Woldt, A.L. and Toman, S.M. (2005) *Gestalt Therapy: History, Theory and Practice*. London: Sage.

Yontef, G.M. (2005) Gestalt therapy theory of change. In A.L. Woldt and S.M. Toman (eds), *Gestalt Therapy: History, Theory and Practice*. London: Sage.

Person-Centred Therapy

(Carl R. Rogers, 1902–1987)

KEITH TUDOR

BRIEF HISTORY

'Person-centred therapy' (PCT) or 'client-centred therapy' (CCT) (here I use 'therapy' to refer to both psychotherapy and counselling) was originally developed by Carl Rogers in the USA from the late 1930s onwards. For a short while the approach now known as PCT was referred to as 'non-directive therapy', a term that fell out of use, although 'non-directivity' as a concept and a principled attitude has remained at the centre of PCT and has been the subject of some recent revival (see Levitt, 2005). A key date in the history of the PCA is 10 December 1940, when Rogers spoke at the University of Minnesota on 'Some newer concepts of psychotherapy'. CCT was further expanded by Rogers and his colleagues at the University of Chicago and included the development of a theory of personality and behaviour, as well as a more detailed description of the characteristics of person-centred therapy (see Rogers, 1951).

Between 1953 and 1954 and based on his research, Rogers formulated his now famous hypothesis of certain necessary and sufficient conditions of therapeutic personality change (published in 1957 and 1959). These papers established Rogers and his colleagues as innovators in the field of therapy, and stimulated a great deal of debate and research, for a summary of which see Patterson (1984/2000) and Tudor and Merry (2002). Rogers himself identified more with an emerging 'third force' of psychology, i.e. humanistic psychology, and is widely recognised as one of its founders; and PCT became established as one of the most influential of the humanistic approaches to therapy. Mearns and Thorne, however, have suggested that, in 'its forsaking of mystique and other "powerful" behaviours of therapists' (2000: 27), PCT is as different from many humanistic therapies as it is from other traditions such as behaviourism and psychoanalysis. In the later years of his life Rogers became interested in the wider application of the principles of person-centred psychology (PCP) to education and learning; groups, group facilitation and conflict resolution; and politics. PCT is now viewed as one application of what has become more broadly referred to as the 'person-centred *approach*' (PCA), for a contemporary outline and development of which see Embleton Tudor et al. (2004).

Although its influence in the USA has diminished in recent years, currently PCT is widely practised and studied in Europe, Japan and South America, and there is a thriving World Association of Person-Centered and Experiential Psychotherapy and Counseling (www.pce-world.org) which has individual and organisational members in many countries; holds a biennial international conference; and publishes a quarterly journal *Person-Centred and Experiential Psychotherapies*. English language publications have been fostered by the presence of PCCS Books (www.pccs-books.co.uk), and there is a considerable and growing international literature, including publications and journals in Dutch, French, German, Italian, Japanese, Portuguese and Spanish.

BASIC ASSUMPTIONS

A number of basic assumptions underlie PCT. Here they are clustered under three core principles (see Sanders, 2000; Tudor and Worrall, 2006):

1 The human organism tends to actualise.
2 In order to support growth and change, the therapist/facilitator needs to embrace and embody a non-directive approach and attitude.
3 Together, therapist and client co-create certain facilitative conditions which promote growth, challenge and change.

Actualisation

The view that the human organism, as other organisms, tends to actualise – i.e. maintain, enhance and reproduce the experiencing organism – represents the sole motivational construct in PCP. The theory of actualisation is a natural science theory, not a moral theory. Whilst no specific moral values are implied by the theory, two values implicit in the person-centred approach to the person are fluidity (as distinct from fixity or rigidity) and creativity.

One function of the fact that we tend to actualise is that we differentiate a portion of our experience into an awareness of self and the organisation of a self-concept. The self-concept or self-structure is a fluid but consistent pattern of perceptions of the 'I', 'me' and 'we' in relation to the environment, personal and social values, goals and ideals. One aspect of organismic actualising, self-actualising, appears after the development of the self-concept and acts to maintain that concept. Self-actualising – or, more commonly, 'self-actualisation' – does not always result in optimal functioning because each person, whether psychologically healthy or unhealthy, is self-actualising to the extent that each has a self-structure to maintain and enhance. Thus, if an aspect of someone's self-concept is to be pleasing, s/he may act socially to support that, at the expense of her/his organismic direction.

Awareness of self is termed 'self-experience'. When any self-experience is evaluated by others as being more or less worthy of positive regard, a person's self-regard becomes vulnerable to these external judgements. When self-experiences become sought after or avoided because they are more or less deserving of self-regard, the individual is said to have acquired conditions of worth, which are the basis of person-centred theories of psychopathology (see Bozarth, 1996; Joseph and Worsley, 2005; Tudor and Worrall, 2006).

Non-directive Approach and Attitude

This follows from the first assumption. If you think that the fact that the organism tends to actualise is an expression of an inherent and trustworthy directionality, then, as a therapist or facilitator, you would tend to support the client's direction.

The view of human nature underlying this approach is positive, constructive and co-creative. It does not, however, deny the capacity for harmful, destructive and antisocial behaviour. It focuses, rather, on the potential for positive, personal and social change to occur throughout life; and takes the view that environmental influences, particularly those concerning relationships with others, including therapeutic and facilitative relationships, are critical factors in determining either positive or negative self-concepts and, hence, healthy or unhealthy functioning. PCP recognises that the outward and, indeed, inward manifestations of harmful behaviour can have serious and extreme consequences. In response, the practice of PCT understands or attempts to understand, and helps the client to understand, the motivation and needs which underlie her/his behaviour; and, generally, views behaviour as a needs-driven expression of a unitary theory of motivation (see Rogers, 1951).

Facilitative Conditions

In PCP, people are regarded as trustworthy, creative, social, contactful, congruent or integrated in themselves and in relationships, loving, understanding, receptive and resourceful. Given the right conditions, we are able to admit all experiencing into awareness without distortion or denial, which are the two defence mechanisms postulated in PCP. Everyone has the capacity to rediscover their organismic valuing process and direction in a relationship in which power and control are shared between therapist and client, and this capacity can be nurtured in a climate of facilitative psychological attitudes or conditions (described below). This climate can exist within a therapeutic setting or elsewhere, for example in groups, families, tribes, communities, schools and workplaces.

ORIGIN AND MAINTENANCE OF PROBLEMS

Disturbance exists whenever there is antagonism between a person's tendency to actualise in one direction and self-actualisation which may lie in another direction. Incongruence exists to the extent that these two tendencies diverge.

At the beginning of life, a person is fully congruent, that is, able to allow all experiencing into awareness without distortion or denial. Later – and developmental studies show that this can take place *in utero* – the person encounters threat, disruption, disapproval and rejection and, as a result, becomes anxious in the face of the continuing need for positive regard from significant others. The formation of the person's self-concept becomes conditioned by these negative experiences, conditions of worth become internalised, and the person seeks protection from further negative experiences. The conditioned self-concept can become so reinforced that the person becomes completely alienated from any sense of themselves and their organismic direction – which is why 'psychopathology' is best understood in terms of alienation (see Tudor and Worrall, 2006). The dichotomy between the self-concept and experiencing leads to increasingly distorted perception. A condition of incongruence now exists, and the person's psychological functioning is disturbed.

Disturbance is maintained through the continuation of a high degree of reliance on the evaluations of others for a sense of self-worth or self-esteem. Anxiety, threat and confusion are created whenever incongruence is experienced between the self-concept, with its internalised conditions of worth, and actual experience. Whenever such anxiety arises, or is threatened, the person will continue to default to defences of distortion or denial of experiencing. If experiences are extremely incongruent with the self-concept, a person's defence system may be unable to prevent such experiences from overwhelming the self-concept. Resulting behaviour may be destructive, disorganised and chaotic.

CHANGE

Effective therapy occurs in a relationship in which the therapist holds certain attitudes or conditions and the client receives and perceives these. In addition, Rogers identified certain client conditions which prefigure more recent concerns about the relational, dialogic and co-creative nature of therapy. Indeed, Rogers first referred to his work as 'relationship therapy'.

The therapist's conditions (based on Rogers, 1959: 213) are:

1   'Two persons are in contact', a condition which requires both therapist and client to be actively present, both in a social sense of meeting and agreeing to work together (or not), and in a more psychological sense. Clearly some, more disturbed clients are less contactful or contactable and, with advances in the theory and practice of 'pre-therapy' (Prouty, 1994), this condition is currently receiving more attention in PCT.
2   The therapist is congruent within the relationship, that is, authentic, genuine or real, putting

up no professional façade. This includes the therapist admitting into awareness all experience of the relationship so that such experiencing is available for direct communication to the client, when appropriate. This condition is more about experiencing than self-disclosing. It is not necessary for the therapist directly to communicate any particular experience of the relationship, except when the failure to do so impedes the practitioner's ability to experience unconditional positive regard and to understand the client empathically, in which circumstances it may become necessary for the therapist to communicate their experiencing.
3   The therapist experiences unconditional positive regard for the client, that is, s/he maintains a positive, non-judgemental and accepting attitude.
4   The therapist experiences an empathic understanding of the internal, subjective frame of reference of the client.

There is a difference between Rogers's two formulations of these hypotheses (1957; 1959) about the extent to which the therapist should communicate the last two conditions.

The requirements of a client, which we may refer to as the 'client's conditions' (see Tudor, 2000; 2011) are:

1   'Two persons are in contact' (as above).
2   By virtue of being vulnerable or anxious, the client is in some way incongruent or (as discussed above) experiencing a discrepancy between organismic and self-actualising tendencies.
3   The client perceives the therapist's unconditional positive regard and empathic understanding 'at least to a minimal degree' (whether the therapist directly or explicitly communicates this or not). In one paper Rogers (1958/1967) refers to this as the 'assumed condition', by which, in effect, all therapy is evaluated or assessed.

As discussed above, a major characteristic of PCT is that it is non-directive. In other words, the therapist has no specific goals for the client and does not suggest the client attend to any particular form of experiencing. The therapist refrains, for example, from interpreting clients' experience, but focuses on non-judgemental acceptance and understanding of her/his experience.

It is important to note that being in contact, congruent, acceptant and understanding are not conceptualised in terms of skills, strategies or techniques. Rather, PCT is better thought of as a relationship in which the client experiences another person – the therapist – as one who is acceptant of the client's subjective world, and who endeavours to understand the client's experiencing and meaning system. Therapeutic progress follows from the client experiencing being empathically understood without judgement.

A skilled therapist is one who can communicate her/his contactfulness, authenticity, positive regard and empathic understanding in ways that the client experiences as non-threatening. Experiencing these conditions without threat enables the client to become increasingly free of the need for denial or distortion.

Moments of therapeutic movement consist of experiences of self-acceptance and integration. Typically, such moments have the following characteristics:

* They are immediate and consist of total experiences, not thoughts or intellectual understandings, although these may follow or accompany the experience.
* They are new in that, whilst they may have been experienced before, at least in part, they have never been experienced completely or with awareness combined with appropriate physiological reactions.
* They are self-accepting in that they are owned as a part of the self.
* They are integrated into the self-structure without distortion.

SKILLS AND STRATEGIES

All skills are based on theory and, ultimately, on principles and values. The person-centred therapist's role is to maintain an attitude of acceptance or unconditional positive regard and empathic understanding, coupled with being open to contact and to personal congruence or integration. It is unhelpful to conceptualise PCT in terms of behavioural strategies since the therapist's only intention is to maintain and enhance a way of relating with the client, based on the conditions described above (and 'strategies' suggest a certain direction based on the therapist's frame of reference).

The skill most commonly associated with PCT is sometimes referred to as reflection of feelings. Although this is useful in that it describes some aspects of the therapist's behaviour in the relationship, it can be misleading in that it is only a partial description. In understanding the client's internal, subjective frame of reference and in communicating that understanding, the therapist does not focus on feelings at the expense of other experiences that may be present within the client's frame of reference – experiences

that may include, for example, thoughts, bodily sensations, fantasies and memories, etc.

Although opinions among person-centred and experiential therapists vary, many would agree that it is possible, even within the strictest theoretical understanding of PCT, to utilise techniques associated with other forms of counselling and psychotherapy *providing* that such techniques, as Rogers put it, 'serve as channels for fulfilling one of the conditions' (1057: 102). Clearly such techniques would not be imposed by the therapist; they would be used only when requested by the client to further a particular purpose; and the client should retain control over the extent of their use. The use of such techniques by person-centred practitioners, however, is minimal.

RESEARCH EVIDENCE

Rogers himself was one of the leading pioneers of research into counselling and psychotherapy (see Rogers and Dymond, 1954), conducting a major research study of psychotherapy with schizophrenics (Rogers et al., 1967). Partly because of its longevity, PCT itself has both been the subject of and generated more research than many other approaches. In the 1950s, using the Q-sort technique, Rogers and Dymond (1954) showed that person-centred therapy results in changes to the self-concept, whereby the perceived self becomes closer to the ideal self, and the self as perceived becomes more comfortable and adjusted.

Research evidence that the therapeutic conditions are both necessary and sufficient is not unequivocal, though much of it suffers from inadequate methodology and the possibility of poorly reported and discussed results; for a useful summary of four decades of research on this see Bozarth (1993). Most research strongly supports the hypothesis that the conditions are necessary for effective counselling, whether this is person centred or not; this research forms the basis of the mainstream view in therapy that the therapeutic relationship is the key factor in successful outcome, and that Rogers's conditions describe significant 'common factors' across theoretical orientations.

Two independent studies, based on randomised controlled assessments (Friedli et al., 1997; King et al., 2000), have concluded that person-centred, non-directive psychotherapy/counselling more than holds its own in comparison with other forms of therapy and helping. A recent book *Person-Centered and Experiential Therapies Work* (Cooper et al., 2010) offers a review of research on counselling, psychotherapy and related practices. A lot of research into person-centred, experiential and humanistic-existential approaches to therapy is being conducted in the Counselling Unit at the University of Strathclyde.

REFERENCES

Bozarth, J. (1993) Not necessarily necessary, but always sufficient. In D. Brazier (ed.), *Beyond Carl Rogers* (pp. 92–105). London: Constable.

Bozarth, J.D. (1996) A theoretical reconceptualization of the necessary and sufficient conditions for therapeutic personality change. *The Person-Centered Journal*, 3 (1): 44–51.

Cooper, M., Watson, J.C. and Hölldampf, D. (eds) (2010) *Person-Centered and Experiential Therapies Work: A Review of the Research on Counseling, Psychotherapy and Related Practices*. Ross-on-Wye: PCCS.

Embleton Tudor, L., Keemar, K., Tudor, K., Valentine, J. and Worrall, M. (2004) *The Person-Centred Approach: A Contemporary Introduction*. Basingstoke: Palgrave.

Friedli, K., King, M., Lloyd, M. and Horder, J. (1997) Randomised controlled assessment of non-directive psychotherapy versus routine general practitioner care. *Lancet*, 350: 1662–5.

Joseph, S. and Worsley, R. (2005) Psychopathology and the person-centred approach: building bridges between disciplines. In S. Joseph and R. Worsley (eds), *Person-Centred Psychopathology: A Positive Psychology of Mental Health* (pp. 1–8). Ross-on-Wye: PCCS.

King, M., Lloyd, M., Sibbald, B., Gabbay, M., Ward, E., Byford, S. and Bower, P. (2000) Randomised controlled trial of non-directive counselling, cognitive behaviour therapy and usual general practitioner care in the management of depression as well as mixed anxiety and depression in primary care. *Health Technology Assessment*, 4 (19).

Levitt, B.E. (ed.) (2005) *Embracing Non-Directivity: Reassessing Person-Centered Theory and Practice in the 21st Century* (pp. i–iii). Ross-on-Wye: PCCS.

Mearns, D. and Thorne, B. (2000) *Person-Centred Therapy Today: New Frontiers in Theory and Practice*. London: Sage.

Patterson, C.H. (1984/2000) Empathy, warmth and genuineness in psychotherapy: a review of reviews (first published 1984). In C.H. Patterson, *Understanding Psychotherapy: Fifty Years of Client-Centred Theory and Practice* (pp. 161–73). Ross-on-Wye: PCCS.

Prouty, G. (1994) *Theoretical Evolutions in Person-centered/Experiential Therapy: Applications to Schizophrenic and Retarded Psychoses*. Westport, CT: Praeger.

Rogers, C.R. (1951) *Client-Centered Therapy*. London: Constable.

Rogers, C.R. (1957) The necessary and sufficient conditions of therapeutic personality change. *Journal of Consulting Psychology*, 21: 95–103.

Rogers, C.R. (1958/1967) A process conception of psychotherapy (first published 1958). In *On Becoming a Person* (pp. 125–59). London: Constable.

Rogers, C.R. (1959) A theory of therapy, personality and interpersonal relationships, as developed in the client-centered framework. In S. Koch (ed.), *Psychology: A Study of Science. Vol. 3: Formulation of the Person and the Social Context* (pp. 184–256). New York: McGraw-Hill.

Rogers, C.R. and Dymond, R.F. (eds) (1954) *Psychotherapy and Personality Change*. Chicago: University of Chicago Press.

Rogers, C.R., Gendlin, E.T., Kiesler, D.J. and Truax, C.B. (eds) (1967) *The Therapeutic Relationship and Its Impact: A Study of Psychotherapy with Schizophrenics*. Madison, WI: University of Wisconsin Press.

Sanders, P. (2000) Mapping person-centred approaches to counselling and psychotherapy. *Person-Centred Practice*, 8: 62–74.

Tudor, K. (2000) The case of the lost conditions. *Counselling*, 11 (1): 33–7.

Tudor, K. (in press) Rogers' therapeutic conditions: a relational conceptualization. *Person-Centered and Experiential Psychotherapies*, 10 (3): 165–80.

Tudor, K. and Merry, T. (2002) *Dictionary of Person-Centred Psychology*. London: Whurr.

Tudor, K. and Worrall, M. (2006) *Person-Centred Therapy: A Clinical Philosophy*. London: Routledge.

5.21

Psychodrama

(Jacob Levy Moreno, 1889–1974)

CLARK BAIM

BRIEF HISTORY

Psychodrama is a holistic method of psychotherapy in which people are helped to explore their psychosocial and emotional difficulties using sensitively guided enactment. Psychodrama uses a wide range of action-based techniques to help people examine troubling episodes from their life, their current or past relationships, unresolved situations, desired roles or inner thoughts, feelings and conflicts. The aims are to help the person to understand and transform the impact of these experiences and relationships, to test out new responses, and to promote insight, emotional release, resolution of trauma and loss, and integration.

Psychodrama was first devised in the 1920s and 1930s by the psychiatrist Dr Jacob Levy Moreno, and further elaborated over several decades in collaboration with his wife Zerka Toeman Moreno. Among Moreno's extensive writing, his essential texts include *Who Shall Survive* (1934) and *Psychodrama* (1946–1969, three volumes, Volumes 2 and 3 co-authored with Zerka Moreno).

Psychodrama was the first recognised method of group psychotherapy. It has gained wide acceptance as an effective approach to psychological and emotional healing, and is practised in more than 100 countries by more than 10,000 professionals. It has an extensive literature of more than 6300 publications, with many national and regional journals, associations and training organisations around the world. A comprehensive bibliography of world psychodrama can be found at www.pdbib.org.

Moreno was born in Romania and spent his formative years as a young doctor in Vienna during its renowned period of cultural ferment. During the First World War he was a medical superintendent at a resettlement camp. After emigrating to the USA in 1925, Moreno lived the rest of his life in New York City and in upstate New York, where he founded a private sanatorium in Beacon, which also served as a training centre for the early generations of psychodramatists. A full account of his inspiring life and ideas can be found in Hare and Hare (1996).

In addition to being a medical doctor and psychiatrist, Moreno was also a philosopher and visionary. He was a highly ebullient and charismatic figure, with an inspirational vision that human beings have the potential to be – in his terms – co-creators of the cosmos, with vast reserves of untapped creative power to change the world for the better. His far-reaching vision was that therapy should be for all humankind just as much as it is for individual human beings. He coined the term *sociatry* – the healing of society – as a counterpart to the term *psychiatry* – the healing of the individual mind. His development of methods such as sociodrama and sociometry were important contributions to his broader aim of sociatry for all of humanity.

Psychodrama uses a very wide array of active techniques, and many of these have been incorporated into other therapies. The far-reaching influence of psychodrama led Eric Berne, the creator of transactional analysis, to observe:

> In his selection of specific techniques, Dr Perls shares with other 'active' psychotherapists the 'Moreno

problem': the fact that nearly all known 'active' techniques were first tried out by Dr Moreno in psychodrama, so that it is difficult to come up with an original idea in this regard. (1970: 163–4)

BASIC ASSUMPTIONS

Spontaneity and Creativity

In his young adulthood, Moreno first became interested in the healing potential of spontaneity and creativity when watching children play in the parks of Vienna and joining them as a storyteller. He observed that children often appeared able to solve their conflicts with play and without adult intervention. He also noted that children who repeatedly took the same roles in their play had more difficulty in showing creativity and making friends. With encouragement to try new roles, the children became more spontaneous and vital in their interactions and better integrated with the group.

These observations led Moreno to the underlying premise of psychodrama, which is that all human beings are born with an innate will to survive, which includes the drives of spontaneity and creativity. Spontaneity is the capacity to find adequate responses to new situations or new responses to old situations in order to best meet the challenges and opportunities that life presents.

Moreno often wrote about the many forces within families and society that constrain spontaneity and creativity from infancy onwards, resulting in robot-like thinking, feeling and behaviour. One way to encapsulate the purpose of psychodrama is that it is a process of rediscovering and unblocking our innate spontaneity in order to 'heal ourselves' and free ourselves from the tendency towards becoming automatons. To further develop this point, we see that in the terminology of psychodrama, the client is called the 'protagonist,' a term borrowed from the ancient Greek theatre meaning 'the first actor'. Psychodrama is intended to help each person find the courage to act with authenticity and to take centre stage as the primary actor in their own life story.

Encounter

An important aspect of psychodrama is that the client is part of the action. As part of the action, they are encouraged to encounter the other people in the group. (Psychodrama is normally a group process, although it also used effectively in one-to-one sessions.) The challenge and energy of encounter are among the prime healing forces in psychodrama; it is through authentic here-and-now encounter with other people that we are best able to gain an understanding of how our behaviour affects other people, to get feedback from others about how they perceive us, and hence to know if we are 'getting better'. The spontaneously offered hug from a fellow group member, or being held and accepted by another group member even when experiencing a 'messy' emotion, can generate profound emotional healing. At the same time, to hear another group member tell you that they perceive you in a different way than you intend – while often challenging and frustrating – can be a valuable source of insight about how you relate to other people.

Catharsis and Integration

Catharsis is a term first used by the Greek philosopher Aristotle to describe how drama can lead to emotional purging among audience members and in the characters in the drama. In psychodrama, it is common for group members to experience *catharsis of emotion*, particularly a release of deeply held emotions such as sadness, fear or anger. It should also be noted that, for some people, particularly those who are typically overwhelmed by emotion, psychodrama can be used just as effectively to help them contain rather than express emotion, or to help them express the 'forbidden' emotion that they are not able to express (such as the anger behind sadness, or the fear beneath a defiant exterior).

There is another important form of catharsis, which is the *catharsis of integration*. Emotional release may have limited value if it is not then integrated into the person's psychosocial functioning. The catharsis of integration usually takes place towards the end of a psychodrama, when the protagonist is helped to put into practice their new learning and apply it to daily living.

ORIGIN AND MAINTENANCE OF PROBLEMS

Psychodrama is deeply rooted in role theory (Moreno, 1946). One of the principles of role theory is that, in the course of our lives, we carry out many roles. When we know how to perform a given role, it can be said to be in our *role repertoire*. In general, the greater the number of integrated roles we have in our repertoire, the better able we are to meet our needs and function successfully because we have a wide variety of strategies from which to choose. This flexibility of roles is essential if we are to meet the demands of the moment, because our behaviour may need to alter radically when we move from one context to another.

Somatic Roles

Role theory also provides a way of understanding the origin and maintenance of emotional and psychosocial problems. For example, Moreno observed that, in order to survive, a baby must carry out somatic roles (*somatic* meaning 'of the body') such as the role of breather, drinker, eater, crier or signaller of distress, excreter, sleeper, self-soother, and other roles necessary to stay alive. These roles may develop smoothly and instinctively, or they may be full of conflict and distress, depending on a wide range of variables influencing the baby, the parents and their environment. If there are significant disturbances in the development of somatic roles, this may lead to illness or vulnerability related to breathing, eating, intestinal function, mobility, bodily shape and posture, sensory processing, emotional self-regulation and expression, and other somatic processes. The body remembers even if the mind forgets. This is where psychodrama comes into its own as an action method, because many of the problems people face are literally 'beyond words'. For this reason, psychodrama focuses on emotion and action just as much as the higher functions of thinking, speaking and reflection.

Social/cultural Roles

The next category of roles includes the social/cultural roles, such as son, daughter, mother, father, shopper, commuter, partner, lover, teacher, etc. Each role consists of a constellation of behaviours that are associated with that role in a given cultural context. Most of these roles are subject to social learning, and are heavily influenced by role models within the family and within the broader culture. Given a sufficiently stable and conducive environment, a person can develop appropriate and effective social roles that help them survive and that best suit them, their abilities and their goals. Problems may develop, however, if the person is allowed only to learn and carry out a very restricted range of roles, or if one role is over-developed to the detriment of other roles. Another type of problem arises when roles are in conflict and the person is faced with a dilemma.

Fantasy/psychodramatic Roles

The next category of roles is the fantasy/psychodramatic roles. These are the roles that develop through imagination and through myths, stories and dreams. When used in an integrated way, the psychodramatic roles can strengthen and inspire us. (Think of the strength one may find in stories, music, art, poetry, film and drama.) However, these roles can also become over-developed; if we are too identified with our psychodramatic roles, we may lose touch with reality.

Roles and The Emergence of The Self

Summarising the relationship between roles and the development of our sense of self, Moreno (1946) observed that *roles do not emerge from the self, but the self may emerge from roles*. In other words, the person that we are – our deepest sense of what constitutes our self – develops out of all the roles we are encouraged and permitted to carry out. This idea runs counter to what is generally our more instinctive view of the self, which is that there is some irreducible core self from which our roles and abilities develop. Moreno states exactly the opposite, that the roles come first, and then – possibly – a sense of self. This description of the formation of self-identity has disturbing implications when we consider what sort of self emerges from conflicted roles, from over-rigid roles, or from self-doubting, antisocial or victim roles. Psychodrama can help people to develop new roles and to 'relieve from duty' the roles that once served a purpose but which are no longer needed.

CHANGE

Psychodrama offers a medium for 'rewriting the script' of our lives and rehearsing new behaviours and roles. Where the issue is unresolved trauma and loss, it is necessary that the person should have his or her suffering acknowledged and believed. Resolution is often achieved by revisiting the scene of the hurt in a structured way and providing an opportunity for emotional release and also a comforting and empowering new experience.

In its so-called 'classical' form, a psychodrama often begins with a current problem or difficulty and traces it back to earlier life situations. Here, the participant (the protagonist) may have the chance to experience what was missing but needed at that time. The enactment then returns to the present, where new learning can be integrated and put into practice. At the end of the drama, the group members share how they relate to the participant's issues and problems. The sharing portion of the session is very important, as it offers the group members an opportunity to speak about their own emotional burdens. It also lets the protagonist know that they are not alone in their suffering.

Examples of Psychodramas (anonymised)

Gerry has suffered a string of relationship breakdowns. During his psychodrama, he traces his difficulties back to his early relationship with his mother, whom he experienced as cold and distant. Speaking to a group member who is in the role of his mother, Gerry angrily expresses his unmet need for love and care from her. Within the drama, Gerry then experiences an emotionally attuned mother. He allows himself to be held, and he weeps. He speaks about all the times he has run away from intimacy, or treated women badly because he could not bear to be vulnerable and then rejected by them. His more attuned, psychodramatic mother encourages him to form intimate relationships and to allow himself to love and be loved, without fear. Following this, Gerry is given time to practise a new way of being in intimate relationships, drawing from this experience of attuned mothering.

Meredith chooses a group member to represent the child she never had. In the drama, she holds the child she always wanted, but could not have for medical reasons. She expresses her grief and longing, while gently stroking the child's hair and face. After a long and sensitive encounter with this much-wanted child, she is helped to explore ways in which she can still carry out her desired role of 'loving mother' with her nieces and nephews and in her community. She finds hope for her future, beyond her despair, as she interacts with an immigrant family of two children and their struggling mother (played by group members) who live in her street. She reflects that there are creative and valuable ways to carry out her mothering role that don't involve being a biological mother.

As a child, Tom was sexually assaulted by a neighbour who had 'befriended' him. Twenty years later, he is still terrified by the memory of this event. In the psychodrama, Tom expresses his fear and grief, and summons up his rage about the abuse. Tom takes back his ability to say 'No!' as he accuses his abuser and sees him brought to justice in a psychodramatic 'courtroom'.

Tom receives supportive hugs from the group members and tells them it is a relief to be believed and understood. He feels relieved of the pressure to keep secrets and the burden of guilt and shame that he has held onto for so long.

SKILLS AND STRATEGIES

Psychodrama is notably different from talk-based therapy, because in psychodrama all aspects of life are not only discussed but re-created, worked through in action and integrated in the here-and-now of the therapy session. This active involvement can deepen learning, recovery and growth.

Elements of Psychodrama

Five elements are present in a psychodrama session:

- *The protagonist.* The person whose story or issue is the primary focus of the session.
- *The auxiliary egos.* Group members or trained members of staff who assume the roles of significant others in the drama. This may include significant people, objects or even aspects of the self or a person's internal world, e.g. 'my optimistic self' or 'my negative thoughts'.
- *The audience/group.* Group members who witness the drama and who may become involved as auxiliary roles. The emphasis is on creating a safe and supportive environment where each person is a potential therapeutic agent for the others.
- *The stage.* The physical space in which the drama is conducted. It may be an actual stage or simply a designated space.
- *The director.* The trained therapist who guides participants through each phase of the session.

Techniques

Key psychodrama techniques include:

- *Role reversal.* In this technique, one person reverses roles (changes places) with another person and speaks from their point of view. It is a fundamental technique for encouraging empathy and insight into the mind of other people.
- *Doubling.* In this technique, we try to become the 'double' of another person by speaking what we imagine to be their inner thoughts, feelings and beliefs. Doubling can be helpful when people struggle to voice their authentic thoughts and feelings.

- *Parts of self or internal roles.* In this technique, the client is encouraged to speak from the various 'parts' of himself, such as 'the part of me that hates myself and doesn't care about having a decent life' and 'the part of me that likes myself and wants to live a better life'.
- *Role training and role play.* This is perhaps the most widely adopted of the techniques derived from psychodrama. As the name implies, in role training the client is encouraged to learn and practise virtually any human skill.
- *Empty chair.* The client speaks directly to a person or concept being represented by an empty chair. This technique can be used to address unfinished business from the past or to have a 'conversation with myself', to offer just two of the myriad applications of this technique. A chair is often useful when it is too difficult to speak directly to a person.
- *Concretisation.* In psychodrama, it is common to find ways of putting the 'inner world outside' by making the intangible real or 'concrete.' So, objects, symbols, drawings, chairs or other group members may be used to represent internal processes.

There are scores of psychodramatic and action-based techniques. Many of these are described in Moreno (1959) and Blatner (1997).

RESEARCH EVIDENCE

In recent years, there has been an increasing number of systematic quantitative and qualitative analyses of psychodrama's effectiveness in the treatment of addictions, offending behaviour, unresolved trauma and loss, and a wide range of mental health disorders. These studies have shown that psychodrama can be an effective therapeutic method, although there is significant variation in the types of instruments and the criteria used to measure effectiveness. A summary of studies into psychodrama's effectiveness can be found in Weiser (2007). A meta-analysis of psychodrama research conducted by Kipper and Ritchie (2003) documented an improvement effect similar to or better than that commonly reported for group psychotherapy. The techniques of role reversal and doubling emerged as the most effective interventions. Hudgins and Toscani (2011) have found increasing consensus among therapists focusing on post-traumatic stress disorder (PTSD) that active methods, including psychodrama, are not only effective in working with unresolved trauma, but are indeed the treatment of choice for people suffering with unresolved trauma.

One important finding from the research is that psychodrama needs adaptation to meet the needs of different groups and people with different diagnoses. Given the very wide range of techniques available in psychodrama, it is a method that is particularly amenable to such flexible application. It is always possible for a skilled practitioner to find the 'shoe that fits' a particular person and group.

Psychodrama has been applied in every type of therapeutic and mental health setting, and is also used in personal development, relationship and marital counselling, community building, professional training, and business and industry. While there is still much room for additional evidence of psychodrama's effectiveness in these areas and in the clinical domain, it is fair to say that much of the research into the effectiveness of all group therapy is likely to apply to psychodrama as well.

REFERENCES

Berne, E. (1970) Book review. *American Journal of Psychiatry*, 126.

Blatner, A. (1997) *Acting-In: Practical Applications of Psychodramatic Methods* (3rd edn). London: Free Association.

Hare, A. Paul and Hare, June R. (1996) *J.L. Moreno*. London: Sage.

Hudgins, K. and Toscani, F. (2011) *Stories at the Frontlines: The Global Therapeutic Spiral Model*. In press.

Kipper, D.A. and Ritchie, T.D. (2003) The effectiveness of psychodramatic techniques: a meta-analysis. *Group Dynamics: Theory Research and Practice*, 7 (1): 13–25.

Moreno, J.L. (1934) *Who Shall Survive? A New Approach to the Problem of Human Interrelations*. Washington, DC: Nervous and Mental Disease Publishing.

Moreno, J.L. (1946) Psychodrama and group psychotherapy. Address to the American Psychiatric Association Meeting, 30 May.

Moreno, J.L. (1946) *Psychodrama* (Vol. 1). New York: Beacon.

Moreno, J.L. (1946–1969) *Psychodrama* (Vols 1–3; Vols 2 and 3 with Z.T. Moreno). New York: Beacon.

Moreno, Zerka T. (1959) A survey of psychodramatic techniques. *Group Psychotherapy*, 12: 5–14.

Weiser, M. (2007) Studies on treatment effects of psychodrama psychotherapy. In C. Baim, J. Burmeister and M. Maciel (eds), *Psychodrama: Advances in Theory and Practice*. London: Routledge.

Psychosynthesis Therapy

(Roberto Assagioli, 1888–1974)

HELEN SIERODA

BRIEF HISTORY

Roberto Assagioli, the founder of psychosynthesis, was a student of Freud and Bleuler, a contemporary of Jung, and a pioneer of psychoanalysis in Italy. He was actively involved in the birth of depth psychology, writing articles and participating in the Zurich Freud Society, but his participation in the psychoanalytic movement between 1909 and 1912 was brief. Assagioli's conception of the person was radically different from Freud's and as early as 1910, in his doctoral thesis, he was beginning to develop psychosynthesis. He argued that Freud's vision of the person was incomplete because it did not include the healthy or spiritual aspects of being human. He envisioned a holistic psychology which could integrate psychoanalysis with psychosynthesis and 'depth psychology' with 'height psychology'. Psychosynthesis builds upon Freud's theory of the unconscious; it addresses psychological distress, and intra-psychic and interpersonal conflict, *as well as* actualisation of human potential, the capacity for wholeness and the search for deeper meaning and purpose.

Assagioli drew inspiration for his approach to human development from diverse sources (a full account of these can be found in Hardy, 1978). He was influenced by Western philosophical and mystical thinking and had a serious interest in Eastern traditions. In order to gain a deeper understanding of the development of psychosynthesis it is necessary to appreciate the broader currents of European culture at the end of the nineteenth century. This was a period characterised by anticipation of radical change. Assagioli's vision of personal transformation and cultural revitalisation and his attempt to marry the emerging science of psychology with mysticism reflect both the spiritual and scientific quests of the *fin de siècle*. The creative tensions and contradictions of this period seem fundamental to the birth and later development of the synthetic, integrative vision of psychosynthesis.

The Istituto di Psicosintesi was founded in Rome in 1926. Following this a number of other centres were established in Europe and in 1957 the Psychosynthesis Research Foundation was founded in the United States. Although Assagioli did not enjoy wide recognition until the late 1950s, he developed and practised his ideas 50 years before 1960s counterculture and the birth of humanistic and transpersonal psychology. He played a part in the development of both of these movements, serving on the board of editors for the *Journal of Humanistic Psychology* and the *Journal of Transpersonal Psychology*.

Assagioli envisaged psychosynthesis as an approach (rather than a school) with no central, formal authority, structure or institute. Shortly before his death he issued a statement indicating that the relationship of centres 'should be not that of a "solar system" but that of a "constellation'" (Assagioli, 1974). Whereas this undoubtedly created a context where immense richness, diversity and creative freedom could flourish, it does make keeping track of the international development and impact of psychosynthesis a challenge.

Psychosynthesis has moved on in the decades since Assagioli's death and is flourishing in numerous centres worldwide. There are well-established training centres throughout Europe and in the UK.

BASIC ASSUMPTIONS

Assagioli outlined seven core principles underpinning the psychosynthesis approach, which together convey its essence. Although by no means limited to these, their inclusion is central to any full account of psychosynthesis. These are:

- transpersonal self or 'Self'
- superconscious
- dis-identification
- personal self or 'I'
- the will
- ideal model
- synthesis.

Central to psychosynthesis is a celebration of the vast potential of the human spirit. Both human suffering and potential are held in a broad psychospiritual context, based on the understanding that a deeper connection with our spiritual source or transpersonal self (often referred to simply as 'self') is at the heart of the human condition and is the foundation of psychological health. Transpersonal self is not psychologised, understood as a God concept, archetype or symbol; Assagioli maintained that self is a spiritual, metaphysical reality. Psychosynthesis holds that each of us essentially *is* a self and has the potential to develop a relationship with this source, not only at times of mystical or 'peak' experiences at the higher levels of the superconscious but also in the midst of our everyday lives.

One fundamental proposition is that the transpersonal infuses all levels of the personality and all levels of consciousness through every stage of life. Just as we have a lower unconscious containing sexual and aggressive drives, instincts, complexes and pathological symptoms, we also have a higher unconscious or superconscious which is the source of creative imagination, inspiration, intuition, ethical imperatives and the pull towards spiritual maturity. The latter is as basic to human nature as the former. Spiritual development is not conceived of as a linear journey from here outward to some lofty and distant destination. It is described as an unfolding process which includes all of life participating in a spiritually evolving cosmos. The goal is a regenerated personality aligned with this wider context, and the process combines attending to the lower unconscious with utilising superconscious energies and the imagination to create a realistic and attainable ideal (as opposed to idealised) model of what we can become.

Though psychosynthesis has an optimistic view of the person, it actively addresses the destructive potential in human nature, whilst holding the possibility for positive change. Much of the work of psychosynthesis involves increasing awareness or uncovering the 'split-off' or disowned parts of ourselves and facilitating the integration of contradictions and multiplicity within the personality. This includes the psychological functions: desires, sensation, feeling, thinking, imagination and intuition. It is an approach which sees the person as carrying within themselves the resources to become whole.

Assagioli frequently stressed that superconscious or mystical experiences are not to be seen as an end in themselves. Rather, these experiences should be a source of inspiration for engaging with the world in pragmatic ways, in a spirit of service similar to the bodhisattvic endeavour of Buddhism. He conceived of society as a reflection of human consciousness, with psychosynthesis playing a part in social and political transformation. This orientation has facilitated the emergence of social or applied psychosynthesis and 'ecopsychosynthesis' which offer a pragmatic response to the psychological reductionism and socio-political disconnection of which counselling and psychotherapy in general are often accused.

Psychosynthesis embraces a transpersonal context for our life journey and is often linked with the transpersonal movement. Like transpersonal psychology it has developed a variety of techniques for working with the symbolic, with images, dreams and the realm of the superconscious. Like transpersonal psychology it addresses the 'dark night of the soul', spiritual emergence and emergency. However, the transpersonal movement and some New Age offshoots are often associated with an exclusive focus on the attainment of spiritual experiences and the cultivation of superconscious energies; this emphasis can make an association with the transpersonal movement problematic. This movement does not accurately reflect the work of the majority of psychosynthesis practitioners when there is a valuing of transcendence or higher states of consciousness *to the exclusion of other perspectives*, or where repression of our earthly lives is confused with transpersonal development. An overemphasis on height creates a problem of duality and an uneasy polarisation of higher and lower, personal and transpersonal, psyche and spirit, self and world. For this reason many practitioners adopt the term 'psychospiritual'.

Nevertheless, psychosynthesis has historically made an important contribution to the development of the transpersonal movement and is also enriched by transpersonal thinkers. Wilber's (2000) quadrant model is routinely found on the curriculum of psychosynthesis training. Jorge Ferrer's (2002) participative view of the transpersonal, A.H. Almaas's (2001) approach to fundamental narcissism, and the work of other transpersonal theorists are all recognised within psychosynthesis.

ORIGIN AND MAINTENANCE OF PROBLEMS

From a psychosynthesis perspective, psychological disturbances are not merely disturbances to self-concept but crucially are a disconnection from self. Assagioli asserted that much psychological dysfunction stems from a case of mistaken identity, an estrangement from our essential nature which leads to a lack of meaning and purpose in our lives. He proposed that the purpose of psychosynthesis was to recognise a deeper pull to meaning in our lives and to connect with this deeper source of identity. The personal self or I is the point of connection with self at the level of the personality and makes possible the integration and synthesis of the various (often competing) pulls within the personality.

From a developmental perspective, early environment frequently contributes to a failure to develop into all that we might be in later life. This happens where parents or caregivers require us to become radically different from who we truly are. For example, we may grow up in a repressive environment where our emotions, drives and impulses are not accepted and are driven underground, or when our unique individuality, qualities and gifts are not recognised, encouraged and sustained. We could say that under circumstances like these, the seed of self lacks vital conditions to support its emergence and development. Under these conditions our growth is stunted; as children we adapt to our surroundings in order to survive. As time goes on, most of us habitually settle for living far short of all that we can be, making choices based on what others want or expect, or what causes least discomfort or disruption. To the extent that we are not being true to ourselves, this creates a rupture in the relationship between soul and self. Here the work of personal development and that of transpersonal development are not seen as separate processes; the task is to work with blocks and obstacles that prevent the emergence of self wherever they occur.

Every human life is confronted with tragedies, loss, change and uncertainty. Sometimes our usual defences and coping mechanisms don't work, leading to a sense of powerlessness, trepidation or alarm as our lives seem to be unravelling. In psychosynthesis, this psychological distress is understood in the context of a larger mystery which unfolds over time. The lifelong journey of navigating pain, crisis and failure presents an opportunity for awakening to the deeper psychospiritual context of our lives.

CHANGE

Life is uncertain; it confronts us all with the challenge of change. Often we attempt to maintain the illusion of permanence in the face of a dynamic and changing world, experiencing enormous resistance and anxiety at the prospect of change. Psychosynthesis recognises two different orientations towards change. The first is *regressive* – trying to hold on to a situation, behaviour or worldview which we have outgrown or is no longer serving us; this orientation generates more pain. The second is *progressive* – taking responsibility for our lives, choosing to let go of (or dis-identify from) a pattern of thinking, behaviour or state of affairs, or conversely choosing to engage with a tough, challenging situation which we might prefer to avoid. This orientation can also be challenging and disruptive, with painful awakenings; but it leads to inner freedom, for it involves the perspective of the I, the essential spark or seed of the self which is available to us all at the core of our personality. Access to this centre opens the possibility to transform, through the engagement of awareness and will (basic functions of the I), both ourselves and the situation. Even in conditions like sickness, ageing and death, where we have no power over external circumstances, we can choose how we respond to the inevitable.

SKILLS AND STRATEGIES

Psychosynthesis practitioners respond to the client's own understanding of their experience, adapting strategies, techniques and the application of core principles contextually.

The empathic support provided within the therapeutic relationship is fundamental to the work of helping the client to experience and understand how they have been betrayed by their early environment and/or turned from their true nature or self in order to survive. A vital component within this process is the ability of the therapist to hold what is sometimes called a 'bifocal' perspective: seeing the client as more than their problems, as *both* a spiritually whole self *and* at the same time a personality with pain, problems and pathology.

Psychosynthesis is often associated with subpersonalities. Subpersonalities are a way of making sense of the sometimes bewildering complexity of the human condition and the stormy juxtaposition between different parts of ourselves. Working with subpersonalities creates an awareness of the multiplicity of our inner world, making our inner conversations explicit. It provides a powerful and effective tool for working with intra-psychic conflict whilst simultaneously addressing the pushes and pulls from the wider world in which we live. Central to this is the development of non-judgemental awareness and the technique of dis-identification which facilitates integration or synthesis within the personality. This brings depth and power to a psychosynthesis approach to subpersonalities. Psychosynthesis has made a great contribution to developing and refining a dialogical approach to working with subpersonalities; however, subpersonalities *per se* are not essential to the practice of psychosynthesis.

A goal of psychosynthesis is to cultivate the ability to purposefully direct psychological energies through the I in line with our highest values, deepest aspirations and a sense of meaning. This includes subpersonalities as well as other psychological functions: desire, sensation, feeling, thinking, imagination, intuition. Working with meaning and purpose might take the form of asking what legacy we wish to leave, what difference we choose to make in the lives of those we touch, or what deeply matters to us, 'what makes our heart sing'. This is an area for challenging clients to engage their vision, gifts and talents. The goal is to develop the courage, insight and vision to grow through both the successes and the difficulties of life.

To sum up, in psychosynthesis the development and refinement of the personality or 'personal psychosynthesis' involve gaining a wide-ranging knowledge of one's personality, learning to direct and coordinate its diverse constituents. This work involves the discovery of the unifying centre or I and the integration of the personality around this centre. The transpersonal aspect of this process involves strengthening the relationship between I and self in the midst of life and engaging with the energies of the superconscious. These are not separate stages that happen in a particular order, but rather interweaving elements in a complex emergent process.

RESEARCH

Like many humanistic-existential and integrative approaches, published research in psychosynthesis is sparse. This is despite partnerships with universities offering masters-level qualifications in psychosynthesis. Academic research would seem to be happening; research-oriented summer schools and conferences take place, but little finds its way into peer reviewed journals.

Whereas it is possible that research is abandoned once training is completed and private practice established, a more likely reason is a historic ambivalence towards traditional research methods. These methods, relying as they do on statistical data analysis, are commonly seen as hyper-rational and reductionist. From the perspective of the quantitative world of data and statistics, this subjective, soft, contextual approach lacks academic rigour. From a psychosynthesis perspective, therapy is a creative, emergent process – more improvisation than set piece. The mystery of life and human development cannot easily be squeezed into narrow predetermined models or step-by-step tick-box recipes. Arguably, the research dilemma goes beyond epistemological issues of whether we are qualitative and quantitative researchers and beyond theoretical and methodological issues to encompass competing philosophical paradigms. Nevertheless, the importance of engaging in research and the need to demonstrate a credible epistemological basis for psychosynthesis is increasingly being recognised.

One important example of current qualitative and quantitative research is taking place within the field of social or 'applied' psychosynthesis in the Teens and Toddlers teenage pregnancy prevention programme. Although not overtly publicised as psychosynthesis, both the vision and the approach of this project are deeply grounded in psychosynthesis principles and incorporate counselling and the related fields of mentoring and coaching. Teens and Toddlers research delivers a solid and methodical evaluation, which surveys the effectiveness of both short- and long-term impacts. To date, over 70 Teens and Toddlers projects have been delivered to 1500 at-risk young people. Retrospective studies found that over six years, the programme has had a pregnancy rate of 2.7 per cent, far lower than the national rate of 4.1 per cent; this is despite working *only* with young people most at risk of teenage pregnancy. The project has been recognised by the Department for Children, Schools and Families as a successful programme for early intervention, building skills and resilience in vulnerable young people who are at risk of dropping out of education and helping to prevent early pregnancy. In addition, using questions which reflect the government's Every Child Matters criteria, attitudes were measured with positive outcomes for all five criteria, concluding that Teens and Toddlers is successful in affecting the attitudes, behaviour and personal development of participants. The consensus would seem to be that this psychosynthesis-based approach is effective in addressing the problems of teenage pregnancy and social exclusion and in reaching young people who are notoriously difficult to reach.

REFERENCES

Almaas, A.H. (2001) *The Point of Existence*. Boston: Shambhala.

Assagioli, R. (1974) Training. Unpublished paper.

Ferrer, J.N. (2002) *Revisioning Transpersonal Theory*. New York: SUNY Press.

Hardy, J. (1987) *A Psychology with a Soul: Psychosynthesis in Evolutionary Context*. London: Routledge and Kegan Paul.

Wilber, K. (2000) *Integral Psychology*. Boston: Shambhala.

www.teensandtoddlers.org/evaluationandesearch/index.htm.

RECOMMENDED READING

Assagioli, R. (1965) *Psychosynthesis: A Collection of Basic Writings*. Wellingborough: Turnstone.

Assagioli, R. (1974) *The Act of Will*. Wellingborough: Turnstone.

Ferrucci, P. (1982) *What We May Be*. London: Aquarian/Thorsons.

Firman, J. and Gila, A. (2002) *A Psychology of the Spirit*. New York: SUNY Press.

Whitmore, D. (1991) *Psychosynthesis Counselling in Action*. London: Sage.

Young Brown, M. (1993) *Growing Whole: Self-Realisation on an Endangered Planet*. Center City, MN: Hazelden.

Transactional Analysis

(Eric Berne, 1910–1970)

KEITH TUDOR AND CHARLOTTE SILLS

BRIEF HISTORY

Transactional analysis (TA) is a theory of personality, including theories of child development and psychopathology, all of which provide the basis for a theory of psychotherapy. It also provides a theory of communication which may be applied to individuals and systems such as groups and organisations.

TA was founded by Eric Berne, a Canadian psychiatrist who originally trained as a psychoanalyst. TA has its theoretical roots in the psychoanalytic tradition, although it is also substantially influenced by the cognitive-behavioural approach and social theory, while being philosophically rooted in a humanistic-existential tradition that believes in the power of the individual to take charge of his life, to make changes and to live in harmony with himself and others. Berne was particularly influenced by Paul Federn who, from 1941, was his training analyst in New York. Federn's system of ego psychology was seminal in Berne's later development of the ego state theory of personality (see Tudor, 2010). In 1943 Berne, by then an American citizen, joined the United States Army Medical Corps where, as a psychiatrist, he conducted group psychotherapy and pursued his studies in the field of intuition, the results of which again may be seen in his later development of TA theory, especially the importance of checking intuitive judgements against objective observations. On leaving the army

Berne moved to California and in 1947 became an analysand of Eric Erikson, from whom he learned about sequential life stages and the importance of social influences in psychosocial development. In the early 1950s Berne was beginning to take a more critical view of psychoanalysis and its conceptualisation of the unconscious; his break with it came in 1956 with the rejection of his application for membership of the San Francisco Psychoanalytic Institute. Berne threw himself into activity – in his public psychiatric posts and, by now, his private practice as well as his writing – and, by 1958, had published articles which contained all the principal terms and concepts of TA. In 1956 Berne had established a series of weekly meetings of mental health professionals interested in TA, under the name the San Francisco Social Psychiatry Seminar; in 1960 this became an incorporated educational body which, in turn, led to the foundation in 1964 of the International Transactional Analysis Association (ITAA). In 1961 Berne published *Transactional Analysis in Psychotherapy* which drew together all his previous writings on TA and still presents a complete view of TA personality, psychotherapy and communication theory. The publication in 1964 of Berne's *Games People Play* marked a blossoming of interest in TA especially in the States, demonstrated by the passage into common usage of TA terms such as 'OK' (as in 'I'm OK, You're OK'), 'games' (mutual transferential processes) and 'strokes' (units of recognition).

Since the 1960s, TA has developed its theory, applications and organisation. There are nearly 10,000 members worldwide, located in regional and national organisations in more than 90 countries, which are affiliated to the International TA Association (ITAA), the European TA Association (EATA) or the Western Pacific TA Association (WPATA). These associations provide an international system of accreditation of practitioners, supervisors and trainers. In Britain, TA has grown from initial seminar groups in the early 1960s, through the first national conference of the (UK) Institute of Transactional Analysis in 1974, to a flourishing community comprising over 1000 people with involvement in and recognition by the current national organisations of psychotherapy and counselling (see Tudor and Hobbes, 2007).

BASIC ASSUMPTIONS

- People are born with a basic drive for growth and health – in TA terms, 'OKness'. To the 'positions' or internal psychological conditions understood by Melanie Klein and object relations theory – that is, the paranoid ('I'm OK, You're not OK'), depressive ('I'm not OK, You're OK') and schizoid ('I'm not OK, You're not OK') – Berne added a fourth 'I'm OK, You're OK' life position. Later, in his last book *What Do You Say After You Say Hello*, Berne (1972/1975) also explored a third-handed position, involving 'They', thereby acknowledging the wider social context of such life positions.
- Similarly, Berne asserted that there is a creative force in nature which strives for growth and completion. Alongside Freud's instinctual drives – *thanatos* (death instinct) and *eros* (sexual instinct) – Berne proposed that there is a third drive, *physis*, which describes the creative life instinct. In his work and writing Berne also referred to *vis medicatrix naturae* or the curative power of nature.
- A general goal in life for people is autonomy, a word that has a particular meaning in TA. Berne defined autonomy as the release or recovery of our capacity for awareness, spontaneity and intimacy. In this sense autonomy is not a selfish, individual goal; it is an outcome which requires relationship with others and, indeed, one which may be viewed as a social goal not only for individuals but also for groups, organisations, communities and societies.
- Everyone has the capacity to think – and, therefore, to take responsibility for their actions.
- People decide their own destiny and, therefore, these decisions can be changed. These decisions may be cognitive and conscious in the ordinary sense of the word; they can also be unconscious, preverbal, bodily or visceral 'decisions'. This assumption is the basis of redecision work in TA.

PRINCIPLES OF PRACTICE

TA is distinguished by its emphasis and reliance on the 'contractual method', by which all decisions about therapy (administrative, professional and psychological) are framed. A contract is a bilateral agreement or commitment between therapist and client to a well-defined course of action. In recent years, there have been some developments in thinking about contracts and the process of contracting (see Sills, 2006), with a greater emphasis on the contractual *method* as reflecting an important process between client and therapist.

TA practitioners are committed to 'open communication' in their transactions. Berne was one of the first psychiatrists, if not the first, to hold case conferences which were open to clients, and is reported as having said, 'Anything that can't be said in front of a patient isn't worth saying' – a radical statement even these days. This is not to imply that *everything must* be said, but that *anything can* be said. An authentic meeting between psychotherapist and client is at the heart of TA practice.

CENTRAL THEORETICAL CONCEPTS

Most theoretical concepts in TA fall into four main areas: ego states (which describe personality); transactions (communication and relationships); life scripts (identity and relational patterns); and games and rackets (ways of confirming our scripts).

Ego States

Following the work of Berne, who in turn drew on the work of Federn, Weiss and Glover, transactional analysts think about personality in terms of ego states. An ego state is 'the subjectively experienced reality of a person's mental and bodily ego with the original contents of the time period it represents' (Clarkson et al., 1996: 222). Berne identified three types of ego state: Parent, Adult and Child (see Figure 5.23.1).

The Parent and Child ego states are archaic in that they represent past influences:

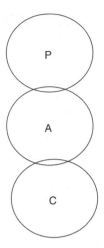

Figure 5.23.1   *Structural diagram of a personality: Parent, Adult and Child ego states*

the Parent ego state is a set of feelings, attitudes, and behavior patterns which resemble those of a parental figure ... The Child ego state is a set of feelings, attitudes and behavior patterns which are relics of the individual's own childhood. (Berne, 1961/1975: 75–7)

By contrast, the Adult ego state is characterised by autonomous, here-and-now feelings, attitudes and behaviours. Ego states may be ascertained or diagnosed by four methods:

1 *behavioural* – based on observable gestures, expressions, words, voice tones, etc.
2 *social* – the reactions the subject elicits from other people
3 *historical* – the experience can be traced to a past which did actually occur
4 *phenomenological* – subjective self-experience (or examination of self-experience).

All four diagnoses are necessary for a sufficient identification of an ego state, and Berne emphasised the need for *both* observable *and* phenomenological verification of intuitive diagnosis.

Transactions

All communication can be analysed in terms of transactions between ego states. This helps to understand how human beings engage with each other, both in achieving real contact and intimacy and also in repeating limited patterns of relating (games). In analysing such transactions, Berne (1966) identified three 'rules' of communication:

1 When we communicate or transact from complementary ego states, i.e. between Parent and Parent, Adult and Adult, Child and Child, and Parent and Child, communication can continue indefinitely. As Berne put it: 'as long as the vectors are parallel, communication can proceed indefinitely' (1966: 223).
2 A break in communication is described as a crossed transaction. As Stewart and Joines have described it: 'When a transaction is crossed, a break in communication results and one or both individuals will need to shift ego-states in order for communication to be re-established' (1987: 65) Crossed transactions can be problematic; they can also be therapeutic, for example, when a therapist or a client 'crosses' an unhelpful, repetitive communication.
3 'The behavioural outcome of an ulterior transaction is determined at the psychological and not at the social level' (Berne, 1966: 227). This is based on the idea that non-verbal or 'ulterior' psychological communications often have more impact than social-level communications. Berne's understanding of an ulterior transaction was that it is likely to be driven by script. Novellino (2003) identified a fourth rule or type of communication by which an unconscious message is transmitted from Adult to Adult (for example from client to therapist), not as a script enactment but in order to communicate an important but unacknowledged emotion.

Life Scripts

In TA the origin of problems is understood as the result of a person's life script, which has several elements:

• It is a *specific life plan*, laid out in the form of a drama with a beginning, a middle and an end.
• It is *decided* or developed *in early childhood*, based on predispositions and needs balanced against the demands of the environment. Such decisions or survival conclusions are made on the basis of the infant's emotions and reality testing and her/his basic need to be in relationship. The script is understood to be the best decision or survival conclusion the infant can make at the time.
• It is *reinforced by parental influence*, i.e. through actual, specific, observable transactions with the parents or carers. Such script messages are both non-verbal and verbal.
• It *directs behaviour* in the most important aspects of a person's life, in that the person's script culminates in a chosen (decided) alternative and, *out of awareness*, we choose behaviours which lead to the conclusion or 'script payoff'.

Psychological disturbance is understood in terms of *child development*, i.e. ego state development, and of *psychopathology*, i.e. in terms of the structure of the personality, e.g. the exclusion or contamination (unaware influence) of ego states or symbiosis when two (or more) individuals develop a co-dependent relationship based on script decisions.

Again, there is a lively debate in TA about the nature of script, with some theorists and practitioners advancing definitions of script which allow that it can be positive or, at least, an essential part of life (for example Cornell, 1988; English, 1977; 1988; Summers and Tudor, 2000).

Games and Rackets

Disturbance is maintained through the development of a system of beliefs about self, others and the world; repressed authentic feelings; observable behaviours, internal experiences and fantasies; and reinforcing memories. This is known as the 'racket system' (after the notion of a protection racket: Erskine and Zalcman, 1979) or a 'script system'. This system is closely linked to the relational concept of *games*, which are repeating patterns of interaction with others in which script beliefs are enacted relationally and lead to a reinforcement of the script payoff, normally for both or all people involved.

CHANGE

Health may be viewed as the manifestation of *physis* and the expression of autonomy. More specifically, Berne defined change in terms of 'cure' as a progressive process involving four stages:

1 *social control* – the control of dysfunctional social behaviours
2 *symptomatic relief* – the personal relief of subjectively experienced symptoms
3 *transference cure* – when the client can stay out of their script, as long as the therapist is around either literally or 'in their head'
4 *script cure* – by which the person's own adult ego state takes over the previous role of the therapist and the person makes autonomous decisions.

In recent years, the understanding of change, cure and health is generally considered in the context of cultural and social attitudes, pressures and circumstances. The notion of a progression from behavioural change through to characterological transformation is, nevertheless, still useful.

SKILLS AND STRATEGIES

A central skill of the TA practitioner is detailed observation. In discussing the requirements of the group therapist, Berne summarised them as an ability to use ideally 'all five senses in making a diagnosis, assessing the situation, and planning the treatment: sight, hearing, smell, touch and taste' (1966: 65) – although he acknowledged that the sense of taste is seldom used! Berne paid particular and detailed attention to facial expressions and gestures. This is not to say that the therapist comments on all that they observe; it is to suggest that all this is available to their awareness. Observing in such detail has direct implications for the training of therapists in general and of group therapists in particular.

TA originally took an operational, actionistic approach to change and 'treatment'. Based on the contractual method and their diagnosis of the client, TA practitioners negotiated, defined and generally followed a mutually agreed treatment plan. TA has developed a sophisticated approach to treatment planning sequences comprising a number of stages including: agreeing the contract, decontamination (of the Adult ego state), building inner support, impasse resolution, therapy with the Parent ego state, integration, etc.

Berne (1966) identified eight 'therapeutic operations' which characterise TA therapy:

1 *Interrogation or enquiry*: inviting the client to talk about himself.
2 *Specification*: categorising and highlighting certain relevant information.
3 *Confrontation*: using previously specified material to point out inconsistencies; often this has the purpose and effect of disconcerting the client's Parent, Child, or contaminated Adult.
4 *Explanation*: explaining a situation with a view to strengthening the client's Adult.
5 *Illustration*: using an anecdote, simile or comparison to reinforce a confrontation or explanation.
6 *Confirmation*: using new confrontations to confirm the issues and patterns that emerge in the client's discourse.
7 *Interpretation*: offering ways of understanding a client's underlying motives, designed to stabilise the client's adult control and 'deconfuse' his child.
8 *Crystallisation*: making summary statements to help the client make autonomous choices.

Since the early days, the original methodology has been developed in a number of ways. The early approaches relied on the 'concrete' analysis of script elements that were amenable to conscious cognitive awareness. Later developments have reflected changes in the wider field of psychotherapy. These include narrative or constructivist approaches that take account of new understandings in relation to memory and meaning making. They also include psychoanalytic TA (for example Moiso and Novellino, 2000) and relational TA, where the relationship between therapist and client is the vehicle in which the client can express his, sometimes unconscious, self-experience and patterns of relating. Relational approaches to TA (see Summers and Tudor, 2000; Hargaden and Sills, 2002) also introduce the intersubjective into their understanding of the therapeutic endeavour, the former describing a present-centred theory of expanding the Adult (see also Tudor, 2003), and the latter examining the 'deconfusion' of the Child, elaborating Berne's therapeutic operations into 'empathic transactions'. The relational turn in psychotherapy in general is reflected and well articulated in TA in these and other publications (see Cornell and Hargaden, 2005) and in the development of an International Association for Relational TA (see www.relationalta.com).

RESEARCH EVIDENCE

Berne (1966) argued that research and therapy must be clearly separated, to the extent that a research group should be designated as such and any therapeutic results regarded as secondary. He also discussed issues of motivation and possible psychological games involved in research, as well as the effect of the presence of the investigator. Nevertheless, Berne himself prefigured the more recent concept of the reflective practitioner who is more aware of research. Berne's own writing, as well as that of other TA practitioners, reflects a broad concern in the TA community to observe the external manifestations of internal, phenomenological realities and to operationalise the conclusions.

It follows that most TA concepts are amenable to research: the life script through questionnaires; functional modes of ego states through the egogram; passivity and discounting through the discount matrix; the stroke economy through the stroking profile; and so on (for explanation of these and other TA concepts see Stewart and Joines, 1987; Lapworth and Sills, 2011). In the last 20 years research articles have appeared in the *Transactional Analysis Journal* (the official journal of the international TA world) and the *EATA News* on for example: self-esteem in a self-reparenting program; the impact of TA in enhancing adjustment in college students; ego states; the effects of TA psychotherapy on self-esteem and quality of life; stress amongst high school students; egograms; functional fluency (using the functional modes of ego states); and the use of TA in treatment centres for addiction and others. Relational TA has been the springboard for some qualitative action research (van Rijn et al., 2008; Fowlie, in preparation). In 2010 the TA organisations launched the *International Journal of Transactional Analysis Research*; an article in the first issue provided a reference list of TA research published in TA journals since the 1960s (Ohlsson, 2010a; 2010b).

REFERENCES

Berne, E. (1961/1975) *Transactional Analysis in Psychotherapy* (first published 1961). London: Souvenir.

Berne, E. (1966) *Principles of Group Treatment*. New York: Grove.

Berne, E. (1972/1975) *What Do You Say After You Say Hello?* (first published 1972). London: Corgi.

Clarkson, P., Gilbert, M. and Tudor, K. (1996) Transactional analysis. In W. Dryden (ed.), *Handbook of Individual Therapy* (pp. 219–53). London: Sage.

Cornell, B. and Hargaden, H. (eds) (2005) *From Transactions to Relations: The Emergence of a Relational Tradition in Transactional Analysis*. Chadlington: Haddon.

Cornell, W.F. (1988) Life script theory: a critical review from a developmental perspective. *Transactional Analysis Journal*, 18 (4): 270–82.

English, F. (1977) What shall I do tomorrow? Reconceptualising transactional analysis. In G. Barnes (ed.), *Transactional Analysis after Eric Berne* (pp. 287–347). New York: Harper's College Press.

English, F. (1988) Whither scripts? *Transactional Analysis Journal*, 30 (1): 294–303.

Erskine, R.G. and Zalcman, M. (1979) The racket system. *Transactional Analysis Journal*, 9 (1): 51–9

Fowlie, H. (in preparation) Reflective inquiry in relational TA training. In H. Fowlie and C. Sills (eds), *Relational Transactional Analysis in Practice*. London: Karnac.

Hargaden, H. and Sills, C. (2002) *Transactional Analysis: A Relational Perspective*. London: Brunner Routledge.

Lapworth, P. and Sills, S. (2011) *An Introduction to Transactional Analysis*. London: Sage.

Molso, C. and Novellino, M. (2000) An overview of the psychodynamic school of transactional analysis and its epistemological foundations. *Transactional Analysis Journal*, 30 (3): 182–91.

Novellino, M. (2003) On closer analysis: a psychodynamic revision of the rules of communication within the framework of transactional analysis. In C. Sills and H. Hargaden (eds), *Ego States* (pp. 149–68). London: Worth.

Ohlsson, T. (2010a) Scientific evidence base for transactional analysis in the year 2010. Annex 1. The big list: references to transactional analysis research 1963–2010. *International Journal of Transactional Analysis Research*, 1 (1): 12–23.

Ohlsson, T. (2010b) Scientific evidence base for transactional analysis in the year 2010. Annex 2. The psychotherapy list: references to research on transactional analysis psychotherapy effects 1963–2010. *International Journal of Transactional Analysis Research*, 1 (1): 24–9.

Sills, C. (ed.) (2006) *Contracts in Counselling and Psychotherapy* (2nd edn). London: Sage.

Summers, G. and Tudor, K. (2000) Cocreative transactional analysis. *Transactional Analysis Journal*, 30 (1): 23–40.

Stewart, I. and Joines, V. (1987) *TA Today*. Nottingham: Lifespace.

Tudor, K. (2003) The neopsyche: the integrating adult ego state. In C. Sills and H. Hargaden (eds), *Ego States* (pp. 201–31). London: Worth.

Tudor, K. (2010) The state of the ego: then and now. *Transactional Analysis Journal*, 40 (3 and 4).

Tudor, K. and Hobbes, R. (2007) Transactional analysis. In W. Dryden (ed.), *The Handbook of Individual Therapy* (5th edn, pp. 256–86). London: Sage.

Van Rijn, B., Sills, C., Hunt, J., Shivanath, S., Gildebrand, K. and Fowlie, H. (2008) Developing clinical effectiveness in psychotherapy training: action research. *Counselling and Psychotherapy Research*, 8 (4): 261–8.

PROFESSIONAL ORGANISATIONS

European Association for Transactional Analysis: www.eatanews.com

International Transactional Analysis Association (ITAA): www.ita-net.org/

Institute of Transactional Analysis: www.ita.org.uk.

Western Pacific Association of Transactional Analysis: www.wpata.com.au/

PART V

THEORY AND APPROACHES

INTEGRATIVE AND ECLECTIC APPROACHES

5.24

Cognitive Analytic Therapy

STEPHEN KELLETT

BRIEF HISTORY

Cognitive analytic therapy (CAT) was originally developed by Dr Anthony Ryle (psychiatrist and consultant psychotherapist) in the 1980s at the United Medical and Dental Schools of Guy's and St Thomas's Hospitals in London. There were three main motivations for development of a new psychotherapy (1) to establish a 'common language' for the psychotherapies (Ryle, 1978), (2) to help therapists avoid the dilemma of adopting either an overly cognitive or an overly analytic approach (Ryle, 1995) and (3) to design a psychotherapy suited to the needs of the public sector (Ryle, 1995). CAT has evolved as a widely used, structured, brief and integrative form of psychotherapy, which has a well-developed self-contained methodology, backed by a fully structured theory of mental functioning and therapeutic change (Ryle, 2004). CAT has evolved from an approach to help clients with neurotic problems, to a therapy for clients with personality disorder (Ryle, 1997) and psychosis (Kerr et al., 2003). CAT has also been applied as an organisational intervention to help community mental health (Thompson et al., 2008), assertive outreach (Kellett et al., 2009) and surgical teams (Walsh, 1996) function more effectively. This is achieved by using CAT theory to map the dysfunctional dynamics that can occur between clients and teams and within teams (Carradice, 2004).

BASIC ASSUMPTIONS

The hallmark of CAT is active collaborative – the notion of doing therapy with a client, rather than doing therapy to a client. CAT demands a great deal from the therapist in terms of focused therapeutic activity. There are specific tasks (such as writing letters to clients that reformulate their psychological distress, producing maps of how problems originate and are maintained, and writing goodbye letters) to complete at specific points in CAT. This is done whilst consistently managing the alliance and working within the relationship using CAT theory. CAT is therefore not suited to a passive therapeutic style. The delivery of CAT occurs in three sections (1) reformulation (the development of shared and collaborative narrative and diagrammatic reformulations of the client's distress), (2) recognition (providing the client with the structure and skills to be able to notice when they are about to be or are in specified patterns) and (3) revision (enabling the client to explore exits from such patterns).

ORIGINS AND MAINTENANCE OF PROBLEMS

The CAT therapist during the reformulation phase arrives at an agreed list of target problems (TPs) with the client. These become the focus of the therapy and are the means of evaluating the effectiveness of the therapy. TPs are therefore rated at each CAT session in terms of (1) recognition (how rapidly a client can spot the problem pattern attached to the target problem) and (2) revision (how effectively a client can halt the problem or replace it with a healthier pattern). Target problems in CAT are maintained by target problem procedures (TPPs), which are the means by which the client fails to learn over time more effective ways of coping. The three TPPs in CAT are (1) dilemmas (taking up 'either–or' positions), (2) traps (the maintenance of negative beliefs via the action of vicious circles) and (3) snags (the abandonment of appropriate goals). Figure 5.24.1 contains diagrammatic examples of dilemmas, snags and traps, as they would be fed back to the client.

In the reformulation letter, TPPs are presented to the client in the first person to enable more accurate recognition. For example, the TP of 'trust in relationships' would have the following TPP as a dilemma: *'I either hold people at arm's length and they tire of this and leave or I get too close too quickly and smother the other person, causing them to leave.'* The CAT therapist needs to be continuously aware to avoid (1) corroborating and colluding with clients' target problem procedures, and (2) enacting their own target problem procedures with the client. The psychotherapy file is a specific CAT tool that is completed in the assessment stage, with client completion set as a piece of 'homework' after the first session. The psychotherapy file gives examples of snags, traps and dilemmas and asks the client to rate themselves in terms of their frequency. The file also gives instructions on self-monitoring of mood states and symptoms, and screening questions on personality integration.

In CAT psychological problems and symptoms arise from the development of inflexible, stereotyped and dysfunctional interpersonal positionings or *roles*. Such roles are typically in response to the manner in which the client was parented as a child, the presence of early neglect or trauma, and any damaging peculiarities of the early life environment. Two key aspects of early learning of roles therefore take place (1) learning of how to 'be' or 'do' the manner in which the child is currently being treated, and (2) establishment of the affect(s) arising from how the child is being treated. These positions are interactive and are known in CAT as *reciprocal roles*.

For example, a child growing up with a consistently caustic and critical mother learns how to be critical of self and/or others and also how to feel crushed and/or demoralised. In CAT this might be summarised on the diagrammatic reformulation as the reciprocal role of 'harshly critical' to 'crushed and criticised'. Both ends of each reciprocal role are available to the client as an adult. For example, in terms of the 'harshly critical' role the client might (1) be perfectionistic and intolerant of any actions which are less than faultless, (2) be critical of others that don't live up to their high standards, (3) elicit criticism from others through inflexibility, (4) choose partners who occupy the 'harshly critical' role so that they can maintain the familiar 'crushed and criticised' position, (5) be overly sensitive to criticism, and (6) perceive any feedback from people (crucially, including the CAT therapist) as an attack. For example, in terms of the 'crushed and criticised' end of the role, the client might (1) become overly hurt at any feedback that contains any aspect of negativity, (2) always feel that they are never good enough, (3) focus on negative aspects and fail to see positives, and (4) be pessimistic concerning change. This internalisation of early experience is the keystone of the analytic aspect of CAT. The constellation of typical dysfunctional and functional reciprocal roles is described and listed in Table 5.24.1.

CAT therapists reformulate the coping styles that were useful for 'survival' during childhood, and indicate how these styles remain unrevised in adult life and can become active in the therapeutic relationship. For example, if a client is used to treating people with an air of disdain by emotional distancing, then the CAT therapist would notice the client's engagement in the therapeutic relationship in such a manner and bring their awareness to this whenever it occurred. Where chronic or severe abuse has taken place the client can only develop a partial and restricted reciprocal role repertoire. Each reciprocal role operates as an independent 'self-state' separated by dissociation, creating a fragmented and disintegrated personality structure (Ryle, 1997; 2004), perhaps best characterised as borderline personality disorder. The degree of fragmentation of personality structure is measured in CAT via the Personality Structure Questionnaire (Pollock et al., 2001).

SKILLS AND STRATEGIES

A major aspect of CAT practice and philosophy is *transparency*, and this is perhaps most apparent in practice with the preparation and delivery of a narrative reformulation letter. The information for the letter is gleaned from semi-structured assessment interviewing of the client (typically over three sessions) and the content of the psychotherapy file. A typical three-session CAT assessment would cover; session 1, functional analysis and mapping of current TPPs; session 2, developmental history and

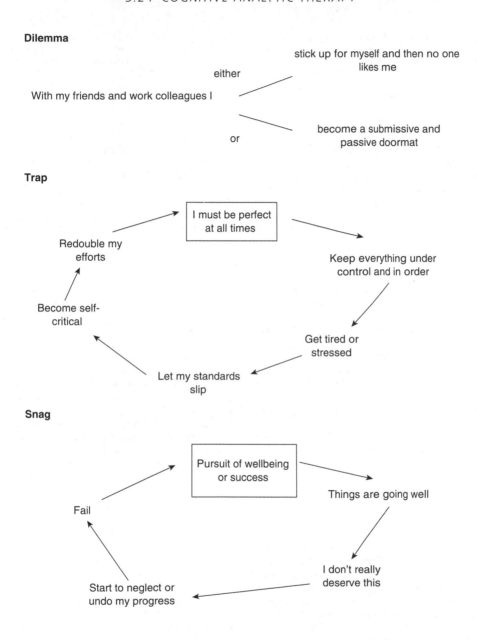

Dilemma

With my friends and work colleagues I

either → stick up for myself and then no one likes me

or → become a submissive and passive doormat

Trap

I must be perfect at all times

Keep everything under control and in order

Get tired or stressed

Let my standards slip

Become self-critical

Redouble my efforts

Snag

Pursuit of wellbeing or success

Things are going well

I don't really deserve this

Start to neglect or undo my progress

Fail

Figure 5.24.1   *Clinical examples of diagrammatic feedback of dilemma, trap and snag in CAT*

session 3, relational history. A provisional letter is typically delivered at session 4 of 16- and 24-session contracts (CAT is offered in either format according to patient need and complexity) and presents a summary and integration of the evidence collated across the first three sessions. CAT therefore adopts a rapid and transparent engagement approach to alliance formation. The client adds to and corrects the reformulation letter as a between-session 'homework' task. The completed and agreed letter therefore ensures a 'shared understanding' of the history, development and current expression of chronically endured emotional difficulties and pain.

The main purposes of the narrative reformulation in CAT are as follows:

Table 5.24.1   *Description and examples of typical malignant and positive reciprocal roles*

Malignant reciprocal roles	Positive reciprocal roles
Smothering – Dependent	Caring – Nurtured
Unreliable – Anxious and needy	Compassionate – Connected
Criticising – Undermined	Empathic – Understood
Conditionally caring – Striving	Supporting – Encouraged
Abusing – Shamed	Patient – Calm
Abandoning – Abandoned	Warm – Comfortable
Rejecting – Alone	Encouraging – Encouraged
Controlling – Crushed	Boundaried – Held
Mocking – Humiliated	Containing – Safe
Conditionally approving – Performing	Freeing – Autonomously exploring
Bullying – Passive victim	Empowering – Motivated

- to state what brought the client to therapy
- to make connections between past neglect, abuse and trauma and current patterns of functioning
- to demonstrate overt sympathy, empathy and understanding for the current plight of the client
- to identify repeated themes, roles and patterns across the client's life and relationships
- to state the typical dysfunctional roles that the client takes up in the present and to link these to past events
- to clearly state the current target problem procedures
- to highlight and predict how that client may take up certain roles in the therapeutic relationship
- to highlight and predict how the client may rely on old procedural sequences during the therapy
- to offer a realistic notion of what might be attainable during therapy and to state the identified goals of the work.

A major skill of CAT is the diagrammatic reformulation of client distress, termed the sequential diagrammatic reformulation (SDR). The function therefore of the SDR is to summarise and integrate a full description of the core reciprocal role repertoire and current target problem procedures. Figure 5.24.2 describes a simple SDR for a client with low self-esteem and poor assertiveness.

The SDR therefore serves as an explanatory and reflective model for the client; it explains why the client experiences psychological distress, and is a comprehensive means of accounting for and reflecting upon chronically endured emotional pain. The SDR is in essence a cognitive tool in CAT, but is highly informed by the analytic concept of reciprocal roles. CAT therapists have the completed SDR visible in the room at each session following completion, as a means of navigating the content of the sessions and crucially the therapeutic relationship. Therefore, if the

client appears overly resistant or avoidant within the therapeutic relationship or there appears to have been some sort of therapeutic rupture, then the SDR enables both therapist and client to reflect on the possible reciprocal roles that may have been enacted in the therapeutic relationship. SDRs therefore function as a 'route map' of the client's psychopathology and alert the therapist to the manner in which they are possibly colluding with or clashing with the client. As the exits from dysfunctional reciprocal roles and TPPs are placed on the SDR, the SDR also therefore functions as a means of remaining theoretically coherent and consistent when planning change and agreeing between-session homework tasks.

Towards the end of the 16- or 24-session contract, the client and the therapist discuss and prepare 'goodbye letters' that are exchanged at the final session. The writing of a goodbye letter from the client is an explicitly agreed piece of homework, with the client given guidance on completion, if such scaffolding is indicated and necessary. The typical guidance for the client goodbye letter is as follows:

- What have been the highlights of this piece of work for you?
- What have you learnt about yourself and others in this therapy?
- What thoughts and feelings does this particular ending bring up for you?
- What are the most important exits that you have learnt?
- How can you keep your progress going and avoid relapse?
- What do you want to say about our therapeutic relationship?
- Were there any moments in which you negotiated difficulties within the therapeutic relationship that you want to reflect on?

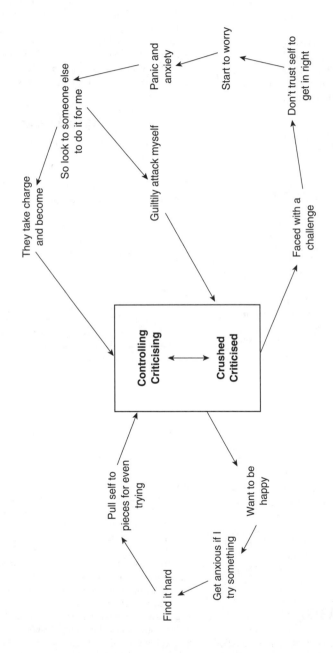

Figure 5.24.2   *Example of a sequential diagrammatic reformulation in CAT*

- What is the work that has been left uncompleted, and how can this be a new goal?
- How would you like to remember this time together?

Typically, when the alliance has been effective between client and therapist, the content of the goodbye letters is very similar. The use of goodbye letters particularly enables effective endings for clients for whom endings are an issue. This will also have been signalled early in the CAT in the reformulation letter and via the use of a reciprocal role on the SDR (typically abandoning to abandoned).

CHANGE

In CAT, change is defined as the client's ability to reflectively notice when they are in or about to enter a TPP, and then to exit that pattern by being able to behave, think or relate to self and others in a new and more compassionate, balanced, integrated and self-caring manner. This creates the new reciprocal roles that are detailed in Table 5.24.1. Change methods in CAT are catholic and frequently draw on change techniques from other therapies (e.g. facilitating the development of more balanced and rational thinking). However, such change techniques are always planned and conducted through the SDR to ensure that they are (1) driven by the formulation, (2) theoretically consistent with CAT and (3) consistent with the diagnosis.

In CAT the therapeutic relationship is a major vehicle for change, as the theory recognises that the reciprocal role repertoire of the client will often be enacted within the therapeutic relationship. CAT therapists therefore use the therapeutic relationship as a means of exploring and behaviourally experimenting with the development of new interpersonal styles and the establishment therefore of new reciprocal roles. For example, clients with an abandoning to abandoned reciprocal role will find the end of focal and short-term CAT typically painful and will experience the therapist as abandoning. The acknowledgement of this by the therapist via the SDR enables the dyad to plan for any dysfunctional enactments, such as wishing to abandon the therapy, in a much more psychologically informed manner – with this stated and summarised in the goodbye letter.

RESEARCH

When CAT was originally conceived it was designed in a manner to enable it to be 'researchable' (Ryle, 1995). The hourglass model (Salkovskis, 1995) of clinical research envisages any new therapy going through three stages of evaluation (1) initially developed experimentally or theoretically, then tested via case reports and single-case experimental designs, (2) tested in a range of efficacy RCT type studies, and (3) tested in a range of clinical effectiveness studies via field trials and service evaluations. CAT appears to be generically progressing through the hourglass model, as evidenced by the research listed below. The weakness of the CAT evidence base is that the model has not progressed through the hourglass in terms of specific diagnoses.

Stage 1 Evidence

Ryle et al.'s (1992) early case studies provided evidence for the effectiveness of CAT with patients who had had extensive previous treatment. Subsequent CAT case studies noted the therapy facilitating symptom resolution in dissociative psychosis (Graham and Thavasotby, 1995) and BPD (Kerr et al., 2003; Ryle and Beard, 1993). Pollock and Belshaw (1998) highlighted the usefulness of CAT for offenders, based on two case studies. Yeates et al. (2008) presented two case studies using CAT with clients with dysexecutive deficits following brain injury. Kellett (2005; 2007) presented single-case experimental designs of the CAT treatment of dissociative identity disorder and histrionic personality disorder, respectively. Both studies empirically indexed the impact of reformulation and the long-term effectiveness of CAT.

Stage 2 Evidence

Fosbury et al. (1997) compared CAT to diabetes specialist nurse education (DSNE) in a controlled trial of chronically poorly controlled adult type 1 diabetes. Whilst there was no statistical difference between outcomes in the two types of therapy, CAT produced a more prolonged effect with regard to diabetes management. Treasure et al. (1995) compared educational behavioural treatment and CAT for anorexia nervosa. Whilst patients receiving CAT reported significantly greater subjective improvement, there were no differences in other outcome parameters. Dare et al. (2001) compared focal psychoanalytic psychotherapy, CAT, family therapy, and treatment as usual (TAU) for anorexia nervosa. Psychoanalytic psychotherapy and family therapy were significantly superior to TAU, but CAT did show some clinical benefit. Chanen et al. (2008) compared CAT to manualised good clinical care and TAU for BPD. CAT emerged as an efficacious early intervention for BPD, producing a faster rate of improvement, with good outcomes at two year follow-up.

Stage 3 Evidence

Ryle and Golynkina (2000) studied the effectiveness of CAT with BPD in routine practice and observed a low dropout rate and found that over half of patients no longer met BPD criteria at follow-up. Marriott and Kellett (2009) compared CAT outcomes to matched clients receiving person-centred therapy or CBT for common mental health problems in routine practice and demonstrated broad similarities between therapies, with comparable rates of clinically significant improvement. Dunn et al. (1997) conducted an audit of CAT and found high adherence to treatment and a satisfactory outcome rate.

Summary

CAT is a focal, short-term, contracted and integrative form of psychotherapy that has been designed for the public sector. The hallmarks of CAT are an active, collaborative and transparent therapeutic style, in which narrative and diagrammatic reformulations facilitate initial client recognition of dysfunctional roles and procedures and then eventual revision of these via cognitive, behavioural and interpersonal exits. CAT therapists place equal emphasis on cognitive and analytic concepts and work in an explicitly integrative therapeutic manner. The therapeutic relationship in CAT is a potent vehicle for change, as the roles and procedures which disable client functioning are often apparent within the therapeutic dyad, with ruptures in the alliance repaired via use of the relationship and the SDR. CAT therapists frequently work within the therapeutic relationship and use the therapeutic relationship as a means of facilitating change. The practice of CAT requires a high degree of therapist ability in managing sessions, self-awareness, recognising collusion and unhelpful reciprocation, maintaining an open collaborative stance, agreeing homework, and maintaining the focus on the possibility for change and growth. CAT is a popular therapy in secondary care services in the NHS that has as yet untapped potential. This requires greater research support to refine the model and evaluate its efficacy and effectiveness across disorders and as an organisational development and change tool.

REFERENCES

Carradice, A. (2004) Applying cognitive analytic therapy to guide indirect working. *Reformulation*, 23: 16–23.

Chanen, A.M., Jackson, H.J., McCutcheon, L.K., Jovev, M., Dudgeon, P., Yuen, H.P., Germano, D., Nistico, H., McDougall, E., Weinstein, C., Clarkson, V. and McGorry, P.D. (2008) Early intervention for adolescents with borderline personality disorder using cognitive analytic therapy: randomised controlled trial. *British Journal of Psychiatry*, 193: 477–84.

Dare, C., Eisler, I., Russell, G., Treasure, J. and Dodge, L. (2001) Psychological therapies for adults with anorexia nervosa: randomised controlled trial of out-patient treatments. *British Journal of Psychiatry*, 178: 216–21.

Dunn, M., Golynkina, K., Ryle, A. and Watson, J.P. (1997) A repeat audit of the Cognitive Analytic Therapy Clinic at Guy's Hospital. *Psychiatric Bulletin*, 21: 165–8.

Fosbury, J., Bosley, C.M., Ryle, A., Sonksen, P.H. and Judd, S.L. (1997) A trial of cognitive analytic therapy in poorly controlled type I diabetes patients. *Diabetes Care*, 20: 959–64.

Graham, C. and Thavasotby, R. (1995) Dissociative psychosis: an atypical presentation and response to cognitive-analytic therapy. *Irish Journal of Psychological Medicine*, 12: 109–11.

Kellett, S. (2005) The treatment of dissociative identity disorder with cognitive analytic therapy: experimental evidence of sudden gains. *Journal of Trauma and Dissociation*, 6: 55–81.

Kellett, S. (2007) A time series evaluation of the treatment of histrionic personality disorder with cognitive analytic therapy. *Psychology and Psychotherapy: Theory, Research and Practice*, 80: 389–405.

Kellett, S., Wilbram, M. and Davis, D. (2009) Using CAT as a consultation tool: qualitative and quantitative results from a controlled study. Paper presented at 3rd International CAT Conference, Bath, UK.

Kerr, I.B., Birkett, P.B.L. and Chanen, A. (2003) Clinical and service implications of a cognitive analytic therapy (CAT) model of psychosis. *Australia and New Zealand Journal of Psychiatry*, 37: 515–23.

Marriott, M. and Kellett, S. (2009) Evaluating a cognitive analytic therapy service: practice-based outcomes and comparisons with person-centred and cognitive-behavioural therapies. *Psychology and Psychotherapy: Theory, Research and Practice*, 82: 57–72.

Pollock, P. and Belshaw, T. (1998) Cognitive analytic therapy for offenders. *Journal of Forensic Psychiatry*, 9: 629–42.

Pollock, P.H., Broadbent, M., Clarke, S., Dorrian, A.J. and Ryle, A. (2001) The Personality Structure Questionnaire (PSQ): a measure of the multiple self-states model of identity disturbance in cognitive analytic therapy. *Clinical Psychology and Psychotherapy*, 8: 59–72.

Ryle, A. (1978) A common language for the psychotherapies? *British Journal of Psychiatry*, 132: 585–94.

Ryle, A. (1995) *Cognitive-Analytic Therapy: Developments in Theory and Practice*. Chichester: Wiley.

Ryle, A. (1997) *Cognitive Analytic Therapy and Borderline Personality Disorder: The Model and the Method*. Chichester: Wiley.

Ryle, A. (2004) The contribution of cognitive analytic therapy to the treatment of borderline personality disorder. *Journal of Personality Disorders*, 18: 3–35.

Ryle, A. and Beard, H. (1993) The integrative effect of reformulation: cognitive analytic therapy with a patient with borderline personality disorder. *British Journal of Medical Psychology*, 66: 249–58.

Ryle, A. and Golynkina, K. (2000) Effectiveness of time-limited cognitive analytic therapy of borderline personality disorder: factors associated with outcome. *British Journal of Medical Psychology*, 73: 197–210.

Ryle, A., Spencer, J. and Yawetz, C. (1992) When less is more or at least enough: two case examples of 16-session cognitive analytic therapy *British Journal of Psychotherapy*, 8: 401–12.

Salkovskis, P.M. (1995) Demonstrating specific effects in cognitive and behavioural therapy. In M. Aveline and D.A. Shapiro (eds), *Research Foundations for Psychotherapy Research* (pp. 191–228). Chichester: Wiley.

Thompson, A.R., Donnison, J., Warnock-Parkes, E., Turpin, G., Turner, J. and Kerr, I.B. (2008) Multidisciplinary community mental health team staff's experience of a 'skills level' training course in cognitive analytic therapy. *International Journal of Mental Health Nursing*, 17: 131–7.

Treasure, J., Todd, G., Brolly, M., Tiller, J., Nehmed, A. and Denman, F. (1995) A pilot study of a randomised trial of cognitive analytic therapy vs educational behavioral therapy for adult anorexia nervosa. *Behaviour Research and Therapy*, 33: 363–7.

Walsh, S. (1996) Adapting cognitive analytic therapy to make sense of psychologically harmful work environments. *British Journal of Medical Psychology*, 69: 3–20.

Yeates, G., Hamill, M., Sutton, L., Psaila, K., Gracey, F., Mohamed, S. and O'Dell, J. (2008) Dysexecutive problems and interpersonal relating following frontal brain injury: reformulation and compensation in cognitive analytic therapy. *Neuro-Psychoanalysis*, 10: 43–58.

Emotional Freedom Techniques

(Gary H. Craig, 1940–)

JOHN BULLOUGH

BRIEF HISTORY

Emotional freedom techniques (EFT) is the popular name for a therapeutic approach that combines the well-proven techniques of exposure and cognitive restructuring with a crucial new component, namely simultaneous somatic stimulation. In EFT, this somatic stimulation takes the form of tapping certain electromagnetically sensitive points on the body while at the same time focusing conscious attention on the issue presented for therapy. The procedure is unconventional, yet can produce empirically demonstrated improvements with profound psychological and/or physiological consequences in a relatively small number of sessions, sometimes a single session (Church et al., 2009). It also often works where other approaches do not.

EFT was developed in the 1990s by Stanford engineer Gary Craig following a lifelong interest in techniques for building self-confidence and emotional health. EFT is derived from thought field therapy (TFT), developed in the 1980s by psychologist Roger Callahan. Craig not only simplified TFT, making it more accessible to the layperson, but also offered a free instruction manual and 140 hours of low-cost video recordings of client sessions and instruction via the internet over a 15 year period. This led to a rapid rise in the approach's popular use worldwide and the accumulation of a large body of anecdotal evidence (thousands of cases) documenting the effectiveness of the approach, all made freely available on Craig's website.

EFT, TFT and many other similar techniques are classified under the general heading of energy psychology, which in turn forms part of the broader field of energy medicine (Eden, 2008). In common with traditional Chinese and Hindu/yogic medical practices (and indeed the medical practices of many ancient cultures closer to nature than we in the West), such techniques treat the mind/body as an 'energy system', and somatic stimulation is generally focused on points on the skin (acupoints) which coincide with the endpoints of acupuncture or acupressure 'meridians'. EFT thus has its roots in medical practices dating back more than 5000 years.

Despite growing acceptance of acupuncture by the Western medical establishment and the World Health Organization, mainstream practitioners initially tended to treat anecdotal reports of EFT's efficacy with some suspicion, not least because the quoted levels of success were difficult to believe when seen through the lens of conventional medical and psychotherapeutic experience. However, in recent years, as more reliable data from controlled trials have begun to accumulate (see below), this picture is rapidly changing. And since EFT is non-invasive and appears to have no known side effects in a clinical setting, increasing numbers of physicians, psychologists and psychotherapists worldwide are now beginning to incorporate and integrate techniques such as EFT into their work (Feinstein et al., 2006), often with startling improvements in the speed, efficacy and durability of treatment. In common with acupuncture, potential applications include virtually the whole range of psychological and physiological disorders, including the amelioration/alleviation of chronic and acute pain and the symptoms and side effects of illness and its associated medical treatment. EFT is also used to good effect in sports and business by reducing the anxiety that impedes performance.

BASIC ASSUMPTIONS

EFT is based not on any particular theoretical model or set of assumptions concerning the human psyche, but rather on the serendipitous discovery of the efficacy of certain treatments. The principles and assumptions of EFT are thus highly empirical, based on observation and experimentation.

ORIGIN AND MAINTENANCE OF PROBLEMS

Implicit in EFT's procedures and protocols is the assumption that the principal cause of psychological/physiological distress is life trauma, particularly in early childhood. Such trauma may result from one or more major life shocks, or represent the cumulative effect of many apparently less dramatic events (Scaer, 2005). A key factor in this process is the *meaning* consciously or subconsciously attributed to the life events, and this in turn is governed by the individual's genetic predisposition and prior life experience. What is traumatic for one person may not be for another, and the associated negative effects may be quickly discharged or may persist for a whole lifetime if left untreated.

Many authors have described the biological and psychological mechanisms of such trauma and conditioning. The interested reader is referred to Scaer (2005) for a detailed description of the full spectrum of trauma from the perspective of a neurologist/traumatologist, and to LeDoux (2002) for an explanation of how memories are formed, encoded with emotion and conditioned through repetition.

Whilst none of this relies on the existence of an 'energy system' *per se*, in recent years the latest developments in quantum physics and the implications of the 'new biology', particularly the emerging fields of epigenetics ('the study of the molecular mechanisms by which environment controls gene activity': Lipton, 2005: 26), psychoneuroimmunology (the interplay between psychological processes and the body's nervous and immune systems) and neuroplasticity (the ability of the brain to change with experience throughout life), have begun to build a bridge between Eastern philosophy and mainstream Western science (Lipton, 2005; Church, 2007; Braden, 2007; Sheldrake, 2009; Edwards, 2010). Church (2007: 107–49) in particular makes a compelling case for the central role of the piezoelectric

qualities of connective tissue and collagen, allowing a close correlation with ancient Eastern models.

CHANGE

Almost anyone can use EFT to good effect as a self-help tool. But for complex issues, or to approach the 86–90 per cent success rates in only six sessions recorded in recent trials of EFT for war veterans suffering from PTSD (Church et al., 2010), it is usually more productive to work with a skilled practitioner. Following successful treatment with EFT, the mind/body is normally able to hold the previously troubling thought (or be in the previously troubling circumstance) without the unwanted emotional response.

Rather than trying to diagnose which acupoints to stimulate and in what order (as in TFT), EFT works on the principle of overhauling *all* points over and over again (each application or 'round' taking less than a minute) until the emotional charge is seen to subside. Craig (2008) refers to this as the '100% overhaul principle'.

Although psychotherapeutic factors such as insight, positive expectation and the quality of the relationship can play a role in therapeutic change, particularly when working with complex issues requiring multiple sessions, the often startling success of EFT in comparison to conventional talk-based therapies is attributed principally to the direct electro-biochemical consequences of somatic stimulation when combined with appropriate imaginal exposure and cognitive restructuring. These effects include rapid changes in brain electro-biochemistry, as measured by MRI, SPECT and PET scans and EEG brain wave monitors, and equally rapid changes in the expression of stress-related genes, particularly 'immediate early genes', as confirmed by gene assays (which can be used to assess the instantaneous expression of any combination of genes in the human body during any given activity). Feinstein and Church (2010) hypothesise that treatments such as EFT can serve to reduce or eliminate exaggerated limbic response to innocuous stimuli, correct distortions in learning and memory, help restore balance to the autonomic nervous system (including the promotion of cardiac coherence), balance the expression of stress and anti-ageing hormones, and boost the functioning of the immune system. Feinstein and Church go on to speculate that careful measurement of factors such as these, particularly via gene assays, could offer 'a new framework for assessing the effects of psychotherapy' (2010: 11).

Concerning the mechanism of change in EFT, Feinstein and Church speculate that:

the exposure increases arousal while the simultaneous acupoint stimulation reduces arousal. These conflicting inputs are resolved, assuming nothing aversive occurs in the environment, with arousal being reduced. The triggering cue then becomes associated with a neutral emotional state. This leads to conditioned fear pathways being overridden ... or depotentiated ... eliminating long-standing signal transmissions between neurons. (2010: 19)

As to *how* the acupoint stimulation reduces arousal, Church (2007) describes the creation of a piezo-electric charge within the body's network of connective tissue which in turn precipitates a cascade of neurological and physiological effects. In particular, research indicates that manual stimulation of acupoints:

> produces opioids, serotonin and gamma-aminobutyric acid (GABA) and regulates cortisol. These neurochemical changes reduce pain, slow the heart rate, decrease anxiety, shut off the fight/flight/freeze response, regulate the autonomic nervous system and create a sense of calm. This relaxation response reciprocally inhibits anxiety and creates a rapid desensitization to traumatic stimuli. (Lane, 2009: 31)

For a comprehensive review of the research literature concerning the mechanisms thought to be involved, the interested reader is referred to a paper by Feinstein (2010).

Although the above mechanisms of change and their associated measurable physiological effects have been well documented in the treatment of anxiety-related disorders, the electro-biochemical and epigenetic mechanisms of change for the many other apparently successful applications of EFT (particularly related to physical illness) appear as yet to be less well understood.

SKILLS AND STRATEGIES

The 'basic recipe' for EFT is described by Craig (2008), noting that practitioners should master this simplest form of EFT before moving on to more complex variations. In essence, the process begins with a number of repetitions of an acceptance statement such as: '*Even though I feel so angry with the driver of the car, I deeply love and accept myself anyway*', followed by reminder phrases such as '*this anger*', all accompanied by tapping on appropriate acupoints. Progress on any particular issue is monitored using a Likert-type scale (from 0 minimum to 10 maximum, referred to as subjective units of distress, SUD) as the work progresses, and it is normal to test the results with a suitable challenge (for example, presentation of a real spider in the case of spider phobia) to ensure that the emotional charge has really declined to zero. Amended wording is used as SUD levels reduce.

Although in its simplest form EFT may be applied mechanically with good success by almost anyone with minimal training (even a young child), in the hands of a qualified and experienced practitioner it can become much more sophisticated. Central to high success rates with complex issues are the ability and willingness of the practitioner to allow intuition to guide the words used, accepting that the healing comes *through* you, not *by* you. The practitioner should also be focused on excellence of process, working mindfully rather than being invested in any particular outcome. In EFT parlance, this is referred to as 'getting yourself out of the way' and generally involves a lifetime practice of personal development by the practitioner to ensure that neither counter-transference nor a practitioner need to fix the client interferes negatively with intuition or the therapeutic process.

It has generally been found much more effective to apply EFT to specific events than to generalities. For example, instead of working with a thought such as '*My mother was bad to me*', it is generally more effective to work with specific memories such as '*The time my mother screamed at me in front of my friends at my sixth birthday party*'. Allied to this, a client's unwanted thought, feeling, emotion or behaviour may be simple in nature, but equally it may have numerous aspects associated with it. For example, a phobia may simply involve the look of spiders, or it may be much more complex, involving traumatic memories of specific incidents as well as a wide variety of emotions, thoughts and physiological reactions. In EFT it is important to treat each of these aspects individually, often helping the client to become mindfully aware of physiological responses to the emotion as well as cognitive interpretations, and to facilitate the use of these as a potential bridge to earlier memories or pictures. Whereas the positive effects of EFT are generally found to be permanent, if the unwanted emotion, thought, feeling or behaviour does return, it is usually because one or more aspects have been neglected in the treatment.

Imaginal exposure is a key element of the work, often using a mental movie of the traumatic event or feared experience followed by positive visualisation once the negative emotional charge has been released. However, in contrast to some other approaches involving exposure, it is possible with EFT to 'creep up' slowly on the presenting issue, dealing with and neutralising each subaspect or event or cognition step by step, thus limiting the risk of emotional flooding or abreaction. On the rare occasions when this does occur, continuous tapping without words usually restores equilibrium in short order. Persistence is the watchword with EFT, together with a high level of practitioner congruence with the process. Interestingly, healthy client scepticism seems to have no effect on efficacy.

Cognitive restructuring is another key element. Skilled practitioners are at pains not to lead or direct their clients, but aim instead to guide and facilitate as the work progresses, often using humour or gentle provocation to encourage alternative interpretations and meanings to emerge in the dialogue. When properly done, such reframes generally hold firm (or 'stick') over time, provided the emotional charge of the original aspect(s) has been dissolved with EFT.

When EFT does not seem to be working, it is often because a mechanism such as 'psychological reversal' is interfering with the process. Although the *basic recipe* includes a routine treatment for this, it is sometimes necessary to look for issues that may be standing in the way of progress such as secondary gain, or issues of safety, identity, deserving or possibility, and apply EFT directly to these first. Alternatively, the presenting issue may sometimes be a smokescreen for a subconsciously held core issue that is the real cause of the client's emotional discomfort. It can take considerable detective work to discover, 'creep up on' and subsequently apply EFT to this maintaining core issue, which may for example be an old suppressed memory, trauma or gestalt.

In addition to the procedures described in such detail by EFT's originator Gary Craig, other skilled practitioners are continually adding to the power of EFT with new ideas and procedures. Notable among these are the 'choices method', 'matrix reimprinting', 'EFT imagineering' and 'deep state repatterning'. Details of these and numerous other important innovations in EFT as described by their originators are now available in one volume (Bruner and Bullough, 2009).

Clearly the potential for integrating EFT with other psychotherapeutic modalities is considerable, particularly CBT and EMDR which already contain similar elements. In a review of TFT and its derivatives, Mollon concludes that combining acupoint tapping with talk therapy 'vastly enhances the effectiveness of psychotherapy' (2007: 127).

RESEARCH EVIDENCE

Studies of EFT-related techniques have been ongoing for a number of years now, and the number of randomised controlled trials with peer review is steadily growing. Based on a review of existing trials, Feinstein states that in his opinion:

energy psychology has reached the minimum threshold for being designated as an evidence-based treatment, with one form [EFT] having met the APA Division 12 criteria as a 'probably efficacious treatment' for specific phobias; another [TAT] for maintaining weight loss The limited scientific evidence, combined with extensive clinical reports, suggests that energy psychology holds promise as a rapid and potent treatment for a range of psychological conditions. (2008: 199)

In a more recent review of clinical trials, Feinstein and Church (2010) conclude that progress with EFT in anxiety disorders can be significantly faster than with other psychotherapeutic approaches (including CBT), and may be more durable when reassessed at follow-up. Comorbid conditions such as depression and insomnia can also show marked improvement even though not worked on specifically, and EFT appears to offer much reduced risk of retraumatisation in cases of PTSD.

Based on the results and analysis presented in this article, further scientific research is clearly warranted across a wide range of presenting issues in the interests of bringing the potential of EFT to the attention of a wider proportion of health professionals worldwide.

ACKNOWLEDGEMENTS

I am grateful to Dawson Church, David Feinstein and other colleagues for their valuable comments and suggestions.

REFERENCES

Braden, G. (2007) *The Divine Matrix: Bridging Time, Space, Miracles and Belief*. New York: Hay.

Bruner, P. and Bullough, J. (eds) (2009) *EFT and Beyond: Cutting Edge Techniques for Personal Transformation*. Saffron Walden: Energy.

Church, D. (2007) *The Genie in Your Genes*. Santa Rosa: Elite.

Church, D., Piña, O., Reategui, C. and Brooks, A.J. (2009) Single session reduction of the intensity of traumatic memories in abused adolescents: a randomised controlled trial. Paper presented at the 11th Annual EP Conference, Toronto, Canada, 17 October. Submitted for publication.

Church, D., Hawk, C., Brooks, A., Toukolehto, O., Wren, M., Dinter, I. and Stein, P. (2010)

Psychological trauma in veterans using EFT (emotional freedom techniques): a randomized controlled trial. Poster session at the 31st Annual Meeting and Scientific Sessions of the Society of Behavioral Medicine, Seattle, 7–10 April 2010. www.stressproject.org/documents/ptsdfinal1.pdf, 4 September 2010.

Craig, G. (2008) *The EFT Manual*. Santa Rosa, CA: Energy Psychology Press.

Eden, D. (2008) *Energy Medicine*. London: Piatkus.

Edwards, G. (2010) *Conscious Medicine*. London: Piatkus.

Feinstein, D. (2008) Energy psychology: a review of the preliminary evidence. *Psychotherapy: Theory, Research, Practice, Training*, 45 (2): 199–213.

Feinstein, D. (2010) Rapid treatment of PTSD: why psychological exposure with acupoint tapping may be effective. *Psychotherapy: Theory, Research, Practice, Training*, 47 (3): 385–402.

Feinstein, D. and Church, D. (2010) Modulating gene expression through psychotherapy: the contribution of non-invasive somatic interventions. *Review of General Psychology*, 14 (4): 283–95.

Feinstein, D., Eden, D. and Craig, G. (2006) *The Healing Power of EFT and Energy Psychology*. London: Piatkus.

Lane, J. (2009) The neurochemistry of counter-conditioning: acupressure desensitization in psychotherapy. *Energy Psychology: Theory, Research, Treatment*, 1 (1): 31–44.

LeDoux, J. (2002) *Synaptic Self: How Our Brains Become Who We Are*. New York: Penguin.

Lipton, B. (2005) *The Biology of Belief*. Santa Rosa, CA: Elite.

Mollon, P. (2007) Thought field therapy and its derivatives: rapid relief of mental health problems through tapping on the body. *Primary Care and Community Psychiatry*, 12: 123–7.

Scaer, R. (2005) *The Trauma Spectrum: Hidden Wounds and Human Resiliency*. New York: Norton.

Sheldrake, R. (2009) *A New Science of Life: The Hypothesis of Formative Causation* (3rd edn). London: Icon.

Interpersonal Psychotherapy

ELIZABETH ROBINSON AND GRAHAM DYSON

Interpersonal psychotherapy (IPT) is a manualised brief therapy originally developed for the treatment of depression. In this chapter we present an overview of the approach for depression, and the research evidence in a clinical setting.

BRIEF HISTORY

The interpersonal approach has a long history dating from the work of Adolf Meyer (1957) and Harry Stack Sullivan (1953). Meyer suggested that mental disorders developed as a result of an individual's attempt to adapt to his or her environment. Sullivan proposed that psychiatric evaluation should involve the scientific study of people and the interactions between people, that is, 'interpersonal relations'.

A group of researchers from the New Haven Boston Collaborative Depression Research Project tested variations of interpersonal psychotherapy in several clinical trials (Klerman et al., 1974; Weissman et al., 1979) and developed IPT in its current form. In 1984, an IPT manual was published to facilitate the application of IPT in both clinical and research settings (Klerman et al., 1984).

More recently, Ravitz et al. (2008) looked in depth at the processes underlying the success of IPT as a treatment for depression. They formulated that IPT can be viewed as an integration of attachment theory (Bowlby, 1969), exploring humans' innate tendency to seek attachment relationships, and contemporary interpersonal theory (Kiesler, 1996),

exploring covert aspects of interpersonal situations that mediate overt behaviours.

BASIC ASSUMPTIONS

IPT is a brief structured psychotherapy with a dual focus: to reduce depressive symptoms and to deal with associated social and interpersonal problems. Sixteen 50-minute sessions are provided weekly and involve three phases of treatment: an *initial*, a *middle* and an *end*.

The interpersonal approach focuses its observation and therapeutic intervention on the primary social group, notably the individual's most significant relationship(s) such as partner, close friends, family members and significant wider social networks. Interpersonal psychotherapy makes links between depressed mood and disrupted interpersonal events.

IPT assumes a medical model of depression (Weissman et al., 2007) and deliberately uses the concept of the 'sick role' (Parsons, 1951) as a therapeutic intervention in order to temporarily excuse the client from overwhelming social obligations, which in turn may hamper progress. It helps to ease the guilt or self-blame often associated with depression and reinforces what treatment is needed, as well as helping to provide hope for the future. The therapist explores collaboratively with the client what they can do to bring about a remission. This includes making time for treatment, exploring if work or social activities should be reduced during their initial recovery, and seeking help from their social network.

ORIGIN AND MAINTENANCE OF PROBLEMS

Connections between interpersonal events and the potential impact on the client's mood are explored during the *initial phase* of IPT. During sessions 1–4 the therapist provides an overview of the therapy and sets a framework for treatment. The IPT therapist starts with a comprehensive history, including a timeline focusing on episodes of depression, while simultaneously exploring associated interpersonal events. Particular attention is paid to the current episode of depression. Using standard diagnostic criteria (APA, 2000) a diagnosis of depression is given to the client and the therapist reinforces that their condition is treatable.

A baseline measurement of the severity of the client's depression is assessed by the therapist at the start of treatment. The IPT manual recommends the Hamilton Depression Rating Scale (Hamilton, 1960), although other robust measures of depression can be utilised. The initial assessment provides the therapist with a clear understanding of the incidence, frequency and intensity of the specific depressive symptoms. In fact, the information obtained during the assessment will have given a clear indication of the onset of each particular symptom and the course of the current depressive episode. From this, the therapist can identify collaboratively with the client their own particular symptom signature. The depressive symptoms are then evaluated weekly to monitor progress.

As part of the initial phase the therapist completes an interpersonal inventory, which provides an in-depth exploration of current relationships. The inventory is used to identify helpful relationships, which may provide a positive resource to build on, as well as negative relationships, which may serve as an emotional drain and contribute to the current depression. Detailed information gained about each relationship might include: frequency of contact, level of satisfaction, expectations, disagreements or disharmony, and what the client may like to change. Connections are then made between the onset of the depressive episode and changes in relationships or interpersonal events, which could include: bereavement, redundancy, retirement, promotion, having a baby, leaving home, or marital disharmony.

At the end of the initial phase the therapist offers an interpersonal formulation (Markowitz and Schwartz, 1997). Drawing upon the information obtained from the history, timeline and interpersonal inventory, a link is made between the onset and maintenance of the current depressive episode and the client's social and interpersonal situation. This is a collaborative approach whereby the therapist seeks to reach agreement with the client regarding the possible focal area. The four potential focal areas in IPT are: role transition, role dispute, interpersonal sensitivities and complicated bereavement. When the therapist and client have identified one or a maximum of two linked focal areas, achievable goals linked to the focal areas are agreed and a treatment contract is set.

CHANGE

The *middle phase* of IPT, which usually occurs from sessions 5 to 12, forms the main focus of treatment. Having identified one or two focal areas with the client during formulation at the end of the initial phase, the therapist implements specific treatment approaches for the particular focal area. The IPT manual sets out clearly defined strategies for each focal area (Klerman et al., 1984). The aim for the therapist is to work with the client to reduce depressive symptoms caused and maintained by interpersonal problems.

Role Dispute

Disputes are common and may manifest in various ways. The client may be in open dispute or disagreement with an individual or group of individuals which could include friends, family or work colleagues. Non-reciprocal role expectations may contribute to the role dispute and associated depression.

Role Transition

This is a broad area and could involve any change in role such as promotion, demotion, retirement or redundancy, separation, divorce, moving house, getting married, having a baby, or receiving a diagnosis of a medical illness. It is important to identify the existing role which is a struggle to the client and how adapting to that particular role leads to or maintains the current depressive episode.

Complicated Bereavement

The client has experienced the death of a loved one and for whatever reason has not been able to grieve for this loss. Typically, the therapist will identify with the client how they may not have effectively worked through the mourning process and how this has led to ongoing symptoms of depression.

Interpersonal Deficit

There are some individuals who have limited or no satisfying or rewarding interpersonal relationships, which leads to social isolation and depression. Alternatively, a client who has relationships that are transient, superficial or disruptive can also experience social isolation and depression.

Once the IPT therapist has collaboratively identified and agreed the focal area, he or she will work through the strategies highlighted in the IPT manual, with the aim of reducing depressive symptoms and increasing interpersonal functioning. Specific goals which were linked to the focal area will be worked towards during this process.

SKILLS AND STRATEGIES

Where there is a role dispute, the IPT therapist employs a number of strategies to explore in more detail the disputed relationship with the client, for example, identifying problems with faulty communication, non-reciprocal role expectations, and issues or disagreements within the relationship. Helping the client to consider alternative options for communication, expressing their needs, or evaluating expectations and considering compromises are beneficial at this stage. Role play and communication analysis are used to aid this process. There may be cases where the dispute cannot be resolved, as the relationship has reached an impasse and the client may therefore seek to end the relationship.

In the case of a role transition, the IPT therapist makes the link between the current depressive symptoms and the client's struggle to adapt to a specific role. The aim of IPT is to help the client adapt and view this role in a more satisfying and acceptable way. This in turn will reduce depressive symptoms and improve interpersonal functioning. The therapist will explore circumstances regarding the role change and encourage the client to mourn the loss of the old role, realistically reviewing positive and negative aspects of the role. The therapist helps the client adapt to the new role by aiding recognition of positive and negative aspects of the new role.

Where there is a death of a loved one, which has led to a complicated bereavement, the therapist links the death to a limited ability or opportunity to grieve. Realistic evaluation of the relationship with the deceased, reconstructing events leading up to the death, exploring support from others in their social network, and looking at new activities, are all strategies used with a complicated bereavement. As with any bereavement, complicated or otherwise, emotions associated with grief and loss are very intense and can feel overwhelming and raw. The pace of work may feel slower during this process as the therapist models tolerating painful affect. The aim of IPT is to help the client get started with mourning the loss of a loved one and to use social support to help with their loss and reduce depressive symptoms.

The fourth focal area identifies that a significant lack of sustained quality relationships leads to the onset and maintenance of depressive symptoms. This is often due to reduced social skills and/or confidence in social situations. The aim is to help the client develop social skills in order to build increasingly meaningful relationships. The IPT therapist will focus on previous and current relationships to identify with the client potential areas for development. Again, role play and communication analysis are useful during this phase. Encouragement and support also play a large part in allowing the client to increase interpersonal interaction.

The *end phase* of IPT is provided over the last four weeks of treatment and continues alongside the middle phase strategies. The therapist discusses explicitly the end of therapy and explores how the client may feel. This includes identifying any concerns about terminating treatment and dealing with normal feelings of sadness. A review of progress throughout therapy is made with the client, allowing an opportunity to recognise and consolidate therapeutic gains and look at ways as to how they can be sustained.

Depression runs a high risk of recurrence (APA, 2000) and IPT is proactive in managing this risk. Psycho-education regarding depression is provided, with emphasis on how it can be prevented through the interpersonal gains covered in therapy. This may run concurrently with advice on the need for prophylactic antidepressant medication, depending on the level of risk. The IPT therapist provides advice on how to deal with a potential subsequent episode, ensuring the client is confident about how to access health services. Identification of the client's symptom signature at the start of the initial phase of treatment provides information to recognise early warning signs of a further episode.

RESEARCH EVIDENCE

A brief summary of research evidence on IPT for depression is presented below.

IPT Across all Age Groups

Most of the IPT studies have focused on treatment outcome, with demonstrated efficacy in reducing depressive symptoms in adolescents, adults and older adult depressed clients (Van Schaik et al., 2007; Brunstein-Klomek et al., 2007; Weismann et al., 2007). IPT has been demonstrated as an effective treatment in both moderate and severe depression (NICE, 2010). IPT alone or with medication has been shown to significantly increase the survival time of both highly recurrent depressed adults (Kupfer et al., 1992) and older adults (Miller et al., 2003).

IPT and Medication

Researchers have shown that IPT can improve compliance with pharmacotherapy (Wolfson et al., 1997; Miller et al., 2001). Recent studies have also shown some benefits for chronic or treatment-resistant depression using antidepressant medication in conjunction with IPT (Schramm et al., 2007; Murray et al., 2010).

Types of Depression

IPT has been shown to be effective in treating recurrent depression. Recovery rates are similar in adult and older adult clients, although the latter group tend to demonstrate a slower response to treatment and relapse earlier (Reynolds et al., 1996). Frank et al. (2000) demonstrated how a staged approach to treatment using medication and IPT yielded positive benefits for depressed women with recurrent depression.

IPT has demonstrated efficacy in postpartum and antepartum depression and has been well tolerated (O'Hara et al., 2000; Spinelli and Endicott, 2003). Furthermore, it has also been found to improve social adjustment (O'Hara et al., 2000) and has helped to improve mother and infant interaction in postpartum women (Spinelli and Endicott, 2003).

Delivery of Interpersonal Psychotherapy

IPT has been successfully delivered by telephone (Miller and Weissman, 2002) and within a group setting (MacKenzie and Grabovac, 2001; Zlotnick et al., 2001). Group IPT (Wilfey et al., 2000) may have the added benefits of being cost-effective and provides an ideal forum for social support and to develop social skills.

REFERENCES

APA (2000) *Diagnostic and Statistical Manual of Mental Disorders* (4th edn text rev.). Washington, DC: American Psychiatric Association.

Bowlby, J. (1969) *Attachment and Loss*. Vol. 1: *Attachment*. London: Hogarth.

Brunstein-Klomek, A., Zalsman, G. and Mufson, L. (2007) Interpersonal psychotherapy for depressed adolescents (IPT–A). *Israel Journal of Psychiatry & Related Sciences*, 44 (1): 40–6.

Frank, E., Grochocinski, V.J., Spanier, C.A., Buysse, D.J., Cherry, C.R., Houck, P.R., Stapf, D.M. and Kupfer, D.J. (2000) Interpersonal psychotherapy and antidepressant medication: evaluation of a sequential treatment strategy in women with recurrent major depression. *Journal of Clinical Psychology*, 61 (1): 51–7.

Hamilton, M. (1960) A rating scale of depression. *Journal of Neurology, Neurosurgery and Psychiatry*, 23: 56–62.

Kiesler, D.J. (1996) *Contemporary Interpersonal Theory and Research: Personality, Psychopathology and Psychotherapy*. New York: Wiley.

Klerman, G.L., Dimascio, A., Weissman, M., Prusoff, B. and Paykel, E.S. (1974) Treatment of depression by drugs and psychotherapy. *American Journal of Psychiatry*, 131 (2): 186–91.

Klerman, G.L., Weissman, M.M., Rounsaville, B.J. and Chevron, E. (1984) *Interpersonal Psychotherapy for Depression*. New York: Basic.

Kupfer, D.J., Frank, E., Perel, J.M., Cornes, C., Mallinger, A.G., Thase, M.E., McEachran, A.B. and Grochocinski, V.J. (1992) Five-year outcome for maintenance therapies in recurrent depression. *Archives of General Psychiatry*, 49: 769–73.

MacKenzie, K.R. and Grabovac, A.D. (2001) Interpersonal psychotherapy group (IPT–G) for depression. *Journal of Psychiatric Research*, 10 (1): 46–51.

Markowitz, J.C. and Schwartz, H.A. (1997) Case formulation in interpersonal psychotherapy of depression. In ELSTD (ed.), *Handbook of Psychotherapy Case Formulation* (pp. 192–222). New York: Guilford.

Meyer, A. (1957) *Psychobiology: A Science of Man*. Springfield, MA: Thomas.

Miller, M.D., Cornes, C., Frank, E., Ehrenpreis, L., Silberman, R., Schilernitzauer, M.A., Tracey, B., Richards, V., Wolfson, L., Zaltman, J., Bensasi, S. and Reynolds, III C.F. (2001) Interpersonal psychotherapy for late-life depression past, present and future. *Journal of Psychotherapy Practice and Research*, 10: 231–8.

Miller, M.D., Frank, E., Cornes, C., Houck, P.R. and Reynolds, III C.F. (2003) The value of maintenance interpersonal psychotherapy (IPT) in older adults with different IPT foci. *American Journal of Geriatric Psychiatry*, 11 (1): 97–102.

Miller, L. and Weissman, M. (2002) Interpersonal psychotherapy delivered over the telephone to recurrent depressives: a pilot study. *Depression and Anxiety*, 16: 114–17.

Murray, G., Michalak, E.E., Axler, A., Yaxley, D., Hayashi, B., Westrin, A., Ogrodniczuk, J.S., Tam, E.M., Yatham, L.N. and Lam, R.W. (2010) Relief of chronic or resistant depression (Re-ChORD): a pragmatic, randomized, open-treatment trial of an integrative program intervention for chronic depression. *Journal of Affective Disorders*, 123 (1–3): 243–8.

NICE (2010) *The Treatment and Management of Depression in Adults* (updated edn). National Clinical Practice Guideline 90. National Collaborating Centre for Mental Health. Commissioned by the National Institute for Health and Clinical Excellence. London: British Psychological Society and The Royal College of Psychiatrists.

O'Hara, M.W., Stuart, S., Gorman, L.L. and Wenzel, A. (2000) Efficacy of interpersonal psychotherapy for postpartum depression. *Archives of General Psychiatry*, 57: 1039–45.

Parsons, T. (1951) Illness and the role of the physician: a sociological perspective. *American Journal of Orthopsychiatry*, 21: 452–60.

Ravitz, P., Maunder, R. and McBride, C. (2008) Attachment, contemporary interpersonal theory and IPT: an integration of theoretical, clinical, and empirical perspectives. *Journal of Contemporary Psychotherapy*, 38 (1): 11–21.

Reynolds, C.F., Frank, E., Perel, J.M., Mazumdar, S., Dew, M.A., Begley, A., Houck, P.R., Hall, M., Mulsant, B., Shear, M.K., Miller, M.D., Cornes, C. and Kupfer, D.J. (1996) High relapse rates after discontinuation of adjunctive medication in elderly persons with recurrent major depression. *American Journal of Psychiatry*, 152: 1418–22.

Schramm, E., van Calker, D., Dykierek, P. et al. (2007) An intensive treatment programme of interpersonal psychotherapy plus pharmacotherapy for depressed inpatients: acute versus long term results. *American Journal of Psychiatry*, 164: 768–77.

Spinelli, M.G. and Endicott, J. (2003) Controlled clinical trial of interpersonal psychotherapy versus parenting education program for depressed pregnant women. *American Journal of Psychiatry*, 160 (3): 555–62.

Sullivan, H.N. (1953) *The Interpersonal Theory of Psychiatry*. New York: Norton.

Van Schaik, A., Van Marwijk, H., Beekman, A.T., De Haan, M. and Van Dyck, R. (2007) Interpersonal psychotherapy (IPT) for late-life depression in general practice: uptake and satisfaction by patients, therapists and physicians. *BMC Family Practice*, 13: 8–52.

Weissman, M.M., Prusoff, B.A., Dimasccio, A., Neu, C., Goklaney, M. and Klerman, G.L. (1979) The efficacy of drugs and psychotherapy in the treatment of acute depressive episodes. *American Journal of Psychiatry*, 136 (4B): 555–8.

Weissman, M.M., Markowitz, J.C. and Klerman, G. (2007) *A Clinician's Quick Guide to Interpersonal Psychotherapy*. New York: Oxford University Press.

Wilfey, D.E., Mackenzie, K.R., Welch, R.R., Ayres, V.E. and Weismann, M.M. (2000) *Interpersonal Psychotherapy for Groups*. New York: Basic.

Wolfson, L., Miller, M., Houch, P., Ehrenpreis, L., Stack, J.A., Frank, E., Cornes, C., Mazumdar, S., Kupfer, D.J. and Reynolds, III C.F. (1997) Focus of interpersonal psychotherapy (IPT) I. Depressed elders: clinical and outcome correlates in a combined IPT/nortriptyline protocol. *Psychotherapy Research*, 7 (1): 45–55.

Zlotnick, C., Johnson, S.L., Miller, I.W., Pearlstein, T. and Howard, M. (2001) Postpartum depression in women receiving public assistance: pilot study of an interpersonal therapy oriented group intervention. *American Journal of Psychiatry*, 158 (4): 638–40.

Multimodal Therapy

(Arnold A. Lazarus, 1932–)

STEPHEN PALMER

BRIEF HISTORY

During the 1950s Arnold Lazarus undertook his formal clinical training in South Africa. The main focus of his training was underpinned by Rogerian, Freudian and Sullivanian theories and methods. He attended seminars by Joseph Wolpe about conditioning therapies and reciprocal inhibition and in London he learned about the Adlerian orientation. He believed that no one system of therapy could provide a complete understanding of either human development or the human condition. In 1958 he became the first psychologist to use the terms 'behavior therapist' and 'behavior therapy' in an academic article.

Lazarus conducted follow-up inquiries into clients who had received behaviour therapy and found that many had relapsed. However, when clients had used both behaviour and cognitive techniques more durable results were obtained. In the early 1970s he started advocating a broad but systematic range of cognitive-behavioural techniques, and his follow-up inquiries indicated the importance of breadth if therapeutic gains were to be maintained. This led to the development of multimodal therapy, which places emphasis on seven discrete but interactive dimensions or modalities which encompass all aspects of human personality.

BASIC ASSUMPTIONS

Individuals are essentially biological organisms (neurophysiological and biochemical entities) who behave (act and react), emote (experience affective responses), sense (respond to olfactory, tactile, gustatory, visual and auditory stimuli), imagine (conjure up sights, sounds and other events in the mind's eye), think (hold beliefs, opinions, attitudes and values) and interact with one another (tolerate, enjoy or suffer in various interpersonal relationships). These dimensions of personality are usually known by the acronym BASIC ID, derived from the first letters of each modality, namely Behaviour, Affect, Sensations, Images, Cognitions, Interpersonal and Drugs/biology.

Modalities may interact with each other: for example, a negative image or cognition may trigger a negative emotion. Modalities may exist in a state of reciprocal transaction and flux, connected by complex chains of behaviour and other psychophysiological processes.

The multimodal approach rests on the assumption that unless the seven modalities are assessed, therapy is likely to overlook significant concerns. Clients are usually troubled by a multitude of specific problems which should be dealt with by a similar multitude of specific interventions or techniques.

Individuals have different thresholds for stress tolerance, frustration, pain, and external and internal stimuli in the form of sound, light, touch, smell and taste. Psychological interventions can be used to modify these thresholds but often the genetic predisposition has an overriding influence in the final analysis.

Individuals tend to prefer some of the BASIC ID modalities to others. They are referred to as 'cognitive reactors' or 'imagery reactors' or 'sensory reactors', depending upon which modality they favour.

Human personalities stem from interplay among social learning and conditioning, physical environment and genetic endowment. Therefore each client is unique and may need a personalized therapy.

Individuals usually benefit from a psycho-educational approach to help them deal with or manage their problems.

Although the therapist and client are equal in their humanity (the principle of parity), the therapist may be more skilled in certain areas in which the client has particular deficits. It is not automatically assumed that clients know how to deal with their problems or have the requisite skills, and the therapist may need to model or teach the client various skills and strategies.

No one theory has all the answers when helping clients. Multimodal therapy is underpinned by a broad social and cognitive learning theory, while drawing on group and communications theory and general systems theory. However, multimodal therapists can choose not to apply these theories obsessively to each client.

Technically speaking, 'multimodal therapy' *per se* does not exist; multimodal counsellors and psychotherapists, as technical eclectics, draw from as many other approaches or systems as necessary. To be accurate, there is a multimodal assessment format and a multimodal framework or orientation.

ORIGIN AND MAINTENANCE OF PROBLEMS

Human problems are multilevelled and multilayered. Few problems have a single cause or simple solution.

According to Lazarus, psychological disturbances are the product of one or more of the following:

- conflicting or ambivalent feelings or reactions
- misinformation
- missing information which includes ignorance, *naïveté* and skills deficits
- maladaptive habits including conditioned emotional reactions
- issues pertaining to low self-esteem and lack of self-acceptance
- inflexible and rigid thinking styles and attitudes
- unhelpful core schemas
- tendency to cognitively or imaginally 'awfulize' events and situations
- unhelpful beliefs maintaining a low frustration tolerance (e.g. 'I can't stand it-itis')
- information-processing errors (cognitive distortions)
- interpersonal inquietude such as misplaced affection, undue dependency or excessive antipathy
- biological dysfunctions.

Individuals avoid or defend against discomfort, pain, or negative emotions such as shame, guilt, depression and anxiety. This is known as 'defensive reactions' and should not be confused with psychodynamic concepts.

The principal learning factors which are responsible for behavioural problems and disorders are conditioned associations (operant and respondent); modelling, identification, and other vicarious processes; and idiosyncratic perceptions.

Non-conscious processes are often involved in learning. Stimuli that can influence feelings, conscious thoughts/images and behaviours may go unrecognized by the person concerned.

Interactions between two or more people involve communications and meta-communications (i.e. communication about their communication). Communication can disintegrate when individuals are unable to stand back from the transaction, thereby failing to examine the content and process of ongoing relationships.

Individuals may have a genetic predisposition or vulnerability to certain disorders or distress.

CHANGE

A good therapeutic relationship, a constructive working alliance and adequate rapport are usually necessary but often insufficient for effective therapy. The therapist–client relationship is considered as the soil that enables the strategies and techniques to take root. The experienced multimodal therapist hopes to offer a lot more by assessing and treating the client's BASIC ID, endeavouring to 'leave no stone (or modality) unturned'.

Usually an active-directive approach to therapy is taken. However, this depends upon the issues being discussed and upon the client concerned.

The process of change commences with the counsellor explaining the client's problems in terms of the seven modalities, that is the BASIC ID, and then negotiating a counselling programme which uses specific techniques or interventions for each particular problem. This is usually undertaken in the first or second session and the completed modality profile is developed (see Table 5.27.1).

Multimodal therapists take Paul's mandate very seriously: '*What* treatment, by *whom*, is most effective for *this* individual with *that* specific problem and under *which* set of circumstances?' (1967: 111). In addition *relationships of choice* are also considered.

Positive, neutral or negative change in any one modality is likely to affect functioning in other modalities.

The approach is psycho-educational and the therapist ensures that the client understands why

Table 5.27.1   *John's full modality profile (or BASIC ID chart)*

Modality	Problem	Proposed programme/treatment
Behaviour	Eats/walks fast, always in a rush, hostile, competitive; indicative of type A behaviour	Discuss advantages of slowing down; disadvantages of rushing and being hostile; teach relaxation exercise; dispute self-defeating beliefs
	Avoidance of giving presentations	Exposure programme; teach necessary skills; dispute self-defeating beliefs
	Accident proneness	Discuss advantages of slowing down
Affect	Anxious when giving presentations; guilt when work targets not achieved	Anxiety management; dispute self-defeating thinking
	Frequent angry outbursts at work	Anger management; dispute irrational beliefs
Sensation	Tension in shoulders	Self-message; muscle relaxation exercise
	Palpitations	Anxiety management, e.g. breathing relaxation technique, dispute catastrophic thinking
	Frequent headaches	Relaxation exercise and bio-feedback
	Sleeping difficulties	Relaxation or self-hypnosis tape for bedtime use; behavioural retraining; possibly reduce caffeine intake
Imagery	Negative images of not performing well	Coping imagery focusing on giving adequate presentations
	Images of losing control	Coping imagery of dealing with difficult work situations and with presentations; 'step-up' imagery (Palmer and Dryden, 1995)
	Poor self-image	Positive imagery
Cognition	I must perform well otherwise it will be awful and I couldn't stand it	Dispute self-defeating and irrational beliefs; coping statements; cognitive restructuring; ABCDE paradigm
	I must be in control	
	Significant others should recognize my work	(REBT) bibliotherapy
	If I fail then I am a total failure	Coping imagery (Palmer and Dryden, 1995)
Interpersonal	Passive/aggressive in relationships; manipulative tendencies at work; always puts self first; few supportive friends	Assertiveness training
		Discuss pros and cons of behaviour
		Friendship training (Palmer and Dryden, 1995)
		Improve sleeping and reassess; refer to GP
Drugs/biology	Feeling inexplicably tired	Refer to GP; relaxation exercises
	Taking aspirins for headaches	
	Consumes 10 cups of coffee a day	Discuss benefits of reducing caffeine intake
	Poor nutrition and little exercise	Nutrition and exercise programme

Source: Palmer (1997: 159–60)

each technique or intervention is being used. Bibliotherapy is frequently used to help the client understand the methods applied and also to correct misinformation and supply missing information. A self-help coaching book provides details regarding the majority of multimodal techniques and how to develop a modality profile (Palmer et al., 2003).

The approach is technically eclectic as it uses techniques and methods taken from many different psychological theories and systems, without necessarily being concerned with the validity of their theoretical principles.

Multimodal therapists often see themselves in a coach/trainer–trainee or teacher–student relationship as opposed to a doctor–patient relationship, thereby encouraging self-change rather than dependency.

Flexible interpersonal styles of the therapist which match client needs can reduce dropout rates and help the therapeutic relationship. This approach is known as being an 'authentic chameleon'. The term 'bespoke therapy' has been used to describe the custom-made emphasis of the approach.

Lazarus summed up briefly the main hypothesized ingredients of change when using the multimodal approach:

- *behaviour*: positive reinforcement; negative reinforcement; punishment; counter-conditioning; extinction
- *affect*: admitting and accepting feelings; abreaction
- *sensation*: tension release; sensory pleasuring
- *imagery*: coping images; changes in self-image

- *cognition*: greater awareness; cognitive restructuring; modification of unhelpful core schema and information-processing errors
- *interpersonal*: non-judgemental acceptance; modelling; dispersing unhealthy collusions
- *drugs/biology*: better nutrition and exercise; substance abuse cessation; psychotropic medication when indicated.

SKILLS AND STRATEGIES

Therapists should practise humility; Lazarus stresses that therapists should know their limitations and other therapists' strengths. The therapist tries to ascertain whether a judicious referral to another therapist may be necessary to ensure that the client's needs are met. In addition, a referral to other health practitioners such as medical doctors or psychiatrists may be necessary if the client presents problems of an organic or a psychiatric nature.

Therapists take a flexible interpersonal approach with each client to maximize therapeutic outcome and reduce dropout rates.

Techniques and interventions are applied systematically, based on client qualities, therapist qualities, therapist skills, therapeutic alliance and technique specificity. For example, research data will suggest various techniques that could be applied for a specific problem although the counsellor may only be proficient in using a number of them; while the client may only be able to tolerate one or two of the suggested interventions due to having a low tolerance to pain or frustration. Finally, a poor therapeutic alliance may increase the chances of attrition (dropout) occurring if a high-anxiety-provoking technique is applied.

A wide range of cognitive and behavioural techniques is used in multimodal therapy. In addition, techniques are taken from other therapies such as gestalt therapy (e.g. the empty chair). Table 5.27.2 illustrates the main techniques used in therapy.

A 15-page Multimodal Life History Inventory (MLHI: Lazarus and Lazarus, 1991) is often but not invariably used to elicit information about each of the client's modalities, general historical information, and expectations about counselling and the counsellor. The client usually completes the MLHI at home between sessions 1 and 2. If the client is not up to undertaking the task due to inadequate skills or severe depression, the therapist can use the MLHI questions as a guide in the session (Palmer and Dryden, 1995).

Second-order BASIC ID is a modality profile which focuses solely on the different aspects of a resistant problem. It is undertaken when the interventions or techniques applied to help a specific problem do not appear to have resolved it.

To obtain more clinical information and also general goals for therapy, a structural profile is drawn up (Lazarus, 1989). This can be derived from the MLHI or by asking clients to rate subjectively, on a scale of 1 to 7, how they perceive themselves in relation to the seven modalities. The counsellor can ask a number of different questions that focus on the seven modalities:

- *Behaviour*: How much of a 'doer' are you?
- *Affect*: How emotional are you?
- *Sensation*: How 'tuned in' are you to your bodily sensations?
- *Imagery*: How imaginative are you?
- *Cognition*: How much of a 'thinker' are you?
- *Interpersonal*: How much of a 'social being' are you?
- *Drugs/biology*: To what extent are you health conscious?

Then in the session the therapist can illustrate these scores graphically by representing them in the form of a bar chart on paper (see Figure 5.27.1). Then clients are asked in what way they would like to change their profiles during the course of therapy. Once again the client is asked to rate subjectively each modality on a score from 1 to 7 (see Figure 5.27.2).

Tracking is another procedure regularly used in multimodal therapy. Here the 'firing order' of the different modalities is noted for a specific problem. Therapy interventions are linked to the sequence of the firing order of the modalities. This is particularly useful for dealing with panic attacks.

Multimodal therapists deliberately use a 'bridging' procedure to initially 'key into' a client's preferred modality, before gently exploring a modality (e.g. affect/emotion) that the client may be intentionally or unintentionally avoiding (Lazarus, 1997).

RESEARCH EVIDENCE

The majority of techniques used are taken from behaviour and cognitive therapy. These approaches, and more recently the techniques that are applied to specific problems and disorders, have been shown to be more effective than other forms of therapy.

Controlled outcome studies have supported the benefits of multimodal assessment and counselling programmes. In addition, Kwee's (1984) outcome study on 84 hospitalized clients suffering from phobias or obsessive compulsive disorders resulted in substantial recoveries and durable follow-ups.

The application of the multimodal approach to coaching is a new area for research (Palmer, 2008; Palmer and Gyllensten, 2008). Research is currently being undertaken into multimodal health coaching (see Rose et al., 2010).

Table 5.27.2 *Frequently used techniques in multimodal therapy and training*

Modality	Techniques and interventions
Behaviour	Behaviour rehearsal Empty chair Exposure programme Fixed role therapy Modelling Paradoxical intention Psychodrama Reinforcement programmes Response prevention/cost Risk-taking exercises Self-monitoring and recording Stimulus control Shame attacking
Affect	Anger expression/management Anxiety management Feeling identification
Sensation	Bio-feedback Hypnosis Meditation Relaxation training Sensate focus training Threshold training
Imagery	Anti-future shock imagery Associated imagery Aversive imagery Compassion-focused imagery Coping imagery Goal-focused imagery Implosion and imaginal exposure Motivation imagery Positive imagery Rational emotive imagery Time projection imagery Trauma-focused imagery
Cognition	Bibliotherapy Challenging faulty inferences Cognitive rehearsal Coping statements Correcting misconceptions Disputing irrational beliefs Focusing Positive self-statements Problem-solving training Rational proselytizing Self-acceptance training Thought stopping
Interpersonal	Assertion training Communication training Contracting Fixed role therapy Friendship/intimacy training Graded sexual approaches Paradoxical intentions Role-play Social skills training
Drugs/biology	Alcohol reduction programme Lifestyle changes, e.g. exercise, nutrition Referral to physicians or other specialists Stop smoking programme Weight reduction and maintenance programme

Source: adapted from Palmer (1996: 55–6)

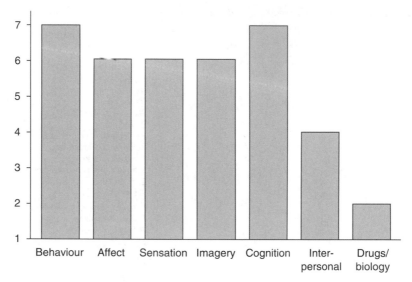

Figure 5.27.1   *Natalies's structural profile*

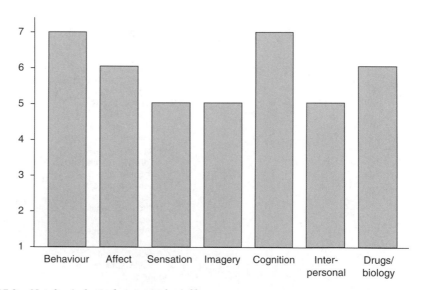

Figure 5.27.2   *Natalies's desired structural profile*

REFERENCES

Kwee, M.G.T. (1984) *Klinische Multimodale Gegragtstherapie*. Lisse: Swets and Zeitlinger.

Lazarus, A.A. (1989) *The Practice of Multimodal Therapy: Systematic, Comprehensive and Effective Psychotherapy*. Baltimore: Johns Hopkins University Press.

Lazarus, A.A. (1997) *Brief but Comprehensive Psychotherapy: The Multimodal Way*. New York: Springer.

Lazarus, A.A. and Lazarus, C.N. (1991) *Multimodal Life History Inventory*. Champaign, IL: Research.

Palmer, S. (1996) The multimodal approach: theory, assessment, techniques and interventions. In S. Palmer and W. Dryden (eds),

Stress Management and Counselling: Theory, Practice, Research and Methodology. London: Cassell.

Palmer, S. (1997) Modality assessment. In S. Palmer and G. McMahon (eds), *Client Assessment*. London: Sage.

Palmer, S. (2008) Multimodal coaching and its application to workplace, life and health coaching. *The Coaching Psychologist*, 4 (1): 21–9.

Palmer, S. and Dryden, W. (1995) *Counselling for Stress Problems*. London: Sage.

Palmer, S. and Gyllensten, K. (2008) How cognitive behavioural, rational emotive behavioural or multimodal coaching could prevent mental health problems, enhance performance and reduce work related stress. *The Journal of Rational Emotive and Cognitive Behavioural Therapy*, 26 (1): 38–52.

Palmer, S., Cooper, C. and Thomas, K. (2003) *Creating a Balance: Managing Stress*. London: British Library.

Paul, G.L. (1967) Strategy of outcome research in psychotherapy. *Journal of Consulting Psychology*, 331: 109–18.

Rose, S., Palmer, S. and O'Riordan, S. (2010) A HEALTHY development from the multimodal approach to coaching. *The Coaching Psychologist*, 6 (2): 88–96.

Pluralistic Counselling and Psychotherapy

JOHN MCLEOD AND MICK COOPER

BRIEF HISTORY

The emergence of counselling and psychotherapy in the middle of the twentieth century was associated with a proliferation of different and competing therapeutic approaches. Such diversity did much to foster creativity and growth within the field. However, the development of 'schools' has also tended to lead to an unproductive 'schoolism', with adherents of particular approaches becoming entrenched in the 'rightness' of their model, and blind to ways of working that might be more helpful for particular clients.

As a response to this, therapists from the 1930s onwards have attempted to develop more integrative and eclectic practices. Yet these, too, can end up as relatively discrete and fixed models of therapy (e.g. Egan's skilled helper model). Moreover, in most of these approaches, the decision as to which methods or understandings to use tends to remain primarily with the therapist.

Pluralistic therapy, as developed by Cooper and McLeod (2007; 2011), is an attempt to construct a framework for therapy that can overcome some of these limitations, while drawing on the most valuable features of these previous models. It is not one specific therapeutic practice, but a set of principles and meta-strategies that can be adopted by therapists from a wide range of backgrounds.

Pluralistic counselling and psychotherapy were developed at the beginning of the twenty-first century, and reflect some of the key cultural developments in this era. Pluralistic therapy reflects a postmodern suspicion of 'grand narratives' such as all-encompassing psychological theories, and a preference instead for 'local' solutions. It builds on the increasing tendency for people to be informed consumers of health care, whose use of the internet and other media enables them to develop their own ideas about what ails them and how they might be helped. Also relevant is a high level of global or multicultural sensitivity, that takes the form of acknowledgement of the potential value of healing practices from other cultures. Finally, there is an appreciation of the value of non-hierarchical social networking and knowledge-building structures, such as the various wiki systems.

BASIC ASSUMPTIONS

Pluralism is a term that is widely used in politics, theology and philosophy, and refers to the idea that, in the arena of social life, any substantial problem admits to a multiplicity of reasonable and plausible answers. A pluralistic stance implies that a person is willing to accept the validity of other answers to a question, even while adopting a specific position (e.g. atheist, Christian or Islamic). Pluralism is associated with a strong moral and ethical commitment to the intrinsic value of connection and dialogue between people – active curiosity and interest rather than disengaged tolerance. In relation to models of therapy integration, the concept of pluralism represents a form of theoretical integration that is not constructed around any specific set of psychological concepts, but instead is held together by a philosophical and ethical valuing of diversity. Theoretical integration on the basis of any psychological concept always has the effect of privileging that idea while downplaying other psychological ideas. By contrast, the concept of pluralism opens a conceptual space in which all psychological theories (and other ideas, from sociology, human ecology and other disciplines) can coexist.

Within the domain of counselling and psychotherapy, the application of pluralism takes the form of an acceptance that there are many factors that contribute to the problems for which people seek help, and many mechanisms of change through which therapeutic help can be delivered. Moreover, it holds the view that a plurality of perspectives – the client's as well as the therapist's – should inform the direction of the therapeutic work. If a client comes to see a counsellor or therapist with questions such as 'What is wrong with me?' or 'How can I get better?', it is likely that *both* of them will have some ideas about how to answer these questions. In addition, there are other potential answers available within the wider culture that may be valuable to this client and therapist but which they have not yet discovered. Pluralistic counselling and psychotherapy involve the therapist finding ways to enable his or her client to select from all of these possibilities, in order to address their specific problem.

Pluralistic counselling and psychotherapy are based on further assumptions about the characteristics of clients and therapists. Clients are viewed as active agents, with important personal strengths, who are engaged in using whatever tools and resources are available to them in order to construct a more satisfying life (Bohart and Tallmann, 1999). In responding to the needs of their clients, pluralistic therapists are required to possess a solid foundation of counselling skills and self-awareness, an overview and critical appreciation of a range of therapy approaches, and in-depth practical knowledge of at least one approach (e.g. person centred, psychodynamic, CBT). Pluralistic therapists are expected not to be omnicompetent, but to be open-minded and curious about all therapy ideas and methods, and to be committed to a process of ongoing lifelong learning in which they continue to incorporate ideas and methods from different therapy approaches into their practice.

ORIGIN AND MAINTENANCE OF PROBLEMS

Within the counselling and psychotherapy literature, and the wider stock of cultural knowledge, there exists a multiplicity of ideas and theories around the origins of personal, emotional and behavioural problems. A pluralistic stance implies that any of these accounts, or a combination of them, may be valid in any particular case. For example, if a person seeks counselling because of fearfulness around meeting other people, it may be that this pattern is due to previous trauma (being humiliated in front of peers at school), lack of social skills (growing up in a reclusive family), biological factors (being too tall or too fat to be accepted by others), and so on. A therapist who works pluralistically seeks to keep an open mind about the possible origins of their clients' problems. As a means of keeping the options open, in respect of the nature of a client's problems, some pluralistic therapists use the very general term 'problems in living' as their starting point. The process of pluralistic therapy involves the therapist and client being willing to share their ideas about the origins of the client's problems, and to work together to evaluate and test out which explanations seem most relevant.

Just as there exists a multiplicity of possible origins for the problems presented by clients, so there are a multiplicity of factors that contribute to the maintenance of these problems. The role of the client in maintaining problems is of particular relevance because it is assumed that he or she would have done all they could to resolve their problems in advance of seeking help from a therapist. It may be that the coping strategies that the client has adopted have been ineffective, have not been pursued vigorously enough, or require to be modified. It may be that the client has an absence of appropriate strategies, or that there are strengths and resources that are potentially available to him or her but are being disregarded for some reason. By inviting discussion with the client around the issue of how their problems are being maintained, and their sense of what might help, a pluralistic therapist seeks to identify ways of making a difference that are grounded in the client's worldview and life experience, rather than externally imposed.

CHANGE

From a pluralistic perspective, there are many processes of change that may be relevant within therapy and may be activated through the work that the client and therapist do together. The counselling and psychotherapy theoretical literature includes descriptions of a wide range of different change processes: insight, altering patterns of behaviour through reinforcement, acquiring new social or cognitive skills, developing new relationships, working through the impact of trauma and loss, and so on. There are further change processes that may be meaningful to some clients, such as beginning or ending medication, participation in exercise or spiritual activity, and making changes to life situation (e.g. leaving home, starting a new job). It is likely that several of these change processes will occur at the same time, no matter which therapy intervention is used. For example, a standard CBT intervention such as training the client in relaxation skills as a means of counteracting anxiety may also be interpreted by the client in terms of greater connectedness in – and trust of – a therapist who cares about them, and/or as a shift in self-definition ('Yes, I can take responsibility for doing something different in my life'). Ultimately, the aim of pluralistic therapy is to facilitate the client in engaging with the change processes or mechanisms that make a difference for them, in terms of allowing them to move on in their life. Pluralistic therapists therefore need to discipline themselves to retain an open mind about the pathways of change that may be right for an individual client, and also the pace, location and extent of change. Some clients can get what they need in one session, while others require a lot of time. Some clients can be observed undergoing moments of insight or catharsis in the therapy room, while for others the change happens in everyday life and the therapist is someone who is used as a source of support and an aid to reflection.

SKILLS AND STRATEGIES

The core therapeutic skills and strategies that are used by pluralistic practitioners are drawn from established theories of counselling/psychotherapy and models of counselling skills. For example, the skill of empathic reflection is well defined within person-centred counselling, and the strategy of using a case formulation to structure planned cognitive and behavioural change is similarly well defined within the CBT literature. However, working pluralistically requires the development of a number of meta-strategies that are necessary in order to facilitate the effective combination of ideas and methods from different therapy approaches. These are as follows.

Capacity to Deconstruct Existing Therapy Approaches

To function as a pluralistic therapist it is essential to appreciate that existing therapy approaches consist of assemblages of ideas and practices that reflect the personal interests of the founders of the approach and the socio-historical context in which the approach was first developed. Often, there is no fundamental or necessary logical coherence to any of the mainstream therapy approaches; they each comprise bundles of ideas and practices that can be dismantled and used separately. For example, empathic reflection is a core skill within person-centred counselling but can be used by any therapist without necessarily buying into other person-centred ideas such as the notion of an actualising tendency. This kind of conceptual flexibility is essential if pluralistic therapy is to be tailored to the specific preferences of particular clients.

Enabling Clients to Participate Actively in Therapy

It is unrealistic to expect that clients will enter therapy with clearly formed ideas about what will help them, and how they want to work. Nevertheless, from a pluralistic perspective it is assumed that the client will have spent a lifetime being a 'self-therapist', and will have various ideas and preferences around what has been useful (or otherwise) for them. In addition, when presented with different options, most clients are drawn to some possibilities and intuitively know that other possibilities are not appropriate for them. A key skill in pluralistic therapy involves being able to assist the client to be more aware of their own preferences, and the broader 'therapy menu' that is potentially available to them. Strategies for achieving this outcome include:

- providing the client with information about how they can be involved in the therapy process, during intake or assessment, and through written materials, and reinforcing these inputs by regularly checking out with the client that they have read and understood the material
- taking opportunities within therapy to engage in conversations with clients around key choice points in the therapy process, such as their goals, the immediate tasks that need to be accomplished in order to achieve these goals, and the methods or activities that might help them in making progress.

Routine Monitoring of What Works

If therapy is to be constructed around what works for each particular client, it is important to know about whether the way that the therapist and client are working together is producing satisfactory results. This can be carried out through inviting the client on a weekly basis to complete an outcome scale such as one of the CORE questionnaires, or a problem rating scale in which they evaluate the severity of problems that they have defined in their own language. Other instruments that can be used to monitor whether the client is getting what they want from therapy include the Helpful Aspects of Therapy scale, measures of the client's perception of therapeutic alliance, or the Therapy Personalisation Form. Further information on these techniques can be found in Cooper and McLeod (2011). The aim is to use such instruments as 'conversational tools' that supplement and extend what emerges from review sessions and the ongoing feedback that clients offer to their therapists. An assumption that informs the use of these tools is that some clients may lack a language for conveying their experience of therapy, or may feel inhibited in passing comment by the professional status of their counsellor. These instruments therefore function to give clients a voice, and to externalise their evaluations of the therapy in a form in which client and therapist can reflect together on what it implies.

RESEARCH EVIDENCE

The pluralistic approach to therapy was specifically developed as a framework that could incorporate the widest possible range of findings on what clients might find helpful in therapy. Furthermore, a growing body of evidence indicates that attuning therapeutic interventions to clients' individual wants *does* lead to improved outcomes. For instance, in a study by Berg et al. (2008), client preferences for particular types of change process were assessed before they entered therapy. At the end of treatment, those who reported that they had received the kinds of therapeutic experiences that they preferred were found to have benefited more from therapy than those whose preferences had not been fulfilled. In a review of relevant research literature, Swift and Callahan (2009) found that clients whose preferences were reflected in the therapy they received were less likely to drop out of therapy.

REFERENCES

Berg, A.L., Sandahl, C. and Clinton, D. (2008) The relationship of treatment preferences and experiences to outcome in generalized anxiety disorder (GAD). *Psychology and Psychotherapy: Theory, Research and Practice*, 81: 247–59.

Bohart, A.C. and Tallman, K. (1999) *How Clients Make Therapy Work: The Process of Active Self-Healing*. Washington: APA.

Cooper, M. and McLeod, J. (2007) A pluralistic framework for counselling and psychotherapy: implications for research. *Counselling and Psychotherapy Research*, 7 (3): 135–43.

Cooper, M. and McLeod, J. (2011) *Pluralistic Counselling and Psychotherapy*. London: Sage.

Swift, J.K. and Callahan, J.L. (2009) The impact of client treatment preferences on outcome: a meta-analysis. *Journal of Clinical Psychology*, 65 (4): 368–81.

The Skilled Helper Model

(Gerard Egan, 1930–)

VAL WOSKET

BRIEF HISTORY

Since it first emerged on the counselling scene in the mid 1970s, the skilled helper model developed by Professor Gerard Egan of Loyola University, Chicago has been continuously revised and expanded. The model has evolved from Egan's early writings on interpersonal skills in group and individual contexts and has moved through presenting a sequential process model of individual counselling to the development of change agent models and skills within the broader field of organisational change. In this chapter we will consider the model as it applies to the field of one-to-one counselling.

Early and enduring influences on the skilled helper model include the work of Rogers and Carkhuff, which provide its person-centred values and principles. The model's cognitive-behavioural elements are closely informed by figures such as Bandura, Beck, Ellis, Seligman and Strong. While a three-stage map of the helping process (see below) has remained a constant during the various editions of the model, there have been a number of significant adjustments that take account of emerging research and developments in integrative practice. For instance the third edition, published in 1986, evidenced a shift from problem management to opportunity development; and in 1990 the fourth edition carried an increased emphasis on challenge and action, as running through all stages of the counselling process. In 1994 the fifth edition engaged more forcefully with debates about eclecticism and integrationism. In this text the fundamentally flexible, non-linear characteristics of the model and the importance of addressing shadow-side elements of the helping process were highlighted.

In the book's seventh edition Egan incorporated a positive psychology (Carr, 2004) approach to helping, with more emphasis on clients' resourcefulness, resilience and capacity for constructive change. In the eighth edition there was an evident shift in focus from the problem management process to a greater emphasis on relationship and dialogue. Additionally, more attention was given to issues of difference and diversity. This theme was further developed in a booklet 'Skilled Helping around the World' written to accompany *Essentials of Skilled Helping* (Egan, 2006) – a more compact version of the skilled helper model written to appeal particularly to para-professional helpers. The model is now in its ninth edition (Egan, 2010) and continues to build on a positive psychology, solution-focused theme. Greater attention is given to the collaborative nature of the helping relationship; for instance, empathy is viewed as a process of mutuality involving both client and counsellor. Additional research elements include discussion of debates around evidence-based practice.

The skilled helper model has been expanded and updated for counsellors working in the UK by Wosket (2006) in consultation with Gerard Egan. Wosket's approach illustrates how the model can be applied in a variety of clinical settings and emphasises how it can be used as an integrative framework for developing a personally authentic style of counselling. The model is 'dejargoned' and translated from the American idiom into terminology more commonly used by therapists (and their clients) in the UK. How the model can be applied to supervision and training is discussed and a number of guidelines and exercises are included which can be used in training. This version of the skilled helper model also endeavours to address some of the perceived omissions in the conceptualisation and development of the model through a consideration of how it can evolve and adapt to fit a range of client issues and counselling contexts. These include working long term with complex issues such as trauma and abuse; adopting a more relational approach that takes account of the client's past inter- and intra-personal history; and working with unconscious and dissociated processes.

Stated in simple terms, the three stages of the skilled helper model are concerned with:

1 problem definition
2 goal setting
3 action planning.

Egan has used different terminology in the various editions of *The Skilled Helper* to describe the three stages. In the current edition these are as follows:

- Stage 1: 'What's going on?'
- Stage 2: 'What solutions make sense to me?'
- Stage 3: 'How do I get what I need or want?'

Underpinning the three stages of the model is an emphasis on action: 'How do I make it all happen?'

It is sometimes debated whether the model, as currently practised, is integrative or eclectic, as such divisions are not always clear cut (Wosket, 2006). The model can be thought of as integrative in that it provides an overarching framework for the helping process, yet it does not have an over-reliance on theory. It is derivative in that it draws on person-centred values and principles and cognitive-behavioural approaches. Egan himself has described the model as atheoretical – meaning it moves beyond theory in searching for a framework or map which is built on pragmatism (what has been shown to work) rather than on theoretical constructions.

The model is designed to provide a versatile and adaptable framework for developing a personal style of working that takes proper account of different client populations, issues and contexts (Wosket, 2006). At its best, it is a shared map that helps clients participate more fully in the helping process. The stages and steps of the model become orientation devices that keep the helping process on course and prevent it deteriorating into a random set of events.

BASIC ASSUMPTIONS

As noted above, Egan has explicitly adopted a positive psychology approach to helping in more recent editions of *The Skilled Helper*. This involves taking the view that managing problems is more a proactive than a reactive process. As such, problem management is considered to provide opportunities for clients to learn effective, life-enhancing skills.

Two core functions of the skilled helper model are: (1) providing a 'geographical' map for the terrain of helping, and (2) outlining the tasks of helping and how these tasks interrelate. Egan describes the three principal goals of helping encompassed by the model as follows:

> GOAL 1: Life-Enhancing Outcomes. Help clients manage their problems in living more effectively and developing unused or underused resources and opportunities more fully.
>
> GOAL 2: Learning Self-Help. Help clients become better at helping themselves in their everyday lives.
>
> GOAL 3: Prevention Mentality. Help clients develop an action-oriented prevention mentality in their lives.
> (2010: 7–10)

In the service of these three goals for the helping process, counsellors need to be both skill learners and skill trainers.

The key values that underpin the culture of helping as understood by Egan are client empowerment and the Rogerian core qualities of respect, genuineness and empathy. These core values suffuse the communication skills that drive the model. While Rogers considered empathy to be a facilitative condition and one of the core qualities of the helping relationship, Egan views empathy both as 'a basic value that informs and drives all helping behavior' and as an interpersonal communication skill (2010: 44). As a value, empathy places a requirement on the counsellor to understand clients as fully as possible in three particular ways:

1 understanding the client from his or her point of view
2 understanding the client in and through the context (the social setting) of her or his life
3 understanding the dissonance wherever it appears to exist between the client's point of view and current reality.

Client empowerment is linked to the three goals of helping outlined above. According to Egan, helpers do not empower clients, 'rather they help clients discover, acquire, develop, and use the power they have at the service of constructive life change' (2010: 54). It is recognised that counsellors are, by virtue of their role and status, in a more powerful position than those who seek their help. On the negative side, helpers can misuse their power wherever they encourage deference or dependency and when they oppress others. More positively, helpers can use the power inherent in their position within a social-influence process that can enable clients to become more effective at managing their own problems. A positive psychology approach encourages helpers not to see their clients as victims even 'if victimising circumstances have diminished a client's degree of freedom' but instead to 'work with the freedom that is left' (Egan, 2010: 55). Egan therefore suggests that helpers who use the model think of themselves as consultants and facilitators who provide as much or as little assistance as the client needs in order to better manage the problem situations in their lives. Minimum intervention is considered to be the optimum way of working.

ORIGIN AND MAINTENANCE OF PROBLEMS

Egan's view of the person comprises a 'deficit' rather than a pathology model. The problems that clients bring to counselling arise, in most part, from their difficulties in harnessing energy and resources (both internal and external) to realise their best potential. Egan considers that unused human potential constitutes a more serious social problem than psychological or emotional disorders because it is more widespread.

Egan identifies the healthy and functional personality as someone who has the necessary knowledge, skills and resources to successfully complete developmental tasks and to handle upsets and crises when they occur. The individual's ability to accomplish life's challenges will be affected by external factors in the environment and may be reduced by these. Such limiting factors might include economic and social constraints, racism and oppression of minority populations, and dysfunctional family environments.

Psychological disturbance is mainly attributed to:

- being out of community, i.e. isolated or alienated from key social systems
- the inability to successfully negotiate developmental tasks
- being out of touch with developmental resources (intrapersonal, interpersonal and environmental).

The helper is dealing with unique human beings at particular points in their lives. Pathologising clients through general diagnostic labels is seen as unhelpful and perpetuates a remedial rather than a positive psychology approach to helping. Psychiatry and psychoanalysis have been too much focused on the individual at the expense of the social and cultural context in which the individual exists. Egan argues that the horizons of the helper need to be expanded to include these systems and settings.

People become estranged from their capacity to realise their full potential through factors such as passivity, learned helplessness and their experience of undermining social systems and environmental conditions. Abnormal behaviour and emotional disturbance are seen as ineffective behaviour and its consequences, arising from lack of knowledge or skills. Skills and knowledge have to be acquired at each stage of development in order for the individual to accomplish increasingly complex tasks and fulfil new roles. Helpers need to be accomplished skill trainers or act as points of referral to external sources of information and skills that clients may need to make progress through developmental impasses. For instance, the counsellor might spend time helping the client to develop and practise the interpersonal skills of conflict management to help them move out of established patterns of passivity or deference to others.

CHANGE

Changes in self-concept come about through empowerment as clients learn to be more effective at problem management and opportunity development. Therapy can help to overcome early developmental deficits by enabling the client to acquire skills in living, in particular interpersonal and problem management skills.

Counselling is seen as a social influence process. People are capable of realising their potential and rising above 'the psychopathology of the average' when given optimum amounts of supportive challenge within a strong therapeutic relationship. Helpers aim to be directive of the process but not the content of therapy. The model is collaborative and designed to be 'given away' to clients so that the process is shared with them and owned by them. The client is considered to be the expert on himself or herself and the counsellor acts as consultant to, and facilitator of, the client's process. The quality of the therapeutic relationship importantly mediates the effectiveness of the change process but is not an end in itself. Reluctance and resistance are seen as natural aspects of the change process.

The skilled helper model is one of a number of models that view the process of counselling as unfolding over definable stages. The emphasis on skills learning that is apparent in the skilled helper can suggest a disjointed and mechanistic approach. To guard against this, Egan is at pains to emphasise the need for helpers to mediate their use of skills through spontaneous engagement with the client.

Egan further asserts that it is a mistake to over-identify the helping process with the communication skills that are merely the tools that serve it. Communication skills do not, in themselves, constitute the problem management process, and 'being good at communication skills is not the same as being good at helping' (Egan, 2007: 136). Communication skills are principally helpful in establishing a good working relationship with the client. The working alliance provides a solid foundation for intentional counselling which Egan views, first and foremost, as a systematic process of 'social-emotional reeducation' (2007: 136).

Change comes about through action. However, action is not limited to behavioural change outside counselling sessions. Action can be understood as both internal (an inner shift or change in thinking or feeling) and external (observable action in behavioural terms) and as happening both within and between sessions.

SKILLS AND STRATEGIES

The first stage of the counselling process is about helping clients to construct a coherent personal narrative or story. Stories may consist of both problems and missed opportunities. The counsellor enables the client to tell their story through the active listening skills of attending (verbal and non-verbal), listening, reflecting back (content, thoughts and feelings), summarising and clarifying. These communication skills help to convey the key quality of empathy, through which the counsellor demonstrates their understanding and acceptance of the client.

In order to elicit as clear a story as possible, the counsellor encourages the client to give concrete examples of behaviours, experiences and feelings. Empathic challenges are introduced to invite the client to begin to explore possible blind spots and to develop new perspectives on their situation. In the eighth edition of *The Skilled Helper* the term 'new perspectives' was introduced in preference to 'blind spots' in line with the shift to positive psychology. Here the emphasis is more on the 'task' of helping clients reframe their stories and develop new perspectives than on the notion of the helper challenging the client's lack of awareness. Through a balance of support and challenge the counsellor helps the client search for what is termed 'value' in the ninth edition and was called 'leverage' in previous editions. This task described is to 'help clients work on issues that will add value to their lives' (Egan, 2010: 260) and the helper does this through using the skills of advanced empathy, immediacy, probing, questioning, summarising and clarifying.

The second stage of the counselling process is about helping the client gain a clearer view of what they need and want. Where people have difficulty managing problems, this is frequently down to a tendency to link problems to actions, as in 'What do I *do* about this?', rather than to link action to outcomes, as in 'What do I need to do to get what I want?' An axiom that Egan continuously emphasises is that goals, not problems or strategies, should drive action.

The second stage involves helpers assisting their clients first to see options for a better future and then to turn these into workable objectives that can drive action. The additional skills needed by the helper here are those related to goal setting, including future-oriented questioning, goal shaping, and working with reluctance and resistance to generate hope and commitment. In the eighth edition the term 'preferred picture' was introduced in preference to the 'preferred scenario' used in previous editions as this phrase is considered to be clearer and more understandable for clients and helpers.

The third stage of the helping process is concerned with enabling the client to identify and implement strategies for action that will result in positive and sustainable outcomes. Here the helper assists the client in achieving their identified goals using the skills of creative and divergent thinking, force field analysis and sequential action planning.

Although this brief summary is presented in a linear fashion for ease of understanding, it is important to emphasise that in skilled hands the model is rarely applied in this fashion. The truly skilled helper learns to offer the stages of the model in a flexible and fluid manner, where steps frequently overlap and merge into one another as counsellor and client move back and forth in the ebb and flow of the helping process.

RESEARCH EVIDENCE

As with any integrative model that is largely mediated by the way the individual therapist adapts and applies it, the skilled helper model is not accessible to outcome research in the way that a more singular approach might arguably be. The model is a framework that provides a 'geographical' map for the terrain of helping while also outlining the tasks of helping and how these tasks interrelate. Within this framework the helper utilises their own unique blend of skills and awareness so that one counsellor's way of working with the model may be very different to another's. The model is not a set of treatment techniques that exists in any useful way independently of the practitioner who uses it. As such it is not accessible to empirical research in the way that a therapeutic approach with strictly definable techniques that can be replicated using a treatment manual might be. That said, the model has been used as the basis for researching client change in longer-term counselling (Jinks, 1999), while Sutton (1989) has drawn on the skilled helper model in developing a 'goal-attainment' approach for outcome evaluation that is client centred and can be adapted to a range of counselling approaches.

Wosket's (2006) publication on the skilled helper model engages in depth with the critical debate around the perceived lack of research activity relating to the model. She argues that Egan 'has developed a process for counselling that makes use of sequential patterns in problem management that have been empirically validated by researchers' (2006: 171) and discusses at length research elements underpinning the model. This publication includes a wealth of qualitative data on the client's experience of the model through a range of clinical case studies showing its application to different contexts and client populations.

While empirical studies into the effectiveness of the model may be lacking, the model itself is built on a firm foundation of research into the helping process. Egan is at pains to point out the bedrock of research upon which the various components of the model are founded. So, for instance, he draws extensively on research into cognitive dissonance theory, social learning, motivation and positive psychology that inform past and current versions of the model. That the skilled helper model continues to be highly influential in the training and supervision of therapists in the UK and beyond (Connor, 1994; Page and

Wosket, 2001; Wosket, 2006) attests to its enduring popularity as a pragmatic and adaptable framework for both students and established practitioners.

REFERENCES

Carr, A. (2004) *Positive Psychology: The Science of Happiness and Human Strengths*. Hove: Brunner-Routledge.

Connor, M. (1994) *Training the Counsellor: An Integrative Model*. London: Routledge.

Egan, G. (2006) *Essentials of Skilled Helping: Managing Problems, Developing Opportunities*. Pacific Grove, CA: Brooks/Cole.

Egan, G. (2007) *The Skilled Helper: A Problem Management and Opportunity-Development Approach to Helping* (8th edn). Belmont, CA: Brooks/Cole.

Egan, G. (2010) *The Skilled Helper: A Problem Management and Opportunity-Development Approach to Helping* (9th edn). Belmont, CA: Brooks/Cole.

Jinks, G.H. (1999) Intentionality and awareness: a qualitative study of clients' perceptions of change during longer term counselling. *Counselling Psychology Quarterly*, 12 (1): 57–71.

Page, S. and Wosket, V. (2001) *Supervising the Counsellor: A Cyclical Model* (2nd edn). London: Brunner-Routledge.

Sutton, C. (1989) The evaluation of counselling: a goal attainment approach. In W. Dryden (ed.), *Key Issues for Counselling in Action*. London: Sage.

Wosket, V. (2006) *Egan's Skilled Helper Model: Developments and Applications in Counselling*. London: Routledge.

PART V

THEORY AND APPROACHES

CONSTRUCTIVIST APPROACHES

Narrative Therapy

JOHN MCLEOD

BRIEF HISTORY

Narrative approaches to counselling and psychotherapy initially emerged in the 1980s. Within psychology as a whole, theorists such as Jerome Bruner,
Theodore Sarbin and Donald Polkinghorne had
argued that storytelling represented a fundamental
human means of communication and sense making
(McLeod, 1997). These writers proposed that it was
essential for psychologists to become more sensitive
to the actual stories people told, and the way they
told these stories. This 'narrative turn' within psychology, which reflected similar developments
within philosophy and the social sciences in general,
soon began to have an impact on psychotherapy and
counselling. The writings of Lester Luborsky,
Donald Spence, Roy Schafer (1992) and others
demonstrated how a narrative perspective could be
integrated into psychoanalytic and psychodynamic
therapies. During the 1990s, a proliferation of narrative-
informed approaches were developed, within all
mainstream therapy orientations (Angus and
McLeod, 2004). However, the most significant contribution to the evolution of narrative-informed
therapy is associated with the work of Michael
White and David Epston in the field of family therapy. An excellent introduction to their *narrative
therapy* model can be found in Morgan (2000). The
present chapter offers an introduction to the key
assumptions and skills of the narrative therapy tradition that grew from the publication of *Narrative
Means to Therapeutic Ends* by White and Epston
(1990), and which is now applied in therapy with
individuals and couples as well as with families.

BASIC ASSUMPTIONS

Narrative therapy has been influenced by the ideas of
the French poststructuralist philosopher Michel
Foucault and other postmodern writers who are critical
of the assumption that is made within contemporary
psychology that cognitive, biological and emotional
structures within the individual person are the source
of human action and decision-making. These writers
propose an alternative way of making sense of people,
in terms of relationships and connections between
individuals and participation in a shared language
which incorporates and conveys layers of historical
meaning. Within this perspective, stories play a crucial
role in mediating between the person and the culture
within which he or she lives their life. As a result, narrative counselling and psychotherapy are based on a
complex set of ideas or assumptions about the role of
narrative in human communication, identity and
meaning making. These ideas are as follows.

Stories are the basic way in which people make
sense of their experience. Relating a story about an
event conveys the intentionality and purpose of the
teller and their understanding of relationships and
the social world, expresses feelings, and communicates a moral evaluation of what has happened.

We tell our own personal tales, but do so by
drawing on a cultural stock of narrative forms. We
are born into the story of our family and community, and the story of who we are (e.g. our birth
story, the story behind our name). As we grow up
we adopt narrative templates provided by myths,
films, novels and other cultural resources to give
shape and meaning to our individual life narrative.

People are social beings, and have a basic need to tell their story. Holding back on telling the story involves a process of physiological inhibition that can have negative effects on health. Telling one's story promotes a sense of knowing and being known, and leads to social inclusion.

Personal experience and reality are constructed through the process of telling stories. The stories that we tell are always co-constructed, and are told in the presence of a real or implied audience. There is a dialogic aspect to stories. Constructing a story is a situated performance, a version of events created at a particular time and place to have a specific effect. A story is something that is created *between* people rather than existing in one person's mind. The narrativization of experience is an open-ended process. There are always other stories that can be told about the same events or experiences.

The concept of *voice* refers to the way in which a story is told. The life narrative represents a weaving together of multiple voices. For example, the story of someone's life, or episodes in that life, can be narrated through an official, psychiatric/medical voice, a personal and vulnerable voice, or the harsh critical voice of an angry parent. One of the tasks of therapy is to distentangle these voices. The concept of voice also conveys something of the embodied nature of storytelling, by drawing attention to the physical qualities of *how* the story is told, in terms of volume, tone, rhythm and the use of speech forms such as metaphor, repetition and contrast.

It is useful to distinguish between oral and literary (written) forms of narration. Writing down a story tends to produce a more logically structured version, which can function as a permanent record. People attribute authority and legitimacy to written stories. Oral versions of stories, by contrast, are generally more relational, improvised, emotionally involving and transient.

ORIGIN AND MAINTENANCE OF PROBLEMS

These underlying assumptions suggest a distinctive narrative perspective on the origins and maintenance of the problems that can lead people to seek therapy. The elements of this perspective are as follows.

The experience of being *silenced* is emotionally painful and problematic for most people. Silencing can be a consequence of the social isolation that can result in many situations, such as bereavement, emigration/exile, illness and disability. Silencing can also be produced through purposeful oppression of persons, for example those who may have been sexually, physically or emotionally abused by family members

or those who are members of political, ethnic, religious or sexual orientation minority categories.

A life story that is silenced or that is habitual minimizes the possibility of dialogical engagement with other persons. 'Problems' can be understood as being those areas of personal experience around which the person is not able, or willing, to engage in conversation.

The life narrative templates available within a culture, community or family may be difficult or impossible to reconcile with the circumstances of actual lived experience. For example, the *dominant narratives* within a culture may prescribe gender, age or social class 'scripts' which deny many or most of the possibilities for creative human encounter.

The trajectory of some lives may contribute to the production of narratives which are *incomplete* or *incoherent*.

Some people can develop a style of telling personal stories that is almost wholly *problem saturated*. This tendency can be exacerbated by over-involvement with mental health ideologies.

CHANGE

The change process in narrative therapy involves the construction of opportunities for stories to be told, leading to a phase of reflection and then finally the possibility that the story might be modified or changed. White and Epson (1990) use the term *reauthoring* to characterize this change process.

People find it helpful to have an opportunity to tell their story in a setting in which what they have to say is accepted and valued by others. The basic experience of another person becoming a witness to one's account of troubles is meaningful and worthwhile.

It can be useful to be given the opportunity to generate different versions of a story concerning life issues. Usually, the telling and retelling of the story produces *solution-focused* narratives alongside the more habitual problem-saturated accounts of troubles which people bring into therapy.

The ritual of therapy makes it possible for the person to articulate their life narrative with support and without interruption or competition. This gives the person a chance to reflect upon their story, and to consider whether there are any parts of it that perhaps they might seek to articulate in different ways. Unfolding the story in its entirety is a means of retrieving and preserving the meaning of that life narrative, and in itself leads to a more meaningful life.

The notion of *externalizing* the story (a key technique within White and Epson's 1990 narrative therapy) conveys the idea that the person creates the stories he or she tells (and therefore can tell different stories). The person is not identified with their story but has a relationship with it.

Narrative therapy methods involve the construction of a more satisfying or coherent life narrative through a process of broadening the narrative horizon. The person may find that stories of current troubles may make sense when understood in the light of earlier 'chapters' in the life story.

People who are seeking to change aspects of their life story may engage in a search for examples of more convivial or suitable narrative forms they can live within. This search may involve exploring literary sources, meeting new people, or learning from fellow members of a therapy or self-help group.

The act of narrating a life in a changed way may necessitate disrupting or deconstructing habitual narratives. This process can be facilitated by the use of figurative and concrete language and different modes of telling (e.g. writing). Therapists encourage the telling of vivid, meaningful and emotionally resonant personal stories rather than bland, abstract reports.

Telling a different story about oneself can require recruiting new audiences, and challenging the ways in which pre-existing audiences and communities promote problem-saturated narratives.

SKILLS AND STRATEGIES

The skills and strategies employed in narrative therapy can be understood as comprising two broad dimensions: a poststructuralist worldview, and the use of specific narrative interventions. Narrative therapy practice requires sensitivity and awareness in relation to language use and narrative forms, and genuine curiosity about the stories through which people create and maintain their identities and relationships. In narrative therapy, the role of the counsellor or psychotherapist includes being both witness to, and co-editor of, the stories told by the person seeking help. The client–therapist relationship is not regarded as being at the centre of the therapy process (as it would be in psychodynamic or person-centred therapy). Instead, the aim is to 'decentre' the therapy relationship, in ways that invite the client to become aware of how they relate to other people in their real everyday life. The narrative therapy worldview is critical of oppression and inequality in society. Narrative therapists seek to minimize the danger that the therapeutic experience will function as a means of reinforcing dominant cultural narratives. One of the ways in which they do this is by adopting a *not-knowing* stance, which involves honouring the teller as the expert on their own story. Users of therapy are seen as consultants to the therapeutic process, and are asked for advice on what is helpful.

The second dimension of narrative practice concerns the specific interventions or procedures that have been developed within the narrative therapy tradition. Some narrative-informed therapists use techniques based on writing, such as a letter written to clients or documents written by clients, rather than relying solely on spoken dialogue (Bolton et al., 2004). The purpose of writing is to exploit the value of a communication format that is permanent, and allows reauthored stories to be recorded and reread. Most narrative therapists make use of the technique of *externalizing* the problem, based on inviting the client to find a way of talking about their problem as something separate from them (example: 'I allowed the *fog of panic* to take over my life', rather than 'I panicked'). This strategy opens up a space for exploring the influence of the person on the problem, and the problem on the person. It also enables the therapist to invite the client to consider times when they were problem free (unique exceptions) and to build an alternative narrative around these hitherto silenced or disregarded 'glittering moments'. An important aspect of narrative therapy involves the recruitment of new audiences for the reauthored story that is emerging from therapy; the aim is not to be able to tell this story in the therapy room, but to make it part of everyday life. Some narrative therapists will invite family or community members into therapy sessions to act as *witnesses* to the client's new story, or will encourage the client to seek opportunities within their life to recruit friends, family and work colleagues as witnesses. In some situations, where the social pressure and control of the dominant narrative is particularly strong, the therapist may facilitate the creation of support groups of people who are engaged in similar reauthoring 'projects'. An example of this kind of social action approach can be found in the 'anti-anorexia league' (Maisel et al., 2004), a support network and political action group for people fighting to free themselves from a 'voice of anorexia' that is powerfully reinforced through media images. Further information on recent developments in narrative therapy skills and strategies can be found in Brown and Augusta-Scott (2007) and White (2007).

RESEARCH EVIDENCE

The philosophical stance adopted by narrative therapists makes them sceptical of the value of mainstream research based on measurement and randomized controlled trials, because these methodologies sustain the hegemony of dominant groups within society and narratives that are destructive of the possibility of dialogue and relationship. For example, studies that rely on psychiatric diagnostic categories have the effect of disseminating and supporting a 'language of deficit'. As a result, there is little conventional research evidence regarding the effectiveness of narrative therapy. The research base for narrative therapy consists of a number of participatory action research studies that document the efforts of particular groups of people to overcome specific problems (see for example Denborough, 2008) and to communicate what they have learned to others who are engaged in similar struggles.

REFERENCES

Angus, L.E. and McLeod, J. (eds) (2004) *Handbook of Narrative and Psychotherapy: Practice, Theory and Research*. Thousand Oaks, CA: Sage.

Bolton, G., Howlett, S., Lago, C. and Wright, J.K. (eds) (2004) *Writing Cures: An Introductory Handbook of Writing in Counselling and Psychotherapy*. London: Brunner-Routledge.

Brown, C. and Augusta-Scott, T. (eds) (2007) *Narrative Therapy: Making Meaning Meaning, Making Lives*. Thousand Oaks, CA: Sage.

Denborough, D. (2008) *Collective Narrative Practice: Responding to Individuals, Groups, and Communities Who Have Experienced Trauma*. Adelaide: Dulwich Centre.

Maisel, R., Epston, D. and Borden, A. (2004) *Biting the Hand that Starves You: Inspiring Resistance to Anorexia/Bulimia*. New York: Norton.

McLeod, J. (1997) *Narrative and Psychotherapy*. London: Sage.

Morgan, A. (2000) *What Is Narrative Therapy? An Easy-to-Read Introduction*. Adelaide: Dulwich Centre.

Schafer, R. (1992) *Retelling a Life: Narration and Dialogue in Psychoanalysis*. New York: Basic.

White, M. (2007) *Maps of Narrative Practice*. New York: Norton.

White, M. and Epston, D. (1990) *Narrative Means to Therapeutic Ends*. New York: Norton.

5.31

Neuro-Linguistic Programming

(Richard Bandler, 1950– and John Grinder, 1940–)

JO COOPER AND PETER SEAL

When the originators of neuro-linguistic programming (NLP) came together in the early 1970s their interest was in finding out how the way that we structure our subjective experience informs our behaviour. They were searching for what made the difference between people whose work was generally perceived as brilliant and others whose work was competent but less remarkable. Their form of study was to 'model' people who were experts in their fields and to design 'models' that they could use to achieve similar results themselves and that they could teach to others.

To put it simply, NLP offers a model – and a modelling process – of how humans function, as well as ways of applying the models to facilitate change. Whilst NLP is not in itself a therapy, it can be remarkably effective when used therapeutically.

BRIEF HISTORY

Neuro-linguistic programming was founded in the early 1970s by Richard Bandler, a mathematician and information scientist, and John Grinder, an associate professor of linguistics at the University of California at Santa Cruz. They were interested in communication and influence and modelled people in many different fields.

Bandler and Grinder's best-known modelling was of the work of three major therapists: the gestalt therapist Fritz Perls, the family therapist Virginia Satir, and Milton H. Erickson, doctor and founder of the American Society of Clinical Hypnosis. Bandler explains:

> We watched them at work, and instead of getting caught up in the content of what they were doing, we looked at the syntax of what they were saying and doing. As soon as we looked at it in that way, the patterns popped out everywhere – in the questions they asked, the words they used, the gestures they made, the tonality and rate with which they spoke. (2010: 22)

Bandler and Grinder's first books *Structure of Magic I* (1975a) and *Structure of Magic II* (1976) were the result of their modelling of Perls, Satir and others and were primarily directed towards therapists. The first volume dealt with the way in which people use language to code, sequence and represent their experience and presented the *meta model*, a language model for therapists and other communicators. The second volume dealt with the intuitions and systematic behaviour of the therapists modelled, in relation to 'other ways a human being can both represent and communicate their world'. Bandler and Grinder's modelling of the work of Milton Erickson was set out in *Patterns of the Hypnotic Techniques of Milton H. Erickson, MD, Volumes 1 and 2* (Bandler and Grinder, 1975b; Grinder et al., 1977) and again more recently by Bandler (2010).

BASIC ASSUMPTIONS

The name that Bandler and Grinder chose for their work can be thought of as descriptive:

- *Neuro* refers to neuro-physiology, the functioning of the nervous system within the physiological structure of the human body, taken to be 'one system'.
- *Linguistic* refers to the use of language to communicate – both verbal and non-verbal.
- *Programming* refers to the patterns and sequences evident in neurological processing, demonstrated in behaviour, which can be thought of as representing personal 'programmes'.

The domain of NLP is the functioning of the human system within its environment. At its simplest, NLP assumes that human beings use their senses (seeing, hearing, feeling, smelling and tasting – or, as usually referred to in NLP, visual, auditory, kinaesthetic, olfactory and gustatory) to perceive and process information – their subjective experience. As they continuously process their experience, individuals develop their own unique models of their world.

For practical purposes, human modelling (the individual's creating and updating of their model of the world) can be thought of as the systemic interrelationship of neuro-linguistic patterning and behaviour. A key assumption in NLP is that experience has structure – it is never random – and that all behaviour is informed by the individual's model of the world, however bizarre or extreme it may seem to others. Bandler and Grinder (1975) said that identifying the assumptions in a client's modelling is the equivalent of understanding how the client's behaviour 'makes sense'.

Similarly, NLP itself 'makes sense' when its basic assumptions are understood. These were initially identified by its originators and have become known as the *NLP presuppositions*.

Perhaps the best known of the NLP presuppositions is that 'the map is not the territory': the individual's *model of the world* is not the world. Many problems and misunderstandings occur when people confuse their model of the world with the world itself, believing that their model is 'true' and that it is, or should be, shared by others. NLP presupposes that each individual's model of the world is *unique* and is no more real or true than any other.

NLP is a systemic model. This is difficult to describe in our 'linear' language; at best we can say that the 'body/mind' (or 'mind/body') is one system and that life and mind are *systemic processes*. Two other NLP presuppositions follow from this. The first is the idea that any change in one element of a system will, in some way, be *detectable throughout the system*. The second is that the element of the system with the greatest *flexibility of behaviour* will be the most influential in the system.

Cybernetic models were central in the development of NLP. A key conceptual model adopted by the originators was the test–operate–test–exit (TOTE) model, developed by Miller et al. (1960). The TOTE model maintains that all behaviour is goal oriented, and feedback is provided by testing the goal against the evidence criteria for its achievement. This is encapsulated in the NLP presuppositions that all behaviour has a *positive intention* (in which 'positive' refers to purposeful, not to a value judgement as to its worth) and that in communication there is no failure, only *feedback*, the constant evaluating of the goal and evidence.

The NLP presuppositions, taken together, generate the possibility of choice, in that a particular behaviour is chosen to accomplish a purpose. NLP presupposes that individuals will make the *best choice* they can, given their model of the world and the resources they perceive to be available to them. Implicitly, individuals may be limited as much by their models of the world and the choices they make as by the world itself.

Internal resources are a function of the development and sequencing of representational systems in internal processing. So provided that they have the necessary neuro-physiology, everyone either has, or has the potential to develop, *all the resources they need*.

ORIGIN AND MAINTENANCE OF PROBLEMS

The domain of NLP is subjective experience – how human beings model and structure their experience. Bandler and Grinder proposed that three sets of 'filters' affect this modelling process:

1   neurological constraints, the limits imposed by the human nervous system
2   social genetic factors, which are shared by members of the same socio-linguistic community
3   individual constraints, which provide the basis for the most far-reaching differences between individuals.

It is the combination of these filters that ensures that the experience of each individual is unique and, therefore, that each individual generates their own unique model of the world. Bandler and Grinder said that 'these uncommon ways [in which] each of us represents the world will constitute a set of interests, habits, likes, dislikes and rules for behaviour which are distinctly our own' (1975: 12).

In NLP a 'problem' occurs when an individual is aware of a difference between their present state and desired state but perceives that they have little or no choice. NLP does not attribute causes to problems, but explores how a problem is being maintained in the structure of the client's subjective experience. The NLP practitioner's intention is to help their client to enrich their model of the world and to restructure their experience in such a way as to enhance choice.

CHANGE

Over the years NLP modelling has become more detailed and precise as finer distinctions have been made. In the early days, for example, it was recognized that human beings process their experience in sensory modalities. People see images in their mind's eye, hear internal sounds and voices (including their own voice) and have feelings that are internally generated, as well as taking in information from the 'outside world'.

The significance of changes in 'submodalities' was explored later. Submodalities are the finer distinctions within each representational system, for example the colour, brightness, shape and location of an image; the tone, pitch, volume and tempo of a sound; and the location and intensity of a feeling.

In principle, deliberate and systematic NLP modelling can enable the practitioner to identify specific neuro-linguistic patterns and sequences in order to make sense of, and re-create, aspects of the behaviour of their 'subject'. In the therapeutic context, this process is used to elicit how the client maintains their 'problem' and to design potential ways of facilitating change.

Bandler and Grinder (1975) claimed that all successful therapy, whatever its emphasis or method of treatment, characteristically involves a change in the client's representation or model of the world.

Individuals process vast amounts of sensory information while creating and maintaining their models of the world. Some of this is in conscious awareness but most is processed unconsciously (in NLP 'unconscious' is used simply to refer to processing that is outside conscious attention).

Sensory experience is transformed by what Bandler and Grinder have referred to as the three universal modelling processes: deletion, generalization and distortion. Deletion occurs when information is left out, generalization when information is expanded so as to exclude counter-examples, and distortion when there is assumption of causal connections and equivalencies. These are natural processes that are essential for the processing and coding of information. They can be both limiting and empowering.

In *Structure of Magic I* Bandler and Grinder showed how the universal modelling processes can be identified in an individual's language patterns. The words and phrases that people use can be regarded as 'surface structure', which is derived from 'deep structure' (full linguistic representation), which in turn is derived from the sensory representation of the individual's model of the world.

By observing the client's behaviour and listening to their language patterns, an NLP practitioner can identify deletion, generalization and distortion in the client's modelling. By using language and behaviour in specific and precise ways, the NLP practitioner can help the client enrich their model and expand its boundaries.

When an NLP practitioner and client work together it is always with the active, creative participation of the client. The practitioner uses sensory acuity, an understanding of modelling processes and behavioural flexibility to influence the system and to create a context in which the client is able to access new choices. Provided that the NLP practitioner has integrated the NLP presuppositions in their own behaviour, and has the skills to model the client's processing and to detect the limits of the client's model, they can use whatever behaviour they choose to influence the system and create a context for change.

SKILLS AND STRATEGIES

The skills needed by the NLP practitioner can be thought of from three perspectives: conceptual, analytical and behavioural. Conceptual skills include the understanding of, and ability to apply, NLP models. Analytical skills include the ability to analyse the system (including the practitioner's own and the client's behaviour). Behavioural skills include the practitioner's ability to vary their own behaviour to influence the system and to facilitate the client's ability to change.

NLP is a systemic model and the TOTE model described earlier is a key concept. Other conceptual models in NLP are language models (the meta and Milton models), representation systems (the way in which human beings process their experience in the different sensory systems), accessing cues (signalling how individuals access information in their internal experience), anchors (the patterns of association between external cues and internal experience) and rapport (pacing and leading).

Analytical skills can be thought of as the ability to analyse the 'system'. Practitioners make use of the TOTE when they model the client's behaviour and as a structure for their own participation in the system (Dilts, 1998; Dilts and DeLozier, 2000). They need to chunk information at different levels, to identify patterns and sequences of behaviour, language patterns and naturally occurring anchors.

Behavioural skills include the use of sensory acuity to be aware of what is happening in the system as it occurs. There is always external evidence of internal processing, including posture, gesture, breathing rate and location, eye movements, language patterns, voice tone, tempo and pitch, and much more in every sensory system. The more highly developed the acuity of the practitioner and the better the feedback in the system, the more the practitioner will be able to vary their behaviour to influence the system. Behavioural skills also include the ability to match the client's behaviour in a variety of ways and to lead the client to change their behaviour, to anchor specific states and to use language precisely to achieve specific outcomes.

In the early days of NLP, Bandler and Grinder summed up the necessary components of NLP as to gather information, to evolve the system and to solidify change. Over the years there has been a tendency for the methodology of modelling to be set aside and for the application of recipe-like formats to be confused with NLP. Bandler is often quoted as saying that NLP is an attitude (of curiosity) and a methodology (of modelling), which leave behind a trail of techniques.

Many effective change formats have evolved from NLP, but skilled practitioners tailor their approach to the individual they are working with, rather than merely applying a 'recipe' and limiting what can be an exciting, inventive and creative process. NLP actually provides limitless opportunity for applying the attitude of curiosity and the methodology of modelling to bring about change.

RESEARCH EVIDENCE

There have been many efforts to research NLP and related topics, and many of them are listed in a database of NLP research compiled and edited by PD Dr Daniele Kammer and associates at the University of Bielefeld and published on the internet.

NLP research can be thought of in two categories: first, research into the conceptual models formulated by Bandler and Grinder; and second, research into the efficacy of the application of NLP 'techniques'.

The conceptual models present a difficulty for researchers in that Bandler and Grinder used the word *model* advisedly. They said in *Frogs into Princes*:

> We call ourselves *modelers* … We are not psychologists, and we're also not theologians or theoreticians. We have *no* idea about the 'real' nature of things, and we're not particularly interested in what's 'true'. The function of modelling is to arrive at descriptions which are *useful*. So, if we happen to mention something that you know from a scientific study, or from statistics, is inaccurate, realize that a different level of experience is being offered you here. We're not offering you something that's *true*, just things that are *useful*. (1979: 7)

In his introduction to a recent book introducing NLP to health professionals, Bandler (2008) has written: 'I have for years been very good at modelling successful healers, but have fallen short on providing the science … It seems obvious to me that the more we know about the brain and how it works well, the better off we will be.'

Neuroscience has indeed brought validation to key concepts of NLP. The essence of NLP – Bandler and Grinder's modelling process – has been supported by the 1990s discovery of mirror neurons. Ramachandran writes that within the brain:

> there is a special class of nerve cells called mirror neurons. These neurons fire not only when you perform an action, but also when you watch someone else perform the same action. This sounds so simple that its huge implications are easy to miss. What these cells do is effectively allow you to empathise with the other person and 'read' her intentions – figure out what she is really up to. (2011: 23)

Some of the key presuppositions of NLP are also gaining credibility in neuroscience. The ideas that individuals operate from their unique, individual map or model of the world, and that behaviour is intentional rather than reactive, were radical in the early 1970s, but now neuroscientists are reporting similar conclusions.

In their book about the emerging science of body maps, Blakeslee and Blakeslee write: 'Perception and action are inherently predictive. Your brain creates mental models of your body and the world, and is constantly updating those models with newly arrived information from the senses and constantly extrapolating predictions from them' (2008: 62).

Research into the application of NLP, and especially into NLP 'techniques', is difficult to design. Skilled NLP practitioners who have integrated NLP into their own models of the world are aware of sensory feedback within the system and vary their behaviour accordingly to achieve their outcomes. Their choice of behaviour is made in relation to the way the client is structuring their own experience, rather than the application of a standardized format.

Traditional research, however, has typically required the construction of a boundary around some particular aspect of behaviour in the belief that it is possible to measure the effectiveness of one element of behaviour in isolation. When NLP practitioners are working with their clients it is not their behaviour in isolation that is NLP; the NLP is in the intentional and purposeful application of the model.

REFERENCES

Bandler, R. (2008) Introduction. In G. Thomson and K. Khan (eds), *Magic in Practice*. London: Hammersmith.

Bandler, R. (2009) *Get the Life You Want*. London: Harper Element.

Bandler, R. (2010) *Richard Bandler's Guide to Trance-Formation*. London: Harper Element.

Bandler, R. and Grinder, J. (1975a) *Structure of Magic I*. Palo Alto, CA: Science and Behavior.

Bandler, R. and Grinder, J. (1975b) *Patterns of the Hypnotic Techniques of Milton H. Erickson, MD, Vol.1*. Cupertino, CA: Meta Publications.

Bandler, R. and Grinder, J. (1979) *Frogs into Princes*. Moab, UT: Real People.

Blakeslee, S. and Blakeslee, M. (2008) *The Body Has a Mind of Its Own*. New York: Random House.

Dilts, R. (1998) *Modeling with NLP*. Capitola, CA: Meta.

Dilts, R. and DeLozier, J. (2000) *Encyclopedia of Systemic NLP and NLP New Coding*. Santa Cruz, CA: NLP University Press.

Grinder, J. and Bandler, R. (1976) *Structure of Magic II*. Palo Alto, CA: Science and Behavior.

Grinder, J., Delozier, J. and Bandler, R. (1977) *Patterns of the Hypnotic Techniques of Milton H. Erickson, MD, Vol. 2*. Capitola, CA: Meta Publications.

Miller, G.A., Galanter, E. and Pribram, K.H. (1960) *Plans and the Structure of Behavior*. New York: Holt, Rinehart and Winston.

Ramachandran, V.S. (2011) *The Tell-Tale Brain*. London: Heinemann.

The NLP Research Data Base at www.nlp.de/research/ is compiled and edited by PD Dr Daniele Kammer, Bielefeld, Germany, and published by Dr Franz-Josef Hücker, Berlin, Germany.

Personal Construct Counselling and Psychotherapy

(George A. Kelly, 1905–1967)

FAY FRANSELLA AND DAVID WINTER

BRIEF HISTORY

Personal construct counselling and psychotherapy are based directly on George Kelly's *The Psychology of Personal Constructs* set out in his two volumes published in 1955. His first degrees were in physics and mathematics, followed by postgraduate degrees in sociology, education and, eventually, psychology. He spent much of his academic life at Ohio State University and overlapped there with Carl Rogers for a short time. In his theory of personal constructs, George Kelly aimed to encompass the person's experiencing of the world in its entirety. Feeling involves thinking and behaving just as behaviour involves feelings and thoughts. The theory had a mixed reception on its publication as it was explicitly against the current climate in psychology of behaviourism on the one hand and psychoanalytic theories on the other. Its influence, both as a theory of personality and as an approach to counselling and psychotherapy, was felt first in Great Britain and spread into Europe before being taken up in any substantial way in its birthplace, the United States of America. (See Fransella, 1995 for more details of the man and his theory and Walker and Winter, 2007 for details of how personal construct psychology has been developed and applied since Kelly introduced it.)

Early critics of the theory insisted that it explained 'cognitions' very well but did not deal adequately with emotions. In spite of arguments to the contrary, in 1980 Walter Mischel called George Kelly the first cognitive psychologist. He said, 'There is reason to hope that the current moves toward a hyphenated cognitive-behavioral approach will help fill in the grand outlines that Kelly sketched years before anyone else even realized the need.' The argument about this issue continues today, but suffice it to say that many personal construct psychologists would not be happy with the present chapter's inclusion in a section on cognitive-behavioural approaches, instead considering that personal construct theory has more in common with humanistic or integrative approaches.

Of great influence has been George Kelly's philosophy of *constructive alternativisim*, which underpins the theory throughout. That philosophy is seen as one of the main precursors of the movement of *constructivism* that has swept through psychology as well as psychotherapy and counselling (Chiari and Nuzzo, 2010; Neimeyer, 2009) during the last few years. The philosophy sees reality as residing within the individual. While 'true' reality may indeed be 'out there', we, as individuals, are only able to place our own personal interpretations on that external reality.

Personal construct counselling and psychotherapy are practised around the world, but are not as popular as some other approaches. The main reason, no doubt, is the fact that the personal construct approach is based on a very complex theory about how all individuals experience their worlds. Personal construct therapy is one application of that theory, designed to help those who are experiencing problems in dealing with their world.

BASIC ASSUMPTIONS

Constructive alternativism states that there are always alternative ways of looking at events. That means no one need be the victim of their past since that past is always capable of being seen in a different way – it can be *reconstrued*. However, we can trap ourselves by our past if we construe it as fixed.

The philosophy gives a positive and optimistic view of life since there is always the possibility of change – no matter how difficult that change may be. We have created the person we now are, and so can re-create ourselves.

Personal constructs are essentially discriminations. We see some events, or people, or behaviours as being alike and, thereby, different from other events. These dichotomous personal constructs are formed into a system and it is through that system of personal constructs that we peer at the world of events milling around us.

We place an interpretation on an event by applying certain of our repertoire of personal constructs to it and, thereby, predict an outcome. You see someone smiling at you across the street and predict, perhaps, that he is about to cross the road to say hello. You act accordingly.

Behaviour is the experiment we conduct to test out our current prediction of a situation. The man does cross the street and you put out your hand to shake his, only to find he is smiling at someone behind you. In the language of personal construct theory, you have been invalidated.

The theory is couched in the language of science. Kelly suggested we might look at each person 'as if' we were all scientists. We have theories (personal construing), make predictions from those theories and then test them out by behaving.

The person is a form of motion. No sooner have we conducted one behavioural experiment than the answer leads us into another situation and another cycle of construing.

'Negative' feelings are experienced when we become aware that our current ways of construing events are not serving us well. We become aware that the current situation means we are going to have to change how we see our 'self': we are threatened; or we become aware that we cannot make sense of what is happening and, until we do, we experience anxiety; or we become aware that we have behaved in a way which is 'not me', and feel guilty.

Personal construct therapists know some of the ways of helping the client find alternative ways of construing events and life that will enable them to conduct more productive behavioural experiments. But the client is the expert and the client has the answers. However, those answers may well not be available to conscious awareness.

Construing takes place at different levels of cognitive awareness. The lowest level of cognitive awareness is what is termed *pre-verbal*, that is, discriminations that have been made before the acquisition of language.

An essential feature of personal construct theory is its reflexivity. It accounts for the construing of the counsellor and therapist as well as of the client.

ORIGIN AND MAINTENANCE OF PROBLEMS

There is no list for the personal construct therapist of ways in which problems start. The answer lies with the client who is presenting a problem.

A person decides they have a psychological problem when their present way of construing and predicting events is not working well. Predictions and behavioural experiments are being invalidated but the person is not able to modify those predictions and behaviours in the light of experience.

In all cases, the client has the answer to the question, 'Why do you go on behaving in this way when you would rather not?'

CHANGE

Since each person is a form of motion, change is the norm. The person with a psychological problem is seen as being 'stuck'. The goal of therapy and counselling is to help the person 'get on the move again'. At the most superficial level, this might involve the client changing the use of their existing constructs, but more fundamental changes include modification of these constructs or their replacement by new constructs (see Fransella and Dalton, 2000 for more detail of the change process).

A collaborative therapist–client relationship, which Kelly saw as analogous to that between a research supervisor and their student, is necessary to facilitate change. As part of this, the therapist uses the 'credulous approach'. He or she takes at face value everything the client relates – even if it is known to be a lie. Credulous listening helps the therapist get a glimpse into the client's world. A therapeutic plan cannot be drawn up and certainly cannot be put into action until the practitioner has some idea of what certain changes may mean to the client. The therapist essentially provides a climate of sufficient validation to enable the client to risk experimentation with, and the possibility of some invalidation of, their construing.

Somewhere in the client's construing system are the reasons why he or she cannot get on with the business of living. The therapist uses the theory of personal constructs to make a temporary *diagnosis* of why the client has the problem.

That theoretical diagnosis leads to the therapeutic plan of action. It may, for instance, focus on the *looseness* of the client's construing process. The client cannot make enough sense of events to conduct meaningful behavioural experiments. Or the client may be thought to be resisting any change because that change has some unacceptable implications. For instance, being *anxious all the time* may be seen as indicating that one is a *sensitive*, *thoughtful* and *caring* person whereas being *anxiety free* means one is the opposite.

The focus of the process of change is mostly in the here-and-now. It is how the client construes things now that is important. Sometimes, the client links the present with a past event. In that case, the counsellor explores, with the client, that past event. But there is nothing in the theory that makes it mandatory to explore the past with the client.

SKILLS AND STRATEGIES

Personal construct counselling and psychotherapy are largely value free. There is little in personal construct theory that dictates how a person should be. Therefore, the therapist or counsellor needs to be able to suspend his or her own personal construct system of values. Without that ability, it is not possible to step into the client's shoes and look at the world through the client's eyes, because the therapist's personal values get in the way. In the place of a personal system of constructs, the therapist peers through the system of professional constructs provided by personal construct theory. That means the therapist needs to be well versed in the use of theoretical constructs.

Kelly (1955/1991) suggests the personal construct practitioner needs several other skills, including creativity and good verbal ability. The need for creativity stems from the fact that the theory is eclectic in terms of tools available to the counsellor or therapist.

The aim is to help the client find alternative ways of dealing with personal events and any means may be used to attain that goal. Kelly put it like this:

> Creation is therefore an act of daring, an act of daring through which the creator abandons those literal defenses behind which he might hide if his act is questioned or its results proven invalid. The … [therapist] who dares not try anything he cannot verbally defend is likely to be sterile in a [counselling/psychotherapy] relationship.

Kelly described two specific tools that allow the exploration of the client's construing:

- *Self-characterization*. This stems from Kelly's first principle: 'If you want to know what is wrong with a person, ask him, he may tell you.' It consists of a statement written by the client, in the third person, describing him/herself in a sympathetic way. The client is free to say whatever he or she likes.
- *Repertory grid technique*. This is a method which can assess both the content and the structure of the client's personal construct system, by such means as indicating the strength of mathematical relationships between personal constructs, between the elements to which they may be applied, and between constructs and elements. It was a way Kelly suggested psychologists could 'get beyond the words'. This technique has been widely used in counselling and psychotherapy, for example, as a means of identifying the client's dilemmas, which may then be the focus of therapy (Feixas and Saúl, 2005). However, as with all else, its use is by no means a requirement (see Fransella et al., 2004 for details on how to use this technique).

A specific therapeutic technique developed by Kelly for use with some, but by no means all, clients is *fixed-role therapy*. It involves the therapist or counsellor writing a sketch of a new character whom the client is invited to become for a week or more. This character is not the opposite of the client, but rather will involve the elaboration of some new theme which it might be valuable for the client to explore. The client must agree that the character portrayed is understandable and acceptable. The new role that the client plays shows him or her that making changes to oneself also produces changes in how others respond to us, how we feel and so forth. Most importantly, it shows we can re-create ourselves (see Epting et al., 2005). Fixed-role therapy is but one of many ways by which the personal construct counsellor or psychotherapist may facilitate the client's experimentation.

Over the years, personal construct counselling and psychotherapy have been employed with a wide range of client groups throughout the age range, and in individual, couple, family and group settings (Winter, 1992; Winter and Viney, 2005).

RESEARCH EVIDENCE

There is a not inconsiderable evidence base for personal construct counselling and psychotherapy (Metcalfe et al., 2007; Winter, 2005). This includes research, mostly using the repertory grid, into changes in construing resulting from personal construct interventions, and evidence that the outcome of this form of counselling and psychotherapy is comparable to that of other major therapeutic approaches.

REFERENCES

Chiari, G. and Nuzzo, M.L. (2010) *Constructivist Psychotherapy: A Narrative Hermeneutic Approach*. London: Routledge.

Epting, F., Germignani, M. and Cross, M.C. (2005) An audacious adventure: personal construct counselling and psychotherapy. In F. Fransella (ed.), *The Essential Practitioners' Handbook of Personal Construct Psychology*. Chichester: Wiley.

Feixas, G. and Saúl, L.A. (2005) Resolution of dilemmas by personal construct psychotherapy. In D.A. Winter and L.L. Viney (eds), *Personal Construct Psychotherapy: Advances in Theory, Practice and Research*. London: Whurr.

Fransella, F. (1995) *George Kelly*. London: Sage.

Fransella, F. and Dalton, P. (2000) *Personal Construct Counselling in Action* (2nd edn). London: Sage.

Fransella, F., Bell, R. and Bannister, D. (2004) *A Manual for Repertory Grid Technique* (2nd edn). Chichester: Wiley.

Kelly, G.A. (1955/1991) *The Psychology of Personal Constructs* (Vols I and II). New York: Norton, 1955. Republished Routledge, 1991.

Metcalfe, C., Winter, D. and Viney, L. (2007) The effectiveness of personal construct psychotherapy in clinical practice: a systematic review and meta-analysis. *Psychotherapy Research*, 17: 431–42.

Neimeyer, R.A. (2009) *Constructivist Psychotherapy*. London: Routledge.

Walker, B.M. and Winter, D.A. (2007) The elaboration of personal construct psychology. *Annual Review of Psychology*, 58: 453–77.

Winter, D.A. (1992) *Personal Construct Psychology in Clinical Practice: Theory, Research and Applications*. London: Routledge.

Winter, D. (2005) The evidence base for personal construct psychotherapy. In F. Fransella (ed.), *The Essential Practitioners' Handbook of Personal Construct Psychology*. Chichester: Wiley.

Winter, D.A. and Viney, L.L. (eds) (2005) *Personal Construct Psychotherapy: Advances in Theory, Practice and Research*. London: Whurr.

Solution-Focused Therapy

BILL O'CONNELL

BRIEF HISTORY

The key founders of solution-focused therapy (SFT) in the 1980s were the family therapists Steve de Shazer, Insoo Kim Berg and their colleagues at the Brief Family Therapy Center in Milwaukee, USA. Bill O'Hanlon, a therapist in Nebraska, also made a significant contribution. Other influential ancestors in the solution-focused family tree include George Kelly (founder of personal construct theory); John Weakland, Paul Watzlawick and Robert Fisch, who developed a problem-focused model at the Mental Research Institute (MRI) in Palo Alto, California; and Gregory Bateson and Milton Erickson whose ideas and clinical practice were seminal to the philosophy and application of SFT.

The approach has branched out from its origins in family therapy to applications in many other fields, such as mental health, psychology, group work, education, nursing, drug and alcohol work, counselling, social work and business. It is important to recognise that context shapes how the ideas and interventions are implemented. Practitioners need to adapt the model to the norms, goals and ethics of their workplace setting. A good example of this is John Henden's (2008) work with suicidal clients.

In the early days of the model's evolution, the Milwaukee team of family therapists, headed by Steve de Shazer and Insoo Kim Berg, observed that their clients made significant changes following conversations about their preferred futures, even when there had been minimal attention to their problems or complaints. When clients described their solutions, these sometimes related directly to the problem, but often not. When clients articulated their solutions, they often saw the original problem in a different light. The more they focused upon their solutions, the less time and attention they paid to the 'problem'.

Following the clients' lead, the therapy team suspended judgement about the reported problems and focused upon the clients' non-problematic behaviour, competences and personal strengths. They discovered that by skilful prompting they could evoke solutions from clients. These standard interventions ('skeleton keys') could be used with all clients, irrespective of their presenting problems.

These interventions included:

- seeking exceptions to the problem – paying attention to what works when the problem is being managed better
- encouraging clients to 'do something different' – on the basis that many people become entrenched in their problems because they keep repeating the same failed solutions
- using the miracle question – to engage clients in imagining their preferred future without the problem dominating their lives
- scaling – to measure progress and build motivation
- taking small steps – to encourage clients to be realistic and not to be overwhelmed by the scale of change required
- giving feedback about the client's strengths, qualities and accomplishments based on the evidence of the session
- negotiating between-session tasks.

BASIC ASSUMPTIONS

The solution-focused approach aims to help clients achieve their preferred outcomes by evoking and co-constructing solutions to their problems (O'Connell, 2005). Its primary emphasis is upon clients' resources, strengths and personal qualities. It makes a number of assumptions:

- Clients have ideas about their preferred futures.
- Clients are already carrying out constructive and helpful actions (otherwise things would be worse!).
- Clients have many resources and competences, many of which go unacknowledged by themselves and by others.
- It is usually more helpful to focus on the present and the future. The past can be useful as a source of evidence for prior successes and skills.
- Constructing solutions is a separate process from problem exploration.
- The 'truth' of a client's life is negotiable within a social context. Fixed objective 'truths' are unattainable. There are many truths about the client's life.

ORIGIN AND MAINTENANCE OF PROBLEMS

Solution-focused therapy is not an 'explanatory' approach. It does not use a theoretical map to develop a rationale for problems. It is deeply suspicious of theories which claim to make causal links in people's behaviours. It rejects the notion that there is an objective truth about the client out there to be uncovered. Even if it considered such a task desirable and possible, it doubts whether it is necessary for real and enduring change to take place.

Solution-focused therapists take the social constructionist view that 'reality' is socially negotiated by people through language. Conversation shapes 'reality' and makes 'new meaning' with the client. This epistemological stance explains why many solution-focused therapists feel uneasy about professional assessment processes which define and diagnose problems and the 'treatment' required. When professional authority figures control the linguistic agenda and thereby define 'reality', the client voice is unheard or marginalised.

Professional control of the 'problem agenda' is likely to make clients defensive. SF therapists listen to, acknowledge and validate clients' problems and concerns without trying to classify or define them. At the appropriate moment the therapist will guide the conversation away from further problem exploration to enquire about life beyond the problem and what the client is already doing that is helpful. As they explore hopes, strengths and solutions, a dynamic partnership evolves. Clients begin to shift their perceptual priorities away from seeing problems everywhere to becoming aware of what they are already doing that works for them. Even when there is an organisational requirement to make an assessment of the client, a solution-focused approach which balances strengths with weaknesses can give the client an immediate therapeutic experience (Duncan et al., 2007).

In order for clients to find their own specific and unique pathways to change they are invited to pay particular attention to:

- their hopes for their immediate and long-term future
- how they manage to make exceptions to the problem happen
- skills, qualities and strengths they show in one area of their lives that can be transferable
- the first steps they need to take.

The solution-focused understanding of the nature of problems is that they are an integral part of the human condition – they happen! They are 'normal'. In fact, overcoming adversity is what helps people to become resilient, creative and courageous.

Solution-focused therapists see clients as the experts in their lives. Their 'local' knowledge (i.e. what they know works in their particular context) is privileged above 'professional' knowledge. Clients need solutions that fit them. There are times when it is helpful for therapists to share possible solutions with clients as long as they are offered in a tentative and collaborative spirit.

CHANGE

Observation of clinical practice led solution-focused therapists to conclude that certain types of conversation were more effective in motivating and supporting client change. These conversations stressed the competence, skills and qualities that clients were already using. Optimistic, hopeful and respectful interactions created an awareness in clients that change is always happening and that they have the ability to determine, at least to some extent, the direction of change.

Fletcher Peacock (2001) talks about high-speed, medium-speed and low-speed clients. The high-speed ones are ready to take action; the medium-speed ones can be encouraged to observe, reflect and consider what they could do; and low-speed ones want to take things slowly and need positive feedback and encouragement. A skilled therapist will gauge the pace required to match the needs of the client. The cardinal sin of the solution-focused practitioner is to become a solutions pusher who pressurises clients towards solutions, but only ends up alienating them

The solution-focused approach generates *descriptions* of clients' experiences, rather than diagnoses and definitions. It privileges language that conveys the ever-changing experience of the client. By breaking down depression, for example, into a series of specific behaviours – e.g. can't get out of bed in the morning, not taking care of appearance, neglecting the children, watching daytime television – it is easier to find leverage for change.

SKILLS AND STRATEGIES

- *Pre-session change.* On initial contact with an agency or a therapist, clients are asked to notice any changes that take place between then and the time when they come for their appointment. At the first session many clients report that they have managed to contain their problem, or indeed improve their situation. When this happens, therapy can 'hit the ground running'.
- *Problem-free talk.* In a sense, all solution-focused interventions encourage problem-free talk, but therapists also give clients the specific opportunity to talk about themselves and their interests, without reference to the problem. These conversations often yield information that is helpful to the therapist in knowing (1) how to work with the client, (2) which metaphors or examples will connect with the client's world, and (3) clients' strengths, qualities and values pertinent to solution construction. Another form of problem-free talk is to ask questions such as, 'Would you say you are the kind of person who likes to be told what to do all the time?', 'Would you say you do not give up easily if you really want something?' Questions such as these can provide useful clues to the therapist on ways to cooperate with a client, as well as raising the client's self-awareness. SF therapists tend to find out more about the person than the problem (Bliss and Edmonds, 2008: 26).
- *Listening for evidence of clients' strengths, qualities and skills.* While acknowledging clients' experiences and feelings, therapists specifically listen for evidence of the client's resources. Throughout a session the therapist will give feedback and invite reflection from the client

about these resources. The therapist supports the client to move from perceived 'conscious incompetence' to 'conscious competence'.
- *Building on exceptions.* Instead of focusing upon the times when clients 'do' their problems, therapists question them about times when they manage the problem better. There are always times when the problem is less a concern or even disappears entirely, to be replaced with something better. These occasions reveal clients' constructive strategies. By highlighting and exploring these, clients can find ways to expand exception times and thus reduce the problem times.
- *The miracle question.* The miracle question is an intervention used by therapists to help clients bypass 'problem talk' and generate a description of life without the problem. Their answers identify goals and strategies they would like or have already begun to use. The question originated with de Shazer (1988) and his colleagues. Its standard form is: 'Imagine one night when you are asleep, a miracle happens and the problems we've been discussing disappear. As you were asleep, you did not know that a miracle had happened. When you wake up, what will be the first signs for you that a miracle has happened?' Therapists question clients in some detail about what is happening that tells them that something has changed for the better. They explore the impact of the client's miracle on significant people and situations. As clients enter into their miracle they become more aware and motivated to achieve this preferred scenario. It is important however for the therapist to keep the client grounded, even if the preferred reality is for the moment slightly out of reach.
- *Scaling.* Therapists use a scale of 0 to 10 to help clients measure progress, set small identifiable goals and become aware of strategies they are already employing. A score of 10 represents 'the best it could be' and 0 the worst. Therapists invite clients to explore where they are on the scale, what that means to them and where they would like to get to. They identify small steps which could help them to move up the scale. Scaling is a simple, practical technique which clients are encouraged to use between sessions.
- *Feedback.* As the session comes to a close, the therapist gives brief feedback to the client. This consists of relevant compliments, a summary of the client's achievements and, where appropriate, the negotiation of a between-session task.
- *Tasks.* In negotiating tasks, therapists follow principles such as:

  - If it works, keep doing it.
  - If it doesn't work, invite them to stop doing it.

- Take small steps, as small changes can lead to a big difference.
- Give the client space to do something different from what was agreed.

RESEARCH EVIDENCE

According to Alasdair Macdonald (www.solutionsdoc.co.uk/) there are, at the time of writing, 89 relevant studies: two meta-analyses; 13 randomised controlled trials showing benefit from solution-focused brief therapy, with six showing benefit over existing methods. Of 30 comparison studies, 23 favour SFT. Effectiveness data are available from more than 3000 cases with a success rate exceeding 60 per cent, requiring an average of three to five sessions of therapy time. More detail on these is available in Macdonald's (2007) book or on his website.

CONCLUSION

Solution-focused practices have become popular in many different settings and with many diverse client groups. The popularity of the approach as a therapeutic model is due perhaps to its simplicity, brevity and elegance, but also because therapists report that the majority of their clients find it extremely practical. A form of therapy which is time-efficient, user-friendly and effective is clearly one which fits with the spirit of the times.

REFERENCES

Bliss, E.V. and Edmonds, G. (2008) *A Self-Determined Future with Asperger Syndrome: Solution Focused Approaches*. London: Jessica Kingsley.

De Shazer, S. (1988) *Clues: Investigating Solutions in Brief Therapy*. New York: Norton.

Duncan, L., Guhl, R. and Mousley, S. (2007) *Creating Positive Futures: Solution Focused Recovery from Mental Distress*. London: BT Press.

Henden, J. (2008) *Preventing Suicide: The Solution-Focused Approach*. Chichester: Wiley.

Peacock, F. (2001) *Water the Flowers, Not the Weeds*. Montreal: Open Heart.

Macdonald, A. (2007) *Solution-Focused Therapy: Theory, Research and Practice*. London: Sage.

O'Connell, B. (2005) *Solution-Focused Therapy*. London: Sage.

PART VI

CLIENT PRESENTING PROBLEMS

Introduction

COLIN FELTHAM AND IAN HORTON

This part of the book examines a selection of some of the most common problems presented to counsellors and psychotherapists in and across different settings. To some extent this reflects what may be found in the *DSM* or elsewhere, although a notable difference perhaps is that some of these categories of problem are specific to situations, agencies, gender, the British experience and so on. Obviously it is not exhaustive, but hopefully it is representative. The selection is based mainly on the extensive practice experience of counsellors and psychotherapists. Writers come from a wide variety of clinical professions and their individual perspectives usefully reflect the catholicity of views in the therapy field. The term 'problems' has been chosen as common parlance, but of course different practitioners may prefer to think of psychodiagnostic categories, disorders, symptomatology, presenting problems, issues or concerns, goals, aspirations or simply different areas of clients' ongoing experience. A focus of this kind has become more common with the increasing influence of the evidence-based lobby, IAPT and progress towards statutory regulation. For ease of reference, an alphabetical ordering has been adopted here.

While each of these problem categories has been presented from a particular perspective, and with some emphasis on impressionistic and indicative themes, this part of the book is intended broadly to raise awareness of some of the following:

- description and recognition of a fairly distinct problem
- nature of the problem – signs and symptoms, degrees of severity, accompanying psychological or physical problems
- extent or prevalence of the problem, including, for example, social contexts, gender specificity, etc.
- aetiology – single or multiple causes or associated exacerbating factors
- contra-indications of therapy or treatment
- therapeutic procedures, i.e. 'treatments of choice', including medication, etc.
- clinical management, course, prognosis, time factors
- relevant research findings, evidence and indications
- debates concerning the reality and distinctiveness of the problem
- (optional) recommended further reading.

Conceptualizing Clients' Problems

COLIN FELTHAM

How we understand and conceptualize clients' distress, presenting problems and goals is a subject filled with interestingly conflicting views. Means of classifying different kinds of distress or problems in living, and associated terminology, have differed widely and changed significantly historically, culturally and according to the different clinical professions and their various theoretical orientations. Critics have also added to the debate by querying the very principle of classifying people in terms of 'psychopathology' – psychological disease or sickness (Bentall, 2009; Graham, 2010; Joseph and Worsley, 2005). Counsellors and psychotherapists must balance allegiance to training-oriented theoretical loyalties against a wide range of factors idiosyncratic to each client. Arguably, the focus on 'clinical reasoning' shown by certain other helping professions (medicine, speech therapy, etc.: see Feltham, 2010; Higgs and Jones, 2000) has not been well developed within our own profession due to training loyalties (Davies and Bhugra, 2004; Milner and O'Byrne, 2004), competing knowledge claims and an emphasis on the therapeutic relationship rather than on the actual, complex cluster of client characteristics calling for attention.

HISTORICAL VIEWS OF PSYCHOPATHOLOGY

Probably the first kinds of human 'psychological' problems were those related to fear of natural threats, including environmental hazards, fierce or abruptly changing weather conditions, and hostile animals and humans, combined with an acute awareness of mortality. In addition, competition for resources and for sexual mates, along with anxious protection of the young, may all have begun to sow the seeds of later susceptibility to the counterproductively extended emotions of anxiety, hypervigilance, etc. (Cantor, 2005; Stevens and Price, 2000). While names for these states would have taken a considerable time to develop, early cave paintings, charms and rituals testify to non-verbal attempts to ward off evil spirits. All long-established religions contain allegories or theories about the origins of suffering and propitiatory methods, and much 'psychopathology' was and is, in religious terms, understood as aspects of divine testing, as evil, karma, and so on.

Hippocrates in the fourth century BC devised a system of classification of illnesses into the humours of blood (sanguinity), phlegm (dullness), black bile (melancholy) and yellow bile (choler). Later Greeks applied more philosophical analyses, remedies and terminologies to problems of human distress. The Buddha had spoken in the sixth century BC of 'all worldlings as deranged' (Goleman, 2003: 341) and Buddhism developed the concept of *kleshas* (mental afflictions). The Middle Ages saw in Europe the gradual replacement of the idea of demonic possession (and the occasional admiration of those believed to be possessed as visionaries) with concepts of madness. Burton's *Anatomy of Melancholy*, published in 1621, interpreted depression and allied states as forms of divine retribution for sin. Concepts of lunacy, idiocy and insanity have waxed and waned, but by the end of the eighteenth century the Frenchman Pinel had arrived at a classification of mania, melancholia, dementia and idiotism. Westphal named agoraphobia in 1871. (Interestingly, in 1870 it was named *Platzschwindel*, 'dizziness in public places', but this coinage, although descriptively accurate, has not survived.) The 1880 United States census led to the seven categories of mania, melancholia, monomania, paresis, dementia, dipsomania and epilepsy. In 1898 the German Kraepelin coined the term 'dementia praecox', which was largely replaced by 1908 with Bleuler's term 'schizophrenia'.

This highly condensed selection is intended only to suggest that religion, philosophy, medicine and other disciplines have variously staked their claims to understanding and naming human beings' multifaceted problems of distress and demoralization. But it also shows that interpretations and names change (Berrios and Porter, 1995; Lane, 2007). Even within the relatively short span of time from the late nineteenth century to the beginning of the twenty-first century, the following psychopathological labels have come and mostly gone: neurasthenia, hysteria, shell shock, nymphomania, inferiority complex, neurosis. In other words, diagnostic entities are to a considerable extent constructs of their own time and place. Hence, post-traumatic stress disorder (PTSD) came into being as an official (APA, 2000) clinical entity only in 1980, and the Vietnam War seems heavily implicated in its 'invention' (Young, 1997). Homosexuality was until 1972 (*DSM*) and 1992 (WHO, 1992) classified as a psychopathological condition, and alcoholism remains a disputed term. 'Road rage' has yet to become a recognized impulse control disorder, nor has 'technophobia' yet become a recognized species of anxiety disorder.

TRANSCULTURAL VIEWS OF PSYCHOPATHOLOGY

While all cultures recognize signs of 'something awry' with individuals' minds or souls and have their own terminology for varieties of distress, there is usually no exact correspondence between these and traditional Western, scientific classifications. There is also considerable scope for misunderstanding the signs and symptoms presented to Western therapists working in multicultural societies (Watters, 2010).

Social and medical anthropologists have charted some of what are often called *culture-bound syndromes*. Indeed, the *DSM-IV-TR* (APA, 2000) includes a specific outline section for culture-bound syndromes. As an illustration, an anthropological study of the Chewong (aboriginal Malaysians) found a very limited vocabulary for emotions, and showed that distress for the Chewong is conceptualized in *socially* oriented terms. Hence, transgression of rules and customs leads to shame: *tola* is an illness arising from disrespect; *maro* is a kind of dizziness associated with meanness.

Gopaul-McNicol and Brice-Baker (1998: 83) draw from several sources to demonstrate culture-bound syndromes. These include: *ataque de nervios* (Hispanic, 'an out-of-consciousness state resulting from traumatic events'); *falling-out* (African American, 'seizure-like symptoms resulting from traumatic events'); *Taijinkyofusho* (Asian, 'guilt about embarrassing others; timidity resulting from the feeling that one's appearance, odor, facial expressions are offensive to other people'); *Wacinko* (American Indian, 'anger, withdrawal, mutism, suicide resulting from reaction to disappointment and interpersonal problems'). Indigenous classifications may refer to supernatural causes and environmental factors. Hence, the Yoruba of Nigeria may speak of *Inarun* ('a condition which comes from God', involving weakness, skin rashes, memory loss, irrational talking, etc.) and of *Ori ode* ('hunter's head', involving the psychosomatic symptoms of a burning sensation, thumping in the head, visual problems, insomnia, etc.). A small-scale research survey of depressed Asian women in Britain includes discussion of what the women called 'thought sickness' (*soochne ke bimaari*), which often comprised a mixture of bereavement, isolation, poverty, racism and other contributing factors. As the publication reporting on this challengingly puts the diagnostic dilemma: 'Depression, or just life?' (CRE, 1993: 4).

Transculturally, reports of spirit possession and somatic symptoms are common, and easily misconstrued by Western mental health professionals. The continuing disproportionate number of black people in British psychiatric hospitals and prisons is often attributed to such misunderstandings. Almost by definition, the loss, dislocation, trauma and problems of adaptation and poverty, as suffered by many migrants and refugees in a new cultural environment, are too easily misunderstood (Van der Veer, 1998). A tortured refugee, for example, will find it hard to trust strangers (e.g. mental health professionals), and may be legitimately suspicious, but this could easily be misconstrued as paranoia. It is also true to say that the number and kinds of psychopathologically oriented labels used for the distress or emotional difference experienced by or associated with women is a cause for concern. Psychiatric abuses in the former Soviet Union, whereby political dissidents were often hospitalized for holding 'incorrect' views, should have alerted us to such dangers. More recently, the North American vogue for diagnosing multiple personality disorder (now dissociative identity disorder) has raised questions about different (and perhaps sometimes erroneous) diagnostic patterns in different countries. Practitioners claiming that their practices are 'colour blind' or neutral regarding race, culture and gender should pause to consider the implications of the transcultural challenge. Additional helpful guidelines may be found in Eleftheriadou (1999), Paniagua (1998) and Ridley (1995).

BIOMEDICAL VIEWS OF PSYCHOPATHOLOGY

Just as organized religion gradually displaced the dominance of magical practices, so science in the last three centuries has eroded the territory of religious practice. Physical and mental sickness and their definitions have been regarded as legitimate territory for scientific conceptualization, research and treatment. Many believe that our understanding – scientific or otherwise – of emotional or psychological problems or disorders is still at a fairly primitive, somewhat hit-or-miss stage. Clare (1980) argued that we might think in terms of four approaches to understanding mental distress: (1) organic (biological); (2) psychotherapeutic (or psychological in the sense of having a focus on inner, subjective, mental and emotional life); (3) sociotherapeutic (relating to social functioning and change); and (4) behavioural (psychology which concerns itself purely with symptoms and their removal). Ridley (1995) discusses alternative models of mental health in relation to multicultural awareness and the need to overcome unintentional racism in therapy by adopting models which are not inherently racist.

Psychiatrists are often attacked for their alleged adherence solely to the first of the above approaches, and have often been vilified for the practices of psycho-surgery, electro-convulsive therapy (ECT), and use of psychotropic medications. While this is probably not a balanced portrayal, it is true to say that the medical and psychiatric professions are enormously powerful in leading research, influencing policies and dictating what is and is not psychopathology. Hence, a great deal of energy and public and private funds are dedicated to genetic, psychopharmacological and related research. The scientific model of mental distress based on biology and behaviour (approaches 1 and 4 above) is clearly differently oriented from typical models of counselling and psychotherapy which are concerned with subjectivity and context. In other words, reflecting 2 and 3 above, psychological therapies (especially the psychodynamic and humanistic) tend to 'assess' individuals more in terms of their holistic existence: inner (psychic) functioning; self-determination; (non-dualistic) body–mind system; psychosocial factors; spirituality; and potentiality as well as problem focus.

The Western scientific tradition led inexorably, it seems, to the systematic categorization of forms of mental illness or disorder. The first edition of the *DSM*, now in its fourth edition with the fifth due out in 2013, was published in 1952. Of very similar status and aims is the *International Classification of Diseases and Related Health Problems* (*ICD*, 10th edition), published by the World Health Organization (WHO, 1992). We now have a 2000 'text revised' edition of *DSM* but, for simplicity's sake, the *DSM-IV International Version with ICD-10 Codes* is focused upon here. The *DSM-IV* is an extremely influential text, indeed an institution – a necessity to most North American mental health professionals but also of considerable importance in Britain. Its aim is to offer comprehensive standardized categories for diagnosis that can be shared by all clinicians and agreed by third parties such as health agencies and funders. Acknowledging that *mental disorder* is an unsatisfactory term, the editors of the *DSM* nevertheless define it as

> a clinically significant behavioral or psychological syndrome or pattern that occurs in an individual and that is associated with present distress … or disability … or with a significantly increased risk of suffering death, pain, disability, or an important loss of freedom. (APA, 2000: xxi)

To qualify as a disorder, the client's condition must 'cause clinically significant distress or impairment in social, occupational, or other important areas of functioning' (1995: 7).

The *DSM* is a huge collaborative endeavour that attempts to set out some 340 mental disorders in the following groups:

- disorders usually first diagnosed in infancy, childhood or adolescence
- delirium, dementia, and amnestic and other cognitive disorders
- mental disorders due to a general medical condition not elsewhere classified
- substance-related disorders
- schizophrenia and other psychotic disorders
- mood disorders (mainly depressive and bipolar disorders)
- anxiety disorders (includes PTSD and phobias)
- somatoform disorders (e.g. hypochondriasis)
- factitious disorders (feigned illnesses, etc.)
- dissociative disorders
- sexual and gender identity disorders
- eating disorders
- sleep disorders
- impulse control disorders not classified elsewhere (e.g. kleptomania)
- adjustment disorders (extreme negative reactions to stressors)
- personality disorders
- other conditions that may be a focus of clinical attention (e.g. sexual abuse, bereavement, phase of life problems).

The *DSM* gives criteria and guidelines as to severity and course of disorder: mild, moderate, severe, in partial remission, in full remission. Prior history, recurrence, principal diagnosis or 'reason for visit' are also key concepts. Concepts of prevalence, specific culture, gender and age features are given. It does not focus on treatment or therapy (see, however, Bellack and Hersen, 1990; Reid et al., 1997; Roth and Fonagy, 1996). The *DSM* commends multi-axial assessment, and the axes are: clinical disorders, and other conditions that may be a focus of clinical attention; personality disorders and mental retardation; general medical conditions; psychosocial and environmental problems; global assessment of functioning. The realities of 'diagnostic uncertainty' are acknowledged.

The *DSM*, it must be said, is regarded as a clinical bible by some, and as anathema by others (Kutchins and Kirk, 1997). It quite clearly suits the ethos of psychiatry and clinical psychology, particularly since many of the 'disorders' referred to are severe and more likely to come to the attention of statutory mental health professionals. However, in terms of discretionary clinical judgement, therapeutic tradition and ideology, client presentation and preferences, agency brief and so on, the *DSM* may be seen as at best one among many useful but fallible guides to understanding and assessment. What it does do, along with similar influential clinical traditions, is to call attention to problems that may be beyond the remit and power of counselling and psychotherapy to address successfully. In other words, it raises the question of limitations and contra-indications. Certain conditions such as very entrenched depression may benefit from medication as well as psychological therapy; some may benefit primarily from biomedical treatment; and others will benefit primarily from psychological therapy or alternatives.

LAY OR CLIENT VIEWS OF PSYCHOPATHOLOGY

For the most part ordinary people – non-professionals, sometimes referred to as 'lay' – do not use the vocabulary of psychopathology (except where influenced by prevalent therapeutic discourse to present as 'depressed' or as having 'panic attacks', etc.). Rather, their first words and phrases to therapists may often include: 'I don't know where to begin'; 'I'm unhappy'; 'I can't cope'; 'I can't stop crying'; 'I think I'm cracking up, having a breakdown, going mad, losing my mind'; 'I can't face going to work'; 'I'm having trouble sleeping'; 'I can't seem to pull myself together'; 'I don't know what's wrong with me, what to do.'

Clients also quite often present using borrowed terminology: 'The doctor thinks it's a stress reaction'; 'I think perhaps I'm in shock'; 'Am I having a nervous breakdown?', etc. Such usage may be a combination of terms from the media and popular psychology, and is not necessarily helpful. Clients' own stories, faltering narratives in their own words, probably offer a better guide than pseudo-diagnostic language. When such terms *are* used, it is important to try and discover exactly how they are being used. 'I'm depressed' can mean 'I've been told I'm depressed' or 'I just can't cope with my job' or 'I'm really sad' or have many other nuances. Sometimes, as humanistic therapists have recognized, the core of a client's 'problem' – their deep inner pain, profound sorrow or self-loathing, for example – is best identified and most usefully conveyed experientially, by non-verbal and emotional expressions rather than by inexact, standardized pathological terms. Very often images and metaphors too are more effective personal labels than generalized medically oriented terms.

CRITICS' VIEWS OF PSYCHOPATHOLOGY

Most practitioners of the humanistic and existential therapies are opposed to psychodiagnostic concepts, terms and procedures on the grounds of *inaccuracy*, *gratuitousness*, *stigmatization*, *disempowerment*, *abuse* and *shrinkage* (this last colloquialism refers to the tendency of psychiatric labels to shrink or reduce the totality of the human being to a spuriously named *part* of themselves, to dissect them psychologically and treat them accordingly). Many humanistic therapists are largely unconvinced by or uninterested in diagnostic assessment, and may commence therapy on the basis of non-judgemental acceptance and 'trial therapy'. Usually emphasizing the importance of clients' self-determination and self-knowledge, as well as the trustworthiness of authenticity and emotional experience, some of these therapists have been known as 'anti-psychiatric', and many counsellors are opposed to the '(bio)-medical model' of diagnosis and treatment, with its perceived unwarranted use of medical or psychiatric nomenclature and uncritical use of psychotropic drugs. In spite of such critiques, somewhat paradoxically, some therapists have spoken of 'the trauma of eventlessness' (psychological damage done by an oppressively under-stimulating environment); of 'hypophobia' (being less than appropriately anxious or fearful); and of 'the psychopathology of the average' (the tendency towards unhealthy conformity, the common failure in self-actualization).

Although psychodynamically affiliated therapists have closer links with the medical model, their assessments are often more influenced by clients' 'psychological mindedness and quality of object relationships'. This is sometimes referred to as *dispositional assessment* rather than diagnostic. According to Roth and Fonagy, 'some orientations – particularly psychodynamic – consider that "suitability for therapy" is more important than formal diagnosis when considering which patients to accept into therapy' (1996: 29). However, the North American turn to empirically supported managed care, which influences even psychodynamic practitioners to adapt their therapy to brief treatments for diagnostic categories (Barber and Crits-Christoph, 1995), combined with increasing emphasis on evidence-based practice, may yet affect psychodynamic assessment and therapy in Britain (Fonagy, 2003).

Thomas Szasz is one of the most outspoken critics of psychopathology, arguing that 'mental illness' as such cannot exist because illness is physical, and furthermore that psychiatry and psychotherapy overreach themselves self-servingly when their ideologies colonize ordinary 'problems of living'. Szasz argues that psychiatry has taken over from religious domination and oppression; our version of the persecution of witches is the 'manufacture of madness', the unjustified labelling and involuntary incarceration or medicalization of people simply suffering, to different degrees, from a world that is often difficult to live in. See also Graham (2010).

Experiments in which professionals have reported to psychiatric services with minimal or transient symptoms of mental illness (e.g. Rosenhan: see Clare, 1980) have resulted in detention on the basis, for example, of a single symptom (hearing voices) and subsequent difficulty in obtaining release. Concerns about the potential for misdiagnosis are very natural. It was at one time the habit of many psychiatrists to commit to hospital women who had had children outside marriage, and community care measures as late as the 1990s led to the 'decarceration' (release) of many such women, in some cases after 40 or more years in hospital, mainly on the basis of an implied pathological promiscuity.

Hare-Mustin and Maracek (1997), Parker et al. (1995) and Bentall (2009) point out that psychodiagnosis has always been abnormality oriented, and has frequently led to stereotyping 'mad people' as completely beyond the range of normal humanity and often beyond help. Alternatively, they have been regarded as objects of medical and psychiatric analysis, and have been benignly *pathologized* instead of being empathically understood or helped. Willingness to listen to their stories, to understand and value their differences (including 'delusions'), is recommended as a better way forward. As Parker et al. and other writers (e.g. Szasz, Cooper, Gergen) have noted, the official language of madness, abnormality, psychopathology and clinical treatment tends

subtly to spread so that ordinary people unwittingly think of themselves, when sad or demoralized, as depressed or stressed, or as in need of 'being in touch with my inner child' and so on.

Some clients no doubt seek the reassurance of official labels (and the associated understanding and 'cure' implied in them) and a small proportion are known to abuse such classificatory systems. 'Factitious PTSD' (fabricated PTSD symptoms), for example, can lead to financial compensation and the psychosocial rewards of adopting a 'sick role' (Young, 1997). In all such ways, therapeutic discourse may be consciously exploited, or unwittingly internalized and made to seem natural, but this cultural tendency is not necessarily in the true interests of individuals' welfare.

In recent years many new, critical and culturally informed commentators on various conditions have not only questioned traditional accounts but have offered alternative, thought-provoking explanations for how different forms of suffering arise or are constructed, for example shyness (Lane, 2007), mania (Healy, 2008) and obsession (Davis, 2008).

INFORMED AND FLEXIBLE ASSESSMENT

Having weighed up some of the complex issues involved in the conceptualization of clients' problems, therapists obviously have to develop their own appropriate style of assessment. This will depend on the effect of the variables of training, profession and setting on the abilities and preferences of therapist and client, and on the uniqueness of each therapeutic encounter. Certain facets of practical assessment have been referred to in Chapter 3.5 in this volume. Here, an informed and flexible model of assessment is briefly outlined.

A simple classical model of assessment is given by Lemma (1996: 46) and is reproduced in Figure 6.2.1. Added to such a model are some proposed variations, complexities and problems for consideration.

PROCEDURAL VARIATIONS

According to various theoretical allegiances, the therapist may conduct a full formal assessment (using *DSM*-like criteria and possibly involving a good many questions), or may eschew assessment altogether, or devise an approach that is midway between these. A useful alternative to a full, formal, written assessment is an informal mutual assessment session or sessions. Therapists may rely more on clinical experience, impressions and intuition than on objective criteria. Alternatively, they may

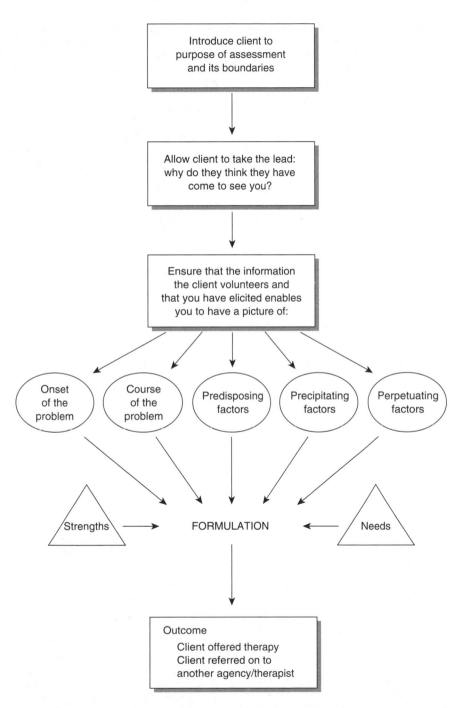

Figure 6.2.1   *The content of assessment*

Source: Lemma (1996)

utilize multiple-item inventories that are not classification centred but aim to gather comprehensive information, such as the Multimodal Life History Inventory (Palmer and McMahon, 1997: 188–96). They may engage in ongoing assessment, in which the client's active participation forms an integral part, possibly with regular reviews and evaluation mechanisms built in (1997: 168–86). Trial therapy – inviting the client to try or taste the therapy – is a typical variation that serves to test out the match between client problem and therapeutic offer.

Another variation is to place real emphasis on assessment of the client's strengths, resources and aspirations rather than on problems or psychopathology (Milner and O'Byrne, 2004). Many brief therapists, for instance, allow for the possibility that the client may need either *no therapy* or only *very brief therapy*, which is partly assessed by a question like, 'Why is this otherwise reasonably well-functioning person presenting for help only *now*?' Alternatively, problematic character traits and everyday problems of living, or hassles, may be construed by humanistic therapists as of equal (but no more) interest than clients' other experiences, stories and goals.

Assessment also includes, of course, the therapist's judgement as to their own competence to tackle the client's problem. This is often best decided in consultation with a supervisor. Where onward referral is decided upon, careful consideration obviously has to be given to the suitability of an alternative therapist or service (Leigh, 1998). The concept of *prescriptive matching* (optimum match of client and client problem with appropriate therapist, therapeutic approach, therapeutic modality, etc.), while attractive in some ways, is extremely difficult to accomplish in practice (Palmer and McMahon, 1997: 93–114).

PROBLEMS OF ASSESSMENT

There is an unhelpful tendency for some texts to disguise the fact that diagnosis and assessment are inexact procedures, involving as much art and educated guesswork as science (Mace, 1995). Although a warning is given in the *DSM* against 'excessively flexible and idiosyncratic' assessments (APA, 2000: xxiii), potential pitfalls lie in wait for *all* practitioners. The client may be opposed to diagnostic assessment (sometimes due to previous bad experiences) and/or the therapist, due to training orientation, ideology or temperament, may be opposed to formal assessment. An ideology of non-directiveness inevitably precludes assessment made from an 'external locus of evaluation'.

In some cases, the client *may* be 'resistant' and 'non-compliant' and/or the therapist may indulge in covert clinical conjectures. Varieties of collusion, impasse or mismatch can result from such unpredictable interplays of differences. Accordingly, assessment of likely therapeutic alliance (often based on the client's previous relational history) is always a crucial procedure. The range of possible presenting problems, complicated by the need to judge severity, and to factor into the assessment equation a knowledge of therapeutic specificity, contra-indications, the therapist's own competence, etc., must lead to some inevitable degree of uncertainty (see also Chapter 3.5 in this volume).

In problem-specific agencies (e.g. alcohol treatment centres, rape crisis centres, HIV/AIDS counselling agencies) a tendency can exist to take the presenting problem for granted as the singular, real, significant problem. Often enough, however, a drinking problem, for example, can *mask* or *compound* other serious problems or conditions, such as depression, PTSD or childhood sexual abuse. Community-based services often attract clients whose problems are multiple, not only in psychological but also in psychosocial terms. Such agencies may have particular assessment challenges when access to their services is easy, yet therapy is necessarily time limited, and alternative local mental health services may have long waiting lists. Sometimes clients are then seen and worked with as a compromise. A degree of compromise also exists where practitioners need to stretch their competence by taking on clients whose kind or severity of problem they have not worked with before, in order to gain clinical experience.

It is more than likely, in an era of increasing emphasis on evidence, that more stringent training and practice in assessment will be called for, as well as far better understanding of the clinical reasoning of practitioners which underpins assessment and early therapeutic decisions (Higgs and Jones, 2000). See also Churchill (2011) for an excellent example of a pluralistic model for understanding client distress.

REFERENCES

APA (2000) *Diagnostic and Statistical Manual of Mental Disorders* (4th edn text rev.). Washington, DC: American Psychiatric Association.

Barber, J.P. and Crits-Christoph, P. (eds) (1995) *Dynamic Therapies for Psychiatric Disorders (Axis I)*. New York: Basic.

Bellack, A.S. and Hersen, M. (eds) (1990) *Handbook of Comparative Treatments for Adult Disorders*. New York: Wiley.

Bentall, R.P. (2009) *Doctoring the Mind: Why Psychiatric Treatment Fails*. London: Allen Lane.

Berrios, G. and Porter, R. (eds) (1995) *A History of Clinical Psychiatry: The Origin and History of Psychiatric Disorders*. London: Athlone.

Cantor, C. (2005) *Evolution and Posttraumatic Stress*. London: Routledge.

Churchill, S. (2011) *The Troubled Mind: A Handbook of Therapeutic Approaches to Psychological Distress*. Basingstoke: Palgrave.

Clare, A. (1980) *Psychiatry in Dissent: Controversial Issues in Thought and Practice* (2nd edn). London: Tavistock.

CRE (1993) *The Sorrow in My Heart: Sixteen Asian Women Speak about Depression*. London: Commission for Racial Equality.

Davies, D. and Bhugra, D. (2004) *Models of Psychopathology*. Maidenhead: Open University Press.

Davis, L.J. (2008) *Obsession*. Chicago: Chicago University Press.

Eleftheriadou, Z. (1999) Assessing the counselling needs of the ethnic minorities in Britain. In S. Palmer and P. Laungani (eds), *Counselling in a Multicultural Society*. London: Sage.

Feltham, C. (2010) *Critical Thinking in Counselling and Psychotherapy*. London: Sage.

Fonagy, P. (2003) The research agenda: the vital need for empirical research in child psychotherapy. *Journal of Child Psychotherapy*, 29 (2): 129–36.

Goleman, D. (2003) *Destructive Emotions: And How We Can Overcome Them*. London: Bloomsbury.

Gopaul-McNicol, S. and Brice-Baker, J. (1998) *Cross-Cultural Practice: Assessment, Treatment, and Training*. New York: Wiley.

Graham, G. (2010) *The Disordered Mind: An Introduction to Philosophy of Mind and Mental Illness*. New York: Routledge.

Hare-Mustin, R. and Maracek, J. (1997) Abnormal and clinical psychology: the politics of madness. In D. Fox and I. Prilleltensky (eds), *Critical Psychology: An Introduction*. London: Sage.

Healy, D. (2008) *Mania: A Short History of Bipolar Disorder*. Baltimore: Johns Hopkins University Press.

Higgs, J. and Jones, M. (2000) *Clinical Reasoning in the Health Professions*. Edinburgh: Butterworth-Heinemann.

Joseph, S. and Worsley, R. (eds) (2005) *Person-Centred Psychopathology: A Positive Psychology of Mental Health*. Ross-on-Wye: PCCS.

Kutchins, H. and Kirk, S.A. (1997) *Making Us Crazy: DSM – The Psychiatric Bible and the Creation of Mental Disorders*. London: Constable.

Lane, C. (2007) *Shyness: How Normal Behavior Became a Sickness*. New Haven, CT: Yale University Press.

Leigh, A. (1998) *Referral and Termination Issues for Counsellors*. London: Sage.

Lemma, A. (1996) *Introduction to Psychopathology*. London: Sage.

Mace, C. (ed.) (1995) *The Art and Science of Assessment in Psychotherapy*. London: Routledge.

Milner, J. and O'Byrne, P. (2004) *Assessment in Counselling: Theory, Process and Decision-Making*. Basingstoke: Palgrave.

Palmer, S. and McMahon, G. (eds) (1997) *Client Assessment*. London: Sage.

Paniagua, F.A. (1998) *Assessing and Treating Culturally Diverse Clients* (2nd edn). Thousand Oaks, CA: Sage.

Parker, I., Georgaca, E., Harper, D., McLaughlin, T. and Stowell-Smith, M. (1995) *Deconstructing Psychopathology*. London: Sage.

Reid, W.H., Balis, G.U. and Sutton, B.J. (1997) *The Treatment of Psychiatric Disorders: Third Edition Revised for DSM-IV*. Bristol, PA: Brunner-Mazel.

Ridley, C. (1995) *Overcoming Unintentional Racism in Counseling: A Practitioner's Guide to Intentional Intervention*. Thousand Oaks, CA: Sage.

Roth, A. and Fonagy, P. (1996) *What Works for Whom? A Critical Review of Psychotherapy Research*. New York: Guilford.

Stevens, A. and Price, J. (2000) *Evolutionary Psychiatry: A New Beginning* (2nd edn). London: Routledge.

Van der Veer, G. (1998) *Counselling and Therapy with Refugees and Victims of Trauma* (2nd edn). Chichester: Wiley.

Watters, E. (2010) *Crazy Like Us: The Globalization of the American Psyche*. New York: Free.

WHO (1992) *International Classification of Diseases and Related Health Problems* (10th edn). Geneva: World Health Organization.

Young, A. (1997) *The Harmony of Illusions: Inventing Post-Traumatic Stress Disorder*. Princeton, NJ: Princeton University Press.

Psychopharmacology

DIGBY TANTAM

Psychopharmacology is the generic term for the study and use of drugs to alter brain functioning with the aim of changing mental function. This definition includes the study and use of recreational drugs; of mind or pleasure enhancers that are supposed to improve on normal functioning; of drugs that are intended to complement other medical or psychological treatments, including drugs designed to enhance the efficacy of psychotherapy; of drugs that are intended to treat physical disorders, but have incidental or occasional effects on the mind; of drugs that are intended to restore people to normal functioning; and of drugs that counteract the effects of other drugs. I shall give at least one example from each of these classes, but will give most examples from the latter classes since these include the prescribed drugs and therefore the drugs or medication that psychotherapists will most often encounter in their clients.

I shall concentrate on the impact of drugs on the experience of being a client in therapy. However, taking medication may also affect the therapist and so questions may sometimes arise about the ethics of taking a particular drug at all or in a particular dose whilst performing therapy.

A considerable amount of information about drugs is available on the internet, much of it published by reputable bodies for the benefit of practitioners or patients. Careful research may provide reliable information even if no access can be gained to the carefully edited information available to professionals, for example that provided in the online version of the *British National Formulary*. I shall not therefore write in detail about any particular drug, but try to address some of the more general issues that might arise when drug use or abuse are combined with psychotherapy and to consider some of the principles that underlie prescribing decisions.

IS PSYCHOPHARMACOLOGY EVER JUSTIFIED?

Radical criticisms of the use of drugs in psychiatry have often been made, sometimes extending to complete opposition to the use of drugs at all. These views are often endorsed by the public who, in surveys, regularly prefer talking treatments to drug treatments in psychological disorders.

One kind of argument is a theological one: man is created in God's image, and is therefore already perfect in form. To believe that one can improve upon God's perfection by the use of drugs is a kind of heresy. Many people would endorse this argument when it comes to cognitive or other enhancements, for example the use of stimulants to help people to study or of amyl nitrate to increase sexual pleasure. However, although some would argue that illness is also part of God's design for the world, and should not be tampered with, it is difficult to argue that illness is a kind of perfection. In fact most people would probably accept that wounds or diseases render a person imperfect and that treatment of them is in pursuit of God's purposes. My intuition is that most people would say that treatment of, say, a child with pneumonia with an antibiotic is also in line with God's purpose or, to put it in humanistic terms, enables the child to have their true destiny or to reach their full potential. But some people might argue that this does not apply to a condition that is 'purely' mental, such as a person who is stricken with grief.

Some psychiatric disorders do approximate to the disease model: the inexorable course of schizophrenia in some people is one example; another is the onset of self-destructive episodes of mania or of profound depression in some people with bipolar disorder. Although psychotherapists may contribute to the amelioration of these conditions, their primary treatment is usually medical. This may be considered inappropriate by a few critics of psychopharmacology, but the strongest criticism is reserved for psychopharmacology in anxiety-related disorders or unipolar depression (i.e. depression not associated with a past history of being high or 'hypomanic').

Objections to the use of medication in these conditions are made not just on the ethical or religious grounds mentioned, but on moral and practical grounds too.

DOES TAKING DRUGS PREVENT PEOPLE FROM OVERCOMING THEIR OWN PROBLEMS?

The moral objections to psychopharmacology often rest on the concept of agency or responsibility. At the height of the use of benzodiazepines by doctors during the 1980s in the UK, one of the feminist arguments against their use was that women who were distressed by adverse home circumstances – an abusive husband for example – were sedated by their doctors and so lost the will to try to rectify the situation. Use of antidepressants or anxiolytics may be seen to be a voluntary abrogation of the responsibility to change one's life, or a denial of the power or agency to do so, because taking medication is to frame the problem as a kind of disease in oneself. Not only that, but taking tranquillizers quells or suppresses the negative emotions that might power a change.

Related to this is the perception by some psychotherapists that taking medication might be a kind of escape from the work of self-reflection and therefore from being honest about oneself and one's situation. This may be linked to the common idea that counselling and psychotherapy are undermined by combining them with psychoactive medication. I consider this later.

People who have regularly taken medication for emotional problems do seem more likely to think of medication as their first-line strategy when new problems emerge. So it seems likely that the use of psychoactive drugs does alter a person's preferred choice of coping strategy. But whether this makes them, in the long run, less resilient in the face of future adversity, as many psychotherapists might argue, cannot be assumed; I shall consider the evidence in a later section.

ARE PSYCHOACTIVE DRUGS A KIND OF PSYCHOTHERAPY?

Comparisons of the response to drugs and to psychotherapy in people with unipolar depression or anxiety disorders suggest that the outcomes are much more similar than might be expected (Tyrer et al., 1988). The most likely explanation is that both act through a process of what Jerome Frank (1961) memorably called 'remoralization'. When medicine was more paternalistic, doctors would sometimes capitalize on this by giving their patients sugar-coated pills that were psychopharmacologically inert. To conceal this from their patients, they would term these pills 'placebos' (from the Latin *placebo*, 'I will please') and the pharmacist would have a stock of these inert pills to dispense. The placebo effect remains an important hidden element in psychiatry. A recent reanalysis of the effects of antidepressants that included unpublished as well as published studies demonstrated, for example, that the outcome of antidepressants and the outcome of placebo was no different in people with mild or moderate depression, even though the published studies suggested otherwise (Kirsch et al., 2008).

The passage of time might account for some of the placebo effects: sharp dips in mood or rises in anxiety may just remit given change in the circumstances that caused the dip in the first place. But in many studies, outcome is compared to being on a waiting list and the outcome of the treated group is normally better than that of the waiting list group, indicating that the placebo effect is a real treatment effect.

Frank argued that the placebo effect accounted for the therapeutic effect of psychotherapy as well as of drugs. There has been continual interest in how it is produced, and what factors increase or decrease it. It is plausibly assumed that believers in drugs benefit more from drug placebos and believers in therapy more from talking treatments: however, there is some evidence against this (Chilvers et al., 2001).

COST–BENEFIT ANALYSIS

Drugs cost money, sometimes a lot of money. New drugs cost more than old ones, often because old ones can be made in factories by companies who just make drugs rather than go to the additional expense of developing them. These generic drugs are the pharmacological equivalent of the eclectic or non-branded therapies, provided by psychotherapists who have not gone to the expense of acquiring the licence to provide an acronymic treatment like CBT. Money is not the only cost. Psychotherapy and counselling have time costs. It has been argued that they may cost more than that. Fay Weldon argued in her novel *Affliction* that they may cost relationships, too. (*Affliction* was written after Weldon broke up with her second husband Ron Weldon who, according to Wikipedia, left her after being told by an 'astrotherapist' that their star signs were incompatible.)

These costs have to be set against benefits. Benefits, too, may be varied: there may be offset effects in a reduction of the need for other treatment, a decrease in disability leading to increased income, and, of course, a reduction of symptoms. In order to compare symptoms one with another, they are often recast as increments of quality of life.

As placebos are inert, it is sometimes assumed that they have no costs, but this is not so. There may be travel costs, time off work costs, the reduced quality of life for people who get worse with placebos (the 'nocebo' effect), the costs of delaying more active treatment, and most importantly the costs of reducing resilience if, indeed, treatment may do that.

SHOULD PSYCHOTHERAPISTS KNOW ABOUT DRUGS?

A little knowledge is a dangerous thing, so people say. So is it better for psychotherapists to have no knowledge at all about drugs? The answer to this partly depends on the practice of the psychotherapist or counsellor. Working in private practice will often mean working with a clientele who is rarely taking psychoactive drugs; working in a general practice, the opposite. Working in a school or college setting may often mean working with students who are using street drugs, and working in a substance misuse clinic will almost always mean this.

I would argue that any therapist or counsellor who is likely to work with people taking psychoactive drugs needs to know about them. My primary reason is that I think of counselling or therapy as a kind of primary care, and not as a specialized add-on to other health services. So a counsellor's role will include recognizing possible side effects of medication and recommending to a client that they have these investigated. It will also include evaluating if the use of a psychoactive drug is adversely affecting counselling, and more rarely, but no less importantly, if a client might benefit from psychotherapy.

The justification that I have just given for knowing about drugs focuses more on knowing the costs of psychoactive drugs and less on the benefits. This is the inverse of psychopharmacology training for doctors, and rather unusually, I will therefore consider drugs according to the categories of their side effects rather than the customary classification of drugs by the expected benefits – antidepressants, anxiolytics and so on. Fortunately this side effect classification is actually simpler than a classification according to main effects. The reason for this is that most of the drugs currently used in psychiatry are presumed to act by either augmenting or competing with naturally occurring chemicals – transmitters – that mediate electrical transmission in brain, spinal cord, and smooth muscle.

THE TRANSMITTER HYPOTHESIS OF PSYCHOPHARMACOLOGY

Nerve cells conduct signals electrically, but there is always a gap between the membrane at the end of one nerve cell and the membrane at the beginning of another. This tiny gap or synapse normally prevents the electrical current in one nerve from jumping to the next nerve, or to the muscle or end organ. The spark is carried forward by a chemical, released from the nerve carrying the current and acting on the next nerve to create a new spark, leading to a current in that nerve. A surprising range of chemicals are used in the body as 'transmitters' in this way. They include gases such as nitric oxide, simple organic compounds such as amino acids, and more complex chains of amino acids or polypeptides. Nitric oxide leads to the widening or dilation of blood vessels, and this is its main therapeutic use in treating angina and impotence (Viagra works this way). Its effects on the brain are only just being understood. This is true of many of the polypeptides too. Often these also act on the gastro-intestinal system as well as on the brain.

Most psychoactive drugs are thought to have their effect by influencing chemical transmission in the synapse (treatments for epilepsy and mania may be exceptions). They may mimic the transmitter and combine with the place or receptor where they attach, or bind, on the nerve to which the spark is being transmitted. If they do, they may stimulate a spark themselves ('agonists') or act as an inert 'blocker' or 'antagonist'. Normally transmitters are quickly destroyed so that their effects are very short lived, but drugs may delay this inactivation either by blocking enzymes that normally break the transmitter down or by blocking the pump that reabsorbs the transmitter ('reuptake inhibitors'). The effect of this is to prolong or potentiate the action of the transmitter.

TOLERANCE AND DEPENDENCE

One further complication is that the receptors on the nerve to which the spark is being transmitted (the post-synaptic receptor) or in the pump that sucks up the transmitter again (the pre-synaptic receptor) in the nerve down which the spark is travelling may reduce or increase in number. This may be in response to an increase in transmission, and therefore counteract the effect of a drug. Many psychoactive drugs lead to this kind of 'up regulation' or 'down regulation'. So many psychoactive drugs, if they are stopped, particularly if they are stopped suddenly, may leave transmission in a more parlous state than it was before the drug was started. As a result, some psychiatric disorders may recur or relapse if treatments are stopped suddenly (a 'rebound' effect) and, even if this does not happen, more and more drugs may be required to produce the same effect ('tolerance'). Tolerance, coupled with symptoms recurring more and more intensely when the drug's effects have worn off, may lead to dependence.

Dependence seems to be a particular problem for drugs that have an immediate effect on pain, anxiety or low mood – sometimes collectively called dysphoria. Tolerance and dependence are not generally a problem with drugs that take several weeks to work, as is the case with most treatments for depressive illness or psychosis. One does not need to be an existential psychotherapist to conclude that evolution has worked to ensure that dysphoria persists even if it is artificially abolished, and that therefore dysphoria has an important signal function that is necessary for survival or successful reproduction or both.

Dependence bedevils psychopharmacology because it contributes to one of the most damaging myths: that psychopharmacology should always be avoided because of the risk of dependence.

WHEN ARE DRUGS INDICATED?

There is strong evidence that severe depression, mania, psychosis, and attention deficit disorder improve with drug treatment. Panic disorder and obsessive compulsive disorder may also respond. The first three are disorders that I have previously mentioned are most 'disease-like' in the minds of many people. Treatability is not in itself an indication that drugs should always be used in these conditions. Depression, for example, spontaneously remits in as many as 85 per cent of people. However, this eventual recovery may take years, and without treatment it is associated with an increased mortality. This is also true of schizophrenia and even ADHD.

Mortality is not the only indication that doctors give for treatment. Increasing quality of life (that is, reducing dysphoria and/or reducing disability) is also often given as an indication by doctors but is one that has more opponents. One argument is that dysphoria may be the driver for personal initiatives that might lead to a resolution of the condition and not just an amelioration. One such initiative is psychotherapy or counselling. So some psychotherapists believe that psychotherapy is less likely to be successful if people are taking prescribed psychoactive drugs for this reason. Another contra-indication to medication sometimes given by psychotherapists or counsellors is that psychoactive drugs may affect thinking and feeling and so interfere with the process of therapy.

Psychotherapists do not have to prescribe drugs and are not in a position to either recommend or counsel against their use. What they do need to know, though, are the side effects of medication, particularly as these may affect the therapy or counselling itself.

TYPES OF PSYCHOPHARMACOLOGICAL TREATMENTS

The types of psychopharmacological treatment are shown in Table 6.3.1. The psychopharmacology of the common psychiatric disorders and their 'normalization' is dominated by the pharmacology of a limited number of types of drugs acting on an even more limited number of transmitters (Table 6.3.2). Many new drugs turn out to be variants of old ones.

The effect of benzodiazepines is on a fifth transmitter, gamma-aminobutyric acid or GABA, that is released by short inhibitory neurons in many parts of the brain. GABA is derived from another amino-acid transmitter, glutamate. Oddly, glutamate is the main excitatory transmitter in the brain. 'Inhibitory' in this context means that the transmitter makes a neuron less sensitive to the effects of another transmitter, and therefore less likely to carry forward a spark from another neuron. Excitatory transmitters have the opposite effect.

Table 6.3.1   *Types of psychopharmacological treatment*

Enhancers	These drugs aim to increase function above normal. They include stimulants like caffeine and khat, and disinhibitors like ethanol. They also include nitric oxide sexual stimulants like Viagra and amyl nitrite (both potentiators of nitric oxide), amphetamine and cocaine (for reduced fatigue and greater focused attention), Ecstasy for better clubbing, and anticholinesterase inhibitors for enhanced memory
Normalizers	This class of drugs overlaps with the previous one but is justified on the basis that they do not increase function but 'correct' dysfunction. They include anticholinesterases that reduce the early effects of Alzheimer-type dementia; dopamine precursors that reduce the early symptoms of Parkinson's disease including those of early dementia; dopamine blockers that reduce some of the symptoms of schizophrenia; drugs that increase frontal lobe function in ADHD by combining an enhancement of both dopamine and serotonin function; and drugs that reduce low mood in depression by enhancing catecholamine and serotonin function in depression. There are also peptide drugs that may prove of value in the future, including opiates that some think may reduce the likelihood of repeated self-injury through stimulating endorphin transmission, and a possible class of future drugs for attachment disorders that will work through oxytocin or vasopressin transmission
Treatments	Most psychological disorders are 'endogenous'. Those that are not are most often the result of psychosocial adversity for which there is no drug treatment. The number of psychological disorders that are caused by a remediable cause are few, and many of those are the consequences of drug treatments (iatrogenic disorders) or of drug misuse rather than caused by some external, physical agent that can be counteracted by medication. Some inflammations of the brain may present as mental disorders, and so treatment of, for example, cerebral malaria presenting as psychosis constitutes a treatment of a mental disorder. Gene therapies or drugs that can directly affect neuronal growth or connectivity may provide treatments in the future

Table 6.3.2   *'Normalizers' by condition*

Condition	Supposed cause	Treatment
Alzheimer's disease (the most common cause of dementia)	Destruction of nerve cells, selectively affecting nerves that release acetyl choline (cholinergic neurons)	Drugs that block the enzymes (cholinesterases) that break down acetylcholine, and so increased acetylcholine release
Depression	Reduced catecholamine release (release of norepinephrine particularly) and reduced serotonin release	Drugs that enhance norepinephrine, serotonin, or both
Schizophrenia	Over-production of dopamine in the cerebral cortex relative to an under-production of other transmitters such as glutamate or HDMA	Drugs with complex effects on transmitters but commonly block dopamine and enhance acetylcholine
Anxiety	Complex and probably depend on type of anxiety	Drugs that enhance gamma-aminobutyric acid (GABA) transmission Drugs that enhance serotonin transmission Drugs that block histamine receptors, e.g. several of the antipsychotics Drugs that block specific symptoms such as drugs for sleep, or drugs for tremor, by blocking the effects of epinephrine and norepinephrine

Some transmitters may be excitatory in one synapse and inhibitory in another. This happens when there is one receptor in one synapse but a different one in the other synapse. Glutamate has three different receptors, with one subtype, the NMDA receptor, being the most studied in psychiatry. Norepinephrine and serotonin have many more. Norepinephrine has an alpha and a beta subtype, and each has variants. Serotonin has seven families of receptor subtypes, each family having several variant subtypes within it. Despite this complexity, many of the side effects of drugs can be inferred from their enhancement or inhibition of these six transmitters: acetylcholine, serotonin, dopamine, norepinephrine, GABA and glutamate (Table 6.3.3).

Table 6.3.3 *Transmitters, drugs affecting them, their mode of action on the transmitter, and side effects**

Transmitter	Enhance (+) or counteract (−)	Common drugs affecting this transmitter	Side effects with particular impact on therapy	Other selected side effects
Dopamine (D$_2$ receptor)	+	Drugs for Parkinson's disease, e.g. L-dopa		Increased gambling, increased libido, addiction to the drug itself
		Drugs for ADHD, e.g. amphetamine, methylphenidate	Lack of reward seeking, reduced task-driven behaviour, with a reduction of thoughts and 'blunting' of feelings, inner restlessness, sedation	Stiffness, tremor, other symptoms similar to Parkinson's disease; over-activity of the breast
	−	Antipsychotics, especially high-potency antipsychotics		
Serotonin (5-HT$_{2c}$ receptor)	+	Some antidepressants and anxiolytics, e.g. selective serotonin reuptake inhibitors (SSRIs), some antipsychotics	Possible impulsivity, dominant behaviour	'Toxic confusion' may lead to death in rare cases
	−	Lipid lowering drugs, e.g. statins, diet	Panic attacks in predisposed individuals with sensitivity to suffocation, low mood (Miller et al., 2000)	Cravings
Catecholamines (epinephrine and norepinephrine)	+	Serotonin and norepinephrine reuptake inhibitors (SNRIs), e.g. venlafaxine, duloxetine, sympathomimetic drugs such as some first-generation tricyclic antidepressants, e.g. amitryptiline	Sometimes conflicting effects, depending on whether alpha or beta receptors blocked more, but may be agitation, anxiety, rapid heart, irritability	Conflicting effects but blood pressure may be raised along with other physical symptoms associated with stress
	−	Some atypical antipsychotics, e.g. quetiapine, clozapine, sertindole, zotepine, some antidepressants, e.g. mianserin, mirtazepine	Sedation	Conflicting effects but may include weight gain, rapid heart rate, dizziness on standing
Acetylcholine (muscarinic receptor)	+			Constipation, dry mouth, blurred vision, difficulty in passing water, eyes more sensitive to light
	−	A very large number of commonly prescribed drugs including the low-potency antipsychotics (usually dose over 50 mg per day), e.g. chlorpromazine, clozapine, loxapine, quetiapine, and some tricyclics, e.g. amitryptiline	Sedation	Increase in heart problems, possible increase in cognitive decline, and possibly increased risk of Alzheimer's disease in elderly, risk of death in overdose
Glutamate (NMDA receptor)	+	Drugs to alter conscious level, e.g. methadone (also an opiate), alcohol, phencyclidine, ketamine	Disinhibition, reduced ability to store current events in memory, dissociation, psychotic symptoms	Linked to cell death
	−	Drugs for Parkinsonism, e.g. amantadine		
GABA (A receptor)	+	Antiepileptic drugs, benzodiazepine anxiolytics, barbiturates	Impaired memory of current events, sedation (Czubak et al., 2010)	
	−	Benzodiazepine antagonists, but only used in emergencies		

*This is not a complete list of the side effects of each medication mentioned. This can be found on guides to drugs such as the *British National Formulary* or on the drug packaging.

CONCLUSIONS

Psychopharmacology is now an industry as well as a major research area. Given this, it is perhaps surprising that more is not known about the action of commonly used drugs in psychiatry. One reason might be that so much research has focused on a few transmitters while other possible modes of drug action have continued to be refractory to investigation. Another is that these few transmitters interact. Another reason is the placebo effect, by which expectations rather than the drug itself produce the effect.

Even less is known about the subtle side effects of drugs, such as the reflection or exploration of feeling that are required by psychotherapy or counselling. Since many people who seek psychotherapy and counselling because of a mental disorder are likely to be taking, or at least to have been offered, drug treatment for their condition, psychotherapists do need to know if psychotherapy and pharmacotherapy conflict, as many might assume.

I have considered the possible prejudices that may lead psychotherapists or patients to be suspicious of drug therapy, but I think that there may sometimes be contra-indications when the side effects of drugs might interfere with psychotherapy or counselling. What is known about this is summarized in Table 6.2.3.

REFERENCES

Chilvers, C., Dewey, M., Fielding, K., Gretton, V., Miller, P., Palmer, B., et al. (2001) Antidepressant drugs and generic counselling for treatment of major depression in primary care: randomised trial with patient preference arms. *British Medical Journal*, 322 (7289): 772–5.

Czubak, A., Nowakowska, E., Burda, K., Kus, K. and Metelska, J. (2010) Cognitive effects of GABAergic antiepileptic drugs. *Arzneimittelforschung*, 60 (1): 1–11.

Frank, J. (1961) *Persuasion and Healing*. Baltimore, MD: Johns Hopkins University Press.

Kirsch, I., Deacon, B.J., Huedo-Medina, T.B., Scoboria, A., Moore, T.J., Johnson, B.T. (2008) Initial severity and antidepressant benefits: a meta-analysis of data submitted to the Food and Drug Administration. *PLoS Medicine*, 5 (2): e45.

Miller, H.E.J., Deakin, J.F.W. and Anderson, I.M. (2000) Effect of acute tryptophan depletion on CO_2-induced anxiety in patients with panic disorder and normal volunteers. *The British Journal of Psychiatry*, 176 (2): 182–8.

Tyrer, P., Seivewright, N., Murphy, S., Ferguson, B., Kingdon, D., Barczak, P., et al. (1988) The Nottingham study of neurotic disorder: comparison of drug and psychological treatments. *Lancet*, 2: 235–40.

PART VI

CLIENT PRESENTING PROBLEMS

SPECIFIC PROBLEMS

Alcohol Problems

RICHARD VELLEMAN

WHY IS ALCOHOL AN ISSUE?

Very many people, both in the UK and across the world, drink at an excessive level, and are causing themselves and others immense problems. On a typical day in the UK, some 10,000 individuals seek help for their own or someone else's drinking problem; on a typical day in the USA, more than 700,000 people are treated for 'alcoholism'. The World Health Organization estimates that about 140 million people throughout the world suffer from alcohol dependence. Alcohol causes nearly 10 per cent of all ill-health and premature deaths in Europe.

A quick examination of some of the huge range of available statistics (references to all of these statistics are given in Velleman, 2011: Chapter 1) reveals that:

- More than a third of British adults (37 per cent in 2007) drink in excess of sensible limits: 41 per cent of men in 2007 drank more than 3–4 units of alcohol on at least one day of the week, and 34 per cent of women exceeded their limit of 2–3 units. This is a huge rise in less than 10 years: in 1988 around a quarter of men and 10 per cent of women drank more than the recommended limits.
- More than 75 per cent (in 2008) of both boys and girls aged 14–15 had drunk alcohol. Almost 40 per cent of 15-year-olds drank in the previous week, and the average amount consumed by these children exceeded the recommended levels for adults. Underage consumption of alcohol is often a precursor to smoking and the use of illicit drugs, and the risk of smoking and drug use is particularly high in adolescents who report high levels of drunkenness.
- In England, 26 per cent of adults aged 16–64 have an alcohol use disorder (38 per cent of men and 16 per cent of women). This is equivalent to approximately 8.2 million people in England. Over 17.5 million people in the US have alcohol-related problems.
- Each of these individuals will have contact with and will influence a wide range of others: family members, friends, workmates and members of the public (who, for example, share the same roads as intoxicated drinkers).
- Therefore, the number of people who may need information, advice and counselling related to their own or someone else's alcohol problems is huge, representing people at all points on a continuum from relatively early and mild difficulties at one end to serious and life-threatening concerns at the other.

The seriousness of some of these issues cannot be overstated:

- Deaths attributable to alcohol consumption are estimated to be in the region of 40,000 per year in England and Wales, and 100,000 per year in the US. In the UK, the rate of male deaths attributable to alcohol consumption has more than doubled from 9.1 per 100,000 in 1991 to 18.7 per 100,000 in 2008; the rate for females has risen from 5.0 per 100,000 in 1991 to 8.7 in 2008 – less than half of the male rate. By comparison the total number of deaths in England and Wales related to illicit drug use has ranged from 829 in 1993 to 1805 in 2001 (2004 figures were 1495; 2005 figures were 1608); deaths in the USA related to illicit drugs are around 15,000 per year.

- Within these figures of alcohol-related deaths, up to 63 per cent of all deaths following falls, up to 61 per cent of all deaths by fire, up to 47 per cent of all deaths by drowning, and around 40 per cent of all deaths following assaults are alcohol-related.
- About 50 per cent of all crime is alcohol related, as is around 60 per cent of stranger violence and 46 per cent of domestic violence. Between one-third and one-half of all child abuse cases dealt with by social services are alcohol related.
- In 2005–6 there were over a quarter of a million admissions to NHS hospitals in England for alcohol-related diagnoses; hospital admissions for these diagnoses have virtually doubled since 1997. Up to 35 per cent of all accident and emergency attendances and ambulance costs are alcohol related; between 12 midnight and 5 a.m., 70 per cent of A&E attendances are alcohol related.

WHAT ARE ALCOHOL PROBLEMS?

So, alcohol is related to lots of different types of problem. But as counsellors, what do we mean when we say that someone has an alcohol problem? The statistics listed above about the amounts consumed imply that alcohol problems are related to this. But in fact, my own definition (Velleman, 2011) of an alcohol problem is much simpler than this. My definition is that, if someone's drinking causes problems for him or her, or for someone else, in any area of their lives, then that drinking is problematic. So if someone's drinking causes problems with his or her health, finances, the law, work, friends or relationships, then that drinking is problematic; and if it causes problems for husbands, wives, children, parents, bosses or subordinates, then it is also the case that that drinking is problematic.

There are many implications of such a simple definition. It means that whether or not someone has a drinking problem is not determined by fixed quantities of alcohol, or timings (e.g. early morning drinking), but instead is a matter of negotiation by the individual with himself or herself, and with family, friends, workplace, and society as a whole. And the definition is based on consequences of drinking (for the individual, for their families or work colleagues, or for society) and not simply on amount consumed or frequency of consumption.

Other Definitions

A very commonly used term is *alcoholism*. Here, alcohol problems are seen as a disease or psychiatric condition. 'Alcoholics' are ill, and hence need psychiatric care. Another form of this idea is that alcoholism is an allergic reaction to alcohol: this view is held by Alcoholics Anonymous, and by many health and other care practitioners.

Although this disease view has been with us for a long time, it was helped along by the formation of Alcoholics Anonymous (AA) in the 1930s, and especially within the helping professions by the publication of a book entitled *The Disease Concept of Alcoholism* (Jellinek, 1960), in which the author suggested there were five different types of alcoholism.

There are both advantages and disadvantages to using the term 'alcoholism'. Many people find the disease concept useful; and conceptualising it as an illness has allowed a far more helpful approach to be developed within the workplace, where people with alcohol-related problems can be helped to overcome their difficulties as opposed to being sent immediately down the disciplinary route. Disadvantages include the fact that 'alcoholism' is often used as a generic label, implying a single entity; this in turn has led to expensive and fruitless searches for both a single cause and an all-embracing cure. Furthermore the idea of the 'disease' of alcoholism suggests a medical problem, where people are physically addicted and are subject to powerful cravings for alcohol. This medicalisation links it with a whole range of beliefs concerning diseases and illnesses held in our society: treatment is the job of the medical profession; there is nothing I can do about my drinking; the solution is not my responsibility, it is the doctors'; and so on. The term also dissuades many people from seeking help, either because they do not want to be labelled an 'alcoholic', or because they are sure their drinking, even though it may be causing some 'slight' problems, is nothing like their stereotype of what an alcoholic is like.

Due to some of these reasons, the World Health Organization (WHO) in 1977 suggested replacing the term 'alcoholism' with *alcohol dependence syndrome* (ADS). In many ways, this is an improvement. It suggests that a drinking problem can be described in terms of three factors, that is the degree to which: a person's drinking behaviour is abnormal; they feel there is something wrong with their drinking; and they have an altered physiological response to alcohol (tolerance and withdrawal symptoms). Hence the definition accepts that there are three indices which need to be measured, namely behavioural, subjective and physiological; these are all continua running from normal to highly abnormal, and it is possible for a person to be high on one or two dimensions without necessarily being high on all. However, although officially ADS has replaced 'alcoholism', it is the latter term which is commonly used by both the general public and many counsellors.

Many people argue that, although the development of the ADS is an improvement, it is still a medical, disease notion of what is fundamentally a non-medical problem. However, others argue that because people do develop problems with their consumption of an addictive drug, it is reasonable to use such a medical notion.

What is clear is that the terminology which we use to describe our clients with alcohol problems does reveal important values about the ways in which we think that clients change. I use 'problems' because I believe that people can change the ways that they think and feel about, and behave towards, alcohol; whereas the term 'alcoholism' implies that a client has some irreversible disease or malfunction which is not really amenable to a counselling intervention.

WHAT DIFFICULTIES DO CLIENTS WITH ALCOHOL-RELATED PROBLEMS POSE FOR US AS COUNSELLORS?

Clients who have problems with their drinking come to us in a wide variety of ways, bearing a wide variety of difficulties. Because these clients with alcohol problems are individuals living within our society, they are prey to the same stresses and strains as we all are. The difficulties they present, then, will be similar to those which clients with any other sort of problem show. So as counsellors, when we work with clients with alcohol-related problems, we confront exactly the same set of difficulties as we do when working with any other client group. That is, there are problems which all clients share, irrespective of their presenting problem; and there are difficulties which are specific to the presenting problem (which could be bereavement, debt, marital crisis and so on, but which in this case is alcohol).

Similarities Common to all Counselling

Wherever we work, the types of emotional difficulties with which clients present are similar; whatever type of agency we work within, and whatever sort of initial problem a client brings, people living in today's society in the UK have similar problems. So clients with alcohol problems may also present with any combination of other problems: emotional, cognitive, behavioural or practical. They may be overcome with grief, depression, anger, uncertainty, bewilderment, anxiety and so on. They may have problems with their social lives, their relationships, the law, their jobs, their health, their finances or their housing. People who have developed a problem with alcohol are still people; seeing a client with an alcohol problem does not mean that you as a counsellor will be faced with an entirely different set of issues than if you worked with any other sort of presenting problem.

Specific Difficulties with Alcohol Problems

There are, however, particular issues which relate specifically to clients' alcohol consumption. These are usually concerned with two elements. The first is that, because alcohol is an addictive drug, it can give rise to problems of tolerance and withdrawal, dependency, craving, and a strong ambivalence about whether or not giving up or reducing use is either possible or desirable. The second is that public and professional attitudes to drinking problems are so negative that clients will often find it difficult to get help when they need it.

WHY DO PEOPLE DEVELOP ALCOHOL PROBLEMS?

There are a large number of theories purporting to explain the causes of alcohol problems (Orford, 2001; Velleman, 2011; West, 2006). Some are based on factors within the individual, some on factors within the social context, and others on overall cultural factors.

My own view is that there is no single cause for all alcohol problems. People must be dealt with on an individual basis, not according to some pre-existing formula based on any single theory of causation. Any person's vulnerability towards developing an alcohol problem will exist on a continuum, from highly vulnerable to highly invulnerable. Even highly invulnerable individuals could develop a problem with their use of alcohol, given the right circumstances. And even those people who are most vulnerable will need some triggering factor (such as easy availability of cheap alcohol, or some other personal problem such as bereavement or relationship crisis) to push them towards developing a problem.

The most important insight into helping people with their alcohol problems is to realise that people drink for reasons. They may not understand what these reasons are, or else they would change without our help. Our two most important tasks as the counsellor are to help our clients understand what their reasons are for behaving in the ways that they do, and then to empower them to change, so that they no longer need to behave in these ways.

INTERVENTIONS

Five simple principles should underpin our counselling of people with alcohol problems (Velleman, 2011):

- People drink problematically for reasons.
- Working with alcohol-misusing clients means we need to deal simultaneously with their alcohol use and other difficulties.
- People cannot be dealt with in isolation from the rest of their lives (family, friends).
- Counselling clients with these problems is no different to working with people with other types of difficulty.
- It is not necessary to be a specialist counsellor to help clients with alcohol-related problems.

There are also four simple assumptions which are useful (Velleman, 2011):

- Alcohol use lies along a continuum: there is no simple dividing line between 'alcoholic' drinkers and the rest of the population.
- Individuals can move along this continuum, in either direction.
- Individuals learn how to behave towards alcohol, and this is open to change.
- We know from a lot of research that most people who develop alcohol problems go on to change without recourse to outside professional help. This implies of course that the ones who need our assistance will have perpetuating factors in their lives which block them from changing under their own steam.

These principles and assumptions can be used to help us counsel people with alcohol problems. We help these clients by using the same skills that we use in counselling any person with any problem, and the same understanding of the counselling process that we use with any other kind of presenting problem.

This counselling process needs to go through a number of steps or stages as we work through our tasks in counselling. We need to develop trust, help the client to explore the problem, help to set goals, empower clients to take action, help them to maintain changes, and agree when the time comes to end our counselling relationship. In counselling, we are responsible for this process and for ensuring that these tasks are undertaken and fulfilled. The main responsibility for the content of the sessions (instead of the process) lies with the client.

In exploring and assessing a client's alcohol problems, we should examine the client's alcohol use; their drinking behaviour; the effects on them of their use of alcohol; the client's thinking concerning the alcohol use (their expectations, values, definition of the problem, understanding of its cause); and the context (family, employment, social) within which the client has been drinking.

There are other techniques which are especially relevant to problem drinkers: giving clients information and simple advice as to how to cut down or give up; helping the client to set intermediate, short-term goals which are (and seem to the client to be) achievable; helping problem drinkers to become more aware of the forces within their environments which push them towards drinking; and using more active techniques to help them to rethink what they can do.

Other important techniques and ideas which have been developed within the alcohol field have proved very effective. Key amongst these are the Prochaska and DiClemente cycle of change (DiClemente, 2003; Prochaska and DiClemente, 1983; 1994; Prochaska et al., 1995) and motivational interviewing (Miller and Rollnick, 1991).

The *cycle of change* was underpinned by two important ideas: that *change has various stages*, and that *the change process is a cycle*: people usually make more than one attempt before succeeding. This clear and commonsensical model suggests that when clients arrive for counselling, they may be at one of a variety of stages, to each of which the authors gave a name: *pre-contemplation* (an individual may not be aware that his/her drinking is causing problems; or may not really think about the problematic side of their drinking); *contemplation* (an individual acknowledges the link between behaviour and problems; they try to work out what is going wrong; they start to think about their inappropriate use); *preparation* (a serious commitment to action, and to a change plan to be implemented in the short term, is made); *action* (the client implements the proposed action or change, and constantly practises new skills which have been learnt to enable change, so as to maintain the new habits or behaviours); *maintenance* (an attempt to integrate the behaviour change into their lifestyle, trying to maintain the chosen direction); *termination* or *lapse/relapse* (either the new behaviour has been successfully learnt, and the new coping methods are successfully incorporated into the client's repertoire; or the person succumbs to the pressures to resume problematic drinking).

Motivational interviewing is a powerful technique that accepts that ambivalence about changing behaviour is normal. We need to work with this ambivalence from the outset, as opposed to ignoring it until a client 'fails', whereupon explanations are couched in terms of 'lack of willpower' or 'lack of motivation'.

Effective interventions will almost always include working with this ambivalence, and working with clients at whichever stage of the cycle of change that they are at. We will always have to work with clients' expectations and ambivalence, give them information, focus on their goals, help them to believe they can change (which will involve both raising awareness and restructuring the way they think about their behaviour), and teaching them new skills to deal with old problems and new strategies to overcome anticipated problems.

Skills

To help clients to develop their own abilities to solve the problems in their lives, it is of paramount importance that clients acquire and practise relevant skills, as opposed to merely discussing the issues with us. Our clients must learn and practise alternative ways of coping with the triggers which normally push them into drinking. Those clients who can engage in alternative ways of behaving, and who can adopt a positive style of coping with problems, appear to do well in the long term.

Many of the techniques outlined above are based on cognitive-behavioural therapy (CBT) ideas. These are very helpful and I use them a lot in my own counselling work. But it is important to remember that research which has looked at the relative efficacy of different sorts of therapy has found that *all* therapies with a good evidence base and which are well delivered seem to be equally effective. The phrases 'good evidence base' and 'well delivered' are key: I am not arguing that all therapies or all therapists are equally effective. But it seems clear that the important issues are whether the therapist or counsellor:

- has the key counselling skills
- is using an intervention which he or she is happy with and confident about
- is using an intervention which is evidence based.

I look at this issue again, later in this chapter, in examining the 'matching' of clients to treatments.

As well as the techniques mentioned above, there also will be specific issues relating to alcohol which we ought to understand. This will increase *our* self-confidence in working with the clients. So it is useful to know a bit about alcohol's effects, to understand that alcohol is an addictive drug, but also to understand that people with drinking problems can control their behaviour; they are not overcome by an impossible-to-resist urge to consume alcohol.

It is also useful to know that 'controlled drinking' goals are legitimate ones for clients to aim towards (if the client wishes to), although both we and our clients should realise that controlled drinking is more difficult than abstaining. Related to that, if we think clients are aiming for the wrong goal (drinking or otherwise), we should tell them that, on the one hand, we are happy to back them up and help them to achieve this goal, but, on the other hand, we personally think they have chosen incorrectly, and why we think this.

Another key area in counselling for alcohol problems (in common with all addictive problems, and most other problems within mental health) is relapse: the situation where a client is making progress towards achieving their goals and then they gradually (or, more commonly, suddenly) take a number of steps backwards. Clients need to know that even if they do relapse, we want them to return and discuss the situation with us.

Relapse management is like the other parts of counselling: understanding the reasons for a client's behaviour; understanding the central role a client's expectations and beliefs play in determining his or her behaviour; and enabling a client to learn new skills and utilise those already learnt.

Myths

There are many myths which increase the negative way in which people perceive working with clients with drinking problems. These myths include beliefs that 'all alcoholics are liars or in denial', 'one can't work with someone unless he/she has admitted he/she is an alcoholic', 'one can't work with people unless they have reached rock-bottom', 'one can't work with people until they are ready to be helped or admit they have a problem', 'abstinence is the only answer to a serious drinking problem', 'there's no point in trying to help alcoholics, treatment successes are a real rarity', 'the only people who can help problem drinkers are those who have an alcohol problem themselves'. There is good evidence that all of these beliefs are myths (see Velleman, 2011). Furthermore, if one adopts the stance towards counselling problem drinkers outlined above, it becomes very difficult to agree with any of these myths. That stance is that:

- People are individuals who do things for individual (or familial or social) reasons.
- There *are* reasons for people's behaviour: it is up to us to help clients understand these reasons.
- Counselling draws out the client through a process of reflecting, clarifying, challenging, exploring.
- These activities are done with, not to, the client.
- Alcohol use lies along a continuum: there is no simple dividing line between 'alcoholic' drinkers and the rest of the population.
- Individuals can move along this continuum in either direction.
- Individuals learn how to behave towards alcohol, and this is open to change.
- If people continue to use alcohol despite developing problems, this must occur for reasons as well.

Families

Most counselling of problem drinkers is undertaken in individual sessions. However, there is increasing evidence (Copello et al., 2005; McCrady and Epstein, 2008; O'Farrell and Fals-Stewart, 2006; Smith and Meyers, 2004) that the involvement of family members (spouses, parents, other close and affected people) can lead to better outcomes. Sometimes relatives of problem drinkers do not wish to get involved; they often have had very negative experiences while living with a problem drinker and may just want the drinker to 'sort themselves out'. Indeed, often these relatives need help in their own right, although frequently they do not receive it. But if we can involve interested and affected family members in our counselling of clients with alcohol problems, it is likely that help to both the drinker and the relative will be more effective.

TREATMENT SETTINGS

Most people who develop problems related to their consumption of alcohol never receive any form of official or professional help. There are many reasons for this, but mostly it is because they find help and advice from family, friends, colleagues and so on.

For those who do turn to helping agencies, there exists a wide range. Services are provided by volunteers, non-statutory agencies, statutory authorities, private bodies, and via workplaces.

In theory, problem drinkers should be able to receive help from any of a wide range of primary care professionals such as GPs, social workers, health visitors and probation workers. In practice, many such professionals do not feel confident working with alcohol and other addictive problems and hence tend not to identify them unless they are very extreme. Many clients therefore either present to more specialist agencies such as alcohol advisory centres or seek help from private counsellors or residential centres. Because much more money has been put into drug treatment than into alcohol treatment, in many places it is easier to access help from agencies which provide treatment for 'addiction' or 'substance misuse' rather than 'alcohol'. It is difficult to get public funding to access residential centres, although some health or social services organisations do still fund places. These centres commonly follow some variation of the 'Minnesota model', which broadly follows the AA/12-step tradition. However, many residential projects aim to be holistic in their approach, often emphasising spiritual dimensions as well as social skills, education about alcohol and the development of psychological insight.

Services which might be offered by any of these agencies include medical, individual counselling, group, and couple or family-oriented interventions. What is usually offered in the UK has changed over the past decades from a relatively fixed programme of intervention, usually including therapeutic groups, social skills sessions and – in some settings – an emphasis on following a 12-step/AA-based approach to recovery, to a more individually based counselling approach. If someone is a very physically dependent drinker (i.e. they show withdrawal symptoms when they abruptly stop drinking such as sweats, shakes, nausea, agitation, disrupted sleep patterns or more rarely hallucinations or paranoia) they may need to be prescribed medication to help them safely through this period – normally a reducing dose of diazepam for a period of four to 10 days. In addition, some drugs are also prescribed as part of an intervention package to help people remain abstinent from alcohol. The most common type of drug used is Antabuse (disulfiram), although newer drugs such as acamprosate and naltrexone are also becoming more widely used. Antabuse is a drug that has no physical effect unless someone consumes alcohol, whereupon it has very unpleasant effects. Antabuse works not only because of these physical effects, but also because of the *expectation* of the negative effects if alcohol is drunk.

Self-help is also an important intervention. The most widely available self-help group is AA, which many severely dependent drinkers find extremely helpful. It has a clear philosophy, is readily available, and offers vital mutual support, although some people are put off by its belief in alcoholism as a disease. 'Al-Anon' is a network of self-help groups for the partners and spouses of people with an alcohol problem, and can be a useful source of support for many people.

MATCHING CLIENTS TO INTERVENTIONS

There is clear evidence that some forms of help are better than others. Bill Miller in the USA has been at the forefront for many years of an approach where the outcomes of different types of help are compared, and hence where we can see what is more likely to work and what less (see for example Miller and Wilbourne, 2002). From the work of Miller and his colleagues, and of others working in this same tradition, it has been shown that some interventions (such as brief interventions, motivational approaches, or social and family approaches) are far more effective than are others (such as educational films or lectures, confrontational counselling, or relaxation training).

However, what is also becoming evident is that, as long as one uses interventions which *do* have good evidence, then any of these 'good interventions' is as effective as any other. Project MATCH was the largest, most statistically powerful and most methodologically rigorous psychotherapy trial ever undertaken – not just in the alcohol field but in any area of psychotherapy. It was conducted in the USA over a number of years, starting in 1989 (Project MATCH, 1997a; 1997b). It compared three major and rather different methods of helping people with serious alcohol problems, all of which had good empirical support: cognitive-behaviour therapy (CBT), motivational enhancement therapy (MET), and 12-step facilitation (TSF). Project MATCH showed that there were no major differences in how well people did, irrespective of which form of help they received. The United Kingdom Alcohol Treatment Trial (UKATT Research Team, 2005a; 2005b) built upon the findings of MATCH, comparing one of the therapeutic methods that had been used in that project (MET) with results from using a quite different method, based around ideas related to family and social support and social networks (Social Behaviour and Network Therapy, SBNT: Copello et al., 2009). Again, UKATT showed that there were no differences in how well people did, irrespective of which form of help they received.

Importantly, as well as showing that all these well-evidenced interventions seem to work as well as each other, what both Project MATCH and UKATT also showed was that *treatment works*. In both trials, substantial reductions in alcohol consumption, dependence and problems, and better mental-health-related quality of life, were reported.

Many organisations now *do* offer some of these ways of helping. There has been a move over the past few years for those who commission services (such as commissioners in health authorities or primary care trusts, or in local authorities) to insist that organisations do offer evidence-based ways of helping. Unfortunately, all too often commissioning authorities have been pushing for only those evidence-based interventions which are cheap to deliver, such as brief interventions. Whilst these do work very well with many people, there are also many others for whom such an intervention does not work, and who need a much greater level of input. Unfortunately, commissioners are not so enthusiastic about funding agencies to provide these interventions! However, it is the case that almost all commissioning authorities *are* insisting that agencies need to have good record keeping mechanisms and can provide some evidence, although this is still much more about processes than outcomes.

REFERENCES

Copello, A., Velleman, R. and Templeton, L. (2005) Family interventions in the treatment of alcohol and drug problems. *Drug and Alcohol Review*, 24: 369–85.

Copello, A., Orford, J., Hodgson, R. and Tober, G. (2009) *Social Behaviour and Network Therapy for Alcohol Problems*. London: Routledge.

DiClemente, C. (2003) *Addiction and Change: How Addictions Develop and Addicted People Recover*. New York: Guilford.

Jellinek, E. (1960) *The Disease Concept of Alcoholism*. New Jersey: Hill House.

McCrady, B. and Epstein, E. (2008) *Overcoming Alcohol Problems: A Couples-Focused Program. Therapist Guide: A Cognitive-Behavioral Therapy Approach (Treatments That Work)*. New York: Oxford University Press. Also *Overcoming Alcohol Problems: Workbook for Couples*. New York: Oxford University Press.

Miller, W. and Rollnick, S. (1991) *Motivational Interviewing: Preparing People for Change* (2nd edn 2002). London: Guilford.

Miller, W. and Wilbourne, P. (2002) Mesa Grande: a methodological analysis of clinical trials of treatments for alcohol use disorders. *Addiction*, 97 (3): 265–77.

O'Farrell, T. and Fals-Stewart, W. (2006) *Behavioral Couples Therapy for Alcoholism and Drug Abuse*. London: Guilford.

Orford, J. (2001) *Excessive Appetites* (2nd edn). Chichester: Wiley.

Prochaska, J. and DiClemente, C. (1983) Transtheoretical therapy: toward a more integrative model of change. *Psychotherapy: Theory, Research and Practice*, 19: 276–88.

Prochaska, J. and DiClemente, C. (1994) *The Transtheoretical Approach: Crossing Traditional Boundaries of Therapy*. New York: Krieger.

Prochaska, J., Norcross, J. and DiClemente, C. (1995) *Changing for Good: A Revolutionary Six-Stage Program for Overcoming Bad Habits and Moving Your Life Positively Forward*. New York: Harper.

Project MATCH Research Group (1997a) Matching alcoholism treatments to client heterogeneity: project MATCH post-treatment drinking outcomes. *Journal of Studies on Alcohol*, 58: 7–29.

Project MATCH Research Group (1997b) Project MATCH secondary *a priori* hypotheses. *Addiction*, 92: 1671–98.

Smith, J. and Meyers, R. (2004) *Motivating Substance Abusers to Enter Treatment: Working with Family Members*. New York: Guilford.

UKATT Research Team (2005a) Effectiveness of treatment for alcohol problems: findings of the randomised UK Alcohol Treatment Trial (UKATT). *British Medical Journal*, 331: 541–4.

UKATT Research Team (2005b) Cost effectiveness of treatment for alcohol problems: findings of the randomised UK Alcohol Treatment Trial (UKATT). *British Medical Journal*, 331: 544–8.

Velleman, R. (2011) *Counselling for Alcohol Problems* (3rd edn). London: Sage.

West, R. (2006) *Theory of Addiction*. Oxford: Wiley Blackwell.

Anger Management

EMMA WILLIAMS, MICHAEL SCOTT AND COLIN FELTHAM

Anger is a common emotion experienced at times by us all. Indeed, if used constructively, it can be a positive and empowering emotion. Anger can be defined as an *emotional state* experienced as the impulse to behave in order to protect, defend or attack in response to a threat or a challenge. Of itself, anger is not classified as an emotional disorder (APA, 2000). It becomes problematic only when experienced with such a frequency or intensity that, for example, it frustrates the attainment of desired goals, interferes with the ability to connect with others, or is detrimental to health. Problematic anger, associated with poor impulse control, is commonly evidenced in domestic violence and other forms of criminal behaviour, and sometimes in premenstrual syndrome. Some problematic anger (for example, associated with couple conflicts and alcohol abuse) may well be presented to counsellors, while anger resulting in police intervention and criminal convictions will more often be presented to probation staff individually or in anger management groups.

NATURE, SIGNS AND SYMPTOMS

Anger, like all other emotional states, is influenced by our cognitions (thoughts, images or values), our behaviours and our physiology.

Cognitions involved in an angry response commonly include thinking errors such as personalizing, 'He did that deliberately to upset me', and catastrophizing, 'I'll never get another job.' Common anger-inducing beliefs typically include, for example, that life should be fair or that one is entitled to take revenge for perceived injustice. Brondolo (1998) has suggested that anger arises when a person perceives that his core values have been violated.

The behavioural response to anger can include 'adaptive' responses such as problem solving, assertiveness and tactical withdrawal, and 'maladaptive' responses such as social withdrawal, self-harm, and verbal and physical aggression, the latter two being the target of most anger control/management therapies.

The physiological response is that triggered in the autonomic nervous system by adrenalin which produces symptoms such as increased heart rate, sweating and flushing, common to all emotions. It is the individual's labelling of these symptoms as 'anger' which differentiates it from other emotions, and of course there are cross-cultural variations.

Rasmussen (2010), from an Adlerian perspective, considers anger to be one of the 'protest and fighting emotions' that are typically felt when obstacles or threats are present; it springs from a 'felt minus position' and commonly develops in childhood. Most humanistic therapies probably share this view of anger.

Aggression, perhaps the most important sequela of anger, can be defined as any form of *behaviour* directed towards the goal of harming or injuring another living being or object.

TYPICAL ACCOMPANYING PSYCHOLOGICAL, SOCIAL AND PHYSICAL PROBLEMS

People with anger control problems frequently experience associated problems with interpersonal

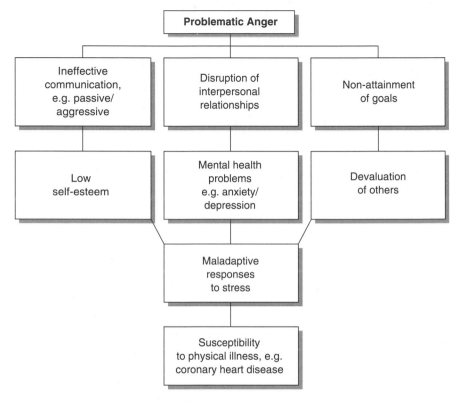

Figure 6.5.1 *Anger and its associated problems*

relationships, low self-esteem and mental and physical health problems. The interrelationships of these problems are illustrated in Figure 6.5.1.

Treatments might focus on the various associated problems as well as on anger control *per se*, for example enhancement of self-esteem, ability to cope with stress, and communication skills, or examination of the person's goals and values.

EXTENT/EPIDEMIOLOGY

Compared with emotional disorders such as anxiety and depression, a great deal of the psychological research has largely ignored anger as an emotional disorder, and few researchers have addressed anger as an important emotion in psychological disturbance. The extent of anger control problems is difficult to define as it is dependent on the levels of expressed anger and aggressiveness tolerated in our (or any) society. Aggressive behaviours in the form of arguments, indirect hostility, threats and displaced aggression are commonplace. However, the

more severe consequences of loss of anger control are legally defined by criminal offences. Although not all acts of aggression are anger related, crime statistics can give an indication of the extent of the problem. The police recorded 1,391,000 violent offences in England and Wales for 2009–10. In a significant number of cases of violent incidents, offenders are known to the victim in some way (Smith and Allen, 2004). To disabuse readers of the idea that most violence is part of 'street (or criminal) culture', consider that the Health and Safety Executive's figures for 2009–10 show that there were 366,000 threats of violence in the workplace, with 6017 reported injuries resulting. Forty-three percent of all those assaulted were repeat victims. Warnings against violence in the workplace and on pubic transport have proliferated in recent years, and incidents of so-called road rage, air rage and supermarket checkout rage (as well as football 'hooliganism') have received (perhaps disproportionate) media attention.

With regard to domestic violence, it has been estimated that in the UK up to 43 per cent of all women have been victims of domestic violence, sexual assault and stalking. It was found that physical violence between spouses occurs in almost one-third of marriages in the USA (Straus et al., 1980). Other statistics also illustrate the enormous extent of the problem of anger and aggressive behaviour. For example, typically a woman may be physically abused 35 times before she reports to police. Seventy-five per cent of domestic violence may never be reported to police; 27 per cent of abused women have said their partner also physically assaulted their children; and 3000–5000 children die each year in the USA from parental abuse (Pagelow, 1984).

There is a notable gender difference in anger expression, and hence in referrals to anger management programmes or anger control therapy, with men being highly predominant. In recent years great concern has been expressed about the increase in gun and knife crime, particularly among young people, only some of which is associated with impulsive anger. The expression of anger is strongly socially and culturally determined: women tend to suppress anger, to become depressed or to self-injure. Those women who do behave aggressively are more likely to be seen as suffering from a mental disorder.

AETIOLOGY

The major origin or causes of anger control problems for any individual are likely to be an interaction of both internal and external factors. Internal determinates are often rooted in childhood formative experiences. These commonly include a family history of violence or aggression, experience of bullying, or experience of physical, sexual, emotional abuse or neglect. In addition, biological predisposition or vulnerability factors might also play an important role.

External or social factors also have a role in determining aggression, for example, frustration, provocation and peer influence. Environmental factors such as noise, overcrowding and poor living conditions can also be influential determinants.

TREATMENTS OF CHOICE

The aim of therapy for anger problems is greater awareness and *control* of anger, not its suppression.

The treatment approach chosen will in part be dependent upon the theoretical background of the therapist. The development of treatments for anger control problems has generally followed the course of the development of psychological treatments for other emotional disorders: from the early instinct and evolutionary theories to motivational and drive theories, and more latterly to social learning and cognitive-behavioural theories.

The treatment implications stemming from psychological theories of anger and aggression are briefly summarized below:

- *Instinct theory* (e.g. Freud). The positive redirection of aggressive drives, for example, into combative sports, the displacement of aggressive urges and use of catharsis.
- *Evolutionary theory* (e.g. Lorenz). The prevention of accumulation of anger by engaging in lower-level non-injurious behaviour, the experience of emotions incompatible with aggression, for example, happiness.
- *Motivational theory* (e.g. Berkowitz). Modification of cues to aggression, cognitive restructuring, reduction of physiological arousal.
- *Social learning theory* (e.g. Bandura). Cognitive reappraisal, relearning, examination of consequences of aggression.
- *Feminist theories* (e.g. Rohrbaugh). Challenging gender identity and sex-role stereotypes.
- *Humanistic theories* (e.g. Rogers). Accepting and changing the subjective experience of anger, re-experiencing and catharsis, enhancing understanding, ownership, examining personal values.
- *Stress-inoculation theories* (e.g. Meichenbaum). Exposure to manageable levels of stress, cognitive preparation, skills acquisition, application training, self-instructional training.
- *Cognitive-behavioural theories* (e.g. Beck). Anticipation of triggers to aggression, reduction of physiological arousal, challenging thoughts, modifying beliefs, changing behaviours.
- *Relapse prevention theories* (e.g. Marlatt and Gordon). Increasing awareness, antecedents, behaviour and consequences of aggression, use of early warning signs, high-risk situation management, behavioural rehearsal, relapse prevention planning.

The treatments of anger with the strongest research database are cognitive/relaxation approaches (Edmondson and Conger, 1996). These authors concluded, from their review of 18 studies, that it was difficult to recommend one treatment approach – be it relaxation training, cognitive restructuring or social skills training – above another because different anger treatments produce large effects for some aspects of anger and small effects for others. Thus treatment should be targeted to specific presenting problems, for example, focusing on the reduction of physiological arousal for clients who are habitually tense, or on emotional regulation through mindfulness for some clients labelled with borderline personality disorder. Focusing on cognitive techniques such as distraction, self-calming statements, rationalizing and task focusing would be appropriate for clients who tend to ruminate or present with significant cognitive distortions.

Brondolo (1998) has suggested that listening to clients' stories about anger-evoking situations gives a clue to their core values. The therapeutic task is to make the values explicit, identify their origins, and elaborate a viable expression of these values. Brondolo points out that values might compete, for example 'to achieve' and 'to care', and that the values may have to be expressed sequentially rather than simultaneously.

Williams and Barlow (1998) have presented a comprehensive treatment programme for clients with anger problems. Their programmes include:

1 motivational techniques, including an examination of the consequences of anger and aggressive behaviour for self and others
2 an understanding of anger as an often self-defeating coping strategy by addressing clients' personal predisposing factors, triggers and anger aetiology
3 the development of more adaptive coping strategies by modifying core beliefs and thinking errors that underlie the expression of anger
4 the identification of early warning signs, high-risk situations, escalating and defusing behaviours, lifestyle balance, and the detailing of relapse prevention strategies such as self-statements, reducing physiological arousal, emergency tactics, challenging beliefs and increasing repertoire of responses.

Feindler (2006) has presented an excellent comparative text for this field. Suggested components for the treatment of problematic anger are presented in Table 6.5.1.

Table 6.5.1 *Suggested components for the treatment of problematic anger*

Phase 1

Engagement, motivation and preparation for change
Educate about the cycle of anger, thoughts, feelings, beliefs and behaviour
Focus on acceptance of and responsibility for anger control problem
Clarify expectations, help clients to set personal goals
Promote clients' motivation to change their behaviour, e.g. decision matrix, cost–benefit analysis
Encourage practice of self-monitoring techniques, e.g. personal anger diaries, trigger events, anger charts, hassle logs

Phase 2

Anger- and aggression-focused interventions
Develop individual formulation of the factors underlying problematic anger for the client, e.g. beliefs, social, familial and environmental influences, common triggers, anger cycle and coping strategies
Develop coping strategies to deal with anticipated triggers, e.g. escape, de-escalation techniques and alternative responses
Help client to recognize and manage automatic thoughts and cognitive distortions by applying a range of cognitive strategies, e.g. thought stopping, self-talk, replacement thoughts, cognitive restructuring, reattribution, decentring, reframing, decatastrophizing
Identify, understand and challenge key beliefs that underlie and maintain anger control problem
Increase clients' repertoire of responses to conflict situations, e.g. defusing, assertiveness, conflict resolution, problem solving, negotiation, compromise
Construct behavioural experiments to enable client to test their predictions and learn about their thoughts, their behaviour and the consequences
Enhance clients' control of physiological responses, e.g. tension release techniques, relaxation and stress management

Phase 3

Relapse prevention, maintaining gains
Review clients' personal aims and set new ones
Develop a comprehensive relapse prevention plan, including high-risk situations, early warning signs and coping strategy enhancement
Focus on lifestyle change
Develop 'problem profiles': what to change and how to do it

WHAT WORKS FOR WHOM?

No treatment intervention for anger will work unless the client is enabled to recognize it as a problem and indeed as *their* problem. Motivational work is often a prerequisite to successful engagement in anger control treatments. Clients who deny they have any problem with anger control, who have no motivation to change, or who have very significant impulse control problems might benefit from pre-treatment preparation, such as building a therapeutic relationship, gaining insight into past incidents and situations, enhancing self-esteem, competency and control recognition, personal anger awareness, and basic anger and aggression monitoring. Recent publications have indicated treatment successes with clients previously thought to have intractable anger control problems, for example seriously assaultive violent populations (Novaco, 1997) and violent psychotic forensic patients (Becker et al., 1997). In some cases there might be physical reasons, such as head injury, that interfere with the person's ability to benefit from psychological treatment. The general rule in the treatment of any psychological condition is that alcohol and substance abuse have to be controlled before the underlying condition can be addressed, and this applies equally to the treatment of anger. Obviously, the more other conditions are associated with anger (e.g. personality problems, mental illness, impulse control problems), the more difficult it will be to effect successful treatment.

Anger control is often an important component of marital therapy, focusing on moving the couple from an 'I win, you lose' to a 'both win' framework. However, with regard to domestic violence, caution should be exercised to ensure that issues such as perpetrator accountability and responsibility are successfully addressed before anger control strategies are employed as one part of a comprehensive treatment approach. Similarly, anger control training can be an important component of teaching child management strategies to parents within the framework of understanding the parent–child relationship, and adult acceptance of responsibility for non-violence (Potter-Efron, 2005). Generating 'emergency tactics' and aggressive incident analysis can be particularly useful. The development of uncharacteristic irritability is one of the diagnostic features of post-traumatic stress disorder, and strategies for tackling this are outlined in Scott and Stradling (2001). Some support has been demonstrated for the person-centred approach with domestic violence offenders (Wilkinson and O'Keeffe, 2006).

CLINICAL MANAGEMENT AND TYPICAL PROGNOSIS

From primary referral source (e.g. the general practitioner) to attendance at therapy, the dropout rate might be expected to be between 30 and 60 per cent. Good professional liaison, explicit client suitability criteria and provision of information regarding the therapy can reduce inappropriate referrals and dropout rates. Those clients who do engage in therapy, and who are motivated, can be expected to show lasting improvements in anger control.

Following therapy, clients might be offered:

- maintenance sessions to focus on their relapse prevention plans, to formally examine incidents of loss of anger control and to rehearse coping strategies
- support or self-help groups
- supplementary sessions to focus on associated problems, such as low self-esteem, confidence building, assertiveness training and coping with stress
- referral to other agencies or colleagues to explore specific problems identified in anger control therapy, for example, experience of childhood sexual or physical abuse.

Clients with anger control problems, more than any other emotional disorder, are a risk to others. The clinical management of anger should therefore focus not only on helping the client to maintain control over their anger, and potential aggressive behaviour, but also on assessment and management of their risk of violence and aggressive behaviour. Once assessed, the client's potential risk to others should be managed by isolating the critical factors identified and drawing up a treatment or supervision plan to attempt to reduce the risk. Good liaison and communication with other professionals involved with the client are usually essential. The limits of confidentiality should be made explicit to the client.

Increasingly, self-help resources (e.g. Bloxham, 2010; Davies, 2009) and web-based resources (e.g. www.nhs.uk/conditions/anger-management, www.angermanage.co.uk) are available.

REFERENCES

APA (2000) *Diagnostic and Statistical Manual of Mental Disorders* (4th edn text rev.). Washington, DC: American Psychiatric Association.

Becker, M., Love, C.C. and Hunter, M.E. (1997) Intractability is relative: behaviour therapy in the elimination of violence in psychotic forensic patients. *Legal and Criminological Psychology*, 2 (1): 89–101.

Bloxham, G. (2010) *Anger Management for Dummies.* Chichester: Wiley.

Brondolo, E. (1998) Affirming core values: a cognitive approach for use in the treatment of anger and anxiety problems. *The Behaviour Therapist*, 21: 60–87.

Davies, D. (2009) *Overcoming Anger and Irritability.* London: Robinson.

Edmondson, C.B. and Conger, J.C. (1996) A review of treatment efficacy for individuals with anger problems: conceptual, assessment and methodological issues. *Clinical Psychology Review*, 16 (3): 251–75.

Feindler, E.L. (ed.) (2006) *Comparative Treatments of Anger Related Disorders.* New York: Springer.

Novaco, R.W. (1997) Remediating anger and aggression with violent offenders. *Legal and Criminological Psychology*, 2 (1): 77–88.

Pagelow, M.D. (1984) *Family Violence.* New York: Praeger.

Potter-Efron, R.T. (2005) *Handbook of Anger Management: Individual, Couple, Family and Group Approaches.* London: Routledge.

Rasmussen, P.R. (2010) *The Quest To Feel Good.* New York: Routledge.

Scott, M.J. and Stradling, S.G. (2001) *Counselling for Posttraumatic Stress Disorder* (2nd edn). London: Sage.

Smith, C. and Allen, J. (2004) *Violent Crime in England and Wales.* Home Office online report 18/04. London: HMSO.

Straus, M.A., Gelles, R.J. and Steinmetz, S.K. (1980) *Behind Closed Doors: Violence in the American Family.* Garden City, NY: Doubleday/ Anchor.

Wilkinson, K. and O'Keeffe, C. (2006) *Raging Anger Within Me: An Evaluation of a Person-Centred Service for Male Victims and Perpetrators of Domestic Violence at Doncaster Prison 2005–2006.* Project Report. Sheffield: Sheffield Hallam University.

Williams, E.E. and Barlow, R.S. (1998) *Anger Control Training: A Practitioner's Guide.* Bicester: Speechmark.

RECOMMENDED READING

Beck, A.T. (1999) *Prisoners of Hate: The Cognitive Basis of Anger, Hostility and Violence.* London: Harper Collins.

Davies, D. (2009) *Overcoming Anger and Irritability.* London: Robinson.

Kassinove, H. (ed.) (1995) *Anger Disorders: Definition, Diagnosis and Treatment.* Washington, DC: Taylor and Francis.

Williams, E.E. and Barlow, R.S. (1998) *Anger Control Training: A Practitioner's Guide.* Bicester: Speechmark.

Anxiety and Panic

GILL DONOHOE AND TOM RICKETTS

Problematic anxiety is a common and pervasive difficulty which manifests in many ways. Phobic conditions, obsessive compulsive disorders, and the specific difficulties resulting from severe trauma are dealt with elsewhere. Here the focus will be on 'pure' anxiety difficulties as represented by the conditions labelled panic disorder and generalized anxiety disorder. Given the increasing effectiveness of cognitive-behavioural approaches to these disorders, this is the perspective which will be taken throughout.

This chapter will first outline the features of panic disorder and generalized anxiety disorder. Models for understanding these difficulties will be introduced, and the treatment implications deriving from these models outlined. Finally, research into the area will be briefly reviewed, and areas of contention discussed.

CLINICAL FEATURES

Two different types of anxiety disorder can be distinguished. In the first, panic disorder, the main problem is recurrent panic attacks which occur unexpectedly at times when the individual does not anticipate anxiety. A panic attack is a discrete period of intense fear or discomfort that is accompanied by a range of somatic or cognitive symptoms (see Table 6.6.1). Panic attacks are often accompanied by a sense of imminent danger or impending doom and an urge to escape. They may be cued, that is triggered by specific situations, such as in phobic conditions or following trauma, or may be spontaneous. Unexpected or spontaneous panic attacks are important in the *diagnosis* of panic disorder, where at least two attacks need to have occurred spontaneously, that is, not in situations which commonly cause the individual anxiety. Panic disorder and agoraphobia commonly occur together, with the fear and avoidance of a wide range of situations common in agoraphobia often being linked to a fear of the recurrence of panic attacks. Other features of panic disorder are that sufferers experience persistent concern about having additional attacks, worry about the implications of the attack or its consequences, or a significant change in behaviour related to having had a panic attack.

Individuals may also experience panic attacks as a result of substance use, or as part of a medical condition such as hyperthyroidism. These possible explanations for symptoms should be explored in assessment.

In the second type of anxiety disorder, generalized anxiety disorder (GAD), the main defining feature is excessive anxiety and worry. To meet diagnostic criteria these feelings must be experienced more days than not for at least six months, must be about a range of different events or activities, and must cause significant interference with the individual's functioning. Table 6.6.2 shows other diagnostic features for generalized anxiety disorder.

Overall, the symptoms experienced in generalized anxiety disorder are less intense than in panic disorder, onset is more gradual, and the central

Table 6.6.1   *Criteria for a panic attack*

A discrete period of intense fear or discomfort, in which four (or more) of the following symptoms developed abruptly and reached a peak within 10 minutes:

1	palpitations, pounding heart, or accelerated heart rate
2	sweating
3	trembling or shaking
4	sensations of shortness of breath or smothering
5	feeling of choking
6	chest pain or discomfort
7	nausea or abdominal distress
8	feeling dizzy, unsteady, lightheaded, or faint
9	derealization or depersonalization
10	fear of losing control or going crazy
11	fear of dying
12	paresthesias (pins and needles in extremities)
13	chills or hot flushes

Table 6.6.2   *Diagnostic features of generalized anxiety disorder*

Excessive anxiety and worry, occurring more days than not for at least six months, about a number of events or activities (such as work or school performance). At least three out of the following symptoms:

1 restlessness or feeling keyed up or on edge
2 being easily fatigued
3 difficulty concentrating or mind going blank
4 irritability
5 muscle tension
6 sleep disturbance

The anxiety, worry or physical symptoms must lead to significant distress or impairment in important areas of functioning
The focus of the anxiety or worry is not exclusively related to another psychiatric disorder

feature is the repeated experience of excessive worry. Although less intense, GAD can be very difficult to control (which is in itself one of the defining features) and the condition tends to be under-recognized, although prevalence rates, difficulties in diagnosis and the chronic course of the untreated disorder have been recognized (McManus et al., 2009).

UNDERSTANDING PANIC DISORDER AND GENERALIZED ANXIETY DISORDER

In the cognitive model of panic disorder, it is proposed that panic attacks result from the misinterpretation of certain bodily sensations, with the sensations being perceived as much more dangerous than they actually are. Examples would be an individual perceiving palpitations as evidence of an impending heart attack, or perceiving a shaky feeling as evidence of loss of control and insanity.

Figure 6.6.1 illustrates the model. Triggers can be either external (e.g. a department store for a client suffering from agoraphobia) or internal (e.g. bodily sensations, thoughts or images). If the trigger is experienced as threatening, a mild state of apprehension occurs. This is accompanied by a range of bodily sensations, which are then interpreted as catastrophic. This interpretation becomes the next perceived threat, and the vicious circle continues, culminating in a panic attack.

Once panic attacks have become established, the individual develops further responses to panic which serve to maintain the problem, namely selective attention, safety behaviours and avoidances. Selective attention relates to the way in which clients are watching out for physical symptoms constantly, and therefore notice them more, activating the panic cycle. Safety behaviours develop to prevent the feared catastrophic consequence from occurring, and include such things as holding on to walls or sitting down to prevent collapse. These behaviours give the individual an

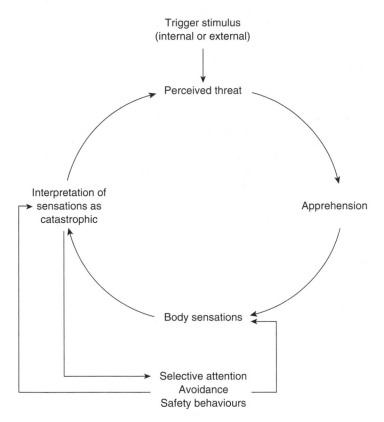

Figure 6.6.1   *Cognitive model of panic disorder*

Source: adapted from Clark (1986), Wells (1997)

alternative explanation for why the feared event did not occur, and prevent changes in thinking during panic attacks. An example would be the individual thinking that they did not collapse because they sat down. Avoidances develop which restrict the individual's contact with anxiety-inducing situations, thereby reducing opportunities for discovering that the feared consequences do not occur.

The cognitive model proposes that panic disorder develops as a result of the triggering of pre-existing learnt assumptions about physical symptoms such as 'bodily symptoms are always an indication of something being wrong'. These assumptions are viewed as being developed through a range of routes such as parental response to illness, perceived medical mismanagement, and sudden deaths of significant others. Such assumptions are argued to be relatively stable (Beck, 1976), but to become more pertinent when triggered by events such as the individual experiencing illness themselves, or a first panic attack.

Models of generalized anxiety disorder (Borkovec and Sharpless, 2004; Dugas et al., 1998; Wells, 1997; Zinbarg et al., 2006) all share a focus on the central element of worry. This is consistent with developments in the understanding of the nature of the disorder, which is in turn evidenced in revisions of the last two editions of the *Diagnostic and Statistical Manual of Mental Disorders* (*DSM*: American Psychiatric Association, 1987; 1994). Diagnostic revisions supported the need to categorize GAD as a chronic and disabling disorder, identifiable even if coexisting with another anxiety disorder, and present for at least six months (instead of just one month).

A model outlined by Dugas and colleagues represents the considerable advancement in the understanding of GAD over the last 15–20 years, and forms the basis of a step-by-step treatment approach now recommended by the Department of Health in the UK (IAPT, 2007). Figure 6.6.2 outlines this model. Central to the Dugas model is the tendency of the individual to have a set of negative beliefs around uncertainty and its implications; an example is the belief that uncertainty is unfair or upsetting and should be avoided at all costs. This enduring tendency is described as an 'intolerance of uncertainty' and is usually overtly manifested in the 'what if?' style of thinking which feeds the worry, and a range of possible approach or avoidance behaviours. These can include, among others, repeated checking, reassurance seeking, not being able to delegate, procrastination or avoidance of commitment. Consistent with previous models (e.g. Wells, 1997), the beliefs the individual holds about the worry itself have an important part to play in the development and maintenance of the problem. These can be either negative or positive. An example of a negative belief would be that the 'worrying will send me crazy', whereas a positive belief may be that 'worrying can prevent bad things from happening' or 'I need to worry to help me solve my problems.' Although both negative and positive beliefs may require targeting in therapy, Dugas and colleagues have helped to focus attention on the key role that positive beliefs may have in that if the act of worrying leads to a desired outcome (even if this may be coincidental), then the beliefs and in turn

the worry will be reinforced. An example of negatively reinforced worry would be where a negative outcome is avoided.

The two other key aspects of the Dugas model are negative problem orientation and cognitive avoidance. Cognitive avoidance incorporates emotional and cognitive features and can be usefully outlined as implicit/automatic or explicit/voluntary. To explain implicit avoidance, in the late 1980s the work of Borkovec provided the theoretical ground for understanding how worry, which is primarily a verbal-linguistic mental activity, seemed to suppress mental imagery associated with stronger emotional and physiological responses. Worry can therefore be reinforced through a process of avoidance of emotional or physiological arousal. Examples of the explicit and more deliberate forms of avoidance include the conscious suppression of worrisome thoughts or replacement with neutral or positive thoughts, the use of distraction, or the avoidance of situations associated with worry. The role of cognitive avoidance has had important implications for the treatment of GAD as it has led to the incorporation of exposure approaches where appropriate – methods traditionally associated

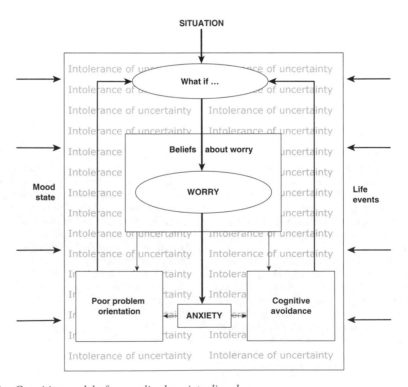

Figure 6.6.2 *Cognitive model of generalized anxiety disorder*

Source: Dugas et al. (1998), reprinted with permission from Elsevier

primarily with phobic anxiety. This will be addressed in the next section. Negative or poor problem orientation seems to be closely linked to the intolerance of uncertainty and relates to the way an individual approaches problems, for example viewing them as threatening with associated doubts regarding their confidence to solve them or to have a positive outcome.

These explanations of panic disorder and generalized anxiety disorder have led to the development of specific interventions, which will be outlined below.

TREATMENT

In both conditions cognitive-behavioural approaches deriving from the work of Beck (1976) have been shown to be effective, along with earlier methods based upon conditioning and learning theories (see Hawton et al., 1989; Craske and Barlow, 2007). Treatment is based upon detailed assessment and analysis of the presenting difficulty along with any other associated problems. This includes the client keeping a diary of their symptoms, and the taking of a history of the development of the problem. The assessment information is then discussed with the client within a cognitive-behavioural framework. This forms the first stage of therapy, the main purpose of which is to educate the client on the principles of the approach and the rationale for the treatment plan based upon their difficulties.

A considerable proportion of individuals with anxiety may be managed within primary care, adopting a self-help approach with more limited therapist involvement but still within the framework described in this section. The National Institute for Health and Clinical Excellence guidance on anxiety (NICE, 2007) is currently being updated and, in line with the recommendations for other conditions such as depression, a stepped care framework is outlined to assist in the management of GAD. Self-management approaches provide the client with access to guidance and information on panic and anxiety and how to apply therapeutic strategies. These methods are considered in further detail later within the research section.

APPROACHES TO PANIC DISORDER

- *Education about anxiety*. Given the importance of catastrophic misinterpretations of bodily symptoms in panic disorder, education regarding the features of normal anxiety is a first stage in treatment.

- *Dealing with misinterpretations of physical symptoms*. This part of the treatment focuses on enabling the client to identify thoughts associated with concerns about physical symptoms, and then to begin to develop alternative perspectives on those same symptoms. The previous educational intervention regarding the nature of anxiety and panic provides the client with a starting point for identifying an alternative perspective. Once an alternative perspective has been developed, current evidence for each of the two perspectives should be considered in detail, and a behavioural experiment agreed. Within this process the therapist is directive in engaging the client in consideration of their thoughts regarding symptoms, but the alternative views need to be elicited from the client, rather than presented by the therapist. An example would be the client who views palpitations as indicating the risk of an imminent heart attack coming to recognize that the symptom can be understood as being the result of the release of adrenalin into the bloodstream. The behavioural experiment could take the form of exercising when the person is anxious, thereby reducing the belief in the dangerousness of the symptom.

- *Dealing with avoidance*. Following a reduction in the degree of belief in the dangerousness of physical symptoms, the client should gradually resume all avoided behaviours, utilizing a graded exposure approach as described within the chapter on phobias in this volume (Chapter 6.17).

- *Reduction of safety behaviours*. The use of safety behaviours by panic sufferers helps to explain how, despite the repeated failure of the feared consequence to occur during panic attacks, they continue to believe that it may occur next time. Safety behaviours will therefore prevent the cognitive approach outlined earlier from being effective. As for avoidances, safety behaviours should be gradually reduced as the client becomes more confident in the alternative explanations for their symptoms.

- *Relapse prevention*. Consideration of the patterns of unhelpful behaviours which the client had engaged in, together with discussion and reconsideration of any long-standing assumptions regarding the dangerousness of physical symptoms, should occur towards the end of treatment, with a view to maintenance of change.

- *Breathing retraining*. Where hyperventilation is a feature of an individual's symptoms, it may be helpful to teach the client a diaphragmatic breathing technique. Instructions on breathing retraining are outlined in Figure 6.6.3. This

1. Place one hand on your stomach (little finger level with your waistband) and the other over your breast bone. See diagram opposite.
2. Notice which hand is moving as you breathe.
3. If it is the hand on your chest that is moving, then try and switch your breathing so the hand on your stomach is moving. Perhaps try to imagine that you have something tight around your chest so that you have to breathe from your stomach.
4. Breathe in and out gently through your nose. Feel the movement under the lower hand as your stomach expands. The upper hand should be still.
5. Breathe out for longer than you breathe in, at about 10 breaths a minute.
6. Once aware of how you are breathing, take the hands away from the rib cage. When you fill your lungs with air your stomach should push out too. If your breathing is too shallow your chest will move up and down. This should not be happening if you have mastered the technique.

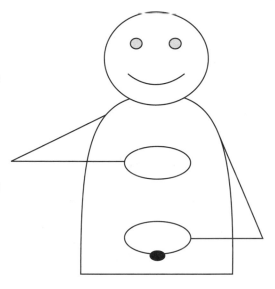

Figure 6.6.3   *Breathing retraining instructions*

is particularly helpful with clients who have beliefs regarding the uncontrollability of panic symptoms. Caution should be exercised to ensure that the technique is not overused, as it may become another safety behaviour.

APPROACHES TO GENERALIZED ANXIETY DISORDER (GAD)

- *Education*. As with panic disorder, educating the client about the normal features of anxiety is a first component of treatment. This should include an explanation of the model, for example, as outlined above, and the central role of worry. Anxiety and worry in GAD should be explained as the extreme end of a normal and universal mental phenomenon. Dugas and colleagues suggest that the treatment model and approach should be presented to the client in a step-by-step fashion. Following and alongside psycho-education, the client is instructed to keep a 'worry diary'. This helps the client to recognize the triggers for worry and the types of worry they experience. Worries are then classified into two main types: worries about current problems and worries about future hypothetical situations.

- *Modifying beliefs about worry*. As with panic disorder, a process of identifying and then reconsidering beliefs about the nature of symptoms, in this case worry, is central to treatment of generalized anxiety disorder. Other strategies seek to disconfirm beliefs, both positive and negative, about worry, specifically through behaviour change. Behavioural experiments can be used to increase tolerance of uncertainty by targeting avoidance or reducing other behaviours such as checking or reassurance seeking. To engage the client in experiments they are first helped to identify the range of behaviours which they have been adopting in an attempt to be more certain but which in effect fuel the worry. Tolerating uncertainty experiments are planned and recorded. For example, a homework experiment may be to go to an unknown restaurant without first checking or to invite a colleague or friend out for the evening. Other more internal behaviours such as thought control can also be abandoned in a controlled therapeutic experiment. Challenging thoughts about the usefulness of worry (targeting positive beliefs about worry) may follow. Beliefs should be identified and sensitively challenged through non-judgemental questioning and discussion. See Dugas and Robichaud (2007) for a list of possible approaches. Negative beliefs can also be targeted. An example of a strategy which may be incorporated here includes the use of controlled worry periods, in which a 15-minute period each day is set aside to actively worry about issues. Throughout the rest of the day, when worry is identified, it is deferred until the planned worry period. This can be utilized to challenge perceptions of the uncontrollability of worry. Another example could be where the client is encouraged to 'lose control' of worry, or actively exaggerate their worries, so that the possible feared consequence of mental illness or complete loss of control is disconfirmed.

- *Problem solving training.* In line with recent developments in the understanding of worry and GAD (Dugas et al., 1998; Dugas and Robichaud, 2007), two aspects to problem solving approaches should be considered – problem solving orientation and problem solving skills. Strategies to improve problem orientation incorporate a number of cognitive and behavioural approaches such as assisting the individual to view problems as opportunities rather than threats and identifying and approaching problems earlier (rather than putting off or avoiding). Actual problem solving skills can then follow with a step-by-step method for identifying and dealing with problems and decision making.
- *Imaginal/cognitive exposure.* The roles of avoidance, thought suppression and neutralization are explained to clients along the lines of that which would be considered in the treatment of a phobia. The individual is then helped to identify core fears associated with worry. A scenario is then developed with the client, which can then be drafted and eventually recorded on to, for example, a compact disc. This then forms the material for exposure sessions repeatedly presented until anxiety levels reduce. It is important that the exposure scenario does not include neutralization, for example, self-reassuring statements, and that core fears are addressed but without them being taken to a ridiculous extreme. Sessions are initially conducted in clinic but can be repeated for homework.
- *Relaxation training.* Given the tension and restlessness evident in GAD, there is a place for the teaching of progressive and applied relaxation for clients. It is important to recognize applied relaxation as a stand-alone approach which if utilized should adhere to a standard protocol and, like CBT, be delivered over approximately 12–15 sessions (see NICE, 2011; Davis et al., 1995). This does not mean, however,

that relaxation skills may not be utilized with other approaches (see Borkovec and Sharpless, 2004). Caution should be exercised that doing the relaxation 'right' does not become another source of worry for the client.

RESEARCH

Treatment outcome studies into the cognitive treatment of panic disorder have shown generally good results, despite some studies having relatively small sample sizes. Cognitive therapy has been shown to be more effective than supportive therapy (Beck et al., 1992), applied relaxation (Clark et al., 1994), and imipramine (Clark et al., 1994). Cognitive therapy targeting catastrophic misinterpretations of physical symptoms, and excluding all exposure elements, has been found to be successful in reducing panic frequency. The addition of exposure-based approaches does appear to strengthen treatment effects, however. Where research has focused on panic disorder with agoraphobia, the superiority of cognitive therapy over exposure therapy alone is less clear cut, with Bouchard et al. (1996) finding no significant difference.

Research into the treatment of generalized anxiety disorder by cognitive therapy is more recent, but results are promising. Cognitive-behaviour therapy has been found to be more effective than behaviour therapy alone (Butler et al., 1991), having good effects on thoughts, expectations and beliefs about worry in something less than half the clients. Borkovek and Costello (1993) have shown superior outcomes for cognitive therapy over applied relaxation. More recently, Hunot et al. (2007) conducted a Cochrane review into the effectiveness of psychological therapies for GAD and found that CBT was effective for short-term treatment of anxiety. The studies were included within the recent review for guidance update by NICE.

For both panic disorder and generalized anxiety disorder, if medication is to be offered, an antidepressant from the selective serotonin reuptake inhibitor (SSRI) group has generally been shown to be most effective. The National Institute for Health and Clinical Excellence (NICE, 2007) recommends that psychological therapy (cognitive-behavioural therapy, applied relaxation) or drug treatment should be offered if a less intensive approach, e.g. self-help or psycho-educational group, is not effective, and this should be before a referral is made to specialist mental health services.

The inclusion of self-help within the recommendations reflects increasing evidence on the value and range of methods which are more readily acces- sible to clients and less demanding on services. Over the last few years there has been a significant investment in the national Improving Access to Psychological Therapies (IAPT) programme and a stepped care approach is firmly embedded within many services. Self-management approaches can include the use of written materials (bibliotherapy), access to relevant charities and organizations, large psycho-education groups, and limited or remote (e.g. telephone) access to a therapist for advice. Computerized therapy programmes have also been developed and show considerable promise. However, further research is recommended before these are fully introduced into routine health service settings (Kaltenthaler et al., 2004). Indeed, it is recognized that although a stepped care approach is recommended and makes both therapeutic and eco- nomical sense, there is a need to gather more evi- dence on the effectiveness of stepped care, incorporating variations on service models. Views of patients are also just starting to emerge (Richards, 2010). Further specific recommendations include the need to evaluate the use of primary-care-based collaborative care in the treatment of GAD and to compare computerized CBT with an individual face- to-face format.

DEBATES

Two main areas of continuing debate in the treat- ment of panic disorder and generalized anxiety disorder can be identified. These are the differential benefit of the cognitive approach over exposure alone, and the use of control rather than discon- firmatory strategies in treatment.

Cognitive therapy for both panic disorder and generalized anxiety disorder includes what are termed 'behavioural experiments'. There is a con- tinuing debate as to whether the active elements in treatment are those claimed by the model, that is disconfirmation of beliefs, rather than the reduction in fear resulting from exposure. As with any therapy with a number of elements, the impact of any spe- cific approach is difficult to distinguish. Evaluation of the effectiveness of individual elements of ther- apy, specifically through the comparison of cogni- tive and behavioural techniques, is required to clarify this issue. However, as behavioural aspects are central to cognitive therapy, such studies may be difficult to undertake. With regard to the under- standing and treatment of GAD, the field has advanced considerably, and evidence-based proto- cols (Dugas et al., 1998; Dugas and Robichaud, 2007; Zinbarg et al., 2006) clearly recommend the

inclusion of both behavioural experiments and exposure. Research into panic disorder with agora- phobia indicates the clear effectiveness of exposure alone, which indicates the need for an individual- ized approach following assessment.

A second issue is that in the treatment of both panic disorder and generalized anxiety disorder there are competing treatment models which include control strategies for symptoms. In panic disorder, these take the form of the breathing retraining strategy (outlined earlier). In generalized anxiety disorder, the use of controlled worry could be understood as a control strategy (although work- ers could argue that this could alternatively be employed as a means of challenging negative thoughts regarding worry). Use of control strategies does not readily fit with the cognitive model, where the focus is on the misinterpretation of normal phe- nomena. As such, the inclusion of these elements in therapy is the subject of debate.

REFERENCES

APA (1987) *Diagnostic and Statistical Manual of Mental Disorders* (3rd edn, text rev.). Washington DC: American Psychiatric Association.

APA (1994) *Diagnostic and Statistical Manual of Mental Disorders* (4th edn, text rev.). Washington DC: American Psychiatric Association.

Beck, A.T. (1976) *Cognitive Therapy and the Emotional Disorders*. New York: International Universities Press.

Beck, A.T., Sokol, L., Clark, D.A., Berchick, B. and Wright, F. (1992) Focused cognitive therapy for panic disorder: a crossover design and one-year follow-up. *American Journal of Psychiatry*, 147: 778–83.

Borkovec, T.D. and Costello, E. (1993) Efficacy of applied relaxation and cognitive-behavioral therapy in the treatment of generalized anxi- ety disorder. *Journal of Consulting and Clinical Psychology*, 61: 611–19.

Borkovec, T.D. and Sharpless, B. (2004) Generalized anxiety disorder: bringing cogni- tive behavioural therapy into the valued present. In S. Hayes, V. Follette and M. Linehan (eds), *New Directions in Behavior Therapy* (pp. 209–42. New York: Guilford.

Bouchard, S., Gauthier, J., Laberge, B., French, D., Pelletier, M.H. and Godbout, C. (1996)

Exposure versus cognitive restructuring in the treatment of panic disorder with agoraphobia. *Behaviour Research and Therapy*, 34: 213–24.

Butler, G., Fennell, M., Robson, P. and Gelder, M. (1991) A comparison of behavior therapy and cognitive behavior therapy in the treatment of generalized anxiety disorder. *Journal of Consulting and Clinical Psychology*, 59: 167–75.

Clark, D.M. (1986) A cognitive approach to panic disorder. *Behaviour Research and Therapy*, 24: 461–70.

Clark, D.M., Salkovskis, P.M., Hackmann, A., Middleton, H., Anastasiades, P. and Gelder, M.G. (1994) A comparison of cognitive therapy, applied relaxation and imipramine in the treatment of panic disorder. *British Journal of Psychiatry*, 164: 759–69.

Craske, M.G. and Barlow, D.H. (2007) *Mastery of Your Anxiety and Panic (Therapist Guide)* (4th edn). Oxford: Oxford University Press.

Davis, M., Eshelman, E.R. and McKay, M. (1995) *The Relaxation and Stress Reduction Workbook* (4th edn). Oakland, CA: New Harbinger.

Dugas, M.J. and Robichaud, M. (2007) *Cognitive-Behavioural Treatment for Generalized Anxiety Disorder: From Science to Practice*. London: Routledge.

Dugas, M.J., Gagnon, F., Ladouceur, R. and Freeston, M.H. (1998) Generalized anxiety disorder: a preliminary test of a conceptual model. *Behaviour Research and Therapy*, 36: 215–26.

Hawton, K., Salkovskis, P.M., Kirk, J. and Clark, D.M. (eds) (1989) *Cognitive Behaviour Therapy for Psychiatric Problems: A Practical Guide*. Oxford: Oxford University Press.

Hunot, V., Churchill, R., Silva de Lima, M., et al. (2007) Psychological therapies for generalised anxiety disorder. *Cochrane Database of Systematic Review* CD001848.

IAPT (2007) *The Competencies Required to Deliver Effective Cognitive and Behavioural Therapy for People with Depression and with Anxiety Disorders*. Improving Access to Psychological Therapies. London: Department of Health.

Kaltenthaler, E., Parry, G. and Beverley, C. (2004) Computerized cognitive behaviour therapy: a systematic review. *Behavioural and Cognitive Psychotherapy*, 32: 31–55.

NICE (2007) *Anxiety (Amended): Management of Anxiety (Panic Disorder, with or without Agoraphobia, and Generalized Anxiety Disorder) in Adults in Primary, Secondary and Community Care*. London: National Institute for Health and Clinical Excellence.

NICE (2011) *Generalised Anxiety Disorder and Panic Disorder (with or without Agoraphobia) in Adults: Management in Primary, Secondary and Community Care*. Clinical Guideline 113. London: NICE.

McManus, S., Meltzer, H., Brugha, T., et al. (2009) *Adult Psychiatric Morbidity in England, 2007: Results of a Household Survey*. Leeds: NHS Information Centre for Health and Social Care.

Richards, D.A., Weaver, A., Utley, M., et al. (2010) *Developing Evidence-Based and Acceptable Stepped Care Systems in Mental Health Care: An Operational Research Project*. Final report. NIHR Service Delivery and Organisation programme.

Wells, A. (1997) *Cognitive Therapy of Anxiety Disorders*. Chichester: Wiley.

Zinbarg, R.E., Craske, M.G. and Barlow, D.H. (2006) *Mastery of your Anxiety and Worry*. Oxford: Oxford University Press.

Attention Deficit Hyperactivity Disorder in Children and Adults

PAM MARAS

DEFINING AD/HD

Attention deficit hyperactivity disorder (AD/HD) is a developmental disorder with a neurobiological basis. It is affected by environmental factors and may be heritable; it is now recognised as having biopsychosocial features (Cooper, 1997); and it is often described under the broad umbrella of social, emotional and behavioural difficulties (SEBDs). The disorder may be referred to as AD(H)D, ADHD and ADD as it can occur with and without hyperactivity, which is the 'H' in AD/HD.

Three main features are central to the identification of AD/HD. Problems must be: (1) pervasive across contexts, (2) persistent over time and (3) typified by developmentally inappropriate behaviour. Although AD/HD was described by a Dr Still in *The Lancet* as long ago as 1902, in recent years there has been heated debate linked to the use of medication with children, a growth in parent pressure groups and differing inter-professional views (e.g. Maras et al., 1997). There is now agreement that assessment is best carried out by a multidisciplinary team and across contexts (BPS, 1996; 2000).

AD/HD is typically categorised by inattention and impulsivity, often manifested, especially in children and young people, in outbursts of 'unreasonable' and/or unexpected behaviour. Detrimental effects of AD/HD for children and young people are often seen in academic achievement (Raggi and Chronis, 2006);

AD/HD typically affects school-aged children, but can present during the preschool years and persist into adulthood (Vaughan et al., 2008). Limited research evidence on AD/HD in adulthood suggests that adults tend to respond to treatment and have a common neuropathology that may be distinct from children and young people; there is however a need for further research with adults.

AETIOLOGY

The *DSM-IV-TR* (APA, 2000) and *ICD-10* (WHO, 1994) provide definitions of AD/HD in behavioural and descriptive terms (Tables 6.7.1, 6.7.2). Evidence from neuroscience provides further useful insights into underlying aetiology and can be more useful for assessment and interventions. For example, Goldstein and Naglieri (2008) describe AD/HD as a condition resulting from impaired behavioural inhibition leading to executive function deficits. The authors describe people with AD/HD as presenting deficits in impulsivity and planning, inattention, hyperactivity, modulation of gratification and emotional regulation.

AD/HD Subtypes

Two main neuropsychological theories dominate current thinking: (1) AD/HD as a disorder of

Table 6.7.1   *DSM-IV-TR diagnostic criteria for AD/HD*

1	Either A or B
A	*Inattention*
	Six or more symptoms persisting for at least 6 months to a degree that is maladaptive and inconsistent with developmental level
	Often fails to give close attention to details or makes careless mistakes in schoolwork, work, or other activities
	Often has difficulty sustaining attention in tasks or play activities
	Often does not seem to listen when spoken to directly
	Often does not follow through on instructions; fails to finish schoolwork, chores or workplace duties (not due to oppositional behaviour or failure to understand instructions)
	Often has difficulty organising tasks and activities
	Often avoids, dislikes, or is reluctant to do tasks requiring sustained mental effort
	Often loses things necessary for tasks or activities
	Is often easily distracted by extraneous stimuli
	Is often forgetful in daily activities
B	*Hyperactivity-impulsivity*
	Six or more symptoms persisting for at least 6 months to a degree that is maladaptive and inconsistent with developmental level
	Hyperactivity
	Often fidgets with hands or feet or squirms in seat
	Often leaves seat in classroom or in other situations where remaining seated is expected
	Often runs or climbs excessively where inappropriate (feelings of restlessness in young people or adults)
	Often has difficulty playing or engaging in leisure activities quietly
	Is often 'on the go' or often acts as if 'driven by a motor'
	Often talks excessively
	Impulsivity
	Often blurts out answers before questions have been completed
	Often has difficulty awaiting turn
	Often interrupts or intrudes on others (for example, butts into conversations or games)
2	Some hyperactive-impulsive or inattentive symptoms that caused impairment were present before age 7 years
3	Some impairment from symptoms is present in two or more settings (for example, at school or work and at home)
4	There must be clear evidence of significant impairment in social, school or work functioning
5	The symptoms do not happen only during the course of a pervasive developmental disorder, schizophrenia or other psychotic disorder. The symptoms are not better accounted for by another mental disorder (for example, mood disorder, anxiety disorder, dissociative disorder, or a personality disorder)

Source: APA (2000)

inhibition dysfunction and (2) AD/HD as a maladaptive functional response or motivation style to avoid delay. Sonuga-Barke (2002) proposed a dual-pathway model in which environmental factors, such as chaotic parenting, family history and diet, interact with genetic components. Adams et al. (2008) considered potential differences between two subtypes of AD/HD which they describe as AD/HD/I (inattentive) and AD/HD/C (deficient behavioural inhibition). The authors suggest that there are potential differences between the subtypes with respect to how important contextual information from the environment is processed, such as preparatory cues that precede responses and rewarding or punishing feedback following behaviour, and that these differences need to be reflected in differential interventions to target each specific subtype.

Table 6.7.2   *ICD-10 diagnostic criteria for AD/HD*

1   *Inattention*

At least six symptoms of attention have persisted for at least 6 months, to a degree that is maladaptive and inconsistent with the developmental level of the child

Often fails to give close attention to details, or makes careless errors in schoolwork, work or other activities

Often fails to sustain attention in tasks or play activities

Often appears not to listen to what is being said to him or her

Often fails to follow through on instructions or to finish schoolwork, chores or duties in the workplace (not because of oppositional behaviour or failure to understand instructions)

Is often impaired in organising tasks and activities

Often avoids or strongly dislikes tasks, such as homework, that require sustained mental effort

Often loses things necessary for certain tasks and activities, such as school assignments, pencils, books, toys or tools

Is often easily distracted by external stimuli

Is often forgetful in the course of daily activities

2   *Hyperactivity*

At least three symptoms of hyperactivity have persisted for at least 6 months, to a degree that is maladaptive and inconsistent with the developmental level of the child

Often fidgets with hands or feet or squirms on seat

Often leaves seat in classroom or in other situations in which remaining seated is expected

Often runs about or climbs excessively in situations in which it is inappropriate (in adolescents or adults, only feelings of restlessness may be present)

Is often unduly noisy in playing or has difficulty in engaging quietly in leisure activities

Often exhibits a persistent pattern of excessive motor activity that is not substantially modified by social context or demands

3   *Impulsivity*

At least one of the following symptoms of impulsivity has persisted for at least 6 months, to a degree that is maladaptive and inconsistent with the developmental level of the child

Often blurts out answers before questions have been completed

Often fails to wait in lines or await turns in games or group situations

Often interrupts or intrudes on others (for example, butts into others' conversations or games)

Often talks excessively without appropriate response to social constraints

4   *Onset*

Onset of the disorder is no later than the age of 7 years

5   *Pervasiveness*

The criteria should be met for more than a single situation, for example, the combination of inattention and hyperactivity should be present both at home and at school, or at both school and another setting where children are observed, such as a clinic. (Evidence for cross-situationality will ordinarily require information from more than one source; parental reports about classroom behaviour, for instance, are unlikely to be sufficient.)

6   The symptoms in 1 and 3 cause clinically significant distress or impairment in social, academic or occupational functioning

Source: WHO (1994)

Research based on the planning, attention, simultaneous, successive processes theory (PASS) contributes to understanding of the intellectual and neuropsychological processes implicated in AD/HD (Goldstein and Naglieri, 2008). The authors found that people with AD/HD had a distinctive profile of PASS processes, in line with the expected cognitive nature of their disorder, including deficits in planning and associated anxiety disorders. Children with AD/HD were found to have problems with behavioural inhibition and self-control, with their PASS profile differentiating them from children with other developmental disorders such as dyslexia (Goldstein and Naglieri, 2008).

Comorbidity

Daley (2006) provides a useful overview of the aetiology of AD/HD including comorbidity and associated problems, developmental trends and potential interventions. AD/HD is often described as comorbid with other emotional and behavioural difficulties, the most common being oppositional defiant disorder, conduct disorder, depression, and anxiety. Problems with motor coordination, impaired academic functioning, low IQ, psychosocial functioning, unintentional injury, and sleep problems have also been described as comorbid. Given diagnosis is not always clear and often entails the use of behavioural checklists, it may be more accurate to refer to 'other problems associated with AD/HD' or 'co-occurring' rather than comorbid (Sonuga-Barke, 2002).

ASSESSMENT, DIAGNOSIS AND IDENTIFICATION

AD/HD is a medical diagnosis and can only therefore be made by a qualified medic in the UK. For children this is likely to be through child and adolescent mental health services (CAMHS) via a specialist paediatrician or psychiatrist; in the case of adults a diagnosis would be given by a psychiatrist or a suitable qualified medic, again through mental health services. Diagnostic measures are most often applied to children and young people, and it has been suggested that preschoolers and adults require adaptation of the current diagnostic criteria to account for differences in symptomatology across the age span. The differential diagnosis of AD/HD and the pattern of psychiatric comorbidity vary with each age group and complicate diagnosis and management (Vaughan et al., 2008). Clinicians must therefore be able to accurately identify AD/HD across the lifespan, and to develop comprehensive, collaborative treatment plans to reflect this.

Assessments leading to diagnosis are increasingly carried out by psychologists. School is the most common place that children and young people first come to be identified with AD/HD, often following incidences of repeated behaviour that has affected their own and more often other children's learning and classrooms.

Behavioural Checklists and AD/HD

Notwithstanding the convincing evidence from neuroscience, behavioural measures are the most common means of assessment of AD/HD and comorbid and other behavioural disorders such as oppositional defiance disorder and conduct disorder. There are a number of measures including the Achenbach scales (Child Behaviour Checklist, Achenbach, 1991a; Youth Self Report, Achenbach, 1991b; Teachers Report Form, Achenbach, 1991c) and the Goodman Strengths and Difficulties Questionnaire (SDQ: Goodman, 1997; Goodman et al., 1998).

The Conners Teacher, Parent and Child Rating Scales are the most frequently used screening tool for AD/HD (Conners, 2000). They may be used with the Conners Continuous Performance Test (CPT), which assesses attention and impulsivity and is one of the most frequently used measures in relation to AD/HD (Conners et al., 2000). It is worth noting however that both the CPT and the Conners behavioural checklists are most often used in research studies rather than diagnostic settings. Deb et al. (2008) used the Conners Parent Rating Scale–Revised (CPRS–R) and the Conners Teacher Rating Scale–Revised (CTRS–R) with children with AD/HD and with or without intellectual disabilities. The authors found that the CPRS–R distinguished between children with ID with or without AD/HD but that the CTRS–R did not. The authors suggested that many items on the two scales were not applicable to children with severe disabilities and lack of speech. They also found that teacher and parent scores (CPRS–R and CTRS–R) did not correlate one or each other.

Alloway et al. (2009) looked at the diagnostic utility of behavioural checklists in identifying children with AD/HD including those with working memory deficits, which are commonly assumed to be related to AH/HD. The authors compared the Conners Teacher Rating Scale (CTRS), the Behaviour Rating Inventory of Executive Function (BRIEF) and a working memory rating scale. They also included the Conners Continuous Performance Test (CPT). The authors found that the first three scales differentiated between the two samples and typical developing peers but did not differentiate between children with working memory impairments and children with AD/HD. They also found that CTRS and BRIEF could partially differentiate between children with working memory deficits and AD/HD; children with AD/HD were characterised by more oppositional and hyperactive disorders whilst children with working memory deficits were more inattentive.

Many behavioural measures are self-report and it has been suggested that children with SEBDs may not be self-aware; however, this claim is not supported by evidence. Klimkeit et al. (2006) reported that findings from a self-report measure (the Self-Evaluation Scale for Children) completed by children with AD/HD showed that the children recognised that they had more disorganised, poor, disruptive behaviour; they had a worse self-perception and poorer communication skills than their peers without AD/HD. It is interesting to note that the authors found no difference in self-reported interest in school activities or anxiety between children with and without AD/HD.

Findings from this and similar work suggest a strong need for care when applying behavioural checklists. They also show the importance of ensuring that behavioural checklists should be sensitive to possible overlap between potential findings for different disorders (e.g. see Alloway et al., 2009).

INTERVENTIONS

Medication

Although the increase in the use of medication in children and young people with AD/HD has been a topic of debate for at least 20 years (e.g. Wright, 1997), there is now general agreement that in some cases medication may be appropriate, in particular when used in conjunction with psychosocial interventions including psychotherapy and counselling. Medication has been repeatedly shown to increase the ability of some young people to attend, although research on long-term effects is still not clear (Advokat, 2009). For example, Muris et al. (2006) used a behavioural rating scale to look at the effects of medication on children and found that scores for behavioural problems showed a substantial decline after medication had been administered. Pelham and Fabiano (2008) suggest that all interventions are affected by participants' characteristics, strength of treatment and treatment adherence. They conclude that psychosocial and behavioural interventions should be tried before medication and an increasing number of studies have found that combined programmes (that include psychosocial interventions) are more effective than medication alone, and that psychosocial interventions were better in certain groups and setting (Swanson et al., 2002).

Psychosocial Interventions

In a review of the literature, Pelham and Fabiano (2008) concluded behavioural parent training (BPT) and behavioural classroom management were well-established treatments for children with AD/HD. Intensive peer-focused behavioural interventions implemented in recreational settings (e.g. summer programmes) were also found to be effective. The authors suggest that problem-solving communication training might also be a promising intervention, especially with adolescents. The authors found less evidence for the efficacy of cognitive therapies, which is surprising given the social-cognitive mechanisms associated with the development of SEBDs (Dodge, 1993).

Shalev et al. (2007) tested the efficacy of a computerised progressive attentional training programme (CPAT) which was composed of four sets of structured tasks designed to activate sustained attention, selective attention, orienting of attention, and executive attention. The authors found that experimental participants showed a significant improvement in reading comprehension and passage copying. In addition, parents reported a reduction in inattentiveness in children who took part in the study whilst no significant improvements were observed in the control group.

Teacher- and School-based Interventions

Gai et al. (2008) conducted a meta-analysis of 62 studies looking at cognitive, social, behavioural and academic interventions for children and young people with AD/HD across 1994–2005. The authors found that interventions had the greatest effect on academic outcomes.

Sayal et al. (2006) suggest that although teachers may be well placed to identify unrecognised children and to facilitate their referral to specialist services, teachers' identification of AD/HD has been limited. Teachers' views have been found to be based on both the severity of symptoms and the impact of these problems on the teacher and the class.

School-based interventions for children and young people

Children with AD/HD are at risk for academic failure. It is surprising therefore that, although interventions to alleviate AD/HD symptoms have focused on behavioural outcomes, little attention has been given to academic impairments as the consequence of executive functioning deficits.

Trout et al. (2007) reviewed 41 studies on the impact of non-medication interventions on the academic functioning of students with AD/HD. The authors found that although a broad range of traditional and non-traditional interventions had been used to improve students' academic outcomes, the research was generally unsystematic. For example, important demographic and descriptive information, such as participant characteristics and classroom settings, were often poorly defined and generally did not reflect the current population of students with AD/HD.

Educational interventions that have been found beneficial include class-wide peer tutoring and parent tutoring, self-monitoring task and instructional modifications, strategy training, use of functional assessment, and homework management programmes. A main goal of such interventions should be to decrease distractions and the amount of competing non-relevant stimuli available, thus ensuring that the task or stimulus in hand holds an optimal level of attention. This can be enhanced by providing immediate feedback and smaller chunks of information.

School-based interventions for AD/HD have been shown to be effective in the short term for reducing disruptive behaviours and improving on-task behaviour and academic performance of children with AD/HD. However, multimodal interventions that may include concurrent medication in addition to parent training, school interventions and child interventions have been found to be more effective than school-based interventions alone for children and young people with the most severe difficulties (Miranda et al., 2006). DuPaul and Weyandt (2006) reviewed three major types of interventions: behavioural, academic and social.

Behavioural interventions can involve antecedent- or consequence-based strategies, and both require some self-management. Antecedent-based strategies involve choice making, reduction in size of assigned tasks, and active teaching of classroom rules. Consequence-based strategies aim to discourage disruptive behaviour by applying consequences (including verbal reprimands) and have not been used effectively. Contingent management strategies, where an outcome is contingent on certain behaviours, are commonly used, though they have not been found to be effective in the long term. Token reinforcement is often used in schools and has been found to decrease disruptive behaviour; variants include the use of home-based reinforcement for school behaviour (daily school report card, as in the Summer Treatment programme developed by Pelham et al., 2002).

The combination of token reinforcement and cost response is highly effective for on-task behaviour, seatwork productivity and academic accuracy, but is less likely to result in generalised behaviour change.

Academic interventions include peer tutoring (Greenwood et al., 2002), teacher-mediated academic intervention, class-wide peer tutoring (CWPT: Greenwood et al., 1988) and computer-assisted instruction (CAI). The CWPT is one of the most commonly used techniques; it has been used to enhance maths, reading and spelling skills and has been found to improve attentional behaviour and academic performance. Notwithstanding limited empirical evidence, CAI seems to be effective on off-task behaviour, and academic improvement is also possible.

Social interventions such as social skills training have been used extensively with children and young people with AD/HD who typically present aggressive behaviour, enter ongoing peer activities abruptly and do not follow implicit rules of good conversation because of an inability to delay responses to the environment and impulsive behaviour. Social skills training has been found to improve conversation skills, problem-solving and anger control in specific situations, but changes are often not lasting or generalised. A main reason for this is that social skills training most often takes place in school rather than therapeutic settings: see for example the Tough Kids Social Skills (Sheridan, 1995), Cunningham and Cunningham's (1995) student-mediated conflict resolution programme, and the Challenging Horizons Program (Evans et al., 2006). A growing number of parent and teacher training approaches have been developed for children and young people with AD/HD (e.g. Sanders, 1999; Webster-Stratton et al., 2004).

Teacher interventions

Teacher factors, including teachers' attitudes and beliefs about AD/HD and treatment options, have been found to influence students' behavioural and learning outcomes (Sherman et al., 2008). For example, gesture use by teachers can influence performance on certain academic puzzles by students with AD/HD, and teachers' opinions about specific treatment options can impact student behaviour and the types of interventions implemented in the classroom.

Teachers in Sherman et al.'s study were found to prefer interventions with daily report procedure, followed by response cost and then medication. Medication combined with other strategies was preferred to medication only. Teachers who demonstrate patience, knowledge of intervention techniques, an ability to collaborate with an interdisciplinary team, and a positive attitude towards children with special needs can have a positive impact on student success. Teachers' attitudes are associated with the peer social acceptance of AD/HD students. According to these authors, more research should test more directly and more often, the relationship between critical outcomes

Tymms and Merrell (2006) carried out a large study comparing different school-based interventions. One involved naming pupils with AD/HD-like behaviour, another provided evidence-based advice for teachers about how to teach pupils with AD/HD-like behaviour, and a third included both strategies. The authors found that labelling children to teachers had no significant impact, whilst providing research-based advice had a significant positive but small effect even two years later on AD/HD children's attitudes, behaviour and teacher-reported quality of life. Interestingly, the third intervention, the combination of labelling and research-based advice, had a negative impact on the AD/HD-like children's reading and maths skills, but a positive effect on reading skills in the general sample (children with and without AD/HD-like symptoms).

Parent and Family Interventions

Although the empirical base for evaluating parent training interventions is relatively small, they have been shown to result in improved behavioural outcomes in children and young people. Deault (2010) carried out a systematic review of 22 studies on parenting and AD/HD from 2000 to 2008. The author noted that most of the studies had a correlational design, and parenting variables such as stress in the family, higher rate of parental psychopathology and conflicted parent–child relationships were related to AD/HD with behavioural disorders.

Stroh et al. (2008) examined North American parents' knowledge, attitudes and information sources about AD/HD, including treatment with stimulant medication and behavioural interventions. The authors found that parents who had a child diagnosed with AD/HD rated the effects of stimulant medication more positively, were aware of short-term improvements in academic performance and behaviour because of the medication, and rated side effects (physical growth rate and development of tics) as less severe than other

parents. They also rated behavioural interventions as less effective.

A main issue in respect of measuring outcomes of parent training is differences in parents' and children's views on the goals of training. For example, Traywick et al. (2006) found that children's desired outcomes were to be 'better at school, listen and be good' whilst parents were preoccupied with affective outcomes, e.g. for their children to feel good and have high self-esteem.

CONCLUSIONS

AD/HD is a developmental disorder with a biological basis. It can be heritable and is affected by environmental factors. Although there is a growing body of neuroscientific evidence on its biological basis, AD/HD is most often diagnosed using behavioural checklists which are best applied across situations and contexts. To be identified as such, AD/HD must be persistent over time and context; it is mainly referred to in children and young people and is often linked to problems in school. It can though persist into adulthood and is now diagnosed more often in late adolescence and early adulthood than it was in the past. In some instances medication is appropriate when used in conjunction with other interventions, the most common being behavioural; however, these have been found to be most effective when combined with psychosocial interventions, some of which have been used effectively with parents and teachers.

REFERENCES

Achenbach, T.M. (1991a) *Manual for the Child Behavior Checklist 14–18 and 1991 Profile.* Burlington, VT: University of Vermont, Department of Psychiatry.

Achenbach, T.M. (1991b) *Manual for the YSR and 1991 profile.* Burlington, VT: University of Vermont, Department of Psychiatry.

Achenbach, T.M. (1991c) *Manual of the Teacher's Report Form and 1991 Profile.* Burlington, VT: University of Vermont, Department of Psychiatry.

Adams, Z.W., Derefinko, K.J., Milich, R. and Fillmore, M.T. (2008) Inhibitory functioning across ADHD subtypes: recent findings, clinical implications, and future directions.

Developmental Disabilities Research Reviews, 14 (4): 268–75.

Advokat, C. (2009) What exactly are the benefits of stimulants for ADHD? *Journal of Attention Disorders*, 12 (6): 495–8.

Alloway, T.P., Gathercole, S.E., Holmes, J., Place, M., Elliott, J. and Hilton, K. (2009) The diagnostic utility of behavioural checklists in identifying children with ADHD and children with working memory deficits. *Child Psychiatry and Human Development*, 40 (3): 353–66.

APA (2000) *Diagnostic and Statistical Manual of Mental Disorders* (4th edn text rev.). Washington, DC: American Psychiatric Association.

BPS (1996) *Attention Deficit/Hyperactivity Disorder (AD/HD): A Psychological Response to an Evolving Concept.* Leicester: British Psychological Society.

BPS (2000) *Attention Deficit/Hyperactivity Disorder (AD/HD): Guidelines and Principles for Successful Multi-Agency Working.* Leicester: British Psychological Society.

Conners, C.K. (2000) *Conners' Rating Scales–Revised Technical Manual.* North Tonawanda, NY: Multi-Health Systems.

Conners, C.K. and MHS Staff (2000) *Conners' Continuous Performance Test II: Computer Program for Windows Technical Guide and Software Manual.* North Tonawanda, NY: Multi-Health Systems.

Cooper, P. (1997) Biology, behaviour and education: ADHD and the bio-psycho-social perspective. *Educational and Child Psychology*, 14 (1): 31–9.

Cunningham, C.E. and Cunningham, L.J. (1995) Reducing playground aggression: student mediation programs. *The ADHD Report*, 9–11.

Daley, D. (2006) Attention deficit hyperactivity disorder: a review of the essential facts. *Child: Care, Health and Development*, 32 (2): 193–204.

Deault, L.C. (2010) A systematic review of parenting in relation to the development of comorbidities and functional impairments in children with attention-deficit/hyperactivity disorder (ADHD). *Child Psychiatry and Human Development*, 41 (2): 168–92.

Deb, S., Dhaliwal, A.-J. and Roy, M. (2008) The usefulness of Conners' Rating Scales–Revised in screening for attention deficit hyperactivity disorder in children with intellectual disabilities and borderline intelligence. *Journal of Intellectual Disability Research*, 52 (11): 950–65.

Dodge, K.A. (1993) Social-cognitive mechanisms in the development of conduct disorder and depression. *Annual Review of Psychology*, 44 (1): 559–84.

DuPaul, G.J. and Weyandt, L.L. (2006) School-based intervention for children with attention deficit hyperactivity disorder: effects on academic, social, and behavioural functioning. *International Journal of Disability, Development and Education*, 53 (2): 161–76.

Evans, S.W., Timmins, B., Sibley, M., White, L.C., Serpell, Z.N. and Schultz, B. (2006) Developing coordinated, multimodal, school-based treatment for young adolescents with ADHD. *Education and Treatment of Children*, 29 (2): 359–78.

Gai, X., Lang, G. and Liu, X. (2008) A meta-analytic review on treatment effects of attention deficit/hyperactivity disorder children in China. *Acta Psychologica Sinica*, 40 (11): 1190–6.

Goldstein, S. and Naglieri, J.A. (2008) The school neuropsychology of ADHD: theory, assessment, and intervention. *Psychology in the Schools*, 45 (9): 859–74.

Goodman, R. (1997) The Strengths and Difficulties Questionnaire: a research note. *Journal of Child Psychology and Psychiatry*, 38: 581–6.

Goodman, R. (1998) The Strengths and Difficulties Questionnaire: a pilot study on the validity of the self-report version. *European Child and Adolescent Psychiatry*, 7: 125–30

Greenwood, C.R., Delquadri, J.C. and Carta, J.J. (1988) *Classwide Peer Tutoring (CWPT).* Delray Beach, FL: Education Achievement Systems.

Greenwood, C.R., Maheady, L. and Delquadri, J. (2002) Classwide peer tutoring programs. In M. Shinn, H.M. Walker and G. Stoner (eds), *Interventions for Academic and Behavior Problems II: Preventive and Remedial Approaches* (pp. 611–49). Bethesda, MD: NASP.

Klimkeit, E., Graham, C., Lee, P., Morling, M., Russo, D. and Tonge, B. (2006) Children should be seen and heard: self-report of feelings and behaviours in primary-school-age children with ADHD. *Journal of Attention Disorders*, 10 (2): 181–91.

Maras, P., Redmayne, T., Hall, C., Braithwaite, D. and Prior, P. (1997) 'Helicopter children' and 'butterfly brains'. ADHD: perceptions, issues and implications. *Educational and Child Psychology*, 14 (1): 39–50. Leicester: BPS.

Miranda, A., Jarque, S. and Tarraga, R. (2006) Interventions in school settings for students with ADHD. *Exceptionality*, 14 (1): 35–52.

Muris, P., Vaesen, H., Roodenrijs, D. and Kelgtermans, L. (2006) Treatment sensitivity of a brief rating scale for attention-deficit hyperactivity disorder (ADHD) symptoms. *Journal of Child and Family Studies*, 15 (2): 223–30.

Pelham, W.E. and Fabiano, G.A. (2008) Evidence-based psychosocial treatments for attention-deficit/hyperactivity disorder. *Journal of Clinical Child and Adolescent Psychology*, 37 (1): 184–214.

Pelham, W.E., Hoza, B., Pillow, D.R., Gnagy, E.M., Kipp, H.L., Greiner, A.R., Trane, S.T., et al. (2002) Effects of methylphenidate and expectancy on children with ADHD: behavior, academic performance, and attributions in a summer treatment program and regular classroom setting. *Journal of Consulting and Clinical Psychology*, 70 (2): 320–35.

Raggi, V.L. and Chronis, A.M. (2006) Interventions to address the academic impairment of children and adolescents with ADHD. *Clinical Child and Family Psychology Review*, 9 (2): 85–111.

Sanders, M.R. (1999) Triple P-positive parenting program: towards an empirically validated multilevel parenting and family support strategy for the prevention of behavior and emotional problems in children. *Clinical Child and Family Psychology Review*, 2 (2): 71–90.

Sayal, K., Hornsey, H., Warren, S., MacDiarmid, F. and Taylor, E. (2006) Identification of children at risk of ADHD: a school-based intervention. *Social Psychiatry and Psychiatric Epidemiology*, 41 (10): 806–13.

Shalev, L., Tsal, Y. and Mevorach, C. (2007) Computerized progressive attentional training

(CPAT) program: effective direct intervention for children with ADHD. *Child Neuropsychology*, 13 (4): 382–8.

Sheridan, S.M. (1995) *The Tough Kid Social Skills Book*. New York: Sopris West Educational Services.

Sherman, J., Rasmussen, C. and Baydala, L. (2008) The impact of teacher factors on achievement and behavioral outcomes of children with attention deficit/hyperactivity disorder (ADHD): a review of the literature. *Educational Research*, 50 (4): 347–60.

Sonuga-Barke, E.J.S. (2002) Psychological heterogeneity in AD/HD: a dual pathway model of behaviour and cognition. *Behavioural Brain Research*, 130 (1–2): 29–36.

Still, G.F. (1902) Some abnormal psychical conditions in children. *Lancet*, 1: 1008–12, 1077–82, 1163–8.

Stroh, J., Frankenberger, W., Cornell-Swanson, L.V., Wood, C. and Pahl, S. (2008) The use of stimulant medication and behavioral interventions for the treatment of attention deficit hyperactivity disorder: a survey of parents' knowledge, attitudes, and experiences. *Journal of Child and Family Studies*, 17 (3): 385–401.

Swanson, J.M., Arnold, L.E., Vitiello, B., Abikoff, H.B., Wells, K.C., Pelham, W.E., March, J.S., Hinshaw, S.P., Hoza, B., Epstein, J.N., Elliott, G.R., Greenhill, L.L., Hechtman, L., Jensen, P.S., Kraemer, H.C., Kotkin, R., Molina, B., Newcorn, J.H., Owens, E.B., Severe, J., Hoagwood, K., Simpson, S., Wigal, T. and Hanley, T. (2002) Response to commentary on the multimodal treatment study of ADHD (MTA): mining the meaning of the MTA. *Journal of Abnormal Child Psychology*, 30: 327–32.

Traywick, T.B., Lamson, A.L., Diamond, J.M. and Crawan, S. (2006) A comparison of preferred treatment outcomes between children with ADHD and their parents. *Journal of Attention Disorders*, 9 (4): 590–7.

Trout, A.L., Ortiz Lienemann, T., Reid, R. and Epstein, M.H. (2007) A review of non-medication interventions to improve the academic performance of children and youth with ADHD. *Remedial and Special Education*, 28 (4): 207–26.

Tymms, P. and Merrell, C. (2006) The impact of screening and advice on inattentive, hyperactive and impulsive children. *European Journal of Special Needs Education*, 21 (3): 321–37.

Vaughan, B.S., Wetzel, M.W. and Kratochvil, C.J. (2008) Beyond the 'typical' patient: treating attention-deficit/hyperactivity disorder in preschoolers and adults. *International Review of Psychiatry*, 20 (2): 143–9.

Webster-Stratton, C., Reid, M.J. and Hammond, M. (2004) Treating children with early onset problems: interventions outcomes for parent, child and teacher training. *Journal of Clinical Child and Adolescent Psychology*, 33 (1): 105–24.

WHO (1994) *International Statistical Classification of Diseases and Related Health Problems (10th revision)*. Geneva: World Health Organization.

Wright, S.F. (1997) A little understood solution to a vaguely defined problem: parental perceptions of Ritalin. *Educational and Child Psychology*, 14 (1): 50–60.

Bereavement

GABRIELLE SYME

During most people's lives at least one person close to them will die. In 2008, 509,090 people died in England and Wales: 491,042 from natural causes, 12,231 accidentally, and 3858 through suicide or self-inflicted harm. Further details are given in Table 6.8.1. This makes it surprising that most people know so little about the normal grieving process until they or close friends are bereaved. A major reason may be denial of mortality. In ordinary speech, 'if I die' rather than 'when I die' is the more common expression.

Bereavement is the reaction to the loss of someone or something that really matters both personally and emotionally. Thus bereavement is part of a much broader phenomenon: the response of social animals to loss. While this chapter will centre on bereavement through death, it is important to realize that the emotional response to any other major loss and the appropriate therapeutic interventions will probably be similar. Examples of other major losses are: amputation, separation and divorce, emigration, moving house, burglary, miscarriage, infertility, imprisonment, a major life-threatening illness, disability, redundancy, retirement, rape, abortion, leaving home, and disfigurement.

Grief is the complex emotional response to bereavement. A number of people have sought theoretical explanations of grief, while others have attempted to produce a model of grief by describing and categorizing the responses to loss. The psychological process involved in recovery is known as mourning. It is this process that can be helped by people who will listen and understand in a sustained way. Obviously well-trained counsellors and therapists can do this, but often the bereaved have their own network of support who must not be sidelined if the bereaved are to remain part of their own social group. On occasions, the best intervention by the professionals is to support and possibly inform the concerned family and friends as they journey with someone who is grieving.

THEORIES OF GRIEF

The main theories of grief, all derived from Western cultures, seek to explain the origin of grief. Although developed independently, none is self-sufficient. They need to be integrated to get the most complete understanding of the psychological process involved in grieving. Stress theory (Cannon, 1929) sees the response to bereavement as one example of the complex physiological and psychological responses of animals to danger. These responses were essential when early humans were hunter-gatherers living in a hostile world of unforeseen dangers and predators. To survive in a dangerous and terrifying situation the response was fright, then fight, and if the worst came to the worst, flight (Cannon's 'fright, fight and flight' response). Nowadays human beings still respond both physiologically (their metabolism responds so they can run away at high speed) and psychologically (they think more quickly and try to avoid the situation again by being hypersensitive to it) when fight and flight are not appropriate responses. This theory partly, but not totally, explains the occurrence of post-traumatic stress

Table 6.8.1 *Deaths from all causes, England and Wales, 2008*

Age	Male	Female
All ages	243,014	266,076
<1	1,920	1449
1–4	284	270
5–14	370	277
15–24	2,034	809
25–34	3,088	1,445
35–44	6,419	3,811
45–54	12,269	8,291
55–64	27,098	18,187
65–74	47,862	33,883
75–84	79,805	77,827
85	61,876	119,827

Source: data supplied by the Office for National Statistics

disorder (PTSD) after being involved in a life-threatening event, such as a major fire, the sinking of a ship, a car crash or a mass murder.

The stress theory was elaborated further by Caplan (1964) to take into account that almost any stressful event happens to not just one person but a group of people who can help each other live through dangerous situations. He also observed that people respond less severely if they have some preparatory knowledge of how to deal with a crisis and the effects of trauma, and that survivors are helped considerably by the support of others who have also been through the same or a similar traumatic event. However, the addition of crisis theory to stress theory is not sufficient to explain the response to loss in general.

The psychoanalyst Lindemann (1944), on observing the survivors of a fire in a nightclub in which almost 500 people died, noticed that some people had a delayed or distorted grief reaction. This led him to propose that in these situations grief was being repressed and this was causing the delayed response. Thus repression was added to the theories to explain grief, but of course repression was only being observed in a tiny minority of people. It is not a major component of the normal grief reaction.

Bowlby (1979) developed with his co-workers a theory to explain the immediate reaction to separation and loss. Their observation of infants separated from their mothers led them to propose that the formation of an attachment between these two in the first year of life was critical for survival. If a baby is separated from its mother, its first urge is to cry until she returns or, in other words, until she is found (see Chapter 5.9 in this volume). This is the basis of the immediate reaction to separation and loss at any point in our lives. Extensive studies have shown four attachment patterns in infants: secure, and insecure with three subcategories, namely avoidant, ambivalent, and disorganized/disoriented. There are corresponding attachment patterns in adults: secure, and insecure with three subcategories, namely dismissing, preoccupied, and unresolved/disorganized. The quality of attachment, whether it is secure or insecure, has a profound effect on the parenting styles of people in adulthood, with attachment styles being transmitted from parent to child. Thus secure parents have secure infants, dismissing parents have avoidant infants, and so on. The ability to manage loss is also influenced by attachment patterns. Those with an insecure attachment are much more likely to show prolonged and chronic grief when a relationship is lost. More recent research by psychoneurobiologists such as Eisenberg, Hobson, Schore and Trevarthen has produced neurological evidence for the crucial role of attachment behaviour and emotional communication in the growth of the orbito-frontal area of the brain and in emotional development. This is the socio-emotional part of the brain – the area responsible for empathy and attunement (Schore, 2001).

What attachment theory does not do is attempt to explain recovery from bereavement (though not all people do recover), and the way in which some people change, develop a new identity and in some instances noticeably mature as a result. This possible change is called the psychosocial transition by Parkes (1971) and is based on the work of Marris (1974). Bereavement, along with a number of other life events, challenges people's presumptions about their world. Many assumptions that had been made on the grounds of previous experience are no longer correct. For instance, the world is less predictable; some plans are no longer relevant; the person who has died is no longer a natural reference point. Part of the grief work is coming to terms with a different relationship with the deceased, the world and oneself. In many ways the work is learning about and coming to terms with a new 'I'.

MODELS OF GRIEF

Many people have described and systemized the reactions to bereavement. One of the first was Lindemann (1944), who described five characteristics of the normal acute grief response:

1 somatic or bodily distress of some type
2 preoccupation with the image of the dead person
3 guilt relating to the deceased or circumstances of the death
4 hostile reactions
5 the inability to function as one had before.

Anyone who has worked with the bereaved would recognize these responses and know that, alongside these, there are characteristic feelings, physical sensations, behaviours and ways of thinking.

A number of writers, the most notable being Bowlby and Parkes, separated all these responses into phases. Bowlby (1979) identified three phases when a child was separated from their parent or significant caregiver. These were angry pining, depression and despair, followed by detachment if the parent did not return soon enough or at all.

Parkes (1996), on the basis of interviews with London widows, added an additional phase of numbness before the pining or yearning. These phases, and the associated feelings, are shown in Table 6.8.2. Though this pattern of response was constructed from interviews with women, it is essentially the same for men.

There has been a lot of unjust criticism of these phases on the grounds that they suggest that grieving is a linear process, something that Parkes never suggested. The process is very much one of two steps forward and one step back, and the phases overlap. One moment it seems to the griever that life is improving and there are things to enjoy again – the acceptance phase – and then the next moment the mourner is plunged back into acute grief – the phase of despair and disorganization. Another criticism is that the phases also suggest a time scale. While for many the numbness lasts about two weeks, the acute yearning six months, and the whole process approximately two years, there are huge variations which, when they occur, should not be interpreted as abnormal. On the other hand, counsellors and therapists must be able to assess what parts of the grief have been experienced and whether they have been worked through, and also to recognize when the grieving is complicated and severely delayed. For this reason it is important that counsellors and therapists know what to expect but not to have rigid expectations of the process. The different phases and their suggested timings offer a checklist and no more.

It will be noted that Parkes's phases of grief focus exclusively on feelings. Stroebe and Schut (1995) studied grieving in a variety of cultures and

Table 6.8.2   *Phases of adult mourning and related feelings*

Phases		Predominant feelings	Time from death
1	Numbness Disbelief	Shock	2 weeks to 1 month
2	Yearning	Reminiscence Searching Hallucination Anger Guilt	6 months
3	Disorganization and despair	Anxiety Loneliness Ambivalence Fear Hopelessness Helplessness	1 year
4	Reorganization	Acceptance Relief	2 years or more

Source: based on Parkes (1996)

realized that there are many differences. For instance, in some cultures, such as Muslim communities in Bali, grief is neither confronted nor expressed, with no serious psychological consequences. In others, such as Japan, a family shrine in memory of the dead ancestors is normal, yet in Western communities it is viewed as a sign of unresolved grief. This led Stroebe and Schut to propose the dual-process model of grief. They recognized that the two components of grief are loss orientation (essentially the feeling part of the process observed by Parkes) and restoration orientation. The latter process is the necessary focus on new tasks and the development of new skills to be able to manage the momentous life changes that result from the death of a significant person. Recovery from bereavement involves both loss- and restoration-oriented activities.

A further development has been the recognition by the theoreticians of something that the bereaved always knew: the deceased are never forgotten; the wound, albeit healed, is always present; and there are continuing bonds, both tangible and intangible, with the deceased. The tangible ones are keepsakes, such as letters, personal belongings and photographs of those who have died. Intangible ones are memories held in the heart. Klass et al. (1996) have written extensively on the necessity of continuing bonds and the inappropriateness of terms like 'letting go', which were commonly found in the bereavement literature.

CLINICAL MANAGEMENT: NORMAL GRIEF REACTION

The majority of the bereaved who seek help do so at least two months after the death. This may well be because immediately after the death, family and friends rally round and are very supportive. The combination of their lack of awareness of how long the road of recovery is for the bereaved, and having a less close relationship with the dead person, means that after about two months all but the bereaved have returned 'to normal' and expect that of the bereaved as well. In reality, the bereaved are probably at their lowest ebb, perhaps thinking they are going mad, feeling acute fear and such loss of self-esteem that they do not believe anyone is interested in them. This latter feature may make it extremely difficult to ask for help.

For most bereaved, what is needed is supportive counselling and an environment in which all the emotions associated with the death can be expressed. Many people need help in expressing anger and understanding guilt. Anger, because the person the griever is most likely to be angry with is the dead person, and frequently there is an almost superstitious belief that if 'ill is spoken of the dead' then punishment is inevitable. Guilt, because it is rarely absent and is often expressed as 'if only ...'. To an outside observer, this often seems misplaced when it is only too obvious just what the griever did for the dead person before the death. It is important to allow this guilt to be expressed and linked to reviewing the relationship with all its imperfections, and all the unkind things people say to one another in normal living. For some people, it takes a lot to be honest enough with themselves to admit there were occasions in the past when they had wished their partner or other close relatives and friends absent, if not dead.

Working with the bereaved is different from conventional therapy in that a lot more normalizing of the experience is necessary. This may be because so few people seem to know anything about bereavement unless it has happened to them. There are several powerful feelings and experiences that result in the bereaved fearing or even thinking they are going mad. The initial numbness, which is often both physical and emotional and gives a 'cotton-wool' feeling, seems to be an experience unique to loss. It is often a comfort to know that this is usual. The constant searching, which means going over and over in one's mind (or out loud) the details of the last days, hours or minutes before the death, can be frightening, in particular because some of the images can be very disturbing. To know that this non-stop 'noise' in one's head is usual and not a sign of madness is comforting. Very often, once the terrible image has been shared, it fades. The third common experience which makes the bereaved, and frequently their family, query their sanity is the occurrence of hallucinations, which may be auditory, visual, sensual or olfactory. These are very vivid and can actually be comforting to the bereaved, but they are also disturbing because the person is dead. It is as if the brain has only partly accepted the death and at the same time expects the person to be around. This is also seen in how many routine actions are done unnecessarily, such as laying the table for five people when there are now only four.

What the counsellor or therapist is doing is facilitating the grief work, which in uncomplicated grieving will often be a short piece of work in the range of two to 10 sessions. The grief work (Worden, 2009) will be to help the client to:

- accept the reality of the death
- experience the pain of grief
- adjust to an environment in which the deceased is missing
- relocate the deceased emotionally and move on with life.

Grief work involves facilitating the expression of grief by focusing on feelings and emotions, and also by focusing on the new skills which are necessary distractions from the emotional side of grieving and which need to be acquired. In general, women choose to do the former and men the latter. However, Stroebe and Schut (1995) suggest that both areas need to be attended to and thus men need encouragement to talk about their feelings and women to be more practical.

The tendency for women to focus on their feelings and men to look practically to the future can cause enormous conflict in families. Frequently, a death means several people in a family are affected and they can become very angry with one another if they are grieving differently. Indeed, the person not showing much emotion is often accused of not caring, when that is far from the case. Such families may need a great deal of support. It is common for the death of a child in a family to cause such conflict that the couple separate. Working through a bereavement will only strengthen a sound relationship.

When a death happens in a family, children need special help. They are often ignored because they move very rapidly through Bowlby's three stages and attach to another key adult. This misleads the adults into thinking the child is unaffected, but this is unlikely to be true. Depending on their age, they may not even understand what dying means, and up to about the age of five they expect the dead person to return. Between eight and 10 years of age, children develop an adult's concept of death. It is most important to understand that children up to at least the age of 10 are likely to think that they 'caused' the death, for instance linking a row with the death and believing that their anger has driven the person away. These irrational beliefs are found in adults too. Any belief of this sort must be explored and the child helped to understand that people do not die because the child has hated them.

Both children and adults need to be encouraged to value the importance of the continuing bonds found in memories, both tangible and intangible. The use of memory books or boxes for photographs, mementoes, significant letters and certificates can be very useful. Another helpful activity is writing a life history or creating a lifeline which helps to encapsulate significant events from the life of the deceased (Lendrum and Syme, 2004).

Another major strand of Stroebe and Schut's work is to draw attention to cultural differences in mourning and to warn against drawing wrong conclusions. For a Buddhist it is usual to erect a shrine to a dead person, while in some Western cultures this is considered to be a sign of a chronic and complicated grief. Likewise, ritualized mourning is still normal in orthodox Judaism; at one time it was usual in Great Britain, but is now unusual and even considered morbid.

It is often assumed that people with a religious belief will be less upset by bereavement. For some this will be true, but it is unhelpful to make such assumptions. The feeling that even God has let them down, and it is useless railing against a spiritual force, drives some people away from any religious beliefs. It is essential in bereavement work to have knowledge of the different religions and cultural groups in the UK as the rituals around death are very varied.

It is particularly important in bereavement work to hold the ending in mind in every session. Obviously, the ending of the therapy is in danger of being yet another loss. The reality of another loss must not be denied, and it is very important that the ending in bereavement counselling is planned with the client. Indeed, a lot of clients find it useful to create their own ritual for the ending of therapy. If the client shows a marked reluctance to end, this would suggest that either the therapist has replaced the 'dead' person – always a danger, as a therapist can seem much more understanding than any family or friends – or some part of the grief work has been omitted. A discussion with a supervisor about the ways to handle this is essential so that the problems can be confronted, understood and worked with.

CHRONIC COMPLICATED GRIEF

A number of factors may predict that the grieving could be greatly complicated and probably prolonged. These factors must be checked in the initial assessment. They are separated into two groups: the external circumstances surrounding the death; and the internal factors linked with the life history and emotional development of the bereaved person. External circumstances that affect the grieving process are shown in Table 6.8.3. Internal factors affecting grief are shown in Table 6.8.4; the first three factors affect the person's capacity to grieve, and the latter three will influence the reaction to the death because of the quality of the relationship which is lost.

It is not possible to predict exactly how the combination of these factors will affect the grieving process, but it is essential they are assessed. Their presence will help alert the therapist to the likelihood of a complex and/or a prolonged grieving process which may include severe, chronic depression, and thus enable a decision to be made on what level of skill will be needed to work with someone and whether a psychiatric referral is necessary. If someone already has a psychiatric history, it would be unwise to work with them as bereavement can greatly exacerbate mental instability.

Table 6.8.3   *External circumstances affecting grief*

Place of death	If person dies far away and particularly if dead body or grave not seen
Coincidental deaths	Simultaneous and multiple deaths in family or community
Successive deaths	If deaths or losses follow one after another in close succession, then the grief reaction and work over one may be incomplete before the next one and the whole process is interrupted
Nature of the death	Where a death is sudden, untimely, violent or traumatic, it is more difficult to grieve Homicide and suicide are particularly difficult
Social networks	Closely knit families and communities can be most helpful. The converse is also true. The attitude of a society to death and dying can help or hinder the grieving process

Source: Lendrum and Syme (2004)

Table 6.8.4   *Internal factors affecting grief*

Attachment history	If securely attached in childhood, can cope with anxiety in adulthood and will have a capacity to express emotion and to grieve
Loss and death history	If an earlier death or loss has been difficult to accept and grieve, then current grief will 'awaken' the earlier unresolved grief. The combination will then be harder to grieve
Age and stage of griever	For children and young people and those in life transitions, grief may be more challenging
Intimacy level	The more intimate the relationship (e.g. spouse, lover, partner, child, parent, sibling), the more intense the grief
Emotional complexity	The more straightforward the relationship, the less complicated the grief. If the relationship had many denied feelings or had unrecognized ambivalence, the grief will be more complex
Social network	If the family and community are supportive and the griever has the capacity to use it, this will aid grieving. Similarly if the attitudes of society are helpful

Source: Lendrum and Syme (2004)

REFERENCES

Bowlby, J. (1979) *The Making and Breaking of Affectional Bonds*. London: Tavistock.

Cannon, W.B. (1929) *Bodily Changes in Pain, Hunger, Fear and Rage*. London: Appleton.

Caplan, G. (1964) *Principles of Preventive Psychiatry*. New York: Basic.

Klass, D., Silverman, P.R. and Nickman, S. (eds) (1996) *Continuing Bonds: New Understandings of Grief*. London: Taylor and Francis.

Lendrum, S. and Syme, G. (2004) *Gift of Tears* (2nd edn). London: Routledge.

Lindemann, E. (1944) The symptomatology and management of acute grief. *American Journal of Psychiatry*, 101: 141.

Marris, P. (1974) *Loss and Change*. London: Routledge and Kegan Paul.

Parkes, C.M. (1971) Psychosocial transitions: a field for study. *Social Sciences and Medicine*, 5: 101.

Parkes, C.M. (1996) *Bereavement: Studies of Grief in Adult Life*. London: Routledge.

Schore, A.N. (2001) Minds in the making: attachment, the self-organising brain, and developmentally-oriented psychoanalytic psychotherapy. *British Journal of Psychotherapy*, 17: 299–328.

Stroebe, M.S. and Schut, H.A.W. (1995) The dual process model of coping with loss. Paper presented at the International Work Group on Death, Dying and Bereavement, St Catherine's College, Oxford, 26–29 June.

Worden, W. (2009) *Grief Counselling and Grief Therapy* (4th edn). London: Routledge.

Depression

PAUL GILBERT

DEPRESSION

In 2009 the National Institute for Health and Clinical Excellence (NICE: www.nice.org.uk) published its revised guidelines for the treatment of depression. This document discusses the nature of depression, and its huge economic and social burden for both sufferers and those who live with them. It offers a useful resource and guideline for understanding the range of different types and severities of depression, different causes of depression, and different evidence-based treatments for depression. It recommends that an individual person's depression emerges from a unique interaction of biological, psychological and social processes (see also Gilbert, 2004). A recent excellent resource book on just about all aspects of depression is Ingram's *International Encyclopaedia of Depression* (2009).

SYMPTOMS

Although the variety of different depressions vary symptomatically (Beckham et al., 1995), psychologically (Arieti and Bemporad, 1980; Beck, 1983) and biologically (Thase and Howland, 1995), its core features are well recognized (Gilbert, 2007) and are given in Table 6.9.1.

EPIDEMIOLOGY

It has been estimated that about one in five people are at risk of suffering a depressive episode at some time in their lives (this figure varies according to social class and social circumstances) and women are over twice as likely to suffer an episode as men (Bebbington, 1998), largely for psychosocial reasons. Once depression has struck there is a high chance of relapse (over 50 per cent), early onset depression (on or before 20 years) being particularly vulnerable to relapse (Giles et al., 1989). Around 50 per cent of depressions are comorbid (e.g. with anxiety disorders and substance abuse), complicating their treatment. Depression is commonly linked to personality disorders such as borderline personality disorders.

VULNERABILITIES

Children growing up with a depressed parent can be affected in both their social and their intellectual development. Rapid diagnosis and treatment are key to helping depressed parents and their children (Compas et al., 2009). Increased vulnerability to depression arises in hostile, low-warmth and neglectful families (Kessler and Magee, 1994), and chronic depression in women is especially associated with childhood sexual abuse (Andrews, 1998). In a series of studies, Brown and his colleagues explored in depth the links between early parental

Table 6.9.1   *The major symptomatic features of depression**

Biological	Sleep disturbance, loss of appetite, loss of weight, fatigue, changes in circadian rhythms, hormones and brain chemicals (Healy and Williams, 1988; Thase and Howland, 1995). People can feel 'ill' and may describe feeling 'heavy and weighed down'. There is also a range of physical conditions that increase risk of depression (e.g. diabetes and hypothyroidism) with new evidence that some people are 'virally' vulnerable due to their raised cytokine immune response (Roque et al., 2009)
Emotional	Low mood, anhedonia, i.e. difficult to enjoy or find pleasure in things (Watson and Clark, 1988; Willner, 1993); struggles with the feelings of affection and affiliation to others and from others (Gilbert, 2007); experiences increases in feelings of emptiness, anger, frustration, irritability, resentment, anxiety, shame, guilt (Gilbert, 1992; 2007)
Motivation	Apathy, loss of energy and interest (Klinger, 1993); things seem pointless, hopeless (Abramson et al., 1989; Alloy et al., 1988)
Cognitive	Poor concentration and memory, commonly with worry about the changes (Miller, 1975; Watts, 1993) and rumination (Fisher and Wells, 2009)
Evaluations	Negative ideas about the self (including self-criticism: Gilbert et al., 2010; Zuroff et al., 2005), feelings of inferiority (Zuroff et al., 2007), the world and the future (Beck et al., 1979), with a sense of defeat and entrapment (Gilbert and Allan, 1998; Trachsel et al., 2010)
Behaviour	Lowered activity, social withdrawal, agitation or retardation. Problems in social relationships are common in depression, as both cause and consequence (Feldman and Gotlib, 1993; Segrin and Abramson, 1994; Dimidjian et al., 2006)

*The key symptom of depression is anhedonia – the loss of pleasure and positive affect. However, negative emotions such as anger, shame, guilt and anxiety typically increase in depression.

experience, life events and vulnerability to depression and their interactions (e.g. Brown et al., 2008).

Life events associated with feeling defeated and entrapped (a perceived impossibility of getting away from a difficult situation) is especially associated with depression (Gilbert, 1992; 2004; Gilbert and Allan, 1998) and more so than loss events (Brown et al., 1995). The importance of people's experience of entrapment and sense of defeat has recently been extended and confirmed (Trachsel et al., 2010) and found to be importantly related to depression in certain ethnic communities (Gask et al., 2011). Zuroff et al. (2007) explored 113 people's interactions over 20 days and found that seeing one's partner as dominant and feeling inferior and submissive were highly linked with depression, highlighting again the importance of how people compare themselves with others (social comparison) and their assertive or submissive styles (Gilbert, 1992; 2007).

Perfectionism, along with self-criticism and shame, play major roles in depression, including increasing vulnerability to depression (Zuroff et al., 2005) and self-harm. Self-criticism also interacts with life events and interferes with treatment (Bulmash et al., 2009). In many studies self-criticism has been shown to be a very important variable in the depression (e.g. Gilbert et al., 2010; Zuroff

et al., 2005) and should be a target for psychological therapy (Gilbert, 2010).

ASSESSMENT

Although depression is a highly heterogeneous disorder (with some depressions, such as bipolar depression, having a high genetic loading) most depressions result from a variety of complex interacting factors, including biological vulnerability, early life history, current relationship problems, and life difficulties (Bifulco and Moran, 1988; Gilbert, 2004) which require biopsychosocial and multimodal assessments and interventions (Gilbert, 1995; 2004; NICE, 2009). Counsellors are not expected to be able to make a specific psychiatric diagnosis based on *ICD-10* or *DSM-IV* but they should be familiar with these symptom profiles. In addition, and especially in the context of fatigue, it is important that an appropriate medical assessment is conducted to rule out physical disorders such as hypothyroidism, diabetes (B12 deficiency, especially in older people) and other disorders that can be linked to fatigue and depression. Counsellors of course will be seeking to understand specific problem areas. Asking questions about the symptoms in

Table 6.9.1 will give you an assessment of the current mental state. This can be done by saying (for example), 'I would just like to ask you a few questions about how you're feeling and functioning at the moment', and then, 'How are you sleeping? What is your energy like?', etc. To explore emotions you might ask, 'How would you describe your current feelings just now?' Elevated rates of anger (frustration and irritation) and anxiety are common in depression and can often be a source of depression where people feel guilty about anger, so one needs to ask about anger. 'Have you noticed any change in your experience of anger, irritation, frustration? Do you find these difficult to express or try and hold them in?', 'Have you noticed any change in anxiety?' Some depressed people have difficulties in acknowledging anger but may need to address this in therapy. Shame and guilt are also very common in depression and should be emotions that are asked about. For example, 'Are there things in your life you would find very hard to talk about?' The various diagnostic criteria for depression do not do a good job in evaluating negative emotions such as anger, anxiety and shame, so you will need to look at these especially. Depressed clients who are very prone to shame may not reveal the key things that are bothering them, so you may need to be sensitive to what is hidden. Unrevealed shame issues can be one reason why therapy gets stuck. Current life events are explored in terms of current difficulties including relationship difficulties.

Sources of social support and having a confidant are important to assess because lack of social support and not having a confidant are associated with depression. Having few friends and being socially isolated, particularly for young mothers, is associated with depression. Some depressions are related to domestic violence, although people might feel shame in acknowledging that. Recent life events such as loss of employment or financial strain or family disputes are often associated with depression. These may require practical interventions from social services, Citizens Advice Bureaux and so on. The important thing about assessment is that we don't just provide the same intervention whatever kind of difficulty the client comes with; rather, we are able to assess their needs in detail and then signpost to other services if they need them, and develop a collaborative relationship that focuses on the internal and external problems.

ASSESSMENT AND CONTEXT

If counsellors are under pressure to provide short-term therapies of say six sessions, then consideration should be given as to whether the client should be referred to a more specialist service. Therefore, some time should be given within the first few sessions to previous history of mental health problems and relational history. It is useful, if even briefly, to find out what kind of relationship clients had with parents and significant others during their formative years. So attention should be given to the degree of warmth, control, neglect, aggression and shaming (such as being criticized, disapproved of, and called names). Peer relationships should also be assessed, such as difficulties in forming friends or experiences of bullying. Clients can be invited to reflect on how these early experiences may have shaped their inner world, and in particular their typical beliefs and feelings about themselves and others. You are getting a feel for whether this is likely to be a short-term case or not; whether the person had reasonable functioning before the depression or has been struggling for a while; whether the person has a reasonable attachment experience and history or whether there are difficulties in the history. The latter nearly always take longer, and setting them up for short-term therapy runs the risk of compounding a sense of failure and not being able to be helped. Managing this dilemma is important.

Having explored something of the symptom profile, nature of the problem and some historical context of the depression, formulation may move to focus on current beliefs about self and others. Beck's (Beck et al., 1979) cognitive triad of negative experiences of the world in the future is a very good guiding framework for exploring beliefs. In regard to the self, depressed people typically see themselves as inferior, worthless and inadequate. Shame and self-criticism are common too. Indeed, these can be a source of continuing to feel depressed, particularly if one is ruminating on them. Negative views of the future are linked to feelings of hopelessness, not been able to see how to cope, feeling trapped and wanting to escape, feeling a lack of the resources one needs. One can also ask about feeling defeated, as if one has failed to sort out certain struggles in life. A sense of defeat can be a powerful predictor of depression and hopelessness (Gilbert and Allan, 1998).

Negative views of the world are often linked to ideas that the world is a difficult place, full of obstacles that are hard to surmount. In addition, some depressed people are very distrusting of others. Those who have felt let down in their lives, or who have possibly been abused or neglected, can find it difficult to form open and trusting relationships with others, including the counsellor. Recent research suggests that fears of compassion, of being open to the compassion of others, and of being self-compassionate are linked to depression (Gilbert et al., in press). It can sometimes be useful to reflect gently on that as a potential area of difficulty.

ASSESSING RISK

Self-harm and suicide risk factors are associated with depression, particularly when it is chronic and/or severe (Worchel and Gearing, 2009). You ask about potential suicide, 'Do things sometimes seem so bad to you that you can't see any way out?' If the answer to this is yes then you might ask, 'Have you had any thoughts about how you might get out?' Then follow up the question with, 'Have you had any thoughts of ending a life?' If the answer to this is yes you might then follow up with, 'Have you had any thoughts about how you might do that or have you made any plans?' Now of course many people, even people who are not that depressed, can have thoughts of suicide; but in the context of the depression, feeling hopeless and seeing no way out should trigger a need for further assessment within specialist services. You might say, 'We need to cover all the angles and I am concerned for you, your distress and these feelings, so I would like this other person (e.g. psychiatrist, CPN or psychologist) to have a talk with you and see if there is anything further we can offer.' Don't feel isolated with clients you are worried about, or not able to ask others for help. If you're working with depressed people you will need to have worked out these routes for support from other professionals and services should the need arise.

Recent major life events such as bereavement, loss of employment, major change of physical health, or living alone can be factors associated with suicide. History of suicide attempts and impulsiveness are especially important in younger cohorts.

Other forms of risk associated with depression can be neglect of self and children, and when depression involves increasing irritability, concern for children is increased. If you have concerns about children then you should contact child protection services within social services who will offer you advice and possibly be able to provide support for the family.

DISCUSSING THE NATURE OF DEPRESSION WITH CLIENTS

Some depressed people like to have a label for their difficulties and some do not. One can, however, talk in terms of exhaustion; of being exhausted in body and mind, and feeling that there is 'no more fight left in you'. This position can make it easier to negotiate for an antidepressant if that is indicated by, for example, the severity of the depression, serious sleep disturbance, somatic symptoms, concentration problems and strong feelings that things can't improve. If you are unfamiliar with these decisions or with assessing suicide risk then contact someone who is, and explain to your client why you may be referring them on for further assessment. You might, for example, talk of how states of mind lead us to think and feel things that we know we do not normally think and feel, and how depression is notorious for making the world seem dark, leading to a strong wish to escape it – even for life itself. Here you are normalizing but not trivializing.

When talking about depression it is very important for the counsellor to constantly advise the client that their depression is not their fault. Depression is common and is a state of mind that can overtake us because of the way our minds and brains are designed. It is linked to becoming exhausted and is absolutely nothing to do with personal weakness or character defects. This deshaming intervention can be very important at the beginning of counselling because depressed patients often fear that it is something about them and that they should be able to cope better than they are doing. Clarity on this issue right at the beginning of counselling can reassure clients.

ASSESSING STRENGTHS AND RESOURCES

Assessments shouldn't just be about problems and deficits; they should also be about the strengths and resources that are available. For example, some depressed people have been very courageous and battled on in difficult circumstances, and so their courage and efforts can be highlighted. There may be friends that they could turn to, but their feelings of burdening others or shame stop them. Sometimes inviting partners into therapy can be helpful, especially if partners want to be helpful but are not sure how to be. If people are feeling suicidal you can validate those feelings but also direct them to thoughts about things they would like to live for, such as: remembering they don't always feel like this; children they would like to see grow up or be there for; recontacting with personal and core values. So it can help to look at the strengths and resources of the person as well, so that you can work with your client how to build on those (Worchel and Gearing, 2009).

FORMULATION

Formulations guide treatments, although the issue of formulation is not without controversy (Bieling and Kyken, 2003; Tarrier, 2006). Counsellors can link background experiences to fears, concerns and drives which lead to safety strategies and ways of acting in the world. These can then have unforeseen consequences, making us vulnerable to a range of difficulties (Gilbert, 2007).

The formulation of a psychiatrist who is going to give medication will be different from that of a counsellor or therapist. Counsellors formulate depression in terms of its psychological and/or social difficulties. The initial focus will be on the specific problem areas (for example, relationship problems), and for the milder depressions this may be enough, but for the moderate or more severe depressions it is important to share your overview with clients. You can take them through early life experiences and explore the way these may have shaped how they feel about and see themselves and others, how these in turn may have shaped how they think about the world and their role in it, and how these affect the way they behave in the world, particularly in relation to interpersonal conflicts or seeking out various opportunities for relating (including employment).

For example, Jane had a critical mother and spent her childhood trying to avoid her mother's criticism and elicit her approval. Key fears were those of being shamed, feeling that 'inner sinking feeling' of rejection and abandonment. As a result she developed a range of safety strategies, focused on trying to please others, on being liked, accepted and avoiding criticism and rejection. The unintended consequences were that she struggled to be assertive, was frightened of anger, struggled to process and express anger assertively, found it hard to be honest about her feelings, thus making it difficult for her to deal with conflicts. In addition she developed the typical self-critical style that people do in these contexts. A combination of being unable to deal with conflicts in her marriage, fear of being rejected and isolated, problems in being unable to recognize and cope with difficult emotions, and a self-critical style gave rise to a depression. The counsellor was able to help Jane recognize that those difficulties are a natural and understandable consequence of her history and efforts to do her best. However, the unintended consequences of her safety and drive strategies made her ill-equipped to deal with difficulties in life. The formulation would of course be quite different from someone who had a fairly secure background but had run into serious financial problems because of unemployment and buildup of financial debt for which they were blaming themselves but feeling trapped.

It is important that the formulation is co-constructed and uses narratives to 'paint the story'. This agreed and co-constructed formulation is a springboard to move on to therapeutic work. Out of the formulation comes an agreement about what would be helpful to change and work with. Sometimes this can be a focus on specific life problems that the counsellor can break down and work through step by step, or on problematic emotions or key beliefs, or on key behaviours (such as difficulties in behaving assertively or working through problems or finding positive activities again), or sometimes it may mean offering an opportunity for clients to explore the issues in their own way, in their own time, in a rather non-structured way.

INTERVENTION

From the formulation, the focus for intervention emerges. There are many types of therapeutic intervention for depression. Some people benefit from antidepressant drugs, whereas others do not. Antidepressant drugs do not help people retrain or understand the origins for the vulnerability to depression, or learn new coping skills – yet poor coping skills are a reason for relapse. On the social side, depressed people may need practical help with finances, housing, children, relationships and legal matters. Counsellors should be aware that sometimes these practical interventions are as helpful as counselling.

Most therapies use a basic system which understands that therapy is conducted in the context of a supportive relationship that invites openness and exploration. This context opens to a set of therapy tasks and goals which depend on the school of therapy. These range across group therapy, family therapy and individual therapy, and each may follow different approaches such as systemic, behaviour, cognitive, interpersonal and psychodynamic. Some therapies suggest various kinds of 'homework' for people to try out during the inter-session period. Others just invite the client to spend time reflecting between sessions. There is a great variety of psychological therapies for depression (Ingram, 2009).

It is, therefore, useful to try to develop a focus with particular clients and to evaluate if certain types of therapy may be more appropriate for them than others. For example, under what conditions might you refer a patient for family therapy or group therapy? Although there is an increasing range of therapies that have some evidence behind them, and currently the evidence favours the more engaging, specifically developed therapies for depression such as CBT, we should also be aware that recent research suggests that psychological therapies may be less helpful than sometimes thought, particularly when people are followed up over the long term (Cuijpers et al., 2008). In addition, the last few years have seen an explosion of different therapies seeking to get good quality research evidence, and it is likely that the future will increase the range of therapies for which there is such evidence. It would be helpful if researchers spent less time comparing therapies and instead researched 'which interventions work for this person with these difficulties'.

The essence of the counselling approach, however, is to create a safe place with a safe relationship where people can begin to explore their feelings, hopes and fears. The counsellor is primarily reflective and helps a person to discover for themselves things that can be helpful. Cognitive therapists will tend to focus on identifying unhelpful and ruminating thoughts and how people become alert to them, stand back from them and consider alternatives. Rumination is an important maintaining process in depression. Behaviour therapists will focus more on changing behaviours, especially because depressed people have a tendency to withdraw and avoid. Here the counsellor will encourage engagement with various activities, both pleasant ones and also those that focus on problem-solving. Clients can be encouraged to focus on what they can do, rather than on what they can't do (many depressed people tend to focus on what they can't do and feel defeated).

Depression can arise in people who are struggling with difficult dilemmas, e.g. 'Should I stay in this relationship or leave?' It is the counsellor's job not to resolve the dilemma but to create the psychological conditions for the client to think about it, talk it over and come to their own resolution. What the counsellor can do is note if unhelpful emotions such as guilt, shame and resentment, or sunk costs ('I've invested so much in this I can't give it up', or 'If I stay with this it will eventually become good' in spite of all the evidence that it isn't going to), are interfering with problem-solving. Emotion-focused therapists are likely to focus on problems with processing certain emotions, particularly those of anger or grief. Depressed people can have fears about the depth of their anger, or they may not even recognize it. Helping the depressed person to validate, understand and work through difficult emotions can be very important. In all of these therapies it can also be useful to be aware of a range of self-help books that people can use to find out more about depression and how they might help themselves (e.g. Gilbert, 2007; 2009).

Sometimes it is important to revisit past traumas and to enable clients to experience certain kinds of emotions while working through those traumas. If these traumas are related to abuse, and you feel unable to deal with them, then it is useful to steer the client in the direction of therapists who do have experience of working with abuse. Try to be open on these issues rather than defensive.

In general, therapists try to assist people to gain a different perspective on themselves and their current situation, so that they are not collapsed in a dark hole of pessimism and a sense of worthlessness. In the compassion-focused therapy approach, whatever 'interventions and techniques' one engages in, one has to ensure that the depressed person experiences these as helpful, supportive, validating and encouraging. It is easy for depressed patients to say, 'I understand the logic but it doesn't help me feel any different.' It is therefore the feeling towards the therapy that is important (Gilbert, 2009; 2010).

OVERVIEW

Depression is a very varied and complex disorder, with many different causes, and presents in many different forms. When we come to treat depression we cannot afford to be 'a one-club golfer'. Sometimes we will need a mixture of treatments. Even when we focus on a psychological treatment it is not always clear which psychological or social treatment would best suit a particular client. It is also the case that some individuals get on better with certain types of therapist, as opposed to certain types of approach. Often it is the way in which counsellors can aid people to deal with problems in their life or pick up on new and fresh starts in their life that is helpful. Helpful relationships are often key to wellbeing, and counsellors can help clients work on those elements of developing helpful rather than critical relationships. Counsellors should also be aware that treatments for depression are developing quite quickly now, with a different focus on emotions, rumination, activation, relationships and so on. Hopefully, in the years to come, as we understand more about the causes and maintenance factors of depression, we will be able to help more people, and to help them to stay well for longer.

REFERENCES

Abramson, L.Y., Metalsky, G.I. and Alloy, L.B. (1989) Hopelessness: a theory-based subtype of depression. *Psychological Review*, 96: 358–72.

Alloy, L.B., Abramson, L.Y., Metalsky, G.I. and Hartledge, S. (1988) The hopelessness theory of depression: attributional aspects. *British Journal of Clinical Psychology*, 27: 5–12.

Andrews, B. (1998) Shame and childhood abuse. In P. Gilbert and B. Andrews (eds), *Shame: Interpersonal Behavior, Psychopathology and Culture* (pp. 176–90). New York: Oxford University Press.

Arieti, S. and Bemporad, J. (1980) The psychological organization of depression. *American Journal of Psychiatry*, 137: 1360–5.

Bebbington, P. (1998) Editorial: sex and depression. *Psychological Medicine*, 28: 1–8.

Beck, A.T. (1983) Cognitive therapy of depression: new perspectives. In P.J. Clayton and J.E. Barrett (eds), *Treatment of Depression: Old Controversies and New Approaches*. New York: Raven.

Beck, A.T., Rush, A.J., Shaw, B.F. and Emery, G. (1979) *Cognitive Therapy of Depression*. New York: Wiley.

Beckham, E.E., Leber, W.R. and Youll, L.K. (1995) The diagnostic classification of depression. In E.E. Beckham and W.R. Leber (eds), *Handbook of Depression* (2nd edn, pp. 36–60). New York: Guilford.

Bieling, P.J. and Kyken, W. (2003) Is cognitive case formulation science or science fiction? *Clinical Psychology: Science and Practice*, 10: 52–69.

Bifulco, A. and Moran, P. (1988) *Wednesday's Child: Research into Women's Experiences of Neglect and Abuse in Childhood, and Adult Depression*. London: Routledge.

Brown, G.W., Harris, T.O. and Hepworth, C. (1995) Loss, humiliation and entrapment among women developing depression: a patient and non-patient comparison. *Psychological Medicine*, 25: 7–21.

Brown, G.W., Craig, T.K.J. and Harris, T.O. (2008) Parental maltreatment and proximal risk factors using the Childhood Experience of Care and Abuse (CECA) instrument: a life-course study of adult chronic depression 5. *Journal of Affective Disorders*, 110: 222–33.

Bulmash, E., Harkness, K.L., Stewart, J.G. and Bagby, R.M. (2009) Personality, stressful life events, and treatment response in major depression. *Journal of Consulting and Clinical Psychology*, 77: 1067–11.

Compas, B.E., Forehand, R., Keller, G., et al. (2009) Randomized controlled trial of a family cognitive-behavioral preventive intervention for children of depressed parents. *Journal of Consulting and Clinical Psychology*, 77: 1007–20.

Cuijpers, P., van Straten, A., Warmerdam, L. and Andersson, G. (2008) Psychological treatment of depression: a meta-analytic database of randomized studies. *BMC Psychiatry*, 8: 36. DOI 10.1186/1471-244X-8-36.

Dimidjian, S., Hollon, S.D., Dobson, K.S., et al. (2006). Randomized trial of behavioral activation, cognitive therapy, and anti-depressant medication in the acute treatment of adults with major depression. *Journal of Consulting and Clinical Psychology*, 74: 658–70.

Feldman, L.A. and Gotlib, I.H. (1993) Social dysfunction. In C.G. Costello (ed.), *Symptoms of Depression* (pp. 65–112). New York: Wiley.

Fisher, P. and Wells, A. (2009) *Metacognitive Therapy*. London: Routledge.

Gask, L., Seem, S., Waquas, A. and Waheed, W. (2011) Isolation, feeling 'stuck' and loss of control: understanding persistence of depression in British Pakistani women. *Journal of Affective Disorders*, 128: 49–55.

Gilbert, P. (1992) *Depression: The Evolution of Powerlessness*. Hove: Erlbaum, New York: Guilford.

Gilbert, P. (1995) Biopsychosocial approaches and evolutionary theory as aids to integration in clinical psychology and psychotherapy. *Clinical Psychology and Psychotherapy*, 2: 135–56.

Gilbert, P. (2004) Depression: a biopsychosocial, integrative and evolutionary approach. In M. Power (ed.), *Mood Disorders: A Handbook of Science and Practice* (pp. 99–142). Chichester: Wiley.

Gilbert, P. (2007) *Psychotherapy and Counselling for Depression* (3rd edn). London: Sage.

Gilbert, P. (2009) *Overcoming Depression* (3rd edn). London: Constable Robinson (also CD 'Talks With Your Therapist').

Gilbert, P. (2010) *Compassion Focused Therapy: The CBT Distinctive Features Series*. London: Routledge.

Gilbert, P. and Allan, S. (1998) The role of defeat and entrapment (arrested flight) in depression: an exploration of an evolutionary view. *Psychological Medicine*, 28: 584–97.

Gilbert, P., McEwan, K., Irons, C., Bhundia, R., Christie, R., Broomhead, C. and Rockliff, H. (2010) Self-harm in a mixed clinical population: the roles of self-criticism, shame, and social rank. *British Journal of Clinical Psychology*, 49: 563–76.

Gilbert, P., McEwan, K., Matos, M. and Rivis, A. (in press) Fears of compassion: development of three self-report measures. *Psychology and Psychotherapy*.

Giles, D., Jarrett, R., Biggs, M., Guzick, D. and Rush, J. (1989) Clinical predictors of recurrence in depression. *American Journal of Psychiatry*, 146: 764–7.

Ingram, R.E. (2009) *The International Encyclopaedia of Depression*. New York: Springer.

Kessler, R.C. and Magee, W.J. (1994) Childhood family violence and adult recurrent depression. *Journal of Health and Social Behaviour*, 35: 13–27.

Klinger, E. (1993) Loss of interest. In C.G. Costello (ed.), *Symptoms of Depression* (pp. 43–62). New York: Wiley.

Miller, W.R. (1975) Psychological deficit in depression. *Psychological Bulletin*, 82: 238–60.

NICE (2009) *Depression in Adults* (update). http://guidance.nice.org.uk/CG/WaveR/24

Roque, S., Correia-Neves, M., Mesquita, A.R., Palha, J.A. and Sousa, N. (2009) Interleukin-10: a key cytokine in depression? *Cardiovascular Psychiatry and Neurology*, 1: 1–5. Article ID 187894, DOI 10.1155/2009/187894.

Segrin, C. and Abramson, L.Y. (1994) Negative reactions to depressive behaviours: a communication theories analysis. *Journal of Abnormal Psychology*, 103: 655–68.

Tarrier, N. (ed.) (2006) *Case Formulation in Cognitive Behaviour Therapy: The Treatment of Challenging and Complex Cases*. London: Routledge.

Thase, M.E. and Howland, R.H. (1995) Biological processes in depression: an update and integration. In E.E. Beckham and W.R. Leber (eds), *Handbook of Depression* (2nd edn, pp. 213–79). New York: Guilford.

Trachsel, M., Krieger, T., Gilbert, P. and Holtforth, M.G. (2010) Testing a German adaption of the Entrapment Scale and assessing the relation to depression. *Depression Research and Treatment*. Article ID 501782. DOI: 10.1155/2010/501782.

Watson, D. and Clark, L.A. (1988) Positive and negative affectivity and their relation to anxiety and depressive disorders. *Journal of Abnormal Psychology*, 97: 346–53.

Watts, F. (1993) Problems with memory and concentration. In C.G. Costello (ed.), *Symptoms of Depression* (pp. 113–14). New York: Wiley.

Willner, P. (1993) Anhedonia. In C.G. Costello (ed.), *Symptoms of Depression* (pp. 63–84). New York: Wiley.

Worchel, D. and Gearing, R.E. (2009) *Evidence-Based Suicide Assessment and Treatment*. New York: Springer.

Zuroff, D.C., Santor, D. and Mongrain, M. (2005) Dependency, self-criticism, and maladjustment. In J.S. Auerbach, K.N. Levy and C.E. Schaffer (eds), *Relatedness, Self-Definition and Mental Representation* (pp. 75–90). London: New York.

Zuroff, D.C., Santor, D. and Mongrain, M. (2007) Depression, perceived inferiority, and interpersonal behaviour: evidence for the involuntary defeat strategies. *Journal of Social and Clinical Psychology*, 26: 751–78.

Counselling Drug-Related Problems

ANDREW GUPPY AND SALLY WOODS

OVERVIEW

This chapter provides an insight into the special challenges and opportunities within the field of drug misuse counselling. The next section outlines what we are referring to by the term 'drug-related problems', describing the types of substances and the expected range of problems. Following this, the types of intervention environments are then explored more deeply, focusing on the main approaches to counselling with some background to their underlying theory. Some practical considerations of counselling substance-related problems are then presented. The final section looks at potential areas for development of this field and suggests ways of integrating drug counselling more closely into other fields.

DEFINING DRUGS, USE AND MISUSE

Initially, it is necessary to clarify what is meant by the concept of 'substance misuse'. According to the American Psychiatric Association (APA, 2000), misuse can include drug-related behaviour that may cause trouble in the short term through accidents, social or legal problems, though this behaviour need not have become a regular pattern. The APA definitions also include two more serious categories of 'substance abuse' (recurrent and continued misuse of a substance over the last 12 months) and 'substance dependence' (presence of tolerance, withdrawal and control loss features as well as

those of abuse). However, a recent announcement from the *DSM-V* Substance Use Disorders Workgroup (APA, 2010) suggests that in future abuse and dependence will be combined into a single disorder of graded clinical severity. In addition to clinical definitions, it may be useful for practitioners to be aware of the various substances that are commonly misused. Useful websites for such information (and much more) are described at the end of the chapter.

COUNSELLING SUBSTANCE-RELATED PROBLEMS

Models of Substance Misuse and their Implications for Treatment

There are several different approaches in the drug and alcohol counselling field (see Wanigaratne et al., 2005). One widely held view may be epitomised by Narcotics Anonymous (NA) and is designed to follow on from the approach pioneered by AA. This approach assumes that drug abuse is a pre-existing physical (biochemical) abnormality, and it is almost as though some individuals have an incurable allergy to their substance of addiction (hence lifelong abstinence being the only answer). Another medically influenced approach views the important element as being the harm that is related to the drug misuse and seeks to minimise this by reducing risks, reducing intake (as opposed to cessation) and possibly changing to another (usually prescribed) substance with reduced harm implications. The third approach may be seen as viewing the drug misuse as principally a pattern of inappropriate coping, and thus focuses on cognitive-behavioural elements to recognise and deal with situations likely to lead to drug use, to reduce unhelpful perceptions, to improve feelings of efficacy, and to increase the range of coping behaviours that may be used as an alternative to drugs. Obviously, there are any number of other approaches that are available and successful, but the following are probably the most commonly encountered within the UK at present.

Narcotics Anonymous

Although this kind of 'intervention' may appear to be different to usual forms of 'counselling', Narcotics Anonymous quite clearly provides a well-known type of support for those with problems. The spread and level of activity of NA in the United Kingdom is considerably less than its sister organisation AA; however, the broad philosophy of this approach can also be found in a number of residential and outpatient treatment facilities.

The principles of the NA (and AA) approach are covered in the 'twelve steps'. These steps principally involve six stages. Firstly, there is an admission of powerlessness over substance use and that life has become 'unmanageable'. The second stage involves an acceptance of assistance from a 'higher power'. Stage three is about becoming aware of the 'nature of our wrongs', with the fourth stage working on removing 'defects of character' and 'shortcomings'. A penultimate stage is about promising to make amends to those who have been harmed, and the final stage emphasises the maintenance of progress through prayer, meditation and a commitment to helping others in similar need. An interesting perspective on the active psychological ingredients embedded within these stages can be found in the review by Moos (2008) which helps to explain the effectiveness of twelve-step approaches.

It has been noted that there are variations across AA (and perhaps more so NA) groups in terms of the emphasis placed on the 'higher power principle' (some are more spiritual than religious). However, the principle that does not vary within the twelve-steps approach concerns the goal behaviour of abstinence. This has some implications for those who are opiate abusers, where a common alternative involves methadone substitution (described below) which may be seen as incompatible with an abstinence approach by some.

Typical Harm Reduction Approach

The essence of the harm reduction approach to substance misuse is a focus of service provision on meeting and working with drug users on their terms. It is a feature of such an approach that at times these terms may be out of line with mainstream social, government or service provision policy. Critics of this approach have long argued that by being supportive, in reality giving drugs to drug users, the services may be encouraging these individuals to maintain their current patterns of use, with no compelling reason to stop (e.g. Edwards, 1969). Supporters of the harm reduction approach would argue that it is an attempt to bridge the gap between the expectations of drug users and service providers with realistic rather than moralistic methods of intervention.

Usually the first step in harm reduction involves the stabilisation of the client's illicit use, which includes provision of sterile equipment and other harm reduction resources (e.g. condoms). The next step would normally involve reduction of use, often paired with GP or specialist prescribing. Generally, counselling is offered throughout this process but is particularly encouraged during periods of change (reduction in script). Group counselling is generally available via most community drug action teams, though the particular approach adopted may be varied. Clients would normally keep close contact with a key worker whose remit includes social and welfare support as well as specific drug-related matters. To some extent, problem-oriented, directive counselling occurs with this key worker. In many environments this relationship may be maintained within a 'contract' situation where support from the key worker is dependent on the client complying with the 'script regime' (e.g. cessation of illicit use). Interesting recent research related to this approach has come from the Drug Treatment Outcome Research Study, indicating that positive outcome can be found even within clients referred via the criminal justice system (Jones et al., 2009).

One of the primary benefits of this approach tends to be in the realistic perspective on relapse management. As the approach does not rely on abstinence as the only acceptable alternative to harmful use, the relapse event may be more accepted within the treatment regime and the re-establishment of the treatment process is much easier. However, one possible drawback to the most commonly encountered harm reduction approach is the potential lack of detailed counselling support. To some extent the process may focus on the management of the intake reduction and ignore underlying deficiencies in terms of self-perceptions and coping skills.

A Typical Psychological Approach to Substance Misuse Counselling

A number of community-based agencies focusing on alcohol and drug misuse could be seen as providing a mixture of intervention methods added to a more traditional counselling approach. Thus, one may see agencies providing certain features core to the harm reduction approach but also advocating a move towards abstinence while featuring a range of group and individual sessions focusing on elements central to cognitive-behavioural and rational emotive behaviour therapies.

The elements of harm reduction education and support in the provision of information and advice (as well as equipment in terms of syringes etc.) would normally occur early on in the process. Later, the discussion of eventual outcome goals could be approached and specific input relating to unhelpful cognitions and behaviours would be the focus of later sessions. In particular, the use of group sessions focuses on the uptake of alternative (to substance use) behaviours in order to positively replace the effects of drug taking.

Beyond the drug-specific information, the main difference in substance misuse counselling concerns the focus of activities (towards abstinence or 'controlled' use) rather than the actual activities themselves (e.g. role playing within a general social skills development package). It is common for some time to be devoted to such obvious substance-related issues as 'saying no'. Additionally, a lot of effort is directed towards 'relapse prevention' within the substance misuse field (see later). Within this general package, material focusing on stress management and assertiveness training could be included, as would other exercises on self-awareness and the development of positive ways of spending leisure time (other than substance use).

Increasing attention has been focused on the benefits of motivational interviewing (Miller and Rollnick, 2002) methods in dealing with substance misuse problems. Motivational approaches seem to be effective at the earlier stages of engagement in promoting the perspective that change is desirable and achievable. There is an increasing evidence base for the effectiveness of this approach across a wide range of substances (Wanigaratne et al., 2005).

PRACTICAL ISSUES IN DRUG COUNSELLING

One of the first lessons learned in substance misuse counselling concerns the difficulties of providing assistance to someone who is too intoxicated to talk coherently or to remember much of what was said.

Although it is unlikely that much progress may be made, there is an opinion that intoxicated clients should not be refused contact with the counsellor. This greatly depends on the situation. In our experience, there may be distinct problems with having intoxicated individuals participating in (or disrupting) group counselling sessions. However, as relapse is a commonly occurring feature of drug misuse, there is a danger that loss of contact and risk of harm may result if a regular client turns up intoxicated on an isolated occasion and is refused contact.

There are also some lessons to be learned in terms of structuring contact around known 'difficult times'.

1   Group sessions late on a Friday night may be useful for many early clients as it reduces the likelihood of weekend-long binges starting after work on Friday.
2   Holding group sessions immediately before script handout when clients may be 'strung out' can lead to sessions being unhelpful with behaviour varying between aggressive and silent.
3   Mixed model group sessions may be more difficult to manage, though can lead to useful discussion. The obvious clash comes between those on an abstinence route and those who are receiving scripts or who are trying to control their substance use.

Polysubstance Abuse

In the field of drug misuse it is clear that while there may be a 'principal drug' that is misused, the client may well be using and misusing other substances. A very common pattern is the occasional or frequent heavy use of alcohol which can remain after use of the main problem drug has reduced (Gossop et al., 2001).

Dual-diagnosis Patients

It is not uncommon to find additional psychiatric problems present in substance misusers. It is similarly likely that such underlying problems may be difficult to detect at the early points of contact when the client is still under the influence of drugs or alcohol. It usually the case that such clients will benefit from psychiatric referral from the counsellor. Other underlying psychological problems may also come to light in the course of a programme of counselling sessions which, depending on the environment, may also be appropriate to refer on. This very much depends on the expertise of the counsellor and the nature of the counselling environment (it may be inappropriate in some substance misuse focused agencies). For a more detailed review of many of the significant issues related to this field see Rassool (2002).

Relapse Management

This has been one of the key features of substance misuse intervention (e.g. see Marlatt and Donovan, 2005). If substance use/misuse has become the most important and reliable method of coping behaviour within the individual over a period of years, it is quite likely that during or after assistance the client may 'return' to a pattern of substance use. The use of inverted commas around 'return' is important as the aim is for the individual to continue to progress such that they are not returning to substance use with the same set of cognitions or perspectives that they started with. Even in successful cases relapse can occur, but the process is more likely to lead to eventual success if it is managed properly and if the individual feels able to call on support as soon as possible. One of the criticisms of the NA/AA philosophy was that it made it difficult to maintain self-esteem following a relapse, and that the distance in days from the last occasion of substance use seemed more important than how you may have developed along the way. However, this perspective is thankfully changing, and one of the very useful elements of the group counselling environments found within NA/AA and elsewhere is the sharing of experience in relapse management such as identifying high-risk situations or times and sharing ideas for alternative cognitions and behaviours.

Contracts and Expectations

A number of substance misuse counselling agencies have developed an approach of agreeing a 'contract' with the client in terms of defining what sort of effort they were required to undertake and, in return, what sort of support may be expected from the agency. While it is felt important to discuss what both sides are expecting and willing to do, this may be developed over time and the use of a formal contract (especially early on) may be over the top.

It may be the case that the client is uncertain of what they actually want from the process and this may be the focus of counselling for some time, developing the client's perspective on themselves and relevant others, their drug use and its advantages and disadvantages. As this develops, the process encourages users to develop perceptions of control over their patterns of use and works towards

realistic decisions over where they are heading. To some extent, this approach does fit in with the notion of harm reduction in the sense that safer drug use (clean equipment from needle exchanges, known content of drug from prescription, move towards non-injected substitute) may be preferred by the user as a treatment goal. There is, however, the alternative perspective that allowing the user to select the relatively easier option of harm reduction rather than abstinence as the treatment goal only delays the inevitable.

OUTCOME AND MAINTENANCE

It is clear that success has been achieved by many different therapeutic approaches in the field of drug misuse (Wanigaratne et al., 2005). However, it is clear that success needs to be carefully defined and must incorporate a number of dimensions rather than simply focusing on the volume or weight of the substance. Thus modern researchers advocate a range of outcome measures to include wider aspects of psychological and social functioning as well as the more usual substance- and symptom-oriented measures (Marsden et al., 1998; Guppy and Marsden, 2002).

Where outcome evidence has been examined in the field of substance misuse, there is support for virtually all the interventions described above (Wanigaratne et al., 2005). Thus twelve-step, harm reduction, REBT and CBT approaches have positive outcomes, though the prognosis tends to be less positive for those with heavier and longer patterns of misuse, perhaps particularly when misuse ranges over more than one substance. From experience, it seems that some individuals need to try a number of intervention approaches before they achieve much success. However, it remains unclear whether such success is necessarily dependent on a strength of that particular intervention or is a result of coincidental changes within the individual achieved largely outside the counselling process.

FUTURE DEVELOPMENTS

It is easy to say, but one of the main difficulties in dealing with illicit drug misuse is the drug itself. For many years, the prescribing of drugs and substitute drugs has developed the possibility of moving the user away from the criminal sections of society and regaining some semblance of normal functioning. The continued development of this approach is viewed quite positively (see Gossop et al., 2001 and

Jones et al., 2009 for treatment outcome success). This is not to say that decriminalisation should or should not be a future consideration; it is merely to suggest that we need to move away from a moral position that dictates that any illicit drug use is against the law and therefore must be clinically construed as misuse. While we have a society that regards non-problem use of alcohol as acceptable, there seems to be no strong psychological argument to support these double standards.

Of course the other main difficulty in dealing with illicit drug use is the person. Much of the policy and practice in relation to drug misuse has focused on the chemical rather than the person. Even the most common interventions struggle to acknowledge the subsidiary role that the substance takes in relation to the person choosing to take it. It may be viewed that all forms of addiction primarily relate to part of a wider model of mental health, that of inappropriate coping behaviour. Recent research and practice have begun to focus on other parts of the model in relation to how we appraise our interactions with the world, including expectations about our control over situations and outcomes and the efficacy of our coping. Thus, it is considered that the long-term development in this field will be to bring it into the fold of other interventions in the promotion of psychological wellbeing to the mutual benefit of practitioners and clients all round.

REFERENCES

APA (2000) *Diagnostic and Statistical Manual of Mental Disorders* (4th edn text rev.). Washington, DC: American Psychiatric Association.

APA (2010) *DSM-V Development: Substance Use Disorder*. American Psychiatric Association. www.dsm5.org/ProposedRevisions/Pages/proposedrevision.aspx?rid=431#, 1 November 2010.

Edwards, G. (1969) The British approach to the treatment of heroin addiction. *The Lancet*, 7598: 768–72.

Gossop, M., Marsden, J. and Stewart, D. (2001) *NTORS after Five Years: Changes in Substance Use, Health and Criminal Behaviour during the Five Years after Intake*. London: Department of Health.

Guppy, A. and Marsden, J. (2002) Alcohol and drug misuse and the organization. In M. Shabracq, J.A. Winnubst and C.L. Cooper (eds), *Handbook of Work and Health Psychology* (2nd edn). Chichester: Wiley.

Jones, A., Donmall, M., Millar, T., Moody, A., Weston, S., Anderson, T., Gittins, M., Abeywardana, V. and D'Souza, J. (2009) *The Drug Treatment Outcomes Research Study (DTORS): Final Outcomes Report*. Home Office Research Report 24. London: Home Office.

Marlatt, G.A. and Donovan, D.M. (2005) *Relapse Prevention* (2nd edn). New York: Guilford.

Marsden, J., Gossop, M., Stewart, D., Best, D., Farrell, M., Lehmann, P., Edwards, C. and Strang, J. (1998) The Maudsley Addiction Profile (MAP): a brief instrument for assessing treatment outcome. *Addiction*, 93 (12): 1857–67.

Miller, W.R. and Rollnick, S. (2002) *Motivational Interviewing* (2nd edn). New York: Guilford.

Moos, R.H. (2008) Active ingredients of substance-use-focused self-help groups. *Addiction*, 103: 387–96.

Rassool, G.H. (2002) *Dual Diagnosis: Substance Misuse and Psychiatric Disorders*. London: Blackwell.

Wanigaratne, S. et al. (2005) *The Effectiveness of Psychological Therapies on Drug Misusing Clients*. National Treatment Agency for Substance Misuse. London: NHS. www.nta.nhs.uk/uploads/nta_effectiveness_psycho_therapies_2005_rb11.pdf.

WEBSITES

Alcoholics Anonymous: www.alcoholics-anonymous.org/

Drugscope UK Information Service: www.drugscope.org.uk

European Monitoring Centre for Drugs and Drug Abuse: www.emcdda.europa.eu/

Home Office: www.homeoffice.gov.uk/drugs/

Narcotics Anonymous: www.ukna.org/index.php

National Institute of Drug Abuse: www.nida.nih.gov

National Treatment Agency for Substance Misuse: www.nta.nhs.uk/

6.11

Eating and Exercise Disorders

SUZANNE ABRAHAM

Eating disorders are psychosomatic disorders and their treatment involves ongoing supportive psychotherapy, crisis intervention and counselling. Other therapies are employed depending on the needs of the patient. All patients are different and have different histories and problems. They may require medical or psychiatric intervention, couple or family assessment and treatment, management of childhood and adolescent trauma or abuse issues, and drug and alcohol counselling.

WHAT IS AN EATING DISORDER?

Eating disorders most commonly appear in young women, within a few years of their first menstrual period. They will usually have been eating less than their body requires for normal functioning. This may have occurred because they had:

- increased their exercise to train for a sporting event and not increased their food intake commensurately
- learnt that to prevent obesity they should be eating less and exercising more
- wanted to lose weight to achieve the 'ideal' body image to gain a happy life and respect from others
- been diagnosed with a condition like diabetes or coeliac disease and needed to be careful with what they ate
- suffered a traumatic and depressing event such as loss of a parent
- developed depression or anxiety (see gender differences).

What triggers the onset of an eating disorder is not necessarily what is responsible for its continuation. Many young women go through a phase of dieting during adolescence in response to the deposition of fat on their breasts, thighs, bottoms and hips during development, and may restrict their food or increase their exercise and avoid family meals. However, after a short period they accept some dissatisfaction with their body weight or shape, become distracted by other things and do not develop an eating disorder which affects their day-to-day living. It is frequently the things that maintain the disordered eating behaviour and their thoughts that require most treatment.

DO GENES PLAY A PART?

There appears to be a large genetic component involved in the development and maintenance of eating disorders. It is not uncommon for there to be female family sufferers. For example, with identical twins, if one twin has an eating disorder the other twin is likely to develop an eating disorder but not necessarily with the same presentation; one may be more anorexic and the other more bulimic. It may be this genetic propensity to develop or be protected from developing an eating disorder that is responsible for the maintenance and chronicity of eating disorders in some people.

WHAT MAINTAINS AN EATING DISORDER?

Eating disorder behaviour helps manage and control unpleasant and anxious feelings. This is believed to be the major reason for these behaviours, particularly as self-induced vomiting and excessive exercise are so addictive, since they unfortunately provide short-lived relief, and the behaviour needs to be repeated to maintain 'control'. There are other benefits for different people: eating disorders can allow a person to be looked after, to control others, to gain attention, and to avoid social and anxiety-provoking situations. Patients can usually provide a long list of advantages and disadvantages of keeping their eating disorder. Even when the person is no longer ambivalent about recovery and commits to treatment, it can take some years to achieve freedom from their eating disorder.

WHAT IS AN EXERCISE DISORDER?

'Exercise disorder' is not an official diagnosis but can be useful in making treatment plans for some individual patients. Exercise disorders occur when there are all-consuming thoughts about control of exercise, the amount of exercise each day is excessive, and the person feels they must undertake a certain amount each day. Frequently the amount increases over time despite the discomfort. Eating and body weight or shape issues may play a part and become a bigger issue if people are involved in sports requiring low weight or weight ranges for competition, or if they are preparing for a career such as dancing.

People with exercise disorders may be involved in physical activities before any eating disordered behaviour commences, or the exercise disorder may follow an effort to try to control eating behaviour. It is often a solitary activity such as jogging or running. Encouraging group social activities can help lessen the preoccupying thoughts.

Helping patients withdraw from excessive exercise can take some time and requires a lot of support as they need to find other ways to cope with their feelings and moods. It is hard for people to think of exercise as being 'bad' as it is always promoted as being good for both physical and mental health: 'the more the better'. Exercise is used in the treatment of depression and for eating disordered patients who do not exercise.

HOW IS AN EATING DISORDER DIAGNOSED?

Eating disorders are characterised by a preoccupation with control over body weight, eating, body image, the body or exercise. The current diagnostic criteria are fairly loose and a lot is left to clinical experience. It is likely that there is only one type of eating disorder that manifests in different ways, with some being more 'anorexic' (low weight) and some more 'bulimic' or 'purging' (most commonly, self-induced vomiting or abusing laxatives). Patients can move between the current diagnoses depending on their behaviour or their body weight; for example, a patient can become dehydrated on one day and, because of the slightly lower body weight, could move from a diagnosis of bulimia nervosa to anorexia nervosa. It is also confusing when clinicians use different BMI kg/m² values to diagnose anorexia nervosa, most commonly BMI 17.5 or BMI 18.5 kg/m².

A diagnosis of anorexia nervosa is given priority over bulimia nervosa and both are given priority over eating disorder not otherwise specified (EDNOS). Binge eating disorder (BED) can be included as a separate diagnosis or as part of EDNOS.

Anorexia Nervosa

Anorexia nervosa is characterised by:

1 weight loss and persistent failure to maintain a weight consistent with normal body function appropriate for age and gender
2 a preoccupation with control over the body, manifested by the persistent presence of weight controlling behaviour.

BMI is useful as a guide but its usefulness is limited by the amount of muscle present, pubertal development, and ethnicity (particularly those from some Asian backgrounds, where a BMI of 18.5 kg/m² can be normal for a woman).

The diagnosis should not depend on the presence of a demonstrated disturbance in the person's perception of their body size.

Evidence of failure to maintain a body weight consistent with normal functioning can include amenorrhoea in women not taking hormonal contraception, high white blood cell count, low heart rate, low blood pressure, poor temperature control or dehydration. In other words, the physical symptoms are those of semi-starvation. The symptoms also include psychological symptoms of semi-starvation such as irritability, poor concentration and attention, depressed mood, increased obsessionality and self-absorption.

Subclassifications of anorexia nervosa are restricting, vomiting, excessive exercising, binge eating and atypical (chewing and spitting). Frequently only two classifications are used: restricting type and binge/purge.

Bulimia Nervosa

Bulimia nervosa is characterised by:

1 frequent episodes of overeating a large amount of food that the person feels is outside their control
2 preoccupation with food, eating and counteracting the effects of food intake on the body by using extreme methods of weight control (commonly episodes of starvation or extreme food restriction, self-induced vomiting, excessive exercise).

The frequency of these features used to qualify for a diagnosis of bulimia nervosa can vary from an average of one or two times a week over the previous month to an average of once a week over three months if the person has episodes of binge eating for several weeks and then is free from binge eating for a period.

What qualifies as a large amount of food must be objectively assessed. For example, people with anorexia nervosa may consider eating a whole apple to be a large amount as it is not included in what they set themselves to eat. This is a subjective binge.

Most people consider purging to include abusing stimulant laxatives and diuretics as weight losing behaviours. Men, women and sports people may use and abuse these for a variety of reasons but they are not weight losing behaviours; they simply dehydrate and move faeces more quickly through the colon (not the small intestine, where absorption of nutrients takes place) to create a false low weight. Withdrawal from laxatives can cause fluid retention. If laxatives or diuretics are being abused this is usually in conjunction with one of the other methods.

Subclassifications of bulimia nervosa are: restricting, vomiting, excessive exercising, binge eating and atypical (prescription slimming tablets/stimulants, social stimulant drugs).

Eating Disorder not Otherwise Specified (EDNOS)

This diagnosis is given when there is clearly disordered eating affecting the person's quality of life, but they do not have the presence or frequency of behaviours or the body weight to qualify for a diagnosis of anorexia nervosa or bulimia nervosa. Preoccupation with body weight, eating, body image or exercise is present.

This does not mean EDNOS patients are not physically or mentally unwell. A patient who is normal weight, is vomiting many times a day, frequently resulting in electrolyte disturbances, but is only binge eating on occasions, would be considered as EDNOS. Before a diagnosis of anorexia nervosa or bulimia nervosa is made, and during recovery from an eating disorder, patients are likely to fulfil the criteria for EDNOS. Many patients with medical and psychiatric comorbidity are also likely to receive this diagnosis and may never fulfil the criteria for anorexia nervosa or bulimia nervosa.

Subclassifications of EDNOS are: anorexia nervosa like, bulimia nervosa like (can include BED) and atypical.

Binge Eating Disorder

Binge eating disorder is characterised by:

1 binge eating (as defined for bulimia nervosa) on average at least once per week over the previous 3 months
2 binge eating associated with distress but not with compensatory weight control methods.

As a result, people with BED will be overweight or obese and potentially at risk for symptoms associated with obesity.

AGE AND GENDER DIFFERENCES

Males also develop eating disorders, with approximately 1 in 10 to 1 in 20 sufferers being male. Eating disorder onset in males is usually later than for females, probably because they continue to develop and lay down muscle and do not experience the weight challenge accompanying female puberty. Puberty is also a time when females are more likely to develop depression than males and the number of females diagnosed with clinical depression becomes twice that of males. This may contribute to the onset of eating disorders in females.

The eating disorder symptoms are similar in males and females; the only differences are a history of excessive exercise present in nearly all men with an eating disorder, and a greater degree of psychopathology and comorbidity. Although men may want to be 'bigger' or more muscular, this is often accompanied by a desire for less fat to achieve their 'ideal'.

Eating disorders also occur in prepubertal male and female children. In older men and women over 50 years the prevalence is approximately the same and is predominantly binge eating disorder. Approximately one-third of obese people binge eat, but what proportion also have or have had an eating disorder is unknown.

TREATMENT

Treatment can take a long time. Eating disorders are very insidious and a person can go for many years without recognising or accepting they have a problem which is affecting their life. It can be unrecognised or kept hidden from their family or partners. After this a patient may be very ambivalent about 'giving up' their eating disorder as disordered behaviours can help them to feel in control of their life, including their body, and to cope with anxious and dysphoric feelings.

Initial Treatment

A thorough medical, psychiatric, psychological, social and family history must be taken and appropriate investigations made. Medical management must be addressed and any psychiatric interventions for comorbid problems considered. When the person is physically stable, the next step is nutritional rehabilitation. An assessment by a dietician who has experience with eating disorder patients is important. All patients need to learn to work with a dietician as part of treatment, particularly early in treatment, as their perception of what constitutes a normal amount of food for them will be inaccurate. Later in treatment the dietician will help the person gain the necessary confidence to continue eating normally until they are in their normal weight range. People fear they will continue to gain weight when they reach a weight in the healthy range and start to cut back on their food intake; this in turn can trigger off binge eating. This is also important for people who have been overweight as they may continue to undereat for fear of rapid weight gain. Experiences of binge eating in response to inadequate energy intake can be associated with a relapse or change in the type of eating disorder.

Nutritional Rehabilitation

The important aspects of learning to eat 'normally' are:

- to learn to eat sufficient food to fulfil their body's needs, at regular discrete times that are not too far apart
- to gain confidence in their body's ability to regulate itself

- to learn appropriate amounts and types of foods for each meal or snack
- to learn to eat alone, with people, in food courts, in restaurants, including food from all cultures and to participate in social eating
- to learn to eat normal foods (the selection of low-energy food may trigger off a psychological relapse in both underweight and overweight people: 'I can eat more', 'a little less will not matter').

Once a person has become used to the structure of regular episodic eating, the concept of flexibility needs to be addressed so that the food eaten and the times food is eaten can fit in with the family, social activities and lifestyles.

Medication

There are no convincing studies to suggest any medications help in treatment or the prevention of relapse of eating disorder thinking or behaviour. If someone also has a depressive illness then an antidepressant will help. The anti-anxiety effects of the newer antipsychotic medications, when used at very low doses, can be useful for some patients who are very anxious and at low weight, and are having problems with the intensity of their thoughts.

AFFECTIVE DISORDERS

Anxiety and depressive mood are common symptoms associated with eating disorders and it can be very hard to diagnose a depressive disorder if it was not present before the apparent onset of the eating disorder. Until a person has recovered from their eating disorder, the presence of a depressive disorder may be missed. Comorbidity can become apparent in low-weight patients as refeeding is proceeding. Anxiety disorders, post-traumatic stress, panic disorder, obsessive compulsive disorder, and alcohol and drug disorders are more common than in the general population. Continual psychological and psychiatric assessment is indicated during treatment.

Personality Disorder

There is a myth that all people with eating disorders have a personality disorder. This is not true; some do, but most do not. Patients may show features of a personality disorder, the most common being anxious/avoidant. If people do have a personality disorder or conduct disorder, management may be integrated into the treatment plan.

PSYCHOLOGICAL INTERVENTION

Throughout treatment, supportive psychotherapy and counselling are ongoing. Treatment over the long term will range from the current 'crisis' such as breakdown in a relationship, or the death of someone close, to family problems, work/study problems, and problems with friends, and may include addressing earlier issues of abuse or early poor attachment and unavailable parents.

A number of psychological therapies will help. These are the cognitive-behaviour therapies (CBT), interpersonal therapy (IPT), relaxation therapies and mindfulness meditation. After a few years it may be that being in therapy and being introduced to a range of therapies rather than a specific therapy are important for recovery.

At very low weights, probably below 15.5 kg/m^2, most psychological therapies are of limited success until nutritional status and body weight are improved. This does not mean that no therapy should be introduced in low-weight patients but simply means that not too much should be expected until weight is also regained.

Relaxation, either passive or more active such as tai chi or yoga, to help with anxious feelings, and mindfulness meditation to help people get in touch with their feelings and not be afraid of them, also appear to be helpful. Nowadays patients receive a lot of help and introduction to different types of therapies/skills from a range of sources including leadership, school and tertiary education courses, and the media.

It is important to be aware of specific treatments that may help different individuals because of their current or past experiences. Dialectical behaviour therapy (DBT) and acceptance and commitment therapy (ACT) are variations that can be useful in addition to the other therapies for patients with a history of abuse or poor impulse control or identity issues. Marital or family therapy may also be included.

FAMILY THERAPY

If the patient is living with their family or if they would like their family to be seen and assessed, family therapy is advisable. If the patient is a child or in the very early teen years, the available family will be involved in helping with treatment. Again it depends on the special needs of the person and the family.

If the patient is living with a partner, including the partner in some sessions may be of benefit. Support groups for carers provide information and allow people to develop skills to cope with their role.

WHO SHOULD TREAT?

Self-help is good. Encouraging people to discuss the books they read, the internet sites they visit, and what they learn allows discussion and can give balance to some of the more unhelpful ideas that abound. Self-help manuals or web-based programmes are effective and useful, and may be all that is available to someone who lives a long distance from where help is available. Self-help guided by a therapist is usually more effective.

It is preferred that the patient's management be carried out by a team of health professionals. The team will ideally consist of a general practitioner who is able to assess the person and to refer appropriately for tests and to other health-care professionals, dietician, psychiatrist, psychologist, social worker, and other professionals relevant for the accompanying problems or conditions. The general practitioner may remain the coordinator of treatment or that role may be transferred to another professional, for example a psychiatrist if there is significant psychiatric comorbidity. It is best when the team works together so the individual patient needs can be met. The patient should be encouraged to keep in touch with at least one person in the team, even when the eating disorder appears to be quiet; it is usually best if they choose which therapist they would like to remain in contact with.

LEVEL OF TREATMENT

Outpatient treatment is the recommended initial approach; if progress is not made, referral for day patient or inpatient treatment is warranted. Day patient treatment involves attending one to five days each week during which some meals are supervised and patients attend groups. Day patient treatment can provide a step down from inpatient treatment and allows patients to integrate back to school, study or work. Inpatient treatment can be recommended for a variety of reasons, as outlined later in this chapter in the section on recovery and outcome. The reasons do not always reflect the failure of other treatments or the presence of a more severe form of the eating disorder.

INDIVIDUAL TREATMENTS

Women's Health

Women can lose their menstrual periods (amenorrhoea) or fail to have their first period until after 16 years if they are at low body weight, exercising excessively at any weight, or losing weight even if normal or high weight. Amenorrhoea can occur in normal weight, non-exercising women who are binge eating and starving or vomiting. If the body does not have the reserves of energy it needs to function optimally it can switch off those functions that are not needed, such as the reproductive system. The only problem with this is that without sufficient oestrogen, available calcium is not taken up into bone and so bones become thin (osteopenia). If this continues for some time the bones may start to lose their structure (osteoporosis). The only way to replace bone is to be, and stay, in the normal weight range, reduce exercise, and stop other extreme eating disorder behaviours such as vomiting. The earlier this occurs the better the recovery, as it is easier to lay down bone in the teens and early twenties. The oral contraceptive pill or hormone replacement does not help bone loss or recovery.

The bleeding experienced when taking oral contraceptives is a 'withdrawal bleed'; it occurs in response to the hormones being taken away. It does not indicate that periods will occur if 'the pill' is not being taken.

Women with a history of an eating disorder should be monitored during and after pregnancy as they have a higher incidence of pregnancy loss, are more likely to deliver an intrauterine growth restricted baby, and are more likely to suffer perinatal depression. During pregnancy they may relapse or be completely free of any eating disorder thoughts or behaviours. After delivery they may relapse as a result of mood changes, and their behaviour and thinking may be aimed at rapid weight loss.

Women with regular menstrual cycles may find they are likely to have more problems with eating during the premenstrual phase of the menstrual cycle, particularly if they also experience moderate premenstrual mood and physical symptoms. Most women find it easy to reduce food intake in the early part of the cycle but will binge eat in the premenstruum. Eating sufficiently in the first part of the cycle reduces the urge to binge eat in the premenstrual phase. Some women will also find the deposition of fat centrally in middle age a challenge and find the eating disorder thinking returning along with symptoms of menopause.

GASTROINTESTINAL PROBLEMS

Gastrointestinal problems are very common, with over 80 per cent of patients having at least one functional gastrointestinal disorder, but the type and presence do not necessarily relate to the eating disorder behaviours or psychological symptoms present. When people are at low weight or have not been eating regularly, their stomach may empty slowly and their colon may take some weeks to return to normal; this can cause discomfort and a sensation of bloating. This can make the early stages of refeeding of anorexia nervosa patients unpleasant, and they need to be reassured that they will become used to eating again and the symptoms will decrease.

WHAT IS RECOVERY?

After 5 to 10 years:

- 40 per cent recover completely
- 40 per cent recover with good quality of life but are still weight/shape concerned
- 20 per cent remain with an eating disorder, or are deceased.

The long-term outcome data from recent and older studies remain fairly similar, irrespective of how outcome is defined. As most five and 10 year outcome studies have involved patients treated as inpatients in hospital, the data were thought to reflect only those patients with severe eating disorders. However, more recent studies involving patients treated in primary care have given similar results. This may reflect the varied reasons people seek or are encouraged to receive inpatient treatment, such as: having a break from the family or giving the family a rest; living too far away from access to treatment of any kind; living with a person also struggling with an eating disorder; or preferring to receive concentrated treatment in a shorter period to prevent time away from study or career.

Outcome is better if the person has never been at a very low or a very high body weight; if they receive treatment early in their illness; if they do not induce vomiting; if they do not have a personality disorder; and if there is no other comorbid psychiatric or medical illness.

Relapses are common until the person learns what is associated with their relapses and is able and motivated to make changes to prevent relapse. Motivation to change depends on many things including resilience and wanting a 'normal life'.

RECOMMENDED READING

Abraham, S. (2008) *Eating Disorders: The Facts* (6th edn). Oxford: Oxford University Press.

Treasure, Janet, Schmit, Ulrike and MacDonald, Pam (2009) *The Clinician's Guide to Collaborative Caring in Eating Disorder Patients.* London: Taylor and Francis.

WEBSITES

NICE: www.nice.org.uk

Eating Disorders Section, Institute of Psychiatry, South London and Maudsley NHS Trust, guide to the medical risk assessment for eating disorders, by Professor Janet Treasure: www.eatingresearch.com

HIV/AIDS

JILL BALMONT AND IDA WAKSBERG

INTRODUCTION

The human immuno-deficiency virus (HIV) first began to spread amongst groups of gay men and intravenous drug users in the late 1970s in the UK. This was followed by the first report of the constellation of symptoms known as acquired immune deficiency syndrome (AIDS) in 1981. AIDS is the disease of the immune system caused by HIV, and individuals are said to have AIDS when they have very advanced HIV infection. Illnesses commonly seen as AIDS defining are pneumocystis pneumonia, wasting syndromes, tuberculosis, and cancer of the lymphatic system. In the context of widespread public ignorance and panic, people tended to be blamed for their own illness and suffering on account of their lifestyles, and efforts were initially focused on reducing HIV transmission.

Throughout the 1980s and 1990s, it was clear that HIV continued to disproportionately affect the disempowered and poor in society: those growing up marginalised because of their sexuality, mental health difficulties, impoverished social backgrounds and lifestyles. Young people were mostly affected, and both voluntary and statutory sector services were developed in response to the medical, psychological, support and advocacy needs of patients and carers. By the late 1990s new medications had instilled some hope, although prevention remained a major concern as the virus continued to spread into new populations, both geographically and in terms of age and social/cultural groupings.

The estimated number of people infected through heterosexual contact doubled in the four years between 2003 and 2007 in the UK. Today, heterosexually acquired infections are gradually declining but infection rates amongst gay men remain at a high level; and as better medical treatments enhance survival, people are increasingly growing older with HIV. Despite better public knowledge, however, the stigma of the illness has not gone away.

In this chapter, we describe HIV and its treatment, common psychological issues and problems, factors influencing psychological adjustment, and how psychological therapies might help. The chapter builds upon the work of Ratigan (1991; 2006) and draws on our experience of delivering psychological therapy in UK NHS genito-urinary medicine clinics over the past 12 years. It is also written from a psychodynamically informed perspective.

WHAT IS HIV?

HIV is a systemic viral infection which is, at present, incurable. The virus uses the cells it has infected to replicate, and as levels of viral infection in the blood increase, the immune system is weakened such that it cannot function effectively. This leaves the HIV positive person susceptible to developing HIV-related systemic complications such as renal disease, opportunistic infections such as pneumocystis pneumonia (PCP), and malignancies such as the characteristic skin cancer Kaposi's sarcoma. Infection of the central nervous system by the HIV virus commonly results in neurological complications, ranging from subtle to moderate cognitive impairments, to severe and disabling HIV-associated dementia, CNS infections such as encephalitis, and other neurological dysfunctions.

Since the first AIDS diagnosis some 30 years ago, HIV has remained one of the most serious communicable diseases in the UK. Whilst medical advances have improved the efficacy of HIV treatments, and the quality of life of many HIV infected people, the disease continues to be associated with serious morbidity, significant mortality and numbers of potential years of life lost, and high costs of treatment and care.

By 2010 there were over 110,000 reported cases of people living with HIV in the UK (this number is likely to increase as further reports come in). In 2009, over 6500 new cases were reported. A small number of these (a little more than 20) were children infected perinatally by vertical transmission from their mothers, and a similar number of people were probably infected as a result of receiving infected blood or bodily tissue products abroad. Small but rising rates of infection were reported amongst intravenous drug users, with a prevalence rate in this population of about 1 in 75 currently infected with HIV in the UK.

The vast majority of people with HIV are infected through unprotected vaginal or anal sexual intercourse, with over 50 per cent of new diagnoses in 2009 probably acquired through heterosexual contact, and over 40 per cent through sex between men. (Infection through oral sex is also possible, but it is probably rare to acquire HIV in this way.) Approximately two-thirds of all diagnosed heterosexually acquired infections were among black Africans living in the UK, whilst 80 per cent of men infected through sex with men were white. A third of black Caribbeans living with HIV in the UK were estimated to have acquired their infection through sex with men (HPA, 2010).

As HIV infection has a prolonged 'silent' period it often remains undiagnosed. It is estimated that 25–30 per cent of people are unaware of their infection and, as a result, almost a third of people are being diagnosed late. This means that they are missing out on the benefits of starting treatment early, which includes the possibility of prolonged life expectancy.

MEDICAL TREATMENT

Since 1996, HIV has been treated with highly active anti-retroviral therapy (HAART); this comprises combinations of drugs which suppress viral replication and restore immune functioning. The discontinuation of HAART results in the rapid resurgence of viral replication and so, to be optimally effective, HAART needs to continue uninterrupted

over the course of a person's lifetime. This can be difficult to achieve as the combinations of drugs to be taken, and the frequencies and strict timetables to be adhered to, can result in complicated regimens to maintain. This is all the more so for those people struggling with cognitive impairments which affect their attention, memory and problem-solving capabilities.

The drugs themselves may be poorly tolerated and can build to toxic levels, they can interact negatively with other drugs, and they can give rise to serious adverse side effects. It is not uncommon for some drugs, and their combinations with others, to cause nausea, vomiting and sometimes diarrhoea, insomnia and vivid dreams, mood disturbances including mania, depression and even psychosis, skin rashes, or jaundice.

Pharmaceutical advances are resulting in simpler and more convenient dosing schedules which, if effective and tolerated well, can facilitate people's consistent management of the demands of treatment. This is, however, just one of the many challenges of living with HIV. People are faced not just with the uncertain physical impact of a complex, life-threatening, chronic condition and its treatment, but also with the profound and uncertain psychological impact, compounded by fears of strongly negative social reactions.

FACTORS INFLUENCING PSYCHOLOGICAL ADJUSTMENT

Many factors influence the ease or otherwise by which people adjust to having and living with an HIV diagnosis. A previous history of emotional or psychological disturbance is probably the most significant and may have been a factor in increasing a person's vulnerability to becoming infected. For example, responses to early experiences of deprivation, abuse and traumatic loss can leave someone predisposed to taking sexual risks, failing to negotiate safer sexual relating, or being vulnerable to sexual exploitation. Negative reactions to those with HIV and the manner by which HIV was transmitted can compound earlier deprivations and abuses, undermining perceptions of and the availability of support at a time of need.

Good social support can provide a buffer against being overwhelmed by the emotional impact of the diagnosis and its implications. Consequently, those who are more isolated or find it difficult to access and make use of support can be particularly at risk of experiencing psychological difficulties. Young people for example, infected at birth and living in areas of low prevalence, may struggle to find a similar sense of belonging with their peer group in safely negotiating the transition to establish an adult sexual identity of their own, which includes being HIV positive. Partners infected within their committed relationships are also vulnerable on account of the scale of the breach of trust, and consequent loss of support involved.

Those who are already members of marginalised groups in society often have limited support and may be vulnerable to experiencing psychological problems. Being gay may mean, for some, accepting and/or having to conceal a stigmatised identity, and in some cultures, homosexuality is still regarded as a valid reason for persecution. Drug users are another socially stigmatised group who can also be at an increased risk of psychological disturbance as a direct result of their drug use.

People living in some form of exile from the support of home can be vulnerable to experiencing psychological problems, and especially when the underlying reason for their exile is traumatic, and possibly linked to the transmission of the virus. For many immigrants, refugees and asylum seekers, an HIV diagnosis can compound the sense of loss associated with their departure from their own country and community, and their struggle to resettle here. This is all the more traumatic if HIV was acquired as the result of sexual violence, possibly in the context of war or persecution, and/or if they come from countries where an HIV diagnosis is associated with certain early death. Uncertainty regarding their claims to settle in the UK further compound the trauma and isolation.

COMMON PSYCHOLOGICAL PROBLEMS AND CHALLENGES

There are times in the course of HIV infection and disease progression where people are more vulnerable to experiencing distress, providing opportunities for psychological, supportive and practical interventions. These commonly include:

- pre- and post-testing, and at the time of diagnosis (the time between testing and diagnosis can be a period of great uncertainty for many people)
- after the initial shock has subsided, and adjustment to managing the practical demands of the illness has been achieved, or when someone who has been very ill is in a reliably more stable condition and feeling better
- when faced with disruption to relationships or problems of disclosure, loss of valued social roles, or when faced with having to let go, mourn and/or modify personal aspirations
- when the medical markers of disease progression indicate the need to start medication, or

- when experiencing difficulties with deciding to take medication
- when struggling with the side effects of medication or taking medication consistently, or having to change medication
- when faced with the onset of physical or neurological symptoms and/or disability associated with disease progression
- in anticipation of the terminal stages of disease, or in preparation for death.

To understand the problems people encounter and the challenges they face, we need to know the subjective meanings of the diagnosis for them in terms of their past personal history, their relationships, their current situation and their future. Important issues may be thought about as in the following sections.

The Prospect of Early Mortality and Associated Losses

Although HIV no longer carries a 'death sentence', there is no cure, and an HIV diagnosis confronts someone with the long-term presence of an infection, potentially reminding them of the finiteness of time and opportunity available to them, culminating eventually in death. Feared associated losses along the way may include a reduction or loss of sexual potency and its impact on relationships; the possibility of redundancy and loss of a valued sense of identity; increasing dependence on others as a consequence of illness and disability; loss of control and dignity in ill health; and perhaps the growing realisation that some of their personal goals may no longer be realisable.

Pre-morbid history and functioning are the most important factors in determining how well a person's psychological adjustment following the threat of diagnosis will facilitate their coping with the losses, both real and anticipated, that follow. A sense of psychic integrity is achieved through being able to value and hold on to the positive and affirming aspects of oneself and one's experiences. This includes being loved and being able to love. Having had their own dependency needs met well in the past, they are more likely to have confidence that they will continue to be looked after well in the future, both in sickness and in death.

Those more likely to be overwhelmed by terror at the prospect of their mortality may be unconsciously anticipating a repeat of failures of dependency in the past. This may also be coloured by images of how others have died before them. Sickness and death can then be dreaded as a state of continued lonely suffering and neglect, of being rejected, humiliated and hated. Powerful defensive measures can be drawn on to manage such over-whelming dread and anxiety.

The emotional impact may be averted by denying and neglecting the realities of the illness, which may include the need for medication to keep them alive, for sexual partners at risk to be protected, and for consent for dependent children at risk to be tested. This can raise difficult ethical dilemmas and concerns for the clinical team, including the counsellor or therapist, on becoming aware of the ways in which a person might be putting themselves or others at risk. There can be a pressure to act, especially when the risks are high and confidence in being able to help them understand and manage their risky behaviour is low.

Here is an example of how one woman's defences were worked with in therapy.

Mrs M, who came to the UK after imprisonment and rape by boy soldiers in her country, was advised to be tested for HIV by her solicitor who thought this might have a bearing on her asylum case. Mrs M tested positive but refused to know the result of the test, putting the team looking after her under considerable strain as she needed treatment. She was referred to the psychotherapist and for many meetings she sat shivering, wearing a coat and hat although it was a warm summer.

She talked about the awful things that had happened to her, focusing on her various physical complaints. The therapist listened, and sometimes talked with her about how she protected herself by not wanting to know about things, to which Mrs M quietly agreed. After several weeks she decided to find out the results of the test, and later she told the therapist that she felt strengthened by her understanding and support. She wanted to join a woman's HIV support group, started to take antiretroviral medications, and did well in her treatment despite many setbacks in her asylum application.

Fears of Contamination

HIV, as an infectious disease which is easily transmitted, means that people can feel dangerous to themselves and others, and therefore intimacy becomes troublesome and unsafe. Since the virus was acquired as a result of the desire for intimacy, and this need does not diminish, sex becomes linked with death. Intimacy thus becomes associated with fears of contamination and dread.

The fear and discomfort generated by HIV and the manner of its transmission become attached to the person suffering it so that others can distance themselves from its emotional significance and impact for them. This is stigma – an isolating mark of shame and disgrace which constantly reminds the infected person of their social unacceptability. This can compound their own self-reproach and self-rejection if they also struggle to accept themselves, the choices available to them and/or the decisions they have made in the past, which might have also contributed to their becoming infected.

Psychological therapy can thus offer a space where socially unacceptable feelings can be safely explored, and changes in how people come to know themselves can be made.

Mrs G, in her early 50s and a member of the bourgeoisie in her country of origin, was referred two years after her HIV diagnosis, as distressed as she had been when first diagnosed. She gave a false name in the clinic, and found it very painful to sit in the reception area in case she was recognised. No one else knew she was HIV positive, and she felt isolated, remembering how she had previously pitied those with HIV. She had felt that they were contagious and untouchable, and now she felt horrified to feel the same. She was deeply religious and had heard that in her country, where HIV was a sign of promiscuity, someone with HIV had been stoned to death. She often wished she was dead, and thought she would die soon, although physically she was responding well to antiretroviral medication.

Therapy provided a setting in which she did not have to pretend that everything was alright. This challenged her sense of isolation as she now found herself able to discuss things that were of real concern to her. She gradually started to consider a less catastrophic view of HIV, and began to take in some of the positive messages she read in the self-help literature.

She looked forward to her sessions, started to feel better, and after about eight weeks, with great trepidation about the prospect of disclosing her status, she applied for a job. Her success proved to have great therapeutic potential and she later acknowledged that HIV had given her something important: it had brought her down to earth.

Note that it is unlawful for people with HIV to be discriminated against in employment. Although it is not necessary to disclose to employers, it is advisable to inform occupational health when applying to work in health-care settings.

Trauma

For many, becoming infected with HIV is traumatic. People can variously feel aggrieved, deeply wounded, guilty and complicit in their own suffering, and furious or ashamed at having this confirmed by the attitudes of others. Facing such feelings is painful and can uncover deeper layers of hurt, isolation and loss.

Mr S, a 30-year-old white gay man, was referred for psychotherapy for his problems with depression and difficulties with physically tolerating the side effects of his HIV medication. After his first appointment, he complained that the meeting had upset him too much. After talking about this he continued to come but less frequently, then he decided to stop his HIV medication altogether. In his therapy, he disclosed in a detached way a history of sexual abuse as a child by a male teacher, at a time when his home life had been unpredictable and violent.

He often seemed to struggle to feel safe with the therapist, equating help with abuse. They explored together whether a helping activity could have other meanings for him. The frequency of the sessions gradually increased at his request, and he brought his poems for her to read. He appeared to be enjoying her attention, and she wondered if he was feeling a little safer with her. A few weeks later he decided to start another antiretroviral regimen after discussing its possible side effects with his consultant, and this time he seemed to tolerate it better.

THE PROCESS OF THERAPY

The main therapeutic modalities of practice have all been reported to be helpful: cognitive-behavioural, psychodynamic, interpersonal, systemic, humanistic and psycho-educational interventions, provided in individual, couple, family and group formats. If we take an integrative stance, focusing on what tends to take place in a therapy, we can identify three main components: the creation of a safe relationship, the exploration of meanings to arrive at an understanding, and the promotion of change. These three components can be expressed in different ways, in different theoretical languages, placing a different emphasis or priority on each.

We would suggest that many psychological therapies with people infected with HIV explore, within a safe relationship, themes of mortality, trauma, stigma, shame and guilt in order to achieve changes in areas such as disclosure of HIV status, adherence to medication, negotiating safe sex in relationships, and working towards finding an increased investment in life and purpose in living. A life-threatening illness brings opportunities as well as threats, and therapy can help people find or reconnect with their own inner resources, re-evaluate their priorities and live more creatively.

In the vignettes above, feeling safe and understood allowed Mrs M to face her diagnosis. The therapeutic attachment and opportunity to explore the meanings of her experiences helped Mrs G to feel less isolated, ashamed and untouchable such that she could participate in life again, more fully. With Mr S, it was not until the meanings of help were linked to his previous trauma that he felt able to attempt to take medication again.

These examples are with people who engaged in the process, yet therapists must also be prepared for the possibility that many can struggle to engage in therapy, and for some it may even not be appropriate.

CHALLENGES AND CONTRA-INDICATIONS

Therapy often involves participating in a partial identification with the person seeking help. For example, therapists' capacity to imagine and experience their own vulnerability and fears of mortality can help in understanding and sharing to some extent the other's experience. Therapists can however, be prone to over-identification and can become overwhelmed, wishing to omnipotently rescue the other from their predicament, and blaming or devaluing themselves when they are unable to do so.

Reacting against these feelings can lead to a distancing and emotional detachment. This is similar to a stigmatising process whereby the therapist's reactions imply 'the problem is in you'. For example, therapists' personal beliefs about homosexuality, injection use or unsafe sex practices may, in more or less subtle ways, prevent an empathic relationship developing. The importance of supervision in which such issues are honestly explored cannot be underestimated in helping therapists to deepen their understanding of the issues facing the people they are trying to help.

A careful assessment is necessary if psychological help is to be of benefit. Resistance to exploring problems in psychological terms is self-protective, and we need to respect this when the stakes for unsettling someone's psychological equilibrium are high. Much needed social, self-help or practical support might be more appropriate.

We need to recognise when someone may be heading towards a suicidal crisis or developing serious psychiatric symptoms which might require the skilled intervention and resources of colleagues in generic mental health services. We also need to ask ourselves if cognitive impairments might be influencing the problems with which someone is presenting, and whether or not a neuropsychometric assessment might be helpful.

CONCLUSIONS

People often minimise the risks of unprotected sex against what they hope to gain, and it only takes one exposure to become infected. That is why HIV continues to be a challenging public health concern which is not helped by the stigma and secrecy which still surround it. In writing this chapter we have reviewed our practice and reflected on both how demanding and how rewarding this work can be. The aim for psychological therapy that stands out most strongly for us is to help change the meanings of the HIV virus from something toxic and contagious that resides in certain people from certain social groups, into something perhaps more acceptable and reflective of the universal risks and precariousness of life.

REFERENCES

HPA (2010) Unpublished HIV Diagnoses Surveillance Tables 01:2010. Health Protection Agency Centre for Infections, Health Protection Scotland and UCL Institute of Child Health.

Ratigan, B. (1991) On not traumatising the traumatised: the contribution of psychodynamic psychotherapy to work with people with HIV and AIDS. *British Journal of Psychotherapy*, 8 (1): 39–47.

Ratigan, B. (2006) HIV/AIDS. In C. Feltham and I. Horton (eds), *The Sage Handbook of Counselling and Psychotherapy* (2nd edn, pp. 406–9). London: Sage.

RECOMMENDED READING

Barret, B., Anderson, J. and Barret, R. (2001) *Ethics in HIV-Related Psychotherapy: Clinical Decision-Making in Complex Cases.* New York: American Psychological Association.

Steinberg, J. (2009) *Three Letter Plague: A Young Man's Journey through a Great Epidemic.* London: Vintage.

FURTHER INFORMATION AND SELF-HELP

Body and Soul, a self-help organization which supports women, heterosexual men, children and families living with or affected by HIV: 020 738 37678.

National Aids Manual (NAM): www.aidsmap.com

National Aids Trust (NAT): www.nat.org.uk

Positively Women, a national organization providing peer support to HIV positive women and their children: 020 771 30444

Terence Higgins Trust: www.tht.org.uk

Low Self-Esteem

ALISON WAINES

WHAT IS SELF-ESTEEM?

Self-esteem is based on the opinion a person has of himself or herself and the degree to which they value themselves. It is one of the most important aspects of self-concept: the multi-dimensional construct or 'inner map' that creates a person's individual perception of 'self'. This self-concept involves a range of characteristics such as likes, dislikes, abilities, strengths, beliefs and values, but self-esteem seems to have the most impact on how worthy a person feels engaging in everyday living. Even when clients present with seemingly unrelated issues in counselling, such as relationship difficulties, depression, anxiety, obesity, substance dependency or even infertility, more often than not a lack of self-esteem is at the source. As such, it is a 'symptom' mentioned in many of the problems discussed in this chapter.

Low self-esteem can leave people feeling inadequate and unworthy, ashamed, awkward and unable to handle everyday situations with confidence. Healthy self-esteem refers to feelings of worthiness, liking oneself and feeling powerful and significant. The term 'healthy self-esteem' is used here as a desirable outcome, as opposed to 'high self-esteem', as it can be argued that the latter term also involves an inherent 'rating' of the self instead of an unconditional acceptance of the self (Ellis, 2007).

A reduction in self-esteem can occur after any circumstance that leaves a person feeling rejected, powerless or hurt, such as infidelity, a dysfunctional relationship, divorce, redundancy, ill health, disability or an unexpected loss or failure. Sometimes even the ageing process itself, which might involve weight gain, loss of previous skills, loss of sexual functioning, or loss of status, can bring about this reduction. There are also people who feel that their self-esteem has been low ever since they were children. This may be due to perceived beliefs of being unworthy, or significant childhood events (bullying, parents' divorce, neglect, abandonment) that lead a child to regard themselves as having little value (Dalgas-Pelish, 2006; Salmon et al., 1998).

Essentially, self-esteem is the kind of relationship people have with themselves – the way they regard themselves on a day-to-day basis. It is difficult for a person to be fulfilled and satisfied if he or she does not feel worthwhile or good about themselves.

Self-esteem Versus Self-confidence

Self-confidence, also known as self-efficacy, exists alongside self-esteem but is a separate aspect of self-concept. People with self-confidence know that they have particular skills, such as being able to drive, give presentations, play a sport or make people laugh, and believe that they are able to engage successfully in those areas. People who know and trust they have an ability in a particular skill tend to value themselves. Self-esteem, however, is more complex and consists of more factors than simply self-confidence. Self-esteem is the way we feel about our *whole* person, not only our skills and talents. It is something we wake up with in the morning that governs our general sense of wellbeing. Healthy self-esteem is about feeling valuable and worthy just as we are *right now*, without having to prove or change anything.

The American psychologist Maslow (1987/1943) devised a hierarchy of needs, identifying self-esteem as a key component to wellbeing once our practical needs for survival, safety and a sense of belonging are satisfied. People with low self-esteem tend to spend a lot of their lives making comparisons with other people and drawing the conclusion that they are inadequate: not attractive enough, clever enough, funny enough, talented enough or generally 'not good enough' as human beings. They invariably regard themselves in a negative light, being overly critical about aspects of their character, appearance or behaviour. This can affect their body language (such as difficulty making eye contact), their behaviour (the inability to speak up for themselves or ask for what they want) and also the life choices they make (such as the kind of job or career they might aim for or the kind of relationships they might have).

WHERE DOES SELF-ESTEEM COME FROM?

Inner Self-talk

One aspect of our thinking – our 'inner self-talk', also known as 'internal monologue' or 'conversation with oneself' – has a direct bearing on our self-esteem (Beck and Alford, 2009). This inner self-talk starts the moment we wake up each day. If it is negative, it can sound like: 'There I go making a fool of myself – I'm such an idiot.' If it is positive, it might sound like: 'Well done – you didn't win, but you gave it your best shot.' People with low self-esteem tend to put themselves down through this inner self-talk and often do not realise that they are doing so, whereas those with healthier self-esteem tend to support themselves and take care of themselves through this constant inner chit-chat.

Upbringing

Upbringing plays a significant part in the development of inner self-talk and thus self-esteem (Finzi-Dottan and Karu, 2006; Wilding and Palmer, 2010). Children learn how to self-evaluate through the ways in which others have responded to them in the past. Parents or main carers act rather like a mirror, letting a child know how he or she is perceived. In this way, the opinions of significant adults and the ways in which they respond to a child subconsciously contribute to the child's self-identity. Imagine the level of self-esteem a five-year-old child might have if she has been told many times each day that she is naughty, difficult, a nuisance or unwanted. Compare this to the child who is told as many times that she is clever, good, loved and doing well. Children tend to internalise this feedback, whether it is negative or positive, and regard it as 'the truth' about themselves. This internalisation of judgements received from parents, school, siblings and friends from an early age forms the basis of a person's self-esteem.

When establishing a sense of self, however, people often fail to take into account hidden factors that may influence the way others respond to them. As a child, if someone significant picks fault, the child may simply see themselves as 'bad' or 'difficult'. If they are ignored or neglected, the child may regard themselves as 'unlovable', but they may not realise that the person who conveys this negativity might be directing it inappropriately and at the wrong person. A range of unseen reasons may lie behind the negative feedback, which makes it unreliable. A carer may be anxious, for example, due to money worries, or may be snapping at the child because they have a migraine. Children are unable to see the broader picture; the context and mitigating factors influencing the feedback they receive from those around them.

The Way Feedback is Interpreted

In addition to this, people have different ways of *interpreting* external circumstances and responses from others. Interpretation is the personal meaning we make of certain events or interactions, which often do not represent the truth (Ellis, 2001). For example, a young boy whose mother was largely absent during his infant years (perhaps due to pressure to earn a living) may interpret this absence to mean he was not sufficiently valued. His interpretation generates the belief that his mother did not love him enough to want to spend time with him. Despite her attempts to convince him of her love, it is the absence that the boy remembers, and he may take the feelings and expectation of 'being unlovable' into his adult life. Counselling can help clients to examine how they may have misinterpreted events, often helping them to reframe situations from the past in an altogether new and more positive light, which can then transform the client's view of themselves.

Living a Meaningful Life

Significant events in adulthood can also challenge a person's self-esteem, even if it has been healthy until that point, such as an unexpected redundancy. Gradual changes over time can also erode self-esteem, especially if these changes involve broader losses involving three existential elements: making a difference, a sense of identity and purpose in life (Deurzen, 2002; Maslow, 1987/1943). These three elements help create meaning in life and are essential for healthy self-esteem.

1   *Making a difference.* Most people need to feel that they are 'making a difference', making some kind of contribution in life or feeling valued in some way. This might come about through their job, such as believing they are a competent teacher, or in any other way, such as being a loving father. This also applies on a small, everyday scale, such as knowing they have listened to someone, made a person smile or eased someone's pain. When absent: there can be the belief that being in the world makes no difference to anyone and that their life has no meaning to themselves or others.
2   *Sense of identity.* This refers to a person's ego; an aspect of the psyche which brings about the need to feel seen and noticed, to belong and have significance. It comes about when a person feels recognised for their individual personality and what they have to offer. This can be established through their position at work, as long as this role helps a person feel appreciated, or it can apply to any role where they feel part of something they value, such as a member of a club or community, or leader of a group. When absent: there can be a sense of feeling invisible, anonymous, isolated, as if a person believes they have no part to play in anything.
3   *Sense of purpose.* The third essential element for self-esteem depends on a person's belief that their life is going somewhere meaningful, with a sense of achievement and fulfilment, rather than feeling they are living the same day, over and over. With purpose comes passion and a sense of development and being on a journey. When purpose is absent, there is a feeling of emptiness and pointlessness about life and the future.

In combination, these three elements provide a foundation that contributes to a feeling of healthy self-esteem and wellbeing. If any of them are missing or 'damaged' for whatever reason, self-esteem is likely to suffer. The counsellor can help the client to identify which elements may be depleted (if this is not obvious) and to explore the impact this has had on the client. This can then lead to an exploration of the client's history to identify where the client used to find meaning and then move on to discovering ways in which the client may be able to reintroduce or discover new sources or expression of those elements.

ASSESSING LOW SELF-ESTEEM

Most people are familiar with the term 'self-esteem' and can make their own self-assessment about how high or low it is. Counsellors can offer clients a simple rating scale from 0 to 10 to help them assess their current level of self-esteem. The language clients use to describe themselves will also offer clues, and words such as 'should', 'ought', 'bad', 'failure', 'unworthy', 'unloveable' or other forms of negative self-judgement will indicate how hard a client is being on himself or herself. A more detailed assessment can be obtained through using established inventories designed to measure self-esteem (Fennell, 2009; Rosenberg, 1965; Sorensen, 2006).

COUNSELLING FOR SELF-ESTEEM ISSUES

There are a number of therapeutic approaches that can help to build or rebuild self-esteem. Cognitive-behavioural therapy (CBT) can help a client to develop self-awareness and to tune into their inner self-talk (Wilding and Palmer, 2010). In doing so, the client can assess how they respond inwardly to everyday situations. This process is most usefully carried out by keeping a journal or writing daily records, as it is important to try to capture the exact statements that are 'heard' in the internal monologue (Waines, 2004).

In sessions, the client can be asked to describe the words they use to talk to themselves *about* themselves, identify how often they encourage and praise themselves, and notice whether they put themselves down or are expecting too much. Most people are not aware of how many destructive messages are being fed into their consciousness, through their own thinking, every day. Together with the therapist, these messages are identified and then challenged, and evidence of alternatives or exceptions is explored.

Clients are encouraged to reframe their situation, including examples of how they might support a 'best friend' going through identical circumstances. They are also encouraged to experiment with positive statements and with a new language to describe themselves, such as 'I tried my best' or 'it's okay to make mistakes', instead of 'I failed and I'm useless.'

In a similar way, psychosynthesis involves identifying a critical inner voice and invites the client to create a full persona around this voice, including name, age and physical image (Whitmore, 2004). By visualising this 'inner critic' as a comic demon or a cartoon character its power can be minimised. The essence of this technique is to identify a possible original source of this critical inner voice, to challenge the motives behind the voice and to tone the voice down. The client is then invited to 'turn up the volume' on a nurturing inner voice, by drawing on positive influences from the past or present, such as a kindly grandparent who cherished the client or a current best friend.

Reparative therapy (Clarkson, 2003) aims to provide objective and reliable feedback to the client, separating past from present and separating the person from their behaviour. The statement, 'I like you and I'm very disappointed about your thoughtless behaviour', for example, conveys a completely different message from, 'I'm very disappointed about your thoughtless behaviour and therefore I don't like you.' Understanding this kind of distinction can help to prevent clients from jumping to negative conclusions about themselves and can help them start to challenge old patterns of self-concept. Reparative therapy aims to show the client that they are lovable, with all their faults and difficulties, and helps develop self-acceptance and self-love.

AIMS IN COUNSELLING

The counsellor aims to help clients to:

- notice the way they put themselves down and challenge inner self-talk
- be more objective about their positive qualities and achievements
- identify, reinforce and feel more confident about their abilities and the way they handle situations
- be more assertive; ask for what they want or deserve
- feel more accepting and valuing of themselves; allow mistakes and failings, apply self-forgiveness and stop aiming to be perfect
- take better care of themselves.

THE REWARDS OF HEALTHY SELF-ESTEEM

Clients sometimes imagine that people with healthy self-esteem are able to rise above the trials and tribulations life seems to throw at everyone else. Healthy self-esteem, however, does not mean being immune to problems and upsets. People with healthy self-esteem still have difficulties, get let down or make terrible mistakes, but they allow themselves to experience all the feelings that are involved and have better ways of bouncing back from disasters (Csikszentmihalyi, 2002). They honour the whole range of human emotions, such as sadness, fear, hurt or anger, when they face difficult situations and they look after themselves as they experience those feelings. They know how to pick themselves up after a setback by being a good friend to themselves. When they perform less well than they had hoped, they find out what went wrong and aim to put it right without berating themselves. They know how to congratulate themselves when they score a success (Seligman, 2006).

Healthy self-esteem includes effective coping skills, assertiveness and resilience to setbacks. Self-esteem also embraces how well we understand, accept and forgive ourselves. It usually gives us an inner security and stability, where we can trust ourselves and our judgement. Healthy self-esteem is not about getting everything right, but about reminding ourselves that we are still learning and giving ourselves permission to try again. It means being able to see choices and possibilities and make clear decisions for ourselves.

REFERENCES

Beck, A.T. and Alford, B.A. (2009) *Depression: Causes and Treatment* (2nd edn). Philadelphia: University of Pennsylvania Press.

Clarkson, P. (2003) *The Therapeutic Relationship* (2nd edn). Chichester: Wiley-Blackwell.

Csikszentmihalyi, M. (2002) *Flow: The Classic Work on How to Achieve Happiness*. London: Rider.

Dalgas-Pelish, P. (2006) Effects of a self-esteem intervention program on school age children. *Pediatric Nursing*, 32 (4): 341–7.

Deurzen, E. van (2002) *Existential Counselling and Psychotherapy in Practice* (2nd edn). London: Sage.

Ellis, A. (2001) *Overcoming Destructive Beliefs: New Directions for Rational Emotive Behavior Therapy*. New York: Prometheus.

Ellis, A. (2007) *The Practice of Rational Emotive Behaviour Therapy* (2nd edn). New York: Springer.

Fennell, M. (2009) *Overcoming Low Self-Esteem: A Self-Help Guide Using Cognitive Behavioural Techniques*. London: Robinson.

Finzi-Dottan, R. and Karu, T. (2006) From emotional abuse in childhood to psychopathology in adulthood: a path mediated by immature defence mechanisms and self-esteem. *The Journal of Nervous and Mental Disease*, 194: 616–21.

Maslow, A.H. (1987/1943) *Motivation and Personality* (3rd edn). Quarry Bay, Hong Kong: Longman Asia.

Rosenberg, M. (1965) *Society and the Adolescent Self-Image*. Princeton, NJ: Princeton University Press.

Salmon, G., James, A. and Smith, D.M. (1998) Bullying in schools: self-reported anxiety, depression and self-esteem in secondary school children. *British Medical Journal*, 317: 924–5.

Seligman, M.E.P. (2006) *Learned Optimism: How to Change Your Mind and Your Life*. New York: Vintage.

Sorensen, M.J. (2006) *Breaking the Chain of Low Self-Esteem* (2nd edn). Sherwood, OR: Wolf.

Waines, A. (2004) *The Self-Esteem Journal: Using a Journal to Build Self-Esteem*. London: Sheldon.

Whitmore, D. (2004) *Psychosynthesis Counselling in Action* (3rd edn). London: Sage.

Wilding, C. and Palmer, S. (2010) *Beat Low Self-Esteem with CBT*. London: Teach Yourself.

RECOMMENDED READING

Ellis, A. (2005) *The Myth of Self-Esteem: How Rational Emotive Behavior Therapy Can Change Your Life Forever*. New York: Prometheus.

Helmstetter, S. (1991) *What to Say When You Talk to Yourself*. London: Thorsons.

McKay, M. and Fanning, P. (2006) *Self-Esteem: A Proven Program of Cognitive Techniques for Assessing, Improving and Maintaining Your Self-Esteem* (3rd edn). Oakland, CA: New Harbinger.

Waines, A. (2004) *The Self-Esteem Journal: Using a Journal to Build Self-Esteem*. London: Sheldon.

Waines, A. (2005) *Making Relationships Work: How to Love Others and Yourself*. London: Sheldon.

6.14

Medically Unexplained Symptoms

DANIEL ZAHL AND DIANA SANDERS

As many as half of people attending general practitioner and medical outpatient clinics have symptoms which cannot be clearly medically diagnosed. The majority find these symptoms transient, are reassured that there is nothing seriously wrong, and one way or another find their own solutions. However, a proportion continue to believe that there is something seriously wrong, and remain worried and concerned. They may seek medical help numerous times, and have numerous tests and investigations, over perhaps many years. These people have traditionally been poorly managed by the medical profession, using up considerable resources in investigations and treatments that have not resolved the problems but have contributed to further distress and disability. They often invoke negative reactions, being described in the medical and psychiatric literature as the 'hard to help', 'difficult to manage', 'fat-file' and 'heart-sink' patients. Their symptoms may be dismissed as medically unexplained, psychosomatic or all in the mind, and therefore not real.

Many of these people face considerable disability and hardship as a consequence of their symptoms and may be apprehensive about a referral to counselling or psychotherapy services. This can lead to issues of engagement, requiring the therapist to adapt their therapeutic style. This chapter aims to offer an overview of the definition of medically unexplained symptoms (MUS), to identify the range of patients within this category, to discuss psychological conceptualizations of MUS and to describe ways of working with these clients.

DEFINING MEDICALLY UNEXPLAINED SYMPTOMS

Many terms are used to refer to the presentation of unexplained somatic symptoms. The terms *somatization* and *psychosomatic* suggest that symptoms are due to underlying psychological problems, and are considered the most pejorative by patients. The terms *medically unexplained symptoms* (MUS) and *functional somatic symptoms* (FSS) have been adopted by clinicians and researchers because of their aetiological impartiality. The term MUS acknowledges that medicine is currently unable to explain symptoms, and leaves open the possibility that it may do in the future. The term FSS is used to describe a group of syndromes that people with MUS may be diagnosed with.

The range of symptoms that are commonly found to be medically unexplained (see Table 6.14.1) includes very common symptoms which many people have experienced, such as stress-induced headaches, aches and pains, rashes and tiredness. Each of the functional somatic syndromes has specific diagnostic criteria, and includes many of these common symptoms; it is the number, severity and duration of symptoms and the exclusion of a medical cause that typically constitutes the diagnosis. For example, essential to a diagnosis of chronic fatigue syndrome or myalgic encephalomyelitis (CFS/ME) is that physical and mental fatigue have significantly compromised functioning more than 50 per cent of the time for at least the last six months. Diagnoses of FSS do not require the presence or suspicion of a psychological problem, and

Table 6.14.1   *Symptoms, syndromes and diagnoses that may be medically unexplained*

Somatic symptoms	Associated diagnoses and syndromes	Medical speciality
Breathlessness	Dysmorphophobia	Infectious diseases
Diarrhoea	Factitious syndromes	Neurology
Dizziness	Hyperventilation syndrome	Cardiology
Dysphagia (difficulty swallowing)	Post-traumatic syndromes	Ear nose and throat
Dysphonia, aphonia (vocal impairments)	Premenstrual syndrome	Gastroenterology
Fatigue	Somatization disorder	Rheumatology, anaesthetics
Incontinence and urgency	Chronic fatigue syndrome or myalgic encephelomyletis (CFS/ME)	
Nausea	Chronic headache, dizziness	
Pain (abdominal, chest, muscle and joint, low back, headache, facial, pelvic, neuropathic)	Non-cardiac chest pain	
	Globus pharyngis, dysponia	
Palpitations	Irritable bowel syndrome (IBS)	
Pruritis (itching)	Chronic pain syndromes/fibromyalgia	
Tinnitus		
Tremor		
Worry about benign tissue lumps and inconsistencies		

Source: adapted from Sanders (1996)

can be a reason for excluding a diagnosis. The diagnosis of specific FSS is usually made in specialist medical outpatient clinics without the consultation of a mental health practitioner. Following diagnosis, patients are sometimes referred by these clinics to counselling and psychology services.

Medically unexplained symptoms may occur in association with physical illness: for example, people with angina caused by diseased coronary arteries may also experience non-cardiac chest pains. They may also occur following a serious physical illness: for example, many people with chronic fatigue syndrome (CFS) experience a viral illness such as glandular fever prior to diagnosis, and in irritable bowel syndrome (IBS) bacterial gastroenteritis is a common precursor to diagnosis. Very occasionally, medically unexplained symptoms later turn out to have a measurable organic basis.

Regardless of the relation to organic factors, psychological factors play an important role both in the individual's distress and in the decision to seek help. Somatic symptoms characterize many psychological problems too, particularly depression and anxiety. Around one-fifth of new consultations for physical symptoms in primary care are found to be due to primary, or coexisting, psychological problems, most commonly anxiety and depression. An emotionally distressed individual is far more likely to consult a general practitioner with physical symptoms than to consult directly with emotional or social problems; and while the majority will,

with appropriate questioning, disclose relevant psychological explanations for their distress, a number will not wish to make the links with psychological or social difficulties, and will continue to seek help in the medical realm.

'Somatization' was originally defined as the hypothetical process whereby a deep-seated neurosis could cause a bodily disorder. The concept of somatization arises from earlier ideas from Freud and Breuer, who developed concepts such as unconscious conflict, defences and resistance. Unexplained physical symptoms were considered to be outward signs of psychological disturbance, which became transduced into somatic forms via hysteria and conversion. Patients' insistence that their symptoms were 'real' and organic was taken to represent their defence against the outpouring of intra-psychic conflict. The definition has moved on since then, losing some of its psychoanalytic overtones: somatization is generally defined as the process whereby people with psychosocial and emotional distress articulate their problems primarily through physical symptoms (Hotopf, 2004).

A common problem within the field of medically unexplained symptoms is health anxiety or hypochondriasis, where clients are extremely anxious about the possibility of serious illness and disease; become convinced, often with little or no evidence, that they are ill; and may repeatedly seek medical reassurance which they then disbelieve (Salkovskis and Bass, 1996). Health anxiety may be a primary problem, or may accompany other MUS as well as a range of physical difficulties. It is not always the case that clients with MUS are also anxious; many are reassured that they are not suffering from serious disease, but remain understandably puzzled and disabled by their symptoms.

CONCEPTUALIZING MEDICALLY UNEXPLAINED PROBLEMS

The research literature is abundant with observations of elevated rates of mental health problems amongst those with MUS. Many researchers have suggested that childhood experience of parental illness and physical and sexual abuse are risk factors for developing MUS in later life. Associations have also been made between the experience of adverse life events and onset of MUS. There is broad consensus that fixed organic illness beliefs, unhelpful responses to symptoms, such as excessive rest and avoidance, coupled with high estimates of personal vulnerability, contribute to the perpetuation of symptoms. The contribution of physiological and social variables is also crucial in informing our understanding of MUS.

The presence of adverse life events and early experience may be particularly relevant because of the impact they can have on us psychologically and physiologically through stress and anxiety. Chronic stress has well-documented short- and long-term physiological effects on cardiovascular and gastroenterological systems, and on immunity and cognitive function (Shoenberg, 2007), and can generate many of the symptoms commonly reported by people with MUS.

Social learning theory suggests that many people move into the 'sick role' when they are unwell, which may involve certain exemptions and exonerations from normal expectations and responsibilities. The stigma attached to psychological problems ensures that the most acceptable sick role involves having somatic dysfunction. The theory suggests that those who inhabit this role for long periods are likely to grow more disabled over time as they focus on symptoms and withdraw from productive life. The idea that there are rewards and exemptions associated with the sick role is often referred to as secondary gain; Fishbain (1994) lists some of these which include financial compensation, avoidance of unsatisfactory life roles or activity, and avoidance of sex.

These research findings and ideas have informed the development of specific and generic models of MUS. Specific multifactorial models have been

developed for FSS such as CFS (Suraway et al., 1995), IBS (Toner et al., 2000), and fibromyalgia (Bennett and Nelson, 2006). The CFS model suggests that for those who are vulnerable, life events (or a virus) can lead to a self-perpetuating cycle in which illness beliefs, physiological changes, reduced/inconsistent activity, medical uncertainty and lack of guidance interact to maintain symptoms. Specific models can be enormously helpful in clinical practice, when faced with a patient with an array of presenting problems, as they draw attention to specific cognitive and behavioural elements that may otherwise be overlooked. However, on a theoretical level it continues to be hotly debated whether FSS really represent discrete phenomena (Wesseley et al., 1999; White, 2010).

A detailed overarching CBT model of MUS which integrates much of the above research has been proposed by Deary et al. (2007), but as the relative contribution of these factors is likely to vary wildly between patients, it provides only a useful reminder of the factors that ought to be considered in any conceptualization.

The biopsychosocial model provides a practical template within which clinicians can map relevant physiological, cognitive, affective and behavioural components that may precipitate and/or perpetuate the problem (see Abramowitz and Braddock, 2008 for an explanation of how it can be applied to treat health anxiety).

The psychoanalytic idea that particular somatic symptoms have symbolic meaning continues to hold currency in this field, although it lacks an evidence base. The concept of alexithymia, a deficit in the ability to put emotions into words, came out of more recent attempts to determine if there were particular personality characteristics that patients with MUS shared. This is a popular notion, and while some patients score highly on measures of alexithymia, many also score highly on measures of neuroticism, suggesting that they have no difficulty expressing thoughts and emotions. Woolfolk and Allen (2007) suggest that patients with somatization disorder often have difficulty appropriately regulating emotion, and it is only through a thorough assessment that one can arrive at an individualized conceptualization of the problem.

PRINCIPLES OF THERAPY FOR MEDICALLY UNEXPLAINED SYMPTOMS

Working with clients with MUS often involves careful adaptation of the therapist's usual model of working. The majority of clients are likely to welcome the opportunity to talk through their problems and make links between psychological difficulties and life events. However, some may be reluctant to come for therapy, seeing it as irrelevant and as implying that the symptoms are 'all in the mind'. As a result, a structured approach can be very helpful, giving time to develop an individualized model of the problems and negotiating specific goals for therapy. Where specific treatment protocols exist (e.g. for health anxiety, somatization disorder, fibromyalgia and CFS), much can be gained. Some of the principles of therapy when working with this client group are outlined below.

The Therapeutic Relationship and Engaging the Client

Many patients report feeling misunderstood or having their symptoms ignored by health professionals. Time is always well spent building a strong therapeutic alliance at the start of therapy; it is likely to be a key factor in determining the outcome of therapy. One of the particular challenges for the practitioner can be how to engage the client actively in a way that does not threaten the individual's view of the self, takes account of misgivings about counselling or therapy, and offers an understanding of the problems without either colluding with or rejecting the client's beliefs.

Listening to the Symptoms and Broadening the Agenda

One way to begin to engage the client is to take a very full assessment of the physical symptoms and medical problems, gain an understanding of the client's medical treatment, and finally broaden the agenda to look at psychological factors. Many patients will have been used to short medical appointments, and feel that no one has ever taken the time to listen to and understand the whole story; thus careful listening and the appropriate expression of empathy can help to quickly build a good therapeutic relationship. Once the client has been given the opportunity to describe and discuss the somatic symptoms and medical treatment, it is useful to ask about their own explanation of the symptoms, such as abdominal pain caused by a food allergy or virus, or chest pain caused by spasm in the heart. Rather than attempting to challenge this assumption directly, it is more helpful to build on the client's view and work on the idea that precipitating factors, causing the symptoms in the first place, may differ from maintaining factors.

Therefore, an illness or a disease may have caused symptoms in the first place, but are no longer responsible for keeping it going.

Developing Alternative Hypotheses

Once the client's views about their symptoms have been discussed, it can be helpful to explore a number of hypotheses about what is causing the problems, other than physical illness. One technique commonly used in CBT treatment for health anxiety is the use of hypothesis testing to introduce the idea that there may be an alternative explanation for symptoms. This can be introduced by proposing that there are two ways of seeing the situation (theory A and theory B): the first is that the client does indeed have a serious physical illness, and that the doctors so far have not been able to diagnose or treat it; the second is that the individual is *concerned and anxious* about the possibility of illness, and that the anxiety is the central problem. The evidence for and against and the usefulness of each hypothesis are reviewed with the client. The therapist then proposes that they work together for a set time on the alternative theory; after that time, if they have had a good try at a psychological approach and the problem has not improved, then it would be reasonable to review their original hypothesis. This can be a useful way of avoiding 'getting into an argument' about the cause of the symptoms, and the client's beliefs are respected. For other MUS this approach may need to be carefully adapted based on the particular presentation; for those who do not report being anxious, discussion of 'stress' or other unhelpful coping behaviour, such as excessive rest in response to symptoms, may be more relevant. Being clear that therapy is principally concerned with helping people to overcome or better manage their problems rather than with understanding the origin of their symptoms can help avert unproductive discussions about the cause of symptoms.

Offering Alternative Explanations for the Symptoms

People with MUS may say they understand that symptoms are not caused by serious disease; however, clients with health anxiety in particular are unlikely to accept that there is 'nothing wrong' in the absence of a convincing explanation for their distressing symptoms. There are a number of ways of demonstrating links between physical symptoms and psychological and other maintaining factors, such as keeping diaries of symptoms and stress, and demonstrating how stress or paying attention to symptoms can make them appear worse (Sanders and Wills, 2003; Sanders et al., 2010). In addition, the client can be encouraged to experiment with discovering alternative explanations by using 'behavioural experiments' devised in cognitive therapy.

Dealing with Maintaining Factors

Symptoms can be exacerbated and maintained by a range of activities which the client uses to attempt to cope, such as seeking medical reassurance and further tests, illness behaviour, avoiding exercise, and checking or poking sore areas. It is important to identify what kind of unhelpful coping strategies the client may have evolved, and carefully negotiate with the client to reduce or stop, and to monitor how helpful this is. Again, behavioural experiments enable the client to discover the role of maintenance factors, and to experiment with alternative ways of dealing with the symptoms (Sanders et al., 2010; Silver et al., 2004a; 2004b). For example, the client can be encouraged to exercise gradually rather than rest, or to stop seeking reassurance or checking the internet, and monitor the impact on how he or she feels. Taking a systemic approach, looking at the role of the client's family and wider social context, is important; for example, while a client may be trying to get better, the spouse may be inadvertently reinforcing the sick role, or encouraging the individual to seek medical reassurance to allay their own fears.

Coping Strategies

For some clients, learning appropriate ways of coping with symptoms and other factors such as stress may be helpful, such as breathing and relaxation exercises, learning to distract from symptoms rather than pay attention to them, and dealing with low mood, stress or anxiety. Mindfulness meditation has been shown to help clients with physical health problems as well as stress, anxiety and depression (see Kabat-Zinn, 2005; Williams et al., 2007), and may be a valuable adjunct to psychological therapies for clients with health anxiety and medically unexplained symptoms.

Working with Other Issues and Difficulties

Once the client has acknowledged that psychological factors may be important, therapy can move on to focus on other difficulties. Life difficulties and stress may well be involved; problem-solving and solution-focused therapy (see Chapter 5.33 in this volume) can be helpful, enabling the client to look for solutions to the issues which may underlie and maintain the difficulties. Clients' assumptions and beliefs, as discussed above, can maintain the problems, requiring focus during therapy. A proportion of this client group will have experienced physical, emotional or sexual abuse in earlier years, and illness may be one means the individual has developed to cope with such trauma. The counsellor, therefore, needs to proceed with care and caution, only gently exploring these areas as and when the client is ready. It is sometimes the case that it is preferable for the client to experience physical distress than to look at the pain from the past.

EFFECTIVENESS OF THERAPY FOR MEDICALLY UNEXPLAINED SYMPTOMS

There is a growing evidence base for the use of psychological therapies for a range of medically unexplained problems and health anxiety (Hotopf, 2004; Kleinstäuber et al., 2011). Reviews of the literature suggest that CBT is moderately beneficial for MUS in general (e.g. Martin et al., 2007), with stronger support found in randomized controlled trials (RCTs) of CFS and fibromyalgia than in IBS (Deary et al., 2007). CBT has also been found to be beneficial for somatization disorder (Kroenke, 2007). There is an absence of RCTs that have found psychodynamic therapy to be beneficial in MUS, though some studies are supportive (Creed et al., 2003). Brief dynamic therapy, group psychotherapy and cognitive-behavioural therapy have been shown to be effective for a range of psychosomatic problems, chronic pain and health anxiety (Kroenke and Swindle, 2000; Lidbeck, 2003).

WHEN COUNSELLING IS NOT APPROPRIATE

It is also important to consider when psychological approaches, particularly brief therapy, might not be helpful. One danger in working with this client group is that the therapist becomes yet another 'expert' who has not been able to help the client, thus compounding their distress and dissatisfaction with the 'helping' professions.

Counselling and psychological therapies are more likely to be helpful if the client accepts that psychosocial factors affect their somatic problems, such as the symptoms being aggravated by stress or emotion, thus lending more credibility to a psychological model; if the client reports being psychologically distressed; if the symptoms were preceded by identifiable life events; and if client and counsellor are able to negotiate mutually agreed goals and work collaboratively towards these goals. Factors which may indicate a poor response to psychological approaches include an attempt by the client to claim compensation for the symptoms, an inability on the part of the client to see any link with psychological difficulties or stresses, the presence of persistent dysfunctional beliefs about illness, and if the client does not experience psychological difficulties. In many cases it is helpful for the counsellor to work very closely with those involved in the client's medical treatment, and, for some long-term somatizing clients, a structured, long-term medical management plan is most appropriate. Counsellors and psychologists working in medical settings have a great deal to offer in helping medical professionals to manage such clients.

REFERENCES

Abramowitz, J.S. and Braddock, A.E. (2008) *Psychological Treatment of Health Anxiety and Hypochondriasis: A Biopsychosocial Approach*. Cambridge, MA: Hogrefe.

Bennett, R. and Nelson, D. (2006) Cognitive behavioural therapy for fibromyalgia. *Nature Clinical Practice*, 2: 416–24.

Creed, F., Fernandes, L., Guthrie, E., Palmer, S., Ratcliffe, J., Read, N., Rigby, C., Thompson, D. and Tomenson, B. (2003) The cost-effectiveness of psychotherapy and Paroxetine for severe irritable bowel syndrome. *Gastroenterology*, 124: 303–17.

Deary, V., Chalder, T. and Sharpe, M. (2007) The cognitive behavioural model of medically unexplained symptoms: a theoretical and empirical review. *Clinical Psychology Review*, 27: 781–97.

Fishbain, D.A. (1994) Secondary gain concept: definition problems and its abuse in medical practice. *American Pain Society Journal*, 3: 264–73.

Hotopf, M. (2004) Preventing somatization. *Psychological Medicine*, 34: 195–8.

Kabat-Zinn, J. (2005) *Coming to Our Senses: Healing Ourselves and the World through Mindfulness*. London: Piatkus.

Kleinstäuber, M., Witthöft, M. and Hiller, W. (2011) Efficacy of short-term psychotherapy for multiple medically unexplained symptoms: a meta-analysis. *Clinical Psychology Review*, 31 (1): 146–60.

Kroenke, K. (2007) Efficacy of treatment for somatoform disorders: a review of randomized controlled trials. *Psychosomatic Medicine*, 69: 881–8.

Kroenke, K. and Swindle, R. (2000) Cognitive behavioral therapy for somatization and symptom syndromes: a critical review of controlled clinical trials. *Psychotherapy and Psychosomatics*, 69 (4): 205–15.

Lidbeck, J. (2003) Group therapy for somatization disorders in primary care: maintenance of treatment goals of short cognitive-behavioural treatment one and a half year follow-up. *Acta Psychiatrica Scandinavica*, 107 (6): 449–56.

Martin, A., Rauh, E., Fichter, M. and Rief, W. (2007) A one-session treatment for patients suffering from medically unexplained symptoms in primary care: a randomized clinical trial. *Psychosomatics*, 48: 294–03.

Salkovskis, P.M. and Bass, C.M. (1996) Hypochondriasis. In D.M. Clark and C.G. Fairburn (eds), *Science and Practice of Cognitive Behaviour Therapy* (pp. 313–39). Oxford: Oxford University Press.

Sanders, D. (1996) *Counselling for Psychosomatic Problems*. London: Sage.

Sanders, D. and Wills, F. (2003) *Counselling for Anxiety Problems*. London: Sage.

Sanders, D., Surawy, C., Zahl, D. and Salt, H. (2010) Physical health settings. In M. Mueller et al. (eds), *Oxford Guide to Surviving as a CBT Therapist* (pp. 253–73). Oxford: Oxford University Press.

Shoenberg, P. (2007) *The Effects of Stress in Psychosomatics: The Uses of Psychotherapy*. Basingstoke: Palgrave Macmillan.

Silver, A., Sanders, D., Morrison, N. and Cowie, C. (2004a) Health anxiety. In J. Bennett-Levy et al. (eds), *The Oxford Guide to Behavioural Experiments in Cognitive Therapy* (pp. 87–105). Oxford: Oxford University Press.

Silver, A., Surawy, C. and Sanders, D. (2004b) Physical health. In J. Bennett-Levy et al. (eds), *The Oxford Guide to Behavioural Experiments in Cognitive Therapy* (pp. 327–47). Oxford: Oxford University Press.

Suraway, C., Hackmann, A., Hawton, K. and Sharpe, M. (1995) Chronic fatigue syndrome: a cognitive approach. *Behavioural Research Therapy*, 33 (5): 535–44.

Toner, B.B., Segal, Z.V., Emmott, S.D. and Myran, D. (2000) *Cognitive-Behavioral Treatment of Irritable Bowel Syndrome: The Brain–Gut Connection*. New York: Guilford.

Wesseley, S., Nimnuan, C. and Sharpe, M. (1999) Functional somatic syndromes: one or many? *Lancet*, 354: 935–6.

White, P.D. (2010) Chronic fatigue syndrome: is it one discrete syndrome or many? Implications for the 'one vs. many' functional somatic syndromes debate. *Journal of Psychosomatic Research*, 68: 455–9.

Williams, M., Teasdale, J., Segal, Z.V. and Kabat-Zinn, J. (2007) *The Mindful Way through Depression*. New York: Guilford.

Woolfolk, R.L. and Allen, L.A. (2007) *Treating Somatization: A Cognitive Behavioural Approach*. New York: Guilford Press.

Obsessive Compulsive Disorder

TOM RICKETTS AND GILL DONOHOE

Obsessive compulsive disorder (OCD) is a serious mental health problem whose defining features are the presence of obsessions and/or compulsions. These features are defined and described later. Until recently, the disorder was considered to be relatively uncommon, but this appears to have been due to the large extent of under-reporting by sufferers. Over 2 per cent of the population will experience OCD at some time (Roth and Fonagy, 2005), with an average age of onset in the mid 20s. OCD commonly has a chronic course, with untreated individuals suffering difficulties for decades. Developments in understanding, and particularly behavioural and cognitive-behavioural treatment models, have improved the prognosis for sufferers. Therefore a priority is for the early identification of sufferers, and the offering of appropriate therapy.

This chapter will first outline the clinical features of OCD, exploring the range of common presentations. A behavioural model will then be introduced, and the link between this model and the approaches deriving from it outlined. Research supporting the utilization of exposure and response prevention will be briefly reviewed. Finally, the developments and debates in the area of therapy of OCD will be discussed.

CLINICAL FEATURES

Obsessions

Obsessions are defined in the *DSM-IV* (APA, 2000) as recurrent, persistent and distressing ideas, thoughts, impulses or images. These are experienced (at least at some point during the disorder) as intrusive and senseless, and do not represent excessive worries about real-life problems. The person attempts to suppress or neutralize such thoughts or impulses with another thought or action. There is a clear recognition by the individual that the obsessions are a product of their own mind, and not imposed from without. Table 6.15.1 gives some examples of obsessions.

Compulsions

Compulsions are defined as repetitive and intentional behaviours or mental acts. These are performed in response to an obsessional thought, according to idiosyncratic rules that have to be applied rigidly, and which aim to reduce distress or prevent a dreadful event or situation. However, the behaviour is not clearly linked to an outcome, or it is clearly excessive. The act is performed with a sense of subjective compulsion, with at least initially some sense of resistance. Table 6.14.1 gives some examples of compulsions and how they link to obsessional thoughts.

Insight

In OCD there is a recognition by the individual, at least at some point during the disorder, that their obsessions are senseless or excessive, and their actions excessive. At the point of assessment there may be wide variability in the degree to which the individual recognizes the inappropriateness of the extent of their behaviour.

Table 6.15.1 *Examples of obsessional thoughts and linked behaviours*

Content of obsessional thought	Nature of compulsive behaviour	Avoidances	Behavioural excesses
I may have come into contact with swine flu or other contamination	Repeated handwashing Showering for several hours at a time	Avoids crowded areas, touching 'dirty people', touching door handles	Scanning others for signs of illness Wearing gloves Covering mouth
Have I made a mistake which may harm others?	Repeated checking of items in home or at work, e.g. gas taps, switches, door locks	Avoids switching on/off high-risk items	Repeatedly requests reassurance from others Engages others in checking
Sexual, aggressive or blasphemous content	Mental neutralizing by repeated praying and efforts to 'put a good thought' in place	Avoids being alone with children	Scanning environment for evidence of own evil

While the different types of obsessive compulsive presentation can usefully be outlined (as in Table 6.14.1), there is much evidence of overlap between the different types, indicating common pathways to their development.

Biochemical Aspects

In a review of personality and individual differences research regarding susceptibility to develop OCD, Macdonald (2003) highlights that evidence for a possible genetic predisposition for OCD remains equivocal. Efforts to find biochemical or genetic markers for OCD have proved inconclusive. This may be because OCD is heterogeneous, meaning that individual susceptibility to particular features of the disorder may need to be the focus for investigation. It is also clear that environmental factors play a large part in the development of OCD.

Comorbidity

OCD often coexists with other disorders, with over 50 per cent of OCD sufferers entering trials commonly reporting another anxiety or mood disorder. Comorbidity with specific phobia, generalized anxiety disorder or panic disorder is common. OCD is also commonly complicated by depression, with studies identifying concurrent major depression in one-quarter to one-third of OCD sufferers. However, suicidal ideation or attempts among clients with OCD is reported to be rare (Steketee and Barlow, 2002). Assessing for depression is important, as severe depression has consistently been found to be a predictor of poorer treatment outcome (Keeley et al., 2008).

UNDERSTANDING OCD

Behavioural models of OCD have been very helpful in enabling effective treatments to be developed. Figure 6.15.1 shows a behavioural model.

Within the model, intrusive thoughts are viewed as normal phenomena which, due to association with fear-inducing stimuli, have become fear inducing themselves. This fear is neutralized through the undertaking of voluntary behaviours (compulsions), either overt or covert, to prevent harm ensuing. For example, an obsessional thought regarding being responsible for harm coming to others through carelessness may be followed by a checking behaviour. The undertaking of compulsive behaviours has a number of effects. First, it prevents the anxiety associated with the intrusive thought spontaneously reducing, a process termed extinction. Second, it increases the perceived importance of the intrusive thought. Because the thought is acted upon, the range of situations that will trigger it are increased, and it occurs more often. Third, as the compulsive behaviours are followed by a reduction in anxiety, they are more likely to occur again in similar situations. For example, an obsessional thought about having come into contact with swine-flu virus may initially only occur where there is evidence of symptoms in others. Where the individual repeatedly responds to the thought by washing themselves thoroughly, an increasing range of situations come to be associated with the perceived contamination risk. Eventually the vicinity of a doctor's surgery, touching door handles, or even being in the same room with others may be sufficient to trigger the obsessional thought, with the individual responding by repeated handwashing or other extensive decontamination activities.

In contrast, if the obsessional thought, discomfort and urge to engage in the compulsive behaviour are provoked but the individual refrains from carrying out the behaviour, the urge and discomfort will dissipate naturally, but more slowly than if the urges had been acted upon. With repeated induction there is a cumulative effect, with progressively less discomfort, and less urge to engage in the compulsive behaviour, and progressively more rapid reduction in the urge to do so.

The process through which intrusive thoughts come to elicit anxiety and discomfort is the subject of some debate, with acquisition through a process of classical conditioning not finding general support (Jones and Menzies, 1997). However, the model of the maintenance of OCD has proved clinically fruitful, particularly in underpinning exposure and response prevention, which remains the treatment of choice, and is explained in the next section.

THERAPY

Assessment

Assessment of OCD is similar to that for other disorders in that the aim is to obtain as full a picture as possible, utilizing a range of data collection techniques. Assessment is guided by the model, so that at the end of assessment a clear formulation of the development and maintenance of the disorder is possible, this being the basis of the individualized therapeutic plan. Data collection techniques include

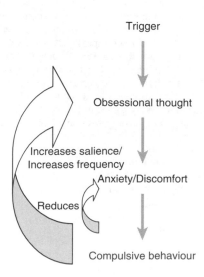

Figure 6.15.1   *A behavioural model of OCD*

clinical interviews, self-monitoring of thoughts, emotions and behaviour, and, where possible, direct observation of the client undertaking their compulsive behaviours.

Client Education

Prior to undertaking exposure and response prevention the client is informed of the outcome of the assessment, as a means of making sense of symptoms that they may previously have found incomprehensible. They are also informed about the beneficial impact of experiencing obsessional thoughts in the absence of undertaking compulsive behaviours. This process should enable them to understand the rationale for the therapeutic plan, and enhance the collaborative relationship with the therapist. As they will be undertaking what may be frightening procedures, it is important that they understand the purpose and process of therapy.

Exposure and Response Prevention

The key elements of exposure and response prevention are that the client is enabled to re-enter previously avoided situations while resisting the urge to undertake behaviours which would rapidly reduce subjective discomfort. This process is most effective when the exposure tasks are challenging but achievable, when the tasks are undertaken for an hour or more, and on a daily basis if possible. Specifics are as follows:

- A list of trigger situations/tasks is developed with the client, and graded according to difficulty. Tasks to be undertaken with the therapist should be as difficult as the client is willing to undertake. Working with the therapist initially, the client is enabled to engage in contact with the previously avoided triggers, for instance holding an item considered contaminated, for a prolonged period, preferably over an hour. Where possible, the perceived extent of exposure should be maximized by such behaviours as touching other items, face, hair with hands considered contaminated. Throughout exposure, the urge to undertake the compulsive behaviour should be monitored, while the client is assisted not to undertake the behaviour. This subjective urge or discomfort should have reduced substantially (by at least 50 per cent) before the exposure session is terminated.
- A high frequency of exposure sessions is associated with more rapid processing of fear. In practice, the implications of this are that enabling clients to undertake self-managed exposure with

response prevention between therapy sessions is essential. Encouraging the client to repeat what has been achieved within the therapy session is often sufficient, but clear written guidance is helpful.

- Therapist modelling of the desired behaviour prior to the client undertaking it increases client compliance and speeds up the process of exposure. Specific messages about the therapist not asking the client to do anything they would not do themselves should be given, with emphasis on a collaborative approach. Care should be taken to ensure that therapist involvement does not become a subtle form of reassurance for the client.

Cognitive Approaches

Cognitive theories of OCD emphasize the importance of faulty appraisals regarding mental intrusions as a core feature (Clark, 2004). Specific appraisals may relate to inflated responsibility for the prevention of harm (Salkovskis, 1985), or the overestimation of the significance of mental events (Rachman, 1997). Cognitive approaches aim primarily to alter these appraisals through addressing thoughts evaluating the content of the obsessions, rather than the obsessions themselves. Studies investigating this approach indicate that cognitive therapy along these lines can be as effective as exposure and response prevention (Clark, 2004).

Medical Treatment

The National Institute for Health and Clinical Excellence (NICE, 2005) recommends that the initial intervention for people suffering from OCD is cognitive-behaviour therapy as described above. Where the client refuses or is unable to engage with therapy, the use of a serotonergic compound (SSRI) such as fluoxetine and fluvoxamine is recommended. As SSRIs may increase the risk of suicidal thoughts and self-harm in people suffering from depression and young people, careful monitoring is recommended following their commencement. This is particularly important for the large group of clients suffering from OCD who will also be suffering from depression, and those under 30. The combining of medication with cognitive-behaviour therapy appears to convey few additional benefits over cognitive-behaviour therapy alone, and should only be considered if there is inadequate response to initial intervention or the client is experiencing severe functional impairment (NICE, 2005).

RESEARCH

In a meta-analysis of multiple randomized controlled trials, Eddy et al. (2004) identified that exposure with response prevention and cognitive therapy were broadly equivalent in their effects, and as effective as serotonergic medications. The addition of cognitive approaches to exposure with response prevention appeared to result in no greater effects than exposure with response prevention alone. However, despite these results a majority of clients continue to suffer significant symptoms following treatment; that is, they improve but do not recover. In addressing this issue Eddy et al. (2004) analysed the same studies used in their meta-analysis using a threshold of 12 or below on the commonly used Yale–Brown Obsessive Compulsive Scale (Goodman et al., 1989) as a definition of recovery. In doing so they identified that approximately two-thirds of clients completing the therapies improved, but only one-third 'recovered'. There is also a subgroup of clients who refuse or do not complete therapy.

Two other issues have been the focus of recent research. The first is whether the results from research trials can be transferred into routine practice. The second is predicting those clients who are less likely to benefit from cognitive-behaviour therapy, so as to adjust treatments to their needs.

The difficulty of generalizing results from research clinics to routine practice settings has been cited as a reason to ignore the evidence for cognitive-behaviour therapy as summarized in practice guidelines such as those produced by the National Institute for Health and Clinical Excellence (Holmes, 2002; NICE, 2005). Studies of what outcomes are achieved in routine practice settings are required. When such studies have been undertaken (Houghton et al., 2010) the results have been encouraging, with the routine delivery of cognitive-behaviour therapy for OCD resulting in effects equivalent to those found in research trials.

Seeking to identify factors that may predict response to cognitive-behaviour therapy has been the subject of a large amount of research. Keeley et al. (2008) reviewed predictors and identified inconsistent findings with regard to much of the literature. Amongst the relatively few consistent findings were those that severe depression, negative family interactions and poorer therapeutic alliance were predictors of worse outcome.

DEBATES IN THE FIELD

The major debate regarding psychological treatment for OCD currently centres around the extent to which less intensive and self-management approaches to treatment can maintain the known efficacy of exposure and response prevention, whilst making the approach available to a wider group of sufferers.

Self-management approaches to anxiety disorders and their application to OCD have been the subject of debate. The OCD guideline from the National Institute for Health and Clinical Excellence (NICE, 2005) recommends low-intensity exposure with response prevention supported by self-help materials, or group-delivered cognitive-behaviour therapy as the first intervention for people suffering from milder forms of OCD. To date there is only limited evidence of the effectiveness of such approaches, but the expansion of cognitive-behavioural approaches in primary care through the Improving Access to Psychological Therapies (IAPT) programme (Clark et al., 2009) has allowed for the widespread delivery and evaluation of these approaches. Results of the national evaluation are that, for at least a percentage of people suffering from milder forms of OCD, guided self-help delivered by a psychological wellbeing practitioner (Clark et al., 2009) can be sufficient to reduce the functional impact of OCD. Further work can be expected on both manual-aided and computer-delivered approaches (Greist et al., 2002).

REFERENCES

APA (2000) *Diagnostic and Statistical Manual of Mental Disorders* (4th edn text rev.). Washington, DC: American Psychiatric Association.

Clark, D.A. (2004) *Cognitive-Behavioral Therapy for OCD*. New York: Guilford.

Clark, D.M., Layard, R., Smithies, R., Richards, D.A., Suckling, R. and Wright, B. (2009) Improving Access to Psychological Therapies: initial evaluation of two UK demonstration sites. *Behaviour Research and Therapy*, 47: 910–20.

Eddy, K.T., Dutra, L., Bradley, R. and Westen, D. (2004) A multidimensional meta-analysis of psychotherapy and pharmacotherapy for obsessive-compulsive disorder. *Clinical Psychology Review*, 24 (8): 1011–30.

Goodman, W.K., Price, L.H., Rasmussen, S.A., Mazure, C., Fleischmann, R.L., Hill, C.L., Heninger, G.R. and Charney, D.S. (1989) The Yale–Brown Obsessive Compulsive Scale I.

Development, use and reliability. *Archives of General Psychiatry*, 46, 1006–11.

Greist, J.H., Marks, I.M., Baer, L. et al. (2002) Behaviour therapy for obsessive compulsive disorder guided by a computer or by a clinician compared with relaxation as a control. *Journal of Clinical Psychiatry*, 63: 138–45.

Holmes, J. (2002) All you need is cognitive behaviour therapy? *British Medical Journal*, 324: 288–94.

Houghton, S., Saxon, D., Bradburn, M., Ricketts, T. and Hardy, G. (2010) The effectiveness of routinely delivered cognitive behavioural therapy for obsessive-compulsive disorder: a benchmarking study. *British Journal of Clinical Psychology*, 49: 473–89.

Jones, M.K. and Menzies, R.G. (1997) The relevance of associative learning pathways in the development of obsessive-compulsive washing. *Behaviour Research and Therapy*, 36: 273–83.

Keeley, M.L., Storch, E.A., Merlo, L.J. and Geffken, G.R. (2008) Clinical predictors of response to cognitive-behavioral therapy for obsessive-compulsive disorder. *Clinical Psychology Review*, 28 (1): 118–30.

Macdonald, A.M. (2003) Personality and individual differences in OCD. In R.G. Menzies and P. de Silva (eds), *Obsessive-Compulsive Disorder: Theory, Research and Treatment*. Chichester: Wiley.

NICE (2005) *Obsessive-Compulsive Disorder: Core Interventions in the Treatment of Obsessive-Compulsive Disorder and Body Dysmorphic Disorder*. London: National Institute for Health and Clinical Excellence.

Rachman, S. (1997) A cognitive theory of obsessions. *Behaviour Research and Therapy*, 35: 793–802.

Roth, A. and Fonagy, P. (2005) *What Works for Whom? A Critical Review of Psychotherapy Research* (2nd edn). New York: Guilford.

Salkovskis, P.M. (1985) Obsessive-compulsive problems: a cognitive-behavioural analysis. *Behaviour Research and Therapy*, 25: 571–83.

Steketee, G. and Barlow, D.H. (2002) Obsessive-compulsive disorder. In D.H. Barlow (ed.), *Anxiety and Its Disorders: The Nature and Treatment of Anxiety and Panic* (2nd edn). New York: Guilford.

Personality Disorders

STEPHEN KELLETT AND DAN TULLY

BACKGROUND

A Personality Disorder (PD), formerly known as a character disorder, is defined as 'an enduring pattern of inner experience and behavior that deviates markedly from the expectations of an individual's culture, is pervasive and inflexible, has an onset in adolescence or early adulthood, is stable over time and leads to distress or impairment' (APA, 2000: 685). PDs are one of the main categories of psychiatric diagnoses, and like any other mental health problem have 'signs' (the consistent behavioural patterns of the client) and symptoms (the subjective distress of the client) that the counsellor or psychotherapist can be usefully aware of at screening or assessment. The recognition of PD in clinical practice is vital as the modality, intensity and duration of treatment will alter accordingly. Clients with PD can be frequently mishandled and the alliance easily fractured, due to lack of knowledge of PD categories and core PD psychological and emotional processes. Clients with PD generally evoke strong and typically negative feelings in any providers of care, with such feelings common in the counsellor or psychotherapist. The feelings evoked in the therapist, or counsellor, during consultations are a valuable piece of information in the assessment of the client and the understanding and formulation of their chronic interpersonal difficulties.

Well into the eighteenth century, the sole 'types' of mental illness – then commonly referred to as 'delirium' or 'mania' – were depression (melancholy), psychoses and delusions. At the turn of the nineteenth century, Pinel (1802) referred to a group of patients with *manie sans delire* (insanity without delusions) who were impulsive, quick to extreme anger and prone to violent outbursts – but in the absence of any delusions. Pritchard (1835) subsequently suggested the new diagnosis of *moral insanity* concerning antisocial patients with labile affect, anger, compulsions and impulse control problems, but crucially without intellectual disability, thought disorder or psychosis. The term was still in wide clinical and legal circulation until Maudsley (1868) criticized its ambiguity and sought a more scientific replacement.

Koch (1891) subsequently coined the phrase *psychopathic inferiority* as a diagnosis for patients who were rigid in their patterns of behaviour, with such patterns being apparent across the life cycle, and in the absence of intellectual disability or psychosis. Kraepelin (1905) suggested six additional types of disturbed personalities: excitable, unstable, eccentric, liar, swindler and quarrelsome. Henderson (1939) hypothesized that psychopaths were defined by lifetime antisocial conduct disorders whose behaviour was unaffected by social, penal and medical attempts to intervene, in the absence of intellectual disability. Henderson (1939) described three types of psychopath: (1) aggressive psychopaths who were violent, suicidal and prone to substance abuse; (2) passive and inadequate psychopaths who were over-sensitive, unstable and hypochondriacal; and (3) creative psychopaths who were dysfunctional but managed to become famous or infamous. Schneider (1959) sought to expand the diagnosis of characterological problems to include people who harm themselves, as well as others; depressed, socially anxious, shy and insecure patients therefore continued to be labelled as 'abnormal'.

Rado (1953) defined PD as gross and persistent disturbances in the organization of higher mental activities that govern a sense of self and others, control and impulses. In 1959, in the Mental Health Act for England and Wales, 'psychopathic disorder' was defined as: '[A] persistent disorder or disability of mind (whether or not including subnormality of intelligence) which results in abnormally aggressive or seriously irresponsible conduct on the part of the patient, and requires or is susceptible to medical treatment' (section 4(4)). Today, most practitioners rely on either the *Diagnostic and Statistical Manual of Mental Disorders* (*DSM-IV-TR*) (APA, 2000) or the *International Classification of Diseases* (*ICD-10*) (WHO, 1992) for categorizing PD. The diagnostic characteristics of PD usually differ only in terms of intensity and frequency from the personality features evident in the majority of the population.

AN OVERVIEW OF PERSONALITY DISORDER

The concept of personality involves consistent interpersonal, behavioural and attitudinal consistencies that are apparent regardless of context or time. The temperament of the client is the inherited personality traits, which are evident and observable in childhood and presumed to be primarily biologically determined. Four main temperaments have been suggested: harm avoidance, novelty seeking, reward dependence, and persistence (Cloninger et al., 1993). These aspects are believed to be independently heritable, become apparent very early in life and to involve preconceptual biases in perceptual memory and habit formation. A 'trait' is considered the 'basic unit' of personality or PD and consists of a cluster of stereotyped and inflexible related behavioural habits. Personality is the sum total and enduring qualities of the manner in which an adult acts and reacts across social and personal circumstances and time. Personality therefore provides a means for the organization, congruence and integration of the attitudes, beliefs, behaviours and affects that govern and influence self-management, relating to others and planning for the future. The manifestation of PD is therefore recognizable by adolescence and continues throughout adult life, although the traits may soften and recede in middle age or later life. It is therefore inappropriate to diagnose PD in people under the age of 16 years. Should an adult undergo a major traumatic event or a series of such events, then it is possible that some disintegration of the extant personality organization takes place and maladaptive enduring personality change can occur. Clients with PD typically view their own deficits or excesses in an 'egosyntonic'

manner, in that they are labeled as both reasonable and appropriate. For example, someone with an antisocial PD would show little concern for the wellbeing of another person if they perceived that that person had wronged them in some way. If the client with an antisocial PD assaulted the person then this would be seen as settling a score. They would view the assault with little guilt or remorse, externalizing the locus of blame.

In both modern diagnostic systems (*ICD-10* and *DSM-IV-TR*), PDs are defined and categorized. There are many justifiable criticisms of such a 'disease concept' approach; a PD diagnosis can be seen as both inherently unreliable and simply a means of attaching a demeaning label to a patient who has outstripped the assessment methods of the therapist. Therefore, the diagnosis of PD is criticized as being more analogous to a moral judgement, as opposed to a valid and reliable summative clinical formulation. *DSM-IV-TR* (APA, 2000) uses a cluster approach with regard to the diagnosis of PD; 10 PDs are listed that are grouped into three clusters. Cluster A (the *odd/eccentric* cluster) contains paranoid, schizoid and schizotypal PD; cluster B (the *dramatic* cluster) antisocial, borderline, histrionic and narcissistic PD; and cluster C (the *anxious* cluster) avoidant, dependent and obsessive compulsive PD. *DSM-IV-TR* also contains a category for behavioural patterns that do not map accurately onto the 10 extant PDs, but nevertheless exhibit characteristics of PD; this diagnosis is termed *PD not otherwise specified*. In order to help the counsellor or psychotherapist recognize typical PD presentations, each cluster is represented in Table 6.15.1, with the core means of relating summarized.

As is evident from Table 6.16.1, there is an emphasis on chronic and pervasive behavioural patterns that are apparent in the absence of stress; such patterns are exacerbated by the presence of high interpersonal or environmental stress. The most common form of PD that is likely to present to counsellors and psychotherapists is that of borderline personality disorder (BPD). This is because (1) clients with BPD frequently seek the care that was typically absent during childhood, (2) they are likely to present in other medical services due to chronic self-harm and are therefore likely to be referred, and (3) the personality organization of other PDs frequently mitigates against active help seeking. For example, clients with schizoid PD will not want to engage with services due to lack of interest in social relationships; clients with narcissistic PD may feel that they are above a talking approach; and clients with paranoid PD would be too suspicious of services to be able to form a therapeutic alliance. In part, the confusion over the definition of BPD is one of semantics, as the term suggests that clients with such a diagnosis have

Table 6.16.1　*DSM-IV personality disorder clusters, diagnoses and main clinical characteristics (key feature in italics)*

Cluster A: odd/eccentric	
Paranoid personality disorder	A pervasive and unwarranted tendency to interpret the actions of others as *demeaning or threatening*
Schizoid personality disorder	A pervasive pattern of *indifference to social relationships and a restricted range of emotional experience and expression*
Schizotypal personality disorder	A pervasive pattern of *deficits in interpersonal relatedness and peculiarities of ideation, experience, appearance and behaviour*
Cluster B: dramatic/impulsive	
Antisocial personality disorder	Evidence of a *childhood conduct disorder* before the age of 15 and a pattern of *irresponsible and antisocial behaviour* post 15 years
Borderline personality disorder	Pervasive pattern of *instability of mood, interpersonal relationships and self-image*
Histrionic personality disorder	Pervasive *pattern of excessive emotionality and attention-seeking*
Narcissistic personal disorder	Pervasive pattern of grandiosity, lack of empathy and hypersensitivity to the evaluation of others
Cluster C: anxious	
Avoidant personality disorder	A pervasive pattern of *social discomfort, fear of negative evaluation and timidity*
Dependent personality disorder	A pervasive pattern of *dependent and submissive* behaviour
Obsessive compulsive personality disorder	A pervasive pattern *of perfectionism and inflexibility*

'half' a personality disorder. The term 'borderline' has a long heritage and refers to people that exist on the borderline between psychosis and neurosis (see diagnostic feature 9 below). However, it is the ability of clients with BPD to exhibit both neurosis and pseudopsychosis that represents the core diagnostic feature of the disorder. The *DSM-IV-TR* (APA, 2000) lists nine discrete features and requires five of these to be pervasive across time and context. The nine features are as follows:

1　frantic efforts to avoid real or imagined abandonment
2　typically unstable and intense personal relationships
3　identity disturbance
4　impulsivity in two areas of life that are potentially self-damaging
5　recurrent suicidal behaviour, gestures, threats, or self-mutilating behaviour
6　affective instability due to marked reactivity of mood
7　chronic feeling of emptiness
8　inappropriate intense anger
9　transient stress-related paranoid ideation or severe dissociative symptoms.

RECOGNIZING PERSONALITY DISORDER

In this section we will consider the complex combination of chronic intrapersonal difficulties (the manner in which the client treats and relates to themselves) and chronic interpersonal difficulties (the relational milieu – how others are treated and seen and the manner in which the client is seen and treated by others). Due to the egosyntonic nature of their difficulties, clients with PD have difficulty recognizing when they are eliciting behaviours from others that actually maintain their core conception of social relationships. For example, the client with paranoid PD would find it hard to see that being distrustful of others makes people pull away and therefore reinforces the sense that people can't be trusted. In terms of the origin and maintenance of problems, Beck and Freeman (1990) proposed that PD could be understood in terms of chronic interpersonal styles or vectors. Therefore in relation to others, clients with PD habitually move or place themselves *against* (e.g. antisocial), *towards* (e.g. dependent), *away from* (e.g. schizoid and paranoid), *above* (e.g. narcissistic) or *below* (e.g. obsessive compulsive) others, or show an impulsive mix of all five styles (e.g. borderline). The manner in which a person with a PD relates to others will be replicated in the therapeutic relationship: against (untrusting), towards (eliciting over care and smothering), away from (distancing), above (dismissive) or chaotic (alternating between seeing the counsellor or psychotherapist as the perfect rescuer or the cold technician). Table 6.16.2 describes the manner in which the ten PDs tend to relate to the world, people and themselves, which therefore summarizes and differentiates the origins and maintenance of emotional distress across the PDs. The table contains for each PD the most common behavioural trait, the least likely or most difficult behaviour for each PD to exhibit, and the particular stress points for each PD that the counsellor or psychotherapist can be usefully aware of.

TREATMENT OF PERSONALITY DISORDER

The mechanism of therapeutic change can be difficult to identify across the diagnostic family of PD. There is ongoing debate within the literature as to whether psychotherapeutic treatments change core personality constructs, or rather ameliorate their impact on the client's life and wellbeing.

For the purposes of this section we will consider the subjective experience of the client and draw out key recommendations common to the various treatment approaches. We will focus primarily on BPD due to the frequency of this presentation to services and the wider community. As discussed earlier, people with BPD are more likely to present to services perhaps as a function of, or reparation for, early neglect.

As with any mental illness or disorder, a holistic approach to care and treatment is more likely to encourage change for the better. A broad approach to multidisciplinary care can be split into four main categories: social, psychological, occupational and medical.

Social

People with BPD (and PD generally) can often find it difficult to maintain satisfying, fulfilling interpersonal relationships and manage the activities of daily living. As a consequence this can lead to isolation, lack of agency and a tendency to withdraw from community life. Support and encouragement to engage in community groups, service user organizations, drop-in centres and support services

Table 6.16.2 *Typical intrapersonal and interpersonal strategies of personality disorder*

	The world is ...	People are ...	I am ...	Commonest behavioural approach	Least likely to be ...	Emotional hot-spot
OCD PD	Sloppy	Irresponsible	Responsible	Control	Flexible	Making a mistake
Paranoid PD	A conspiracy	Devious	Always on guard	Watchfulness	Trusting	Being discriminated against
Schizoid PD	Uncaring	Pointless, replaceable	The only person I can depend on	Withdrawal	Emotionally available and close	Being over-cared-for and smothered by others
Narcissistic PD	A competition	Inferior	Special	Competitiveness	Humble	Loss of face or social rank or social status
Antisocial PD	Predatory	Weak	Autonomous and alone	Crushing	Gentle and sensitive	Perceiving exploitation
Histrionic PD	My audience	In competition for attention	Vivacious	Exhibitionism	Able to listen to others	Being actively or passively sidelined
Borderline PD	Contradictory	Untrustworthy	Ashamed	Self-harm	Able to show self-compassion	Abandonment
Dependent PD	Overwhelming	Stronger, more competent than me	Needy	Clinging	Self-sufficient	Making a decision
Avoidant PD	Evaluative	Judgemental	Inept	Inhibition	Assertive	Exposed ridicule or rejection
Schizotypal PD	Watchful	Peculiar	Confused	Yes rumination	Connected with others	When events mirror or conflict with fixed beliefs

helps to build interpersonal confidence and effective behavioural structures.

Adequate housing and advice around finances or benefits act to reduce stress and allow people to focus on other aspects of their difficulties or even to consider readiness for a formal psychotherapy.

Psychological

Psychological assessment and formulation, and their explicit use in developing individual treatment plans, guide both the client and care team (or professionals involved) on likely routes to achieving positive change. They can be an opportunity to learn about the different models of psychotherapy available and to explore whether the client is suited to, or able to make use of, a particular formal psychotherapy. In some situations, a formal psychological therapy may not be indicated or may represent more risk than likely benefit. This can be a useful outcome of assessment, encouraging choice, autonomy and responsibility, balancing risk and refocusing a care plan on, for instance, social or occupational interventions.

Individual and group psychotherapy, using a range of different models, can improve wellbeing, although, at present, evidence of efficacy is sparse (see below).

Occupational

An assessment of barriers to meaningful and sustainable employment facilitates thought towards education and training opportunities and ultimately employment.

Medical

Medical assessment from either GP or psychiatrist can help to identify the core problem, offer a diagnosis and make treatment decisions based on the available evidence. A diagnosis can also give access to further or more specialist treatment. To some clients 'naming' the problem can be helpful; to others it can seem a 'reductionist' or stigmatizing label.

Clients with a diagnosis of BPD (and PD) are more likely to have both physical and mental health comorbidity, which medical assessment can highlight and treat. There is a recognized tendency to neglect the physical health care of those with a mental disorder (Phelan and Stradin, 2001). Paying attention to these areas of neglect also helpfully challenges psychological procedures rooted within the core problem. Pharmacological

therapy for BPD will be discussed in the research section.

PSYCHOTHERAPEUTIC APPROACHES TO BORDERLINE PERSONALITY DISORDER

Different models or approaches to the psychotherapeutic treatment of BPD (and other personality disorders) vary in the detail of managing oneself and the therapeutic relationship. Despite this variety, there are core skills, values and strategies that run across the models that enable us to remain in a therapeutic position in relation to this client group. Adherence to the model or psychological framework can be containing for the client. This implicitly highlights therapeutic boundaries, offers consistency and guards against enactment of unhelpful responses. In opposition to the strict adherence to a model, it is widely acknowledged that professionals with rigidity to their working style or low tolerance to chaos are less likely to be helpful to clients with BPD. This represents a dialectic that can in some ways be seen as a reflection of the often changing states of mind that people with BPD can display across and within sessions. Essential to maintaining a therapeutic position, and managing this dichotomy, is the ability to stand back and reflect on our part in the relationship, and consider our own thoughts, feelings, impulses and motivations. This highlights the importance of supervision and the use of a safe, containing, non-judgemental space in which we can consider both the positive and (perhaps sometimes more importantly) the negative responses we may have to clients. From a wider perspective, in recent years an understanding has emerged of the importance of an explicit, collaborative approach between all the professionals, teams and organizations involved in BPD service provision:

> When providing psychological treatment for people with borderline personality disorder, especially those with multiple comorbidities and/or severe impairment, the following service characteristics should be in place: an explicit and integrated theoretical approach used by both the treatment team and the therapist, which is shared with the service user. (NICE, 2009)

This reduces the likelihood of 'splitting' and mitigates against increasing the fragmentation of the client's internal world (a goal of treatment often

Table 6.16.3 *Prevalence of borderline personality disorder*

Setting	Prevalence
People living in the community	5–13%
People in the prison population	50–70%
Service users in community mental health teams	30–40%
Psychiatric inpatients	40–50%

Source: NIMHE (2003)

being integration of separate aspects of the self). Within the therapeutic frame, working explicitly and using one's own genuine emotional responses offers an opportunity for a client to explore their part in the perpetuation of their difficulties and challenge their own sense of what might be in someone else's mind.

RESEARCH

In comparison with other mental disorders, e.g. schizophrenia, there is a dearth of research concerning the aetiology, epidemiology, phenomenology and efficacy/effectiveness of interventions in PD. For the benefit of this review we will consider the most common presentation, BPD. Estimates of the prevalence of BPD vary widely (Table 6.16.3). Despite these wide estimates of prevalence of BPD across populations, controversies around treatability, stigma and the validity of the diagnosis remain and have discouraged further research.

Pharmacology

Currently there is little evidence to support pharmacological treatment for the core symptoms of BPD. The NICE (2009) guideline for BPD drew evidence from a variety of sources, including meta-analyses of available trials (Binks et al., 2006a).

Medication can be used to treat a wide range of comorbid illness, for instance depression or obsessive compulsive disorder; however, its success can be limited.

Psychotherapy

There is a large body of research evidence that supports a variety of different approaches to BPD including psychodynamic psychotherapy, cognitive-behavioural therapy (CBT), dialectical behavioural therapy (DBT), cognitive analytic therapy (CAT) and others. Currently there is a national trend prioritizing measurable outcomes in line with cost effectiveness, and the majority of research in psychotherapy and BPD does not fall into this category. There are very few 'gold standard' randomized controlled trials comparing different psychotherapeutic models to each other or to treatment as usual. At present the only research which would fit into this category indicates weak evidence for DBT for women with BPD and associated high levels of self-harm or parasuicide, as cited in Binks et al. (2006b).

In summary, there is a paucity of understanding of the treatments and approaches that are most likely to help people with a diagnosis of BPD. There is possibly even less known about other PDs. This has a major impact on both the clients and families who experience the condition and the range of health, legal and social services that have contact with people with PD. For counsellors and psychotherapists in contact with this type of referral, a working model of risk assessment, good clinical supervision, organizational support and good enough fidelity to the treatment model appear to be the building blocks of effective PD practice.

REFERENCES

APA (2000) *Diagnostic and Statistical Manual of Mental Disorders* (4th edn text rev.). Washington, DC: American Psychiatric Association.

Beck, A.T. and Freeman, A. (1990) *Cognitive Therapy of Personality Disorders*. New York: Guilford.

Binks, C.A., Fenton, M., McCarthy, L., Lee, T., Adams, C.E. and Duggan, C. (2006a) Pharmacological interventions for people with borderline personality disorder. *Cochrane Database of Systematic Reviews 2006*, CD005653.

Binks, C.A., Fenton, M., McCarthy, L., Lee, T., Adams, C.E. and Duggan, C. (2006b) Psychological therapies for people with borderline personality disorder. *Cochrane Database of Systematic Reviews 2006*, CD005652.

Cloninger, C.R., Svrakic, D.M. and Przybeck, T.R. (1993) A psychobiological model of temperament and character. *Archives of General Psychiatry*, 50: 975–90.

Henderson, D.K. (1939) *Psychopathic States*. New York: Norton.

Koch, J.L.A. (1891) *Die psychopatischen minderwertigkeiter*. Ravernsberg: Dorn.

Kraepelin, E. (1905) *Lectures on Clinical Psychiatry* (2nd edn, trans. T. Johnstone). London: Bailliere-Tindall.

Maudsley, H. (1868) *The Physiology and Pathology of Mind*. London: Macmillan.

NICE (2009) *Guideline for Borderline Personality Disorder*. National Institute for Health and Clinical Excellence. www.nice.org.uk: CG78.

NIMHE (2003) *Personality Disorder: No Longer a Diagnosis of Exclusion*. National Institute for Mental Health in England. London: Department of Health.

Phelan, M. and Stradin, L. (2001) Physical health of people with severe mental illness. *British Medical Journal*, 2001: 322–443.

Pinel, P. (1802) *La Médecine Clinique*. Paris: Bayreuth.

Pritchard, J.C. (1835) *Treatise on Insanity and Other Disorders of the Mind*. Philadelphia: Harwell, Barrington and Harwell.

Rado, S. (1953) Dynamics and classification of disordered behaviour. *American Journal of Psychiatry*, 110: 406–16.

Schneider, K. (1959) *Clinical Psychopathology* (trans. M.W. Hamilton). London: Grune and Stratton.

WHO (1992) *ICD-10 Classification of Mental and Behavioural Disorders: Clinical Descriptions and Diagnostic Guidelines*. New York: World Health Organization.

Phobias

GILL DONOHOE AND TOM RICKETTS

A phobia can be described as a marked and persistent fear that is excessive or unreasonable, cued by the presence or anticipation of a specific object or situation (APA, 2000). There is a strong desire to avoid the feared situation despite a recognition, when the phobic stimulus is not present, that the fear is irrational.

Phobic disorders can be broadly categorized into three main groups: specific phobias, agoraphobia and social phobia. Although in theory an individual can become phobic about any stimulus, and rare cases do exist, the list of five categories for specific phobias, as indicated later, addresses all types seen in clinical practice.

The aims of this chapter are to introduce readers to the various phobic disorders, focusing upon shared and specific clinical features and to provide a conceptual base for understanding phobias by outlining key theories. The main treatment approaches will be outlined with an emphasis on cognitive-behavioural methods, as indicated by research and current clinical practice. Recent advances and ongoing debates in the field will conclude this chapter.

DESCRIPTION AND CLINICAL FEATURES

Phobic disorders all share the central feature of anxiety, which is experienced in anticipation of and/or upon confrontation with the feared situation or stimulus. Anxiety responses are intense and extreme and can present in the form of panic. Although symptoms are often negligible when the feared objects or situations are not encountered, some anxiety may occur at other times, for example in association with anticipation of confrontation. In addition, it is common for individuals with a phobic disorder to have at least one other anxiety disorder, with generalized anxiety being particularly common (Roth and Fonagy, 2005).

Individuals with phobic disorders may also experience panic attacks. These may only occur when faced with the phobic situation, and are referred to as situationally bound panic attacks. Panic attacks are more common in the case of agoraphobia, where they are often a central feature. Reference will therefore be made to panic attacks in this chapter, although for a more comprehensive account readers should refer to the chapter on anxiety and panicm (Chapter 6.6 in this volume).

In order to satisfy diagnostic criteria for a phobic disorder, the individual must experience difficulties carrying out daily activities impacting on the domestic, personal, occupational and relationship areas of their lives. If the person is able to avoid the feared stimulus, for example snakes or plane travel, then treatment may not be warranted or sought.

Individuals with phobic conditions commonly suffer difficulties for many years, with little evidence of spontaneous remission. At the same time, with current behavioural and cognitive-behavioural approaches, they are readily treated. Identification and the offer of intervention for sufferers is therefore a priority. Table 6.17.1 gives details of the prevalence, course and gender distributions of the different types of phobic disorder.

Table 6.17.1   *Epidemiological data for phobias*

Phobic disorder	Prevalence (lifetime risk)	Onset and course	Gender and distribution
Specific phobia	7.2–11.3%	Childhood	Depends upon subtype but generally higher proportion of women
Agoraphobia	1–2% (panic with or without agoraphobia) of whom one-third to one-half with panic disorder also have agoraphobia (with higher rates in clinical samples)	Late adolescence to mid thirties (agoraphobia usually within first year of panics)	Three times more frequent in women (panic without agoraphobia twice as frequent)
Social phobia	3–13%	Mid to late teens	More frequent in women in epidemiological samples but equal in clinical samples

Source: APA (2000)

SPECIFIC PHOBIAS

Specific phobias have in the past been referred to as simple phobias as the fear is confined to one main stimulus. Specific phobias can be further categorized according to the following types:

- animal type, including mammals, insects and reptiles
- natural environment type, for example storms, water, heights
- blood/injection/injury type
- situational type, for example, aeroplanes, lifts
- other type, for example, illness, choking or vomiting (APA, 2000).

In the case of specific phobias, the extreme fear is experienced immediately upon contact with the feared stimulus and is usually proportionate to the proximity.

The symptoms of anxiety experienced upon anticipation or actual contact with the phobic stimulus include the usual range of autonomic symptoms. However, the pattern of arousal seems to differ in one particular type of specific phobia, namely, blood/injection/injury. These individual sufferers commonly experience a vasovagal response whereby the blood pressure may rise as usual initially, but then drops rapidly causing a fainting response. It has been suggested that approximately 75 per cent of individuals with blood/injection/injury phobias report a history of fainting in phobic conditions (APA, 2000).

Agoraphobia

Agoraphobia is a complex phobia as it involves a wide range of feared situations. Anxiety symptoms occur on entering a variety of public situations, for example, crowded places such as shops, queues, public transport; open spaces; confined places; and any situations from which escape may be difficult or embarrassing and help unavailable. Distance from home or other places of safety and being alone are often key factors.

Agoraphobia appears to be closely linked to panic. This is reflected in diagnostic manuals (APA, 2000) which make the classification of 'panic disorder with or without agoraphobia'.

Panic attacks are characterized by the sudden onset of intense symptoms along with fears associated with the symptoms, for example, of dying or losing control. Symptoms include palpitations, sweating, trembling or shaking, shortness of breath or choking sensations, dizziness or feeling faint, numbness or tingling sensations, derealization (feelings of unreality) or depersonalization (feeling detached from self). The experience of at least four of these symptoms is required to meet the diagnostic criteria (APA, 2000).

Social Phobia

Social phobia is another more complex type of phobia, although some individuals present with more specific social fears. Although triggered by social interaction, the nature of the fear is associated with prediction of less observable events, such as being rejected or viewed negatively by others. Specific fears may include public speaking or eating in public.

UNDERSTANDING PHOBIAS

There has been, and remains, much debate about how and why phobias develop. Although one single theory does not appear to account for the acquisition and maintenance of all phobias, most of the progress in understanding has arisen from conditioning and learning theory accounts. Learning theories suggest that emotional responses such as fear can be learnt in a similar way to other aspects of human development.

The learning theory of phobias incorporates the principles of classical and operant conditioning. Pavlov and other Russian physiologists conducted animal experiments in the early to middle part of the last century which demonstrated that dogs, for example, could be conditioned to salivate at the sound of a bell. It was shown that by repeatedly pairing food (an unconditioned stimulus resulting in the unconditioned response of salivation) with the sound of a bell, the bell eventually became a conditioned stimulus resulting in salivation (conditioned response) even in the absence of food. Thus, the principles are based upon the notion that previously neutral stimuli can develop stimulating properties and provoke new responses if repeatedly presented with another stimulus. In the case of phobias, the new or conditioned response is fear.

The second learning principle is based upon operant conditioning, whereby learning is dependent upon the consequences following the behaviour. For example, if a behaviour is rewarded, then it is more likely to occur in the future. Similarly, a behaviour which is followed by the removal of something the individual finds unpleasant is also rewarded, and is also more likely to occur again in future. These examples are termed positive and negative reinforcement respectively.

In applying these principles to the development and maintenance of phobias, they can be understood to be acquired through the process of classical conditioning and maintained by the effects of negative reinforcement, specifically the rapid reduction of anxiety which follows escape from or avoidance of the phobic situation.

To acquire a phobia through the above process, the individual must experience and associate traumatic or aversive stimuli with the phobic object until the latter develops these properties. While this is reportedly the case for many individuals suffering from phobias, there are cases where such conditioning events have not occurred. This has prompted the suggestion that phobic anxiety may also arise simply through the observation of fearful others, or through being told about potentially fear-invoking stimuli or circumstances. This 'three pathways to fear' model (Rachman, 1977) has found good empirical support, suggesting that the acquisition of phobic anxiety may come about through multiple routes.

Maintenance of phobias through negative reinforcement of escape and avoidance is best understood as preventing the spontaneous reduction of fear. In the absence of escape and avoidance, repeated contact with the phobic stimulus reduces the link between the situation and fear. After repeated contact, the previously fearful stimulus becomes neutral, no longer triggering an anxiety response.

THERAPY

Research studies and reviews on the effectiveness of therapies for phobic disorders have found exposure therapy to be the primary treatment of choice, with the incorporation of cognitive approaches and other strategies such as applied relaxation in some cases (see below). There seems to be no indication and little evidence for the use of non-directive counselling approaches or for the use of medication as the main approach (Roth and Fonagy, 2005).

Treatment is based upon a detailed assessment and analysis of the presenting difficulty along with any other associated problems. This includes a history of the development of the problem. The assessment information is then discussed with the client within a cognitive-behavioural framework. This forms the first stage of therapy, the main purpose of which is to educate the client on the principles of the approach and the rationale for the treatment plan based upon their difficulties.

EXPOSURE THERAPY

Exposure therapy involves repeated, prolonged confrontation with the feared stimuli until the discomfort reduces and is no longer evoked by further contact. Exposure therapy should be *in vivo* (live) wherever possible and also should be graded, prolonged and repeated regularly (Marks, 1981). To achieve this, exposure tasks should be practised by the client as homework, either with or without the help of a partner or spouse.

The components of exposure can be summarized as follows:

1   *Education and instruction on the nature and principles of exposure therapy.* As homework practice is essential for successful therapy, the client's full understanding and active involvement are required. The therapist must enable the client to be their own therapist, giving them all the tools and knowledge available.

2   *Construction of a hierarchy for graded tasks.* This should be negotiated with the client based on agreed overall goals and assessment outcome. The hierarchy should represent the

range of phobic and avoided situations in order of difficulty. Each situation can be rated according to the anxiety evoked or degree of avoidance (for example, on a 0–8 scale). Each step should be practical and realistic with equal spacing between steps where possible.

3 *Exposure tasks.* Exposure therapy may be therapist assisted or self-directed. It can be conducted in a group or with a friend or spouse. If therapist-assisted exposure is the chosen method, it is important to consider the effects of the therapist's (or relevant others') presence and plan to phase this out. Ultimately, the client must be able to manage phobic situations alone and not have to depend on the presence of others. Whether alone or accompanied, within each session, the client monitors his/her level of anxiety and remains within the situation until this has reduced (at least two points on a 0–8 scale). The client is encouraged to focus upon the phobic object (e.g. spider) or the situation (e.g. supermarket) rather than distract themselves. The client may refer to other strategies if utilized, for example, applied relaxation or helpful self-talk (see below).

4 *Homework tasks.* If the exposure task has been conducted within a treatment session, whether accompanied or alone, this should be followed by further practice, which must be specified and agreed between client and therapist along with any relevant others. It is preferable that the task is based upon that which has already been completed so that the client can consolidate their learning.

ADDITIONAL AND ALTERNATIVE STRATEGIES

Although some form of exposure therapy should be the first treatment of choice in the majority of cases, some individuals and types of phobia may require additional strategies or a focus on cognitive approaches.

Applied Tension

Individuals with blood/injection/injury phobias frequently experience fainting when presented with blood- or injury-associated stimuli due to the unique physiological response. Applied tension is a technique developed specifically for these individuals in order to control the fainting response and is therefore used in conjunction with exposure therapy. Individuals are taught to tense key muscle groups which in turn increases cerebral blood flow and helps to control fainting (see Ost and Sterner, 1987).

Cognitive Therapy

Cognitive factors are clearly implicated in the maintenance of certain phobias and, in the case of panic and social phobias, specific cognitive models have been developed (Clark, 2005; Clark and Beck, 2009). Whether cognitive approaches are superior to or enhance traditional exposure therapy programmes for phobias has been the focus of research, but so far real benefit has only been shown in the case of social phobia (Clark et al., 2006). Cognitive therapy has demonstrated significant benefits for depression (see Beck et al., 1979) and therefore should be considered if this is a major difficulty.

Cognitive strategies, as initially developed by Beck, focus upon identification and modification of faulty thinking styles by a variety of means, including verbal disputation and behavioural experimentation. For further reading, see Wells (1997) and Clarke and Beck (2009).

Skills Training

Social skills and assertiveness training approaches may have an important role to play, particularly in the case of social phobia. Social skill deficits often accompany social phobic difficulties; therefore skill levels should be assessed and training approaches used if appropriate. Skills training may incorporate education, modelling, role play and rehearsal of specific skills, feedback and real-life practice.

Drug Treatment

Antidepressant and anxiolytic drugs have been utilized, although they have only demonstrated short-term benefits and have not been found to be superior to cognitive-behavioural therapy programmes. Medication is certainly not indicated for specific phobias and most of the research has focused upon agoraphobia. This research has found that medication is not as effective as cognitive-behavioural approaches and relapse is more likely. There is some suggestion, however, that antidepressants may have some slight benefits when combined with psychological methods (Roth and Fonagy, 2005).

ADVANCES AND DEBATES

The efficacy of exposure-based approaches is well established, but there is increasing recognition of the insufficiency of conditioning theories alone to explain fear processes (Barlow, 2004).

Developments in cognitive psychology and cognitive therapy have led to models and interventions to help clients who have not benefited from purely exposure-based methods. In practice, the majority of clinicians now claim to be utilizing cognitive-behavioural methods, demonstrating how well these approaches have been integrated. However, research is still required to determine which aspects of therapy have what effect on which symptoms. For example, although we know that in the majority of cases exposure works, how does it work? Is it through the deconditioning process or is it as a result of the client's reappraisal of the stimulus? Research has focused on the differences between specific approaches (e.g. cognitive versus exposure therapy) in order to determine which has more potency with which type of difficulty or symptom. As cognitive therapy would normally incorporate some aspect of fear confrontation, it has not always been easy to achieve. As suggested previously, for those with a diagnosis of social phobia or panic disorder, cognitive models have been developed and have received good research support. However, further research is required on the effectiveness of therapy, particularly in the case of social phobia.

The emphasis on tailoring treatment to individual clients has developed in conjunction with the need to investigate more efficient and client-led approaches. In the UK the Improving Access to Psychological Therapies programme (Clark et al., 2009) has enhanced access to 'low-intensity' approaches (Richards and White, 2009) such as guided self-help, telephone interventions, computerized cognitive-behaviour therapy (NICE, 2006) and large-group interventions (White, 1995) for clients suffering from anxiety disorders. Initial results indicate that large numbers of people with phobic conditions can be assisted through the implementation of such approaches, when the outcomes for individuals are closely monitored (Clark et al., 2009). Further evaluation of these approaches is being undertaken as they are being implemented.

REFERENCES

APA (2000) *Diagnostic and Statistical Manual of Mental Disorders* (4th edn text rev.). Washington, DC: American Psychiatric Association.

Barlow, D.H. (2004) *Anxiety and Its Disorders: The Nature and Treatment of Anxiety and Panic.* New York: Guilford.

Beck, A.T., Rush, A.J., Shaw, B.F. and Emery, G. (1979) *Cognitive Therapy of Depression.* New York: Guilford.

Clark, D.M. (2005) A cognitive perspective on social phobia. In W.R. Crozier and L.F. Alden (eds), *The Essential Handbook of Social Anxiety for Clinicians.* Chichester: Wiley.

Clark, D.M. and Beck, A.T. (2009) *Cognitive Therapy of Anxiety Disorders.* New York: Guilford.

Clark, D., Ehlers, A., McManus, F., Fennell, M., Grey, N., Waddington, L. and Wild, J. (2006) Cognitive therapy versus exposure and applied relaxation in social phobia: a randomised controlled trial. *Journal of Consulting and Clinical Psychology*, 74: 568–78.

Clark, D.M., Layard, R., Smithies, R., Richards, D.A., Suckling, R. and Wright, B. (2009) Improving access to psychological therapy: initial evaluation of two UK demonstration sites. *Behaviour Research and Therapy*, 47: 910–20.

Marks, I.M. (1981) *Cure and Care of Neurosis.* Chichester: Wiley.

NICE (2006) *Technology Appraisal 97: Computerised Cognitive Behaviour Therapy for Depression and Anxiety (Review).* London: National Institute for Health and Clinical Excellence.

Ost, L.G. and Sterner, U. (1987) Applied tension: a specific behavioural method for treatment of blood phobia. *Behaviour Research and Therapy*, 25 (1): 25–9.

Rachman, S. (1977) The conditioning theory of fear acquisition: a critical examination. *Behaviour Research and Therapy*, 22: 109–17.

Richards, D. and Whyte, M. (2009) *Reach Out: National Programme. Student Materials to Support the Delivery of Training for Psychosociological Wellbeing Practitioners Delivering Low Intensity Interventions* (2nd edn). London: Rethink.

Roth, A. and Fonagy, P. (2005) *What Works for Whom? A Critical Review of Psychotherapy Research* (2nd edn). New York: Guilford.

Wells, A. (1997) *Cognitive Therapy of Anxiety Disorders: A Practice Manual and Conceptual Guide.* Chichester: Wiley.

White, J. (1995) Stresspac: a controlled trial of a self-help package for the anxiety disorders. *Behavioural and Cognitive Psychotherapy*, 23: 89–107.

Post-Traumatic Stress Disorder

CLAUDIA HERBERT

Trauma can shatter lives. Of people experiencing a traumatic event, 25–30 per cent may go on to develop post-traumatic stress disorder (PTSD: NICE, 2005). Davidson (2000) suggested that for those affected, the costs of PTSD are so heavy that it must be viewed as the most serious of all psychiatric problems. Although professional and public awareness of PTSD has significantly increased in recent years and scientific research has flourished, assessing, diagnosing and treating trauma-related problems remains a challenge for many therapists, and clients can go unnoticed, misdiagnosed or untreated for their PTSD for many years. This chapter offers therapists an overview of the major clinical issues relevant to understanding, recognizing and assessing PTSD and provides guidance as to its effective treatment.

WHAT IS POST-TRAUMATIC STRESS DISORDER?

Historical Perspective

While PTSD has been around for centuries under the guise of different names, only as recently as 1980 was it officially described by the American Psychiatric Association (APA) as an emotional disorder in the third edition of the *Diagnostic and Statistical Manual of Mental Disorders* (*DSM-III*). In the past, most commonly PTSD has been associated with soldiers, but increasingly it has been recognized that it can develop in any person at any age in response to overwhelming and threatening life events. Most of the early advances in PTSD research and practice took place in the US. In 1992 the term complex post-traumatic stress disorder (C-PTSD) was coined by American psychiatrist Judith Herman, who described it as a separate diagnostic entity to PTSD. In 1994 a seminal paper entitled 'The body keeps the score', written by American psychiatrist and neuroscientist Bessel van der Kolk, influenced the change towards a whole new understanding of trauma and PTSD, which began to acknowledge the role of neurobiology and the body in trauma. In 1995 the first ever therapeutic self-help book for trauma survivors and their families (Herbert, 1995/2007) was published in the UK, leading the way towards increased client understanding and education about PTSD (Herbert and Wetmore, 1999/2008; Collard, 2003; Herbert, 2011). In the last decade neuroscientific research has advanced understanding of PTSD further; it is increasingly being recognized as a psycho-neurobiological condition, largely determined by the responses of the autonomic nervous system in the body.

Classification of Post-traumatic Stress Disorder

Two different systems are used for the diagnosis of PTSD: the *ICD-10* (*International Classification of Mental and Behavioural Disorders*: WHO, 1993), often used by psychiatrists within the health service, and the *DSM* classification system, currently in its fourth revised edition (*DSM-IV-TR*: APA, 2000), soon to be replaced by *DSM-V* (expected 2013). Interestingly, concordance between the two diagnostic systems has been found to be only 35 per cent, with clients having a 6.9 per cent PTSD prevalence when diagnosed with *ICD-10* criteria compared to a 3 per cent PTSD prevalence when diagnosed with *DSM-IV-TR* criteria (Andrews et al., 1999). Due to the more stringent standards, the APA's *DSM* classification system seems to be preferred in PTSD research and will guide the PTSD diagnostic criteria referred to in this chapter.

What Classifies as a Trauma?

The proposed revision for *DSM-V* (APA *DSM-V* Task Force, 2010) states as criterion A that in order to qualify for a diagnosis of PTSD, a person has to have been exposed to one or more of the following event(s): death or threatened death, actual or threatened serious injury, or actual or threatened sexual violation, in one or more of the following ways:

1   experiencing the event(s) him/herself
2   witnessing in person the event(s) as they occurred to others
3   learning that the event(s) occurred to a close relative or close friend; in such cases, the actual or threatened death must have been violent or accidental
4   experiencing repeated or extreme exposure to aversive details of the event(s) (e.g. first responders collecting body parts; police officers repeatedly exposed to details of child abuse); this does not apply to exposure through electronic media, television, movies or pictures, unless this exposure is work related.

These revisions provide a more encompassing description of the means by which a person may have been exposed to trauma when compared to *DSM-IV* classification criteria; condition 2 of criterion A in *DSM-IV*, which states that a person's response needs to have involved intense fear, helplessness and horror, has been lifted. This is helpful as it allows for the diagnosis of PTSD in people who were unconscious at the time of a trauma or who developed PTSD as a result of waking up during anaesthesia, but cannot report experiencing any of these responses at the time. Currently, the proposed revisions for *DSM-V* do not make provision for C-PTSD as a separate disorder, and therefore diagnostically this has to be accounted for within the specified criteria for PTSD. However, these fail to capture some of the core characteristics of C-PTSD, which arise out of (1) situations of prolonged and repeated severe threat or danger, often spanning months or years, from which the victim cannot escape, for example, torture, hostage taking or living in war zones and conflict-ridden territories and/or dictatorships; and/or (2) pervasive relational- or attachment-based trauma, for example, domestic, institutional, ritual and/or childhood sexual, physical or emotional abuse. Sufferers of C-PTSD may not remember any or all of the traumatic event(s), depending on their developmental age, the severity, multiplicity and longevity of the exposure and the support system available at the time.

CLINICAL ASSESSMENT OF PTSD

Clinical assessment of PTSD usually involves a person fulfilling the requisite number and severity of symptoms specified by the diagnostic system used, obtained either during clinical interview, often combined with administration of standardized questionnaires, or through self-administered questionnaire measures taken on their own. However, this widely accepted PTSD assessment practice does not automatically ensure accuracy, and many trauma clients remain misdiagnosed or are not recognized as suffering from PTSD because they report 'coping alright'. Conferring an accurate diagnosis of PTSD is greatly influenced by a client's ability to perceive and report their symptoms correctly and a therapist's ability to hear and understand the client's symptoms and to determine whether a client meets the required diagnostic threshold. Additionally, therapists need to be able to distinguish between PTSD and C-PTSD and they need to be able to recognize the symptoms of avoidance and those falling into the spectrum of dissociation. Further, therapists need to be able to establish a therapeutic environment of safety and trust in order for a trauma client to feel secure enough to report their symptoms accurately and fully without feeling retraumatized by the assessment. This requires specialist clinical skills that move far beyond mere knowledge of the prevailing diagnostic criteria, but require acute sensitivity and an astute knowledge of the psychoneurobiological factors underlying PTSD, which need to guide assessment and subsequent trauma therapy.

What are the Diagnostic Symptoms of Post-Traumatic Stress Disorder?

If a person meets the conditions for trauma under criterion A, the proposed revision of *DSM-V* states that seven further criteria have to be met in order to qualify for a diagnosis of PTSD. Four of these criteria (B, C, D and E) describe four different symptom clusters out of which a particular number of symptoms have to be met, and three criteria state additional requirements which have to be fulfilled. The proposed *DSM-V* revisions of four symptom clusters reflect research studies (Amdur and Liberzon, 2001) which have found evidence for four clusters but never for the three clusters used in previous *DSM-IV* classifications for PTSD.

Criterion B: intrusion symptoms

These are associated with the traumatic event(s) and began after the traumatic event(s), as evidenced by one or more of the following:

1　spontaneous or cued recurrent, involuntary, and intrusive distressing memories of the traumatic event(s) (in children, repetitive play may occur in which themes or aspects of the traumatic event(s) are expressed)
2　recurrent distressing dreams in which the content and/or affect of the dream is related to the event(s) (in children, there may be frightening dreams without recognizable content)
3　dissociative reactions (e.g. flashbacks) in which the individual feels or acts as if the traumatic event(s) were recurring; such reactions may occur on a continuum, with the most extreme expression being a complete loss of awareness of present surroundings (in children, trauma-specific re-enactment may occur in play)
4　intense or prolonged psychological distress at exposure to internal or external cues that symbolize or resemble an aspect of the traumatic event(s)
5　marked physiological reactions to reminders of the traumatic event(s).

Criterion C: persistent avoidance

This is of stimuli associated with the traumatic event(s) and began after the traumatic event(s), as experienced by efforts to avoid one or more of the following:

1　avoiding internal reminders (thoughts, feelings, or physical sensations) that arouse recollections of the traumatic event(s)
2　avoiding external reminders (people, places, conversations, activities, objects, situations) that arouse recollections of the traumatic event(s).

Criterion D: negative alterations in cognitions and mood

These are associated with the traumatic event(s) and began or worsened after the traumatic event(s), as evidenced by three or more of the following (in children, as evidenced by two or more of the following):

1　inability to remember an important aspect of the traumatic event(s) (typically dissociative amnesia; not due to head injury, alcohol or drugs)
2　persistent and exaggerated negative expectations about one's self, others, or the world (e.g. 'I am bad', 'no one can be trusted', 'I've lost my soul forever', 'my whole nervous system is permanently ruined', 'the world is completely dangerous')
3　persistent distorted blame of self or others about the cause or consequences of the traumatic event(s)
4　pervasive negative emotional state (e.g. fear, horror, anger, guilt or shame)
5　markedly diminished interest or participation in significant activities
6　feelings of detachment or estrangement from others
7　persistent inability to experience positive emotions (e.g. unable to have loving feelings, psychic numbing).

Criterion E: alterations in arousal and reactivity

These are associated with the traumatic event(s) and began or worsened after the traumatic event(s), as evidenced by three or more of the following (in children, as evidenced by two or more of the following):

1　irritable or aggressive behaviour
2　reckless or self-destructive behaviour
3　hypervigilance
4　exaggerated startle response
5　problems with concentration
6　sleep disturbance (e.g. difficulty falling or staying asleep, or restless sleep).

Additional requirements

Additionally, criterion F states that the duration of the disturbance, as evidenced by the required number of symptoms in criteria B, C, D and E, has to have been more than one month in order for it to qualify for a diagnosis of PTSD. Criterion G requires that the disturbance causes clinically significant distress or impairment in social, occupational or other important areas of functioning. Criterion H postulates that the disturbance is not due to the direct physiological effects of a substance (e.g. medication or alcohol) or a general medical condition (e.g. traumatic brain injury, coma). Lastly, if the above symptoms and requirements are not fully met until six months or more after the traumatic event(s), a diagnosis of PTSD with delayed onset needs to be made (although onset of some of the symptoms can occur sooner than this).

The proposed revisions provide some improvement on earlier *DSM-IV* versions of PTSD diagnostic criteria. However, they still fail to address one of the greatest areas of confusion from the perspective of a practising clinician (Herbert, 2006), which is the distinction between the psychological effects of a single isolated traumatic event (type I) or multiple such events (type II) and those of long-term, enduring trauma during early childhood, critical stages of development or adult situations of extreme duress (type III). While all of these groups may meet diagnostic criteria for PTSD, the assessment needs of the third group differ and require extensive therapeutic skill and knowledge of additional symptoms, such as severe psychological fragmentation into different, often separate personality structures, alterations in perception of the perpetrator (Stockholm syndrome), absence of internal self-regulatory ability, and attachment problems, e.g. problems with relationship boundaries and lack of empathy (see Herbert, 2006 for a more extensive review). These are not outlined in the current diagnostic criteria for PTSD and move beyond the scope of this chapter.

PTSD COMORBIDITY

Research has indicated that PTSD shows a severe and diverse pattern of comorbidity (Keane et al., 2007). Of individuals diagnosed with PTSD, 92 per cent met criteria for another, current axis I disorder, most frequently major depression (77 per cent), generalized anxiety disorder (38 per cent) and alcohol abuse/dependence (31 per cent). Studies examining veterans diagnosed with PTSD (Dunn et al., 2004; Bollinger et al., 2000) found high comorbidity with an axis II disorder (between 50 and 79 per cent). It is not uncommon in clinical practice that clients are initially referred by their GP to a therapist for help with their comorbid symptoms and, depending on the level of the treating therapist's own knowledge of PTSD, this gets diagnosed during the assessment stage or remains undiagnosed and untreated.

NEUROBIOLOGICAL FACTORS UNDERLYING PTSD

Our brain can be understood to be organized into three brain structures (triune brain: MacLean, 1990) which must interact and affect each other in order to ensure cohesive and integrated functioning. Each of these three brain structures is interconnected by nerves to the other two, but each operates with its own distinct capacities.

Lanius et al. (2006) outline the importance of the hypothalamus as the primary sensory gateway for all information reaching the neocortex. All sensory information, except olfaction, is routed through the hypothalamus to the neocortex. This enables the resonance between lower brain structures (reptilian brain complex and limbic system) and top brain structures (neocortex) and integrates top-down and bottom-up processing.

In order to protect and increase a person's chances of survival from the emotional and/or physical pain of traumatic experiences, a split in consciousness takes place in a person, whereby the traumatic material becomes disconnected (dissociated) from active consciousness (disconnected from or only partially connected to certain neocortical structures of the brain). Recent research indicates decreased hypothalamic activity in sufferers of PTSD and complete shut down of hypothalamic activity in complex trauma sufferers (Lanius et al., 2006).The hypothalamic shutdown would explain why traditional talking therapies or cognitive approaches, which rely on change through rational, top-down processing, cannot tackle the trauma memories that are held in the body.

When an experience is registered as overwhelming and possibly life threatening, the amygdala (part of the limbic system) is activated, functioning like an internal security camera, signalling alarm within 7–20 milliseconds while at the same time taking 'snapshots' of the sensory, somatic and emotional details of a person's frightening experience. Such alarm activates the innate arousal system through the brain stem (part of reptilian brain), which together with the amygdala prepares the body initially for 'fight' or 'flight' reactions; if this is not possible in a particular situation, it initiates the 'freeze' response, the most serious of all trauma-related responses (Levine, 1997; Rothschild, 2000; 2010). The rise in sympathetic nervous system activity releases specific neurochemicals, which close down activity of the frontal lobes (part of the neocortex), and cortisol shuts down the hippocampus (another part of the limbic system) (Lanius et al., 2006).

While arrest of higher-order brain structures, which operate more slowly and are not necessary for the immediate survival of the organism, is a highly adaptive solution to situations of threat in evolutionary terms, it hinders processing and integration of the emotional, sensory and bodily responses attached to the traumatic event(s) into a person's conscious memory system, and instead these stay stored as 'fragmentary snapshots' in non-verbal body memory systems. They become 'timeless', which means that although an event may have happened a long time ago, a person re-experiencing these 'snapshots' feels as if they were happening in the here-and-now despite the memory's actual content belonging to the past. While unprocessed, retriggering of these memories and associated emotional, sensory and somatic arousal symptoms can occur through external and internal stimuli that resemble aspects of the original traumatic experience. Retriggering is controlled by autonomic nervous system functioning and thus takes place outside a person's conscious control, and can feel overwhelmingly strong and significantly interfere with day-to-day life.

THERAPEUTIC APPROACHES WITH PTSD

It will already have become apparent to the reader of this chapter how complex the work with PTSD and trauma-related problems actually is. This stands in the face of currently promoted 'so-called' effectiveness- and cost-driven fast fixes and cures for PTSD, which if applied incorrectly could do more damage than good. Due to the underlying psychoneurobiological nature of PTSD, the resulting arousal and survival responses driven by the autonomic nervous system, and the increased sensitivity to threat, specific therapeutic factors must be adhered to in order to ensure safe and successful PTSD assessment and therapy.

Therapeutic Skills in the Assessment and Treatment of PTSD

Successful assessment and therapy for PTSD can only take place under conditions that feel safe to a PTSD client, as anything else will immediately retrigger uncomfortable autonomic arousal reactions and survival-based coping responses, which maintain or even increase the PTSD severity and block any possibility of processing and integrating the traumatic content held in split-off memories. Safety in this context will be determined both by factors in the therapeutic environment and by factors relating to the therapist and the therapeutic relationship.

In order to determine factors in the therapeutic environment, each client's particular needs have to be understood. For example, a PTSD client who survived torture may not feel very safe in a small therapy room without a window, in which the door is shut; or a PTSD client who has experienced medical trauma may not feel very safe being assessed and treated in a hospital setting or rooms that have a sterile medical feel to them. It is important that careful planning goes into the environment in which trauma assessment and therapy are offered,

that the needs of individual PTSD clients are considered, and that adverse client reactions are validated as indicators of something feeling unsafe that may need to be changed, rather than being dismissed as a client's unreasonable 'acting-out' behaviour. This is especially important during the initial assessment and the early treatment stages of therapy, when trust and a safe therapeutic relationship are still being established and it is unlikely that a therapist will know of a PTSD client's exact traumatic experiences.

Factors Contributing to the Perceived Safety of a Therapist

These include:

- ability to tolerate uncertainty and unexpected 'interference' (e.g. sudden flashbacks)
- flexibility and responsiveness to each client's needs, including patience
- emotional maturity, integrity and authenticity
- ability to form safe, empathic, non-threatening and non-threatened relationships, even in the face of highly charged client emotions and accounts of potentially horrific and dehumanizing trauma
- sensitive attunement to each PTSD client's emotional and bodily dysregulation symptoms to help them reground.

Additionally, it is important that trauma therapists have processed their own traumatic experiences, as these could otherwise interfere with and limit their ability to be helpful to their clients.

Another factor determining safety relates to session length and pacing of sessions. Due to the high levels of autonomic arousal in PTSD, clients often require considerable time before they feel calm enough to engage safely in any assessment or therapeutic work. PTSD clients frequently report that the traditional 50- to 60-minute session time framework doesn't work for them, as it does not give them enough time to safely open up, process and then safely close and contain some of the painful content they are bringing. It is therefore important that session length is individually tailored to each PTSD client's needs (rather than the therapist's convenience) in order for therapy to have a positive therapeutic effect and not to retraumatize them (Herbert, 2006).

Lastly, therapists must also be aware of helping each of their clients during assessment and therapy to stay within their individual 'window of tolerance' (Ogden and Minton, 2000; Siegel, 1999), which describes the level of autonomic and emotional arousal that is most effective for the creation of wellbeing and good functioning. This requires significant therapist skill, because of PTSD clients' tendency to have too much arousal (hyperarousal) or too little (hypoarousal) or to swing erratically between the two.

Therapeutic Approaches for the Treatment of PTSD

Since 2005, national guidelines (NICE) have existed in Britain for the care and treatment of people suffering from PTSD. These recommend:

- People at potential risk of developing PTSD following a traumatic event should be screened one month after the event.
- Trauma-focused psychological treatment should be offered to all people with PTSD.
- Drug treatments should not be used as a routine first-line treatment for adults in preference to a trauma-focused psychological therapy.
- Trauma-focused cognitive-behavioural psychotherapy (T-CBT: Friedman et al., 2007) and eye movement desensitization and reprocessing (EMDR: Shapiro, 1989; 2001; 2002) are the only two psychological treatments shown as effective in randomized controlled trials (RCTs) to specifically address PTSD sufferers' troubling memories and the personal meanings of the traumatic event and its consequences.
- All clients suffering from single-event PTSD should be offered a course of initially 8–12 sessions (longer sessions of at least 90 minutes are recommended when the trauma is discussed) of either T-CBT or EMDR on an individual outpatient basis regardless of the time that has elapsed since the trauma.
- If several problems need to be addressed in the treatment of PTSD, particularly after multiple traumatic events or traumatic bereavement, or where chronic disability resulting from the trauma, significant comorbid disorders or social problems are present, the duration of treatment should be extended beyond the recommended 12 sessions.
- For those PTSD sufferers who may initially find it difficult and overwhelming to disclose details of their traumatic events, it is recommended that health-care professionals should consider devoting several sessions to establishing a trusting therapeutic relationship and emotional stabilization before addressing the traumatic event.

It moves beyond the scope of this chapter to give a detailed outline of the elements entailed in T-CBT and EMDR. Both forms of therapy aim to reconnect the client with traumatic material which has been so distressing that the client's system has been unable to integrate it and had to shut it out. T-CBT utilizes a collaborative approach with clients, which includes an element of psycho-education about common reactions to trauma that normalizes the PTSD sufferer's symptoms, and a rationale for the interventions. Additionally, T-CBT includes one or more of the following groups of treatment techniques: exposure, cognitive therapy and stress management. When clients are deemed ready to reconnect with the traumatic material, either imaginal or *in vivo* exposure to the traumatic event(s) or the most distressing aspects of it is used. Negative thoughts, beliefs and assumptions in relation to the trauma and the client's PTSD responses are noted, and therapist and client aim to work together to modify these during the course of treatment.

EMDR follows an information processing approach which is aligned with the neurobiological processes related to PTSD and allows for top-down and bottom-up processing, enabling processing of traumatic body memories. EMDR can be integrated as a therapeutic modality into any type of psychotherapy, including psychodynamic, integrative, CBT and others. Therefore, the initial phases of EMDR will to a certain extent be determined by each individual therapist's therapeutic orientation. However, in EMDR therapists would then follow a standard treatment protocol, which proceeds through eight different phases. Phase 1 involves taking a detailed client history and also an educational component, explaining to clients the information processing model of EMDR and how it can help with PTSD. EMDR recognizes the need for stabilization and safety building in PTSD and, during phases 2–7, EMDR therapists would firstly install a safe place as an inner stabilization resource, and only subsequently target and reprocess the disturbing traumatic memories. A form of bilateral stimulation, tailored to the client's preferences, would be employed for this by the therapist. This can be bilateral eye movements, or bilateral tapping, touch or movement, or bilateral sound. Throughout processing, changes in clients' subjective levels of distress (SUDS) are monitored, and also their ability to replace their negative cognition in relation to the targeted memory with a more positive cognition (VOC). Phase 8 entails re-evaluation of the targeted processed memories to determine whether the next steps need to involve further processing of the chosen target or completion of the chosen target has been achieved, which would allow either moving to a new target or completing the session.

Several alternative EMDR treatment protocols are available and can be utilized to work with more complex PTSD presentations.

Whatever the treatment approach, it does require considerable sensitivity, pacing and clinical skill on behalf of the therapist to help a PTSD client reconnect with the traumatic material safely. Such reconnection is achieved through the client's internal feelings of safety in the here-and-now of the therapeutic relationship. For some single-event PTSD clients it is relatively easy to experience safety in their relationship with the therapist; however, for those who have experienced sudden traumatic loss or experienced multiple traumatic events, and also for C-PTSD clients, this can be very difficult to achieve. In both T-CBT and EMDR, a client can be retraumatized if the above described conditions for safety are not met during treatment, which is usually recognized by either a worsening in PTSD symptoms or the client's premature termination of therapy.

Despite the existence of several other models of trauma therapy – some of which, for example sensorimotor psychotherapy (Ogden and Minton, 2000), have been specifically developed to address the neurobiological and somatic effects of trauma – according to NICE guidelines PTSD sufferers should be informed that there is as yet no convincing evidence for a clinically important effect of any other treatments for PTSD. While scientific research and examination of therapies for their effectiveness in the treatment of PTSD should be welcomed, the overemphasis on RCTs as the only perceived gold standard for an evidence base makes it very difficult for other newer and potentially also effective psychotherapies to be established and validated. Further, it could be argued that the apparent overemphasis on measuring therapies' effectiveness with single-event PTSD is misleading, because in clinical practice it is rarely found that clients suffer from a single-event trauma only. Frequently, although referred as a result of having experienced a single-event trauma, for example a road traffic accident, a much more multifaceted and complex trauma picture emerges in the course of the trauma processing. This can potentially be very disconcerting for the novice trauma therapist, who may not be sufficiently skilled to deal with the clinical scenario of multiple-event PTSD emerging once Pandora's box has opened, potentially putting the client at significant clinical risk.

In light of the actual complexity of PTSD-related trauma work, Herbert (2006) suggested in her therapeutic spectrum for trauma and positive growth therapy (Herbert, 2002; 2006; revised in Herbert and Wetmore, 2008) that, rather than measuring individual therapeutic modalities with each other for comparative effectiveness, it would be far more

useful to design a model which incorporated different therapeutic factors, based on current psychoneurobiological understanding of trauma and PTSD, which should be part of all effective trauma therapies. These factors would then need to be tailored to each PTSD client's individual needs and requirements, depending on the complexity of their traumatic experiences and PTSD. Such a model moves away from the assumption that any singular modality can serve all PTSD clients and allows for a more holistic and integrative approach to the treatment of trauma, which for many clients provides the stepping stone toward recovery and positive growth.

REFERENCES

Amdur, R.L. and Liberzon, I. (2001) The structure of posttraumatic stress disorder symptoms in combat veterans: a confirmatory factor analysis of the impact of event scale. *Journal of Anxiety Disorders*, 15: 345–57.

Andrews, G., Slade, T. and Peters, L. (1999) Classification in psychiatry: ICD-10 versus DSM-IV. *British Journal of Psychiatry*, 174: 3–5.

APA (2000) *Diagnostic and Statistical Manual of Mental Disorders (DSM-IV-TR)*. Arlington, VA: American Psychiatric Association.

APA *DSM-V* Task Force (2010) *Proposed Draft Revisions to DSM Disorders and Criteria, Diagnostic and Statistical Manual of Mental Disorders (DSM-V)*. Arlington, VA: American Psychiatric Association.

Bollinger, A., Riggs, D., Blake, D. and Ruzek, J. (2000) Prevalence of personality disorders among combat veterans with posttraumatic stress disorder. *Journal of Traumatic Stress*, 13: 255–70.

Collard, P. (2003) Interview with Dr Claudia Herbert. *Counselling Psychology Quarterly*, 16 (3): 187–93.

Davidson, J.R.T. (2000) Introduction to new strategies for the treatment of posttraumatic stress disorder. *Journal of Clinical Psychiatry*, 61 (7): 3–4.

Dunn, N.J., Yanasak, E., Schilaci, J., Simotas, S., Rehm, L., Souchek, J., et al. (2004) Personality disorders in veterans with posttraumatic stress disorder and depression. *Journal of Traumatic Stress*, 17: 75–82.

Friedman, M.J., Resick, P.A. and Keane, T.M. (2007) PTSD: twenty-five years of progress and challenges. In M.J. Friedman, T.M. Keane and P.A. Resick (eds), *Handbook of PTSD, Science and Practice*. New York: Guilford.

Herbert, C. (1995/2007) *Understanding Your Reactions to Trauma: A Guide for Survivors of Trauma and Their Families* (3rd rev. edn). Gloucester: Blue Stallion.

Herbert, C. (2002) A CBT-based therapeutic alternative to working with complex client problems. *European Journal of Psychotherapy, Counselling and Health*, 5 (2): 135–44.

Herbert, C. (2006) Healing from complex trauma: an integrated 3-systems' approach. In J. Corrigal, H. Payne and H. Wilkinson (eds), *About a Body: Working with the Embodied Mind in Psychotherapy*. London: Taylor and Francis.

Herbert, C. (2011) *Overcoming Traumatic Stress: An Audio Companion*. London: Constable and Robinson.

Herbert, C. and Wetmore, A. (1999/2008) *Overcoming Traumatic Stress: A Self-Help Guide Using Cognitive Behavioural Techniques* (2nd rev. edn). London: Constable and Robinson.

Herman, J. (1992) *Trauma and Recovery*. New York: Basic.

Keane, T.M., Brief, D.J., Pratt, E.M. and Miller, M.W. (2007) Assessment of PTSD and its comorbidity in adults. In M.J. Friedman, T.M. Keane and P.A. Resick (eds), *Handbook of PTSD, Science and Practice*. New York: Guilford.

Lanius, R., Lanius, U., Fisher, J. and Ogden, P. (2006) Psychological trauma and the brain: toward a neurobiological treatment model. In P. Ogden, K. Minton and C. Pain (eds), *Trauma and the Body*. New York: Norton.

Levine, P. (1997) *Waking the Tiger: Healing Trauma*. Berkeley, CA: North Atlantic.

MacLean, P.D. (1990) *The Triune Brain in Evolution: Role in Paleocerebral Functions*. New York: Plenum.

NICE (2005) *Post-Traumatic Stress Disorder (PTSD): The Management of PTSD in Adults and Children in Primary and Secondary Care*. National Clinical Practice Guideline number 26. National Collaborating Centre for Mental Health. Commissioned by the National Institute for Health and Clinical Excellence (NICE). The Royal College of Psychiatrists and The British Psychological Society.

Ogden, P. and Minton, K. (2000) Sensorimotor psychotherapy: one method for processing traumatic memory. *Traumatology*, 6: 1–20.

Rothschild, B. (2000) *The Body Remembers: The Psychophysiology of Trauma and Trauma Treatment*. New York: Norton.

Rothschild, B. (2010) *8 Keys to Safe Trauma Recovery: Take-Charge Strategies to Empower Your Healing*. New York: Norton.

Shapiro, F. (1989) Eye movement desensitization: a new treatment for post-traumatic stress disorder. *Journal of Behavior Therapy and Experimental Psychiatry*, 20: 211–17.

Shapiro, F. (2001) *Eye Movement Desensitization and Reprocessing: Basic Principles, Protocols and Procedures* (2nd edn). New York: Guilford.

Shapiro, F. (2002) EMDR twelve years after its introduction: a review of past, present, and future directions. *Journal of Clinical Psychology*, 58: 1–22.

Siegel, D. (1999) *The Developing Mind*. New York: Guilford.

Van der Kolk, B. (1994) The body keeps the score: memory and the evolving psychobiology of posttraumatic stress. *Harvard Psychiatric Review*, 1: 253–65.

WHO (1993) *The ICD-10 Classification of Mental and Behavioural Disorders. Diagnostic Research Criteria*. Geneva: World Health Organization.

The Psychoses

BRIAN MARTINDALE

This chapter will give a brief historical and cultural perspective to psychosis. It will then discuss psychosis from categorical, dimensional and aetiological perspectives and describe the most common phenomenology before outlining psychological, social and pharmacological interventions.

HISTORICAL PERSPECTIVES AND CLASSIFICATION ISSUES

The definitions of the broader concepts of psychosis and narrower concepts such as schizophrenia and bipolar disorder with psychotic features continue to shift according to culture, context and research. Contemporary debate focuses on whether classifications should be based on categories or dimensions or on putative causes.

In 1896 Kraepelin separated out dementia praecox and manic depression from other neuropsychiatric disorders. In 1911 Eugen Bleuler realised not only that there was not the inevitable deterioration implied by the term 'dementia praecox', but that there was considerable clinical heterogeneity within those so defined, leading him to rename the conditions as 'the group of schizophrenias'. This name reflected his awareness of the mental splitting processes involved. His close contact with his patients and their lives made him realise that the conditions were often psychologically understandable. Subsequent paradigms reflected both differing emphases on the role of nature and nurture in the theoretical understanding of the bases for the disorders, and the question of whether the disorders fall into discrete categories or are best thought of as dimensional issues no different from phenomena seen in the 'normal' population but coming to clinical attention because of the distress or problems posed to others.

Contemporary thinking has been helped by developments such as the epidemiological work of van Os et al. (2009) who have shown the considerable incidence of 'psychotic' phenomena in the general public. Van Os (2010) has also shown that the categorisation into distinct disorders has little scientific validity. There have also been considerable developments within cognitive psychology, depth psychologies, neuropsychology, genetics, neurochemistry and neuroimaging fields, which have contributed to the current utility of the stress vulnerability model of the psychoses as being the most embracing framework if used in a sophisticated way (Zubin and Spring, 1997).

DEFINITIONS

For this chapter, I define psychoses as disturbances in which reality testing has been lost in order to distinguish the disorders from non-psychotic conditions where people suffer but *remain in connection* with the realities of their lives.

There are a host of organic conditions that are uncommonly the primary cause of these disturbances, such as hormonal disturbances and certain medications such as steroids. Other brain disorders including dementias commonly lead to psychotic phenomena. These conditions are classified separately according to the primary aetiological agent or disorder, e.g. steroid induced psychosis, myxoedema psychosis or Alzheimer's disease, and will not be further considered here.

Splitting of reality is central to those in a borderline psychotic state. The reality, especially of the self and of others, is seriously distorted by powerful emotions; this leads to splitting, usually into unrealistic positive and negative views, and often results in idealisation or unbrokered hatred of self and others, associated with poor impulse control. (These conditions are considered in Chapter 6.16 in this volume.) People with borderline personality are as prone as others to further disintegration into the spectrum of psychotic states from 'schizophrenia' to manic-depressive psychoses.

In manic-depressive states, now more commonly called bipolar disorders, the conditions extend from non-psychotic affective states of mind to psychotic states, where voice hearing and delusional beliefs about oneself or one's environment are seemingly driven by and *congruent with* the mood, whether it be unrealistically positive or negative or a mixture.

THE PHENOMENOLOGY OF PSYCHOSIS

The phenomena are the consequence of the mind, for whatever reason, being unable to synthesise or integrate the many realities needed to function in life. The phenomena can be primary manifestations of disintegration or secondary attempts to reconstitute the mind, creating a new 'false' reality to avoid a too painful one. A simple example would be the primary psychotic experience of falling apart after a belittling rejection, followed by a secondary grandiose delusional solution to the rejection, such as believing oneself to be the king.

Hallucinations

Hallucinations in various perceptual modalities are frequent experiences in psychosis. Auditory hallucinations are most common, varying from vague sounds to hearing the clear speech of other persons in external space. Some experience a number of voices; sometimes the voices are pleasant or soothing or emotionally neutral, but more often they are unpleasant and denigratory and are talking about the person or to the person, sometimes giving commands. In psychosis these are experienced as real without an 'as if' quality. Visual, olfactory and tactile hallucinations are not uncommon.

Delusions

Delusional beliefs are frequent phenomena in psychosis. In these states the patient has fixed beliefs that have a minimal basis in objective reality and are out of keeping with cultural beliefs. More bizarre delusions are easy to identify, but some are difficult to differentiate from non-psychotic phenomena, especially if other features of psychosis are not elicited: for example, the person who lives in a violent area and believes that people are trying to break into his house. However, the fact that *the clinician* can see the symbolic significance or personal origins of the delusion does not mean that it is not a delusion.

Loss of Self/other Boundaries

A common phenomenon is the loss of normal boundaries between self and others. This usually refers to the mind of self and other but can apply to the body as well. The psychotic may experience that they are able to read other people's minds or that others can read their own mind, and this can be very distressing. Likewise, there can be the belief that others are putting ideas into one's mind.

Thought Disorder

Thoughts can be disordered in a number of ways. Thoughts can feel blocked, sentences are not strung together with normal syntax, non-existent words (neologisms) can be used freely. Especially in affective disorders, the flow of words is more dictated by linkages of sound or similarity than by coherence of a theme in order to communicate to others.

Affective Psychoses

To distinguish bipolar psychoses (also called manic-depressive psychoses), it is important to recognise hallucinatory and other delusional experiences that are *in keeping* with affect from those that do not appear to be connected with affect. The person with a depressive psychosis may experience voices telling them they don't deserve to live or to have positive experiences, whereas the euphoric patient may experience themselves as having physical and sexual energy and special powers or a sense of entitlement. Bipolar disorders have their own subclassifications according to whether the person suffers from recurrence of only manic or depressive episodes or of both.

Denial and Rationalisation

Denial and rationalisation are the most common phenomena in psychosis. The clinical interview is therefore only one tool in ascertaining the diagnosis. Diagnostic evidence may need to be gathered from many sources. Often it is the family or others close to the patient who are most important in contributing to the overall picture.

The phenomena will often lead to secondary and circular difficulties. In mood (affective) psychoses patients usually come to attention quite quickly, especially through their exuberant behaviour. In other psychoses, people tend to withdraw because of paranoia or other difficulties in social relationships or cannot concentrate so well in study or work.

'Negative' Symptoms

These are quieter but major problems not specific to the psychoses. They manifest themselves as a lack in drive and motivation, flatness of emotions, lack of pleasure, and a slowing of thought and communication.

PSYCHOTIC AND NON-PSYCHOTIC FUNCTIONING

It is important to be aware that a person with a psychosis will have aspects of mental functioning which are completely normal and reality oriented alongside the psychosis. Insight will vary greatly from person to person and from time to time.

> Harry had been under observation in hospital for two weeks and no psychosis had been noted. However, in informal discussions with his psychiatrist he conveyed beliefs that the prime minister was regularly speaking to him via a microchip that had been placed behind his eye. The psychiatrist remarked that he had not spoken of this to the nursing staff. The patient said that if he were to do so they might think he was mad (indicating that that was not his belief)!

In other patients the psychosis has so taken over that it is difficult to find a sane part of the patient to relate to, even though the person may be able to eat and dress themselves and operate the computer; in yet other patients there may be quite a struggle going on between the reality-oriented functioning of the patient who 'knows' (has some insight) that they have a psychotic part, and the psychotic who tries to convince the patient that the psychotic phenomenon is reality. (An example is the patient who is seeking help and talking to the clinician, and at the same time is receiving convincing hallucinatory voice commands to not talk about the voice, saying it will only lead to harm.)

THE BRAIN AND PSYCHOSIS

The Stress-vulnerability Model and Formulation

It is important for the contemporary clinician working with psychosis to be familiar with the likely complexity that lies behind psychotic disorders and not to be caught up in reductionistic ideologies. The stress-vulnerability model (Zubin and Spring, 1997) opens the door to many avenues of understanding from biological to psychological and developmental and other approaches, and is a most useful framework for an individualised therapeutic approach. It is likely that psychoses are the final common pathway of a vast number of interacting phenomena that will vary greatly between individuals although the presenting phenomena may be similar. It is accepted now that genetics and environment have a complex interaction early in life affecting the very structure of the brain and its later interactions and development.

The stress-vulnerability model implies that as a result of a mixture of constitutional (including genetic), negative developmental and earlier traumatic experiences the person is vulnerable to psychosis under particular stresses that connect with the earlier difficulties. For example, it is common for psychosis to have its onset at a time when a young person is not able to manage the stress of individuating from their family because a host of earlier developmental issues necessary for this phase have not been mastered, perhaps exacerbated by changes in the brain during puberty.

Once one becomes familiar with the patient and their family, it is common to find that there has been a long prodromal phase in which brief psychotic experiences have been occurring in the context of decline in functioning.

FORMULATION

It is important in helping persons with psychosis to develop a formulation that best makes sense of that person and their psychosis within the stress-vulnerability model. Formulations often need to be modified as a result of increasing understanding of the patient, and the aspect concerned with vulnerability will require knowledge of the past of the patient to develop understanding of previous personal and interpersonal capacities, interests and limitations. This will assist in formulating why recent stresses have been so particularly 'toxic' for that individual.

This formulation will benefit from information collected from a number of sources, bearing in mind that the person's psychotic state may continue to change (disguise) or deny reality of their current difficult circumstances and painful aspects of their past. The formulation aids the making of realistic shorter- and longer-term interventions and the development of an effective individualised relapse prevention plan.

Although there is a danger of developing a new form of narrow or reductionistic approach, a formulation developed by a team can lead to classification of the psychosis into such groups as post-traumatic psychoses, anxiety or sensitivity psychoses, drug-induced or exacerbated psychoses, and long-standing paranoid psychoses developing from paranoid personalities, and may also incorporate neurobiological correlates.

Here is a simple example of a formulation.

Harry, the patient mentioned above, believes that negative information about him is being spread on the national news and that he is being influenced by a microchip implanted behind his eye during an X-ray years ago. He rarely reveals these beliefs, fearing he would be labelled 'mad'.

He constantly disengages from services, believing (and convincing others) that he would have no trouble now going to college, finding somewhere nice to live and settling down to a family life. In reality he has declined over the years and can barely manage basic care of himself.

Harry's father had always had great expectations of him, hoping Harry would make up for his own resentments at the little help he had had as a child and that Harry would fulfil his own dreams. Father was always very abusive of Harry when he did not meet these expectations. Harry was reasonably competent as a wrestler and father would tell us how famous and

---

wealthy Harry would now be if he had followed this career. Mother feared father and was unable to stand up for her son's actual capacities and against father's abuse of Harry; likewise Harry could not oppose father without being rejected.

Harry had little capacity to develop a sense of realistic self/identity in his formative years and continues to be mentally governed by concrete representations of two aspects of father: his unrealistic (delusional) expectations or the condemning and publicly shaming authority figures (the national news). He cannot readily use the help of the mental health services because of the denial that protects him from being open with them, as he believes this would lead to repetition of the condemnation as 'mad' if he revealed his struggles or would be ineffective like his view of his mother.

THERAPEUTIC INTERVENTIONS FOR PEOPLE WITH THE PSYCHOSES

Cultural Variations in Therapeutic Approaches

In the United Kingdom there continues to be a dominance of the biological approach to psychoses, with pharmacological interventions forming the mainstay of treatment. There are a number of reasons for this, of which perhaps three have greatest explanatory power. First, until a few years ago British psychiatrists had very little exposure to and first-hand experience of other approaches to understanding and treating psychosis, perhaps because UK psychiatric specialists in the psychological approaches tended to focus on non-psychotic disorders. Second, only recently has the discipline of psychology seriously involved itself in psychosis to challenge the relative hegemony of the biological approach (British Psychological Society, 2000). Third, most of the accepted treatment research had been into medications due to massive funding from pharmaceutical companies. There is little question of the effectiveness of pharmacological agents in helping many patients with psychosis, but equally no question that for many the effects are limited and side effects remain very problematic (Lieberman et al., 2005) and many patients soon stop taking medication. However, there is now increasing understanding in the UK of the potential contribution of additional approaches to people with psychosis, and these are recognised in National Institute for Health and Clinical Excellence guidelines (NICE, 2009). Besides medications, supportive therapies, CBT and family interventions are those that have been most evaluated in randomised controlled trials and there has also been a resurgence of the recovery movement.

As already stated, understanding of psychosis varies between cultures and so do therapeutic approaches and outcomes. In the UK, NICE guidelines make no reference to WHO studies consistently demonstrating better outcomes in developing countries and not using neuroleptics, or the cohort studies from Alanen (1997) and Seikulla et al. (2006) from Finland. The latter reports on the training of all mental health staff of a community in a specific family-oriented approach offering immediate and protracted engagement, involving dialogue with family and friends in the patient's home. Their research found that only 30 per cent with a schizophrenic psychosis needed antipsychotic medication in the course of five years. Moreover, outcomes were far superior to a similar cohort treated by a more traditional approach in which neuroleptics were central to treatment. The approach of Seikulla and his predecessor Aaltonen arose out of a predominantly psychoanalytic-oriented developmental understanding of psychosis that later incorporated family systems approaches applied in a very flexible and friendly way. This led to the now well-known Finnish need-adapted approach to psychosis (Alanen, 1997) which eschews randomised controlled trials as perhaps unethical, and considers psychosis not as having a common aetiology such as diabetes or an infection, but as being a condition that varies greatly from individual to individual.

The therapeutic emphasis is on attending to the psychological areas needing help and using medication to support the patient's capacities to engage in the psychological help indicated, which may vary from phase to phase. For example, a psychosis occurring in the context of a young person unable to separate from his family when he starts at college may first benefit from a family intervention, move on to a therapeutic milieu to allow for better capacities to form peer relationships, and later still use an individual therapy to attend to remaining issues related to his sensitive sense of self. This approach requires sophisticated understanding by the managers and leaders of services and the careful development and retention of staff with a range of skills relevant to patients' needs – in contrast to an all-too-common situation where the patient has to fit the limited service.

Coordination of Care and Therapeutic Relationships

It is important that people with psychoses have access to staff with a wide range of skills to match the extensive consequences of psychosis on their lives. In the British National Health Service, patients should have a care coordinator whose task is to form a reliable, durable and trusting relationship with the patient and ideally also with his family and friends. When this wider engagement happens from the beginning, issues of confidentiality are rarely encountered and safety is greatly enhanced due to the sharing of planning at risky times. The care coordinator's task is to ensure that all aspects of the patient's needs are clarified and appropriate responses are organised in a timely and coordinated way. Patients will vary greatly in what they both need and can make use of at different times. The gathering of as much information as possible is indicated so that a comprehensive formulation can be arrived at and treatment planned accordingly.

Some general principles are important to bear in mind. Historically, large percentages of patients drop out of services and often lead very limited isolated lives. The priority of the team is therefore to develop and sustain sufficient trusting relationships and be the link to more specialist interventions when needed.

The establishment of an enduring relationship is much more important than rushing into treatment if the patient is not in imminent danger to himself or others. Engagement is aided by attending closely to what is most troubling to the patient and the family. This is not necessarily the same as the most bizarre phenomena that the clinician notices; it might be difficulty in sleeping.

There is good evidence from a number of countries now that if the patient is otherwise safe, quiet respite housing can contribute greatly to recovery for a good percentage of patients (Bola et al., 2009). The general principle here is that in an acute psychotic crisis the patient needs a calm environment and the hectic atmosphere of inpatient wards may be counterproductive for some.

Early Detection

Many people with psychosis only get help after being psychotic for more than a year or two. This is certainly so with those who are more at the schizophrenia end of the spectrum who tend to withdraw, contrasting with those with manic depressive disorders who more readily come to attention. Early detection and involvement with quality services reduces suicidality, reduces the secondary psycho-social deterioration stemming from psychosis (loss of relationships, capacity for work, tendency to use substances, involvement in crime, etc.), and improves outcomes.

There is increasing evidence that people can be recognised in states where they are at high risk of converting to psychoses and that interventions at this stage may prevent a percentage from conversion.

Medication

Many patients have sleep difficulties that have played a significant part in exacerbating their disturbed mental state and/or anxiety and panic attacks. Although there are other approaches, including attending to the environment, the use of simple sleeping medication and anxiolytics, can often take the urgency out of situations and improve mental states.

Patients who remain actively psychotic in spite of other measures such as reducing the strain of the environment will often benefit from neuroleptic medications. These should not be primarily used for any sedative qualities that they have. They work mainly on the neurotransmitter pathways that have become dysfunctional in psychosis and often make the positive symptoms (delusions and hallucinations and thought disorder) much more manageable and tolerable for the patient, and sometimes will lift them completely. However, for many, improvement is partial and there remains a tendency still to use doses that give side effects that can outweigh the benefits, contributing to large dropout rates. Other patients improve and then too readily discontinue medications hoping they no longer need them; however, relapse rates are considerable in the absence of other interventions.

For patients who have had a single episode of psychosis and have full symptomatic recovery, it can be a difficult decision how long to continue antipsychotic medication. Consideration of the circumstances of the onset of psychosis will help evaluate whether there is now evidence that in similar circumstances they would be or have been able to manage better. Withdrawal of medication should always be very slow and in the context of a trusting personal and/or professional relationship that will pick up early signs of relapse before insight is lost.

Many patients will not make a full personal recovery on medication alone and the availability of a full range of psychological and social interventions is indicated.

Patients with a bipolar psychotic disorder often benefit from the same kind of medications as used in other psychoses. In addition there are medications that have mood stabilising qualities that for many will reduce the frequency and severity of either pole of the disorder. Lithium, valproate, carbamazepine and lamotrigine are the four most commonly used.

Relapse Prevention

It can take a long time for a person to fully recover from a psychosis and a major relapse is a most serious event. The prevention or mitigation of relapse therefore needs considerable attention and there is increasingly good evidence that both medication and psychological interventions and combinations can be effective in reducing relapses.

Relapse prevention depends on developing the belief that this is possible. The best chances of success are when there is active cooperation of the patient and those closest to them in the process of recovery. Carefully and repeatedly going back over the sequence of events leading up to previous episodes is very helpful to jointly identifying the stressful factors, the personal warning signs (relapse signature) and the factors that exacerbated and alleviated these. Discussion and education are needed as to what could be more effective in the face of the beginning of new signs of relapse, in removing stress, other psychological techniques and the role of appropriate medication.

Cognitive-behavioural Therapy

Many patients with psychosis will also have problems common to those who do not suffer from psychosis and will benefit from the indications for CBT such as depression, anxiety, phobias and self-esteem issues, and the same considerations should apply. However, some of these symptoms may relate to their psychotic problems: for example, anxiety about leaving the house could be related to a belief that the government has a hit squad waiting for the patient in the trees behind the nearby park.

CBT has been shown to be useful in residual positive symptoms such as hallucinations and to some extent in delusions and in depression, but less useful in those with other negative symptoms. CBT obviously involves engagement with the non-psychotic aspects of a patient's mind to help them reflect and challenge the power of the psychotic experiences. CBT is especially directed at distressing symptoms and disabling social functioning.

Longer-term Interventions

In the longer term it is important to assist the person to strengthen their inner capacities and/or to help them develop techniques in dealing with adverse situations and feelings. Here, accurate formulation is essential in identifying the particular vulnerabilities that vary so much from one person to another. For example, for one it could be feelings of attachment that provoked psychosis stemming from *fears* of being let down; for another it could be the opposite, i.e. the actual experiences of separation; for yet another person, psychosis could arise in the face of any potential aggression or name calling or 'failure'. Psychodynamic interventions have a long history in some countries in assisting with developing a more robust sense of self and reducing tendencies to give in to psychotic processes. Here, the formulation may be of immense help. Post-traumatic psychoses and anxiety psychoses may need specific interventions

Family Interventions

The effectiveness of family interventions is an area for which there is the most robust evidence. There are family circumstances where there is what is called 'high expressed emotion' or 'high EE' and this is associated with high relapse rates. High EE means either a high frequency of critical comments directed to the patient, a hostile atmosphere, or family members spending 'too much time' with the patient. Altering these factors reduces relapse rates. Understimulation can be equally undesirable. Nearly all family members will find aspects of living with a member who has psychosis stressful, and NICE (2009) guidelines make extensive recommendations for family interventions. There are many ways in which the families can be helped both with their vulnerable relative and in their own right. Working within the stress-vulnerability model of psychosis clearly implies that families are not immune from creating stress for susceptible members, but it is vital that professionals do not get caught up in a blaming approach – a fear that may have previously inhibited professionals and families from working more together.

A development in some countries has been to gather members of several families into what are called multi-family groups. This can be useful both where there has been a first episode of psychosis and for families where a member has a psychosis of longer duration. These groups can be useful as a way of delivering education and information, but if groups meet regularly they can be used as a means of helping families support recovery, develop problem-solving skills and reduce their stigma and isolation.

Group Interventions

Many patients with psychoses have had poor peer relationships, either preceding the psychosis or as consequence of prolonged psychotic states. Being able to function in groups is a very important part of recovery, opening the doors to many aspects of a richer life. A good number of patients with low self-esteem and poor verbal skills will benefit from simple structured activity groups with people of similar age, doing things they may have little previous experience of such as playing pool, bicycle rides, bowling, cinema outings, perhaps ending with a low-key meeting in a café or burger bar. Others may become ready for residential therapeutic communities (Gale et al., 2008), or skilled evaluation by a vocational specialist may help people back into college, training or a manageable work environment.

Substance Misuse

A significant number of young people with psychosis use substances. It is now well established that: (1) a range of street substances can lead to psychosis; (2) young people will use substances to try and deal with the troubling symptoms of psychosis and often get transient relief; (3) substances exacerbate pre-existing psychosis. Amphetamines will give rise to a psychosis indistinguishable from non-drug-induced psychosis. Many patients who have used substances will reluctantly come to accept that unlike their peers they cannot continue to indulge without putting themselves at severe risk; others may need more specialist help in coming to terms with this and adjusting their way of life. Outcomes are better if such expertise is contained within psychosis services (Copello et al., 2007).

CONCLUDING REMARKS

Psychoses are almost certainly a very wide range of conditions where the mind's capacity to integrate the realities of the person's life is impaired. In many of those who come to the attention of health professionals, the disturbance has many distressing consequences for the individual and the family, and a wide range of skills may be needed to minimise the consequences and to support recovery. Securing long-term safe and trusted supportive therapeutic relationships is an essential feature. Most patients will need a coordinated team approach. Unless very experienced, counselling and psychotherapy professionals should ensure they have full team support for their work and have supervisors who are experienced with psychosis. Staff will very often inevitably become involved in a complex way in both the psychotic and non-psychotic world of the individual.

REFERENCES

Alanen, Y. (1997) *Schizophrenia: Its Origins and Need-Adapted Treatment*. London: Karnac.

Bola, J., Lehtinen, K., Cullberg, J. and Ciompi, L. (2009) Psychosocial treatment, antipsychotic postponement, and low-dose medication: a review of the literature. *Psychosis*, 1 (1): 4–18.

British Psychological Society (2000) *Recent Advances in Understanding Mental Illness and Psychotic Experiences*. BPS Division of Clinical Psychology. Leicester: BPS.

Copello, A., Graham, H., Mueser, K. and Birchwood, M. (2007) *Substance Misuse in Psychosis*. Chichester: Wiley.

Gale, J., Realpe, A. and Pedriali, E. (2008) *Therapeutic Communities for Psychosis: Philosophy, History and Clinical Practice*. London: Routledge.

Lieberman, J.A., Stroup, T.S., McEvoy, J.P., Swartz, M.S., Rosenheck, R.A., Perkins, D.O., Keefe, R.S.E., Davis, S.M., Davis, C.E., Lebowitz, B.D., Severe, J. and Hsiao, J.K. (2005) Effectiveness of antipsychotic drugs in patients with chronic schizophrenia. *New England Journal of Medicine*, 353: 1209–23.

NICE (2009) *Schizophrenia: Core Interventions in the Treatment and Management of Schizophrenia in Adults in Primary and Secondary Care*. NICE guideline. National Institute for Health and Clinical Excellence. www.nice.org.uk.

Seikkula, J., Aaltonen, J., Alakare, B., Haarakangas, K., Keranen, J. and Lehtinen, K. (2006) Five-year experience of first-episode nonaffective psychosis in open-dialogue approach: treatment principles, follow-up outcomes. *Psychotherapy Research*, 16 (2): 214–28.

Van Os, J. (2010) Are psychiatric diagnoses of psychosis scientific and useful? The case of schizophrenia. *Journal of Mental Health*, 19 (4): 305–17.

Van Os, J., Linscott, R.J., Myin-Germeys, I., Delespaul, P. and Krabbendam, L. (2009) A systematic review and meta-analysis of the psychosis continuum: evidence for a psychosis proneness–persistence–impairment model of psychotic disorder. *Psychological Medicine*, 39 (2): 179–95.

Zubin, J. and Spring, B. (1977) Vulnerability: a new view of schizophrenia. *Journal of Abnormal Psychology*, 86 (2): 103–26.

RECOMMENDED READING

Alanen, Y., González de Chavez, M., Silver, A.-L. and Martindale, B. (2009) *Psychotherapeutic Approaches to Schizophrenic Psychoses*. London: Routledge.

Cullberg, J. (2004) *Psychoses: An Integrative Perspective*. London: Routledge.

Martindale, B., Bateman, A., Crowe, M. and Margison, F. (2000) *Psychosis: Psychological Approaches and their Effectiveness*. London: Gaskell.

Relationship and Sex Problems

GAIL EVANS

It is useful to read about couple relationships even if you are not intending to be a couple therapist. All people you work with as a therapist (and you yourself) are influenced by couple relationships – their own and those of close family and friends.

DEFINITIONS

As I began to write this chapter the attempt to determine clear definitions, and the consequent mass of questions, threatened to stall progress. For example, what is a relationship in this context? A fairly safe starting point is that we are talking about adults. It seems most adults desire to have at least one adult relationship that is primary or 'special' – in some way marked out as different from other relationships.

A primary relationship is often referred to as an intimate relationship. What exactly is intimacy? Does this have to involve sex or some other defining principle like emotional closeness or shared home life? Expectations or definitions will be affected by gender, orientation, socio-economic status, education and culture amongst many potential influences. How many adults are involved? I imagine most people's preconception in this culture would be two individuals. Many also expect that sexual exclusivity will define an intimate relationship. This is reflected in an example definition of intimacy shown.

A definition of intimacy: communicating openly, non-defensively and spontaneously

- *Responding* with empathy (able to relate to each other).
- *Negotiating* conflicts by accommodating and compromising with each other.
- *Affirming* each other's vulnerabilities.
- *Enjoying* physical contact ranging from affection to sex.
- *Creating* a unique identity from their mutual developmental history derived from shared experiences.
- *Respect and support* for each other's evolution as individuals by accepting their differences in interests, friendships, careers, hobbies and so on.
- *Providing* support for each other in a crisis.
- *Contributing* to mutually shared goals and responsibilities.
- *Playing* together openly and spontaneously.
- *Remaining* monogamous and faithful to each other.

Mills and Turnbull (2004)

However, we have the *ménage à trois*, polyamory and the so-called 'open marriage/relationship' in our own culture as well as the instances of multiple wives, and occasionally husbands, in other cultures. I will not attempt to deal with these questions here, but invite you to bear them in mind. An issue for you as a therapist to examine and challenge is your own preconception about what *constitutes* an adult intimate relationship and how it should function; and also, which clients you are able to work with.

From within a love relationship it may seem unlikely that your individual options and choices are influenced and shaped by wider economic, social, spiritual, political and technological forces. Yet these do impact on the function, dynamics and even the necessity of couple relationships as well as on the potential availability and choice of partners. In the industrialised world, expectations of couple relationships have changed and continue to evolve, especially over the decades since World War II, with greater emancipation, economic independence and fertility control available to women. The free availability of information and open discussion about alternatives to traditional models of couple, family and sexual relationships, via the media, information technology and education, is also modifying expectations, life choices and the influences on individuals. All these affect what defines a 'normal' relationship and what is perceived to be a problem; and they also influence what kinds of problem legitimise the end of a couple relationship and/or whether to seek help.

I will not concern myself here with why most of us appear to wish to be in a couple relationship; there is a complex and fascinating array of explanations that range from metaphysical, romantic, biological and evolutionary, socio-economic and political, to psychosexual and intra-psychic. Rather, the focus is mainly on the issues that may lead to an individual or couple deciding they have 'a relationship problem' and on the theoretical understanding of the issues and how a couple may be helped. Many of the counselling theories that are helpful for understanding individual problems and guiding one-to-one practice may be applied to understanding and working with couple relationships, but there are some that are most commonly used. In terms of practice there are significant differences when working with couples which are addressed in my other contribution to this book (Chapter 7.7 in this volume).

I will use the term *couple relationship* throughout to denote all adult intimate relationships. Not all adult couple relationships are pairings, nor are all subject to the same pressures; *any* that are considered by prevailing powerful opinions as being in some way transgressive are likely to face prejudice, abuse, internalised oppression, ostracism and lack of recognition and support, and often also experience practical obstacles. Sometimes this will lend strength and an alternative community bond and culture, but sometimes it will exert more stress than the couple can hold. Couples within minority communities may experience difficulty in finding appropriate, sympathetic, confidential and unbiased help.

SOME STATISTICAL INFORMATION

The following information is drawn from the Office for National Statistics (www.ons.gov.uk) which compiles information about historical and current marital status and future trends in the United Kingdom.

Since 1979 there has been a steady decline in the numbers of married people, with a commensurate rise in divorce and cohabitation (although the latter is difficult to estimate). However, since 2004 divorce has been falling, cohabitation is believed to have levelled off and the number of single people has been rising. The numbers of remarriages of divorced people has also declined. There has been an increase in the, albeit small, number of people travelling abroad to marry. Civil partnerships began in December 2005 with a peak and have been declining, and dissolutions rising, since then (although overall numbers are small compared with heterosexual marriage and divorce).

Couples are often at their most stressed when they have children, but tend to stay together when the children are young. By contrast, couples caring for a child with a disability are at greater risk of marital problems and divorce. The presence of children in second and subsequent relationships also heightens the likelihood of relationship breakdown.

WHAT MAKES A GOOD COUPLE RELATIONSHIP?

In considering the problems couples face in their relationships it is worth thinking about what brings people together, what needs to be in place or to happen to build a resilient relationship, and potential strengths and pressure points. It is useful to reflect on your own ideas about what constitutes and makes for a good couple relationship and where these ideas come from, as well as consulting relevant research. As with any other branch of therapy your own assumptions may adversely affect the work with clients.

This chapter cannot offer a comprehensive literature review, but examples are offered here.

Longitudinal research into enduring couple relationships is relatively scarce, and particularly so for 'non-standard' relationships.

An early psychotherapeutic attempt to consider couple relationships in depth was made by Henry Dicks (1993). He suggested three levels of influence on couple relationships:

1 *the social* – opportunities to meet, shared cultural norms
2 *the personal* – personal norms and role expectations
3 *the unconscious* – unconscious drives, introjections and splits.

Informed by psychoanalytic and attachment ideas, he was particularly interested in the unconscious. However, we should not overlook the very real impact of the first two (often the focus of marriage and dating agency questionnaires). Shared values and expectations cement the relationship and perhaps explain how arranged marriages are as likely to be as successful as so-called 'love marriages'. The unconscious drivers identified by psychodynamic and attachment approaches become useful when considering problematic relationships and how to help them (see later in this chapter).

Some research identifies *tasks* that need to be successfully negotiated to build a lasting couple relationship, for example (Wallerstein and Blakeslee, 1996):

- separation from the family of origin
- becoming a couple, creating togetherness and autonomy
- coping with crises
- making a safe place for conflict
- exploring sexual love and intimacy
- sharing laughter and keeping interests alive
- providing emotional nurturance
- preserving a double vision: holding onto past positive experiences and present realities.

Largely based on white, Western examples (and some cultural criticism might be levelled against the first item in the above list), nevertheless such ideas are endorsed by research from non-Western cultures (e.g. Rabin, 1996). Another finding is that *fairness* is a key principle (Rabin, 1996) regardless of whether the relationship adopts traditional or other role separations.

Other models suggest *stages* of relationship development. The following stage model of development may help normalisation and threat reduction for gay relationships (McWhirter and Mattison, 1985):

- blending (first year)
- nesting (1–3 years)
- maintaining (3–5 years)
- collaborating (5–10 years)
- trusting (10–20 years)
- repartnering (20 years).

It is significant that if you deviate from what society defines as 'normal', or if you did not experience a positive parental couple relationship, the lack of role models for your own relationship is a potential obstacle to:

- identifying and building on your own positive relationship ingredients
- defining shared expectations of what should be 'normal' in your own relationship
- knowing how to resolve difficulties or differences.

Some research identifies the *elements* needed for creating and maintaining an enduring relationship. For example (Reibstein, 1997):

- *Protective love.* We have needs for protection and dependence which are normal impulses.
- *Focus.* A robust research finding is that couples who do things together and talk to each other are happier together.
- *Gratitude.* Consistent demonstration of gratitude reinforces 'the sense that you are special and supported by you partner'.
- *Balance.* The above three 'engender balance, which also reinforces the protection because it is about mutuality of support' within the couple.
- *Pleasure.* Happy couples have a sense of pleasure which 'keeps providing the glue they need to continue their mutually protective alliance'.

This may be compared with the Mills and Turnbull (2004) suggestions about intimacy given above, and with the following ideas on relationship needs put forward by Gottman (2000):

- build love maps
- share fondness and admiration
- turn towards
- the positive perspective
- manage conflict
- make life dreams come true
- create shared meaning.

Erskine et al. (1999) suggest similar elements:

- security
- validation
- acceptance

- confirmation (of personal experience)
- self-definition
- to have an impact
- to have the other initiate
- expression of love.

WHAT GOES WRONG?

Indicators of the potential for relationships to go wrong can no doubt be spotted in the research and models cited above. Most of us have met couples who are obviously in trouble: public arguments, sniping and negative body language show all is not well. Often though, it comes as a surprise to others. The privacy of a couple relationship, the hurt, pride, humiliation, disloyalty, not wanting to acknowledge the truth, not having a language to discuss it, are among many possible factors that contribute to secrecy and a tendency to leave it too long before addressing issues.

Some baseline factors influence the ability to create a resilient relationship and underlie the development of problems, including:

- individual capacity to tolerate difference, anxiety and frustration
- respect and acceptance for self and others
- communication and defence patterns and the interlocking aspects of these
- communication and problem-solving skills
- shared versus mismatched expectations, attitudes or values
- attachment patterns
- gender myths and assumptions, and gender differences (in heterosexual couples) and similarities (in same-sex couples)
- hidden or unacknowledged traits (e.g. relating to sexuality).

Even assuming a reasonable level of strength develops in the above areas, stress points impact on couples, and tend to have a greater effect when the couple does not have a good foundation. Very often stresses are minimised or overlooked by the couple, who focus on the obvious, for instance the prevalence of arguments, and can be very surprised to hear the therapist point out other issues as relevant, for example:

- health issues
- financial changes (positive and negative)
- life stages and transitions
- life and family events (e.g. house moves; pregnancies, terminations and miscarriages; job changes or loss)

- wider family relationships, including step-family, previous partners etc.
- other external factors, e.g. work stresses, working hours, bullying at work, traumatic incidents
- sexual issues including (increasingly) sexual addiction
- triangular relationships that intrude on the life of the couple (maybe an affair, but also other intense friendships or close family relationships, including with children; and the impact of work demands).

Individual consequences of stress, for example affairs and other 'acting out', depression and other mental health issues, substance misuse, violence and domestic abuse and somatic problems, can exacerbate couple difficulties. Often a couple will report a string of stressful events and experiences but fail to have made the connection between these and their current difficulties.

There is a wide range of ways couples present for help. Commonly there is a precipitating event which highlights that things have not been right for some time. Typically, communication has become fraught, either because it is beset by misunderstanding and argument or paralysed by fear of speaking, or because it has ceased due to lack of interest and shared existence. The sense of 'we' gets lost. The interactive nature of couple personalities and issues creates circular and polarised behaviours: for example, the more one partner retreats, the more the other pursues, and this pushes the retreating partner further away.

Underlying the presenting issues are often deeper ones. I have worked with many couples where differences in intra-psychic needs, values, role and life expectations or sexual orientation only emerged at a later stage of the relationship, often disastrously and usually when negotiating a transition, for example from being a couple to becoming a family. Systems-behavioural theory and concepts (e.g. Crowe and Ridley, 2000) can illuminate such issues with attention to rules, roles and interrelationships.

The idea of 'unconscious fit', referred to above, has been developed by writers in the psychodynamic and attachment traditions, such as Scarf (2008), Clulow (2000) and Clulow and Mattinson (1989). Classic, potentially destructive, pairings are identified and denoted by evocative titles, for example, 'carer and wounded bird', 'cat and dog' and 'babes in the wood'. These identifiers capture a sense of the interactivity of the unconscious motivators of two partners and the nature of the relationship dynamics. These relationships can also be described in transactional analysis terms using the parent–adult–child matrix. Couples can fall into permutations of relating such as parent (nurturing) and child (compliant), parent (critical) and child (free or rebellious), and child–child (where one or both are free or compliant).

Most of us can recognise some of these pairings in our families, friends, selves and clients. It is argued that we tend to seek familiar (archaic) relationships to replay (perhaps with the hope of a more positive outcome) the dramas of our childhood. For some couples, recognising these interactive patterns can lead to finding healthier ways of meeting their own and each other's psychological needs.

WHY DO COUPLES COME FOR COUNSELLING?

Some couples come for therapy to rescue their relationship, others to discover whether there is anything worth rescuing, and some want help to find a way to part. In some couples the agenda is not shared or fully owned and therapy is a way of feeling 'at least we tried before throwing in the towel'. Sometimes one initiator has brought the partner to be told off or to be 'dumped' with the counsellor so they can leave with a clear conscience. Warring couples may be overtly looking for a 'referee' and covertly seeking an ally in the war.

Occasionally couples want to develop or explore an aspect of their relationship, for example the impact of becoming a family, because one or both is aware of their own adverse history, or to improve their sexual relationship. More often, couples recognise that they have reached some impasse that their own resources seem unable to dislodge, and frequently one partner is the initiator. Sadly, this is often at a point of crisis, either following an event or when disagreements have reached an intolerable intensity. Some couples are able to give a fairly coherent account of how they have reached this point and know what they need to do (although they may disagree about it); others are mystified how it got that bad.

The precipitating factors are usually to do with problematic communication in one form or another (verbal or sexual crossed communication or absent communication), 'acting out' behaviours such as affairs or excessive time and energy engaged in non-couple activities, or another precipitating non-containable event such as a death in the family or other trauma. Any, or several, of these may be present and be experienced as overwhelming by the couple.

Some couples initially avoid discussing their sexual relationship in therapy, although it is likely to be implicated in some way – as either cause or casualty of other difficulties. They may need permission and encouragement to explore this aspect of their relationship. Others present with a sexual issue at the forefront, either because it genuinely is the key problem or sometimes because it is easier to acknowledge this contained aspect of their relationship – it being much more threatening to recognise a more general relationship problem. Either way, it is important for the couple therapist to have a good understanding of and be comfortable with discussing the sexual aspects of the relationship and to recognise the limits of their own competence and when specialist help will be more useful. In our psychologically biased theorising about a couple's difficulties we can misattribute sexual problems to a relationship issue.

WHAT APPROACHES COULD BE HELPFUL?

As a therapist you may hold allegiance to particular theories, and these will influence how you approach thinking about and working with the relationship issues of an individual or a couple. Although there is no reliable evidence that any one modality is more effective than another, there is good evidence of the effectiveness of couple therapy (Gurman and Frankel, 2002). Gurman (2008) gives an overview of different possible therapeutic approaches to couple therapy. Often approaches are integrative, for example, Butler and Joyce (1998) and Bobes and Rothman (2002).

Predictors of responsiveness to therapy include couples who are younger, less distressed and polarised, and where there is commitment and active collaboration with early 'softening' of interaction (Gurman and Frankel, 2002). The nature and duration of the work are likely to reflect the degree to which the inner world needs to be addressed. Some couples are readily helped by being provided with a neutral and safe space to talk with minimal guidance. Others may need a mediator using positive interventions to interrupt unhelpful patterns, to teach communication and problem-solving skills, and to offer exercises and creative means of exploring issues. My own observation from practice is that the therapeutic alliance and the therapist's ability to work openly with (and between) the couple's values, aims, communication and attachment patterns, and personality styles are key. Alongside this are some well-tried ideas, techniques and skills for managing couple work (discussed in Chapter 7.7 in this volume).

There are some contra-indicators for successful couple work, for example where there are:

- court hearings (where clients are conscripts rather than volunteers)
- lack of shared goals
- serious individual issues
- ongoing domestic violence episodes
- serious mental health issues
- very heightened, uncontainable emotions.

When couples or individuals present with a sexual relationship problem, a careful assessment is needed to ascertain whether referral to a psycho-sexual therapist for sex therapy would be the most effective form of help. Sometimes it is tricky to work out whether the sexual problem caused the relationship difficulties or is caused by those issues. Two general rules of thumb are: firstly, ask the client(s) which issue they believe to be the most important; and secondly, if in doubt discuss the matter with, or refer to, a sex therapist who can advise.

On occasion the focus of therapy is on what it would mean to the individual or couple to sepa-rate. This can be helpful to consider even if the couple is intent on *not* separating, as it can lead to recognition of positive reasons for staying in the relationship and a renewed commitment. Some couples seem unable to make use of therapy to progress their relationship (towards commitment or separation) and one may speculate about the reasons for this using the different available theo-ries. For example, in behavioural terms there may be less to gain and more to lose by changing the dynamics of the relationship. For some couples the struggles of everyday life militate against find-ing the time, energy and money to make produc-tive use of therapy.

What couples usually discover from therapy is a different set of explanations, a new and shared nar-rative about their relationship and its difficulties. Often there are incomplete stories, laden with blame. Therapy enables the discovery of another, fuller and more balanced, explanation which can help to rebuild trust, for example by understanding that an affair (blame apportioned to one party) was a symptom of other issues (possibly leading to shared responsibility). Therapy frequently uncovers previously hidden or undiscussed issues and reveals the impact of the history of both partners. This increased understanding may lead to greater mutual acceptance and empathy, even if the outcome is a decision to part.

REFERENCES

Bobes, T. and Rothman, B. (2002) *Doing Couple Therapy: Integrating Theory with Practice*. New York: Norton.

Butler, C. and Joyce, V. (1998) *Counselling Couples in Relationships: An Introduction to the Relate Approach*. Chichester: Wiley.

Clulow, C. (2000) *Adult Attachment and Couple Psychotherapy: The 'Secure Base' in Practice and Research*. London: Brunner-Routledge.

Clulow, C. and Mattinson, J. (1989) *Marriage Inside Out*. London: Penguin.

Crowe, M. and Ridley, J. (2000) *Therapy with Couples: A Behavioural-Systems Approach to Marital and Sexual Problems*. Oxford: Blackwell Science.

Dicks, H.V. (1993) *Marital Tensions: Clinical Studies Towards a Psychological Theory of Interaction*. Foreword by F.M. Sander. London: Karnac.

Erskine, R., Moursand, J. and Trautmann, R. (1999) *Beyond Empathy: A Therapy of Contact-in Relationships*. London: Brunner/Mazel.

Gottman, J.M. (2000) *The Seven Principles for Making Marriage Work*. London: Orion.

Gurman, A.S. (ed.) (2008) *Clinical Handbook of Couple Therapy*. London: Guilford.

Gurman, A.S. and Frankel, P. (2002) The history of couple therapy: a millennial review. *Family Process*, 41 (2).

McWhirter, A.M. and Mattison, D.P. (1985) *The Male Couple*. Englewood Cliffs, NJ: Prentice Hall.

Mills, B. and Turnbull, G. (2004) Broken hearts and mending bodies: the impact of trauma on intimacy. *Sexual and Relationship Therapy*, 19 (3): 265–91.

Rabin, C. (1996) *Equal Partners, Good Friends: Empowering Couples through Therapy*. London: Routledge.

Reibstein, J. (1997) *Love Life: How To Make Your Relationship Work*. London: Fourth Estate.

Scarf, M. (2008) *Intimate Partners: Patterns in Love and Marriage*. New York: Ballantine.

Wallerstein, J.S. and Blakeslee, S. (1996) *The Good Marriage*. London: Transworld.

Sexual Abuse in Childhood

MOIRA WALKER

WHAT IS SEXUAL ABUSE?

Any discussion of sexual abuse has to acknowledge that many children who are sexually abused are also abused physically and emotionally, and that many children who are not abused sexually are damaged by other forms of abuse. In working with adult survivors it is particularly important to be aware of this, as some survivors feel their abusive experiences are somehow insignificant if they were not sexual in nature. Indeed, the NSPCC suggests that emotional abuse is the most hidden and underestimated form of child maltreatment (Cawson et al., 2000; Howe, 2006).

My definition of sexual abuse is based on recognizing the essential misuse of power and authority, combined with force or coercion, which leads to the exploitation of children in situations where adults, or children sufficiently older than the victim, have greater strength and power than, and seek sexual gratification through, those who are developmentally immature such that consent from the victim is a non-concept. What is central is the exploitation of the child, the denial of their rights and feelings, and the essential gratification of the abuser through the child, the child being regarded solely as an object for the perpetrator's use and to meet their needs.

Sexual abuse occurs in all communities, ethnic backgrounds, religions, cultures and social and economic classes, and is experienced by both males and females, although to date research suggests that the majority of victims are female and the majority of perpetrators male. Some abuse is particularly violent, long lasting and frequent, while other abuse is a single incident. There is current and serious concern about the use of the internet for child pornography as a form of child sexual abuse that is particularly difficult to police but that horribly involves many children. It is now also increasingly recognized that adolescent abuse of younger children is a serious problem.

It is crucial to recognize the complexities of defining sexual abuse to avoid falling into oversimplified stereotyping that prevents survivors seeking help. For example, although nowadays there is much greater awareness of the needs of male survivors, and many more services geared to their needs, men can still find seeking help difficult. Similarly, abuse by girls and women has been underestimated and denied in the past, making it harder for those abused by women to come forward. Much that was previously firmly believed to be true has been proved wrong in the light of new evidence, and child victims and adult survivors have suffered as a consequence. Working with survivors takes place in a field where much remains unknown and where counsellors are often faced with believing the apparently unbelievable.

The Extent of Sexual Abuse

Statistics for England up to 31 March 2009 show 37,900 children on child protection plans: of these, 2200 were registered for sexual abuse. This gives an indication of the problem, but both retrospective studies and clinical work with survivors suggest that official child protection figures are the tip of the iceberg, with many children suffering in isolation and in silence.

Sexual offences conviction rates can provide another indicator. A 1997 report (National Statistics, 1997) indicates that of men born in England and Wales in 1953, seven in 1000 have a conviction for sexual offences against a child by the age of 40. Home Office figures show that in 1997 the police were notified of 1269 offences of 'gross indecency with a child under 14 years' and that at least one-quarter of recorded rape victims are children. Other studies show that men convicted of sexual offences against a child claim five or more undetected sexual assaults for which they were never caught. Given that many perpetrators will not be honest about the extent of their offending, that many will not be caught and others will not be prosecuted, these figures also provide some idea of the potential extent of the problem.

An adult retrospective study demonstrated that 50 per cent of adults abused as children never reported the abuse and that in 67 per cent of cases the abuse started before the age of 11 years. Another NSPCC study (Ghate and Daniels, 1997) took a national sample of 998 children aged 8–11 years and found that 15 per cent said they would not talk to someone if they had a problem.

Statistics produced by the NSPCC (2007) suggest that 16 per cent of children aged less than 16 experienced sexual abuse during childhood, 11 per cent of boys and 21 per cent of girls. Most had more than one sexually abusive experience. Three-quarters told no one about the abuse at the time, and by early adulthood about a third still kept their painful secret to themselves.

In 2009 the NSPCC collated figures indicating that 20,758 children reported sexual offences to the police in the previous year, including rape, gross indecency and incest (Laville, 2009). The number of sex crimes recorded against girls was six times more than against boys. What is particularly of note is that in order to acquire these crucial and significant statistics the NSPCC had to issue freedom of information requests to all 43 police forces in England and Wales. The Home Office does not collect these figures, and police forces only record them on an individual basis. Therefore, valuable information on the extent of child sexual abuse is effectively hidden from obvious view.

Estimates of abuse do vary considerably. Variations in the figures reflect the real difficulty in defining, researching and measuring sexual abuse. But even if the most conservative of estimates is taken, it is abundantly clear that a very large number of the adult population are survivors of abuse. Although it is difficult to precisely state the size of that problem, what is abundantly clear is that it is a major problem and one that remains frequently hidden from the view of a wider world, and maintained

as a dreadful secret by both the child victim and the adult survivor.

The Impact of Sexual Abuse on the Child

The impact of abuse on the child is well documented and researched (Bray, 1997; Corby, 2006; Walker, 1992; 2003). The basic needs of children for love, security, care and nurture, safety, appropriate boundaries and respect for self and body are consistently undermined by sexual abuse. The abused child learns to confuse love and sex, and love and violence. Life is unpredictable and unsafe; personal boundaries are invaded physically, sexually and emotionally. What should be the safest place for the child – their home – is the most dangerous for many abused children, so nowhere is safe and no time is safe, and bribery serves to effectively silence and frighten the child into submission.

The existence of a safe attachment and a secure base is essential for satisfactory development: children learn who they are and what sort of person they are through their earliest relationships. Safe and secure attachment can be wrecked or damaged by abuse. Children abused by significant caregivers are in an impossible position: the person they need and trust for protection is also the one the child needs protection from, and the impact on development is huge and negative.

Sexually abused children are frequently isolated, mistrustful and deeply confused. They live in a climate of fear and often experience considerable pain; and children who are abused by one parent or carer, but are unable to tell the other, effectively become a psychological orphan. Education frequently suffers and they can become labelled as attention seeking, difficult, naughty or bad – all reinforcing their sense of unacceptability. Feelings of shame, guilt, dirtiness, badness and of being unlovable and unlikeable are often experienced and extend into adulthood.

The Impact of Childhood Abuse on the Adult

Sexual abuse in childhood frequently leaves the adult with a catalogue of losses to deal with that render assimilation into the wider world extremely problematic (Sanderson, 2006). The long-term effects of child sexual abuse have been well documented, and a meta-analysis carried out by Neumann and colleagues (1996) of 38 studies of the impact of child sexual abuse on later adult problems identified these as anxiety, depression, revictimization, sexual problems, self-harm, suicidal tendencies, post-traumatic stress symptoms, dissociation, interpersonal problems, problems of self-esteem and substance abuse. In addition, other studies have shown a high proportion of survivors in the psychiatric population. Ainscough and Toon (1996) state that 50 per cent of women and 23 per cent of men receiving psychiatric help have been sexually abused.

More effects of child sexual abuse become identified as research develops and extends into previously uncharted areas. For example, neurobiology research into the developmental and integrative aspects of the central nervous system describes brain changes occurring in adults sexually abused in childhood (Bremner et al., 2003). Many other studies have similarly reported the negative impact on parts of the brain responsible for learning, memory and processing emotions in those who have experienced child abuse.

This is not to say that all survivors of abuse will experience severe difficulties during adult life. Some clearly do not, raising the interesting question of what are the protecting factors. As a rule of thumb, it appears that the following are likely to intensify the negative long-term effects of abuse:

- the younger the child when abused
- the closer the relationship of the abuser to the child
- the significance of that person as an attachment figure
- abuse that is repeated over many years
- the involvement of others in the abuse (e.g. in an abuse ring)
- the absence of other supportive or loving figures.

If the abuser is a close caregiver and the child is very young, the damage is likely to be considerable and long lasting. But while it is recognized that the extent of the impact of abuse is related to its severity, its duration and the closeness of the victim to the abuser, the impact of single incidents should never be underestimated, particularly when the abuser is a trusted adult on whom the child depends. A girl of 13 who was sexually abused on one occasion only by her previously apparently trustworthy and loved and loving father felt this had destroyed her trust, wrecked her relationship with both parents, and had long-term and very serious consequences for her.

Therapeutic Issues in Counselling Abuse Survivors

These are many and complex. The provision of a safe, trustworthy and appropriately boundaried space is essential for the abuse survivor – remembering that abuse invades the boundaries of the self and damages the child's trust. Being believed and being heard are essential and central. Most children have been abused by a person whom society deems to be trustworthy (e.g. parents, step-parents, other family members and carers) and counsellors and psychotherapists arrive with the same label. Consequently, trust has to be worked at and earned and may be constantly tried and tested and retried by the client.

In early sessions the counsellor may or may not know if abuse is an issue, and even if the client's presentation indicates this, counsellors should never suggest abuse. Even when abuse is on the agenda, words should not be put into the client's mouth. Counsellors need to listen carefully, framing interventions in the client's own language and not pushing the client into revealing what they are not yet ready to reveal.

One of the central dilemmas in working with abuse survivors is that of remaining gently supportive while also being effectively containing. There is always a danger of the therapist being experienced as being ineffective or uncaring or uninterested (just as abuse survivors will have experienced in childhood), or being seen as abusive and invasive (as with their experience of the abuser). It is a delicate therapeutic balance.

While it is crucial to be empathic and connected to the client's experience, it is important to make contact without the client feeling the counsellor is somehow getting inside them, or has magical powers to 'know' about them. This resonates powerfully with the original experience of sexual abuse. Thus, enormous care has to be taken not to be invasive or inappropriate and, while helping the client to recognize a theme, not trapping them into uncomfortable exploration.

Being aware of the misuse of power in the adult's own childhood, and not misusing the power implicit in the counselling situation, is central. The client had no control over their abuse, but should control the pace and development of counselling sessions. It is also significant that women who have been abused in childhood are a particular target for the small but significant group of male therapists who have sexual relations with women clients.

Although gender issues in working with survivors are complex, if the counsellor is the same gender as their abuser, this may be an impossible scenario for the client. A choice of counsellor is important, although difficulties may still remain. For example, a woman abused by a man may consider a woman counsellor to be as helpless and as impotent as she was.

Some survivors will decide while they are in counselling that they wish to take legal action against their abusers. Although counsellors can assist the client in exploring their reasons for doing so, help them to consider what they may hope to achieve, and support them during this process, it is crucial that clients who are seriously considering legal action seek legal advice. Counsellors need to take care to only work within their own area of expertise. They may be called to give evidence in such cases and therefore would need to take appropriate advice themselves.

Therapeutic Approaches

Research on what works best is limited (Dale et al., 1998) but anecdotal evidence from survivors is strong. Although dialectical behaviour therapy (DBT) seems to be having a promising effect in terms of reducing self-harm by abuse survivors, many survivors themselves are not positive about short-term approaches.

Generally speaking, there is not a good match between a survivor struggling to seek help for the first time and short-term or time-limited work, particularly where this is for only six to eight sessions. In short-term work the process does not easily go at the client's pace, since both clear focus and speed are of the essence. However, some survivors find a 'bite-sized chunk' approach helpful, whereby an agreed issue is worked with and further help given later. This can be combined with couple work and group work.

The need for services that provide longer-term help is critical. A research study carried out by the University of York Department of Social Policy and Social Work (1999) recommended 'more resources for free long term psychotherapy and counselling are needed' (1999: 33) and 'secure funding for voluntary organisations, especially for those that offer help lines and self help groups for survivors of abuse, is needed' (1999: 34). The need for longer-term help is also summed up in the following from a survivor: 'I recognise that the NHS has limited resources, but when dealing with chronic physical illness ... treatment continues while the patient needs it. It should be the same for survivors and particularly because they, if given appropriate support and allowed enough time, do become well' (Department of Health, 2006: 221).

Some survivors prefer working in a group, as the one-to-one relationship may replicate too closely the abusive situation and they may not feel safe. Conversely, other survivors cannot initially manage group therapy, but may find this helpful later.

In counselling survivors, counsellors can expect to encounter powerful feelings, both in themselves and from their clients. Distress, anger, horror and hopelessness are often evident and counsellors may feel deskilled, inadequate and overwhelmed. In the light of such powerful emotions and disturbing material there is an obvious question of how much is enough: should the work be time limited or open ended; should clients be seen weekly or more frequently; and how should counsellors react if the client cannot manage between sessions and wants more time and contact? A key feature of abuse is the invasion of the child's boundaries of body, self and psyche, and it is vital that therapy and counselling in no way re-create this, and that secure boundaries are established and safely maintained. These may be challenged by the client, in the same way as theirs were by the abuser, but the counsellor's job is to hold, manage and contain boundaries. Different models have different views on frequency of sessions and ultimate length of the counselling, and, for instance, telephone contact between sessions. What is most important is that there is a model, that there is clarity for the client, and that if any change is made it should be on the basis of carefully considered therapeutic need. It should never be a knee-jerk reaction – an inappropriate response to unprocessed, unconsidered and uncomfortable feelings in the counsellor. Therefore, for example, a desire to rescue, feelings of guilt and inadequacy, and experiencing pressure from the client to give more should always be discussed with a supervisor. Supervisors too need to be aware of the complex dynamics that can be involved (Walker, 2004).

It is absolutely crucial that counsellors do not commit to more than they can safely and realistically give, and that changing the frame and the implications of this are explored before changes are made. To work safely with abuse survivors, counsellors must be able to contain and make therapeutic sense of very difficult feelings.

The approach should match the needs of that particular client, although sadly the opposite is often the experience of survivors (especially those who cannot afford to seek private help). They are offered what is available, not what they need. The voluntary sector, however, has some excellent services in some parts of the country, although others are sadly bereft of these. Many are run by survivors for survivors.

Some survivors have a strong need to work their way through the abuse, to describe it, to explore it, to have the counsellor act as witness to it, and to attempt to make some sense of the awfulness. Others do not find this helpful; while yet others do not have a clear enough recall to enable them to do this. In that event, the therapeutic task is often helping someone to come to terms with, and move on from, uncertainty and not knowing.

A Controversial Field:
Recovered Memory

Working with abuse has always involved controversies, reflecting both societal and individual denial and a genuine difficulty in believing the horrors that can be perpetrated on children. These change over time but controversy is ever present. It has moved from whether sexual abuse is fantasy or real, to difficulty in acknowledging boys as victims and women as perpetrators, to having to face the widespread and often extreme abuse perpetrated by those in the care sector and in religious groups, to the existence or not of satanic and ritual abuse – and to the question of recovered memory and the role of therapy within this.

Recovered memory has been a major controversy in work with abuse survivors (Walker, 1996) and is often highly charged emotionally, making it difficult to think clearly and difficult to get accurate information. Although the term 'recovered memory' is used here, the term 'false memory' was originally coined in the United States of America after Jennifer Freyd recovered memories of childhood sexual abuse whilst in therapy. Her parents disputed the accuracy of her memories and in conjunction with Ralph Underwager (who was later discredited) started the False Memory Syndrome Foundation (FMSF) which then also set up in the UK. It was argued that families were being destroyed by ill-trained therapists actively seeking to discover in therapy repressed memories of abuse that are essentially false, particularly by using hypnosis and 'truth drugs'. The term 'false memory' is in itself emotive, implying that memories *are actually false*. When, as does happen, the term 'syndrome' is also attached, a pseudo-scientific validity is implied that is neither accurate nor helpful. At times bitter disputes have arisen between survivor groups and those who support the 'false memory' groups, and considerable anxiety is caused to those working in this area.

This controversy is closely linked to the debates surrounding the concepts of both repression and dissociation, that is, whether child sexual abuse can cause victims to effectively repress or dissociate from the memories of those experiences. A significant study carried out by Linda Meyer Williams (1992) into women's memories of childhood sexual abuse researched 129 women with previously documented histories of sexual victimization in childhood. In other words, abuse had been proved to take place. In detailed interviews about their abuse histories a large proportion of the women did not recall the abuse, which had been reported 17 years earlier. Women who were younger at the time of the abuse and those molested by someone they knew were more likely to have no recall of the abuse. In one case a woman told the interviewer that she was never sexually abused as a child, and she repeatedly and calmly continued to deny any such experiences throughout the detailed questioning. In fact her uncle had sexually abused her when she had been four, as well as her cousin aged nine, and her friend also aged four.

Recent research in Russia provides an interesting perspective. The FMSF assumes a culture where media exposure and awareness of ideas such as dissociation and recovered memory are prevalent and where both survivors and therapists are in thrall to these ideas – greatly influenced and prejudiced by them, and eagerly seeking out experiences supporting them. This is absolutely not the case in Russia (Dalenberg and Palesh, 2004; Palesh, 2002; Palesh and Dalenberg, 2006) where publicly available information on child abuse, dissociation, or dissociative amnesia is greatly limited. They investigated recovered memory and dissociation in a sample of Russian college students. They report rates of dissociation and memory disturbance for traumatized students in the Russian sample that are higher than in most US college student samples. These findings 'support the argument that dissociation is not a culture-specific phenomenon, created by zealous American/British therapists or an abuse-obsessed media, but instead may be a universal occurrence' (Palesh, 2002: 2).

There is a danger of the 'false memory' issue becoming a therapeutic red herring that once again in the history of abuse acts as a block and defence to facing its appalling extent and effects. And it must always be remembered that perpetrators and denial go hand in hand. However much there are some genuinely distressed and falsely accused families in the false memory groups, inevitably they will also act as a magnet for perpetrators searching for another psychological line of defence against acknowledging to themselves, or their victims, their responsibility for their *violence*. As in all their client work counsellors should not be suggestive; they should not jump to rapid conclusions; and perhaps most importantly they should be able to tolerate and work with uncertainty. It is essential that this controversy is not allowed to distract us from our work with survivors of childhood abuse, or to undermine us in so doing. The history of the denial of abuse is worrying in its power and its tenacity. This debate must not validate and encourage the deepening of denial. Working in this field therefore requires a robustness and an ability to note the controversies, to consider them and to act appropriately as a practitioner, but not to be stopped by them. If practitioners become frightened off in this way, then survivors of sexual abuse will become further alienated and isolated.

REFERENCES

Ainscough, C. and Toon, K. (1996) *Breaking Free: Help for Survivors of Child Sexual Abuse*. London: Sheldon.

Bray, M. (1997) *Sexual Abuse: The Child's Voice. Poppies on the Rubbish Heap*. London: Jessica Kingsley.

Bremner, J.D., Vythilingam, M., Vermetten, E., et al. (2003) MRI and PET study of deficits in hippocampal structure and function in women with child sexual abuse and post traumatic disorder. *American Journal of Psychiatry*, 160: 924–32.

Cawson, P., Wattam, C., Brooker, S. and Kelly, G. (2000) *Child Maltreatment in the United Kingdom: A Study of the Prevalence of Child Abuse and Neglect*. London: NSPCC.

Corby, B. (2006) *Child Abuse: Towards a Knowledge Base* (3rd edn). Maidenhead: Open University Press.

Dale, P., Allen, J. and Measor, L. (1998) Counselling adults who were abused as children: clients' perceptions of efficacy, client–counsellor communication, and dissatisfaction. *British Journal of Guidance and Counselling*, 26 (2): 141–57.

Dalenberg, C.J. and Palesh, O.G. (2004) Relationship between child abuse history, trauma, and dissociation in Russian college students. *Child Abuse and Neglect*, 28: 461–74.

Department of Health (2006) *Victim of Violence and Abuse Prevention Programme: Delphi Report*. London: Department of Health and National Institute for Mental Health in England.

Ghate, D. and Daniels, A. (1997) *Talking about My Generation: A Survey of 8–15-Year-Olds Growing Up in the 1990s*. London: NSPCC.

Howe, D. (2006) *Child Abuse and Neglect: Attachment, Development and Intervention* (3rd edn). Maidenhead: Open University Press.

Laville, S. (2009) NSPCC reveals 53 children are sexually abused every day. *The Guardian*, 19 January.

National Statistics (1997) *Criminal Statistics in England and Wales 1997*. London: Home Office.

Neumann, D.A., Houskamp, B.M., Pollock, V.E. and Brier, J. (1996) The long-term sequelae of childhood abuse in women: a meta-analytic review. *Child Maltreatment*, 1: 6–16.

NSPCC (2007) *Key Child Protection Statistics*. London: NSPCC.

Palesh, O.G. (2002) The study of dissociation in Russia: considerations for the international researcher. *ISSD News*, 20 (6): 2–3.

Palesh, O.G. and Dalenberg, C.J. (2006) Recovered memory and amnesia in Russian college students. In M.V. Landow (ed.), *College Students: Mental Health and Coping Strategies* (pp. 153–65). Hauppauge, NY: Nova Science.

Sanderson, C. (2006) *Counselling Adult Survivors of Childhood Sexual Abuse*. London: Jessica Kingsley.

University of York (1999) *Research on Adult Survivors of Childhood Sexual Abuse: A Report of the Experiences of Services*. North Yorkshire Health Authority.

Walker, M. (1992) *Surviving Secrets: The Experience of Abuse for the Child, the Family and the Helper*. Buckingham: Open University Press.

Walker, M. (1996) Working with abuse survivors: the recovered memory debate. In R. Bayne and I. Horton (eds), *New Directions in Counselling*. London: Routledge.

Walker, M. (2003) Supervising practitioners working with survivors of childhood abuse: counter transference, secondary traumatization and terror. *Psychodynamic Practice*, 10 (2).

Williams, L.M. (1992) Adult memories of childhood abuse: preliminary findings from a longitudinal study. *APSAC Advisor*.

RECOMMENDED READING

British Psychological Society (1995) *Report on Recovered Memory*. Leicester: BPS.

Cawson, P., Wattam, C., Brooker, S. and Kelly, G. (2000) *Child Maltreatment in the UK: A Study of the Prevalence of Child Abuse and Neglect*. London: NSPCC.

Sinason, V. (ed.) (1998) *Memory in Dispute*. London: Karnac.

Walker, M. (2003) *Abuse: Questions and Answers for Counsellors and Therapists*. London: Whurr.

Working with Suicide and Self-Harm in Counselling and Psychotherapy

ANDREW REEVES

INTRODUCTION

Working with suicide and self-harm in counselling and psychotherapy can be both challenging and demanding. While suicide is no longer a criminal act, the demands of organisational working, meeting the requirements of procedural or policy expectations, in addition to responding empathically and appropriately to a potentially highly distressed client, require commensurate skill. Knowing how best to respond to a client's potential suicidal intent or self-harm, or helping a client to begin to explore these potentially highly shameful aspects of their experience, require that the practitioner is aware of both their client's process and their own.

The purpose of this chapter is to explore what is meant by suicide and self-harm, to consider its prevalence and thus the likelihood of counsellors and psychotherapists encountering it in their work, to name the legal and ethical dilemmas that can arise, and to identify key ways in which practitioners can support themselves and their clients in their work. It is important to note, however, that working with suicide and self-harm requires the practitioner to be able to recognise their own anxiety and learn to support themselves effectively with it, rather than develop the capacity to see into the future. It is sometimes assumed that working with suicide risk requires counsellors and psychotherapists to always know what their clients are about to do, i.e. whether or not a client will attempt suicide or self-harm or

not. Until it is possible to acquire the ability to see into the future, the imperative is that practitioners work ethically, professionally and with the client's needs as priority.

DEFINITIONS

Suicide

The World Health Organization defines suicide simply as 'the act of deliberately killing oneself' (WHO, 2010a). For a UK coroner to classify a death as suicide, they must be beyond reasonable doubt that:

- The event which caused the deceased's death must have been self-inflicted, self-enacted and self-administered.
- The intention of the deceased in initiating the fatal event must unequivocally have been to bring about his or her own death (McCarthy and Walsh, 1975; cited in O'Connor and Sheehy, 2000: 15).

Leenaars (2004) notes that defining suicide is altogether a more complex process if a definition is to inform our approach to assessment. A definition of 'suicidal' would be more helpful. Word limits prevent too detailed a discussion here, but a full exploration can be found in Leenaars et al. (1997).

Self-harm

Babiker and Arnold define self-harm as 'an act which involves deliberately inflicting pain and/or injury to one's body, but without suicidal intent' (1997: 2), while the National Institute for Health and Clinical Excellence (NICE) states that self-harm is 'self-poisoning or injury, irrespective of the apparent purpose of the act' and that 'self-harm is an expression of personal distress, not an illness, and there are many varied reasons for a person to harm him or herself' (2004: 7).

Babiker and Arnold's definition draws out a distinction between self-harm and suicidal ideation when they state 'but without suicidal intent'. A generally held view is that self-harm is usually used as a coping strategy against profound or overwhelming feelings of distress (anger, hurt, rage, low self-esteem) and is a means of living rather than dying. A report by the Royal College of Psychiatrists in the UK stated, 'an act of self-harm is not necessarily an attempt or even indicator of suicide, indeed it can sometimes be a bizarre form of self-preservation' (2010: 6). However, it is important to keep in mind that on occasions self-harm can be sufficiently severe or chaotic that the behaviour becomes a risk to life, with or without that intention. Certainly self-harm is correlated with a higher risk of suicide.

PREVALENCE

WHO (2010b) states that internationally, 'Every year, an estimated 900,000 people die by committing suicide. This represents one death every 40 seconds. Worldwide, suicide ranks among the three leading causes of death among those aged 15–44 years.' They also state that suicide rates have increased by 60 per cent over the last 45 years. Bertolote and Fleischmann (2002) estimated that, based on current trends, approximately 1.53 million people will die from suicide in 2020. However, in the UK the trend has been slightly downward over the last few years.

The National Inquiry into Self-Harm is cautious about offering detailed statistics regarding the number of people who self-harm. This is because the majority of self-harmers very probably never present to agencies; self-harm is often hidden and self-treated. Statistics can therefore only be the tip of an iceberg. However, various studies have estimated that 1 in 10 young people have self-harmed at some point in their lives. If the findings of another study were extrapolated to the wider population, estimates would be that more than 1 million

adolescents have considered self-harm, with 800,000 of those actually having inflicted injuries. Full details of these studies with a discussion can be found in the National Inquiry document (Mental Health Foundation, 2004).

ETHICAL AND LEGAL ISSUES

Ethical practice is defined by professional organisations, for example the British Association for Counselling and Psychotherapy (BACP), the United Kingdom Council for Psychotherapy (UKCP) and the British Psychological Society (BPS). As a member of such an organisation, a counsellor or psychotherapist must ensure they work in line with ethical requirements as outlined in codes of practice or frameworks. It is the responsibility of the practitioner to ensure they are aware of, and understand, any particular ethical requirement regarding suicide and self-harm. Additionally, if employed within an organisation, they should ensure that they follow fully any requirements or procedures detailing how clients who are suicidal or are self-harming should be responded to.

As mentioned, suicide is no longer a criminal offence, having been decriminalised in the Suicide Act 1961. The legal requirements surrounding confidentiality are complex, but a full discussion can be found in Bond and Mitchels (2008). Likewise, other Acts of Parliament in the UK inform various aspects of practice, including the Mental Capacity Act 2005, mental health legislation and work with young people.

CLIENT PRESENTATION

Suicide

While some clients may talk openly about their suicidal thoughts, many will not talk about them at all, or will perhaps allude to them through metaphor or imagery. For some clients their suicidal thoughts may be ever present; knowing they have the option to end their life is sufficient to keep them alive. For others, the thought of suicide may be infrequent or in response to crisis; while for others, particularly younger people, the risk of suicide will lie in the impulsivity of their thoughts and responses. Given how many clients are reluctant to begin talking about suicide, it is essential that clients are asked openly about suicide; doing so will more likely reduce rather than increase risk.

Self-harm

Contrary to the myths of self-harm being 'attention-seeking', the overwhelming majority of self harm is hidden and masked, often not coming to the attention of treating or helping organisations. One of the difficulties in researching the prevalence of self-harm is the lack of consistency in definition. As discussed earlier, self-harm may include behaviours that are self-injuring, e.g. cutting, burning, etc., but a wider definition (and thus a more helpful one) would include any activity where 'harm' (direct or indirect) is sustained as a response to particular thoughts or feelings e.g. excessive exercising or risk-taking behaviours such as dangerous driving.

As with suicide potential, it is essential that the practitioner is willing to ask their clients about self-harm, e.g. 'I wonder whether you have ever harmed yourself as a means of coping with how you feel?' Doing so will help reduce the stigma associated with self-harm, and provide the client with an invitation to explore their actions in a way they may never have done elsewhere.

THERAPIST RESPONSES TO SUICIDE AND SELF-HARM

Much is written about how suicide might present in counselling and psychotherapy, with less written about how counsellors and psychotherapists might respond to suicide potential or self-harm. The majority of what has been written focuses only on the client's suicidal process; the practitioner apparently should have the capacity to leave their own responses 'at the door' (as it is often said) and meet the client in some form of *tabula rasa* encounter. Of course, the reality of therapy is that the therapist response to their client or their counter-transferential response – a complex interplay of different responses and experiences – is equally important in determining the process of therapy. The same is true when working with suicide potential or self-harm.

How a therapist responds to the disclosure of self-harm, or the possibility of suicide, will profoundly shape the nature of the discourse client and therapist can have. The therapist will, in virtue of the fact that they are human too, already have a 'position' on suicide; it is a subject that rarely leaves people feeling neutral. Whether the held belief is that every individual retains the right to end their own life or does not have that right, or the view is somewhere between these two positions, will be powerfully present in the therapeutic process if unacknowledged. A number of factors will inform a view of suicide, which may include faith

or spiritually held beliefs, a personal experience of having been suicidal, suicide or potential suicide amongst family or friends, music, films, books, news coverage and so on. The ways in which views about suicide can be shaped and influenced are endless, and the process is a dynamic one, always apt to change.

The same is true for self-harm. Therapists may intellectually understand why an individual may self-harm, but then may experience a very different response in therapy with a client perhaps showing a cut or burn, or providing a description of their self-harming behaviour. The intellectual niceties around suicide and self-harm evaporate quickly when contextualised by a client with whom we have developed an intimate relationship. The potential for therapists to feel angry, hurt, rejected, attacked or undermined by their client's suicide potential or self-harm is high.

The Dangers of Unacknowledged Therapist Responses

There are many ways in which counsellors and psychotherapists might 'act out' their otherwise unacknowledged responses to suicide in a therapy session. Most commonly of course is therapists denying they have a 'response' at all: 'I am fine in working with self-harm, it really doesn't bother me', or perhaps 'I believe that every client has a right to kill themselves if they wish, so it is not for me to get involved.' Both of these examples on the surface might appear to be acceptable; however, I would argue that it is essential for us as therapists to be impacted by our client's potential suicide or self-harm. Anaesthetising ourselves against such pain has the potential to parallel the client's experience of themselves, and potentially undermines the empathy and insight required to offer emotional support.

Leenaars outlines a number of ways 'unacknowledged counter-transference' might present in therapy with suicidal clients, particularly when the therapist's response includes guilt, anger, anxiety or fear, for example:

- underestimation of the seriousness of the suicidal action (or intent)
- absence of a discussion of suicidal thoughts (or intent)
- allowing oneself to be lulled into a false sense of security by the client's promise not to repeat a suicide attempt (or act on suicidal thoughts)
- disregard of the 'cry for help' aspect of the suicidal attempt (or thoughts), and concentration exclusively on its manipulative character
- exaggeration of the client's provocative, infantile and aggressive sides

- denial of one's own importance to the client
- failure to persuade the client to undergo (or continue with) counselling or psychotherapy
- feeling of lacking the resources for the evaluation required by a particular client
- exaggerated sense of hopelessness in response to the client's social situation and abuse of drugs/alcohol
- being pleased with the client's claims to have all problems solved after only a brief period of time
- feeling upset when the client shows resistance after only a brief course of enquiry, despite the therapist's initial profound commitment. (2004: 101–2)

Perhaps however, unacknowledged counter-transferential responses are most often seen in the minutiae of the therapeutic discourse. My own research (Reeves et al., 2004) indicated that, regardless of length of post-qualifying experience or therapeutic orientation, counsellors and psychotherapists can be silenced by suicide potential, not exploring with the client the meaning of their suicidal thoughts and thus not considering, again with the client, the degree of intent and thus the level of risk. Instead, they predominantly used reflective responses. This is not to say that reflective responses are wrong – often a skilfully used reflection can help facilitate a deeper meaning for a client – but when used almost exclusively they have the potential to leave the therapist defined by the client's position, rather than providing an opportunity to explore risk.

The same is true when working with self-harm. In some instances therapists will only focus on the self-destructive aspect of self-harm (as opposed to that part of the behaviour that facilitates coping), and view this as contra-indicatory to growth and development. I have known of some therapy services withdrawing counselling until self-harming stops. Self-harm can often provoke powerful responses in the therapist, including anger, a sense of being attacked by it, revulsion and hopelessness. Literature about self-harm and training often talks of 'people who self-harm', implying that there are people who don't. It is important, and helpful, in establishing and maintaining therapeutic contact with a client around self-harm to be able to recognise how we all self-harm. Perhaps when stressed or angry we drink too much, use other substances, over-exercise, over-eat, spend too much money, and so on. The immediacy of a cut or burn may well be different to shopping excessively, but if both behaviours are triggered as a means of coping with stress or frustration, for example, the process is fundamentally the same.

The more insight a practitioner can have into their own process, the more they will be able to connect with their client's.

The feelings and responses outlined above to both suicide potential and self-harm are not wrong; they are understandable human reactions to another's profound distress. However, they become potentially harmful when unacknowledged and unsupported. The more a practitioner is able to reflect on their own process – their feelings, thoughts, reactions and behaviours in response to suicide potential or self-harm – the more they will be able to support themselves in the work and therefore be available to their clients.

ASSESSING RISK

The previous section highlighted how counsellors and psychotherapists can unwittingly and unexpectedly find themselves disconnected from their clients as a consequence of their own powerful responses and feelings. Assessing risk therefore demands psychological contact and a willingness and ability to remain connected with their client at risk. The prediction–prevention culture is based on the premise that there is sufficient confidence in current research and risk assessment tools to be able to set targets for suicide reduction (Department of Health, 2002; Scottish Executive, 2002; Department of Health, Social Services and Public Safety, 2006; Welsh Assembly, 2008), and that 'failure' to prevent harm might be the 'failure' of the individual practitioner to use such research effectively.

That is not to say that current research into suicide and self-harm is unhelpful, because that is not the case. Understanding factors associated with a higher risk of suicide, for example, can help contextualise the presentation of the individual's experience. Table 6.22.1 outlines a number of key risk factors (Reeves, 2010; and based on Appleby et al., 2001; Battle, 1991; Battle et al., 1993; Bernhard and Bernhard, 1985; Gilliland, 1985; Hazell and Lewin, 1993; Hersh, 1985; Ruddell and Curwen, 2008; Williams and Morgan, 1994).

However, is important that counsellors and psychotherapists engage openly with their clients about suicide, asking such questions as:

- Have you ever thought about harming yourself or killing yourself in response to how you are feeling?
- Have you made any plans about how you might kill yourself?

Table 6.22.1 *Factors associated with higher suicide risk*

Gender, e.g. males generally present with greater risk across age groups

    Age, e.g. males aged 14–25 and people over 75 years

    Relationships: single, widowed, divorced, separated

    Social isolation

    Psychopathology including:

        schizophrenia
        mood disorders, including depression
        psychosis
        post-traumatic stress disorder
        affective disorders, including bipolar
        affective disorder
        organic disorders
        personality disorders, e.g. sociopathy, aggression

    Alcohol and drug use

    Hopelessness

    Occupational factors, e.g. unemployment, retirement

    History of childhood sexual or physical abuse

    Adult sexual assault

    Specific suicide plan formulated

    Prior suicide attempt and/or family history of suicide or suicide attempts

    Physical illness, e.g. terminal illness, biochemical, hormonal

    Bereavement or recent trauma

    Significant and unexplained mood change

    Self-harm

- What has helped you not kill or harm yourself? How do you support yourself at difficult times?
- On a scale of 1–10, 1 being the best, 10 being the worst, how would you rate your feelings and thoughts about suicide or self-harm at the moment?

I would argue this approach most effectively locates risk assessment in the dialogue with the client. As Shneidman states:

> Our best route to understanding suicide is not through the study of the structure of the brain, nor the study of social statistics, nor the study of mental diseases, but directly through the study of human emotions described in plain English, in the words of the suicidal person. The most important question to a potentially suicidal person is not an inquiry about family history or laboratory tests of blood or spinal fluid, but 'where do you hurt?' and 'how can I help you?' (1998: 6).

CONCLUSIONS

Working with suicide and self-harm can be one of the most challenging professional issues encountered by any practitioner. While a knowledge of risk factors and current research into suicide and self-harm is essential, so too is the willingness to engage in a meaningful therapeutic dialogue with clients who present with such problems. Doing so will enable the counsellor or psychotherapist to best understand the level of potential and risk, but will also provide the client with the best opportunity to understand their own distress and take responsibility for their wellbeing.

REFERENCES

Appleby, L., Shaw, J., Sherratt, J., Amos, T., Robinson, J. and McDonnell, R. (2001) *Safety First: Five Year Report of the National Confidential Inquiry into Suicide and Homicide by People with a Mental Illness.* London: HMSO.

Babiker, G. and Arnold, L. (1997) *The Language of Injury: Comprehending Self-Mutilation.* Leicester: British Psychological Society.

Battle, A.O. (1991) Factors in assessing suicidal lethality. Paper presented at the Crisis Center Preservice Volunteer Training, University of Tennessee College of Medicine, Department of Psychiatry, Memphis.

Battle, A.O., Battle, M.V. and Trolley, E.A. (1993) Potential for suicide and aggression in delinquents at juvenile court in a southern city. *Suicide and Life Threatening Behaviour*, 23 (3): 230–43.

Bernhard, J.L. and Bernhard, M.L. (1985) *Suicide on Campus: Response to the Problem.* In E.S. Zinner (ed.), *Coping with Death on Campus* (pp. 69–83). San Francisco: Jossey-Bass.

Bertolote, J.M. and Fleischmann, A. (2002) Suicide and psychiatric diagnosis: a worldwide perspective. *World Psychiatry*, 1 (3): 181–5.

Bond, T. and Mitchels, B. (2008) *Confidentiality and Record Keeping in Counselling and Psychotherapy: Legal Resources for Counsellors and Psychotherapists.* London: Sage/BACP.

Department of Health (2002) *National Suicide Prevention Strategy for England.* London: Stationery Office.

Department of Health, Social Services and Public Safety (2006) *Protect Life: A Shared Vision. The Northern Ireland Suicide Prevention and Action Plan*. Belfast: DHSSPS.

Gilligand, B.E. (1985) Surviving college: teaching college students to cope. Paper presented at the Symposium on Suicide in Teenagers and Young Adults, University of Tennessee College of Medicine, Department of Psychiatry, Memphis.

Hazell, P. and Lewin, T. (1993) An evaluation of postvention following adolescent suicide. *Suicide and Life Threatening Behaviour*, 23 (2): 101–9.

Hersh, J.B. (1985) Interviewing college students in crisis. *Journal of Counseling and Development*, 63: 286–9.

Leenaars, A.A. (2004) *Psychotherapy with Suicidal People: A Person-Centred Approach*. Chichester: Wiley.

Leenaars, A.A., De Leo, D., Diekstra, R.F.W., Goldeny, R.D., Kelleher, M.J., Lester, D. and Nordstrom, P. (1997) Consultations for research in suicidology. *Archives of Suicide Research*, 3 (2): 139–51.

McCarthy, P. and Walsh, D. (1975) Suicide in Dublin: under-reporting of suicide and the consequences for national statistics. *British Journal of Psychiatry*, 126: 301–8.

Mental Health Foundation (2004) *Truth Hurts: A Report on the National Inquiry into Self-Harm among Young People*. London: Mental Health Foundation.

NICE (2004) *Self-Harm: The Short-Term Physical and Psychological Management and Secondary Prevention of Self-Harm in Primary and Secondary Care*. London: National Institute for Health and Clinical Excellence.

O'Connor, R. and Sheehy, N. (2000) *Understanding Suicidal Behaviour*. Oxford: Blackwells.

Reeves, A. (2010) *Counselling Suicidal Clients*. London: Sage.

Reeves, A., Bowl, R., Wheeler, S. and Guthrie, E. (2004) The hardest words: exploring the dialogue of suicide in the counselling process. A discourse analysis. *Counselling and Psychotherapy Research*, 4 (1): 62–71.

Royal College of Psychiatrists (2010) *Self-Harm, Suicide and Risk: Helping People Who Self-Harm*. College Report CR158. London: Royal College of Psychiatrists.

Ruddell, P. and Curwen, B. (2008) Understanding suicidal ideation and assessing for risk. In S. Palmer (ed.), *Suicide: Strategies and Interventions for Reduction and Prevention* (pp. 84–99). London: Routledge.

Scottish Executive (2002) *Choose Life: A National Strategy and Action Plan to Prevent Suicide in Scotland*. Edinburgh: Stationery Office.

Shneidman, E.S. (1998) *The Suicidal Mind*. Oxford: Oxford University Press.

Welsh Assembly (2008) *Talk to Me: A National Action Plan to Reduce Suicide and Self-Harm in Wales 2008–2013*. Cardiff: Stationery Office.

Williams, R. and Morgan, H.G. (eds) (1994) *Suicide Prevention: The Challenge Confronted*. London: HMSO.

WHO (2010a) *Suicide*. World Health Organization. www.who.int/topics/suicide/en/, accessed 6 October 2010.

WHO (2010b) *How Can Suicide Be Prevented?* World Health Organization. www.who.int/features/qa/24/en/index.html, accessed 6 October 2010.

RECOMMENDED READING

Bond, T. and Mitchels, B. (2008) *Confidentiality and Record Keeping in Counselling and Psychotherapy: Legal Resources for Counsellors and Psychotherapists*. London: Sage/BACP.

Leenaars, A. (2004) *Psychotherapy with Suicidal People: A Person-Centred Approach*. Chichester: Wiley.

Reeves, A. (2010) *Counselling Suicidal Clients*. London: Sage.

Reeves, A. and Howdin, J. (2010) *Considerations When Working with Clients Who Self-Harm*. Information Sheet G12. Lutterworth: BACP.

Reeves, A. and Seber, P. (2010) *Working with the Suicidal Client*. Information Sheet P7. Lutterworth: BACP.

Working with Survivors of Rape and Domestic Violence

CHRISTIANE SANDERSON

Working with survivors of rape and domestic violence (DV), while highly rewarding, can be extremely challenging and demanding. Being in the presence of such brutalisation is not only terrifying for the victim and survivor, but inevitably impacts on those who bear witness. To fully understand the impact and long-term effects of rape and DV, counsellors need to view such abuse within the context of interpersonal trauma in which bodily and psychological integrity is threatened and which overwhelms human adaptation to life (Sanderson, 2010a).

When abuse and sexual assault masquerade as love and affection, confusion reigns and reality is compromised. As a result, all relationships are seen as dangerous, even professional ones, making it hard to seek support or therapeutic help for fear of being betrayed again. Such fears can lead to a range of therapeutic challenges which practitioners need to be aware of in order to create a secure base in which traumatic experiences can be integrated, allowing survivors to reconnect to self, others and the world.

The overwhelming terror of rape and DV activates a cascade of neurobiological chemicals and primitive psychobiological defences such as withdrawal, numbing and dissociation. This is accompanied by alterations in perception of self, others and the world, and systems of meaning. The paradox of love conflated with dehumanisation compromises internal and external reality in which the victim feels complicit in his or her violation. This makes it extremely difficult to name or legitimise such abuse.

The secret nature of interpersonal trauma, and the shame associated with rape and DV, render survivors' experiences inchoate (Sanderson, 2010a). Not being able to speak the unspeakable means experiences cannot be named, validated or legitimised. In the abyss of silence the trauma cannot be processed and thus is ossified as a nub of despair in which self and others cannot be trusted. Thus all relationships, including therapeutic ones, are suffused with terror, anxiety and anticipated retraumatisation.

THE DYNAMICS OF RAPE AND DOMESTIC VIOLENCE

The betrayal of trust and dehumanisation in interpersonal trauma commonly lead to a disconnection from self and others. Under threat of physical and psychological annihilation, the individual has to disavow aspects of the self. When such trauma is repeated and prolonged, as in DV, the survivor has no choice but to adapt to the shameless brutality of the abuser by renouncing basic human needs or responses and to suppress 'Knowing what you are not supposed to know and feeling what you are not supposed to feel' (Bowlby, 1988) for fear of further abuse.

Sexual violence, rape and DV often coexist. In the majority of cases of rape the perpetrator is known to the victim, with only 18 per cent of reported rape committed by strangers (Walby and Allen, 2004).

This indicates that rape occurs within a wide range of relationships, including intimate relationships and marriage, making it harder to legitimise or disclose due to attitudes and beliefs around the nature of sexual intimacy. Rape in these instances is invariably used to control and dominate a partner or ex-partner to obtain total submission.

The shame associated with rape and DV, especially around perceived complicity, creates further barriers to disclosure or seeking help. This is compounded by genuine fears of the consequences of disclosure, with women in DV relationships being most at risk of being murdered by their partner when they attempt to leave the relationship (Sanderson, 2010a).

As many survivors are in thrall to their abuser, counsellors need to be aware that interpersonal abuse rarely starts with an act of rape or violence. Many perpetrators initially befriend and entice potential victims over time in order to gain control and power. Rape or the threat of rape is a powerful form of punishment or humiliation in relationships, and as a display of ultimate power and control.

In order to rape or repeatedly brutalise an individual, the abuser must first dehumanise the person. This is done through projective annihilation in which a fantasised identity is projected onto the victim so that they become whoever the abuser wants them to be (Fonagy et al., 2002). The survivor has no choice but to abandon the authentic self to become whatever the abuser wants them to be and take on the false identity imposed by the abuser (Mollon, 2000). The terror of rape and the repeated abuse seen in DV demands either total submission or death, leaving the survivor feeling 'at once dead yet alive in the wake of her own destruction' (Grand, 2000). Once this occurs, surrender is complete and the victim no longer experiences any sense of self-agency.

THE IMPACT OF INTERPERSONAL TRAUMA

The traumatic nature of rape and DV activates primitive psychobiological survival mechanisms, which elicit a range of psychological and emotional responses such as terror, loss of control and self-agency, shame and self-blame. In the presence of overwhelming and life-threatening danger the body's alarm system is activated through the release of a cascade of neurochemicals to prepare the body for fight or flight. If the danger is inescapable as in rape and DV the only option is to freeze, which prevents these powerful neurochemicals from being discharged, so they become trapped in the body.

When such danger is repeated and prolonged, the alarm system remains on high alert, making it harder to shut off (Sanderson, 2010b). This gives rise to many of the post-traumatic stress reactions such as hyperarousal and hypervigilance seen in survivors of rape and DV (van der Kolk et al., 2005).

As the alarm system is on constant high alert there is a sense of heightened danger which is easily tripped by external cues that resemble the original trauma, or by internal triggers such as thoughts or feelings, even in the absence of external danger (Sanderson, 2010a; 2010b). This accounts for associated traumatic reactions such as irritability, outbursts of anger, flashbacks, panic attacks, intrusive memories and nightmares.

Alternatively, the disruption to the alarm system can lead to complete shutdown or hypoarousal in which the person becomes detached or dissociated from their surroundings and internal state to anaesthetise their pain, making it easier to survive emotionally. This is aided by compartmentalisation in which the abuse is split off, allowing the survivor to retain a positive image of the abuser.

As disruptions to the alarm system make it harder to regulate emotions, additional trauma reactions are activated such as avoidance, numbing, and alterations in attention and perception. Impaired affect regulation and avoidance prevent the survivor from processing the trauma and integrating their experiences, which further intensifies the trauma reactions (Sanderson, 2010b). To manage these pervasive trauma reactions the survivor may resort to self-medication to alter internal mood states through food, alcohol, drugs, work, exercise or sex (Sanderson, 2010b).

When the interpersonal trauma is repeated and prolonged, sometimes over many years as in DV, it can lead to post-traumatic stress disorder (PTSD) and complex PTSD (C-PTSD) (Herman, 1992b) in which alterations in perception of self and others and alterations in systems of meaning predominate, leading to relational disturbances as well as compromised physical health (Pelcovitz et al., 1997).

As these trauma reactions are biologically mediated they occur outside conscious awareness and are perceived to be outside the survivors of control. This leads many survivors to believe they are 'going crazy', which generates further anxiety. Changes in perception lead to shame, guilt and self-blame and a concomitant need to conceal. Survivors of rape and DV learn that to be visible is dangerous as they are likely to be attacked, so they feel compelled to become invisible, even though this threatens their very existence. This existential conflict pervades all future relationships in which the survivor oscillates between 'approach' and 'avoid' behaviours.

Survivors of interpersonal trauma commonly conceal the vulnerable aspects of the self and their needs to create a protective barrier between self and others. As feelings are repudiated they become imprisoned in an unassailable fortress, and vulnerability is replaced by a façade of strength and invulnerability. This can lead to fierce self-reliance and fear of dependency which have a considerable impact on relational dynamics, including the therapeutic relationship (Sanderson, 2010a). This can lead to disconnection from others, making it harder to make sense of the trauma. In addition, meaningless acts of brutalisation make it impossible to derive meaning, which can lead to shattered assumptions about self, others and the world and a loss of hope, faith and spirituality, which reinforces a sense of hopelessness and despair.

The lack of meaning and control is mirrored in the psychobiological responses which are often experienced as involuntary reactions outside the victim's control, not unlike the lack of control during the rape or DV. An example of this is sexual arousal during rape. While this is an involuntary biological reaction which protects against tissue damage, it is experienced as a source of shame which gives rise to a false belief that the survivor is complicit in the rape and therefore to blame. The concomitant shame can lead to fears of not being believed, which in combination can hinder the victim from legitimising the rape. The fear of re-experiencing the trauma can also impede survivors from seeking appropriate help, leading them to further isolation and withdrawal from what they perceive as a hostile world. If the rape occurs within a relationship, or marriage, it can be even more difficult to legitimise due to social and cultural constructions and expectations of sexual intimacy.

Such beliefs also influence the perception of relationships and whether they are loving or abusive. Perceptions are further altered through repeated acts of brutalisation and traumatic bonding (Sanderson, 2010a). Traumatic bonding occurs in the presence of life-threatening fear with no means of escape, which evokes fearful dependency and denial of rage as the abuser has the power to preserve or destroy life. Traumatic bonding is conditioned through intermittent reinforcement wherein abusive behaviour alternates with loving and caregiving behaviour as seen in the cycle of abuse (Dutton and Painter, 1981). Such oscillation and unpredictability result in extremely strong emotional attachment that acts as a superglue to bond the relationship (Allen, 2001). The cycle of abuse also intensifies feelings of fear and love which are often misinterpreted as evidence of abiding love and passion (Herman, 1992a; Sanderson, 2008).

In order to manage the repeated abuse, and ensure survival, the survivor is forced to change his or her beliefs about the abuser. To do this the survivor has to separate or split off the abuse in order to retain only positive aspects of the abuser and the relationship. Such knowledge isolation or 'betrayal blindness' enables the survivor to humanise rather than demonise their partner and allows for a semblance of functioning. Such compartmentalisation also allows the survivor to seal off anger and rage, as the expression of such feelings could elicit further threat or danger. It also allows the survivor to manage the paradox of *knowing* and yet *not knowing*, to tolerate the intolerable and bear the unbearable (Sanderson, 2010a).

The shame, self-blame and guilt that accompany such compromised integrity lead to withdrawal and social isolation, which reduce opportunities for talking about and processing the abuse experience or challenging the abuser's behaviour. Ultimately, this reinforces the abuser's power and control, and increases the survivor's entrapment and captivity.

WORKING WITH SURVIVORS OF RAPE AND DV

Counsellors need to be aware of the impact of interpersonal trauma on relational functioning to minimise the replication of abuse dynamics in the counselling process. Survivors of rape and DV find it difficult to trust and can oscillate between hostility and extreme neediness. Practitioners need to be mindful that trust is not finite and that survivors may regularly test the commitment of the counsellor, which can create ruptures in the therapeutic relationship. Counsellors must understand these within the context of the survivor's experience and not personalise such ruptures, in order to remain connected and engaged. Healing is in withstanding such ruptures, not rejecting, shaming or punishing the survivor.

The pervasive fear of others makes it extremely difficult for survivors to risk connection only to have their trust betrayed again. This fear renders some survivors highly suspicious, hostile and resistant to any therapeutic engagement. In contrast some survivors invest trust too easily and indiscriminately, in order to be rescued. Practitioners need to honour survivors who risk connection and see this as a testament to hope in which the essence of the self has not been annihilated.

To facilitate the reconnection to self and others, counsellors need to provide an authentic human relationship to truly 'see' and understand the survivor and undo the effects of dehumanisation. It is only in the 'human to human' relationship that inter-subjectivity can be restored and the survivor can be released from the debasement of interpersonal abuse to permit post-traumatic growth which allows both survivor and practitioner to access a deeper appreciation of what it is to be human and to be alive.

CORE THERAPEUTIC GOALS

The core therapeutic goals when working with survivors of rape and DV are to establish external and internal safety. External safety consists of assessing and minimising external danger and encouraging survivors to access other resources and agencies that can offer support such as medical attention, police, advocacy, housing, and specialist support groups. Alongside this, internal safety from the tyranny of out-of-control trauma-related symptoms such as hyperarousal, flashbacks, panic attacks and intrusive memories must be restored.

This can be achieved through normalisation of symptoms and psycho-education by linking physiological responses to the interpersonal trauma (Sanderson, 2010b). This reassures the survivor that flashbacks, intrusive memories and dreams are not evidence of loss of sanity but arise out of fear and anxiety and are signals of unprocessed aspects of their experience. In the case of rape it is critical that survivors understand that sexual arousal during rape is normal to minimise tissue damage, and that it is a response to the sexual act *not* an indicator of sexual desire (Preble and Groth, 2002). Most importantly, survivors need to be reassured that their sexuality is not compromised, and to understand that it is not sexuality that is objectionable but the lack of consent. This will help the survivor to reduce shame and self-blame, and help them to reclaim their sexuality.

Counsellors will also need to focus on restoring control through affect regulation. Affect regulation reduces the intensity of trauma reactions and enhances distress tolerance, which help the survivor to manage a high level of arousal without resorting to self-medication or self-harm. Once the survivor has gained mastery over their physiological and emotional responses, the process of integrating the traumatic experiences can begin. In exploring the trauma and developing a more coherent narrative the survivor can begin to gain meaning and make sense of his or her experience. In this process, survivors will also need to grieve any losses associated with rape and DV (Sanderson, 2008; 2010a).

A fundamental goal is the building and maintenance of a therapeutic relationship in which the survivor can learn and practise relational skills.

This is pivotal to rebuilding relational worth and to discovering more authentic ways of relating in which needs, feelings and thoughts can be expressed without fear of being punished or humiliated. It is through the therapeutic relationship that the survivor can begin to reconnect to self and others with renewed trust (Sanderson, 2010a). This will enable the survivor to restore reality and challenge distorted perceptions. In addition, counsellors need to restore power and control to the survivor so that they can regain autonomy and self-agency.

While some survivors of rape or DV enter therapy immediately after being traumatised, many survivors remain silent for many years as they are too ashamed to talk about their experiences until trust has been established. In such cases, counsellors need to work on two parallel levels: one which focuses on rape or DV experience in the past, and the other which works to alleviate stress and symptoms in the present (Allen, 2001).

Some survivors may be so traumatised by rape or DV that pharmacological intervention is indicated, and counsellors may need to establish links with local medical and psychiatric services that can offer such options. In order to ascertain the best form of intervention, counsellors need to conduct an in-depth assessment on how the rape or DV has impacted on the survivor, and identify symptoms that have resulted from the rape and DV and pre-existing symptoms that have been reactivated.

Counsellors may combine their own therapeutic model with more specific therapeutic interventions that have been found to be effective when working with survivors of rape, such as prolonged exposure therapy (Foa and Rothbaum, 2002; Foa et al., 1991), cognitive processing therapy (Resick and Schnicke, 1993), dialectical behavioural therapy (Linehan, 1993), eye movement desensitisation and reprocessing (EMDR: Shapiro, 1995), or anxiety management training and psycho-education (Kilpatrick et al., 2007). While some of the techniques employed in these models are also efficacious in working with survivors of DV, they need to be conducted within a safe and secure base and a sensitively attuned therapeutic relationship (Sanderson, 2008; 2010a).

THE ROLE OF THE COUNSELLOR

A prerequisite to working with survivors of sexual and domestic violence is to have a comprehensive understanding of the dynamics of interpersonal trauma, especially the falsification of reality and collusive secrecy, and how these impact on relational dynamics and sexuality. Counsellors also need to be mindful of the socio-psychobiological sequelae of rape and DV and the socio-political, cultural and economic factors that prevent survivors from speaking the unspeakable (Sanderson, 2008).

Counsellors will also need a high level of awareness of their own socially constructed meanings around gender, race, ethnicity, power, control, domination and submission, sexuality and the hierarchical structure of families. In addition, they need to understand their own relational experiences, both past and present, and examine any interpersonal abuse they may have experienced. Such increased awareness will enhance understanding of any counter-transference reactions and how these might manifest when working with survivors of rape or DV. It will also help the practitioner to understand any feelings of shame, sexual arousal or abuse fantasies that may be evoked in the therapeutic process (Sanderson, 2006; 2010a).

Counsellors also need to be aware of their own relational or attachment style, to ensure that they provide a warm, compassionate and empathic therapeutic relationship in which they are comfortable in being present and engaged without blaming, recoiling or hiding behind clinical protocols. To avoid replicating the ubiquitous masquerade in interpersonal abuse, counsellors need to be scrupulously authentic, transparent and honest and not hide behind clinical façades. It is only through the warmth of human connection that brutalisation and dehumanisation can be undone and relational worth restored. To minimise misattunement and distortion, counsellors need to be explicit and mindful of language. Being explicit also reduces uncertainty and the need for 'mind reading'.

Counsellors also need to be flexible in permitting the survivor to pace the therapeutic process at a level that is manageable for them and to minimise retraumatisation. Alongside this, counsellors must ensure they do not reinforce false beliefs that shame the survivor. To this effect, they need to validate the survivor's strengths and existing resources rather than see him or her as a passive victim. To have survived, survivors will have employed a range of active survival strategies to minimise the impact of the abuse (Sanderson, 2008). Counsellors will also need to remain realistic and honest about what can and cannot be done, and be mindful of not making assurances or promises that they cannot fulfil.

THERAPEUTIC CHALLENGES WHEN WORKING WITH SURVIVORS OF RAPE AND DV

There are a number of therapeutic challenges that counsellors face when working with survivors of rape and domestic violence. A significant challenge is to be able to bear the pain of listening to the details of rape and DV without being overwhelmed, or disconnecting from the survivor. Counsellors need to ensure that they can manage their own responses and contain any fears that may emerge. Bearing witness to traumatic experiences can be highly distressing, and counsellors may feel voyeuristic or experience witness guilt (Herman, 1992a) or become sexually aroused. While such responses are normal, counsellors need to ensure that their reactions do not impede or contaminate the therapeutic process (Sanderson, 2010a).

Counsellors also need to possess considerable sensitivity to avoid shaming or alienating the survivor. This includes an awareness of how society and culture perceive victims of rape and DV and how this compounds the trauma. In some cultures the protection of honour lies with the victim, and when this is violated the victim is held responsible. In such instances counsellors need to understand and acknowledge the difficulties around disclosure and any repercussions in the community.

Given the lack of consent and self-agency in rape and DV, counsellors must be vigilant not to coerce or persuade the survivor toward their own preferred course of action. The survivor must be empowered to make their own informed choices about whether to report any sexual assault to the police, or to leave an abusive relationship. Counsellors will need to support the survivor in that decision and continue to remain supportive and engaged. This can present ethical dilemmas around duty of care, boundaries, when to break confidentiality and tolerating uncertainty (Sanderson, 2008).

COUNSELLOR SELF-CARE

Bearing witness to the destructive nature of interpersonal trauma can be highly stressful and give rise to terror, revulsion and disbelief, which can activate a need to detach, disengage or retreat into a rigid professional role or hide behind prescriptive techniques or protocols. To minimise 'compassion fatigue' (Figley, 2002), 'burnout' or secondary traumatic stress (STS) counsellors need to ensure that they are adequately supported through appropriate training, regular discussion with colleagues and peers, and supervision, and that they balance the level of trauma work (Sanderson, 2010a).

Counsellors will also need to prioritise self-care by seeking regular connection with family and friends and by engaging in life-sustaining activities that are pleasurable and revitalising. To counteract the traumatic impact of the work, counsellors will benefit from physical exercise such as martial arts, tai chi or yoga to ensure that they remain embodied. To remain grounded, counsellors will benefit from making a commitment to regularly engage in activities that are fun, stimulate all the senses, and enhance creativity and spirituality. It is through joy and laughter that counsellors can ensure that they maintain their vitality, hope and zest for life.

Working with survivors of rape and DV is transformative for both client and counsellor and can lead to post-traumatic growth. In the presence of trauma and resilience, counsellors become more sentient practitioners who not only understand but come to 'know' their clients (Bromberg, 1998) and truly appreciate what it means to be alive.

REFERENCES

Allen, J.G. (2001) *Traumatic Relationships and Serious Mental Disorders*. Chichester: Wiley.

Bowlby, J. (1988) *A Secure Base*. London: Routledge.

Bromberg, P. (1998) *Standing in the Spaces: Essays on Clinical Process, Trauma, and Dissociation*. Hillsdale, NJ: Analytic.

Dutton, D.G. and Painter, S.L. (1981) Traumatic bonding: the development of emotional attachment in battered women and other relationships of intermittent abuse. *Victimology: An International Journal*, 6: 139–55.

Figley, C.R. (2002) *Treating Compassion Fatigue*. New York: Brunner-Mazel.

Foa, E. and Rothbaum, B.O. (2002) *Treating the Trauma of Rape: Cognitive Behavioural Therapy for PTSD*. New York: Guilford.

Foa, E.B., Rothbaum, B.O., Riggs, D.S. and Murdock, T. (1991) Treatment of posttraumatic stress disorder in rape victims: a comparison between cognitive behavioral procedures and counseling. *Journal of Consulting and Clinical Psychology*, 59: 715–23.

Fonagy, P., Gergely, M., Jurist, E.L. and Target, M. (2002) *Affect Regulation, Mentalisation and the Development of the Self*. New York: Other.

Grand, S. (2000) *The Reproduction of Evil: A Clinical and Cultural Perspective*. Hillsdale, NJ: Analytic.

Herman, J.L. (1992a) *Trauma and Recovery*. New York: Basic.

Herman, J.L. (1992b) Complex PTSD: a syndrome in survivors of prolonged and repeated trauma. *Journal of Traumatic Stress*, 5: 377–92.

Kilpatrick, D., Amstadter, A., Resnick, H. and Ruggerio, K. (2007) Rape related PTSD: issues and interventions. *Psychiatric Times*, 7: 24.

Linehan, M.A. (1993) *Skills Training Manual for Treating Borderline Personality Disorder*. New York: Guilford.

Mollon, P. (2000) Is human nature intrinsically evil? In U. McCluskey and C. Hooper (eds), *Psychodynamic Perspectives on Abuse: The Cost of Fear*. London: Jessica Kingsley.

Pelcovitz, D., van der Kolk, B.A., Roth, S., Mandel, F., Kaplan, S. and Resick, P. (1997) Development of a criteria set and a structured interview for the disorders of extreme stress (SIDES). *Journal of Traumatic Stress*, 10: 3–16.

Preble, J.M. and Groth, A.N. (2002) *Male Victims of Same Sex Abuse: Addressing their Sexual Responses*. Baltimore: Sidran.

Resick, P. and Schnicke, M. (1993) *Cognitive Processing Therapy for Rape Victims*. London: Sage.

Roth, S., Newman, E., Pelcovitz, D., van der Kolk, B. and Mandel, F.S. (1997) Complex PTSD in victims exposed to sexual and physical abuse: results from the *DSM-IV* field trial for post-traumatic stress disorder. *Journal of Traumatic Stress*, 10: 539–56.

Sanderson, C. (2006) *Counselling Adult Survivors of Child Sexual Abuse* (3rd edn). London: Jessica Kingsley.

Sanderson, C. (2008) *Counselling Survivors of Domestic Abuse*. London: Jessica Kingsley.

Sanderson, C. (2010a) *Introduction to Counselling Survivors of Interpersonal Trauma*. London: Jessica Kingsley.

Sanderson, C. (2010b) *The Warrior Within: A One in Four Handbook to Aid Recovery from Childhood Sexual Abuse and Sexual Violence*. London: One in Four.

Shapiro, F. (1995) *Eye Movement Desensitisation and Reprocessing: Principles, Protocols and Procedures*. New York: Guilford.

Van der Kolk, B.A., Roth, S., Pelcovitz, D., Sunday, S. and Spinazzola, J. (2005) Disorders of extreme stress: the empirical foundation of a complex adaptation to trauma. *Journal of Traumatic Stress*, 18: 389–99.

Walby, S. and Allen, J. (2004) *Domestic Violence, Sexual Assault and Stalking: Findings from the British Crime Survey*. Home Office Research Study no. 276. London: Home Office.

PART VII

SPECIALISMS AND MODALITIES

7.1

Introduction

COLIN FELTHAM AND IAN HORTON

There are a number of therapeutic approaches or applications that do not fall into the category of a distinct theoretical orientation, yet have significant identities or areas of specialism of their own. This part of the book brings together some of the most significant such specialisms and modalities. In principle it might be possible to organize these into subgroups but we have decided simply to present them in alphabetical order for ease of reference. Traditionally, couple, family, group and systems therapies are often presented as alternative arenas to individual therapy. Some writers have added to these the subjects of child psychotherapy and brief therapy (Bloch, 2006).

Therapy with older clients is increasingly recognized as an essential focus for provision. Therapies relating to clients with disabilities, multicultural therapy and feminist therapy have some affinity as areas of attention in terms of anti-oppressive and affirmative practice. Co-counselling or peer therapy appears here in order to challenge its neglect in many textbooks.

Sometimes found grouped together as 'settings', the subjects of counselling/therapy in NHS primary care, student counselling, and workplace counselling are presented here in order to identify and honour the particular challenges posed by their contexts. Telephone counselling or therapy, once neglected or subtly demeaned, has a special place here and is an increasingly significant medium. The inclusion in this edition of electronically delivered therapies marks the growth – not without some resistance and problems to be overcome – of forms of therapy that are not face to face; for some, this may represent one of the greatest challenges to the tradition of the direct therapeutic relationship. Finally, since they are so commonly needed in our still fast-moving and arguably dehumanizing society, stress management has been retained here and coaching and hypnotherapy have been added to reflect the growth of those important sector approaches.

REFERENCE

Bloch, S. (ed.) (2006) An Introduction to the Psychotherapies (4th edn). Oxford: Oxford University Press.

Counselling People Labelled with Asperger Syndrome

NICK HODGE

DEFINING AND RECOGNISING ASPERGER SYNDROME

Asperger Syndrome (AS) is the diagnosis given to people who have modes of thinking and experiencing that result in profound and fundamental difficulties with negotiating the neurotypical social world. Neurotypical (NT) and predominant neurotype (PNT) are terms that are used by many people with AS to describe those who have what is generally considered as a more 'typical' system of social thinking and understanding. Asperger Syndrome is one of the 'conditions' that come within the umbrella title of the autism spectrum. Whether Asperger Syndrome is distinct from 'high-functioning autism' (HFA) is contested; some argue that the two conditions differ in that people with AS desire friendship but cannot identify or apply the necessary social processes to achieve this, whereas people with HFA are usually emotionally unconcerned by social isolation. Whilst the causes of AS have not been specifically identified, they are accepted as being organic in origin: AS results from physiology and not from developmental experience. It is a lifelong way of being that is different but not lesser and it is not something that can or should be 'cured'.

Estimates of incidence of AS vary widely, but if a conservative figure of 1:200 is used then the population of people who have AS in the UK will be at least 300,000. Although it still appears that significantly more males than females have AS, this is partly due to under-recognition of the syndrome in women. There is no medical test for AS: it is diagnosed by observation of behaviour and accounts of experience. AS is evidenced by pervasive, fundamental and ongoing differences (compared with the predominant neurotype) in three categories: social communication, social interaction and flexibility of thinking, sometimes referred to as social imagination. AS can make it highly problematic to understand oneself; also problematic can be managing or recognising one's emotions and those of others; understanding and employing PNT social rules and etiquette; being able to predict or monitor how others might react to social exchanges; and identifying, and fitting in with, social and cultural trends that differ from one's own. Other common characteristics include having very strong but narrow and dominating interests and unusual sensory experiences that can make environments highly challenging and stressful. However, people are of course individuals with their own distinct profile of interests, abilities and challenges. Ways of experiencing the world are rich and varied and it should not be assumed that all people with AS will have a prescribed set of concerns or will demonstrate similar responses to counselling approaches.

People with AS are likely to have average or above average intellectual abilities and they are often articulate. These strengths can mask the extent of the difficulties that they experience. As a result, people with AS may not receive a diagnosis until well into adulthood and frequently not at all. They may arrive at counselling because of years of being bullied and ostracised for being perceived as 'different'; because of trying to manage environments that are overwhelmingly stressful; and/or because partners are seeking help with managing the lack of empathy, comfort and appreciation within the relationship. So significant are the tensions of trying to exist in a socially oriented world that these are often demonstrated in people with AS through forms such as extreme anxiety and depression. Other associated conditions include eating disorders, substance abuse and bipolar disorder.

Clients may not have a diagnosis of AS at the time of seeing a counsellor or may not disclose it. Indeed, many counsellors will have encountered Asperger Syndrome without either the counsellor or the client realising it. For those who have acquired a diagnosis, identifying to others as having AS is something that is often tightly controlled by individuals who have internalised a view of Asperger Syndrome as a negative and lesser way of being and/or who fear how association with this label might impact on how others perceive and respond to them. Clients are likely to have established different positions in relation to this, from embracing and promoting the label to trying to 'pass' as neurotypical. Counsellors, therefore, may need to recognise the AS modes of thinking and experiencing from how a client expresses his or her life account. Likely signposts will include a profound lack of understanding of others and feelings of marginalisation; people with AS may well express a need to belong but will be employing strategies to engage that encounter constant rejection from others, the reasons for which often seem inexplicable to the client. Some clients with AS will experience fundamental difficulty with reflecting on their own behaviour, emotions and feelings in a way that makes sense to a counsellor who is neurotypical. A further signpost may be that the client does not use a typical range of body and facial gestures: counsellors may find it harder to 'read' the client with AS or may feel that their own gestural communications are not being responded to.

BARRIERS TO ACCESSING COUNSELLING

People with AS may well experience a number of barriers to accessing counselling services. Generally they will have fewer financial resources than those who are non-disabled and so the cost of counselling is frequently prohibitive (Reeve, 2000). Professionals or carers may assume that anxiety and depression are characteristic of the syndrome, rather than a response to stressful environments, and so not support people with AS in accessing counselling services.

Additional barriers for people with AS may include their lack of awareness of the availability and purpose of counselling; a perspective that the problem always lies 'out there' in society and it is that which needs to change rather than the individual with AS; fear of revealing oneself as having AS; and difficulty with practical and organisational processes such as locating a counsellor, making an appointment and finding a venue (Tantam, 2003). Counsellors' perceptions of their own competence can also lead them to reject potential clients because they have a label signifying a 'condition' that the counsellor feels needs specialist help (Raffensperger, 2009). Unfortunately there are very few specialist services available and so this position can then leave people with AS without any access to counselling services.

There are a number of strategies that counsellors can employ to help to remove some of these barriers. These include promoting their services through AS support networks; identifying potential sources of funding; reporting on how counselling has supported clients with AS; and being flexible about where sessions might take place and in what form. Counsellors should also consider working, where it seems in the best interests of the client and/or the counsellor, as part of a team with a supporter who knows the client well. This raises ethical issues for counsellors including confidentiality and client consent, but research has shown that this type of teamworking is likely to make a positive contribution to counselling outcomes for people with AS (Raffensperger, 2009).

EFFECTIVE APPROACHES

There have been relatively few research studies and accounts of counselling-related interventions with clients who have AS. To date there is no definitive study that establishes either the general effectiveness of counselling for people with AS or the primacy of any particular approach. Many people with AS are themselves dismissive of psychotherapy, viewing their difficulties with social understanding and engagement as being the result of how they are 'wired' rather than having a psychological causation rooted in their past (Singer, 1999). However, psychotherapy might have something to offer people with AS if it uses their strengths with logical and systematic thinking to identify and understand how environments and relationships with others might have disabled and disempowered them. Psychotherapy, if based upon an acceptance of the nature of autistic development, does have the potential to help people with AS to return to the authentic Asperger self.

More claims are made within the research literature and practice accounts for the effectiveness of programmes such as cognitive-behaviour therapy and solution-focused therapy that are carried out 'in the context of solving real problems in everyday life' (Tantam and Girgis, 2009: 56) and which 'address the situations about which the person with AS is concerned, however idiosyncratic those concerns might be to others' (Tantam, 2003: 157). The literature suggests that these more directive counselling approaches, for people with AS, should include explicit guidance on how to manage social situations and emotions. Attwood (2004) in particular suggests a number of useful, practical and accessible strategies that can support people with AS by presenting abstract concepts in more visual, concrete forms. Information that is written down is often much more accessible to people with AS as text can be referred to, and processed, over time. These strategies focus on enabling people with AS to identify and understand their emotions and to find new ways of behaving that might achieve their goals more effectively. Examples of these include using social stories (Gray, 2001) that give explicit written advice on how to manage situations which a client can then use repeatedly to rehearse situations. Social skills training sessions can be useful but social engagement is spontaneous and fluid and it is difficult to prepare someone for all eventualities. It is often more helpful to support a client with formulating practical strategies for managing breakdowns in communication. These might include identifying whom to go to for guidance or using a phrase to 'buy processing time', such as 'let me think about that and I will get back to you'. Selecting appropriate forms of support will depend upon a counsellor being able to understand the client's 'subjective experience of Asperger Syndrome' (Tantam, 2000: 61) and to position this in relation to the person's capacity for empathy and reflection. Psychological 'disorder' – caused by unwanted isolation, lack of meaningful occupation, living on benefits, being subject to victimisation now and/or in the past – may not be easily resolved unless there is a realistic chance of improving the underlying environmental factors.

Impairment and disability attract a wide range of 'therapies' and/or 'interventions' that are professionally packaged and often sold as 'the cure' or 'the answer' to 'the problem'. Although some might be well intentioned, such approaches are usually expensive to access and not supported by any reliable body of empirical research. Swimming with dolphins, for example, might well be a pleasurable and motivating activity for some but there is no reliable evidence to support some of the more spurious claims that are associated with the practice. There are more reliable accounts available of the benefits to wellbeing of pet ownership, horse riding and the use of animals as assistive supports within the community (Burrows et al., 2008), but clients are likely to have definite perspectives on whether animals, for them, are sources of comfort, enablement or stress.

Counsellors may help the person with AS to identify and articulate the barriers to their personal wellbeing but enabling solutions might well require the support of a team around the person with AS. Counsellors should not be discouraged from engaging with people with AS, however, if access to a support team is not immediately apparent. People with AS often experience a very limited number of positive relationships; the act of regular and predictable engagement with another person within a framework of clearly articulated rules and processes that enable being heard, feeling understood and being reminded of your skills and capabilities might go a long way to raising self-esteem and improving quality of life.

Working with people with less typical modes of thinking, experiencing and engagement can challenge and enrich the practice of counselling. Counsellors may well be challenged to present themselves differently to meet the requirements of the client with AS. People with AS often rely upon clearly expressed expectations from others and the boundaries around particular relationships being made explicit. This is good counselling practice anyway but it may help to record this agreement – to make a visual account that the client can revisit, as required, until sure of what is expected and permitted. An assessment of the client's needs may also lead the counsellor to work with approaches that might feel outside her/his immediate comfort zone, such as using technology in sessions (Abney and Maddux, 2004) or even conducting the whole process over the internet (Barak et al., 2009): engagement via computers is reported frequently as especially suited to the communicative and processing style of people with AS. Linking people with AS into internet support groups where they might be able to share interests and life management strategies and/or local support groups can also make significant differences to levels of wellbeing.

CONCLUSION

Although there are no studies that definitively demonstrate the effectiveness of counselling for people with AS, the value of therapy as a general practice is now well established: there is no reason to think that these benefits would not apply equally to clients with AS. All effective counselling will depend on a detailed assessment of a person's worldview and the adoption of an approach which will fit with this mode of being. For clients with AS a successful strategy is likely to be one that involves validating the experience of the client, identifying together his/her skills and abilities, and then using these to develop a programme of change with a focus on problem solving within the real-life context. The strategies adopted may also require a focus on changing disabling environments rather than the client. Counsellors may need to seek support for this process from those who know the client well and who might be able to work with him or her outside the sessions. Outside organisations that can inform about AS will also be a useful resource. Counsellors may need to adapt their own style of communication and also engage with a wider range of approaches than they are used to; many such developments in their practice may well benefit all of a counsellor's clients, not just those with AS. Specialist counselling services for people with AS are rare and it would not be helpful if the lack of practical access to these denies people with AS the benefits of counselling. The counsellor who embraces the challenge of working with clients who have AS is likely to find this an enriching and personally developing experience. The ability to identify, appreciate, learn about and accommodate different ways of being in the world is really the essential requirement for effective counselling with people with AS.

ACKNOWLEDGEMENTS

Thank you to Luke Beardon and Katherine Runswick-Cole for comments on the draft version of this chapter.

REFERENCES

Abney, P.C. and Maddux, C.D. (2004) Counseling and technology: some thoughts about the controversy. *Journal of Technology in Human Services*, 22 (3): 1–24.

Attwood, T. (2004) Cognitive behaviour therapy for children and adults with Asperger's syndrome. *Behaviour Change*, 21 (3): 147–61.

Barak, A., Klein, B. and Proudfoot, J.G. (2009) Defining internet-supported therapeutic interventions. *Annals of Behavioural Medicine*, 38: 4–17.

Burrows, K.E., Adams, C. and Spiers, J. (2008) Sentinels of safety: service dogs ensure safety and enhance well-being for families with autistic children. *Qualitative Health Research*, 18 (12): 1642–9.

Gray, C. (2001) *The New Social Story Book.* Arlington: Future Horizons.

Raffensperger, M. (2009) Factors that influence outcomes for clients with an intellectual disability. *British Journal of Guidance and Counselling*, 37 (4): 495–509.

Reeve, D. (2000) Oppression within the counselling room. *Disability and Society*, 15 (4): 669–82.

Singer, J. (1999) 'Why can't you be normal for once in your life?' From a 'problem with no name' to the emergence of a new category of difference. In M. Corker and S. French (eds), *Disability Discourse.* Buckingham: Open University Press.

Tantam, D. (2000) Psychological disorder in adolescents and adults with Asperger Syndrome. *Autism*, 4 (1): 47–62.

Tantam, D. (2003) The challenge of adolescents and adults with Asperger Syndrome. *Child and Adolescent Psychiatric Clinics of North America*, 12: 143–63.

Tantam, D. and Girgis, S. (2009) Recognition and treatment of Asperger Syndrome in the community. *British Medical Bulletin*, 89: 41–62.

RESOURCES

Specialist counselling services for people with Asperger Syndrome are extremely rare. One example is the Sheffield Asperger Syndrome Counselling Service (www.sct.nhs.uk/aspergersservice). There are also some individual specialist counsellors such as Maxine Aston (www.maxineaston.co.uk).

Attwood, T. (2007) *The Complete Guide to Asperger Syndrome.* London: Jessica Kingsley. An excellent introduction for anyone wanting to know more about AS.

Blomfield, R. (2010) *Doing Therapy with Children and Adolescents with Asperger Syndrome.* Hoboken, NJ: Wiley. Uses case material to illustrate issues involved with doing talk and play therapy with young people with AS.

Paxton, K. and Estay, I.A. (2007) *Counselling People on the Autism Spectrum: A Practical*

Manual. London: Jessica Kingsley. Contains lots of practical advice, illustrated with examples from practice.

Thompson, B. (2008) *Asperger Counselling for Couples.* London: Jessica Kingsley. Offers a seven-stage programme of support for counsellors and their clients.

There is also a useful information sheet by Maxine Aston for the BACP entitled *Recognising AS and Its Implications for Therapy* (no. G9).

AS community websites that can provide information and social and emotional support for people with AS include:

Wrong Planet: www.wrongplanet.net
Asperger Info: www.aspergerinfo.com

Other useful information websites for people with AS and their supporters include:

National Autistic Society: www.nas.org.uk
Tony Attwood: www.tonyattwood.com.au

Brief/Time-Limited Therapy

COLIN FELTHAM

The title of brief/time-limited therapy is used here generically to refer to the many varieties of brief psychotherapy and counselling, time-limited therapies, short-term therapies and the question of time-conscious design and delivery of therapeutic services.

HISTORY AND CONTRIBUTING FACTORS

Relatively little interest in brief and time-limited counselling or psychotherapy was apparent in Britain before the 1990s. Commentators usually trace the development of brief therapy from Freud's own early short-term cases through to the work of Alexander and French in the 1940s, combined with the US experience of administering help to war veterans, also in the 1940s, and an increasing interest in helping people suffering from crises, rather than the kind of 'neurotic populations' of Freud's time. The 1950s and 1960s witnessed the advent of new humanistic and cognitive-behavioural approaches, and the rediscovery and modification of hypnotherapy; and the 1960s in the USA saw the introduction of health legislation that encouraged exploration of short-term approaches. Pioneers in the USA included Mann, Sifneos, Budman and Gurman, Cummings, de Shazer and many others. In the UK, the work of Balint and Malan has been highly influential. The rise of time-limited cognitive analytic therapy (Ryle), and research into very brief interventions by Shapiro, Barkham and others in the 1990s, attempted to answer some of the problems of waiting lists in the NHS. The growth of counselling schools suggests that brief therapy is the most natural fit for many young people (Lines, 2006) and also lends itself to the growing coaching market (e.g. Berg and Szabo, 2005).

As quite widespread public acceptance of and demand for therapeutic services took hold in Britain in the 1990s and 2000s, witnessed for example in the spread of counselling in the NHS and in employee assistance programmes (EAPs), so a number of trends combined to focus on time-conscious, accountable and rationally delivered therapy. These were:

- should the concerns of funders and service providers that thought be put into realistic and accountable provision of therapy and reduction of waiting lists?
- the influence of North American systems of managed care through public health services and in association with insurers and employers
- research findings suggesting that actual take-up of therapy frequently averages at around six sessions, based on consumers' apparent preferences, in a variety of settings
- the rise of evidence-based cognitive-behavioural therapies, group therapies, counselling by telephone, therapeutic writing, online counselling and other new forms of focused therapeutic practices
- an increasing awareness of therapeutic failures, the question of therapeutic specificity, and consumers' demands for effective therapies
- the changing pace of modern working life, uncertain economics, and a turn towards a harsher

work ethic, which spawned respect for stress management and crisis intervention but perhaps little sympathy for extensive psychological explorations with vague or unknown outcomes

- the implementation of IAPT and recommendations from NICE as to not only evidence-based treatment of choice but also indicative length of therapy.

MODELS OF BRIEF THERAPY

Brief therapies can be understood as falling roughly into three categories:

1 Any therapy that is intrinsically concerned with efficiency, pragmatism, parsimony, rapid symptom amelioration, circumscribed aims, etc. Examples are behaviour therapy, cognitive therapy, multimodal therapy, rational emotive behaviour therapy (REBT), reality therapy, neuro-linguistic programming (NLP), etc.
2 Therapies designed or intended to be brief but where brevity is not defined and therapy may in fact be open-ended or intermittent. Examples are short-term dynamic psychotherapy, solution-focused therapy, focused-expressive psychotherapy, depth-oriented brief therapy, etc.
3 Therapies designed to be, and delivered as, time limited, in other words holding to a *pre-designated* time limit. Examples are Mann's time-limited psychotherapy (12 sessions), cognitive analytic therapy (16 sessions), Macnab's contextual modular therapy (six sessions), the '2 + 1 model', single-session therapy, etc.

The late 1990s saw the gradual birth of time-conscious adaptations of traditional models, for example many varieties of short-term dynamic therapies, brief REBT, etc. Of those implementing time limits, many settled on six as a workable minimum number of sessions, especially in the NHS and in EAPs. Anything from one to about 40 sessions has been put forward as 'brief', obviously depending on previous traditions, but typically brief therapy is considered to be up to around 12 sessions. (In medicine and, for example, in community mental health nursing, *minutes or half-hours* spent with a client may be the norm for thinking temporally.) As well as time limits, the issues of optimal, conscious use and organization of valuable therapeutic time, and of the *meaning* of time in therapy, have been raised (Elton Wilson, 1996; Feltham, 1997). Approaches and practitioners most opposed to shortening and rationing are probably independent therapists,

who may recognize that their livelihood would be compromised by too rapid a turnover, but also by those in the humanistic tradition who eschew psychodiagnostic thinking and defend clients' rights to define their own personal growth goals and to work at their own pace (see however, Tudor, 2008).

KEY PRINCIPLES AND INTERVENTIONS

Classical psychoanalysis by its own admission is based on respect for the unconscious and its timeless nature. The 'lengthening factors' inherent in this tradition are thought to include: searching for putative origins of symptoms; preoccupation with clients' early histories; perfectionism; dwelling on mainly in-session phenomena; infantilization and dependency; the apparent aimlessness of free association; transference neurosis; and recognition of the economic convenience of long-term paying clients (Budman and Gurman, 1988; Molnos, 1995). It is no surprise then that many of the key operating principles common to most brief therapies are reversals of these factors. Many psychodynamic therapists have in fact responded creatively to the challenge of brief work (Coren, 2009).

Assessment

Views differ on exactly which conditions do and do not benefit from brief therapy, but a degree of consensus suggests that the most suitable clients may have mild-to-moderate problems, crises, and well-defined symptoms; motivation, readiness, social support, and a reasonable level of everyday functioning; and the ability to make a rapid, good enough therapeutic alliance. Clients with long-standing personality and/or multiple problems, those with histories of childhood sexual abuse, substance or alcohol misuse, and those who attend reluctantly, referred by third parties, may not be suitable (but see Tudor, 2008). Assessment should ideally include realistic estimates of the fit between time available and severity of distress (Burton, 1998), and contracts with clients must always be clear and honest about time limitations and what can be achieved.

Commitment to Brief Therapy

In common with open-ended therapies, brief therapy must be delivered by practitioners who believe in the possibility and usefulness of brief therapy. Covert therapist resistance, including doubts about the rationale for brief work, is likely to adversely permeate the therapeutic work. Concern for client preferences, rapid reduction of distress, elimination of waste, addressing waiting lists, realism about the costs of therapy to clients or funders, are all factors likely to be embraced by brief therapy enthusiasts. The therapist's commitment should also engender the sense of expectancy in the client that can be a vital ingredient in change.

Rapid Therapeutic Alliance

It has been inferred from research on attrition that failure to make strong working alliances within the first three sessions is one reliable predictor of clients dropping out of therapy. Therefore, in order to engage the client and initiate an immediate sense of hope, collaboration and necessary action, the therapist must actively mobilize the client by clear contracting, early identification of transference factors, and pinpointing of possible relational obstacles. *Collaboration* is emphasized in cognitive therapy and cognitive analytic therapy especially and is identified by research as a key variable in the strength of the therapeutic alliance and successful outcomes in *all* therapy.

Focal and Active Concerns

In very brief work, time is not available for extreme non-directiveness, lengthy exploratory or speculative discussion, and free association. Instead, early identification of crisis, symptoms, key personal issues or needs is crucial. This may entail what has been referred to as 'skilful neglect' of certain underlying or dormant issues, and concentration on live problematic issues. Focal concerns may be obvious (e.g. a phobia) or may require work to identify (e.g. a recurring pattern of self-destructive behaviour). Initial contracting must be linked with realistic focal concerns.

Flexible, Creative and Informed Skills

To some extent adherence to traditional theoretical models needs to be adapted or even sometimes abandoned, allowing for the primacy of each client's pressing needs. A certain pragmatism may be required to address psychosocial, decision-making needs, for example, and therapists may need to be prepared to teach relaxation or assertiveness skills, utilize and/or improvise simple cathartic or cognitive techniques, or be prepared – on the basis of research awareness – to refer elsewhere for specialized therapy (e.g. eye movement desensitization and reprocessing (EMDR) may be indicated for PTSD). Brief

therapy – as in the emerging pluralistic paradigm (Cooper and McLeod, 2011) – particularly challenges therapists to fit the therapy to the client, not the client to the therapeutic tradition.

Parsimony

This refers to the practice of making the least radical intervention necessary and the most obviously indicated. Many clients (up to 25 per cent) attend for, and/or find satisfactory resolution in, only one session, and up to 62 per cent may improve significantly by 13 sessions (see Feltham, 1997: 140). Consumer surveys have produced some evidence that many clients have far less extensive agendas for personal change than do their therapists. Also, advocates of intermittent (as opposed to 'all at once') therapy argue that sporadic therapy may be more realistic and economic. Interventions may therefore include non-therapy (assuring the client that she needs no therapy at this time), referral elsewhere, very short sessions, supportive work, and practical and decision-making guidance.

Challenge

Contrary to the above, some brief therapists argue for the validity and desirability of highly challenging short-term work (Ecker and Hulley, 1996; Molnos, 1995). Brief dynamic therapy as practised by Malan, Davanloo, Molnos and others may entail 'trial therapy' from the very outset, which judiciously confronts defences in order to test out tolerance for this kind of therapy. Transferential behaviour may be noted and addressed immediately, and therapy may have a purposefully anxiety-arousing character. Ecker and Hulley propose working authentically with deep emotions and the unconscious immediately, in their depth-oriented constructivist approach; cognitive analytic therapy may include challenging, transference-interpreting work; and Mahrer's experiential therapy works with deep feelings from the first session. In the cognitive-behavioural tradition, clients may be challenged to undertake homework and various self-challenging exercises.

Time Itself as Containing and Challenging

Contrary to common belief among some therapists, many clients have reported feeling contained (made safe) by firm time limits, and being less likely to drop out. Therapists informed by existentialist and other views on death anxiety (e.g. Mann) consider that the finiteness and less-than-ideal frame of a small number of sessions fixed in advance usefully arouses existential anxiety. Many brief therapists explicitly utilize notions of time as precious and therapy as a valuable chance for change, applying these factors as leverage. Available time is also often enhanced by encouraging the client to take seriously their own between-session change attempts and their post-therapy lives as full of further such opportunities.

Specific Techniques

While many brief therapy techniques are simply sharpened or more rapidly applied techniques from traditional approaches, some are peculiar to or have evolved from within the brief therapy tradition. In the solution-focused therapy (often referred to simply as 'brief therapy') of de Shazer and others, so-called *miracle questions* may be used, requiring clients to imagine and describe in detail their circumstances if they were magically transformed overnight. Such catalytically designed challenges can unleash or restore clients' optimism and forgotten constructive abilities. Similarly, asking for *exceptions* to the presenting problem can be powerful (e.g. requiring the client to identify times when they are *not* depressed or anxious). *Paradoxical interventions* have been advocated (e.g. asking clients to escalate a problem; 'prescribing the symptom'). *Scaling questions* require clients to self-score their problems, degrees of severity, and amount of change, and to predict what would be necessary to progress one point on their scale. Variations on *hypnotherapeutic techniques* have been utilized by Milton Erickson and are advocated by Budman and Gurman (1988). Dramatic phobia-eliminating techniques based on behavioural and NLP principles involving hypnotherapy and exposure have been reported as successful in single sessions (e.g. a long-standing bee phobia resolved in seven minutes). Implied in this is a possible eclectic imperative: that effective brief therapists may need to add to their technical repertoires or be willing to refer on. (Readers may refer back to Chapter 3.4 of this volume, on specific strategies and techniques, for further details; and see also O'Connell, 1998.) Wright (2003) shows the value of combining therapeutic writing with brief therapy.

Preparation for Ending

It is responsible, ethical and effective practice to incorporate into brief therapy elements of the following: (1) realism about end results and willingness to discuss likely degrees of disappointment; (2)

discouragement of dependency on the therapist and reinforcement of coping self-images; (3) preparation for possible relapse by, for example, devising and rehearsing coping strategies; (4) discussion of possible follow-up sessions or extendable contracts (Elton Wilson, 1996; 2006), or alternative forms of help (e.g. self-help groups, bibliotherapy, co-counselling, etc.); (5) evaluation of outcomes – verbally, by questionnaire or other evaluation instruments, and with 'goodbye letters'.

THERAPISTS' PROFESSIONAL DEVELOPMENT NEEDS

Brief therapy probably remains under-developed in theoretical and training terms, but see Feltham (1997: 131–9) for relevant issues. Views differ on whether beginners or experienced practitioners are most likely to find brief therapy difficult to learn (since it may demand a good deal of 'unlearning' of traditional attitudes), but there is an emerging consensus that some specific training or reorientation from long-term work *is* necessary. Problematic, too, is supervision for brief therapy, particularly for very short-term (e.g. six-session) therapy, the rapid client turnover associated with it, the contexts in which it is increasingly obligatory, and the current evidence suggesting that the cognitive-behavioural therapies are most likely to be effective in a short time (Mander, 1998; Roth et al., 2006).

CRITIQUES AND LIMITATIONS

Short-term therapy is still sometimes regarded as a faddish, merely politically and economically motivated development; as a second best or even damaging practice, cheating clients of what they *really* need; as encouraging superficial, transient 'flight into health' and possible symptom substitution; as overly problem focused instead of growth promoting; as inviting dubious compliance with therapists; and as likely to result in a false economy (i.e. clients will return with the same or worse distress later). Critics of the IAPT approach often make this charge.

Much research has indicated equivalent outcomes across short-term and long-term therapies, and has validated claims of phobia cures, of removal of post-traumatic stress symptoms, and of significant positive impact on some personality disorders. However, early enthusiasm has given way to some extent to acknowledgement of research findings that therapeutic gains do not necessarily hold up reliably over time, that clients do sometimes outwardly comply with brief therapy but inwardly suppress some of their significant concerns, and so on. Many therapists and counsellors in primary care express frustration at unhelpfully inflexible time limits and, in some cases, a limit of six sessions is extended to eight or 12 in the interests of clients. The tendency for innovative approaches to be hailed as panaceas is strong, and brief therapy should be placed in perspective.

CONCLUSIONS

The time-conscious lobby has forced all therapists to reconsider implicit philosophies of time in the therapeutic context. It is not only about time rationing, but also about the optimal organization of therapeutic time as a scarce resource. Traditional 50-minute hours do not necessarily provide what is best for all clients; longer, intensive sessions, very brief but frequent sessions, intermittently distributed sessions might all be considered on their merits. Strictly time-limited therapy is not necessarily desirable or perhaps even ethically defensible for all clients, and judiciously extended temporal contracts are to be recommended. It is important to regard brief therapy as one therapeutic option among others, and to use assessment skilfully to this end (Burton, 1998; Shipton and Smith, 1998). Finally, better clinical guidelines *vis-à-vis* temporal factors are awaited.

REFERENCES

Berg, I.K. and Szabo, P. (2005) *Brief Coaching for Lasting Solutions.* New York: Norton.

Budman, S.H. and Gurman, A.S. (1988) *Theory and Practice of Brief Therapy.* New York: Guilford.

Burton, M.V. (1998) *Psychotherapy, Counselling and Primary Health Care: Assessment for Brief or Longer-Term Treatment.* Chichester: Wiley.

Cooper, M. and McLeod, J. (2011) *Pluralistic Counselling and Psychotherapy.* London: Sage.

Coren, A. (2009) *Short-Term Psychotherapy: A Psychodynamic Approach.* Houndmills: Palgrave.

Ecker, B. and Hulley, L. (1996) *Depth-Oriented Brief Therapy.* San Francisco: Jossey-Bass.

Elton Wilson, J. (1996) *Time-conscious Psychological Therapy.* London: Routledge.

Elton Wilson, J. (2006) Choosing a time-limited counselling or psychotherapy contract. In C. Sills (ed.), *Contracts in Counselling and Psychotherapy* (2nd edn). London: Sage.

Feltham, C. (1997) *Time-Limited Counselling.* London: Sage.

Lines, D. (2006) *Brief Counselling in Schools: Working with Young People from 11 to 18* (2nd edn). London: Sage.

Mander, G. (1998) Supervising short-term psychodynamic work. *Counselling*, 9 (4): 301–5.

Molnos, A. (1995) *A Question of Time: Essentials of Brief Dynamic Psychotherapy.* London: Karnac.

O'Connell, B. (1998) *Solution-Focused Therapy.* London: Sage.

Roth, A., Fonagy, P., Parry, G. and Target, M. (2006) *What Works for Whom? A Critical Review of Psychotherapy Research* (2nd rev. edn). New York: Guilford.

Shipton, G. and Smith, E. (1998) *Long-Term Counselling.* London: Sage.

Tudor, K. (ed.) (2008) *Brief Person-Centred Therapies.* London: Sage.

Wright, J. (2003) Five women talk about work-related brief therapy and therapeutic writing. *Counselling and Psychotherapeutic Research*, 3 (3): 204–9.

Counselling Children

KATHRYN GELDARD AND DAVID GELDARD

Counselling children is different in a number of ways from counselling adolescents or adults. Whereas many adolescents and most adults seek counselling of their own volition, children are usually brought to see counsellors by their parents or significant other adults. The adults involved are likely to have agendas of their own. It is therefore imperative when counselling children that significant adults involved in the child's life are also involved in the therapeutic process in some way. The situation is also complicated because children live in families and their emotional and behavioural problems may relate to the family system. Their problems certainly occur within the family system and will almost inevitably result in some consequences for the system. Therefore, when counselling children a counsellor will usually need to address not only the intrapersonal issues of the child in individual counselling, but also systemic issues involving the child's parents and/or family which may be causing and/or maintaining the child's problems or be a consequence of these problems.

Another important difference between counselling adults and counselling children is that adults are generally comfortable and able to explore and resolve their issues in a conversational relationship with a counsellor. Although some children may be able to do this, many are unable to share the things that trouble them with a counsellor who uses only conversational strategies. Consequently, most counsellors trained in counselling children will make use of media and activity to engage the child, to enable the child to talk about what is troubling them and to help the child find resolution of their issues.

Although many, if not most, of the children who are brought to counselling have underlying emotional problems, it is common for adults to bring children to counselling only after noticing behavioural problems. However, for successful therapeutic outcomes the counsellor needs to address both the emotional and the behavioural issues.

An additional difference between counselling adults and counselling children relates to confidentiality. With adults, confidentiality can be offered subject to the usual limitations imposed by ethical considerations, whereas with children the confidentiality issue is confounded by the rights of the parents to have information about their children. Clearly, if a child is to talk freely, he or she must have some confidence that the information they share will be treated respectfully and will not be disclosed to others without good reason (Fox and Butler, 2007; Jenkins, 2010).

THERAPEUTIC APPROACHES

Several therapeutic approaches can be used when counselling children, including:

- non-directive play therapy
- creative and expressive therapy
- gestalt therapy
- time-limited play therapy
- cognitive-behavioural therapy
- family therapy.

Each of these approaches has some advantages and some limitations. The literature suggests that there is not one preferred way of working which is appropriate for all children. Some counsellors believe that they need to be flexible enough to select a method of working which is specifically suitable for a particular child and relevant for the child's issues. This idea was originally proposed by Millman and Schaefer (1977), who called it a 'prescriptive approach'. An alternative which is gaining acceptance is an integrative approach incorporating ideas from a number of therapeutic frameworks. Whatever approach is used, there are a number of goals which can usefully be achieved when counselling children. These include:

- To help the child gain mastery over issues and events.
- To enable the child to feel empowered.
- To help the child develop problem-solving and decision-making skills.
- To build the child's self-concept and self-esteem.
- To improve the child's communication skills.
- To help the child develop insight.

We will now discuss the range of individual approaches previously listed and will then explain how these can be combined in an integrative approach.

Non-directive Play Therapy

It has been widely documented that the use of non-directive play therapy can be a viable therapeutic means of assisting children with self-expression, when facilitated by the play therapist (Axline, 1989; Ray et al., 2001; Landreth, 2002). This approach emphasizes non-directive approaches to therapeutic play, based on supporting the child's developing self within the safe boundaries provided by the setting and the worker's emotional holding and containment (McMahon, 2009).The counsellor observes the child as the child plays without direction in an environment which contains suitable media. This material is likely to include typical children's toys, toy furniture, and materials such as clay, paint and crayons. The counsellor's observations might include observation of mood or affect, intellectual functioning, thinking processes, speech and language, motor skills, play, and the relationship with the counsellor.

Creative and Expressive Therapy

Some theorists propose that from birth the child experiences emotional reactions to their internal needs, and it is through these emotional reactions that a child develops internal working models (IWMs) of their social world (Johnson et al., 2007). As the child matures they continue to develop their emotional understanding, expression, and regulation skills by building on their IWMs. Accessing and modifying unconscious IWMs have been suggested as an important component of counselling children who have experienced abuse and/or neglect in order to limit maladaptive emotional outcomes. It has been proposed that strategies which address the underlying physiological dimension of emotional processing, and hence target unconscious IWMs, may be useful when working with children by intentionally using strategies which focus on reorganizing brain function (Wright et al., 2009). Unlike more cognitive or behavioural therapies, literature provides evidence that creative techniques can be used to access and modify unconscious aspects of self, such as implicit emotional memories and IWMs (Gantt and Tinnin, 2009; Glover, 1999; Harris, 2009; Herman, 1997; Walker, 1998). Sand play and symbol work are powerful therapeutic tools that utilize the child's creativity and can access and allow expression of the child's inner world. Sand play and symbol work can reveal unconscious processes and dilemmas, bringing them into a representational form that allows resolution. This approach was pioneered by Margaret Lowenfeld in an attempt to find a way of helping children to communicate without the use of language (Schaefer and O'Connor, 1994). She used a variety of small objects as symbols in a sand tray to encourage non-verbal expression which was less influenced by rational thinking (Ryce-Menuhin, 1992). Many contemporary counsellors use sand tray work as a tool to engage the child and to enable the child to talk openly and thus explore their issues (Sweeney et al., 2009). Sand tray work is very useful in helping a child to tell their story, explore issues, and express emotions.

Gestalt Therapy

Oaklander (1988; 2003) and Blom (2006) have demonstrated a particular way of combining the use of gestalt therapy principles and practice with the use of media when working with children. Oaklander works therapeutically with children by encouraging them to use fantasy and/or metaphor, and believes that usually the fantasy process will be the same as the life process in the child. She therefore works indirectly in bringing out what is hidden or avoided and relies on what is essentially a projective process. A limitation of Oaklander's approach is that it is an indirect projective technique. Although this works well for some children, others may have difficulty in making the connection between their fantasy and real life. Other counsellors use a gestalt therapy approach in a more direct way. While engaging the child in the use of media and/or activity they will use gestalt techniques to help the child experience raised awareness while they are telling their story. For example, Blom (2006) uses a stage-related process to build a relationship and assess and develop a treatment plan followed by contact-making and building self-support in children, emotional expression, self-nurturing, addressing inappropriate processes and termination.

Time-limited Play Therapy

This approach uses ideas from brief therapy with a psychodynamic orientation (Sloves and Belinger-Peterlin, 1986). A brief assessment of the child's issues is made. The counsellor then selects a central theme and the therapeutic work is limited to this theme. The work with the child focuses on empowerment, adaptation and strengthening the ego. It focuses on the future rather than the past. Generally, individual work with the child is limited to 12 sessions. This form of therapy is both directive and interpretive. It is effective for some children and not useful for others (Schaefer and O'Connor, 1994). In particular, it has been found to be effective for children with recent post-traumatic stress disorder and adjustment disorders, and for children who have lost a parent due to a chronic medical condition (Christ et al., 1991).

Cognitive-behavioural Therapy

An educational model, as described by Beck (1995) and developed by more recent practitioners (Friedberg et al., 2009), cognitive-behavioural therapy is used to describe the connection between thoughts, emotions and behaviours. The child's current thoughts, which are driving their emotions and behaviours, are explored. The counsellor's goal is to enable the child to replace unhelpful thoughts with more adaptive ones. When working with children using cognitive-behavioural therapy, media and activity are useful. For example, worksheets, drawing and role-playing might be used in order to help the child explore their current thoughts and behaviours and practise new ways of thinking and behaving.

Cognitive-behavioural therapy tends to be popular with health services which have limited financial resources as the process is short term, involving only a few counselling sessions. Cognitive-behavioural techniques are useful in enabling many children to gain a level of control over their emotions and behaviours. Limitations of this approach are that it does not directly target emotions or encourage emotional release. Also, the approach requires the child to have reasonably good language skills, and a level of cognitive development and emotional maturity. Without this, the child will not be able to make sense of the educational model, and may not be able to interrupt emotional outbursts by making changes to their thinking. Consequently, it is not suitable for very young children.

Cognitive-behavioural therapy is often used in conjunction with behavioural psychotherapy where incentives are used to reinforce positive behaviour, and there are consequences for undesirable behaviour. Behaviour therapy can be used with children of all ages.

Family Therapy

This approach is discussed in Chapter 7.11 in this volume. Some counsellors believe that it is sufficient to explore and resolve a child's emotional and behavioural problems within the context of the family system. This can be a very effective way of working with some children. However, many children who come for counselling are troubled by emotional issues and/or thoughts which are of a highly personal nature and which they may not be able to talk about in the context of the family.

ECLECTIC AND INTEGRATIVE COUNSELLING

The previous discussion has highlighted the advantages and limitations of a number of differing ways of working with children. Some counsellors like to use a particular therapeutic approach, but others prefer to work in an integrative or eclectic way. Some integrative counsellors will choose to select and use the particular therapeutic approach which they think is most appropriate for helping a particular child with specific issues, in the way that was described as prescriptive by Millman and Schaefer (1977). Other eclectic counsellors will select and make use of strategies from more than one therapeutic approach with the goal of meeting a child's specific needs as they arise. Both of these approaches can have positive outcomes. However, although some eclectic counsellors have success in using the approaches described, it can be argued that there is a risk that the process of counselling might be compromised by the inappropriate selection and/or sequence of strategies used. An alternative is to use an integrative model where strategies from particular therapeutic approaches are intentionally used at particular points in the therapeutic process.

The SPICC Model

An example of an integrative model is the 'sequentially planned integrative counselling for children' model (the SPICC model), which we developed and use ourselves (Geldard and Geldard, 2008). This model divides the counselling process into a sequence of stages.

Wherever possible before using the SPICC model we try to engage the family in family therapy so that we can have a full understanding of the family dynamics and can see the child in the context of the family system. Sometimes after family therapy we will discover that the problem has been resolved and no further therapeutic work is required. At other times we will recognize that the child with the presenting problem, or another child in the family, may be experiencing emotional distress. We will then proceed to work individually with the child using the SPICC model.

The SPICC model involves the following sequence: joining with the child, enabling the child to tell their story, raising the child's awareness so that they get in touch with and express emotions, helping the child to cognitively restructure, helping the child to look at options and choices, and enabling the child to rehearse and experiment with new behaviours.

Sand play work

In the initial stage the counsellor joins with and engages the child. To do this, use will be made of media and/or activity. Typically, a counsellor might use symbols in the sand tray, or with older children who are cognitively able to use a projective technique, miniature animals can be used to represent family members. If working in the sand tray, the child can be encouraged to use objects as symbols to make a picture in the sand of their world as they perceive it, and/or their family. The activity component of the exercise enables the child to feel relaxed rather than pressured to talk. As the picture in the sand tray develops, the counsellor is able to explore its meaning for the child and help the child to talk openly about their life.

Use of gestalt therapy

Once a trusting relationship has been established the counsellor can begin to use creative media and/or activity together with gestalt therapy awareness-raising techniques to help the child connect with troubling emotions. The use of suitable media and/or activity maintains the child's interest, allows them to anchor their story, and ensures that the child has time to process thoughts in silence rather than to feel pressured to talk. As the child's awareness is raised the counsellor might encourage the release of troubling emotions. This might be done through the use of media such as clay, or activity such as painting and drawing. The goal of therapy up to this point has been to facilitate a process which will allow the child to share their story, to get in touch with troubling issues and emotions, and to release those emotions in the safety of the therapeutic environment.

Use of cognitive-behavioural therapy and behaviour therapy

The next stage in the process is to target any unhelpful and/or maladaptive thoughts and behaviours. It is not sufficient just to help the child get in touch with and express emotions. Unhelpful thinking patterns need to be restructured using cognitive-behavioural therapy. The child is unlikely to change and emotional distress will probably recur if this stage in the process is overlooked. Similarly, the child needs to be encouraged to explore their options and choices regarding current and future behaviour. The new behaviour can then be reinforced using a behaviour therapy approach with the parents' cooperation.

Integration of individual and family work

During the individual counselling process with the child there may be times when it will be useful for the child to share information either with their parents or with the family. Certainly, towards the end of the therapeutic process it can be useful to re-engage the whole family in family therapy so that any changes can be reinforced and supported and remaining problems can be addressed.

CONCLUSION

Counselling children involves a range of specialist skills which can only be developed under the guidance of a counselling supervisor who is trained and experienced in working with children. Additionally, as with all counselling, ongoing supervision is necessary and essential to ensure good practice. Although there are several different approaches to counselling children it is generally advantageous for counsellors to combine the use of media and activity with suitable counselling skills to enable the child to feel at ease and to maximize positive outcomes of the counselling process.

Finally, the importance of ongoing research into the practice of child counselling and psychotherapy cannot be ignored. A review of research papers and current practices focusing on child psychotherapy can contribute towards enhanced practice. For example, Midgley et al. (2009) have compiled a review of research papers focusing on current practices and how they and similar studies contribute to the now all-important evidence-based practice and are useful when considering working with emotionally troubled children.

REFERENCES

Axline, V. (1989) *Play Therapy*. London: Ballantine Books. (Original work published 1947.)

Beck, A.T. (1995) *Cognitive Therapy: Basics and Beyond*. New York: Guilford.

Blom, R. (2006) *The Handbook of Gestalt Play Therapy: Practical Guidelines for Child Therapists*. London: Jessica Kingsley.

Christ, G.H., Siegel, K., Mesagno, F. and Langosch, D. (1991) A preventative program for bereaved children: problems of implementation. *Journal of Orthopsychiatry*, 61: 168–78.

Fox, C. and Butler, I. (2007) If you don't want to tell anyone else, you can tell her: young people's views on school counselling. *British Journal of Guidance and Counselling*, 35 (1): 97–114.

Friedberg, R.D., McClure, J. and Garcia, J. (2009) *Cognitive Therapy Techniques for Children and Adolescents: Tools for Enhancing Practice*. New York: Guilford.

Gantt, L. and Tinnin, L.W. (2009) Support for a neurobiological view of trauma with implications for art therapy. *The Arts in Psychotherapy*, 36 (3): 148–53.

Geldard, K. and Geldard, D. (2008) *Counselling Children: A Practical Introduction* (3rd edn). London: Sage.

Glover, N.M. (1999) Play therapy and art therapy for substance abuse clients who have a history of incest victimization. *Journal of Substance Abuse Treatment*, 16 (4): 281–7.

Harris, D.A. (2009) The paradox of expressing speechless terror: ritual liminality in the creative arts therapies' treatment of posttraumatic distress. *The Arts in Psychotherapy*, 36 (2): 94–104.

Herman, L. (1997) Good enough fairy tales for resolving sexual abuse trauma. *The Arts in Psychotherapy*, 24 (5): 439–45.

Jenkins, P. (2010) Having confidence in therapeutic work with young people: constraints and challenges to confidentiality. *British Journal of Guidance and Counselling*, 38 (3): 263–74.

Johnson, S.C., Dweck, C.S. and Chen, F.S. (2007) Evidence for infants' internal working models of attachment. *Psychological Science*, 18 (6): 501–2.

Landreth, G.L. (2002) *Play Therapy: The Art of the Relationship* (2nd edn). New York: Bruner Routledge.

McMahon, L. (2009) *The Handbook of Play Therapy and Therapeutic Play* (2nd edn). New York: Routledge/Taylor.

Midgley, N., Anderson, J., Grainger, E., Nesic-Vuckovic, T. and Urwin, C. (eds) (2009) *Child Psychotherapy and Research: New Approaches, Emerging Findings*. London: Routledge,

Millman, H. and Schaefer, C.E. (1977) *Therapies for Children*. San Francisco: Jossey-Bass.

Oaklander, V. (1988) *Windows to Our Children*. New York: Center for Gestalt Development.

Oaklander, V. (2003) Gestalt play therapy. In C.E. Schaefer (ed.), *Foundations of Play Therapy* (pp. 143–55). Hoboken, NJ: Wiley.

Ray, D., Bratton, S., Rhine, T. and Jones, L. (2001) The effectiveness of play therapy: responding to the critics. *International Journal of Play Therapy*, 10 (1): 85–108.

Ryce-Menuhin, J. (1992) *Jungian Sand Play: The Wonderful Therapy*. New York: Routledge, Chapman and Hall.

Schaefer, C.E. and O'Connor, K.J. (eds) (1994) *Handbook of Play Therapy*. Vol. 2: *Advances and Innovations*. New York: Wiley.

Sloves, R. and Belinger-Peterlin, K. (1986) The process of time-limited psychotherapy with latency-aged children. *Journal of the American Academy of Child Psychiatry*, 25: 847–51.

Sweeney, D.S., Homeyer, L.E. and Drewes, A. (2009) Blending play therapy with cognitive behavioral therapy: evidence-based and other effective treatments and techniques. In Daniel Sweeney and Linda Homeyer (eds), *Sandtray Therapy* (pp. 297–318). Hoboken, NJ: Wiley.

Walker, S.C. (1998) Stories of two children: making sense of children's therapeutic work. *The Arts in Psychotherapy*, 25 (4): 263–75.

Wright, M.O., Crawford, E. and Del Castillo, D. (2009) Childhood emotional maltreatment and later psychological distress among college students: the mediating role of maladaptive schemas. *Child Abuse and Neglect*, 33: 59–68.

Coaching

JANET LAFFIN

WHAT IS COACHING?

'Contemporary professional coaching is a cross-disciplinary methodology for fostering individual and organizational change, which comprises both personal or "life" coaching and workplace coaching with staff, managers and executives' (Grant, 2006a: 13). Definitions of coaching are usually built on the following assumptions: there is an absence of serious mental health problems in the client; the client is resourceful and willing to engage in finding solutions to her problems; coaching is an outcome-focused rather than an insight-focused activity which is client centred and aims to facilitate learning through collaborative goal setting and action planning. Most proponents of coaching are at pains to distinguish it from therapy: 'High performance athletes are coached; sick, weak, or crazy people get therapy' (Peltier, 2001: xix). While some authors question whether coaching is merely a more socially acceptable form of therapy, others recognize that defining coaching as exclusively for the mentally healthy is unsatisfactory for many practical and ethical reasons.

Although coaches broadly agree that coaching is not therapy, the lack of an agreed definition has led to problems, particularly in distinguishing coaching from mentoring, counselling and psychotherapy. The different conceptualizations of coaching, its multidisciplinary and eclectic mix of models, techniques and approaches, have induced one expert to call it 'a rag bag subject' (Garvey, in Sparrow, 2008: 1). Coaching has emerged in response to a wide variety of needs and, as such, it is an umbrella term which takes on different meanings in the social contexts in

which it is delivered. Consequently, coaches, in contrast to counsellors or psychotherapists, do not typically label their style of coaching in terms of a theoretical tradition, rather the different coaching brands relate to the contexts in which they offer their services. These are very diverse and include sports, education, business, working and personal life, counselling and psychotherapy and, currently, health coaching in the field of medicine is on the rise.

A VERY BRIEF HISTORY OF COACHING

It is difficult to know when coaching first began as a practice. Some writers link coaching to classical times and especially Socratic dialogue. William James, Carl Jung, Alfred Adler, Carl Rogers and Abraham Maslow have been cited as influences on modern-day coaching. Most writers agree that the origins of coaching are in humanistic psychology and its various fields of self-development. Grant (2007) links coaching and the human potential movement (HPM) of the 1960s, as the philosophy of 'eclectic pragmatic utilitarianism' – the 'use of whatever works, and if it works, do more of it' – heavily influenced the early development of the contemporary commercial coaching industry (2007: 24). Also, 'The uncritical, anti-intellectualism of the HPM and an accompanying suspicion of scientific debate and rigorous evaluation have been noticeable aspects of many early commercial proprietary life coaching schools' (2007: 24–5). More recent influences on modern-day coaching include the growth of the talking therapies, consulting and organizational development, industrial psychology, and popular personal development training initiatives such as the Landmark Forum seminars and Lifespring. High-profile personalities include Anthony Robbins and Thomas Leonard, the founder of the main international coaching association, the International Coach Federation (ICF), which held its first convention in 1996.

Historically, coaching is associated with academic learning and performance, particularly in sports such as rowing and cricket. It was transferred to business throughout the 1970s and 1980s, where it became a popular and widely used resource for personal development and the fastest-growing field within consulting. Coaching is often presented as a 'feelgood' industry and promoted as a dynamic, future-focused and strengths-based form of human helping (Spence et al., 2006). It has a wide-ranging appeal and is used to encompass a variety of activities and approaches including:

> coaching individuals to fake malingering on psychological tests, peer coaching in educational settings, cognitive training for learning difficulties and disabilities, resolving relationship difficulties, coping with infertility, premature ejaculation, career coaching, job coaching to help disadvantaged individuals gain and retain employment, improving performance in interviews, executive coaching and sales performance. (Grant, 2004: 10)

Executive coaching is by far the most dominant form of coaching and the platform from which personal coaching has evolved. The Bresser (2009) consulting survey estimates that there are between 45,000 and 50,000 business coaches worldwide, and the Chartered Institute of Personnel and Development Learning and Development Survey (CIPD, 2009) found that 90 per cent of respondent organizations are using coaching. Executive coaching is becoming one of the fastest-growing interventions in the development of managers, especially managers in large organizations. Potential topics include everything in the life-coaching agenda plus any and every aspect of running organizations, career/business relationship and work/life balance issues, and niches such as coaching for new leaders. The rise of psychological coaching in organizations has been attributed to the competitiveness of the business world and the increased pressures on executives to perform and boost their individual employability.

THE FIELD OF COACHING

The field of coaching is divided into distinct camps, almost tribal in nature, which emphasize particular characteristics of coaching and represent the experience, views and interests of the writer but do not distinguish it from other helping professions or provide it with a unique identity (Cox et al., 2010). This has led to a phenomenal growth in coaching approaches and methodologies which may be attributed to a healthy pluralism and a postmodernist respect for diversity as coaching is delivered to meet a wide variety of needs in an increasingly diverse range of contexts. More cynically, perhaps, the lack of agreement about what coaching is and is not may be due to the vested financial and professional interests of coaches and coaching interest groups. The proliferation of approaches has been linked to the general widespread commercialization and commodification of coaching (Garvey et al., 2009) as the different coaching brands draw on different knowledge frameworks and a wide range of practice methodologies to vie for expenditure on coaching, demonstrate its impact and justify their own approach.

THE DEVELOPMENT OF COACHING THEORY

Whilst there has been exponential growth in the practice of coaching, the body of evidence-based literature on coaching is still rather small, so most popular coaching models owe more to the experience of coaches than to evidence-based practice. Coaches come from a wide variety of prior professional backgrounds and their level of education also varies. Until several years ago there were no standards of training for coaches which would guarantee quality and consistency. Most coach training programmes are offered by commercial institutes which deliver a few days training based on proprietary models of coaching with little or no theoretical grounding, and finish by granting some kind of coaching certification, e.g. a 'Certified Master Life Coach'. Therefore it is no wonder that coaches tend to conduct theoretical one-size-fits-all coaching interventions (Grant, 2006b). The chaos arising from vastly different standards of practice and the resulting risks for the buyer faced with a bewildering array of different types of coach certification have led to the executive coaching industry being dubbed 'the Wild West of yesteryear' (Sherman and Freas, 2004: 82).

In contrast to the commercial training programmes that dominated the market during the late 1990s and 2000s, now there are a number of universities that offer postgraduate programmes in coaching. The coaching profession is still self-regulating but there are some professional associations which were established several years ago that have developed professional standards for their membership so as to guarantee the quality of coaching. These include the International Coach Federation (ICF), the oldest and biggest professional body with an estimated 17,000 coaches in 90 countries, which sees its credentialling programme as the gold standard in the world of coaching; and the Worldwide Association of Business Coaches (WABC), founded in 1997, which has declared itself to be the first international association to represent business coaching. The main professional bodies in the UK include the Association for Coaching, the Association for Professional Executive Coaching and Supervision, the European Mentoring and Coaching Council (EMMC: UK membership 2700 in 2008), the Chartered Institute for People Development, the British Psychological Society and within it the Special Interest Group in Coaching Psychology. Recently, representatives of the various bodies met in Dublin to align definitions and standards and provide more coherence to the collective marketplace. In particular, the Dublin declaration of 2008, while acknowledging the multidisciplinary roots and nature of coaching, pointed to the 'need to add to the body of coaching knowledge by conducting rigorous research into the processes, practices and outcomes of coaching, in order to strengthen its practical impact and theoretical underpinnings' (Mooney, 2008: 5).

THE INTRODUCTION OF PSYCHOLOGY INTO COACHING

The rise of coaching psychology has been attributed to coaching's coming of age. Until quite recently, coaches tried to differentiate themselves from any association with in-depth psychological work. The recent U-turn in attitudes to psychology in relation to coaching is due to a newly recognized need for psychological underpinnings for coaching interventions and to bring greater depth to the coaching relationship.

For the past 30 years, the dominant model of coaching has been that of the sports model. The development of coaching as a business tool, particularly for management and leadership development, has been traced to the influential tennis coach turned business guru Timothy Gallwey (1974), whose coaching theory was based on his personal insights into what produces peak performances which he termed the inner game process. His discovery that our outer game (our performance) is affected and influenced by our fears, doubts, self-limiting beliefs and assumptions (our inner game) led to a new focus on psychology and therapeutic approaches to coaching.

BEHAVIOURISM AND COACHING

The GROW (goal, reality, options, will) model was popularized by Whitmore in the 1990s. Traditionally, it has been viewed as a non-psychological model suitable for coaches without psychological training, and many coaches are unaware of its behaviourist roots. It appeals to managers because of the dominance of behaviourist thinking within organizations. It is used by most business coaches and involves a simple four-stage problem solving approach which focuses exclusively on the behaviour of the coachee. The coach uses Socratic questioning to help the coachee move through the four action-focused stages and to identify the specific behaviours that will lead to improved performance or achievement of a specific goal. The main interventions are setting goals to inspire high performance, reviewing current and past performance to identify gaps for improvement, brainstorming ideas, and drawing on learning from previous successes and failures. Berglas says that coaches using behaviourist approaches often ignore unconscious conflict in the client and 'tend to fall into the trap of treating the symptoms rather than the disorder' (2002: 90). He outlines the very real dangers of using non-psychologically trained coaches in organizations and argues that coaching as a fledgling profession risks being seen as Machiavellian, unethical, unregulated, unprofessional and dangerous.

De Haan considers behaviourist approaches unsuitable for leadership/executive coaching, as 'Underpinning even the simplest of leadership issues are emotions, anxieties and personal traits which need a deeper and more sensitive approach' (Sparrow, 2008: 1). Drawing on psychotherapy research, De Haan's (2008) relational coaching model focuses on the coach/coachee relationship as the main vehicle for change. The shift of focus to the coaching relationship has led to psychodynamic approaches being used particularly in executive coaching to examine conflicts, object relations, attachment styles, coachee defences and the dynamics of the coach/coachee relationship (Kilburg, 2004).

POSITIVE PSYCHOLOGY COACHING (PPC)

Like other humanistic models of coaching (person centred, existentialist, motivational interviewing, gestalt, transactional analysis), *positive psychology* is presented to the coaching marketplace as an established brand. The rise of coaching psychology parallels that of positive psychology. They both emerged to redress the perceived practice and research imbalance in psychology between psychopathology and disease (the deficit model) relative to human strengths and wellbeing (the human strengths model) (Linley et al., 2006: 4). Their aim is to build performance and enhance wellbeing in non-clinical populations and they have three main shared interests: the search for a scientifically rooted approach to increase wellbeing, improve performance and achieve valued goals; the need to establish theoretical and research foundations; and the development of an arsenal of empirically validated models and interventions to help clients to achieve directed, purposeful change (Kauffman et al., 2010: 158). In short, positive psychology offers rich research and practice pickings for coaching, and coaching is an ideal vehicle through which the science of positive psychology can be applied. Many coaches look to positive psychology coaching to satisfy the increasingly vociferous demands of commissioning organizations for evidence that expenditure on coaching can be justified in terms of return on investment. Positive psychology's vast large-scale research base offers coaching a rich resource of knowledge and coaching interventions. For example, the character strengths inventory (Values in Action Institute Inventory of Strengths, VIA–IS) has identified 24 strengths of character that are valued by most of the world's cultures. The coach can use the self-report questionnaire and VIA survey which are available free of charge online (www.AuthenticHappiness.org) to assess the coachee's strengths and wellbeing and help her to build on these to enhance life satisfaction and identify potential routes to peak performance. Other PPC interventions include powerful and inspirational questioning to help coachees identify a broader range of choices and find ways to apply their strengths to achieve desired outcomes, e.g. by using visualization techniques and brainstorming (Kauffman et al., 2010).

METHODOLOGICAL INTEGRATION AND MANAGED ECLECTICISM IN COACHING

Increasingly, coaches are adopting integrative approaches to coaching, and some have argued for a return to coaching's eclectic practice beginnings. Bachkirova and Cox's (2007) cognitive-developmental approach to coaching draws on cognitive psychology and adult learning theories. Other integrative coaching models include Grant's (2006b) integrative goal- and solutions-focused approach to executive coaching; Kilburg's (2004) and Brunning's (2006) psychodynamic and systems approaches; and Orenstein's integrative model for executive coaching which is based on the assumption that 'the consultant's most crucial tool in the executive coaching process is the use of self' (Grant, 2008a: 19).

Some experts reject the exclusivity claims of powerful meta-models of coaching on the grounds that coaching using one-model approaches can become mechanistic and can miss critical clues to the client's context, and the client can easily become manipulated to fit the coach's agenda (Clutterbuck, 2010: 73). Clutterbuck argues that 'managed eclecticism' (also known as the 'British eclectic model'), which involves 'an intelligent, sensitive ability to select a broad approach, and within that approach, appropriate tools and techniques, which meet the particular needs of a particular client at a particular time' (2010: 75), is a measure of the relative maturity of a coach. Megginson and Clutterbuck's (2009) four levels of coaching maturity framework compares four main coaching approaches (models based, process based, philosophy based and managed eclectic) which relate to the coach's style of coaching (control, contain, facilitate, enable) and the critical questions the coach poses to himself during the coaching conversation. These four approaches represent the cognitive and socio-emotional developmental stages that the coach must pass through in order to achieve maturity and 'managed eclecticism' (2009: 5).

THE SCIENTIST-PRACTITIONER MODEL OF COACHING

The introduction of the scientist-practitioner model of coaching can be seen as a response by coaching psychologists to the growing demands for evidence of the effectiveness of different types of coaching; a move to enhance the acceptance and credibility of coaching amongst corporate and private clients by utilizing up-to-date research findings to support decisions about practice (Cox, 2003); and an attempt to develop coaching from a service industry towards a respected cross-disciplinary profession with a solid research base (Grant, 2004). The aim is to inspire confidence in the efficacy of coaching across the diverse contexts in which it is practised and among practitioners and clients alike. In this view, coaches are expected to be informed consumers rather than significant producers of research, and the professionalization of their coaching practice is dependent on their ability to utilize relevant research. The adoption of the scientist-practitioner model has been promoted as vital for the professionalization of coaching and the consolidation of its links with the behavioural sciences (Grant, 2004).

THE DEVELOPMENT OF COACHING RESEARCH

With an estimated $2 billion per annum market for coaching (Fillery-Travis and Lane, 2007) the pressure is on coaches to differentiate their offering, enhance their credibility in the eyes of their clients, and convince clients of the distinctiveness and effectiveness of their approach. Some writers argue that research can help distinguish coaching from its close relatives (mentoring, counselling and psychotherapy) and drive up standards of practice. Research into coaching has been growing at a substantial rate since the first peer-reviewed paper was published in 1937. Between 2000 and July 2008 a total of 335 articles were published, compared to the previous 62 years between 1937 and 1999 when only 93 articles appeared. Between 1980 and 2008, 59 PhDs and 150 empirical studies were produced (Grant, 2008a). However, given the relative youth of coaching compared to its counselling and psychotherapy cousins, theory is still lagging behind practice, and coaching research is at best variable in quality and at worst rudimentary, often due to weaknesses and gaps in the research methodology. To date there has been little outcome research; some notable examples, mainly evaluation studies, seek to address bottom line or other business-critical variables.

Two impact studies which meet the criteria for good research are Smither et al. (2003) and Wasylyshyn (2003). In a large-scale study Smither et al. (2003) investigated the impact of coaching on 404 senior managers who received 360-degree multi-rater feedback and coaching and found that this enhanced performance and re-evaluation scores.

Wasylyshyn's (2003) research underscores the distinctive assets that psychologists possess as executive coaches and points to the heightened scrutiny of coach competencies and credentials by business clients. He argues strongly that further outcome research is needed or executive coaching in particular runs the risk of being seen as a costly fad.

Kampa and White summarized the five known empirical studies of executive coaching across the 1990s to early 2000s, and stated that 'coaching may positively impact individual productivity at the most senior levels and that coaching results in increased learning, self-awareness and development and more effective leadership' (2002: 153).

Bono et al. (2009) compared the practices of psychologist and non-psychologist coaches as well as the practices of coaches from various psychological disciplines (counselling, clinical and industrial/organizational) and found as many differences between psychologists of differing disciplines as were found between psychologist and non-psychologist coaches. Moreover, differences between psychologist and non-psychologist coaches were generally small and related to key competencies identified by the coaches. A recent survey of the membership of the BPS Special Interest Group in Coaching Psychology found that the most popular frameworks that psychologists are using in their coaching are cognitive behavioural, person centred and solution or goal focused (Whybrow and Palmer, 2006).

In terms of life coaching, the empirical literature is almost silent. However, in the two peer-reviewed published empirical evaluations of the impact of life coaching conducted by Grant, life coaching was found to be effective in facilitating goal attainment, well-being and purposeful change in normal, non-clinical populations (Grant, 2003), and personal life coaching for coaches in training reduced anxiety, enhanced cognitive hardiness and increased goal attainment and levels of personal insight (Grant, 2008b).

Academic coaching research conducted at the University of Sydney found that between 25 and 50 per cent of those seeking coaching have clinically significant levels of anxiety, stress and depression (Grant, 2009). This suggests that coaching is attracting some individuals who wish to address an array of mental health issues without the stigma often associated with therapy and counselling. It has also given rise to debate about how well equipped coaches are for dealing with mental health issues that may emerge in coaching and raised ethical questions in relation to duty of care, particularly for the coaching profession and for organizations which employ non-psychologically trained coaches.

KEY CHALLENGES FOR COACHING

In spite of the claims that coaching has now reached a state of maturity, the industry is a long way from meeting even the basic requirements of a true profession because it lacks a holistic theoretical framework derived from a sound empirical base and a unique body of knowledge (Vaartjes, 2005). If coaching is to become a profession, it must adopt criteria such as the development of an agreed and unified body of knowledge, professional standards and qualifications, and codes of ethics and behaviour. Following the Dublin declaration, some headway has already been made in this direction; 'However, the multiplicity of coaching associations suggests that the pathway of coaching to professionalization may be at best bumpy, and at worst derailed' (Gray, 2011: 1).

Coaches come from numerous backgrounds and disciplines, have a wide variety of education and training, and are applying their skills and knowledge from other fields. The challenge for coaching is to develop coaching-specific training, research and practice. As in related disciplines like counselling and psychotherapy, coaching needs to develop explicit evidence of what works in coaching, why it works and how it can deliver return on investment (Stober et al., 2006).

To date, much evidence is anecdotal or descriptive and extrapolates from other fields such as counselling and psychotherapy. There is a need to evaluate this evidence's applicability to coaching and then to begin to adapt it for particular coaching interventions and techniques. Coaching-specific research is the lifeblood of the emerging profession of coaching (Grant, 2004). If there is no research base to support the ongoing development of practitioners and the profession, coaching runs the risk of exacerbating the tension between theory and practice which exists at the heart of the discipline and potentially of fading or becoming a fad.

REFERENCES

Bachkirova, T. and Cox, E. (2007) A cognitive-developmental approach for coach development. In S. Palmer and A. Whybrow (eds), *Handbook of Coaching Psychology: A Guide for Practitioners*. Hove: Routledge.

Berglas, S. (2002) The very real dangers of executive coaching. *Harvard Business Review*, June: 86–92.

Bono, J.E., Purvanova, R.K., Towler, A.J. and Peterson, D.B. (2009) A survey of executive coaching practices. *Personnel Psychology*, 62: 361–404.

Bresser, F. (2009) *Global Coaching Survey*. Frank Bresser Consulting. www.frank-bresser-consulting.com.

Brunning, H. (2006) The six domains of executive coaching. In H. Brunning (ed.), *Executive Coaching: Systems-Psychodynamic Perspective* (pp. 131–51). London: Karnac.

CIPD (2009) *Learning and Development Annual Survey Report: Taking the Temperature of Coaching*. Chartered Institute of Personnel and Development, Learning and Development Survey, June.

Clutterbuck, D. (2010) Coaching reflection: the liberated coach. *Coaching: An International Journal of Theory, Research and Practice*, 3 (1): 73–81.

Cox, E. (2003) The new profession (editorial). *International Journal of Evidence Based Coaching and Mentoring*, 1 (1).

Cox, E., Bachkirova, T. and Clutterbuck, D. (eds) (2010) *The Complete Handbook of Coaching*. London: Sage.

De Haan, E. (2008) *Relational Coaching: Journey Towards Mastering One-to-One Learning*. Chichester: Wiley.

Fillery-Travis, A. and Lane, D. (2007) Research: does coaching work? In S. Palmer and A. Whybrow (eds), *Handbook of Coaching Psychology: A Guide for Practitioners*. Hove: Routledge.

Gallwey, W.T. (1974) *The Inner Game of Tennis*. London: Pan.

Garvey, B., Stokes, P. and Megginson, D. (2009) *Coaching and Mentoring Theory and Practice*. London: Sage.

Grant, A.M. (2003) The impact of life coaching on goal attainment, metacognition and mental health. *Social Behavior and Personality*, 31 (3): 253–64.

Grant, A.M. (2004) Towards a profession of coaching: sixty-five years of progress and challenges for the future. *International Journal of Evidence Based Coaching and Mentoring*, 2 (1): 1–16.

Grant, A.M. (2006a) A personal perspective on professional coaching and the development of coaching psychology. *International Coaching Psychology Review*, 1 (1): 12–22.

Grant, A.M. (2006b) An integrative goal-focused approach to executive coaching. In D.R. Stober and A.M. Grant (eds), *Evidence Based Coaching Handbook*. Hoboken, NJ: Wiley.

Grant, A.M. (2007) Past, present and future: the evolution of professional coaching and coaching psychology. In S. Palmer and A. Whybrow (eds), *Handbook of Coaching Psychology: A Guide for Practitioners* (pp. 23–39). Hove: Routledge.

Grant, A.M. (2008a) *Workplace, Executive and Life Coaching: An Annotated Bibliography from the Behavioural Science Literature*. Coaching Psychology Unit, University of Sydney, Australia.

Grant, A.M. (2008b) Personal life coaching for coaches-in-training enhances goal attainment, insight and learning. *Coaching: An International Journal of Theory, Research and Practice*, 1 (1): 54–70.

Grant, A.M. (2009) Coach or couch? In D. Coutu and C. Kauffman (eds), *What Can Coaches Do for You? Harvard Business Review*, January: 26–32.

Gray, D.E. (2011) Journeys towards the professionalization of coaching: dilemmas, dialogues and decisions along the global pathway. *Coaching: An International Journal of Theory, Research and Practice*, pending publication in 2011.

Kampa, S. and White, R.P. (2002) The effectiveness of executive coaching: what we know and what we still need to know. In R.L. Lowman (ed.), *Handbook of Organizational Consulting Psychology* (pp. 139–58). San Francisco: Jossey-Bass.

Kauffman, C., Boniwell, I. and Silberman, J. (2010) The positive psychology approach to coaching. In E. Cox, T. Bachkirova and D. Clutterbuck (eds), *The Complete Handbook of Coaching*. London: Sage.

Kilburg, R.R. (2004) When shadows fall: using psychodynamic approaches in executive coaching. *Consulting Psychology Journal: Practice and Research*, 56 (4): 246–68.

Linley, P.A., Joseph, S., Harrington, S. and Wood, A.M. (2006) Positive psychology: past, present and (possible) future. *The Journal of Positive Psychology*, 1 (1): 3–16.

Megginson, D. and Clutterbuck, D. (2009) *Further Techniques for Coaching and Mentoring*. Oxford: Elsevier Butterworth-Heinemann.

Mooney, P. (2008) *The Dublin Declaration on Coaching, Version 1.3*. Global Community of Coaches, Dublin. www.pdf.net/Files/Dublin%20 Declaration%20on%20Coaching.pdf.

Peltier, B. (2001) *The Psychology of Executive Coaching*. New York: Routledge.

Sherman, S. and Freas, A. (2004) The Wild West of executive coaching. *Harvard Business Review*, November.

Smither, J.W., London, M., et al. (2003) Can working with an executive coach improve multisource feedback ratings over time? A quasi-experimental field study. *Personnel Psychology*, 56 (1): 23–44.

Sparrow, S. (2008) Origins of coaching: origins of the species. www.personneltoday.com, 8 July 2010.

Spence, G.B., Cavanagh, M.J. and Grant, A.M. (2006) Duty of care in an unregulated industry: initial findings on the diversity and practices of Australian coaches. *International Coaching Psychology Review*, 1 (1): 71–85.

Stober, D.R., Wildflower, L. and Drake, D. (2006) Evidence-based practice: a potential approach for effective coaching. *International Journal of Evidence Based Coaching and Mentoring*, 4 (1): 1–8.

Vaartjes, V. (2005) Integrating action learning practices into executive coaching to enhance business results. *International Journal of Evidence Based Coaching and Mentoring*, 3 (1): 1–17.

Wasylyshyn, K.M. (2003) Executive coaching: an outcome study. *Consulting Psychology Journal: Practice and Research*, 55 (2): 94–106.

Whybrow, A. and Palmer, S. (2006) Taking stock: a survey of coaching psychologists' practices and perspectives. *International Coaching Psychology Review*, 1 (1).

Co-Counselling

ROSE EVISON AND RICHARD HOROBIN

Co-counselling is a personal growth method involving participants working in reciprocal role pairs, exchanging client and counsellor roles halfway through the session time. Theory and practice have evolved around the core experience that inbuilt emotionally expressive processes provide the means of transforming maladaptive rigid responses into adaptive flexible feeling, acting and thinking. The rigidities involve the whole person, though single aspects may be salient, e.g. distressed feelings, destructive actions, negative thinking. Dealing with such rigid responses is central to all therapeutic and personal growth methods, although few distinguish clearly between flexible and rigid responses, or work with all aspects of the person. Current research into connections between emotions and physical and mental health validates the perspective that rigid or flexible responses correlate with poor or good mental health respectively (Thayer and Brosschot, 2005).

Co-counselling can be used by anyone who is able to learn the techniques, and also able to fulfil the counsellor role as well as work as client. Whilst some heavily distressed people are excluded by these criteria, others are not. Co-counselling can result in therapeutic changes ranging from emotional first aid and problem solving to emerging from internalized oppression. For ongoing growth using co-counselling techniques, most people need to work within a supportive community of co-counsellors.

KEY CONCEPTS

The present authors link the key concepts and working methods of co-counselling to an embodied and embedded theory of emotions, in which inbuilt emotions constitute our motivating system, and organize our mind and body resources appropriately to meet task demands. This research-supported theory (Evison, 2001) distinguishes three organizing modes. *Learning mode* facilitates problem solving and learning, with resources organized by inbuilt positive/pleasurable emotions; *emergency mode* enables us to react rapidly to threats to our physical, psychological and social wellbeing, with resources organized by inbuilt negative/painful emotions; and *rigid mode* is driven by redundant emotional pain. Co-counselling uses strategies that reliably facilitate changing from rigid mode to learning mode.

In learning mode, pleasurable core emotions of interest and joy motivate us to problem-solve and learn; whilst love and pride motivate us to care for, and to act confidently with, others. These emotions form our basic way of interacting with our physical and social environments, with positive feelings, relaxed bodies and alert minds. Learning mode is the most flexible mode, providing maximum choice of actions with full access to our skills and knowledge. Learning mode enables adaptability to our ever-changing environment.

In emergency mode, painful core emotions motivate us to overcome physical and psychological threats to wellbeing. Body and mind resources are organized for short-term survival, narrowing our attention to focus on the threat and, according to the threat's nature, activating appropriate muscles: to repair threatened relationships; to cry for help to replace lost loved ones; to retch out poisons; to flee dangers; and to fight to overcome obstacles. These preparations are associated with inbuilt core emotions of shame, grief, disgust, fear and anger respectively. Because emergency mode needs rapid responses, options are limited to existing skills and knowledge.

After successfully overcoming threats, our emergency mode – with its high energy demands and narrowed attention – is redundant. For tackling the next task with maximum effectiveness, and to minimize physical wear and tear, emergency mode resources need rapid reclaiming. Consequently, inbuilt processes exist for reclaiming redundant resources by returning body and mind to learning mode. Mastering a threat results in the emotion of joy which, being incompatible with painful emotional arousal, provides the necessary rapid return to learning mode.

When we fail to master a threat but survive – an everyday occurrence, especially in childhood – the negative emotion activated by the threat remains, locking up attentional and body resources. Because redundant negative emotion reduces resources available for new tasks, and causes wear and tear on bodies, a reset to learning mode is again needed. Such a reset is spontaneously triggered by becoming aware there is no immediate threat, while experiencing mind and body resources still oriented to a now-past distressing situation. Co-counsellors term these conditions a *balance of attention*, and the reset processes as *emotional discharge*.

Discharge processes have observable bodily aspects, namely non-purposive movements of the aroused muscles, such as laughing for shame, crying for grief, retching for poisonous ideas, shaking for fear, storming – a tantrum-like process – for anger. The resulting muscular relaxation releases attention trapped by the threat, producing learning mode.

Unfortunately the metaphoric term *discharge* is a source of confusion. This term encourages the belief that something damaging needs to be lost or expelled from our persons; whereas the metaphor of emotional reset suggests that resources are being reclaimed or reassigned. The vaguer term *catharsis* encourages the same confusion, along with the belief that the process is artificial, a purgative rather than a natural process. Psychologists add to this confusion by continuing to use a venting metaphor for strong expressions of emotion.

However, these specific emotional reset processes, occurring naturally after failure experiences, are often interfered with using physical punishment and/or shaming when emotional expressiveness is socialized in childhood. With reset inhibited, we experience the pain of our aroused bodies. Seeking to minimize such pain results in the inadequate responses, occurring when the threat ceased, becoming conditioned. Co-counsellors term these

conditioned responses *patterns*. Any reminders of the past threat will trigger these patterns – a process termed *restimulation*.

Patterns affect the whole person, and are usefully modelled as rigidly connected gestalts of key aspects of experience, i.e. feelings, actions, thoughts and the body states that support these aspects. The co-counselling experience is that everyone has patterns, they are not restricted to people with psychiatric diagnoses. Patterns vary in complexity, from nauseous responses to specific pain-associated smells, via shame–anger cycles of humiliated rage, to complex knots of internalized oppression. Such responses may be unique to individuals, or shared within a subculture, where patterns trigger acting as agents or targets of oppression.

To escape from patterns we must set up the appropriate reset conditions – crucially, awareness of the absence of current threats plus re-experiencing the emotion that was not reset in the past. When such a balance of attention is achieved, spontaneous discharge occurs; and pain-triggered rigid responses are changed into the high-potential processes of learning mode. The result is a disabling of pattern triggers, and the occurrence of spontaneous insights – termed *re-evaluation* – with new learning replacing maladaptive responses.

As Scheff (1979) has pointed out, whilst the term 'catharsis' has been used in a variety of ways – rarely clearly defined – the concept of discharge provides a sufficiently explicit model to be experimentally testable. Although critical investigation of the discharge model in psychotherapeutic settings is still lacking, research into discharge-related phenomena such as 'mirthful laughter' and 'emotion with tears' is now being carried out (respectively, Kimata, 2006; Miller and Fry, 2009). Consequently various health-promoting effects of discharge, including lowered blood pressure, have now been experimentally documented.

STRATEGIES AND SKILLS

Co-counselling uses two major strategies. First, participants agree to a contract, which provides the foundation for a peer working relationship. Peerness is established by participants alternating client and counsellor roles, and changing those roles halfway through the time. The contract minimizes restimulations from the counsellor; providing a non-threatening relationship which maximizes clients' ability to change rigid life responses into flexible ones.

The contract specifies the client is always free to choose the distresses/patterns they want to address, and the level of counsellor support they want.

Levels run from supportive attention only, via reminders of appropriate techniques, to direct suggestions of what to say and do derived from techniques likely to produce discharge. The counsellor agrees to provide ongoing supportive attention to the client, and avoid verbal and non-verbal judgemental messages, interpretations, and advice about life situations. The reciprocal role relationship enables co-counsellors who become skilled at offering supportive attention and keeping the basic contract to provide high levels of non-judgemental warmth, empathy, and genuineness for each other.

The second strategy involves noticing the pattern cues the client displays at any moment, and utilizing a technique likely to move the client into a balance of attention, so they discharge. The overarching technique for reaching a balance of attention is contradicting salient features of the pattern currently operating, i.e. those aspects perceived by the client and/or the counsellor at any moment, termed *pattern cues*. Contradicting means enacting the opposite to the verbal and bodily pattern cues. Thus a contradiction to 'You're dreadfully lazy' would be 'You're delightfully hard working', said in a delighted tone of voice. Again, sitting with arms folded and legs crossed could be contradicted by uncrossing the legs and opening the arms wide. Clients do not have to believe what they are saying, or feel comfortable with the contradictory body gestures/postures adopted. They are putting some part of their whole person totally outside the pattern they are working on, becoming aware that the pattern is irrelevant in the present, and so producing a balance of attention. However, clients are encouraged to make suggestions to themselves, to develop their inner counsellor. Depending on the agreed contract, the counsellor may make suggestions to the client. Ongoing development of inner counsellors results from actively learning skills in both roles.

The type of contradiction needed varies according to which side of the balance of attention the pattern cues fall. The client may be too distant from the emotion driving the pattern – patterns that inhibit emotional expressiveness. Common cues for inhibited patterns are a low monotonous voice, restricted gestures and body movements, using past tense, or third-person talk about problems and distresses, using 'reasonable' words. For example, 'I think you sometimes don't hear what I'm saying', said in a low voice, could be contradicted by saying in a forceful tone, 'You're a lousy listener.'

Alternatively, the client may be engulfed by a pattern, which is experienced as present reality. Here the threat triggering the pattern is perceived as present in the counselling session. Such uninhibited patterns are labelled as 'acting out' by our culture. Cues are a loud monotonous voice, uncontrolled gestures and movements, strongly derogatory verbal descriptions. Thus, 'You're an arrogant bastard' said aggressively could be contradicted by, 'You relate to me as a peer' said appreciatively. For expanded accounts of co-counselling concepts and techniques see Evison and Horobin (1990; 1994).

VARIATIONS IN UK CO-COUNSELLING

Co-counselling grew from a USA counselling agency, Personal Counselors. In the 1960s, the Re-evaluation Counseling (RC) organization was set up, which spread beyond the USA, first reaching the UK in 1971. Currently, RC exists in organized form in 60 countries. Co-Counselling International (CCI) was set up by RC dissidents in the USA in 1974, and in the UK in 1975, with co-counselling coming into use as a generic term for the process. CCI has a presence in some 15 countries.

RC uses central control to maintain coherence in theory, practice and organizational form. Major developments include working with oppressive distresses (e.g. sexism, racism, classism), tackling them within RC and out in the world. Their counselling strategies and campaigning in the world provide a model for how to carry out such work – something not yet taken up by CCI. The organizational style adopted can result in difficulties in identifying and working on authoritarian patterns. Although RC encourages the client to take charge of their own progress, an emphasis on skilled counselling encourages rapid client change, with the possibility of unbalancing the reciprocal relationship in favour of the counsellor role. The search for a good counsellor can replace individuals developing their inner-counsellor skills. For an account of this variant by two of its experienced teachers, see Kauffman and New (2004).

CCI, a loose network without formal membership criteria, provides an umbrella for a variety of ways of using reciprocal pairs for personal growth. CCI groups in different countries – and within the UK – have diverged in theory, practice and organization from both RC and each other. Some common variants:

1 Some teachers have moved from a focus on discharge to include techniques from other therapies (e.g. from cognitive therapy, gestalt and meditation). Such techniques can be diluting, or even contradictory, of traditional co-counselling, e.g. dropping the concept of patterns, and teaching that discharge can be damaging in some circumstances.

2 An individualistic style has developed, with some teachers making the client role the expert one, reducing the attention paid to counsellor skills beyond providing supportive attention, or doing exactly what the client dictates – more like co-clienting than co-counselling. Such deskilling of the counsellor role can make identifying and working on strong patterns, like internalized oppression or isolation, difficult. Development of inner counsellors, which occurs best when counsellor and client skills are treated as of equal importance, is likely to be stunted.

3 An emphasis on clients' right to use any techniques from other therapies they find helpful can result in the loss of a common pool of techniques. When differences are major, contracts may be limited to supportive attention only, reducing client growth opportunities.

4 The traditional strategy of establishing supportive groups, in which patterned interpersonal behaviour arising outside sessions is treated as material to be worked on, has changed. Some teachers and groups now espouse group dynamics models, in which participants are encouraged to personally challenge destructive behaviour in other co-counsellors outside sessions.

With such variants in mind, the present authors now use the phrase 'traditional co-counselling' to describe their own practice and teaching, and that of others with similar orientations. We continue to use supportive group cultures, considering them optimal for learning and personal change, as indicated by Evison's (2001) research review. Emphasis is also placed on participants viewing the reciprocal roles as teamworking, which supports skill development in both client and counsellor roles. We consider client–counsellor teamwork makes change processes more efficient, and in particular facilitates tackling strong patterns. However, the authors' use of current emotion theories to provide an intellectual underpinning is not traditional.

TRAINING AND SUPERVISION ISSUES

RC runs its own training and supervision, regarding both professionals and institutions as oppressive. Beginners' classes are conducted by teachers accredited by the central organization. For full membership, RC participants are required to continue taking classes and attending workshops to develop their skills as clients and counsellors. Regional, national and international workshops are held. Teachers are expected to become skilled in the counsellor role, and to do demonstration counselling of class participants. Personal growth and supervision are combined in a system of teachers and leaders being counselled by their organizational superiors, including during workshop demonstrations. Teachers are encouraged to work on what gets in the way of becoming better teachers. Teachers and members who deviate from accepted theory and practice, and who are unwilling to fall into line, are ejected from the organization. A journal, *The RC Teacher*, is devoted to co-counselling teachers' skills and interests.

Within CCI, the teaching role is recognized as needed for passing on the skills. There is much variability in the content and methods of teacher training, though apprenticeships and short training courses predominate. Regional, national and international workshops provide opportunities for exchange of skills and ideas, but these occasions seem little used for advancing teacher skills. While there are skilled co-counselling teachers in CCI, there is no overall system for maintaining teacher quality. Individual or group supervision is rare, probably due to a critical stance to hierarchy and authority. The increasing variations in theory and practice between groups have the potential consequences of loss of theoretical understanding and loss of techniques.

BENEFITS OF CO-COUNSELLING FOR THERAPEUTIC PRACTITIONERS

For therapeutic practitioners, using traditional co-counselling provides ways to:

1 participate in a peer support system, independent of professional and job hierarchies, which can reduce the stresses inherent in the practitioner role, and accelerate personal growth

2 experience being clients, noticing the large overlaps in distresses between practitioners and their clients, seeing trust-building from a client's viewpoint, and having first-hand experience of the processes of discharge and re-evaluation

3 work as both client and counsellor in the reciprocal relationship, which enables the development of the participants' inner counsellors, who then operate in life situations outside co-counselling sessions

4 increase practitioner counselling skills, particularly their ability to offer non-judgmental warmth; to recognize the differences between emotional expressiveness and emotional acting out; and to add methods of assisting, or at least

not suppressing, emotional reset to their repertoire of therapeutic techniques
5 understand that balance of attention and discharge are significant phenomena in facilitating therapeutic change, even in therapeutic methods which do not intentionally seek them.

Practitioners who use co-counselling variants which de-emphasize discharge, and/or reduce the need to develop counsellor skills, are unlikely to gain all the above benefits.

REFERENCES

Evison, R. (2001) Helping individuals manage emotional responses. In R.L. Payne and C.L. Cooper (eds), *Emotions at Work: Theory, Research and Applications in Management* (pp. 241–68). Chichester: Wiley.

Evison, R. and Horobin, R.W. (1990) *How to Change Yourself and Your World: A Manual of Co-counselling Theory and Practice* (2nd edn). Pitlochry: Co-counselling Phoenix, Change Strategies.

Evison, R. and Horobin, R.W. (1994) *Co-counselling as Therapy* (2nd edn). Pitlochry: Co-counselling Phoenix, Change Strategies. An expanded version of a chapter in J. Rowan and W. Dryden (eds), *Innovative Therapies in Britain*, Milton Keynes: Open University Press, 1988.

Kauffman, K. and New, C. (2004) *Co-counselling: The Theory and Practice of Re-evaluation Counselling*. Hove: Brunner-Routledge.

Kimata, H. (2006) Emotion with tears decreases allergic responses to later in atopic eczema patients with latex allergy. *Journal of Psychosomatic Research*, 61: 67–9.

Miller, M. and Fry, W.F. (2009) The effect of mirthful laughter on the human cardiovascular system. *Medical Hypotheses*, 73: 636–9.

Scheff, T.J. (1979) *Catharsis in Healing, Ritual and Drama*. Berkeley, CA: University of California Press.

Thayer, J.F. and Brosschot, J.F. (2005) Psychosomatics and psychopathology: looking up and down from the brain. *Psychoneuroendocrinology*, 30: 1050–8.

The RC Teacher: a journal for people interested in the theory and practice of teaching re-evaluation co-counseling. Seattle: Rational Island Press. Issues 28 and 29 (2009 and 2010 respectively) comprise a handbook for RC teachers.

WEBSITES

Co-Counselling International UK: www.co-counselling.org.uk
Re-evaluation Counseling: www.rc.org

Couple Counselling

GAIL EVANS

The therapy process with couples can be draining, intense, challenging and frustrating – but also liberating and exciting. Because it is very different from working with individuals, specialised training is recommended. Whatever theoretical approach is used to understand the clients and the therapy process, there are some common themes.

PREPARING THE SCENE

Whether in private practice or working in an organisation, you need to consider how to advertise what you do and to whom you are appealing. Bear in mind that disadvantaged and minority groups need active encouragement that their needs will be understood and welcomed. Organisations need to train staff to respond differentially to enquiries, taking into account some of the issues referred to below. If you have a sexual therapy or other specialised service, clients need to be openly asked which type of help they are seeking.

Consider which partner makes contact and arranges an appointment: inevitably one person takes responsibility, but behind this is a sequence that may prove telling. How have you been selected; has the decision been motivated and taken jointly and equally or has one partner 'brought' the other, perhaps to be changed or to be abandoned to the therapist's care? As with any therapy, the freer you are from internal conversations and concerns, the better able you are to notice clues to the nature of the relationship dynamics. It is useful to have thought through how you take referrals and what information you do or do not ask for at both the enquiry and assessment stages.

Look at your therapy room and its layout for working with two clients. What messages and choices do the seating and surroundings convey? Do you allow your clients free choice of where they sit; what happens when one claims the only chair and you are left to share the sofa with their partner? In such interchanges the power dynamics of the couple relationship and the relationship triad are played out. This raises a key difference between one-to-one therapy and working with more than one client: whatever your therapeutic orientation, to some degree working with couples is likely to involve more direction from the therapist.

From the moment you meet, greet and seat your clients, much is communicated or inferred about your position in the triad: for example, whose side are you on; is your role that of parent (nurturing or critical), friend, sibling, expert, collaborator (with one side)? Initially, as far as possible, and maybe very explicitly, you need to engage with both partners equally. However, a thought-provoking idea put forward by Claire Rabin (1997) is that, when there is a power imbalance, by maintaining neutrality you *de facto* collaborate with the stronger party. This raises an ethical dilemma and a possible conflict of therapeutic values. Conscious choices need to be made about how you approach and present yourself, and later as you engage in session.

ASSESSMENT, REFERRAL AND CONTRACTING

The assessment process resembles, of course, the beginnings of other therapy relationships. Here, though, you will be trying to establish a relationship with two people and deciding whether the couple is willing and able to work well enough and together with you, albeit that there may be hurt, animosity and differences. There needs to be a shared agenda for the therapy, so the assessment process may continue until it is established that a shared agenda does or does not exist. Part of my agenda as a couple therapist is that the relationship is the client and this has an impact on the nature of the contract and the interaction between us.

In settings where short-term work is required, a decision has to be made whether it is in the clients' interests to offer therapy or refer. There are examples of short-term couple therapy models (e.g. Gilbert and Shmuckler, 1996). As with one-to-one work, some clients are on the cusp of change and the actions of arranging and coming to a therapy session galvanise their own resources. An opportunity to air issues in a supportive environment launches the couple into working together to find their own resolution, sometimes one session being enough for this. However, there are many instances where the issues are more complex or long standing and less easily resolved. In a setting where only short-term work can be offered, the therapist needs to be alert to signs that a couple can quickly respond to facilitation of effective communication and to engage in cooperative work where both parties can lower their defences to hear and respect each other's point of view and take shared responsibility for change. One indicator is that the narratives that each tells about the history of their relationship and difficulties are broadly similar and/or can adapt during dialogue to create a shared narrative.

In addition, the assessment process aims to uncover whether there is an area of work which needs a specific approach, like sexual therapy. General relationship problems may be caused by, or be the cause of, sexual difficulties and this needs to be teased out. Whilst it may appear from the media that there is openness about sexual matters, in practice many couples will need an invitation and encouragement to discuss this aspect of their relationship. Conversely, some couples will discuss their sexual difficulties freely but be reluctant to examine their general relationship, probably because to admit that the global relationship is in trouble is more disturbing than picking out a part of the relationship for blame – 'if only this was ok then everything would be fine'.

Where there are specific sexual difficulties it is advisable to:

1 recommend the client to consult their GP or a sexual health clinic to rule out physical causes
2 consult with a sexual therapist about the appropriateness of referral.

Specific sexual issues which are likely to benefit from specialised therapy include:

- pain (either partner) at, during or preventing penetration, e.g. vaginismus
- desire and arousal problems (loss of or inhibited desire or arousal in either partner) including erectile problems
- orgasmic problems including inability to orgasm (either partner), premature and retarded ejaculation
- fetishes and addictions.

Depending on your knowledge and experience you may be able to help with general sexual problems (e.g. sexual ignorance, doubts about orientation). In Relate's training the acronym PLISSIT is referred to as a guide:

P	**Permission**
	Many couples merely need an invitation and support to discuss sexual matters, possibly including some familiarisation with language
LI	**Limited Information**
	Some basic education in sexuality and sexual functioning may be within your knowledge and comfort to discuss
SS	**Specific Sexual tasks**
	If you have sufficient knowledge and some training you may feel able to negotiate specific things the couple could do to reduce anxiety and enhance their sexual relationship
IT	**Intensive Therapy**
	Referral to a sexual therapist is indicated because there is a specific sexual dysfunction

In all instances you need to feel comfortable with and knowledgeable about sexual issues and sexual language so you can facilitate a free and frank exchange, both with you and between the couple. There are many publications available to expand your knowledge and understanding, and the numerous television programmes (such as 'Embarrassing Bodies') and documentaries on sexuality are very informative and challenging of attitudes.

THE ETHICAL DIMENSION

Working with couples demands another set of ethical considerations and poses different challenges, dilemmas and decisions compared with one-to-one work. Some of these emerge straight away on contact or during the assessment process. Examples from my own practice include being asked to work with 'affair couples' (e.g. a couple engaged in an affair for 20 years; a bigamous marriage; a couple where the man's wife had been in a home with a degenerative disease for years) and being told about an affair with a request not to reveal this to the client's partner in couple therapy. You may also be approached by lawyers and other professionals involved in divorce and custody cases wanting information or supporting letters or asking for your notes. It is useful to think through some of your attitudes prior to starting couple work but, as with many ethical dilemmas, these situations can take you unawares; so it is advantageous to have a way of deferring decisions until you have a chance to think them through, and access to supervision with an experienced couple-work supervisor is recommended.

The contract requires negotiation around confidentiality and being clear about your attitude to different permutations of working with the couple. Will you insist that both partners attend all appointments together as some couple therapists do? Whether you do or not, what will happen if one partner turns up alone for an appointment? If you and the couple think that some separate appointments would be useful, you need an agreement about what may or may not be shared from a one-to-one conversation back into the triad: do you want to be left holding secrets, and if you do hold a secret, what will be the impact on the ensuing work with the couple? It is worth considering that the solution is not necessarily your responsibility; the client who has revealed the secret to you has a responsibility. There will also be considerations about the impact of developing your relationship with one partner whilst the other partner is more distant from the therapeutic process. Such issues often come up during the first appointment, so the couple therapist should have thought through some likely situations in principle, to be clear what the consequences of alternative courses of action might be and how flexible you are prepared to be. Being clear about your own principles and the rationales that underpin your responses to these requests will help you to handle the situation sensitively and calmly when put on the spot.

Another ethical dimension is responsibility for safety. Domestic violence and abuse are, sadly, commonplace; they cross class, gender and orientation boundaries, and the chances of domestic violence are higher when the relationship is strained or when the victim leaves or threatens to leave the relationship. Arguments can get overheated and threatening behaviour deployed. One partner may relentlessly pursue the other for a response, culminating in the pursued partner lashing out. People are frequently unaware of how their behaviour escalates, how intimidating their actions may be to their partner, and also the impact on children (often wrongly thought to be unaware). Relationship therapists need to be alert for signs and it should be ascertained, routinely, whether such incidents are or have been happening. Clearly it takes skill to 'hold' the couple and convey acceptance whilst also being firm that continued violence or emotional abuse is not acceptable.

Couple therapists may refuse to work with a couple on the relationship until a domestic abuse contract is in place, even when incidents are described as 'minor' or not recent. Therapy may inflame and exacerbate difficulties. A partner who has been subjected to violence is unlikely to be able to speak openly and honestly without running the risk of a consequent assault outside the therapy room. A specific domestic violence contract aims to identify a workable plan of action for situations of potential violence where each party takes some responsibility for safety, before therapy commences. This may include discussion of expectations of behaviour within the therapy room and with respect to breaching confidentiality and safeguarding children.

Other issues that may emerge during an initial meeting, and all of which in some way may affect the balance, include:

- Who pays, and the symbolism of money in the relationship.
- How appointments are negotiated with three diaries and multiple commitments.
- Timing of appointments: issues of childcare, etc. may limit availability as a couple.
- The therapist's gender will potentially create an imbalance in the counselling room.
- Ensuring opportunities for feedback from both partners: one may act as spokesperson for the couple.
- Negotiating tasks, homework, etc. means ensuring both parties have the same information, and that both understand and subscribe to the intention and meaning of such exercises.
- Issues that impact on the power in the counselling room, for example if one partner's lack of proficiency in English means the other acts as go-between or translator.

THE TASKS AND COURSE OF THERAPY

Whilst a therapist's particular approach to a couple's issues will be influenced by their theoretical allegiance, the tasks may be summed up as follows:

- Raising awareness of the nature of the problem as each partner experiences it and creating a different narrative.
- Developing couple communication with the aim of leading to improved emotional intimacy and the capacity to problem solve, have fun and share sexual gratification.
- Exploring the compatibility of values, beliefs and frames of reference.
- Improving problem-solving and conflict resolution.
- Strengthening couple bonds, care and support for each other by developing mutual empathy, and ultimately acceptance through some of the above.

From the outset of therapy a message should be conveyed that both partners will be heard. This may mean taking charge of the interaction to enable each to speak and not allowing a pattern to become established that one speaks for both or that one speaks most of the time. It may also be necessary to intervene to maintain the couple focus (as opposed to focusing on individual issues or third parties). In this, couple therapy has a very different and unfamiliar feel compared with many one-to-one approaches.

Associated with this is a commitment to encouraging the couple to talk to, and develop their relationship with, *each other*. This may sound obvious but can be trickier than it sounds because as a one-to-one therapist you are used to your client talking and relating to you. You might overtly ask a couple to face each other and speak to one another. A way of subtly influencing this to happen is to 'decentre'. When one partner is speaking you turn your attention and gaze to the other partner, which encourages the speaker to also address their partner. As soon as the conversational turn passes to the other partner you switch your attention to the listening partner. This will feel odd and runs counter to all your one-to-one training! Try practising it on friends and family to get the hang of it.

When a couple seems unable to listen to each other they may not be ready to because they are individually too defensive. You then need to focus on building a relationship with each (rather like a parent having to share their attention between siblings) before they can be encouraged to have empathy for each other. This may be done by dividing sessions between the partners, formally or informally, for example by offering separate sessions or by agreeing that you will work with one partner with the other present as silent witness.

STRENGTHENING COUPLE BONDS

Mutual empathy is a key to successful couple relationships. The therapeutic process with couples often centres on developing such mutual understanding and acceptance (e.g. Greenberg and Johnson, 1988) and gaining, or regaining, a sense of being a couple. Some of this will be learned from the therapist as model, whilst some will be deliberately encouraged by the therapist. A beginning to mutuality can be developed by highlighting shared emotional experiences and values, especially during the initial meeting. Although displayed behaviour differs, much of the internal emotional experience and many values will be similar. Normalising and contextualising difficulties also helps: many couple difficulties are associated with life and couple/family changes or stages. Frequently there are clusters of such events that even individually would engender stress and a process of re-evaluation. Some history exploration can assist couples to contextualise their situation, improve communication and develop mutual empathy, and is sometimes a helpful way to distract from damaging exchanges and to identify strengths.

A tool borrowed from systems theory and family therapy can be helpful to therapist and couple. The geneogram, a form of family tree, identifies actors in the family history and the relationships between them, and also notes repeating patterns across generations, expectations, rules, roles, conflicts and boundaries and how these are similar or different between the couple. Using a large piece of paper and marker pens to create the tree facilitates a sense of common purpose and distraction from destructive differences. Couples are often surprised and enlightened by this exploration which offers an opportunity to develop mutual understanding, open up areas of negotiation and strengthen the couple bond. Whatever your theoretical orientation you can use this tool for exploration.

DEVELOPING COUPLE COMMUNICATION

When couples are in distress, a major cause and/or casualty is communication. Some couples never establish helpful communication patterns while others lose the capacity to communicate constructively. This allows projections and assumptions to develop and exacerbate difficult issues. The model of the therapist demonstrating careful listening skills is helpful, but the aim of the therapy is to assist them to establish constructive communication patterns and they may need direct teaching and practice. A tool I find useful is a simple, step-by-step listening exercise. It is important to explain any exercise carefully, explore specific times to do it and potential pitfalls, and try it in the therapy room first. If a couple cannot do it with you there to act as umpire

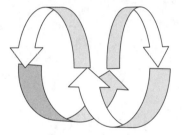

| A
When I
experience attack
I get scared
When I get
scared I
withdraw | | B
When I experience
withdrawal I feel
rejected
When I feel
rejected I
get angry (attack) |

Figure 7.7.1   *Figure of eight pattern of interaction in couple counselling*

or referee they will certainly not be able to manage it at home.

Using such an exercise in the therapy room is an example of how liberating couple counselling can be. The emphasis is not all on the relationship between the client and the therapist. While the couple talk you can sit back and observe and see very clearly some unhelpful habits they are unaware of, including how unproductive arguments (as opposed to productive ones) develop. One common pattern is a repeating loop of interactions (see Figure 7.7.1, showing partners A and B) which replays deeper attachment wounds. This may be understood theoretically as interactive projection and projective identification, learned behaviour or fragile process, or in other terms depending on your theoretical orientation. Clients can find it helpful and illuminating to see this on paper without needing to understand any underlying theoretical explanations.

The figure of eight pattern of interaction shown in Figure 7.7.1 is a graphic demonstration of interactive attachment patterns. Attachment theory offers some useful insights into some of the destructive or unhealthy dynamics that may be operating in a relationship, and they may also be explored through the geneogram described above. These are examples of how couple therapy may be more directive and psycho-educational in approach than individual therapy: for instance, Wile (1993) advocates teaching couples how to argue effectively, and sex therapy usually includes psychosexual education. As with individual therapy, once emotive issues are ventilated many couples' own resourcefulness re-emerges and the wise therapist will encourage a couple's own solutions which fit their values; some couple therapies particularly focus on this emotional ventilation (e.g. Greenberg and Johnson, 1988).

With the advent of easy-to-use video technology I believe more therapists will incorporate this resource into their work with clients so that a couple can see for themselves, in a very immediate way, how they interact. Several television shows over recent years have demonstrated how powerful this can be in highlighting helpful and unhelpful patterns of interaction and also suggest that it may be advantageous on occasion to take the work outside the limitations of the therapy room.

REFERENCES

Gilbert, M. and Shmuckler, D. (1996) *Brief Therapy with Couples: An Integrative Approach*. Chichester: Wiley.

Greenberg, L.S. and Johnson, S.M. (1988) *Emotionally Focused Therapy for Couples*. New York: Guilford.

Rabin, Professor Claire (1997) Intimacy in an age of changing gender roles. BASRT Conference on Intimacy in the 90s, November.

Wile, D.B. (1993) *Couples Therapy: A Nontraditional Approach*. Chichester: Wiley,

Disability

SIMON PARRITT

Little information is gathered on the number and demographic of disabled people who seek or use professional counselling services, despite there being reference to the fact that disabled people are more likely than the general population to experience comorbidity, such as anxiety and depression. Indeed, a large study in the US found that serious psychological distress among adults 'with disabilities' was over 14 per cent, being seven times greater than among non-disabled adults (Okoro et al., 2009). Increasing survival rates due to medical advances, social moves towards independent living and social integration suggest that disabled people could present for therapy more often. It is therefore becoming more important to have an understanding of disability.

Whatever context or situation you find yourself working within, you are likely to encounter clients who are disabled or living with long-term conditions. As impairments are sometimes hidden, counsellors should be aware that a client may be disabled and living with an impairment, though this may not be obvious. The referral may not mention disability or even seem central to the referral but this may emerge as therapy continues. There can be a tendency to avoid, or refer on, because working with disability can be perceived as a specialist or challenging area to work in.

Many previously non-disabled people choose not to identify themselves as 'disabled', preferring to refer to themselves as 'being ill' or 'suffering from' a particular condition, such as epilepsy, arthritis or MS. Despite advances in attitudes, government initiatives and there being a greater disability awareness, it is worth noting that 'disability' is still, to some extent, considered a low-status and stigmatised label. This may be an issue for many clients who are now seen as 'different', and working with this 'difference' and what it means for the client can be useful if and when they are ready to address it, both within the therapeutic relationship and in the wider world.

Counselling and psychotherapy can be problematic for those disabled people who have lived with their impairments from birth or for many years. It is true that you may encounter fewer of this group than those who have more recently become disabled. However, contact with other health and social care professionals will usually have been characterised by assessments and medical treatment. Coming from a medical model, it is a relationship which is characterised by a power differential quite different from that within the therapeutic encounter. Being aware of how you are perceived, whilst key with any client, requires special attention in relation to the life experienced by the disabled client, as you may be seen as someone who is 'treating' them and/or assessing them. Do not assume that the client understands the level of confidentiality or trusts you easily. Confidentiality and even consent, as we know it, may be unique concepts and yet all the more powerful and valuable a part of what you can offer.

Often, one of the first casualties of becoming or being born a disabled person is privacy and autonomy. There is an assumption of access to body and person that few ever experience. Medical interventions, physical assistance and the need for support in day-to-day activities, such as dressing and washing, only reinforce the context in which a disabled person has to manage their own identity in relation to others, especially in a one-to-one relationship but also in family and the wider community. Whilst not dismissing the physical dimension and impact, one of the issues that brings people to therapy is emotional distress, often in relationship to others or their environment. How counsellors and disabled people relate in the room will also reflect the way that impairment disrupts and distorts relationships in the wider world. We should therefore be brave enough to learn from our client about their real experience; never be afraid to ask what you don't know, as the client is the expert. Balancing societal attitudes, behaviour and prejudice with the personal internal relationship within themselves is a task that can be undertaken collaboratively within a good empathic therapeutic relationship.

As therapists, we need to understand and empathise with the world within which our clients live. The lived experience of being disabled in an essentially non-disabled world can take its toll. It is unrealistic and uneconomic to expect, as some have demanded, that counselling for disabled people should be by disabled people. However, it is regrettable that despite some improvement in disability being represented amongst the ranks of counsellors and psychotherapists, they remain very under-represented and also silent. It is also wrong to 'ghettoise' disabled people and counsellors who are disabled people. Even if disabled counsellors and psychotherapists may have an initial advantage in sharing something of the same world, a disabled client can misconstrue such common experience as being more than it is, as diversity exists within the disabled community as much as it does in the non-disabled world. You should not, therefore, take being non-disabled as a reason not to enjoy and embrace working in this area effectively.

SUPERVISION

The concept of disability is not well covered within counselling courses, let alone supervision training. In a study by a disabled counsellor, 75 per cent of trainee counsellors on a course were surprised, following some awareness exposure, that they viewed disability in terms of tragedy and loss (Parkinson, 2006). Counsellors have fewer opportunities, in training or placements, to incorporate disability as an area where they develop good supervision skills once they qualify. It is thought useful to have some access to a disabled supervisor if possible, if only on a short-term basis, especially if you are not experienced in working with disabled people. Failing that, seek access to a supervisor experienced in working in this area from an empowerment perspective.

Evidence shows also that exposure to disabled people, either professionally or sometimes through personal life experiences, will mitigate some of the pitfalls and produce a more open, empowering and constructive approach to working with this client group (Parritt and O'Callaghan, 2000).

The circumstances that bring disabled clients to therapy can in themselves be distressing for the counsellor. There are issues that are not necessarily germane to the client and can prove challenging and even distressing for the counsellor. A client who has become impaired as a result of a violent incident or crime may evoke strong personal feelings within the counsellor. Such feelings and reactions can more usefully be explored with a supervisor familiar with disability issues. Equally, aspects of living as a disabled person, such as the constant presence of assistants and carers, can also prove both alien and confusing for the counsellor. Some disabled people also present with a physical difference which can disrupt or unsettle a counsellor who is unfamiliar with dealing with difference, be that a facial or bodily difference.

ASSISTANTS AND ASSISTANCE

It is unusual for most counsellors to work with someone else in the room. However, a client may be accompanied by a personal assistant (PA) or carer, and whilst in most cases they will not be present in the session, in some circumstances they may need to act as a facilitator to aid communication. It may be that the client has some communication impairment that requires an interpreter to be present during the session. Whilst this is not ideal and will alter the dynamic that you are used to when doing one-to-one work with your clients, access is a real practical issue for some clients and sometimes a facilitator may be the only way to access a therapeutic relationship. However, before acceding to this, it is also worth considering that for some disabled clients, as stated earlier, the concept of privacy may be alien and consequently the therapeutic value of being in a private and confidential relationship may not initially be understood.

VENUE AND ACCESS

It is part of the requirement of the original Disability Discrimination Act 1995, now largely superseded by the Equalities Act 2010, that it is illegal to discriminate against disabled people in areas such as the provision of goods and services. You are therefore expected to make reasonable adjustment to accommodate your clients. This is a vague phrase, and what is reasonable is not always clear. However, many counselling services outside the NHS are located in places that are difficult to access because of stairs, transport or other barriers including cost. Whilst you cannot be expected to anticipate all the access requirements of a disabled client, it is good practice to enquire prior to the initial visit what adjustments or help might be needed to access your service. For instance, you may be able to arrange a ground floor room or some parking accommodation or perhaps vary your session times to take account of the unpredictability of community transport such as dial-a-ride. The location of such amenities as accessible toilets is also important to consider.

HOME VISITS

Opinions, practices and codes of practice vary in respect of home visits and can often impose barriers to making them. Indeed, the safety of both client and counsellor are important considerations. The 'cosy' therapeutic space and environment within which many of us are used to working is absent. Those who have worked within a hospital ward will be well aware of the challenges that present in more open and less private spaces. There are, though, positives to visiting a client who has severe mobility issues and a home visit might be the only viable option. It also gives you a real insight into the day-to-day environment in which a severely impaired client might exist.

Online counselling in its many forms is also increasingly important for a number of disabled clients. The online community, with all its pros and cons, has given a freedom to the outside world which has become an important part of many disabled people's lives. The internet offers communication in a form that gives access where it would otherwise be denied. Having some experience in and possible training around online counselling and the issues of the internet would therefore be a valuable addition to your skills.

ASSESSMENT

There is nothing essentially different in assessing disabled clients and the general rule is to follow your own theoretical and practical training and practice. There are, however, some aspects of a disabled person's history and social context that may be important. The dislocation of past and present lives can be stark and accompanied by a gradual loss of previous friends, work and social life. Understanding and working with what it now means to belong is

nearly always an aspect of working with any marginalised group. Indeed, the dynamics within a family or couple are altered sometimes overnight by the onset of an impairment, whether that be slow and progressive as with some neurological conditions, or more sudden and traumatic when it is the result of injury, assault or accident. The age of onset is also important for social and emotional development. Those who have been disabled people from an early age have often had little opportunity to form close relationships and may become reliant upon professionals as substitutes for a social life and see them as friends, or indeed even potential partners.

COUNSELLING

A disabled person can seek or be referred for psychotherapy or counselling at any time in their lives and for a variety of reasons and not necessarily because of their impairment. In fact, many may not see or classify themselves as disabled and, of those who do, most will have recently acquired an impairment. It is less common for those who have been a disabled person for a long time to seek or want counselling. They will likely have been subjected to far too many health professionals in their lives already and be familiar with a professional relationship based upon treatment and cure, and aimed at 'overcoming' or 'reducing' the physical aspects of their impairments. Challenging the misconception that counsellors are just another health professional is an important task in the early stages of the therapeutic relationship. Hence, when and at what time in their life a disabled person arrives for counselling can be very important.

For newly impaired clients, many are seeking to reclaim the person they once were or the life they previously lived or the future they had hoped for. Traditionally, psychotherapy has thought of this as the same process as loss and bereavement. Whilst there is a place for this, counsellors need to be cognisant of the risks of using a tragedy or loss model. It may be hard for some clients to even use the term 'disabled' in reference to themselves, often preferring to say they are 'ill' or have a 'condition'. It is important to understand that disability is still a low-status attribute and that people bring with them, in this new identity, all the negative feelings and prejudices they held as a non-disabled person. This goes some way to explain the struggle that many face in accepting who they are now, which is compounded by societal reactions to disability. Whilst pain, fatigue and restriction of physical abilities may be the context within which a client seeks help or is referred, clients come to explore how they experience themselves as a disabled person in the social world. Living in a non-disabled world is challenging for any disabled person but, for many, reconciling who they are and can be, with who they once were and hoped to be, can be a complex negotiation between the real world out there and the new self. Integrating a positive disabled identity alongside the reality of an impairment with the new self and the wider society is an ongoing core issue.

A balancing act is required for both the counsellor and the client. The real impact of physical impairment cannot and should not be dismissed or ignored during the therapeutic process. An understanding of the amount of mental and physical energy that is taken up with planning and organising life is essential for the therapist. It means that there will be much less available energy to devote to social and leisure activities, however accessible they may be. Fatigue and/or pain can dominate and others will not necessarily understand what it feels like to require physical support and assistance for large parts of your daily existence. The quantity of different factors and to what extent any of them are applicable to any one client and their particular experiences are part of the collaborative discovery that has to take place.

All this needs to be understood and acknowledged by and with the counsellor for a beneficial therapeutic relationship to develop. The balance, then, is working with what is a real restriction or limitation of an impairment and what is a function of living as a disabled person in a world which has so many barriers to being a fully autonomous person. Helping a client overcome a trauma or an accident can be part of working with this client group, but the underlying work may lie in helping bring into being a new self-affirming identity, a major part of which is being a disabled person. Negotiating this path is an ongoing day-to-day struggle, and yet offering a space where this can be explored, beyond the trauma and loss agenda, can be the most rewarding and positive aspects of this work for both the client and counsellor alike.

CONCLUSION

Ultimately there is nothing different or unusual about disabled people, whether born with an impairment or acquiring one later in life. Whatever theoretical background or model is employed, the same skills and abilities are required to work with disabled people. We work and love within a world of diversity, however; unlike nearly all other minority groups, anyone, at any time, can 'join the club' and become a disabled person. As such, there are many differences such as religion, culture and gender which are important variables in how any individual disabled person experiences their world. It is essential to always acknowledge the reality of the pressures – social, economic and physical – faced by disabled people. This includes fundamental changes in the attitudes of family, partners, friends and society in general towards the client now they are seen as 'disabled'. Indeed, such basic issues as housing needs, living with professional carers, loss of income and employment are all social pressures that are faced by clients. It is also important not to ignore the personal and sexual relationship aspects of a client.

Few if any impairments prevent or remove sexual identity and a need for sexual expression. This is an aspect of disability that is often overlooked or sidelined as professionals, as well as the public at large, find it difficult to address. To the client it may be the most important and yet silent aspect of their lives but they feel unable to address it, even in therapy. However problematic it may seem, without incorporating this aspect of a client's identity and life we are failing to address and meet with the whole person and, as such, ultimately we diminish the full humanity of the client and society.

REFERENCES

Okoro, A., Strine, T., Balluz, L., Crews, J., Dhingra, S., Berry, J. and Mokdad, A. (2009) Serious psychological distress among adults with and without disabilities. *International Journal of Public Health*, 54 (supp. 1): 52–60.

Parkinson, G. (2006) Counsellors' attitudes towards young people with disabilities: how may we ensure equality of service delivery? *British Journal of Guidance and Counselling*, 34 (1): 93–105.

Parritt, S. and O'Callaghan, J. (2000) Splitting the difference: an exploratory study of therapists' work with sexuality, relationships and disability. *Sexual and Relationship Therapy*, 15 (2): 151–69.

RECOMMENDED READING

Shakespeare, Tom (2006) *Disability Rights and Wrongs*. Oxford: Routledge.

Shakespeare, Tom, Davies, Dominic and Gillespie-Sells, Kath (1996) *The Sexual Politics of Disability: Untold Desires*. New York: Continuum.

Wilson, Shula (2003) *Disability, Counselling and Psychotherapy: Challenges and Opportunities*. Basingstoke: Palgrave Macmillan.

Electronically Delivered Therapies

KATE ANTHONY

The concept of delivering psychotherapeutic services via technology has traditionally been a controversial one. However, the body of evidence that was slowly increasing when the second edition of this handbook was published is now established, and it is increasingly rare to find a mental health service that does not have an internet presence in some form – from a simple website or directory listing to a fully developed e-clinic or presence in a virtual environment.

Fifteen years on from the first appearance of commercial websites that offered email and chat for therapeutic communication, many publications have provided a wealth of information and literature around the topic. Perhaps the most comprehensive of these, for further textbook reading, are Hsiung (2002), Goss and Anthony (2003), Kraus et al. (2004; 2010), Derrig-Palumbo and Zeine (2005), Evans (2009), Jones and Stokes (2009), Anthony and Nagel (2010) and Anthony, Nagel and Goss (2010; and see Chapter 7.10 in this volume).

As well as the work of international experts in the field, publishing literature and collaborating on research projects, the area of electronically delivered therapy (and in particular the ethical and legal side of it) has been addressed by mental health organizations worldwide. Professional bodies such as the British Association for Counselling and Psychotherapy (Anthony and Goss, 2009; Anthony and Jamieson, 2005; Goss et al., 2001), the National Board of Certified Counselors (2001), and the American Counseling Association (1999) have addressed and published guidelines for their members who wish to offer an online presence. The International Society for Mental Health Online (www.ismho.org) was formed in 1997 and offers

suggested principles for working online; the Association for Counselling and Therapy Online (www.acto-uk. org) was formed in 2006 for UK practitioners and offers a code of ethics; and in 2008, the formation of the Online Therapy Institute (www.onlinetherapyinstitute. com) led to the Ethical Framework for the Use of Technology in Mental Health (Nagel and Anthony, 2009), a framework designed to be applicable to as many areas of mental health provision as possible.

This chapter describes the most essential elements that practitioners need to be aware of before considering an online presence, from a theoretical stance. It will concentrate on the use of *text*, via email, chat, forums and mobile phone texting (SMS), for conducting an individual client–practitioner therapeutic relationship. Of course, many of these elements of working in cyberspace can be extended to online group work, supervision, training and research. In addition, they can be applied to other uses of technology which are covered in Chapter 7.10 in this volume.

TYPES OF ELECTRONICALLY DELIVERED THERAPY

Using Block-text Email (asynchronous) for Therapy

This is most people's perception of using email for therapeutic use: the exchanging back and forth of emails between two people within a contract, which is (usually) short term and (usually) weekly, and which utilizes encryption software for privacy and confidentiality.

Using Narrative Dynamic Email (asynchronous) for Therapy

This type of email is where the practitioner inserts his/her responses *within* the client's email using different fonts and/or colours, and the client reciprocates in the same way, usually for a small number of exchanges before the dynamic text becomes too unwieldy and a new narrative is required. Again, it is (usually) short term and (usually) weekly, and utilizes encryption software for privacy and confidentiality.

Using Chat Rooms (synchronous) for Therapy

This method involves a dialogue between client and practitioner in real time, using an encrypted internet chat room or encrypted instant messaging software. The contracted sessions are usually weekly, and often incorporate a weekly exchange of asynchronous email (this is a useful function to allow the client to expand upon actual descriptive situations that would otherwise take up valuable time within the sessions).

Using Forums (asynchronous) for Therapy

More secure than any other form of electronically delivered therapy within this context, forums are held on the internet itself behind a password protected access system so that client and therapist visit a website to view and post responses to each other.

Using Mobile Phone Texting (asynchronous) for Therapy

Mobile phone texting (short message service, SMS) is often reserved for making and cancelling face-to-face appointments, but is increasingly used as part of the therapeutic process and is useful if used with care within a boundaried relationship. It is increasingly also used for crisis intervention by organizations such as Samaritans (Goss and Ferns, 2010).

THE ESSENTIAL CONCEPTS OF ONLINE TEXTUAL THERAPY

The first aspect of working with text that may seem obvious but bears clarifying is that it is a distance method of communication. There are obvious benefits to those who cannot access therapy, for example because of disability or geographical reasons, but apart from practical reasons it is important to understand the disinhibition effect (Suler, 2004) that makes for a more open and honest relationship. The ability for the client to reveal much more when working at a certain perceived distance (the one with which they feel comfortable) is significant. It also means that the level of disclosure occurs at a much faster pace than it usually does in a face-to-face relationship or even within other methods of distance therapy, such as the telephone. This intensity of disinhibition is peculiar to using typed text over the internet for communication, and should not be underestimated, particularly when taking care of the self and the client. Many clients find that a one-off outpouring of emotion and narrative, due to the disinhibition that affords a cathartic experience, means that they feel better and can disappear into cyberspace – a particularly distressing experience for the practitioner (also known as a black hole experience). For the most part, though, the disinhibition effect is a positive empowering experience, and one that is important to clients who cannot reveal sensitive information due to shame, embarrassment or being unable to 'look someone in the eye' while doing so.

The distance of the client also means that self-revelation of practitioner material, where appropriate within the work, can be a useful tool to facilitate a second aspect of working online – the concept of presence, described by Lombard and Ditton (1997) as 'the perceptual illusion of non-mediation'. This is described in my original research as occurring when 'the media used (in this case the computer and keyboard) is unimportant and you are interacting with another person in a separate space' (Anthony, 2000: 626). In this way, the medium used to conduct a therapeutic relationship is secondary to the therapeutic relationship actually taking place as a mutual journey towards the client's recovery. Despite the lack of any body language, so often cited as the reason that online work via text can never be 'real' therapy, the practitioner is able to enter the client's mental constructs of their world through their text, respond in a similar manner, and so develop a rapport that transcends the hardware used to support the communication as *well* as the 'white noise' that a physical presence can induce.

The white noise of the physical presence, which can introduce bias and judgement into a face-to-face therapeutic relationship, is bypassed when working online. Rather than seeing this as a negative part of the method, many online practitioners believe that it is not only positive, but also essential to the development of the therapeutic relationship to encourage a fantasy of the other person via a visual, auditory and kinaesthetic representation system. In this way, the client can build an overall sense of their counsellor or psychotherapist and develop that fantasy to fit their perception of the person they are most able to work with. It can be argued that the person behind each other's defences is found and the therapeutic relationship becomes stronger much more quickly.

Finally, we must consider how all this building of the therapeutic relationship can occur without the gestures, vocal interventions and eye contact that make up the traditional face-to-face relationship. The quality of the practitioner's written communication and their ability to convey the nuances of body language that facilitate the client's growth (empathic facial gestures, for example) are paramount when working online. However, it should be noted that respect for the client means that their ability to communicate in this way need not be expert (although the practitioner's work is made much easier if it is). The use of text to replicate body language takes many forms online, as does the use of netiquette (a combination of 'net' and 'etiquette'), but both aspects are integral to the success of the communication and therefore the client's recovery. Both these aspects are also sometimes considered facile within the conventional profession, and yet their contributions to the online therapeutic relationship being established, developed and maintained are vital. While in no way exhaustive, the following should give the reader some insight into what is possible within the remit of using typed text:

- There are different ways of communicating in an appropriate manner, depending on the context of that communication. Danet (2001) identified two types of textual communication: business and personal. However, in Goss and Anthony (2003) I explain how a third definition is necessary because the 'therapeutic textual communication' is at once both a business transaction (contracted between therapist and client) and a personal communication (because of the nature of the content).
- One rule of netiquette that it is essential to be aware of is that the use of CAPITALIZATION for an entire sentence or block of text is considered to be shouting and is usually disrespectful and rude.
- There are many ways of emphasizing certain words where necessary, such as *italicizing*, **bold**, underlining, _underscoring_, and *asterisks*.
- Overuse of exclamation marks generally makes the text difficult to read and is considered poor form.
- There are thousands of emoticons that are used to convey facial expressions. Most are supplied in email and chat software and some have to be (or are preferred to be) created using keyboard

characters and read by holding the head to the left (this does not apply in Asian countries – a cultural issue practitioners need to be aware of). Some of the more frequently used in online therapeutic work are:

☺ or :o)   or :)   smiles (smileys)
☹ or :o(or >:o{   frowns
;) or ;o)   winks (winkies)

The winky, in particular, is essential to indicate irony or a non-serious statement.

- Abbreviations and acronyms are also widely used. Some of the more frequently used in online therapeutic work are:

LOL   laugh out loud
BTW   by the way
PFT, k?   pause for thought, OK?

The latter is particularly useful for the client to use silence within a synchronous session.

- Emotional bracketing is also used to clarify emotion. As well as being able to hug your client by using parentheses, as in ((((Kate)))), some other uses are:

<<crying>>
[[sigh]]

- Automatic signature files, greetings and sign-offs also need careful consideration and the use of personal style *within the appropriate context of the communication.*

CONCLUSION

As well as the above facets of using typed text for therapeutic communication, there is, of course, a wealth of both practical and ethical considerations that need to be taken into account when setting up an online presence to work with clients. In-depth analysis of these facets is available in Anthony and Goss (2009) and Anthony and Nagel (2010), but some of the more obvious considerations are:

- confidentiality and data protection
- limitations of the method
- contracting and informed consent
- encryption
- fee structure
- assessment skills, suitability of client and referring on
- verification of parties (identity management)
- practitioner competence (both within IT and online work)

- boundaries
- licensing, regulation and quality control
- virus, worm and trojan management
- crisis intervention and the suicidal client
- cultural differences
- technical breakdown.

Training in online work is now considered essential (Anthony and Goss, 2009; Anthony and Nagel, 2010; Gehl et al., 2010), and there are now a variety of online trainings available in the form of long or modular courses, such as those of the Online Therapy Institute (www.onlinetherapyinstitute.com) and others as itemized at the International Society for Mental Health Online (www.ismho.org) resource pages.

The world of technological development is one that moves and develops extremely quickly, and it is well known that the counselling and psychotherapy profession in particular has been playing catch-up with the arrival of technology for therapeutic use over the last 15 years. What is certain, however, is that the profession has had to come to terms with the idea that sometimes the client is in a situation that means that they not only *cannot* sit with us face to face, but also that *they don't want to*. It is these clients that practitioners can now stop excluding from our services, ensuring that the world of counselling and psychotherapy becomes more accessible to our potential clients worldwide.

REFERENCES

American Counseling Association (1999) *Ethical Standards for Internet Online Counselling*. www.counselling.org/resources/internet.html, accessed 12 June 2004.

Anthony, K. (2000) Counselling in cyberspace. *Counselling Journal*, 11 (10): 625–7.

Anthony, K. and Goss, S. (2009) *Guidelines for Online Counselling and Psychotherapy* (3rd edn). Lutterworth: British Association for Counselling and Psychotherapy.

Anthony, K. and Jamieson, A. (2005) *Guidelines for Online Counselling and Psychotherapy* (2nd edn). Rugby: British Association for Counselling and Psychotherapy.

Anthony, K. and Nagel, D.M. (2010) *Therapy Online [A Practical Guide]*. London: Sage.

Anthony, K., Nagel, D.M. and Goss, S. (eds) (2010) *The Use of Technology in Mental Health: Applications, Ethics and Practice*. Springfield, IL: Thomas.

Danet, B. (2001) *Cyberplay*. Oxford: Berg.

Derrig-Palumbo, K. and Zeine, F. (2005) *Online Therapy: A Therapist's Guide to Expanding Your Practice*. New York: Norton.

Evans, J. (2009) *Online Counselling and Guidance Skills: A Practical Resource for Trainees and Practitioners*. London: Sage.

Gehl, N., Anthony, K. and Nagel, D.M. (2010) Online training for online mental health. In K. Anthony, D.M. Nagel and S. Goss (eds), *The Use of Technology in Mental Health: Applications, Ethics and Practice*. Springfield, IL: Thomas.

Goss, S. and Anthony, K. (2003) *Technology in Counselling and Psychotherapy: A Practitioner's Guide*. Basingstoke: Palgrave.

Goss, S. and Ferns, J. (2010) Using cell/mobile phone SMS to enhance client crisis and peer support. In K. Anthony, D.M. Nagel and S. Goss (eds), *The Use of Technology in Mental Health: Applications, Ethics and Practice*. Springfield, IL: Thomas.

Goss, S., Anthony, K., Palmer, S. and Jamieson, A. (2001) *Guidelines for Online Counselling and Psychotherapy*. Rugby: British Association for Counselling and Psychotherapy.

Hsiung, R. (ed.) (2002) *e-Therapy*. New York: Norton.

Jones, G. and Stokes, A. (2009) *Online Counselling: A Handbook for Practitioners*. Basingstoke: Palgrave Macmillan.

Kraus, R., Zack, J. and Stricker, G. (eds) (2004) *Online Counseling*. San Diego, CA: Elsevier.

Kraus, R., Stricker, G. and Speyer, C. (eds) (2010) *Online Counseling* (2nd edn). San Diego, CA: Elsevier.

Lombard, M. and Ditton, T. (1997) At the heart of it all: the concept of presence. *Journal of Computer Mediated Communication*, 3 (2). http://jcmc.indiana.edu/vol3/issue2/lombard.html, accessed 22 September 2011.

Nagel, D.M. and Anthony, K. (2009) *Ethical Framework*. Online Therapy Institute. www.onlinetherapyinstitute.com/ethical-training, accessed 22 September 2011.

National Board of Certified Counsellors (2001) *The Practice of Internet Counseling*. www.nbcc.org/Assets/Ethics/nbcccodeofethics.pdf, accessed 22 September 2011.

Suler, J. (2004) The online disinhibition effect. http://users.rider.edu/~suler/psycyber/disinhibit.html, accessed 22 September 2011.

Wider Uses of Technologies in Therapy

STEPHEN GOSS, KATE ANTHONY AND DEEANNA MERZ NAGEL

Every therapist now needs to be able, at least, to understand the ramifications of technologically mediated relationships for their clients, lest they fail to appreciate that such things are real and not merely 'virtual' (Anthony, 2001), and to be able to utilize the opportunities technologies now afford.

Use of technology is not for every client or every therapist. Dangers exist – such as touching deeply sensitive parts of a client's life while not physically present to help contain the experience – and are evident in the specialist ethical guidance that is required (Anthony and Goss, 2009; Nagel and Anthony, 2009a). The growth in technological means of receiving psychological help has frequently been led by clients rather than therapists, who have often had strongly polarized reactions to introducing technologies of any kind to their work (Goss and Anthony, 2003; Caspar, 2004).

This chapter briefly considers a small sampling of technologies that can be of assistance in providing therapy, either as an adjunct to it or to support client development and self-help. Telephones, email and internet chat are considered in other chapters in this volume.

COMPUTERIZED COGNITIVE-BEHAVIOURAL THERAPY

Computerized cognitive-behavioural therapy (CCBT) has been one of the most successful general uses of computer technology in therapy, at least in terms of the evidence base it has gathered (Marks and Cavanagh, 2009; Kaltenthaler et al., 2010; Cavanagh, 2010).

Typically, CCBT distils the key elements of cognitive-behavioural therapy (CBT) into software made available to clients screened as appropriate for this type of intervention by a professional. Typically, clients undertake tasks to ensure identification, monitoring and evaluation of negative thought patterns and are guided through strategies such as graded exposure, problem solving and behavioural experiments.

There is variation in CCBT programs, from single-session anonymous use to more complex systems facilitating more sophisticated relationships with the user. Some CCBT programs require no therapist input while others are designed to be used as an adjunct to therapy or to be used with the support of a professional by telephone, by email or in person. Good programs will monitor risk (such as suicidality) and will provide appropriate alerts to the user, the responsible practitioner or both.

Among numerous others, examples of CCBT programs include Beating the Blues and FearFighter, both of which have been recommended as appropriate treatments, for depression and phobia/panic respectively, by the UK National Institute for Health and Clinical Excellence (NICE) in their 2006 technology appraisal. NICE recommendations now include a 'class effect' acceptance of any competently designed CCBT package for depression (NICE, 2009). Just what would qualify a program as sufficiently well designed is, at the time of writing (August 2011), less clear, however (Cavanagh, 2010). Nonetheless, the quantity, quality and clarity of research into the outcomes achieved by CCBT mean that it has a less qualified recommendation than many talking therapies do generally.

PSYCHOLOGICAL TESTING AND WEB ASSESSMENT

Provision of psychological tests over the internet does nothing to alter the general principle that their use must remain grounded in sound clinical principles (Klion, 2010). Computerized psychological assessment dates back over 40 years (Butcher et al., 2004) but expanded rapidly with the development of the internet in the 1990s with applications extending beyond personnel selection (Wiskoff, 1997) and the limited range of tests previously available.

Advantages include cost, ease of access, automated scoring and, for more sophisticated tests programs, clinical indicators and aids to interpretation of test scores. Web-based tests can also be updated (or corrected) easily and in some instances scores can be recorded and collated centrally, allowing the development of large datasets. There is less need for assessments of this type to take up clinical time and they are also suited to pre-intake assessment, repeated measures and situations where information from multiple respondents is desirable (e.g. in child or family therapy). Some populations (e.g. younger and higher socio-economic groups) may actively prefer computerized assessments (Berger, 2006).

Debate flourishes on the ethics of online test administration (Association of Test Publishers, 2000; International Test Commission, 2005; Naglieri et al., 2004). In addition to the factors to be considered for any psychological testing, the proliferation of poorly designed and tested tests available on the web may mislead clients, and clinicians must ensure that tests are valid for the population with which they are being used (e.g. children). Appropriate levels of professional support should also be available, especially if distressing material may be a focus. Web-based tests do not reduce the need for clinical judgement or the responsibilities of the clinician. While concerns have been expressed about the psychometric equivalency of tests in computer format, and clinicians should be aware of them (Barak and English, 2002; Buchanan, 2003), they recede as tests become increasingly designed for electronic delivery and, furthermore, the issue of equivalency does not seem to be an issue for many common measures, such as the Minnesota Multi-phasic Personality Inventory (MMPI: Finger and Ones, 1999). Another factor is that of security, privacy and appropriate use of centrally stored data (along with intellectual property rights protection). It is essential that only trusted providers, employing the latest privacy protection standards, are used.

Self-help online tests can be effective forms of help in themselves when used appropriately. Examples include Qwitter.tobaccofreeflorida.com and Psychtracker.com (Dombeck, 2010).

TELEHEALTH GAMING

Computer games can have psychoactive effects. While the negative effects often gain most attention (e.g. Gentile et al., 2004), research suggests that positive outcomes can also be obtained (Coyle et al., 2005; Matthews and Coyle, 2010). Consequently, there is increasing interest in the positive uses of suitably designed games (Griffiths, 1997; Parkin, 2000), often as an adjunct to other forms of therapy.

Examples include Personal Investigator, in which the player hunts for clues to help solve a personal problem following solution-focused therapy principles (Matthews et al., 2008; Matthews and Coyle, 2010), and biofeedback-based games to treat anxiety (Pope and Paisson, 2001), among several others (Griffiths, 1997). Research has suggested that games can

- help develop problem solving skills
- displace aggression and deal with negative and positive outcomes as they arise
- engage otherwise difficult-to-reach populations, such as adolescents
- improve attendance rates
- decrease stigma associated with mental-health-related activities
- increase self-confidence, a sense of mastery and the willingness to accept responsibility
- increase cooperation with the therapist and improve therapeutic relationships.

MOBILE/SMS TEXT MESSAGING

Also noted in Chapter 7.9 in this volume, despite being restricted to a mere 160 characters per message, anecdotal and limited research evidence suggests that it is possible to create helpful therapeutic services based on short message service (SMS) interactions (Merz, 2010), commonly referred to as mobile phone text messages or texts. This is a popular means of communication with many clients, especially younger populations (Kaseniemi and Rautiainen, 2002). The UK Samaritans' SMS service, for example, received 413,000 messages from over 7500 unique mobile numbers in its first 36 months (Goss and Ferns, 2010).

In addition to providing access to a professional response – possibly at a time of crisis such as during a suicide attempt – text messaging offers a psychologically and physically involving activity, itself of value, for example for people who self-harm. Mobile devices (like smartphones) can also act as a platform for other interventions (Preziosa et al., 2009), are accessible during peak stress periods, and are well suited to semi-automated interventions such as post-therapy follow-up (e.g. Bauer et al., 2003), symptom monitoring (e.g. Elliott, 2008) or reinforcing treatment protocol adherence (e.g. Neville, 2002). Mobile-phone-based services are of particular relevance for emerging economies, typified by poor mental health care provision but burgeoning mobile phone availability.

WEBSITES

The internet is one of the world's most popular sources of health information, with more people turning to that than their own doctor or even a personal friend (iCrossing, 2008). Websites may be single pages of information (e.g. advertising a mental health service) or can be vast information sources containing many thousands of items (like WebMD.com, PsychCentral.com or www.mentalhealth.com). They may contain static information or any of the interactive elements described elsewhere in this chapter, including self-help interventions with or without therapist support (e.g. Botella et al., 2009).

The greatest single issue in using or providing mental-health-related websites is that of ensuring that information and services are of sufficiently high standards and remain up to date. Use of only the most reputable sources and seals of approval such as HONcode (see www.hon.ch/) or that provided by the Online Therapy Institute (see www.onlinetherapyinstitute.com/get-verified/) can help to identify those sites that seek to ensure that suitable standards are maintained. Nonetheless, it is often advisable to check information from websites, unless of impeccable provenance, against other sources (Grohol, 2010).

PODCASTING

A podcast is an audio or video recording that can be downloaded or viewed over the internet. Numerous mental-health-related podcasts are available, many of which are directly psycho-educational in intent.

The extent to which the information they contain can be relied upon is variable and care must be taken to ensure that they are from a reputable, well-informed source.

Examples can be found at www.thejoveinstitute.org/podcast.html, www.mentalhealth.org.uk/information/wellbeing-podcasts/ and www.iop.kcl.ac.uk/podcast/?id=64&type=artist.

BLOGGING

A web log or 'blog' contains a series of entries, usually arranged in date order, somewhat like an online diary. Most blogs are interactive to some degree, often allowing responses to posts, facilitating conversations between readers and authors and, in some cases, fostering the development of distinctive communities focused around the blog's themes (Nagel and Anthony, 2009b).

While many blogs are overtly psycho-educational or designed to keep practitioners informed of developments in the field (e.g. www.onlinetherapy-instituteblog.com/ or www.psychcentral.com/blog), writing about one's experiences has long been known to have therapeutic potential (Pennebaker, 1997; Thompson, 2004). There may be specific additional advantages to writing in electronic form (Hyland et al., 1993) and in sharing that work in a blog, so long as it is done with sufficient care and attention to self-protection. Tan (2008) reported that around 50 per cent of blogs are kept at least in part for the therapeutic effects experienced by the author.

Privacy issues can easily arise, however, even where a blog is apparently anonymous. Even where pseudonyms are used, with some effort content can often be traced back to the real author. Practitioners should be aware of the potential for clients to blog about their therapy and consider including discussion of this in contracting with clients, especially if they practise online, to ensure adequate protection of privacy for both parties (Anthony and Goss, 2009; Grohol, 2010; see also www.onlinetherapyinstitute.com/ethical-training/).

WIKIS

A wiki is a web page that can be edited or added to by any user to provide an evolving information resource, potentially comprising the combined expertise of the entire internet community. While the best known is Wikipedia, a number of smaller wikis exist designed specifically for mental health service users or practitioners (e.g. www.onlinetherapyinstitute.com/wiki/).

Wikis and blogs are excellent examples of Web 2.0 thinking in which the content of the web becomes less controlled by centralized or commercial interests and is increasingly in the hands of the community of users as a whole.

VIDEOCONFERENCING

Videoconferencing applications (sometimes referred to as voice over internet protocol, VOIP), such as Skype, are effectively an extension of familiar audio telephony (discussed in Chapter 7.21 in this volume) (Simpson, 2009). They have been used effectively to extend the reach of mental health services in many parts of the world. Simpson and Morrow (2010) note that evidence suggests that video therapy, as with many therapeutic technologies, can particularly benefit marginalized groups such as those in prison, the elderly, rural communities and the disabled as well as hard to reach groups who may avoid face-to-face interventions as a result of perceived stigma or anxiety.

VIRTUAL REALITY, VIRTUAL EXPOSURE THERAPY AND AVATAR THERAPY

Virtual reality environments allow users to experience synthetically created environments with which they can interact and, often, communicate with other users. A virtual world may be limited, like a single room or set of objects, or extensive, like the infinitely expandable world of Second Life, within which relationships, businesses – and therapy – can all flourish. Virtual worlds were estimated to have 30 million active users in 2008, expected to rise to 50 million by 2011 (Schwartz, 2008) and a billion by 2018, with real clients paying for real services in a US\$8 billion services sector (Gilbert, 2008). Even if you do not intend to practise in a virtual setting, it is increasingly likely your clients will bring issues that originated online (Anthony, 2001; Wilson, 2010).

Virtual worlds with a community of users – massively multiplayer online (MMO) environments – can offer vastly increased social opportunities (Deeley, 2008; Live2Give, 2005) with an equality not restricted by the users' gender, race or disability, including social skills deficits (Nagel, 2009).

Avatars – the digital representation of the user – can be created to express one's actual or ideal self or different 'configurations of self' (Mearns and Thorne, 2000) – a child, a different gender or even an animal – in what has been termed 'avatar therapy' (Anthony and Lawson, 2002), a model that holds greater potential than has been explored thus far. It is possible to construct conversations with deceased family members (Nagel and Anthony, 2010), allowing clients to process 'unfinished business', or to address other parts of their selves, extending familiar 'empty chair' techniques (Ivey and Ivey, 1999).

While communications in some virtual worlds, including Second Life, are not currently sufficiently secure to conduct therapy, it can be combined with more thoroughly encrypted services such as Skype to allow properly private conversations. Other virtual environments, such as NeuroVR Editor (Riva, 2010) or EMMAs World (Baños et al., 2009), have been created with therapeutic levels of safety and benefit in mind (Riva, 2005; 2010).

Examples of clinical applications include virtual exposure therapy in which clients address problematic situations within the safety of a virtual environment. Sexual disorders (Optale, 2003), stress management (Villani et al., 2007), eating disorders (Riva et al., 2006), fear of spiders (Emmelkamp et al., 2001) or public speaking can be addressed by placing the client – or an avatar representing them – in a simulation of the feared situation. By monitoring reactions and rehearsing behaviours in simulated situations, clients can be helped to address them in real life. Behavioural rehearsal, it should be noted, has the potential for negative effects when conducted outwith a safe therapeutic frame: examples have been noted of suicidal behaviours being rehearsed in Second Life, leading to increased suicidality in the everyday physical world.

WEB 2.0, SOCIAL MEDIA AND HEALTH 2.0

Web 2.0 capabilities mark a shift in the philosophy of internet use (rather than a new technology as such) away from central control of web-based information towards shared control among communities of users – and they are changing the way mental health practitioners do their work even further. McDonald (2010) describes the hallmarks of Web 2.0 facilities, already more than a decade old, as rapid development of interactive applications, ease of combining data from different systems, and independence from specific types of device or operating systems. McDonald stresses that Web 2.0 refers to the ways people can use the web to easily publish information online, share that information with others and, perhaps most importantly, develop relationships and communicate interactively with people who share common interests. Often these behaviours are individualistic, spontaneous and highly decentralized.

'Social media' refers to the increasingly open and social nature of web-based communications, often seen as an essential feature of Web 2.0. Sometimes traditional media adopt 'social media' characteristics, as when a newspaper not only publishes its original content online but also encourages readers to discuss its articles online or to report events alongside postings by professional journalists.

Landro (2006) defines Health 2.0 as the result of the social networking revolution being applied in health care such that consumers can locate personalized health information quickly and with ease, and notes that patients who once connected mainly through email discussion groups and chat rooms are building more sophisticated virtual communities that enable them to share information about treatment and coping and build a personal network of friends. At the same time, traditional websites that once offered cumbersome pages of static data are developing blogs, podcasts, and customized search engines to deliver the most relevant and timely information on health topics.

However, more and more we are seeing the concept of Health 2.0 not just as a way in which social networking occurs in the health professions, but as a new wave into the future that changes how health care, including counselling and psychotherapy, is delivered (Porter, 2009).

In summary, with the advent of Web 2.0 and social media, many practitioners are utilizing the internet more and more. Not only has the internet become a platform for delivering therapeutic interventions, but it also offers very practical and increasingly necessary tools for the delivery of care as well as practice management and service development (Truffo, 2007; Giurleo, 2010). Blogging can be used to reach an audience of potential clients but can also serve as a vehicle for delivering positive mental health care information and discussion (Nagel and Palumbo, 2010).

CONCLUSION

With all the technologies noted here, it is essential that practitioners are aware of the ethical issues that arise in their use (Anthony and Goss, 2009; Nagel and Anthony, 2009a). Proper training and preparation are prerequisites to ensure client safety and optimal use. More extensive discussion of these technologies, and others such as social networking (Thomson, 2010), telehealth (Kim, 2010), the use of film and media (Sutherland, 2010) and technologically facilitated training and supervision (Coursol et al., 2010; Gehl et al., 2010; Groman, 2010), can be found in Anthony et al. (2010), Goss

and Anthony (2009) and Anthony and Nagel (2010). Additional up-to-date discussion can also be found at www.onlinetherapyinstituteblog.com/.

Given the rapid development typical of the field, we can be assured that new uses of technology will continue to emerge. Whether and how to use them will, naturally, be up to the individual practitioner.

REFERENCES

Anthony, K. (2001) Online relationships and cyberinfidelity. *Counselling Journal*, 12 (9): 38–9, online, accessed 26 May 2009. Available at: www.kateanthony.co.uk.

Anthony, K. and Goss, S. (2009) *Guidelines for Online Counselling and Psychotherapy Including Guidelines for Online Supervision* (3rd edn). Lutterworth: BACP.

Anthony, K. and Lawson, M. (2002) The use of innovative avatar and virtual environment technology for counselling and psychotherapy. www.kateanthony.co.uk, accessed 10 March 2010.

Anthony, K. and Nagel, D.M. (2010) *Therapy Online [A Practical Guide]*. London: Sage.

Anthony, K., Nagel, D.M. and Goss, S. (2010) *The Use of Technology in Mental Health: Applications, Ethics and Practice*. Springfield, IL: Thomas.

Association of Test Publishers (2000) *Guidelines for Computer-Based Testing*. Washington, DC: Association of Test Publishers.

Baños, R.M., Botella, C., Guillen, V., García-Palacios, A., Quero, S., Bretón-López, J. and Alcañiz, M. (2009) An adaptive display to treat stress-related disorders: EMMA's World. *British Journal of Guidance and Counselling*, 37 (3): 347–56.

Barak, A. and English, N. (2002) Prospects and limitations of psychological testing on the internet. *Journal of Technology in Human Services*, 19 (2/3): 65–89.

Bauer, S., Percevic, R., Okon, E., Meerman, R. and Kordy, H. (2003) The use of text messaging in the aftercare of patients with bulimia nervosa. *European Eating Disorders Review*, 11 (3): 279–90.

Berger, M. (2006) Computer assisted clinical assessment. *Child and Adolescent Mental Health*, 11 (2): 64–75.

Botella, C., Gallegoa, M.J., García-Palacios, A., Baños, R.M., Quero, S. and Alcañiz, M. (2009)

The acceptability of an internet-based self-help treatment for fear of public speaking. *British Journal of Guidance and Counselling*, 37 (3): 297–311.

Buchanan, T. (2003) Internet-based questionnaire assessment: appropriate use in clinical contexts. *Cognitive Behaviour Therapy*, 32 (3): 100–9.

Butcher, J.N., Perry, J. and Hahn, J. (2004) Computers in clinical assessment: historical developments, present status and future challenges. *Journal of Clinical Psychology*, 60 (3): 331–45.

Caspar, F. (2004) Technological developments and applications in clinical psychology: introduction. *Journal of Clinical Psychiatry*, 60 (3): 221–38.

Cavanagh, K. (2010) The use of computer-aided cognitive behavioural therapy (CCBT) in therapeutic settings. In K. Anthony, D.M. Nagel and S. Goss (eds), *The Use of Technology in Mental Health: Applications, Ethics and Practice*. Springfield, IL: Thomas.

Coursol, D., Lewis, J. and Seymour, J. (2010) The use of videoconferencing to enrich counselor training and supervision. In K. Anthony, D.M. Nagel and S. Goss (eds), *The Use of Technology in Mental Health: Applications, Ethics and Practice*. Springfield, IL: Thomas.

Coyle, D., Matthews, M., Sharry, J., Nisbet, A. and Doherty, G. (2005) Personal Investigator: a therapeutic 3D game for adolescent psychotherapy. *International Journal of Interactive Technology and Smart Education*, 2 (2): 73–88.

Deeley, L. (2008) Is this a real life, is this just fantasy? *TimesOnline*. women.timesonline. co.uk/tol/life_and_style/women/body_and_soul/article1557980.ece, accessed 26 May 2009.

Dombeck, M. (2010) The use of online psychological testing in mental health. In K. Anthony, D.M. Nagel and S. Goss (eds), *The Use of Technology in Mental Health: Applications, Ethics and Practice*. Springfield, IL: Thomas.

Elliott, J. (2008) Monitoring mental health by text. *BBC WorldNews America*, 31 December. news.bbc.co.uk/2/hi/health/7797155.stm, accessed 10 August 2009.

EmmelKamp, P.M., Bruynzeel, M., Drost, L. and van der Mast, C.A.P.G. (2001) Virtual reality treatment in acrophobia: a comparison with exposure *in vivo*. *CyberPsychology and Behavior*, 4 (3): 335–40.

Finger, M.S. and Ones, D.S. (1999) Psychometric equivalence of the computer and booklet forms of the MMPI: a meta-analysis. *Psychological Assessment*, 11 (1): 58–66.

Gehl, N., Anthony, K. and Nagel, D.M. (2010) Online training for online mental health. In K. Anthony, D.M. Nagel and S. Goss (eds), *The Use of Technology in Mental Health: Applications, Ethics and Practice*. Springfield, IL: Thomas.

Gentile, D.A., Lynch, P.J., Linder, J.R. and Walsh, D.A. (2004) The effects of violent video game habits on adolescent hostility, aggressive behaviors and school performance. *Journal of Adolescence*, 27 (1): 5–22.

Gilbert, B. (2008) Virtual worlds projected to mushroom to nearly one billion users. *Strategy Analytics*. www.strategyanalytics.com/default.aspx?mod=PressReleaseViewer&a0=3983, accessed 26 May 2009.

Giurleo, S. (2010) Marketing toolbox. *Therapeutic Innovations in Light of Technology*, 1: 42–4. issuu.com/onlinetherapyinstitute/docs/premier/43, accessed 31 September 2010.

Goss, S. and Anthony, K. (eds) (2003) *Technology in Counselling and Psychotherapy: A Practitioner's Guide*. London: Palgrave Macmillan.

Goss, S. and Anthony, K. (2009) Developments in the use of technology in counselling and psychotherapy. *British Journal of Guidance and Counselling*, 37 (3): 223–30.

Goss, S. and Ferns, J. (2010) Using cell/mobile phone SMS to enhance client crisis and peer support. In K. Anthony, D.M. Nagel and S. Goss (eds), *The Use of Technology in Mental Health: Applications, Ethics and Practice*. Springfield, IL: Thomas.

Griffiths, M. (1997) Video games and clinical practice: issues, uses and treatments. *British Journal of Clinical Psychology*, 36 (4): 639–41.

Grohol, J. (2010) Using websites, blogs and wikis within mental health. In K. Anthony, D.M. Nagel and S. Goss (eds), *The Use of Technology in Mental Health: Applications, Ethics and Practice*. Springfield, IL: Thomas.

Groman, M. (2010) The use of telephone to enrich counselor training and supervision. In K. Anthony, D.M. Nagel and S. Goss (eds), *The Use of Technology in Mental Health:*

Applications, Ethics and Practice. Springfield, IL: Thomas.

Hyland, M., Kenyon, C.A., Allen, R. and Howarth, P. (1993) Diary keeping in asthma: comparison of written and electronic methods. *British Medical Journal*, 306 (6876): 487–9.

iCrossing (2008) *How America Searches: Health and Wellness*. www.icrossing.com/research/how-america-searches-health-and-wellness.php, accessed 6 May 2009.

International Test Commission (2005) *International Guidelines on Computer-Based and Internet Delivered Testing*. www.intestcom.org/itc_projects.htm, 27 November 2009.

Ivey, A.E. and Ivey, M.B. (1999) *Intentional Interviewing and Counseling*. Pacific Grove: Brooks/Cole.

Kaltenthaler, E., Cavanagh, K. and McCrone, P. (2010) Evaluating the role of CCBT within mental health. In K. Anthony, D.M. Nagel and S. Goss (eds), *The Use of Technology in Mental Health: Applications, Ethics and Practice*. Springfield, IL: Thomas.

Kaseniemi, E. and Rautiainen, P. (2002) Mobile culture of children and teenagers in Finland. In J.E. Katz and M. Aakhus (eds), *Perpetual Contact*. Cambridge: Cambridge University Press.

Kim, T. (2010) The role of behavioral telehealth in mental health. In K. Anthony, D.M. Nagel and S. Goss (eds), *The Use of Technology in Mental Health: Applications, Ethics and Practice*. Springfield, IL: Thomas.

Klion, R.E. (2010) Web based clinical assessment. In K. Anthony, D.M. Nagel and S. Goss (eds), *The Use of Technology in Mental Health: Applications, Ethics and Practice*. Springfield, IL: Thomas.

Landro, L. (2006) Social networking comes to health care: online tools give patients better access to information and help build communities. *Wall Street Journal Digital Network*. online.wsj.com/article/SB116717686202159961.html, accessed 31 September 2010.

Live2Give (2005) *All About Live2Give*. braintalk.blogs.com/live2give/2005/01/all_about_live2.html, 9 January 2005.

Marks, I.M. and Cavanagh, K. (2009) Computer-aided psychotherapy: state of the art and state of the science. *Annual Review of Clinical Psychology*, 5: 121–41.

Matthews, M. and Coyle, D. (2010) The role of gaming in mental health. In K. Anthony,

D.M. Nagel and S. Goss (eds), *The Use of Technology in Mental Health: Applications, Ethics and Practice*. Springfield, IL: Thomas.

Matthews, M., Doherty, G., Sharry, J. and Fitzpatrick, C. (2008) Mobile phone mood charting for adolescents. *British Journal of Guidance and Counselling*, 36 (2): 113–29.

McDonald, D.D. (2010) On attempting an updated definition of 'Web 2.0'. socialmedia-today.com/dennismcdonald/139517/attempting-updated-definition-web-20, accessed 31 September 2010.

Mearns, D. and Thorne, B. (2000) *Person Centred Therapy Today*. London: Sage.

Merz, T. (2010) Using cell/mobile phone SMS for therapeutic intervention. In K. Anthony, D.M. Nagel and S. Goss (eds), *The Use of Technology in Mental Health: Applications, Ethics and Practice*. Springfield, IL: Thomas.

Nagel, D.M. (2009) People with Asperger's syndrome learn social skills in Second Life. *Telehealth World*, 2 (1): 1–8. www.telehealthworld.com/images/Spring09.pdf, accessed 1 May 2009.

Nagel, D.M. and Anthony, K. (2009a) *Ethical Framework for the Use of Technology in Mental Health*. Online Therapy Institute. www.onlinetherapyinstitute.com/id43.html, accessed 26 May 2009.

Nagel, D.M. and Anthony, K. (2009b) Writing therapies using new technologies: the art of blogging. *Journal of Poetry Therapy*, 22 (1): 41–5.

Nagel, D.M. and Anthony, K. (2010) Conclusion: innovation and the future of technology in mental health. In K. Anthony, D.M. Nagel and S. Goss (eds), *The Use of Technology in Mental Health: Applications, Ethics and Practice*. Springfield, IL: Thomas.

Nagel, D.M. and Palumbo, G. (2010) The role of blogging in mental health. In K. Anthony, D.M. Nagel and S. Goss (eds), *The Use of Technology in Mental Health: Applications, Ethics and Practice*. Springfield, IL: Thomas.

Naglieri, J., Drasgow, F., Schmitt, M., Handler, L., Prifitera, A., Margolis, A. and Velasquez, R. (2004) Psychological testing on the internet: new problems, old issues. *American Psychologist*, 59 (3): 150–62.

Neville, R., Greene, A., McLeod, J., Tracy, A. and Surie, J. (2002) Mobile phone text messaging can help young people manage asthma. *British Medical Journal*, 325 (7364): 600.

NICE (2006) *Guidance on the Use of Computerised Cognitive Behavioural Therapy for Anxiety and Depression*. Technology Appraisal no. 97. London: National Institute for Health and Clinical Excellence.

NICE (2009) *Depression: Management of Depression in Primary and Secondary Care*. Guidance CG90. London: National Institute for Health and Clinical Excellence.

Optale, G. (2003) Male sexual dysfunctions and multimedia immersion therapy. *CyberPsychology and Behavior*, 6 (3): 289–94.

Parkin, A. (2000) Computers in clinical practice: applying experience from child psychiatry. *British Medical Journal*, 321 (7261): 615–18.

Pennebaker, J.W. (1997) Writing about emotional experiences as a therapeutic process. *Psychological Science*, 8 (3): 162–6.

Pope, A.T. and Paisson, O.S. (2001) Helping video games 'rewire our minds'. Presented at Playing by the Rules Conference, Chicago, IL, 26–27 October.

Porter, M.E. (2009) A strategy for health care reform: toward a value-based system. *New England Journal of Medicine*, 361: 109–12. www.nejm.org/doi/full/10.1056/NEJMp0904131, accessed 31 September 2010.

Preziosa, A., Grassi, A., Gaggioli, A. and Riva, G. (2009) Therapeutic applications of the mobile phone. *British Journal of Guidance and Counselling*, 37 (3): 313–25.

Riva, G. (2005) Virtual reality in psychotherapy: review. *CyberPsychology and Behavior*, 8 (3): 220–40.

Riva, G. (2010) Using virtual reality immersion therapeutically. In K. Anthony, D.M. Nagel and S. Goss (eds), *The Use of Technology in Mental Health: Applications, Ethics and Practice*. Springfield, IL: Thomas.

Riva, G., Bacchetta, M., Cesa, G., Conti, S., Castelnuovo, G., Mantovani, F. and Molinari, E. (2006) Is severe obesity a form of addiction? Rationale, clinical approach and controlled clinical trial. *CyberPsychology and Behavior*, 9 (4): 457–79.

Schwartz, D. (2008) Noted Gartner analyst Steven Prentice updates his predictions on virtual worlds. *Fast Company*. www.fastcompany.com/blog/donald-schwartz/fc-technology-moderator-blog/noted-gartner-analyst-steven-prentice-updates-his-, accessed 26 May 2009.

Simpson, S. (2009) Psychotherapy via videoconferencing: a review. *British Journal of Guidance and Counselling*, 37 (3): 271–86.

Simpson, S. and Morrow, E. (2010) Using videoconferencing for conducting a therapeutic relationship. In K. Anthony, D.M. Nagel and S. Goss (eds), *The Use of Technology in Mental Health: Applications, Ethics and Practice*. Springfield, IL: Thomas.

Sutherland, J.-A. (2010) The role of film and media in mental health. In K. Anthony, D.M. Nagel and S. Goss (eds), *The Use of Technology in Mental Health: Applications, Ethics and Practice*. Springfield, IL: Thomas.

Tan, L. (2008) Psychotherapy 2.0: MySpace® blogging as self-therapy. *American Journal of Psychotherapy*, 62 (2): 143–63.

Thompson, A. (2010) Using social networks and implications for the mental health profession. In K. Anthony, D.M. Nagel and S. Goss (eds), *The Use of Technology in Mental Health: Applications, Ethics and Practice*. Springfield, IL: Thomas.

Thompson, K. (2004) Journal writing as a therapeutic tool. In G. Bolton, S. Howlett, C. Lago and J. Wright (eds), *Writing Cures*. Hove: Brunner-Routledge.

Truffo, C. (2007) *Be a Wealthy Therapist: Finally You Can Make a Living While Making a Difference*. Saint Peters, MO: MP Press.

Villani, D., Riva, F. and Riva, G. (2007) New technologies for relaxation: the role of presence. *International Journal of Stress Management*, 14 (3): 260–74.

Wilson, J. (2010) Using virtual reality to conduct a therapeutic relationship. In K. Anthony, D.M. Nagel and S. Goss (eds), *The Use of Technology in Mental Health: Applications, Ethics and Practice*. Springfield, IL: Thomas.

Wiskoff, M. (1997) R&D laboratory management perspective. In W.A. Sands, B.K. Waters and J.R. McBride (eds), *Computer Adaptive Testing: From Inquiry to Operation*. Washington, DC: American Psychological Association.

Family and Systemic Therapy

MARK RIVETT

There is an old Albanian proverb which summarises the focus of family and systemic therapy very well: 'No problem is an orphan.' This encapsulates the approach taken by the family and systemic therapies which see all psychological difficulties, indeed all of human life, as embedded in a relational web which both constructs and is constructed by those difficulties. The focus therefore is on human 'systems' and the most significant of these: the family. In these therapies, the 'family' is defined broadly (Carter and McGoldrick, 1999) with a deep respect for themes of diversity (McGoldrick and Hardy, 2008) and an emphasis on generational connectedness. Most family psychotherapists therefore help families who are dealing with the many stresses of family life: coping with children and adolescents, family separation and caring for the elderly. These stresses become further compounded by additional 'vertical stressors' (Carter and McGoldrick, 1999) such as disability, mental health concerns, substance misuse or ill health. However, the systemic perspective also informs therapy with individuals (Hedges, 2005), institutions (Campbell et al., 1989) and private sector firms (Wynne et al., 1986).

SYSTEMS THEORY AND THE FAMILY/ SYSTEMIC THERAPIES

The family tree (geneogram) of family therapy is generally seen as starting from the insights brought into psychotherapy by Gregory Bateson (1972; 1979) who was an anthropologist and systems scientist. Bateson encouraged his co-researchers at the Mental Research Institute (MRI) in post-war America to view individual problems within a relational context. This radical perspective contradicted the normal therapy practice of working only with an individual (the one with a 'problem') and working with relationships only via that individual's understanding of them. Bateson was particularly interested in the patterns of interaction in families where an individual had a diagnosis of schizophrenia or alcohol abuse. He and his co-workers hypothesised that these patterns contributed to the development and maintenance of difficulties and therefore 'recovery' depended on altering those patterns.

The application of systems theory to human systems (families, communities, organisations) includes a number of notable ideas. Firstly, it asserts that human beings manifest themselves within relational patterns that have built up over time. This means that who we are is often only understandable when we consider our closest relationships. A phrase credited to Bateson summarises this view: 'It takes two to know one.' Secondly, these relational patterns will themselves be influenced by other human systems such as inter-generational expectations, wider cultural meanings, and institutional processes. This means that no individual is to 'blame' for any particular interactional process. The third, and perhaps more contentious, point is that within relationships a personal 'problem' is often a form of communication about those relationships, or it functions to regulate those relationships. This has led some family therapists to talk about 'the interactional function of a problem'. This form of description is circular in nature because it does not assume that a 'problem' functions only for one individual; it serves a function for all individuals in the system as well.

The systemic perspective also provides an understanding about personal change. A commonly quoted phrase expresses this perspective: 'It is the people we love who keep us the way we are.' Thus change is unlikely to occur unless the human system in which the difficulty is embedded is helped to change. At the 'dawn' of the systemic therapies, this idea was supported by the clinical experience of many therapists who found that work with an individual did not lead to lasting change once that individual returned to their context/family. Bateson and others argued that human systems are more likely to change if the therapist respected the integrity of the system (e.g. the way relationship patterns balanced each other) and introduced difference into the system by altering meanings, behaviours or feelings. Bateson himself talked about finding a 'difference that made a difference' to the interactive patterns. He believed that this difference was often stimulated by finding multiple perspectives on a difficulty.

We can see how these ideas might help therapists if we look at common relationship patterns: a woman becomes depressed within a heterosexual relationship in which the male partner relies on her for all his own emotional needs; a child behaves badly in a family where the parental couple constantly argue; an elderly man retreats into solitude after the death of his wife while his daughters try harder and harder to engage with him. In all these situations, the behaviour of the 'presented symptom bearer' acts to balance as well as challenge the relational system within which they are embedded.

A BRIEF REVIEW OF THE HISTORY OF THE FAMILY/SYSTEMIC THERAPIES

These axioms of systems theory contributed to the initial 'generation' of family therapy models. These are frequently described as 'first-order' models because these clinicians looked for 'dysfunction' within the family system and tried to change it. Pioneers such as Minuchin (1974), Haley (1976) and Watzlawick et al. (1974) established the structural, strategic and MRI schools of family therapy. These therapists were interested in the family scripts that therapists brought to therapy but had not fully understood the influence of gender and culture to this process. The second wave of family therapy models evolved from the work of the Milan Associates (Palazzoli et al., 1978) and the Galveston Institute (Anderson and Goolishian, 1988). These therapies

are called 'second order' because they acknowledge that the therapist could never be an expert on the family system. He or she could only describe what their experience was of that system. This generation of family/systemic therapists emphasised another Batesonian idea: that the 'map is not the territory'. For example, what the therapist sees and describes is not what is experienced by members of the system. Equally, the second-order therapist could not predict how their engagement with the family system would influence or change it (Keeney, 1983). The view was that if the therapist retained a curiosity about the family system, this would generate new perspectives that would lead to change. Within this generation of family/systemic practitioners, more attention was given to the person of the therapist, with a special place given to how culture and gender inform what the therapist sees, does and says.

The 'third wave' of family/systemic therapies was ushered in as postmodernism entered the therapeutic world. Family therapy probably embraced postmodernism in a more enthusiastic way than any other therapy. Indeed one writer claimed that family therapy was the natural therapeutic expression of postmodernism in the same way that psychoanalysis was modernism's natural expression (Parry, 1991). There are many reasons why a social constructionist understanding of human systems would suit family therapy (McNamee and Gergen, 1992; Rivett and Street, 2003; 2009) but this new impetus gave rise to the next generation of family therapists who are represented by Hoffman (1993) and Anderson (Anderson and Gehart, 2007). This third wave of family therapies expanded with the arrival of both narrative therapy (White and Epston, 1990) and brief solution-focused therapy. Both of these have roots within other models of family therapy. This 'third-wave' generation integrated the practices of previous generations but emphasised the 'non-expert' stance of the therapist as well as concentrating on helping change meanings and stories rather than relying on tasks and *in vivo* change in the session.

THERAPEUTIC TECHNIQUES

The techniques that family therapists use draw their inspiration from systems theory itself (Rivett and Street, 2009). The first one to note is the fundamental therapeutic attitude adopted by family therapists. Because systems theory suggests that any family system is complex and can be understood from many different angles, none of which will be 'true', family therapists approach families with a stance of curiosity (Cecchin, 1987). This is designed to evoke curiosity in the family members themselves. On one level this approach encourages family members to question their own certainty. Most families for instance come to therapy 'knowing' what is 'wrong' and wanting the therapist to 'do something about it'. It is not uncommon for parents to want the therapist to 'tell their child to stop doing X' and yet they have tried this themselves to no avail and no doubt have asked others to do the same. The uncertainty of the therapist (variously described as 'authoritative doubt' or 'safe uncertainty': Mason, 1993) helps perturb this systemic certainty and gradually helps family members begin to see that their own behaviour or understandings are connected to each other. Curiosity allows the therapist to 'enter' the family system without alienating any family member and without perturbing the system too much. It also allows the therapist to ask open questions from a position of naivety (such as, 'When you first had a child, what kind of a family did you want to create?').

However, curiosity is also balanced by hypothesising. Because any human system is complex and can be understood from many different perspectives, the therapist (and his/her team) will construct a number of ideas about how the family works and the role of the difficulties in this process. The interview will be guided by these hypotheses which will be collaboratively developed and explored. There are a number of qualities to the hypotheses that family therapists use. Firstly, the hypotheses are systemic and circular: they do not lay the blame for the problem on any individual but rather they explore relational/interactive patterns. Secondly, family therapists seek to develop a number of hypotheses because they wish to ensure that they retain their curiosity and uncertainty. Lastly, and very much connected to this, family therapists are encouraged 'not to fall in love' with their hypotheses.

Very much associated with the curious stance are the questions that family therapists ask. Again various authors have provided typologies of these (Penn, 1982; Tomm, 1988) but here we wish to emphasise the use of circular or relational questions. These ask family members to connect meanings, behaviours or feelings that they experience with the relational pattern within which these are exhibited or experienced. Again the intention is to help family members widen their understanding so that they see what might be maintaining a problem within family relationships. Examples of circular questions might be 'When you try to stop X doing Y, whose example in your family are you most likely to follow?', or, 'When your wife wakes up in the morning and says she is sad, what do you think she wants you to do for her?'

Systems theory suggests that human systems adapt ('change') more constructively when they are faced, not with extreme pressure to change, but by gentle 'perturbations'. This gives rise to the techniques of positive connotation and reframing (O'Brian and Bruggen, 1985). Positive connotation was a concept of the Milan team, who asserted that 'no one changes under a negative connotation' (e.g. criticism). Accordingly, the Milan school constantly sought to ascribe positive intentions to family members. For instance, a father who rows with his daughter might be described as 'loving her too much'. Reframing, variously viewed as a structural or strategic technique, looks at finding alternative explanations for the feelings, behaviour or thoughts that family members have. Reframing may not necessarily be to a 'positive' description. An example might be where a family member who is described as being 'angry' might be reframed as 'hiding sadness'.

Techniques from early schools of family therapy are also very common, such as setting families tasks between sessions to help alter the interactive process within the home. A common task for parents who cannot decide on how to manage a child's tantrums, for instance, might be to ask one parent to 'be in charge' on some days of the week and the other parent to 'be in charge' on other days. Such a paradoxical task is designed to force the parents into collaboration (or separation) and if collaboratively designed it can add humour, creativity and difference. Most family therapists will also map out family structure via a family tree or geneogram (McGoldrick et al., 1999). Drawing such a geneogram might take more than one session and will include adding major family traumas as well as important family 'rules' and ties of closeness to the physical diagram. This process if done well is therapeutic in itself: it encourages a collective view of family issues and helps family members place their own issues within generational patterns.

CONTEMPORARY FAMILY THERAPY/ SYSTEMIC PRACTICE

Not surprisingly, a therapy that favours the concept of 'context' has been radically altered by the context within which it functions. A number of major influences within institutional practice have impacted upon family therapy. On the one hand the professionalisation of family therapy (Rivett and Street, 2003) has ensured that some of the earlier, rather strident claims for family therapy have become outdated; family therapists now work with other therapists and integrate ideas from CBT, counselling, and newer therapies like EMDR within their work. On the other hand, working in mostly NHS settings has meant that family therapists have adapted to the demands of evidence-based practice. From this perspective, family therapists and family researchers have amassed a large body of evidence that family therapy is effective (Carr, 2009a; 2009b) and it is now recommended in the UK and USA as an evidence-based psychological intervention.

With the increasing proliferation of family interventions there have come an increasingly complex number of terms describing these. Thus, the literature will now include terms such as 'family management' (normally equated to work with severe mental illness), 'family treatment', 'family intervention' as well as specific models such as 'functional family therapy' and 'multi-systemic therapy'. Although most of these will share in common many of family therapy's ideas (such as treating the family as an essential aspect of treatment), they may not all share the assumption that symptoms are caused or maintained by family interactional patterns. It is also noticeable that governments of various hues have continued to find it necessary to encourage welfare professionals to 'think family', yet many interventions (such as cognitive-behavioural therapy) continue to appear to encourage a concentration on the individual, not on the relational patterns within which the individual functions.

STATUTORY REGULATION AND TRAINING

Because most registered family therapists work for the NHS, as a group they are generally understood to favour statutory rather than voluntary regulation (via the Health Professions Council or equivalent). The Association for Family Therapy (www.aft.org.uk) was instrumental in establishing standards of training and ethical practice in the early 1990s and has continued to promote both the wider systemic model of therapy and family therapy posts. While this development has been controversial at times (Rivett and Street, 2003), family therapists now work in the NHS as a profession equivalent both to clinical psychology and child psychotherapy. Institutionally therefore, with professional recognition and evidence to support their practice, family therapists are established members of multidisciplinary teams in adult and children's mental health services, in older adult services and in disability services. With this acceptance have come a number of institutional developments such as national occupational standards (Fonagy, 2010) and core competencies (Pilling et al., 2010; Stratton et al., 2011).

Training to become a family therapist continues to be rigorous and retains many of the original hallmarks of the early practice. Thus, family therapists must complete a number of hours of direct work, all of which is both supervised live (usually by use of a one way mirror) and videotaped. In this way learning is immediate and also reflective. Training is a four-year, part-time process. The assumption is that attention to relationship patterns is a complex learning task which can only be learnt when the student is already a qualified professional in nursing, social work, psychology or counselling. Learning to attend to relationship patterns in a therapy session is a challenge for those therapists who have been trained in an individual-focused modality.

CONTEMPORARY PRACTICE AND FUTURES

Within this chapter, reference has been made to systemic and family therapies in the plural. It is important to note both that systemic ideas and techniques are applicable in many settings other than families (Rivett and Street, 2009) and also that there is no one version of family therapy. Each clinician uses skills and ideas from first-, second- or third-wave theories as well as integrating techniques from other modalities (Rivett, 2008). Each practitioner also brings to their therapeutic work their own interests, their own family/cultural experiences and their own unique twists to the practice. This rich system is further sweetened by each therapist interpreting the evidence for their work differently: some may follow manuals, others may refer to 'guidelines', and yet others will have a bias to the creative and innovative. This diversity is reflected in the variety of terms that systemic therapists will call themselves: 'family psychotherapist', 'systemic psychotherapist' or 'family therapist'. It is highly likely that this diversity will continue to typify this modality of psychotherapy that values multiple perspectives and favours a curious stance on truth.

REFERENCES

Anderson, H. and Gehart, D. (2007) *Collaborative Therapy*. New York: Routledge.

Anderson, H. and Goolishian, H. (1988) Human systems as linguistic systems. *Family Process*, 27: 371–93.

Bateson, G. (1972) *Steps to an Ecology of Mind*. New York: Ballantine.

Bateson, G. (1979) *Mind and Nature*. New York: Dutton.

Campbell, D., Draper, R. and Huffington, C. (1989) *A Systemic Approach to Consultation*. London: Karnac.

Carr, A. (2009a) The effectiveness of family therapy and systemic interventions for child-focused problems. *Journal of Family Therapy*, 31: 3–45.

Carr, A. (2009b) The effectiveness of family therapy and systemic interventions for adult-focused problems. *Journal of Family Therapy*, 31: 46–75.

Carter, B. and McGoldrick, M. (1999) *The Expanded Family Life Cycle*. Boston: Allyn and Bacon.

Cecchin, G. (1987) Hypothesizing, circularity and neutrality revisited: an invitation to curiosity. *Family Process*, 26: 405–13.

Fonagy, P. (ed.) (2010) *Digest of National Occupational Standards for Psychological Therapies*. Skills for Health. DOH.

Haley, J. (1976) *Problem Solving Therapy*. San Francisco: Jossey-Bass.

Hedges, F. (2005) *Systemic Work with Individuals*. London: Palgrave.

Hoffman, L. (1993) *Exchanging Voices*. London: Karnac.

Keeney, B. (1983) *The Aesthetics of Change*. New York: Guilford.

Mason, B. (1993) Towards positions of safe uncertainty. *Humans Systems*, 4: 181–200.

McGoldrick, M. and Hardy, K. (eds) (2008) *Re-visioning Family Therapy*. New York: Guilford.

McGoldrick, M., Gerson, R. and Shellenberger, S. (1999) *Genograms: Assessment and Intervention*. New York: Norton.

McNamee, S. and Gergen, K. (1992) *Therapy as Social Construction*. London: Sage.

Minuchin, S. (1974) *Families and Family Therapy*. Cambridge, MA: Harvard University Press.

O'Brian, C. and Bruggen, P. (1985) Our personal and professional lives: learning positive connotation and circular questioning. *Family Process*, 24: 311–22.

Palazzoli, M.S., Boscolo, L., Cecchin, G. and Prata, G. (1978) *Paradox and Counter-Paradox: A New Model in the Therapy of the Family in Schizophrenic Transaction*. Northvale, NJ: Aronson.

Parry, A. (1991) A universe of stories. *Family Process*, 30: 37–54.

Penn, P. (1982) Circular questioning. *Family Process*, 21: 267–80.

Pilling, S., Roth, A. and Stratton, P. (2010) The competencies required to deliver effective systemic therapies. www.ucl.ac.uk/clinical-psychology/CORE/systemic_framework.htm.

Rivett, M. (2008) Metamorphosis: towards the transformation of family therapy. *Child and Adolescent Mental Health*, 13: 102–6.

Rivett, M. and Street, E. (2003) *Family Therapy in Focus*. London: Sage.

Rivett, M. and Street, E. (2009) *Family Therapy: 100 Key Points and Techniques*. London: Routledge.

Stratton, P., Reibstein, J., Lask, J., Singh, R. and Asen, E. (2011) Competences and occupational standards for systemic family and couples therapy. *Journal of Family Therapy*, 33(2): 123–43.

Tomm, K. (1988) Interventive interviewing: intending to ask lineal, circular, strategic or reflexive questions? *Family Process*, 27: 1–15.

Watzlawick, P., Weakland, J. and Fisch, R. (1974) *Change: Principles of Problem Formation and Problem Resolution*. New York: Norton.

White, M. and Epston, D. (1990) *Narrative Means to Therapeutic Ends*. New York: Norton.

Wynne, L., McDaniel, S. and Weber, T. (1986) *Systems Consultation*. New York: Guilford.

Feminist Psychotherapy

M. COLLEEN HEENAN

WHAT IS FEMINIST PSYCHOTHERAPY?

Feminist therapy has a 40-year history in both North America and the United Kingdom. However, feminist therapy is neither unitary nor coherent. It integrates complex bodies of knowledge about social structures and models of personality, as well as diverse therapy techniques, preventing it from becoming monolithic and unified. It is more appropriate to think about feminist therapy as a pluralistic set of techniques hinged on some shared fundamental beliefs and principles (Seu and Heenan, 1998).

The term 'feminist therapy' is usually used when referring to the 'empowerment' model of therapy rooted in humanistic and cognitive-behavioural models of personality, dominated by practitioners from the United States (Worell and Remer, 2002). In the United Kingdom, however, the term references the work of feminist object relations therapists mainly associated with the psychoanalytic model of The Women's Therapy Centre in London (Ernst and Maguire, 1987). Clearly there are notable differences between these models, which I describe later.

I begin with the origins and commonalities of feminist therapy across continents and cultures. One key conviction is that many of women's problems are related to injustices and inequalities rooted in patriarchal society. Coupled with this is the principle of understanding the impact of the social construction of gender on psychological development, therapeutic theory and practice. Therapeutic technique thus evolves from integrating these beliefs within adaptations of existing models of personality and practice, for the common cause of empowering women.

The initial focus of feminist therapy was almost entirely on gender-related issues. Indeed, early radical feminist therapists argued that women's psychological suffering results specifically from contradictions between the egalitarian ideology of North American society and the social reality of its patriarchal system. However, contemporary contributions could be described as more postmodern in that they focus on how power and dominance intersect in relation to a number of complex and interrelated identity issues such as class, racism, sexuality, etc., coalescing with gender.

ORIGINS

During the women's liberation movement in the early 1970s, feminist therapists joined the challenge to eliminate the social and cultural barriers oppressing women.

Enns (2004) offered a comprehensive history of the origin of feminist therapy arising from within women-only consciousness-raising groups associated with the early years of the feminist movement. These C-R groups rejected the gendered assumptions dominating beliefs about women's lives and problems, arguing instead that 'the personal is political': that is, personal problems could be better understood as political problems. Crucially, the 'personal' experience of women was considered to be a more reliable source of information than the male-dominated or patriarchal structures of knowledge prevalent in medicine, psychiatry and psychology. Attempting to overturn these structures, women in C-R groups turned to the direct exploration and examination of their feelings, with the support of other women, in order to examine how these patri archal knowledge bases functioned to silence and deny their experiences. With their redefined understanding of these issues, C-R groups also explored ways of taking action at both a political and a personal level, to gain liberation from gender oppression. Through their participation in these groups, a number of women therapists also realized the potential of utilizing their therapeutic skills for political as well as therapeutic aims, leading to the development of an emerging 'feminist' therapy.

This alternative 'feminist' approach to counselling, psychotherapy and psychology focused on two gender-related areas. First, there was a rejection of traditional theories of female and male development, behaviour and sex-role stereotypes. Instead it was argued that if there were sex differences, they arose from inequalities in social status and interpersonal power between women and men. Second, there was a challenge to the sexist biases of theories of personality and psychopathology. Feminists regarded traditional psychological theories as androcentric, gender centric, heterosexist, intra-psychic and deterministic. The focus was predominantly on promoting gender as an overarching social identity around which *all* women could be grouped.

THEORY AND PRACTICE

Seu (2006) summarizes the theory and practice of feminist therapy as containing the following general principles.

The Personal is Political

As mentioned above, this principle is based on the assumption that women's problems are almost entirely rooted in inequalities in patriarchal societies. This key component of feminist therapy reframes what would be seen by traditional psychologists, psychotherapists and psychiatrists as *pathology*, into creative solutions or coping tools for socially determined problems. Thus, instead of decontextualizing and viewing women's problems as intra-psychic processes, feminist therapists encourage their clients not only to distinguish between internal/psychological and external/social aspects of the issues they are dealing with, but also to understand how 'the external comes to be internalized'. For instance, a woman who berates herself because she is regarded as 'over' weight would be encouraged to challenge stereotypical notions of

fatness and thinness. In this way the client is not *blamed* but recognized and validated in her struggle, and is thus empowered to find social and personal solutions to her problems.

The Therapist–Client Relationship is not Value-free

Feminist therapists believe that it is impossible for any therapist to practise value-free therapy. Research shows that even when one's values remain unstated, the therapist's techniques, roles, non-verbal behaviour and attitudes are likely to reveal important aspects of their views (Enns, 2004). Nevertheless, therapists vary in their approach to this type of self-disclosure: some consider it essential to clarify their beliefs to their clients; others feel more cautious and would not even define themselves as 'feminist' to their clients. Regardless of the implicit or explicit nature of each therapist's statement, it is agreed that careful attention should be paid to how one's beliefs and values affect clients.

Respect and Power

Feminist therapists believe that the client is the main expert and should be treated as such. Thus, 'symptoms' should be validated as creative attempts at coping and surviving. In this way the client's self-reliance is enhanced and strengthened.

The issue of the therapist's power presents a more complex dilemma. Although an attempt at sharing power with the client is recommended, it is also recognized that some power imbalances are impossible or inappropriate to erase (the issue of fees may be one of these power imbalances). As a result, humanistic principles like genuineness, congruence, empathy and self-disclosure have been advocated as ways of making the relationship more equal. I return to this issue later.

'Clients' not 'Patients'

Feminist therapists feel that to position women as 'patients' pathologizes and disempowers them. Thus, feminist therapists promote their clients' rights as consumers. This involves the use of clear, jargon-free language and the establishment of a clear contract at the beginning of therapy which is regularly reviewed. The therapist should also provide clear information regarding her training and theoretical orientation. In addition, a safe atmosphere should be fostered to allow the client to feel entitled to ask questions about the direction of the therapy and about the therapist's interventions.

Liberation Versus Adjustment

Feminists have criticized traditional psychology for functioning as a subtle but powerful instrument of oppression by manipulating women into not only blaming themselves for their suffering, but at the same time regarding adjustment to their oppression as an indicator of improved mental health. In contrast, feminist therapists regard enhancing their clients' awareness of oppression, and helping them find psychological as well as practical means of liberating themselves, as clear therapeutic aims. For example, the client might be encouraged to become financially independent and less bound to gender-stereotypical roles in her relationships. Some feminist therapists also feel it is their duty to provide the client with information and encouragement to join political groups and participate in action which will contribute to her and other women's liberation (Marecek and Kravetz, 1998).

Empowerment and Self-nurturance

Expressions of anger and emotional needs are identified by feminists as particularly difficult for women because they bring up shame and self-hatred, thus clashing with traditional stereotypes of women as passive and selfless. Feminist therapists aim to help women feel more comfortable with experiencing their anger   viewed not as negative but as a self-empowering feeling – and to find more effective ways of expressing it. In this way women's sense of competence and self-esteem is enhanced. Feminists are also aware how rarely women feel entitled to and comfortable with their 'neediness', tending to focus their energies into looking after others' needs instead. Orbach (1978; 1988) argued, for instance, that the emergence of 'eating problems' amongst women may arise from women's emotional 'starvation'. Feminist therapy aims to redress this imbalance, encouraging women not to feel selfish when nurturing themselves, but also to redefine the boundaries between themselves and others more clearly.

EPISTEMOLOGICAL DIFFERENCES

Notwithstanding the above common principles, Enns (2004) groups feminist therapists into categories using criteria based on a range of feminist political positions. She suggests that these differing epistemologies also influence how practitioners emphasize these principles:

- *Non-sexist/humanistic therapists* emphasize personal choice and growth issues. They do not focus explicitly on gender issues or external factors.
- *Liberal/gender-role feminist therapists* encourage the client to consider how socialization has influenced their choices and to change traditional gender-role definitions if alterations are consistent with her personal goal. Their focus is on individual development rather than social change. The major goal in this group is to resocialize the client and to facilitate her personal growth.
- *Radical feminist therapists* believe that in order for women's psychological health and status to improve, society must be changed at its roots. They explicitly communicate their beliefs about the importance of equality in human relationships and encourage the client to become aware of the common issues that influence women. The major goal in radical feminist therapy is to equalize women's and men's power in all of society's institutions.

PSYCHOANALYTIC FEMINIST THERAPY

As mentioned earlier, in the United Kingdom the psychoanalytic feminist object relations model of therapy, popularized by practitioners from The Women's Therapy Centre in London, is mainly identified as 'feminist' therapy. While many feminists and feminist therapists regard the intrapsychic model of psychoanalysis as antithetical to many of the key principles, Eichenbaum and Orbach (1982) argued that it was essential for feminists to understand the interrelationship between the social world and unconscious processes. They also argued that the use of psychoanalytic theory, albeit deconstructed in relation to its theory of gender, could act to *liberate* rather than oppress women. Orbach's (1978; 1988) seminal writings on eating 'problems' have not been superseded.

CRITIQUING FEMINIST THERAPY

Marecek and Kravetz (1998) suggested there is a confusion between the process and goals of feminist therapy. In their research they found that often therapists would describe their feminist stance in terms of *process* rather than goals and outcome: that is, containing more warmth and allowing more 'crossing of boundaries' than in traditional therapy. They question whether the presence of these qualities changes the power dynamic or just makes it more hidden.

Seu (2006) notes that therapist self-disclosure of negative experiences and sexist behaviour, as a way to make the client feel that the therapist is 'equal', is a controversial technique which has elicited fierce criticism. There is also concern that attempts to deny or eliminate the power differential might also restrict the full benefits of the therapist bringing into the relationship her skills and professional expertise; these cannot be shared, but can be used for the client. Generally speaking, it is still being debated whether it is actually beneficial to deny or attempt to eliminate power imbalance in the therapy situation, or whether it should be openly acknowledged and used as a creative opportunity for the exploration of strategies for dealing with similar situations elsewhere as well as in the therapy. For instance, O'Connor and Ryan argue for the use of the term 'patient' in working therapeutically with lesbians, because 'client' 'can seem to reduce the complexities of the therapeutic relationship to a service provided. It also fails to acknowledge the centrality of suffering and the search for help of some kind that the term "patient", despite its other drawbacks, does convey' (1993: 27).

CONTEMPORARY FEMINIST THERAPY

It has been suggested that feminist therapy needs to enter into a further stage of development, one that involves naming biases within the profession and adopting a reflexively deconstructive stance in clinical practice. The challenge comes from postmodern feminism, which questions the most taken-for-granted beliefs about power, knowledge and the self as well as the Eurocentric and heterosexist biases which have come to dominate and thus represent 'feminism' as singular. Because postmodern feminists believe that knowledge can never be neutral, they warn feminist researchers and practitioners against theories that ignore issues of difference by generalizing what it means to be a woman. It has also been argued that issues of race, class, ethnicity, age and sexual orientation should be as important as gender for feminists.

Since the last 10 years feminist psychotherapy has taken up these challenges. Porter describes contemporary approaches as having a common commitment to:

> the deconstruction of patriarchy in the service of understanding the lived experience of women, the assertion that the multiple contexts of women's lives must be addressed in theory and in therapy, and the recognition that feminist therapy

theory must involve the reconstruction of therapeutic goals, values, frameworks, and theory. (2005: 144)

In addition, there is an extension of the therapist's critical interrogation of her 'position' beyond gender politics to include a reflexive interrogation of how the power dynamics of gender, race, class, economic status and sexual orientation may be re-created in the therapist–client situation. Landrine and Russo (2010) have identified a range of contemporary work within feminist psychology which will influence the therapeutic practice of feminist therapists (who, in the United States, come from the discipline of psychology; in the United Kingdom, feminist therapists have differing professional backgrounds). There is also a rich body of work exploring ways in which gender and cultural issues intersect in family dynamics and mental health (Ballou and Brown, 2002; Zimmerman, 2001).

REFERENCES

Ballou, M.B. and Brown, L.S. (eds) (2002) *Rethinking Mental Health and Disorder: Feminist Perspectives*. New York: Guilford.

Eichenbaum, L. and Orbach, S. (1982) *Outside In, Inside Out: Women's Psychology, a Feminist Psychoanalytic Approach*. Harmondsworth: Pelican.

Enns, C.Z. (2004) *Feminist Theories and Feminist Psychotherapies: Origins, Themes, and Variations* (2nd edn). New York: Haworth.

Ernst, S. and Maguire, M. (eds) (1987) *Living with the Sphinx: Papers from the Women's Therapy Centre*. London: Women's Press.

Landrine, H. and Russo, N.F. (eds) (2010) *Handbook of Diversity in Feminist Psychology*. New York: Springer.

Marecek, J. and Kravetz, D. (1998) Power and agency in feminist therapy. In I.B. Seu and M.C. Heenan (eds), *Feminism and Psychotherapy: Reflections on Contemporary Theories and Practices* (pp. 13–29). London: Sage.

O'Connor, N. and Ryan, J. (1993) *Wild Desires and Mistaken Identities: Lesbianism and Psychoanalysis*. London: Virago.

Orbach, S. (1978) *Fat is a Feminist Issue*. London: Paddington.

Orbach, S. (1988) *Hungerstrike*. London: Faber and Faber.

Porter, N. (2005) Location, location, location: contributions of contemporary feminist theorists to therapy theory and practice. In M. Hill and M. Ballou (eds), *The Foundation and Future of Feminist Therapy* (pp. 143–60). New York: Haworth.

Seu, I.B. (2006) Feminist psychotherapy. In Feltham, C. and Horton, I.E. (eds), *The SAGE Handbook of Counselling and Psychotherapy* (pp. 527–31). London: Sage.

Seu, I.B. and Heenan, M.C. (eds) (1998) *Feminism and Psychotherapy: Reflections on Contemporary Theories and Practices.* London: Sage.

Worell, J. and Remer, P. (2002) *Feminist Perspectives in Therapy: Empowering Diverse Women.* New York: Wiley.

Zimmerman, S.T. (ed.) (2001) *Integrating Gender and Culture in Family Therapy Training.* New York: Haworth.

Gender and Sexual Minority Therapy

OLIVIER CORMIER-OTAÑO AND DOMINIC DAVIES

GENDER AND SEXUAL MINORITIES

This chapter will focus on working with gender and sexual minorities (GSM). This is a more inclusive term than the more traditionally used LGBT (IQ) (lesbian, gay, bisexual, transgender/sexual, intersex, questioning). It encompasses a wider range of gender and sexual minority identities including, but not restricted to, people who engage in kink/BDSM (bondage, dominance, discipline, submission, sadism and masochism) practices or lifestyle – irrespective of sexual orientation (Langdridge and Barker, 2007) – as well as people who may identify anywhere across the gender spectrum and not simply as intersex or transgender.

Gender and sexual minorities are also opening up the debate on different possibilities in relationships such as asexuality (Rothblum and Brehony, 1993) and celibacy or polyamory, swingers and other forms of non-monogamy (Barker and Langdridge, 2010).

Recent theories (Diamond, 2008) around sexual orientation elaborate on its natural fluidity. Sexual preference is best thought of as a continuum and may vary according to the social context and over time: some same-sex attractions may occur at various points in one's life, whilst libido or desire for sex may also vary in degree. Diamond's research indicates that women are more fluid than men as they tend to be attracted to an individual rather than a sexual object. Gay men tend to be more rigid in their choice of partner type (Diamond, 2008; see also Davies, Chapter 2.6 in this volume). Individuals often identify their gender or sexuality differently from one stage of their life to another; for instance, gender variance may manifest late in adult life (Lev, 2004).

Clients present with different ways of experiencing romantic and/or sexual relationships. Often the issues are about interpersonal rather than intrapsychic factors. The asexual population (whether in romantic relationships or not) is struggling to be out and accepted: individuals not engaging in sexual activities are frequently pathologised and discriminated against. When disclosing their asexuality they face social opprobrium and pressure to partner up and have sex (Cormier-Otaño, unpublished research). At the other end of the spectrum are polyamorous relationships, where individuals are concurrently having more than one romantic and sexual relationship. Polyamory – like asexuality – embraces heterosexual, homosexual and bisexual individuals.

The possible combinations of sexual preferences, sexual orientation, gender identity, gender preferences and relationship choices are varied and each becomes an individual narrative. Some of these narratives come with varying degrees of difficulty, but of course most GSMs never present for therapy and lead happy and fulfilled lives. Helping clients to identify and name their own sexuality highlights the complexity faced by gender-variant clients, who challenge society's definition both of gender and of sexual orientation: is a lesbian couple still in a same-sex relationship when one of them transitions to become a man (Lev, 2004)?

GENDER AND SEXUAL MINORITY THERAPY

Gender and sexual minority therapy (GSMT) is a recent and deliberate move away from gay affirmative therapy

(GAT) to encompass and support all forms, aspects and issues around gender and sexual minorities. It is a trans-theoretical approach where all theoretical models (psychodynamic, humanistic, cognitive-behavioural, etc.) can operate within their central organising principles and tenets (Davies and Neal, 2000).

The name 'gay affirmative therapy' was problematic in a number of ways. On a political level it may appear to exclude (among others) lesbians and bisexuals or the gender variant. It also ignores subcultures and groups where opposite-sex attractions are present (kink, fetishism, swingers, etc.). Finally the concept of 'gay affirmation' implies an agenda for clients' self-actualisation.

HYPERVIGILANCE: A KEY CONCEPT

GSMs have a long history of being considered 'mad, bad or dangerous to know'. This results in hypervigilance against pathologisation or negative judgements, and GSMs will scan their environment for signs of hostility or safety (Carroll, 2010): am I going to be (mis)read? Am I going to be accepted or understood? Is it safe to reveal myself? This very sensitive state is a source of anxiety and distress that will also be present in the counselling room. GSM clients will often unconsciously or directly question their therapists around their understanding of gender and sexual differences. Consequently, some clients may benefit from or request to work with a therapist who is also from a gender or sexual minority; others may benefit from, or prefer to work with, someone from outside their community. The client's choice of therapist is charged with meaning, and it is well worth exploring the assumptions that lie behind the request for a minority therapist or indeed a non-minority therapist. However, the clients' wishes need to be respected and accommodated where possible. This issue also raises the question of whether GSM therapists are comfortable and willing to reveal their sexual orientation or gender history.

GOOD PRACTICE

Most counsellors and psychotherapists are unlikely to be specifically trained to work with GSMs (Davies, 2007). Virtually all developmental models and many counselling theories privilege heterosexuality, both as a social norm and as a sign of psychological health. Recent UK research found that 17 per cent of counsellors would agree to help a client suppress their same-sex attractions (Bartlett et al., 2009). So-called 'conversion' or reparative therapies are unethical because they collude with social and internal oppression based on the belief that same-sex desire equals pathology, and they have been shown to be harmful to individuals who undergo them (Daniel, 2009).

Good practice in GSMT requires a subtle curiosity and interest in the client's life, and an ability to work sensitively with their hypervigilance. It is not the client's place to educate the therapist with regard to the social context of their experience. However, the client's own perspective on that social context is, of course, entirely relevant and appropriate. This requires therapists to have a wide understanding of the social context in which gender and sexual minorities are living their lives, as well as how multiple identities can interact and sometimes conflict. There is a wealth of books and information online that deal with gender and sexual minority clients. Much of the current literature is American, although the UK is now making a good contribution to the field.

It is also paramount for any therapists to develop their awareness of their own prejudices, beliefs and assumptions about what is 'healthy' and 'normal' in terms of sex, gender role, relationships, etc. All of us have been socialised within mainstream culture, in which heteronormative beliefs are an inherent and perpetuated given, and therefore none of us is entirely free of heterosexism and homophobia – in the same way as it is hard to be free of racist or sexist attitudes.

UK therapy trainings rarely offer adequate training around gender and sexual minority issues. Often these issues are included in a single lecture on diversity and rarely exceed three hours of teaching. A common training experience is that GSM issues are included only upon the demand of LGBT trainees and these students are expected to facilitate their peers' learning. This can result in their own learning needs (to work effectively within their own communities) remaining unattended to, and they are forced to seek post-qualification specialist training elsewhere (Davies, 2007).

A third area for learning and developing good practice is to understand more about gender and sexual minority psychology, and the impact of stigma on the development of the self. Therapists should not fall into the trap of denying the very real differences that exist between those of a minority identity and those of the heterosexual mainstream or majority. Lesbian relationships are quite different from gay male relationships, which differ again from heterosexual couplings. There are many differences between each of the GSM identities as well as some sharing of common features. It is the authors' view that training is essential to have a sufficient understanding of the intrapsychic, as well as socially constructed, elements of GSM experience.

Personal experience and clinical practice are helpful ways of gaining knowledge. Volunteering as a counsellor in GSM charities is a unique way to learn but these organisations may require their counsellors to identify as GSM. Meeting with other therapists and sharing information, books, supervision and support is another way to maintain good practice. Just having a gay friend is not enough; nor is it sufficient simply to hold a GSM identity. Training is essential for all wanting to work in this area.

Supervision is undoubtedly a key factor in good practice – as it is in all other aspects of the therapist's work. Although it can be difficult to make enquiries of a long-term supervisor, or to challenge their knowledge and awareness, therapists working with gender and sexual minority clients are best served if their supervisor has had some specific training in this area as well. A therapist reflecting on his or her own prejudices around issues affecting gender and sexual minority clients needs a supervisor who has worked on these prejudices as well. Otherwise, issues such as erotic transference and counter-transference or angry feelings in the counselling room will remain unexplored or ill advised (Pope et al., 2000). An uncomfortable example would be a kink-aware (someone who takes a non-pathologising attitude to BDSM/kink) therapist who wants to think about their work with a client whose sexual practices usually involve domination, and who is faced with a supervisor who understands BDSM as the acting out of self-harming tendencies resulting from childhood abuse or pathology.

UNDERSTANDING SOCIAL CONTEXT AND PARTICULAR ISSUES

GSM clients may well come to therapy with issues not so different from those presented by all clients, but the social context will bring an extra dimension and different layers to their narrative.

It is important to consider the power of the heteronormative, patriarchal and Eurocentric society in which we have evolved. External oppression and negative messages around sexual orientation, gender and ethnicity lead to internalised oppression. A young boy pressured to behave in a way stereotypical of his own gender (e.g. wearing blue or having short hair) can lead to the internalised belief that it is wrong for a man to dress in pink or have long hair. Such beliefs, if not challenged, may lead to this adult man accepting the idea that a feminine side to himself is wrong or socially unacceptable. Similarly, messages that sex and its expression should be limited to heterosexual, procreative activities, remote from consensual experimentation, can lead to feelings of guilt and shame. This kind of internalised oppression can result in self-loathing, low self-esteem, isolation, fear of rejection and other psychological difficulties.

Gender and sexual minorities experience higher levels of mental health distress, depression, self-harm and substance misuse than heterosexuals (King et al., 2008).

In urban environments the majority of socialising between individuals of gender or sexual minority groups takes place in clubs and bars. Many new designer drugs have been introduced on the gay club scene first, thus becoming a very common ingredient to a night out – prior to becoming mainstream on the general club scene. This use of drugs and alcohol among gender and sexual minority groups can be understood in part as a response to pressure and oppression. There is an urge to escape from external pressures, to lower inhibitions, and to experience a sense of community with one's peers. The misuse of drugs and alcohol can also lead to unsafe sexual practices or risky situations.

Isolation, hiding and shame are common amongst GSM clients and can lead to a lack of access to accurate information. This means that the counsellor may need to employ psycho-educational methods, bibliotherapy, homework and so on to help with relationship skills, sex education and other issues. In cases where the therapist's sexual orientation matches the client's and is disclosed, the therapist can sometimes be seen as a role model whether they want that or not. This of course is one of the dynamics to be discussed in supervision.

IDENTITY AND BELONGING

Individuals carrying such strongly internalised self-oppressive thoughts may well question their own identity and sense of belonging. Only by exploring their own narratives or in finding kindred spirits does the client experience an integration of these different parts. The GSM-aware therapist can help to empower clients to find the words to describe and make sense of their own sexuality and sexual expression. Having gained a sense of their own sexual identity, clients will often move to a position where the need to belong to a community then becomes more important. However, difficulties can arise when the pressure to embrace cultural norms within the GSM communities is very strong and oppressive (fashion, lifestyle, peer pressure) and leads to the development of a false self where the client again feels only conditionally accepted.

Many GSM individuals want to marry (civil partnership) and adopt children, thus re-creating a lifestyle more attuned to the heterosexual mainstream. For some people this is looking towards the dominant majority for a seal of approval; for others they might see their minority identity as an insignificant feature in their lives.

GSM clients belong to many communities (spiritual, cultural, professional, political, families, gender, etc.) and may experience the impact of conflicting beliefs or ideologies. Most religions or faiths do not tolerate same-sex relationships. Similarly, within the various GSM communities, not all individualities, ethnicities, sexual practices or gender identities are embraced. Ableism, ageism and racism are just some of the very real discriminations operating from within a broadly GSM culture.

MOVING TIMES AND 'OLDEN DAYS'

Historically, in order to negotiate a place in society, gender and sexual minority individuals had to 'pass' as heterosexual or to come out: either to pretend to be what they were not (reinforcing external and internal oppression) or to disclose to self and others their own sexual preferences or gender identity and put themselves at great risk. This is a process of self-acceptance and exposure that heterosexual individuals do not have to undergo.

Coming out is a process and not a single event. It is complex and recurrent: there is a well-founded fear of being rejected, victimised or abused (trans and homophobic hate crime is on the rise), and the constant decision of whether to come out or not in each new social or professional situation (work, friends, family, neighbours, authorities, institutions, GPs, etc.) is very stressful and anxiety provoking for some individuals, particularly where the level of internalised and externalised oppression is too high (Carroll, 2010).

Universal 'coming out' is also a Western concept that may have little relevance for people from other social and ethnic groups. Coming out can result in exclusion from the family and community – especially for members of black and minority ethnic communities where other ways of negotiating the integration of minority sexual identities are more relevant (Beckett, 2010; Nair, 2006). Nair describes a process of people stepping in and out of the closet, sometimes having to manage their gay identity more covertly and alongside cultural expectations to marry and have children. Beckett, relating her work with a young Muslim man, eloquently describes the process of 'inviting in' rather than coming out, where significant people are selectively invited into knowing more about the client's life and sexuality.

Fortunately, the coming out experience (or 'emerging' as it has come to be known for trans people: Lev, 2004) and the acceptance of GSM by significant others and society have for a larger number of people changed for the better in recent years. New generations may be more comfortable with a 'queer' identity rather than a gay or lesbian one and may be completely at ease with their identity as 'other'. The notion of making a declaration of a fixed sexual or gender identity is breaking down among many young

people for whom nailing their sexuality to a post is irrelevant. This so-called 'Rainbow Generation' may experience their identities more fluidly.

On the other hand, the older GSM population might still be struggling with internalised oppression and repression from past experience (electroconvulsive therapy, criminalisation of same-sex practices, public naming and shaming, etc.).

Active listening and empathy are key skills to allow the client to develop their narrative in order to realise the impact of the social context on their identity. The difficulties experienced by people with GSM identities will often have common causes, but as ever it is the reflective, aware, respectful and non-judgemental clinical approach to each client's unique situation that is at the core of good practice and will ultimately support their wellbeing and mental health (Davies, 1996).

The skilled and ethical GSM practitioner needs to be flexible enough to work with all clients regardless of the client's stage of accepting their sexuality. Therapeutic work around sexual or gender identity may well help the client work through unease about difference, but does not take on an agenda to alter this integral part of a person's lived experience.

Finally, GSM therapists should be ready to work with clients presenting with requests for 'cure' or reduction of their same-sex attractions, or who have been damaged or abused by 'reparative' therapies.

SEXUAL PRACTICES

Pleasure, procreation and play are the three aims for sex, and imagination can be fertile when it comes to sexual practices. It is the therapist's responsibility to have an open mind and an understanding of diverse sexual practices should they choose to work with gender and sexual minority clients.

Language and communication between client and therapist should be on a similar level or register; the therapist's vocabulary should mirror the client's and unfamiliar words should be congruently explored by the therapist. The impact of using medical or anatomical terms by the therapist in response to informal, colloquial or slang terms used by the client may well send messages of discomfort or disapproval from the therapist.

It is also helpful for the therapist to have current knowledge of sexual health, HIV awareness, treatments and safer sex.

CONCLUSION

Gender and sexual minority therapy is cognisant of the social context in which gender and sexual minorities live as well as the particular concerns of each individual. It works with the hypervigilance and consequences of living within a society which is biased towards heteronormativity and a binary conception of gender. It helps clients understand their experiences and the impact of external oppressions, how they are internalised, and a range of issues specific to these populations and communities. It stresses the need for clients to self-define and to develop personally relevant values and moral codes.

GSMT good practice requires a thorough working through of the therapist's prejudices around sex and gender and a minimum knowledge of how these minorities live, not only in a Western, heteronormative and patriarchal society but also in different settings around the world. Therapists will continuously be challenged, provoked and educated by clients whose presenting issues confront two of the world's biggest and most sacred taboos: sexuality and gender.

REFERENCES

Barker, M. and Langdridge, D. (eds) (2010) *Understanding Non-Monogamies*. Hove: Routledge.

Bartlett, A., Smith, G. and King, M. (2009) The response of mental health professionals to clients seeking help to change or redirect sexual orientation. *BMC Psychiatry*, 9 (11). Available at: www.biomedcentral.com/1471-244X/9/11.

Beckett, S. (2010) Azima ila hayati: an invitation into my life. Narrative conversations about sexual identity. In Lyndsey Moon (ed.), *Counselling Ideologies: Queer Challenges to Heteronormativity*. Farnham: Ashgate.

Carroll, L. (2010) *Counselling Sexual and Gender Minorities*. Columbus, OH: Merrill.

Daniel, J. (2009) The gay cure? *Therapy Today*, October: 10–14.

Davies, D. (1996) Towards a model of gay affirmative therapy. In D. Davies and C. Neal (eds), *Pink Therapy: A Guide for Counsellors and Therapists Working with Lesbian, Gay and Bisexual Clients*. Buckingham: Open University Press.

Davies, D. (2007) Not in front of the students. *Therapy Today*, February 2007.

Davies, D. and Neal, C. (eds) (2000) *Therapeutic Perspectives on Working with Lesbian, Gay and Bisexual Clients*. Buckingham: Open University Press.

Diamond, L. (2008) *Sexual Fluidity: Understanding Women's Love and Desire*. Cambridge, MA: Harvard University Press.

King, M., Semlyen, J., Tai, S.S., Killaspy, H., Osborn, D., Popely, D. and Nazareth, I. (2008) A systematic review of mental disorder, suicide, and deliberate self-harm in lesbian, gay and bisexual people. *BMC Psychiatry*, 8 (70). Available at: www.biomedcentral.com/1471-244X/8/70.

Langdridge, D. and Barker, M. (eds) (2007) *Safe, Sane and Consensual*. Basingstoke: Palgrave.

Lev, A.I. (2004) *Transgender Emergence: Therapeutic Guidelines for Working with Gender-Variant People and Their Families*. New York: Haworth.

Nair, R. (2006) Coming out, staying in, and stepping in and out of the closet: questions of black and minority ethnic-queer identities. Paper presented to BPS Lesbian and Gay Psychology Conference, 1 December, London.

Pope, K.S., Sonne, J.L. and Holroyd, J. (2000) *Sexual Feelings in Psychotherapy*. Washington, DC: American Psychological Association.

Rothblum, E.D. and Brehony, K.A. (1993) *Boston Marriages: Romantic but Asexual Relationships among Contemporary Lesbians*. Amherst, MA: University of Massachusetts Press.

RECOMMENDED READING

Finnegan, D.G. and McNally, E.B. (2002) *Counseling Lesbian, Gay, Bisexual, and Transgender Substance Abusers: Dual Identities*. New York: Haworth.

Moon, L. (2008) *Feeling Queer or Queer Feelings: Radical Approaches to Counselling Sex, Sexualities and Genders*. Hove: Routledge.

Pattatucci Aragón, A. (2006) *Challenging Lesbian Norms: Intersex, Transgender, Intersectional and Queer Perspectives*. New York: Haworth.

Sue, D.W. (2010) *Microaggressions in Everyday Life: Race, Gender and Sexual Orientation*. Hoboken, NJ: Wiley.

Group Counselling and Therapy

STEPHEN PAUL

WHY GROUPS?

We all live in relation to others. Our self-concept is formed as a result of our experiences with others. We learn to value ourselves in relation with others. So many life problems people bring to individual therapy evolve from trauma experienced in relation to others. One may wonder therefore why individual therapy has been the therapy in ascendancy.

In this chapter I will explore the difference between individual and group therapy, the development of group therapy, what research says, models of therapy and implications for practice.

THE CONTEXT

I have for over 30 years been involved in therapy groups, personal development groups for trainee counsellors, and training in group therapy for qualified counsellors. It has become clear to me over this time that many good counsellors:

1 have trouble relating in therapeutic groups
2 have difficulty with 360° perception
3 are fearful about communicating in a group.

Considering that so many life problems evolve from trauma experienced in relation to others, it is of concern that many counsellors may struggle with group dynamics.

There are significant differences between individual and group therapies (Table 7.14.1):

1 The therapist–client relationship is not central in group therapy. Counsellor training, with its focus on the unidimensional therapeutic relationship, may lead the counsellor to some degree to be blind to other communications that take place in a group.

2 The group has a unique pattern of dynamics related exponentially to the number of members. Complex process issues may predominate and the group therapist needs to be able to work with process issues at individual and group level.

3 There may be different levels of intrapsychic, interpersonal and intragroup relationships in play at any one time. The therapist needs to be aware of and competent to work with them.

4 Boundary issues are often of added importance as the therapist works with the group. Clients often test boundaries and challenge the therapist in quite different ways to individual therapy.

5 Particular social phenomena occur in groups which are not necessarily pathological or interpretable psychotherapeutically (for example groupthink, conformity, influence, cognitive dissonance, etc.). There is a real potential for stereotyping to take place in groups which a therapist needs to be aware of and able to work with.

6 There are a number of 'experts' who may question the therapist or offer their own therapeutic insights and support to each other.

DEVELOPMENT OF GROUP WORK

Group therapy developed from the beginning of the twentieth century. Initially, it was the only

Table 7.14.1   *Summary of differences for therapists between individual and group therapy*

Group	Individual
Variety of relationships possible	Therapist–client relationship central
Process issues may be more central in activating live material in the group	Content issues may predominate
Group can replicate outside experiences	One relationship processes all outside material
Therapist trained in interpersonal dynamics	Therapist trained typically in self-focused therapy
Plethora of interactions that the therapist has to work with. Therapist may have less personal influence or power as expert	Therapist may hold more expert power and have more influence over interactions
Therapist open to feedback at any time from any member about any things	Feedback to therapist only from one person
No clear research evidence as to what heals. Cohesiveness most important factor	Research indicates therapeutic relationship most important in-therapy factor

psychological therapy available for those people who could not afford individual psychotherapeutic help which was accessed by the upper classes. The start of modern group work is credited to Pratt in the United States. He was a physician working with tuberculosis sufferers. He started an outpatient therapy programme for patients who could not afford individual help. With a formula reminiscent of the modern Weight Watchers programmes he used encouragement and support and the didactic delivery of practical information to help patients cope with and alleviate their suffering. Pratt then realized the psychotherapeutic benefits of supportive groups.

After the First World War, Marsh, who worked with the chronically mentally ill, developed group methods. He was one of the first to realize the therapeutic value of the psychiatric hospital. Concurrently, Lazell worked with groups of mentally disturbed combatants using a didactic-instructional approach.

New insights into the human psyche which sprang from the work of Freud led to the understanding of transference (Wender, 1936) and free association (Schilder, 1936) in groups. Burrow (1927) coined the term 'group analysis', noting that in groups individuals behaved as they believed others wanted them to. Maintaining these social images impeded spontaneity and maintained rigid ways of behaving.

Around the same time in Vienna, Moreno (1958) developed psychodrama. He introduced role-playing, working with group members to re-enact past experiences and resolve repressed feelings. It was Moreno who introduced the term 'group psychotherapy' in 1932. Adler (1958) developed a model of group work which focused on the social and interactional empowerment of the individual.

With the upsurge of Nazism in Europe Klein came to the UK and was central in the development of object relations theory which influenced Bion (1959) who formulated classical group analysis. Foulkes (1964), who founded the modern British group analysis school, worked under Goldstein alongside Perls, the founder of gestalt therapy

(Perls et al., 1959). Goldstein (1939), whose research led to the founding of humanistic psychology, discovered individual neurones always functioned as part of a network. This led Foulkes to postulate that the individual is a nodal point within the network of relationships within any group and that psychoanalysis should view all the relationships the individual is involved in. There are no rigid delineations between the individual and the environment, the inner and the outer.

During the 1950s Rogers (1970) developed encounter groups as a means of developing psychological growth. He criticized the psychoanalytic concept of 'homeostasis' – that is, that the person is a closed adaptive system with no potential for growth. He believed that the desire for change and growth is the healthy result of inner sickness. Maslow (1964) developed the notion of synergy: the idea that an individual has more potential for development in a healthy group than alone.

The 1960s saw the development of family therapy (Slipp, 1993), with the notion that the disturbed family member was a symptom of a dysfunction in the family unit as a whole. Laing (1985) popularized the therapeutic community approach based on existential philosophy and family systems theory as an alternative to psychiatric treatment. Laing saw that it was not an individual's perception of the world that was faulty but that social pressure led to the falsification of the self. Psychotic behaviour was, literally, a sane response to an insane situation. The therapeutic community enabled the reparation of early family trauma.

Yalom (1981) is considered the main modern writer on the existential approach to group work, although his later writing on group therapy is now considered within an interpersonal, relational frame.

Cognitive and behavioural groups have been mostly developed in mental health settings. Task-focused group work has been used. The outcomes of such groups were more measurable quantitatively and thus lend themselves to research. A mushrooming of evidence-based practice research in this field and the development of wide-ranging group approaches for a variety of psychological problems have greatly enhanced the use of CBT in health service practice.

In the modern era a more theoretically generic interpersonal approach to group therapy has also developed (Ratigan and Aveline, 1988; Yalom, 2005). This approach is more often used by therapists of different professional disciplines who work more relationally and are not formally trained within one core model paradigm.

WHAT WORKS?

Social Psychology and Group Dynamics

Research by social psychologists (e.g. Feld and Radin, 1982) gives insights into interpersonal interaction in group settings. This research is important because it is not based within a therapeutic paradigm but is research about how people function in groups. Key factors that have been found to affect the experiences of individuals in groups are interpersonal attractiveness, attitudes, cohesiveness, conformity and norms. This research can help group therapists understand group phenomena.

Interpersonal attractiveness

The more people like each other, the more they will communicate with each other and the less stress they will report. Alternatively where people report disliking others they communicate with them less and their stress levels rise.

Attitudes

People are more likely to change their attitudes with the minimum of inducement. We attribute others' behaviour to internal factors whilst attributing our own to external situational factors. A person will change their values when inconsistencies between what they say, and what they actually do, are pointed out. Discrepancies between attributed and actual traits of group members can be recognized and changed. However, if the group culture is not healthy, attitudes may develop that are not psychologically positive. A group member confronted with attitudes different to his/her own may feel justified to withdraw from group interaction.

Cohesiveness

Cohesiveness is now considered a central factor in therapy group effectiveness (Bednar and Kaul, 1994). Cohesiveness is identified by Burlingame

et al., in their summary of group therapy research, as 'the therapeutic relationship in group psychotherapy' (2004: 683).

A low-cohesive group performs less well than a high-cohesive group. An individual in a low-cohesive group may not benefit as well as in a high-cohesive group. A new member may be scapegoated or alienated. Alternatively, members of a high-cohesive group may indeed attack members who threaten the cohesiveness which may block therapeutic change.

Conformity

Many studies have shown the power of group members to make individuals conform to group norms against their personal better judgement (e.g. Ash, 1956). Janis (1972) proposes that groupthink takes over and that a group will aim at a consensus unanimity at the expense of a realistic approach. There is higher conformity amongst 'like' people. A person is more likely to conform more with group members who are perceived as more competent or who have higher status. An individual's decision making in a group is affected by the desire to protect the self and others in the group, by self-interest, and by normative pressures to conform.

Norms

Social groups develop their own norms. Groups apply pressure to achieve conformity by rewarding members who conform, by encouraging deviants to conform, and by punishing or rejecting members who do not. A group member may receive such negative feedback that s/he may be psychologically damaged and/or may withdraw from interaction within the group to avoid such feedback. Group members who refuse to or are unable to conform to group norms are liable to be scapegoated. In fact, minority groups within a therapeutic group are liable to be adversely affected by the experience (Hulse, 1985). The same can be said of subgroups. A member of a minority in a group may become the object of projections and fantasies by other group members.

Studies by Fielding and Llewellyn (1986) and others have indicated different dimensions in group participation which will affect group relations:

- intragroup factors
- intergroup factors
- interpersonal factors
- intrapersonal factors.

This and similar research can inform the group therapist in their understanding of the behaviour of individuals in groups. Clarkson and Fish (1988) and

Tudor (1999) explore the notion of the client in context. Every group member brings with them their family, work and social systems, all of which filter and illuminate how they view the therapist and the group.

Social psychological research indicates therefore that the individual does not come to the group alone and that their behaviour in the group is dependent on their relations with other members. The group therapist has a responsibility therefore to be aware of the different and unique dimensions present in the group.

Social Psychology and Group Leadership

The facilitation of the group therapist is central to change in group therapy.

Bales (1958) found two necessary functions for a group leader:

- *Instrumental task function*: initiating action, keeping members focused on the task, organizing the group, and emphasizing the need to meet original aims.
- *Socioemotional function*: meeting expressed needs of the group, being sensitive to members' feelings, mediating disputes, encouraging and supporting other members, using humour to relieve tension.

Research indicates that a good group therapist will be aware of both the task of the group and socioemotional factors, ensuring that members feel comfortable and supported. A good group therapist will pay attention to both dimensions of their own behaviour in the group. The research further indicates that a therapist may be better suited to change the model of practice to their own leadership style rather than faithfully trying to follow ways of behaving. Rigid adherence to chosen ways of behaving may actually cause harm to group members.

RESEARCH INTO GROUP THERAPY

The research tends to fall into two approaches to group therapy. The first is interpersonal group therapy as exemplified by Yalom (1975) and Rogers (1970); Aveline and Dryden (1988) suggested that many practitioners with no formal group therapy training work in this way. It is probably the case that it is generally the most practised approach to group therapy overall. The focus is more on the process and interpersonal relationships in the here-and-now.

The other type of group therapy is the more structured, with a focus on goals. This approach lends itself more to quantifiable research than the first by its very nature, which compounds the problem researchers have in comparing effectiveness.

Table 7.14.2 summarizes Johnson's (2008) review of effective group therapy treatments.

Yalom goes on to question those approaches which rely on technique and are driven by goals of efficiency rather than effectiveness: for him the 'interactional focus is the engine of group therapy' (2005: xvi). The therapeutic factors developed by Yalom have been recognized as a benchmark in group therapy research (Bednar and Kaul, 1994; Burlingame et al., 2004). These are variously described and are shown in Table 7.14.3.

Research has indicated that the relationship is the most important factor in the therapy setting in individual therapy (Paul and Haugh, 2008). As noted above, cohesiveness is identified by Burlingame et al. as the therapeutic relationship of group psychotherapy and thus the central factor of change.

Burlingame et al. further consider that group therapy is blighted with too many models. Meta-summaries of research do concur that group members who experience acceptance, belonging and support, regardless of therapeutic model, typically report more improvement (Burlingame et al., 2002). Attributes such as warmth, openness and empathy have been associated with increased cohesion and better outcomes. Research into person-centred group therapy not surprisingly concurs with these outcomes (Paul, 2008).

Apart from these findings it is difficult to quantify other significant factors. We can summarize thus:

- Group therapy works as a whole.
- There is not significant evidence to suggest that one modality is better than any other.
- Modality-based intervention may pathologize normal behaviours.
- Therapists should check recent research into group therapy with the client group they are working with.
- Therapists may be more effective working in a way which they are comfortable with rather than trying to 'fit' into a modality.
- Cohesiveness is central to group therapy and the therapeutic relationship is central to outcome.
- Many social factors may affect group members. Therapists should not pathologize them and should be mindful of the human rights of members of therapy groups.
- A group leader is in a position of power and needs to be mindful of this.

Table 7.14.2   *Effective group therapy treatments*

Type of approach	Methods	Success
Alcohol abuse and dependence		
Community reinforcement approach	Social group work using CBT	Some evidence of general success
Cue exposure treatment	Desensitization to stimuli	Well established
Project CALM (treating alcoholism in the family unit)	Group work with couples	Some evidence of general success
Social skills training	Developing communication skills	Probably proven effective
Anxiety disorders		
CBT for generalized anxiety disorder	CBT in groups	Too few studies to indicate generalized success
Exposure and response prevention for obsessive compulsive disorder	Behaviour therapy in groups	Probably proven effective
CBT for panic disorder and agoraphobia	CBT in groups	Probably proven effective
Depression		
Cognitive therapy	Includes CBT	Well established
Behaviour therapy	In groups	Too few studies to indicate generalized probability
Interpersonal therapy		Well established
Eating disorders		
CBT for binge eating disorder	In groups	Well established
Interpersonal therapy for binge eating disorder		Probably proven effective
CBT for bulimia nervosa	In groups	Too few studies to indicate generalized probability

Source: after Johnson (2008)

Table 7.14.3   *Yalom's curative factors*

Interpersonal input	Learning through the input of others in the group
Catharsis	Letting out feelings in the group
Cohesiveness	A sense of belonging and feeling accepted in the group
Self-understanding	Linking past experiences to present thoughts and feelings
Interpersonal output	Learning how to behave in relation to others in the group
Existential factors	Coming to terms with the fact that some things cannot be changed but have to be faced up to, and that we are all in the same life situation and can find mutual support in this
Instillation of hope	The realization that as others in the group can improve, so the group member can
Altruism	The gains to self-esteem through helping others in the group
Family re-enactment	The group somehow re-creates the family experience and can help members understanding of behaviour patterns from their past
Guidance identification	Getting helpful advice from others in the group

MODELS

Psychoanalytic Group Therapy

There are traditionally three approaches to psycho-analytic group work, as follows.

Psychoanalysis in the group

Practitioners apply wholesale concepts drawn from individual psychoanalysis, e.g. resistance, transference and interpretation. The individual remains the central focus. This approach is commonly used by classically trained individual therapists where the therapist is expert and does not engage relationally with members.

Psychoanalysis of the group

In this approach, developed by Bion (1959), the task of the analyst is to interpret the group phenomena. The group learns as the analyst identifies for the group what is happening to the group. The analyst works with resistances and transferences in the group and not individual members. Ezriel (1952) developed a more commonly used approach called the Tavistock model, in which the focus is on the 'here-and-now' interactions in the group.

Psychoanalysis through the group

Foulkes (1964), drawing on the work of Lewin, saw the individual as a social animal whose psychological disturbances have their roots in relationships. In new situations people behave in ways which seek to reduce their anxieties based on self-perceptions they believe to be true. A group has a 'group tension' which is the conflict between individuals' needs and the group's needs. As a result of this tension individuals take up roles. Foulkes dismissed the notion of the 'group mind' as an entity. Group members can make meaningful insights. The role of the therapist is as conductor, who makes subtle, informing contributions. This approach has been significantly refined and developed in Britain.

Existential-humanistic Approaches

Existential position

The existential approach places phenomenology and the subjective experience of the individual at its core (Walsh and McElwain, 2002). The freedom of the individual to choose how to respond to life's limitations, the intersubjectivity of living, temporality, acceptance of the givens of life, and a focus on authenticity are all central tenets. The existential therapist emphasizes the therapeutic relationship as a focus for corrective emotional experiences and sees therapy as a partnership (Corey, 2003). Change comes from relationship. The therapist works to foster meaningful relationships between group members. The therapist will also work with members in confronting and working through existential life issues, common in some way to all members, and find meaning and authenticity.

Person-centred therapy

The work of Rogers is central to the development of humanistic group therapy. The place of facilitative factors is seen as central to the development of the therapeutic relationship in the group. Genuineness, unconditional positive regard, and empathy are seen as core conditions for the facilitation of the therapeutic process. Person-centred group work enables and facilitates the emergence of personal power. The person-centred group therapist is present in the group, and is willing to take part as an equal member of the group and to share their struggles with group issues as appropriate.

Gestalt Therapy

Gestalt group therapy (Hinksman, 1988; Perls et al., 1959) aims to enable the individual to become more fully alive, to overcome the blocks and unfinished issues that prevent the individual from being fully aware and fulfilled in the here-and-now, and to enable the individual to take responsibility for their situation. Group members are encouraged to make contact with others in the group to explore and work through blocks to full contact with self and others. The group is the medium for therapy as it is the multifaceted 'therapeutic field' members inhabit. The main focus of the therapist in this approach is to enable 'contact'. The therapist aims to meet others and work with members around their boundaries and defences at making contact with themselves and other group members. Whilst techniques (e.g. two-chair work) may be used to some degree, technique is seen as a medium for individuals to explore relational contact.

Cognitive-behavioural Therapy

CBT group therapy was originally developed to facilitate the treatment of individuals in groups. Group processes and dynamics were not considered important or helpful to the task in hand. The therapist's role was to assess and treat group members. However, an underlying assumption was the importance of a good working relationship (Meichenbaum, 1985; Lazarus, 1986; 1989). Particular human characteristics were indicated with successful therapists, notably respect for others, a non-judgemental attitude, warmth, humour, congruence and authenticity. More recently CBT group therapists have recognized and worked with group dynamic processes in their work (White, 2000). Many CBT programmes are psycho-educational and didactic in nature. Within this context however research indicates the therapeutic relationship is pivotal.

Interpersonal Group Therapy

The work of Sullivan and the later prolific contributions of Yalom are important in the development of an interpersonal group therapy. This approach is used by many professionals (Ratigan and Aveline, 1988) but with little common, conceptual methodology.

The underlying assumptions are threefold:

1 Existential factors (Yalom, 1975; 2005) including self-determination, choice and responsibility.
2 Interpersonal and social psychology, with the notion that I define myself through my relations with others.
3 Group analytic theory (Ezriel, 1952): group members behave normatively (the required relationship) because if they said and did what they really wanted to (the avoided relationship), something terrible would happen (the calamitous relationship).

Sullivan (1953) proposed that personality is developed by social forces not innate or determined in childhood and that psychopathology is based on maladaptive interpersonal experience. Therapy works by interpersonal learning (see Yalom's curative factors), the group as social microcosm, and the here-and-now focus of the group. The therapist will work with the relationships between members and the therapist, relationships between group members themselves, and relationships between group members and the group. The therapist processes individual (intrapsychic), interpersonal and group phenomena as a whole. Paul and Pelham (2000) articulated a relational paradigm in which they propose that the focus of therapy is relational and that a range of theoretical perspectives can assist the therapist in the task of working with the individual in making sense of the individual in her/his social relationships. The therapeutic relationship itself is considered 'central to change' (2000: 110).

More recent developments in psychology (Owusu-Bempah and Howitt, 2000) and increasing awareness of non-Eurocentric ways of being, suggest movement away from the focus on the self and more emphasis on the person in the group.

GROUP OR INDIVIDUAL?

Burlingame et al. (2004), in their review of comparative meta-studies, find little to suggest that one is any better than the other. There is some evidence to suggest that group therapy is more effective where social interaction and support are a desired outcome (Tschuschke, 1999).

More consideration needs to be given to the suitability of individuals for group therapy. Whilst there is no definitive research in this area, people who may not benefit from group therapy include (after Burlingame et al., 2002; Yalom, 2005):

- those who are actively psychotic or similarly organically impaired
- those who have severe limitations in interpersonal skills or the ability to receive feedback
- those who are in acute crisis
- those with poor ego strength
- those whose problems might be more easily resolved by one-to-one therapy.

Those who might benefit from group therapy include:

- those whose problems are interpersonal in nature
- those who are able to give and receive feedback and be empathic to others
- those who are not helped by the one-to-one relationship
- those who are experiencing something missing in their lives.

IN SUMMARY: WHAT MAKES AN EFFECTIVE GROUP THERAPIST?

An effective group therapist needs to attend to the following in order to maximize their potential to work effectively:

1 training in working in groups within a coherent theoretical model
2 significant experience as a member of a therapeutic group
3 prior exploration of personal issues relating to groups
4 an ability to work at a number of dynamic levels
5 an ability to manage own personal material in group settings
6 an awareness of group dynamics and how to work with them
7 an awareness of how to work anti-oppressively and to work with oppressive behaviour of group members towards others in the group.

REFERENCES

Adler, A. (1958) *What Life Should Mean to You*. New York: Capricorn.

Ash, S.E. (1956) Studies of independence and conformity: a minority of one against a unanimous majority. *Psychological Monographs*, 70.

Aveline, M. and Dryden, W. (eds) (1988) *Group Therapy in Britain*. Milton Keynes: Open University Press.

Bales, R.F. (1958) Task roles and social roles in problem-solving groups. In E.E. Maccoby, T.M. Newcomb and E.L. Hartley (eds), *Readings in Social Psychology* (3rd edn, pp. 437–7). New York: Holt.

Bednar, R.L. and Kaul, T. (1994) Experiential group research. In A.E. Bergin and S.L. Garfield (eds), *Handbook of Psychotherapy and Behavior Change* (pp. 631–63). New York: Wiley.

Bion, W.R. (1959) *Experiences in Groups*. New York: Basic.

Burlingame, G.M., Fuhriman, A. and Johnson, J. (2002) Cohesion in group psychotherapy. In J. Norcross (ed.), *A Guide to Psychotherapy Relationships that Work*. Oxford: Oxford University Press.

Burlingame, G.M., Mackenzie, K.R. and Strauss, B. (2004) Small-group treatment: evidence for effectiveness and mechanisms of change. In M.J. Lambert (ed.), *Bergin and Garfield's Handbook of Psychotherapy and Behaviour Change* (5th edn). New York: Wiley.

Burrow, T. (1927) *The Social Basis of Consciousness*. New York: Harcourt Brace and World.

Clarkson, P. and Fish, S. (1988) Systematic assessment and treatment considerations in TA child psychotherapy. *Transactional Analysis Journal*, 18: 123–52.

Corey, G. (2003) *Theory and Practice of Group Counseling* (6th edn). Belmont, CA: Wadsworth.

Ezriel, H. (1952) Notes on psychoanalytic therapy. II: Interpretation and research. *Psychiatry*, 15: 119–26.

Feld, S. and Radin, N. (1982) *Social Psychology for Social Work and the Mental Health Professions*. New York: Columbia University Press.

Fielding, R.G. and Llewelyn, S.P. (1986) Applying the social psychology of groups in clinical settings. *British Journal of Psychotherapy*, 2 (4): 281–91.

Foulkes, S.H. (1964) *Therapeutic Group Analysis*. New York: International Universities Press.

Goldstein, K. (1939) *The Organism: A Holistic Approach to Biology Derived from Pathological Data in Man*. New York: American Book Company.

Hinksman, B. (1988) Gestalt group therapy. In M. Aveline and W. Dryden (eds), *Group Therapy in Britain* (pp. 65–87). Milton Keynes: Open University Press.

Hulse, D. (1985) Overcoming the social-ecological barriers to group effectiveness: present and future. *Journal for Specialists in Group Work*, 10 (2): 92–7.

Janis, I.L. (1972) *Victims of Groupthink*. Boston: Houghton Mifflin.

Johnson, J. (2008) Using research-supported group treatments. *Journal of Clinical Psychology: In Session*, 64 (11): 1206–24.

Laing, R.D. (1985) *Wisdom, Madness and Folly: The Making of a Psychiatrist*. London: Macmillan.

Lazarus, A.A. (1986) Multimodel therapy. In J.C. Norcross (ed.), *Handbook of Eclectic Therapy* (pp. 65–93). New York: Brunner/Mazel.

Lazarus, A.A. (1989) Multimodal therapy. In R.J. Corsini and D. Wedding (eds), *Current Psychotherapies* (4th edn). Itasca, IL: Peacock.

Maslow, A.H. (1964) Synergy in society and the individual. *Journal of Individual Psychology*, 20: 153–64.

Meichenbaum, D. (1985) *Stress Inoculation Training*. New York: Pergamon.

Moreno, J.L. (1958) Fundamental rules and techniques of psychodrama. In J.H. Masserman and J.L. Moreno (eds), *Progress in Psychotherapy*. New York: Grune and Stratton.

Owusu-Bempah, K. and Howitt, D. (2000) *Psychology beyond Western Perspectives*. Chichester: Wiley-Blackwell.

Paul, S. (2008) The relationship in group therapy. In S. Haugh and S. Paul (eds), *The Therapeutic Relationship: Perspectives and Themes* (pp. 230–46). Ross-on-Wye: PCCS.

Paul, S. and Haugh, S. (2008) The relationship not the therapy? What the research tells us. In S. Haugh and S. Paul (eds), *The Therapeutic Relationship: Perspectives and Themes* (pp. 9–22). Ross-on-Wye: PCCS.

Paul, S. and Pelham, G. (2000) A relational approach to therapy. In S. Palmer and R. Woolfe (eds), *Integrative and Eclectic Counselling and Psychotherapy*. London: Sage.

Perls, F.S., Hefferline, R.F. and Goodman, P. (1959) *Gestalt Therapy: Excitement and Growth in the Human Personality*. Harmondsworth: Penguin.

Ratigan, B. and Aveline, M. (1988) Interpersonal group therapy. In M. Aveline and W. Dryden (eds), *Group Therapy in Britain*. Milton Keynes: Open University Press.

Rogers, C. (1970) *Carl Rogers on Encounter Groups*. New York: Harper and Row.

Schilder, P. (1936) The analysis of ideologies as a psychotherapeutic method. *American Journal of Psychiatry*, 93: 601.

Slipp, S. (1993) Family therapy and multiple family therapy. In H. Kaplan and B. Sadock (eds), *Comprehensive Group Therapy*. Baltimore: Williams and Wilkins.

Sullivan, H.S. (1953) *The Interpersonal Theory of Psychiatry*. London: Norton.

Tschuschke, V. (1999) Gruppentherapie versus Einzeltherapie: gleich werksam? [Group therapy versus individual therapy: equally effective?]. *Gruppenpsychotherapie und Gruppendynamik*, 35: 257–74.

Tudor, K. (1999) *Group Counselling*. London: Sage.

Walsh, R.A. and McElwain, B. (2002) Existential psychotherapies. In D.J. Cain and J. Seeman (eds), *Humanistic Psychotherapies: Handbook of Research and Practice* (pp. 253–78). Washington, DC: American Psychological Association.

Wender, L. (1936) The dynamics of group psychotherapy and its application. *Journal of Nervous and Mental Disease*, 84: 55.

White, J. (2000) Introduction. In J. White and A. Freeman (eds), *Cognitive-Behavioural Group Therapy for Specific Problems and Populations*. Washington, DC: American Psychological Association.

Yalom, I.D. (1975) *The Theory and Practice of Group Psychotherapy* (2nd edn). New York: Basic.

Yalom, I.D. (1981) *Existential Psychotherapy*. New York: Basic.

Yalom, I.D. with Leszcz, M. (2005) *The Theory and Practice of Group Psychotherapy* (5th edn). New York: Basic.

Hypnotherapeutic Skills

KATHY STEPHENSON

DEFINITIONS

Clinical hypnosis has no precise single agreed definition. There have been many different descriptions of the broad concepts and techniques of hypnosis. It is commonly described as an altered state of consciousness and is regarded as a naturally occurring everyday state similar to daydreaming. This view of hypnosis suggests that hypnotic trance is a relaxed hyper-suggestible state whereby the client is in a very relaxed state of mind and body, has a reduction in critical faculties and is more responsive to suggestion. This is just one of several views as to the nature of hypnosis; however, the neurophysiology rationale is still not clearly understood. Hypnosis has also been described as an altered state of consciousness whereby the client enters a state called hypnosis which is distinct from a normal state of being and involves shifts in perception (Barber, 1991). A different emphasis comes from Hilliard (1977) who suggests that humans have multiple cognitive systems capable of functioning simultaneously. He described hypnosis as a dissociated state whereby the client has a disconnection between unconscious and conscious mental processes, allowing the unconscious mind to be more receptive to positive suggestions made by the therapist.

Despite the lack of precise definition, it is generally agreed that in hypnosis clients become focused and receptive to positive suggestion. Therapeutic intervention such as hypnosis involves skilled communication between the client and the therapist. Erickson's definition of hypnosis concisely sums this up:

> Hypnosis is essentially a communication of ideas and understandings to an individual in such a fashion that he will be most receptive to the presented ideas and therefore be motivated to explore his body potential for control of his psychological and physiological responses and behaviour. (quoted in Battino, 1999)

Hypnosis is commonly associated with the induction of trance state during which behavioural modification may be suggested. The therapist acts as a facilitator helping the client towards a desired behaviour modification (Rankin-Box, 2010). This chapter focuses on the concept of trance phenomena which are naturally occurring states and, when harnessed via hypnotherapeutic intervention, can lead to beneficial changes in clients with a wide range of conditions. It explores how hypnotherapy can be utilized to help clients change cognition and behaviour. It can help clients to reconstruct belief systems, redefine memories and establish new confidence (Gilligan, 1999).

HISTORICAL CONTEXT

Historically, various forms of hypnotic trance can be found in a number of different cultural settings. Indeed Hippocrates, Plato and Aristotle all spoke of the effects of the mind on the physical body. As

Rossi and Cheek (1988) point out, since ancient times healers have been aware of the effects of words and ideas upon our physical wellbeing. Ideas can evoke real dynamic physiological responses. It is documented that the ancient Greeks had healing shrines and the Egyptians had sleep temples in which patients were given healing suggestions whilst in induced sleep. Anthropologists and archaeologists have documented numerous cases of different cultures throughout the world using various hypnotic practices for physical and spiritual benefits and using dancing and drumming to hypnotic effect during religious and healing ceremonies. Over the centuries various hypnotherapeutic interventions have been conceived, developed and modified from Mesmer, Charcot, Esdaile and Braid (Waterfield, 2004). Hypnosis as a therapeutic tool evolved over the course of the twentieth century and expanded into many different areas due to the work of innovative doctors and psychologists who began to explore the application of hypnosis to a wide range of conditions including pain relief, behavioural issues and anxiety-related conditions. Traditional hypnotherapeutic intervention involved quite direct suggestions such as 'now close your eyes … you will begin to feel relaxed' and generally directing clients into trance.

There has been a general shift over the past few decades from the authoritarian, direct approach in the field of hypnotherapy to more indirect, permissive approaches. The use of a more permissive style of hypnosis was developed by psychiatrist and psychotherapist Milton Erickson, who is widely regarded as the founding father of modern hypnosis. He regarded trance as a special psychological state which was characterized by the functioning of the client at a level of awareness other than an ordinary state, which has been conceptualized as the unconscious (Battino, 1999). Erickson pioneered techniques which highlighted the natural ability of the individual to alter states of consciousness and awareness in order to effect therapeutic change. He developed an indirect style of induction, characterized by words such as 'allow yourself' and 'imagine, if you will', using ambiguous and cooperative rather than directional language to guide the unconscious mind into trance.

Erickson developed a way of working therapeutically that integrated hypnosis into a wider therapy using an artfully vague permissive language framework which is known as the Milton model. This model aims to bypass the client's conscious critical condition through the use of deletion, distortion and generalizations which allow the client freedom to access their own unconscious resources. The term 'unconscious' as used by him is a metaphorical expression of the function performed by the mind/ body as a whole. Erickson viewed the unconscious as a storehouse of infinite resources and believed clients already held the necessary resources to overcome their problems. He regarded the role of the therapist as to guide clients towards finding their own answers. Decades after Erickson's innovative approach there is now an increasing understanding of the extent to which unconscious mental processes influence physiological states (Lipton, 2008; Pert, 1997).

ETHICS AND THE THERAPEUTIC RELATIONSHIP

Most professional codes of ethics within health and therapeutic settings recognize specific ethical responsibilities which include the following: undertaking professional development and supervision; maintaining confidence and keeping good records; empowering clients so they fully understand and consent; creating professional boundaries and responding appropriately to complaints (Stone, 2010). Hypnotherapeutic techniques should be provided by appropriately trained, regulated practitioners working within the limits of their competencies in safe practice settings. One of the key ethical concerns when using hypnosis is the variability of the training as hypnotherapy is currently a voluntary self-regulated profession, although it is moving towards establishing a single register with a coherent standard of training and practice. To date this has not yet been achieved although there are a number of registering bodies within the UK which have comprehensive training accreditation and codes of professional practice. Many therapists use hypnotherapeutic techniques in addition to their other trained discipline such as counselling, psychotherapy or health care and therefore work in line with their own regulatory body. Another consideration when working hypnotherapeutically with clients is that as hypnosis is used widely to alleviate physical symptoms, it is important, when appropriate, to involve qualified health professionals (Cummings and Cummings, 2000).

One useful analogy for the hypnotherapeutic relationship between therapists and clients is hypnosis as a dance (Voit and Delaney, 2004). If a person were to have a dance partner who is unconscious, is unable to hear the music and has no sense of rhythm, the encounter would be unsatisfactory. A good hypnotherapeutic relationship suggests a sharing of the movement whereby the therapist takes the lead, responding and guiding the dance partner who tenses and relaxes along with the leader. As the music plays they both find rhythm and get into a groove and the client is led into their own dance, movement and style. This metaphorical reference presupposes the client has all the necessary resources to move in the right direction rather than someone for whom the therapist is responsible for teaching step by step.

Therapeutic intervention of any type inevitably involves skilled communication between the client and the therapist in order to develop rapport and a trusting cooperative therapeutic alliance. As Yapko points out, 'The study of hypnosis offers substantial insights into how human beings construct their individual realities and how various interpersonal components of human experience can be assembled to generate wellness at one end of the continuum and pathology at the other' (2003: 6). Erickson was highly skilled at developing rapport with clients and adapted his style to each client. He was renowned for his ability to develop strong therapeutic relationships with clients based upon trust and cooperation which enhanced rapport, enabling him to optimize hypnotic responsiveness (Lyn and Hallquirst, 2004). He was able to work with the client's experiences and resources and he developed the theory of utilization. Once a client was in trance, he would use any external stimulus in the room to deepen the trance and emphasize the journey of the client through using the experiences and emotions that the client brought with them, resulting in a positive therapeutic outcome. Erickson worked from the premise that the experience of trance is a natural everyday experience.

TRANCE PHENOMENA

If we take the premise that trance is a naturally occurring phenomenon and clinical hypnosis is in a sense an extension of natural states of awareness, it is useful to explore the everyday context in which such states naturally or spontaneously occur. In everyday life individuals enter trance-like states on many different occasions throughout the day (Rossi and Cheek, 1988). If we take daydreaming for example, individuals look off into the distance appearing to reflect inwards. Other altered states include the so-called automatic pilot activities such as driving home, where such activities are carried out while the mind appears to be elsewhere. Time can often lose its usual meaning and appear to pass quickly when one is deeply engrossed in an enjoyable pastime. Conversely it can seem to drag when, say, waiting in the cold for a bus. Trance occurs both effortlessly and spontaneously in everyday events. Hypnotic phenomena can be regarded as aspects of unconscious functioning that are evident in everyday experience and are often exaggerated in the trance state.

Apart from the everyday experiences of naturally occurring trance phenomena, it could be argued that all therapeutic intervention involves some degree of trance (Battino, 1999). When a client focuses inwards to think or process, such internal focus closes out external input and the client enters light trance states. Much deeper trance states can be witnessed during various therapeutic interventions such as the gestalt therapy two-chair exercise. The difference with hypnosis is the intent on the part of the therapist to induce trance.

There are a number of different trance phenomena, and various ways in which they can be utilized in direct or indirect suggestions to help clients in a wider range of conditions. These phenomena will now be described. Many of these are evident in many models of psychotherapy, often in the form of other names and characteristics.

The trance phenomenon of time distortion allows clients to alter their perception of time and therefore they experience time as either expanded or condensed. Classically, a client experiencing time condensation may feel as though they never have enough time. The experience of time is subjective and time can be experienced as flying by or passing much more quickly. It can also be experienced as dragging by more slowly than usual. This time distortion ability has many therapeutic applications: for example, a client can experience time contracting so physical pain does not appear to last as long, or time expanding so a pleasant experience lasts for longer.

Positive hallucination is another trance phenomenon. It allows the client to see something which isn't there, to hear something, or even to touch, smell or taste something. It may also allow the client to perceive something that is there in a particular way, such as someone with a fear of public speaking seeing the audience looking positive. The term 'positive' is used as it refers to the capacity to insert something that is not present. Positive hallucination is a trance phenomenon which is used widely with performance anxiety as it helps to instil confidence and expectation of success.

Negative hallucination in contrast allows the client in hypnosis to eliminate something that can be seen, heard or felt. Emotional denial may be regarded as a form of negative hallucination; this is where the client has failed to acknowledge something that is there because it may be considered too distressing. A classic example of this is clients caught in a cycle of abusive relationships (Voit and Delaney, 2004). The term does not imply something negative but means only that something is being removed; the hypnosis uses suggestions which cause the client to not notice something in their environment.

Various forms of sensory distortion can also be utilized in hypnosis so that clients may experience changes to the sensory awareness of one or more of their senses. The information from any of the client's auditory, visual or kinaesthetic senses may be distorted in terms of being either magnified or diminished in some way so that a feeling can be given a different meaning. Examples of auditory distortion include a critical voice being changed in hypnosis into something non-threatening. Other senses such as taste and smell, the gustatory or olfactory senses, can be distorted so that, for example, a taste can be made unpleasant.

Amnesia is the full or partial loss of memory. This phenomenon may manifest itself in clients repressing memories and filtering out aspects of the past. Eliciting amnesia in hypnosis is beneficial in terms of clients forgetting particular things connected to their problem. It can be used to avoid overwhelming a client and to lessen the impact of a traumatic situation. It is also important when using this trance phenomenon to encourage the client to learn any lessons from the problematic experience so that it can be avoided in the future.

Dissociation is a familiar concept to most therapists in the context of dissociative disorders and is considered a basic response of clients to repress traumatic experiences such as abuse. However, all dissociation is not negative and the psychological capacity of an individual to separate from a feeling or an experience can also be potentially beneficial. Indeed, all hypnosis by its very nature is a dissociative experience and this phenomenon can be used as a pain management strategy, to dissociate the client from a part of their body. This enables the client to put a barrier or some distance between the self and any discomfort. This is particularly useful in childbirth.

There can also be full dissociation, where the person is led to observe themselves during a situation which they perceive as being problematic, for example watching themselves public speaking at a large event which would normally generate performance anxiety. It can be used generally to help clients with a range of presenting problems to lessen physical or emotional distress by removing themselves from the experience. Dissociative techniques used in hypnosis operate from the premise that the condition has a component which the client feels they are not in control of when they are experiencing the problematic condition.

Age regression takes place when the client is taken back to a specific time to re-experience various events so that they can be therapeutically revivified and re-experienced. Regression can be used to recall positive resources and situations from the past and access forgotten abilities as well as reprocessing negative emotional events. The trance phenomenon of age regression can be utilized in hypnosis to allow the client to experience a past event through which they can gain insights into their current problematic situation. It is particularly useful in helping clients deal with traumatic events to regress the client to a more functional ego state than existed before trauma was experienced (Voit and Delaney, 2004). This enables the client to retrieve and reconnect with past psychological resources that will facilitate their present situation.

In contrast to age regression is age progression. This phenomenon allows for a subjective feeling of moving forward in time in order to experience a future event. This phenomenon occurs in everyday life when a person images something that is going to happen, or could happen, in a negative way. This is often the basis of a client's state of anxiety. Someone who is age progressed would be apprehensive about the future or an anticipation of rejection. Within hypnosis the client is guided by suggestion towards the future to imagine a forthcoming event in a positive way, and then the anxiety about that event will diminish. Imagining the positive consequences of a change of behaviour, such as walking into an examination in a calm and focused manner, can make that change seem significantly more achievable.

The various trance phenomena discussed in this chapter are the key foundations for the therapeutic application of hypnosis. Trance is a naturally occurring phenomenon and hypnosis is in part an extension of natural states of awareness. Therapists using hypnosis as a therapeutic tool for change can take processes and events which are already part of the client's everyday experiences and utilize them to create positive suggestion to enable beneficial change to be facilitated. In hypnosis, everyday trance states of consciousness are harnessed to allow the client to access their own inner resources, enabling their unconscious creative problem-solving potential to be enhanced for therapeutic purposes.

HYPNOSIS RESEARCH

In recent years there has been a growth in evidence-based practice research undertaken to demonstrate the benefits of hypnotherapeutic intervention. The highly effective use of hypnosis for the treatment of irritable bowel syndrome (IBS) has been widely studied (Gonsalkorale, 2003; Whorwell, 2008). The use of hypnosis for both acute and chronic pain management in the form of hypo-analgesic was shown to be effective in the majority of cases studied by Paterson and Jenson (2003). The beneficial effects of combining hypnosis with cognitive-behaviour therapy (CBT) in the management of acute stress disorder was demonstrated by Bryant et al. (2005). Hawkins and Polemikos (2002) found that school-aged children who were experiencing sleep disturbances following trauma benefited from learning self-hypnosis. Extensive research has been conducted into the therapeutic application of hypnosis for the treatment of depression (Yapko, 2006; 2010).

Hypnosis can be a powerful tool in a therapist's toolbox. However, as Yapko (2003) argues, hypnosis by itself does not cure anything. It is what happens during the hypnosis that has the potential to be helpful. Hypnosis can help clients to step outside their usual experience of themselves, allowing new associations to be formed in their inner world on many levels including cognitive, behavioural and physical. Identifying and utilizing clients' natural hypnotic abilities enable the therapist to match solutions to symptoms and bypass the resistance that can be met by challenging a symptom directly.

REFERENCES

Barber, J. (1991) The locksmith model: accessing hypnotic response. In S. Lyn and J. Rhue (eds), *Theories of Hypnosis: Current Models and Perspectives*. New York: Guilford.

Battino, R. (1999) *Ericksonian Approaches: A Comprehensive Manual*. New York: Crown.

Bryant, R.A., Moulds, M.L., Guthrie, R.M. and Nixon, R.D. (2005) The additive benefit of hypnosis and cognitive-behavioral therapy in treating acute stress disorder. *Journal of Consulting and Clinical Psychology*, 73 (2): 334–40.

Cummings, N. and Cummings, J. (2002) *The Essence of Psychotherapy*. New York: Academic.

Gilligan, S. (1999) *Therapeutic Trances: Cooperation Principle in Ericksonian Hypnotherapy*. London: Routledge.

Gonsalkorale, W. (2003) Long term benefits of hypnotherapy for irritable bowel syndrome. *Gut*, 52 (11): 1623–9.

Hawkins, P. and Polemikos, N. (2002) Hypnosis treatment of sleeping problems in children experiencing loss. *Contemporary Hypnosis*, 19 (1): 18–24.

Hilliard, J. (1977) *Personality and Hypnosis*. Chicago: Chicago University Press.

Lipton, B. (2008) *The Biology of Belief: Unleashing the Power of Consciousness, Matter and Miracles*. London: Hay House.

Lyn, S. and Hallquirst, M. (2004) Towards a scientifically based understanding of Milton Erickson's strategies and tactics: hypnosis and common factors in psychotherapy. *Contemporary Hypnosis*, 21 (2): 63–78.

Paterson, D. and Jenson, M. (2003) Hypnosis and clinical pain control. *Psychology Bulletin*, 129 (4): 495–521.

Pert, C. (1997) *Molecules of Emotion*. New York: Pocket.

Rankin-Box, D. (2010) The development of hypnotherapy in healthcare. In A. Cawthorne and P. Mackereth (eds), *Integrative Hypnotherapy*. Oxford: Churchill Livingstone.

Rossi, E. and Cheek, D. (1988) *Mind Body Therapy*. New York: Norton.

Stone, J. (2010) Professional, ethical and legal issues in hypnotherapy. In A. Cawthorne and P. Mackereth (eds), *Integrative Hypnotherapy*. Oxford: Churchill Livingstone.

Voit, R. and Delaney, M. (2004) *Hypnosis in Clinical Practice*. Hove: Brunner-Routledge.

Waterfield, R. (2004) *Hidden Depths: The Story of Hypnosis*. London: Pan-Macmillan.

Whorwell, P.J. (2008) Hypnotherapy for irritable bowel syndrome: the response of colonic and noncolonic symptoms. *Journal of Psychosomatic Research*, 64 (6): 621–3.

Yapko, M. (2003) *Trancework: An Introduction to the Practice of Clinical Hypnosis*. Hove: Brunner-Routledge.

Yapko, M.D. (ed.) (2006) *Hypnosis and Treating Depression: Applications in Clinical Practice*. New York: Routledge.

Yapko, M.D. (2010) Special Issue. Hypnosis in the Treatment of Depression: An Overdue Approach for Encouraging Skillful Mood Management. *International Journal of Clinical and Experimental Hypnosis*, April.

Counselling Older People

ANGELA HARRIS AND KEN LAIDLAW

The age distribution of society is undergoing change. It is estimated that there are 3 million people in the UK who experience mental illness and Age Concern estimates that, by 2021, 1 in 15 of these will be an older person. More therapists will come into contact with older people resulting, in the need for a focus on the oldest and most vulnerable members of society (Laidlaw and Pachana, 2009).

There are two schools of thought about counselling older adults: one is that their needs should be met by integrated services; and the second is that they require specialist services. Both recognize that older adults have been poorly served in getting access to psychological therapy. As Knight (2004) states, older people often come into therapy for the same reasons that younger people do so. However, where therapists possess inadequate knowledge of ageing, or hold negative views of ageing, psychotherapy is likely to be ineffectual and disempowering. In some services there may be no age bar but barriers remain in the bias of adult mental health professionals who under-appreciate the needs of older people. Some argue that specialist geriatric services are better equipped to cope with age integration than adult working-age services (Bucks et al., 2007). There is a likelihood that an increased drive towards age-integrated services in mental health will result in some older people being seen by non-geropsychologists (Knight et al., 2009).

The second school point to the heterogeneity of older people where some may need counsellors with specialist training in gerontology (Zeiss and Steffen, 1996). Sadavoy (2009) labelled a toxic combination of geriatric client features as the five

Cs – chronicity, complexity, comorbidity, continuity and context – and suggested that these can be the challenging part of geropsychology, especially for the oldest-old age group of clients aged 85 and older. For while people are living longer and remaining healthier, it is the oldest old (people aged 80 years and above) that achieve the most rapid increase in numbers, so that by 2050 there will be an almost fourfold increase, resulting in 395 million oldest-old people alive in the world (UN, 2009).

THE EVIDENCE BASE

There are few specific models of psychotherapy developed for use with older people with depression and anxiety. Individual therapy appears to be superior to group (Pinquart and Sorensen, 2001; Scogin et al., 2005) and psychotherapy seems comparable in efficacy to medication (Gerson et al., 1999; Pinquart et al., 2006). Evidence for CBT is stronger than for other forms of therapy (Gatz et al., 1998; Laidlaw, 2001; Pinquart et al., 2006; Scogin et al., 2005). CBT has begun to develop process-type research that has considered treatment modifications designed to enhance treatment outcome (Laidlaw et al., 2004; Laidlaw and McAlpine, 2008) and these studies may be useful to working-age psychotherapy practitioners who will treat older people. Most of the evidence for other forms of psychotherapy with older people comes as an indirect result of CBT outcome studies. Interpersonal psychotherapy (IPT) with older people is an evidence-based intervention that is often underrepresented in evidence-based and systematic reviews of psychotherapy (Gatz et al., 1998; Scogin et al., 2005). This appears to be as a result of many of the data for IPT with older people coming from drug maintenance outcome trials. A recent book on IPT with older people (Hinrichsen and Clougherty, 2006) suggests that this is an efficacious approach.

The most common anxiety disorder in later life is generalized anxiety disorder (GAD), and as a result many of the outcome studies have evaluated treatment outcome for this disorder. There are studies that have evaluated psychological therapies for panic disorder in later life but limited studies have evaluated treatment for obsessive compulsive disorder (OCD) and post-traumatic stress disorder (PTSD). Highly specialized CBT for anxiety in people with executive dysfunction is a newly developed intervention that shows promise. CBT for late life anxiety disorder has been criticized because the studies have tended to be conducted with a generally young (55+) older adult group of healthy and active volunteers in university settings (Hendriks et al., 2008). A recent randomized controlled trial by Stanley et al. (2009) has answered many of these criticisms in a study conducted in primary care settings showing good outcome.

The overall conclusion about psychotherapy with older people is that there is good evidence that it is effective for a range of common mental health problems, but many more studies need to be conducted. Conditions that are associated with age such as dementia, stroke and Parkinson's disease are being recognized as having significant psychological consequences for the individual and their caregivers. The evidence base for psychotherapies in these conditions reflects an emerging literature that is rich with promise but is at very early stages (Wilson et al., 2008).

The therapeutic relationship is considered important for treatment outcome (Beck et al., 1979). The next section considers some of the issues that might impact the formation of the relationship with older clients.

THERAPEUTIC ENGAGEMENT

The relationship between client and counsellor is important for most psychotherapeutic endeavours. There are some factors that might make this harder when the client is older such as: cognitive changes; sensory impairment; beliefs about ageing; generational cohort values; the mask of ageing; and the maintenance of boundaries.

The Cognitive and Sensory Signs of Ageing

Cognitive impairment can occur as a result of many causes such as stroke, traumatic brain injury, dementia and, to a variable extent, the normal ageing brain (Craik et al., 1987). Functions that can be affected are memory; problem solving; attention; and reading, linguistic, verbal, mathematical and visual comprehension. It can be advantageous for counsellors working with older adults to have some knowledge of the normative and non-normative physical aspects of ageing so that they can adapt their therapy and also make more accurate interpretations of the meaning of their client's behaviour. For example, understanding the nature of working memory, executive functioning and activation of unconscious processes could help the counsellor understand the reason for the client with early stage dementia repeating the story of their spouse dying as being the activation of a sequence of activities that are stored as a memory sequence or script rather than unfinished business (James, 2010).

As people age, there is likely to be sensory decline in sensitivity and speed of response. It is helpful to understand what this means for therapy. For example, some therapists use a style of speaking to older people to aid comprehension and retention. However, Kemper and Harden (1999) discovered that being spoken to in a slower than normal speed, in shorter phrases, with exaggerated pitch and intonation was not helpful in enhancing the older adult's comprehension. What helped was using simpler grammar and semantic elaboration.

Beliefs About Ageing

Counsellors will need to become knowledgeable about longevity statistics and demographic change (Knight et al., 2009). Equipped with information contained in practice guidelines (see APA Working Group on the Older Adult, 1998), counsellors will be better equipped to identify and challenge erroneous age-related negative cognitions (e.g. growing older is depressing) that could sound understandable and realistic to counsellors inexperienced in working with older people (Laidlaw et al., 2004). Depressed older people may erroneously appraise their remaining years as bound up with negativity, loss and decrepitude. Thus, depressed older people often view their age as being against them when it comes to managing depressive symptoms. When one speaks with a depressed older adult about increased lifespan, their view about ageing may be mood congruent, and hence negative. For instance when an older person says, 'Old age is a terrible time', or 'All my problems are to do with my age', or 'I'm too old to change my ways now', this can appear difficult to challenge from the naïve perspective of a younger therapist (Laidlaw and Pachana, 2009). Pioneers such as Bob Knight, Dolores Gallagher Thompson and Larry Thompson started research programmes that demonstrated that depression was not a necessary condition of the ageing process. From investigating depression outcomes in therapy, clinicians started investigation into psychological treatments for older adults with anxiety, personality and psychotic disorders and dementias.

Generational cohort beliefs

As L.P. Hartley (1953) wrote: 'The past is a foreign country; they do things differently there.'

Knight (2004) states that working with older adults means learning something of the folkways of people born many years before. The major sources of beliefs are family, friends, religion, school, geography, economics and media. It can be important to understand the historical context in which your client formed their beliefs as this can be a barrier in forming a therapeutic relationship. Laidlaw et al. (2004) refer to this as 'cohort beliefs' in their comprehensive framework for older people. Cohort beliefs can be rigid and inflexible and are more attributable to social rather than personal developmental experiences. For example, understanding that, before the 1970s, women found it difficult to get mortgages and credit without the signature of their father or husband, helps the counsellor understand the poignant meaning for an elderly woman having to relinquish the ownership of her home as she moves into a care home. Also, the psychological expectations of the baby boomer cohort are likely to be more evident in client caseloads and older people may become more sophisticated about using counselling in years to come.

The mask of ageing

Generational differences between client and therapist also have another impact. Most psychological therapists will be significantly younger than their clients. One important phenomenon that emerges repeatedly in geriatric psychotherapy is that the way in which older patients experience and view themselves often lags far behind their chronological age and physical appearance. However, counsellors and others may not see this inner world and only see the older person. The counsellor will need to tune in to the dual realities of old age: old body, young identity. For many clients there will be a disturbing realization that they have become old and that their true self has become invisible to other people and society as a whole.

Theoretical Models of Ageing

To mention all the theoretical models of ageing is beyond the scope of this chapter. There are three models that we have found particularly useful when working with older people: Levy's (1996) negative self-stereotyping theory; selective optimization with compensation (SOC: Baltes and Baltes, 1990); and socioemotional selectivity (Carstensen et al., 1999).

Levy's research suggested that older people have an internalized negative stereotype about ageing that becomes a negative self-stereotype. Older people then can develop negative expectations about ageing and can become fearful about ageing and, if problems are attributed to age rather than to depression, this can produce high levels of hopelessness that can be very challenging for counsellors to deal with (Laidlaw, 2010).

Healthy ageing research points to three key processes that people use to adapt to the losses and gains experienced through the life course: selection, optimization and compensation. Baltes (1997) illustrates SOC with the example of concert pianist Artur Rubinstein who retired from the stage aged 89. He reduced his repertoire (selection); practised the repertoire more intensely (optimization); and slowed down immediately before playing faster segments, giving the impression of greater dexterity (compensation). When in old age the losses outweigh the gains due to chronic illness, the counsellor may want to make an assessment of a number of elements: psycho-education to orient the client to focus on realistic goals; collaborative empiricism to test out the limits; active problem solving to manage behavioural disturbances and cognitive distortions; evaluation of the nature and quality of supports; and enhancement of the adjustment to the new reality of life. Laidlaw et al. (2004) provide clinical examples that illustrate the use of this model of successful ageing in practice.

When a client explains that the reason for seeking therapy is because they have lost interest in the hobbies and pastimes that they regularly enjoyed, the counsellor might consider an interpretation based on the emotion and values shift that occurs when time is perceived as finite rather than open-ended. Carstensen et al. (1999) suggest that they will seek more emotionally meaningful goals and interests as opposed to novel information-seeking.

CONCLUSION

These are welcome and exciting times to be a counsellor working with older people (Laidlaw and Pachana, 2009). Counselling for older clients should ideally be delivered by an appropriate skill mix of trained practitioners working at different levels of complexity. Many counsellors can offer therapy to a broad age range of their clients by taking account of the issues raised in this chapter. Counsellors wanting to provide specialist interventions for complex cases will seek significant additional training in working with older people.

REFERENCES

APA Working Group on the Older Adult (1998) *What Practitioners Should Know about Working with Older Adults*. Brochure. Washington, DC: American Psychological Association.

Baltes, P.B. (1997) On the incomplete architecture of human ontogeny: selection, optimization, and compensation as foundation of developmental theory. *American Psychologist*, 52: 366–80.

Baltes, P.B. and Baltes, M.M. (1990) Psychological perspectives of successful aging: the model of selective optimization with compensation. In P.B. Baltes and M.M. Baltes (eds), *Successful Aging: Perspectives from the Behavioral Sciences*. Cambridge: Cambridge University Press.

Beck, A.T., Rush, A.J., Shaw, B.F. and Emery, G. (1979) *Cognitive Therapy of Depression*. New York: Guilford.

Bucks, R.S., Burley, C. and McGuinness, P. (2007) *To Merge or Not To Merge? That Is the Question*. A survey of the PSIGE membership regarding pressure to amalgamate older adult and adults of working age services in their localities. www.psige.org/publications.php.

Carstensen, L., Isaacowitz, D. and Charles, S.T. (1999) Taking time seriously: a theory of socioemotional selectivity. *American Psychologist*, 54: 165–81.

Craik, F.I.M., Byrd, M. and Swanson, J.M. (1987) Patterns of memory loss in three elderly samples. *Psychology and Aging*, 2: 79–86.

Gatz, M., Fiske, A., Fox, L.S., Kaskie, B., Kasl-Godley, J.E., McCallum, T.J. and Wetherell, J.L. (1998) Empirically validated psychological treatments for older adults. *Journal of Mental Health and Aging*, 4: 9–4.

Gerson, S., Belin, T.R., Kaufman, M.S., Mintz, J. and Jarvik, L. (1999) Pharmacological and psychological treatments for depressed older patients: a meta-analysis and overview of recent findings. *Harvard Review of Psychiatry*, 7: 1–28.

Hartley, L.P. (1953) *The Go-Between*. London: Hamish Hamilton.

Hendriks, G.J., Oude Voshaar, R.C., Keijsers, G.P.J., Hoogduin, C.A.L. and Van Balkom, A.J.L.M. (2008) Cognitive-behavioural therapy for late-life anxiety disorder: a systematic review and meta-analysis. *Acta Psychiatrica Scandinavica*, 117: 403–11.

Hinrichsen, G.A. and Clougherty, K.F. (2006) *Interpersonal Psychotherapy for Depressed Older Adults*. Washington, DC: American Psychological Association.

James, I.A. (2010) *Cognitive Behavioural Therapy with Older People: Interventions for Those with and without Dementia*. London: Jessica Kingsley.

Kemper, S. and Harden, T. (1999) Experimentally disentangling what's beneficial about elderspeak from what's not. *Psychology and Aging*, 14: 656–70.

Knight, B.G. (2004) *Psychotherapy with Older Adults* (3rd edn). Thousand Oaks, CA: Sage.

Knight, B.G., Karel, M.J., Hinrichsen, G.A., Qualls, S.H. and Duffy, M. (2009) Pikes Peak model for training in professional geropsychology. *American Psychologist*, 64: 205–14.

Laidlaw, K. (2001) An empirical review of cognitive therapy for late life depression: does research evidence suggest adaptations are necessary for cognitive therapy with older adults? *Clinical Psychology and Psychotherapy*, 8: 1–14.

Laidlaw, K. (2010) Enhancing cognitive behaviour therapy with older people using gerontological theories as vehicles for change. In N.A. Pachana, K. Laidlaw and B.G. Knight (eds), *Casebook of Clinical Geropsychology: International Perspectives on Practice*. Oxford: Oxford University Press.

Laidlaw, K. and McAlpine, S. (2008) Cognitive behaviour therapy: how is it different with older people? *Journal of Rational-Emotive Cognitive-Behavior Therapy*, 26: 250–62.

Laidlaw, K. and Pachana, N. (2009) Aging, mental health and demographic change: psychotherapist challenges. *Professional Psychology: Research and Practice*, 40: 601–8.

Laidlaw, K., Thompson, L.W. and Gallagher-Thompson, D. (2004) Comprehensive conceptualization of cognitive behaviour therapy for late life depression. *Behavioural and Cognitive Psychotherapy*, 32: 1–8.

Levy, B. (1996) Improving memory without awareness: implicit self-stereotyping in old age. *Journal of Personality and Social Psychology*, 71: 1092–107.

Pinquart, M. and Sorensen, S. (2001) How effective are psychotherapeutic and other psychosocial interventions with older adults? A meta-analysis. *Journal of Mental Health and Aging*, 7: 207–43.

Pinquart, M., Duberstein, P.R. and Lyness, J.M. (2006) Treatments for later-life depressive conditions: a meta-analytic comparison of pharmacotherapy and psychotherapy. *American Journal of Psychiatry*, 163: 1493–501.

Sadavoy, J. (2009) An integrated model for defining the scope of psychogeriatrics: the five Cs. *International Psychogeriatrics*, 21: 805–12.

Scogin, F., Welsh, D., Hanson, A., Stump, J. and Coates, A. (2005) Evidence-based psychotherapies for depression in older adults.

Clinical Psychology: Science and Practice, 12: 222–37.

Stanley, M.A., Wilson, N.L., Novy, D.M., Rhoades, H.M., Wagener, P.D., Greisinger, A.J., Cully, J.A. and Kunik, M.E. (2009) Cognitive behavior therapy for generalized anxiety disorder among older adults in primary care: a randomized controlled trial. *JAMA*, 301: 1460–7.

UN (2009) *World Population Prospects: The 2008 Revision, Highlights*. Working Paper no. ESA/P/WP.210. United Nations, Department of Economic and Social Affairs, Population Division.

Wilson, K., Mottram, P.G. and Vassilas, C.A. (2008) Psychotherapeutic treatments for older depressed people. *Cochrane Database of Systematic Reviews*, issue 1. Art. No. CD004853. DOI: 10.1002/14651858. CD0044853.pub2.

Zeiss, A.M. and Steffen, A. (1996) Treatment issues with elderly clients. *Cognitive and Behavioral Practice*, 3: 371–89.

Counselling in Primary Care

LOUISE ROBINSON, SARA PERREN AND PAT SEBER

DEFINING COUNSELLING IN PRIMARY CARE

The term 'counselling in primary care' can mean different things to different people. While the public uses 'counselling' as a generic term for talking therapies, in the NHS the term is often used to describe a smaller range of therapies (such as humanistic or person-centred counselling, psychodynamic counselling and relationship counselling). NHS workers tend to regard modalities such as interpersonal therapy (IPT), cognitive-behavioural therapy (CBT) and psychotherapy as distinct from counselling, using the term 'psychological therapies' to describe all therapies including counselling.

The NHS is a system formed by several organisations and individuals providing health services to the public. Primary care services are those which provide treatments that do not require a hospital visit, and the most widely accessed services in primary care are GP practices. Counselling in primary care sits within a part of the NHS system that provides psychological therapies intended for people with mild to moderate levels of emotional and psychological distress and/or mental health problems such as depression and anxiety.

HOW COUNSELLING IS PROVIDED IN PRIMARY CARE

Decisions are made about what services to provide through a process of decision-making called commissioning, which has four main steps:

- analysing the health needs of a local population
- deciding the services required to meet these needs
- reviewing services that already exist and identifying gaps
- making the necessary changes to ensure the right services are in place.

The commissioning process is informed by the following:

- guidance from central government
- local priorities and available funding
- clinical judgement (the current government intends that GPs will lead commissioning in England by 2013)
- developments in best practice, i.e. the evidence base.

Commissioning is a cycle; this means that all commissioned services are subject to review. It is therefore essential that such services meet the terms of their contract, are effective, deliver value for money, and keep evolving with local commissioning priorities, or they may face closure.

There are four main types of commissioning arrangements for primary care counselling:

- services set up and managed by the NHS
- commissioned organisations in the third sector (such as charities and voluntary organisations)
- commissioned organisations in the private sector
- individual counsellors contracted by GP practices.

In any one locality there may be all or none of these services available. Where there is more than one provider they may need to work in partnership. Commissioning arrangements are also different in each of the four UK nations because of political devolution.

DEVELOPMENTS AFFECTING COUNSELLING IN PRIMARY CARE

There are three main areas of development affecting primary care counselling: clinical guidelines, patient choice and the economic case.

The NHS is expected to use clinical guidelines to develop the most clinically effective and cost-effective treatments. Clinical guidelines published by organisations such as the National Institute for Health and Clinical Excellence (NICE) in England and the Scottish Intercollegiate Guidelines Network (SIGN) make recommendations on treatments for various health problems. These guidelines often present the treatment options using a stepped-care approach. This approach is about providing an appropriate level of treatment for the level of need: for example, someone with mild depression may benefit from guided self-help and it may be inappropriate to prescribe medication. The stepped-care approach (also called the stepped-care model) is revolutionising counselling in primary care.

There is evidence that providing patients with choice can have a positive impact on the outcomes of treatment; offering choice can also help ensure patient satisfaction. In response to this, UK governments have indicated a commitment to delivering patient choice. One area where patient choice has differed extensively by locality is access to psychological therapy; in recent years UK governments have sought to address this by publishing guidelines for the provision of such services and, in some cases, providing further funding.

In order for funding to be secured an economic case for psychological therapy has to be made, such as the case presented by Lord Richard Layard in his *Depression Report* (2006). This report suggested funding additional services for patients with depression in accordance with NICE guidelines for depression and anxiety. Layard indicated that the cost of providing these services could be met by savings made in incapacity benefit payments as people with long-term depression would be assisted to regain employment following their recovery. The report was successful in gaining funding from the English government for the Improving Access to Psychological Therapies (IAPT) programme; it also influenced policy development across the UK.

The IAPT programme has funded over 100 new psychological therapy services; in some cases they have developed alongside counselling services, in others they have merged. The key distinction between the IAPT workforce and counsellors working in primary care is that IAPT workers are trained to work with patients who have depression or anxiety, whereas trained counsellors work with people who have a wide range of needs.

OTHER KEY FACTORS INFLUENCING HOW SERVICES ARE DESIGNED AND PROVIDED

UK government health departments have published policy, guidelines and/or targets that relate to themes which impact on all services provided or commissioned by the NHS. These themes are:

- public protection and patient safety
- clinical governance
- collaborative working
- data collection
- outcome measurement
- patient and public involvement.

Counsellors working in primary care should receive training to help them understand the relevance of these terms and meet their responsibilities in ensuring that the relevant protocols and policies of the services are met.

MAIN FEATURES OF PATIENTS REFERRED FOR PRIMARY CARE COUNSELLING

Patients who are emotionally or psychologically distressed are most likely to talk to their GP. The GP may use questionnaires such as the PHQ-9, GAD-7 or CORE to help them decide whether there is an underlying mental health problem, such as depression and/or anxiety. Such a questionnaire can also show the level of severity and whether the patient is at risk of suicide. The GP will also use clinical judgement and their knowledge of the patient to determine other possible causes for the distress. The GP will then discuss with their patient whether they think a referral for therapy might be helpful. If the patient is in agreement the GP will make a referral to the most appropriate service.

In many localities there is a range of psychological therapy services with a diversity of practitioners; for example, some may offer counselling, others may offer guided self-help and/or CBT. In such localities it is becoming increasingly common for GPs to send referrals to one service acting as a central hub. Practitioners in the central hub, also described as a single point of access, assess patients before referring them to the most appropriate service.

It is possible for patients to approach some psychological therapy services directly, i.e. without being referred by their GP. There are relatively few services that allow such self-referrals but the number is rising. These services have their own assessment process, which will inform how the patient is treated, or referred to other more appropriate services.

Regardless of the route that referrals take, counsellors in primary care are likely to work with people who have a range of problems, symptoms and diagnoses. These may include (based on Clark et al., 2008) people who have:

- mild, moderate or severe anxiety or depression
- been assessed as unsuitable for other treatments or therapies
- been offered counselling following different treatment or therapy that did not improve their symptoms
- identified unresolved issues – historic or developmental – that are impacting on their current coping methods and personal development
- relationship difficulties
- problems with adjustment (e.g. to parenthood, retirement, diagnosis of illness)
- low focus and low motivation towards implementing changes
- a prolonged or complex grief reaction or other high level of emotional distress
- a high requirement for risk management
- a complex history, with significant risk and/or high impairment of functioning
- a number of previous interventions with unhelpful outcomes.

This list demonstrates that a counsellor in primary care may find themselves working with people who have complex problems. Counsellors may work with such patients over several weeks but it is more common for primary care counselling to be short term and focused. For example, NICE (2009) guidelines are based on studies that indicate six to 10 sessions of counselling are needed over eight to 12 weeks to treat someone with mild to moderate depression. Practice-based evidence drawn from studies of the outcomes of therapy indicate that the average number of sessions of primary care counselling across the range of patients and the problems they present is 5.9 per patient (Mellor-Clark et al., 2001).

It is essential to bear in mind these figures are guidelines based on averages. Some services do impose a limit of six sessions on primary care counselling, which does not allow counsellors much autonomy or flexibility to work over the longer term with patients who need it. In services that do allow counsellors to use their clinical judgement

when deciding the duration of therapy, they may see some patients for one session and others for many more. Evidence indicates the average number of sessions will still be around six.

SPECIFIC TRAINING FOR COUNSELLORS WORKING IN PRIMARY CARE

Graduate training is available to qualified counsellors who want to acquire specific training in health-care counselling, but this is limited. It is more common that counsellors acquire health-care experience, training and development while on counselling placements.

Counsellors who gain employment in the NHS can expect to receive support from their employer to ensure they develop knowledge in the following areas:

- an understanding of NHS structure and policy
- clinical governance
- NHS multidisciplinary working and collaborative care
- knowledge of mental health referral pathways and procedures
- assessment, including risk assessment and risk management
- time-limited/brief therapy
- psychotropic medication and the effects of other medication on health and wellbeing
- chronic illness and its impact on mental health
- focused, evidence-based practice
- audit, evaluation and research.

The availability of formal training in NHS England has recently been influenced by the IAPT programme. In the first three years, IAPT focused on training a new workforce of CBT practitioners. Some primary care counsellors were successful in applying for these posts as an opportunity to step into CBT practice.

In 2010 the IAPT training programme was extended to include top-up training in: humanistic counselling, dynamic interpersonal therapy (DIT), relationship counselling and interpersonal psychotherapy (IPT). The focus of these trainings is learning to adopt a manualised approach in order to treat a patient's depression. They are brief trainings and will only be available to therapists who already hold a recognised qualification.

The coalition government indicated in its mental health strategy, *No Health without Mental Health* (Department of Health, 2011), that expanding the provision of talking therapies will remain a priority in England. In parallel, the health bill of 2011 is redefining and restructuring the NHS as we know it. The extent of planned change within the NHS means it is currently unclear how the expansion of talking therapy provision will be achieved, and how this will impact on counsellors. It is also unclear how the other UK nations will progress their plans to improve access to psychological therapies, and whether this will provide opportunities for trained counsellors.

Regardless of how the IAPT, or talking therapies, agenda develops across the UK, there will continue to be a need for counsellors in primary care. Counsellors who are keen to develop skills that are attractive to employers might consider bolt-on training in modalities such as IPT and CBT that are widely recommended in clinical guidelines.

PROFESSIONAL SUPPORT

Support for professionals in the workplace is a shared responsibility between employer and individual. The employer should provide quality in-service training and supervision in order to ensure staff wellbeing and performance delivery; while the employee should be committed to ethical practice and their own continuing professional development (CPD).

Standards for employment and professional support are essential in any profession where the public is at risk of harm. Counselling is not regulated by government; therefore employers rely on professional bodies to set and monitor standards for safe and ethical practice. Consequently, there is an expectation that NHS counsellors will maintain membership of a professional body; furthermore, most NHS advertisements for counsellors specify that applicants are accredited by the British Association for Counselling and Psychotherapy (BACP) or equivalent.

One of the standards set by BACP to help ensure members are professionally supported is the requirement for regular clinical supervision. In NHS-managed services it is common practice for supervision to be provided by the employer; in other instances, they may fund an external provider. Where an external supervisor is used it is important they thoroughly understand the NHS context; there is also a need to ensure confidentiality in accordance with NHS protocols. Regardless of which supervision model is used, it is essential the supervisor is appropriately trained and has an awareness of different counselling modalities.

Effective supervision is both supportive and developmental. Other beneficial activities include reading books and professional journals, attending events, networking, accessing information on good practice and ultimately applying learning. Many primary care counsellors choose to belong to a specialist organisation such as BACP Healthcare (formerly the Faculty of Healthcare Counsellors and Psychotherapists) to help them access the resources they need.

BACP Healthcare is a division of BACP and is the largest and longest-standing professional organisation for counsellors working in health care. There are other professional bodies in the sector, such as the Association of Counsellors and Psychotherapists in Primary Care (CPC), which is part of the United Kingdom Council for Psychotherapy (UKCP). As an employee, additional support can be achieved by having indemnity insurance cover and belonging to a recognised union.

WORKING AS A PRIMARY CARE COUNSELLOR

As part of the NHS Agenda for Change agreement in 2004, national job profiles for counsellors were established which helped develop awareness of the role of NHS counsellors and strengthened their terms and conditions of employment. Today, counsellors are employed by the NHS at Agenda for Change pay bands 5, 6, 7 or 8 depending on their level of responsibility and the skills required by their role. The health bill that is currently under development (2011) is likely to lead to a significant reduction in the number of NHS employees; this means that the future of pay scales for counsellors working in primary care, and other health-care workers, is uncertain.

The work of a primary care counsellor is challenging, demanding, exciting and rewarding. Anyone wishing to work in this environment needs to be robust enough, physically and mentally, to withstand the pressure that comes from constant change and new initiatives.

Some of the challenges stem from the knock-on effect of the changes in government policies mentioned elsewhere in this chapter. Never before have services been required to provide so much information to government bodies; as part of this process organisations require staff to gather comprehensive data to demonstrate their effectiveness.

Referrals for counselling made by GPs have not changed much over the years, only increased. We still see clients who are adjusting to life events such as redundancy, illness, infertility, relationship breakdown and bereavement. Although loss issues make up a good proportion of referrals, others such as self-harm, childhood sexual abuse, rape, trauma, medically unexplained symptoms and the psychological impact of long-term conditions are also prevalent.

As far as counselling and mental health are concerned we live in interesting times. Multidisciplinary teams are now commonplace – an approach that is seen as beneficial to clients, team members and the service. It is therefore essential that primary care counsellors are skilled at teamworking.

THE FUTURE OF PRIMARY CARE COUNSELLING

We are in a new political climate of spending cuts. However, the government has published an action plan for the expansion of talking therapies in England over the next four years. This is due to a growing recognition that such therapies are an important part of mental health provision because of their potential to create long-term savings: for example, by keeping people in work and helping couples and families to stay together.

There is also growing interest in developing more effective psychological therapy provision for people who have poor physical health that cannot be explained by a medical diagnosis (medically unexplained symptoms). For such patients there can be an underlying psychological cause for their ill-health, and treating this underlying problem will alleviate their symptoms and save the NHS money in the long term.

Another area where psychological therapies may help the NHS become more efficient is in improving outcomes for people with long-term conditions such as diabetes. For these patients there is a psychological component to their condition; by exploring this with a trained therapist they can be helped to come to terms with their condition and manage it better. Complementing this, there is increasing emphasis on working to prevent mental distress and the associated negative impact on people's lives.

As the NHS implements the government's vision it will make decisions based on clinical judgement, patient choice and, crucially, the best available evidence. The NHS considers some forms of evidence to hold greater significance than others, with randomised controlled trials (RCTs) generally holding the greatest significance. RCTs follow a rigid method to test whether a treatment or therapy is effective. Counselling in primary care has been tested using RCTs but these are relatively few in number. There is a need now and in the future to add to the RCT evidence for counselling in order to make the most of the opportunities ahead.

REFERENCES

Clark, D.M., Layard, R. and Smithies, R. (2008) *Improving Access to Psychological Therapy: Initial Evaluation of the Two Demonstration Sites*. LSE Centre for Economic Performance Working Paper no. 1648.

Department of Health (2011) *No Health without Mental Health. A Cross-Government Mental Health Outcomes Strategy for People of All Ages: A Call to Action*. London: Department of Health.

Mellor-Clark, J., Simms-Ellis, R. and Burton, M. (2001) *National Survey of Counsellors Working in Primary Care: Evidence of Growing Professionalisation*. Occasional paper 79. London: Royal College of General Practitioners.

NICE (2009) *Depression: The Treatment and Management of Depression in Adults*. NICE Clinical Guidance 90. p. 29. www.nice.org.uk/nicemedia/live/12329/45888/45888.pdf.

Clinical Applications of Working with Race, Culture and Ethnicity

HARBRINDER DHILLON-STEVENS

This chapter builds on the earlier theoretical chapter regarding race, culture and ethnicity (Chapter 2.8 in this volume) and discusses the clinical issues that practitioners need to consider.

The connections between race, culture and ethnicity having been made, the intention in this chapter is to raise critical questions so the reader can arrive at his/her own integrative framework in terms of an anti-oppressive practice stance.

It is worth noting that currently UKCP recognises this as a key clinical issue and has appointed a diversity, equalities and social responsibility officer who is in the process of formulating a UKCP diversity, equality and social responsibility framework. This involves reviewing UKCP's policies, procedures and structures in relation to issues of difference.

Diversity, equalities and social responsibility work groups have been formulated in the following areas:

- training (supervision and CPD) issues
- the image of psychotherapy in minority communities
- children's issues
- diversity support groups
- environmental concerns
- asylum, immigration and institutional discrimination
- class, economic inequality and access to psychotherapy.

It is important to recognise that psychological therapies are still a white middle-class profession, and statistics distributed in June 2010 by UKCP

Table 7.18.1   *Ethnic origin of UKCP membership, 2010**

Asian		0.79%
White	British	75.61%
	Irish	5.15%
	other	15.73%
Black	British	2.66%
Mixed race		0.00%
Other		0.05%

*Categories are those used by UKCP.

showed its membership as in Table 7.18.1. BACP too has appointed an equalities officer.

CONTEXTUAL FRAMEWORKS

Human beings, from the moment they are born, are defined in relationship with others (Stern, 1985). A person's context (environmental, social, cultural, political, religious, linguistic) is an important part of the development of their identity, and to understand that identity one needs to understand and have an awareness of context (Sills et al., 2001). These authors refer to the relationship and contextual framework of psychotherapy and counselling. Therapists need to see the interrelationship between the structural (external) world and the psyche (internal world) of the client.

Samuels notes that 'depth psychology must face the problem that it is not possible to depict a person divorced from his cultural, social, gender, ethnic and above all, economic and ecological contexts' (1993: 201). Again it is interesting to note the omission of race.

In taking account of this, Evans and Gilbert (2005) add the contextual relationship to Clarkson's five-relationship model. Arguably, a contextual relationship is not an additional relationship but one that provides an overarching framework for the other five relational stances (Dhillon, 1979).

The multiple oppression model (Dhillon, 1979; Dhillon-Stevens, 2004b; 2011) has arisen out of ongoing academic and clinical work with issues of oppression and working within an anti-oppressive practice (AOP) framework. The ideology of such a model has existed in the combined works of authors such as Friere (1990), Lorde (1984) and Begum (1994). This model is an integrative relational model focusing on the active use of the dialogic relationship in working with issues of oppression in psychotherapy and counselling.

The framework focuses on oppressions of race, ethnicity, gender, disability, sexual orientation, age, class, religion, language and culture, though obviously other oppressions exist. I accept that in naming certain oppressions others are excluded, but the intention in naming these oppressions is to provide a platform for understanding the complexities involved and transferring the knowledge gained to other areas of discrimination or oppression.

WHAT IS ANTI-OPPRESSIVE PRACTICE?

As a model that works in terms of empowerment and liberation (Phillipson, 1992), anti-oppressive practice recognises power dynamics as central to the relationship and considers both the internal and the external world of the client. It requires a fundamental rethinking of values, institutions and relationships: therapists are seen as change agents and are proactive in considering these issues rather than reactive. Therapists accept that they can have influence at the individual-to-individual level but also are aware of their contribution at the structural level in terms of institutional levels and the cultural norm. Therapists have an understanding of structural inequalities of oppression (social, economic, historical, political, cultural and psychological) and how these dimensions impact on clients from specific oppressed groups.

Therapists are aware of the differences between prejudice, discrimination and oppression and consider how systematic oppression works at an individual and structural level for clients of certain groups, thus raising awareness of differences between discriminated and oppressed groups.

THE MULTIPLE OPPRESSION MODEL

Working in an AOP framework promotes a multiple oppression model (Dhillon, 1979). This model considers the interconnectedness of oppressions but also acknowledges the differences, and this is the area that is highlighted in the therapeutic relationship and dialogue. This model does not accept that all oppressions are the same. Neither does it promote a hierarchical view of oppressions. The idea that some oppressions are visible (race) and others invisible (sexual orientation) is explicit and understood in terms of power between oppressions, and the potential to be oppressed as well as to be an oppressor is central to the model (Dhillon-Stevens, 2004a).

RACE AND RACISM

The issues need to be discussed in terms of black-client/white-therapist and black-therapist/white-client dyads.

Ridley defines 'racism as any behaviour or pattern of behaviour that systematically tends to deny access to opportunities or privilege to one social group while perpetuating privilege to members of another group' (1989: 60). Racism is a belief that black people are inferior to white people.

The starting point is to acknowledge and accept that black people have historically faced disadvantage and oppression. Race and racism target visible differences, so when black clients enter the therapeutic space they do not want to be further marginalised or disempowered. As Mann (2002) asserts, although interpersonal therapy has always been considered ideal for work between individuals of differing cultures with the aim of getting to know the 'stranger', the cultural (and racial) context is still left largely unaddressed by interpersonalists.

Curry, in his 1964 paper 'Myths, transference and the black psychotherapist', discusses the concept of the 'pre-transference'. He describes this as the ideas, fantasies and values ascribed to the black therapist and his race which are held by the white patient long before the two meet for the first time in the consulting room. Later writers (Comas-Diaz and Jacobsen, 1991; Thomas, 1992) examined the dynamics which may arise in black–white, white–black and black–black therapist–client dyads. I am always aware of the pre-transference over the initial phone conversation. Clients have all sorts of views about me, whether they refer to me as Harbrinder, Mrs Stevens or Dr Dhillon-Stevens; my English accent betrays my race, culture and ethnicity. In a phone conversation with a white professional about a Sikh family where there were child protection concerns, the professional commented, 'How do you work with these foreigners?' My response was, 'I am one of these foreigners.' The pre-transference is always present in the clinical context.

Although there is little available literature on cultural transference in a white–white dyad, research is being conducted in this area in terms of white-Irish/white-British therapeutic dyads.

In a questionnaire distributed to psychotherapists in 2002 (Dhillon-Stevens, 2004a), respondents were asked, as part of a training programme for therapists, whether there should be a competency framework or clear learning outcomes for therapists in working with clients who are different to them. Yes, stated 73 per cent. One respondent's comments were: 'Therapists in training need most help to recognise their own blind spots and limitations and support to become more fully present with all clients (from marginalised groups) they see.'

So how should the question of race be brought into the room? Whose responsibility is it to raise this difference? Is it the therapist's or the client's? Should these issues be addressed from the start or later in the therapeutic relationship? How do therapists bring this issue into the room? What is it that they say?

In research (Dhillon-Stevens, 2004a) these are questions therapists find difficult. Either therapists ignore the issue, as they feel that if it was important then the client would raise it; or they raise the questions of difference, but put the onus back onto the client to name what this difference means. As Kareem states: 'I believe that it is the responsibility of the therapist, from the outset, to facilitate the expression of any negative transference which is based on historical context, and not leave the onus on the patient' (Kareem and Littlewood, 1992: 23). The client may be too needy or too afraid to raise these issues or may not want to raise these issues immediately in an attempt to build a good relationship. First-generation clients from India and Africa, due to the experience of colonialism and imperialism, have an internalised schema of being grateful to white people, not rocking the boat and when offended turning the other cheek. In research, black clients reported they avoided such issues in order not to upset the white therapist (Dhillon-Stevens, 2004a; 2011). Kareem further states: 'For the therapist who is working with a patient of a different background, it is a fundamental clinical issue which

must be acknowledged and brought out into the open' (Kareem and Littlewood, 1992: 23).

Black clients carry intergenerational and historical experiences of racism, colonisation and imperialism and therefore these issues are always present whether articulated or not. Addressing these issues is important in developing a working alliance and in developing trust. The client's mistrust of the therapist in a historical and socio-political context needs to be acknowledged and worked with. This is where the literature on whiteness and what it means to be white is crucial. White therapists need to own their ancestral oppression of black people and the intergenerational legacy of racism and racist ideology. In my opinion this is where the difficulty is, as many white therapists feel that if they accept or ally themselves with racism this is not who they are and feel very threatened in accepting or acknowledging such issues. Ryde in her reflections states:

> I found that some of how I felt about being English, including a pervasive sense of 'nothingness' about it, applied even more when I thought about being white. Although it seemed quite possible to write in theory about a western hegemony I found it almost impossible to 'feel' what being white was like ... I wonder if 'white' also seems to imply an absence of race. (2009: 35)

In research (Dhillon-Stevens, 2004a) black and white participants in dialogue reported that individuals of the 'norm' (white populations) have no point of reference regarding oppressions and therefore minimise the experience in their contact with others who are oppressed. There is a genuine issue of competence here: how do you engage in dialogue when you have no experience of race, culture, ethnicity? A white therapist in undertaking a clinical viva exam in 2010, following a four-year training, was asked how she worked with issues of difference. The therapist stated that the geographical area she worked in contained white populations and had no experience of black populations. The therapist did not see issues of culture and ethnicity in relation to white populations.

Tuckwell (2002) lists interesting ways in which white people tend to resist acknowledging their whiteness. These are:

1 focusing on experiences of gender and culture rather than race
2 focusing intellectually on structural issues such as racism
3 challenging the concept of race at an intellectual level
4 referring to relationships with neighbours or friends who are black
5 wishing to protect black people from hurt

6   wishing to identify with black people (and I would say, in AOP, concentrating on the similarities between them and the client rather than working with the difference).

On one occasion we were teaching anti-oppressive practice to a group of therapists and academics in Ireland. We had previously talked about being white and being British, and in this conversation the Irish participants accepted the racism, colonialism and imperialism of the British. When we moved on to discuss being white and being Irish, I noticed the Irish participants' resistance and their investment in identifying with the black students and populations. I named this resistance, and a rich dialogue followed about how the Irish participants saw the British as oppressors and therefore in their psyche they could not identify with the aggressor. This fixed schema was stopping them from accepting their whiteness and their racism towards black students, who saw them as white and oppressive. Hence, from this positioning they could not fully appreciate the experience of black students and populations. The theme of being oppressed as well as being an oppressor emerges in such dialogue.

In research (Dhillon-Stevens, 2004a) a white therapist raised the issue of the racial difference between her and the black client, who stated: 'I am aware that I am black and you are white, I wonder how that feels for you?' The therapist undertook an interpersonal process recall (IPR: Kagan, 1984) whilst viewing the videoed session. She reported that once she had named this issue she did not know how to proceed. The black client in her IPR stated: 'Noticing is not enough. I wanted her to show me. Why was she raising this issue? What was she trying to convey to her client?' The therapist needed to be explicit, especially about her whiteness and its potential to impact upon the work. The client clearly wanted the therapist to take responsibility for the issue and not to put it back onto the client by asking, 'How is it for you?'

What also became clear was that the therapist censored herself from engaging in the real relationship and being explicit as a result of an 'internal voice' that said, 'I'm the therapist, I'm not supposed to say things like that.' Her congruence was avoided, and her sense of how to be was influenced by her training, which stressed such issues should be explored by the client and not the therapist.

Later in the cooperative inquiry group the white therapist realised she was coming to terms with her veil of hypocrisy, owning the murderous parts of her, the very archaic parts that accepted the dynamics around AOP but never had the opportunity to explore, question or discuss them. The absence of dialogue had meant these feelings were being stored elsewhere and coming out in her work.

Black participants reported comments such as, 'I am aware that I am black and you are white, I wonder how that feels for you?' evoked feelings by black participants that they are exploited in dialogue with white participants. They have to engage in helping someone else through this – someone who, as they see it, has a problem with them and their race. In Dhillon-Stevens (2011) a more expansive view of issues for psychological therapists from black and minority ethnic groups is presented.

INTERNALISED RACISM AND A RUPTURED SENSE OF SELF

Many authors who have researched black people's experiences of racism write about the trauma of racism and how clients develop a ruptured sense of self (Alleyne, 2004; Dhillon-Stevens, 2011; Mckenzie-Magava, 2010; Straker, 1992), and that in working with racism this is a developmental trauma.

I also want to raise the concept of internalised racism. Many therapists say that when they raise issues of racism some black clients will negate the issue and say this is not important to them as they have never faced racism. The conversation ends. Black and white therapists need to be mindful of this concept.

Internalised racism occurs when people targeted by racism are coerced and pressured to agree with the distortions of racism. Each of us targeted by racism fights, from childhood, as long and as hard as we can, to maintain a sense of ourselves as good, smart, strong, important and powerful. However, racist attitudes can be so harsh, so pervasive and so damaging that each of us is forced at times to turn racism in upon ourselves and seemingly agree with some of the conditioning, internalising the messages of racism. We come to mistreat ourselves and other members of our group in the same ways that we have been mistreated as the targets of racism. This is a psychological process that is strongly linked to identity development; other psychological terms that help us understand this come from gestalt psychotherapy, where the literature refers to retroflection.

If we think of racism as trauma, as when the boundary between self and other becomes unclear, lost or impermeable, this results in a disturbance of the distinction between self and other, a disturbance of both contact and awareness (Perls, 1973). In good boundary functioning, people alternate between connecting and separating, between being in contact with the current environment and withdrawing attention from the environment. Retroflection is a split within the self, a resisting of aspects of the self by the self. This substitutes self for environment, as in doing to self what one wants to do to someone else, or as in doing for self what one wants someone else to do for self. This mechanism leads to isolation. The mechanisms of introjection and projection are also evident.

Object relations theory also provides a useful way of understanding this. Whiteness is all around oneself and, as discussed in the literature, the majority of white people do not think about whiteness. Whiteness is associated with positive notions: cleanliness and purity; favoured, favourable and favourite; turning bad into good; legitimate and honest (Dalal, 2002). In contrast, black is associated with negative connotations: soiled or stained with dirt; gloomy; pessimistic; dismal, a black outlook; harmful; inexcusable, a black lie; hostile; threatening, black words; black looks; without any moral quality or goodness; evil; wicked; indicating censure, disgrace or liability to punishment, a black mark on one's record; marked by disaster or misfortune; wearing black or dark clothing or armour, the Black Prince; based on the grotesque, morbid or unpleasant aspects of life, black comedy. If this is what is projected at conscious and unconscious levels then black people take in whole a very negative self-concept. In understanding this process of identity development, it is helpful to consider the work of Cross (1971; 1978; 1991) and the development of a five-stage model of what he called 'Nigrescene', which refers to the process some individuals go through toward a secure and confident black identity. The stages characterise a demoralised black person in the process of positive change:

- *Pre-encounter stage*. At this level the person's worldview is white oriented (Eurocentric). He or she will even deny racism exists.
- *Encounter stage*. The person now experiences or observes a situation that brings him/her face to face with racism. The experience is so shattering that it forces the individual to reinterpret his/her world.
- *Immersion–emersion stage*. This stage encompasses the most sensational aspects of black identity development (Cross, 1971). This is the most sensitive stage. The person struggles to remove all semblance of the old identity process while intensifying 'blackness'.
- *Internalisation stage*. The individual has now managed to separate the old identified self and the new self, thus moving towards a positive identity.
- *Internalisation–commitment stage*. The individual involves him/herself in black groups and community issues.

This work has been developed and referred to by Maxime (1993) and Richards (1997).

Helms (1984; 1990; 1995) developed the people of colour racial identity model and the white racial identity model. His models offer a theoretical framework which is made up of a number of ego statuses/stages that describe the developmental process of racial identity.

In summing up, visible differences (race: black and white) need to be named, but therapists need to be clear about why they are raising issues and what it is they want to communicate to the black client about their difference, and the implications of this in the therapeutic space/relationship.

CULTURE AND ETHNICITY

Culture and ethnicity can be considered in terms of black-client/white-therapist, black-therapist/white-client, black-therapist/black-client and white-therapist/white-client dyads. A culture can be defined variously as follows:

> The set of unique characteristics that distinguishes its members from another group. (Rosinski, 2003)

> The shared history, practices, beliefs and values of a racial, regional, or religious group of people. (d'Ardenne and Mahtani, 1989: 4)

Ethnicity can be defined as belonging to a group of humanity sharing common national or cultural traditions. The key characteristics of an ethnic group are: a long shared history, a cultural tradition of their own, a common geographical origin or descent, a common literature, a sense of being a minority, shared traditions, and nationality.

The difficulty in therapists seeking cultural/ethnic knowledge is the application of this to all clients from one group. Although my ethnic origins remain the same, my culture is not the same as my grandmother or mother. Culture is fluid, so how does having cultural knowledge help us in working with clients? Cultural differences can be cited in the therapeutic space with an attempt to embrace 'difference', but racism is still present and perpetuated in the client's world. Multiculturalism attempts to superficially embrace difference through targeting differences such as food, clothes, festivals, etc. but ignores issues of race and racism, and the power dynamics remain unchanged. Dominelli (1997) refers to this willingness to learn about black people's cultures in order to practise culturally competently as the 'new racists'.

In ascertaining cultural/ethnic issues that are figural for the client whilst incorporating his or her own individual/family culture, it is the way therapists attune to the client's material and the way we inquire into the significance of this for the client that is the most effective strategy.

In assessing a white Russian, Jewish single mother, where there were concerns around her parenting, I asked her about her experiences in Russia of her own upbringing, about the views she held of how children should be brought up. It became clear that she had been brought up by governesses and would spend one hour in the evening with her mother. In interviewing her mother, she explained that the elite in Russia did not bring up children and she, too, had been brought up by a governess. What became evident was a clear cultural philosophy located in class, culture and ethnic roots about how children should be raised. I was able to identify the intergenerational pattern, culture, values and beliefs and in doing so I was able to present the mother in a different light by establishing cultural notions of child rearing. Previously, professionals involved had seen her as a self-centred, preoccupied person interested in her career with little concern for her child.

In working with a young white Irish woman, she joked at our first meeting that she thought I would have worn 'Indian clothes and smelt of curry' (pre-transference). As the work progressed, what became clear was that she had chosen me because she identified me as someone born in the Indian subcontinent, an immigrant who had managed to retain her culture, ethnicity and language within the British context. She felt she had assimilated into British society and the only remnant of her Irish identity was her accent. In exploring her loss of identity, as a therapist I needed to be attuned to the politics of assimilation, similarities in immigrant experience between the Irish and Indians, dislocation, loss and the differences in our race, culture and ethnicity. In the interpersonal dynamics, the therapist held that although Irish people may be seen as the dominant white majority, in historical terms in the British context Irish people have suffered racism too. The therapist's understanding and communication of this created empathic resonance. This work involved showing my client aspects of my identity in order for her to find her own identity. At the end of the therapy she decided to return to her Irish homeland.

Therapists may want to consider their attitudes and beliefs towards race, culture and ethnicity and how these develop into a strategy for working with the issues. The following may be strategies adopted by therapists:

ignore the difference
avoidance strategies: deny differences exist
recognise differences but evaluate them in a negative way
patronising approach (feeling superior)
recognise differences but minimise their importance

colour-blind approach: 'I treat everyone the same', 'everyone is equal'
dumping strategies (putting the responsibility on to minority groups)
other strategies (you may have others not listed above).

KEY PRINCIPLES IN FORMULATING AN ANTI-OPPRESSIVE PRACTICE FRAMEWORK

The following are some key principles in working with issues of race, culture and ethnicity.

Language and Use of Language

Language has the power to empower or disempower people. One must be aware of professional jargon in the therapeutic relationship and the impact of words on different groups, e.g. 'black', 'coloured'. Black clients have reported the intentional use of certain words to ascertain if they and the therapist are a good match. Words used can have the effect of either attuning to the client or misattuning and possibly causing ruptures. A white therapist working with a black client continually used the word 'explore'. The therapist was unaware of the impact of this word and how it linked to the client's narrative of oppression. The use of the word 'explore' evoked all sorts of historical, namely colonial, feelings that were not safe for the client. The client reported that it was as if 'we're going to explore you, the white therapists are going to explore me. These feelings were exploring me in a sort of taking over rampaging, what do you call it plundering kind of way' (Dhillon-Stevens, 2004a).

Communication Patterns

It is necessary to think about interpersonal styles and intrapersonal styles, to be aware of using our own preferences of interpersonal communication styles to evaluate others' behaviour. McAvoy and Donaldson (1990) give a list of criteria to consider when communicating with clients, especially if English is not a first language.

Stereotypes

One must be aware of stereotypes and how these can be presented in a positive way but yet have an underlying negativity. For example, the African-Caribbean grandmother is often perceived as strong and therefore not needing support. Common misperceptions are that Asian women are not assertive; that African-Caribbean women are aggressive; and that white European women are assertive.

Non-verbal Behaviours

Non-verbal behaviours include eye contact (direct, indirect, avoidance), gestures, touch, and voice tone. (In my family when I speak Punjabi my voice goes up several decibels; others may perceive me as arguing or being angry, but this is not the case.) One must be aware of the use of silences, and of body distance. It is easy to misread non-verbal behaviour.

Definitions of Identity

Therapists need an awareness of 'I' versus 'we' constructs. Western cultures very much promote the development of the self and the individual. Eastern cultures promote the 'we' (group, family system, community); the needs of the 'we' are greater than those of the 'I' and decisions are made on this basis. One's individuality is subordinated to collective solidarity; one's identity and knowledge of oneself comes from being part of a family. In supervision, a white male therapist working with a female Asian client reported that he felt he was missing his client. In his attempts to develop the 'I' he asked her what she wanted, what she thought, and her reply always began with 'my family feel …'. The goals for psychotherapy also need to be defined in terms of the 'we'.

Islam is in no sense a race, an ethnicity or a single culture; it is a worldwide religion. However, while there is no *prima facie* case for referring to Islam in isolation, events since 9/11 and their repercussions and implications in the UK mean that Muslims have faced additional discrimination and stereotyping. Clients who identify as Muslim may sometimes be preoccupied with national and religious identity issues, and practitioners need to be mindful of this in therapeutic exchanges.

Personal Versus Professional Boundaries

In my work with people from the same culture I have to engage in certain dialogue and self-disclosure before the client feels we have a working alliance. This dialogue is about understanding the other's background; so questions like where were you born? what village? who is your father, grandfather? are you married? do you have children? are seen as a necessary prerequisite to engaging in the work. This is a form of interpersonal etiquette. I see self-disclosure as necessary in working with difference (Dhillon-Stevens, 2004a).

What you say about yourself demonstrates you are open and willing to be reflective about your work.

Concept of Empathy

If you are dealing with someone who is distressed, the demonstration and communication of empathy are differently understood. The resonance is different and has to be communicated in an indirect way (Dhillon-Stevens, 2011). This becomes even more problematic with the use of interpreters.

Working in a Strengths Model

A strengths model requires looking at a client's strengths in terms of culture, race and ethnicity rather than seeing behaviours as negative. The client's frame of reference is paramount, and working in a strengths model opens up our critical reflexivity as practitioners. For example, in working with refugees, often the themes of loss and dislocation are prevalent, and overcoming these and surviving is a feature in terms of strengths and the client's perception of their own capacity. Soloman (1976) describes work with black communities and her approach to utilising a strengths model.

Working Alliance

Discussing issues of 'difference' is an important factor in building a working alliance, and valuing difference demonstrates an understanding of identity formulation and how these issues relate to self-esteem and self-confidence in clients. Therapists need to develop the skills of how to raise these issues and when in the therapy. A supervisee recently discussed her work with a client of mixed-race parentage. She had been working with this man for five months. In our first supervision session we had discussed issues of difference between us and how contextual issues were important in clinical work. This exploration had made her aware that the client had an Indian mother and an English father. The client looked Indian and these issues had never been discussed. The supervisee became aware the client was very reluctant to talk about his mother, who had died in very tragic circumstances. She thought that this part of his identity was crucial in terms of his presentation and could not find a way into this conversation. I hypothesised about the nurturing the client would have received from his Indian mother and wondered if that part of him had died with his mother. We explored the racial and cultural material in relation to his trauma and how this had not been considered in his diagnosis of paranoid schizophrenia that had its onset following his mother's death. I encouraged my supervisee, who was a white woman with a vast experience of living and working interculturally, to focus on the difference between her and the client in the here-and-now and how she felt that she was not attending to all of him by not acknowledging this. The dialogue helped to build a bridge between the issues of race, culture and ethnicity in the here-and-now and the back-there issues related to his identity and the painful death of his mother.

Practise 'Both/and' Thinking

Therapists should be aware of holding different ideas together and avoiding the 'yes but' syndrome that puts ideas into a competitive and superior framework.

Intention Versus Impact

We should be aware of our intentionality and its impact, especially when this is different, and find a way of communicating this when we experience ruptures and difficult moments.

Making Mistakes

Do expect to make mistakes and feel uncomfortable. This is an area that requires us to feel uncomfortable so we can reflect on this and learn from our mistakes.

Power and Power Dynamics

Be alert to these in relation to our power as psychological therapists, and in terms of who our clients are and their experiences at both personal and structural levels of power and powerlessness.

CONCLUSION

This chapter has examined the key clinical issues in terms of race, culture and ethnicity. Anti-oppressive practice requires a critically reflexive stance by the therapist and a development of competence in this area. Clearly supervision is an important development in one's competence in this area, and I refer you to Dhillon-Stevens (2001) to think further about the supervisory relationship and AOP.

In working with race, culture and ethnicity, psychological therapists need to develop their own expertise; it will be hard to counsel effectively beyond stages you have not first mastered

yourself. It is paramount to be proactive about your learning, to integrate this learning into your practice and to consider these issues as good ethical practice.

REFERENCES

Alleyne, A. (2004) The internal oppressor and black identity wounding. *Counselling and Psychotherapy Journal*, 15 (10): 48–50.

Begum, N. (1994) Mirror, mirror on the wall. In N. Begum, M. Hill and A. Stevens (eds), *Reflections: The Views of Black Disabled People on Their Lives and Community Care*. Cambridge: CCETSW.

Comas-Diaz, L. and Jacobsen, F.M. (1991) Ethnocultural transference and countertransference in the therapeutic dyad. *American Journal of Orthopsychiatry*, 61 (3): 392–402.

Cross, W.E. (1971) The negro-to-black conversion experience: toward a psychology of black liberation. *Black World*, 20 (9).

Cross, W.E. (1978) The Cross and Thomas models of psychological nigrescence. *Journal of Black Psychology*, 5 (1).

Cross, W.E. (1991) *Shades of Black Diversity in African-American Identity*. Philadelphia: Temple University Press.

Curry, A. (1964) Myths, transference and the black psychotherapist. *Psychological Review*, 51 (1): 7–14.

Dalal, F. (2002) *Race, Colour and the Process of Radicalization*. Hove: Brunner-Routledge.

D'Ardenne, P. and Mahtani, A. (1989) *Transcultural Counselling in Action*. London: Sage.

Dhillon, H. (1979) *Integrative Psychotherapy Dissertation*. MSc in Integrative Psychotherapy, Middlesex University.

Dhillon-Stevens, H. (2001) Anti-oppressive practice in the supervisory relationship. In M. Carroll and M. Tholstrup (eds), *Integrative Approaches to Supervision*. London: Jessica Kingsley.

Dhillon-Stevens, H. (2004a) *Healing Inside and Out: An Examination of Dialogic Encounters in the Area of Anti-Oppressive Practice in Counselling and Psychotherapy*. Doctorate in Psychotherapy by Professional Studies, Middlesex University.

Dhillon-Stevens, H. (2004b) Personal and professional integration of anti-oppressive practice and the multiple oppression model in psychotherapeutic education. *United Kingdom Association for Psychotherapy Integration (UKAPI) Journal*, 2: 47–62.

Dhillon-Stevens, H. (2011) Issues for psychological therapists from black and minority ethnic groups. In C. Lago (ed.), *Transcultural Counselling and Psychotherapy: Bridging the Divide*. Maidenhead: Open University.

Dominelli, L. (1997) *Anti-Racist Social Work* (2nd edn). London: Macmillan.

Freire, P. (1990) *Pedagogy of the Oppressed*. New York: Continuum.

Evans, K. and Gilbert, M. (2005) *An Introduction to Integrative Psychotherapy*. Hampshire: Palgrave Macmillan.

Helms, J.E. (1984) Toward an explanation of the influence of race in the counselling process: a black–white model. *The Counselling Psychologist*, 12: 153–65.

Helms, J.E. (ed.) (1990) *Black and White Racial Identity: Theory, Research and Practice*. Westport, CT: Greenwood.

Helms, J.E. (1995) An update of Helms' white and people of colour racial identity models. In J.G. Ponterotto, J.M. Casas, L.A. Suzuki and C.M. Alexander (eds), *Handbook of Multicultural Counselling*. Thousand Oaks, CA: Sage.

Kagan, N. (1984) Interpersonal process recall: basic methods and recent research. In D. Larson (ed.), *Teaching Psychological Skills: Models for Giving Psychology Away*. Monterey: Brooks/Cole.

Kareem, J. and Littlewood, R. (1992) *Inter-cultural Therapy*. Oxford: Blackwell.

Lorde, A. (1984) *Sister Outsider: Essays and Speeches*. Freedom, CA: Crossing.

Mann, D. (ed.) (2002) *Love and Hate: Psychoanalytic Perspectives*. London: Brunner-Routledge.

Maxime, J. (1993) The therapeutic importance of racial identity in working with black children who hate. In V. Varma (ed.), *How and Why Children Hate*. London: Jessica Kingsley.

McAvoy, B.R. and Donaldson, L.J. (1990) *Health Care for Asians*. Oxford: Oxford University.

Mckenzie-Magava, I. (2010) *Black Issues in the Therapeutic Process*. Basingstoke: Palgrave Macmillan.

Perls, F. (1973) *The Gestalt Approach and Eye Witness to Therapy*. Palo Alto, CA: Science and Behavior.

Phillipson, J. (1992) *Practising Equality: Men, Women and Social Work*. London: Central Council for Education and Training in Social Work.

Richards, G. (1997) *Race, Racism and Psychology: Towards a Reflexive History*. London: Routledge.

Ridley, C.R. (1989) Racism in counselling as an adverse behaviour process. In P.B. Pedersen, J.G. Draguns, W.J. Lonner and J.E. Trimble (eds), *Counseling Across Cultures* (3rd edn). Honolulu: University of Hawaii Press.

Rosinski, P. (2003) *Coaching Across Cultures*. London: Intercultural Press.

Ryde, J. (2009) *Being White in the Helping Professions: Developing Effective Intercultural Awareness*. London: Jessica Kingsley.

Samuels, A. (1993) *The Political Psyche*. London: Routledge.

Sills, C., Lapworth, P. and Fish, S. (2001) *Integration in Counselling and Psychotherapy: Developing a Personal Approach*. London: Sage.

Soloman, B. (1976) *Black Empowerment: Social Work in Oppressed Communities*. New York: Columbia University Press.

Stern, D. (1985) *The Interpersonal World of the Infant*. New York: Basic.

Straker, G. (1992) *Faces in the Revolution: The Psychological Effects of Violence on Township Youth*. Johannesburg and Athens, OH: David Philip and Ohio University Press.

Thomas, L. (1992) Working with racism in the consulting room. In J. Kareem and R. Littlewood (eds), *Inter-cultural Therapy*. Oxford: Blackwell.

Tuckwell, G. (2002) *Racial Identity, White Counsellors and Therapists*. Buckingham: Open University Press.

Managing Stress

ROWAN BAYNE

The term 'stress' is generally used to mean feeling overwhelmed, 'It's all too much, I can't cope'; and sometimes to describe having too little to do, or too little that's engaging or fulfilling, 'I'm so bored'. Much has been written about how to manage or cope with stress in both senses, with a recent emphasis on interpreting this body of ideas and evidence more positively and preventively as 'developing resilience' – the capacity to persist in the face of stressful challenges and to recover well from them (e.g. Reivich et al., 2011; Skovholt and Trotter-Mathison, 2011).

How responsible is each of us for our stress levels? 'Managing stress' and 'developing resilience' both emphasize the role of individuals rather than their organizations, social contexts or cultures. However, if for example an organization expects employees to regularly work for 60 hours a week or accepts bullying, then the organization is arguably the main source of stress and can make the most effective interventions. Providing stress management workshops or access to an employee assistance programme (EAP) won't tackle the real problem. On the other hand, we generally do contribute significantly to our own stress, and working on ourselves is therefore helpful. It should also make well-considered and productive political action more likely.

The symptoms or signs of stress are often also possible symptoms of illness (see Sapolsky, 2004 for a review of stress and health). Feeling 'tired all the time', aches, irritability, sleeping difficulties, lack of concentration and 'negative' mood are among the most common symptoms. Another, unfortunately, is ignoring such symptoms. Ideally, each person will notice *early* symptoms of stress and take action to reduce or remove them. The advantages of early action are obvious: less energy wasted and less damage done. Working out the source(s) of stress, internal and external, may also be more feasible.

The rest of this chapter will touch on ideas and findings about (1) sources of stress for therapists and (2) several approaches to developing resilience, first briefly reviewing two which seem particularly effective in their own right – relaxation and exercise – and then reviewing a current major programme. Other strategies that can work well include supervision, music, expressive writing and of course counselling itself (Norcross and Guy, 2007; Skovholt and Trotter-Mathison, 2011).

SOURCES OF STRESS

Several sources of stress for therapists are discussed by Norcross and Guy (2007). Perhaps the most obvious are clients who are suicidal, hostile, etc., as well as clients who end therapy abruptly or who do not turn up. Each therapist is likely to be affected more by some of these ways that clients behave than others. Other sources of stress include emotional depletion, physical isolation, psychic isolation and working conditions. This is a bleak list and may raise the question, 'Why become a therapist?' However, there are strategies for trying to cope with each of these stresses and therapy can be very rewarding too.

A further, underlying source of stress is when therapists conceal from themselves one or more of their motives for being a therapist. The idea here is that it is not so much our motives themselves that are a problem but how aware we are of them and how we express or moderate them. Motives for being a counsellor can include trying to help, trying to avoid loneliness, seeking praise, fear of intimacy, seeking power, and playing various unhelpful roles such as those of victim, persecutor and rescuer (Bayne and Jinks, 2010). Skilful use of supervision, and reflection during and after therapy sessions, are probably the most effective safeguards.

It is also worth mentioning some more apparently mundane factors which can contribute to stress. Sleeping badly, eating certain foods (including, unfortunately, chocolate and other sources of sugar), and going without food for more than a few hours, can all be sources as well as symptoms of stress. It may be helpful to consider such factors the next time you or a client are trying to understand and cope with stress.

DEVELOPING RESILIENCE

There is a substantial body of research on stress and resilience. However, much of the time we are not yet justified in saying, 'This technique has been shown to be the most likely to be effective with this kind of problem and for someone with these characteristics.' Rather, it is a matter of discussing options, perhaps modifying one or more of them, and then undertaking individual experimentation and follow-up. Lapses are quite likely and best treated with compassion (Leary et al., 2007).

However, there can of course be deeper, motivational problems. Why does X, who knows all the arguments, continue to overwork and ignore her feelings of futility and emptiness? Why does Y, who knows all the arguments and wants to eat more healthily and exercise, do quite well for a few days and then, as he sees it, fail again? The crucial factors here are the wish to change (or not) and the obstacles if we do wish to change. We have the right, for example, to work much longer hours than most people, smoke, and not exercise, though some of the writing on stress seems to assume otherwise and has a moralizing, patronizing tone. Conversely, when someone does want to exercise more, say, and gets frustrated and demoralized with their attempts, therapists can draw on theories of change and motivation.

Relaxation

The strategy of physical relaxation illustrates some of the points above well. Generally it has a positive and cumulative effect, but for some clients, at least

at a particular time in their lives, it may actually add to stress. For example, someone may try too hard to relax or may be afraid of losing control of certain images or emotions. Relaxation can also be boring and therefore stressful. The client and the therapist can then try either shaping the strategy accordingly, or another strategy, or a combination, for example several very brief sessions rather than the more standard two 10-minute sessions per day; or meditation, mindfulness or visualization as possible ways of relaxing mentally; and so on (see Rosenthal, 1993 for a particularly lively, open-minded and empirical discussion of a wide range of relaxation techniques, including guided imagery, pets, etc.).

Exercise

Exercise is another strategy which is particularly effective (Taylor, 2009). Some general principles are to become more active gradually and comfortably in ways that you enjoy and to have rest days. A few years ago, the government's recommended minimum amount of exercise was being slightly out of breath for 30 minutes most days, but the 2008 British Association of Sport and Exercise Sciences (Bases) guideline is 'vigorous exercise' for several minutes two or three times a week, with 'vigorous' defined as making it difficult to speak in sentences. Much more demanding! However, although the evidence for the benefits of vigorous exercise for health and reducing stress is strong, some people thrive with very little exercise.

RESILIENCE TRAINING

Several programmes for resilience training have been developed and evaluated, e.g. the Penn Resilience Program, which is for teachers and has been shown to reduce anxiety and depression in their students. Reivich et al. (2011) drew on this programme and on positive psychology and CBT for their response to a request from the American army for help with record rates of suicide, depression, PTSD and divorce in their soldiers. The resulting resilience training programme will be experienced by over a million soldiers, their families and the army's civilian workforce over the next decade or so (i.e. up to about 2020) and, if the outcomes are sufficiently positive, could be used widely in the general population too.

Many of the ideas, strategies and techniques in the programme will be familiar to some or all counsellors, e.g. self-awareness, empathy, thinking traps, 'icebergs' (deeply held and undermining beliefs such as 'asking for help shows weakness'), energy management and assertiveness skills. Others may be less familiar, at least in their latest forms, e.g. identifying character strengths in self and others, 'active constructive responding' (which sounds deceptively like empathy but is not) and 'cultivating gratitude'.

The programme emphasizes prevention and positive psychology. It seemed to me *not* to be relentlessly and one-sidedly positive in the way some contributions to this area are; for example, it does seem to recognize the value and inevitability of 'negative emotions'. Considering what soldiers experience in wartime, and that their trainers are drill sergeants (the programme is initially being run to train the trainers), this is probably not surprising. However, its ideas, philosophy and tone do strike an optimistic note, and they reframe ideas about managing stress.

REFERENCES

Bayne, R. and Jinks, G. (2010) *How to Survive Counsellor Training: An A–Z Guide*. Basingstoke: Palgrave Macmillan.

Leary, M.R., Tate, E.B., Adams, C.E., Allen, A.B. and Hancock, J. (2007) Self-comparison and reactions to unpleasant self-relevant events: the implications of treating oneself unkindly. *Journal of Personality and Social Psychology*, 92: 887–904.

Norcross, J.C. and Guy, J.D. (2007) *Leaving It at the Office: A Guide to Psychotherapists' Self-Care*. London: Guilford.

Reivich, K.J., Seligman, M.E.P. and McBride, S. (2011) Master resilience training in the US army. *American Psychologist*, 66 (1): 25–34.

Rosenthal, T. (1993) To soothe the savage breast. *Behaviour Research and Therapy*, 31 (5): 439–62.

Sapolsky, R. (2004) *Why Zebras Don't Get Ulcers* (3rd edn). New York: Holt.

Skovholt, T. and Trotter-Mathison, M. (2011) *The Resilient Practitioner: Burnout Prevention and Self-Care Strategies for Counselors, Therapists, Teachers, and Health Professionals* (2nd edn). London: Routledge.

Taylor, S.E. (2009) *Health Psychology* (7th edn). San-Francisco: Jossey-Bass.

Counselling and Psychotherapy with Students

ANDREW REEVES

DEFINITIONS

The purpose of this chapter is to explore the form and nature of counselling and psychotherapy within education. This statement immediately raises a number of important issues about definition. For the purposes of this chapter, education refers to post primary and secondary education (ages 5–16 years), i.e. tertiary education in further or higher educational settings such as colleges and universities. While there is growing research evidence for the efficacy of counselling in schools (Cooper, 2009), many of the issues and challenges for the practitioner will be different across these two settings.

The differences between counselling and psychotherapy, if any, have been discussed elsewhere in this book. Certainly, the activities of counselling and psychotherapy both take place within further and higher education settings. However, historically and currently, the provision of therapy within education is usually referred to generically as counselling. Colleges and universities typically offer their students a counselling service (or increasingly a wellbeing and counselling service, or a variant thereof), encompassing a range of therapeutic activity.

A HISTORICAL OVERVIEW

Bell notes the difficulty in identifying the point at which student counselling developed, stating that, 'searching for the source of student counselling is a little like searching for the source of a river with many tributaries' (1996: 1). However, Bell (2006: 555) suggested three main influences on the formation of the Association for Student Counselling (ASC: later the Association for University and College Counsellors, AUCC):

- the work of psychodynamic/psychoanalytic counsellors such as Mary Swainson, whose work in education helped develop the service at the University of Leicester
- changes in North America with the development of person-centred counselling and the provision of counselling in US colleges and universities
- the work of specific individuals in the UK (e.g. Nick Malleson).

The early professional standards developed by the ASC helped inform the early work of the then British Association for Counselling (now BACP). As a division of BACP, AUCC has always retained its own strong identity, taking responsibility for the development of counselling in student settings, including the publication of its own guidance on standards (Lawton et al., 2010).

THE INSTITUTIONAL SETTING

Like students themselves, there is no such thing as a 'typical' education institution. Broadly speaking, in the UK such institutions can be divided into two categories: further education and higher education. Further education traditionally has offered non-graduate programmes, including A levels and a range of diplomas, while higher education has offered graduate and postgraduate programmes. These areas of demarcation are no longer as clear, with both settings offering a range of educational opportunities that sometimes overlap.

Further education settings have traditionally attracted 16- to 18-year-olds looking for an alternative to a school setting to complete their non-graduate education (although again this demographic is changing). As such, counsellors and psychotherapists in these institutions have to be familiar with safeguarding (child protection) procedures relating to their clients, and engage in the ethical and moral quagmire that is capacity, consent and confidentiality. Generally, students in higher education settings are 18 years or over, and therefore in the UK at least are not subject to the law determining the safeguarding of children (other than where concerns regarding the wellbeing of a child are reported). While there is no statutory requirement in the UK to report child protection concerns, the majority of counsellors and psychotherapists, through conscience or institutional policy requirement, would do so. General legislative requirements around mental health and capacity apply universally, and therefore all counsellors and psychotherapists would need a working knowledge of how the law informs and influences their practice.

STUDENT SUPPORT NETWORKS

The nature and form of student support services within education institutions will be dependent on the available funding and the culture and size of the institution, for example. Smaller colleges may have one 'welfare officer', who is additionally trained to offer some limited counselling. Larger institutions may have a number of bigger teams delivering specific advice or support around particular problems or issues, for example, accommodation, finance, advice for international students.

In addition to counselling services, some larger institutions employ allied staff, such as clinical psychologists or sessional psychiatrists, to assess students with more complex mental health problems. Such professionals might offer consultative advice and support to the counselling service, or carry their own caseload of people requiring particular types of intervention, e.g. eating disorders.

The task of any counselling service is to understand the nature of the institution it is serving: the culture of learning; the profile of other staff, e.g. academics, support staff, administrative staff; the profile of students, e.g. age, culture, diversity; the community in which it is located; the socio-economic climate of the area; competitor institutions; and so on. By understanding these issues, the counselling service will be well placed to develop a service that is a 'best match' for the institution and the clients it supports, as well as increasing the potential for supporting the institution in ways beyond the delivery of individual or group work, e.g. consultative support to staff, delivery of training, etc. (May, 1999). It will also be able to develop policies and procedures, e.g. around referral, assessment and confidentiality, that appropriately complement other available services, avoiding duplication.

COUNSELLING AND PSYCHOTHERAPY IN EDUCATION SETTINGS

Many services in smaller institutions are staffed by 'lone counsellors', i.e. where there is only one counsellor employed to deliver counselling. In larger institutions the counselling team may be much larger, often constituted by a mix of full-time and part-time counsellors and psychotherapists. Often working in a dedicated counselling service, counsellors and psychotherapists may also be situated in a larger, generic student services team. I shall discuss later the particular challenges faced when working in a more generic team.

Bell (1996) noted that the working orientation of counsellors in education settings tended to divide between psychodynamic and person centred. Many years on this is still probably the case. However, the resurgence of other models over the last decade in the UK, such as cognitive-behavioural therapy (CBT), solution-focused therapy or cognitive analytic therapy (CAT), is now reflected in education counselling services. The majority of services that employ a number of counsellors now have the capacity to offer a variety of interventions, which might additionally include transactional analysis (TA), gestalt, etc.

Because of this eclectic mix, training placements in education counselling services tend to be in high demand. They have the potential to offer the trainee counsellor or psychotherapist with a rich and diverse training experience, working with male and female clients with diverse backgrounds and presenting issues. Additionally, a proportion of qualified practitioners in such settings are also educators, familiar with current thinking and research. Bell (2006: 559), citing Butcher et al. (1998), identified the following areas of competence for student counsellors:

- general management
- information management
- information giving

- facilitating self-help groups
- advising
- liaison with, and giving feedback to, providers
- teaching and training
- advocacy
- supporting other key pastoral workers in the institution.

I would add: supporting and advising parents; crisis response; consultative support regarding individual or institutional dynamics; supervision; writing; and research.

A PROFILE OF CLIENT WORK

My own myths about student counselling were dispelled quickly after my move from a secondary care psychiatric service into a higher education counselling service. Coming from mental health crisis work with people with severe and enduring mental health problems, I held a belief that student counselling was probably more concerned with late assignments and homesickness. My first client in higher education, an 18-year-old medical student with an eating disorder who was additionally self-harming, helped refocus my attention. While, very occasionally, clients will present with late assignments and homesickness, they are the exception rather than the rule.

It is difficult to clearly define a 'typical' client who presents to a student counselling service. The presenting issues are so diverse, the stories so different, that each individual needs careful assessment. Most common perhaps are students who present with depression and anxiety. However, other presentations might include:

- eating disorders
- low self-esteem and low self-confidence
- trauma
- abuse
- body dysmorphia
- other mental health problems, e.g. bipolar affective disorder, other mood disorders
- panic attacks
- obsessive compulsive disorder (OCD)
- early onset psychosis
- attachment issues
- family breakdown
- relationship problems
- pregnancy and termination
- sexual problems
- sexuality and identity
- self-harm
- suicide potential

- bereavement
- procrastination and academic issues.

Alongside the variety of presenting issues will be the differences in demographic: male and females (although female students are more regularly seen); a range of ages (there is no longer a 'typical' school leaver undergraduate, with many people returning to education later on in life, or studying at postgraduate levels); diversity around culture (many international students choose to study in the UK); and diversity around sexuality, disability, etc.

The challenge for a counsellor or psychotherapist therefore in the education setting is competency and flexibility in thinking when responding appropriately to such different presentations. For example, in a drop-in service (often available in education settings, where students can attend for short sessions without appointment), a practitioner might offer techniques and support around procrastination to one student; then support another following a sexual assault; and then see a student with deteriorating mental health or possible early onset psychosis. The Royal College of Psychiatrists' report into student mental health concluded that, 'University counselling services are, in effect, the primary mental health care option for many students' (2003: 8).

ETHICAL AND PROFESSIONAL CHALLENGES

Assessment

The demand for a timely assessment of a client's needs is a particular problem in education settings where the population is much more transient than the 'static' population found in primary or secondary care services, for example. In HE settings, students may only be in the area for a number of weeks, before often returning home some distance away for extended periods. A vulnerable or distressed client self-referring to a counselling service midway through term may only be available for five or six more weeks. The problem becomes more acute towards the end of an academic year in May or June, when students who have presented at risk may be leaving the area permanently, and in the meantime are facing end-of-year examinations. The imperative to see clients quickly then transcends targets, and is driven more by urgency of time and availability.

The majority of counselling services assess students in a first-appointment face-to-face interview before deciding with the student the best form of support. Such assessments are often supplemented by the use of self-report assessment or benchmarking questionnaires, e.g. the Clinical Outcomes in Routine Evaluation (CORE) tool, widely used in the UK (Barkham et al., 2006). More specifically, such tools may be used to help determine levels of priority for assessment, particularly around risk. A fuller discussion around the factors that might inform a therapeutic assessment can be found in Reeves (2008).

Working Briefly

Working briefly, e.g. to a time-limited model of eight sessions or fewer, is a requirement of many agencies managing high demands for counselling. For many counsellors and psychotherapists, working briefly is not an imposition but instead is a preferred way of working. Many counselling services within education settings offer brief contracts for therapy for several reasons, including: management of high demand for counselling; availability of students for counselling within the context of academic terms/semesters; high numbers of part-time staff employed within counselling services; and the fact that many students, regardless of age, opt into counselling for help with a specific problem, or at a time of transition or change as well as personal and professional development.

Counsellors and psychotherapists can often maintain a small caseload of longer-term work (because most counselling is offered briefly), but increasingly services are opting for a brief model. These models vary, ranging from assessment plus eight to 10 sessions, through to some single-session or dual-session models. Many services see their role as triage: assessing needs, meeting them where appropriate and possible, but typically referring on to other internal or community support services.

Confidentiality

Traditionally counsellors and psychotherapists have agreed a very exclusive contract of confidentiality with their clients, limited only by risk to self and others, together with statutory limitations in the UK, e.g. terrorism, notes subpoenaed in court hearings. As counsellors and psychotherapists have found themselves increasingly working in multidisciplinary settings, e.g. in health-care settings, the agreements made around confidentiality have evolved. The challenge for practitioners working in education settings is achieving the correct balance of confidentiality: where the client's autonomy and privacy are respected, but where a wider student support system can also be taken into account.

The traditional boundaries to confidentiality have additionally been challenged by the practicalities of counselling in busy education settings. For example, many counselling services are now located in generic student services buildings, as opposed to dedicated or discrete venues. Clients cannot necessarily expect anonymity when accessing counselling alongside accommodation or finance advice, for example. The challenge therefore for student counsellors is to fine tune confidentiality agreements so that the therapeutic relationship and the dignity of the client are respected, but not in a way that leaves the client, counsellor or counselling isolated.

Fitness to Practise/study

Following the case of Harold Shipman, a UK GP convicted of murdering hundreds of his own patients, attention has been given to the fitness to practise of students studying for health-care degrees, e.g. medicine, nursing, etc. Educators are now tasked with the responsibility of determining the fitness of any given student to undertake professional training, and to determine whether they are fit to practise. This is crucial given that the majority of health-care students will undertake a practice placement during their study.

The pressures of training and the demands of practice will bring many such students to counselling services. There is often a tension for counsellors and psychotherapists in working with such students between the confidentiality of counselling – respecting the individual student's right to explore their mental health distress in the privacy of therapy – and the institution's duty of care in determining fitness to practise.

Aligned with fitness to practise are concerns around fitness to study. All students have the potential to experience at some point in their studies a crisis or deterioration in their mental health that significantly impairs their capacity to study effectively. For most students these impairments may be short term and transient, but for others their capability to study over a longer period can become seriously jeopardized.

In considering the wellbeing of students, and protecting their studies, an institution has a duty to respond to such situations quickly and effectively. In most instances the student will make an informed decision to suspend their studies, perhaps returning the following academic year to recommence or resit a year of their programme. Occasionally however, perhaps when the student has little insight into their difficulties because of an emerging mental health problem, the institution may require the student (if allowed to do so procedurally) to suspend.

Counsellors and psychotherapists are usually very clear that they do not see themselves as having a role in assessing, and therefore determining, an individual student's fitness to study or practise. However, increasingly services or individual counsellors are being approached for their professional opinion. The role of professional organizations and associations, e.g. BACP, is key in offering advice and guidance in such situations. In the UK a division of BACP, the Association for University and College Counsellors (AUCC), mentioned earlier, lead in the area of student counselling. Through their advisory committee, regular updated guidance is offered to services to help in such situations (Lawton et al., 2010).

Dual Roles

Ethical requirements for the provision of counselling and psychotherapy typically warn against the dangers of dual roles, i.e. where a counsellor or psychotherapist has contact with their client in a capacity other than therapy. While colleges and universities can be large institutions, sometimes with many thousands of students, they also have the potential to become surprisingly small communities in which the potential for dual roles is high.

Many counselling services engage with the institution in ways beyond the provision of individual or group therapy. Heads of services or practitioners can often be found on key institutional committees, e.g. student welfare, international students, and therefore meet with the students, or perhaps the staff, to whom they are offering counselling. It is essential therefore that counselling services pay particular attention to how counselling is contracted initially with clients so that, when such a scenario arises, it is not necessarily a shock, and practitioner and client can explore the implications in a way that protects the therapeutic relationship and the autonomy of both the client and the therapist.

Staff Counselling

Although this chapter is specifically considering the work of student counsellors, it is worth briefly mentioning that many counselling services in education settings also offer counselling to members of staff. Sometimes staff services are delivered separately, perhaps in a different building, but often staff are seen in the same building by the same practitioners who are also delivering student counselling. This makes further demands on the counsellor, both in the increase in presenting issues, e.g. bullying, harassment and employment matters, but also in managing the privacy of students and staff alike and in 'holding' different perspectives of the same institution. For example, a counsellor might be seeing a student

of English, but also be seeing an English lecturer. It is important to ensure that when there are overlaps where unethical practice is a potential, e.g. seeing a tutor who is a personal adviser to a student being seen by the same counsellor, these are responded to quickly and effectively, perhaps through reallocation to a different counsellor where possible.

Evaluation

I have already mentioned the CORE benchmarking system. This is widely used across the UK in a variety of counselling and psychotherapy services, including primary and secondary care. Adopted by counsellors (with a university 'spoke' containing education-specific statements), the CORE outcome measure is a popular instrument used by many to facilitate therapy or therapy assessment, but also as a benchmarking tool. Services now have the capability to determine the psychological profile of their clients benchmarked against a national 'clinical' population, and provide a measure of the efficacy of their service.

Given the business model that now permeates the education field in the UK, it is essential that counselling services articulate their worth in a language that policy makers and fund holders in institutions can understand: student retention, numbers, grants, the 'student experience' and so on.

THE FUTURE FOR COUNSELLING AND PSYCHOTHERAPY IN EDUCATION

At the time of writing the UK is in the process of political change. Major changes are proposed for the funding of further and higher education and there is a potential for significant cuts. Not only are counselling services in education settings under threat, but in some instances whole institutions.

The challenge is for counselling services to adapt and change, or face the ongoing threat of extinction. Some education-based counselling services in the UK have closed over recent years. While all services are under threat, counselling and psychotherapy in education remain arguably one of the most vibrant, energetic and imaginative centres of excellence in the UK. While renowned for innovative practice, counselling services in educational settings have to integrate the new 'business model' of education institutions and demonstrate efficacy, efficiency and responsiveness, with the onus of responsibility on counsellors and psychotherapists to show how invaluable they are to students and institutions alike.

CONCLUSIONS

Student counselling is a highly respected division of counselling and psychotherapy in the UK, based within world-leading institutions and contributing to the growing research evidence base for counselling and psychotherapy generally. Responding to a vast array of student demographic and presenting need, counsellors and psychotherapists in student counselling have helped shape and influence counselling provision at a national level. The future is uncertain, however, with services increasingly having to embrace an emerging ideology of educational business, and integrate benchmarking and evaluation, while at the same time retaining and protecting the soul of therapy.

REFERENCES

Barkham, M., Mellor-Clark, J., Connell, J. and Cahill, J. (2006) A CORE approach to practice-based evidence: a brief history of the origins and applications of the CORE-OM and CORE system. *Counselling and Psychotherapy Research*, 6 (1): 3–15.

Bell, E. (1996) *Counselling in Further and Higher Education*. Buckingham: Open University Press.

Bell, E. (2006) Student counselling. In C. Feltham and I. Horton (eds), *The Sage Handbook of Counselling and Psychotherapy* (2nd edn, pp. 554–60). London: Sage.

Butcher, V., Bell, E., Hurst, A. and Mortensen, R. (1998) *New Skills for New Futures: Higher Education Guidance and Counselling Services in the UK*. Cambridge: Careers Research and Advisory Centre.

Cooper, M. (2009) Counselling in UK secondary schools: a comprehensive review of audit and evaluation data. *Counselling and Psychotherapy Research*, 9 (3): 137–50.

Lawton, B., Bradley, A.M., Collins, J., Holt, C. and Kelley, F. (2010) *AUCC Guidelines for University and College Counselling Services*. Lutterworth: BACP.

May, R. (1999) Doing clinical work in a college or university: how does the context matter? In J. Lees and A. Vaspe (eds), *Clinical Counselling and Further and Higher Education*. London: Routledge.

Reeves, A. (2008) Assessment. In W. Dryden and A. Reeves (eds), *Key Issues for Counselling in Action* (2nd edn). London: Sage.

Royal College of Psychiatrists (2003) *The Mental Health of Students in Higher Education*. Council Report CR112. London: RCP.

RECOMMENDED READING

Lawton, B., Bradley, A.M., Collins, J., Holt, C. and Kelley, F. (2010) *AUCC Guidelines for University and College Counselling Services*. Lutterworth: BACP.

Telephone Counselling

MAXINE ROSENFIELD

HISTORY

The use of the telephone for counselling, as distinct from befriending or the incidental use of counselling skills, was almost unheard of until the late 1990s in the UK, which is surprising since more than 90 per cent of the UK population in 1990 had access to a telephone in their place of residence. This figure has not changed. UK government statistics from 2008 still quote 90 per cent of households as having a telephone, with mobile phone ownership at 79 per cent. Across income groups this percentage varies widely, with 61 per cent of households in the lowest-income decile group having a mobile phone compared with 88 per cent in the highest-income decile group (Office for National Statistics, 2010). With such familiarity with phones, it could be expected that people would choose to use the phone for counselling.

Over the past decade in particular, telephone counselling has become an accepted mode of counselling. The 'old-school' objections to telephone counselling, relating to the imagined impossibility of successful counselling when there is a lack of the visible perspective, have been challenged further with the rapid development of e-counselling. E-counselling has been made more accessible by the increase in home computer ownership, which was quoted as 72 per cent in 2008 (Office for National Statistics, 2010). There also remains the option to work by textphone with hearing-impaired clients, which is confidential as long as both parties have access to a private textphone.

For over 40 years there has been an increasing acceptance of the use of telephone helplines for talking about feelings, finding information and seeking advice. The proliferation of helplines in the UK, which between them respond to millions of calls each year, has helped to encourage people to seek support by telephone. There are helplines for almost any social-, health- or welfare-related situation or condition, and for anyone in a crisis who is seeking help or information or who wants to be listened to then and there.

The demand for in-depth work by telephone has come from the public seeking more than any helpline can offer, as well as from counsellors seeking to explore the medium. The telephone offers a versatile counselling medium because, in addition to individual telephone counselling sessions, some counsellors run closed counselling groups by teleconference.

Working as a counsellor by telephone is significantly different from face-to-face work, as this chapter will highlight. It will also consider the standards and ethical considerations that should be taken into account to ensure that clients receive the best possible service from their counsellors and that the counsellors develop high-quality practice.

THEORY OF TELEPHONE COUNSELLING

The key concept of telephone counselling is that appropriately trained counsellors use the telephone to conduct entire therapeutic relationships with clients.

Telephone counselling can have many advantages over face-to-face counselling. The lack of the impact of any visual impressions and assumptions or prejudices that occur when client and counsellor see each other in a formal counselling room, at home or in an office, makes both parties focus on each other's voice tones and words. The anonymity of the medium is liberating for many clients (and counsellors!). The intensity of the interaction, because there is less opportunity for distractions during the session since both parties are focused on words and voice tone alone, further enhances the development of the relationship. This usually enables a deeper therapeutic relationship to become established sooner than occurs in much face-to-face work. The entire process of counselling is generally 'accelerated' so that fewer sessions are indicated for the client to gain insight, awareness, understanding and/or empowerment.

Telephone counselling is an excellent example of an integrative approach to counselling. It can utilise aspects of psychodynamic orientations, person-centred approaches, brief therapeutic interventions and other humanistic methods of working. Cognitive-behavioural techniques may be used alongside interpretive psychotherapeutic disciplines. There is no doubt that transference and counter-transference occur, triggered by language, by subject matter and, perhaps most important of all, by voice tones, pitch and accents. Psycho-education, goal setting and action planning may be as much a part of some sessions as is exploring the emotional aspects of the client's situation. Much effective work by telephone can focus on helping the client to draw on their own strengths-based orientation or on the client's 'self-healing potential'.

The telephone is excellent for crisis intervention and one-off interactions because of its immediacy and the fact that the clients only need say what they want to say, retaining some degree of anonymity or privacy if they wish. Indeed, one of the key reasons why people say they phone telephone helplines is because they are in crisis and want to talk anonymously and confidentially.

When someone contracts for telephone counselling sessions, some of their anonymity and confidentiality goes. As with helpline work, a point of crisis may be the trigger for the person to seek counselling but, unlike calling a helpline, the client is not totally anonymous. The client has to agree a contract for the work (see later) and therefore provide some personal details which they might not reveal if they are calling a helpline for a one-off call. The counselling relationship will last more than one session but may be relatively brief in comparison with face-to-face work; for example, often a block of six sessions is all that is used with a client who has a specific issue or concern to discuss and explore.

Telephone counselling is an excellent way of equalising the power relationship between the counsellor and the client. Both parties have to work with the unknown in ways that face-to-face counselling does not present. This is no bad thing for broadening the horizons of any counsellor. Further, it could be argued that the ultimate power lies with the client, who can choose to hang up at any time.

ACCESSIBILITY AND FINANCIAL CONSIDERATIONS OF TELEPHONE COUNSELLING

Many people can have relatively easy access to a telephone, but for a one-hour counselling session, finding a place that is private, quiet and uninterrupted is more difficult. Public phones are clearly not ideal, so for some people there is a practical deterrent to using telephone counselling. Similarly, mobile phones are not always ideal as they may be neither as confidential nor as reliable in sound quality as regular phone lines. Whilst many helplines are free or offer subsidised call charges, the cost of calls between a private counsellor and a client, on regular phone lines or mobile, can impact on the consideration of both parties to enter into a therapeutic relationship. Technology is, however, coming to the aid of this potential financial constraint. The increasing use of voice over internet protocol (VOIP) enables people to talk at low cost over internet networks, although there may be data limitations for heavy usage. Software such as Skype enables users to make voice calls over the internet. Skype calls are free to other Skype users but calls can be made to both landlines and mobiles for a fee.

If one has access to a phone and a quiet room, telephone counselling makes it unnecessary for the client to have to travel to see a counsellor, which means that the session can take place without the client or counsellor having to be in the same locations for each session. This makes it a very accessible medium for people who travel in their working lives, for example. It also makes counselling more accessible for someone who has limited mobility or limited time.

Illness does not always prevent telephone counselling sessions from taking place, whereas face-to-face sessions might be cancelled. People who are terminally ill or limited in their ability to go out of doors can still receive counselling. Carers who might wish to go out but cannot guarantee to be able to find respite care regularly at a specific time for an appointment can benefit from telephone counselling.

The cost of a regular phone call is likely to be less than the cost in time and travel to go to a counsellor, making telephone work more financially accessible in many cases (see later on contracting). Clients can choose to work by telephone with counsellors who are not geographically accessible to them. This enables people to find a specific counsellor for a specific purpose if they wish. Some counsellors and clients work together when one party is outside their own country.

From the counsellor's perspective, the telephone can be liberating, enabling them to operate from any environment that is quiet and where they are uninterrupted. It may also mean that the counsellor can work with a wider variety of clients at a greater range of times.

For telephone group work, the teleconference can bring together people from all over the UK and include people from overseas, as long as each can be in a quiet, private place. This can lead to groups being created for people who are linked through rarer situations, specific illnesses, age or any other common theme.

CONTRACTING AND ETHICS

Some of the issues to be considered for contracting have already been addressed, such as location and time.

A contract must be agreed at an assessment session, which may be free of charge except for perhaps the cost of the phone call, and can last for up to an hour. The contract should include:

- terms of reference for both parties, outlining the goals or aims of the sessions
- the length of each session, which should be fixed at no longer than an hour and no less than 30 minutes
- the time interval between sessions, ideally a week or two
- the number of sessions before a review: a block of six with a review during the fifth is suggested, and further blocks of four to six sessions can be agreed as desired
- the location, to ensure privacy and no interruptions
- who calls whom and therefore pays if there is any cost for the call
- what is considered a late start or no-show and what happens in these instances
- what type of notes or other means of recording the sessions would be acceptable: if recording is to happen, both parties must give overt consent
- what the client might do to 'leave the room' in a practical sense after the session ends, given there is no travelling which helps the session to 'end' or 'close' psychologically
- methods of payment: how much, when and how it will be received

- what the terms are for the cancellation of a session
- whether or not photographs will be exchanged to provide a visual image (some counsellors prefer not to do this and work instead with the impact of the lack of any visual clues if it is appropriate)
- what would constitute a breach of confidentiality and why
- how confidentiality relates to technological issues for both parties (see later on technology)
- what happens if the client calls between sessions.

Ethical issues include the counsellor explicitly adhering to existing codes of conduct such as those published by BACP. There is also an ethical consideration regarding payment. It is possible for a counsellor to purchase a premium rate tariff telephone line. In this case, the client calling the counsellor pays more than the cost of a regular phone call and the 'profit' could constitute all or part of the counsellor's fee. If this is to be the case, the counsellor must inform the client or the potential client of the likely cost per session in advance. Ethically, it is inappropriate for the counsellor to use this premium rate telephone line for the assessment session. In addition, such a tariff does not permit any discretionary rate for clients.

Mixing face-to-face sessions and telephone sessions is not acceptable for telephone counselling. This is because the mixing of the media will affect the transference issues, power balance and dynamics of the relationship, with visual assumptions or judgements or prejudices changing the phone relationship thereafter. When a counselling relationship is being established, this could have quite an impact on the trust within and the development of the partnership. It might be agreed when contracting that photos could be exchanged, with an awareness that this can bring judgements into being which could impact on the development of the relationship. This could, of course, be addressed during subsequent sessions.

Confidentiality comes into both contracting and ethics. If the client calls the counsellor who operates anything other than a freephone service, the counsellor's phone number will be itemised on the client's telephone bill. This might not always be desirable for the client, and the counsellor cannot prevent this from happening unless the service is provided as a freephone service. Further, the last number dialled out – in this case the client calling the counsellor – can be found by anyone who subsequently uses the phone at the client's location. Clients need to be mindful of this potential breach of their confidentiality and counsellors should make this an explicit part of the contracting session.

TELEPHONE TECHNOLOGY AND THE CONFIDENTIALITY OF THE RELATIONSHIP

Confidentiality is one key factor of which both parties need to be aware with regards to technology. For the client, this includes the itemised telephone bill mentioned above.

If the counsellor is calling the client and the counsellor's number is not permanently barred, they may wish to use the 141 one-off block (number withhold) code. This may not be a concern in the usual course of events, but perhaps the counsellor is calling at a time when the client would not expect the call, and therefore the counsellor wishes to preserve the confidentiality of the relationship from anyone else who might answer the phone. The block will enable the counsellor's number to be anonymous.

There are other technological developments and services available, such as anonymous call reject (ACR), where if either party has their number permanently blocked, in this case the client, and the counsellor has ACR, the client's call will not get through in the first place. It is possible to cancel ACR but it might be more effective and less of a concern if a counsellor simply has a phone number specifically and only for their counselling clients to use. Then the only concern for the client is whether or not they wish to keep the contact confidential from others who can access the landline they use, in which case the client needs to be aware of how their phone stores last numbers dialled and take steps to ensure the counsellor's number is not immediately apparent to anyone looking at those numbers. Other technology options, such as call waiting, should not be used by the counsellor at all, since the tone that comes on the line if another call is trying to get through can be distracting. The implications of these and other technological developments should be fully explored by any counsellor seeking to work by telephone as they may affect the ability of either party to make safe and confidential contact.

TRAINING AND SUPERVISION

One assumption throughout this chapter is that the counsellor should hold at least a full graduate diploma or degree in counselling and have experience of face-to-face counselling practice before they commence telephone work. Currently there is no specific accredited training in the UK solely for telephone counselling, although there is plenty of training for helpline counselling skills. The Telephone Helplines Association, for example, offers a range of training courses suitable for helpline work rather than in-depth telephone counselling work.

Group facilitation requires additional skills for telephone groups and, again, there is no specific training qualification applicable to this at present.

It is not enough to assume that a good face-to-face counsellor will have, or be able to develop, the necessary skills for telephone counselling. There is a worrying trend in trained counsellors or therapists developing a telephone practice without ever receiving qualitative feedback about their voice, style and manner – things that could have been assessed during a telephone counselling training course.

A SKILLS CHECKLIST FOR THE TRAINED COUNSELLOR/THERAPIST STARTING TELEPHONE WORK

- How do you sound?
- Is your accent pronounced, or could it be off-putting to the client group you seek to attract?
- Are you able to work with silence on the phone? Be aware that a silence of a few seconds on the phone often seems like minutes, and the usual counselling/therapeutic interpretations of silence and methods of responding to silence need to be adapted for successful work on the phone.
- Are you confident and skilled at handling distress by phone?
- Are you confident at interrupting the client's flow if needs be because the session is almost over?
- How can you confidently keep the boundaries you adhere to in face-to-face work?

SUPERVISION BY TELEPHONE

This is growing as counsellors seek out supervisors for specific reasons. The issues relating to skills transfer and voice tones are the same as for the client–counsellor relationship, and not all supervisors can or should adapt to the phone. At the very least, a supervisor might ask a fellow supervisor to do an objective assessment for voice tone, manner and style before offering themselves to work this medium.

COUNSELLOR ACCREDITATION

It is possible to include some telephone counselling work as part of the individual counsellor accreditation process of the BACP. However, there are no specific criteria that acknowledge the specialism of the medium, and casework will be presented in the same way as for face-to-face work, which seems to me to negate the impact of the specialism.

CULTURAL ISSUES

Helpline statistics have shown that among some black and minority ethnic (BME) communities there is less use of the phone for support. While there is no reason to doubt this, it is essential not to make any assumptions, and so discussion of the ethnic origin and cultural identity of both client and counsellor should preferably form part of the assessment session.

Prejudice and/or assumptions can form a large part of telephone work based on voice alone, and the counsellor should always discuss their frame of reference with a new client to reduce or, ideally, prevent this.

One example of what happens when this does not take place is linked to accents or dialects. An accent or dialect often sounds more pronounced on the phone than it would do if the person was face to face. If, for example, English is the counsellor's first language and the client has English as a second language, or vice versa, this could inhibit someone from attempting to explore the medium.

CONCLUSION

The telephone is an excellent medium for enabling the client to feel free to talk about anything. It is also an excellent way of broadening the counsellor's horizons. It is one of very few counselling techniques that enable an equalising of power in the client–counsellor relationship. Further, it constantly reminds the counsellor of the skills of listening and *really* hearing.

RECOMMENDED READING

Rosenfield, M. (1997) *Counselling by Telephone*. London: Sage.
Telephone Helplines Association: www.helplines. org.uk

Workplace Counselling

KEVIN FRIERY

BRIEF HISTORY AND DEVELOPMENT OF WORKPLACE COUNSELLING

The history of workplace counselling is very much tied up with the recent history of social development in the UK. From the beginnings of the nineteenth century we can begin to trace a change in the way employees were viewed. From a state of employees being considered merely 'units of production' there developed a realisation that they were human and, as such, required their basic needs to be met in order to support their productivity. Gradually we can trace the introduction of works doctors, nurses and social welfare staff into the workplace. At first, this was piecemeal and most workplaces did not benefit from such largesse. The chocolate manufacturing families of Cadbury and Fry were amongst the first to identify the need for and benefit of a more philanthropic approach to the workforce, and of course the Lever family were hugely influential, but it took decades of social and legal changes to induce a significant number of employers to address the 'welfare' agenda.

Two elements were particularly relevant in this regard. The rise of trade unionism helped to shift the focus from outputs to people and challenged many of the undesirable components of work. This brought about some demonstrable change, and to some extent this is an influence that continues today, albeit in a rather different context. The First World War, however, had a particular significance because it brought so many women into the world of work. Whilst women had always worked, particularly in factories and mills, the war saw the need to recruit a large number of women who had not hitherto considered themselves to be 'workers' and who brought with them some expectations and needs that had not previously been expressed or addressed on such a large scale. Some of the elements that emerged – works social clubs, pensions, welfare officers, canteens, rest rooms – became embedded in the workplace culture for many, particularly in the manufacturing sector, and the concept of 'looking after the workers' became part of an emergent sense of corporate social responsibility.

From the beginning of the twentieth century, we begin to see evidence of people whose role included the social wellbeing of employees, who would help workers deal with domestic, financial, education and other needs. These early precursors of workplace counsellors were not necessarily trained in any recognisable way, but they were seen as having an important part to play in the maintenance of a healthy and productive workforce. Most counselling at work, in those times, did not sit with a dedicated counsellor; rather it was part of the role of a welfare officer, a personnel officer, an occupational health nurse or someone with other roles to fulfil. It was only very slowly that the idea of actually employing or contracting with professional counsellors started to take hold. As it did, we saw the emergence of a more structured approach to the psychological wellbeing of employees. These UK developments were also part of a growing awareness in other countries of the benefits of providing employee support. The employee assistance movement had already grown in the United States, but was often seen as a tool of management, particularly with substance use and misuse. In the UK, more organisations preferred to use their own counsellors and welfare staff – often on self-employed arrangements rather than by employed contract – and the confidentiality of counselling was recognised as a key determinant of a positive outcome.

Cullup (2005) provides an excellent description of the growth of workplace counselling in the UK in the latter part of the twentieth century. She describes how the first workplace counselling skills training in the UK was launched in 1978. From this point forward, the concept of workplace counselling as a professional activity supported by training began to gain ground; whilst neither universal nor standardised, counselling was beginning to be identified as a credible resource in its own right and this in turn led to the development of a clearer professional framework.

KEY CHARACTERISTICS

One of the key factors that distinguishes workplace counselling from other forms is that there is an 'entry ticket', which is that the client is an employee accessing a service that is paid for by his or her employer. It creates a context for the work, even if much of the counselling is about non-work issues. The skill of the workplace counsellor lies partly in an ability to understand this context yet provide effective counselling within a sound ethical framework.

Friery (2006) looked at the reasons why organisations provide counselling and compared these with the issues presented by clients. He identified nine discrete motivations for the provision of a service (along with a number of other outlying factors): these ranged from protection from litigation through to a desire to be an exemplar employer. The top five commissioning reasons were, in descending order:

1   to provide additional support for employees
2   to meet the employer's duty of care
3   to support employees through times of organisational change
4   to help alleviate stress
5   to enhance the employer's welfare package.

For people accessing workplace counselling, however, the presenting issues were entirely different. In descending order, the most frequent presentations were:

1   relationship problems
2   health
3   work/career issues
4   family problems
5   bereavement.

The relevance of this research to the modern workplace counsellor is the realisation that, in providing the service, there are two distinct customers – the employer and the employee – and that effective counselling will understand and acknowledge this.

For almost all counsellors in the UK a core professional training revolves around the counsellor and client in a room together, with a supervisor somewhere in the background; these relationships are relatively straightforward and easily mapped. In workplace counselling the picture is different. The counselling context may include a whole multitude of relationships – often upwards of 12 identifiable stakeholders – and most workplace counsellors develop their skills in managing this complexity by working within it; it is rarely a taught skill.

Workplace counselling services can be structured in a number of ways. According to EAPA (2008), employee assistance providers (EAPs) work with approximately 5000 UK employers, and counselling is normally only a fraction of their activity, but there are other ways in which workplace counselling is provided. Many organisations have a directly employed counselling team, whilst others will contract with individual local counsellors on a case-by-case basis; some employers incorporate workplace counselling into their occupational health provision, and still others will use a mixed model, with some internal resource augmented by additional referral routes. There is an important factor in almost all workplace counselling, in that it is a managed service. Whether in-house or external, the counselling takes place within a managed structure, and this is a quite different experience for the counsellor whose background is as a self-employed independent practitioner. It creates reporting requirements and requires a good appreciation of the boundaries of counselling coupled with a pragmatic approach to appropriate information sharing.

COMPETENCIES OF WORKPLACE COUNSELLORS

The concepts of competency, experience and qualification run throughout workplace counselling. Increasingly in the UK counsellors are expected, if not required, to be BACP accredited, COSCA registered, BPS chartered (as counselling psychologists), UKCP registered or IACP accredited. There are a plethora of other accrediting bodies, but these are considered the mainstream core.

As with NHS counselling, the normal delivery contract is for a maximum of six sessions. Although this can vary, it is the most commonly occurring. For the workplace counsellor, competency in short-term work is critical. To provide ethical, effective counselling within a small number of sessions the counsellor needs to be able to identify a therapeutic purpose, a delivery framework and an end point; without these the counselling risks arriving at the final session with the parties unable to identify whether any real therapeutic work has been undertaken. For many people who are relatively new to the profession, this is a process that can be difficult unless it is well supported by an understanding supervisor and excellent case management – the latter being a function of managed services that is absent in independent practice.

One of the great complications of workplace counselling is that the counsellor may be asked to fulfil a number of roles. Mediation, coaching, mentoring, defusing, critical incident management, conflict resolution and a number of other needs are sometimes directed at the counsellor, who has to determine whether or not it is possible to engage with these activities. What is clear is that they sit outside counselling; they are sometimes related activities that a counsellor may include in a repertoire of professional skills, but counselling remains the core activity of the workplace counsellor who may well decide that any other activities create too many boundary conflicts and may decline to get involved. Kinder et al. (2008) provide an in-depth exploration of the various themes that may emerge in the workplace.

CONFIDENTIALITY

No discussion of workplace counselling can be complete without spending time exploring confidentiality. Nothing in the peculiarities of workplace counselling overrides the ethical framework as described by the appropriate professional bodies – normally taken to mean BACP and EAPA – but there are a number of areas in which the counsellor (and those responsible for managing the service) may be asked to consider the exact limits of confidentiality.

Taking three real examples:

- A line manager rings the counsellor and says she has just come away from a meeting with an employee who says he is having counselling. All the manager wants to know is whether the counsellor can offer a different appointment next week because there is a key meeting and she doesn't want to disadvantage the employee.
- An HR manager rings on a Saturday morning and says that he has received a call from the husband

of an employee whose wife has not returned home since work the previous day. He knows the wife has been distressed so wants to know whether he should call the police or whether the counsellor knows something that might help.
- A client, who is facing dismissal for taking frequent unexplained absences, reveals in counselling that she is being violently abused at home and her absences are a result of her injuries.

These three scenarios highlight some of the demands on confidentiality that can be posed. In a large organisation these are almost daily occurrences, and the ability of the counsellor to maintain the ethical boundaries of the profession can be sorely tested. One of the aspects of workplace counselling that is ever present is the link to absence management. This immediately creates an issue for the counsellor, who needs to be clear about what agenda is being pursued. If the workplace counselling service has been initiated as a tool to support attendance and reduce absence, the employer is likely to expect the counsellor to take some proactive steps in relation to this. Many counsellors, on the other hand, may feel disinclined to have such an agenda imposed and will want to limit the extent to which this impacts on the therapeutic work.

One of the elements of workplace counselling that can vary is the referral route. Often employees can self-refer, but many employers also operate only through a direct referral system involving line manager, human resources or occupational health. In these situations the counsellor needs to be clear, as does the client, about the limits of confidentiality and any reporting pathways. Confidentiality may change according to the referral route or the presenting issue; it is rarely possible to maintain a rigid boundary around everything that a workplace counsellor encounters. One aspect that can bring this into focus is the 'sent' client. In workplace counselling it is not unusual to encounter clients who have been sent for counselling because of some performance concern. In these cases there can be a clear conflict of interest – a variance between the intent of the employer and that of the client. In a recent case, for example, a manager was sent for counselling because of perceived inappropriate behaviour at work; in her eyes she had done nothing wrong, but the employer wanted to be reassured that the behaviour would not recur. The workplace counsellor has a challenge in deciding whether to take the work in the first place – and this might be exacerbated if the employer indicates that the only other option is dismissal – and beyond this the limits of confidentiality must be very explicit to all parties if the work does proceed. Part of the problem is that, as a profession, counselling is quite good at defining confidentiality and boundaries to its practitioners, but service purchasers are not so clear and can be baffled by the insistence on confidentiality.

If there is one key thought that may help the workplace counsellor when struggling with these issues it is this: counselling is a confidential activity; confidentiality and secrecy are not the same thing. Understanding this, and knowing where the counsellor stands with it, help to create a good ethical structure within which good therapy can take place.

EVALUATION

Workplace counselling is a business activity. Organisations fund it because they believe that, ultimately, it is a business benefit; implicit in this is the belief that a workplace counselling service needs to be able to demonstrate its value. The phrase in common currency is 'return on investment' (ROI): a workplace counsellor needs to be able to demonstrate that there has been a return on the investment made by the company. One of the more obvious ways of achieving this is to use a recognised clinical effectiveness measurement; Carroll (1996) described the need for counselling evaluation, and Mellor-Clark et al. (1999) have been instrumental in the development of the CORE (Clinical Outcomes in Routine Evaluation) system (CORE System Group, 1998; and see Chapter 4.11 in this volume), a tool that is widespread throughout services delivering psychological therapies in the UK. There are literally hundreds of evaluation tools, but many employers prefer to use one that can be benchmarked nationally on a large scale, and CORE provides this.

There is a strong movement within counselling to shift the focus from evidence practice towards practice-based evidence. In the workplace setting this can be particularly relevant because it is the effectiveness of individual programmes, individual interventions, that holds more relevance than the straitjacketed delivery of a single model of counselling. Research by Friery (2008) showed that as many as 12 different core modalities of counselling were used in the workplace in one EAP service, with little to choose between them in terms of clinical outcome as measured by CORE. The individual practitioner, working within or outside a managed service, needs to be willing to provide evidence of the efficacy of their particular practice.

TRENDS IN WORKPLACE COUNSELLING

There have been some major changes in the way workplace counselling sits within a wider agenda in the workplace. Government and organisations have developed a clearer understanding of the benefits of counselling as part of a strategy to increase productivity and improve wellbeing – not only in the workplace but as a psychosocial construct. Black (2008) described the importance of addressing wellness in the workplace and this report formed the basis of political policy, augmented by other significant research including the Foresight (2008) report. The focus has shifted from counselling as a remedial activity to a more proactive intervention, aimed at developing a resilient, engaged workforce. Counselling as a strategic tool to improve engagement requires counsellors who understand the factors that influence this, as addressed by Schroeder-Saulnier (2009) from an organisational perspective. In addition, there has been strong political will expressed to reduce the number of people who are classed as 'incapable of work' and to create employment opportunities instead. This will inevitably bring into the workplace a population of people with mental health issues that had previously kept them away from employment, creating a need for appropriate support for individuals and organisations in order to achieve successful integration.

Notwithstanding the desire to improve wellbeing and resilience, there is still evidence of major gaps in service provision. HSCIC (2009) showed that, in any one week, the incidence of common mental disorders stands at 16 per cent of the adult population, with only 15 per cent of these having access to treatment. This working-age population experiences exactly the level of problems for which counselling has a strong evidence base of effectiveness, and it is inevitable that this will lead to a greater demand for access to services.

For employers, whose key role is to fulfil the organisation's aims in either production or service delivery, the importance of engaging with the counselling profession has never been more powerfully highlighted, whilst for counsellors the importance of engaging with employers and employees is clear.

REFERENCES

Black, C. (2008) *Working for a Healthier Tomorrow: Review of the Health of Britain's Working Age Population*. London: Stationery Office.

Carroll, M. (1996) *Workplace Counselling*. London: Sage.

CORE System Group (1998) *CORE System (Information Management) Handbook*. Leeds: CORE System Group (www.coreims.co.uk).

Cullup, S. (2005) *Little Acorns*. www.bacp.co.uk/admin/structure/files/doc/3785_acw_history.doc.

EAPA (2008) *Market Research*. www.eapa.org.uk/page--research.html.

Foresight (2008) *Final Project Report: Foresight Mental Capital and Wellbeing Project*. London: Government Office for Science.

HSCIC (2009) *Adult Psychiatric Morbidity in England, 2007*. London: NHS Information Centre.

Friery, K. (2006) Workplace counselling: who is the consumer? *Counselling at Work*, Autumn: 24–6. Rugby: BACP.

Friery, K. (2008) *State of the Workforce*. London: Right Management.

Kinder, A., Hughes, R. and Cooper, C.L. (2008) *Employee Well-being Support: A Workplace Resource*. Chichester: Wiley.

Mellor-Clark, J., Barkham, M., Connell, J. and Evans, C. (1999) Practice-based evidence and the need for a standardised evaluation system: informing the design of the CORE systems. *European Journal of Psychotherapy, Counselling and Health*, 2: 357–74.

Schroeder-Saulnier, D. (2009) *Employee Engagement: Leading the Way to an Engagement Culture*. Philadelphia: Right Management.

Counselling Young People

KATHRYN GELDARD AND DAVID GELDARD

This chapter describes the principles and practices required for counselling young people who are in the adolescent stage of their lives. These principles and practices are in many ways different from those required for counselling either children or adults. In order to help young people effectively we need to use a counselling approach which is specifically designed to fit comfortably with their developmental stage and to take account of the typical communication processes used by young people. Doing this enables the counsellor to join appropriately with the young person to achieve a collaborative working relationship.

THE ADOLESCENT STAGE OF DEVELOPMENT

Young people experience many challenges during adolescence including biological, cognitive, psychological, social, moral and spiritual challenges. Two major challenges of particular importance to consider when counselling a young person are the need for them to individuate and establish a personal identity, and the struggle many young people have in re-evaluating their constructs about their world.

Individuation and the Establishment of a Personal Identity

Whereas a child is primarily joined with parents and family, in the stage of adolescence it is appropriate for a young person to begin a process where they progressively develop a level of relative independence from family relationships and an increased capacity to assume a functional role as a member of adult society (Nelson and Nelson, 2010). Young people are in the process of establishing a personal identity and the struggle for individuation will have implications socially. Thus, their process of socialization is based on a balance between individuation together with the formation of personal identity, on the one hand, and integration with society on the other (Fadjukoff and Pulkkinen, 2006). Unless this balance is achieved, there are likely to be personal crises which may result in the need for counselling.

Continual re-evaluation of Constructs

According to Piaget (1948/1966), during the early adolescent stage young people typically move from the limitations of concrete thinking to being able to deal cognitively with ideas, concepts and abstract theories. They are able to become passionately interested in abstract concepts and notions and are therefore able to discern what is real from what is ideal.

When counselling young people it can be useful to take account of constructivist theory which helps explain how we set about trying to make sense of the world in which we live (Fransella et al., 2007). In trying to make sense of the world in which they live, young people use their personal experiences to conceptualize and develop ideas or beliefs about their world. In other words, they form constructs which encapsulate their concepts about the world in which they live. These constructs or personal interpretations of the world will not be fixed, but will be revised and replaced as new information becomes available to the individual concerned. Thus, personal construct theory is based upon the philosophical assumption that all of our present interpretations of the universe are subject to revision or replacement (Kelly, 1955). Each of us behaves like a scientist, formulating hypotheses, using our experiences to test them out, and if necessary revising them (Winter, 2003). Typically this is how young people behave.

The young person is in a stage of development which involves a high level of exploration, so that new, previously unmet experiences challenge the young person to revise and replace inappropriate and/ or inadequate constructs with new ones. As Kelly (1955) pointed out, constructs can be reconstructed at any time and reconstruction usually occurs when constructs are invalidated by experience.

Because young people are continually revising their constructs as they encounter new experiences, a counsellor needs to actively listen to the young person's personal and individual narrative, and explore, understand and respect the constructs on which the narrative is based. Such a process provides an opportunity for the counsellor to select therapeutic strategies and techniques which fit with the young person's personal constructs. The narrative therapy work of Michael White and David Epston (Becvar, 2008) highlights the significance and value of this process when working with young people.

ESTABLISHING AND MAINTAINING A THERAPEUTIC ALLIANCE

It is widely accepted that the outcome of any counselling intervention is determined by the quality of the relationship between the counsellor and client. This is certainly true for young people where the quality of the relationship is critical in influencing outcomes and client satisfaction (Safran and Muran, 2000). For successful outcomes, it is desirable that the counselling relationship should be an authentic person-to-person relationship, be accepting and understanding, and have appropriate levels of warmth and empathy.

Acceptance and understanding are particularly important when counselling young people because sometimes they are inclined to feel judged and criticized, particularly by adults, and tend to be very quick to recognize disapproval. They are unlikely to talk freely if they believe that negative judgements are being made about them. Consequently counsellors need, as far as they are able, to accept and validate the young person's story and constructs without judgement.

There are two important ways in which a counsellor can enhance their opportunity to establish and maintain a positive working relationship with a young person. These are by:

- making use of typical adolescent communication processes
- using a proactive approach.

MAKING USE OF TYPICAL ADOLESCENT COMMUNICATION PROCESSES

Many counsellors find it difficult to join with young people and engage them in a way that enables them to talk freely. This is understandable because there is evidence in the literature to support the notion that young people are generally reluctant to talk to adults about sensitive issues in the first instance (Boldero and Fallon, 1995; Gibson-Cline, 1996). One way to address this problem is to make use of strategies commonly employed by young people when they communicate with each other.

When young people meet with and join with peers at a personal level they usually engage in some of the following behaviours (Seiffge-Krenke et al., 2010)

- They positively connote aspects of the other person's presentation, including appearance, behaviours and adornments or possessions.
- They use direct closed questions to get information.
- They disclose information about themselves and assume that the other person will similarly self-disclose.
- They validate the other person's views, if possible.
- They use praise when relevant.
- They are very direct about what they like and do not like.
- They match and exaggerate the other person's emotional expressions in response to story-telling.

Additionally we have noticed that many young people tend to:

- frequently digress, move away from a topic of interest, and then return to it
- take the lead in a conversation and feel as though they are in control of it
- give and receive advice.

If, as counsellors, we are to engage young people in conversation, we can learn from their communication processes so that we ourselves can make use of these processes when appropriate as described below.

Believing and Accepting the Young Person's Constructs

Generally, but not always, young people will validate each other's points of view. By doing this their conversations become collaborative explorations rather than one-sided and argumentative. Together, they will share their beliefs, attitudes and constructs, examine these together, and quite possibly revise them (Geldard, 2006). Even if we do not agree with a young person's point of view, if we can validate what they are telling us by letting them know that we understand their beliefs, attitudes and constructs, and accept the young person for who they are, then collaboratively we have the opportunity to help them explore, review and revise their constructs. By letting them know that we understand their point of view, even though we may also let them know that we have a different point of view, we show them that they are valued as a person. In this way we can join with them and create a genuine, open and honest relationship, where they can feel safe in exploring their own ideas with us.

Positively Joining in Digressions

A common feature of adolescent conversation is that young people tend to frequently digress from a topic of interest, talk about something else, and then return to the topic. Of course, some adults do the same. However, we believe that, especially for young people, this tendency to digress and then return to the topic of conversation serves some useful purposes.

Because young people are continually revising their constructs, they are often trying to grapple with many differing thoughts and ideas at the same time. By digressing they are able to deal with new thoughts without putting them on hold.

Digression also has a very useful function in that it provides a young person with the opportunity to move away from discussing issues that may be troubling for them. Often after a period during which the conversation has been less intense they may return to talking about the emotionally troubling issues. Rather than shut down the conversation altogether to avoid talking about issues which were distressing for them, digression provides them with some respite.

Similarly, young people are often troubled by extremely powerful emotions as they confront new and challenging experiences. As a consequence, in a counselling situation they may at times worry about getting in touch with strong emotions, or feel overwhelmed by their emotions. At these times they can find it very helpful to have opportunities to move away from the intensity of these emotions by digressing. If they know that they have the opportunity to digress when they want, they are more likely to feel safe in the counselling environment rather than finding it threatening or worrying.

When talking about a serious issue, sometimes a young person will become distracted and temporarily withdraw from the counselling process. They may play with their shoes or jewellery, or look out the window at something that is happening outside. This distraction may serve the same purpose as a digression. It may allow the young person to escape from continuing to talk about an important but very troubling issue. However, we also need to recognize that they may have just lost the energy and desire to continue talking, and consequently have become distracted.

When a young person becomes distracted the counsellor has an opportunity to introduce a digression and by doing so to join more closely with the young person. For example, if the young person starts to play with their shoes, the counsellor might comment on their shoes and ask about them, saying something such as, 'They're colourful; where did you get them?', or, 'I had some shoes rather like those, but mine weren't very comfortable. What are yours like?' Notice that, if the counsellor digresses in this way, the conversation will no longer involve addressing issues, but instead a low-key conversation will develop which will be likely to help the young person relax. Also, the young person is likely to experience a closer connection with the counsellor through this mutual sharing and self-disclosure about something of common interest. Consequently, the climate in the counselling room will change. A friendly and relaxing conversation will take place which will enable the young person to regain energy, and join more effectively with the counsellor. After having such a conversation, it is easy for the counsellor to help the young person return to addressing an important issue. This can be done by using a transitional question such as, 'Earlier we were talking about ... would you like to tell me more about that?'

As counsellors of young people we should not be worried if at times a counselling session becomes an enjoyable chat about irrelevancies. This may help establish a good relationship.

Appropriate Use of Self-disclosure

Most counsellors who work with adults believe that counsellor self-disclosure should either be strictly limited or not occur at all. However, we believe that the situation is quite different when working with young people, and that there are good reasons for deliberately making use of appropriate counsellor self-disclosure.

We believe that appropriate counsellor self-disclosure enables young people to feel more comfortable when self-disclosing to us. When a counsellor shares personal information with a young person the young person is implicitly invited to relate to the counsellor as an equal. They are likely to see the counsellor as a real person who has feelings and experiences which may have some similarity with their own. However, there do need to be some clear limits to counsellor self-disclosure. It is not appropriate or ethical for the counselling process to lead to undesirable closeness with the client and over-involvement by the counsellor.

Generally, counsellor self-disclosure should not involve talking about the counsellor's own past or present problems, unless these are both minor and resolved, and are useful for joining or are directly related to demonstrating a depth of understanding of the young person's situation. For example, if a young person is discussing their response to a recent parental separation and the pain involved in that experience, and if the counsellor has had a similar experience, then disclosure might be appropriate. Through such self-disclosure by the counsellor the grief experience can be normalized and the young person may be encouraged to disclose more information. Such disclosure should only occur if the counsellor's own issues relating to the relevant events have been fully resolved by the counsellor, in counselling for themselves, or in supervision. Otherwise, the counselling session might be inappropriately used to enable the counsellor to work through their own problems. The focus must always be on the young person's problems.

Counsellors need to know, and let their young clients know, that there will inevitably be differences between the client's experiences and responses and their own. This acknowledgement indicates to the young person that full understanding is impossible because two people's experiences will never be identical and provides an opportunity for the young person to talk more fully about their own personal experience. In addition, young people may be tempted to match their own responses inappropriately to those of the counsellor in an attempt to normalize their experience.

Being Direct

Most young people are very direct about what they like and what they don't like. If we are to build a useful counselling relationship with them, they need to see us as real people who are open in our communication with them about who we are.

However, when working with adults, most counsellors are cautious about disclosing information about their values and beliefs. When working with young people it can be very useful to be more direct in this regard. In doing this, we need to be respectful of the young person by letting them know that we accept them fully with their own values and beliefs, even though they may be different from our own.

Young people typically make use of direct closed questions in their conversations with peers. Similarly, in the counselling situation, many young people like to have a direct approach from the counsellor. In contrast adults prefer counsellors to be more circumspect in the questions they ask, giving them more opportunity to reveal only the information they choose.

Matching and Exaggerating

As discussed previously, young people typically match and exaggerate each other's emotional expressions when they are talking to each other about things that have happened to them or others. As counsellors, we can learn from the lively and dynamic ways in which young people communicate. Young people generally put a great deal of energy into conversations with their peers. We can learn from this, and ourselves be energized when we communicate with them.

Use of Praise

Because of their developmental stage, most young people are continually questioning themselves and their achievements. They generally use praise in a natural way when communicating with each other. Similarly, counsellors can usefully endorse a young person's beliefs or behaviour by providing positive feedback when appropriate. Clearly, when we do this we need to be careful to ensure that we are seen to be genuine and not patronizing.

Giving Advice

Typically, when young people are uncertain about what to do, or what decision to make, they will talk to a peer or a number of peers, and will ask for advice (Geldard, 2006). This is something that they would be less likely to do with a parent, because they want to make their own decisions without parental direction. When they ask for advice from a friend of their own age, it is unlikely that either they, or their friend, will expect that they will necessarily take the advice (Geldard, 2006). This is different from parent or adult advice-giving. When adults are asked for advice and give it, they usually have an expectation the advice will be taken and may feel aggrieved if it is not. In contrast, when young people seek advice from peers they are usually just trying to get another point of view, and to draw on another person's experience. Advice-giving then, for young people, involves the sharing of ideas about possible solutions rather than an injunction that these solutions should be adopted.

Most counsellors who work with adults try to avoid giving advice and instead try to empower their clients to find their own solutions. It is obvious that this is also a good policy with young people, as they don't want to be told what they should do. However, it is well documented that young people generally have expectations that counsellors will give advice (Gibson-Cline, 1996). Additionally, they have expectations that counsellors have experience and knowledge which they do not have themselves.

Counsellors working with young people can contribute to the formation of useful constructs by sharing information with them which has been gained through either education or life experience. When a young person asks for advice, we believe that, rather than declining to give it, it is better to join with the young person and offer them an invitation to explore their situation with us, so that together we might come up with a possible solution. By doing this, the young person is invited to join in a collaborative process in which there is a mutual sharing of ideas and information. Solutions can be explored, together with their consequences.

USING A PROACTIVE APPROACH

When compared with counselling children or adults, counselling young people needs to be more flexible and freer in structure. The counselling process will generally not be as well defined and predictable. Young people are less likely to stay engaged in a counselling process which follows sequentially through the stages of therapy over time. They may have difficulty in articulating their difficulties and may only be able to focus on, and describe, discrete parts of their world which tend to be disconnected from the broader picture. The counselling process therefore needs to take account of this, with counsellors using strategies which will enable young people to draw their ideas and beliefs together to form constructs which will help them to make sense of their world.

The counselling process needs to allow young people to explore in ways which are similar to those which they use generally. Therefore, the counsellor

might expect that the young person may move from subject to subject and wish to explore seemingly disconnected parts of their world and experiences. This requires the counsellor to be proactively spontaneous, creative, flexible and opportunistic, while continually attending to the counselling relationship.

Being proactive involves taking responsibility for responding to the young person by intentionally introducing new direction and strategies into the counselling process when appropriate.

Just as with peer conversations between young people, an effective and comfortable counselling conversation with a young person involves alternating the direction of the conversation between the two participants. However, at all times, it is essential to try to ensure that the young person understands that they have *choice* about what they say and do, so that they do not feel inappropriately controlled during those times when the counsellor takes the initiative by intentionally focusing the process.

It is preferable that the relationship between a young person and counsellor should not be predominantly intense or serious. It should be balanced, so that although serious and distressing matters may be discussed, there can additionally be some pleasant times involving friendly conversation and/or the use of humour. It is interesting to note that humour has been found to be a useful treatment technique when working with young people (Radomska, 2007; Yuan et al., 2008).

Figure 7.23.1 illustrates diagrammatically a proactive process for counselling young people. The central feature of the counselling process involves having regard to the therapeutic alliance by carrying out the primary counselling functions of attending to the relationship, and collaboratively assessing and addressing the issues presented. While continually focusing on the primary counselling functions the counsellor is able to proactively introduce commonly used counselling skills as described in Geldard and Geldard (2005; 2009) and can whenever appropriate parallel typical adolescent communication processes as described previously. Additionally, the counsellor may choose to introduce, at appropriate times, a symbolic, creative, behavioural, or psycho-educational strategy. These strategies are briefly discussed below and are described in detail in Geldard and Geldard (2010).

Symbolic, Creative, Behavioural and Psycho-Educational Strategies

Symbolic strategies include the use of metaphor, ritual, symbols, sand tray and miniature animals. These strategies can be particularly useful in

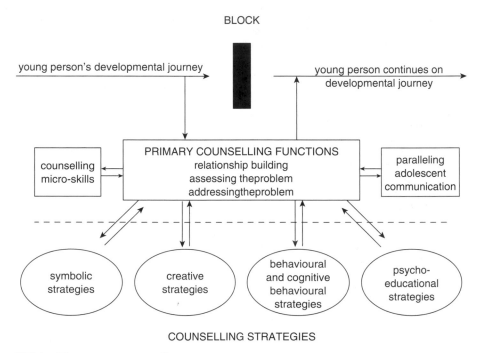

Figure 7.23.1   *The proactive counselling process*

enabling a young person to talk about sensitive issues in a non-threatening way. Additionally, they may enable a young person to get more fully in touch with their experience and as a consequence to re-evaluate their constructs in a useful way. Creative strategies involve the use of art, role-play, journals, relaxation, imagination and dream work. These strategies appeal to many young people who like to use artistic methods to express themselves. Behavioural strategies are particularly useful for addressing issues involving self-regulation, unhelpful beliefs, anger management, assertiveness training, lifestyle goals and decision-making. Psychoeducational strategies can be used to enable the young person to share information, explain relationships and/or behaviour, and examine ways to change behaviour.

During a counselling session, one or more strategies may be utilized. The counsellor can be proactive in selecting and introducing relevant strategies at particular times. Being proactive involves taking responsibility for orchestrating the counselling process to fulfil the primary counselling functions, while allowing the young person freedom within the process to explore and resolve issues. Counselling strategies are selected in response to the young person's cognitive, emotional, somatic, verbal and non-verbal behaviours and the issues being discussed.

The introduction of a particular strategy may significantly influence the young person's level of interest and engagement in the counselling process.

Making Each Session Complete in Itself

Making each counselling session complete in itself is particularly important for young people. This is because many young people will come to see a counsellor at a time of crisis but will not believe it is helpful to continue once the crisis is over. Young people often return when a new crisis occurs, particularly if they have had a positive experience of counselling on the first occasion. When counselling young people it is useful to remember that because of their developmental stage in life they may be unreliable with regard to keeping appointments. Consequently, it can be useful to assume that each appointment with a young person may be the final appointment. Achieving a level of completion in single-session therapy (SST) is a useful goal when counselling young people. In a study examining the benefits of planned SST for child and adolescent clients with mental health problems, Perkins and Scarlett (2008) demonstrated that the short-term benefits of SST, for children and adolescents with a range of mental health problems, were maintained over an 18-month period. However, some clients benefited from booster sessions. Overall, SST appears to be an empirically supported, cost effective and beneficial form of therapy for children and adolescents with mental health problems.

It is important to note here that the counsellor is sometimes the first to notice and act as gatekeeper in relation to onset of mental health problems in adolescence.

REFERENCES

Becvar, D.S. (ed.) (2008) The legacy of Michael White. *Contemporary Family Therapy: An International Journal*, 30 (3): 139–40.

Boldero, J. and Fallon, B. (1995) Adolescent help-seeking: what do they get help for and from whom? *Journal of Adolescence*, 18: 193–209.

Fadjukoff, P. and Pulkkinen, L. (2006) Identity formation, personal control over development, and well-being. In Lea Pulkkinen, Jaakko Kaprio and Richard Rose (eds), *Socioemotional Development and Health from Adolescence to Adulthood* (pp. 265–85). New York: Cambridge University Press.

Fransella, F., Dalton, P., Weselby, G. and Dryden, W. (2007) Personal construct therapy. In W. Dryden (ed.), *Handbook of Individual Therapy* (5th edn, pp. 173–94). Thousand Oaks, CA: Sage.

Geldard, K. (2006) *Adolescent Peer Counselling*. Doctoral dissertation, Queensland University of Technology, Brisbane, Australia.

Geldard, K. and Geldard, D. (2005) *Practical Counselling Skills: An Integrative Approach*. Basingstoke: Palgrave Macmillan.

Geldard, K. and Geldard, D. (2009) *Basic Personal Counselling: A Training Manual for Counsellors* (6th edn). Frenchs Forest: Pearson Education Australia.

Geldard, K. and Geldard, D. (2010) *Counselling Adolescents: The Proactive Approach for Young People* (3rd edn). London: Sage.

Gibson-Cline, J. (1996) *Adolescents: From Crisis to Coping. A Thirteen Nation Study*. Oxford: Butterworth-Heinemann.

Kelly, G.A. (1955) *The Psychology of Personal Constructs*. New York: Norton.

Nelson, T. and Nelson, J.M. (2010) Evidence-based practice and the culture of adolescence. *Professional Psychology: Research and Practice*, 41 (4): 305–11.

Perkins, R. and Scarlett, G. (2008) The effectiveness of single session therapy in child and adolescent mental health. Part 2: An 18-month follow-up study. *Psychology and Psychotherapy: Theory, Research and Practice*, 81 (2): 143–56.

Piaget, J. (1948/1966) *Psychology of Intelligence*. New York: Harcourt.

Radomska, A. (2007) Understanding and appreciating humour in late childhood and adolescence. *Polish Psychological Bulletin*, 38 (4): 189–97.

Safran, D.J. and Muran, J.C. (2000) *Negotiating the Therapeutic Alliance: A Relational Treatment Guide*. New York: Guilford.

Seiffge-Krenke, I., Kiuru, N. and Nurmi, J. (2010) Adolescents as 'producers of their own development': correlates and consequences of the importance and attainment of developmental tasks. *European Journal of Developmental Psychology*, 7 (4): 479–510.

Winter, D.A. (2003) The constructivist paradigm. In R. Woolfe and W. Dryden (eds), *Handbook of Counselling Psychology* (2nd edn, pp. 241–59). London: Sage.

Yuan, L., Zhang, J. and Chen, M. (2008) Moderating role of sense of humor to the relationship between stressful events and mental health. *Chinese Journal of Clinical Psychology*, 16 (6): 576–8.

Postscript: Summary and Future Forecasting

COLIN FELTHAM AND IAN HORTON

Counselling and psychotherapy have gained in acceptance by the general public, in spite of initial cultural resistances and undermining by critics (see, for example, Furedi, 2004). This is not to say that the public understands the ongoing plethora of different therapeutic models and the meaning of different professional titles in the field. In 2004, the Future Foundation found somewhat surprisingly – in a telephone survey of 1008 people – that an estimated 21 per cent of people in the UK had now had counselling or psychotherapy. Previous estimates had been around 5 per cent at most. The BACP (2004) summarized this and similar trends towards greater acceptance:

- 83 per cent of British adults have had or would consider having counselling or psychotherapy.
- 72 per cent believed that people would be happier if they talked more about their problems to a counsellor or psychotherapist.
- Over 90 per cent consistently agreed that anyone can suffer from depression.
- 63 per cent agreed that they know someone who could benefit from counselling and psychotherapy.
- 45 per cent of employees expressed a desire for the opportunity to avail themselves of a confidential counselling service provided by their employer.

Counselling remains strong but certain factors in recent years have had a significant impact. Economic circumstances have caused a few courses to close or contract (yet foundation degrees in counselling have grown). The advent of IAPTs, along with the promotional work of the health economist Richard Layard, has raised the profile of CBT and to some extent threatened employment for counselling, although this may be changing. To some extent the IAPT and other health service procedures have increased the bureaucratic burden on counsellors. Psychotherapy continues to maintain a separate identity and to flourish and be modified in somewhat different ways, but it is also inevitably affected by wider trends. In 2004, a sharp tension appeared between the British Psychoanalytical Society and the newly formed College of Psychoanalysts, with serious questions raised about the rights to ownership and training in psychoanalysis. Simultaneous expansions and adaptations of mental health nursing, psychiatry, psychoanalysis, clinical psychology and counselling psychology are accompanied by some inevitable misunderstandings and tensions between all these professions. In most respects the mental health professions have not chosen to move forward on the agenda of professional convergence since the challenge issued by James and Palmer (1996).

The professionalization agenda came to an impasse in recent years over various matters: disputed distinctions between counselling and psychotherapy, frictions and altercations between professional bodies, disagreement over the best way forward *vis-à-vis* voluntary or statutory regulation, and so on. At the time of writing, statutory regulation via the Health Professions Council had quite surprisingly been abandoned due to changing government policy and ongoing difficulties in reaching agreement on protection of title and other matters.

A voluntary register now seems to be the way forward for counselling and psychotherapy, while clinical and counselling psychology opted into the HPC.

One of the most significant planks of the professionalization agenda has been evidence-based practice (EBP), which has been heavily promoted by NICE. Counselling and psychotherapy have to some extent followed medicine and other health-care professions in engaging in and promoting research to establish the effectiveness and efficacy of the psychological therapies (Rowland and Goss, 2002). This may yield short- to medium-term gains for this profession – in public relations, parity with other health-care professions, enhanced employment opportunities, clinical guidelines, and clearer information available to clients – but it also contains dangers. While EBP adherents reassure us that therapeutic creativity and individuality will not be stifled, the tendencies for available evidence to favour short-term and cognitive-behavioural therapies is clear. In the long term, EBP holds many dangers and threats that require critical analysis (Feltham, 2004; 2010). It remains important that some maintain a critical opposition to this trend, whether at the level of promoting alternative research methods or as an eloquent defence of the values of humanistic therapy.

Debates continue among therapists as to the needs for, and benefits of, empirical research, supervision, personal therapy and continuing professional development (Feltham, 1999; 2010). It is often taken for granted that continuous refinements in ethical underpinnings, complaints procedures, public relations and other endeavours bolster the value and effectiveness of therapy. A former emphasis on 'good enough', humanly fallible practice subtly concedes to the government-driven ethos of continuous improvement, value for money, efficient use of time, professional and clinical excellence. Counselling and psychotherapy – and their valuing of genuineness, difference and holistic aspirations – do not necessarily dovetail seamlessly with government socio-economic, health and educational policies, or indeed with the pressures of increasingly globalized capitalism.

Integration of models of therapy has partly continued but has also partly been resisted. Hence, more and more practitioners identify themselves as integrative, and recently as pluralistic. To some extent this tendency has been fostered by the day-to-day pressures and prompts of working in primary care settings and by short-term contracts with clients: practitioners have, in the best interests of clients, frequently looked for and forged the most practical therapeutic packages. But in parallel with this, many 'new' models of therapy, including new brief models and models targeting specific client groups, have arisen. Expediency, market forces and innovation combine to produce a continuing abundance of new models in a manner that works against integrative convergence. Solution-focused therapy has now become well established as one of the most widely practised models of therapy, due not only to its brevity but also to its hopeful, anti-pathologizing, forward-looking ethos and interventions. Beginning to make an impression on the UK scene from the USA are models like interpersonal psychotherapy, dialectical behaviour therapy (DBT) – both now included in this volume – and mindfulness-based cognitive therapy (MBCT), with the promise of addressing the needs of many 'difficult' clients in particular (often, those diagnosed with borderline personality disorder). Interestingly, DBT and MBCT both incorporate meditational features, a development that could signal a hitherto unlikely resonance between cognitive-behavioural, humanistic and transpersonal models.

It remains the case that the UK is primarily a recipient of American models rather than an exporter. It is also to the credit of the BACP that many countries still developing a counselling profession turn to the BACP frameworks and norms for guidance. It is of some concern that despite continuing calls for models and interventions that are non-American and non-Eurocentric, no truly multicultural model – or even modest experiments in culturally specific therapies or interventions – has emerged. There remains little available formally to underpin Islamic values for Muslim clients, for example. Client-centred 'non-directiveness' remains the dominant value base and therapeutic style in much counselling despite voiced dissatisfaction from some quarters. There is continuing emphasis on verbal exchange in therapy instead of more creative and diverse forms of delivery and exploration, including online counselling and body psychotherapy at different ends of a spectrum. The health, spiritual and socio-economic-related needs of specific client groups have still not been focused upon as concertedly as they might have been. (For an excellent discussion of the poorly explicated topic of human needs, see Doyal and Gough, 1991.) While a certain amount of UK literature has brought a welcome focus on some of the above areas, typical training curricula do not appear to have altered substantially. Tensions do, however, exist between aspirations to respond creatively to such needs, and the real limitations of funding, time and suitable personnel.

While therapists develop research (mainly small-scale empirical studies) into the subtleties of the client–therapist relationship and the multifaceted micro-processes of therapeutic practice, developments in science slowly impinge on our field. In evolutionary psychology, neuroscience, genetics and psychopharmacology, significant advances are still being made. All such endeavours hold potential for helping to explain parts of the aetiology of human distress and dysfunction, and all might potentially offer suggestive remedies of their own and/or challenges to the conversational norms of counselling and psychotherapy. Equally, it remains possible that some of their findings will confirm therapists' long-standing practice knowledge of the importance of early childhood experiences, the quality of parent–child interaction, emotional needs, and the potency of certain corrective emotional experiences in therapy. Difficult though it may be, it seems crucial that therapists are aware of scientific developments that could sometimes threaten and sometimes support their work.

As therapists we tend to react to present human need rather than to anticipate or forecast future scenarios. Arguably, however, we might be drawing on the values of therapy and the insights gained from practice, training and supervision, in order to visualize and attempt to address future social needs, trends and problems. It is predicted that we will have an increasingly ageing population, probably with extended employment, growing pensions problems and health-care demands accompanying longevity. Alongside this, it is predicted that a population of fewer young people will have to support older citizens economically, and that immigration may have to be well maintained to make good the shortage in the workforce. Economic and cultural tensions at the time of writing make all this quite uncertain. Varieties of conflict between young and old and different ethnic groups have been predicted. As we know, marriage and similar but less formal partnerships have been enduring for a shorter time than traditionally; typical family size has fallen, and family constitution has changed. Pressures and expectations have increased on students at all levels, with mental health problems escalating accordingly. Work stress has remained a fairly high-profile issue for much of the early twenty-first century. Depression increases across populations and, while therapy has gained in acceptance, powerful pharmacological companies gain much more from such trends in problematic mental health (Ritzer, 2004). Concern has been expressed about the continuing rise in prescribed drugs for young people.

This general scenario, if accurate, challenges us in two main ways. First, it behoves us to consider how theory and practice may have to adjust to meet new and greater demands. A greater number of older clients may well seek help, for example, with attitudes and dilemmas that differ from those associated with traditional prospects for retirement and later life aspirations. Better and more accessible knowledge of our genetic profiles will generate a need for more specifically informed genetic counselling. An increasingly multicultural society will demand changing content in counselling and psychotherapy training. Increasing knowledge of the benefits of psychopharmacology, of neuroscientific understanding and of the interplay between different available and documented therapies will probably require of counsellors and psychotherapists more stringent updating and/or choice of specialized further training modules. As yet, counsellors and psychotherapists have not had to 'think epidemiologically' (and strategically) in the way that many psychiatrists and clinical psychologists have begun to (Abernathy and Power, 2002).

Second, and much more difficult for therapists to respond to, perhaps, is the problem of how human suffering and psychological need should be conceived. A gradual shift from traditional aetiological models focusing primarily on individual psychology, parent–child interactions, personal traumas and so on is an almost inevitable prospect. Demographic changes, cultural and religious pluralism, geopolitical uncertainties, environmental degradation, terrorist threats and pervasive (if low level in many societies) death anxiety may come to be seen to drive compromised mental health as much as, if not more than, traditional analyses of clinical, psychic or cognitive dysfunctional tendencies. In other words, 'social contexts' should feature more prominently in our thinking, theorizing and training. We may also be forced rather uncomfortably to concede that therapy is not quite the panacea we have perceived it as being and does not hold quite the position of eminence in addressing personal insecurities that we may hope. In the UK population of about 61 million, even if there are, as estimated, around 250,000 therapists, and even if all therapy had a great deal of reliable and durable success, exponential happiness expansion is still an unlikely scenario. In a world population climbing towards 7 billion, many of whom do not have even basic needs met and suffer from untreated diseases, shortened life expectancy, war and terror, and associated traumatic effects, there is far greater cause for caution (Ritzer, 2004; Williams, 2004). Concerns about climate change have yet to impinge much on everyday life or therapy, but one or two models of ecotherapy are beginning to appear. Therapy quite naturally addresses the near at hand, and seems likely to experience high demand and professional success in the short to medium term. But alongside this, long-term forecasting suggests that responses to human problems may need to emerge that are more socially potent than one-to-one therapeutic work.

Accepting that therapy is a meaningful but relatively modest part of the answer to our human problems is an arguably necessary step in the maturity of therapy, whether regarded as a profession or as a vocation. Balancing hope and enthusiasm for the growth of professional norms against vigilance and sensitivity to emergent social and global trends may be said to parallel the task faced by the individual therapist in believing in her or his work while remaining profoundly receptive to the client's subtly changing material, insights and experiences.

REFERENCES

Abernathy, J. and Power, M. (2002) The epidemiology of mental distress. In C. Feltham (ed.), *What's the Good of Counselling and Psychotherapy? The Benefits Explained*. London: Sage.

BACP (2004) Press release, October. Rugby: British Association for Counselling and Psychotherapy.

Doyal, L. and Gough, I. (1991) *A Theory of Human Needs*. Basingstoke: Macmillan.

Feltham, C. (ed.) (1999) *Controversies in Psychotherapy and Counselling*. London: Sage.

Feltham, C. (2004) Evidence-based psychotherapy and counseling in the UK: critique and alternatives. *Journal of Contemporary Psychotherapy*, 35 (1): 131–43.

Feltham, C. (2010) *Critical Thinking in Counselling and Psychotherapy*. London: Sage.

Furedi, F. (2004) *Therapy Culture: Cultivating Vulnerability in an Uncertain Age*. London: Routledge.

Future Foundation (2004) *The Age of Therapy: Exploring Attitudes Towards and Acceptance of Counselling and Psychotherapy in Modern Britain*. London: Future Foundation and British Association for Counselling and Psychotherapy.

James, I. and Palmer, S. (eds) (1996) *Professional Therapeutic Titles: Myths and Realities*. Leicester: British Psychological Society.

Ritzer, G. (ed.) (2004) *Handbook of Social Problems: A Comparative International Perspective*. Thousand Oaks, CA: Sage.

Rowland, N. and Goss, S. (eds) (2002) *Evidence-Based Counselling and Psychological Therapies: Research and Applications*. London: Routledge.

Williams, J. (2004) *50 Facts That Should Change the World*. Duxford: Icon.

List of Abbreviations

ACT	acceptance and commitment therapy	CPC	Association of Counsellors and Psychotherapists in Primary Care
AD/HD	attention deficit hyperactivity disorder		
ADS	alcohol dependence syndrome	CPD	continuing professional development
AIDS	acquired immune deficiency syndrome	DBT	dialectical behaviour therapy
AMHP	approved mental health professional	DDA	Disability Discrimination Act
AOP	anti-oppressive practice	DIT	dynamic interpersonal therapy
APA	American Psychiatric Association	DNA	did not attend
AS	Asperger syndrome	DRG	diagnostic-related group
ASC	Association for Student Counselling	DSM	*Diagnostic and Statistical Manual of Mental Disorders*
AUCC	Association for University and College Counsellors	EAP	employee assistance programme/ provider
BACP	British Association for Counselling and Psychotherapy	EATA	European Transactional Analysis Association
BASPR	British Association for Supervision Practice and Research	EBP	evidence-based practice
BED	binge eating disorder	ECHR	European Convention on Human Rights
BOP	body-oriented psychotherapy		
BPC	British Psychoanalytic Council	ECT	electro-convulsive therapy
BPD	borderline personality disorder	EDNOS	eating disorder not otherwise specified
BPS	British Psychological Society		
BPT	behavioural parent training	EFT	emotional freedom techniques
CAMHS	child and adolescent mental health services	EMDR	eye movement desensitization and reprocessing
CAT	cognitive analytic therapy	EMMC	European Mentoring and Coaching Council
CBT	cognitive-behavioural therapy		
CCBT	computerized cognitive-behavioural therapy	FDAP	Federation of Drug and Alcohol Professionals
CCI	Co-Counselling International	FSS	functional somatic symptoms
CCRT	core conflictual relationship theme	GAD	generalized anxiety disorder
CCT	client-centred therapy	GAT	gay affirmative therapy; gender-aware therapy
CFS	chronic fatigue syndrome		
CMHT	community mental health team	GSM	gender and sexual minorities
CORE	Clinical Outcomes in Routine Evaluation	GSMT	gender and sexual minority therapy
COSCA	Counselling and Psychotherapy in Scotland	HFA	high-functioning autism
		HIV	human immuno-deficiency virus

HPC	Health Professions Council	PCT	person-centred therapy
HRA	Human Rights Act	PD	personality disorder
IACP	Irish Association for Counselling and Psychotherapy	PPC	positive psychology coaching
		PPS	Psychologists Protection Society
IAPT	Improving Access to Psychological Therapies	PT	primal therapy
		PTSD	post-traumatic stress disorder
IBS	irritable bowel syndrome	RC	Re-evaluation Counseling
ICD	*International Classification of Diseases*	RCT	randomized controlled trial
ICF	International Coach Federation	REBT	rational emotive behaviour therapy
IMHA	independent mental health advocate	RFT	relational frame theory
IPN	Independent Practitioners' Network	ROI	return on investment
IPR	interpersonal process recall	SEBDs	social, emotional and behavioural difficulties
IPT	interpersonal psychotherapy		
ITAA	International Transactional Analysis Association	SFT	solution-focused therapy
		SIGN	Scottish Intercollegiate Guidelines Network
IWM	internal working model		
LGBT (IQ)	lesbian, gay, bisexual, transgender/ sexual, intersex, questioning	SMS	short message service
		SOAD	second opinion appointed doctor
MBCT	mindfulness-based cognitive therapy	SOC	selective optimization with compensation
MBTI	Myers–Briggs Type Indicator		
MCT	multicultural counselling and therapy	SST	single-session therapy
MET	motivational enhancement therapy	STS	secondary traumatic stress
MSE	mental state examination	TA	transactional analysis
MUS	medically unexplained symptoms	TFT	thought field therapy
NICE	National Institute for Health and Clinical Excellence	TSF	twelve-step facilitation
		UKCP	United Kingdom Council for Psychotherapy
NLP	neuro-linguistic programming		
OCD	obsessive compulsive disorder	VOIP	voice over internet protocol
PCP	person-centred psychology	WHO	World Health Organization

Index

Notes: Page numbers in **bold** indicate a more comprehensive coverage of the topic.
Page numbers in *italic* refer to figures and diagrams.